PRENTICE HALL
WORLD HISTORY
CONNECTIONS TO TODAY

Elisabeth Gaynor Ellis and Anthony Esler
With Senior Consultant Burton F. Beers

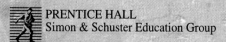

PRENTICE HALL
Simon & Schuster Education Group

The World History Team

Core Team: Lynda Cloud, Kathryn Dix, Anne Falzone, Monduane Harris, Carol Leslie, Emily Rose, Frank Tangredi, Elizabeth Torjussen

Advertising and Promotion: Carol Leslie, Rip Odell

Art and Design: Laura Jane Bird, Paul Gagnon, Monduane Harris, AnnMarie Roselli, Gerry Schrenck, Kira Thaler

Computer Test Bank Technology: Greg Myers, Cleasta Wilburn

Editorial: Tom Barber, Jim Doris, Anne Falzone, Nancy Gilbert, Mary Ann Gundersen, Barbara Harrigan, Rick Hickox, Naomi Kisch, Marion Osterberg, Kirsten Richert, Luess Sampson-Lizotte, Amit Shah, Frank Tangredi

Manufacturing: Rhett Conklin, Matt McCabe

Marketing: Laura Asermily, Lynda Cloud

Media Resources: Martha Conway, Libby Forsyth, Vickie Menanteaux, Emily Rose

Pre-Press Production: Carol Barbara, Kathryn Dix, Annette Simmons

Production: Christina Burghard, Joan McCulley, Marilyn Stearns, Elizabeth Torjussen, Cynthia Weedel

Text Permissions: Doris Robinson

ISBN 0-13-435915-1

4 5 6 7 8 9 10   03 02 01 00 99

 PRENTICE HALL
Simon & Schuster Education Group

Upper Saddle River, New Jersey
Needham, Massachusetts

ACKNOWLEDGMENTS

Grateful acknowledgment is made to the following for permission to reprint copyrighted material:

Excerpt from "Requiem," translated by Robin Kemball, Copyright © 1974 by Robin Kemball, from *Selected Poems* by Anna Akhmatova, edited and translated by Walter Arndt. Reprinted by permission of **Ardis.** Excerpt from "No Time" by Nguyen Sa, from *A Thousand Years of Vietnamese Poetry*, translated by Nguyen Ngoc Bich with Burton Raffel and W. S. Merwin, edited by Nguyen Ngoc Bich. Copyright © 1962, 1967, 1968, 1969, 1970, 1971, 1974 by The Asia Society, Inc. Reprinted by permission of Nguyen Ngoc **Bich.** From "A Doll's House," from *The Complete Major Prose Plays of Henrik Ibsen* by Henrik Ibsen, translated by Rolf Fjelde. Translation copyright © 1965, 1970, 1978 by Rolf Fjelde. Used by permission of **Dutton Signet, a division of Penguin Books USA Inc.** From *Book of Songs*, translated by Arthur Waley. Copyright © 1937 by Arthur Waley. Used by permission of **Grove/Atlantic, Inc.** From "The Heirs of Stalin," from *The Collected Poems, 1952–1990*, Yevgeny Yevtushenko, edited by Albert C. Todd with the author and James Ragan. Copyright © 1991 by Henry Holt and Co. Reprinted by permission of **Henry Holt and Co.** From *Casualties* (**Longmans**, 1970). Lines from "Year after year I have Watched," by Li Ch'ing Chao, translated by Kenneth Rexroth from *Love and the Turning Year: One Hundred More Poems from the Chinese* by Kenneth Rexroth. Copyright © 1970 by Kenneth Rexroth. Reprinted by permission of **New Directions Publishing Company.** Excerpts from "The Prologue" to *The Canterbury Tales* by Geoffrey Chaucer, translated by Nevill Coghill (Penguin Classics, 1951, Fourth revised edition, 1977), copyright © Nevill Coghill, 1951, 1958, 1960, 1975, 1977. Reprinted by permission of **Penguin Books Ltd.** From *The Misadventures of Alonso Ramirez*, translated by Edwin H. **Pleasants** (Mexico, 1962). From *Sundiata: An Epic of Old Mali* by D. T. Niane, translated by G. D. Pickett. © Présence Africaine 1960 (original French version: *Soundjata, ou l'Epopée Mandingue*). © Longman Group Ltd. (English Version) 1965. Reprinted by permission of **Présence Africaine.** Four lines of "In Memory of W. B. Yeats," from *W. H. Auden: Collected Poems* by W. H. Auden. Copyright © 1940 and renewed 1968 by W. H. Auden. Reprinted by permission of **Random House, Inc. and Faber and Faber Limited.** From "We Crown Thee King" by Rabindranath Tagore from *The Hungry Stones and Other Stories*, published by The Macmillan Company, 1916. Reprinted by permission of **Simon & Schuster, Inc. and Macmillan Publishers Ltd.** Four lines

(Acknowledgments continue on page 634.)

PRENTICE HALL WORLD HISTORY

CONNECTIONS TO TODAY

Authors

Elisabeth Gaynor Ellis

Elisabeth Gaynor Ellis is a historian and writer. She is a co-author of *World Cultures: A Global Mosaic*. Ms. Ellis, a former social studies teacher and school administrator, has taught world cultures, Russian studies, and European history. She holds a B.A. from Smith College and an M.A. and M.S. from Columbia University.

Anthony Esler

Anthony Esler is Professor of History at the College of William and Mary. He received his Ph.D. from Duke University and received Fulbright Fellowships to study at the University of London and travel to Ivory Coast and Tanzania. Dr. Esler's books include *The Human Venture: A World History* and *The Western World: A History*, as well as seven historical novels.

Senior Consultant
Burton F. Beers

Burton F. Beers is Professor of History at North Carolina State University. He has taught European history, Asian history, and American history. Dr. Beers has published numerous articles in historical journals and several books, including *The Far East: A History of Western Impacts and Eastern Responses*, with Paul H. Clyde, and *World History: Patterns of Civilization*.

Program Reviewers

AREA SPECIALISTS

Africa Abraham Kuranga, Department of History, Cincinnati State, Technical and Community College, Cincinnati, Ohio

Ancient World Maud Gleason, Department of Classics, Stanford University, Palo Alto, California

Chicano/a Studies Shirlene Soto, California State University, Northridge, California

East Asia Burton F. Beers, Department of History, North Carolina State University, Raleigh, North Carolina

Economics Richard Sylla, Department of Economics, Stern School of Business, New York University, New York, New York

Medieval Europe Kathryn Reyerson, Department of History, University of Minnesota, Minneapolis, Minnesota

Modern Europe Douglas Skopp, Department of History, State University of New York, Plattsburgh, New York

Religion Michael Sells, Department of Religion, Haverford College, Haverford, Pennsylvania

South Asia David Gilmartin, Department of History, North Carolina State University, Raleigh, North Carolina

Susan Wadley, Department of Anthropology, Syracuse University, Syracuse, New York

Southwest Asia Linda T. Darling, Department of History, University of Arizona, Tucson, Arizona

Women's History Lyn Reese, Women in the World: Curriculum Resource Project, Berkeley, California

Program Reviewers
Continued

CONTENT REVIEWERS

David Beaulieu, Minnesota Department of Human Rights, St. Paul, Minnesota

Samuel Chu, Department of History, The Ohio State University, Columbus, Ohio

Susan Douglass, Educational Consultant, Falls Church, Virginia

Shabbir Mansuri, Director, Council on Islamic Education, Fountain Valley, California

José Morales, Department of Puerto Rican and Hispanic Caribbean Studies, Rutgers University, New Brunswick, New Jersey

Mark Peterson, Coordinator of Asian Studies, Brigham Young University, Provo, Utah

Charlotte Stokes, Supervisor of Social Studies, K–12, Prince Georges County Public Schools, Prince Georges County, Maryland

TEACHER ADVISORY PANEL

Colleen Anderson, Del Campo High School, Fair Oaks, California

Trudy Bantle, Fairport High School, Fairport, New York

Richard A. Birdie, John F. Kennedy High School, Bellmore, New York

John Boglioli, Holy Trinity High School, Hicksville, New York

Alice D'Addario, Walt Whitman High School, Huntington, New York

Herbert R. Duncan, Roosevelt High School, Dallas, Texas

Donald Gatian, Lanier High School, San Antonio, Texas

Taddie Hamilton, Lewisville School District, Flower Mound, Texas

Dorcas Helms, Birdville School District, Haltom City, Texas

Maria Elena Estrada, Martin High School, Laredo, Texas

Jean Fleet, Riverside University High School, Milwaukee, Wisconsin

Sara Hamm, Palo Duro High School, Amarillo, Texas

Al Kniss, Traverse City High School, Traverse City, Michigan

Manuel Lopez, Thomas Jefferson High School, Dallas, Texas

Linda Massey, Seagoville High School, Dallas, Texas

Edward Michels,* Ridgefield Park Junior/Senior High School, Ridgefield Park, New Jersey

Richard C. Morris, Saratoga Springs High School, Saratoga Springs, New York

Robert Orth, L. G. Pinkston High School, Dallas, Texas

Swanya Howell Pitts, Riverside High School, El Paso, Texas

Harvey Plaut, Bowie High School, El Paso, Texas

Cynthia Ramirez, J. W. Nixon High School, Laredo, Texas

Lela Roberts, Booker T. Washington High School, Houston, Texas

Victoria Robinson, Price Laboratory School, University of Northern Iowa, Cedar Falls, Iowa

Dr. Michael J. Romano, Northport High School, Northport, New York

Eddie Sewell, Cleburne High School, Cleburne, Texas

Priscilla Watkins, Scarborough High School, Houston, Texas

Steven Weiner, Gateway High School, Aurora, Colorado

STUDENT REVIEW BOARD

Caleb Cutwright, Price Laboratory School, University of Northern Iowa, Cedar Falls, Iowa

Erika Menanteaux, Bogota High School, Bogota, New Jersey

Christopher Ostuni, Holy Trinity High School, Hicksville, New York

Megan Scheuer, Ridgefield Park Junior/Senior High School, Ridgefield Park, New Jersey

Dawnyeala Washington, Gateway High School, Aurora, Colorado

Franklin A. Williams, Roosevelt High School, Dallas, Texas

ACCURACY PANEL

Victoria Robinson, Price Laboratory School, University of Northern Iowa, Cedar Falls, Iowa

With William O'Dell

* Contributing editor

Contents

THE BIG PICTURE

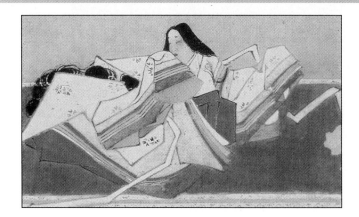

723

Olympe de Gouges:
Declaration of the Rights of Woman and the Female Citizen

DOCUMENT IN BRIEF

In this document French journalist Olympe de Gouges demands equal rights for women.

Born Marie Gouze, Olympe de Gouges did not believe the Declaration of the Rights of Man had gone far enough. In 1791 she wrote the Declaration of the Rights of Woman demanding equal rights for women. De Gouges was guillotined in 1793 in part because of her royalist politics and in part because of her ideas about women's rights.

1. *Woman is born free and lives equal to man in her rights. . . .*

2. *The purpose of any political association is the conservation of the natural and imprescriptible rights of woman and man; these rights are liberty, property, security, and especially resistance to oppression.*

6. *The law must be the expression of the general will; all female and male citizens must contribute either personally or through their representatives to its formation. It must be the same for all. . . .*

. . . accused, arrested, and detained in . . . , like men, obey this rigorous law.

. . . lty, complete rigor is [to be] exercised . . .

. . . very basic opinions; woman has the . . . must equally have the right to mount . . . emonstrations do not disturb the . . .

. . . hout the guarantee of rights and the . . . ution is null if the majority of individ- . . . not cooperated in drafting it.

. . . hether united or separate. . . . . . . rm bell] of reason is being heard . . . iscover your rights. . . . When will . . . antage have you received from the . . . scorn, a more marked disdain. . . . . . . ny [inheritance], based on the wise . . . u to dread from such a fine under-

▲ Women's march on Versailles

. . . lowing

. . . y states a

. . . onstitu-

A Women have not cooperated in drafting it.

B It does not guarantee property rights to women.

C Women are not treated with respect.

D Women are subject to unjust arrest.

3. *Critical Thinking:* **Recognizing Causes and Effects** Why do you think de Gouges included article 9 above which implies that women should not be given special treatment if found guilty of a crime?

Historical Documents 1011

Europe: Political

▲ Capital City
• Major City

DOCUMENTS

Special Features

PARALLELS THROUGH TIME

Going Shopping

Some complain that the marketplace is loud, busy, crowded. But for merchants selling their wares, shoppers looking for bargains, and people who just want to be with people, this is the place to be.

Linking Past and Present What advantages does an enclosed mall have over an open-air marketplace? Why are some open-air markets still popular?

PAST Muslim bazaars, or marketplaces, sold local goods as well as imports made available by a vast trading network. In major cities, such as Baghdad and Istanbul, the bazaar consisted of miles of streets enclosed by a roof. In this illustration, we see, from left to right, a jeweler, a druggist, a butcher, and a baker.

PRESENT The giant, multilevel, indoor mall is a modern version of the bazaar. Within its great expanse, you may shop, dine, see a movie, or perhaps even ice skate.

Up Close

▶ *In-depth stories bring history alive.*

Art History

▶ *Works of art reveal the talents and creativity of artists and artisans around the world.*

World Literature

▶ *Literature selections offer insights into diverse world cultures throughout history.*

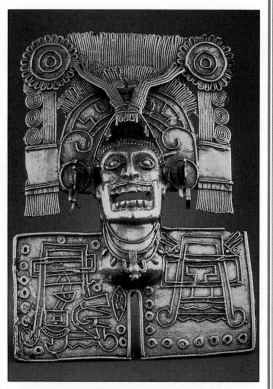

Gold Ritual Ornament Like Native American artists throughout Central and South America, Mexican artists crafted elaborate works of gold. Their creations were rich in religious symbolism, representing gods and incorporating sacred objects and animals, such as jaguars, serpents, eagles, and suns. The golden ornament shown here probably portrays the god of the dead. **Economics and Technology** How do you think the fine quality of the gold work produced in Central and South America reinforced Europeans' desire to conquer the area?

Skills for Success

SKILLS FOR SUCCESS   ANALYZING FINE ART

Works of fine art, such as paintings and sculptures, can show us what famous people looked like, what a culture's beliefs were, and what people wore. As with written sources, a historian must determine the reliability of an artwork. For example, a painter might have tried to flatter the king who was paying for a portrait by making him look more imposing than he was in real life.

At right is a section of a large painting called *Children's Games*, by Pieter Bruegel. (See page 350.) Study the painting and answer the following questions.

Charts and Graphs

Time Lines and Maps

Regional Time Lines

Maps

Geography of the Ancient Middle East

GEOGRAPHY AND HISTORY

Like the Nile River in Egypt, the Tigris and Euphrates rivers gave rise to early civilizations. The rivers made the land fertile and provided avenues for trade.

1. **Location** On the map, locate (a) Tigris River, (b) Euphrates River, (c) Fertile Crescent, (d) Sumer, (e) Akkad, (f) Mesopotamia, (g) Egypt.
2. **Place** What physical features may have helped limit the expansion of Akkad?
3. **Critical Thinking** **Comparing** Look at the map on page 25. Compare the location, physical features, and size of the Egyptian and Babylonian empires.

Time Lines and Maps

Maps

Documents

Confucius: *Analects*

The *Analects* are a collection of 497 verses recorded by Confucius' followers long after his death (perhaps in the fourth century B.C.). Confucius' teachings emphasize duty and responsibility as a means of ensuring social order and good government.

*T*he Master said, He who rules by moral force is like the pole-star, which remains in its place while all the lesser stars do homage to it.

The Master said, If out of the three hundred Songs I had to take one phrase to cover all my teaching, I would say 'Let there be no evil in your thoughts.'

Mêng Wu Po asked about the treatment of parents. The Master said, Behave in such a way that your father and mother have no anxiety about you, except concerning your health.

Tzu-kung asked about the true gentleman. The Master said, He does not preach what he practices till he has practiced what he preaches.

The Master said, A gentleman can see a question from all sides without bias. The small man is biased and can see a question only from one side.

The Master said, Yu, shall I teach you what knowledge is? When you know a thing, to recognize that you know it, and when you do not know a thing, to recognize that you do not know it. That is knowledge.

Chi K'ang-tzu asked whether there were any form of encouragement by which he could induce the common people to be respectful and loyal. The Master said, Approach them with dignity, and they will respect you. Show piety towards your parents and kindness towards your children, and they will be loyal to you. Promote those who are worthy, train those who are incompetent; that is the best form of encouragement.

◆ DOCUMENT IN BRIEF

The *Analects* are a collection of sayings that emphasize education and self-sacrifice as the keys to becoming a superior person.

DOCUMENTS

▲ Confucius and his students

Documents

◆ **DOCUMENT IN BRIEF**

In his *Discourses*, Machiavelli describes methods for establishing and preserving republics.

DOCUMENTS

Niccolò Machiavelli: *Discourses*

Niccolò Machiavelli (1469-1527) is best known for a system of power politics in which "the ends justify the means," as described in his book *The Prince*. However, in his book *Discourses on the First Ten Books of Titus Livy*, Machiavelli concludes that the best-governed state is ruled by the people rather than by a ruthless prince.

In short, to bring this topic to conclusion, I say that, just as princely forms of government have endured for a very long time, so, too, have republican forms of government; and that in both cases it has been essential for them to be regulated by laws. For a prince who does what he likes is a lunatic; and a populace which does what it likes is unwise. If, therefore, it be a question of a prince subservient to the laws and of a populace chained up by laws, more virtue will be found in the populace than in the prince; and if it be a question of either of them loosed from control by the law, there will be found fewer errors in the populace than in the prince, and these of less moment and much easier to put right. For a licentious [disregarding rules] and turbulent populace, when a good man can obtain a hearing, can easily be brought to behave itself; but there is no one to talk to a bad prince, nor is there any remedy except the sword. . . .

When the populace has thrown off all restraint, it is the not the mad things it does that are terrifying, nor is it of present evils that one is afraid, but of what may come of them, for amidst such confusion there may come to be a tyrant. In the case of bad princes it is just the opposite: it is present evils that are terrifying, but for the future there is hope, since men are convinced that the evil ways of a bad prince may make for freedom in the end. . . . The reason why people are prejudiced against the populace is because of the populace anyone may speak ill without fear and openly, even when the populace is ruling. But of princes people speak with the utmost trepidation and the utmost reserve.

▲ Lorenzo de Médici, Renaissance Prince

ANALYZING THE DOCUMENT

Use the excerpt above to answer the following questions.

1. Machiavelli states that the only way to bring an unruly prince under the law is to—

   A obtain a hearing.

   B use physical combat.

   C discuss the people's legal rights.

   D choose a tyrant.

2. Machiavelli concludes that the greatest threat posed by an unlawful populace is—

   A the rise of a dictator.

   B the violence of the mob.

   C the loss of a prince.

   D the destruction of property.

3. *Critical Thinking:* **Making Inferences** Why do you think Machiavelli believes that the populace is more subject to criticism than a prince?

About This Book

World History: Connections to Today is organized into 5 units, made up of 21 chapters. The Table of Contents lists the units and chapters, special features and graphics, and the Reference Section at the back of the book.

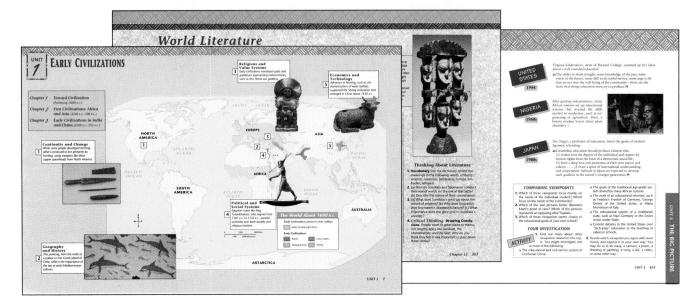

IN EACH UNIT

- **Unit Opener:** a two-page introduction that includes a map and illustrations.
- **World Literature:** a two-page literature excerpt from the time period of the unit.
- **The Big Picture:** a six-page wrap-up to each unit, including:
    - **Unit-in-Brief**, a short summary of each chapter in the unit;
    - **A Global View**, a thematic essay and timeline;
    - **You Decide**, a document-based look at an enduring global issue.

IN EACH CHAPTER

- **Chapter Opener:** a two-page introduction that includes a locator map, theme questions, and timeline.
- **Guide for Reading:** an introduction to each section, including questions to guide your reading and a list of vocabulary terms in the section.
- **Section Reviews:** questions at the end of each section that test your understanding of what you have read.
- **Issues for Today:** questions linking content in the chapter to enduring issues that face us today.

- **Global Connections:** historical notes that show how events and ideas are connected over time and place.
- **Maps, Graphs, and Charts:** graphics that provide essential information and also teach important critical thinking and graphics skills.
- **Chapter Review:** two pages that present a Skills for Success skill lesson and review your understanding of the chapter content, plus providing opportunities for critical thinking and activities.
- **Special Features:**
    - **Parallels Through Time**, on links between past and present;
    - **Art History**, presenting artistic masterpieces from around the world;
    - **Up Close**, an in-depth look at an interesting person or event;
    - **Cause-and-Effect Charts** on key historical developments;
    - **Quick Study Charts**, providing graphic overviews of historical developments.

REFERENCE SECTION

- Includes an Atlas, Glossary, Historical Documents, Literature and Science Connections, and an Index.

Researching on the Internet

The Internet and the World Wide Web

The **Internet** is a global computer network that began in the 1960s as a U. S. Department of Defense project linking university computer science departments. The Internet has since grown to include millions of business, governmental, educational, and individual computers around the world. The **World Wide Web**, or "the Web" for short, is a collection of linked electronic files. Using programs called browsers, Internet users can find out what files are available on the Web and then access those files.

Searching the Internet

There are two basic ways to find information on the Internet. The first is to go directly to the Web site that contains the information you want. Each Web site has its own address, called a **URL**, or Universal Resource Locator. (For example, http://www.phschool.com is the URL of the Prentice Hall Web site.) Of course, this method only works if you know the appropriate URL. Also, Web sites sometimes change URLs or disappear altogether.

The second way is to search the Web for information on your chosen topic. Using a **search engine**, such as Infoseek or Yahoo!, you type the key words representing the topic you want to research. The search engine will then scan the Internet and list all of the Web sites with information on your topic.

Whichever method you choose, you will encounter Web sites containing **hyperlinks**. These appear on your screen as colored or underlined text or as icons. Hyperlinks act as doorways to other documents. When you click your mouse on hyperlinked text or graphics, an entirely new document appears on your screen. That document may come from the same computer as the Web site you just left, or from one thousands of miles away.

As you search the Internet, you should pay careful attention to the source of the information you find—is it from a government agency, or a university, or a private company, or an individual? Not all sources are equally accurate or reliable.

Visit the Prentice Hall Home Page!
http://www.phschool.com

Tips for Successful Searches

- **Keep your search focused**. Because the Internet contains so much interesting and varied information, it is easy to "wander off" into other parts of the Internet and forget about the information that you are trying to locate. To avoid this, you should establish a specific research goal *before* you begin your Internet research.

- **Make bookmarks for your favorite Web sites.** A bookmark is a note to your computer to "remember" the location of the Web site. You can reach any bookmarked site from any other site with a simple click of your mouse.

- **Use specific key words.** If your key words are too general, your search might turn up thousands of Web sites. To search for information on ancient Egypt, for example, the key words "ancient Egypt" are preferable to "history" or "Egypt." Many search engines have useful tips on searching with key words.

- **Evaluate the quality of Internet information.** Not all of the information available on the Internet is appropriate for your research. Ask a teacher, parent, or librarian for help in evaluating the reliability and appropriateness of Web sites and information.

Analyzing Documents

Many of today's issues and events are connected to the past in such a way that they can only be understood by examining history. One way to do this is to analyze written documents. There are two basic types of written documents: *primary sources* and *secondary sources.*

A primary source is a record of an event written by someone who witnessed or participated in the event. This could include newspaper articles, diaries, interviews, speeches, autobiographies, or church and government records.

Secondary sources are usually based on primary sources. Authors of secondary sources did not witness the events, but studied evidence left behind by those who did. Many history books are secondary sources, including this textbook.

POINTS TO REMEMBER

When analyzing documents, there are important points you need to remember. To help you understand these points, analyze the quote below from Frederick Lugard.

> 66There are some who say we have no *right* to Africa at all, that 'it belongs to the natives.' I hold that our right is the necessity that is upon us to provide for our ever-growing population—either by opening new fields for emigration, or by providing work and employment . . . and to stimulate trade by finding new markets.99

- **Basic Message** Summarizing the main idea of a document helps you understand what the author is trying to say. One summary of Lugard's quote is that expansion into Africa was necessary for Europe's survival. This is his basic message. While you may not agree with Lugard, his message is clear.

- **Author Viewpoint** The author of a document, even an eyewitness, may have personal, political, or religious opinions that affect what is written. In this case, it is important to understand Lugard's personal interest. He was a businessman. He knew that expansion into Africa would help his business and this may have influenced what he wrote.

- **Identifying Fact and Opinion** Distinguishing between fact and opinion is important if we want to make intelligent decisions. Lugard based his argument for expansion partly on the "ever-growing population" in Europe. This was a fact. Europe's population was growing. However, Lugard's argument that expansion would solve the problems associated with an increase in population is opinion. Seizing land that belongs to another may not solve the problems of increased population.

Analyzing Documents

World History: Connections to Today, Volume I provides many opportunities for you to analyze documents. The documents you will examine are all *primary sources.*

REFERENCE SECTION

Pages 572–603 contain **Historical Documents.** Each document has a set of questions that will guide you in analyzing primary sources. (See the example on this page.)

IN EACH CHAPTER

In every chapter review, you will find **Analyzing Primary Sources.** This is a set of questions that refer to a quote in the chapter. (See the example on this page.)

A SYSTEM FOR ANALYZING DOCUMENTS

Each time you analyze a document, begin by reading any introduction that may be provided. Then read the selection, noting the basic message, author's viewpoint, and any facts or opinions. This will be helpful when answering the questions that accompany each primary source. Be sure to read each question carefully before answering. Refer back to the quote or document to help you find the answer.

Magna Carta

◆ DOCUMENT IN BRIEF

The Magna Carta— or Great Charter— established the principle that the king or queen must obey the law.

A group of barons forced King John of England to sign the Magna Carta at Runnymede in 1215. The barons were tired of the king's military campaigns and heavy taxes. The purpose of the document was to limit the power of the monarch and to secure rights such as trial by jury, due process of law, and protection against the arbitrary taking of life, liberty, or property. Below are excerpts from 5 of its 63 articles.

2. We also have granted to all the freemen of our kingdom, for us and for our heirs [those who inherit a title or property] forever, all the underwritten liberties, to be had and holden by them and their heirs, of us and our heirs forever. . . .

12. No scutage [tax] or aid shall be imposed in our kingdom, unless by the general council of our kingdom; except for ransoming our person, making our eldest son a knight and once for marrying our eldest daughter; and for these there shall be paid no more than a reasonable aid.

14. And for holding the general council of the kingdom concerning the assessment of aids, except in the three cases aforesaid, and for the assessing of scutage, we shall cause to be summoned the archbishops, bishops, abbots, earls, and greater barons of the realm, singly by our letters. And furthermore, we shall cause to be summoned generally, by our sheriffs and bailiffs all others who hold of us in chief, for a certain day, that is to say, forty days before their meeting at least, and to a certain place. And in all letters of such summons we will declare the cause of such summons. And summons being thus made, the business shall proceed on the day appointed, according to the advice of such as shall be present, although all that were summoned come not.

39. No freeman shall be taken or imprisoned, or diseised [deprived], or outlawed, or banished, or in any way destroyed . . . unless by the lawful judgment of his peers, or by the law of the land.

40. We will sell to no man, we will not deny to any man, either justice or right.

▲ King Edward I and the Great Council

ANALYZING THE DOCUMENT

Use the excerpt above to answer the following questions.

1. In article 2 the king grants the rights described in the document to—
   A only those freemen who have heirs.
   B his own heirs.
   C all freemen and their heirs for all time.
   D all freemen currently living in England.

2. Article 14 forces the king to consult a great council before raising new taxes. The article also prevents the king from—
   A holding unannounced meetings or meetings on short notice.
   B summoning the general council to make laws regarding taxation.
   C consulting with the general council before calling a meeting.
   D summoning the sheriffs and bailiffs.

3. *Critical Thinking:* Making Inferences What does article 40 imply about royal corruption during this period of English history?

Historical Documents   1003

DOCUMENTS

ANALYZING PRIMARY SOURCES

Use the quotation about Mongol battle tactics on page 315 to answer the following questions.

1. How did the Mongols trick their opponents in battle?

2. Why were the Mongols able to use this tactic effectively?

3. How would you describe the writer's attitude toward the Mongol warriors?

The Big Picture

FOCUS ON THEMES

Events that happened hundreds of years ago, or thousands of miles away, can have a powerful impact on our lives. Ancient Greeks pioneered democratic ideas that influenced the framers of our Constitution. American rock 'n' roll grew out of the music brought to North America by Africans in the time of slavery. Today, decisions made by a Brazilian planter, a Saudi Arabian oil minister, or a Japanese manufacturer can have a direct impact on our daily lives.

This textbook can help you understand how today's complex world came to be. To make the past easier to comprehend, this text emphasizes nine themes. They can help you to focus on key features of each society you read about. The nine themes are

- Continuity and Change
- Geography and History
- Political and Social Systems
- Religions and Value Systems
- Economics and Technology
- Diversity
- Impact of the Individual
- Global Interaction
- Art and Literature

In the following pages, you will learn what these themes are and how they can help you to understand world history.

ACTIVITY Turn to the following pages in your textbook and identify how one or more of the themes listed above is highlighted on that page: pages 74–75, page 282, page 429, page 542.

CONTINUITY AND CHANGE

Human history is a story of change. Some changes are quick. For example, in 1532, Spanish conquerors toppled the vast Incan empire of Peru, transforming South America forever. Other changes take place over centuries, such as the spread of democratic ideas or the shifting role of women in many societies. While change is always happening, enduring traditions and concerns link people across time and place. In India, current politics are affected by a social system more than 3,000 years old. And the question of how to get a good education was as important to a youth in ancient Egypt, Rome, or China as it is to you.

ACTIVITY

Interview a parent or any other older acquaintance. Ask them to identify three ways in which your community or the world has changed in the last 25 years.

Migration has been taking place since the beginning of history. One of the most common migrations has been the movement from farming villages (left) to crowded industrial cities (right).

In the 1940s, the government of South Africa imposed apartheid, a system of strict racial separation. In the 1990s, apartheid was abolished, and Nelson Mandela, far right, became president of South Africa.

GEOGRAPHY AND HISTORY

Geography influences the work people do, the clothes they wear, the food they eat, and how they travel. Since the time of the pharaohs, for example, Egyptians have used the Nile River to transport people and goods. But people also try to master their surroundings. They have built dams to control flooding and cut highways through rugged mountains. More recently, pollution and other environmental issues have caused heated debate. The uneven distribution of vital natural resources, such as oil or gold, is another way geography has helped to shape history.

ACTIVITY

With a partner, create a Geographic Profile for your local area. You might list location, climate, type of land, nearest waterways, plant and animal life, resources, and outstanding geographic features.

▷ Geography plays a key role in military strategy. Using knowledge of geographic conditions, the French general Napoleon Bonaparte seized control of the high ground to win the Battle of Austerlitz.

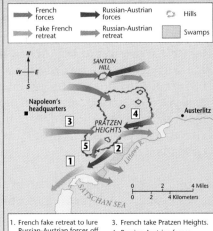

Battle of Austerlitz, 1805

⇒ French forces	⇒ Russian-Austrian forces	⟳ Hills
⇒ Fake French retreat	⇒ Russian-Austrian retreat	▨ Swamps

1. French fake retreat to lure Russian-Austrian forces off Pratzen Heights.
2. Russian-Austrian forces chase French.
3. French take Pratzen Heights.
4. Russian-Austrian forces attack, but are repulsed.
5. More French troops join in to defeat Russian-Austrian forces.

GEOGRAPHY AND HISTORY

In December 1805, Napoleon's forces fought a combined Russian-Austrian army at the Battle of Austerlitz. Thanks to Napoleon's superior leadership, his outnumbered troops won an outstanding victory.

1. **Location** On the map, locate (a) Austerlitz, (b) Pratzen Heights, (c) Satschan Sea, (d) Napoleon's headquarters.
2. **Movement** How were Napoleon's troops able to defeat the Russian-Austrian forces south of Pratzen Heights?
3. **Critical Thinking** *Making Generalizations* Why is control of the high ground important in a battle?

◁ The cutting down of tropical rain forests, like this one in Costa Rica, has become an urgent economic and environmental issue of our time.

◁ The Sahara is the world's largest desert. Since early times, it has served as a highway for trade and migration among widely separated African civilizations.

POLITICAL AND SOCIAL SYSTEMS

Kings and queens, presidents and dictators, elected congresses and tribal councils—each society has a way to govern itself. A government tries to keep order within a society and protect it from outside threats. Societies have other important institutions, including the most basic one of all, the family. Social classes—which rank people based on wealth, ancestry, occupation, or education—are also important. Nobles, priests, merchants, workers, and slaves were common social classes in early societies. In addition, most societies have made sharp distinctions between the roles of women and men.

ACTIVITY

Draw a political cartoon describing a current political issue in your country, state, or community.

Modern democracy has its roots in the Greek city-state of Athens, left, where every adult male citizen was expected to take part in government. In 1994, Haitians celebrated a return to democratic government after years of military rule.

Describe the type of political system you think this cartoon represents.

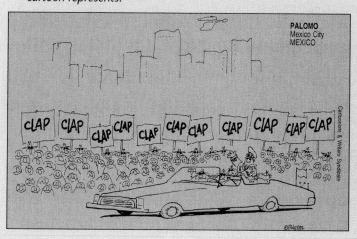

PALOMO
Mexico City
MEXICO

CLAP CLAP CLAP CLAP CLAP CLAP CLAP CLAP CLAP CLAP CLAP

Cartoonists & Writers Syndicate

©Palomo

A feudal social system is based on rigid classes and mutual obligations. This chart shows the feudal system developed in Japan in the 1100s.

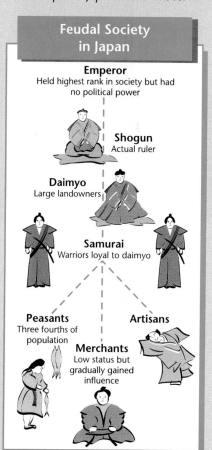

Feudal Society in Japan

Emperor
Held highest rank in society but had no political power

Shogun
Actual ruler

Daimyo
Large landowners

Samurai
Warriors loyal to daimyo

Peasants
Three fourths of population

Artisans

Merchants
Low status but gradually gained influence

RELIGIONS AND VALUE SYSTEMS

How was the world created? How can we tell right from wrong? What happens to us after death? Since early times, people have turned to religion for answers to such questions. Religious ideas—such as the belief in a single true God, shared by Jews, Christians, and Muslims—have exerted a powerful influence on human life. Other kinds of value systems have also shaped societies. The ancient Chinese thinker Confucius preached duty, respect for parents, and loyalty to the state. In the 1800s, a strict code of "middle-class values"—including hard work, thrift, and good manners—came to dominate western society. Through their religions and value systems, people define their vision of a good society.

ACTIVITY Make a list of 10 values that you think are shared by most people in your community. Compare your list with those of others in the class.

Jesus, pictured at left, the founder of Christianity, was born in Palestine about 4 B.C. Today, Christianity is the most widely practiced religion in the world, with over a billion followers.

Sacred books help pass religious beliefs and values from one generation to the next. Above, a Jewish boy studies the Torah. Below, Muslim children learn to read the Quran.

Two major world religions emerged in India: Hinduism, below left, and Buddhism, below right. Buddhism gradually became the dominant religion in much of East Asia and Southeast Asia.

ECONOMICS AND TECHNOLOGY

Early humans lived by hunting animals and gathering plants. When people learned how to grow crops, they settled in farming villages. Thousands of years later, the steam engines of the Industrial Revolution created millions of factory jobs. These examples all show the impact of technology. Technology is often related to economic questions. Who controls vital resources? How are goods exchanged? Are people fairly rewarded for the work they do? Economic motives have forged trading networks, caused wars, and contributed to the rise or decline of nations.

ACTIVITY Skim through a recent news magazine. Locate two advertisements or articles that deal with advances in technology and two articles that deal with economic issues. Identify the topics addressed by each article in a one-sentence summary.

Inventions that changed the course of history include, in clockwise order, wheeled vehicles, block printing, the magnetic compass, the steam engine, and the automatic machine gun.

What do you think is the meaning of this cartoon?

Hazelbrook
AUSTRALIA

SPORTS

TECHNOLOGY 56
HUMAN RACE 3

Cartoonists & Writers Syndicate

Somerville

Advances in transportation during the Industrial Revolution greatly reduced travel time between major cities.

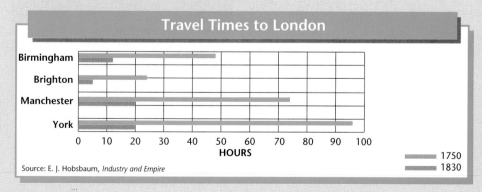

Travel Times to London

Birmingham
Brighton
Manchester
York

0 10 20 30 40 50 60 70 80 90 100
HOURS

—— 1750
—— 1830

Source: E. J. Hobsbaum, *Industry and Empire*

DIVERSITY

How many languages can you think of? English, Spanish, and Japanese are easy. But what about Urdu, Quechua, Gaelic, or Wolof? Today, as in the past, the diversity of human culture is shown by the hundreds of languages people speak. Diversity is also reflected in religions, social systems, art, customs, and forms of government. Within each nation, there may also be a mix of cultures. India, for example, has 16 official languages and hundreds of other regional languages. While diversity has enriched human experience, cultural or ethnic differences can also lead to conflict.

ACTIVITY

Make a list of six examples that show diversity in your community. The list might include languages, religions, buildings, clothing styles, foods, or cultural events.

Comparing Languages

English	month	mother	new	night	nose	three
German	Monat	Mutter	neu	Nacht	Nase	drei
Persian	māh	mādar	nau	shab	bini	se
Sanskrit	mās	matar	nava	nakt	nās	trayas
Spanish	mes	madre	nuevo	noche	nariz	tres
Swedish	månad	moder	ny	natt	näsa	tre

◀ Many diverse languages—stretching from Western Europe to India—came from a common root. Word similarities show the relationship of these "Indo-European" languages.

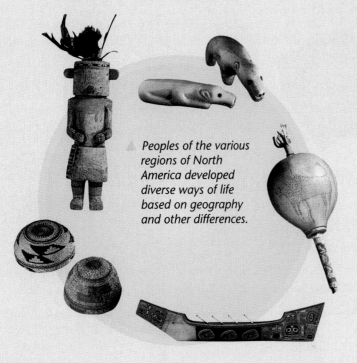

▲ Peoples of the various regions of North America developed diverse ways of life based on geography and other differences.

▲ Russia is the world's largest country, spanning both Europe and Asia. This drawing from the early 1800s shows the diverse peoples of Russia.

IMPACT OF THE INDIVIDUAL

Some people have such an impact on events that we remember them long after they die. Vietnam still honors the Trung sisters who fought against Chinese invaders nearly 2,000 years ago. In the 1400s, the voyages of Christopher Columbus and Vasco da Gama launched new patterns of world trade and conquest. The 1900s saw such important political leaders as Mohandas Gandhi, Adolf Hitler, Franklin Roosevelt, Mao Zedong, Juan and Eva Perón, Gamel Abdel Nasser, and Margaret Thatcher. For good or for ill, these individuals have shaped our world.

ACTIVITY Skim the Index of this book and find three people whose names you recognize. Try to identify the reason that each of these people is famous. Then check your responses against the book.

Nearly 4,000 years ago, the Babylonian king Hammurabi became the first person in history to collect all the laws of one civilization into a single legal code.

In the 1300s, Mansa Musa built the West African kingdom of Mali into one of the most prosperous empires in the world.

In the 600s, Tang Taizong became Emperor of China, establishing the Tang Dynasty and uniting China for the first time in 400 years.

In the 1400s, Joan of Arc, a teenage peasant woman, led French troops to battle in an effort to liberate France from its English conquerors.

Benjamin Franklin was an inventor, writer, diplomat, and political thinker whose ideas helped shape the young United States of America.

As Queen of England, Elizabeth I reigned during the religious wars in Europe and skillfully guided England away from war by promoting religious tolerance.

Simón Bolívar led the battle to liberate Venezuela, Ecuador, Bolivia, and other South American nations from Spanish rule in the early 1800s.

GLOBAL INTERACTION

Coffee was first grown in the 1300s in the Middle East. Two hundred years later, Portuguese settlers carried coffee beans to Brazil. Today, Brazil is the world's leading exporter of coffee. This is one example of global interaction. Nations may interact in many ways—through trade, through migration, or through war and conquest. When people traveled by oxcart or sailing ship, interaction was slow. Today, communication and transportation networks can instantly link all parts of the globe. Organizations such as the United Nations and the World Bank show the growing interdependence of the world.

ACTIVITY Look through a current newspaper and find three articles concerning interaction between the United States and other countries. Locate these countries on the maps at the back of the book.

◀ How can a war in one part of the world affect people living in other parts of the world?

▲ Starting in the 1400s, European powers gained outposts along the African coast. This ivory carving from Benin depicts Portuguese soldiers and was probably sold to them.

▼ For 1,500 years, the city of Constantinople (present-day Istanbul, Turkey) was a center of world trade, attracting merchants from as far away as China and Britain.

ART AND LITERATURE

From early times, people have created art and literature to reflect their lives and values. Stone by stone, Europeans of the Middle Ages raised soaring cathedrals dedicated to the glory of God. In West Africa, griots, or professional poets, recited ancient stories, preserving both histories and traditional folk tales. In the 1920s, the murals of the Mexican painter Diego Rivera depicted the history of Mexico and the lives of its people. Throughout this book, you will see what poems, stories, songs, paintings, sculpture, and architecture show us about other times and other places.

ACTIVITY Skim through the pages of this book and find one example of painting, sculpture, or architecture that appeals to you. Freewrite a brief description of how you respond to it.

▶ *During the Renaissance, Italian artists such as Michelangelo developed new ways to represent humans in a realistic way. This statue of Moses is almost eight feet tall.*

▲ *Japanese paintings such as this one give us a detailed look at life during a time when Japan was isolated from the rest of the world.*

▼ *The ancient Chinese poem at left describes the emotions of parents whose children have gone off to war. Almost 2,500 years later, the German artist Käthe Kollwitz explored the same theme in her print* The Parents, *at right.*

> ❝My mother is saying,
> 'Alas, my young one
>   is on service;
> Day and night he gets
>   no sleep.
> Grant that he is being
>   careful of himself,
> So that he may come
>   back, and not be cast
>   away.'❞

UNIT 1

EARLY CIVILIZATIONS

Continuity and Change

1 *While some people developed farming, others continued to live primarily by hunting, using weapons like these copper spearheads from North America.*

NORTH AMERICA

1

ATLANTIC OCEAN

PACIFIC OCEAN

SOUTH AMERICA

N
W—E
S

Geography and History

2 *This painting, from the walls of a palace on the Greek island of Crete, reflects the importance of the sea to early Mediterranean cultures.*

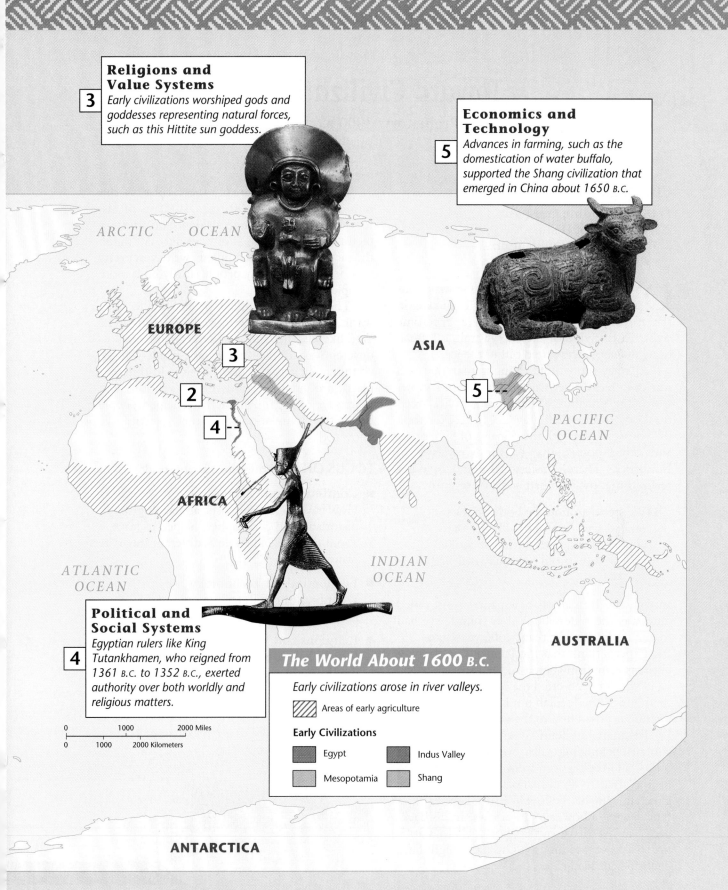

Religions and Value Systems

3 Early civilizations worshiped gods and goddesses representing natural forces, such as this Hittite sun goddess.

Economics and Technology

5 Advances in farming, such as the domestication of water buffalo, supported the Shang civilization that emerged in China about 1650 B.C.

Political and Social Systems

4 Egyptian rulers like King Tutankhamen, who reigned from 1361 B.C. to 1352 B.C., exerted authority over both worldly and religious matters.

ARCTIC OCEAN

EUROPE

3

2

4

ASIA

5

PACIFIC OCEAN

AFRICA

INDIAN OCEAN

ATLANTIC OCEAN

AUSTRALIA

The World About 1600 B.C.

Early civilizations arose in river valleys.

Areas of early agriculture

Early Civilizations

Egypt	Indus Valley
Mesopotamia	Shang

0   1000   2000 Miles
0   1000   2000 Kilometers

ANTARCTICA

Toward Civilization

(Prehistory–3000 B.C.)

CHAPTER OUTLINE

1 **Understanding Our Past**
2 **The Dawn of History**
3 **Beginnings of Civilization**

On an autumn day in 1991, a German couple was tramping through a high pass in the Alps when they came upon a gruesome sight. At one side of the snowy trail, a human head and shoulders jutted out of the ice.

At first, the couple thought that the man was an unlucky hiker who had frozen in a snowstorm the previous winter. Soon, police freed the body from its icy grave. A helicopter took the corpse, along with the remains of his clothes and other possessions, to the University of Innsbruck. There, Professor Konrad Spindler realized that the man had not died recently:

&& We stood around the body on the table. I saw the stone tools and the copper ax and said: 'I think it could be 4,000 years old.' Nobody believed me. 99

In fact, the Iceman, as newspapers soon called him, was the oldest body ever found. He had frozen to death more than 5,000 years ago.

Experts think that the Iceman was sleeping near his campfire when a sudden storm struck. Cold winds freeze-dried the body. Winter snows then buried the Iceman until 1991, when heavy melting exposed him to the gaze of the world.

Fascinated, scientists studied the Iceman and his belongings. His deerskin coat, warm boots, and cape woven from long grass showed he was used to a cold climate. Other evidence gave clues to his skills. He had a copper ax, a flint dagger, a bow, and 14 arrows. In his backpack, he may have carried hot coals to start a fire. Flakes of tree fungus in his pack might have been ancient medicines.

Few discoveries are as spectacular as this one. Yet in the past 200 years, students of history have found enough evidence to create a picture of life thousands of years ago. Although the picture remains incomplete, we have a pretty clear idea of how early people slowly built more complex ways of life.

The Iceman, huddled by his fire to keep warm, may seem far removed from our lives. Yet, like us, he and his descendants had to develop ways to meet their basic needs—food, clothing, shelter, and good health. In different places around the world, new inventions and new ways of organizing activity helped people build the foundations for the societies we know today.

FOCUS ON these questions as you read:

■ **Continuity and Change**
  How have anthropologists, archaeologists, historians, and geographers helped us learn about the lives of people at different stages in history?

■ **Economics and Technology**
  What breakthrough technologies did Stone Age peoples develop?

■ **Religions and Value Systems**
  What religious beliefs and practices were developed by early peoples?

■ **Political and Social Systems**
  What are the basic features of civilization?

TIME AND PLACE

"Cave of the Hands" People of the Paleolithic age, or Old Stone Age, relied on gathering and hunting for their existence. In this South American cave painting, ancient hands seem to reach out for a herd of guanaco. The guanaco, an animal closely related to the llama, provided early Native Americans with meat and wool for clothing. **Political and Social Systems** Why do you think Paleolithic hunters needed to unite in small bands?

HUMANITIES LINK

Art History Lascaux cave paintings (page 10).
Literature In this chapter, you will encounter passages from the following works of literature: Agatha Christie, *Come, Tell Me How You Live* (page 4); *Hymn to Varuna* (page 14).

2,000,000 B.C. First use of stone tools	**18,000** B.C. Coldest period of last ice age	**15,000** B.C. Lascaux cave paintings	**9,000** B.C. Neolithic agricultural revolution	**3000** B.C. River valley civilizations emerge; recorded history begins

B.C. 2,000,000	20,000	16,000	12,000	8000	4000 B.C.

Understanding Our Past

Guide for Reading

- What methods do scientists use to find out about early peoples?
- How do historians reconstruct the past?
- How are geography and history linked?
- **Vocabulary** *prehistory, archaeologist, artifact, anthropology, technology, historian, geography, latitude, longitude*

They knew they were standing on a mountain of hidden treasure. Eagerly, they set up their equipment and began drilling. A 1,300-pound bucket plunged into the mountain, bringing up heaps of "wonderful things." Despite the foul smell that rose from the mound, the scientists sorted eagerly through each pile.

These treasure hunters were members of the University of Arizona Garbage Project. On this day, they were exploring the Fresh Kills landfill on Staten Island, New York—the world's largest garbage dump. Layer by layer, the drill bored into the recent past. At 35 feet, the bucket was bringing up newspapers, grass clippings, and hot dogs from 1984. At 60 feet, the drill had reached debris from the 1940s. From each layer, the team carefully collected and labeled samples.

Members of the Garbage Project learn about our society by studying the things we have thrown away. In a similar way, other scientists find and study the objects left behind by early peoples, from their garbage to their artwork. Through such research, we are slowly learning how people lived at the dawn of human history.

How Do We Know?

The search for our ancient past has led us all over the globe and far back in time. The Iceman, whom you read about on page 2, lived in prehistoric times. Prehistory refers to the long period of time before people invented systems of writing. Prehistoric people had no cities, countries, organized central governments, or complex inventions.

About 5,000 years ago, some people in different parts of the world began to keep written records. That event marked the beginning of recorded history. Although these early records are often scanty, they do give us a narrative of events, as well as a number of names and dates.

Evidence from the past. Prehistoric evidence is of special interest to archaeologists (ahr kee AHL uh jists), scientists who find and analyze the physical remains left by early people. Such remains include bone fragments of early people or animals. Archaeologists also study artifacts, objects made by human beings. Artifacts include tools, weapons, pottery, clothing, or jewelry.

Archaeology is a branch of anthropology, the study of humans and the societies they create. Archaeologists focus on the remains of past cultures. Other anthropologists may investigate societies in different parts of the world today.

By analyzing artifacts and other items, archaeologists draw conclusions about the beliefs, values, and activities of our ancestors. Mystery writer Agatha Christie, who was married to an archaeologist, wrote that artifacts are just a way for people of the past to tell us how they lived:

> 66 'With these bone needles we sewed our clothes.' 'These were our houses, this our bathroom, here our system of sanitation!' . . . 'Here, in this little jar, is my make-up.' 'All these cook-pots are of a very common type. You'll find them by the hundred. We get them from the potter at the corner.' 99

Archaeologists at work. Analyzing ancient artifacts is difficult, but archaeologists have devised many useful techniques. In the 1800s and early 1900s, archaeologists picked a likely site, or place, to look for human remains. Then they began digging. The farther down they dug, the older the artifacts they found. Some long-buried objects crumbled as soon as they were exposed to light and air. Today, scientists have ways to preserve such fragile artifacts.

By studying thousands of items, archaeologists have traced how early people developed new technologies. Technology refers to the skills and tools people use to meet their basic needs. The first stone tools, for example, were

Unearthing the Past *In order to reach the remains of past civilizations, archaeologists must often dig through layers of sand or dirt. This photo shows a team of workers carefully uncovering one section of an ancient Middle Eastern city.* **Economics and Technology** *At what level of an excavation site would archaeologists find the most primitive artifacts? Explain.*

crudely made with jagged edges and rough surfaces. Stone tools from later times are smooth and polished, showing improved skills.

Archaeologists today also make detailed maps locating every artifact they find. By analyzing this evidence, they can tell what went on at different locations within a site. Flint chips, for example, might suggest the workplace of a toolmaker. Piles of shells or gnawed bones may show where prehistoric people threw their garbage.

Technology and the past. Archaeologists use modern technology to study and interpret their findings. Computers can be used to store and sort data or to develop accurate site maps. Aerial photography can reveal patterns of how people used the land. Techniques for measuring radioactivity help chemists and physicists determine the age of objects.

Geologists, or experts on earth science, help archaeologists date artifacts by determining the age of nearby rocks. Botanists and zoologists, experts on plants and animals, examine seeds and animal bones to learn about the diet of early people. Experts on climate determine what conditions early people faced on the plains of Africa

or in ice-covered parts of Europe. Biologists analyze human bones, as well as bloodstains found on old stone tools and weapons.

Historians Reconstruct the Past

While archaeologists have uncovered useful information about the past, most of what goes into a textbook like this one comes from the work of historians. Historians study how people lived in the past. Like archaeologists, historians study artifacts, from clothing and coins to artwork and tombstones. However, they rely even more on written evidence, such as letters or

GLOBAL CONNECTIONS

Today, most historians and nations officially use the Christian Era calendar, based on the life of Jesus Christ. Years are dated either B.C. (before Christ) or A.D. (*anno domini*, "year of the Lord"). But the Christian calendar is not the only one used in the world. For example, the Chinese, Jews, and Muslims have their own dating systems. The year 2000 on the Christian calendar will overlap the Muslim year 1371, the Chinese year 4637, and the Jewish year 5761.

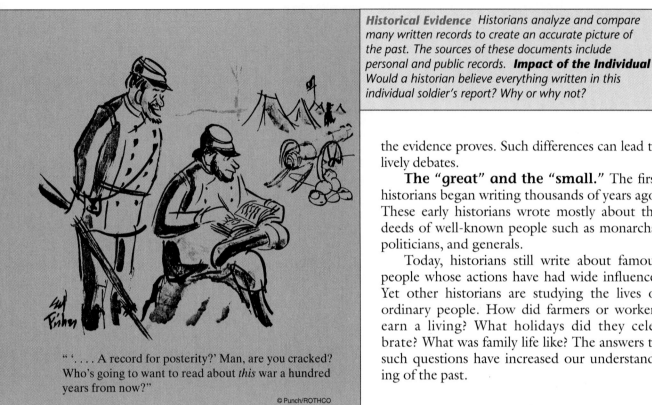

" '. . . . A record for posterity?' Man, are you cracked? Who's going to want to read about *this* war a hundred years from now?"

© Punch/ROTHCO

tax records. Historians of the recent past also use such evidence as photographs or films.

Historical detection. Like a detective, the historian must evaluate the evidence to determine if it is reliable. Do records of a meeting between two officials tell us exactly what was said? Who was taking notes? Does a videotape of an event show everything that happened? Was a letter writer really giving an eyewitness report or just passing on rumors? Could the letter even be a forgery? The historian tries to find the answers.

Historians then must interpret the evidence, explaining what it means. Often, the historian's goal is to determine the causes of a certain development or event, such as a war or an economic collapse. By explaining why things happened in the past, the historian can help us understand what is going on today and what may happen tomorrow.

Generally, historians try to give a straightforward account of events. Sometimes, though, their personal experiences, cultural backgrounds, or political opinions may affect their interpretations. At times, historians disagree about what

the evidence proves. Such differences can lead to lively debates.

The "great" and the "small." The first historians began writing thousands of years ago. These early historians wrote mostly about the deeds of well-known people such as monarchs, politicians, and generals.

Today, historians still write about famous people whose actions have had wide influence. Yet other historians are studying the lives of ordinary people. How did farmers or workers earn a living? What holidays did they celebrate? What was family life like? The answers to such questions have increased our understanding of the past.

Geography and History

Geography is one key to understanding history because it is the stage on which all history takes place. In its broadest sense, geography is the study of people, their environments, and the resources available to them. Like archaeologists and historians, geographers must often draw conclusions from limited evidence. For example, tons of river mud found in the ruins of an ancient city may indicate that the city was wiped out by a flood. Similarities in language and art in widely separated regions may suggest that there was once contact between the two places.

Five themes sum up the impact of geography on the human story. They are location, place, human-environment interaction, movement, and region.

Location. Location tells where a place is on the surface of the Earth. You can locate any place on a map using latitude and longitude. Latitude measures distance north or south of the Equator. Longitude measures distance east and west of the Prime Meridian, an imaginary line that runs north to south through Greenwich, England. For example, you can locate the city of Seoul, South Korea, at 37° N latitude and

127° E longitude. These numbers give its exact location.

Relative location, where one place is located in relation to another, is sometimes more important than exact location. Ancient Athens, for example, was located on the eastern Mediterranean Sea, near much older civilizations in Egypt and the Middle East. This relative location influenced the Athenians' way of life because they acquired valuable skills and ideas from their neighbors.

Place. Geographers describe places in terms of their physical features and human characteristics. Physical features of a place include landforms, bodies of water, climate, soil quality, resources, and plant and animal life. Human characteristics include where most people live, their economic activities, religious beliefs, and languages.

Human-environment interaction. Since prehistoric times, people have interacted with their environment. That is, they have shaped and been shaped by the places in which they lived. Early farmers, for example, used water from rivers to irrigate their crops. Much later, European settlers in the Americas cut down trees to clear land for farms. As technology has advanced, we have changed the environment in

Geography Makes a Difference Where people live affects how they live. Differences in landforms, bodies of water, climate, and natural resources help shape a variety of human cultures. Note some of the differences between life in Siberia (right) and life in Vietnam (above).
Diversity Identify two cultural differences shown by these photos. How might geography help create this cultural diversity?

more complex ways. Today, roads slice through deserts, and canals link distant bodies of water. The impact of these changes has led people to look at the environment in new ways.

Movement. The movement of people, goods, and ideas is another key link between geography and history. In early times, people followed herds of deer or buffalo on which they depended for food. In more recent times, people have migrated, or moved, from farms and villages to cities in search of jobs. Others have fled from war or religious persecution.

In ancient times, as today, traders have carried goods from one part of the Earth to another. Ideas also move, carried by people like missionaries or settlers. Today, communications satellites and television cables carry ideas faster and farther than ever before.

Region. Geographers divide the world into many types of regions. Some regions are based on physical features. The Gulf States, for example, are those countries bordering the Persian Gulf. They are part of a larger region of southwestern Asia, which we today call the Middle East. Regions may also be defined by political, economic, or cultural features. Culturally, the Gulf States are part of two larger regions, the Arabic-speaking world and the Muslim world.

SECTION 1 REVIEW

1. **Define** (a) prehistory, (b) archaeologist, (c) artifact, (d) anthropology, (e) technology, (f) historian, (g) geography, (h) latitude, (i) longitude.
2. How do archaeologists learn about the lives of prehistoric people?
3. What kinds of evidence do historians use to study the past?
4. Give two examples of how people interact with their environment.
5. *Critical Thinking* **Linking Past and Present** Historians and archaeologists have worked to piece together the human story from prehistory up to today. Why do you think it is important to understand our past?
6. *ACTIVITY* Make a list of artifacts that you might find in the weekly trash from your community. Then, describe what archaeologists of the future might learn from these artifacts.

The Dawn of History

Guide for Reading

■ What advances did people make during the Old Stone Age?

■ What can we learn about the religious beliefs of early people?

■ Why was the agricultural revolution a turning point in history?

■ **Vocabulary** *nomad, glacier*

A small band of hunters and food gatherers were camped on the shore of Lake Turkana in East Africa. One member of the group picked up a stone and chipped it with another stone to make a sharp, jagged edge. The toolmaker may have used this simple tool to cut meat from a dead animal or to sharpen a stick for digging up edible roots.

The toolmaker left the chipped stone near the lake. Some three million years later, archaeologist Richard Leakey picked it up. Leakey later described how he felt holding the tool:

66It is a heart-quickening thought that we share the same . . . heritage with the hand that shaped the tool that we can now hold in our own hands, and with the mind that decided to make the tool that our minds can now contemplate.99

Very slowly, early people learned to make better tools and weapons from stone, bone, and wood. They also developed new skills. Technological advances like these helped more people to survive.

Hunters and Food Gatherers

Historians call the earliest period of human history the Old Stone Age, or Paleolithic age. This long period dates from the time of the first stone toolmakers to about 10,000 B.C.

African beginnings. In the last few decades, anthropologists have found startling evidence of early human life in East Africa. In 1959, Mary and Louis Leakey found pieces of

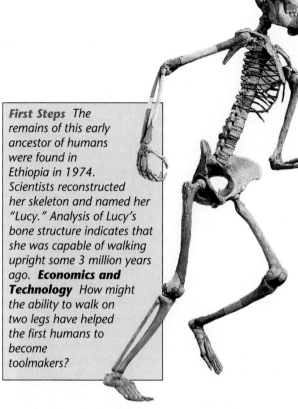

First Steps *The remains of this early ancestor of humans were found in Ethiopia in 1974. Scientists reconstructed her skeleton and named her "Lucy." Analysis of Lucy's bone structure indicates that she was capable of walking upright some 3 million years ago.* **Economics and Technology** *How might the ability to walk on two legs have helped the first humans to become toolmakers?*

bone embedded in ancient rock at Olduvai (OHL duh way) Gorge in Tanzania. After careful testing, they determined that the bone belonged to early humans. In 1974, Donald Johanson found part of a humanlike skeleton in Ethiopia. He named his find "Lucy" after a Beatles song.

Because of such evidence, scientists think that the earliest people lived in East Africa. Later, their descendants migrated north and east into Europe and Asia. In time, people reached the Americas, Australia, and the islands of the Pacific.

Nomads on the move. Paleolithic people lived in small hunting and food-gathering bands numbering about 20 or 30 people. Everyone contributed to feeding the group. In general, men hunted or fished. Women, with their small children, gathered berries, fruit, nuts, wild grain, roots, or even shellfish. This food kept the band alive when game was scarce. Paleolithic people were nomads, moving from place to place as they followed game animals and ripening fruit.

People depended wholly on their environment for survival. At the same time, they found ways to adapt to their surroundings. Men and women made simple tools and weapons such as digging sticks, spears, and axes out of the materials at hand—stone, bone, or wood. At some point, Stone Age people developed spoken language, which let them cooperate during the hunt and perhaps discuss plans for the future.

Environmental changes. Prehistoric people faced severe challenges from the environment. During several ice ages, the Earth cooled. Thick glaciers, or sheets of ice, spread across parts of Asia, Europe, and North America. To endure the cold, Paleolithic people invented clothing. Wrapped in animal skins, they took refuge in caves or under rocky overhangs during the long winters. They also learned to build fires for warmth and cooking. In this harsh life, only the hardy survived.

Early religion and art. About 30,000 years ago, people began to leave evidence of their belief in a spiritual world. To them, the world was full of spirits like those of the animals they hunted. Ancient artists may have expressed those beliefs in the pictures that they painted on cave walls.

In France, Spain, and northern Africa, cave paintings vividly portray animals such as deer, horses, and buffalo. Some cave paintings show stick-figure people, too. The paintings lie deep in the caves, far from a band's living quarters. Cave paintings may have been part of religious rituals in which hunters sought help from the spirit world for an upcoming hunt. (See the picture on page 10.)

Archaeologists have also found small stone statues that probably had religious meaning. Statues of pregnant women, for example, may have been symbols meant to ensure survival of the band. They suggest that early people worshiped earth-mother goddesses, givers of food and life.

Belief in an afterlife. Toward the end of the Old Stone Age, some people began burying their dead with great care. This practice suggests a belief in life after death. They probably believed the afterlife would be similar to life in this world, so they provided the dead with tools, weapons, and other needed goods. Burial customs like these survived in many places into modern times.

Lascaux Cave Paintings *This dramatic view of an ancient hunt exists deep within a cave in Lascaux, France. Religious beliefs probably inspired the Stone Age artists who created the scene by using paints made from crushed minerals and plants. The artists lighted their way by burning animal fats in stone dishes, and climbed wooden scaffolds to reach high walls and ceilings.* **Art and Literature** *What religious purpose do you think this cave painting might have served?*

The First Farmers

About 11,000 years ago, nomadic bands made a breakthrough that had far-reaching effects. They learned to farm. By producing their own food crops, they could remain in one place. Farmers thus settled into permanent villages and developed a whole new range of skills and tools. This change from nomadic to settled farming life ushered in the New Stone Age, or Neolithic age.

Planting seeds. No one knows when and how people began to plant seeds for food. Some scholars think that farming started in the Middle East and then spread. Others argue that farming developed independently in different regions. No matter which way it occurred, the change had such dramatic effects that historians call it the Neolithic agricultural revolution.

Food-gathering women may have made the crucial discovery. They may have noticed that if seeds were scattered on the ground, new plants would grow the next year. They may also have seen that removing some plants enabled nearby ones to grow stronger. Perhaps if game animals were scarce, a band might camp at a place where plants grew and might begin cultivating them season after season.

Domesticating animals. The Neolithic revolution included a second feature. People learned to domesticate, or tame, some of the animals they had once hunted. Rather than wait

ISSUES *For* **TODAY**

Farming technology transformed the lives of Neolithic people. How does technology change the way that people meet their basic need for food?

for migrating animals to return each year, hunters rounded them up. Then they herded the animals to good grasslands or penned them in rough enclosures. The animals provided people with a source of protein.

The Neolithic agricultural revolution enabled people to become food producers for the first time. It led to a growth in population, which in turn led to more interaction among human communities. No greater change in the way people lived took place until the Industrial Revolution, which began in the late 1700s.

Skara Brae, A Neolithic Village

On a windy blue bay in the Orkney Islands, north of Scotland, lies a cluster of half-buried stone houses. Their roofs are long gone. Sheep browse on a green hillside to one side of the houses. On the other side, the chilly waters of the bay wash against the gravel shore.

About 5,000 years ago, a Neolithic village stood on this site. Buried among the ruins of Skara Brae (SKA ruh BRAY), archaeologists have found artifacts that give us clues to the lives of these early farmers.

Skara Brae is tiny. The entire village covers an area about equal to three classrooms. Each house is similar to its neighbor, showing that people were relatively equal in social status. Its single room contains a central, square fireplace, two or three stone shelves against the wall, and a sleeping area set off by stone slabs.

At work and play. If you had visited Skara Brae in the New Stone Age, you would have seen some people planting barley or wheat in the fields near their homes. Children might be tending pigs, cows, or sheep like the ones that graze there today. Other villagers might have been fishing along the shore. In a village such as Skara Brae, cooperation was essential. Families lived close together and depended on one another for survival.

At nightfall, each family probably gathered around its own hearth. They cooked meat or fish in clay pots and baked bread in a small stone oven. Smoke quickly filled the tiny hut, but its walls protected the family from the blustering winds outside.

Gathered around the fireplace, the family might talk over the day's events or make plans for the next day. Perhaps an adult told stories passed down from generation to generation. Children and adults might also have played games. Among the artifacts archaeologists found at Skara Brae were two bone cubes with markings like those on modern dice.

In the village workshop. At one end of the village, chips of flint and chert, a local stone,

A Neolithic Home This photograph shows the remains of a one-room house at the Neolithic village of Skara Brae. To the rear of the house are stone shelves for storing possessions, and to the left is a sleeping area. The house was buried within a mound of dirt for protection from the harsh climate.
Geography and History *What role did geography play in the use of stone rather than wood for buildings in Skara Brae?*

indicate the location of a workshop. There, villagers made tools, including smooth, polished ax heads and chipped arrowheads.

Like Neolithic people elsewhere, the villagers of Skara Brae made clay pots. They had not, however, mastered another basic technology, weaving cloth. In other parts of the world, Neolithic people had learned to weave cloth from animal hair or vegetable fibers. The people of Skara Brae, on the other hand, sewed together animal skins to make clothing, as their Paleolithic ancestors had.

Archaeologists have found many bone beads at Skara Brae. Some were strung into necklaces, while others may have decorated fur or leather clothing. Some stone objects remain mysterious. They are smooth, polished, and marked with patterns of lines, bumps, and hollows. Possibly village religious leaders used these stones in their ceremonies.

Respect for the dead. Villagers buried their dead in earthen tombs surrounded by stone walls. Like other Neolithic people, they showed respect for the dead and may have called on the spirits of their buried ancestors to help them in this world. ▪

Changing Ways of Life

How did the lives of Neolithic farmers differ from those of Paleolithic hunters and gatherers? They probably divided up the work much as their ancestors had done, by gender and age. Still, important differences began to emerge. In settled farming communities, the status of women declined as men came to dominate family, economic, and political life.

Village leaders. Heads of families, probably older men, formed a council of elders. They were responsible for important decisions, such as when to plant or harvest. In time, a village headman, or chief, may have emerged.

During times of economic scarcity, warfare increased and some men gained great prestige as warriors. These elite warriors asserted power over both women and other men. The changes did not mean that women lost all their influence or rights. Rather, they show that village life was reshaping the roles of both women and men.

More possessions. Settled people accumulated more personal property than their no-

madic ancestors. The beads, pottery bowls, and other prized objects displayed on the stone shelves at Skara Brae may have made some families feel wealthier than their neighbors. Great differences among social classes did not yet exist, however.

New technologies. To farm successfully, people had to develop new technologies. Like farmers today, they had to find ways to protect their crops and measure out enough seed for the next year's harvest. They also needed to measure time accurately so that they would know when to plant and harvest. Gradually, they created the first calendars. In some places, farmers learned to use animals such as oxen or water buffalo to plow the fields.

Inventions did not take place everywhere at the same time. Technologies might travel slowly from one area to another, taking thousands of years to spread across continents. Other technologies may have been invented separately in different parts of the world.

By about 5,000 years ago, the advances made by early farming communities led people to a new stage of development—the emergence of civilizations.

SECTION 2 REVIEW

1. **Identify** (a) Paleolithic age, (b) Neolithic age, (c) Skara Brae.
2. **Define** (a) nomad, (b) glacier.
3. How did Paleolithic people learn to adapt to their environment?
4. What do burial customs suggest about the beliefs of early peoples?
5. (a) What were the key features of the agricultural revolution? (b) How did it change people's lives?
6. *Critical Thinking* **Recognizing Causes and Effects** (a) Why might economic scarcity lead to increased warfare? (b) Why do you think this change may have affected the status of women in Stone Age societies?
7. *ACTIVITY* With a classmate, prepare and act out a conversation between someone who lived in Paleolithic or Neolithic times and someone living today. Discuss what you each do every day, what you eat, how you dress, or how you spend your leisure time.

3 Beginnings of Civilization

Guide for Reading

- What are the basic features of civilizations?

- How did the first cities emerge?

- What developments can cause cultures to change?

- **Vocabulary** *bureaucracy, polytheistic, artisan, pictogram, scribe, city-state, empire, steppe, cultural diffusion*

Perhaps the best-known monuments of the ancient world are the great pyramids of Egypt. More than 100,000 workers labored for years under the hot North African sun to build these giant tombs. Without modern machinery, they fit into place more than two million stones *weighing an average of 2 1/2 tons each!*

Clearly, pyramid building required a society more highly organized and technologically advanced than Neolithic farming villages. In fact, the pyramids were created by one of the world's first civilizations. In Egypt, as in other parts of the world, people were taking a giant step from prehistory into history.

Dawn of Civilization *The development of cities marked the beginning of civilization. In the Americas, cities such as this Mayan one at Uxmal served as political and religious centers. The temple-pyramid towering above the surrounding landscape offers lasting evidence of Mayan devotion to their gods.* ***Religions and Value Systems*** *Why do you think nature gods were so important to people of early civilizations?*

Features of Civilization

What do we mean by civilization? What did the early civilizations that rose in different parts of the globe have in common? Historians distinguish eight basic features found in most early civilizations. These eight features are (1) cities, (2) well-organized central governments, (3) complex religions, (4) job specialization, (5) social classes, (6) arts and architecture, (7) public works, and (8) writing.

Rise of cities. The central feature of civilization was the rise of cities. The first cities emerged after farmers began cultivating fertile lands along river valleys and producing surplus, or extra, food. These surpluses in turn helped populations to expand. As populations grew, some villages swelled into cities.

River valley civilizations. Cities rose independently in the valleys of the Tigris and Euphrates rivers in the Middle East, the Nile River in Egypt, the Indus River in India, and the Yellow River, or Huang He, in China. (See the map on page 1.) Conditions in these river valleys favored farming. Flood waters spread silt across the valleys, renewing the soil and keeping it fertile. The animals that flocked to the rivers to drink were another source of food. In addition, rivers provided a regular water supply and a means of transporting people and goods.

Rivers also posed challenges. Farmers had to control flooding and channel waters to the fields. To meet these challenges, cooperation was needed. Early farmers worked together to build dikes, dig canals, and carve out irrigation ditches. Such large-scale projects required leadership and a well-organized government.

Civilizations in the Americas. Unlike the civilizations in Asia, Africa, and Europe, civilizations in the Americas often did not rise in

river valleys. Two major civilizations, the Aztecs and Incas, eventually emerged in the highlands of Mexico and Peru.

In the Americas, the first cities may have begun as religious centers. There, powerful priests inspired people from nearby villages to build temples to their gods. Villagers would gather at the temples for regular worship. In time, many may have remained permanently, creating cities like those elsewhere.

Organized Governments

As cities grew, they needed to maintain a steady food supply. To produce large amounts of food and oversee irrigation projects, new forms of government arose. City governments were far more powerful than the councils of elders and local chiefs of farming villages.

At first, priests probably had the greatest power. In time, warrior kings emerged as the chief political leaders. They took over the powers of the old councils of elders and set themselves up as hereditary rulers who passed power from father to son.

Almost always, rulers claimed that their right to rule came from the gods. They thus gained religious power as well. Darius the Great, ruler of the vast Persian empire, proclaimed that his power came directly from Ahura Mazda, the supreme Persian god:

> 66Ahura Mazda bestowed the kingdom
> upon me. Ahura Mazda bore me aid
> until I got possession of this kingdom.
> By the favor of Ahura Mazda I hold
> this kingdom.99`

Government became more complex as rulers issued laws, collected taxes, and organized systems of defense. To enforce order, rulers relied on royal officials. Over time, government bureaucracies evolved. A bureaucracy is a system of managing government through departments run by appointed officials. Separate departments oversaw tax collection, irrigation projects, or the military.

Complex Religions

Like their Stone Age ancestors, most ancient people were polytheistic. That is, they be-lieved in many gods. People appealed to sun gods, river goddesses, and other spirits that they believed controlled natural forces. Other gods were thought to control human activities such as birth, trade, or war.

In ancient religions, priests and worshipers sought to gain the favor of the gods through complex rituals such as ceremonies, dances, prayers, and hymns. In one hymn of ancient India, a sick man humbly appeals to the god Varuna for help:

> 66Let me not go to the House of Clay,
> O Varuna!
> Forgive, O gracious Lord,
> forgive! . . .
> Whatever sin we mortals have
> committed against . . . the gods,
> If, foolish, we have thwarted your
> commands,
> O god, do not destroy us in your
> anger!99

To ensure divine help, people built temples and sacrificed animals, crops, or sometimes other humans to the gods. Sacrifices and other ceremonies required the full-time attention of priests, who had special training and knowledge.

Job Specialization and Social Classes

The lives of city dwellers differed from those of their Stone Age ancestors. Urban people developed so many new crafts that a single individual could no longer master all the skills needed to make tools, weapons, or other goods.

Skilled artisans. For the first time, individuals began to specialize in certain jobs. Some became artisans, or skilled craftworkers, who made pottery or finely carved or woven goods. Among the crafts that developed in cities, metalworking was particularly important. People learned to make tools and weapons, first out of copper, then later out of bronze, a more durable mixture of copper and tin.

Cities had other specialists, too. Bricklayers built city walls. Soldiers defended them. Merchants sold goods in the marketplace. Singers, dancers, and storytellers entertained on public occasions. Such specialization made people dependent on others for their various needs.

PARALLELS THROUGH TIME

Jewelry

Since the rise of civilization, skilled artisans have engaged in many different crafts. One such craft is the creation of jewelry for the personal adornment of both men and women. With the passage of time, styles may change, but the human desire for beauty endures.

Linking Past and Present What precious materials have artisans of both the past and present used in their jewelry? Why do people consider these materials so valuable?

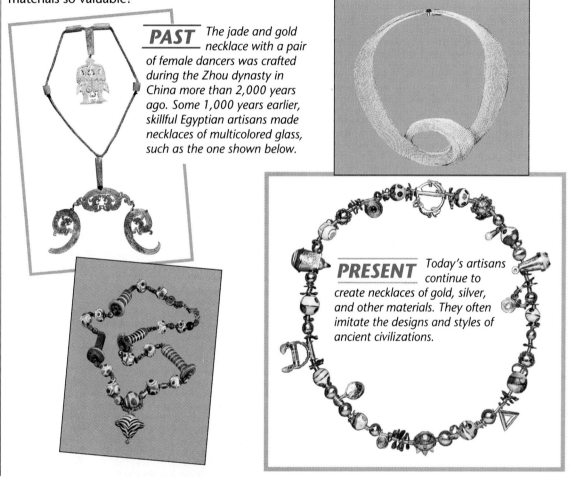

PAST *The jade and gold necklace with a pair of female dancers was crafted during the Zhou dynasty in China more than 2,000 years ago. Some 1,000 years earlier, skillful Egyptian artisans made necklaces of multicolored glass, such as the one shown below.*

PRESENT *Today's artisans continue to create necklaces of gold, silver, and other materials. They often imitate the designs and styles of ancient civilizations.*

Social ranking. In cities, social organization became more complex. People were ranked according to their jobs. Such ranking led to the growth of social classes. Priests and nobles usually occupied the top level of an ancient society. Next came a small class of wealthy merchants, followed by humbler artisans. Below them stood the vast majority of people, peasant farmers who lived in the surrounding villages and produced food for the city.

Slaves occupied the lowest social level. Slaves sometimes came from poor families who sold themselves into slavery to pay their debts. Others were prisoners captured in war. Since male captives were often killed, women and children made up the largest number of these slaves.

Arts, Architecture, and Public Works

The arts and architecture of ancient civilizations expressed the beliefs and values of the people who created them. Temples and palaces dominated the city scenery. Such buildings reassured people of the strength and power of their government and religion.

Skilled workers built and decorated these massive buildings. In museums today, you can see statues of gods and goddesses, temple wall paintings, as well as furniture and jewelry found in ancient tombs from around the world. They give ample evidence of the artistic genius of the first civilizations.

Closely linked to temples and palaces were vast public works that strong rulers ordered to be built. Such projects included irrigation systems, roads, bridges, and defensive walls. Although they were costly in human labor and even lives, such projects were meant to benefit the city, protecting it from attack and ensuring its food supply.

Writing

A critical new skill developed by the earliest civilizations was the art of writing. It may have begun in temples, where priests needed to record amounts of grain collected, accurate information about the seasons, and precise rituals and prayers.

Archaeologists have found masses of ancient writings, ranging from treaties and tax rolls to business and marriage contracts. Early writing was made up of pictograms, or simple drawings to show the words represented. In time, symbols were added. They might stand for sounds of words or for ideas that could not be expressed easily in pictures.

As writing grew more complex, only specially trained people called scribes learned to read and write. Scribes were educated in temple schools and kept records for priests, rulers, and merchants. In only a few societies were women permitted to attend temple schools. As a result, women were generally excluded from becoming scribes, an occupation that could lead to political power.

Spread of Civilization

As ancient rulers gained more power, they conquered territories beyond their cities. This expansion led to the rise of the city-state, a political unit that included a city and its surrounding lands and villages. Rulers, nobles, and priests often controlled the land outside the city and forced peasants to grow crops on it. A large portion of each harvest went to support the government and temples.

The first empires. Rival leaders often battled for power. Sometimes, ambitious rulers conquered many cities and villages, creating the first empires. An empire is a group of states or territories controlled by one ruler. For the conquered people, defeat was painful and often cruel. At the same time, empire building also brought benefits. It helped end war between neighboring communities and created common bonds among people.

Interactions with nomadic peoples. The first cities were scattered islands in a sea of older, simpler ways of life. Most peoples lived as their Stone Age ancestors had. They hunted, gathered food,

▲ *Replica of ancient Egyptian reed boat*

or lived in simple farming villages. On some less-fertile lands or on sparse, dry grasslands, called steppes, nomadic herders tended cattle, sheep, goats, or other animals. Because the lands were poor in water and grass, these nomads had to keep moving to find new pasture.

Nomadic cultures were not "civilized," in the sense that they did not exhibit the characteristics of city life. However, many nomadic peoples developed sophisticated traditions in oral poetry, music, weaving, animal raising, and other areas of the arts and sciences.

Throughout history, relations between nomads and city dwellers have been complex. At times, the two groups cooperated in political, economic, or military matters. At other times, they have been in conflict, with cities subduing nomadic peoples or nomads overrunning cities. You will read about such encounters in later chapters.

Civilizations and Change

All societies and civilizations change. In fact, history itself might be defined as the story of these changes. Ancient civilizations changed in many ways over the centuries. Among the chief causes of change were shifts in the physical environment and interactions among people.

Environmental changes. Like their Stone Age ancestors, people of early civilizations depended heavily on the physical environment. They needed rain and fertile soil to produce crops. Resources such as stone, timber, or metals were also essential. Changes in the environment could have an immediate impact on people's lives.

At times, sudden, drastic events devastated a community. A tremendous volcano may have wiped out Minoan civilization on the island of Crete in the Mediterranean Sea. (See Chapter 5.) Overfarming could destroy soil fertility, or rivers might become too salty. Cities would then suffer famine, and survivors would be forced to move away.

If people used up nearby timber or ran out of other building resources, they would have to adapt to this scarcity. They might, for example, trade with areas where such resources were available. Or they might use alternate building materials such as reeds.

Interactions among people. An even more important source of change was cultural diffusion, the spread of ideas, customs, and technologies from one people to another. Cultural diffusion occurred through migration, trade, and warfare.

As famine, drought, or other disasters led people to migrate, they came into contact with others whose lives differed from their own. As a result of such interactions, people often shared and adapted customs. Trade, too, introduced people to new goods or better methods of producing them. In ancient times, skills such as working bronze and writing, as well as religious beliefs, passed from one people to another.

Warfare also brought change. Often, victorious armies forced their way of life upon the people they defeated. On other occasions, the victors adopted the ways of conquered people. Sometimes, nomadic rulers would become absorbed in city life. At other times, they would rule from camps outside the city limits, keeping their own customs.

Looking ahead. In the next two chapters, you will read about the earliest civilizations that developed in the river valleys of Africa and Asia. They differed in significant ways, each developing its own traditions. At the same time, the civilizations of Egypt, Mesopotamia, India, and China all fit our definition of a civilization.

SECTION 3 REVIEW

1. **Define** (a) bureaucracy, (b) polytheistic, (c) artisan, (d) pictogram, (e) scribe, (f) city-state, (g) empire, (h) steppe, (i) cultural diffusion.
2. How did conditions in some river valleys favor the rise of civilization?
3. How were government and religion linked in early civilizations?
4. What are three causes of cultural change?
5. *Critical Thinking* **Recognizing Causes and Effects** How did job specialization lead to the emergence of social classes?
6. *ACTIVITY* Draw a three-column chart. In the first column, list the eight basic features of a civilization. In the second column, describe each feature. In the third column, give an example of each feature from modern society.

CHAPTER REVIEW

REVIEWING VOCABULARY

Review the vocabulary words in this chapter. Then, use *ten* of these words to create a crossword puzzle. Exchange puzzles with a classmate. Complete the puzzles and then check each other's answers.

REVIEWING FACTS

1. List some kinds of modern technology that can be used to study and interpret the past.
2. What are the five themes of geography?
3. What change marked the beginning of the New Stone Age?

4. How did the change from a nomadic to settled lifestyle affect the number of personal possessions that people owned?
5. List the eight features found in most early civilizations.
6. In which four river valleys did early civilizations emerge?
7. How can interactions among people cause changes in civilizations?

REVIEWING CHAPTER THEMES

Review the "Focus On" questions at the start of this chapter. Then select *three* of those questions and answer them, using information from the chapter.

SKILLS FOR SUCCESS RECOGNIZING CAUSES AND EFFECTS

Causes are the reasons why an event happened. Effects are what followed as a result of the event. The words *since* and *because* often indicate causes. The words *therefore* and *as a result* often indicate effects.

Cause-and-effect charts, like this one, organize information on causes and effects into usable form. You will encounter other, more complex cause-and-effect charts throughout this book. Those charts will show both long-term and short-term causes and effects, as well as connections to today.

Use the chart and the information in Chapter 1 to answer the following questions.

1. **Identify the causes and effects.** (a) What is the subject of the chart? (b) What were the causes? (c) What were the effects?
2. **Analyze the causes and effects.** (a) What role did technology play in the rise of civilization? (b) How did the rise of civilization lead to a more complex system of social classes?
3. **Draw conclusions based on the cause-effect relationship.** (a) What do you think was the most important effect of the rise of civilizations? (b) Why do you think cities can now exist far from fertile river valleys?

CAUSE AND EFFECT

Causes

New technologies improve farming
Food surpluses support rising populations
First cities built in fertile valleys
Farmers cooperate to control flooding and channel water

RISE OF RIVER VALLEY CIVILIZATIONS

Effects

Complex forms of government develop
Arts become more elaborate
Job specialization leads to social classes
Writing is invented

CRITICAL THINKING

1. **Recognizing Points of View** Thomas Carlyle, a Scottish writer of the 1800s, defined history as "the biography of great men." Ibn Khaldun, a Muslim historian of the 1300s, wrote that history was "information about human social organizations." (a) What is the main difference between Khaldun's definition of history and Carlyle's? (b) How might their viewpoints have affected the way each man wrote about history? (c) Which of these two points of view do you support? Explain.

2. **Applying Information** (a) Describe the area where you live in terms of each of the five themes of geography. (b) Explain two ways that geography affects your own way of life.

3. **Recognizing Causes and Effects** Make a list of five major social or technological developments of the Old Stone Age and the New Stone Age. Then, for each development, identify one short-term and one long-term effect.

4. **Linking Past and Present** (a) Describe three ways that cultural diffusion occurs. (b) Give three examples of cultural diffusion in today's world. (c) Why do you think that cultural changes occur more quickly today than ever before?

FOR YOUR PORTFOLIO

CONDUCTING AN INTERVIEW   Together with a classmate, prepare a segment for a television news magazine on major archaeological discoveries. First select a well-known archaeologist and research his or her life and work. Then write a series of questions that an interviewer might ask the archaeologist, along with answers. Prepare visual aids, such as maps, photographs, and drawings, to show during the interview. Then conduct the interview, with one of you playing the part of the archaeologist.

ANALYZING PHOTOGRAPHS

Use this photograph of the Iceman, as well as the text description on page 2, to answer the following questions.

1. Where and when was the Iceman found?
2. What role did climate play in the preservation of the Iceman's body?
3. What can scientists learn about prehistoric times from the belongings of the Iceman?

ANALYZING PRIMARY SOURCES

Use the quotation on page 14 to answer the following questions.

1. What did the man ask the god Varuna to do?
2. What might the "House of Clay" represent?
3. Why did the man ask for forgiveness of whatever sins he had committed, rather than list specific sins?

INTERNET ACTIVITY

WRITING AN ARCHAEOLOGICAL LOG
Use the Internet to research archaeological discoveries of human ancestors, such as "Lucy" or discoveries at Olduvai Gorge, in Africa. Then imagine that you were present when a site was first discovered. Write an archaeological log describing what you found.

First Civilizations: Africa and Asia

(3200 B.C.–500 B.C.)

CHAPTER OUTLINE

1 Ancient Kingdoms of the Nile
2 Egyptian Civilization
3 City-States of Ancient Sumer
4 Invaders, Traders, and Empire Builders
5 The World of the Hebrews

The dying man listened intently as the scribe read the words written on the scroll. The scroll contained the Book of the Dead, which Egyptians believed would prepare them for the perilous journey after death. Without knowing the right magical spells, the dead soul could not defeat fearsome monsters, cross a lake of fire, or outwit the sinister ferryman who piloted the dead through the underworld. One mistake and the journey was over.

Yet a still greater ordeal lay ahead. With dread, the deceased entered the hall of Osiris, god and judge of the dead. Osiris and his tribunal weighed the conscience of each soul. Eternal happiness awaited all who passed the test. To fail meant torture and extinction.

Fearfully, the deceased offered his defense:

> **66**I have made no man to suffer hunger. I
> have made no one to weep. I have
> done no murder. . . . I have not en-
> croached upon the fields of another.
> I have not added to the weights of the
> scales to cheat the seller. I have not
> misread the pointer of the scales to
> cheat the buyer.
>
> I have not turned back water when it
> should flow. I have not cut a cutting in
> a canal of running water. . . . I am pure.
> I am pure. I am pure.**99**

Like people in every society throughout history, the ancient Egyptians grappled with questions of life and death. Through the spells in the Book of the Dead, they tried to overcome earthly mortality and gain a blissful afterlife.

Egyptian civilization emerged more than 5,000 years ago. At about the same time, another center of civilization emerged in the Middle East, in Sumer. Both rose in river valleys and had the basic features of civilization that you read about in Chapter 1. While they differed from each other in significant ways, both made distinct contributions to our world today.

FOCUS ON these questions as you read:

- **Geography and History**
  What role did rivers play in shaping the first civilizations of Egypt and Mesopotamia?

- **Global Interaction**
  How did trade, warfare, and migration spread ideas and inventions among early civilizations?

- **Impact of the Individual**
  How did powerful rulers influence political, military, and religious developments in Egypt and the Fertile Cresent?

- **Diversity**
  What contributions to civilization were made by small groups such as the Phoenicians and the Hebrews?

TIME AND PLACE

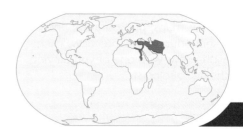

Egyptian Tomb Painting *Paintings found in the tombs of Egypt's rulers provide evidence of Egyptian religious beliefs. Here, the goddess Hathor, protector of lovers, sits next to the hawk-headed sun god Re-Harakhti. In his right hand, Re-Harakhti holds an ankh, symbol of eternal life.* **Religions and Value Systems** *What other symbols appear to have been important in ancient Egyptian religion? What are some important symbols in present-day religions?*

HUMANITIES LINK

Art History Queen Nefertiti (page 30).
Literature In this chapter, you will encounter passages from the following works of literature: Book of the Dead (page 20); *Instructions of the Vizier Ptah-hotep* (page 23); *The Tale of Sinuhe* (page 30); *The Epic of Gilgamesh* (pages 31, 34); Book of Exodus (page 45).

| **3200** B.C. Sumerians develop writing | **2700** B.C. Pyramid age begins in Egypt | **1790** B.C. Hammurabi's Code | **1503** B.C. Queen Hatshepsut of Egypt begins reign | **1000** B.C. Kingdom of Israel established | **600** B.C. Zoroaster founds new religion |

| B.C. | 3500 | 3000 | 2500 | 2000 | 1500 | 1000 | 500 | B.C. |

1 Ancient Kingdoms of the Nile

Guide for Reading

- How did geography influence Egyptian life?

- What were the main periods of early Egyptian history?

- How did trade and warfare affect the Egyptians?

- Vocabulary *silt, cataract, delta, dynasty, pharaoh, vizier*

Every year, the great Nile River in northeastern Africa flooded its banks. As the waters rose, the people of ancient Egypt offered thanks: "Hail to thee, O Nile, that issues from the earth and comes to give life to Egypt." They praised the Nile for nourishing their land and cattle and for filling their storehouses with food.

The fertile lands of the river valley attracted Stone Age farmers. In prehistoric times, migrating people reached Egypt from the Mediterranean area, from hills and deserts along the Nile, and from other parts of Africa. As these early farmers produced more food, populations grew. In the Nile Valley, a powerful civilization emerged that depended on the control of river waters.

Geography: The Nile Valley

Egypt, said the ancient Greek historian Herodotus, "is wholly the gift of the Nile." Without the Nile, Egypt would be swallowed up by the barren deserts that surround it. While the desert protected Egypt from invasion, it also limited where people could settle.

In ancient times, as today, farming villages dotted the narrow band of land watered by the Nile. Beyond the rich, irrigated "Black Land," generally no more than 10 miles (16 km) wide, lay the "Red Land," a sun-baked desert that stretches across North Africa.

Farmers took advantage of the fertile soil of the Nile Valley to grow wheat and flax, a plant whose fibers were used for clothing. By the time of Herodotus, Egypt had been producing large amounts of food for thousands of years. It had become known as a "breadbasket," exporting food to other parts of the Mediterranean world.

Yearly floods. The Nile rises in the highlands of Ethiopia and the lakes of central Africa. Every spring, rains in this interior region send water racing down streams that feed the Nile River. In ancient times, Egyptians eagerly awaited the annual flood. It soaked the land with life-giving water and deposited a layer of rich silt, or soil. An Egyptian hymn expressed the happiness of the people during this season:

❝If the Nile smiles, the Earth is joyous,
 Every stomach is full of rejoicing,
 Every spine is happy
 Every jawbone crushes its food.❞

People had to cooperate to control the Nile floods. They built dikes, reservoirs, and irrigation ditches to channel the rising river and store water for the dry season.

Uniting the land. Ancient Egypt had two distinct regions, Upper Egypt in the south and Lower Egypt in the north. Upper Egypt stretched from the first cataract, or waterfall, of the Nile northward to within 100 miles (160 km) of the Mediterranean. Lower Egypt covered the delta region where the Nile empties into the Mediterranean. A delta is a triangular area of marshland formed by deposits of silt at the mouth of some rivers.

About 3100 B.C., Menes, the king of Upper Egypt, united the two regions. He and his successors used the Nile as a highway linking north and south. They could send officials or armies to towns along the river. The Nile thus helped make Egypt the world's first unified state.

The river also served as a trade route. Egyptian merchants traveled up and down the Nile in sailboats and barges, exchanging the products of Africa, the Middle East, and the Mediterranean world.

The Pyramid Age

The history of ancient Egypt is divided into three main periods: the Old Kingdom (about 2700 B.C.–2200 B.C.), the Middle Kingdom (about 2050 B.C.–1800 B.C.), and the New

Kingdom (about 1550 B.C.–1100 B.C.). During these periods, power passed from one dynasty, or ruling family, to another, but the land generally remained united.

Old Kingdom. During the Old Kingdom, pharaohs (FAIR ohz), as Egyptian rulers were called, organized a strong, centralized state. Pharaohs claimed divine support for their rule. Egyptians believed the pharaoh was a god. The pharaoh thus had absolute power, owning and ruling all the land.

Pharaohs of the Old Kingdom took pride in preserving justice and order. A pharaoh depended on a vizier, or chief minister, to supervise the business of government. Under the vizier, various bureaus looked after matters such as tax collection, farming, and the all-important irrigation system. Thousands of scribes carried out the vizier's instructions.

A wise vizier, Ptah-hotep (tah HOH tehp), took an interest in training young officials. Based on his vast experience of government, he wrote a book, *Instructions of the Vizier Ptah-hotep*. In it, he advised ambitious young people to avoid the errors he had seen all too often among officials:

> 66 Let not your heart be puffed up because of your knowledge; be not confident because you are wise. Take counsel with the ignorant as well as the wise. 99

Majestic tombs. The Old Kingdom is sometimes called the Pyramid Age because during this period the Egyptians built the majestic pyramids that still stand at Giza, near present-day Cairo. The pyramids were tombs for eternity. Because Egyptians believed in an afterlife, they preserved the bodies of their dead rulers and provided them with everything they would need in their new lives.

To complete the pyramids, workers hauled and lifted millions of limestone blocks that weighed an average of 2½ tons each. The pyramid builders had no iron tools or wheeled vehicles. Workers quarried each stone by hand, pulled them on sleds to the site, and hoisted them up earthen ramps to be placed on the slowly rising structure. Building a pyramid took so many years that often a pharaoh would begin building his tomb as soon as he inherited the throne.

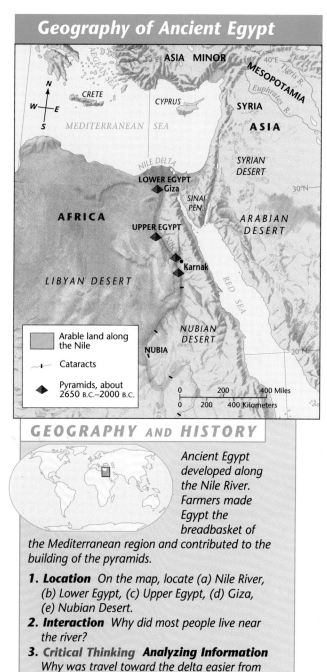

Geography of Ancient Egypt

Arable land along the Nile

Cataracts

Pyramids, about 2650 B.C.–2000 B.C.

0   200   400 Miles
0   200   400 Kilometers

GEOGRAPHY AND HISTORY

Ancient Egypt developed along the Nile River. Farmers made Egypt the breadbasket of the Mediterranean region and contributed to the building of the pyramids.

1. **Location** On the map, locate (a) Nile River, (b) Lower Egypt, (c) Upper Egypt, (d) Giza, (e) Nubian Desert.
2. **Interaction** Why did most people live near the river?
3. **Critical Thinking** *Analyzing Information* Why was travel toward the delta easier from the northernmost cataract?

The pyramids suggest the strength of ancient Egyptian civilization. These costly projects took years to complete and required enormous planning and organization. Thousands of farmers, who had to be fed each day, worked on the pyramids when not planting or harvesting crops.

The Middle Kingdom

Power struggles, crop failures, and the cost of building the pyramids contributed to the collapse of the Old Kingdom. After more than a century of disunity, new pharaohs eventually emerged to reunite the land, ushering in the Middle Kingdom.

The Middle Kingdom was a turbulent period. The Nile did not rise as regularly as it had. Corruption and rebellions were common. Still, strong rulers did organize a large drainage project, creating vast new stretches of arable, or farmable, land. Egyptian armies occupied part of Nubia, the gold-rich land to the south. Traders also had greater contacts with the peoples of the Middle East and the Mediterranean island of Crete.

Catastrophe struck about 1700 B.C. when foreign invaders, the Hyksos (HIHK sohs), occupied the delta region. They awed the Egyptians with their horse-drawn war chariots. In time, the Egyptians would master this new military technology. The Hyksos, in turn, were so impressed by Egyptian civilization that they soon adopted Egyptian customs, beliefs, and even names.

The Hyksos dominated Egypt for more than 100 years. Finally, new Egyptian leaders arose, drove out the foreigners, and set up the New Kingdom.

The Egyptian Empire

During the New Kingdom, powerful and ambitious pharaohs created a large empire. At its height, the Egyptian empire reached the Euphrates River. This age of conquest brought Egypt in greater contact with the Middle East as well as other parts of Africa.

Queen Hatshepsut. Among the outstanding rulers of the New Kingdom was Hatshepsut (hat SHEHP soot), daughter of one pharaoh and widow of another. Like some earlier Egyptian queens, Hatshepsut began by ruling in the name of a male heir too young to take the throne. However, she then took the bold step of declaring herself pharaoh and won the support of key officials. Because Egyptians saw kingship as a male privilege, she donned a false beard as a sign of authority.

Great Sphinx at Giza The Great Sphinx silently guards the pyramid tombs of Egyptian pharaohs. Originally painted in vivid colors, this figure of a crouching lion bears the face of King Khafre. **Political and Social Systems** What does the portrayal of the king as a lion suggest about the nature of kingship in ancient Egypt?

On the walls of her beautiful funeral temple, Hatshepsut left a record of her reign from 1503 B.C. to 1482 B.C. Carvings and writings proclaim her power and right to rule:

66Lo, the god knows me well,
    Amon, Lord of Thrones-of-the-
    Two Lands.
He made me rule Black Land and Red
    Land as a reward.
No one rebels against me in all lands.99

Other carvings describe how she encouraged trade with eastern Mediterranean lands. Her greatest triumph was an expedition sent to Punt, down the Red Sea coast of Africa. We do not know exactly where Punt was, but ships returned loaded with ebony, ivory, spices, leopard skins, and live monkeys for private zoos. They also brought back incense, medicines, and myrrh trees, much valued for their perfume. Hatshepsut had the fragrant trees planted near her temple.

Ramses II. A later pharaoh, Ramses II, won fame for his military victories. Between 1290 B.C. and 1224 B.C., he pushed Egyptian rule northward through Palestine and as far as Syria. On temples and other monuments, he boasted of his conquests, though his greatest victory may not have actually taken place. In a battle against the Hittites of Asia Minor, only the desperate bravery of Ramses himself prevented a crushing defeat. Back home, however, Ramses had inscriptions carved on a monument that made the near defeat sound like a stunning victory.

After years of fighting, the Egyptians and Hittites finally signed a peace treaty, the first such document to have survived in history. The treaty declared

66Egypt, with the land of Hatti [the Hittites], shall be at peace and in brotherhood forever. Hostilities shall not occur between them forever.99

Decline. After Ramses II, Egyptian power slowly declined. Invaders, such as the Assyrians and Persians, conquered the Nile region. (See the map on page 39.) Later, Greek and Roman armies marched into the rich Nile Valley. Each new conqueror was eager to add the Egyptian breadbasket to a growing empire.

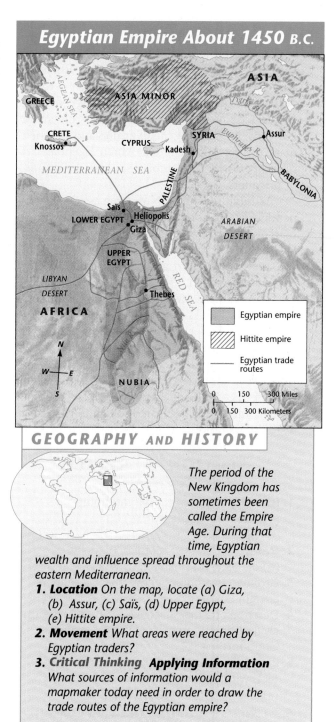

Egyptian Empire About 1450 B.C.

Egyptian empire
Hittite empire
Egyptian trade routes

0   150   300 Miles
0 150 300 Kilometers

GEOGRAPHY AND HISTORY

The period of the New Kingdom has sometimes been called the Empire Age. During that time, Egyptian wealth and influence spread throughout the eastern Mediterranean.

1. **Location** On the map, locate (a) Giza, (b) Assur, (c) Saïs, (d) Upper Egypt, (e) Hittite empire.
2. **Movement** What areas were reached by Egyptian traders?
3. **Critical Thinking** **Applying Information** What sources of information would a mapmaker today need in order to draw the trade routes of the Egyptian empire?

Egypt and Nubia

To the south, the Nile kingdom of Nubia (also known as Kush) developed in the shadow of Egypt. You will read more about Nubian civilization in Chapter 12. Here, we will look at the relationship between the two kingdoms.

For centuries, Egyptians traded or fought with their southern neighbor. From Nubia, they acquired ivory, cattle, and slaves. Egyptian armies conquered Nubia during the New Kingdom. The pharaoh Ramses II used gold from Nubia to pay foreign charioteers in his army. Nubians served in Egyptian armies and left their mark on Egyptian culture. Much Egyptian art of this period shows Nubian soldiers, musicians, or prisoners.

As Egypt declined, Nubia regained its independence. In about 750 B.C., Nubian kings marched north, adding Egypt to their own lands. For 100 years, Nubian kings ruled an empire that stretched from what is today Sudan to the Mediterranean.

The Nubians saw themselves not as foreign conquerors but as restorers of Egyptian glory. They ruled Egypt like the pharaohs of earlier centuries, respecting ancient Egyptian traditions. About 650 B.C., Assyrians, armed with iron weapons, descended on Egypt. They pushed the Nubians back into their original homeland, where Nubian monarchs ruled for 1,000 years more.

SECTION 1 REVIEW

1. **Identify** (a) Menes, (b) Ptah-hotep, (c) Giza, (d) Hatshepsut, (e) Punt, (f) Ramses II.
2. **Define** (a) silt, (b) cataract, (c) delta, (d) dynasty, (e) pharaoh, (f) vizier.
3. Give two examples of how the Nile shaped ancient Egypt.
4. Describe one major achievement of Egyptian civilization during each of the three ancient kingdoms.
5. Explain how Egypt was affected by its contacts with each of the following groups: (a) Hyksos, (b) Hittites, (c) Nubians.
6. *Critical Thinking* **Drawing Conclusions** How are colossal monuments such as the pyramids a source of information about ancient Egypt?
7. *ACTIVITY* Write an instruction of your own that the vizier Ptah-hotep might have written to advise a political leader of today. The topic might be how to work effectively with other people or how to govern fairly.

Egyptian Civilization

Guide for Reading

- How did religious beliefs shape the lives of Egyptians?
- How was Egyptian society organized?
- What advances did Egyptians make in learning and the arts?
- **Vocabulary** *mummification, hieroglyphics, demotic, papyrus*

From an early age, Egyptian children heard stories about their gods and goddesses. A popular tale concerned the god Osiris (oh SĪ rihs), who had ruled Egypt until he was killed by his jealous brother, Set. The wicked Set then cut Osiris into pieces, which he tossed all over Egypt.

Osiris was saved by his faithful wife, the goddess Isis (Ī sihs). She reassembled her husband's body and brought him back to life. Since Osiris could no longer rule over the living, he became god of the dead and judge of the souls seeking admission to the afterlife.

The symbol of the goddess Isis was the ankh, a cross with a loop above the bar. To Egyptians, an ankh placed on a dead person assured the soul of eternal life. "The blood of Isis," they prayed, "the charms of Isis, the power of Isis are a protection unto me." The Egyptians' belief in eternal life had a profound effect on their civilization.

Egyptian Religion

Egyptians inherited from their earliest ancestors a variety of religious beliefs and practices. Inscriptions on monuments and wall paintings in tombs reveal how Egyptians appealed to the divine forces that they believed ruled this world and the afterlife.

Chief gods and goddesses. In the sun-drenched land of Egypt, the chief god was the sun god Amon-Re (AH muhn RAY). The pharaoh, whom Egyptians viewed as a god as well as a monarch, was closely linked to Amon-Re.

Only the pharaoh could conduct certain ceremonies for the sun god.

Most Egyptians identified more easily with Osiris and Isis, whose story touched human emotions such as love, jealousy, and fear of death. According to the myth of Osiris and Isis, their son, Horus, later took revenge on the wicked god Set, killing his uncle.

To Egyptians, Osiris was especially important. Not only did he rule over the underworld, but he was also god of the Nile. In that role, he controlled the annual flood that made the land fertile. Isis had special appeal for women, who believed that she had first taught women to grind corn, spin flax, weave cloth, and care for children. Like Osiris, Isis promised the faithful they would have life after death.

A fateful test. Belief in the afterlife affected all Egyptians, from the highest noble to the lowest peasant. To win eternal life, each soul had to pass a test. Osiris weighed a soul's heart against the feather of truth. Those he judged to be sinners were fed to the crocodile-shaped Eater of the Dead. Worthy souls entered the Happy Field of Food. Egyptians believed that the afterlife would be much like life on Earth, so they buried the dead with everything they would need for eternity.

To give a soul use of its body in the afterlife, Egyptians perfected skills in mummification (muhm mih fih KAY shuhn), the preservation of the dead. Skilled embalmers removed vital organs, then dried and wrapped the body in strips of linen. This costly process took months to complete. At first, mummification was a privilege reserved for rulers and nobles. Eventually, ordinary Egyptians also won the right to mummify their dead.

Evidence of the tombs. Many pharaohs were buried in the desolate Valley of the Kings. Their tombs, filled with fantastic riches, were a temptation to robbers in ancient times. As a result, most royal tombs were stripped of their treasures long ago. Then, in 1922, the British archaeologist Howard Carter unearthed the tomb of the pharaoh Tutankhamen (too tahng KAH muhn), which had remained almost untouched for more than 3,000 years. The tomb and its treasures have provided a wealth of evidence about Egyptian civilization.

The body of the 18-year-old "King Tut" had been placed in a solid-gold coffin, nested within richly decorated outer coffins. Today, the dazzling array of objects found in the tomb fills several rooms in the Egyptian Museum in Cairo. They include chariots, weapons, furniture, jewelry, toys, games, and food. Tutankhamen was a minor king. Imagine the treasures that must have filled the tombs of great pharaohs like Ramses II.

A religious rebel. About 1380 B.C., a young pharaoh challenged the powerful priests of Amon-Re. He devoted his life to the worship of Aton, a minor god whose symbol was the sun's disk. The pharaoh took the name Akhenaton (ah kuh NAH tuhn), meaning "he who serves Aton." With the support of his wife, Queen Nefertiti, Akhenaton tried to sweep away all other gods in favor of Aton.

Scholars disagree about whether or not Akhenaton was trying to introduce a new religion based on worship of a single god. Akhenaton's radical ideas had little success, however. Priests of Amon-Re resisted the revolutionary changes. Nobles also deserted the pharaoh because he paid little attention to defending the empire. After Akhenaton's death, the priests of the old gods reasserted their power.

Mummified Cat Archaeologists have discovered an ancient Egyptian cemetery filled with mummified cats, like this one. Some Egyptians prayed to the cat goddess Bastet for protection against diseases and demons. The religious significance of cats greatly intensified Egyptians' devotion to their pets. **Continuity and Change** Can you think of any interesting beliefs that some people have about cats today?

Board Games

A benefit that accompanied the rise of civilization was an increase in leisure time. People invented games of skill and chance to occupy their free time. Many board games today are similar to their ancient ancestors.

Linking Past and Present What games today resemble the ancient Egyptian game of "twenty squares"? Explain the similarities.

PAST *The Egyptian game of "twenty squares" had a set of specially shaped game pieces that were stored in a built-in drawer. Players threw sticks to determine how they might move their pieces. We do not know the exact rules of the game, but players probably needed both luck and skill to win. The game board shown here was found in the tomb of Tutankhamen.*

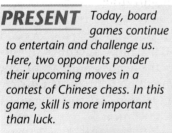

PRESENT *Today, board games continue to entertain and challenge us. Here, two opponents ponder their upcoming moves in a contest of Chinese chess. In this game, skill is more important than luck.*

Egyptian Society

Like other early civilizations, Egypt had its own class system. As both a god and an earthly leader, the pharaoh stood at the top of Egyptian society. Directly under the pharaoh were the high priests and priestesses, who served the gods and goddesses. Next came the nobles, who fought the pharaoh's wars. A tiny class of merchants, scribes, and artisans developed slowly. They provided for the needs of the rich and powerful.

The life of the farmer. Most Egyptians were peasant farmers. Many were slaves. Men and women spent their days working the soil and repairing the dikes. In the off-season, peasants were expected to serve the pharaoh, laboring on palaces, temples, and tombs. Besides working in the fields, women also spent much time raising children, collecting water, and preparing food—similar to the tasks of peasant women today.

An ancient record describes the life of a typical Egyptian peasant:

> 66When the water is full he irrigates [the fields] and repairs his equipment. He spends the day cutting tools for cultivating barley, and the night twisting ropes. Even his midday hour is spent in farm work.99

Social changes. During the New Kingdom, society grew more fluid as trade and warfare increased. Trade offered new opportunities to the growing merchant class. Foreign conquests brought riches to Egypt, which in turn meant more business for artisans. These skilled craftsworkers made fine jewelry, furniture, and fabrics for the palaces and tombs of pharaohs and nobles.

Women. Egyptian women generally enjoyed a higher status and greater independence than women elsewhere in the ancient world. Ramses II declared, "The foot of an Egyptian woman may walk where it pleases her and no one may deny her." Under Egyptian law, women could inherit property, enter business deals, buy and sell goods, go to court, and obtain a divorce.

Although there were often clear distinctions between the occupations of women and men, women's work was not confined to the home. They manufactured perfume and textiles, managed farming estates, and served as doctors. Women could also enter the priesthood, especially in the service of goddesses. Despite this equality of rights, few, if any, women learned to read and write. Even if they were literate, they were excluded from becoming scribes or holding other government jobs.

Lasting Records

Like other early civilizations, the ancient Egyptians developed a form of picture writing. Hieroglyphics (hī er oh GLIHF ihks) were used to keep important records. Early on, priests and scribes carved hieroglyphics on stone. Inscriptions on temples and other monuments preserved records of Egyptian culture for thousands of years.

Scribes. Besides learning to read and write, scribes also acquired skills in mathematics, medicine, and engineering. Temple scribes kept records of ceremonies, taxes, and gifts. Other scribes served nobles or the pharaoh. With skill and luck, a scribe from a poor family might become rich and powerful.

Over time, scribes developed demotic, a simpler form of writing for everyday use. They also learned to make a paperlike writing material from papyrus (puh PĪ ruhs), a plant that grows along the banks of the Nile. (Paper would not be invented until about A.D. 100, in China.) Writing with reed pens and ink on the smooth surface of papyrus strips was much easier than chiseling words onto stone. When writing official histories, however, scribes continued to carve hieroglyphics.

The Rosetta Stone. After the New Kingdom declined, Egyptians forgot the meanings of ancient hieroglyphics. Not until the early 1800s did a French scholar, Jean Champollion (ZHAHN shahm poh LYOHN), unravel the mysterious writings on Egypt's great monuments.

Champollion managed to decipher, or decode, the Rosetta Stone. This flat, black stone has the same message carved in three different forms of script—hieroglyphics, demotic, and Greek. By comparing the three versions, Champollion patiently worked out the meanings of many hieroglyphic symbols. As a result of that breakthrough, scholars could begin to read the thousands of surviving records from ancient Egypt.

The Wisdom of the Egyptians

The records reveal that the ancient Egyptians accumulated a vast store of knowledge in fields such as medicine, astronomy, and mathematics. They were a practical people. When they had a problem, they used trial and error to find a solution.

Medicine. Like most doctors until recent times, Egyptian physicians believed in various

Queen Nefertiti *This painted limestone sculpture of Nefertiti, wife of the pharaoh Akhenaton, reflects a change in Egyptian art. For centuries, Egyptian artists had been preoccupied with scenes of death and the afterlife. During the New Kingdom, artists turned toward portraits and representations of living people. This likeness of the queen also shows the artist's concept of an ideal of beauty.* **Art and Literature** *How did the artist use exaggeration to emphasize the beauty of Nefertiti?*

kinds of magic. Yet, through their knowledge of mummification, they learned a lot about the human body. They also became skilled at observing symptoms, diagnosing illnesses, and finding cures. Doctors performed complex surgical operations, which they described on papyrus scrolls. Many medicines that Egyptian doctors prescribed are still used, including anise, castor beans, and saffron.

Astronomy. Egyptian priest-astronomers studied the heavens, mapping constellations and charting the movements of the planets. With this knowledge, they developed a calendar that had 12 months of 30 days each and 5 days added at the end of each year. With a few changes, this ancient Egyptian calendar became the basis for our modern calendar.

Mathematics. Nile floods forced Egyptians to redraw the boundaries of fields each year. To do this, they developed practical geometry to survey the land. Egyptian engineers also used geometry to calculate the exact size and location of each block of stone to be placed in a pyramid or temple. Huge building projects such as pyramids and irrigation systems required considerable skills in design and engineering.

Literature and the Arts

Literature and art tell us much about Egyptian values and attitudes. The oldest literature includes hymns and prayers to the gods, proverbs, and love poems. Other writings tell of royal victories in battle or, like *Instructions of the Vizier Ptah-hotep*, give practical advice.

The Tale of Sinuhe. Folk tales were popular, especially *The Tale of Sinuhe*. It relates the wanderings of Sinuhe (sihn oo HAY), an Egyptian official forced to flee into what is today Syria. He fights his way to fame among the desert people, whom the Egyptians consider uncivilized. As he gets older, Sinuhe longs to return home. The story ends happily when the pharaoh welcomes him back to court. As Sinuhe sheds the life of the desert nomad for that of an Egyptian noble, he says:

> 66Years were made to pass away from my body. I was shaved, my hair was combed. . . . And I was dressed in the finest linen and anointed with the best oil. I slept on a bed, and gave up the sand to those who live [in the desert].99

The story helps us see how Egyptians viewed both themselves and the people of the surrounding desert.

Painting and sculpture. The arts of ancient Egypt included statues, wall paintings in tombs, and carvings on temples. Some show everyday scenes of trade, farming, family life, or religious ceremonies. Others boast of victories in battles.

Painting styles remained almost unchanged for thousands of years. The pharaoh and gods were always much larger than any other human figures. Artists usually drew people with their heads and limbs in profile but their eyes and shoulders facing the viewer.

Statues often depicted people in stiff, standard poses. Some human figures have animal heads that represent special qualities. The Sphinx, which crouches near the pyramids at Giza, portrays an early pharaoh as a powerful lion. (See the photograph on page 24.)

Besides the pyramids, Egyptians erected other great buildings. The magnificent temple of Ramses II at Karnak contains a vast hall with towering 80-foot columns. Much later, the Romans would adopt building techniques like those used at Karnak.

Looking Ahead

Long after its power declined, Egypt remained a center of learning and culture in the African and Mediterranean worlds. It also retained economic importance as a source of grain and other riches. In later ages, new Egyptian cities like Alexandria and Cairo would attract scholars, traders, and other visitors. Yet, from ancient times to today, foreigners have gazed in awe at the monuments of a culture that flourished for 3,000 years.

SECTION 2 REVIEW

1. **Identify** (a) Osiris, (b) Isis, (c) Amon-Re, (d) Tutankhamen, (e) Akhenaton, (f) Jean Champollion, (g) Rosetta Stone, (h) *The Tale of Sinuhe.*
2. **Define** (a) mummification, (b) hieroglyphics, (c) demotic, (d) papyrus.
3. (a) Which gods and goddesses were especially important to the ancient Egyptians? (b) What role did they play in Egyptian life?
4. (a) What social classes existed in Egypt? (b) What rights did women have?
5. Describe three achievements of ancient Egyptians in the arts or learning.
6. *Critical Thinking* **Synthesizing Information** How were religion, government, and the arts linked in ancient Egypt?
7. *ACTIVITY* Write a headline and brief news account about the decoding of the Rosetta Stone. Include quotations from historians or archaeologists explaining why this discovery is so valuable.

3 City-States of Ancient Sumer

Guide for Reading

- How did geographic features encourage the rise of civilization in the Fertile Crescent?

- How were Sumerian government and society organized?

- What were the main achievements of Sumerian civilization?

- **Vocabulary** *ziggurat, hierarchy, cuneiform*

To the northeast of the Nile lay the cities of Sumer, in the ancient Middle East. There, people passed down stories about a hero named Gilgamesh. In time, these stories were collected into a long narrative poem, *The Epic of Gilgamesh,* which is one of the oldest works of literature in the world.

The epic tells of his fantastic adventures and daring exploits. At one point, the goddess Inanna falls in love with the young hero and proposes marriage:

66 Come to me, Gilgamesh, and be my bridegroom. . . . I will harness for you a chariot of lapis lazuli [a semiprecious stone] and of gold, with wheels of gold and of copper; and you shall have mighty demons of the storm for draft mules. 99

When Gilgamesh rejects Inanna's offer, her love turns to rage and Gilgamesh suffers miseries and heartaches.

The Epic of Gilgamesh is filled with supernatural figures and events. Yet it offers a glimpse into Sumerian civilization. We learn that the people believed in powerful goddesses who exhibited very human emotions. The Sumerians valued gold, copper, and gems, rode in wheeled chariots, and used mules to carry goods. Archaeologists have confirmed much of what the epic tells us about Sumer, the oldest civilization of the Middle East.

Geography of the Ancient Middle East

[Map: Geography of the Ancient Middle East showing BLACK SEA, CAUCASUS MTS, CASPIAN SEA, ASIA MINOR, ARMENIAN PLATEAU, TAURUS MTS, MESOPOTAMIA, ZAGROS MTS, MEDITERRANEAN SEA, SYRIAN DESERT, Euphrates R., Tigris R., Babylon, Kish, Erech, Ur, ARABIAN DESERT, SINAI PEN., EGYPT, RED SEA, PERSIAN GULF, NILE R. Compass rose showing N, W, E, S. Scale: 0 150 300 Miles / 0 150 300 Kilometers. Legend: Fertile Crescent, Sumer, Akkad, Babylonian empire]

GEOGRAPHY AND HISTORY

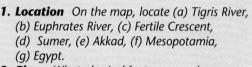

Like the Nile River in Egypt, the Tigris and Euphrates rivers gave rise to early civilizations. The rivers made the land fertile and provided avenues for trade.

1. **Location** On the map, locate (a) Tigris River, (b) Euphrates River, (c) Fertile Crescent, (d) Sumer, (e) Akkad, (f) Mesopotamia, (g) Egypt.
2. **Place** What physical features may have helped limit the expansion of Akkad?
3. **Critical Thinking** **Comparing** Look at the map on page 25. Compare the location, physical features, and size of the Egyptian and Babylonian empires.

Geography: The Fertile Crescent

If you look at the map above, you will notice an arc of land that curves from the Persian Gulf to the eastern Mediterranean coast. The dark, rich soils and golden wheat fields earned it the name the Fertile Crescent.

Nomadic herders, ambitious invaders, and traders easily overcame the few natural barriers across the Fertile Crescent. As a result, the region became a crossroads where people and ideas met and mingled. Each new group that arrived made its own contributions to the turbulent history of the region.

The land between the rivers. The first known civilization in the Fertile Crescent was uncovered in the 1800s in Mesopotamia. The Tigris and Euphrates rivers define Mesopotamia, which means "between the rivers" in Greek. The two rivers flow from the highlands of modern-day Turkey through Iraq into the Persian Gulf.

In Sumer, as in Egypt, the fertile land of a river valley attracted Stone Age farmers from neighboring regions. In time, their descendants produced the surplus food needed to support growing populations. More than 5,000 years

ago, busy cities emerged in the southern part of Mesopotamia.

Floods and irrigation. Just as control of the Nile was vital to Egypt, control of the Tigris and Euphrates was key to developments in Mesopotamia. The rivers frequently rose in terrifying floods that washed away topsoil and destroyed mud-brick villages. To survive and protect their farmland, villages along the riverbanks had to work together. Even during the dry season, the rivers had to be controlled to channel water to the fields.

Temple priests or royal officials provided the leadership to ensure cooperation. They organized villagers to build dikes to hold back flood waters and irrigation ditches to carry water to their fields.

Gradually, Sumerian civilization emerged as the first of many to flourish in the Fertile Crescent. Its achievements would influence all later Mesopotamian civilizations.

Sumerian Civilization

The Sumerians made remarkable strides. They had few natural resources, but they made the most of what they had. They lacked building materials, such as timber or stone, so they built with earth and water. They made bricks of clay, shaped in wooden molds and dried in the sun. These bricks were the building blocks for great cities like Ur and Erech.

The first cities. Sumerian cities were often rectangular in shape, surrounded by high, wide walls. Inside the city gates were broad avenues used for religious processions or victory parades. The largest buildings were ziggurats (ZIHG uh rats), pyramid-temples that soared toward the heavens. Their sloping sides had terraces, or wide steps, that were sometimes planted with trees and shrubs. On top of each ziggurat stood a shrine to the chief god or goddess of the city.

Rulers lived in magnificent palaces with spacious courtyards. Most people, though, lived in tiny houses packed in a tangled web of narrow alleys and lanes. Artisans who practiced the same trade, such as weavers or carpenters, lived and worked in the same street. These shop-lined streets formed a bazaar, the ancestor of today's shopping mall.

Economic life. Trade brought riches to the cities. Traders sailed along the rivers or risked the dangers of desert travel to carry goods to distant regions. (Although the wheel had been invented by some earlier unknown people, the Sumerians made the first wheeled vehicles.) Archaeologists have found goods from as far away as Egypt and India in the rubble of Sumerian cities.

Government. Sumer included many independent city-states. Rival cities often battled for control of land and water. For protection, people turned to courageous and resourceful war leaders. Over time, these war leaders evolved into hereditary rulers.

In each city-state, the ruler was responsible for maintaining the city walls and the irrigation

Stairway to the Gods Sumerian ziggurats were artificial mountains reaching skyward toward the heavens. At the summit of each was a shrine where priests honored their city's chief god or goddess. The sketch reconstructs a ziggurat to the goddess Inanna in the city of Ur. **Continuity and Change** Are there religious structures of today that also seem to reach to the heavens? Explain.

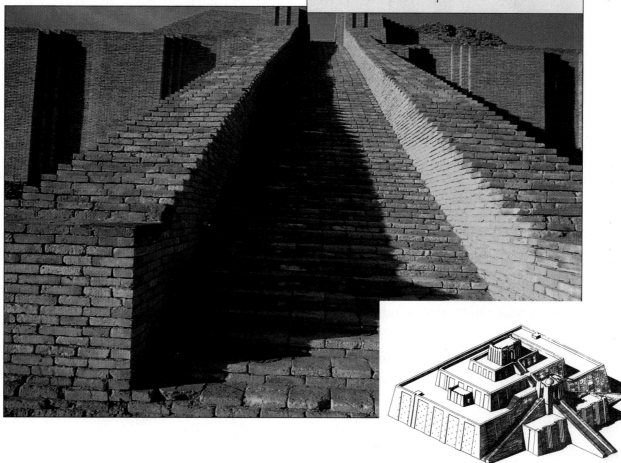

systems. He led its armies in war and enforced the laws. As government grew more complex, he employed scribes to carry out functions such as collecting taxes and keeping records. The ruler also had religious duties. He was seen as the chief servant of the gods and led ceremonies designed to please them.

Social classes. Each Sumerian city-state had a distinct social hierarchy (HĪ uh rahr kee), or system of ranks. The highest class included the ruling family, leading officials, and high priests. A small middle class was made up of merchants, artisans, and lesser priests and scribes.

At the base of society were the majority of people, peasant farmers. Some had their own land, but most worked land belonging to the king or temples. Sumerians also owned slaves. Most slaves had been captured in war. Some, though, had sold themselves into slavery to pay their debts.

Women. In the earliest Sumerian myths, a mother-goddess was the central figure of creation. She may have reflected the honored role of mothers in early farming communities. An ancient proverb advised, "Pay heed to the word of your mother as though it were the word of a god."

As large city-states emerged with warrior-leaders at their head, male gods who resembled early kings replaced the older mother-goddess. Still, in the early city-states, wives of rulers enjoyed special powers and duties. Some supervised palace workshops and ruled for the king when he was absent. One woman, Ku-Baba, became a ruler herself, rising from the lowly position of tavern owner to establish a ruling family in Kish.

Over time, as men gained more power and wealth, the status of women changed. Because they devoted their time to household duties and raising children, women became more dependent on men for their welfare. Despite these changes, women continued to have legal rights. Well-to-do women, for example, engaged in trade, borrowed and loaned money, and owned property.

Sumerian Religion

Like most ancient peoples, the Sumerians were polytheistic, worshiping many gods. These gods were thought to control every aspect of life, especially the forces of nature. Sumerians believed that gods and goddesses behaved like ordinary people. They ate, drank, married, and raised families. Although the gods favored truth and justice, they were also responsible for violence and suffering.

To Sumerians, their highest duty was to keep these divine beings happy and thereby ensure the safety of their city-state. Each city-state had its own special god or goddess to whom people prayed and offered sacrifices of animals, grain, and wine.

People celebrated many holy days with ceremonies and processions. The most important ceremony occurred at the new year when the king sought and won the favor of Inanna, the life-giving goddess of love. The king participated in a symbolic marriage with the goddess. This ritual, Sumerians believed, would make the new year fruitful and prosperous.

Like the Egyptians, the Sumerians believed in an afterlife. At death, they believed, a person descended into a grim underworld from which there was no release. In *The Epic of Gilgamesh,* which you read about on page 31, a character describes the underworld as

❝the house where one goes in and
    never comes out again,
the road that, if one takes it, one never
    comes back, . . .
the place where they live on dust,
    their food is mud;
. . . and they see no light, living
    in blackness:
on the door and door-bolt, deeply
    settled dust.**❞**

The gloomy Sumerian view of an afterlife contrasts with the Egyptian vision of the Happy Field of Food. Possibly differences in geography help account for this contrast. The floods of the Tigris and Euphrates were less regular and more destructive than the Nile floods. As a result, Sumerians may have developed a more pessimistic view of the world.

In Sumer, as in Egypt, rulers fulfilled important religious duties. How do religious values and institutions influence government?

School for Scribes

The scribe bent over the clay tablet. His hand held a stylus, or reed pen, and moved swiftly across the wet clay, leaving small wedge-shaped marks. When he had finished, he read over the text and then called an assistant to place the tablet to dry.

The first writing. By 3200 B.C., the Sumerians had invented the earliest known form of writing. This type of writing was later called cuneiform (kyoo NEE uh form) from the Latin word *cuneus* for "wedge."

Cuneiform grew out of a system of pictographs that priests used to record goods brought to temple storehouses. Later, priests developed symbols to represent more complicated thoughts. (See the chart below.) As their writing evolved, the Sumerians were able to use it to record not only grain harvests but also myths, prayers, laws, treaties, and business contracts.

School days. Sumerian scribes had to go through years of strict schooling to acquire their skills. One scribe wrote an essay describing his school days in the *edubba*, or "tablet house."

"When I arose early in the morning," he recalled, "I faced my mother and said to her: 'Give me my lunch, I want to go to school!'" He then hurried to school, knowing that if he were late he could be beaten with a cane:

> 66The fellow in charge of punctuality said: 'Why are you late?' Afraid and with pounding heart, I entered before my teacher and made a respectful bow.99

With that hurdle cleared, the boy worked hard copying his tablets. The "school-father" (teacher) and "big brother" (assistant teacher) monitored his work with a sharp eye. If he wrote untidily or talked without permission, he could be "caned." Once he even begged his father to pay the teacher more so that he would be treated more kindly.

Cuneiform Writing

Meaning	Outline character about 3000 B.C.	Sumerian about 2000 B.C.	Assyrian about 700 B.C.	Babylonian about 500 B.C.	
Sun					
God or heaven					
Mountain					
Ox					
Fish					

Interpreting a Chart *Sumerian writing developed gradually, from simple outline pictures to the wedged symbols of cuneiform. Later Mesopotamian peoples, like the scribes shown here, adapted Sumerian cuneiform to their own needs.* ■ *Based on this chart, describe how cuneiform changed between 2000 B.C. and 500 B.C.*

Each day had its routine, the student later recalled:

> **"**I recited my tablet, ate my lunch, prepared my [new] tablet, wrote it, finished it . . . and in the afternoon my exercise tablets were brought to me. When school was dismissed, I went home, entered the house, and found my father sitting there. I explained my exercise-tablets to my father, recited my tablet to him, and he was delighted.**"**

Advances in learning. Young scribes-in-training learned by copying and reciting. Most students were boys, but a few girls from wealthy families learned to read and write. Some students left school after learning simple arithmetic so that they could keep accounts. Gifted students went on to gain a wide range of knowledge about religion, medicine, mathematics, geography, astronomy, and literature.

Over the centuries, inventive Sumerians made advances in mathematics. To measure and solve problems of calculation, they developed basic algebra and geometry. They based their number system on six, dividing the hour into 60 minutes and the circle into 360 degrees, as we still do today.

Priests studied the skies, recording the movement of heavenly bodies. This knowledge enabled them to make accurate calendars, which are so essential to a farming society. In Sumerian society, as in most early civilizations, educated scribes enjoyed respect and could sometimes reach high positions. Such benefits made the long, difficult years of schooling worthwhile.

Looking Ahead

Armies of conquering peoples swept across Mesopotamia and overwhelmed the Sumerian city-states. Often the newcomers settled in the region and adopted ideas from the Sumerians. The myths and gods of these people became mingled with those of Sumer. In the process, names changed. The Sumerian goddess Inanna, for example, became Ishtar.

The newcomers adapted cuneiform to their own languages and helped spread Sumerian learning across the Middle East. Building on Sumerian knowledge of the constellations and planets, later Mesopotamian astronomers developed ways to predict eclipses of the sun and moon.

Later peoples also elaborated on Sumerian literature, including *The Epic of Gilgamesh*. In other episodes, Gilgamesh travels the world in search of eternal life. On his journey, he meets the sole survivor of a great flood that destroyed the world. (Archaeologists have found evidence suggesting that a catastrophic flood devastated Mesopotamia somewhere about 4,900 years ago.) By the end of the story, Gilgamesh has learned the greatest truth of all—that even heroes must die.

By means of the various peoples who conquered the Middle East, Sumerian knowledge passed on to the Greeks and Romans. They, in turn, had a powerful impact on the development of the western world.

▼ *Gilgamesh holding a lion*

SECTION 3 REVIEW

1. **Identify** (a) *The Epic of Gilgamesh,* (b) Inanna, (c) Ku-Baba.
2. **Define** (a) ziggurat, (b) hierarchy, (c) cuneiform.
3. How did geography influence the city-states of Sumer?
4. (a) What were the duties of Sumerian rulers? (b) How were religion and government linked?
5. Describe three accomplishments of Sumerian civilization and explain how each influenced later peoples.
6. *Critical Thinking* **Comparing** Compare school life in ancient Sumer to life in your school. How are they similar? How are they different?
7. *ACTIVITY* Review the chart on page 35. Then, create pictographic and cuneiform symbols for three objects or concepts that are important in your own life.

4 Invaders, Traders, and Empire Builders

Guide for Reading

- How did strong rulers shape the civilizations of the Fertile Crescent?

- What advances in government and technology did early civilizations make?

- How did warfare and trade influence the ancient Middle East?

- **Vocabulary** *civil law, satrap, barter economy, colony*

If you had visited the palace of the ancient Assyrian king Assurbanipal (ah soor BAH nuh pahl), you would have found the walls decorated with magnificent carvings. One scene shows Assurbanipal and his queen enjoying a picnic in their lush palace garden. Nearby, musicians entertain the royal couple.

The scene is relaxed and elegant. Look carefully, though, and you will see something startling. Hanging from a tree branch, just behind a harp player, is the head of a defeated king.

In the ancient Middle East, as elsewhere, bloody warfare and advanced culture went hand in hand. In this section, we will look at the accomplishments of Middle Eastern civilizations across 3,000 years of war and peace.

Ruling a Large Empire

Invasion and conquest were prominent features in the history of the ancient Middle East. Again and again, nomadic peoples or ambitious warriors descended on the rich cities of the Fertile Crescent. While many invaders simply looted and burned, some stayed to rule. Powerful leaders created large, well-organized empires, bringing peace and prosperity to the region.

The first empire builder. About 2300 B.C., Sargon, the ruler of neighboring Akkad, invaded and conquered the city-states of Sumer. He built the first empire known to history. His astonishing achievement did not last long, however. Soon after his death, other invaders swept into the wide valley between the rivers, tumbling his empire into ruin.

In time, the Sumerian city-states revived, and their power struggles resumed. Eventually, however, new conquerors followed in the footsteps of Sargon and imposed unity over the Fertile Crescent.

Hammurabi. About 1790 B.C., Hammurabi (hah moo RAH bee), king of Babylon, brought much of Mesopotamia under his control. He took steps to unite the Babylonian empire by publishing a remarkable set of laws, known as the Code of Hammurabi.

Hammurabi was not the author of the code. Most of the laws had been around since Sumerian times. Hammurabi, however, wanted people to know the legal principles his government would follow. So he had artisans carve the 300 laws on a stone pillar for all to see. On it, he proclaimed his goals:

> 66 To cause justice to prevail in the land,
> To destroy the wicked and evil,
> That the strong may not oppress the weak. 99

Code of Hammurabi *"If a man breaks into a house, he shall be killed in front of that break-in and buried there." This law and the rest of Hammurabi's code were cut into a seven-foot-tall pillar nearly 4,000 years ago. At the top of the pillar, this carving shows King Hammurabi standing before the god Shamash, patron of justice.* **Political and Social Systems** *Why do you think Hammurabi displayed his laws in such a public way?*

Crime and punishment. Hammurabi's Code was the first major collection of laws in history. It listed both criminal laws, dealing with murder and theft, and civil laws, dealing with private rights and matters, such as business contracts, property inheritance, taxes, marriage, and divorce.

By today's standards, the laws often seem cruel, following the principle of "an eye for an eye and a life for a life." For example, if a house collapsed because of poor construction and the homeowner was killed, the builder of the house could be put to death. Still, such a legal code was more orderly than older traditions, which permitted unrestricted personal vengeance. (▰ See *You Decide,* "How Should Society Deal With Lawbreakers?" pages 72–73.)

Laws for women. Hammurabi's Code did try to protect the powerless, including women and slaves. One law spelled out the rights of a married woman:

> ❝If a woman so hated her husband that she has declared, 'You may not have me,' her record shall be investigated at her city council, and if she . . . was not at fault . . . that woman, without incurring any blame at all, may take her dowry and go off to her father's house.❞

If the woman was not found blameless, she could be thrown into the river. Still, under Hammurabi's Code, divorce laws were fairer to women than those found in many countries until recent times. Other laws allowed a woman to own property and pass it on to her children.

In general, the code strictly regulated the behavior of women. It expected a woman to remain in her husband's home and be dependent on him. A husband, however, had a legal duty to support his wife. The code also gave a father nearly unlimited authority over his children. The Babylonians believed that an orderly household headed by a strong father was necessary for a stable empire.

Other accomplishments. Although most famous for his law code, Hammurabi took other steps to unite his empire. He improved irrigation and organized a well-trained army. He had temples repaired and promoted the chief Babylonian god, Marduk, over older Sumerian gods.

Warfare and the Spread of Ideas

Later empires shaped the Middle East in different ways. Often, conquerors uprooted the peoples they defeated. By forcing people to move elsewhere, these invaders helped spread ideas. Other conquerors, like the Hittites, brought new skills to the region.

The secret of ironworking. The Hittites pushed out of Asia Minor into Mesopotamia about 1400 B.C. While they were less advanced than the peoples of Mesopotamia, they had learned to extract iron from ore. The Hittites heated iron ore and pounded out impurities before plunging it into cold water. The tools and weapons they made with iron were harder and had sharper edges than those made out of bronze or copper. Because iron was plentiful, the Hittites were able to arm more people at less expense.

The Hittites tried to keep this valuable technology secret. But as their empire collapsed about 1200 B.C., Hittite ironsmiths migrated to serve customers elsewhere. The new knowledge thus spread across Asia, Africa, and Europe, ushering in the Iron Age.

Fierce warfare. The Assyrians, who lived on the upper Tigris, learned to forge iron weapons. By 1100 B.C., they began expanding across Mesopotamia. For 500 years, they terrorized the region, earning a reputation as one of the most warlike people in history.

No one knows why warfare was so central to Assyrian culture. Was it to keep others from attacking or to please their god Assur by bringing peace and order to the region? Assyrian rulers boasted of their brutal treatment of conquered lands. One told of capturing Babylon:

> ❝The city and its houses, from top to bottom, I destroyed and burned with fire. The walls, temples and gods, temple towers of brick and earth, as many as there were, I destroyed.❞

Assyrian society. Despite their brutality, Assyrian rulers encouraged a well-ordered society. They were the first rulers to develop extensive laws regulating life within the royal household. Riches from trade and war loot paid for the splendid palaces in well-planned cities. The women of the palace, though, were confined

Assyrian and Persian Empires

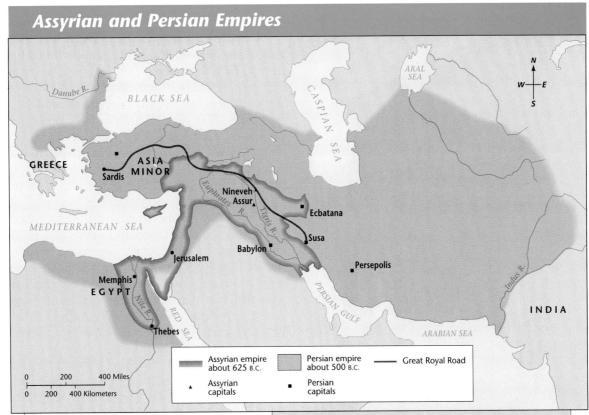

GEOGRAPHY AND HISTORY The Assyrians and Persians built huge empires in the ancient Middle East. The Persians administered their far-flung empire by building four capital cities.

1. **Location** On the map, locate: (a) Assyrian empire, (b) Persian empire, (c) Assur, (d) Susa, (e) Asia Minor.
2. **Movement** What land and water routes might a person have taken to travel from Memphis to Nineveh?
3. **Critical Thinking** **Synthesizing Information** Look at the map on page 32. What lands did the Assyrians control in about 625 B.C. that were not controlled by the Babylonians in the 1700s B.C.?

in secluded quarters and had to be veiled when they appeared in public.

At Nineveh (NIHN uh vuh), King Assurbanipal founded one of the first libraries. He ordered his scribes to collect cuneiform tablets from all over the Fertile Crescent. Those tablets have given modern scholars a wealth of information about the ancient Middle East.

Babylon revived. In 612 B.C., shortly after Assurbanipal's death, neighboring people joined forces to crush the once-dreaded Assyrian armies. An aggressive and ruthless king, Nebuchadnezzar (neh buh kuhd NEHZ uhr), revived the power of Babylon. His new Babylonian empire stretched from the Persian Gulf to the Mediterranean Sea.

Nebuchadnezzar rebuilt the canals, temples, walls, and palaces of Babylon. Near his chief palace were the famous Hanging Gardens, known as one of the wonders of the ancient world. The gardens were probably made by planting trees and flowering plants on the steps of a huge ziggurat. According to legend, Nebuchadnezzar had the gardens built to please his wife, who was homesick for the hills where she had grown up.

Astronomy. Under Nebuchadnezzar, the Babylonians pushed the frontiers of learning into new areas. Priest-astrologers were especially eager to understand the stars and planets, which they believed had a great influence on all events on Earth. Their observations of the

Royal Guardian *This huge, bull-like figure guarded the palace of an Assyrian king. Such mythical creatures stood in front of all Assyrian palaces as protection against evil spirits. Sculptors carved the bull with five legs so that, seen from the front, it appeared to be standing, while seen from the side, it appeared to be walking.* **Art and Literature** *Based on what you have read, how does this sculpture reflect the values of Assyrian society?*

heavens contributed to the growing knowledge of astronomy.

The Persian Empire

The thick walls built by Nebuchadnezzar failed to hold back new conquerors. In 539 B.C., Babylon fell to the Persian armies of Cyrus the Great. Cyrus and his successors went on to conquer the largest empire yet seen. The Persians eventually controlled a wide sweep of territory from Asia Minor to India, including what is today Turkey, Iran, Egypt, Afghanistan, and Pakistan. (See the map on page 39.)

In general, the Persians were tolerant of the people they conquered. They respected the customs and religious traditions of the diverse groups in their empire.

Uniting many peoples. The real unification of the Persian empire was accomplished under the Persian emperor Darius, who ruled from 522 B.C. to 486 B.C. A skilled organizer, Darius set up a government that became a model for later rulers. He divided the Persian empire into provinces, each headed by a governor called a satrap. Each satrapy, or province, had to pay taxes based on its resources and wealth. Special officials, "the Eyes and Ears of the King," visited each province to check on the satraps.

Like Hammurabi, Darius adapted laws from the people he conquered and drew up a single code of laws for the empire. To encourage unity, he had hundreds of miles of roads built or repaired. Roads made it easier to communicate with different parts of the empire. Darius himself kept moving from one royal capital to another. In each, he celebrated important festivals and was seen by the people.

Economic life. To improve trade, Darius set up a common set of weights and measures. He also encouraged the use of coins, which the Lydians of Asia Minor had first introduced. Most people continued to be part of the barter economy, exchanging one set of goods or services for another. Coins, however, brought merchants and traders into an early form of a money economy, replacing barter with the exchange of money. By setting up a single Persian coinage, Darius created economic links among his far-flung subjects.

A new religion. Religious beliefs put forward by the Persian thinker Zoroaster (zoh roh AS tuhr) also helped to unite the empire. Zoroaster lived about 600 B.C. He rejected the old Persian gods. Instead, he taught that a single wise god, Ahura Mazda (ah HOO ruh MAHZ duh), ruled the world. Ahura Mazda, however, was in constant battle against Ahriman (AH rih muhn), the prince of lies and evil. Each individual, said Zoroaster, had to choose which side to support.

Zoroaster's teachings were collected in a sacred book, the *Zend-Avesta*. It taught that in the end Ahura Mazda would triumph over the forces of evil. On that day, all individuals would be judged for their actions. Those who had done good would enter paradise. Evildoers would be condemned to eternal suffering. Two later religions that emerged in the Middle East,

Contributions of the Fertile Crescent

Contribution	People	Description	Connections Today
Wheeled vehicles	Sumerians	Sumerians first used wheeled vehicles to transport goods in trade.	A vital development in human history, wheeled vehicles are used by billions today.
Cuneiform	Sumerians	The Sumerian cuneiform was made up of wedge-shaped symbols. Its "alphabet" included about 300 symbols representing syllables.	Writing has developed from cuneiform to hand-writing and mechanical printing to computer-generated images and text.
Alphabet	Phoenicians	This alphabet contained 22 symbols standing for consonant sounds, written in vertical columns from right to left.	Later peoples adapted the Phoenician alphabet to produce our 26-letter alphabet.
Ironworking	Hittites	Hittites learned to extract iron from ore and fashion tools and weapons that were harder than bronze or copper ones. They helped spread knowledge of iron.	Today, iron is used to make steel products—such as cars, building materials, and utensils—and a few iron products—such as decorative railings.
Advanced knowledge of astronomy	Babylonians	Using advanced geometry, astronomers could predict eclipses of the sun and moon and the positions of planets in relation to the sun.	Today, astronomers still use geometry in the study of the moon, stars, and planets. They get much of their data from powerful telescopes and satellites.
Coins	Lydians, Persians	Early coins were made of electrum, an alloy, or natural mix, of gold and silver. The image on a coin showed its value.	Coins replaced barter, leading to the money economy of today. Now we also use paper money, plastic credit cards, and electronic transfers.

Interpreting a Chart Ancient civilizations of the Fertile Crescent made breakthroughs in writing, science, and technology. Trade and warfare spread these ideas to neighboring lands. ■ *Which contribution on the chart do you think was most important? Explain.*

Christianity and Islam, stressed similar ideas about heaven, hell, and a final judgment day.

Brave Sea Traders

While powerful rulers subdued large empires, many small states made their own contributions to civilization. The Phoenicians (fuh NEE shuhns), for example, gained fame as sailors and traders. They occupied a string of cities along the eastern Mediterranean coast, in what is today Lebanon and Syria.

Manufacturing and trade. The coastal land, though narrow, was fertile and supported farming. Still, the resourceful Phoenicians became best known for manufacturing and trade. They made glass from coastal sand. From a tiny sea snail, they produced a widely admired purple dye, called "Tyrian purple" after the city of Tyre. Phoenicians also used papyrus from Egypt to make scrolls, or rolls of paper, for books. The words *Bible* and *bibliography* come from the Phoenician city of Byblos.

Phoenicians traded with people all around the Mediterranean Sea. To promote trade, they set up colonies from North Africa to Sicily and Spain. A colony is a territory settled and ruled by people from a distant land. (★ See *Skills for Success*, page 46.)

Daring voyages. A few Phoenician traders braved the stormy Atlantic and sailed as far as England. There, they exchanged goods from the Mediterranean for tin. About 600 B.C., one Phoenician expedition may have sailed down the Red Sea and then followed the African coast around the southern tip. That historic voyage was forgotten for centuries. (In the late 1400s, Europeans claimed to be the first to round the southern tip of Africa.)

The alphabet. Historians have called the Phoenicians "carriers of civilization" because they spread Middle Eastern civilization around the Mediterranean. Yet the Phoenicians made their own contribution to our world, giving us our alphabet.

Phoenician traders needed a quick, flexible form of writing to record business deals. The wedges of cuneiform were too clumsy, so they adapted the idea of using symbols to represent spoken sounds. Their system of 22 symbols for consonant sounds became the first real alphabet.

Later, the Greeks adapted the Phoenician alphabet and added symbols for the vowel sounds. From this Greek alphabet came the letters in which this book is written. (See the chart on page 109.)

Looking Ahead

The Middle East continued to be a vital crossroads, where warriors and traders met, clashed, and mingled. Under Persian rule, scholars drew on 3,000 years of Mesopotamian learning and added their own advances to this rich heritage. In time, the achievements of this culture filtered eastward into India and westward into Europe. The chart on page 41 summarizes the impact of some Middle Eastern contributions.

Other conquerors would overwhelm the Persian empire, although different leaders revived Persian power at various times down to the present. The Middle East remained a region where diverse peoples came into close contact. Though these people lived thousands of years ago, some of their beliefs and ideas survived to shape our modern world.

SECTION 4 REVIEW

1. **Identify** (a) Sargon, (b) Hammurabi, (c) Assurbanipal, (d) Nebuchadnezzar, (e) Cyrus the Great, (f) Darius, (g) Zoroaster.
2. **Define** (a) civil law, (b) satrap, (c) barter economy, (d) colony.
3. Describe how each of the following leaders unified his empire: (a) Hammurabi, (b) Darius.
4. How did the Hittites introduce a new age of technology?
5. Why are the Phoenicians called "carriers of civilization"?
6. *Critical Thinking* **Making Inferences** Why do you think Darius supported the spread of Zoroastrianism throughout the Persian empire?
7. *ACTIVITY* Using information in this section and Section 3, create a time line of the ancient Middle East. Include the rise and fall of empires, important individuals, and turning points in technology or religion.

5 The World of the Hebrews

Guide for Reading

- What were the main events in the history of the Hebrews?
- How were Hebrew religious beliefs unique in the ancient world?
- What moral values did the Hebrew prophets preach?
- Vocabulary *monotheistic, covenant, prophet, ethics, diaspora*

The Book of Genesis records a vow made by God to the Hebrew leader Abraham:

66 I will give you many descendants, and some of them will be kings. You will have so many descendants that they will become nations. . . . I will keep my promise to you and your descendants in future generations as an everlasting covenant. I will be your God and the God of your descendants. 99

This promise of a unique relationship with God helped shape the history of the Hebrew people to the present.

At the Crossroads

The Hebrews were among the many peoples who occupied the Fertile Crescent. Living at the crossroads of civilization, they came into contact with many people and ideas. Over time, the Hebrews developed their own ideas, which reflected a blend of many traditions.

The early Hebrews came to believe that God was taking a hand in their history. As a result, they recorded events and laws in the Torah,* their most sacred text. Like many Mesopotamian peoples, the Hebrews told of a great flood that devastated the land. They believed that God had sent the flood to punish the wicked.

---

*The Torah contains five books: Genesis, Exodus, Leviticus, Numbers, and Deuteronomy. Christians later adopted these as the first five books of the Old Testament.

A nomadic people. According to the Torah, the Hebrews had lived near Ur in Mesopotamia. About 2000 B.C., they migrated, herding their flocks of sheep and goats into a region known as Canaan (later called Palestine).

The Book of Genesis tells that around 1800 B.C. a famine in Canaan forced many Hebrews to migrate to Egypt. There, they were eventually enslaved. In time, Moses, the adopted son of the pharaoh's daughter, led the Hebrews in their escape, or exodus, from Egypt. For 40 years, the Hebrews wandered in the Sinai Peninsula. After Moses died, they entered Canaan and defeated the people there, claiming for themselves the land they believed God had promised them.

The kingdom of Israel. By 1000 B.C., the Hebrews had set up the kingdom of Israel. Among the most skillful rulers of Israel were David and Solomon. According to Hebrew tradition, David was a humble shepherd who defeated a huge Philistine warrior, Goliath. Later, David became a strong and shrewd king who united the feuding Hebrew tribes into a single nation.

David's son Solomon turned Jerusalem into an impressive capital. He built a

David and Goliath
The story of David's victory over Goliath has had an enduring appeal. In this thirteenth-century French illustration, the Hebrew shepherd boy David prepares to battle the giant Philistine champion. The story provides hope and inspiration for those facing difficult challenges.
Continuity and Change *What is inaccurate about this portrayal of figures from the Bible?*

The Torah *Over time, Jewish people migrated to diverse lands. Nevertheless, Jewish communities around the world remained united by their common traditions and faith in God. Here, the sacred Torah scroll is elevated for all to see.*
Global Interaction *As shown by the illustration, what other element of Jewish culture has helped unite Jews of many lands?*

splendid temple dedicated to God, as well as an enormous palace for himself. King Solomon won praise for his wisdom and understanding. He also tried to increase Israel's influence by negotiating with powerful empires in Egypt and Mesopotamia.

Division and conquest. The kingdom of Israel paid a heavy price for Solomon's ambitions. His building projects required such heavy taxes and so much forced labor that revolts erupted soon after his death about 930 B.C. The kingdom then split into Israel in the north and Judah in the south.

Weakened by this division, the Hebrews could not fight off invading armies. In 722 B.C., Israel fell to the Assyrians. In 586 B.C., Babylonian armies captured Judah. King Nebuchadnezzar destroyed the great temple in Jerusalem and forced many Hebrews into exile in Babylon.

During their captivity, the Hebrews became known as the Jews.

Years later, when the Persian ruler Cyrus conquered Babylon, he released the Jews from captivity. Many Jews returned to Palestine, where they rebuilt King Solomon's temple in Jerusalem. Yet, like other small groups in the region, they continued to live under a series of foreign rulers, including the Persians, Greeks, and Romans.

A Covenant With God

What you have just read is an outline of early Jewish history. To the Hebrews, history and religion were interconnected. Each event reflected God's plan for the Hebrew people. In time, Hebrew beliefs evolved into the religion we know today as Judaism. Judaism differed in fundamental ways from the beliefs of nearby peoples.

Belief in one true God. Judaism was monotheistic, teaching a belief in one God. At the time, most other people worshiped many gods and goddesses. A few religious leaders, like Zoroaster in Persia and the Egyptian ruler Akhenaton, believed in a single powerful deity. However, their ideas did not have the worldwide impact that Hebrew beliefs did.

The ancient Hebrews prayed to God to save them from their enemies. Many other ancient people had also turned to particular gods or goddesses as their special protectors. But they thought of such gods as tied to certain places or people. The Hebrews believed in an all-knowing, all-powerful God who was present everywhere.

A chosen people. As you read, Jews believed that God had made a covenant, or binding agreement, with Abraham. As a result, Jews considered themselves to be God's "chosen people." Moses later renewed this covenant. He told the Hebrews that God would lead them to Canaan, the "promised land," in exchange for their faithful obedience.

The Ten Commandments. At the heart of Judaism are the Ten Commandments, laws that Jews believed God gave them through Moses. The laws set out both religious duties toward God and rules for moral conduct toward other people, such as:

❝I the Lord am your God who brought
you out of the land of Egypt, the
house of bondage: You shall have
no other gods beside Me. . . .
Honor your father and your mother,
as the Lord your God has
commanded. . . .
You shall not murder.
You shall not steal.**❞**

Other laws. The Torah set out many other laws. Some dealt with everyday matters such as cleanliness and food preparation. Others were criminal laws. Like Hammurabi's Code, many Hebrew laws required an eye for an eye. Yet such severe justice was often eased by other legal principles. Preachers, too, urged rulers to enforce laws with justice and mercy.

Some laws were meant to protect women. For example, the Ten Commandments made respect for mothers a basic law. Still, as in many other religions, most laws treated women as subordinate to men. The male head of a family arranged marriages for his daughters. Also, only a man had the right to seek a divorce.

Early in Hebrew history, a few women leaders, such as the judge Deborah, won honor and respect. Later on, however, women were not allowed to participate in many religious ceremonies.

Justice and morality. Often in Jewish history, prophets, or spiritual leaders, emerged to interpret God's will. The prophets warned that failure to obey God's law would lead their people to disaster.

Prophets preached a strong code of ethics, or moral standards of behavior. They urged both personal morality and social justice, calling

GLOBAL CONNECTIONS

As a result of the diaspora, by A.D. 300 Jewish communities existed as far east as India and as far west as Spain. The first Jewish settlers in the Americas arrived in Brazil in the early 1500s. Much earlier, a separate group had converted to Judaism in Ethiopia. These African Jews, now known as the Falasha, strictly observed Jewish laws and traditions for centuries. In the 1980s, most of the surviving Falasha left their famine-stricken homeland to settle in Israel.

on the rich and powerful to protect the poor and weak. All people, they said, were equal before God. Unlike many ancient societies where the ruler was seen as a god, Jews saw their leaders as fully human and bound to obey God's law.

Looking Ahead

Almost 2,000 years ago, many Jews were forced to leave their homeland in Palestine. (See Chapter 6.) This diaspora (di AS puhr uh), or scattering of people, sent Jews to different parts of the world. Wherever they settled, Jews maintained their identity as a people by living in close-knit communities and obeying their religious laws and traditions. These traditions set Jews apart from other people. Yet they also helped them survive centuries of persecution.

Judaism is numbered among the world's major religions for its unique contribution to religious thought as well as its influence on two later religions, Christianity and Islam. Both those faiths, which also emerged in the Middle East, were monotheistic. Jews, Christians, and Muslims all honor Abraham, Moses, and the prophets, and they all teach the ethical world view developed by the Hebrews.

SECTION 5 REVIEW

1. **Identify** (a) Torah, (b) Moses, (c) David, (d) Solomon, (e) Ten Commandments, (f) Deborah.
2. **Define** (a) monotheistic, (b) covenant, (c) prophet, (d) ethics, (e) diaspora.
3. Why did Israel become a divided kingdom?
4. Describe three basic teachings of Judaism.
5. What was the status of women under Hebrew law?
6. *Critical Thinking* **Linking Past and Present** Compare the ethical beliefs of the Hebrews to those commonly accepted in our society today. How are they similar? How are they different?
7. *ACTIVITY* With a partner, act out a conversation between a Hebrew parent and child in Egypt or Babylon. The parent should try to explain why, even though they are in exile, the Hebrews believe they are "the chosen people."

CHAPTER REVIEW

REVIEWING VOCABULARY

Review the vocabulary words in this chapter. Then, use *ten* of these vocabulary words and their definitions to create a matching quiz. Exchange quizzes with another student. Check each other's answers when you are finished.

REVIEWING FACTS

1. Why was the Nile River important to ancient Egyptian civilization?

2. What were the links between Egypt and Nubia?

3. Why did the people of ancient Egypt mummify their dead?

4. How did the Egyptians record events?

5. Where did Sumerian civilization develop?

6. Explain the importance of Hammurabi's Code.

7. How did Judaism differ from the beliefs of other Middle Eastern peoples?

SKILLS FOR SUCCESS   INTERPRETING A THEMATIC MAP

Thematic maps, such as population or battle maps, illustrate characteristics of a place other than physical features and political boundaries. The most important parts of a thematic map are the title, which tells the topic of the map, and the key, which shows the symbols used in the map. Use the following questions in interpreting the map of Phoenician trade and colonies below.

1. **Use the title and key to read the map.**
   (a) What is the topic of the map? (b) What do the arrows on the map show?

2. **Analyze the map and draw conclusions.**
   (a) How does the map support the claim that the Phoenicians were skilled sailors? (b) Why might the Phoenicians have had trouble controlling their distant colonies?

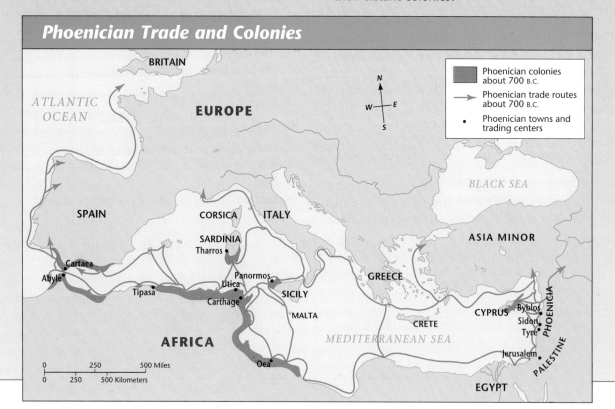

Phoenician Trade and Colonies

REVIEWING CHAPTER THEMES

Review the "Focus On" questions at the start of this chapter. Then select *three* of those questions and answer them, using information from the chapter.

CRITICAL THINKING

1. **Linking Past and Present** (a) How was the building of the pyramids in ancient Egypt similar to public building projects today? (b) How was it different?

2. **Comparing** Compare the view of the afterlife in the Sumerian and Egyptian religions. (a) What differences do you see between the two views? (b) Why do you think they might have been so different?

3. **Drawing Conclusions** One of Hammurabi's laws states, "If outlaws collect in the house of a wine-seller, and she does not arrest these outlaws and bring them to the palace, that wine-seller shall be put to death." (a) What was the purpose of this law? (b) Would you consider this a harsh law? Why or why not? (c) What similar laws do we have in our society today?

4. **Analyzing Information** (a) What rights did women have in Egyptian, Sumerian, and Hebrew societies? (b) How were these rights restricted? (c) What do these facts suggest about the status of women in ancient civilizations?

5. **Predicting Consequences** Review the chart on page 41. Which present-day advances do you think will have the greatest consequences? Explain your choices.

ANALYZING PRIMARY SOURCES

Use the quotation on page 23 to answer the following questions.

1. What fault did the passage warn against?

2. According to Ptah-hotep, from whom should young people learn?

3. Do you think this advice makes sense today? Explain.

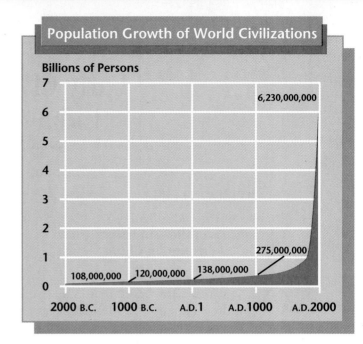

Population Growth of World Civilizations

Billions of Persons

6,230,000,000

275,000,000

108,000,000 120,000,000 138,000,000

2000 B.C. 1000 B.C. A.D.1 A.D.1000 A.D.2000

ANALYZING GRAPHS

Use the graph to answer the following questions.

1. Summarize the trend shown in the graph.

2. Roughly how much larger is the world's population today than it was in 2000 B.C.?

3. What do you think the data line would look like if it were extended in both directions, that is, before 2000 B.C. and after A.D. 2000?

FOR YOUR PORTFOLIO

CREATING A CHART Create a chart illustrating the features of an early African or Asian civilization. First, choose one of the civilizations discussed in this chapter. Then list the ways in which the eight basic features of civilizations, described in Chapter 1, apply to this civilization.

INTERNET ACTIVITY

WRITING IN HIEROGLYPHICS Use the Internet to research hieroglyphics. Then create a *cartouche* (kahr TOOSH) of your name. A cartouche is a hieroglyphic spelling of a name, set within a formal, oval shape. What do the images used in hieroglyphics tell you about the society and environment of ancient Egypt?

Early Civilizations in India and China

(2500 B.C.–256 B.C.)

CHAPTER OUTLINE

1 Cities of the Indus Valley
2 Kingdoms of the Ganges
3 Early Civilization in China

On New Year's Day more than 3,000 years ago, the king, known to his people as the Son of Heaven, mounted the high earth platform and entered the brightly decorated wooden temple. Helped by priests whose prayers echoed his, he made offerings of food and wine to the powerful forces of Heaven and Earth. As cold winds rustled his brilliant green robes, he descended to a nearby field, took up a plow, and cut a furrow into the earth. The people watching these ceremonies felt reassured.

New Year's Day in the Chinese calendar was the beginning of spring. The king's prayers to Shang Di, the Supreme Being, were essential for bringing good harvests.

To the ancient Chinese, the king stood between Heaven and Earth. His sacrifices alone could keep the powerful forces of nature in harmony. An ancient Chinese history explains the link between the king, the powers above, and the people below:

66Heaven and Earth are the parents of
all creatures, and of all creatures,
people are the most highly endowed.
. . . Heaven had to help the inferior
people by providing rulers and teachers that they might be able to aid
Shang Di and secure the peace of the
kingdom. . . . Furthermore, the
One Man [king] having offered
special sacrifice to Heaven and performed the due services to Earth,
leads the people to execute the will
of Shang Di.99

Like leaders in other ancient civilizations, early Chinese rulers served as both priests and kings. Traditions like those surrounding the Son of Heaven continued until A.D. 1911. Every New Year's Day, a Chinese ruler plowed a furrow near the Temple of Heaven to ensure favorable harvests.

As civilizations took shape in the Nile Valley and Fertile Crescent, very different civilizations emerged in India and China. Like ancient Egypt and Sumer, Indian and Chinese civilizations rose in fertile river valleys and influenced nearby lands. These two remarkable civilizations grew up in widely separate areas, one in South Asia and the other in East Asia. In each, people evolved distinct ways of life and thought whose influence can still be seen today.

FOCUS ON these questions as you read:

■ **Geography and History**
How did geographic forces help shape early civilizations in India and China?

■ **Art and Literature**
How do the great epics of ancient India express basic social and religious values?

■ **Continuity and Change**
How did early Chinese traditions form the basis for a long-lasting civilization?

TIME AND PLACE

Dragon's Head *Chinese artisans of the Zhou dynasty crafted this dragon head of bronze overlaid with gold. According to Chinese myth, dragons flew across the heavens, gathering clouds and showering the Earth with life-giving rain. Like other early peoples, the Chinese recognized the importance of nature to their lives and thought that it was controlled by powerful outside forces.* **Art and Literature** *How did the artist convey the image of the dragon as a powerful beast?*

HUMANITIES LINK

Art History Shang bronze sculpture (page 60).
Literature In this chapter, you will encounter passages from the following works of literature: the *Vedas* (pages 54–55); the *Mahabharata* (page 56); *Book of Songs* (pages 63, 64–65).

2500 B.C.	**2000** B.C.	**1650** B.C.	**1500** B.C.	**1027** B.C.	**500** B.C.
Cities built in Indus Valley	Rise of Chinese civilization	Shang dynasty begins	Aryans arrive in India	Zhou dynasty begins	Hindu sacred texts recorded

| B.C. | 2500 | 2000 | 1500 | 1000 | 500 | B.C. |

1 Cities of the Indus Valley

Guide for Reading

- How has geography influenced India?

- How have archaeologists learned about early cities of the Indus Valley?

- Why do so many questions about Indus Valley civilization remain unanswered?

- **Vocabulary** *subcontinent, monsoon*

In 1922, archaeologists made a startling discovery in northwestern India. While digging in the Indus River valley, they unearthed bricks, small statues, and other artifacts unlike any they had seen before. They soon realized that they had uncovered a "lost civilization"—forgotten for some 3,500 years. Though later discoveries have added to our knowledge of the cities of the Indus Valley, many mysteries remain.

Geography: The Indian Subcontinent

The Indus Valley is located in the region known as South Asia or the subcontinent of India. A subcontinent is a large landmass that juts out from a continent. The Indian subcontinent is a huge, wedge-shaped peninsula extending into the Indian Ocean. Today, it includes 3 of the world's 10 most populous countries—India, Pakistan, and Bangladesh—as well as the island nation of Sri Lanka (SREE LAHNG kah) and the mountain nations of Nepal and Bhutan.

Towering, snow-covered mountain ranges arc across the northern border of the subcontinent, including the Hindu Kush and the Himalayas. These mountains limited contacts between India and other lands and helped its people develop a distinct culture. Yet the mountains were not a complete barrier. Steep passes through the Hindu Kush served as gateways to migrating and invading peoples for thousands of years.

Three regions. The Indian subcontinent is divided into three major zones. They are the well-watered northern plain, the dry triangular Deccan plateau, and the coastal plains on either side of the Deccan. (See the map on page 51.)

The northern plain lies just south of the mountains. This fertile region is watered by mighty rivers: the Indus, which gives India its name, the Ganges (GAN jeez), and the Brahmaputra (brahm uh POO truh). These rivers and their tributaries carry melting snow from the mountains to the plains, making agriculture possible. To the people of the Indian subcontinent, rivers are sacred, especially the Ganges. An Indian name for river is *lok-mata,* or "mother of the people."

The most recognizable feature on any map of India is the Deccan, the triangular plateau that juts into the Indian Ocean. The Deccan lacks the melting snows that feed the rivers of the north and provide water for irrigation. As a result, much of the region is arid, unproductive, and sparsely populated.

The coastal plains, India's third region, are separated from the Deccan by low-lying mountain ranges, the Eastern and Western Ghats. Rivers and heavy seasonal rains provide water for farmers in the coastal plains. From very early times, coastal people used the seas for fishing and as highways for trade.

The monsoons. Today, as in the past, a defining feature of Indian life is the monsoon, a seasonal wind. In October, the winter monsoon blows from the northeast, bringing a flow of hot, dry air that withers crops. In late May or early June, the wet summer monsoon blows from the southwest. These winds pick up moisture over the Indian Ocean and then drench the land with daily downpours.

The monsoon has shaped Indian life. Each year, people welcome the rains that are desperately needed to water the crops. If the rains are late, famine and starvation may occur. More than 1,000 years ago, a poet hailed the arrival of monsoon rains after a long dry spell:

66The summer sun, who robbed the
 pleasant nights,
And plundered all the water of the
 rivers,
And burned the earth, and scorched
 the forest-trees
Is now hiding; and the rain-clouds,
Spread thick across the sky to track him
 down,
Hunt for the criminal with lightning
 flashes.99

Yet if the rains are too heavy, rushing rivers unleash deadly floods.

Cultural diversity. India's great size and diverse landscapes made it hard to unite. Many groups of people, with differing languages and traditions, settled in different parts of India. At times, ambitious rulers conquered much of the subcontinent, creating great empires. Yet the diversity of customs and traditions remained.

Indus Valley Civilization

The first Indian civilization is cloaked in mystery. It emerged in the Indus River valley, in present-day Pakistan, about 2500 B.C. This civilization flourished for about 1,000 years, then vanished without a trace. Only in this century have its once prosperous cities emerged beneath the archaeologists' picks and shovels.

Archaeologists have not fully uncovered many Indus Valley sites. Nor have they deciphered the fragments of its writing found on stone seals. We have no names of kings or queens, no tax records, no literature, no accounts of famous victories. Still, we do know that the Indus Valley civilization covered the largest area of any civilization until the rise of Persia more than 1,000 years later. We know, too, that its great cities were as impressive as those of Sumer.

Well-planned cities. The two main cities, Harappa and Mohenjo-Daro (moh HEHN joh DAH roh), may have been twin capitals. Both were large, some three miles in circumference. Each was dominated by a massive hilltop structure, probably a fortress or temple. Both cities had huge warehouses to store grain brought in from outlying villages. Clearly, farmers produced enough surplus food to support tens of thousands of city dwellers.

The most striking feature of Harappa and Mohenjo-Daro is that they were so carefully planned. Each city was laid out in a grid pattern,

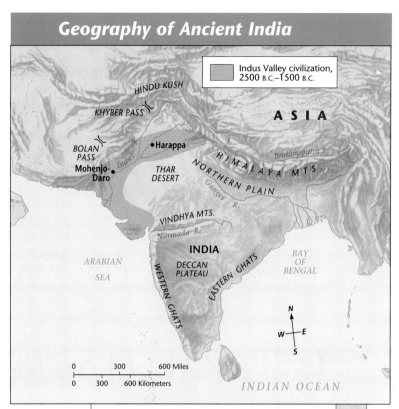

Geography of Ancient India

Indus Valley civilization, 2500 B.C.–1500 B.C.

HINDU KUSH

KHYBER PASS

ASIA

BOLAN PASS

•Harappa

Mohenjo-Daro

Indus R.

THAR DESERT

HIMALAYA MTS.

Brahmaputra R.

NORTHERN PLAIN

Ganges R.

VINDHYA MTS.

Narmada R.

INDIA

ARABIAN SEA

DECCAN PLATEAU

WESTERN GHATS

EASTERN GHATS

BAY OF BENGAL

N E S W

0   300   600 Miles
0   300   600 Kilometers

INDIAN OCEAN

GEOGRAPHY AND HISTORY

As in Egypt and Mesopotamia, the Indus Valley civilization grew up in a fertile river valley. Indus people built great cities and carried on farming and trade.

1. **Location** On the map, locate (a) Himalaya Mountains, (b) Deccan Plateau, (c) Indus River, (d) Ganges River, (e) Mohenjo-Daro, (f) Harappa.
2. **Place** How has India's geography helped protect the people living in the Deccan Plateau?
3. **Critical Thinking** **Making Inferences** Why do you think the Indus River valley was a more inviting location for the development of a civilization than was the Narmada River valley?

with rectangular blocks larger than modern city blocks. All houses were built of uniform oven-fired clay bricks. Over the centuries, houses were built and rebuilt to the same pattern. Houses had surprisingly modern plumbing systems, with baths, drains, and water chutes that led into sewers beneath the streets. Merchants in the marketplaces used a uniform system of weights and measures—additional evidence of careful planning.

From such evidence, archaeologists have concluded that the Indus Valley cities had a well-organized government. Powerful leaders, perhaps priest-kings, made sure the cities had a steady supply of grain from the villages. The rigid pattern of building and the uniform brick sizes suggest government planners at work. These experts must also have developed skills in mathematics and surveying to lay out the cities so precisely.

Farming and trade. As in other early civilizations, most Indus Valley people were farmers. They grew a wide variety of crops, including wheat, barley, melons, and dates. They were also the first people to cultivate cotton and weave its fibers into cloth.

Some people were merchants and traders. Their ships carried cargoes of cotton cloth, grain, copper, pearls, and ivory combs to distant lands. By hugging the Arabian Sea coast and sailing up the Persian Gulf, Indian vessels reached the cities of Sumer. Contact with Sumer may have stimulated Indus Valley people to develop their own system of writing.

Religious beliefs. From clues such as statues, archaeologists have speculated about religious beliefs of Indus Valley people. Like other ancient people, they were polytheistic. A mother goddess, the source of creation, seems to have been widely honored. Indus people also apparently worshiped sacred animals, including the bull. Some scholars think these early practices influenced later Indian beliefs, especially the veneration, or special regard, for cattle.

PARALLELS THROUGH TIME

Seals and Logos

Many artisans and businesses mark their products with a trademark, brand, logo, or other identifying label. In this way, they and their customers can easily distinguish their products from those of competitors.

Linking Past and Present List three animals that are used as company trademarks or logos today.

PAST Archaeologists have recovered more than 2,000 seals from the Indus cities of Harappa and Mohenjo-Daro. They think each merchant family used its own unique seal to stamp labels on its trade goods. The stone seals often bore images of animals, along with symbols whose meaning remains a mystery.

PRESENT

The Sower logo identifies books published by Simon and Schuster. The Seal of Cotton appears on products made of 100 percent United States cotton. Both of these symbols are registered trademarks that cannot be used by other businesses.

Decline and Disappearance

By 1750 B.C., the quality of life in Indus Valley cities was declining. The once orderly cities no longer kept up the old standards. Crude pottery replaced the finer works of earlier days.

We do not know for sure what happened, but scholars have offered several explanations. Ecological disasters may have contributed to the decline. Possibly too many trees were cut down to fuel the ovens of brickmakers. Tons of river mud found in the streets of Mohenjo-Daro suggest that a volcanic eruption blocked the Indus, flooding the city. Other evidence points to a devastating earthquake.

Scholars think that the deathblow fell about 1500 B.C., when nomadic people arrived in ever larger numbers from the north. The newcomers were the Aryans, whose ancestors had slowly migrated with their herds of cattle, sheep, and goats from what is today southern Russia. The Aryans may have completed the destruction begun by nature. With their horse-drawn chariots and superior weapons, the Aryans overran the cities and towns of the Indus region. The cities were soon abandoned.

As the ruined cities disappeared beneath the silt of the Indus, all memory of them faded. Only vague references to the conquest of city dwellers survived in Aryan oral traditions.

SECTION 1 REVIEW

1. **Define** (a) subcontinent, (b) monsoon.
2. Describe two ways in which geography has influenced the people of South Asia.
3. What evidence shows that Indus Valley civilization had a well-organized government?
4. Why do we know so little about Indus Valley civilization?
5. *Critical Thinking* **Linking Past and Present** (a) How could natural disasters have contributed to the decline of Indus Valley civilization? (b) What ecological problems does the world face today?
6. *ACTIVITY* Imagine that you are an archaeologist digging in the Indus region. Write a "wish list" of three items you would like to uncover to learn more about Indus Valley civilization.

2 Kingdoms of the Ganges

Guide for Reading

- How did the Aryans build a new civilization in India?
- How did Aryan life change between 1500 B.C. and 500 B.C.?
- What do India's ancient epics reveal about Aryan life?
- **Vocabulary** *caste, brahman, mystic, rajah*

The Aryans were warlike people. Their hymns praised their warriors as brave heroes and successful looters:

66Hail to the lord of thieves . . . hail to the destructive ones armed with spears, hail to the lord of plunderers.

Hail to the archers, to those who stretch the bowstring, and to those who take aim.99

Over the centuries, the Aryans who destroyed and looted the cities of the Indus Valley became the builders of a new Indian civilization. It rose in the northeast along the Ganges River, rather than in the northwest along the Indus.

The Vedic Age

The Aryans were among many groups of Indo-European people who migrated across Europe and Asia seeking water and pasture for their horses and cattle. (See the map on page 54.) The early Aryans built no cities and left no statues or stone seals. Most of what we know about them comes from the Vedas, a collection of prayers, hymns, and other religious teachings. Aryan priests memorized and recited the Vedas for a thousand years before they were written down. As a result, the period from 1500 B.C. to 500 B.C. is often called the Vedic age.*

---

*Our knowledge about the Aryans is very limited. Historians have re-created a picture of Aryan life from studying their language, but many conclusions are still open to debate.

Indo-European Migrations

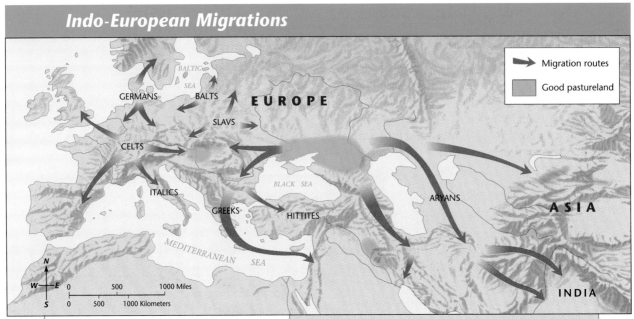

Legend:
→ Migration routes
▨ Good pastureland

Map labels: BALTIC SEA, GERMANS, BALTS, EUROPE, SLAVS, CELTS, ITALICS, GREEKS, HITTITES, BLACK SEA, ARYANS, ASIA, INDIA, MEDITERRANEAN SEA

N / W–E / S
0   500   1000 Miles
0   500   1000 Kilometers

GEOGRAPHY AND HISTORY

Scholars have speculated that the Indo-European peoples originated in north-central Europe. Over thousands of years, they migrated across Europe and into Asia in search of good pastureland. This map shows what many historians think was the route of the Indo-European migrations.

1. **Location** On the map, locate (a) Baltic Sea, (b) Black Sea, (c) Caspian Sea, (d) India.
2. **Movement** (a) Which people migrated to India? (b) To what regions did the Celts migrate?
3. **Critical Thinking** **Linking Past and Present** Look at the maps of modern Europe and Asia on pages 564 and 566. What connections can you see between today's nations and the Indo-European migrations?

In the Vedas, the Aryans appear as warriors who fought in chariots with bows and arrows. They loved eating, drinking, music, chariot races, and dice games. These nomadic herders valued cattle, which provided them with food and clothing. Later, when they became settled farmers, families continued to measure their wealth in cows and bulls.

Aryan society. From the Vedas, we learn that the Aryans divided people by occupation. The three basic groups were the Brahmins, or priests; the Kshatriyas (kuh SHAT ree yuhz), or warriors; and the Vaisyas (VĪS yuhz), or herders, farmers, artisans, and merchants. At first, warriors enjoyed the highest prestige, but priests eventually gained the most respect. Their power grew because Brahmins claimed that they alone could conduct the ceremonies needed to win the favor of the gods.

The Vedas also show that the Aryans felt vastly superior to the Dravidians, the people they conquered. Many scholars think that the Dravidians may have been descended from the original inhabitants of the Indus Valley. Although the Dravidians had built an advanced civilization, the nomadic Aryans had no use for city dwellers. The Aryans therefore separated non-Aryans into a fourth group, the Sudras (SOO druhz). This group included farmworkers, servants, and other laborers who occupied the lowest level of society.

A Vedic hymn explains how Aryans believed their society came to be divided into four distinct classes:

66When the gods divided the Man,
   into how many parts did they
   divide him?

54   *Chapter 3*

> What was his mouth, what were his
> arms, what were his thighs and his
> feet called?
> The Brahmin was his mouth, of his
> arms was made the warrior,
> his thighs became the Vaisya, of his
> feet the Sudra was born.**99**

During the Vedic age, class divisions came to reflect social and economic roles more than racial differences between Aryans and non-Aryans. As these changes occurred, they gave rise to a more complex system of castes,* or social groups into which people are born and from which they cannot change. You will read about the caste system in Chapter 4.

Aryan religious beliefs. The Vedas show that the Aryans were polytheistic. They worshiped gods and goddesses that embodied natural forces such as sky and sun, storm and fire. The Aryans also honored animals, such as monkey gods and snake gods. Fierce Indra, the god of war, was the chief Aryan deity. Indra's weapon was the thunderbolt, which he used not only to destroy demons but to announce the arrival of rain, so vital to Indian life. Other major gods included Varuna, the god of order and creation, and Agni, the god of fire. Agni also served as the messenger who communicated human wishes to the gods.

Brahmins offered sacrifices of food and drink to the gods. Through the correct rituals and prayers, the Aryans believed, they could call on the gods for health, wealth, and victory in war.

As the lives of the Aryans changed, so, too, did their beliefs. Some religious thinkers were moving toward the notion of a single spiritual power beyond the many gods of the Vedas, called brahman, that resided in all things. There was also a move toward mysticism. Mystics are people who devote their lives to seeking spiritual truth. Through meditation and yoga, or spiritual and bodily discipline, Indian mystics sought direct communion with divine forces. The religions that emerged in India after the Vedic age reflected the impact of mysticism as well as the notion of brahman.

---

*Indians use the word *jati* to describe their social system. The Portuguese, who reached India in the late 1400s, used the word *caste,* which other Europeans adopted.

Expansion and Change

Over many centuries, waves of Aryans went through the mountain passes into northwestern India. Aryan tribes were led by chiefs called rajahs. A rajah was often the most skilled war leader, elected to his position by an assembly of warriors. He ruled with the advice of a council of elders made up of heads of families.

From nomads to farmers. Despite their racial pride, Aryans mingled with the people they conquered. Gradually, they gave up their nomadic ways and settled into villages to grow crops and breed cattle. From the local people, they learned farming and other skills and developed new crafts of their own.

In time, Aryans spread eastward to colonize the heavily forested Ganges basin. By about 800 B.C., they had learned to make tools out of iron. Equipped with iron axes and weapons, restless pioneers carved farms and villages out of the rain forests of the northeast.

Cities in the jungle. Tribal leaders fought to control trade and territory across the northern plain. Some rajahs became powerful hereditary rulers, extending their influence over many villages. Walled cities filled with multistory houses rose above the jungle.

By 500 B.C., a new Indian civilization had emerged. Although it consisted of many rival kingdoms, the people shared a common culture rooted in both Aryan and Dravidian traditions. By this time, too, the Indian people had developed a written language, Sanskrit. (See the chart on page 56.) Priests now began writing down their sacred texts.

Heroic Deeds and Moral Lessons

On the eve of battle, the young warrior Arjuna gazes out across a silent battlefield, his heart filled with doubt. These enemies are not invaders from a far-off land. They are friends and relatives, people he has known and loved all his life. Now he must face them in battle and perhaps kill them. Where will he ever find the strength?

For thousands of years, people in India have shared Arjuna's agony. Families today, watching the story on television, are as anxious to know what Arjuna will do as the ancient Aryans were when priests told the story.

India's greatest epic. Arjuna is one of the heroes of the *Mahabharata* (muh HAH bah rah tuh), the greatest Indian epic. Almost 100,000 verses long, the *Mahabharata* was told and retold for centuries before it was written down. Through it, we hear echoes of the battles that rival Aryan tribes fought to gain control of the Ganges region.

Like other epics, such as *The Epic of Gilgamesh* (see page 31), the *Mahabharata* mixes history, mythology, and religion. Characters include mortals, gods, goddesses, animals, and demons. The plot swirls around five royal brothers, the Pandavas, who have lost their kingdom to their cousins but struggle to regain it.

Preparing for battle. Arjuna, one of the Pandavas, at last faces his cousins and rivals in a great battle. Just before the battle, Arjuna confides to Krishna, his charioteer, that he does not want to fight even though he knows that his cause is just:

66O Krishna, when I see my kinsmen thus arrayed for battle, my mind is all awhirl. These I would not kill even though they might seek to kill me.99

Krishna, who is actually a god in human form, then instructs Arjuna about life and death. The soul, Krishna says, cannot be killed:

66It is never born and never dies, nor, once it exists, does it cease to be. Unborn, eternal, abiding, and ancient, it is not slain when the body is slain. . . . Weapons do not destroy it, fire does not burn it, waters do not wet it, wind does not dry it.99

While Arjuna hesitates, Krishna presses his point home. The warrior, he says, has a duty to fulfill. No matter what, he must fulfill that duty: "For there is more joy in doing one's duty badly than in doing another man's duty well." Most important, Krishna advises Arjuna to detach himself from personal desire and ambition and to concentrate on duty. This episode of the *Mahabharata*, known as the *Bhagavad-Gita* (BUHG uh vuhd GEE tuh), reflects important Indian religious beliefs.

Strengthened in resolve, Arjuna goes into battle. The fighting lasts for 18 days and results in the complete victory of the Pandavas. As the *Mahabharata* ends, the brothers have restored peace to India.

Rama and Sita. A much shorter, but equally memorable, epic is the *Ramayana* (rah MAH yuh nuh). It recounts the fantastic deeds of the daring hero Rama and his beautiful bride Sita.

Not long after their wedding, Sita is kidnapped by the demon-king Ravana. The rest of the story tells of Rama's efforts to rescue Sita

Comparing Languages

English	month	mother	new	night	nose	three
German	Monat	Mutter	neu	Nacht	Nase	drei
Persian	māh	mādar	nau	shab	bini	se
Sanskrit	mās	matar	nava	nakt	nās	trayas
Spanish	mes	madre	nuevo	noche	nariz	tres
Swedish	månad	moder	ny	natt	näsa	tre

Interpreting a Chart Similarities in words are one clue that Sanskrit shared a common root with Persian and most modern European languages. These languages are today called the Indo-European family. ■ How might the map on page 54 help explain the word similarities shown on this chart?

Epic Romance *The marriage of the courageous Rama to the beautiful Sita is joyously celebrated in this eighteenth-century illustration from the Ramayana. Excitement and suspense soon follow as the evil, 10-headed Ravana kidnaps Sita, and the noble Rama sets out to rescue his love.* **Diversity** *How does this picture reflect India's ethnic diversity?*

with the aid of the monkey general Hanuman. Ravana tries to ward off the attack by killing a duplicate of Sita before Rama's eyes. But Rama presses on, winning the battle and rescuing his bride.

Like Aryan religion, these epics evolved over thousands of years. Priest-poets added new morals to the tales to teach different lessons about morality. For example, they turned Rama into a model of virtue. In some versions, he appears as an ideal king. Likewise, Sita came to be honored as an ideal woman who remained loyal and obedient to her husband through many hardships. "May you be like Sita" is a common blessing still given to young women in India.

Looking Ahead

The Aryans were the first of many people to filter into India through passes in the Hindu Kush. Even though scholars recognize that our knowledge of the Aryan migrations is very limited, most accept that Aryan traditions and beliefs formed a framework for later Indian civilization.

Aryan religious beliefs would evolve into major world religions. Just as the Middle East gave rise to three world religions—Judaism, Christianity, and Islam—South Asia was the birthplace of two influential faiths, Hinduism and Buddhism. You will read about these religions in Chapter 4.

SECTION 2 REVIEW

1. **Identify** (a) Vedas, (b) Brahmins, (c) Kshatriyas, (d) Vaisyas, (e) Sudras, (f) Indra, (g) Sanskrit, (h) *Mahabharata,* (i) *Bhagavad-Gita,* (j) *Ramayana.*
2. **Define** (a) caste, (b) brahman, (c) mystic, (d) rajah.
3. What do the Vedas tell us about classes in Aryan society?
4. How did Aryan life change in the centuries after the Aryans invaded India?
5. *Critical Thinking* **Analyzing Information** Why might epic poems like the *Mahabharata* and *Ramayana* be good vehicles for teaching moral lessons?
6. *ACTIVITY* According to the *Ramayana,* Rama and Sita possess the qualities of the "ideal" man and woman. Make a list of at least four qualities that you think today's ideal man or woman should have. Do any of the qualities of Rama or Sita appear on your list?

GLOBAL CONNECTIONS

The *Ramayana* bears some resemblance to the *Iliad,* the ancient Greek epic. Both are long heroic tales in verse that were recited for centuries before being written down. Both epics revolve around efforts to recapture kidnapped brides, though Helen of Troy in the *Iliad* bears little resemblance to the admirable Sita. Some scholars think that both the *Ramayana* and the *Iliad* may have derived from a common Indo-European legend.

3 Early Civilization in China

Guide for Reading

- How did geography help shape early Chinese civilization?
- What ideas about government did the Chinese develop?
- What were some achievements of early Chinese civilization?
- **Vocabulary** *loess, clan, ideograph, oracle bone, calligraphy, dynastic cycle, feudalism*

In very ancient times, relates a Chinese legend, flood waters rose to the top of the highest hills. Yu, a hard-working official, labored for 13 years to drain the waters:

> 66 I opened passages for the streams throughout the nine provinces, and conducted them to the sea. I deepened channels and canals, and conducted them to the streams. 99

While taming the rivers, Yu did not once go home to see his wife and children. As a reward for his selfless efforts, he later became ruler of China.

The legend of Yu offers insights into early China. The ancient Chinese valued the ability to control flood waters and to develop irrigation systems for farming. The legend also shows how highly the Chinese prized devotion to duty. Both these values played a key role in the development of Chinese civilization.

Geography: The Middle Kingdom

The ancient Chinese called their land Zhongguo (JONG goo AW), the Middle Kingdom. China was the most isolated of the civilizations you have studied so far. Long distances and physical barriers separated it from Egypt, the Middle East, and India. This isolation contributed to the Chinese belief that China was the center of the Earth and the sole source of civilization.

Geographic barriers. To the west and southwest of China, high mountains—the Tien Shan and the Himalayas—and brutal deserts blocked the easy movement of people. To the southeast, thick jungles divided China from Southeast Asia. To the north lay the forbidding Gobi Desert. To the east, the vast Pacific Ocean rolled endlessly. (See the map on page 59.)

Despite formidable barriers, the Chinese did have contact with the outside world. They traded with neighboring people and, in time, Chinese goods reached the Middle East and beyond. More often, though, the outsiders whom the Chinese encountered were nomadic invaders. To the Chinese, these nomads were barbarians who did not speak Chinese and lacked the skills and achievements of a settled society. Even the invaders accepted the superiority of Chinese culture. Nomads conquered China from time to time, but they were usually absorbed into the advanced Chinese civilization.

Main regions. As the Chinese expanded over an enormous area, their empire came to include many regions with a variety of climates and landforms. The Chinese heartland lay along the east coast and the valleys of the Huang He (HWAHNG HAY), or Yellow River, and the Yangzi (yahng DZEE). In ancient times, as today, these fertile farming regions supported the largest populations. Then, as now, the rivers provided water for irrigation and served as transportation routes.

Beyond the heartland are the outlying regions of Xinjiang (sheen jee AHNG), Mongolia, and Manchuria. The first two regions have harsh climates and rugged terrain. Until recent times, they were mostly occupied by nomads and subsistence farmers. All three outlying regions played a key role in China's history. Nomads repeatedly attacked and plundered Chinese cities. At times, powerful Chinese rulers conquered or made alliances with the people of these regions. China also extended its influence over the Himalayan region of Tibet, which the Chinese called Xizang (shee DZAHNG).

"River of Sorrows." Chinese history began in the Huang He Valley, where Neolithic people learned to farm. As in other places, the need to control the river through large water projects probably led to the rise of a strong central government.

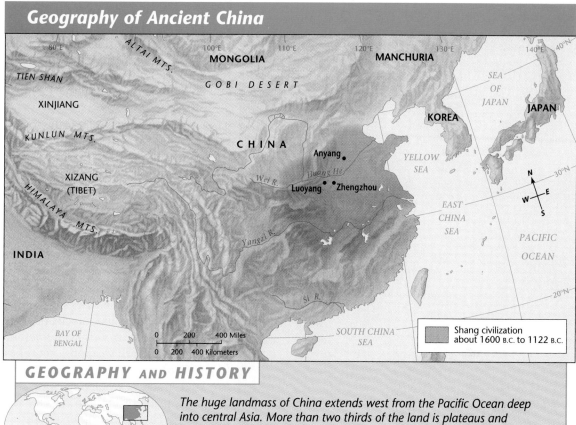

GEOGRAPHY AND HISTORY

The huge landmass of China extends west from the Pacific Ocean deep into central Asia. More than two thirds of the land is plateaus and mountains.

1. **Location** On the map, locate (a) Huang He, (b) Tien Shan, (c) Gobi Desert, (d) Pacific Ocean.
2. **Region** What physical features acted as obstacles to contact with lands outside China?
3. **Critical Thinking** **Synthesizing Information** (a) Which latitudes mark the northern and southern boundaries of China? (b) Use a map of the United States to find the latitude of your community. What part of China is at the same latitude?

The Huang He got its name from the loess, or fine windblown yellow soil, that it carries eastward from Siberia and Mongolia. Long ago, the Huang He earned a bitter nickname, "River of Sorrows." As loess settles to the river bottom, it raises the water level. Chinese peasants labored constantly to build and repair dikes that kept the river from overflowing. However, when heavy rains swelled the river, it ran high above the surrounding plain.

If the dikes broke, flood waters burst over the land. Such disasters destroyed crops and brought mass starvation. Fear of floods is reflected in Chinese writing. The character, or written symbol, for misfortune, 巛, represents a river with a blockage that causes flooding.

China Under the Shang

About 1650 B.C., a Chinese people called the Shang gained control of a corner of northern China, along the Huang He. The Shang dynasty dominated this region until 1027 B.C. During the Shang period, Chinese civilization took shape. Despite many changes, ideas and achievements of this early civilization have survived to the present.

Government. Archaeologists have uncovered large palaces and rich tombs of Shang rulers. Shang kings led other noble warriors in battle. From their walled capital city at Anyang, they emerged to drive off nomads from the northern steppes and deserts.

Shang Bronze Sculpture *This bronze bucket shows the exceptional skill of Shang artists. It is decorated with carved symbolic figures, including serpents, cats, and a small deer. The main figure seems to be some sort of demon in the form of a tiger or bear. Art historians disagree, though, about whether the demon is swallowing the man or protecting him.* **Art and Literature** *What does this bronze suggest about the view of humans in ancient China?*

In one Shang tomb, archaeologists discovered the burial place of Fu Hao (FOO HOW), wife of the Shang king Wu Ding. Artifacts show that she owned land and helped to lead a large army against invaders. This evidence suggests that noblewomen had considerable status during the Shang period.

Shang kings probably controlled only a small area. Princes and nobles loyal to the Shang dynasty governed most of the land. They were most likely the heads of important clans, or groups of families who claimed a common (often mythical)

ancestor. Thus, Shang China probably more closely resembled the small kingdoms of Aryan India or the city-states of Sumer than the centralized government ruled by the Egyptian pharaohs.

Social classes. Shang society mirrored that in other early civilizations. Alongside the royal family was a class of noble warriors who owned the land. Shang warriors used leather armor, bronze weapons, and horse-drawn chariots. The chariots may have come from outside China through contacts with people of western Asia. Noble families lived in large timber or stone houses.

Early Chinese cities supported a class of artisans and merchants. Artisans produced goods for nobles, including bronze weapons, silk robes, and jade jewelry. Merchants organized trade, exchanging food and crafts made by local artisans for salt, cowrie shells, and other goods not found in northeastern China.

Peasant life. Most people in Shang China were peasants. They clustered together in farming villages. Many lived in thatch-roofed pit houses whose earthen floors were dug several feet below the surrounding ground. Such homes preserved the heat in winter and remained cool in summer.

Peasants led grueling lives. All family members worked in the fields, using stone tools to prepare the ground for planting or to harvest grain. When they were not in the fields, peasants had to repair the dikes. If war broke out between noble families, men had to fight alongside their lords. (See *World Literature*, "Book of Songs," pages 64–65.)

Religious Beliefs

By Shang times, the Chinese had developed complex religious beliefs. They prayed to many gods and nature spirits. Chief among them were Shang Di (SHAHNG DEE) and a mother goddess who brought plants and animals to Earth. As you read on page 48, the king was seen as the link between the people and Shang Di.

Veneration of ancestors. Gods as great as Shang Di, the Chinese believed, would not respond to the pleas of mere mortals. Only the spirits of the greatest mortals, such as the ancestors of the king, could get the ear of the Lord of Heaven. Thus, the prayers of rulers and nobles to their ancestors were thought to be essential to the community as a whole, ensuring good harvests or victory in war.

The ruler's power grew out of this veneration of ancestors. At first, only the royal family and other nobles had important enough ancestors to influence the gods. Gradually, other classes shared in these rituals. The Chinese called on the spirits of their ancestors to bring good fortune to the family. To honor their ancestors' spirits, they offered them sacrifices of food and other necessities. When westerners reached China, they mistakenly called this practice "ancestor worship."

Yin and yang. The Chinese believed the universe reflected a delicate balance between two forces, yin and yang. Yin was linked to Earth, darkness, and female forces, while yang stood for Heaven, light, and male forces. To the Chinese, these forces were not in opposition. Rather, the well-being of the universe depended on harmony between yin and yang. People could play a role in maintaining this harmony. For example, the king had to make the proper sacrifices to Heaven while at the same time taking practical steps to rule well.

System of Writing

The ancient Chinese developed a system of writing. It used both pictographs and ideographs, signs that expressed thoughts or ideas.

Consulting the ancestors. The oldest examples of Chinese writing are on oracle bones, used by priests to predict the future. On animal bones or turtle shells, Shang priests wrote questions addressed to the gods or the spirit of an ancestor. These questions generally required a yes or no answer. Priests then heated the bone or shell until it cracked. By interpreting the pattern of cracks, they could provide answers or advice from the ancestors.

A difficult study. Written Chinese took shape almost 4,000 years ago. Over time, it evolved to include tens of thousands of characters. Each character represented a word or idea and was made up of a number of different strokes. In recent years, the Chinese have simplified their characters, but Chinese remains one of the most difficult languages to learn. Students must still memorize up to 10,000 characters to read a newspaper. By contrast, languages based on an alphabet, such as English or Arabic, contain only two dozen or so symbols representing basic sounds.

Not surprisingly, in earlier times, only the well-to-do could afford the years of study needed to master the skills of reading and writing. Working with brush and ink, Chinese scholars turned calligraphy, or fine handwriting, into an elegant art form.

A force for unity. Despite its complexity, the written language fostered unity. Isolated by geographic barriers, people in different parts of China often could not understand one another's spoken language, but they all used the same system of writing.

The Zhou Dynasty

In 1027 B.C., the battle-hardened Zhou (JOH) people marched out of their kingdom on the western frontier to overthrow the Shang. They set up the Zhou dynasty, which lasted until 256 B.C.

The Mandate of Heaven. To justify their rebellion against the Shang, the Zhou promoted the idea of the Mandate of Heaven, or the divine right to rule. The cruelty of the last Shang king, they declared, had so outraged the gods that they had sent ruin on him. The gods then passed the Mandate of Heaven to the Zhou, who "treated the multitudes of the people well."

▲ *Tortoise shell used as an oracle*

The Dynastic Cycle in China

The New Dynasty
Restores peace
Appoints loyal officials
Redistributes land to peasants
Builds canals, irrigation systems,
    and roads
Repairs defensive walls

New dynasty claims the Mandate of Heaven.

After several generations, the new dynasty becomes an aging dynasty.

Problems
Floods, famine, earthquakes
Invasions
Armed bandits in the provinces
Peasant revolts

Aging dynasty loses the Mandate of Heaven.

The Aging Dynasty
Neglects government duties
Ignores corrupt officials
Loses control of the provinces
Imposes heavy taxes to pay for
    luxuries
Allows defensive walls to decay

Interpreting a Chart The Chinese believed that their emperor had received the Mandate of Heaven to rule his people. However, they also believed that the emperor was obligated to govern wisely and preserve order. ■ *According to this flow chart, how did a new dynasty try to repair the problems left by an aging dynasty?*

might seize power and set up a new dynasty. His success and strong government showed the people that the new dynasty had won the Mandate of Heaven. The dynastic cycle would then begin again. (See the chart at left.)

A feudal state. The Zhou rewarded their supporters by granting them control over different regions. Thus, under the Zhou, China developed into a feudal state. Feudalism (FYOO duhl ihz uhm) was a system of government in which local lords governed their own lands but owed military service and other forms of support to the ruler. (In later centuries, feudal societies also developed in Europe and Japan.)

In theory, Zhou kings ruled China, and for about 250 years, they actually did enjoy great power and prestige. After about 771 B.C., though, feudal lords exercised the real power and profited from the lands worked by peasants within their domains.

Economic growth. During the Zhou period, China's economy grew. Knowledge of ironworking reached China about 500 B.C. As iron axes and ox-drawn iron plows replaced stone, wood, and bronze tools, farmers produced more food. Peasants also began to grow new crops, such as soybeans. Some feudal lords organized large-scale irrigation works, making farming even more productive.

Commerce expanded, too. The Chinese began to use money for the first time. Chinese copper coins had holes in the center so they could be strung on cords. This early form of a cash, or money, economy made trade easier. Merchants also benefited from new roads and canals built by feudal lords.

The dynastic cycle. The Chinese later expanded the idea of the Mandate of Heaven to explain the dynastic cycle, or the rise and fall of dynasties. As long as a dynasty provided good government, it enjoyed the Mandate of Heaven. If the rulers became weak or corrupt, the Chinese believed that Heaven would withdraw its support.

Floods, famine, or other catastrophes were signs that a dynasty had lost the favor of Heaven. In the resulting chaos, an ambitious leader

ISSUES For TODAY

According to the dynastic cycle, a dynasty would fall if it failed to fulfill its duties. What services should government provide for its citizens?

Economic expansion led to an increase in population. People from the Huang He heartland overflowed into central China and began to farm the immense Yangzi basin. Feudal nobles expanded their territories and encouraged peasants to settle in the conquered territories. By late Zhou times, China was increasing in size, population, and prosperity.

Chinese Achievements

The Chinese made progress in many areas during the Shang and Zhou periods. For example, astronomers studied the movement of planets and recorded eclipses of the sun. Their findings helped them develop an accurate calendar with 365¼ days. The Chinese also made remarkable achievements in the art and technology of bronzemaking. (See Art History, page 60.)

Silkmaking. By 1000 B.C., the Chinese had discovered how to make silk thread from the cocoons of silkworms. Soon, the Chinese were cultivating both silkworms and the mulberry trees on which they fed. Women did the laborious work of tending the silkworms and processing the cocoons into thread. They then wove silk threads into a smooth cloth that was colored with brilliant dyes. Only royalty and nobles could afford luxurious silk robes.

Silk became China's most valuable export. The trade route that eventually linked China and the Middle East became known as the Silk Road. (See pages 96–97.) To protect this profitable trade, the Chinese kept the process of silkmaking a secret.

The first books. Under the Zhou, the Chinese made the first books. They bound thin strips of wood or bamboo together and then carefully drew characters on the flat surface with a brush and ink.

The earliest Chinese books included histories and religious works. *I Ching*, a handbook for diviners, is still used by people who want to foretell the future.

Among the greatest Zhou works is the lovely *Book of Songs*. Many of its poems describe such events in the lives of farming people as planting and harvesting. Others praise kings or describe court ceremonies. The book also includes tender or sad love songs. In one lyric, a young woman complains that her family is forcing her into a marriage she does not want:

> 66My heart is not a mirror, To reflect
> what others will.
> Brothers too I have; I cannot be
> snatched away.
> But lo, when I told them of my plight
> I found that they were angry
> with me.99

Looking Ahead

By 256 B.C., China was a large, wealthy, and highly developed center of civilization. Chinese culture was already dominant in East Asia. Yet the Zhou dynasty was too weak to control feudal lords who ignored the Son of Heaven and battled each other in savage wars. Out of these wars rose a ruthless leader who was determined to impose political unity on China. His triumphs would leave a lasting imprint on Chinese civilization.

SECTION 3 REVIEW

1. **Identify** (a) Zhongguo, (b) Shang, (c) yin and yang, (d) Zhou, (e) Mandate of Heaven, (f) *Book of Songs*.
2. **Define** (a) loess, (b) clan, (c) ideograph, (d) oracle bone, (e) calligraphy, (f) dynastic cycle, (g) feudalism.
3. How did the Huang He earn the nickname "River of Sorrows"?
4. What role did veneration of ancestors play in ancient Chinese life?
5. How did China's economy expand during the Zhou period?
6. *Critical Thinking* **Predicting Consequences** Give three examples of how your life and schooling might be different if you had had to learn a language written in characters like Chinese rather than a language using an alphabet.
7. *ACTIVITY* Using the simple, direct style of the poems above and on pages 64–65, write a short poem to add to the *Book of Songs*. Your poem might be about floods, rulers, war, or the deeds of an ancestor.

World Literature
Book of Songs

Introduction *The poems in the* Book of Songs *were compiled sometime around 500* B.C., *though many poems are much older. From Zhou times to the present, Chinese have taken pleasure in reciting these ancient songs. In earlier times, scholars had to memorize all 305 poems to show their mastery of Chinese literature.*

Most of these poems were originally folk songs. They offer glimpses into the lives of women and men from all social classes. Men sing of wooing and winning their wives. Women tell of joyful love and heartbreaking losses. Farmers celebrate harvests, while princes reflect on the responsibilities of ruling. The five poems below all deal with the subject of war. Song 100 is the lament of a wife whose husband is away at war; song 117 is a rousing song for the start of a military campaign; while songs 122, 124, and 127 are complaints by common soldiers who have been forced to leave home on a long expedition.

100

My lord is on service;
He did not know for how long.
Oh, when will he come?
The fowls are roosting in their holes,
Another day is ending,
The sheep and cows are coming down.
My lord is on service;
How can I not be sad?

My lord is on service;
Not a matter of days, nor months.
Oh, when will he be here again?
The fowls are roosting on their perches,
Another day is ending,
The sheep and cows have all come down,
My lord is on service;
Were I but sure that he gets drink and food!

117

Firmly set are the rabbit nets,
Hammered with a *ting, ting.*
Stout-hearted are the warriors,
Shield and rampart of our elder and lord.

Firmly set are the rabbit nets,
Spread where the paths meet.
Stout-hearted are the warriors,
Good comrades for our elder and lord.

Firmly set are the rabbit nets,
Spread deep in the woods.
Stout-hearted are the warriors,
Belly and heart of our elder and lord.

122

How few of us are left, how few!
Why do we not go back?
Were it not for our prince and his concerns,
What should we be doing here in the dew?

How few of us are left, how few!
Why do we not go back?
Were it not for our prince's own concerns,
What should we be doing here in the mud?

124

I climb that wooded hill
And look towards where my father is.
My father is saying, "Alas, my son is on service;
Day and night he knows no rest.
Grant that he is being careful of himself,
So that he may come back and not be left behind!"

I climb that bare hill
And look towards where my mother is.
My mother is saying, "Alas, my young one is on service;
Day and night he gets no sleep.
Grant that he is being careful of himself,
So that he may come back, and not be cast away."

I climb that ridge
And look towards where my elder brother is.
My brother is saying, "Alas, my young brother is on service;
Day and night he toils.
Grant that he is being careful of himself,
So that he may come back and not die."

Jade Figures Like the poems in the Book of Songs, these carved jade figures give us a glimpse into the lives of early Chinese people. Actually, human figures like these were rare except in the outlying regions of southern and western China. Most sculptures of the Shang and early Zhou periods represented birds and animals of religious significance. **Economics and Technology** Why do you think museums and private collectors consider such jade sculptures very valuable today?

127
Minister of War,
We are the king's claws and fangs.
Why should you roll us on from misery to
    misery,
Giving us no place to stop in or take rest?

Minister of War,
We are the king's claws and teeth.
Why should you roll us on from misery to
    misery,
Giving us no place to come to and stay?

Minister of War,
Truly you are not wise.
Why should you roll us on from misery to
    misery?
We have mothers who lack food.

Source: Book of Songs, translated from the Chinese by Arthur Waley (New York: Grove Press, 1960).

Thinking About Literature

1. **Vocabulary** Use the dictionary to find the meanings of the following words: stout-hearted, rampart.
2. (a) What does song 117 say about the relationship between soldiers and their feudal lords? (b) How do the soldiers in songs 122 and 127 feel about serving their lords?
3. Give three examples of how these poems show the effects of war on the family.
4. *Critical Thinking* **Linking Past and Present** Do you think the thoughts and feelings expressed in these ancient Chinese poems have meaning for people in our society today? Explain.

CHAPTER REVIEW

REVIEWING VOCABULARY

Select *five* vocabulary words from the chapter. Write each word on a separate slip of paper. Then, write the definition for each word on other slips of paper. Scramble the slips and exchange them with another student. Match the words with their definitions, and then check each other's results.

REVIEWING FACTS

1. How has climate shaped life in the Indian subcontinent?

2. What signs of an advanced civilization can be seen in Harappa and Mohenjo-Daro?

3. Why did the Aryans migrate to India? From where did they come?

4. How did the caste system develop in India?

5. Why was the area between the Huang He and Yangzi the heartland of early China?

6. What was the attitude of the Chinese people toward their ancestors?

7. List Chinese achievements in writing, astronomy, and book printing.

SKILLS FOR SUCCESS   USING THE WRITING PROCESS

Good writers follow three steps. During the **prewriting** stage, the writer decides what to write about and gathers information. During the **writing** stage, the writer decides the purpose of the writing, the audience, and the form of the writing. The writer then prepares a first draft. During the **revising** stage, the writer reviews the draft for sense, style, and errors.

The chart below is a prewriting tool that can help you organize your information.

1. **Develop ideas for writing and organize your information.** Look at the chart below. (a) What is the topic of the writer's essay? (b) How has the writer organized information?

2. **Identify who your audience is and what your purpose is and write a first draft.** (a) In the chart below, who are the likely readers of the writer's work? (b) Would the writer be more likely to use an eyewitness approach, an analytical approach, or a biographical approach? Why?

3. **Review your writing to see if it makes sense.** Ask one of your classmates to listen to your topic sentence. (a) What changes were suggested? (b) Rewrite your sentence based on these suggestions.

Features of Aryan civilization	Features of both civilizations	Features of Shang civilization
• believed in reincarnation	• rigid class system	• power was handed down through family dynasties
• religion moved toward monotheism	• developed written language	• polytheistic
• status of women deteriorated over time	• lived in extended families	• venerated ancestors
• warfare dominated life	• households headed by oldest male	• long period of peace allowed arts and sciences to flourish
• rajahs were elected		• women farmed and practiced some crafts

REVIEWING CHAPTER THEMES

Review the "Focus On" questions at the start of this chapter. Then select *three* of those questions and answer them, using information from the chapter.

CRITICAL THINKING

1. **Linking Past and Present** Based on the evidence uncovered by archaeologists, how were the cities of the Indus Valley similar to and different from today?

2. **Applying Information** In the Vedas, "breaker of cities" is one of the titles of honor given to the god Indra. How might this title have linked Indra to actual events in the history of the Aryans?

3. **Making Generalizations** Based on what you have read about the ancient societies of Egypt, Sumer, China, and the Indus Valley, make three generalizations about the role of religion and priests in early civilizations.

ANALYZING PRIMARY SOURCES

Use the quotation on page 50 to answer the following questions.

1. What was the poet's attitude toward the disappearance of the sun?

2. Why was the sun referred to as a "criminal"?

3. Might this same poet also have thought of the monsoon rains as "criminal"? Explain.

FOR YOUR PORTFOLIO

CREATING A CONTEST ENTRY Create an entry for a contest called "Asian Geography, History, and Life." First, select a specific geographic feature of India or China. Then find out how the feature has affected the history or daily life in that region, and use this information to select a specific topic. Create a contest entry in the form of a brief written report, an illustrated map, or a visual display such as a collage. The class should vote on the winner.

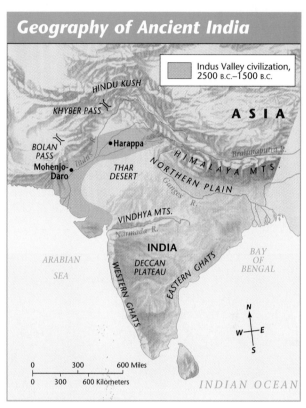

Geography of Ancient India

Indus Valley civilization, 2500 B.C.–1500 B.C.

ANALYZING MAPS

Use the map to answer the following questions.

1. Near what river was the Indus Valley civilization located?

2. Into what sea does that river flow?

3. How does the map show that the Indian subcontinent is not completely isolated from lands to the north?

INTERNET ACTIVITY

COMPARING SETTLEMENT PATTERNS
Use the Internet to research population density in India and China today. Then compare the information you find on the Internet with the information shown in the maps on pages 51 and 59. How do the settlement patterns of ancient India and ancient China compare with the settlement patterns of India and China today?

Unit-in-Brief

UNIT 1

Early Civilizations

Chapter 1 Toward Civilization
(Prehistory–3000 B.C.)

Archaeologists, historians, and other scholars are learning about our ancient human past through careful research. When the evidence that they find is gathered, pieced together, and interpreted, a fascinating story of the emergence of civilization unfolds.

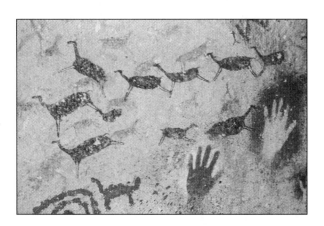

- Archaeologists analyze artifacts to trace how early people developed new technologies and ways of life.
- Historians also study how people lived in the past, but they rely more heavily on written evidence to interpret past events.
- Geographers use the themes of location, place, human-environment interaction, movement, and region to explain the impact of geography on the human story.
- People made tools, learned to build fires, and developed spoken languages during the Paleolithic period, or Old Stone Age, the earliest period of human history.
- About 11,000 years ago, during the Neolithic period, or New Stone Age, people learned to farm, a dramatic breakthrough that transformed the way people lived.

- By about 5,000 years ago, the advances made by early farming communities led to the rise of civilizations.
- Historians define eight basic features common to most early civilizations: (1) cities, (2) well-organized central governments, (3) complex religions, (4) job specialization, (5) social classes, (6) arts and architecture, (7) public works, and (8) writing.
- Cities, the central feature of civilization, first rose in river valleys in the Middle East, Africa, and Asia, where conditions favored farming and a surplus of food could be grown.

Chapter 2 First Civilizations: Africa and Asia
(3200 B.C.–500 B.C.)

The first civilizations to develop emerged in river valleys in Egypt and the Middle East more than 5,000 years ago. In these places, people developed a complex way of life and beliefs that continue to affect our world today.

- A rich civilization emerged in the valley of the Nile River in Egypt that depended on control of the river waters.

- During the Old Kingdom, Egyptian pharaohs organized a strong, centralized state and built majestic pyramids.
- During the Middle Kingdom and the New Kingdom, trade and warfare brought Egypt into contact with other civilizations and helped spread ideas.
- Egyptians worshiped many gods and goddesses and believed in an afterlife.
- Egyptian society was organized into classes with the pharaoh, who was considered both a god and king, at the top of the hierarchy and farmers and slaves at the bottom.
- Independent Sumerian city-states developed in Mesopotamia, an area of rich, fertile land between the Tigris and Euphrates rivers.
- The Sumerians invented the earliest form of writing, known as cuneiform, and made great strides in mathematics and astronomy.
- Mesopotamia's location at a geographical crossroads made it vulnerable to a succession of invaders—including the Babylonians, the Assyrians, and the Persians—who built great empires.
- Warfare and trade in Mesopotamia helped to spread ideas and technology—including codified laws, ironworking, and the Phoenician alphabet—around the Mediterranean.
- The Hebrews developed Judaism, a monotheistic religion based on the worship of one God, whose laws are set out in the Torah and the Ten Commandments.

Chapter 3 Early Civilizations in India and China
(2500 B.C.–256 B.C.)

As civilizations took shape in the Nile Valley and Fertile Crescent, people in India and China carved out their own civilizations. These two remarkable civilizations evolved distinct ways of life and thought that would exert a powerful influence on other civilizations.

- India's first civilization, which emerged in the Indus River valley, flourished for about 1,000 years and then vanished.
- Excavations show that the Indus Valley covered the largest area of any ancient civilization and that its two main cities, Mohenjo-Daro and Harappa, were carefully planned.
- The nomadic Aryans, who overran the Indus Valley, eventually created a new Indian civilization along the Ganges River.
- The Vedas and the great Aryan epic poems, the *Mahabharata* and the *Ramayana,* reveal much about the lives and religious beliefs of the early Aryans.
- Long distances and physical barriers separated China from the other ancient civilizations and contributed to the Chinese belief that it was the sole source of civilization.
- Early on, the Chinese developed the idea of the dynastic cycle, which explained the rise and fall of the many dynasties that came to rule China.
- Chinese religious practices centered around the veneration of ancestors and the concept of balance of two opposing forces, yin and yang.
- During the Shang and Zhou periods, the Chinese made achievements in astronomy and bronzework, discovered how to make silk and books, and developed a complex system of writing.

A Global View

How Did the First Civilizations Evolve?

The first humans were wanderers. Clad in animal skins, equipped with rude spears and digging sticks, they followed game animals and ripening fruit, roots, and wild grain from season to season. Over thousands of generations, they learned to chip stone tools, to make fire, and to decorate cave walls with pictures of animals.

Farming Villages

Then, about 10,000 years ago, some human beings abandoned the wandering life of hunter-gatherers. Settling into tiny villages of stone or mud huts, they raised crops and herded or penned up animals. Thanks to these dependable food sources, agricultural villages grew in number. Some of them began to specialize in arts and crafts, trade, and war.

The next step, from scattered farming villages to city-based civilizations, came a little more than 5,000 years ago. Here and there around the world, cities and city-states emerged. Kings, priests, and traders rose to wealth and power. And the invention of writing symbolized the emergence of a new way of life. We call it civilization.

Ancient Societies

Early civilizations took shape in North Africa, the Middle East, India, and China. Though they emerged in isolation across a widely scattered area, these first civilized societies had much in common.

Politically, the first civilizations turned increasingly to hereditary monarchs for leadership. These rulers depended on priests, officials, aristocrats, or merchants for support.

Priests provided divine sanction for royal rule, asserting that the kings of Sumerian city-states were "stewards of the gods" or that Egypt's pharaohs were gods themselves. Royal officials carried out the ruler's decrees, collected taxes, and supervised large-scale public works, including city walls and irrigation projects. Landowning aristocrats dominated agriculture and often served as military officers in royal armies.

	3000 B.C.	2500	2000
AFRICA	**3100** Menes unites Egypt	**2550** Great Pyramid and Sphinx at Giza	**2050** Middle Kingdom of Egypt begins
THE AMERICAS	**3200** Cultivation of maize and cotton	**2400** Temple platforms in Peru	**2000** Permanent towns in Valley of Mexico
ASIA AND OCEANIA	**3000** Sumerian city-states thrive	**2500** Indus Valley civilization	**2000** Development of Chinese writing
EUROPE	**3100** Skara Brae settlement		**2000** Bronze Age in Europe

The merchants of Mesopotamia, India, and elsewhere grew wealthy from trade, paid taxes, and strengthened the state economically.

Cities like Mohenjo-Daro or Babylon became the centers of political power and economic development. Most people, however, continued to live in small villages and cultivate the soil. These peasant majorities provided a foundation for the more elaborate lifestyles of their social superiors.

Ancient Cultures

These early civilizations built on the cultural achievements of the simpler societies from which they grew. Architects constructed elaborate royal palaces, temples like the ziggurats of Mesopotamia, and royal tombs like the pyramids of Egypt. Sculptors carved beautiful statues of gods, goddesses, and rulers. Painters depicted scenes of everyday life or military victories. The development of writing preserved some of the world's oldest literature, from the Egyptian *Tale of Sinuhe* and the Sumerian *Epic of Gilgamesh* to India's *Mahabharata* and ancient China's *Book of Songs*.

Major advances in science and technology may also be traced to ancient times. From metalworking and textiles to mathematics and astronomy, early civilizations added greatly to humanity's store of skills. Religions also grew more complex, producing early scriptures like the Vedas of India. While most ancient societies were polytheistic, the Hebrew people of Mesopotamia introduced monotheism, the worship of one single, all-powerful God.

Looking Ahead

A thousand years before the time of Jesus, civilization was still a rare phenomenon. Most people on all continents still lived in food-gathering bands, in farming villages, or as nomadic herders. But the future belonged to the islands of civilization that were emerging here and there around the world.

ACTIVITY Choose two events and two pictures from the time line below. For each, write a sentence explaining how it relates to the themes expressed in the Global View essay.

1500   1000   500 **B.C.**

1290–1224
Reign of Ramses II

750–650
Nubian rule over Egypt

1600
Nubian kingdom established

1400
Rise of Olmec civilization

850
Chavín culture in Peru

500
Adena mounds in Ohio

1650
Shang dynasty in China

1100
Assyrians expand power

539
Persian empire created

1700
Height of Minoan civilization

750
Greeks colonize the Mediterranean

You Decide

Exploring Global Issues

How Should Society Deal With Lawbreakers?

"Let the punishment fit the crime." To many people, this seems like the only fair and just way to deal with lawbreakers. The idea appears again and again in the Code of Hammurabi, history's first formal system of law. (See pages 37–38.) To others, though, punishments like Hammurabi's seem primitive and brutal.

The question of how to deal fairly and effectively with lawbreakers is as old as society itself. To begin your own investigation, examine these viewpoints.

CANAAN

700s B.C.

The ancient Hebrews looked to the Torah as God's authority on the law. The book of Leviticus states:

❝When a man causes a disfigurement in his neighbor, as he has done it shall be done to him, fracture for fracture, eye for eye, tooth for tooth; as he has disfigured a man, he shall be disfigured.❞

CHINA

200s B.C.

Hanfeizi, an influential scholar, believed that people were basically corrupt and that the only way to ensure an orderly society was to enforce strict laws:

❝People become naturally spoiled by love, but are submissive to authority. . . . That being so, rewards should be rich and certain that the people will be attracted to them; punishments should be severe and definite so that the people will fear them; and laws should be uniform and steadfast so that the people will be familiar with them.❞

FRANCE

1600s

Artist Jacques Callot depicted the mass hanging of a group of thieves. The caption warns that "it is the fate of vice-ridden men to experience the justice of Heaven sooner or later." ▼

ITALY

1764

Cesare Beccaria was one of the first reformers to argue against torture, capital punishment, and harsh treatment of criminals:

❝The purpose [of punishment] can only be to prevent the criminal from inflicting new injuries on its citizens and to deter others from similar acts. . . . Such punishments and such methods of inflicting them ought to be chosen, therefore, which will make the strongest and most lasting impression on the minds of men, and inflict the least torment on the body of the criminal.❞

GREAT BRITAIN

1969

After decades of heated debate, Great Britain abolished its death penalty in 1969. The picketers shown here were demonstrating outside a prison where a hanging was scheduled to take place. ▶

SINGAPORE

1994

In 1994, an American teenager living in Singapore was sentenced to a painful flogging for acts of vandalism. A Singaporean official defended his country's harsh penalties:

❝Unlike some other societies which tolerate acts of vandalism, Singapore has its own standards of social order as reflected in our laws. We are able to keep Singapore relatively crime free. We do not have a situation where acts of vandalism are commonplace, as in cities like New York, where even police cars are not spared the acts of vandals.❞

COMPARING VIEWPOINTS

1. Which viewpoints here seem closest to Hammurabi's code?
2. On what point would Cesare Beccaria agree with Hanfeizi? With the official in Singapore?
3. How do the two pictures convey opposing messages?

YOUR INVESTIGATION

ACTIVITY

1. Find out more about one of the viewpoints above or another viewpoint related to this topic. You might investigate:
   - Criminal provisions of the Sharia, the Islamic system of law.
   - Other law codes, such as the Code of Justinian or the Napoleonic Code.
   - The work of a prison reformer, such as Elizabeth Fry of England or Dorothea Dix of the United States.
   - The declaration of Pope John Paul II against capital punishment issued in April 1995.
   - Recent articles and editorials about capital punishment or prison conditions.

2. Decide which viewpoint you agree with most closely and express it in your own way. You may do so in an essay, a cartoon, a poem, a drawing or painting, a song, a skit, a video, or some other way.

UNIT 2

EMPIRES OF THE ANCIENT WORLD

Economics and Technology

3 *The Nubian city of Meroë was the center of a prosperous iron industry, which produced pots like this one. Ironworking technology probably spread to the rest of Africa from Meroë.*

NORTH AMERICA

ATLANTIC OCEAN

PACIFIC OCEAN

Diversity

1 *Several early cultures emerged, then vanished, in ancient Peru. This ceramic vessel was a product of the Moche culture that flourished from the 200s to the 500s.*

POLYNESIANS

1

SOUTH AMERICA

N
W—E
S

Religions and Value Systems

2 *By A.D. 200, missionaries and traders had spread Buddhism from India through Southeast Asia and into China. Stupas, or shrines, like this one honored the Buddha.*

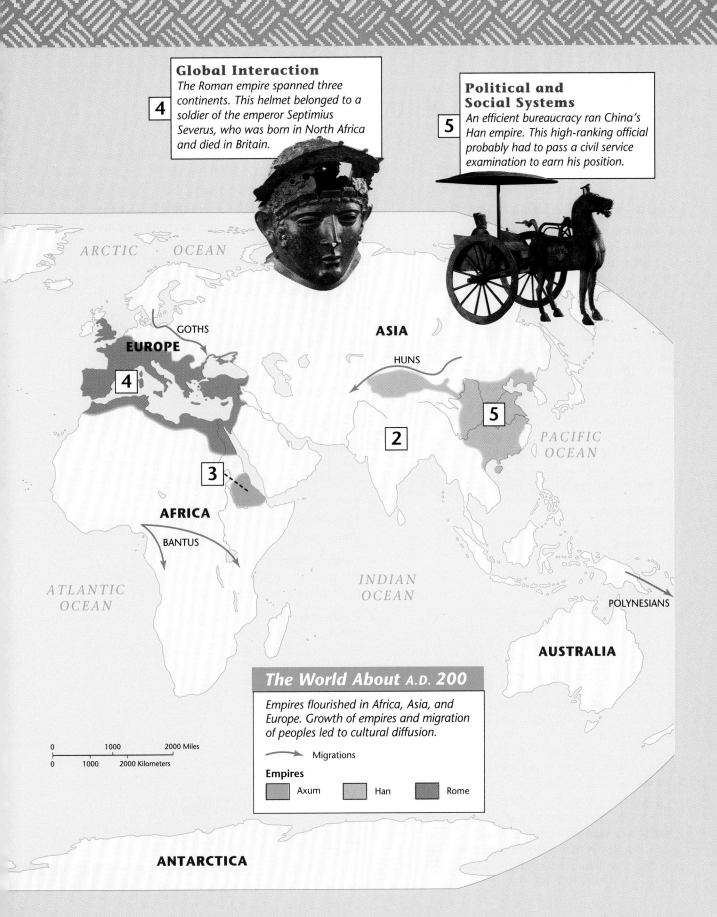

Global Interaction

4 The Roman empire spanned three continents. This helmet belonged to a soldier of the emperor Septimius Severus, who was born in North Africa and died in Britain.

Political and Social Systems

5 An efficient bureaucracy ran China's Han empire. This high-ranking official probably had to pass a civil service examination to earn his position.

ARCTIC OCEAN

GOTHS

EUROPE

ASIA

HUNS

4

AFRICA

BANTUS

2

3

5

PACIFIC OCEAN

INDIAN OCEAN

POLYNESIANS

ATLANTIC OCEAN

AUSTRALIA

The World About A.D. 200

Empires flourished in Africa, Asia, and Europe. Growth of empires and migration of peoples led to cultural diffusion.

Migrations

Empires

Axum   Han   Rome

0   1000   2000 Miles
0   1000   2000 Kilometers

ANTARCTICA

Empires of India and China

(600 B.C. – A.D. 550)

CHAPTER OUTLINE

1 **Hinduism and Buddhism**
2 **Powerful Empires of India**
3 **Pillars of Indian Life**
4 **Three Schools of Thought in China**
5 **Strong Rulers Unite China**

Thousands of years ago, religious teachers in India tried to answer questions about the nature of the universe. Their ideas were later collected into the Upanishads (oo PAN ih shadz). These sacred texts use vivid images to explain complex ideas about the human soul and the connectedness of all life. In one story, a man tries to show his son that the essence of life cannot be seen. He orders the boy to break open the fruit of the banyan, or fig, tree:

66'What do you see?'
  'Very tiny seeds, sir.'
  'Break one.'
  'I have broken it, sir.'
  'Now, what do you see?'
  'Nothing, sir.'
  'My son,' the father said, 'what you do
  not perceive is the essence, and in that
  essence the mighty banyan tree exists.
  Believe me, my son, in that essence is
  the soul of all that is.'99

Stories like this one convey the teachings of Hinduism. Hinduism and Buddhism were two major religions that emerged in ancient India. In China, too, a unique system of thought developed, which was based on the teachings of Confucius. These religions and philosophies spread across Asia, where their influence still affects modern societies from India and Southeast Asia to China, Korea, and Japan.

Complex belief systems were a feature of the civilizations that rose in India, China, and the Mediterranean world between 500 B.C. and A.D. 500. Historians call them classical civilizations because they set patterns in government, philosophy, religion, science, and the arts that served as the framework for later cultures.

Though they differed greatly from one another, classical civilizations had features in common. Strong leaders brought vast territories under their control. To unify their empires, they organized efficient bureaucracies, built strong armies, and improved systems of transportation and communication.

FOCUS ON these questions as you read:

■ **Religions and Value Systems**
  What religious and moral ideas helped shape the civilizations of India and China?

■ **Political and Social Systems**
  How did strong leaders centralize power and impose unity on diverse peoples?

■ **Global Interaction**
  What factors encouraged or limited contacts between peoples across Asia?

■ **Economics and Technology**
  What discoveries and inventions put Gupta India and Han China in the forefront of the world's technology?

TIME AND PLACE

The Buddha Preaching the Law *From India, the Buddha's disciples spread his teachings to China, Korea, Japan, and other Asian lands. This painting from the A.D. 700s was found in a cave temple in China. The Buddha sits under a beautiful canopy as he preaches to his devoted disciples.* **Art and Literature** *How does this painting suggest that the Buddha is a holy and important figure?*

HUMANITIES LINK

Art History Kailasa Temple (page 86).

Literature In this chapter, you will encounter passages from the following works of literature: the Upanishads (page 76); the *Tripitaka* (page 81); Avvaiyar, "The weapons of my king are blunt" (page 85); Kalidasa, *Shakuntala* (pages 86–87); Confucius, *The Analects* (page 90); "My people have married me" (page 95).

551 B.C. Confucius born	**321** B.C. Chandragupta unites northern India	**221** B.C. Shi Huangdi unites China	A.D. **100s** Buddhism spreads from India to China	A.D. **320** Golden age of Gupta empire begins	

B.C.	600	400	200	B.C.	A.D.	200	400	600	A.D.

1 Hinduism and Buddhism

Guide for Reading

- Why is Hinduism such a complex religion?

- What are the central teachings of Hinduism and Buddhism?

- How did Buddhism become a major world religion?

- **Vocabulary** *atman, reincarnation, karma, dharma, ahimsa, nirvana*

As Hinduism evolved over 3,500 years, it absorbed diverse beliefs and forms of worship. If you visited a Hindu temple in India today, you would see people place offerings before the statues of many gods and goddesses. Yet a priest might begin a service with this prayer:

> 66O Lord, forgive the sins that are due to my human limitations. You are everywhere, but I worship you here. You are without form, but I worship you in these forms. You need no praise, yet I offer you these prayers.99

Like Hinduism, Buddhism includes a wide variety of beliefs. The ethical and spiritual message of these religions profoundly shaped the civilization of India.

Hinduism: Unity and Diversity

Unlike most major religions, Hinduism has no single founder and no single sacred text. Instead, it grew out of the overlapping beliefs of the diverse groups who settled India. The process probably began when the Aryans added the gods of the Indus Valley people to their own. Later people brought other gods, beliefs,

and practices. As a result, Hinduism became one of the world's most complex religions, with countless gods and goddesses and many forms of worship existing side by side. Despite this diversity, all Hindus share certain basic beliefs.

Many gods—or one? "God is one, but wise people know it by many names." This ancient proverb reflects a central feature of Hinduism. By the late Vedic age, Hindu thinkers came to believe that everything in the universe was part of the unchanging, all-powerful spiritual force called brahman. (See page 55.) To Hindus, brahman is too complex an idea for most people to understand, so they worship gods that give a concrete form to brahman.

The most important Hindu gods are Brahma, the Creator; Vishnu, the Preserver; and Shiva, the Destroyer. Each represents aspects of brahman. Each of these gods can take many forms, human or animal, and each also has his own family. Some Hindus, for example, worship Shakti, the powerful wife of Shiva. She is both kind and cruel, a creator and destroyer.

The goal of life. To Hindus, every person has an essential self, or atman (AHT muhn). But atman is really just another name for brahman. The ultimate goal of existence, Hindus believe,

Shiva: Lord of the Dance This bronze sculpture portrays the god Shiva dancing to destroy and re-create the universe. With his feet, he crushes a demon into submission. The circle of fire represents the Hindu belief in an endless cycle of creation, death, and rebirth. *Diversity* Why do you think various cultures use the circle to symbolize continuity?

is achieving *moksha* (MAHK shuh), or union with brahman. In order to do that, individuals must free themselves from selfish desires that separate them from brahman. Most people cannot achieve moksha in one lifetime, but Hindus believe in reincarnation, or the rebirth of the soul in another bodily form. Reincarnation allows people to continue working toward moksha through several lifetimes.

Karma and dharma. In each existence, Hindus believe, a person can come closer to achieving moksha by obeying the law of karma. Karma refers to all the actions of a person's life that affect his or her fate in the next life. To Hindus, all existence is ranked. Humans are closest to brahman. Then come animals, plants, and objects like rocks or water. People who live virtuously earn good karma and are reborn at a higher level of existence. Those who do evil acquire bad karma and are reborn into suffering. In Indian art, this endless cycle of death and rebirth is symbolized by the image of the wheel.

To escape the wheel of fate, Hinduism stresses the importance of dharma (DAHR muh), the religious and moral duties of an individual. These duties vary according to class, occupation, gender, or age. By obeying one's dharma, a person acquires merit for the next life. As you will read, the concepts of karma and dharma helped ensure the social order by supporting the caste system.

Sacred texts. Over several thousand years, Hindu teachings were recorded in sacred texts such as the Vedas and Upanishads. The *Bhagavad-Gita* (see page 56) spells out many ethical ideas central to Hinduism. In that poem, you will recall, the god Krishna instructs Prince Arjuna on the importance of duty and the unimportance of the self.

Another key moral principle of Hinduism is ahimsa (uh HIM sah), or nonviolence. To Hindus, all people and things are aspects of brahman and should therefore be respected. Many holy people have tried to follow the path of nonviolence. The teacher Mahavira (muh hah VEE ruh) developed an extreme form of ahimsa. About 500 B.C., he founded Jainism (JIN ihz um), a new religion that grew out of Hindu traditions. Jain teachings emphasized meditation and self-denial. To avoid accidentally killing a living thing, even an insect, Jains carried brooms to sweep the ground in front of their feet.

Opposition to the Brahmins. Mahavira lived in a time of frequent warfare. During this troubled period, Brahmin priests acquired great power by insisting that they alone could perform the sacred rites to bring victory in battle or ensure adequate rainfall. Reformers like Mahavira rejected Brahmin domination and offered other paths to truth. In the foothills of the Himalayas, another reformer, Siddhartha Gautama (sihd DAHR tuh go TUH muh), founded a new religion, Buddhism. His teachings eventually spread across Asia to become one of the world's most influential religions.

Gautama Buddha: The Enlightened One

The facts of Gautama's life are buried in legend. We know that he was born about 566 B.C. into a high-ranking family of the Kshatriya caste. According to tradition, his mother dreamed that a radiant white elephant descended to her from heaven. Because of this dream and other signs, a prophet predicted that the young boy would someday become a wandering holy man. To stop that from happening, Gautama's father kept him in the palace, surrounded by comfort and luxury. Prince Gautama enjoyed a happy life. He married a beautiful woman and had a son who filled his hours with joy.

The search. Then one day, as Gautama rode beyond the palace gardens, he saw for the first time a sick person, an old person, and a dead body. This new awareness of human suffering deeply disturbed him. Late that night, he whispered farewell to his sleeping wife and child and left the palace, never to return. He set out to discover "the realm of life where there is neither suffering nor death."

Gautama wandered for years, vainly seeking answers from Hindu scholars and holy men. He tried fasting, but succeeded only in making himself ill. Eventually, he sat down to meditate under a giant tree, determined to stay there until

ISSUES For TODAY The teachings of both Hinduism and Buddhism emphasize the need to overcome individual desires and ambitions. What value do different cultures place on the individual?

he understood the mystery of life. For 48 days, evil spirits tempted him to give up his meditations. Then, he suddenly believed that he understood the cause and cure for suffering and sorrow. When he rose, he was Gautama no longer, but the Buddha, the "Enlightened One."

Four Noble Truths. The Buddha spent the rest of his life teaching others what he had learned. In his first sermon after reaching enlightenment, he explained the Four Noble Truths that stand at the heart of Buddhism:

1. All life is full of suffering, pain, and sorrow.
2. The cause of suffering is the desire for things that are really illusions, such as riches, power, and long life.
3. The only cure for suffering is to overcome desire.
4. The way to overcome desire is to follow the Eightfold Path.

The Buddha described the Eightfold Path as "right views, right aspirations, right speech, right conduct, right livelihood, right effort, right mindfulness, and right contemplation." The first two steps involved understanding the Four Noble Truths and committing oneself to the Eightfold Path. Next, a person had to live a moral life, avoiding evil words and actions. Through meditation, a person might at last achieve enlightenment. For the Buddhist, the final goal is nirvana, union with the universe and release from the cycle of rebirth.

The Buddha saw the Eightfold Path as a middle way between a life devoted to pleasure and one based on harsh self-denial. He emphasized moral and ethical rules such as honesty, charity, and kindness to all living creatures.

Shared traditions. Buddhism, like Hinduism, grew out of Vedic religious traditions. Both Hindus and Buddhists accepted the law of karma, dharma, and moksha and believed in a cycle of rebirth. Nonviolence was also central to Buddhism.

Yet Buddhism differed from Hinduism in several important ways. The Buddha rejected the priests, formal rituals, and the existence of the many gods of Hinduism. Instead, he urged each individual to seek enlightenment through meditation. Buddhists also rejected the caste system, offering the hope of nirvana to all regardless of birth.

Spread of Buddhism

The Buddha attracted many disciples, or followers, who accompanied him as he preached across northern India. Many men and women who accepted the Buddha's teachings set up monasteries and convents for meditation and study. Some Buddhist monasteries grew into major centers of learning.

Reclining Buddha Traditionally, images of the Buddha lying down represent his achievement of nirvana. Here, a Buddha of carved granite lies amidst the natural beauty of a botanical garden in Sri Lanka. **Religions and Value Systems** Why do you think a garden was chosen as the site for this sculpture?

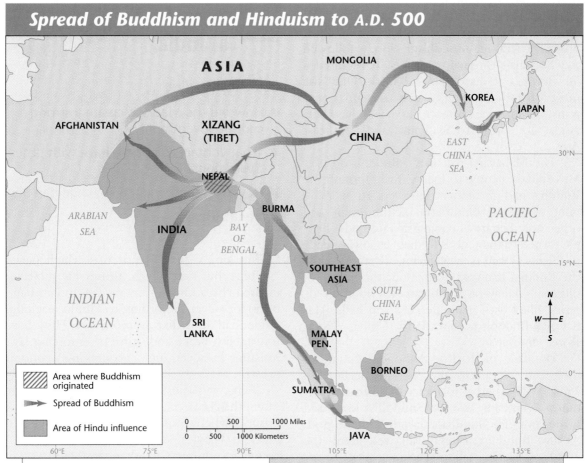

Spread of Buddhism and Hinduism to A.D. 500

ASIA

MONGOLIA

KOREA

JAPAN

AFGHANISTAN

XIZANG (TIBET)

CHINA

EAST CHINA SEA

30°N

NEPAL

PACIFIC OCEAN

ARABIAN SEA

INDIA

BAY OF BENGAL

BURMA

15°N

INDIAN OCEAN

SOUTHEAST ASIA

SOUTH CHINA SEA

N
W   E
S

SRI LANKA

MALAY PEN.

BORNEO

0°

SUMATRA

JAVA

Area where Buddhism originated

Spread of Buddhism

Area of Hindu influence

0   500   1000 Miles
0   500   1000 Kilometers

60°E   75°E   90°E   105°E   120°E   135°E

GEOGRAPHY AND HISTORY

Missionaries and traders carried Buddhism and Hinduism from their birthplace in India. Over time, these religions spread to many parts of Asia.

1. **Location** On the map, locate (a) India, (b) Sri Lanka, (c) Southeast Asia, (d) China, (e) Korea, (f) Japan.
2. **Movement** How did Buddhism spread to Japan?
3. **Critical Thinking** **Drawing Conclusions** Review the information about the spread of Buddhism on pages 81–82. Which arrows on the map probably represent the spread of Theravada Buddhism?

The Buddha's death, like his birth, is clouded in legend. At age 80, he is said to have eaten spoiled food in the home of a poor family. As he lay dying, he told his disciples, "Decay is inherent in all things. Work out your own salvation with diligence."

Sacred texts. After the Buddha's death, some of his followers collected his teachings into a sacred text called the *Tripitaka*, or "Three Baskets of Wisdom." One of the "baskets" includes sayings like this one, which echoes the Hindu emphasis on duty:

66Let no one forget his own duty for the sake of another's, however great. Let a man, after he has discerned his own duty, be always attentive to his duty.99

Other sayings give the Buddha's version of the golden rule: "Overcome anger by not growing angry. Overcome evil with good. Overcome the liar by truth."

Two schools. Missionaries and traders spread Buddhism across India to many parts of

Asia. Gradually, Buddhism split into two major schools, Theravada (ther uh VAH duh) Buddhism and Mahayana (mah huh YAH nuh) Buddhism. Theravada Buddhism closely followed the Buddha's original teachings. It required a life devoted to hard spiritual work. Only the most dedicated seekers, such as monks and nuns, could hope to reach nirvana. The Theravada sect spread to Sri Lanka and Southeast Asia.

The Mahayana sect made Buddhism easier for ordinary people to follow. Even though the Buddha had forbidden followers to worship him, Mahayana Buddhists pictured him and other holy beings as compassionate gods. People turned to these gods for help in solving daily problems as well as in achieving salvation. While the Buddha had said little about the nature of nirvana, Mahayana Buddhists described an afterlife filled with many heavens and hells. Mahayana Buddhism spread to China, Tibet, Korea, and Japan.

Decline in India. Although Buddhism took firm root across Asia, it slowly declined in India. With its great tolerance of diversity, Hinduism eventually absorbed Buddhist ideas and made room for Buddha as another Hindu god. A few Buddhist centers survived until the 1100s, when they fell to Muslim armies that invaded India. (See Chapter 11.)

SECTION 1 REVIEW

1. **Identify** (a) Shiva, (b) Jainism, (c) Siddhartha Gautama, (d) Four Noble Truths, (e) Theravada, (f) Mahayana.
2. **Define** (a) atman, (b) reincarnation, (c) karma, (d) dharma, (e) ahimsa, (f) nirvana.
3. What are three basic teachings of Hinduism?
4. According to the Buddha, what actions would allow people to escape worldly suffering?
5. How did Buddhism spread beyond India?
6. *Critical Thinking* **Drawing Conclusions** How do you think Mahayana teachings increased the appeal of Buddhism?
7. *ACTIVITY* Make a chart or diagram comparing Hinduism and Buddhism. Place a star next to any beliefs or practices that the two religions have in common.

2 Powerful Empires of India

Guide for Reading

■ How did the Mauryas create a strong central government?

■ What contacts did India have with other civilizations?

■ How did Gupta India enjoy a golden age?

■ **Vocabulary** *stupa*

"The king's good is not that which pleases him, but that which pleases his subjects," insisted the author of an ancient Indian handbook for rulers. According to Hindu teachings, a ruler had duties like everyone else. His job was to establish peace and order by enforcing laws, resisting invaders, and encouraging economic growth.

Achieving those goals was difficult. More often than not, northern India was a battleground, where rival rajahs fought for control of the rich Ganges Valley. Then, in 321 B.C., a young adventurer, Chandragupta Maurya (chun druh GUP tuh MOW uhr yuh), forged the first great Indian empire.

The Maurya Empire

Chandragupta first gained power in the Ganges Valley. Building a large army, he then conquered northern India. His son and grandson later pushed south, adding much of the Deccan to their empire. From 321 B.C. to 185 B.C., the Maurya dynasty ruled over a vast, united empire.

Record of the Greek ambassador. We know about Chandragupta largely from reports written by Megasthenes (meh GAS thuh neez), a Greek ambassador to the Maurya court. He described the great Maurya capital at Pataliputra (pah tah lih POO trah), probably the largest and most prosperous city in the world at that time. It boasted schools and a library as well as splendid palaces, temples, and parks. An awed Megasthenes reported that a huge wall surrounding the city "was crowned with 570 towers and had 64 gates."

Chandragupta maintained order through a well-organized bureaucracy. Royal officials supervised the building of roads and harbors to benefit trade. Other officials collected taxes and managed state-owned factories and shipyards. People sought justice in royal courts and from the emperor himself. A brutal but efficient secret police reported on corruption, crime, and dissent within the empire.

Chandragupta's rule was effective but harsh. Fearful of his many enemies, he had specially trained women warriors guard his palace, while servants tasted his food to protect him from poisoning. Secret passages in the palace let him slip about unseen.

The "philosopher king." The most honored Maurya emperor was Chandragupta's grandson, Asoka (uh SOH kuh). A few years after becoming emperor in 268 B.C., Asoka fought a long, bloody war to conquer the Deccan region of Kalinga. Then, horrified at the slaughter— over 100,000 dead—Asoka turned his back on further conquests. He converted to Buddhism, rejected violence, and resolved to rule by moral example.

Asoka had stone pillars set up across India, announcing laws and promising righteous government. On one, he proclaimed:

> **❝**All people are my children, and just as I desire for my children that they should obtain welfare and happiness, both in this world and the next, so do I desire the same for all people.**❞**

Asoka took steps to help his "children" by building roads, rest houses for travelers, and hospitals. "I have had banyan trees planted on the roads to give shade to people and animals," he noted. "I have planted mango groves, and I have had [wells] dug and shelters erected along the roads."

True to the Buddhist principle of respect for all life, Asoka became a vegetarian and limited Hindu animal sacrifices. He sent missionaries, women as well as men, across India and to Sri Lanka. He thus paved the way for the later spread of Buddhism throughout Asia. Although Asoka promoted Buddhism, he preached tolerance for other religions.

Asoka's rule brought peace and prosperity, and helped unite the diverse people within his

Pillars of Asoka *Along roads and near towns all over India, Asoka's massive stone pillars reached skyward for all to see. Atop the columns sat sculptures of lions, elephants, or other symbols. Buddhist virtues and ideals of justice were inscribed into each pillar.* **Political and Social Systems** *What methods do modern governments use to communicate with citizens?*

Maurya and Gupta Empires

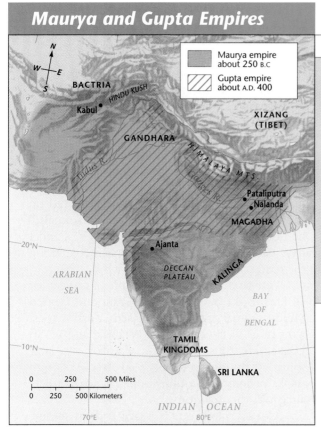

Maurya empire
about 250 B.C

Gupta empire
about A.D. 400

GEOGRAPHY AND HISTORY

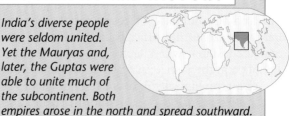

India's diverse people were seldom united. Yet the Mauryas and, later, the Guptas were able to unite much of the subcontinent. Both empires arose in the north and spread southward.

1. **Location** On the map, locate (a) Hindu Kush, (b) Kalinga, (c) Gandhara, (d) Ganges River, (e) Deccan plateau.
2. **Region** What lands included in the Maurya empire were not part of the Gupta empire?
3. **Critical Thinking** *Analyzing Information* What physical features prevented further expansion by the Maurya rulers?

empire. After his death, however, Maurya power declined. By 185 B.C., rival princes again battled for power across the northern plain.

Division and Unity

During its long history, India has seldom been united. In ancient times, as today, the subcontinent was home to many peoples and cultures. Although the Aryan north shared a common civilization, fierce local rivalries kept it divided. In the Deccan south, other cultures thrived. Distance and geographic differences further separated the north and south.

Adding to the turmoil, foreign invaders frequently pushed through mountain passes into northern India. Some came to plunder rich Indian cities but stayed to rule. The divided northern kingdoms could not often resist such conquerors.

Despite invasions and war, India developed into a center of world trade. By 100 B.C., Indian textiles, gems, incense, and spices were widely in demand. Merchants sent Indian goods overland

into Central Asia and China. Others took cargoes by sea to the Middle East, Egypt, East Africa, and Southeast Asia.

Shortly before Chandragupta gained power, Alexander the Great had expanded his empire from Europe across Persia, then into northwestern India. (See Chapter 5.) Alexander controlled the Indus Valley for only a few years, but his conquests opened up a trade corridor between India and the Mediterranean world. After Alexander's death, descendants of his soldiers set up kingdoms in northwestern India, where Greek styles influenced Buddhist art.

Later, during Maurya times and after, Rome conquered much of the Middle East. There, Romans acquired a taste for Indian goods, stimulating trade between the two regions. Indian merchants sent fine textiles and other luxuries westward to eager Roman buyers.

Kingdoms of the Deccan

Most goods produced and shipped to Rome came from Indian cities in the Deccan. Like the northern plain, the Deccan was divided into many kingdoms. Each had its own capital with magnificent temples and bustling workshops. Unlike the peoples of the Aryan north, the peoples of the Deccan were Dravidians with very different languages and traditions. Women, for example, enjoyed a high status and economic power. The Tamil kingdoms, which occupied much of the southernmost part of India, were sometimes ruled by queens.

Over the centuries, Hindu and Buddhist traditions and Sanskrit writings drifted south and blended with local cultures. Deccan rulers generally tolerated all religions as well as the many foreigners who settled in their busy ports.

The Tamil kingdoms have left a rich literature. Tamil poets described fierce wars and festive occasions along with the routines of peasant and city life. One noted Tamil poet, Avvaiyar (ahv vī yahr), praised the virtues of her king:

66My king, when rich, freely gives food away,
    when poor he eats with his men.
    He is the head of the family of the poor,
    yet great is he. . . .99

Golden Age of the Guptas

Although many kingdoms flourished in the Deccan, the most powerful Indian states rose in the north. About 500 years after the Mauryas, the Gupta dynasty again united much of India. (See the map on page 84.) Under the Guptas, who ruled from A.D. 320 to about 550, India enjoyed a golden age. Gupta emperors presided over a dazzling court in the old Maurya capital at Pataliputra. More important, they organized a strong central government that ensured peace and prosperity.

Peace and prosperity. Gupta rule was probably looser than that of the Mauryas. Much power was left in the hands of individual villages and of city governments elected by merchants and artisans.

Faxian (FAH shee EHN), a Chinese Buddhist monk who visited India in the 400s, left behind a detailed record of life under the Guptas. He reported on the mild nature of Gupta rule:

66The people are very well off, without poll tax or official restrictions. Only those who till the royal lands return a portion of the profit of the land as tax. If they desire to go, they go. If they like to stop, they stop. The kings govern without corporal punishment. Criminals are fined, according to circumstances, lightly or heavily.99

The Chinese visitor noted that the wealthy set up hospitals for the poor and that, in accordance with Buddhist teachings, most of the people were vegetarians.

Trade and farming flourished across the Gupta empire. Farmers harvested crops of wheat, rice, and sugar cane. In cities, artisans produced cotton cloth, pottery, and metalware for local markets and for export to East Africa, the Middle East, and Southeast Asia. The prosperity of Gupta India contributed to a flowering in the arts and learning.

Advances in learning. In India, as elsewhere during this period, students were educated in religious schools. In Hindu and Buddhist centers, learning was not limited to religion and philosophy. The large Buddhist monastery-university at Nalanda, which attracted students from other parts of Asia, taught mathematics, medicine, physics, languages, literature, and other subjects.

Indian advances in mathematics had a wide impact on the world. Gupta mathematicians devised the simple system of writing numbers that is used today. These numerals are now called "Arabic" numerals because it was Arabs who carried them from India to the Middle East and Europe. Indian mathematicians originated the concept of zero. They also developed the decimal system based on the number 10, which we still use today.

By Gupta times, Indian physicians had pioneered the use of herbs and other remedies to treat illness. Surgeons were skilled in setting bones and in simple plastic surgery to repair facial injuries. Doctors also began vaccinating people against smallpox about 1,000 years before this practice was used in Europe.

Architecture. Rajahs sponsored the building of magnificent stone temples. Sometimes, cities grew up around the temples to house the thousands of artisans and laborers working there. Hindu temples were designed to reflect cosmic patterns. The ideal shape was a square inscribed in a circle to symbolize eternity.

Buddhists built splendid stupas, large dome-shaped shrines that housed the sacred

Kailasa Temple *Indians considered caves holy and often built temples inside them. Inspired by this tradition, Indian stonemasons cut directly into rock cliffs to create Kailasa Temple and its dark cavernous rooms. Artists decorated the temple with numerous sculptures of Hindu gods, legendary heroes, and mythical creatures.* **Art and Literature** *Where in the temple do you see areas that appear like caves?*

remains of the Buddha or other holy people. The stupas were ringed with enclosed walkways where Buddhist monks slowly walked, chanting their prayers.

Magnificent carvings. While stupas were quite plain, their gateways featured elaborate carvings that told stories of the life of the Buddha. He was portrayed with a gentle smile symbolizing the inner peace of someone who has reached nirvana. Hindu temples, too, were covered with carvings of gods and goddesses, elephants, monkeys, and ordinary people. A familiar figure is the four-armed god Shiva, who dances the world out of existence and then re-creates it again. (See the picture on page 78.)

Paintings at Ajanta. On the walls of the cave temples at Ajanta in western India, Buddhist artists painted rich murals recalling Buddhist stories and legends. The wall paintings also reveal scenes of life in Gupta India, from beg-

gars with bowls to sailors at sea to princes courting princesses in lovely flowered gardens. (See the picture on page 88.)

Literature. During Gupta times, many fine writers added to the rich heritage of Indian literature. They collected and recorded fables and folk tales in the Sanskrit language. In time, Indian fables were carried west to Persia, Egypt, and Greece.

The greatest Gupta poet and playwright was Kalidasa. His most famous play, *Shakuntala,* tells the moving story of a king who marries the lovely orphan Shakuntala. Under an evil spell, the king forgets his beloved bride. After many plot twists, he finally recovers his memory and is reunited with her. At the end of the play, the king's wise adviser blesses the royal couple:

    66For countless ages may the god of
      gods,

Lord of the atmosphere, by plentiful
   showers
Secure abundant harvest to your
   subjects;
And you by frequent offerings
   preserve
The Thunderer's friendship! Thus,
   by interchange
Of kindly actions, may you both
   confer
Unnumbered benefits on Earth and
   Heaven!**"**

Looking Ahead

The Gupta empire reached its height just as the Roman empire in the west collapsed. (See Chapter 6.) Before long, Gupta India also declined under the pressure of civil war, weak rulers, and foreign invaders. From central Asia came the White Huns, a nomadic people who overran the weakened Gupta empire, destroying its cities and trade.

Once again, India split into many kingdoms. It would see no great empire like those of the Mauryas or Guptas for almost 1,000 years. Then, as you will read in Chapter 11, another wave of invaders pushed into India and created a powerful new empire.

SECTION *2* REVIEW

1. **Identify** (a) Chandragupta Maurya, (b) Asoka, (c) Avvaiyar, (d) Kalidasa.
2. **Define** stupa.
3. (a) What steps did Chandragupta take to unite his empire? (b) How did Asoka's rule differ from that of his grandfather?
4. Give three examples of interactions between India and other civilizations.
5. *Critical Thinking* **Defending a Position** "All faiths deserve to be honored for one reason or another," proclaimed Asoka. How do you think Asoka's policy of toleration helped him unite his empire?
6. *ACTIVITY* Imagine that you are either Chandragupta, Asoka, or one of the Gupta emperors. Write a list of three to five "Rules for Governing an Empire."

3 Pillars of Indian Life

Guide for Reading

- How was caste linked to Hindu beliefs?
- How were Indian villages organized?
- What values influenced family life?
- **Vocabulary** *joint family, patriarchal*

Most Indians knew nothing of the dazzling courts of the Mauryas or Guptas. The vast majority were peasants who lived in the countless villages that dotted the Indian landscape. In Gupta times, as today, the village ensured stability and order. Two other pillars of Indian life were the caste system and the family.

A Complex Caste System

In Chapter 3, you read how the Aryans had divided society into four occupational classes. Non-Aryans were considered outcastes and held the lowest jobs. By Gupta times, many additional castes and subcastes had evolved. As invaders were absorbed into Indian society, they formed new castes. Other castes grew out of new trades, occupations, and religions. By modern times, major castes numbered in the hundreds, with thousands of minor or local subcastes.

Complex rules. Caste was closely linked to Hindu beliefs, although other religious groups also accepted it. To Hindus, people in different castes were different species of beings. A high-caste Brahmin, for example, was purer and therefore closer to moksha than someone from a lower caste. To ensure spiritual purity, a web of complex rules developed within the caste system.

Caste rules governed every aspect of life—where people lived, what they ate, how they dressed, and how they earned a living. Rules forbade marrying outside one's caste or eating with members of another caste. High-caste people had the strictest rules to protect them from the spiritually polluted, or impure, lower castes.

For the lowest-ranked outcastes, or "Untouchables," life was harsh and restricted. To them fell the jobs that were considered "impure," such as digging graves, cleaning streets, or turning animal hides into leather. Other castes feared that even the shadow of an Untouchable could spread pollution. Untouchables not only had to live apart, but they also had to sound a wooden clapper to warn of their approach.

Effects. Despite its inequalities, caste ensured a stable social order. People believed that the law of karma determined their caste. While they could not change their status in this life, they could reach a higher state in a future life. The road to improvement lay in faithfully fulfilling the duties of their present caste.

The caste system gave people a sense of identity. Each caste had its own occupation and its own leaders. Caste members cooperated to help one another. Further, each caste had its own special role in Indian society as a whole. Although strictly separated, different castes depended on one another for their basic needs. A lower-caste carpenter, for example, built the home of a higher-caste scholar.

A Diverse People In the Ajanta caves in western India, artists painted murals to illustrate Buddhist beliefs and aspects of Indian life. This mural includes people of the many castes and ethnic groups of Indian society. **Religions and Value Systems** How does this mural reflect the Buddha's rejection of the caste system?

The caste system also adapted to changing conditions, absorbing foreigners and new occupations into their own castes. This flexibility allowed people with diverse customs and practices to live side by side in relative harmony.

Village Life

Throughout India's history, the village was at the heart of life. A typical village included a cluster of homes made of earth or stone. Beyond these dwellings stretched the fields, where farmers grew wheat, rice, cotton, sugar cane, or other crops according to region. In most of India, farming depended on the rains brought by the summer monsoons. Too much or too little rain meant famine. Villagers cooperated to build or maintain vital irrigation systems, as well as roads and temples.

Each village ran its own affairs based on caste rules and tradition. It faced little outside interference as long as it paid its share of taxes. A village headman and council made decisions and dealt with outside authorities when necessary. Members of the council included the most respected people of the village. In early times, women served on the village council, but as Hindu law began to place greater restrictions on women, they were later excluded.

Family Life

Within the village, the basic unit was the joint family, in which parents, children, grandchildren, uncles, and their offspring shared a common dwelling. The joint family was usually achieved only by the wealthy. In poor families, people often died young, so several generations seldom survived long enough to live together. Still, even when relatives did not share the same house, close ties linked brothers, uncles, cousins, and nephews.

The Indian family was patriarchal; that is, the father or oldest male headed the household. Because he was thought to have wisdom and experience, the head of the family enjoyed great authority. Still, his power was limited by sacred laws and tradition. Usually, he made decisions after consulting his wife and other family members. Property belonged to the whole family.

Children and parents. The joint family fostered a sense of security and unity. From an early age, children learned their family duties, which included obeying caste rules. Family interests came before individual wishes.

Children worked with older relatives in the fields or at a family trade. While still young, a daughter learned that as a wife she would be expected to serve and obey her husband and his family. A son learned the rituals to honor the family's ancestors. Such rites linked the living and the dead, deepening family bonds across the generations.

For parents, an important duty was arranging good marriages for their children, based on caste and family interests. Marriage customs varied. In northern India, a bride's family commonly provided a dowry, or payment to the bridegroom, and financed the costly wedding festivities. After marriage, the daughter left her home and became part of her husband's family.

Women. Attitudes and customs affecting women changed over time and varied across India. In early Aryan society, women seem to have enjoyed a higher status than in later times. Women even composed a few Vedic hymns. By early Gupta times, upper-caste Hindu women could still move freely in society and some were well educated.

Women were thought to have *shakti,* a creative energy, that men lacked. Poets acknowledged a woman's power:

> 66The wife is half the man, the best
> of friends,
> the root of . . . all that will help him
> in the other world.
> With a wife a man does mighty deeds,
> with a wife a man finds courage.99

Still, shakti might also be a destructive force. A husband's duty was to channel his wife's energy in the proper direction. For a woman, rebirth into a higher existence was gained through devotion to her husband.

Growing restrictions. By late Gupta times, upper-class women were increasingly restricted to the home. When they went outside the home, they were supposed to cover themselves

Hindu Women *Hindu society valued the creative power of women. In a religious ritual called* dohada, *a woman nurtured a tree with gifts of wine to help increase its fruitfulness. In this sculpture, the two women on the balcony observe a woman who may be performing* dohada. **Religions and Value Systems** *Why do you think one of the women is holding her finger to her lips?*

from head to foot. Lower-class women, however, labored in the fields or worked at spinning and weaving.

As customs changed, a high-caste widow was forbidden to remarry. In parts of India, she was sometimes expected to become a *sati,* or "virtuous woman," by joining her dead husband on his funeral fire. Some widows accepted this painful death as a noble duty that wiped out their own and their husbands' sins. Eyewitness accounts, however, show that other women bitterly resisted the custom.

SECTION 3 REVIEW

1. **Define** (a) joint family, (b) patriarchal.
2. (a) Describe the development of the caste system after Aryan times. (b) How did the caste system provide a sense of order?
3. Describe the government of an Indian village.
4. How did the lives of Indian women change over time?
5. *Critical Thinking* **Analyzing Information** How did the Hindu doctrines of karma and dharma support the caste system?
6. *ACTIVITY* With a partner, act out a conversation between a father and son or a mother and daughter in an Indian village on the child's wedding day. The parent should share information about family and social traditions.

4 Three Schools of Thought in China

Guide for Reading

- What were the teachings of Confucius?
- How did Confucian ideas help shape Chinese life?
- How did Legalist and Daoist views differ?
- **Vocabulary** *filial piety, alchemy*

> 66 Lead the people by laws and regulate them by punishments, and the people will simply try to keep out of jail, but will have no sense of shame. Lead the people by virtue . . . and they will have a sense of shame and moreover will become good. 99

The great philosopher Confucius* offered this advice to China's rulers about 500 B.C. Government, he felt, was more than enforcing laws. Rulers must also set a good example.

Confucius lived in late Zhou times, when war raged across China. Economic and social changes were also disrupting old ways of life. Seeing the chaos, thinkers put forward ideas about how to end conflict and restore social order. Their ideas would shape Chinese civilization for the next 2,500 years.

The Wisdom of Confucius

China's most influential philosopher, Confucius, was born in 551 B.C. to a noble but poor family. A brilliant scholar, Confucius hoped to become an adviser to a local ruler. For years, he wandered from court to court talking to rulers about how to govern. Perhaps because he was too outspoken in his views, he never got a permanent position at court. Instead, he turned to teaching. As his reputation for wisdom grew, he attracted many loyal students.

The Analects. Like two other influential thinkers who lived about the same time,

*The name Confucius is the western version of the name Kong Fuzi, or Master Kong.

Gautama Buddha in India and Socrates in Greece, Confucius never wrote down his ideas. After his death, students collected his sayings in *The Analects.*

Unlike the Buddha, Confucius took little interest in religious matters such as salvation. Instead, he was concerned with worldly goals, especially how to ensure social order and good government. Confucius studied ancient texts to learn the rules of conduct that had guided the ancestors.

Five relationships. Confucius taught that harmony resulted when people accepted their place in society. He stressed five key relationships: father to son, elder brother to younger brother, husband to wife, ruler to subject, friend to friend. Confucius believed that, except for friendship, none of these relationships was equal. Older people were superior to younger ones; men were superior to women. Confucius did bolster the status of women by teaching that mothers of sons should be respected.

According to Confucius, everyone had duties and responsibilities, depending on his or her position. Superiors should care for their inferiors and set a good example, while inferiors owed loyalty and obedience to their superiors. A woman's duty was to ensure the stability of the family and promote harmony in the home. Correct behavior, Confucius believed, would bring order and stability.

Confucius put filial piety, or respect for parents, above all other duties, even loyalty to the state. "While a father or mother is alive, a son should not travel far," he said. Other Confucian values included honesty, hard work, and concern for others, which would promote harmony. "Do not do to others," he declared, "what you do not wish yourself."

Government. Confucius believed that people were naturally good. The best ruler was a virtuous man who led by example:

> 66 If a ruler is upright, all will go well without orders. But if he himself is not upright, even though he gives orders, they will not be obeyed. 99

Confucius put great faith in education for men. "By nature, men are pretty much alike," he said. "It is learning and practice that set them apart." He urged rulers to take the advice of

Confucius and His Students This drawing from the 1700s suggests the Chinese people's lasting respect for Confucius. Confucius sought to replace the conflict of his time with harmony and order. He believed that education should train people in proper values and rules of conduct. **Continuity and Change** Do you think that teachers today should instruct students in values and rules of conduct? Why or why not?

wise, educated men. Education would become the road to advancement in Chinese society.

Spread of Confucianism. In the centuries after Confucius died, his ideas influenced every area of Chinese life. Confucianism never became a religion, as Buddhism did. But Chinese rulers would base their government on Confucian ideas, choosing Confucian scholars as officials. The Confucian emphasis on filial piety bolstered traditional customs such as reverence for ancestors.

As Chinese civilization spread, hundreds of millions of people in Korea, Japan, and Vietnam accepted Confucian beliefs. Close to a third of the world's population came under the influence of these ideas.

The Harsh Ideas of Legalism

A very different school of thought grew out of the teachings of another Chinese philosopher, Hanfeizi (HAHN fay DZEE), who died in 233 B.C. According to Hanfeizi, "the nature of man is evil. His goodness is acquired." Greed, he declared, was the motive for most actions and the cause of most conflicts. Hanfeizi scoffed at the Confucian idea that people would follow the example of a good ruler. The only way to achieve order, he insisted, was to pass strict laws and enforce them with harsh punishments. Because of their emphasis on law, Hanfeizi's teachings were known as Legalism.

To Legalists, strength, not goodness, was a ruler's greatest virtue. "The ruler alone possesses power," declared Hanfeizi, "wielding it like lightning or like thunder."

Many feudal rulers chose Legalism as the most effective way to keep order. It was the official policy of the Qin (CHEENG) emperor who united China in 221 B.C. His laws were so cruel that later generations despised Legalism. Yet Legalist ideas survived in laws that forced people to work on government projects and punished those who shirked their duties.

Daoism: The Unspoken Way

A third Chinese philosophy, Daoism (DOW ihz uhm), differed from both Confucianism and Legalism. Daoists had no interest in bringing order to human affairs. Instead, they sought to live in harmony with nature.

The founder of Daosim was a mysterious figure known as Laozi (LOW DZEE), or "Old Master." He is said to have "lived without leaving any traces" at the time of Confucius. Although we know little about him, he is credited with writing *The Way of Virtue,* a book that had enormous influence on Chinese life.

Seeking "the Way." Laozi looked beyond everyday worries to focus on the *Dao,* or "the way" of the universe as a whole. How does one find the Dao? "Those who know the Dao do not speak of it," replied Laozi. "Those who speak of it do not know it." Daoists often gave such seemingly puzzling answers to show the conflict between human desires and the simple ways of nature.

Daoists rejected the world of conflict and strife. Instead, they emphasized the virtue of yielding. Water, they pointed out, does not resist, but yields to outside pressure. Yet it is an unstoppable force. In the same way, Daoists might give way in a conflict, only to return again, like water, to their natural course. Many Daoists turned away from the "unnatural" ways of society. Some became hermits, mystics, artists, or poets.

Government. Daoists viewed government as unnatural and, therefore, the cause of many problems. "If the people are difficult to govern," Laozi declared, "it is because those in authority are too fond of action." To Daoists, the best government was one that governed the least.

A popular religion. Although scholars kept to Laozi's teachings, Daoism evolved into a popular religion with gods, goddesses, and magical practices. Chinese peasants turned to Daoist priests for charms to protect them from unseen forces. Instead of accepting nature as it was, Daoist priests searched for a substance to bring immortality and experimented with alchemy (AL kuh mee), trying to transform ordinary metals into gold.

To achieve this goal, alchemists mixed chemistry and magic. Sometimes, their experiments led to advances in science. Efforts to find the key to eternal life may have contributed to discoveries in medicine. Daoists are thought to have invented gunpowder, which they first used in firecrackers to frighten ghosts.

A blend of ideas. Confucian and Daoist ideas influenced everyone from nobles and scholars to the poorest peasants. Although the two philosophies differed, people took beliefs and practices from each. Confucianism showed them how to behave. Daoism influenced their view of the natural world.

Buddhism in China

By A.D. 100, missionaries and merchants had spread Mahayana Buddhism from India into China. At first, the Chinese had trouble with the new faith. For example, Chinese tradition valued family loyalty, while Buddhism honored monks and nuns who gave up family life for solitary meditation. In addition, the Chinese language had no word for an unfamiliar, mystical concept like nirvana.

Despite obstacles such as these, Buddhism became more popular, especially in times of crisis. Its great appeal was the promise of escape from suffering. Mahayana Buddhism offered the hope of eternal happiness and presented Buddha as a compassionate, merciful god. Through prayer, good works, and devotion, anyone could hope to gain salvation. Neither Daoism nor Confucianism emphasized this idea of personal salvation.

In China, Buddhism absorbed Confucian and Daoist traditions. Some Chinese even believed that Laozi had gone to India, where he taught the Buddha. Chinese Buddhist monks stressed filial piety and honored Confucius as a person who had achieved enlightenment.

By A.D. 400, Buddhism had spread throughout China. From time to time, Chinese rulers persecuted Buddhists, but the new religion was

Yin and Yang "One must learn to be without desires beyond the immediate and simple needs of nature," wrote Laozi, founder of Daoism. Here, a group of wise Daoists ponder the circular symbol for yin and yang. (See page 61.) **Religions and Value Systems** How does the ancient Chinese concept of yin and yang accord with Daoist beliefs?

▲ *Figures of dancing peasants*

generally tolerated. Large Buddhist monasteries became important centers of learning, literature, and the arts.

SECTION 4 REVIEW

1. **Identify** (a) *The Analects,* (b) Legalism, (c) Daoism.
2. **Define** (a) filial piety, (b) alchemy.
3. Explain how each of these thinkers believed an orderly society could be achieved: (a) Confucius, (b) Hanfeizi, (c) Laozi.
4. What ethical code of conduct did Confucius promote?
5. (a) Why did Buddhism appeal to many people in China? (b) How did Buddhism adapt to Chinese traditions?
6. *Critical Thinking* **Analyzing Information** "Rewards should be rich and certain so that the people will be attracted by them. Punishments should be severe and definite so that the people will fear them." Which of the philosophers discussed in this section expressed these ideas? Explain.
7. *ACTIVITY* Write a dialogue between Confucius, Hanfeizi, and Laozi on the proper role of government.

5 Strong Rulers Unite China

Guide for Reading

■ How did Shi Huangdi unite China?

■ How did Han rulers shape Chinese government?

■ What advances did Han China make?

■ **Vocabulary** *monopoly*

From his base in western China, the powerful ruler of Qin rose to unify all of China. An ancient Chinese poet and historian described how Zheng (JUHNG) crushed all his rivals:

❝Cracking his long whip, he drove the universe before him, swallowing up the eastern and the western Zhou and overthrowing the feudal lords. He ascended to the highest position . . . and his might shook the four seas.❞

In 221 B.C., Zheng proclaimed himself Shi Huangdi (SHEE hoo ahng DEE), or "First Emperor." Though his methods were brutal, he ushered in China's classical age.

Triumph of the First Emperor

Shi Huangdi was determined to end the divisions that had splintered Zhou China. He spent 20 years conquering most of the warring states. Then, he centralized power with the help of Legalist advisers. Using rewards for merit and punishments for failure, he built a strong, authoritarian government.

Sweeping changes. The emperor abolished the old feudal states and divided China into 36 military districts, each ruled by appointed officials. Inspectors, who were actually more like spies, checked on local officials and tax collectors. Shi Huangdi forced noble families to live in his capital at Xianyang, where he could keep an eye on them, and divided their lands among peasants. Still, peasants had to pay high taxes to support Shi Huangdi's armies and building projects.

To promote unity, the First Emperor standardized weights and measures and replaced the diverse coins of the Zhou states with Qin coins. He also had scholars create uniformity in Chinese writing. Workers repaired and extended roads and canals to strengthen the transportation system. A new law even required cart axles to be the same width so that wheels could run in the same ruts on all Chinese roads.

Crackdown on dissent. Shi Huangdi moved harshly against critics. He jailed, tortured, and killed many who opposed his rule. Hardest hit were the feudal nobles and Confucian scholars who despised his laws. To end dissent, Shi Huangdi approved a ruthless campaign of book burning, ordering the destruction of all works of literature and philosophy. Only books on medicine and agriculture were spared.

The Great Wall. Shi Huangdi's most remarkable and costly achievement was the Great Wall. In the past, individual feudal states had built walls to defend their lands against raiders. Shi Huangdi ordered the walls to be joined together. Hundreds of thousands of laborers worked for years through bitter cold and burning heat. They pounded earth and stone into a mountainous wall almost 25 feet high topped with a wide brick road. Many workers died in the harsh conditions.

Over the centuries, the wall was extended and rebuilt many times. Eventually, it snaked for thousands of miles across China.

While the wall did not keep invaders out of China, it did show the emperor's ability to mobilize vast resources. In the long run, the Great Wall became an important symbol to the Chinese, dividing their civilized world from the nomadic bands north of the wall.

Collapse. Shi Huangdi thought his empire would last forever. But when he died in 210 B.C., anger over heavy taxes, forced labor, and cruel policies exploded into revolts. As Qin power collapsed, Liu Bang (LEE OO BAHNG), an illiterate peasant leader, defeated rival armies and founded the new Han dynasty. Like earlier Chinese rulers, Liu Bang claimed the Mandate of Heaven. (See page 61.)

The Han Dynasty

As emperor, Liu Bang took the title Gao Zu (GOW DZOO) and set about restoring order and justice to his empire. Although he continued earlier efforts to unify China, he lowered taxes and eased the Qin emperor's harsh Legalist policies. In a key move, he appointed Confucian scholars as advisers. His policies created strong foundations for the Han dynasty, which lasted from 206 B.C. to A.D. 220.

Strengthening the government. The most famous Han emperor, Wudi, took China to new heights. During his long reign from 141 B.C. to 87 B.C., he strengthened the government and economy. Like Gao Zu, he chose officials from Confucian "men of wisdom and virtue." To train scholars, he set up an imperial university at Xian.

Wudi furthered economic growth by improving canals and roads. He had granaries set up across the empire so the government could buy grain when it was abundant and sell it at stable prices when it was scarce. He reorganized finances and imposed a government monopoly

Army in a Tomb More than 8,000 terra cotta foot soldiers, cavalry, and chariots stand guard inside the tomb of Emperor Shi Huangdi. This life-sized army was expected to protect the First Emperor even after death. The tomb was uncovered accidentally in 1974 by a farmer who was digging a well. *Impact of the Individual* How does this tomb reflect the power of Shi Huangdi?

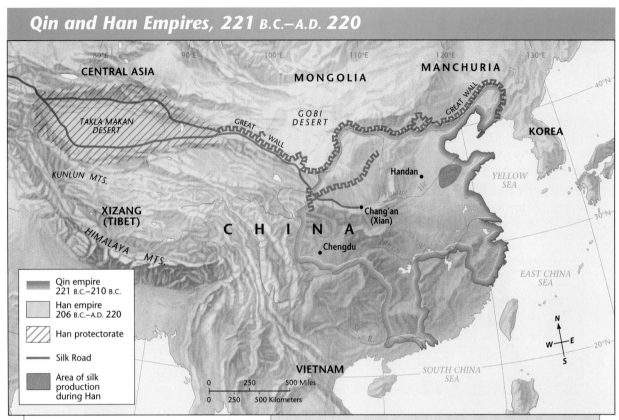

Qin and Han Empires, 221 B.C.–A.D. 220

Qin empire
221 B.C.–210 B.C.

Han empire
206 B.C.–A.D. 220

Han protectorate

Silk Road

Area of silk
production
during Han

GEOGRAPHY AND HISTORY

Under the Qin and Han dynasties, China expanded to roughly its present-day borders. Still, Chinese territory would be lost and regained many times over the centuries.

1. **Location** On the map, locate (a) the Silk Road, (b) the Great Wall, (c) Chang'an, (d) Korea, (e) Qin empire, (f) Huang He.

2. **Region** In which regions of the Han empire was silk production carried on?

3. **Critical Thinking** **Linking Past and Present** Study the map of Asia on page 988. Compare the extent of the Han empire with the extent of China today.

on iron and salt. A monopoly is the complete control of a product or business by one person or group. The sale of iron and salt gave the government a source of income other than taxes on peasants.

Expansion. Wudi earned the title "the Warrior Emperor" because of his endless campaigns to secure and expand China's borders. He fought many battles to drive nomadic peoples beyond the Great Wall. Chinese armies added outposts in Manchuria, Korea, northern Vietnam, Tibet, and Central Asia. Soldiers, traders, and settlers slowly spread Chinese influence across these areas. (See map above.)

To cement alliances with nomads on the western frontier, Wudi and later emperors arranged marriages between nomad chiefs and noble Chinese women. The loneliness of these brides became a popular theme in Chinese poems like this one:

66My people have married me
In a far corner of Earth;
Sent me away to a strange land . . .
A tent is my house,
Of felt are my walls;
Raw flesh my food
With mare's milk to drink.
Always thinking of my own country,
My heart sad within.
Would I were a yellow stork
And could fly to my old home!99

Success Stories

What is the road to success? There are as many answers to that question as there are successful people. Enterprising people have always found new and interesting ways to achieve economic prosperity. Their success is often based on ingenuity, hard work, and perseverance.

Linking Past and Present Do you think one needs to "dress for success"? How do today's attitudes about proper business attire differ from those of the past?

PAST *Sima Qian, a historian of the Han dynasty, studied prosperous business people. He marveled at their many roads to success, which included plowing fields, slaughtering swine, shipping bamboo, making silk, tanning hides, sharpening knives, and drying sheep stomachs.*

"Wealth finds its way to the man of ability like the spokes of a wheel converging upon the hub."
—Sima Qian

PRESENT *Wally Amos of the United States achieved success in the 1970s and 1980s by way of chips—chocolate chips! His cookie business started out as just a way to make a living, but quickly became a multimillion-dollar operation. After selling his first cookie company, Amos started a new one based in Hawaii.*

"I tried really hard to make it. That determination is all it takes."
—Wally Amos

Silk Road to the West

The emperor Wudi listened intently to the tales told by the traveler Zhang Qian (JAHNG chee EHN). Zhang had spent a dozen years among the barbarians of Central Asia. Far to the west, he told the emperor, was a land with an amazing breed of "heavenly horses," stronger than any known in China.

To Wudi, the horses were an irresistible lure. He sent a huge army 2,500 miles (4,025 km) into Central Asia to get some of the marvelous beasts. His forces pushed into the Takla Makan desert, bringing oases under their control. The emperor sent gifts of silk to help secure allies among the nomadic rulers of those distant lands.

Wudi's efforts paid off handsomely—he got his horses. He had also opened up a trade route, later called the Silk Road, that would link China and the west for centuries.

Wondrous goods. Strange and tempting things came to the emperor along the great Silk Road. A Chinese historian reported on one gift from a Persian ambassador:

66To the Chinese court he presented an ostrich egg and some conjurers from

Li-Chien [a Chinese name for the Roman Empire]. The Son of Heaven took great pleasure in these. **"**

During the Han period, new foods such as grapes, figs, cucumbers, and walnuts flowed to China from western Asia. At the same time, the Chinese sent tons of silk westward to fill a growing demand for the prized fabric.

A long, hard journey. Setting out from China along the Silk Road, fearful travelers might begin the journey with a prayer. Beyond the borders of the Middle Kingdom lurked not only bandits and harsh terrain, but evil spirits and strange gods as well. Still, the possible rewards made the risk worth taking. So the travelers would tighten the straps on their pack animals—horses, mules, camels, or yaks laden with bundles of silk or packets of jewels and spices. In a band of 50 or more, protected by a bodyguard of archers, the caravan set forth.

Week after week, month after month, the journey continued. The traders would roast in the deserts of the Takla Makan and freeze in the snowy passes of the Pamirs. Along the way, the caravan passed lonely soldiers huddled in clay-walled forts, ever on the lookout for bands of hostile nomads.

Eventually, the Silk Road stretched for 4,000 miles (6,400 km), linking China to the Fertile Crescent. Still, few traders covered the entire distance. Instead, goods were relayed in stages from one set of traders to another. At the western end, trade was controlled by various people, including the Persians.

Back to China. At the end of the journey, weary merchants could complete their business and begin the journey home. Lucky traders might return to China bearing furs from Central

◀ Woman in silk robe

Asia, muslin from India, or glass from Rome. Unlucky traders might not return at all. Some died of fever under a felt tent on the steppes, or froze in snowy mountain passes, or were killed by bandits. These brave merchants had paid a grave price to keep up the flow of goods on the great Silk Road. ▮

Han Society

Han rulers left their stamp on all areas of Chinese life. Han China made such tremendous advances in so many fields that the Chinese later called themselves "the people of Han."

Scholar-officials. Han emperors made Confucianism the official belief system of the state. They relied on well-educated scholars to run the bureaucracy. A scholar-official was expected to match the Confucian ideal of a gentleman. He would be courteous and dignified and possess a thorough knowledge of history, music, poetry, and Confucian teachings.

Civil service examinations. Han emperors adopted the idea that officials should win positions by merit rather than through family background. To find the most qualified officials, they set up a system of exams. In time, these civil service exams were given at the local, provincial, and national levels. To pass, candidates studied the Confucian classics, a collection of histories, poems, and handbooks on customs that Confucius was said to have compiled.

GLOBAL CONNECTIONS

China and Rome shared goods indirectly by way of the Silk Road. Yet the two empires never made formal contact. They came close in A.D. 97, when a Han general led an army to the edge of the Caspian Sea, the nearest any Chinese army ever came to Europe. He sent an ambassador to learn more about Rome. But when Persian sea captains warned that the journey back would be long and dangerous, the ambassador turned back.

In theory, any man could take the exams. In practice, only those who could afford years of study, such as the sons of wealthy landowners or officials, could hope to succeed. Occasionally, a village or wealthy family might pay for the education of a brilliant peasant boy. If he passed the exams and obtained a government job, he, his family, and his clan all enjoyed immense prestige and moved up in society.

The civil service system had enormous impact on China for almost 2,000 years. It put men trained in Confucian thought at every level of government and created an enduring system of values. Dynasties rose and fell, but Confucian influence survived.

Women. Confucian teachings about filial piety and the superiority of men kept women from taking the civil service exam. As a result, government positions were closed to women. Still, a few women did receive an education, mostly nuns or members of the imperial court.

The proper behavior for both women and men was carefully spelled out. Around A.D. 100, Ban Zhao (BAHN JOW) wrote *Lessons for Women,* an influential handbook of behavior. While she did argue in favor of equal education for boys and girls, Ban Zhao stressed obedience and submission. "Let a woman modestly yield to others," she advised. "Let her respect others."

Han Achievements

The Han period was one of the golden ages of Chinese civilization. Han scientists wrote texts on chemistry, zoology, botany, and other subjects. Han astronomers carefully observed and measured movements of the stars and planets, which enabled them to improve earlier calendars and invent better timekeeping devices.

The scientist Wang Chong disagreed with the widely held belief that comets and eclipses showed Heaven's anger. "On the average, there is one moon eclipse about every 180 days," he wrote, "and a solar eclipse about every 41 or 42 months. Eclipses . . . are not caused by political action." Wang Chong argued that no scientific theories should be accepted unless they were supported by proof.

Advances in technology. In its time, Han China was the most technologically advanced civilization in the world. Cai Lun, an official of the Han court, invented a method for making durable paper out of wood pulp. His basic method is still used to manufacture paper today. The Chinese also pioneered advanced methods of shipbuilding and invented the rudder to steer. Other practical inventions included bronze and iron stirrups, fishing reels, wheelbarrows, suspension bridges, and chain pumps. Some of these ideas moved west slowly, reaching Europe hundreds of years later.

Medicine. Chinese physicians diagnosed diseases, experimented with herbal remedies and other drugs, and developed anesthetics. Some doctors explored the uses of acupuncture. In this medical treatment, the doctor inserts needles under the skin to relieve pain or treat various illnesses.

The arts. The walled cities of Han China boasted splendid temples and palaces amid elegant parks. Although these wooden buildings have not survived, Han poets and historians have described their grandeur. Artisans produced delicate jade and ivory carvings and fine ceramic figures. Bronzeworkers and silkmakers improved on earlier techniques and set high standards for future generations.

Collapse of the Han Empire

As the Han dynasty aged, signs of decay appeared. Court intrigues undermined emperors who could no longer control powerful warlords in the provinces. Weak rulers let canals

A Dutiful Wife This figure of a servant was buried with a Chinese princess. The lamp she is holding symbolizes eternal fidelity. Under Confucianism, wives were expected to give eternal devotion to their husbands. **Political and Social Systems** According to Confucian ideas, how did women contribute to the stability of society?

CAUSE AND EFFECT

Long-Term Causes

Confucian ideas dominate education
China's isolation permits development without
  much outside interference
Common system of writing evolves

Immediate Causes

Zheng conquers eastern and western Zhou and
  overthrows feudal lords
Zheng proclaims himself Shi Huangdi
  ("first Emperor")

UNIFICATION OF CHINA

Immediate Effects

Shi Huangdi standardizes weights and measures
  and money
Roads and canals unify distant provinces
Government cracks down on dissenters

Long-Term Effects

Han dynasty is founded by Liu Bang
China makes advances in government, trade,
  and transportation
Confucian-educated officials gain monopoly
  of government offices
Common culture helps China survive upheavals

Connections Today

Mainland China remains a large, politically
  united country
Chinese still share a common written language

Interpreting Charts Under Shi Huangdi, most of
China united under a single ruler. Although China's
borders continued to shift under later rulers, the
First Emperor's goal of a unified state endured.
■ How did political unification encourage advances in
government, trade, and technology?

and roads fall into disrepair. Burdened by heavy taxes, peasants revolted. In A.D. 220, ambitious warlords overthrew the last Han emperor. After 400 years of unity, China broke up into several kingdoms. Adding to the disorder, invaders poured over the Great Wall and set up their own states. In time, many of these newcomers were absorbed into Chinese civilization.

During this turbulent period, Buddhism took root in China. It appealed to nomads and Chinese alike. A common faith created links among these diverse groups.

Looking Ahead

Shi Huangdi and Gao Zu forged a vast and varied land into a united China. The two rulers established the pattern of government that would survive until 1912.

Han rulers created an empire roughly the size of the continental United States. China would undergo great changes. It would break up and be painfully reassembled over and over. But, on the whole, Chinese civilization flourished in a united land. After periods of disunity, a new dynasty would turn to Confucian scholars to revive the days of Han greatness.

SECTION 5 REVIEW

1. **Identify** (a) Shi Huangdi, (b) Great Wall, (c) Gao Zu, (d) Wudi, (e) Silk Road (f) Ban Zhao (g) Wang Chong.
2. **Define** monopoly.
3. What were three steps Shi Huangdi took to unify China?
4. How did Han emperors increase the influence of Confucianism in China?
5. Why is the Han period considered a golden age of Chinese civilization?
6. *Critical Thinking* **Synthesizing Information** How did the ideas of Wang Chong challenge the ancient Chinese concept of the Mandate of Heaven? (See page 61.)
7. *ACTIVITY* Imagine that you are a Chinese trader traveling along the Silk Road during the Han dynasty. Write a poem or a letter home describing how you feel about your journey.

4 | CHAPTER REVIEW AND SKILLS FOR SUCCESS

CHAPTER REVIEW

REVIEWING VOCABULARY

Write sentences, using *five* of the vocabulary words from this chapter, leaving blanks where the vocabulary words would go. Exchange your sentences with another student and fill in the blanks on each other's lists.

REVIEWING FACTS

1. According to Hinduism, what is the ultimate goal of existence?
2. What are the Four Noble Truths of Buddhism?
3. Describe three advances during the Gupta empire.
4. How did caste rules affect the daily lives of Indians?
5. In the view of Confucius, what duties and responsibilities did superiors and inferiors have toward one another?
6. How did the goal of Daoism differ from the goal of Confucianism?
7. What was the Silk Road?
8. What events caused the collapse of the Han dynasty?

SKILLS FOR SUCCESS   CLASSIFYING SOURCES OF INFORMATION

Primary sources include official documents and first-hand accounts of events by people who witnessed or participated in them. Letters, diaries, and photos are examples of primary sources.

Secondary sources are written after events have occurred by people who did not witness or participate in them. Examples of secondary sources include encyclopedias, biographies, and textbooks.

Below are a list of sources about India and two passages written by Sima Qian, an official historian of Han China. Use them to answer the following questions.

1. **Identify primary sources.** (a) Which items on the list of information sources are primary sources? (b) Why is Reading B a primary source?

2. **Identify secondary sources.** (a) Which items on the list are secondary sources? (b) Why is Reading A a secondary source?

3. **Decide how each kind of source might be used.** What kinds of information about Maurya India might you get from the encyclopedia but not from the laws of Asoka?

Sources of Information About India
One of Asoka's pillars

An encyclopedia entry about Asoka

A report on the Maurya court by the Greek ambassador Megasthenes (see page 82)

The Wonder That Was India, a book written by the scholar A. L. Basham in 1963

A report on Gupta India by the Chinese monk Faxian (see page 85)

Reading A
   ❝Confucius said, 'Bo Yi and Shu Qi never bore old ills in mind and had not the faintest feelings of hatred.' ...The tales of these men state that

Bo Yi and Shu Qi were two sons of the ruler of Kuchu. Their father wished to set up Shu Qi as his heir, but when he died, Shu Qi yielded in favor of Bo Yi.❞

Reading B
   ❝Li Ling and I were both stationed in the palace, but we never had a chance to become friends. Our duties kept us apart; we never shared so much as a cup of wine, let alone enjoyed a closer friendship. But I observed that he conducted himself as no ordinary gentleman. He was filial toward his parents, honest with his colleagues.❞

REVIEWING CHAPTER THEMES

Review the "Focus On" questions at the start of this chapter. Then select *three* of those questions and answer them, using information from the chapter.

CRITICAL THINKING

1. **Comparing** Both Indian and Chinese rulers faced difficult challenges in uniting their lands. How were these challenges similar? How were they different?

2. **Defending a Position** Confucius argued that people were basically good and could be led by virtuous example. Hanfeizi believed that people were basically evil and had to be controlled by strict laws. Express your viewpoint on this issue and support your position with specific examples.

ANALYZING PRIMARY SOURCES

Use the two quotations by Confucius on page 90 to answer the following questions.

1. What did Confucius believe was the most effective method of leading? Why?

2. According to Confucius, how will people react to the orders of an immoral ruler?

3. Do you think it is more important for a ruler to make correct leadership decisions or show proper moral behavior? Explain.

FOR YOUR PORTFOLIO

WRITING AN ARTICLE Write an article for a book entitled *Continuity and Change: The Heritage of India and China.* Begin by choosing a topic, such as Hindu traditions in modern India, the current status of women in India or China, or Chinese medical techniques today. Then research your topic at the public library. Finally, write a two- to three-page article describing what you have learned. You should show both how classical traditions have survived and how they have been adapted.

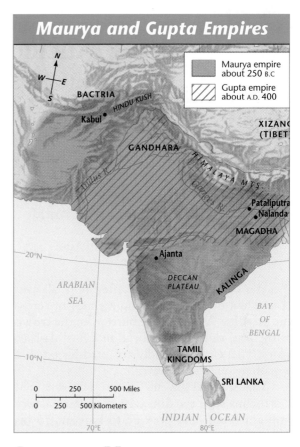

Maurya and Gupta Empires

Maurya empire about 250 B.C

Gupta empire about A.D. 400

BACTRIA
HINDU KUSH
Kabul
XIZANG (TIBET
GANDHARA
HIMALAYA MTS.
Indus R.
Pataliputra
Nalanda
MAGADHA
20°N
Ajanta
DECCAN PLATEAU
KALINGA
ARABIAN SEA
BAY OF BENGAL
10°N
TAMIL KINGDOMS
SRI LANKA
0   250   500 Miles
0   250   500 Kilometers
INDIAN OCEAN
70°E   80°E

ANALYZING MAPS

Use the map to answer the following questions.

1. The city of Kabul was part of which of the two empires shown?

2. What physical features marked the northern boundary of the Maurya empire?

3. Which three rivers were part of both the Maurya and Gupta empires?

INTERNET ACTIVITY

CREATING A TIME LINE Use the Internet to research one or more of the dynasties of ancient China. Then create a time line of ancient China, showing when each dynasty was in power. Include changes in art, technology, or religion that occurred during those times.

Ancient Greece

(1750 B.C. – 133 B.C.)

CHAPTER OUTLINE

1 Early People of the Aegean
2 The Rise of Greek City-States
3 Victory and Defeat in the Greek World
4 The Glory That Was Greece
5 Alexander and the Hellenistic Age

In the hot, dusty summer afternoon, all eyes watched the athletic young men sprint across the meadow. A great cheer burst from the crowd as the lead runner shot ahead in a final dash to glory. The winner proudly accepted his prize, a wreath made of olive leaves.

That summer day in 776 B.C., a cook named Corroebus won the 200-yard dash. His victory brought honor and prestige to him and to his hometown of Elis. His name has survived the centuries as the first recorded victor in the Greek Olympic Games. Centuries later, the poet Pindar captured the joy of victory:

66He who wins, of a sudden,
  some noble prize
In the rich years of youth
Is raised high with hope . . .
He has in his heart what is better
  than wealth. . . .
When god-given splendor visits him
A bright radiance plays over him, and
  how sweet is life.99

Every four years, in the sacred valley of Olympia, the ancient Greeks held athletic contests to honor Zeus (ZOOS), their chief god. The competitive spirit mirrored the rivalries that kept dozens of small Greek city-states in a state of near-constant war. Yet the Olympic Games also helped unify the Greek world. As the time for the games drew near, the Greeks called a truce so that athletes and spectators could reach Olympia safely.

Unlike the other civilizations we have studied so far, Greek civilization did not rise in a fertile river valley. Instead, it emerged in a rugged, remote corner of southeastern Europe. Like the Gupta empire in India and the Han empire in China, Greece gave rise to a classical civilization that set a standard for later civilizations. Faith in the individual strongly influenced Greek thought. The Greeks tried out many forms of government. Among others, they created a system based on the right of each individual citizen to speak out about issues.

FOCUS ON these questions as you read:

- **Geography and History**
  How did geography influence the Greek way of life and interaction between the Greeks and other people?

- **Impact of the Individual**
  What role did individual political leaders, philosophers, and writers play in shaping Greek civilization?

- **Political and Social Systems**
  What Greek ideas about government influenced later societies?

- **Global Interaction**
  How did Greek civilization affect peoples across many regions?

TIME AND PLACE

A Classical Style Artists of ancient Greece developed a style that stressed the search for balance and perfection. This "classical" style had a lasting influence on later European cultures. The two sculptured heads shown here represent Greek ideals of perfect male and female beauty. ***Art and Literature*** What qualities do these two sculptures have in common?

HUMANITIES LINK
Art History Greek vase painting (page 111).
Literature In this chapter, you will encounter passages from the following works of literature: Pindar, *Victory Ode* (page 102); Homer, *the Iliad* (page 107); Herodotus, *History of the Persian Wars* (page 114); Plato, *Euthyphro* and *Apology* (pages 117, 118); Sophocles, *Antigone* (page 120).

1600 B.C.
Height of
Minoan
civilization

460 B.C.
Age of Pericles
in Athens
begins

431 B.C.
Peloponnesian
War
begins

331 B.C.
Alexander
conquers Persia

323 B.C.
Alexander
dies

B.C.   1700   500   450   400   350   300 B.C.

1 Early People of the Aegean

Guide for Reading

- What civilizations influenced the Minoans?

- How did Mycenaean civilization affect the later Greeks?

- What do the epics of Homer tell us about the Greeks?

- **Vocabulary** *strait*

Europa, the beautiful daughter of the king of Phoenicia, was gathering flowers with her friends when she saw a bull quietly grazing with her father's herds. The bull was actually Zeus, king of the gods, who had fallen in love with her. When Europa reached to place flowers on his horns, he suddenly bounded into the air and carried the weeping princess far across the Mediterranean Sea to the island of Crete. Eventually, Europa married the king of Crete and gave her name to a new continent—Europe.

This Greek legend carries seeds of truth. Crete was the cradle of an early civilization that later influenced Greeks on the European mainland. The people of Crete, however, had absorbed many ideas from the older civilizations of Egypt and Mesopotamia. Europa's journey from Phoenicia to Crete thus suggests the diffusion of ideas from east to west.

Minoan Civilization

Washed by the warm waters of the Aegean (uh JEE uhn) Sea, Crete was home to a brilliant early civilization. We do not know what the people who built this civilization called themselves. However, the British archaeologist who unearthed its ruins called them Minoans after Minos, a legendary king of Crete. The success of the Minoans was based on trade, not conquest. Minoan traders set up outposts throughout the Aegean world, including the Greek mainland. (See the map on page 108.)

Location affected these early people. From their island home in the eastern Mediterranean, they crossed the seas to the Nile Valley and the Middle East. Through contact with Egypt and Mesopotamia, they acquired ideas and technology that they adapted to their own culture. Minoan civilization reached its height between about 1750 B.C. and 1500 B.C.

The palace at Knossos. The rulers of this trading empire lived in a vast palace at Knossos (NAHS uhs). It housed rooms for the royal family, religious shrines, banquet halls, and working areas for artisans. Colorful wall paintings show dolphins leaping through Aegean waters or young Minoan nobles strolling through gardens. In another painting, we see men and women practicing for an unusual athletic contest—jumping through the horns of a charging bull.

The paintings suggest that women appeared freely in public and may have enjoyed more rights than women in most ancient civilizations. Perhaps their status was linked to the important role of a mother goddess in Minoan religious beliefs.

A civilization disappears. By about 1400 B.C., Minoan civilization had vanished. Archaeologists are not sure of the cause. A sudden volcanic eruption on a nearby island may have rained flaming death on Knossos. Or an earthquake may have destroyed the palace, followed by a tidal wave that drowned the inhabitants of the island.

However, invaders certainly played a role in the destruction of Minoan civilization. These intruders were the Mycenaeans (mī suh NEE uhnz), the first Greek-speaking people of whom we have a record.

Rulers of Mycenae

The Mycenaeans were an Indo-European people, like the Aryans who swept into India. (See the map on page 54.) The Mycenaeans conquered the Greek mainland before overrunning Crete.

Successful sea traders. Mycenaean civilization dominated the Aegean world from about 1400 B.C. to 1200 B.C. Like the Minoans, the Mycenaeans were sea traders. They reached out beyond the Aegean to Sicily, Italy, Egypt,

and Mesopotamia. The newcomers learned many skills from the Minoans, including the art of writing. They, too, absorbed Egyptian and Mesopotamian influences, which they passed on to later Greeks.

The Mycenaeans lived in separate city-states on the mainland. In each, a warrior-king built a thick-walled fortress from which he ruled the surrounding villages. Wealthy rulers amassed hoards of treasure, including fine gold ornaments that archaeologists have unearthed from their tombs.

The Trojan War. The Mycenaeans are best remembered for their part in the Trojan War, which took place around 1250 B.C. The conflict may have had its origins in economic rivalry between the Mycenaeans and Troy, a rich trading city in present-day Turkey. Troy controlled the vital straits, or narrow water passages, that connect the Mediterranean and Black seas.

Greek legend attributes the war to a more romantic cause. After the Trojan prince Paris kidnapped Helen, the beautiful wife of a Greek king, the Mycenaeans sailed to Troy to rescue her. For 10 years, Greeks and Trojans fought outside the city's well-defended walls. Finally, the Greeks tricked the Trojans into hauling a giant wooden horse inside the city. Hidden inside the "Trojan Horse" were a few Greek warriors. At night, the soldiers slipped out to open the city gates to the Greeks, who quickly overwhelmed Troy and burned the city to the ground.

For centuries, most people regarded the Trojan War purely as a legend. Then, in the 1870s, a wealthy German businessman, Heinrich Schliemann (HĪN rihk SHLEE mahn), set out to prove that the legend was rooted in fact. As he excavated the site of ancient Troy, Schliemann discovered that the city had been rebuilt many times. At the layer dating to about 1250 B.C., he found evidence of fire and war. Though most of the details still remain lost in legend,

modern scholars agree that the Trojan War was an actual event.

The Age of Homer

Not long after the fall of Troy, Mycenaean civilization crumbled under the attack of sea raiders. About the same time, another wave of Greek-speaking people, the Dorians, invaded from the north. As Mycenaean power faded, people abandoned the cities, and trade declined. People forgot many skills, including the art of writing. From 1100 B.C. to 800 B.C., Greek civilization seemed to step backward.

An oral record. We get hints about life during this period from two great epic poems, the *Iliad* and the *Odyssey*. These epics may have been the work of many people, but they are credited to the poet Homer, who probably lived about 750 B.C.

According to tradition, Homer was a blind poet who wandered from village to village, playing his harp and singing of heroic deeds. Like the great Indian epics (see pages 56–57), Homer's tales were passed orally for generations before they were finally written down.

The Hero

In various cultures, epics tell of heroes who overcome obstacles to achieve important goals. The hero succeeds through a special combination of personal characteristics. Legends about the hero endure and inspire others.

Linking Past and Present Name some legendary heroes of the past and present. What special human qualities do they typically possess?

PAST *Odysseus, hero of the* Odyssey, *was known for his cleverness in the face of danger. Here, he outwits the siren, a legendary bird-woman whose bewitching song lured passing sailors to their doom. Odysseus filled his crew's ears with beeswax. He then had himself tied to the ship's mast so that he himself could listen to the siren's song without endangering his ship.*

PRESENT *Indiana Jones is a popular American film hero. By using his wits, he narrowly escapes all obstacles and emerges victorious.*

Epics for all time. The *Iliad* is our chief source of information about the Trojan War, although the story involves gods, goddesses, and even a talking horse. At the start of the poem, Achilles (uh KIHL eez), the mightiest Greek warrior, is sulking in his tent because of a dispute with his commander. Although the war soon turns against the Greeks, Achilles stubbornly refuses to listen to pleas that he rejoin the fighting. Only after his best friend is killed does Achilles again charge into battle to strike down many Trojans.

The *Odyssey* tells of the struggles of the Greek hero Odysseus (oh DIHS ee uhs) to return home to his faithful wife, Penelope, after the fall of Troy. On his long voyage, Odysseus encounters a sea monster, a race of one-eyed giants, and a beautiful sorceress who turns men into swine.

The *Iliad* and *Odyssey* reveal much about the values of the ancient Greeks. The heroes display honor, courage, and eloquence, as when Achilles rallies his troops:

> 66Every man make up his mind to fight
> And move on his enemy! Strong as I am,
> It's hard for me to face so many men
> And fight with all at once. . . .
> And yet I will!99

For almost 3,000 years, the epics of Homer have inspired European writers and artists.

Looking Ahead

For centuries after the Dorian invasions, the Greeks lived in small, isolated villages. They had no writing and few contacts with the outside world. From this unpromising start, they would develop a civilization that influenced many parts of the world. As they emerged from obscurity, they benefited from the legacy of earlier civilizations. Over time, the stories they heard about Crete and Mycenae underwent changes and became part of the Greek heritage.

SECTION *1* REVIEW

1. **Identify** (a) Trojan War, (b) Heinrich Schliemann, (c) Homer.
2. **Define** strait.
3. Describe one similarity and one difference between Minoan and Mycenaean civilizations.
4. How did trade contribute to a blending of cultures in the Aegean world?
5. *Critical Thinking* **Drawing Conclusions** Do you think the epics of Homer are a reliable source of information about the ancient Greeks? Why or why not?
6. *ACTIVITY* Imagine that you are Heinrich Schliemann. Design a newspaper advertisement to attract helpers for your expedition to discover the ruins of Troy.

2 The Rise of Greek City-States

Guide for Reading

- How did geography influence the Greek city-states?
- What kinds of government did the Greeks develop?
- How did Sparta and Athens differ?
- **Vocabulary** *polis, acropolis, monarchy, aristocracy, oligarchy, phalanx, democracy, tyrant, legislature*

"Whatever the Greeks have acquired from foreigners," boasted the Greek thinker Plato, "they have, in the end, turned into something finer." The ancient Greeks absorbed many ideas and beliefs from older civilizations in Mesopotamia and Egypt. At the same time, they evolved their own ways that differed greatly from those of the river valley empires. In particular the Greeks developed unique ideas about how best to govern a society.

Geography: The Greek Homeland

As you have read, geography helped to shape the river valley civilizations early. There, strong rulers organized irrigation works that helped farmers produce the food surpluses needed to support large cities. A very different set of geographic conditions influenced the rise of Greek civilization.

Mountains and valleys. Greece is part of the Balkan peninsula, which extends southward into the eastern Mediterranean Sea. Mountains divide the peninsula into isolated valleys. Beyond the rugged coast, hundreds of rocky islands spread toward the horizon. (See the map on page 108.)

The Greeks who farmed the valleys or settled on the scattered islands did not create a large empire as the Egyptians or Mesopotamians had. Instead, they built many small city-states, cut off from one another by land or water. Each included a city and its surrounding

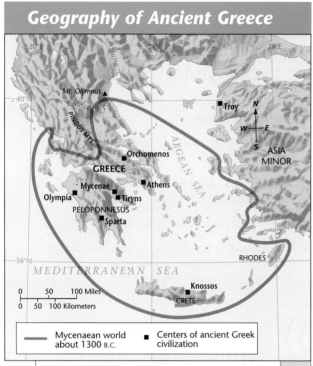

Geography of Ancient Greece

Islands in the Aegean Sea were home to the earliest Greek civilizations. Later, proudly independent Greek city-states, such as Athens and Sparta, arose on the Balkan peninsula.

1. **Location** On the map, locate (a) Aegean Sea, (b) Greece, (c) Knossos, (d) Troy, (e) Athens, (f) Sparta, (g) Pindus Mountains.
2. **Region** How did the geography of Greece present obstacles to the development of a large Greek empire?
3. **Critical Thinking** **Comparing** How did the geography of ancient Greece differ from that of other ancient civilizations?

With its hundreds of bays, the Greek coastline provided safe harbors for ships. Like the Phoenicians, the Greeks became skilled sailors. Carrying cargoes of olive oil, wine, and marble, Greek traders sailed to Egypt, the Middle East, and Asia Minor. They returned not only with grains and metals, but also with ideas, which they adapted to their own needs. For example, the Greeks expanded the Phoenician alphabet. The resulting Greek alphabet became the basis for all western alphabets. (See the chart on page 109.)

By 750 B.C., rapid population growth was forcing many Greeks to leave their own over-crowded valleys. With fertile land limited, the Greeks expanded overseas. Gradually, a scattering of Greek colonies took root all around the Mediterranean from Spain to Egypt. Wherever they traveled, Greek settlers and traders carried their ideas and culture.

The Polis

As their world expanded after 750 B.C., the Greeks evolved a unique version of the city-state, which they called the **polis.** Typically, the city itself was built on two levels. On a hilltop stood the **acropolis** (uh KRAHP uh lihs), or high city, with its great marble temples dedicated to different gods and goddesses. On flatter ground below lay the walled main city with its market-place, theater, public buildings, and homes.

The population of each city-state was fairly small, which helped citizens share a sense of responsibility for its triumphs and defeats. In the warm climate of Greece, free men spent much time outdoors in the marketplace, debating issues that affected their lives. The whole community joined in festivals honoring the city's special god or goddess.

Early governments. Between 750 B.C. and 500 B.C., Greeks evolved different forms of government. At first, the ruler of the polis, like those in the river valley empires, was a king. A government in which a king or queen exercises central power is a **monarchy.** Slowly, though, power shifted to a class of noble landowners. They were also the military defenders of the city-states, because only they could afford bronze weapons and chariots. At first these nobles defended the king. In time, they won power for

countryside. Greeks felt strong loyalty to their tiny city-states and fiercely defended their independence. Endless rivalry led to frequent wars between the city-states—and, in time, to the conquest of Greece by outsiders.

The seas. "We live around the sea like frogs around a pond," noted Plato. The Mediterranean and Aegean seas were as central to the Greek world as the Nile to Egypt. While mountains divided Greeks from one another, the seas provided a vital link to the world outside.

themselves. The result was an aristocracy, or rule by a landholding elite.

As trade expanded, a new middle class of wealthy merchants, farmers, and artisans emerged in some cities. They challenged the landowning nobles for power and came to dominate some city-states. The result was a form of government called an oligarchy. In an oligarchy, power is in the hands of a small, powerful elite, usually from the business class.

Changes in warfare. Changes in military technology contributed to the increased power of the middle class. In about 650 B.C., iron weapons and tools replaced bronze ones. Because iron was cheaper, ordinary citizens could afford iron helmets, shields, and swords. Meanwhile, a new method of fighting emerged. The

phalanx was a massive formation of heavily armed foot soldiers. It required long hours of drill. Shared training created a strong sense of unity among citizen-soldiers.

By putting the defense of the city-state in the hands of ordinary citizens, the phalanx reduced class differences. The new type of warfare, however, led the two most influential city-states to develop very different ways of life. While Sparta stressed military virtues and stern discipline, Athens glorified the individual and extended political rights to more citizens.

Sparta: A Nation of Soldiers

The Spartans were Dorians who conquered Laconia. This region lies in the Peloponnesus (pehl uh puh NEE suhs), the southern part of Greece. The invaders turned the conquered people into state-owned slaves, called helots, and made them work the land. Because the helots greatly outnumbered their rulers, the Spartans set up a brutal system of strict control.

The Spartan government included two kings and a council of elders who advised the monarchs. An assembly made up of all citizens approved major decisions. Citizens were male, native-born Spartans over the age of 30. The assembly also elected five ephors, officials who held the real power and ran day-to-day affairs.

The rigors of citizenship. From childhood, a Spartan prepared to be part of a military state. Officials examined every newborn, and sickly children were abandoned to die. Spartans wanted future soldiers or mothers of soldiers to be healthy.

At the age of seven, boys began training for a lifetime in the military. They moved into barracks, where they endured a brutal existence. Toughened by a coarse diet, hard exercise, and rigid discipline, Spartan youths became excellent soldiers. To develop cunning and supplement their diet, boys were encouraged to steal food. If caught, though, they were beaten.

At the age of 20, a man could marry, but he continued to live in the barracks for another 10 years and to eat there for another 40 years. At the age of 30, after further specialized training, he took his place in the assembly.

Women. Girls, too, had a rigorous upbringing. As part of a warrior society, they were

Early Alphabets

Phoenician	Greek	Roman
Ⱪ	Λ	A
◿	Ᏸ	B
◿	△	D
Ѱ	K	K
⎣	∧	L
⅁	N	N
Φ	Ꮆ	Q
⅁	P	R

Interpreting a Chart *Our alphabet came to us from the Phoenicians by way of the Greeks. The word* alphabet *itself comes from the first two Greek letters, alpha and beta.* ■ *Which of the letters shown here changed the least over time?*

expected to produce healthy sons for the army. They therefore were trained to exercise and strengthen their bodies—something no other Greek women did.

Like other Greek women, Spartan women had to obey their fathers or husbands. Under Spartan law, though, they had the right to inherit property. Because men were occupied with war, some women took on responsibilities such as running the family's estates.

Sparta and its neighbors. The Spartans isolated themselves from other Greeks. They looked down on trade and wealth, forbade their own citizens to travel, and had little use for new ideas or the arts. While other Greeks admired the Spartans' military skills, no other city-state imitated their rigorous way of life. "Spartans are willing to die for their city," some suggested, "because they have no reason to live."

In the long run, Sparta suffered from its rigid ways and inability to change. In time, its warrior class shrank, and its power declined.

Athens: A Limited Democracy

Athens was located in Attica, just north of the Peloponnesus. As in many Greek city-states, Athenian government evolved from a monarchy into an aristocracy. Around 700 B.C., noble landowners held power and chose the chief officials. Nobles judged major cases in court and dominated the assembly.

King Leonidas *This bronze monument honors Leonidas, a great warrior-king of ancient Sparta. It stands today as a reminder of the city's militaristic past. A primary duty of a Spartan king was to lead citizen-soldiers in war.* **Continuity and Change** *Name some government leaders of the past or present who are usually shown in military dress.*

Demands for change. Athenian wealth and power grew under the aristocracy. Yet discontent spread among ordinary people. Merchants and soldiers resented the power of the nobles. They argued that their service to Athens entitled them to more rights. Foreign artisans, who produced many goods that Athens traded abroad, were resentful that Athenian law barred foreigners from becoming citizens.

Demand for change also came from farmers. During hard times, many farmers were forced to sell their land to nobles. A growing number even had to sell themselves and their families into slavery to pay their debts.

As discontent spread, Athens moved slowly toward democracy, or government by the people. As you will see, the term had a different meaning for the ancient Greeks than it does for us today.

Solon's reforms. Solon, a wise and trusted leader, was appointed archon (AHR kahn), or chief official, in 594 B.C. Athenians gave Solon a free hand to make needed reforms. He outlawed debt slavery and freed those who had already been sold into slavery for debt. He opened high offices to more citizens, granted citizenship to some foreigners, and gave the Athenian assembly more say in important decisions.

Solon introduced economic reforms as well. He encouraged the export of wine and olive oil. This policy helped merchants and farmers by increasing demand for their products.

Although Solon's reforms ensured greater fairness and justice to some groups, citizenship remained limited, and only the wealthy landowners could serve in many positions. Widespread and continued unrest led to the rise of tyrants, or people who gained power by force. Tyrants often won support of the merchant class and the poor by imposing reforms to help these groups. (Although Greek tyrants

Greek Vase Painting Most of the ancient Greek painting that survives today is found on vases like this one. It was done in the "red-figure" style of the 400s B.C. The vase itself is made of red clay. The artist then covered the vase with black glaze, letting the red show through to create a detailed scene. Unlike earlier paintings that often depicted gods or warfare, these works focused more on domestic scenes. Here, a group of women prepare a bride for her wedding feast. **Art and Literature** How does this vase painting differ from the painting of Odysseus on page 106?

often governed well, the word *tyrant* has come to mean a vicious and brutal ruler.)

Later reforms. The Athenian tyrant Pisistratus (pi SIHS truh tuhs) seized power in 546 B.C. He helped farmers by giving them loans and land taken from nobles. New building projects gave jobs to the poor. By giving poor citizens a greater voice, he further weakened the aristocracy.

In 507 B.C., another reformer, Cleisthenes (KLĪS thuh neez), broadened the role of ordinary citizens in government. He set up the Council of 500, whose members were chosen by lot from among all citizens. The council prepared laws for the assembly and supervised the day-to-day work of government. Cleisthenes made the assembly a genuine legislature, or lawmaking body, that debated laws before deciding to approve or reject them. All male citizens over 30 were members of the assembly.

Limited rights. By modern standards, Athenian democracy was quite limited. Only male citizens could participate in government, and citizenship was severely restricted. Also, tens of thousands of Athenians were slaves without political rights or personal freedom. In fact, it was the labor of slaves that gave citizens the time to participate in government. Still, Athens gave more people a say in decision making than the other ancient civilizations we have studied.

Women. In Athens, as in other Greek city-states, women had no share in public life. "The loom is women's work, and not debate," observed a Greek man. The respected thinker Aristotle saw women as imperfect beings who lacked the ability to reason as well as men. He wrote:

> **"The man is by nature fitter for command than the female, just as an older person is superior to a younger, more immature person."**

Although some men disagreed, most Greeks accepted the view that women must be guided by men. In well-to-do Athenian homes, women lived a secluded existence, shut off and "protected" from the outside world.

Within their homes, women managed the entire household. They spun and wove, cared for their children, and prepared food. Their slaves or children were sent to buy food and to fetch water from the public well. Poorer women worked outside the home, tending sheep or working as spinners, weavers, or assistant potters.

Education for democracy. Unlike girls, who received little or no formal education, boys attended school if their families could afford it. Besides learning to read and write, they studied music and memorized poetry. They studied to become skilled public speakers because, as citizens in a democracy, they would have to voice their views. Young men received military training and, to keep their bodies healthy, participated in athletic contests. Unlike Sparta, which put military training above all else, Athens encouraged young men to explore many areas of knowledge.

Forces for Unity

Strong local ties, an independent spirit, and economic rivalry led to fighting among the Greek city-states. Despite these divisions, Greeks shared a common culture. They spoke the same language, honored the same ancient heroes, participated in common festivals such as the Olympic Games, and prayed to the same gods.

Religious beliefs. Like most other ancient people, the Greeks were polytheistic. They believed that the gods lived on Mount Olympus in northern Greece. The most powerful Olympian was Zeus, who presided over the affairs of gods and humans. His wife, Hera, was goddess of

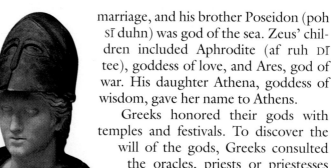

▲ *Athena, goddess of wisdom*

marriage, and his brother Poseidon (poh sī duhn) was god of the sea. Zeus' children included Aphrodite (af ruh DĪ tee), goddess of love, and Ares, god of war. His daughter Athena, goddess of wisdom, gave her name to Athens.

Greeks honored their gods with temples and festivals. To discover the will of the gods, Greeks consulted the oracles, priests or priestesses through whom the gods were thought to speak. Although religion was important, some Greek thinkers came to believe that the universe was regulated, not by the will of gods, but by natural laws.

View of non-Greeks. As trade expanded and Greek colonies multiplied, the Greeks came in contact with people who spoke different languages and had different customs. Greeks felt superior to non-Greeks and called them *barbaroi*, people who did not speak Greek. The English word *barbarian* comes from this Greek root. These "barbarians" included such people as the Phoenicians and Egyptians, from whom the Greeks borrowed important ideas and inventions. Still, this sense of uniqueness would help the Greeks face a threat from the mightiest power in the Mediterranean world—the Persian empire.

SECTION 2 REVIEW

1. **Identify** (a) Solon, (b) Cleisthenes, (c) Zeus.
2. **Define** (a) polis, (b) acropolis, (c) monarchy, (d) aristocracy, (e) oligarchy, (f) phalanx, (g) democracy, (h) tyrant, (i) legislature.
3. Describe how geography affected Greece.
4. (a) How did noble landowners gain power in Greek city-states? (b) How did the development of the phalanx affect Greek society and government?
5. What cultural ties united the Greek world?
6. *Critical Thinking* **Comparing** Compare Athens and Sparta in terms of (a) government, (b) education, (c) the role of women, and (d) values.
7. *ACTIVITY* Create a dialogue between an Athenian and a Spartan in which they discuss the responsibilities of a citizen.

3 Victory and Defeat in the Greek World

Guide for Reading

- What were the results of the Persian and Peloponnesian wars?
- Why did Athens enjoy a golden age under Pericles?
- What led to the outbreak of the Peloponnesian wars?
- **Vocabulary** *direct democracy*

In 492 B.C., King Darius of Persia sent messengers to the Greek city-states, demanding gifts of "earth and water" as a symbol of surrender. Many city-states obeyed. But Athens and Sparta were not so quick to submit. Saying that the Persians could collect their own earth and water, the Athenians threw Darius' messengers into a well, while the Spartans tossed them into a pit.

The Greek historian Herodotus (hih RAHD uh tuhs) told this story of Greek defiance and pride. Despite their cultural ties, the Greek city-states were often bitterly divided. Yet, when the Persians threatened, the Greeks briefly put aside their differences to defend their freedom.

The Persian Wars

By 500 B.C., Athens had emerged as the wealthiest Greek city-state. But Athens and the entire Greek world soon faced a fearsome threat from outside. The Persians, you will recall, conquered an empire stretching from Asia Minor to the border of India. (See page 39.) Their subjects included Greek city-states of Ionia in Asia Minor. When these Ionian Greeks rebelled against Persian rule in 499 B.C., Athens sent ships to help them. As Herodotus wrote some years later, "These ships were the beginning of mischief both to the Greeks and to the barbarians."

Victory at Marathon. The Persians soon crushed the rebel cities. Later, the emperor Darius sent a huge force across the Aegean to punish Athens for its interference. The mighty

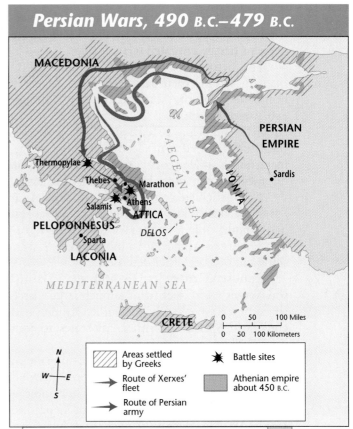

Persian Wars, 490 B.C.–479 B.C.

Areas settled by Greeks
Route of Xerxes' fleet
Route of Persian army
Battle sites
Athenian empire about 450 B.C.

GEOGRAPHY AND HISTORY

By the 400s B.C., the Persians of Asia Minor had forged the largest empire in the world. When the Persians turned their mighty army against Greece, the Greek city-states briefly joined forces to defend their independence.

1. **Location** On the map, locate (a) Athens, (b) Thermopylae, (c) Marathon, (d) Salamis, (e) Persian empire.
2. **Movement** Why do you think Xerxes' fleet hugged the coast instead of sailing across the sea directly to Athens?
3. **Critical Thinking** **Making Inferences** What advantages did the Greeks have in the war against the Persians?

Persian army landed at Marathon, north of Athens, in 490 B.C.

The Persians outnumbered Athenian forces two to one. Yet the invaders were amazed to see "a mere handful of men coming on at a run without either horsemen or archers." Overwhelmed by the fury of the Athenian assault, the Persians hastily retreated to their ships.

The victorious Greeks sent Pheidippides (fī DIHP ih deez), their fastest runner, to carry home news of the stunning victory. Though exhausted, he sprinted 26.2 miles (42 km) to Athens. "Rejoice, we conquer," he gasped—then dropped down dead. In his honor, marathon runners today still cover the same distance that Pheidippides ran 2,500 years ago.

The Athenian leader, Themistocles (thuh MIHS tuh kleez), knew the victory at Marathon had bought only a temporary lull in the fighting. He urged Athenians to build a fleet of warships and prepare other defenses.

Renewed attacks. In 480 B.C., Darius' son Xerxes (ZERK seez) sent a much larger force to conquer Greece. By this time, Athens had convinced Sparta and other city-states to join the fight.

Once again, the Persians landed an army in northern Greece. A small Spartan force guarded the narrow mountain pass at Thermopylae (thuhr MAHP uh lee). Led by King Leonidas, (see page 111), they held out heroically against the enormous Persian force. Herodotus described the heroic stand of the Spartans:

66They defended themselves to the last,
such as still had swords using them,
and the others resisting with their
hands and teeth; till the barbarians . . .
overwhelmed and buried the remnant
that was left beneath showers of missile
weapons.99

The Persians marched south and burned Athens. The city was empty, however. The Athenians had withdrawn to safety, putting their faith in the fleet that Themistocles had urged them to build. In the nearby strait of Salamis, Athenian warships trapped, rammed, and sank the Persian fleet. The following year, the Greeks defeated the Persians on land. In a brief moment of unity, the Greek city-states had saved themselves from the Persian threat.

Results. Victory in the Persian Wars increased the Greek sense of their own uniqueness. The gods, they felt, had protected their superior form of government—the city-state—against invaders from Asia.

Athens emerged from the war as the most powerful city-state in Greece. To meet continued threats from Persia, it organized the Delian League, an alliance with other Greek city-states. Athens dominated the league, slowly using its position to create an Athenian empire. It moved the league treasury from the island of Delos to Athens and forced its allies to remain in the league against their will. Athenians even used money contributed by other city-states to rebuild their own city. Yet, while Athens was enforcing its will abroad, Athenian leaders were championing political freedom at home.

Athens in the Age of Pericles

The years after the Persian Wars were a golden age for Athens. Under the able statesman Pericles (PEHR uh kleez), the economy thrived and the government became more democratic. Because of his wise and skillful leadership, the period from 460 B.C. to 429 B.C. is often called the Age of Pericles.

Political life. Pericles believed that all male citizens, regardless of wealth or social class, should take part in government. Athens therefore began to pay salaries to men who held public office. This reform enabled poor men to serve in government.

By the time of Pericles, the assembly met several times a month and needed at least 6,000 members present before deciding important issues. Athenians had a direct democracy in which a large number of male citizens took part in the day-to-day affairs of government. By contrast, in most democratic countries today, citizens participate in government indirectly through elected representatives. (See *You Decide*, "How Should a Society's Leaders Be Chosen?" pages 180–181.)

The Funeral Oration. Thucydides (thoo SIHD uh deez), a historian who lived in the Age of Pericles, recorded a speech given by Pericles at the funeral of Athenians slain in battle. In this famous Funeral Oration, Pericles praised the Athenian form of government:

66Our constitution is called a democracy
because power is in the hands not of a
minority but of the whole people.
When it is a question of settling private

disputes, everyone is equal before the laws. When it is a question of putting one person before another in positions of public responsibility, what counts is not membership of a particular class, but the ability the man possesses. **"**

Pericles pointed out that Athenian citizens bore a special responsibility. "We alone," he stated, "regard a man who takes no interest in public affairs, not as a harmless but as a useless character."

Economic and cultural life. Athens prospered during the Age of Pericles. With the riches of the Athenian empire, Pericles hired the best architects and sculptors to rebuild the Acropolis, which the Persians had destroyed. Magnificent new temples rose to remind citizens that the gods had favored the Athenians. Building projects further increased prosperity by creating jobs for artisans and workers.

With the help of an educated foreign-born woman named Aspasia, Pericles turned Athens

ISSUES *For* **TODAY** Pericles boasted that it was the duty of every Athenian citizen to participate in government. How have the responsibilities of a citizen changed over time?

into the cultural center of Greece. Pericles and Aspasia surrounded themselves with thinkers, writers, and artists. Through building programs and public festivals, they supported the arts. In the next section, you will read about Greek contributions to the arts, literature, and philosophy.

Greek Against Greek

The power of Athens contained the seeds of disaster. Many Greeks resented Athenian domination. Before long, the Greek world split into rival camps. To counter the Delian League, Sparta and other enemies of Athens formed the Peloponnesian League. Sparta encouraged oligarchy in the cities of the Peloponnesian League, while Athens supported democracy among its allies.

In 431 B.C., warfare broke out in earnest between Athens and Sparta. The 27-year Peloponnesian War engulfed all of Greece.

Peloponnesian War. Despite its riches and powerful navy, Athens faced a serious geographic disadvantage. Sparta was located inland, so it could not be attacked from the sea. Yet Sparta had only to march north to attack Athens by land.

When Sparta invaded Athens, Pericles allowed people from the surrounding countryside to move inside the city walls. The overcrowded conditions soon led to disaster. A terrible plague broke out, killing at least a third of the population, including Pericles himself. His successors were much less able leaders. Their power struggles quickly undermined the city's democratic government.

As the war dragged on, each side committed savage acts against the other. Sparta even allied itself with Persia, the longtime enemy of the Greeks. Finally, in 404 B.C., with the help of the Persian navy, the Spartans captured Athens. The victors stripped Athenians of their fleet and empire.

The aftermath of war. The Peloponnesian War ended Athenian greatness. Although the Athenian economy revived, its spirit and vitality declined. In Athens, as elsewhere in the Greek world, democratic government suffered. Corruption and selfish interests replaced older ideals such as service to the city-state.

Fighting continued to disrupt the Greek world. Sparta itself soon suffered defeat at the hands of Thebes, another Greek city-state. As Greeks fought among themselves, a new power rose in Macedonia (MAS uh dohn ee yuh), a kingdom to the north. By 359 B.C., its ambitious ruler stood poised to conquer the quarrelsome city-states.

SECTION 3 REVIEW

1. **Identify** (a) Marathon, (b) Themistocles, (c) Delian League, (d) Aspasia.
2. **Define** direct democracy.
3. Describe two effects of the Persian Wars.
4. What are three ways in which Pericles contributed to Athenian greatness?
5. How did the growth of Athenian power contribute to the outbreak of the Peloponnesian War?
6. *Critical Thinking* **Linking Past and Present** Compare Athenian democracy under Pericles to American democracy today. (a) How are they similar? (b) How are they different?
7. *ACTIVITY* Draw a political cartoon commenting on the causes or effects of the Peloponnesian War, from the viewpoint of either Athens or Sparta.

4 The Glory That Was Greece

Guide for Reading

- What political and ethical ideas did Greek philosophers develop?
- What were the goals of Greek architects and artists?
- How did Greek theater evolve?
- **Vocabulary** *rhetoric, tragedy, comedy*

Despite wars and political turmoil, Greeks had great confidence in the power of the human mind. "We cultivate the mind," declared Pericles. "We are lovers of the beautiful, yet simple in our tastes." Driven by curiosity and guided by a belief in reason, Greek thinkers, artists, and writers explored the nature of the universe and the place of people in it.

Lovers of Wisdom

As you have read earlier, some Greek thinkers denied that events were caused by the whims of gods. Instead, they used observation and reason to find causes for what happened. The Greeks called these thinkers philosophers, meaning "lovers of wisdom."

Philosophers explored many subjects, from mathematics and physics to music and logic, or rational thinking. Through reason and observation, they believed they could discover laws that governed the universe. Much modern science traces its roots to the Greek search for principles explaining how the universe works.

Other philosophers were more interested in ethics, or moral behavior. Their debates centered on questions such as what was the best kind of government and what standards should govern people's behavior.

In Athens, one group of thinkers, the Sophists, questioned accepted ideas about truth and justice. To them, success was more important than moral truths. They urged students to develop skills in rhetoric, the art of skillful speaking. Ambitious men could use clever words to advance their careers within the city-state. The turmoil of the Peloponnesian War led many young Athenians to follow the Sophists. Older citizens, however, condemned the Sophists for undermining traditional values. An outspoken critic of the Sophists was Socrates, an Athenian stonemason and philosopher, who lived from 469 B.C. to 399 B.C.

Death of a Philosopher

"The unexamined life is not worth living," declared Socrates. True to his word, he encouraged those around him to examine their deepest beliefs and ideas. Eventually, this commitment to truth cost Socrates his life.

A wandering teacher. Most of what we know about Socrates comes from his student Plato. Socrates himself wrote no books. Instead, he lounged around the marketplace, questioning fellow citizens about their beliefs and ideas. In one dialogue reported by Plato, Socrates challenges his friend Euthyphro (yoo THIHF roh) to define what actions are pious, or holy. "What is pleasing to the gods is pious," Euthy-

phro immediately responds. But Socrates refuses to accept this simple answer. Through patient questioning, he gets Euthyphro to contradict himself:

66'Have we not said, Euthyphro, that there are quarrels and disagreements and hatreds among the gods?'
'We have. . . .'
'Then you say that some of the gods think one thing just, the other another; and that what some of them hold to be honorable or good, others hold to be dishonorable or evil; . . . and the same thing will be displeasing and pleasing to them?'
'Apparently.'
'Then, according to your account, the same thing will be pious and impious.'99

Death of Socrates *Socrates urged his students to question and critically examine all around them. For "corrupting the youth" in this way, an Athenian jury sentenced him to death. This French painting of the 1600s shows the condemned Socrates drinking deadly hemlock.* **Impact of the Individual** *Why do you think later artists like this one portrayed Socrates as a heroic figure?*

This questioning process is known today as the Socratic method. To Socrates, it was a way to help others seek truth and self-knowledge. To many of his students, it was an amusing game. To other Athenians, however, it was an annoyance and a threat to accepted traditions.

Trial and execution. When he was about 70 years old, Socrates was put on trial. His enemies accused him of corrupting the city's youth and failing to respect the gods.

Standing before a jury of 501 citizens, Socrates offered a calm defense:

> 66All day long and in all places I am always fastening upon you, stirring you and persuading you and reproaching you. You will not easily find another like me, and therefore I would advise you to spare me.99

To the jurors, Socrates' cool reason seemed like arrogance. They condemned him to death.

His friends urged Socrates to flee. By examining the issue, however, he showed how escape would be morally wrong. "In leaving the prison against the will of the Athenians," he asked, "do I not desert the principles which were acknowledged by us to be just?"

Loyal to the laws of Athens, Socrates accepted the death penalty. He drank a cup of hemlock, a deadly poison. Then, as the poison surged through his body, he chatted with friends and students. According to Plato, his last words were, "Crito, I owe a rooster to Asclepius. Will you remember to pay the debt?" So died the man Plato called the "wisest, justest, and best of all I have ever known."

Ideas About Government

The death of Socrates so shocked and disturbed Plato that he left Athens for 10 years. When he returned, he set up the Academy, a school that survived for almost 900 years. There, he taught and wrote about his own ideas.

Plato. Like Socrates, Plato emphasized the importance of reason. Through rational thought, he argued, people could discover unchanging ethical values, recognize perfect beauty, and learn how to organize an ideal society.

In *The Republic,* Plato described his vision of an ideal state. He rejected Athenian democracy because it had condemned Socrates. Instead, Plato felt the state should regulate every aspect of its citizens' lives in order to provide for their best interests. He divided society into three classes: workers to produce the necessities of life, soldiers to defend the state, and philosophers to rule. This elite class of leaders would be specially trained to ensure order and justice. The wisest of them, a philosopher-king, would have the ultimate authority.

Plato thought that women could rank among the ruling elite of his republic. He claimed that, in general, men surpassed women in mental and physical tasks, but he thought that some women were superior to some men. Talented women, he said, should be educated and put to use by the state. The ruling elite, both men and women, would take military training together and raise their children in communal centers for the good of the republic.

Aristotle. Plato's most famous student, Aristotle, developed his own ideas about the best kind of government. He analyzed all kinds of government—from monarchy to aristocracy to democracy—and found good and bad examples of each. Like Plato, he was suspicious of democracy, which he thought could lead to mob rule. In the end, he favored rule by a single strong and virtuous leader.

Like Plato, Aristotle also addressed the question of how people ought to live. In his view, good conduct meant pursuing the "golden mean," a moderate course between extremes. He promoted reason as the guiding force for learning.

Aristotle set up a school, the Lyceum, for the study of all branches of knowledge. He left writings on politics, ethics, logic, biology, literature, physics, and many other subjects. When the first universities evolved in Europe some 1,500 years later, their courses were largely based on the works of Aristotle.

The Search for Beauty and Order

Plato argued that every object on Earth had an ideal form. The work of Greek artists and architects reflected the same concern with form and order.

The Parthenon *Each year, armies of tourists invade Athens to gaze at the temples on the Acropolis. These buildings have been battered by 2,500 years of weather, war, and pollution. Yet they stand as proud monuments to the Greek quest for order and beauty. The most revered temple on the Acropolis is the Parthenon, shown here.* **Continuity and Change** *Based on this picture, what modern buildings were influenced by the style of the Parthenon?*

Architecture. The most famous Greek temple, the Parthenon, was dedicated to the goddess Athena. Its builders sought to convey a sense of perfect balance to reflect the harmony and order of the universe. The basic plan was a simple rectangle, with tall columns supporting a gently sloping roof. The delicate curves and placement of the columns added dignity and grace.

Greek architecture has been widely admired for centuries. Throughout the United States today, you can see buildings that have adopted various kinds of Greek columns.

Sculpture. In ancient times, a towering figure of Athena, covered in gold and ivory, stood inside the Parthenon. Though this statue has not survived, many other works from this period show Greek sculpture at its best.

Early Greek sculptors carved figures in rigid poses, perhaps imitating Egyptian styles. By 450 B.C., Greek sculptors had developed a new style that emphasized natural poses, such as athletes in motion. While their work was realistic, or lifelike, it was also idealistic. That is, sculptors carved gods, goddesses, athletes, and famous men in a way that showed individuals in their most perfect, graceful form.

Painting. The only Greek paintings to survive are on vases and other pottery. They offer intriguing views of Greek life. Women carry water from wells, oarsmen row trading ships, warriors race into battle, and athletes compete in javelin contests. Each scene is designed to fit the shape of the pottery perfectly. (See the picture on page 111.)

Poetry and Drama

In literature, as in art, the ancient Greeks set the standard for what later Europeans called the classic style. Ever since, writers and artists in the western world have studied the elegance, harmony, and balance of Greek works.

Greek literature began with the epics of Homer, whose stirring tales inspired later writers. Other poets wrote about the joys and sorrows of their own times. Sappho sang of love and of the beauty of her island home. Pindar's poems celebrated the victors in athletic contests. (See page 102.) Perhaps the most important Greek contribution to literature, though, was in the field of drama.

The beginnings of Greek drama. The first Greek plays evolved out of religious festivals, especially those held in Athens to honor Dionysus (di uh NĪ suhs), god of fertility and wine. Plays were performed outdoors in large theaters gouged out of the sides of hills. There was little or no scenery. Actors wore elaborate costumes and stylized masks. A chorus responded to the action by singing or chanting commentary between scenes.

Greek dramas were often based on popular myths and legends. Through these familiar stories, playwrights discussed moral and social issues or explored the relationship between people and the gods.

Tragedy. The greatest Athenian playwrights were Aeschylus (EHS kuh luhs), Sophocles (SAHF uh kleez), and Euripides (yu RIHP uh deez). All three wrote tragedies, plays that told stories of human suffering that usually ended in disaster. The purpose of tragedy, the Greeks felt, was to excite emotions of pity and fear.

Aeschylus drew on tales of the Trojan Wars in *The Oresteia* (ohr eh STEE uh). This series of three plays unfolded hideous crimes of murder and revenge within a powerful family. The plays showed how pride could bring misfortune and how the gods could bring down even the greatest heroes.

In *Antigone* (an TIHG uh nee), Sophocles explored what happens when an individual's moral duty conflicts with the laws of the state. As the play opens, Antigone's brother has been killed leading a rebellion against the city of Thebes. King Creon forbids anyone to bury the traitor's body. When Antigone buries her brother anyway, she is arrested. She tells Creon that duty to the gods is greater than human law:

❝ For me, it was not Zeus who made that order. Nor did I think your orders were so strong that you, a mortal man, could overrule the gods' unwritten and unfailing laws. ❞

For her defiance, Antigone is sentenced to death. Creon, too, is punished when his actions lead to the deaths of his wife and son.

Both Sophocles and Euripides survived the horrors of the Peloponnesian War. That experience probably led Euripides to question accepted ideas. His plays said little about the gods. Instead, they suggested that people were the cause of human misfortune. In *The Trojan Women,* he stripped war of its glamour by showing the suffering of women who were victims of the war.

Comedy. Other Greek playwrights composed comedies, humorous plays that mocked people or customs. Through ridicule, they criticized society, much as political cartoons do today. Almost all surviving Greek comedies were written by Aristophanes (ar ihs TAHF uh neez). In *Lysistrata,* Aristophanes tells what happens when the women of Athens together force their husbands to end a war against Sparta.

The Writing of History

The Greeks applied observation, reason, and logic to the study of history. Herodotus is often called the "Father of History" in the west-

Comic Masks *In this marble relief, the playwright Menander looks at the masks used in one of his comedies. The masks, with their exaggerated facial features, enabled those sitting far from the stage to recognize the characters. A small mouthpiece inside the mask helped project the actor's voice.* **Art and Literature** *What emotions do you see in each of these masks?*

ern world because he went beyond listing rulers or retelling ancient legends. Before writing *The Persian Wars,* Herodotus visited many lands, collecting information from people who remembered the events he chronicled.

Herodotus cast a critical eye on his sources, noting bias and conflicting accounts. Yet his writings reflected his own view that the war was a clear moral victory of Greek love of freedom over Persian tyranny. He also invented conversations and speeches for historical figures.

Thucydides, a few years younger than Herodotus, wrote about the Peloponnesian War, a much less happy subject for the Greeks. He had lived through the war and vividly described its savagery and its corrupting influence on all those involved. Although he was an Athenian, he tried to be fair to both sides.

Both writers set standards for future historians. Herodotus stressed the importance of research. Thucydides showed the need to avoid bias in recording the past.

SECTION 4 REVIEW

1. **Identify** (a) Socrates, (b) Aristotle, (c) Parthenon, (d) Aeschylus, (e) Sophocles, (f) Euripides, (g) Herodotus, (h) Thucydides.
2. **Define** (a) rhetoric, (b) tragedy, (c) comedy.
3. What standards of beauty did Greek artists follow?
4. (a) How were Greek plays performed? (b) What themes did Greek playwrights explore?
5. (a) Why did Plato reject democracy as a form of government? (b) Describe the ideal government set forth in Plato's *Republic.*
6. *Critical Thinking* **Analyzing Information** Review Socrates' statement about an "unexamined life" on page 117. (a) Restate this idea in your own words. (b) How did his actions reflect this belief? (c) Why was Socrates seen as a danger to the state?
7. *ACTIVITY* Thucydides wrote about an event he had lived through because he believed it would still have an impact years later. Choose an event during your own lifetime that you think historians will write about 100 years from now. Write a paragraph explaining the importance of this event.

5 Alexander and the Hellenistic Age

Guide for Reading

■ What were the results of Alexander's conquests?

■ Why was Alexandria a center of the Hellenistic world?

■ How did individuals contribute to Hellenistic civilization?

Again and again, Demosthenes (dih MAHS thuh neez), the finest public speaker in Athens, tried to warn fellow citizens of the danger they faced. Philip II, the ambitious king of Macedonia, was gradually bringing Greece under his control:

66He is always taking in more, everywhere casting his net round us, while we sit idle and do nothing. When, Athenians, will you take the necessary action? What are you waiting for?99

When the Athenians finally took action against Philip, it was too late. Athens and the other Greek city-states lost their independence. Yet the disaster ushered in a new age that saw Greek influence spread from the Mediterranean to the edge of India.

Macedonian Ambitions

To the Greeks, the rugged, mountainous kingdom of Macedonia was a backward, half-civilized land. The rulers of this frontier land, in fact, were of Greek origin and maintained ties to their Greek neighbors. As a youth, Philip lived in Thebes and came to admire Greek culture. Later, he hired Aristotle to tutor his young son Alexander.

When Philip gained the Macedonian throne in 359 B.C., he dreamed of conquering the prosperous, warring city-states to the south. He built a superb army and hired foreign captains to train his troops. Through threats, bribery, and diplomacy, he formed alliances with many Greek city-states. Others he overpowered. In 338 B.C., when Athens and Thebes finally joined forces against Philip, they suffered a crushing defeat at the battle of Chaeronea (kehr uh NEE uh). Philip then brought all of Greece under his control.

Philip had still grander dreams. He proposed to lead a force of Macedonians and Greeks to conquer the Persian empire. Before he could achieve his plan, however, he was murdered at his daughter's wedding feast. Philip's clever and determined wife, Olympias, then outmaneuvered his other wives and children to put her own son Alexander on the throne.

A Mighty Conqueror

Although Alexander was only 20 years old, he was already an experienced soldier. As a boy, he had heard tales of Achilles, hero of the *Iliad*. Alexander saw himself as a second Achilles. In the next 12 years, this confident and reckless young man earned the title Alexander the Great.

From Aristotle, Alexander acquired a love of learning and an interest in the arts. But he was first and foremost a warrior. When Thebes rebelled, his punishment was swift and brutal. He ordered

▲ Alexander and his mother

the city to be burned and its inhabitants to be killed or sold into slavery. He told his soldiers, though, to spare the house where the poet Pindar had once lived.

Conquest of Persia. Like his father, Alexander planned to invade Persia. With Greece subdued, he began organizing the forces needed to achieve that goal. By 334 B.C., he had enough ships to cross the Dardanelles, the strait that separates Europe from Asia Minor.

Persia was no longer the great power it had been. The emperor Darius III was weak, and the satraps who governed the provinces were often rebellious. Still, the Persian empire stretched more than 2,000 miles from Egypt to India.

Alexander won his first victory against the Persians at the Granicus River. He then moved from victory to victory, marching through Asia Minor into Palestine and south to Egypt. In 331 B.C., he took Babylon, then seized the Persian capitals. Before Alexander could capture Darius, however, one of the emperor's satraps murdered him and left his body on the road for Alexander to find. Alexander had the dead emperor buried properly.

On to India. With much of the Persian empire under his control, the restless young conqueror headed further east. He crossed the Hindu Kush into northern India. There, in 326 B.C., his troops for the first time faced soldiers mounted on elephants.

Alexander never lost a battle, but his soldiers were growing tired of the long campaign. At a branch of the Indus River, they refused to go further. Reluctantly, Alexander agreed to turn back. A long, grueling march brought them to Babylon, where Alexander began planning a new campaign.

Sudden death. Before he could set out again, he fell victim to a sudden fever. As Alexander lay dying, his commanders asked to whom he left his immense empire. "To the strongest," he is said to have whispered.

In fact, no one leader appeared who was strong enough to succeed Alexander. Instead, after years of disorder, three generals divided up the empire. Macedonia and Greece went to one general, Egypt to another, and most of Persia to a third. For 300 years, their descendants competed for power over the lands Alexander had conquered.

The Legacy of Alexander

Although Alexander's empire soon crumbled, he had unleashed changes that would ripple across the Mediterranean world and the Middle East for centuries. His most lasting achievement was the spread of Greek culture.

A blending of cultures. Alexander's conquests linked a vast area. Across his far-flung empire, Alexander founded many new cities, most of them named after him. The generals who succeeded him founded still more. Soldiers, traders, and artisans surged out of Greece

Empire of Alexander the Great

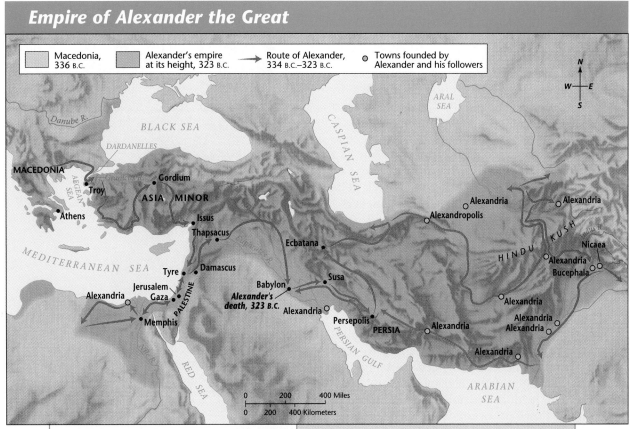

| Macedonia, 336 B.C. | Alexander's empire at its height, 323 B.C. | → Route of Alexander, 334 B.C.–323 B.C. | ○ Towns founded by Alexander and his followers |

N
W—E
S

ARAL SEA

Danube R.

BLACK SEA

DARDANELLES

MACEDONIA

Troy

Gordium

ASIA MINOR

Athens

Issus

Thapsacus

Ecbatana

CASPIAN SEA

Alexandria

Alexandropolis

Alexandria

HINDU KUSH

Nicaea

Alexandria

Bucephala

MEDITERRANEAN SEA

Tyre

Damascus

Jerusalem

Alexandria

Gaza

PALESTINE

Babylon
Alexander's
death, 323 B.C.

Susa

Alexandria

Persepolis

PERSIA

Alexandria

Alexandria

Alexandria

Memphis

RED SEA

PERSIAN GULF

Alexandria

ARABIAN SEA

0   200   400 Miles
0   200   400 Kilometers

GEOGRAPHY AND HISTORY

Alexander sought "opportunities of performing great and illustrious actions." His ambition led him to conquer lands across a wide area.

1. **Location** On the map, locate (a) Aegean Sea, (b) Arabian Sea, (c) Danube River, (d) Indus River, (e) Macedonia, (f) Persia, (g) Athens, (h) Babylon.
2. **Region** Look at the map on page 39. Which parts of Alexander's empire had not been part of the ancient Persian empire?
3. **Critical Thinking Predicting Consequences** Judging from the map, do you think Alexander's empire would be difficult to keep united? Explain.

to settle these new cities. From Egypt to the Fertile Crescent to the borders of India, they built Greek temples, filled them with Greek statues, and held athletic contests as they had in Greece. Local people assimilated, or absorbed, Greek ideas. In turn, Greek settlers adopted local customs.

Gradually, a blending of eastern and western cultures occurred. Alexander had encouraged this blending when he married a Persian woman and urged his soldiers to follow his example. He had also adopted many Persian customs, including Persian dress.

After his death, a vital new culture emerged, which is known as Hellenistic civilization. A blend of Greek, Persian, Egyptian, and Indian influences, Hellenistic civilization would flourish for centuries.

Alexandria. At the very heart of the Hellenistic world stood the city of Alexandria, Egypt. Located on the sea lanes between Europe and Asia, its markets boasted a wide range of goods, from Greek marble to Arabian spices to East African ivory.

A Greek architect had drawn up plans for the city, which would become home to almost a million people. Greeks, Egyptians, Persians, Hebrews, and many others crowded its busy streets. Among the city's marvelous sights was the Pharos, an enormous lighthouse that soared 440 feet into the air. Visitors counted the lighthouse among the Seven Wonders of the World.

Alexander had supported and encouraged learning throughout his empire, and his successors also supported the work of scholars. The rulers of Alexandria built the great Museum as a center of learning. (Its name meant "house of the Muses." The Muses were nine Greek goddesses who presided over the arts and sciences.) The Museum boasted laboratories, lecture halls, and a zoo. Its well-stocked library had thousands of scrolls representing the accumulated knowledge of the ancient world. Unfortunately, the library was later destroyed in a fire.

Opportunities for women. Paintings, statues, and legal codes reveal that women were no longer restricted to their houses in the Hellenistic period. More women learned to read and write. Some became poets and philosophers. Throughout the Hellenistic world, royal women held considerable power, working alongside husbands or sons who were the actual rulers. In Egypt, the able and clever Cleopatra came to rule in her own right.

Hellenistic Civilization

The cities of the Hellenistic world employed armies of architects and artists. Temples, palaces, and other public buildings were much larger and grander than the buildings of classical Greece. The elaborate new style reflected the desire of Hellenistic rulers to glorify themselves as godlike, absolute monarchs.

New schools of thought. The political turmoil of the Hellenistic age contributed to

GLOBAL CONNECTIONS

The list of the Seven Wonders of the World was compiled in the 100s B.C. by a writer who traveled across the Hellenistic world. In addition to the Pharos, the list included the Hanging Gardens of Babylon (see page 39) and the Colossus, a 100-foot bronze statue on the Aegean island of Rhodes. Of all these ancient wonders, only the pyramids of Egypt can still be seen today.

A New Look This bronze head, originally part of a full-length statue, reflects a new realistic approach developed by Hellenistic sculptors. They carved every bone and muscle exactly as it looked in real life. For subjects, they preferred ordinary people to gods and heroes. **Art and Literature** Compare this sculpture to the ones on page 103. What changes in artistic style can you see?

the rise of new schools of philosophy. The most influential, Stoicism, was founded by Zeno. He urged people to avoid desires and disappointments and accept calmly whatever life brought. The Stoics believed that all people, including women and slaves, though unequal in society, were morally equal because all had the power of reason. Stoics preached high moral standards that included protecting the rights of fellow humans. Stoicism later influenced many Roman and Christian thinkers.

Mathematics and the sciences. The Hellenistic age saw important advances in the sciences and mathematics. Hellenistic thinkers built on earlier Greek, Babylonian, and Egyptian knowledge. Pythagoras (pih THAG uhr uhs) derived a formula ($a^2 + b^2 = c^2$) that is still used to calculate the relationship between the sides of a right triangle. In Alexandria, Euclid wrote *The Elements*, which became the basis for modern geometry.

Using mathematics and careful observation, the astronomer Aristarchus (ar ihs TAHR kuhs) argued that the Earth rotated on its axis and or-

CAUSE AND EFFECT

Causes

Rise of civilizations in Persia, Egypt, and Greece

Macedonian conquest of Greece

Growth of Alexander's empire from Greece to northern India

Growing contacts among kingdoms of eastern Mediterranean and Middle East

RISE OF HELLENISTIC CIVILIZATION

Effects

Learning and arts encouraged by Alexander and his successors

Alexandria, Egypt, becomes center of trade and learning

Spread of Greek, Middle Eastern, and Persian religions

Spread of Christianity

Connections Today

Continued practice of Christianity and Judaism in the region

Alexandria, Egypt, still a center of learning

Greek architecture still visible in ruins across Middle East

Interpreting a Chart Alexander the Great's empire split apart soon after his death. Yet, by creating a common civilization over a vast area, he had an impact that endured for centuries. ■ *How did the conquests of Alexander encourage contacts among Mediterranean civilizations?*

bited around the sun. This idea was not accepted until almost 2,000 years later. The astronomer Eratosthenes showed that the Earth was round and accurately calculated its circumference.

The most famous Hellenistic scientist, Archimedes (ahr kuh MEE deez), applied principles of physics to make practical inventions. He mastered the use of the lever and pulley. He boasted, "Give me a lever long enough and a place to stand on, and I will move the world." An awed audience watched as he used his invention to draw a ship onto shore.

Medicine. About 400 B.C., the Greek physician Hippocrates (hih PAHK ruh teez) studied the cause of illnesses and looked for cures. His Hippocratic oath set ethical standards for doctors. Physicians swore to "help the sick according to my ability and judgment but never with a view to injury and wrong" and to protect the privacy of patients. Doctors today take a similar oath.

Looking Ahead

During the Hellenistic period, a powerful new state, Rome, came to dominate the Mediterranean world. By then, the Greeks had already made their greatest contributions.

Greek ideas about law, freedom, justice, and government have influenced political thinking to the present day. In the arts and sciences, Greek works became a standard of excellence for later people of Europe. These achievements were especially remarkable because they were produced by a scattering of tiny city-states whose bitter rivalries cost them their freedom. In the chapters ahead, you will see how the Greek legacy influenced the civilizations of Rome and of Western Europe.

SECTION 5 REVIEW

1. **Identify** (a) Philip, (b) Stoics, (c) Pythagoras, (d) Euclid, (e) Archimedes, (f) Hippocrates.
2. How did Alexander's conquests lead to the rise of a new civilization?
3. Describe three changes in the arts and philosophy during the Hellenistic age.
4. *Critical Thinking* **Ranking** What do you think were the three most important contributions made by Hellenistic scientists and mathematicians? Explain your choices.
5. *ACTIVITY* Imagine that you are a soldier in Alexander's army. Write two postcards to your family. In the first, tell how you feel about the Persian campaign. In the second, tell how you feel about marching into India.

CHAPTER REVIEW

REVIEWING VOCABULARY

Write a sentence comparing each of the following pairs of words or describing the relationship between them: (a) *polis* and *acropolis*, (b) *aristocracy* and *oligarchy*, (c) *legislature* and *democracy*, (d) *comedy* and *tragedy*.

REVIEWING FACTS

1. What were the *Iliad* and the *Odyssey*?
2. How did mountains help shape the development of Greek civilization?
3. How did Spartan males and females serve the military?
4. In what way was Athens a democracy?

5. What were the results of the Persian Wars?
6. How did the Peloponnesian War affect Athens?
7. What is the Socratic method?
8. Describe the extent of the lands conquered by Alexander the Great.
9. What cultures were blended to form Hellenistic civilization?

REVIEWING CHAPTER THEMES

Review the "Focus On" questions at the start of this chapter. Then select *three* of those questions and answer them, using information from the chapter.

SKILLS FOR SUCCESS   WORKING IN A GROUP

Working in a group can help you draw on the ideas and skills of many people. Yet it can also present difficulties, such as making decisions together or ensuring that everyone participates.

Imagine that you are a member of a group that is planning a textbook chapter about ancient Greece. The following techniques can help your group work more productively:

1. **Identify the group's goals.** At the first group meeting, choose a leader to lead the discussion and a recorder to take notes. Then, as a group, answer these questions: (a) What is the group's assignment? (b) What tasks must be done to complete the assignment?

2. **Use brainstorming to generate ideas.** During brainstorming, the members of a group spend a set amount of time freely suggesting any ideas that come to mind. Then the group discuss the ideas until they develop a plan that everyone can accept. Why is it important to encourage people to suggest ideas?

3. **Assign tasks and set deadlines.** The list below gives different ways that your group might per-

form specific tasks. Which plan seems to you to be the most useful, and why?

4. **Communicate progress.** When group members are working at different tasks, they should meet to discuss their progress. Why is it important for the group to communicate regularly?

Ways to Divide Up Work Within a Group

Plan 1. Have the group leader do everything.

Plan 2. Have every person in the group work on every task.

Plan 3. Let each person choose what he or she wants to do.

Plan 4. Have the group leader assign each person a job.

Plan 5. Discuss who should do jobs based on each individual's strengths and talents.

Plan 6. Assign jobs by picking names at random.

Plan 7. Ask someone outside the group to assign tasks.

CRITICAL THINKING

1. **Analyzing Information** (a) How did Greek culture stress the importance of the individual? Give two examples. (b) How do you think the importance given to the individual might have been related to the development of Greek democracy?

2. **Recognizing Causes and Effects** (a) Identify two immediate and two long-range causes of the Peloponnesian War. (b) Why might it be said that all Greeks were losers in the Peloponnesian War?

3. **Synthesizing Information** (a) In what ways was the form of government outlined in Plato's *Republic* similar to the government of Sparta? (b) How was it different?

4. **Linking Past and Present** Reread the description of the Hippocratic oath on page 125. (a) How did Hippocrates address the question of medical ethics? (b) What moral and ethical issues do doctors face today?

ANALYZING PRIMARY SOURCES

Use the quotation on pages 114–115 to answer the following questions.

1. How did Pericles define democracy?

2. What did Pericles mean by the statement, "everyone is equal before the laws"?

3. According to Pericles, how were people chosen for positions of public responsibility?

FOR YOUR PORTFOLIO

CREATING A MAGAZINE Produce a magazine to be called either *Athenian Life* or *Spartan Life*. First, decide which city to write about, and create a list of questions for you and other members of your group to research in the library. Use the information gained in your research to write two articles, one on war or politics and the other on daily life. Assemble your magazine with a cover and table of contents.

Persian Wars, 490 B.C.–479 B.C.

ANALYZING MAPS

Use the map to answer the following questions.

1. Which city, Athens or Sparta, was attacked by the Persians?

2. Did Persian forces reach Thermopylae by land or by sea?

3. What role did the city of Sardis play in the Persian Wars?

INTERNET ACTIVITY

READING A PLAY Use the Internet to find the text of a play by Euripides, Sophocles, or Aristophanes, and read a scene of the play. Then write a summary of the scene. Be sure to describe who the characters are, how they are related, and what is happening in the scene.

Ancient Rome and the Rise of Christianity

(509 B.C. – A.D. 476)

CHAPTER OUTLINE

1 **The Roman World Takes Shape**
2 **From Republic to Empire**
3 **The Roman Achievement**
4 **The Rise of Christianity**
5 **The Long Decline**

The poet Virgil wrote the epic poem the *Aeneid* to remind his fellow Romans of their great heritage. As he set out to celebrate the glories of Rome, though, he faced a dilemma. Educated Romans—the people who would read his poem—viewed Greek culture as superior to all others, including their own. After all, what Roman could match Homer's poetry or Plato's philosophy? How could Romans improve on Greek art, rhetoric, or knowledge of astronomy?

It would be best, the poet decided, to acknowledge Greek greatness at the start:

66Others will . . .
    Bring more lifelike portraits out
        of marble;
    Argue more eloquently, use the
        pointer
    To trace the paths of heaven
        accurately
    And accurately foretell the rising
        stars.99

Having paid his debt to Greece, Virgil reminded Romans of their own special mission in the world:

66Roman, remember by your strength
        to rule
    Earth's peoples—for your arts are to
        be these:
    To pacify, to impose the rule of law,
    To spare the conquered, strike down
        the proud.99

Peace, rule of law, mercy for the conquered—those were the achievements of Rome, Virgil concluded. Practical and solid, those achievements were very important indeed for the millions of people who lived under Roman rule.

From a small village, Rome grew into a superstate that stamped its decrees with the proud words "Rome, the City and the World." Rome expanded across the Mediterranean world to build a huge, ethnically diverse empire ruled by law. Rome's 1,000-year history had many lasting effects, but probably none was more important than the spread of important aspects of the civilizations of Greece, Egypt, and the Fertile Crescent westward into Europe.

FOCUS ON these questions as you read:

■ **Political and Social Systems**
How did Rome conquer and rule a diverse empire?

■ **Global Interaction**
How was Rome a bridge between the civilizations of east and west?

■ **Religions and Value Systems**
How did Christianity become a central institution of western civilization?

■ **Continuity and Change**
Why did Roman power fade?

TIME AND PLACE

Trading Across a Vast Empire At the height of its power, Rome ruled a vast empire stretching over much of Europe, plus parts of northern Africa and the Middle East. A flourishing trade helped spread Roman culture throughout these diverse lands. Here, a merchant ship in the Roman port of Ostia is loaded with grain. **Global Interaction** How does trade help spread culture?

HUMANITIES LINK

Art History Mosaic of Nile delta scene (page 134).
Literature In this chapter, you will encounter passages from the following works of literature: Virgil, the *Aeneid* (page 128); Martial, "By the time the barber Eurus" (page 143); The Gospel According to Matthew (page 145); Paul's Letter to the Romans (page 146); Ovid, *The Metamorphoses* (pages 152–153).

509 B.C.
Romans set up republic

264 B.C.
Punic Wars begin

27 B.C.
Pax Romana begins

A.D. **135**
Romans expel Jews from Palestine

A.D. **392**
Christianity becomes official religion of Roman empire

A.D. **476**
Fall of western Roman empire

| B.C. | 500 | 300 | 100 | B.C. | A.D. | 100 | 300 | 500 | A.D. |

1 The Roman World Takes Shape

Guide for Reading

- How did Italy's geography help the Romans unite the peninsula?

- How did the Roman government become more democratic?

- Why was Rome able to conquer a vast empire?

- **Vocabulary** *republic, patrician, consul, dictator, plebeian, tribune, veto, legion*

Romans loved stories about great heroes of the past. One of their favorite heroes was Horatius, who was said to have single-handedly saved Rome from an invading Etruscan army.

As the enemy approached, Horatius rushed to the far end of the bridge that led into the city. Standing alone, he held off the attackers while his fellow Romans tore down the bridge behind him. As the last timber fell, Horatius flung himself into the river below. Dodging the spears raining down all around him, he swam safely to the other side.

The story of Horatius is more legend than it is history. Still, it helps us to understand the virtues that the Romans admired. Courage, loyalty, and devotion to duty were the pillars on which Romans would build an empire.

The Italian Landscape

Rome began as a small city-state in Italy but ended up ruling the entire Mediterranean world. The story of the Romans and how they built a world empire starts with the land they lived in.

Italy is a peninsula that looks like a boot, jutting into the Mediterranean Sea and kicking the island of Sicily toward North Africa. The peninsula is centrally located in the Mediterranean, and the city of Rome is in the center of Italy. That location helped the Romans as they expanded, first in Italy, and then into lands around the Mediterranean.

Because of its geography, Italy was much easier to unify than Greece. Unlike Greece, Italy is not broken up into small, isolated valleys. In addition, the Apennine Mountains, which run like a backbone down the length of the Italian peninsula, are less rugged than the mountains of Greece. Finally, Italy has the advantage of broad, fertile plains, both in the north under the shadow of the Alps, and in the west, where the Romans settled. These plains supported a growing population.

Roman Beginnings

The Romans, like the Greeks, were an Indo-European people. (See page 53.) Their ancestors, the Latins, had migrated into Italy by about 800 B.C. The Latins settled along the Tiber River in small villages scattered over seven low-lying hills where they herded and farmed. Those villages would in time grow into Rome, the city on seven hills.

The Romans shared the Italian peninsula with other peoples, whose ideas they adapted. Among them were Greek colonists whose city-states dotted southern Italy and the island of Sicily. But closer neighbors, the Etruscans, who lived north of Rome, were the greatest influence.

The Etruscans, who had come from Asia Minor, ruled much of central Italy, including Rome itself. From them, the Romans learned the alphabet that the Etruscans had earlier acquired from the Greeks. They also learned to use the arch in building and adopted Etruscan engineering techniques to drain the marshy lands along the Tiber. Etruscan gods and goddesses merged with Roman deities.

The Early Republic

The Romans drove out their hated Etruscan king in 509 B.C. This date is traditionally considered to mark the founding of the Roman state. By this time, Rome had already grown from a cluster of villages into a small city.

Determined never again to be ruled by a monarch, the Romans set up a new government in which officials were chosen by the people. They called it a republic, or "thing of the people." A republic, Romans thought, would keep any individual from gaining too much power.

Later Romans looked back with enormous pride on the achievements of the early republic. Between 509 B.C. and 133 B.C., Rome adapted its republican form of government to meet changing needs. It also developed the military power to conquer not just Italy but the entire Mediterranean world.

The government takes shape. In the early republic, the most powerful governing body was the senate. Its 300 members were all patricians, members of the landholding upper class. Senators, who served for life, issued decrees and interpreted the laws.

Each year, the senators elected two consuls. Their job was to supervise the business of government and command the armies. Like senators, consuls came from the patrician class. Consuls, however, could serve only one term. They were also expected to consult with the senate. By limiting their time in office and making them responsible to the people through the senate, Rome had a system of checks on the power of government.

In the event of war, the senate might choose a dictator, or ruler who has complete control over a government. Each Roman dictator was granted emergency powers to rule for six months. At the end of that time, he had to give up power. Romans admired Cincinnatus as a model dictator. As he plowed his fields, a messenger arrived to tell him he had been chosen dictator. Cincinnatus left his plow, organized an army, led the Romans to victory over the attacking enemy, attended victory celebrations, and returned to his fields—all within 16 days.

As Rome grew, it elected other officials to oversee finances, justice, city government, and religious matters. A government censor kept an accurate list of citizens, or census.

Plebeians demand equality. At first, all government officials were patricians. Plebeians (plih BEE uhnz), the farmers, merchants, artisans, and traders who made up the bulk of the population, had little influence. The efforts of the plebeians to pry open the doors to power shaped politics in the early republic.

The plebeians' first breakthrough came in 450 B.C., when the government had the laws of Rome inscribed on 12 tablets and set up in the Forum, or marketplace. Plebeians had protested that citizens could not know what the laws

Ancient Italy About 600 B.C.

Greeks
Etruscans
Carthaginians

ALPS
Po R.
Genoa
APENNINE MTS.
Rubicon R.
Arno R.
ADRIATIC SEA
Alalia
CORSICA
Tiber R.
Rome
SARDINIA
TYRRHENIAN SEA
IONIAN SEA
SICILY
Carthage
AFRICA
MEDITERRANEAN SEA

N
W—E
S

0   100   200 Miles
0   100   200 Kilometers

GEOGRAPHY AND HISTORY

Roman civilization developed on the Italian peninsula in southern Europe. The Romans shared the peninsula with Greeks and Etruscans, many of whose ideas they adapted.

1. **Location** On the map, locate (a) Adriatic Sea, (b) Tiber River, (c) Rubicon River, (d) Apennine Mountains, (e) Sicily, (f) Rome, (g) Carthage.
2. **Region** Based on this map, which group had the most influence on the Romans? Explain.
3. **Critical Thinking** **Comparing** Use the map on page 108 to compare the geography of Italy with that of Greece.

were, because they were not written down. The Laws of the Twelve Tables made it possible for the first time for plebeians to appeal a judgment handed down by a patrician judge.

In time, the plebeians gained the right to elect their own officials, called tribunes, to protect their interests. The tribunes could veto, or block, those laws that they felt were harmful to plebeians. Little by little, plebeians forced the senate to choose plebeians as consuls, appoint plebeians to other high offices, and finally to open the senate itself to plebeians who had served the state well.

A lasting legacy. Although the senate still dominated the government, the common people had gained access to power and won safeguards for their rights without having to resort to war or revolution. More than 2,000 years later, the framers of the United States Constitution would adapt such Roman ideas as the senate, the veto, and checks on the power of those who run the government.

Expansion in Italy

As Rome's political system evolved at home, its armies expanded Roman power across Italy. Soon after overthrowing their Etruscan rulers, the Romans gained dominance over their neighbors in central Italy. They then conquered the Etruscans themselves and began moving against the Greek city-states in the south. By about 270 B.C., Rome occupied all of Italy, from the Rubicon River in the north to the tip of the boot in the south.

Masters of war. Rome's success was due partly to skillful diplomacy and partly to its efficient, well-disciplined army. As in Greece, Roman armies consisted of citizen-soldiers who fought without pay and supplied their own weapons. The basic unit was the legion, made up of about 5,000 men.

Well trained in military skills and brought up to value loyalty and courage, Roman soldiers chalked up a series of brilliant victories. To ensure success, Roman commanders mixed rewards with harsh punishment. Young soldiers who showed courage in action won praise and gifts. If a unit fled from battle, however, 1 out of every 10 men from the disgraced unit was put to death.

Conquered lands. Rome generally treated its defeated enemies with justice. Conquered peoples had to acknowledge Roman leadership, pay taxes, and supply soldiers for the Roman army. In return, Rome let them keep their own customs, money, and local government.

To a few privileged groups among the conquered people, Rome gave the highly prized right of full citizenship. Others became partial citizens, who were allowed to marry Romans and carry on trade in the growing city on the Tiber. Such generous treatment created support for Rome, and even in troubled times most of the conquered lands remained loyal.

To protect its conquests, Rome posted soldiers throughout the land. It also built a network of all-weather military roads to link distant provinces to Rome. As trade and travel increased, local peoples incorporated Latin into their languages and adopted many Roman customs and beliefs. Slowly, Italy began to unite under Roman rule.

Rivalry With Carthage

Rome's conquest of the Italian peninsula brought it into contact with a new rival, Carthage. Carthage was a city-state on the northern coast of Africa, in present-day Tunisia. Settled by Phoenician traders, it ruled over a trading empire that stretched across North Africa and the western Mediterranean. As Rome spread into the Mediterranean, conflict between these two powers became inevitable.

Between 264 B.C. and 146 B.C., Rome fought three wars against Carthage. They are called the Punic Wars, from *punicus,* the Latin word for Phoenician. In the First Punic War, Rome defeated Carthage, forcing it to surrender Sicily, Corsica, and Sardinia. Peace was short-lived, however. Carthage was seething with rage at its loss, and 23 years later, led by a general named Hannibal, it sought revenge.

War With Hannibal

According to legend, when Hannibal was nine, his father, the general Hamilcar Barca, had him take a sacred oath. Leading the young boy to the altar of the gods, Hamilcar made him swear himself "an enemy of the Roman people." From that moment, Hannibal dedicated his life to the destruction of Rome.

A daring expedition. Several years after his father's death, Hannibal was selected as leader of the Carthaginian army. He commanded a mixed force of troops from Europe and North Africa. Although they had no language or customs in common, reported a historian, "the skill of the commander was such that these great differences did not disturb their obedience to his will."

In 218 B.C., Hannibal embarked on one of the most daring military expeditions in history. Setting out from Spain, he led his troops, including dozens of war elephants, in a march across the Pyrenees, through France, and over the mighty peaks of the Alps into Italy. The Roman historian Livy (LIHV ee) described the descent down the Alps' steep slopes:

> 66 The whole way was narrow and slippery, so that the soldiers could not prevent their feet from sliding, nor, if they made the least false step could they, on falling, stop themselves in the place; and thus men and beasts tumbled confusedly over one another. . . . Whenever they attempted to rise, either by aid of the hands or knees, these slipping, they fell again; add to this, that there were neither stumps nor roots within reach, on which they could lean for support; so that they wallowed in the melted snow on one entire surface of slippery ice. 99

The trek across the Alps lasted 15 days and cost Hannibal nearly half his army and almost all his elephants. Still, the Carthaginian general had achieved his goal. The Romans had expected an invasion from the south, through Sicily. The bold attack through the Alps caught them completely off guard.

Battle for Italy. For 15 years, Hannibal and his army moved across Italy, winning battle after battle in the Second Punic War. The Carthaginians, however, were never able to capture Rome itself. In the end, the Romans outflanked Hannibal by sending an army to attack Carthage. Hannibal returned to defend his homeland, and at the battle of Zama, the Romans defeated him at last.

Under the peace terms ending the war, Carthage gave up all its lands except those in Africa. It also had to pay a huge tribute, or tax, to Rome. For the Romans, however, the most important result of the Second Punic War was that they were now masters of the western Mediterranean.

Death of Hannibal. At first, the Romans allowed Hannibal to remain free after the war, and under his leadership, Carthage made a rapid recovery. However, the Romans still feared the Carthaginian general and accused him of plotting with their enemies. Learning of these charges, Hannibal fled to the east. When the Romans tracked him down, he took poison rather than surrender to his hated enemy.

Carthage destroyed. Hannibal was dead and Carthage kept to the terms of the peace. Rome, however, still saw Carthage as a rival. Besides, Romans would never forgive the terrible destruction that Hannibal's army had brought to Italy. For years, Cato, a wealthy senator, ended every speech he made with the words "Carthage must be destroyed."

In the end, Rome attacked and completely destroyed the 700-year-old city. Survivors were killed or sold into slavery. The Romans poured salt over the earth so that nothing would grow there again. Carthage and the region surrounding it became the new Roman province of Africa.

War Elephants War elephants, like the one painted on this Roman dish, trampled and crashed through enemy lines. From a tower on the elephant's back, soldiers rained arrows and spears on fleeing enemies. Hannibal hoped his war elephants would terrify Roman armies. *Global Interaction* Why might elephants have been more surprising and terrifying to Roman soldiers than to African and Asian soldiers?

Mosaic of Nile Delta Scene *Like the Greeks before them, Roman artists decorated walls, floors, and ceilings with multicolored mosaics. Each mosaic consisted of thousands of tiny stone and glass pieces. This detail from a mosaic of the first century B.C. re-creates a scene in Roman Egypt.* **Diversity** *How does the mosaic show the diversity that existed within the Roman empire?*

Ruler of the Mediterranean World

"The Carthaginians fought for their own preservation and the sovereignty of Africa," observed a Greek witness to the fall of Carthage; "the Romans, for supremacy and world domination." While Rome fought Carthage in the west, it was also expanding into the eastern Mediterranean. There, Romans confronted the Hellenistic rulers who had divided up the empire of Alexander the Great.

Sometimes to defend Roman interests, sometimes simply for plunder, Rome launched a series of wars in the area. One by one, it brought Macedonia, Greece, and parts of Asia Minor under its rule. Other regions, like Egypt, allied with Rome. By 133 B.C., Roman power extended from Spain to Egypt. Truly, the Romans were justified in calling the Mediterranean *Mare Nostrum*—"Our Sea."

SECTION 1 REVIEW

1. **Identify** (a) senate, (b) Laws of the Twelve Tables, (c) Punic Wars, (d) Hannibal.
2. **Define** (a) republic, (b) patrician, (c) consul, (d) dictator, (e) plebeian, (f) tribune, (g) veto, (h) legion.
3. Describe two ways that the geography of Italy influenced the rise of Rome.
4. (a) Why were plebeians discontented during the early republic? (b) What reforms did they win?
5. *Critical Thinking* **Linking Past and Present** Roman heroes were admired for their courage, loyalty, and devotion to duty. What qualities do American heroes display?
6. *ACTIVITY* Write a series of newspaper headlines announcing the major events in the rise of Rome.

From Republic to Empire

Guide for Reading

- How did winning an empire affect Rome?
- Why did the Roman republic decline?
- What were the strengths and weaknesses of the Roman empire?

The historian Appian, who lived in Alexandria about A.D. 150, wrote about the declining years of the Roman republic. Conquering an empire, he noted, had created strains and conflicts in Roman society:

> 66The powerful ones became enormously rich and the race of slaves multiplied throughout the country, while the Italian people dwindled in numbers and strength, being oppressed by poverty, taxes, and military service.99

In the end, the triumphant Romans tore their state apart. Ambitious generals battled for power, and their struggles crushed the republic. Out of the rubble rose the Roman empire and a new chapter in Rome's long history.

Effects of Expansion

Romans gloried in their successes as they set out to rule the newly acquired provinces. Victory put them in control of busy trade routes, and incredible riches flooded into Rome from the conquered lands. Generals, officials, and traders amassed fortunes from loot, taxes, and commerce. This newly found wealth, however, had disturbing consequences.

Social and economic consequences. A new class of wealthy Romans emerged. They built lavish mansions and filled them with luxuries imported from the east. Wealthy families bought up huge estates, called latifundia, which were worked by slaves captured in war.

The widespread use of slave labor hurt small farmers, who were unable to produce food as cheaply as the latifundia could. The farmers'

problems were compounded when huge quantities of grain pouring in from the conquered lands drove down grain prices. Many farmers fell into debt and had to sell their land.

In despair, landless farmers flocked to Rome and other cities looking for jobs. There, they joined a restless class of unemployed people. As the gap between rich and poor widened, ambitious men aroused angry mobs to riot.

The new wealth also increased corruption. Greed and self-interest replaced virtues such as simplicity, hard work, and devotion to duty so prized in the early republic.

Attempts at reform. Two young patricians, brothers named Tiberius and Gaius Gracchus (GAY uhs GRAK uhs), were among the first to attempt reform. Tiberius, who was elected a tribune in 133 B.C., called on the state to distribute land to poor farmers. He described their plight in moving words:

> 66Even the wild beasts that roam over Italy have a cave to sleep in, but the men who fight and die for Rome enjoy only the air and light, nothing else. They and their wives and children wander about homeless.99

Gaius, elected tribune 10 years later, sought a wider range of reforms, including the use of public funds to buy grain to feed the poor. He also called for extension of full citizenship to some of Rome's allies.

The reforms of the Gracchus brothers angered the senate, which saw them as a threat to its power. The brothers, along with thousands of their followers, were killed in waves of street violence set off by senators and their hired thugs.

A century of civil war. The slayings of the Gracchus brothers showed that the republic was unable to resolve its problems peacefully. During the next 100 years, Rome was plunged into a series of civil wars. At issue was who should hold power—the senate, which wanted to govern as it had in the past, or popular political leaders, who wanted to weaken the senate and enact reforms.

The turmoil sparked slave uprisings and revolts among Rome's allies. At the same time, the endless warfare transformed the old legions

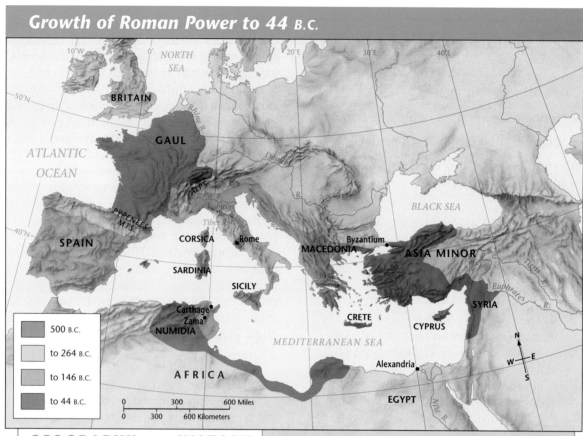

Growth of Roman Power to 44 B.C.

Legend:
- 500 B.C.
- to 264 B.C.
- to 146 B.C.
- to 44 B.C.

GEOGRAPHY AND HISTORY

Through wars and diplomacy, the Roman republic expanded until it surrounded the Mediterranean Sea. The Romans built thousands of miles of roads to unite their sprawling lands.

1. **Location** *On the map, locate (a) Alps, (b) Gaul, (c) Sicily, (d) Egypt, (e) Rome, (f) Byzantium.*
2. **Region** *During which period did Rome gain control of much of Asia Minor?*
3. **Critical Thinking** **Recognizing Causes and Effects** *Why did Rome gain so much territory between 146 B.C. and 44 B.C.?*

---

of citizen-soldiers into highly organized professional armies whose first loyalty was to their commanders. Spurred by their successes abroad, rival generals marched their armies into Rome to advance their ambitions.

Caesar's Bid for Power

Out of this chaos emerged Julius Caesar, an able commander who combined soaring ambition with a determination to make drastic reforms. For a time, Caesar dominated Roman politics with Pompey, one of Rome's most brilliant generals. Then, in 59 B.C., Caesar set out with his army to make new conquests. After nine years of almost constant fighting, he succeeded in bringing all of Gaul—the area that is now France—under Roman control.

Crossing the Rubicon. Back home, Pompey grew jealous of Caesar's successes and fearful of his rising fame. He had the senate order Caesar to disband his army and return to Rome.

Caesar decided to defy the order. Acting swiftly and secretly, he led his army across the Rubicon River into northern Italy and then headed toward Rome. With this act, which was

136   Chapter 6

considered treason, he committed himself to a life-and-death struggle from which there was no turning back.

Once again, civil war erupted across the empire. Caesar crushed Pompey and his supporters. He then swept around the Mediterranean, suppressing rebellious provinces and strengthening Roman power. *"Veni, vidi, vici"*—"I came, I saw, I conquered"—he announced briefly after one victory. Later, returning to Rome, he forced the senate to make him dictator. Although he kept the senate and other features of the republic, he was in fact the absolute ruler of Rome.

Caesar's reforms. Between 48 B.C. and 44 B.C., Caesar pushed through a number of reforms intended to deal with Rome's many problems. He launched a program of public works to employ the jobless and gave public land to the poor. He also reorganized the government of the provinces and granted Roman citizenship to more people. To enact these reforms, however, he packed the senate with his own followers.

Caesar's most lasting reform was the introduction of a new calendar based on Egyptian knowledge. The Julian calendar, as it was later called, was used in western Europe for over 1,600 years, and with minor changes is still our calendar today.

The Ides of March. Caesar's enemies worried that he planned to make himself king of Rome. In order to save the republic, they plotted against him.

According to legend, early in the year 44 B.C., a fortune-teller warned Caesar to "beware the Ides of March," as the Romans called March 15. The day arrived and nothing happened. "The Ides of March have come," Caesar called out mockingly to the fortune-teller. "They have come," the man replied, "but not yet gone." Moments later, as he arrived in the senate, Caesar's enemies stabbed him to death.

The death of Julius Caesar plunged Rome into a new round of civil wars. Mark Antony, Caesar's chief general, and Octavian, Caesar's grandnephew, joined forces to hunt down the murderers. The two men soon quarreled, however, and a

▲ *Julius Caesar*

bitter struggle for power ensued. In 31 B.C., Octavian finally defeated Antony and his powerful ally Queen Cleopatra of Egypt.

End of the republic. The senate proclaimed the triumphant Octavian *Augustus,* or Exalted One, and declared him *princeps,* or first citizen. Although he was careful not to call himself king, a title that Romans had hated since Etruscan times, Augustus exercised absolute power and named his successor, just as a king would do.

Under Augustus, who ruled from 31 B.C. to A.D. 14, the 500-year-old republic came to an end. Romans did not know it at the time, but a new age had dawned—the age of the Roman empire.

Imperial Rome

Through firm but moderate policies, Augustus helped Rome recover from the long period of civil war. At the same time, he laid the foundation for a stable government.

A stable government. While he left the senate in place, Augustus created an efficient, well-trained civil service charged with enforcing the laws. High-level jobs were open to men of talent, regardless of their class. In addition, he cemented the allegiance of cities and provinces to Rome by allowing them a large measure of self-government.

Augustus undertook economic reforms, too. To make the tax system more fair, he ordered a census, or population count, to be taken in the empire. He set up a postal service and issued new coins to make trade easier. He put the jobless to work building roads and temples and sent others to farm the land.

The government that Augustus organized functioned well for 200 years. Still, a serious problem kept arising: Who would rule after an emperor died? Romans did not accept the idea of power passing automatically from father to son. Consequently, the death of an emperor often led to intrigue and violence.

Bad emperors and good emperors. Not all of Augustus' successors were great rulers. Indeed, some were weak and incompetent.

Two early emperors, Caligula and Nero, were downright evil and perhaps insane. Caligula, for example, appointed his favorite horse as consul. Nero viciously persecuted Christians and was even blamed for setting a great fire that destroyed much of Rome.

Between A.D. 96 and A.D. 180, the empire benefited from the rule of a series of "good emperors." The emperor Hadrian, for example, codified Roman law, making it the same for all provinces. He also had soldiers build a wall across Britain to hold back attackers from the non-Roman north. You can still walk along Hadrian's Wall on the border between England and Scotland.

The emperor Marcus Aurelius, who read philosophy while on military campaigns, was close to Plato's ideal of a philosopher-king. His *Meditations* show his Stoic philosophy and commitment to duty: "Hour by hour resolve firmly . . .to do what comes to hand with correct and natural dignity."

The Roman Peace

The 200-year span that began with Augustus and ended with Marcus Aurelius is known as the period of the Pax Romana, or "Roman Peace." During that time, Roman rule brought peace, order, unity, and prosperity to lands stretching from the Euphrates River in the east to Britain in the west, an area equal in size to the continental United States.

The Pax Romana created "a world every day better known, better cultivated, and more civilized than before," glowed one Roman writer. He went on to detail the many benefits of Roman civilization:

> **66** Everywhere roads are traced, every district is known, every country opened to commerce. Smiling fields have invaded the forests . . . the rocks are planted, the marshes drained. There are now as many cities as there were once solitary cottages. Reefs and shoals have lost their terrors. Wherever there is a trace of life, there are houses, well-ordered governments and civilized life. **99**

With legions to maintain the roads and fleets to chase pirates from the seas, trade flowed freely to and from distant lands in Africa, India, and China. Egyptian farmers in the Nile Valley supplied Romans with grain. From other parts of Africa came ivory and gold, as well as lions and other wild animals that were used in public entertainments. From India came spices, cotton, and precious stones. Traveling the great Silk Road, caravans brought exotic goods from China. Iranian merchants, successors to the Persians, were a key link in this long-distance trade between the Mediterranean and Asia.

People, too, flowed across the Roman empire, spreading ideas and knowledge, especially the advances of the Hellenistic east. As you will read, ideas from Greece and Palestine would have tremendous impact on Rome and the western world.

Family and Religion

The family was the basic unit of Roman society. Under Roman law, the male head of the household, usually the father, had absolute power in the family. He enforced strict discipline and demanded total respect for his authority. His wife was subject to his authority and was not allowed to administer her own affairs.

Changing role of women. The ideal Roman woman was loving, dutiful, dignified, and strong. During the late republic and early empire, however, women gained greater freedom.

Patrician women, especially, played a larger role in society than did Greek women. They went to the public baths, dined out, and attended the theater or other public entertainments with their husbands. Some imperial women, such as Livia and Agrippina the Younger, had highly visible public roles and exercised significant political influence.

GLOBAL CONNECTIONS

India was one of Rome's major trading partners. Wealthy Romans dyed their finest purple robes with indigo from India. Indian traders also provided elephants, lions, and tigers to perform in Rome's wild animal shows. For their part, wealthy Indians prized Roman gold, wine, and manufactured goods.

PARALLELS THROUGH TIME

Hairstyles

The art of hairstyling goes back at least 3,500 years, to the ancient Assyrians. They viewed elaborately shaped hair as a sign of wealth and social position, for both men and women. Since then, every society and every generation have evolved their own unique styles.

Linking Past and Present Does Ovid's comment below about fashions in ancient Rome apply to American society today? Explain.

PAST *"I cannot keep track of fashion,"* complained the Roman poet Ovid. *"Every day, it seems, brings in a different style."* Patrician woman, like the ones shown here, were skilled in the use of dyes, curling irons, and other hairdressing technology.

PRESENT

Today, hairstyle is less likely to be a sure sign of social status. Still, individuals find a wide variety of ways to express themselves through their hair.

Women from all classes ran a variety of businesses, from small shops to major shipyards. Those who made their fortunes earned respect by supporting the arts or paying for public festivals. Most women, though, worked at home, raising their families, spinning, and weaving. This memorial pays tribute to an unknown woman named Claudia:

> 66 This is the unlovely tomb of a lovely woman. Her parents named her Claudia. She loved her husband with her whole heart. She bore two sons, one of whom she leaves on Earth; the other she has placed beneath the ground. She was charming in conversation, yet her conduct was appropriate. She kept house; she made wool. 99

Education. Girls and boys alike learned to read and write. Even lower-class Romans were taught to write, as can be seen from the jokes, messages, and other graffiti that archaeologists found scrawled on walls around the city.

By the late republic, many wealthy Romans were hiring private tutors, often Greek slaves, to teach their children. Under their guidance, children memorized major events and developments in Roman history. Rhetoric was an important subject for boys who wanted political careers.

Religion. Roman gods and goddesses resembled those of the Etruscans and Greeks. Like the Greek god Zeus, the Roman god Jupiter ruled over the sky and the other gods. Juno, his wife, like the Greek goddess Hera, protected marriage. Romans also prayed to

Chariot Race *Speed thrilled the fans who crowded into the Circus Maximus for chariot races. Crashes and bloody collisions added even more excitement. The poet Martial once complained that the names of winning horses and charioteers were legendary among the masses, while his own name remained virtually unknown.* **Religions and Value Systems** *What does Martial's comment suggest about Roman values at the time?*

Neptune, god of the sea, whose powers were the same as those of the Greek god Poseidon. On the battlefield, they turned to Mars, the god of war.

The Roman calendar was full of feasts and other celebrations to honor the gods and to ensure divine favor for the city. As loyal citizens, Romans joined in these festivals, which inspired a sense of community.

"Mystery" religions not associated with the official state gods were also popular, especially with women. For example, the cult of Isis, which originated in Egypt, promised life after death and offered women equal status with men. Becoming a priest in such a cult was a way in which a woman could achieve high office.

Bread and Circuses

Rich and poor alike loved spectacular entertainments. At the Circus Maximus, Rome's largest racecourse, chariots thundered around an oval course, making dangerously tight turns at either end. Fans bet feverishly on their favorite teams—the Reds, Greens, Blues, or Whites—and successful charioteers were hailed as heroes.

Gladiator contests were even more popular. Many gladiators were slaves who had been trained to fight. Led into the arena, they battled one another, either singly or in groups. Crowds cheered a skilled gladiator, and a good fighter might even win his freedom. But if a gladiator made a poor showing, the crowd turned thumbs down, a signal that he should be killed.

To the emperors who paid for them with the taxes they collected from the empire, these amusements were a way to control the city's restless mobs. In much the same spirit, the government provided free grain to feed the poor. Critics warned against this policy of "bread and circuses," but no one listened.

During the Pax Romana, the general prosperity hid underlying social and economic problems. Later Roman emperors, however, would face problems that could not be brushed away with "bread and circuses."

SECTION 2 REVIEW

1. **Identify** (a) Tiberius and Gaius Gracchus, (b) Julius Caesar, (c) Augustus, (d) Hadrian, (e) Pax Romana, (f) Circus Maximus.
2. Describe three ways in which empire building affected the Roman republic.
3. What problems did the republic face after the deaths of the Gracchus brothers?
4. (a) What reforms did Julius Caesar undertake? (b) Why did some Romans oppose him?
5. *Critical Thinking* **Analyzing Information** How do you think the founders of the Roman republic would have viewed the Roman empire? Explain.
6. *ACTIVITY* Imagine that you are one of the plotters against Julius Caesar. Create a political cartoon that shows why you oppose him.

3 The Roman Achievement

Guide for Reading

■ How did Roman art and literature blend different traditions?

■ What were Rome's greatest practical achievements?

■ What principles of law did Romans develop?

■ **Vocabulary** *aqueduct*

Marcus Tullius Cicero was a philosopher, politician, essayist, orator, and passionate defender of the law. As the republic declined, Cicero attacked ambitious leaders such as Julius Caesar. When Caesar won power, he forgave Cicero for his attack, noting that his critic's contributions were greater than his own:

> 66How much greater and more glorious to have enlarged the limits of the Roman mind than the boundaries of Roman rule.99

Caesar was modest about the impact of his own deeds. Through war and conquest, he and other Roman generals spread the Latin language and carried Roman civilization to distant lands. Yet the civilization that developed was not simply Roman. Rather, it blended Greek, Hellenistic, and Roman achievements.

Greco-Roman Civilization

In its early days, Rome absorbed ideas from Greek colonists in southern Italy, and it continued to borrow heavily from Greek culture after it conquered Greece. To the Romans emerging from their villages, Greek art, literature, philosophy, and scientific genius represented the height of cultural achievement. Their admiration never wavered, leading the Roman poet Horace to note, "Greece has conquered her rude conqueror."

Over time, Romans adapted and transformed Greek and Hellenistic achievements, just as the Greeks had once absorbed and blended ideas and beliefs from Egypt and the Fertile Crescent. The blending of Greek, Hellenistic, and Roman traditions produced what is known as Greco-Roman civilization. Trade and travel during the Pax Romana helped spread this vital new civilization.

Art. In the field of art, the Romans owed a great debt to the Greeks. They imported shiploads of Greek statues to decorate their homes, gardens, and public buildings. Roman sculptors adapted the realism of Hellenistic works, portraying their subjects with every wart and vein in place. They also broke new ground, however, with portraits in stone or on coins that revealed an individual's character. A statue of a soldier, a writer, or an emperor might capture an expression of smugness, discontent, or haughty pride.

Some Roman sculpture was more idealistic, like the classic Greek statues of gods and athletes. Sculptors, for example, transformed Augustus, who was neither handsome nor imposing, into a symbol of power and leadership.

▲ Sculpture of a Roman senator

Architecture. From England to Spain to North Africa to the Middle East, you can see Roman buildings that combine both Greek and Roman elements and ideas. Roman builders used Greek columns, but where the Greeks aimed for simple elegance, the Romans emphasized grandeur. Immense palaces, temples, stadiums, and victory arches stood as mighty monuments to Roman power and dignity.

The Romans improved on devices such as the arch and the dome, which could roof large spaces. The most famous domed structure is the Pantheon, a temple to all the Roman gods, which still stands in Rome. The Romans also introduced new kinds of buildings, such as the Baths of Caracalla, an enormous structure whose vaulted roofs were supported by arches.

Engineering. The Romans excelled in the practical arts of building, perfecting their engineering skills as they built roads, bridges, and harbors throughout the empire. Roman roads

Roman Engineering *Roman engineers built this bridge, road, and aqueduct across the Gardon River in France. The road stretches across the lowest tier of arches. The aqueduct, a concrete channel that carried fresh water to the town of Nimes, sits atop the entire structure.* **Economics and Technology** *What natural force caused aqueduct water to flow from highlands down to Roman towns?*

were so solidly built that many of them remained in use long after Rome fell.

Roman engineers built many immense aqueducts, or bridgelike stone structures that brought water from the hills into Roman cities. In Segovia, Spain, a Roman aqueduct still carries water along a stone channel supported by tiers of arches.

The availability of fresh water was important to the Romans. Wealthy homes had water piped in, and almost every city boasted both female and male public baths. Here, people gathered not only to wash themselves but to hear the latest news and exchange gossip.

Science. The Romans generally left scientific research to the Greeks, who were by that time citizens of the empire. Alexandria, Egypt, remained a center of learning, where Hellenistic scientists exchanged ideas freely. It was in Alexandria that astronomer-mathematician Ptolemy (TAHL uh mee) proposed his theory that the Earth was the center of the universe, an idea that was accepted in the western world for nearly 1,500 years.

The Greek doctor Galen advanced the frontiers of medical science by insisting on experiments to prove a conclusion. He confessed that "the disease from which I have suffered all my life is to trust . . . no statements until, so far as

possible, I have tested them for myself." Galen compiled a medical encyclopedia summarizing what was known at the time. It remained the standard text for more than 1,000 years.

While the Romans rarely did original scientific investigations, they did put science to practical use. They applied geography to make maps, and medical knowledge to help doctors improve public health. Like Galen, they collected knowledge into encyclopedias. Pliny the Elder, a Roman scientist, compiled volumes on geography, zoology, botany, and other topics, all based on other people's works. In A.D. 79, Pliny's eagerness for knowledge led to his death. He ventured too close to Mount Vesuvius, a volcano that was erupting near Pompeii in southern Italy, and was suffocated by volcanic gases. (★ See *Skills for Success*, page 154.)

Literature, Philosophy, and History

In literature, too, educated Romans admired the Greeks. Many spoke Greek and imitated Greek styles in prose and poetry. Still, the greatest Roman writers used Latin to create their own literature.

Poetry. In his epic poem the *Aeneid*, Virgil tried to show that Rome's past was as heroic as that of Greece. (See page 128.) He linked his epic to Homer's work by telling how Aeneas escaped from Troy to found Rome. Virgil wrote the *Aeneid* soon after Augustus came to power. He hoped it would arouse patriotism and help unite Rome after years of civil wars. Another poet, Ovid, also linked Rome to Greece by retelling tales of Greek and Roman gods. (📖 See *World Literature,* "The Metamorphoses," pages 152–153.)

Roman writers like Horace or Juvenal used verse to satirize, or make fun of, Roman society. In the following verse, the poet Martial laughs at chatty barbers:

❝By the time the barber Eurus
    Had circled Lupo's face,
    A second beard had sprouted,
    In the first one's place.❞

Historians. Roman historians pursued their own theme—the rise and fall of Roman power. Like the poet Virgil, the historian Livy sought to rouse patriotic feeling and restore traditional Roman virtues by recalling images of Rome's heroic past. In his history of Rome, Livy recounted tales of great heroes such as Horatius and Cincinnatus.

Another historian, Tacitus, wrote bitterly about Augustus and his successors, who, he felt, had destroyed Roman liberty. He admired the simple culture of the Germans who lived on Rome's northern frontier and would later invade the empire.

Philosophers. Romans borrowed much of their philosophy from the Greeks. The Hellenistic philosophy of Stoicism impressed Roman thinkers like the emperor Marcus Aurelius. Stoics stressed the importance of duty and acceptance of one's fate. They also showed concern for the well-being of all people, an idea that would be reflected in Christian teachings. (See page 145.)

Roman Law

"Let justice be done," proclaimed a Roman saying, "though the heavens fall!" Probably the greatest legacy of Rome was its commitment to the rule of law and to justice—ideas that have shaped western civilization to today.

Two systems. During the republic, Rome developed a system of law, known as the civil law, that applied to its citizens. As Rome expanded, however, it ruled many foreigners who were not covered under the civil law. Gradually, a second system of law, known as the law of nations, emerged. It applied to all people under Roman rule, citizens and noncitizens. Later, when Rome extended citizenship across the empire, the two systems merged.

During the Roman empire, the rule of law fostered unity and stability. Many centuries later, the principles of Roman law would become the basis for legal systems in Europe and Latin America.

Common principles. As Roman law developed, certain basic principles evolved. Many of these principles are familiar to Americans today. Among them are these ideas:

1. People of the same status are equal before the law.
2. An accused person is presumed innocent until proven guilty.
3. The accused should be allowed to face his or her accuser and defend against the charge.
4. Guilt must be established "clearer than daylight" through evidence.
5. Decisions should be based on fairness, allowing judges to interpret the law.

SECTION 3 REVIEW

1. **Identify** (a) Greco-Roman civilization, (b) Pantheon, (c) Pliny, (d) Virgil, (e) Livy, (f) civil law, (g) law of nations.
2. **Define** aqueduct.
3. How did Roman conquests lead to the birth of a new civilization?
4. Give an example to show how Roman art blended different traditions.
5. What practical skills did Romans develop?
6. *Critical Thinking* **Linking Past and Present** Give two examples of how the principles of law developed by Rome affect life in the United States today.
7. *ACTIVITY* Create a design for a Roman coin celebrating an important achievement of Greco-Roman civilization.

The Rise of Christianity

Guide for Reading

- What attitude did Rome take toward the different religions in its empire?
- What was the basic message of Jesus?
- Why did Christianity spread despite persecution?
- **Vocabulary** *messiah, sect, martyr, bishop, pope, heresy*

Early in the Pax Romana, a new religion, Christianity, sprang up in a distant corner of the Roman empire. At first, Christianity was just one of many religions practiced in the empire. But despite many obstacles, the new faith grew rapidly, and by A.D. 392, it had been declared the official religion of the Roman empire.

As it gained strength, Christianity reshaped Roman beliefs. And when the Roman empire fell, the Christian Church took over its role, becoming the central institution of western civilization for nearly 1,000 years.

Jews and the Roman Empire

Generally, Rome tolerated the varied religious traditions of its culturally diverse empire. As long as citizens showed their loyalty by honoring the gods of Rome and acknowledging the divine spirit of the emperor, they were allowed to worship as they pleased. Since most people at the time were polytheistic, they were content to worship the Roman gods along with their own.

Deep divisions arise. Among the peoples in the empire were the Jews. By 63 B.C., the Romans had conquered Palestine, where most Jews of the time lived, and made it into the province of Judea. As with other citizens of the empire, the Romans tolerated the Jews' religion. They even excused the Jews from worshiping Roman gods. They knew that to do so would violate the Jewish faith, which was based on belief in one God.

Among the Jews themselves, however, religious ferment was creating deep divisions. During the Hellenistic age, many Jews absorbed Greek customs and ideas. Concerned about the weakening of their religion, Jewish reformers rejected these influences and called for strict obedience to Jewish laws and traditions.

The turmoil had a political side, too. While Jewish priests struggled to preserve their religion, other Jews, called Zealots, had a different mission. They called on Jews to revolt against Rome and reestablish an independent Israel. Some Jews believed that a messiah, or savior sent by God, would soon appear to lead the Jewish people to freedom.

Revolt and expulsion. In A.D. 66, discontent flared into rebellion. Roman forces crushed the rebels, captured Jerusalem, and destroyed the Jewish temple. When revolts broke out again in the next century, Roman armies leveled Jerusalem. In A.D. 135, they drove the Jews out of their homeland and forbade them to return. As you recall, this scattering of the Jews is known as the diaspora.

Although they were defeated in their efforts to regain political independence, Jews survived in scattered communities around the Mediterranean. Over the centuries, Jewish rabbis, or scholars, extended and preserved the religious law, known as the Talmud. In the late 1800s, some Jews took steps to rebuild an independent Jewish state in Palestine.

The Life of Jesus

As turmoil engulfed the Jews in Palestine, a new religion, Christianity, rose among them. Its founder was a Jew named Jesus.

What little we know about the life of Jesus comes from the Gospels. These accounts were attributed by early Christians to four followers of Jesus. Jesus was born about 4 B.C. in Bethlehem, near Jerusalem. According to the Gospels, an angel had told Jesus' mother, Mary, that she would give birth to the messiah. "He will be great," said the angel, "and will be called the Son of the Most High God."

Growing up, Jesus worshiped God and followed Jewish law. As a young man, he worked as a carpenter. At the age of 30, the Gospels relate, he began preaching to villagers near the Sea of Galilee. Large crowds gathered to hear him, especially when word spread that he performed miracles of healing. After three years, Jesus and his disciples, or loyal followers, went to Jerusalem to spread his message there.

The message. Jesus' teachings were firmly rooted in Jewish tradition. Jesus believed in one God and accepted the Ten Commandments. He preached strict obedience to the laws of Moses and defended the teachings of the Jewish prophets.

At the same time, Jesus preached new beliefs. According to his followers, he called himself the Son of God and declared that he was the messiah whose appearance Jews had long predicted. His mission, he proclaimed, was to bring spiritual salvation and eternal life to anyone who would believe in him. In the Sermon on the Mount, Jesus summed up his ethical message, which echoed Jewish ideas of mercy and sympathy for the poor and helpless:

> **❝**Blessed are the meek, for they shall
> inherit the Earth. . . .
> Blessed are the merciful, for they will
> be shown mercy. . . .
> Blessed are the peacemakers, for
> they will be called the children
> of God.**❞**

Jesus rejected the principle of "an eye for an eye." Instead, he preached forgiveness. "Love your enemies," he told his followers. "If anyone hits you on one cheek, let him hit the other one, too."

Death on the cross. Some Jews welcomed Jesus to Jerusalem. Others, however, regarded him as a dangerous troublemaker. Jewish priests, in particular, felt that he was challenging their leadership. To the Roman authorities, Jesus was a revolutionary who might lead the Jews in a rebellion against Roman rule.

Jesus was betrayed by one of his disciples, the Gospels state. Arrested by the Romans, he was tried and condemned to be crucified. In crucifixion, a Roman method of execution, a person was nailed to a cross and left to die.

Jesus' disciples were thrown into confusion. But then rumors spread through Jerusalem that Jesus was not dead at all. His disciples, the Gospels say, saw and talked with Jesus, who had risen from the dead. He commanded them to spread his teachings. Then he ascended into heaven.

Jesus Healing a Woman *Jesus promised everlasting life to all who accepted his teachings. Belief in the saving power of Jesus helped early Christians overcome oppression and persecution. This Roman mural depicts Jesus miraculously healing an afflicted woman.* **Religions and Value Systems** *Which social classes do you think were most attracted to Christianity? Why?*

The disciples who spread Jesus' message are known as the Apostles, from the Greek word meaning "a person sent forth." Some preached among the Jews of Judea. Others traveled to the communities of the Jewish diaspora, including Rome. Slowly, a few Jews accepted the teaching that Jesus was the messiah, or the Christ, from the Greek for "the anointed one." These people became the first Christians.

Spread of Christianity

At first, Christianity remained a sect, or small group, within Judaism. Then Paul, a Jew from Asia Minor, began the wider spread of the new faith.

Work of Paul. Paul had never seen Jesus. In fact, he had been among those who persecuted Jesus' followers. Then one day, Paul had a vision in which Jesus spoke to him. Immediately converting to the new faith, Paul made an important decision. He would spread Jesus' teachings beyond Jewish communities to gentiles, or non-Jews.

Paul's missionary work set Christianity on the road to becoming a world religion. A tireless traveler, Paul set up churches from Mesopotamia to Rome. In long letters to the Christian communities, he explained and expanded Christian teachings. For example, he emphasized the idea that Jesus had sacrificed his life out of love for humankind.

> **66**We have complete victory through him who loved us! . . . There is nothing in all creation that will ever be able to separate us from the love of God which is ours through Christ Jesus our Lord. **99**

Paul promised that those who believed Jesus was the son of God and followed his teachings would achieve salvation, or eternal life.

Persecution. Rome's tolerant attitude toward religion did not extend to Christianity. Roman officials suspected Christians of disloyalty to Rome because they refused to make sacrifices to the emperor or to honor the Roman gods. When Christians met in secret to avoid persecution, rumors spread that they were engaged in evil practices.

In times of trouble, persecution increased. Roman rulers like Nero used Christians as scapegoats, blaming them for social or economic ills. Over the centuries, thousands of Christians became martyrs, people who suffer or die for their beliefs. Among them was Paul, who was killed during the reign of Nero.

Survival. Despite the attacks, Christianity continued to spread. The reasons were many. Jesus had welcomed all people, especially the humble, poor, and oppressed. They found comfort in his message of love and of a better life beyond the grave.

As they did their work, Christian missionaries like Paul added ideas from Plato, the Stoics, and other Greek thinkers to Jesus' message. Educated Romans, in particular, were attracted to a religion that incorporated the discipline and moderation of Greek philosophy.

Even persecution brought new converts. Observing the willingness of Christians to die for their religion, people were impressed by the strength of their belief. "The blood of the martyr is the seed of the [Christian] Church," noted one Roman.

Role of women. Women often led the way to Christianity. Many welcomed its promise that in the Church "there is neither Jew nor Greek . . . neither slave nor free . . . neither male nor female." In early Christian communities, women served as teachers and administrators. Even when they were later barred from any official role in the Church, they still worked to win converts and supported Christian communities across the Roman world.

The Catacombs Christians buried their dead in underground vaults and passageways called catacombs. During times of persecution, some worshiped secretly in these hidden tombs. **Religions and Value Systems** How did persecution help strengthen Christianity?

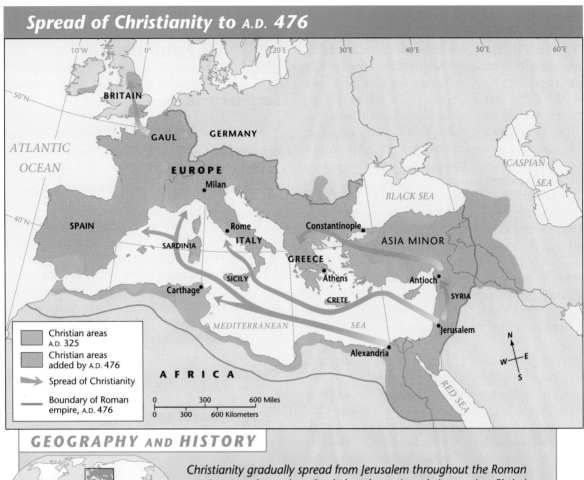

Spread of Christianity to A.D. 476

Christian areas A.D. 325
Christian areas added by A.D. 476
Spread of Christianity
Boundary of Roman empire, A.D. 476

0 300 600 Miles
0 300 600 Kilometers

GEOGRAPHY AND HISTORY

Christianity gradually spread from Jerusalem throughout the Roman empire. Apostles such as Paul played a major role in carrying Christ's message across the region.

1. Location On the map, locate (a) Jerusalem, (b) Constantinople, (c) Alexandria, (d) Spain, (e) Germany.
2. Place Which areas were Christian by A.D. 325?
3. Critical Thinking Synthesizing Information Why do you think the bishop of Rome rather than some other bishop became the pope of the Roman Catholic Church?

The Early Christian Church

Early Christian communities began to organize a formal Church. Each community had its own priest. Priests came under the authority of a bishop, a Church official who was responsible for all Christians in an area called a diocese (DĪ uh sihs).

Later, bishops of important cities gained even greater authority, presiding as archbishops over the other bishops in their area. Bishops traced their spiritual authority to Peter, the chief disciple of Jesus, and through Peter to Jesus himself. The Christian Church thus developed into a hierarchy, or organization in which officials are arranged according to rank. Only men were allowed to become members of the Christian clergy.

Divisions and unity. Rivalry among the bishops of Jerusalem, Antioch, Rome, and Constantinople led to divisions in the Church. In the Latin-speaking west, Christians eventually accepted the bishop of Rome as pope, or head of the Roman Catholic Church. In the Greek-speaking east, Christians acknowledged other leaders, as you will read. (See Chapter 10.)

As the Church grew and evolved, it imposed order and discipline on the scattered

Christian communities. To end disputes over questions of faith, councils of Church leaders met to decide official Christian teachings. They put together the New Testament, the 27 books of the Bible that contain the life and teachings of Jesus. They battled heresies, or beliefs said to be contrary to official Church teachings. The Church also sent out missionaries both within the Roman empire and beyond to convert people to Christianity.

Triumph. The persecution of Christians finally ended in A.D. 313, when the emperor Constantine issued the Edict of Milan. It granted freedom of worship to all citizens of the Roman empire. In making his decision, Constantine was influenced by his mother, who was a devout Christian. Some 80 years later, the emperor Theodosius (thee uh DOH shuhs) made Christianity the official religion of the Roman empire.

As the Christian Church grew in strength and influence, Roman power was fading. When the Roman empire finally collapsed, the Church inherited many of its functions. Along with Christian teachings, the Church preserved, adapted, and spread Greco-Roman civilization. That tradition would be the seedbed for a new western civilization.

SECTION 4 REVIEW

1. **Identify** (a) Jesus, (b) Gospels, (c) Apostle, (d) Paul, (e) New Testament, (f) Edict of Milan.
2. **Define** (a) messiah, (b) sect, (c) martyr, (d) bishop, (e) pope, (f) heresy.
3. (a) How did the Romans treat the Jews of Palestine? (b) Why did divisions arise among the Jews?
4. (a) Describe three basic teachings of Christianity. (b) How were Christian teachings rooted in Jewish traditions?
5. Why did Christianity attract so many diverse converts?
6. *Critical Thinking* **Synthesizing Information** How do you think the unity of the Roman empire, with its extensive system of roads, helped Christianity to spread?
7. *ACTIVITY* Create a diagram showing the hierarchy of the Roman Catholic Church.

The Long Decline

Guide for Reading

- Why did the Pax Romana end?
- How did Diocletian and Constantine try to restore order?
- What led to the fall of the Roman empire?
- **Vocabulary** *mercenary*

More than 1,500 years ago, the western half of the Roman empire stumbled into ruin. Ever since, people have tried to understand why. At the time, the spectacle of decay and defeat left Romans stunned. "For 30 years," lamented one Roman, "war has been waged in the very midst of the Roman empire." Beggars in the street, he noted, had once been "men and women of noble birth." He wondered:

> 66Who would believe . . . that Rome, built upon the conquest of the whole world, would itself fall to the ground?99

The end of greatness was a catastrophe for Romans, but it did not happen overnight. Decay had set in centuries before the final fall.

The Empire in Crisis

After the death of the emperor Marcus Aurelius in 180, the Pax Romana ended. For the next 100 years, political turmoil rocked the Roman empire. One after another, ambitious generals seized power, ruled for a few months or years, and then were overthrown by rival commanders. In one 50-year period, at least 26 emperors reigned. Only one died of natural causes.

At the same time, the empire was shaken by disturbing social and economic trends. High taxes to support the army and the bureaucracy placed heavy burdens on business people and small farmers. Many poor farmers left their land and sought protection from wealthy landowners. Living on large estates, they worked for the landowner and farmed a small plot for themselves. Although technically free, they were not allowed to leave the land.

Efforts at Reform

The political and economic problems underlying the chaos had existed since the late republic. No ruler had been able to solve them, but reforming emperors did try to reverse the decline.

Diocletian. In 284, the emperor Diocletian (DĪ uh KLEE shuhn) set out to restore order. To make the empire easier to govern, he divided it into two parts. He kept control of the wealthier eastern part himself but appointed a co-emperor to rule the western provinces. The co-emperor was responsible to Diocletian, who retained absolute power.

Diocletian tried to increase the prestige of the emperor by surrounding himself with elaborate ceremonies. He wore purple robes embroidered with gold and a crown encrusted with jewels. Anyone who approached the throne had to kneel and kiss the hem of the emperor's robe.

Diocletian also took steps to end the empire's economic decay. To slow the rapid rise of prices, he fixed prices for goods and services. Other laws forced farmers to remain on the land. In cities, sons were required to follow their fathers' occupation. These rules were meant to ensure steady production of food and other goods.

Constantine. In 312, the talented general Constantine gained the throne. As emperor, Constantine continued Diocletian's reforms. More important, he took two steps that changed the course of European history.

First, as you have read, Constantine granted toleration to Christians. By doing so, he encouraged the rapid growth of Christianity within the empire and guaranteed its future success.

Second, he built a new capital, Constantinople, on the Bosporus, the strait that connects the Black and Mediterranean seas. By making his capital there, Constantine made the eastern portion of the empire the center of power. The western Roman empire was in decline, but the eastern Roman empire, which had more people and greater resources, would prosper for centuries to come.

Mixed results. The reforms of Diocletian and Constantine had mixed results. They revived the economy. And by increasing the power of government, they helped hold the empire together for another century. Still, the reforms failed to stop the long-term decline. In the end, internal problems combined with attacks from outside to bring the empire down.

Foreign Invasions

For centuries, Rome had faced attacks from the Germanic peoples who lived along its northern borders. When Rome was powerful, it held back the invaders. As the empire declined, however, it was forced to give up its territories. Under pressure from attacks, it surrendered first Britain, then France and Spain. It was only a matter of time before foreign invaders marched into Italy and took over Rome itself.

A global chain reaction. As early as A.D. 200, wars in East Asia set off a chain of events that would eventually overwhelm Rome, thousands of miles to the west. Those wars sent the Huns, a nomadic people, migrating across Central Asia. By 350, the Huns reached eastern Europe. These skilled riders fought fierce battles to dislodge the Germanic peoples in their path. People like the Visigoths sought safety by crossing into Roman territory. Men armed with spears moved in bands along with women and

Art of the Visigoths *The Germanic peoples who invaded Rome left behind no stone monuments or wall paintings. Instead, they showed their artistic skills in small, portable items, such as the clasps that fastened their clothing. Visigoth artisans crafted these eagle clasps out of gold, bronze, and gemstones.* **Art and Literature** *How are these clasps similar to Greek and Roman mosaics?*

Invasions of the Roman Empire to A.D. 500

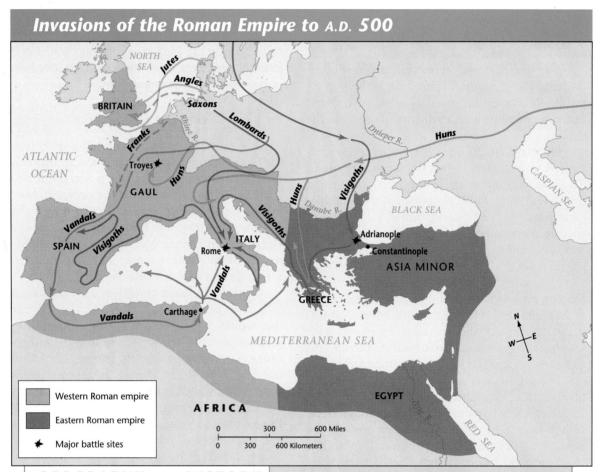

Western Roman empire

Eastern Roman empire

★ Major battle sites

GEOGRAPHY AND HISTORY

Diocletian divided the Roman empire into the western Roman empire and eastern Roman empire. Under Diocletian and Constantine, the eastern empire prospered, but invasions and internal problems led to the gradual decline of the west.

1. **Location** On the map, locate (a) western Roman empire, (b) eastern Roman empire, (c) Rhine River, (d) Danube River, (e) Constantinople.
2. **Movement** (a) Which Germanic tribes entered Italy? (b) Where did the Visigoths originate? (c) Describe the route of the Vandals. (d) To which land did the Angles and Saxons migrate?
3. **Critical Thinking** **Drawing Conclusions** Foreign invasions hurt the western Roman empire more than they did the eastern Roman empire. How does the map help you draw that conclusion?

children, carts and herds, hoping to settle on Roman land.

Retreat. In 378, when a Roman army tried to turn back the Visigoths at Adrianople, it suffered a stunning defeat. Roman power was fading. New waves of invaders were soon hammering at Rome's borders, especially in the west. In 410, the Visigoth general Alaric overran Italy and plundered Rome. Gradually, other Germanic peoples occupied large parts of the western Roman empire.

The "scourge of God." For Rome, the worst was yet to come. Starting in 434, the Hun leader Attila embarked on a savage campaign of conquest across much of Europe. Christians called Attila the "scourge of God" because they believed his attacks were a punishment for the sins of humankind.

Attila died in 453. Although his empire collapsed soon after, the Hun invasion sent still more Germanic peoples fleeing into the Roman empire.

Finally, in 476, Odoacer (oh doh AY suhr), a Germanic leader, ousted the emperor in Rome. Later, historians referred to that event as the "fall" of Rome. By then, however, Rome had already lost many of its territories and Roman power in the west had ended.

The End of Greatness

Why did Rome "fall"? Modern historians identify a number of interrelated causes.

Military causes. Perhaps the most obvious cause of Rome's fall was the Germanic invasions. Still, these attacks were successful in part because Roman legions of the late empire lacked the discipline and training of past Roman armies. To meet its need for soldiers, Rome hired mercenaries, or foreign soldiers serving for pay, to defend its borders. Many were German warriors who according to some historians, felt little loyalty to Rome.

Political and economic causes. Political problems also contributed to Rome's decline. First, as the government became more oppressive and authoritarian, it lost the support of the people. Growing numbers of corrupt officials undermined loyalty, too. Perhaps most important, dividing the empire at a time when it was under attack may have weakened it beyond repair.

Economically, the empire suffered as heavier and heavier taxes were required to support the vast government bureaucracy and huge military establishment. The wealth of the empire itself dwindled as farmers abandoned their land and the middle classes sank into poverty. At the same time, reliance on slave labor discouraged Romans from exploring new technology. Finally, the population itself declined as war and epidemic diseases swept the empire.

Social causes. For centuries, worried Romans pointed to the decline in values such as patriotism, discipline, and devotion to duty on which the empire was built. The upper class, which had once provided leaders, devoted itself to luxury and self-interest. And besides being costly, providing "bread and circuses" may have undermined the self-reliance of the masses.

Did Rome fall? Although we talk of the "fall" of Rome, the Roman empire did not disappear from the map in 476. An emperor still ruled the eastern Roman empire, which later became known as the Byzantine empire and lasted for another 1,000 years. (See Chapter 10.)

The dramatic phrase "the fall of Rome" is, in fact, shorthand for a long, slow process of change from one way of life to another. Roman civilization survived the events of 476. In Italy, people continued to live much as they had before, though under new rulers. Many still spoke Latin and obeyed Roman laws.

Over the next few centuries, however, German customs, ideas, and languages replaced Roman culture. Old Roman cities crumbled, and Roman roads disappeared under mud and weeds. Still, the Christian Church preserved elements of Roman civilization. In Chapters 8 and 9, you will read how Roman and Christian traditions gave rise to a new medieval civilization in western Europe.

SECTION 5 REVIEW

1. **Identify** (a) Diocletian, (b) Constantine, (c) Huns, (d) Visigoths, (e) Alaric, (f) Attila, (g) Odoacer.
2. **Define** mercenary.
3. Describe conditions in the Roman empire after the Pax Romana ended.
4. (a) List two political and two economic reforms of Diocletian. (b) What effect did Constantine's policies have on the Roman empire?
5. Why did the Roman government lose the support of the people?
6. *Critical Thinking* **Linking Past and Present** Imagine that the United States government in Washington no longer existed. What would be the effects on (a) your life, (b) your state, (c) the United States?
7. *ACTIVITY* Create an illustrated booklet for a fifth-grade class explaining why the Roman empire fell. You may use charts as well as pictures to illustrate your booklet.

ISSUES *For* **TODAY**

Historians have identified numerous causes for the fall of Rome. What factors can contribute to the decline of a great power?

World Literature
The Metamorphoses
Ovid

Introduction *Publius Ovidius Naso, known as Ovid, was born near Rome in 43 B.C. He was educated by the best tutors and trained in the law. Much to his father's annoyance, however, he chose to devote his talents to poetry. For much of his career, he enjoyed the sponsorship of the emperor Augustus. Later, though, Ovid lost favor with the emperor and spent the last years of his life in exile.*

The Metamorphoses is one of Ovid's greatest works. In it, he weaves together both Greek and Roman myths about gods and humans. The stories are all connected by a shared theme of metamorphoses, or changes. For example, in one story, a young woman named Arachne boasts that her skills as a weaver are greater than those of the goddess Pallas. After Arachne defeats Pallas in a weaving contest, the angry goddess changes Arachne into a spider. (Arachnid, the scientific term for spiders, comes from the name Arachne.)

The following excerpt from The Metamorphoses *tells the story of Midas, a legendary king known for his foolishness. Midas is a crony of the fun-loving god Bacchus (the Roman name for the Greek god Dionysus). Here, Bacchus agrees to grant the king a wish.*

The Story of King Midas

Then Bacchus, glad to see the old man
  home,
And like a good adopted son, thanked
  Midas,
Gave him the choice of making a wish come
  true:
What would he have? Midas was always sure
To make the worst of every good occasion—
Of turning glory into desperate ill—
So Midas said, "Make everything I touch
  turn gold."

Bacchus gave him the golden touch, yet
  thought
"What foolishness; it almost makes me sad."
  Meanwhile
The Hero Midas danced on his way, and
  touched all things
That flashed before his eyes. Could he be-
  lieve this?
Yes! He plucked a green shoot from a tree—
It was all gold, pure gold, had the right
  weight and color;
Then a handful of wet clay—he had but to
  touch it
And it was gold. His trembling fingers
  plucked
A head of wheat—it might have been the
  promise
Of golden harvest—and next he took an
  apple from a tree,
And in his hand it shone as though it were a
  gift
Transported to him from the Hesperides.[1]
He touched a standing beam that held the
  roof;
Look sharply now! It was a pillar of gold.
And as he dipped his hand in running water,
A stream of gold rushed out. . . .
Midas' imagination, his hopes, his dreams
  grew big with gold:
He called his slaves to bring a feast before
  him,
From wine to meat to bread to fruits to
  wine.
And as he broke bread, that rich gift of
  Ceres,[2]

---

[1] In Greek mythology, the Hesperides were a garden where golden apples were grown.

[2] Ceres was an ancient Italian goddess of agriculture. The Romans later merged Ceres with Demeter, the Greek goddess of fertile land.

It did not break but was of gold itself,
Beautifully hard, not stale, and as his teeth
Ate into meat, the meat was gold, too
And he could not close his jaws. As he
    poured
Water into wine (Bacchus' own wine) red,
    sunset color,
And raised them to his lips, both turned to
    gold.
Dazed, damned by gold, a golden terror
    took him,
Midas began to hate his wealth, tried to
    escape
The very riches that he prayed for. However
    large
The feast laid out before him, he went
    hungry,
And though his throat burned dry, no drink
    could wet it.
By his own choice gold had become his
    torture.
He lifted glittering hands and arms to
    heaven:
"O Bacchus, Father of your unlucky son!
I have done wrong, wrong from the start,
    wrong, wrong forever,
But take away your gift that shines in gold.
It's damned—it curses me." Because he
    seemed to learn
His way was error, the gods took pity on him.
Bacchus reversed him to what he was before;
He said, "Through your own foolishness you
    wear
A golden coffin, your very body is a tomb of
    gold;
Go to the river . . .

To wash your guilt away." The king obeyed;
And gold fell from him to the waters that ran
    gold.
Even now the golden touch has stained the
    river,
And the soil it waters is as hard as gold.
Midas, no longer lured by dreams of riches,
Took to the woods, became a nature lover.

Source: Ovid, *The Metamorphoses, A Complete New Version by Horace Gregory* (New York: The Viking Press, Inc., 1958).

Thinking About Literature

1. (a) What request did King Midas make of the god Bacchus? (b) Why did Midas come to regret his wish?
2. (a) How does *The Metamorphoses* show a blending of Greek and Roman culture? Give two examples. (b) Why were the Romans proud of their cultural ties to Greece?
3. *Critical Thinking* **Making Inferences** (a) What human qualities does the god Bacchus display in "The Story of King Midas"? (b) What does the story suggest about the Roman view of the relationship between gods and people?

CHAPTER REVIEW

REVIEWING VOCABULARY

Review the vocabulary words in this chapter. Then, use *ten* of these words to create a crossword puzzle. Exchange puzzles with a classmate. Complete the puzzles and then check each other's answers.

REVIEWING FACTS

1. What event and date traditionally mark the founding of the Roman state?

2. What were the results of the wars between Rome and Carthage?

3. How did Julius Caesar become leader of Rome?

4. How did Augustus' rise to power mark a change in Rome's form of government?

5. What were the important principles of Roman law?

6. When and where did Jesus live?

7. How did Christianity spread beyond Palestine?

8. What were the major acts of Emperor Constantine?

9. List three reasons for the fall of the Roman empire.

SKILLS FOR SUCCESS   ANALYZING A PRIMARY SOURCE

Primary sources include official documents, as well as firsthand accounts of events by people who witnessed or participated in them.

The excerpt below is from a letter written by the Roman author Pliny the Younger. Pliny witnessed the eruption of Mount Vesuvius in A.D. 79. Read the excerpt and follow the steps below to analyze it.

1. **Identify the document.** What are the author, subject, and date of the document?

2. **Interpret the contents of the document.** How did the eruption threaten Pliny and the other people?

3. **Combine primary and secondary sources to draw conclusions about an event.** According to the *World Almanac,* the eruption of Mount Vesuvius killed about 10 percent of the people in three nearby cities. How do the *World Almanac* and Pliny's letter compare as sources of historical information?

> *From a Letter to Tacitus*
> *by Pliny the Younger*
>
> 66Ashes were already falling, not as yet very thickly. I looked round: a dense black cloud was coming up behind us, spreading over the Earth like a flood. 'Let us leave the road while we can still see,' I said. . . .
>
> We had scarcely sat down to rest when darkness fell, not the dark of a moonless or cloudy night, but as if the lamp had been put out in a closed room. You could hear the shrieks of women, the wailing of infants, and the shouting of men. . . . A gleam of light returned, but we took this to be a warning of the approaching flames rather than daylight. However, the flames remained some distance off; then darkness came on once more and ashes began to fall again, this time in heavy showers. We rose from time to time and shook them off, otherwise we should have been buried and crushed beneath their weight. . . .
>
> At last the darkness thinned and dispersed like smoke or cloud; then there was genuine daylight, and the sun actually shone out, but yellowish as it is during an eclipse.99

REVIEWING CHAPTER THEMES

Review the "Focus On" questions at the start of this chapter. Then select *three* of those questions and answer them, using information from the chapter.

CRITICAL THINKING

1. **Comparing** (a) What geographic differences between Italy and Greece made it easier to unite Italy than Greece? (b) How did those differences make it easier to unite Italy than it was to unite Greece? (c) How did both Greece and Rome benefit from their location on the Mediterranean Sea?

2. **Analyzing Information** Did the Roman republic have a democratic government? Why or why not?

3. **Synthesizing Information** The Roman poet Horace said of Roman civilization, "Greece has conquered its rude conqueror." (a) What did he mean by this? (b) Give three examples that support his statement.

ANALYZING PRIMARY SOURCES

Use the quotation about the Pax Romana on page 138 to answer the following questions.

1. According to the writer, how did the Pax Romana affect commerce?

2. How did farming change under the Pax Romana?

3. How would you expect the end of the Pax Romana to affect daily life?

FOR YOUR PORTFOLIO

MAKING A PRESENTATION Prepare a presentation on the following topic: "The Spirit of Rome Is Alive in the United States." Begin by selecting a subject area, such as government, religion, or architecture. Then use a dictionary to make a list of Latin-based words that are still in use in that subject area. Present these terms in the form of a speech, poster, dictionary, or article.

Some Famous Roman Emperors

Leader/ Years in Office	Major Policies
Augustus 31 B.C.–A.D. 14	Ended civil war; reformed government; established empire
Nero A.D. 54–68	Persecuted Christians after fire destroyed much of Rome
Vespasian 69–79	Authorized building projects in Rome; reorganized government finance
Hadrian 117–138	Built Hadrian's Wall in Britain; codified Roman law
Marcus Aurelius 161–180	Helped unify empire economically; made legal reforms
Constantine 306–337	Ended persecution of Christians; called Nicaea council to settle Church disputes; built new capital of Constantinople

ANALYZING TABLES

Use the table to answer the following questions.

1. Which emperor's reign was the longest? The shortest?

2. How did the religious policies of Nero and Constantine differ?

3. What policy listed above symbolized the growing importance of the eastern part of the Roman empire?

INTERNET ACTIVITY

CREATING A MAP Use the Internet to research the territorial expansion of the Roman empire. Then create a map of the empire at its height. Draw present-day national boundaries on the map to show which nations were once part of the Roman empire.

Civilizations of the Americas

(1400 B.C.–A.D. 1570)

CHAPTER OUTLINE

1 Civilizations of Middle America
2 The World of the Incas
3 Peoples of North America

In a cave outside Mexico City, an archaeologist made an intriguing discovery. He found the remains of plants that had sprouted more than 5,000 years before. Though the plants were less than an inch long, the archaeologist recognized them for what they were—tiny ears of corn. At other levels, the archaeologist discovered slightly larger ears of corn, then still larger ones. Apparently, early farmers in Mexico gradually cultivated a small grass pod into the full-sized corn plant we know today. In the process, corn became the lifeline of civilization in the Americas.

Many Native American religious beliefs reflect the importance of corn, or maize. The Mayan people of Mexico worshiped a handsome maize god, whose profile and flattened forehead resembled an ear of corn. According to Mayan sacred writings, the gods created the first man and woman from corn. "Of yellow corn and white corn they made their flesh; of cornmeal dough they made the arms and legs of people." A Navajo creation story relates that corn was the first plant to appear on Earth:

> 66First Man called the people together.
> He brought forth the white corn
> which had been formed with him.
> First Woman brought the yellow
> corn. They laid the perfect ears side
> by side. . . . [The Turkey] danced
> back and forth four times, then
> shook his feather coat and there
> dropped from his clothing four ker-
> nels of corn, one gray, one blue, one
> black, and one red.99

By 1500 B.C., the technology of growing corn had spread throughout the Americas. With potatoes and manioc in South America, corn supported the large populations that built the first American civilizations. In time, the crops developed in the Americas would feed much of the world.

Three complex civilizations—the Mayas, Aztecs, and Incas—flourished in Middle and South America. Although each had many of the basic features of civilization you read about in Chapter 1, they differed from one another in important ways. Across North America, smaller and less-complex cultures developed their own diverse ways of life.

FOCUS ON these questions as you read:

- **Diversity**
  How did people in different parts of the Americas create distinct civilizations?

- **Continuity and Change**
  How did the Mayas, Aztecs, and Incas build on the achievements of earlier peoples?

- **Political and Social Systems**
  What methods did Aztec and Incan rulers use to organize their large empires?

- **Religions and Value Systems**
  How did religion play a central role in early American societies?

TIME AND PLACE

Sacred Bird of Ancient Mexico *In this colorful mural, a flowery vine pours forth from the mouth of a sacred bird. Murals like this one covered the buildings of Teotihuacán, a city that dominated central Mexico more than 1,000 years ago. In both Central and South America, complex civilizations produced detailed, highly symbolic works of religious art.* **Art and Literature** *How does this mural celebrate nature and fertility? Explain.*

HUMANITIES LINK

Art History Peruvian textile (page 165).

Literature In this chapter, you will encounter passages from the following works of literature: Navajo story of creation (page 156); Nezahualcoyotl, "All the Earth is a grave and nothing escapes it" (page 164); Garcilasco de la Vega, *The Royal Commentary of the Incas* (page 168); *Travel Song* (pages 171 and 173); the Iroquois constitution (page 173).

| 1400 B.C. Olmecs develop first American civilization | A.D. 300 Mayan city-states flourish for next 600 years | A.D. 900s Anasazis build pueblo towns | A.D. 1200 Mississippian center of Cahokia thrives | A.D. 1400s Aztec empire grows | A.D. 1438 Pachacuti founds Incan empire |

| B.C. | 1400 | B.C. | A.D. | 400 | 800 | 1200 | 1600 | A.D. |

1 Civilizations of Middle America

Guide for Reading

- How did the first people reach the Americas?

- What were the main achievements of Mayan civilization?

- How did the Aztecs build a powerful empire?

- **Vocabulary** *tribute*

The Aztecs of Middle America evolved a complex system of religious beliefs. Their religions, like those of many other people, included a belief that the world would someday come to a fiery end.

According to the Aztec Legend of the Five Suns, the universe had been created and destroyed four times in the past. People living under the First Sun had been destroyed by jaguars. People living under the Second Sun were swept away by wind. People living under the Third Sun perished in the fire and ash of volcanoes, while those living under the Fourth Sun had been swallowed by water. The Fifth Sun represented the time of the Aztec empire:

> 66This is our Sun, the one in which we now live. And here is its sign, how the Sun fell into the fire, into the divine hearth. . . . And as the elders continue to say, under the Sun there will be earthquakes and hunger, and then our end shall come.99

The Legend of the Five Suns reflects the important role of the sun in Aztec religion. It also suggests a feeling of helplessness in the face of the harsh forces of nature. Despite this sense of impending doom, the Aztecs were able to create a remarkable civilization. In order to do so, they built on the achievements of earlier peoples. To understand more about these early American civilizations, we must go far back in time to the arrival of the first people in the Americas.

Geography: The Americas

Perhaps as early as 30,000 years ago,* small family groups of Paleolithic hunters and food gatherers reached North America from Asia. This great migration took place during the last ice age. At that time, so much water froze into thick ice sheets that the sea level dropped, exposing a land bridge between Siberia and Alaska. Hunters followed herds of bison and mammoths across this land bridge. Other migrating people may have paddled small boats and fished along the coasts.

Global warming. About 10,000 B.C., the Earth's climate grew warmer. As the ice melted, water levels rose, covering the land bridge under the Bering Strait. The global warming, along with the hunting skills of the first Americans, may have killed off large game animals like the mammoth. People adapted by hunting smaller animals, fishing, and gathering fruit, roots, and shellfish. These nomadic hunter-gatherers slowly migrated eastward and southward across the Americas.

Regions. What lands did the first Americans explore and settle? The Americas are made up of the continents of North America and South America. Within these two geographic regions is a cultural region that historians call Middle America. Middle America, which includes Mexico and Central America, was home to several early civilizations.

Great mountain chains form a spiny backbone down the western Americas. In North America, the Rocky Mountains split into the East and West Sierra Madre of Mexico. The towering Andes run down the length of South America. The continents are drained by two of the world's three longest rivers, the Amazon of South America and the Mississippi of North America.

The first Americans adapted to a variety of climates and resources. Far to the north and south, people learned to survive in icy, treeless lands. Closer to the Equator, people settled in the hot, wet climate and thick vegetation of the Amazon rain forests. Elsewhere, hunters adapted to conditions in deserts like the Atacama of Chile,

---

*Scholars disagree about exactly when the first people reached the Americas. They have proposed dates ranging from 70,000 to 10,000 years ago.

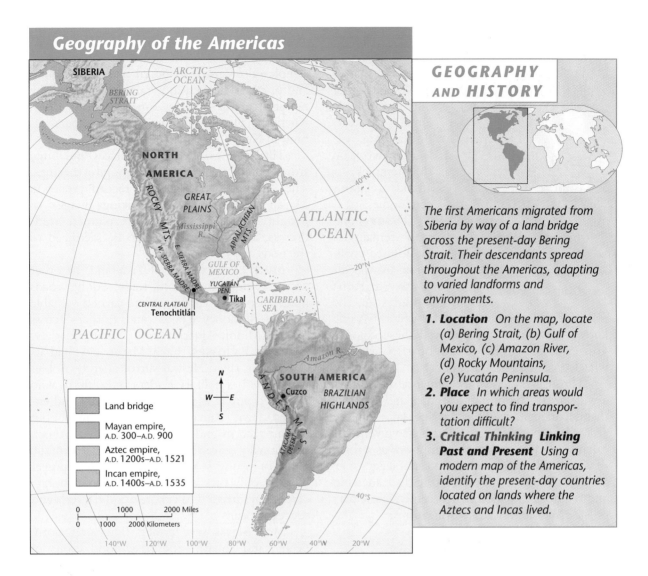

Geography of the Americas

SIBERIA
ARCTIC OCEAN
BERING STRAIT
NORTH AMERICA
ROCKY MTS.
GREAT PLAINS
Mississippi R.
APPALACHIAN MTS.
W. SIERRA MADRE
E. SIERRA MADRE
GULF OF MEXICO
YUCATÁN PEN.
CENTRAL PLATEAU
Tenochtitlán
• Tikal
CARIBBEAN SEA
ATLANTIC OCEAN
PACIFIC OCEAN
40°N
20°N
Amazon R.
0°
ANDES MTS.
SOUTH AMERICA
• Cuzco
BRAZILIAN HIGHLANDS
ATACAMA DESERT
40°S

N
W E
S

Land bridge

Mayan empire,
A.D. 300–A.D. 900

Aztec empire,
A.D. 1200s–A.D. 1521

Incan empire,
A.D. 1400s–A.D. 1535

0   1000   2000 Miles
0   1000   2000 Kilometers

140°W 120°W 100°W 80°W 60°W 40°W 20°W

GEOGRAPHY AND HISTORY

The first Americans migrated from Siberia by way of a land bridge across the present-day Bering Strait. Their descendants spread throughout the Americas, adapting to varied landforms and environments.

1. **Location** On the map, locate (a) Bering Strait, (b) Gulf of Mexico, (c) Amazon River, (d) Rocky Mountains, (e) Yucatán Peninsula.
2. **Place** In which areas would you expect to find transportation difficult?
3. **Critical Thinking** **Linking Past and Present** Using a modern map of the Americas, identify the present-day countries located on lands where the Aztecs and Incas lived.

in woodlands like those in eastern North America, and on the fertile plains of both continents.

The agricultural revolution. In the Americas, as elsewhere, the greatest adaptation occurred when some people learned to cultivate plants and domesticate animals. Archaeologists think that farming was partly a response to the disappearance of the large mammals. With fewer animals to hunt, people came to depend more on other food sources. In Mexico, or perhaps farther south, Neolithic people began cultivating a range of crops from corn and beans to sweet potatoes, peppers, tomatoes, and squash. These changes took place slowly between about 8500 B.C. and 2000 B.C.

Early American farmers learned to domesticate animals. In South America, domesticated animals include the llama and other creatures valued for their wool. However, the Americas had no large animals such as oxen or horses that

were capable of bearing heavy loads or pulling wagons. This lack of draft animals would limit development in some areas.

In the Americas, as in Africa and Eurasia, the agricultural revolution helped to cause other changes. Farming people settled into villages. Populations expanded. Some villages grew into large religious centers and then into the great cities of the first American civilizations.

Legacy of the Olmecs

The first American civilization, the Olmecs, emerged in the tropical forests along the Mexican Gulf Coast and lasted from about 1400 B.C. to 500 B.C. Archaeologists know very little about the Olmecs, but rich tombs and temples suggest a powerful class of priests and aristocrats. The Olmecs did not build true cities, but rather they built ceremonial centers made up

▲ Giant Olmec head

of pyramid-shaped temples and other buildings. People came from near-by farming villages to work on the temples or attend religious ceremonies.

The most dramatic remains of the Olmec civilization are the giant carved stone heads found in the ruins of a religious center at La Venta. No one knows how the Olmecs moved these colossal 40-ton stones from distant quarries without wheeled vehicles or draft animals.

Through trade, Olmec influence spread over a wide area. The grinning jaguars and serpents that decorate many Olmec carvings appear in the arts of later peoples. The Olmecs also invented a calendar and used carved inscriptions as a form of writing. But their most important legacy may have been the tradition of priestly leadership and religious devotion that became a basic part of later Middle American civilizations.

The World of the Mayas

Among the peoples influenced by the Olmecs were the Mayas. Between A.D. 300 and 900, Mayan city-states flourished from the Yucatán in southern Mexico through much of Central America.

Scientists have recently determined how Mayan farming methods allowed them to thrive in the tropical environment. Mayan farmers cleared the dense rain forests and then built raised fields that caught and held rainwater. They also built channels that could be opened to drain off excess water. This complex system produced enough maize and other crops to support rapidly growing cities.

Temples and palaces. Towering pyramid temples dominated the largest Mayan city of Tikal (tee KAHL), in present-day Guatemala. Priests climbed steep temple stairs to perform sacrifices on high platforms, while ordinary people watched from the plazas far below. Some

temples also served as burial places for nobles and priests. The Mayan pyramids remained the tallest structures in the Americas until 1903, when the Flatiron Building, a skyscraper, was built in New York City.

Tikal also boasted large palaces and huge stone pillars covered with elaborate carvings. The carvings, which usually record events in Mayan history, preserve striking images of haughty aristocrats, warriors in plumed head-dresses, and captives about to be sacrificed to the gods.

Much of the wealth of Tikal and the other Mayan cities came from trade. Along roads made of packed earth, traders carried valuable cargoes of honey, cocoa, and feathers across most of Middle America.

Social classes. Each Mayan city had its own ruling chief. He was surrounded by nobles who served as military leaders and officials who managed public works, collected taxes, and enforced laws. Rulers were usually men, but Mayan records and carvings show that women occasionally governed on their own or in the name of young sons. Priests held great power because only they could conduct the elaborate ceremonies needed to ensure good harvests and success in war.

Most Mayas were farmers. They grew corn, beans, and squash—the basic food crops of Middle America—as well as fruit trees, cotton, and brilliant tropical flowers. Men usually cultivated the crops, while women turned them into food. To support the cities, farmers paid taxes in food and helped build the temples.

Advances in learning. Along with their magnificent buildings and carvings, the Mayas made impressive advances in learning. They de-

GLOBAL CONNECTIONS

Maize originated in the Americas and only later arrived in Asia, Europe, and Africa. But how much later? Temples in southern India show stone figures offering maize to the gods. These figures were carved in the A.D. 1000s—more than 400 years before the Spanish arrived in Central America. Some historians take these carvings as evidence that there was earlier contact between the Mayas and people of Asia. But how the maize got to India is still a mystery.

PARALLELS THROUGH TIME

Play Ball!

Kick it. Throw it. Hit it. Roll it. Sink it. Catch it. Dodge it. Through the centuries, sports-minded people all over the world have developed an amazing array of games using a most simple invention—the ball.

Linking Past and Present Which of today's ball games share similarities with the Mayan ball game? Describe the similarities.

PAST *Along with temples and pyramids, ball courts were a key feature of Mayan cities. Spectators watched intently as two teams tried to drive a solid rubber ball through a stone ring that hung from a wall. Opposing players moved the ball across the court by using their bodies, but not their hands or feet. In spite of protective helmets and padding, collisions with other players and the impact of the hard ball resulted in many injuries.*

PRESENT *Ball games today are played on fields, courts, tables, and even in alleys by players using rackets, bats, hammers, cues, clubs, and more. Wherever and however these ball games are played, they thrill both players and spectators alike.*

veloped a hieroglyphic writing system, which has only recently been deciphered. Mayan scribes kept their sacred knowledge in books made of bark. Though Spanish conquerors later burned most of these books, a handful were taken to Europe and survive in European museums.

Mayan priests needed to measure time accurately in order to hold ceremonies at the correct moment. As a result, many priests became expert mathematicians and astronomers. They developed an accurate 365-day solar calendar, as well as a 260-day calendar based on the orbit of the planet Venus. Mayan priests also invented a numbering system and understood the concept of zero long before Europeans acquired this idea from India through the Arabs.

Decline. About A.D. 900, the Mayas abandoned their cities, leaving their great stone

A Look at Mayan Life *Mayan potters fashioned clay figurines depicting people at all levels of society. Here, an aristocrat poses in his robes of state, while a peasant woman holds corn tortillas.* **Political and Social Systems** *What impression of Mayan social classes do you get from these two figures?*

palaces and temples to be swallowed up by the jungle. Not until modern times were these "lost cities" rediscovered.

No one knows for sure why Mayan civilization declined. Possibly, frequent warfare forced the Mayas to abandon their traditional agricultural methods. Or overpopulation may have led to overfarming, which in turn exhausted the soil. Heavy taxes to finance wars and temple building may have sparked peasant revolts. Still, remnants of Mayan culture have survived. Today, millions of people in Guatemala and southern Mexico speak Mayan languages and are descended from the builders of this early American civilization.

The Valley of Mexico

Long before Mayan cities rose to the south, the city of Teotihuacán (tay oh tee wah KAHN) had emerged in the Valley of Mexico. The Valley of Mexico is a huge oval basin ringed by snow-capped volcanoes, located in the high plateau of central Mexico. Teotihuacán dominated a large area from A.D. 100 to 750.

Teotihuacán. The city of Teotihuacán was well planned, with wide roads, massive temples, and large apartment buildings. Along the main avenue, the Pyramid of the Sun and the Pyramid of the Moon rose majestically toward the sky. Citizens of Teotihuacán worshiped a powerful nature goddess and rain god, whose images often appear on public buildings and on everyday objects. Teotihuacán eventually fell to invaders, but its culture influenced later peoples, especially the Aztecs.

Arrival of the Aztecs. In the late 1200s, bands of nomadic people, the ancestors of the Aztecs, migrated into the Valley of Mexico from the north. According to Aztec legend, the gods had told them to search for an eagle perched atop a cactus holding a snake in its beak. They finally saw the sign on a swampy island in Lake Texcoco. Once settled, the Aztecs shifted from hunting to farming. Slowly, they built the city of Tenochtitlán (tay nawch tee TLAHN), on the site of present-day Mexico City.

As their population grew, the Aztecs found ingenious ways to create more farmland. They built *chinampas,* artificial islands made of earth piled on reed mats that were anchored to the shallow lake bed. On these "floating gardens," they raised corn, squash, and beans. They gradually filled in parts of the lake and created canals for transportation. Wide stone causeways linked Tenochtitlán to the mainland.

Conquering an empire. In the 1400s, the Aztecs greatly expanded their territory. Through a combination of fierce conquests and shrewd alliances, they spread their rule over most of Mexico, from the Gulf of Mexico to the Pacific Ocean. By 1500, the Aztec empire numbered about 30 million people.

War brought immense wealth as well as power. Tribute, or payment from conquered peoples, helped the Aztecs turn their capital into a magnificent city.

The World of the Aztecs

When the Spanish reached Tenochtitlán in 1519, they were awestruck at its magnificence. Hernan Cortés described the city as it looked then:

> 66The city has many squares where markets are held and trading is carried on. There is one square . . . where there are daily more than 60,000 souls, buying and selling, and where are found all the kinds of mer-

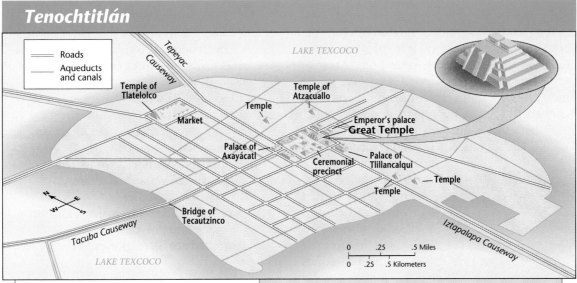

Tenochtitlán

Roads

Aqueducts and canals

Tepeyac Causeway

LAKE TEXCOCO

Temple of Tlatelolco

Market

Temple

Temple of Atzacuallo

Emperor's palace
Great Temple

Palace of Axayácatl

Ceremonial precinct

Palace of Tlillancalqui

Temple

Temple

Bridge of Tecautzinco

Tacuba Causeway

LAKE TEXCOCO

Iztapalapa Causeway

0   .25   .5 Miles
0   .25   .5 Kilometers

GEOGRAPHY AND HISTORY

The Aztec capital, Tenochtitlán, was located in Lake Texcoco and connected to the mainland by causeways. In the center of the city, people gathered at the Great Temple, the emperor's palace, the market, or other public centers.

1. Location On the map, locate (a) Great Temple, (b) market, (c) emperor's palace, (d) Lake Texcoco.

2. Interaction Give two examples of ways the Aztecs adapted their environment to meet their needs.

3. Critical Thinking **Analyzing Information** How can you tell from the map that religion played an important role in Aztec life?

chandise produced in these countries, including food products, jewels of gold and silver, lead, brass, copper, zinc, bones, shells, and feathers.**99**

From its temples and palaces to its zoos and floating gardens, Tenochtitlán was a city of wonders. It was also the center of a well-ordered empire.

Government and society. Unlike the Mayan city-states, each of which had its own king, the Aztecs had a single ruler. The emperor was chosen by a council of nobles and priests to lead in war. Below him, nobles served as officials, judges, and governors of conquered provinces. They enjoyed special privileges such as wearing luxurious feathered cloaks and gold jewelry. Next came the warriors, who could rise to noble status by killing or capturing enemy soldiers. The majority of people were commoners who farmed the land.

At the bottom of society were the slaves, mostly criminals or prisoners of war. Despite their low status, slaves' rights were clearly spelled out by law. For example, slaves could own land and buy their freedom.

Protected by Aztec power, a class of long-distance traders ferried goods across the empire and beyond. From the highlands, they took goods such as weapons, tools, and rope to barter for tropical products such as jaguar skins and cocoa beans. They also served as spies, finding out new areas for trade and conquest.

Religious beliefs. The priests were a class apart. They performed the rituals needed to please the many Aztec gods and prevent droughts, floods, or other disasters. The chief Aztec god was Huitzilopochtli (wee tsee loh POHKT lee), the sun god. His giant pyramid-temple towered above central Tenochtitlán.

Huitzilopochtli, the Aztecs believed, battled the forces of darkness each night and was reborn each morning. As the Legend of the Five Suns (see page 158) shows, there was no guarantee that the sun would always win. To give the sun strength to rise each day, the Aztecs offered human sacrifices. Priests offered the hearts of tens of thousands of victims to Huitzilopochtli and other Aztec gods. Most of the victims were prisoners of war, but sometimes a noble family gave up one of its own members to appease the gods.

Other cultures such as the Olmecs and the Mayas had practiced human sacrifice, but not on the massive scale of the Aztecs. The Aztecs carried on almost continuous warfare, using the captured enemy soldiers for a regular source of sacrificial victims. Among the conquered peoples, discontent festered and rebellion often flared up. When the armies from Spain later arrived, they found ready allies among peoples who were ruled by the Aztec empire.

▲ *Aztec shield decorated with a coyote*

Education and learning. Priests were the keepers of Aztec knowledge. They recorded laws and historical events. Some ran schools for the sons of nobles. Others used their knowledge of astronomy and mathematics to foretell the future. The Aztecs, like the Mayas, had an accurate calendar.

Like many other ancient peoples, the Aztecs believed that illness was a punishment from the gods. Still, Aztec priests used herbs and other medicines to treat fevers and wounds. Aztec physicians could set broken bones and treat dental cavities. They also prescribed steam baths as cures for various ills, a therapy still in use today.

Looking Ahead

The Aztec poet-king Nezahualcoyotl (neh tsah wahl cuh YOH tuhl), or "Hungry Coyote," knew his world would not last forever. His poetry of the 1400s reveals a pessimistic viewpoint:

66All the Earth is a grave and nothing
  escapes it;

Nothing is so perfect that it does not
  descend to its tomb. . . .
Filled are the depths of the Earth
  with dust
Once flesh and bone, once living
  bodies of men
Who sat upon thrones, decided cases,
  presided in council,
Commanded armies, conquered
  provinces, possessed treasure,
  destroyed temples,
Exulted in their pride, majesty, fortune,
  praise and power.
Vanished are these glories.99

In the next century, the doom that Nezahualcoyotl envisioned engulfed the whole Aztec empire. At the height of Aztec power, word reached Tenochtitlán that pale-skinned, bearded men had landed on the east coast. In Chapter 16, you will read about the results of the encounter between the Aztecs and the newcomers from far-off Spain.

SECTION 1 REVIEW

1. **Identify** (a) Olmecs, (b) Teotihuacán, (c) Tenochtitlán, (d) Huitzilopochtli, (e) Nezahualcoyotl.
2. **Define** tribute.
3. (a) Describe the migration and settlement of people through the Americas. (b) Describe how early Americans turned from hunting to agriculture.
4. How were religion and learning linked in Mayan society?
5. (a) How did the Aztecs build and control a huge empire in Mexico? (b) Descibe the social structure of the Aztec empire.
6. *Critical Thinking* **Analyzing Information** How can evidence such as artwork and public buildings help archaeologists trace the influence of a civilization like the Olmecs on later peoples?
7. *ACTIVITY* Write five words that an Aztec noble or priest might use to describe the Aztec empire. Then, write five words that someone in a conquered region might use to describe the Aztec empire.

The World of the Incas

Guide for Reading

■ What regions did the Incas rule?

■ How did the Incas organize their empire?

■ What role did religion play in Incan civilization?

■ **Vocabulary** *quipu*

The Sapa Inca lifted a golden cup to the rising sun, a gesture to honor his divine ancestor. He then entered the temple, where sunlight glinted off the golden statues along the walls. A priest placed a bundle of fibers on the altar. With a copper mirror, he directed the magical power of the sun's rays to explode the fibers into flame.

Other rituals followed. Priests sacrificed a llama and prayed for success in the coming year. When the ceremonies ended, horns blared the news to the crowds outside the temple. A shout rose: "*Hailli!*—Victory!" Reed pipes and flutes echoed the joy as people prepared for a day of feasting and dancing.

This ceremony honoring the sun god took place each year in Cuzco, capital of the Incan empire of Peru. By the early 1500s, the Incas, like the Aztecs, ruled a mighty empire.

Early Peoples of Peru

The Incan empire covered a wide variety of climates and terrains in western South America. The narrow coastal plain is a dry, lifeless desert crossed by occasional river valleys. Further inland, the snow-capped Andes Mountains rise steeply, leveling off into high plateaus that bake by day and freeze at night. East of the Andes lie dense jungles that stretch from Peru into Brazil.

Thousands of years ago, people settled in fishing villages along the desert coast of Peru. Gradually they expanded inland, farming the river valleys up into the highland plateaus. Using careful irrigation, they grew corn, cotton, squash, and beans. On mountain slopes, they cultivated potatoes, eventually producing 700 varieties. In high plateaus, they domesticated

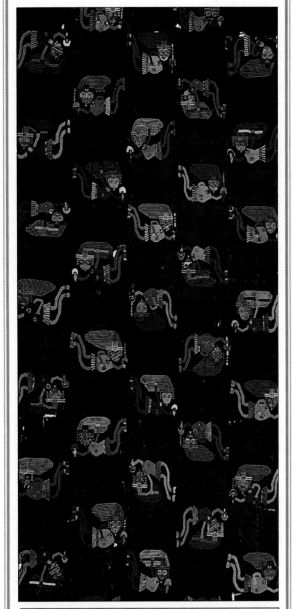

Peruvian Textile Artisans among the Paracas, an early people of Peru, produced this cloak around the 500s B.C. Their work involved many skills. Spinners produced cotton and wool thread, which weavers then turned into cloth. Skillful dyers added color from the more than 150 different shades at their disposal. Finally, embroiderers and painters decorated the fabric with complex and imaginative designs. **Art and Literature** Can you find two identical faces in this design? What does this suggest about the work of the artisans who produced it?

the llama and alpaca. Like the Mayas, they built large ceremonial centers and developed skills in pottery and weaving.

Chavín. Through painstaking work at many sites, archaeologists have pieced together a chronology of various cultures that left their mark on the region. The earliest of these was the Chavín (chah VEEN) culture, named for ruins at Chavín de Huantar in the Andes. There, about 850 B.C., people built a huge temple complex. Stone carvings and pottery show that the Chavín people worshiped a ferocious-looking god, part jaguar and part human with grinning catlike features. The arts and religion of the Chavín culture influenced later peoples of Peru.

Mochica. Between about A.D. 100 and 700, the Mochica people forged an empire along the arid north coast of Peru. Their leaders had roads built and organized networks of relay runners to carry messages, ideas that the Incas would later adopt.

Remains of Mochica cities and temples dot the land. To build one temple, workers had to produce 130 million sun-dried adobe bricks. The people perfected skills in goldwork and woodcarving. They produced remarkable pots decorated with realistic scenes of daily life. On these painted vases, helmeted warriors go into battle, musicians play pipes and drums, and women weave textiles on small portable looms.

Clues, but no answers. Many other cultures left tantalizing clues to their lives and beliefs. In southern Peru, the Nazca people etched giant figures of birds, whales, and other creatures into the sand and gravel hills. These figures may have been family symbols or part of an ancient calendar.

For more than 2,000 years, diverse civilizations rose and fell in Peru. Then, in the mid-1400s, the Incas emerged from high in the Andes. Incan armies rapidly conquered an empire that stretched 2,500 miles (4,025 km) down the Andes and along the Pacific coast. Like the Romans, who also ruled a diverse empire, the Incas drew heavily on the ideas and skills of conquered peoples.

Ruling an Empire

Pachacuti, a skilled warrior and leader, was the founder of the Incan empire. In 1438, he proclaimed himself Sapa Inca, or emperor, and embarked on a policy of conquest. Once he had subdued neighboring peoples, he enlisted them in his armies for future campaigns. In this way, he and his son extended Incan rule from Ecuador in the north to Chile in the south. (See the map on page 159.)

Government. The Sapa Inca exercised absolute power over the empire. Claiming he was divine, the son of the sun itself, he was also the chief religious leader. Like the pharaohs of ancient Egypt, the Incan god-king owned all the land, herds, mines, and people. Gold, the "sweat of the sun," was his symbol. He lived in splendor, eating from golden plates and dressing in richly embroidered clothes. His queen, the Coya, carried out important religious duties and sometimes governed when the Sapa Inca was absent.

From their mountain capital at Cuzco, the Incas ran an efficient government with a chain of command reaching into every village. Nobles ruled the provinces along with local chieftains whom the Incas had conquered. Below them, officials carried out the day-to-day business of collecting taxes and enforcing laws. Specially trained officials kept records on a quipu, a collection of knotted, colored strings. Modern scholars think that quipus noted dates and events as well as statistics on population and crops.

Roads and runners. To unite their empire, the Incas imposed their own language, Quechua (KEHCH wuh), and religion on the people. They also created one of the great road systems in history. It wound more than 12,000 miles (19,300 km) through mountains and deserts. Hundreds of bridges spanned rivers and deep gorges. Steps were cut into steep slopes and tunnels dug through hillsides. Even more impressive than the roads that united the Roman empire, the Incan road system was unmatched until modern times.

The roads allowed armies and news to move rapidly throughout the empire. At regular stations, runners waited to carry messages. Relays of runners could carry news of a revolt swiftly from a distant province to the capital. The Incas kept soldiers at outposts throughout the empire. Within days of an uprising, they would be on the move to crush the rebels. Ordinary people, though, were restricted from using the roads at all.

Cuzco. All roads led through Cuzco. In the heart of the city stood the great Temple of the Sun, its interior walls lined with gold. Like Incan palaces and forts, the temple was made of enormous stone blocks, each polished and carved to fit exactly in place. The engineering was so precise that, although no mortar was used to hold the stones together, Incan buildings have survived severe earthquakes.

Lives of the Incas

The Incas strictly regulated the lives of millions of people within their empire. People lived in close-knit communities, called ayllus (ī looz). Leaders of each ayllu carried out government orders, assigning jobs to each family and organizing the community to work the land. Govern-

ment officials arranged marriages to ensure that men and women were settled at a certain age.

Farming. Farmers expanded the step terraces built by earlier peoples. On steep hillsides, they carved out strips of land to be held in place by stone walls. Terraces kept rains from washing away the soil and made farming possible in places where flat land was scarce.

Farmers had to spend part of each year working land for the emperor and the temples as well as for their own communities. The government took possession of each harvest, dividing it among the people and storing part in case of famine.

Religion. Like other early peoples, the Incas were polytheistic, worshiping many gods linked to the forces of nature. People offered food, clothing, and drink to the guardian spirits of the home and the village. Religion was tied to the routines of life. Each month had its own festival, from the great ripening and the dance of the young maize to the festival of the water. Festivals were celebrated with ceremonies, sports, and games.

"Lost City" of the Andes Some 7,000 feet (2,100 m) above sea level lie the ruins of the Incan city of Machu Picchu. The city's grass roofs are gone, but its sturdy walls have withstood centuries of earthquakes. Incan workers expertly cut and fitted the stones together without the aid of mortar. Abandoned for some 300 years, the ruins of Machu Picchu were not rediscovered until 1911. *Economics and Technology* Where else in the world today must architects design buildings to withstand destructive earthquakes?

A powerful class of priests served the gods, celebrating their special festivals and tending to their needs. Chief among the gods was Inti, the sun god. His special attendants, the "Chosen Women," played a key and honored role in Incan religious rituals.

Chosen Women of the Sun

The royal official carefully examined the girls parading before him. They were young, only eight years old, but he knew what qualities to look for. Nearby, the girls' parents watched with a mixture of pride and anxiety. Who would the Apopanaca, or He-Who-Chooses, choose?

With great ceremony, he made his selections. This girl belonged to the highest-ranking family in the ayllu. That one had great beauty. Another showed great promise as a weaver. Inti would surely approve of such attendants.

The rejected girls returned to their homes. The girls selected by the Apopanaca went with him to the provincial capital—perhaps never to see their homes or parents again. These girls were now Aclla, the Chosen Women.

Years of training. Each provincial capital had its own Acllahuachi, or house of the chosen, not far from the main temple. There, the young Aclla remained in strict seclusion during their period of training. The scholar Garcilasco de la Vega, the son of an Incan mother and Spanish father, later described the house at Cuzco, which admitted only girls of royal blood:

❝There was a narrow passage wide enough for two persons that ran the whole length of the building. The passage had many cells on either side which were used as offices where women worked. At each door were trusted doorkeepers, and in the last apartment at the end of the passage where no one entered were the women of the Sun. . . . There were a score of porters to fetch and carry things needed in the house as far as the second door. The porters could not pass this second door under pain of death, even if they were called from within, and no one was allowed to call them in under the same penalty.**❞**

Within the walls of the Acllahuachi, the young Aclla learned the skills and duties they needed to serve the sun god. They studied the mysteries of the Incan religion, learning the natures and rituals of the many gods and goddesses. They learned to prepare ritual foods and to brew chica, a corn beverage used by priests in their sun ceremonies.

Perhaps most important, the Aclla learned to make the elaborate wool garments and feather headdresses worn by the Sapa Inca and his wife, the Coya. The emperor never wore the same clothing twice, nor could his clothing be passed on to lesser persons. Each garment was worn once, then burned. To meet the constant demand for royal clothing, the Aclla developed legendary skills in the art of weaving. "The luster, splendor, and sheen of the fabrics of featherwork were of such beauty," noted one visitor, "that it is impossible to make them understood, unless by showing them."

A lifetime of service. When a Chosen reached the age of about 16, her long period of training came to an end. Then, her future would be decided. In the provincial capitals, some women might be given in marriage to nobles or other allies and friends of the Incas. At Cuzco, a few Aclla might be selected to serve the emperor or the Coya.

Most of the Chosen Women, however, remained in the house of

The Chosen Women The base of this long-necked vase shows several Aclla in their traditional dress. Each Chosen Woman wears a long gown with a cape draping the shoulders. The rich jewelry and embroidery at the waist and hemline indicate the noble rank of these women who served the Sun. **Religions and Value Systems** Why do you think the potter did not show the faces of individual Aclla on this vase?

seclusion. There, they spent their lives using their skills in the service of the Sun. Some Aclla became *mamacuna,* or "noble mothers," within the Acllahuachi. Their sacred duty was to train new generations of Chosen Women.

In old age, a Chosen Woman might gain permission to return to the home she had left so many years before. There, she lived out her days in comfort, venerated by all for her lifetime of service. ▇

Looking Ahead

At its height, the Incan civilization, like those of Middle America, was a center of learning. Although the Incas were less advanced in astronomy than the Mayas, they did have a calendar. They also excelled in medicine. They used herbs as antiseptics and performed surgery on the skull to relieve swelling caused by wounds.

Then, in 1525, the emperor Huayna Capac (wī nah KAH pahk) died suddenly of an unknown plague that swept across the land. As he had not named a successor, civil war broke out between two of his sons. The fighting weakened the empire at a crucial moment. Like the Aztecs to the north, the Incas soon faced an even greater threat from Spanish invaders.

SECTION 2 REVIEW

1. **Identify** (a) Chavín, (b) Mochica, (c) Pachacuti, (d) Inti, (e) Chosen Women.
2. **Define** quipu.
3. How did geography influence the way the Incas ruled their empire?
4. Describe two steps the Incas took to unite their empire.
5. How did religion affect Incan government and daily life?
6. *Critical Thinking* **Recognizing Points of View** To an ordinary person, what might be the advantages and disadvantages of the absolute rule of the Sapa Inca?
7. *ACTIVITY* Draw a time line of ancient Middle America and Peru. Your time line should show when major civilizations flourished, what advances they made, and which civilizations influenced later peoples.

3 Peoples of North America

Guide for Reading

■ How did Middle American civilizations influence cultures in North America?

■ What has archaeological evidence revealed about the Mound Builders?

■ How did cultural traditions differ across North America?

■ **Vocabulary** *kiva, potlatch*

Hundreds of cultural groups emerged in the present-day United States and Canada. For centuries, they lived by hunting, fishing, and gathering wild plants. As farming spread north from Middle America, many people became farmers, raising corn and other food crops. Some people farmed so successfully that they built large permanent settlements. Here, we will look at the earliest of these farming cultures, in the desert southwest and in the Mississippi Valley.

The Desert Southwest

More than 1,000 years ago, fields of corn, beans, and squash bloomed in the desert southwest. The farmers who planted these fields were called the Hohokams, or "Vanished Ones," by their later descendants, the Pimas and Papagos. To farm the desert, they built a complex irrigation system.

The Hohokams lived near the Gila River in present-day Arizona. They may have acquired skills such as irrigation from the civilizations of Middle America. They built temple mounds and ball courts, as the Mayas did. The Hohokams survived until about A.D. 1500, when

ISSUES *For* TODAY

In both North and South America, geographic differences led to the development of different ways of life. How does geography influence cultural diversity?

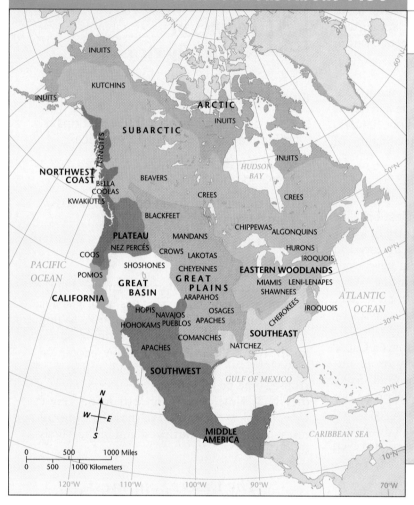

GEOGRAPHY AND HISTORY

As Native Americans spread out to populate North America, they developed varied cultures. The map shows culture areas in which tribes shared similar ways of life.

1. **Location** On the map, locate (a) Northwest Coast culture area, (b) Eastern Woodlands culture area, (c) Great Plains culture area.
2. **Place** (a) Name two tribes in the southwest culture area. (b) With which culture area are the Cherokees associated?
3. **Critical Thinking Making Inferences** Make a list of geographic features, such as natural barriers, climate, or vegetation, that might have led to the development of different ways of life.

drought seems to have forced them to leave their settlements.

Anasazi. The best-known society of the southwest was that of the Anasazi. They lived in what is today the Four Corners region of Arizona, New Mexico, Colorado, and Utah. Between about A.D. 900 and 1300, the Anasazi built large villages, later called *pueblos* by the Spanish.

Remains of Pueblo Bonita still stand in New Mexico. The village consisted of a huge complex with 800 rooms that housed about 6,000 people. Builders used stone and adobe bricks to erect a crescent-shaped compound rising five stories high. Terraces at each level served as streets.

At the center of the great complex was a plaza. There, the Anasazis dug their kiva, a large underground chamber used for religious ceremonies. Men met in the kiva for religious ceremonies to ensure rain and good harvests. Paintings on the walls show their concern with weather, including storms that might damage crops.

Anasazi cliff dwellings. In the late 1100s, the Anasazi began building housing complexes in the shadow of canyon walls, where the cliffs offered protection from raiders. The largest of these cliff dwellings at Mesa Verde, in present-day Colorado, had over 200 rooms. People had to climb up or down ladders to reach their fields on the flatlands above or the canyon floor below. Women farmed, made pottery and cotton cloth, and replastered the walls of their dwellings. Men and older boys cleared the fields and hunted.

In the late 1200s, a long drought forced the Anasazi to abandon their cliff dwellings. Without rain, they could no longer live in large settlements. Attacks by Navajos and Apaches may have contributed further to their decline. Anasazi traditions survived, however, among the Hopi and other Pueblo Indians of the present-day southwestern United States.

The Mound Builders

Far to the east of the Anasazi, in the Mississippi and Ohio valleys, other farming cultures emerged as early as 700 B.C. The Adena and Hopewell people left behind giant earthen mounds. Some mounds were cone-shaped, while others were made in the shape of animals. The Great Serpent Mound in Ohio wriggles and twists for almost a quarter of a mile. This enormous monument is evidence of the Adena people's resources and strong leadership.

Objects found in Hopewell mounds show that traders extended their influence over a wide area. They brought back shells and shark teeth from the Gulf of Mexico and copper from the Great Lakes region. Skilled artisans hammered and shaped the copper into fine ornaments.

▲ *Snake found in Hopewell mound*

Cahokia. By A.D. 800, these early cultures had disappeared, but a new people, the Mississippians, had acquired a greater variety of corn and other crops. With a growing food surplus, their civilization prospered. As their culture spread, the Mississippians built clusters of earthen mounds and ever larger towns and ceremonial centers.

Their greatest center, Cahokia in present-day Illinois, housed as many as 40,000 people by about 1200. Cahokia boasted at least 60 mounds. On top of some mounds stood the homes of rulers and nobles. The largest mound probably had a temple on its summit, where priests and rulers offered prayers and sacrifices to the sun. Archaeologists think that this temple mound shows the influence of Middle American civilizations.

Heirs of the Mound Builders. The Mississippians left no written records, and their cities had disappeared by the time Europeans reached the area. Still, their traditions survived among the Natchez people, whose ruler, the Great Sun, had absolute power. He and his family lived on the top of pyramid mounds.

Diverse Regional Cultures

Many other groups of Native Americans emerged in North America prior to 1500. Modern scholars have identified 10 culture areas based on the environments in which people lived: the Arctic, Subarctic, Northwest Coast, California, Great Basin, Plateau, Southwest, Great Plains, Southeast, and Eastern Woodlands. In each area, people adapted to geographic conditions that influenced their ways of life.

The chart on page 172 summarizes the characteristics and achievements of peoples who lived in each culture area. Here, we will look in greater detail at ways of life in three regions—the Arctic, the Northwest Coast, and the Eastern Woodlands.

A frozen world. In the far north, the Inuits* adapted to a harsh climate, using the resources of the frozen land to survive. Small bands lived by hunting and fishing. Seals and other sea mammals provided them with food, skins for clothing, bones for needles and tools, and oil for cooking. They paddled kayaks in open waters or used dog sleds to transport goods across the ice. An Inuit song describes the life of migrating hunters:

❝Leaving the white bear behind in his
   realm of sea-ice
 we set off for our winter hunting
   grounds . . .

---

* The Inuits were late immigrants from Siberia. Other Native Americans called them Eskimos, "eaters of raw flesh," but they called themselves the Inuits, the "people."

QUICK STUDY Native American Culture Groups of North America

Culture Group/ Selected Tribes	Patterns of Life	Connections Today
Arctic/Subarctic Beavers, Crees, Inuits, Kutchins 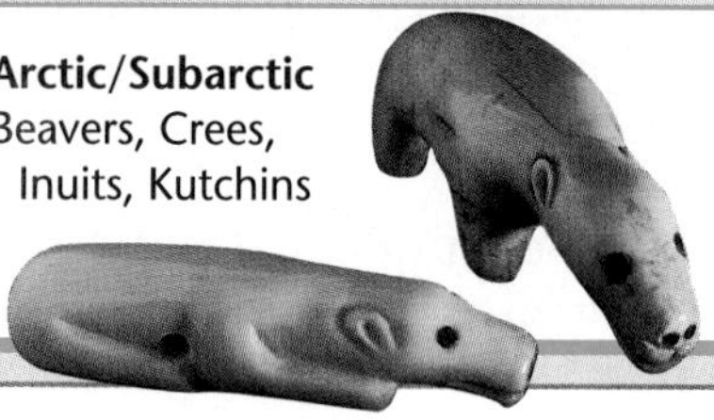	Lived as nomadic hunters and food gatherers in cold climate; honored ocean, weather, and animal spirits	In the 1990s, the Canadian government agreed to restore 140,000 square miles of Inuit lands. The Inuits called the new territory Nunavit, or "our land."
Northwest Coast Bella Coolas, Coos, Kwakiutls, Tlingits 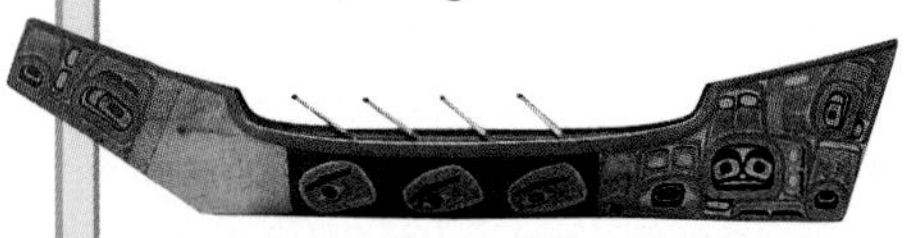	Lived in villages; benefited from rich natural resources in forests, rivers, and ocean; held potlatches, or ceremonial dinners, where host families gave gifts to guests to show wealth and gain status	Artists, such as Jesse Cooday, a Tlingit, are merging many traditional Native American themes with modern styles. Their works are featured in museums and galleries, where they inspire new generations.
California/Great Basin/Plateau Nez Percés, Pomos, Shoshones 	Lived as hunters and gatherers in small family groups; ate mainly fish, berries, acorns	Like many Native Americans, Lillian Valenzuela Robles of southern California is working to stop development of a plot of land that is part of her people's ancestral homeland.
Southwest Apaches, Hopis, Navajos, Pueblos 	Lived in villages in homes made of adobe; built irrigation systems to grow corn and other crops; honored earth, sky, and water spirits	Like many other tribes, Mescalero Apaches in New Mexico have improved the quality of life on their reservation through successful businesses, including a sawmill and a ski lodge.
Great Plains Arapahos, Blackfeet, Cheyennes, Comanches, Crows, Lakotas, Mandans, Osages 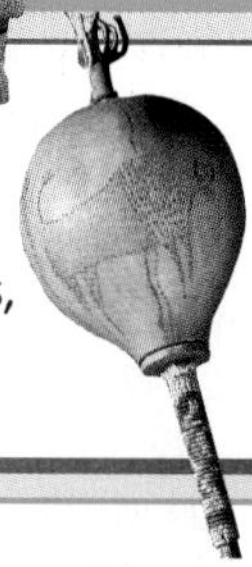	Lived in tepees; animals hunted by men; crops grown by women; relied on buffalo to meet basic needs of food, shelter, and clothing	The Crows in Montana have set up a two-year college that teaches such subjects as math, science, and Crow history. It is one of 28 tribally controlled colleges in the United States.
Eastern Woodlands Algonquins, Chippewas, Hurons, Iroquois, Leni-Lenapes, Miamis, Pequots, Shawnees 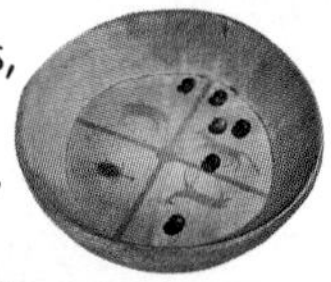	Lived in farming villages, but also hunted for food; long houses shared by several families; women held much social and political power	The Pequots in Connecticut, like other tribes around the country, have built a gambling casino. The profits support education and provide health services.
Southeast Cherokees, Natchez 	Grew corn, squash, beans, and other crops; held yearly Green Corn Ceremony to mark end of year and celebrate harvest	Throughout the country, including the Southeast, Native Americans gather at intertribal pow-wows, to celebrate with singing, dancing, food, games, and sports.

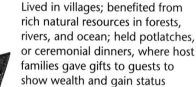

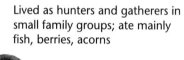

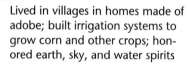

We followed the course of the river
　over the flatlands beyond
Where the sleds sank in the deep snow
　up to the cross slats.
It was sweaty work, I tell you,
Helping the dogs.**"**

In some areas, Inuits constructed igloos, or dome-shaped homes made from snow and ice. In others, they built sod dwellings that were partly underground.

A land of plenty. The people of the Northwest Coast lived in a far richer environment than the Inuits. Rivers teemed with salmon, while the Pacific Ocean offered other fish and sea mammals. Hunters tracked deer, wolves, and bears in the forests. In this land of plenty, people built large permanent villages with homes made of wood. They traded their surplus goods, gaining wealth that was shared in ceremonies like the potlatch. At this ceremony, which continues in Canada today, a person of rank and wealth distributes lavish gifts to large numbers of guests. By accepting the gifts, the guests acknowledge the host's high status.

The Iroquois League. The Eastern Woodlands, stretching from the Atlantic Coast to the Great Lakes, was home to a number of groups, including the Iroquois. They cleared land and built villages in the forests. While women farmed, men hunted and frequently warred against rival nations.

According to Iroquois tradition, the prophet Dekanawidah (deh kan ah WEE dah) urged rival Iroquois nations to stop their constant wars. In the late 1500s, he and his ally Hiawatha formed the unique political system known as the Iroquois League. This was an alliance of five nations who spoke the same language and shared similar traditions. The league's constitu-

tion reflects Dekanawidah's passionate desire to have peace among the nations:

  "I, Dekanawidah, and the confederate lords now uproot the tallest tree and into the cavity thereby made we cast all weapons of war. Into the depths of the earth we cast all weapons of strife. We bury them from sight forever and plant again the tree. Thus shall all Great Peace be established and hostilities shall no longer be known between the Five Nations but only peace to a united people.**"**

The Iroquois League did not always succeed in keeping the peace. Still, it was the best-organized political group north of Mexico. Member nations governed their own villages but met jointly in a council when they needed to resolve larger problems. Only men sat on the council, but every clan had a "clan mother" who could name or depose chiefs and members of the council.

The Iroquois League emerged just at the time when Europeans arrived in the Americas. Encounters with Europeans would take a fearful toll on the peoples of North America and topple the Aztec and Incan empires.

SECTION 3 REVIEW

1. **Identify** (a) Hohokams, (b) Anasazis, (c) Mound Builders, (d) Inuits, (e) Iroquois League.
2. **Define** (a) kiva, (b) potlatch.
3. What evidence suggests that the people of the desert southwest were influenced by Middle American civilizations?
4. How do we know about the lives of the Mound Builders?
5. Give examples of how environmental conditions affected three early cultures of North America.
6. *Critical Thinking* **Linking Past and Present** How do environmental factors affect the way you and others live in your community today?
7. *ACTIVITY* With a partner, create a poster that expresses the ideas behind the formation of the Iroquois League.

CHAPTER REVIEW

REVIEWING VOCABULARY

Write a sentence explaining the significance of each of the following words with respect to the civilizations of the Americas: (a) tribute, (b) quipu, (c) kiva, (d) potlatch.

REVIEWING FACTS

1. How did people first reach the Americas?
2. What were some Mayan advances in learning?
3. In what present-day country was the Aztec empire located?
4. Why did the Incas build an extensive road system?
5. How did the Incas farm on steep hillsides?
6. Why did the Anasazi leave their cliff dwellings in the American Southwest?
7. What was the Iroquois League?

REVIEWING CHAPTER THEMES

Review the "Focus On" questions at the start of this chapter. Then select *three* of those questions and answer them, using information from the chapter.

CRITICAL THINKING

1. **Analyzing Information** (a) What advances in agriculture did the Mayas, Aztecs, and Incas make? (b) Why were these farming methods critical to the development of each civilization?
2. **Comparing** Review Chapter 6. Then, compare the methods used by the Incas and the Romans to unite and control their diverse empires.
3. **Solving Problems** (a) How did the geography of the Valley of Mexico pose a challenge

SKILLS FOR SUCCESS   ANSWERING ESSAY QUESTIONS

Essay questions contain question words or instruction words that are the keys to writing good answers. Some of these words are listed below, with the type of answer that each one requires.

Why:	Give reasons.
How:	Tell in what way or by what means something was done.
What:	Give specific examples that explain or illustrate.
Describe:	Write a detailed account of what happened.
Compare:	Give similarities and differences.

Be sure to look at the question for further clues that limit the topic by identifying specific individuals, events, dates, or areas. Look at the list of sample essay topics given below, then answer the following questions.

1. **Identify the instruction or question words.** (a) What is the instruction word in sample question C? (b) What is it telling you to do?
2. **Look for other clues in the question to focus**

your answer. Which words in question A limit the people your answer should focus on?
3. **Write a thesis statement.** A **thesis statement** is a sentence that presents the main point of your essay. (a) Write a thesis statement for question B. (b) Write a thesis statement for question D.
4. **Organize supporting details.** Supporting details are specific facts that support your thesis statement. List three facts that support your thesis statement for question D.

> ### Sample Essay Questions
> A. Compare the ways the early peoples of North America adjusted to their varied physical environments.
> B. What were the religious beliefs of the Aztecs?
> C. How do historians and scholars account for the decline of the Mayas?
> D. Why was farming critical to the development of early civilizations?

to the Aztecs as they built their civilization? (b) What methods did they develop to overcome this challenge? (c) What does their solution suggest to you about the level of government and learning among the Aztecs?

4. **Synthesizing Information**   Look at the maps on pages 159 and 170 and the chart on page 172. (a) What is the exact location of the land bridge linking Asia and North America? (b) Which North American culture group was located in the region nearest the land bridge? (c) What were the characteristics of this group?

ANALYZING PRIMARY SOURCES

Use the quotation on page 173, second column, to answer the following questions.

1. What was the symbolic meaning of the act of placing weapons into the earth?

2. Who were the "united people" referred to in the excerpt?

3. According to the text, what features did the members of the Iroquois League have in common? How might this have helped the League succeed?

FOR YOUR PORTFOLIO

PREPARING A SLIDE SHOW   Prepare a slide show about an imaginary trip through time that you and two or three classmates make to visit one of the early civilizations of the Americas—the Mayas, Aztecs, Incas, or Anasazis. First, choose a civilization and a date for your visit. Then do research to find information about that civilization that can be shown visually, such as cities, architecture, and clothing styles. Prepare 8–10 pictures to be used as slides, and write a short narrative for each slide. Then write brief opening and closing statements for your presentation, explaining why you chose that civilization and what you learned. Finally, present your "slide show" to the class.

Early Cities of the Americas

City	Description
Tikal	Largest Mayan city; in present-day Guatemala; included pyramid temples
Teotihuacán	Dominated Valley of Mexico; included wide roads and large pyramids
Tenochtitlán	Aztec capital; on site of present-day Mexico City; located on lake with causeways connecting it to mainland
Cuzco	Incan capital; connected by road system to rest of empire
Cahokia	Mississippian center in present-day Illinois; contained temple and wealthy homes built on earthen mounds

ANALYZING TABLES

Use the table to answer the following questions.

1. Which of the cities was located in South America? How do you know?

2. Which cities contained pyramids?

3. What evidence does this table give that early American civilizations had advanced technological skills?

INTERNET ACTIVITY

RESEARCHING ART   Use the Internet to research Aztec, Incan, or Mayan art. Then create a sketch, sculpture, or textile in the style of the civilization you have researched. You can also write a description of a piece of art you have researched, focusing on special features of that civilization's style.

Unit-in-Brief

Empires of the Ancient World

Chapter 4 **Empires of India and China** (600 B.C.–A.D. 550)

Between 600 B.C. and A.D. 550, strong, unified empires with complex belief systems emerged in India and China. These civilizations set patterns in government, religion, and philosophy that influenced later cultures.

- Hindu beliefs, including the concepts of reincarnation, kharma, and dharma, profoundly influenced Indian civilization.
- The Buddha, an Indian religious reformer, sought spiritual enlightenment. His teachings gave rise to a new religion, Buddhism, that eventually spread through Southeast and East Asia.
- Under the Maurya and Gupta dynasties, India developed into a center of trade and had contacts with civilizations in Africa, the Middle East, and Central and Southeast Asia.
- The caste system, the village, and the family influenced many aspects of Indian life.
- The teachings of Confucius, based on ideals of duty and social good, influenced Chinese government and society.
- Legalism and Daoism were two other important philosophies that arose in China.
- Shi Huangdi united all of China and built a strong authoritarian government, which laid the groundwork for China's classical age.

- Under Han rulers, the Chinese made huge advances in trade, government, technology, and the arts.

Chapter 5 **Ancient Greece** (1750 B.C.–133 B.C.)

Despite bitter rivalry, Greek city-states gave rise to a civilization that set a standard of excellence for later civilizations. Greek ideas about the universe, the individual, and government still live on in the world today.

- Through trading contacts, Minoan and Mycenaean culture acquired many ideas from older civilizations of Egypt and Mesopotamia.
- Separated by mountains, the Greek city-states often warred with each other but united to defeat the Persians.
- After the Persian Wars, democracy flourished and culture thrived in Athens under the leadership of Pericles.
- Guided by a belief in reason, Greek artists, writers, and philosophers used their genius to seek order in the universe.
- The conquests of Alexander the Great spread Greek civilization throughout the Mediterranean world and across the Middle East to the outskirts of India.

- Greek culture blended with Persian, Egyptian, and Indian cultures to create the Hellenistic civilization, in which art, science, mathematics, and philosophy flourished.

Chapter 6 Ancient Rome and the Rise of Christianity
(509 B.C.–A.D. 476)

Rome expanded across the Mediterranean to build a huge, diverse empire. In the process, it spread the civilizations of Greece, Egypt, and the Fertile Crescent westward into Europe.

- After the Romans threw out their Etruscan king, they set up a republic. Eventually, commoners were allowed to be elected to the Roman Senate.
- Conquest and diplomacy helped the Romans to extend their rule from Spain to Egypt. However, expansion created social and economic problems that led to the decline of the republic and the rule of an emperor.
- During the Pax Romana, Roman emperors brought peace, order, unity, and prosperity to the lands under their control.
- Rome acted as a bridge between the east and the west by borrowing and transforming Greek and Hellenistic achievements to produce Greco-Roman civilization.
- Christianity, which emerged in Roman-held lands in the Middle East, spread quickly throughout the Roman empire. The new faith reshaped Roman beliefs.
- Foreign invasions, the division of the empire, a corrupt government, poverty and unemployment, and declining moral values finally contributed to the downfall of the Roman empire.

Chapter 7 Civilizations of the Americas
(1400 B.C.–A.D. 1570)

Three advanced civilizations—those of the Mayas, Aztecs, and Incas—developed in Middle and South America. In North America, diverse culture groups emerged.

- The first settlers in the Americas were nomadic hunters who migrated across a land bridge between Siberia and Alaska and gradually populated two vast continents.
- Mayan civilization flourished from southern Mexico through Central America between A.D. 300 and 900. Its system of city-states supported a complex religious structure.
- In the 1400s, the Aztecs conquered most of Mexico and built a highly developed civilization led by a single ruler.
- By the 1500s, the Incas established a centralized government in Peru, ruled by a god-king and a powerful class of priests.
- Ten culture groups developed in the Arctic, Subarctic, Northwest Coast, California, Great Basin, Plateau, Southwest, Great Plains, Southeast, and Eastern Woodlands. Their diverse ways of life were strongly influenced by geography.

A Global View

What Characteristics Were Shared by Ancient Empires Around the World?

Empires combining many cities and small countries emerged in various parts of the world in ancient times. Some of the largest of these empires took shape in India, China, Europe, and, later, the Americas.

These larger political structures had many things in common. Most empires were built by military conquest and ruled by hereditary emperors through appointed governors or lesser kings. Empires everywhere developed powerful centralized bureaucracies like those of China or imposed universal legal codes like Roman law. Emperors protected far-flung trade routes and built large cities, canals, highways, and other public works. They also sponsored the spread of major religions, such as Buddhism in India and Christianity throughout the Roman empire.

Eastern Empires

In India, the Maurya dynasty united the states along the Ganges about 300 B.C. The Hindu faith continued to flourish, but after 500 B.C., followers of a reformer known as the Buddha converted many Indians to Buddhism.

Shi Huangdi unified the states of eastern China around 200 B.C. After that, for most of China's history, the Han and later dynasties ruled a vast united nation. Philosophers like Confucius, as well as Buddhist missionaries, laid the groundwork for many basic Chinese beliefs.

Classical Civilizations of Europe

The earliest European civilizations emerged among the peoples of two neighboring Mediterranean peninsulas. These people were the Greeks and the Romans. The Greeks built a brilliant civilization centered in independent city-states, while the Romans later constructed a huge empire that spanned three continents.

Two earlier societies—those of the sea-trading Minoans and the warlike Mycenaeans—gave

650 B.C.   350 B.C.   50 B.C.

AFRICA

680 B.C.
King Taharqa
rules Nile Valley

500 B.C.
Ironworking flourishes in Meroë

146 B.C.
Destruction
of Carthage

THE AMERICAS

700s B.C.
Chavín gold
carvings made

400s B.C.
Collapse of
Olmec civilization

ASIA AND OCEANIA

566 B.C.
Buddha is born

551 B.C.
Confucius is born

221 B.C.
Shi Huangdi completes
unification of China

EUROPE

700s B.C.
Rise of Greek
city-states

509 B.C.
Roman Republic established

460 B.C.
Age of Pericles
begins

323 B.C.
Hellenistic
age begins

way to the Greek city-states before 500 B.C. Led by Athens and Sparta, the bustling little Greek cities traded with many peoples. Athens also developed an early form of democratic government. Though they often fought with one another, the Greeks created a common body of art, science, and philosophy that laid the foundations of western civilization.

The Romans learned much from the Greeks. Their expanding empire swept around the Mediterranean and then spread northward across western Europe. Dominated first by its aristocratic Senate, Rome came to be ruled by powerful emperors after the reign of Augustus Caesar.

During the reign of Augustus, Jesus was born in the region of Judea. Christianity spread widely in Roman times. The new religion survived the fall of Rome to become the core of European culture in later centuries.

American Civilizations

Across the Atlantic Ocean, civilizations also emerged in the Americas. Hunters and food-gatherers gradually settled into agricultural villages. In places, religious ceremonial centers emerged, then city-states and empires.

In Mexico, the Mayan city-states built magnificent temples and mastered complex mathematics. Peru saw a number of regional empires flourish. In the A.D. 1300s and 1400s, the Aztecs established a powerful empire in Mexico, while the Incas built an even larger one in the high Andes of Peru.

Looking Ahead

Some of these mighty empires of Europe, Asia, and the Americas would serve as models for others to come in later centuries. From the Great Wall of China to the Incan royal road through the Andes, these empires left behind impressive monuments. The civilizations of China and India, Greece and Rome, forged cultural legacies that still influence the world.

ACTIVITY Choose two events and two pictures from the time line below. For each, write a sentence explaining how it relates to the themes expressed in the Global View essay.

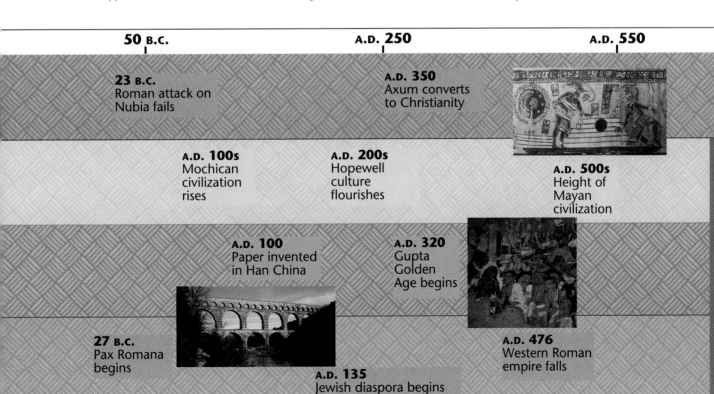

50 B.C.   A.D. 250   A.D. 550

23 B.C.
Roman attack on Nubia fails

A.D. 350
Axum converts to Christianity

A.D. 100s
Mochican civilization rises

A.D. 200s
Hopewell culture flourishes

A.D. 500s
Height of Mayan civilization

A.D. 100
Paper invented in Han China

A.D. 320
Gupta Golden Age begins

27 B.C.
Pax Romana begins

A.D. 476
Western Roman empire falls

A.D. 135
Jewish diaspora begins

You Decide

Exploring Global Issues

How Should a Society's Leaders Be Chosen?

Pericles boasted that under Athenian democracy power was "in the hands not of a minority but of the whole people." More than 2,000 years later, Abraham Lincoln expressed this idea as "government of the people, by the people, and for the people." Yet not everyone has agreed that democracy is the best form of government. More often, leaders have inherited their positions, seized power by force, or been chosen by a small group. To begin your own investigation of leadership, examine these viewpoints.

INDIA

around 200 B.C.

In the *Mahabharata,* a wise man explains that kings became necessary when people grew too greedy to rule themselves:

> To institute order, the gods approached Vishnu, the lord of creatures, and said: 'Indicate to us that one person among mortals who alone is worthy of the highest rank.' Then the blessed lord god Vishnu reflected, and brought forth a glorious son, called Virajas, who became the first king.

RUSSIA

1600s

The theory of divine right was based on the idea that a monarch's authority came directly from God. Many European rulers, like this Russian czar, combined worldly power with religious authority. ▶

UNITED STATES

1787

Alexander Hamilton, a Caribbean-born statesman who helped shape the Constitution, distrusted ordinary citizens:

> All communities divide themselves into the few and the many. The first are the rich and well-born, the other the mass of the people. . . . The people are turbulent and changing; they seldom judge or determine right. Give therefore to the first class a distinct, permanent share in the government.

GREAT BRITAIN

1861

The British philosopher John Stuart Mill was a champion of representative government:

> The ideally best form of government is that in which the sovereignty, or supreme controlling power in the last resort, is vested in the entire . . . community; every citizen not only having a voice in the exercise of that ultimate sovereignty, but being, at least occasionally, called on to take actual part in the government.

TANZANIA

1961

Julius Nyerere, first president of Tanzania, described the practice of government by consensus, or mutual agreement:

“The traditional African society, whether it had a chief or not—and many, like my own, did not—was a society of equals and it conducted its business through discussion. . . . 'They talk till they agree.' That gives you the very essence of traditional African democracy.”

CHILE

1986

Santiago Sinclair, an aide to Chilean military dictator Augusto Pinochet, defended the right of strong leaders to take power into their own hands:

“Command is voice, conscience, justice, and it is made noble by the commitment and personal example of the one who wields it. Command guides spirits and unites wills, carrying them to success in endeavors that often require supreme heroism.”

SOUTH AFRICA

1990s

After years of struggle, the goal of "one person, one vote" was finally achieved by South Africa's black majority. Here, church members learn how to fill out a ballot. ▶

COMPARING VIEWPOINTS

1. Which viewpoints represented here seem closest to the idea of democracy expressed by Pericles? Explain.
2. How is the idea of leadership expressed in the *Mahabharata* similar to divine right?
3. How does a leader emerge according to Hamilton? According to Nyerere? According to Sinclair?

YOUR INVESTIGATION

ACTIVITY

1. Find out more about one of the viewpoints above or another viewpoint related to this topic. You might investigate:

■ The views of government expressed by the Chinese philosopher Confucius.

■ The idea of the "philosopher-king" in Plato's *Republic*.
■ The writings of French bishop Jacques Bossuet on divine right.
■ The Constitution of the United States or another modern constitution.
■ The rise of a charismatic leader such as Napoleon Bonaparte of France, Mustafa Kemal Atatürk of Turkey, or Juan Perón of Argentina.
■ The idea of government expressed by communist thinkers such as Lenin of Russia or Mao Zedong of China.

2. Decide which viewpoint you agree with most closely and express it in your own way. You may do so in an essay, a cartoon, a poem, a drawing or painting, a song, a skit, a video, or some other way.

REGIONAL CIVILIZATIONS

Economics and Technology

1 *The Aztecs were skilled gold-workers, as these earrings show. Gold and other tribute from conquered people would later swell the wealth of the Aztec empire.*

NORTH AMERICA

ATLANTIC OCEAN

1

Tenochtitlán

PACIFIC OCEAN

SOUTH AMERICA

Art and Literature

2 *Calligraphy, ceramics, metalwork, and other arts flourished across the Muslim world. This enameled Persian bowl shows a group of female musicians.*

Political and Social Systems

3 *Ife was one of several kingdoms to emerge in West Africa. The interlocking arms of this royal couple show that they shared political power.*

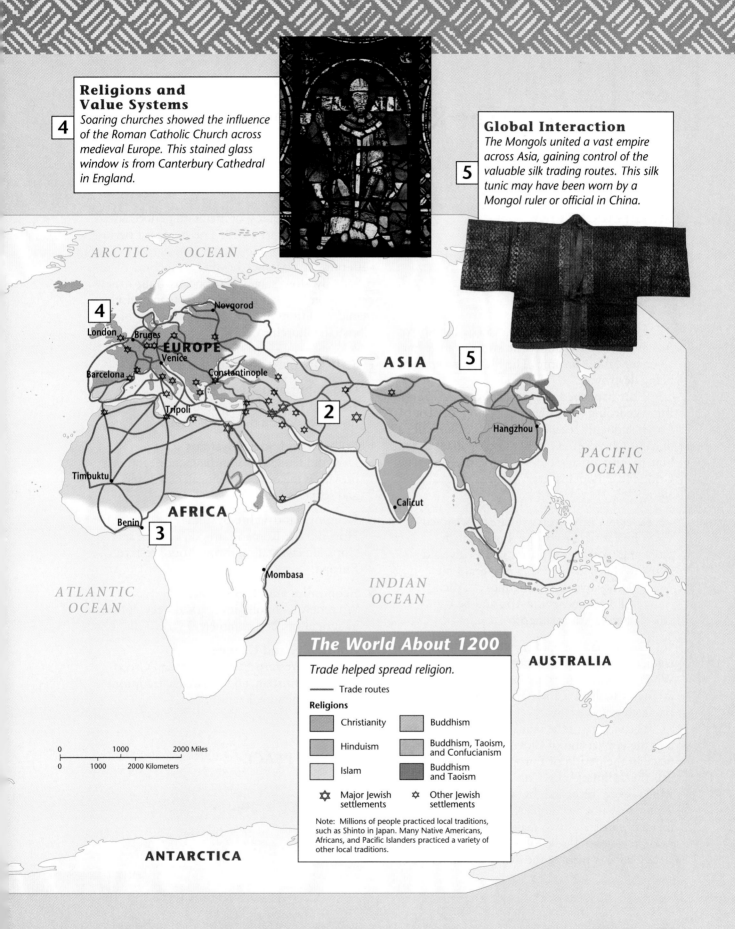

Religions and Value Systems

4 Soaring churches showed the influence of the Roman Catholic Church across medieval Europe. This stained glass window is from Canterbury Cathedral in England.

Global Interaction

5 The Mongols united a vast empire across Asia, gaining control of the valuable silk trading routes. This silk tunic may have been worn by a Mongol ruler or official in China.

4

ARCTIC OCEAN

Novgorod

London

Bruges

EUROPE

Venice

Barcelona

Constantinople

ASIA

5

Tripoli

2

Hangzhou

PACIFIC OCEAN

Timbuktu

Calicut

Benin

3

AFRICA

ATLANTIC OCEAN

Mombasa

INDIAN OCEAN

AUSTRALIA

ANTARCTICA

The World About 1200

Trade helped spread religion.

——— Trade routes

Religions

Christianity

Hinduism

Islam

Buddhism

Buddhism, Taoism, and Confucianism

Buddhism and Taoism

✡ Major Jewish settlements

✡ Other Jewish settlements

Note: Millions of people practiced local traditions, such as Shinto in Japan. Many Native Americans, Africans, and Pacific Islanders practiced a variety of other local traditions.

| 0 | 1000 | 2000 Miles |
| 0 | 1000 | 2000 Kilometers |

The Rise of Europe

(500–1300)

CHAPTER OUTLINE

1 **The Early Middle Ages**
2 **Feudalism and the Manor Economy**
3 **The Medieval Church**
4 **Economic Expansion and Change**

Clovis, king of the Franks, watched in horror as his men fell under the swords of the hated enemy, the Alamanni. The Frankish army was being destroyed.

What happened next is shrouded in legend. But according to Gregory, bishop of Tours, Clovis suddenly recalled the words of his wife, a devout Christian. Queen Clotilde had urged him to give up his old gods for the one true God. He raised his eyes to heaven and cried aloud:

> 66 Jesus Christ: You who are proclaimed by Clotilde to be the Son of the living God, You who are said to give aid to those in distress, if You grant me victory over these enemies . . . then will I also believe in You and be baptized in Your name. 99

Hardly had he spoken when the Alamanni soldiers "turned their backs and began to flee." When Clotilde learned of the miracle, she arranged to have Clovis and his chief warriors baptized as Christians.

The victory of the Franks over the Alamanni and the conversion of Clovis that followed took place in the period of European history that we call the Middle Ages. The details of the story, which were recorded by Gregory, bishop of Tours, may not be completely accurate. Still, the incident illustrates two major themes of the period: the central role of Christianity and the struggle for control of the dying Roman empire.

The Middle Ages, or medieval period, lasted from about 500 to 1500. The medieval period was a time of war and plunder, of hardship and suffering. It was also, however, a period of renewal. By slow stages, Europeans built a new civilization. It blended Greco-Roman and Germanic traditions within the framework of the Christian Church.

FOCUS ON these questions as you read:

■ **Geography and History**
Why did Western Europe develop its own resources during the Middle Ages?

■ **Political and Social Systems**
How did feudalism and the manor economy provide a measure of political, economic, and social order?

■ **Religions and Value Systems**
How did the Roman Catholic Church spread Christian civilization throughout Western Europe?

■ **Economics and Technology**
What new technologies sparked a revolution in agriculture and commerce?

■ **Continuity and Change**
How did Western Europeans blend Greco-Roman, Christian, and Germanic traditions to build a new civilization?

TIME AND PLACE

Age of Faith During the Middle Ages, religion was a central part of everyday living. But the Roman Catholic Church was more than a spiritual guide. It was a powerful organization that helped to unify Western Europe and shaped every aspect of medieval life. This brilliant enamel, portraying Jesus, Mary, and John the Baptist, adorned a medieval church. **Continuity and Change** Why do you think the fall of Rome helped to strengthen the Catholic Church?

HUMANITIES LINK

Art History Illuminated manuscript (page 197).
Literature In this chapter, you will encounter passages from the following work of literature: Geoffrey Chaucer, *The Canterbury Tales* (page 196).

500s	732	800	900s	1100s	1200s
Germanic kingdoms dominate Western Europe	Franks defeat Muslims at Tours	Pope crowns Charlemagne emperor	Viking and Magyar invasions; feudalism develops	Economy revives in Western Europe	Dominican and Franciscan orders founded

500	700	900	1100	1300	1500

1 The Early Middle Ages

Guide for Reading

- Why was Europe a frontier land in the early Middle Ages?
- How did invasions affect the peoples of Western Europe?
- How did Charlemagne blend Roman, German, and Christian traditions?

Pope Gregory the Great sat at his desk in Rome, thinking about the perils facing Italy. The Lombards were attacking from the north, and once again Rome might fall to plundering invaders. In despair, Gregory wrote:

> ❝Where is the senate? Where are the people? The bones are all dissolved, the flesh is consumed, all the pomp and dignities of this world is gone. The whole mass is boiled away.❞

Gregory was writing in about A.D. 600, as waves of invaders swept across Europe. Roman civilization was slowly disappearing. Wars raged constantly. Trade slowed to a trickle, towns emptied, and learning virtually ceased. During the early Middle Ages, from about 500 to 1000, Europe was an isolated, backward region largely cut off from the advanced civilizations that flourished in the Middle East, South Asia, China, and elsewhere.

A Land of Great Potential

Rome had linked its far-flung European territories with miles of fine roads and had spread classical ideas, the Latin language, and Christianity to the tribal peoples of Western Europe. But Rome was a Mediterranean power. The Germanic peoples who ended Roman rule in the West shifted the focus to the north. There, the peoples of Europe began to create a new civilization.

Location. Europe is a relatively small area, although its impact on the modern world has been enormous. It lies on the western end of Eurasia, the giant landmass that stretches from present-day Portugal all the way to China. (See the map on page 187.)

Resources. At the dawn of the Middle Ages, Europe had great untapped potential. Dense forests covered much of the north, and the region's rich black earth was better suited for raising crops than the dry soils around the Mediterranean. Beneath the surface of the soil, from Poland to Britain, lay untapped veins of rich minerals.

The seas that surround much of Europe were important to its growth. Coastal people not only fished for food but also used the seas as highways for trade and exploration. Europe's large rivers were ideal for trade, and its many mountain streams seemed made for turning water wheels.

Germanic Kingdoms

The Germanic tribes who migrated across Europe were farmers and herders. Their culture differed greatly from that of the Romans. They

The Franks *During the early Middle Ages, many Germanic tribes set up small kingdoms in Italy, Gaul, Spain, Britain, and North Africa. They were constantly at war with one another. Gradually, however, the kingdom of the Franks emerged as strongest and established control over much of the western Roman empire. Shown here is a Frankish warrior.* **Geography and History** *How did Germanic peoples help to shift the geographic focus of European civilization?*

Geography and Resources of Europe

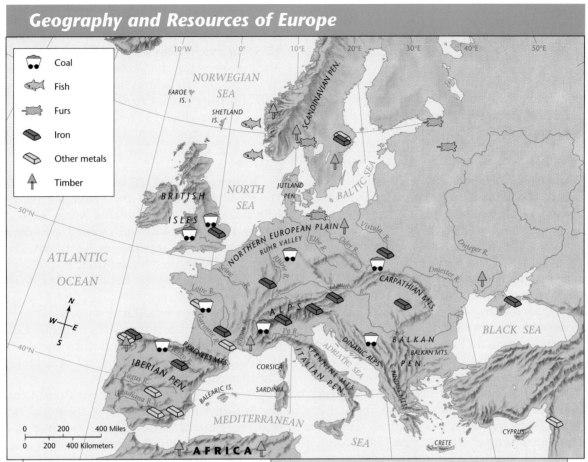

Legend:
- Coal
- Fish
- Furs
- Iron
- Other metals
- Timber

GEOGRAPHY AND HISTORY

Europe extends from the Iberian Peninsula in the west to the Ural Mountains in the east. It contains a wide variety of landforms and many valuable natural resources.

1. **Location** On the map, locate (a) Baltic Sea, (b) Danube River, (c) Seine River, (d) Alps, (e) Northern European Plain, (f) Ruhr Valley.
2. **Movement** a) Name one natural feature of Europe's geography that might have helped bring the people of Europe together. (b) Name one natural feature of its geography that might have kept people apart.
3. **Critical Thinking** **Making Inferences** Based on the map, why do you think that many European nations became important sea powers?

---

had no cities and no written laws. Instead, they lived in small communities governed by unwritten customs. They were ruled by elected kings, whose chief role was to lead them in war. Warrior nobles swore oaths of loyalty and fought for the king in exchange for weapons and booty.

Between 400 and 700, the Germanic tribes carved up Western Europe into small kingdoms. The strongest and most successful kingdom was that of the Franks.

In 481, Clovis, a ruler of great energy and ability, became king of the Franks. Under his brilliant but ruthless leadership, the Franks were able to conquer the former Roman province of Gaul. Clovis ruled his new lands according to Frankish custom. At the same time, however, he managed to preserve much of the Roman legacy in Gaul.

Clovis's reign reached an important turning point when he converted to Christianity, the religion of many of his new subjects. (See page 184.) In doing so, he not only earned the support of the Gauls but also gained a powerful ally, the Roman Catholic Church.

Islam: A New Mediterranean Power

Shortly after the Franks and other Germanic peoples had carved up Western Europe, a powerful new force, Islam, swept out of the Middle East into the Mediterranean world. As you will read in Chapter 11, Islam is a religion that emerged in Arabia in 632. Within 200 years, Muslims, as believers in the Islamic faith are called, had built a great empire and created a major new civilization.

Christians watched with fear as Muslim armies won victories around the Mediterranean. (See the map on page 190.) They overran Christian kingdoms in North Africa and Spain, then headed into France. At the battle of Tours in 732, Frankish warriors led by Charles Martel defeated a Muslim army. Christians saw the victory as a sign that God was on their side. Muslims advanced no farther into Western Europe, although they continued to rule most of Spain.

To European Christians, the Muslim presence was a source of anxiety and anger. Even when Islam was no longer a threat, Christians continued to have a hostile view of the Muslim world. Still, medieval Europeans did learn from the Arabs, whose knowledge in many areas, especially science and mathematics, was superior to their own.

The Age of Charlemagne

For a time around 800, Western Europe had a moment of unity when the grandson of Charles Martel built an empire reaching across France, Germany, and part of Italy. The founder of this empire is known to history as Charlemagne (SHAHR luh mayn), or Charles the Great.

Standing more than six feet tall, Charlemagne towered over most people of his time.

GLOBAL CONNECTIONS

European Christians may have feared the spread of Islam, but they enjoyed many new vegetables and fruits that the Muslims brought with them. Among them were spinach, eggplant, rice, and melons. In addition, the Muslims imported and planted orange, lemon, and mango trees throughout the Mediterranean region.

Astride a war horse, he was an awesome sight. He spent much of his 46-year reign fighting the Muslims in Spain, the Saxons in the north, the Avars and Slavs in the east, and the Lombards in Italy. In many ways, Charlemagne was an old-fashioned war chief. He loved battle and was a successful conqueror who reunited much of the old Roman empire in Europe. (See the map on page 189.)

Emperor of the Romans. Late in 800, Pope Leo III called on the Frankish king for help against rebellious nobles in Rome. Charlemagne marched south and crushed the rebellious Romans. At services on Christmas Day 800, the pope showed his gratitude by placing a crown on Charlemagne's head and proclaiming him "emperor."

The ceremony would have enormous significance. A Christian pope had crowned a Germanic king successor to the Roman emperors. In doing so, he revived the ideal of a united Christian community.

To the emperor of the eastern Roman empire in Constantinople, however, the pope's action was absurd. The eastern emperor saw himself, and not some backward Frankish king, as the sole Roman ruler. In the long run, Leo's crowning of Charlemagne helped to widen the split between the eastern and western Christian worlds. It also laid the ground for desperate power struggles between the Roman Catholic popes and future Germanic emperors.

Government. Charlemagne tried to exercise control over his many lands and create a united Christian Europe. He worked closely with the Church, helping to spread Christianity to the conquered peoples on the fringes of his empire. During his reign, missionaries won converts among the Saxons and the Slavs.

Like other Germanic kings, Charlemagne appointed powerful nobles to rule local regions. He gave them land so that they could offer support and supply soldiers for his armies. To keep control of these provincial rulers, he sent out officials called *missi dominici* (MIH see dohm in NEE kee) to check on roads, listen to grievances, and see that justice was done. He instructed:

66 Let the *missi* make a diligent investigation whenever any man claims that an injustice has been done to him by

anyone . . . and they shall administer the law fully and justly in the case of the holy churches of God and of the poor, of wards and of widows, and of the whole people.**99**

A Revival of Learning

Charlemagne hoped to make his capital at Aachen (AH kuhn) a "second Rome." To achieve this goal, he made determined efforts to revive Latin learning throughout his empire.

Keeping accurate records. Charlemagne himself could read but not write. He is said to have kept a slate by his bed so that he could practice making letters if he had time before going to sleep at night. Although he made little progress with his own writing skills, he saw the need for officials who could keep complete and accurate records and write clear reports. Education had declined so much that even the supposedly educated clergy were often sadly ignorant, as Charlemagne discovered:

> **66**We have had letters sent to us from Church dignitaries that show a painful weakness in composition. On reading these letters and considering their lack of skill, we began to fear that the writers' knowledge and understanding of the Holy Scriptures might also prove to be much less than it ought to be.**99**

Promoting education and learning. To ensure a supply of educated officials, Charlemagne set up a palace school at Aachen. He then asked a respected scholar, Alcuin (AL kwihn) of York, to run the school. Alcuin set up a curriculum of study based on Latin learning, which became the educational model for medieval Europe. It included the study of grammar, rhetoric, logic, arithmetic, geometry, music, and astronomy.

Alcuin also hired scholars to copy ancient manuscripts, including the Bible and Latin works of history and science. These manuscripts served as the textbooks of Europe for the next 700 years.

Charlemagne's Legacy

After Charlemagne died in 814, his empire soon fell apart. His heirs battled for power for

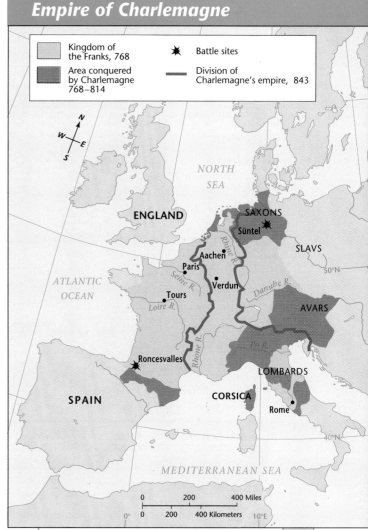

Empire of Charlemagne

Kingdom of the Franks, 768

Area conquered by Charlemagne 768–814

★ Battle sites

— Division of Charlemagne's empire, 843

NORTH SEA

ENGLAND

SAXONS
Süntel ★
Aachen
Paris
Verdun
Tours
Roncesvalles ★

ATLANTIC OCEAN

Rhine R.
Seine R.
Loire R.
Rhone R.
Danube R.
Po R.

SLAVS

AVARS

LOMBARDS

SPAIN

CORSICA

Rome

MEDITERRANEAN SEA

| 0 | 200 | 400 Miles |
| 0 | 200 | 400 Kilometers |

GEOGRAPHY AND HISTORY

By his conquests, Charlemagne nearly doubled Frankish territory. His descendants were unable to hold the empire together, however, and the Treaty of Verdun divided it into three parts in 843.

1. **Location** On the map, locate (a) England, (b) Paris, (c) the Frankish kingdom in 768, (d) Aachen.
2. **Region** Compare the extent of Charlemagne's empire with that of the Roman empire, shown on the map on page 136.
3. **Critical Thinking** Predicting Consequenc[es] What might be one political and one econom[ic] result of the division of Charlemagne's emp[ire]

Invasions of Europe, 700–1000

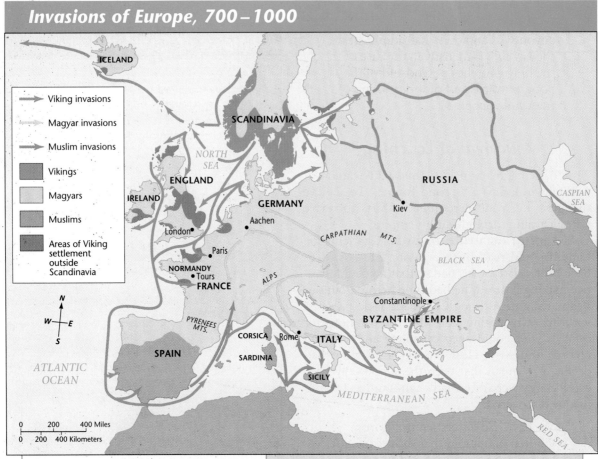

Legend:
- → Viking invasions
- → Magyar invasions
- → Muslim invasions
- Vikings
- Magyars
- Muslims
- Areas of Viking settlement outside Scandinavia

ICELAND

SCANDINAVIA

NORTH SEA

ENGLAND

IRELAND

London

Paris

NORMANDY

Tours

FRANCE

GERMANY

Aachen

RUSSIA

Kiev

CARPATHIAN MTS.

CASPIAN SEA

BLACK SEA

ALPS

Constantinople

BYZANTINE EMPIRE

PYRENEES MTS.

CORSICA

Rome

ITALY

SPAIN

SARDINIA

SICILY

ATLANTIC OCEAN

MEDITERRANEAN SEA

RED SEA

0   200   400 Miles
0   200   400 Kilometers

GEOGRAPHY AND HISTORY

Between 700 and 1000, Western Europe was battered by invaders from other lands. Muslims, Magyars, and Vikings conquered communities and started settlements.

1. Location *On the map, locate (a) North Sea, (b) Scandinavia, (c) Byzantine empire, (d) Tours, (e) Kiev.*

2. Place *(a) Where did the Magyars set out from? (b) Where did the Vikings build settlements? (c) Which parts of Europe were influenced by the Muslims?*

3. Critical Thinking **Comparing** *(a) How did the Viking invasions differ from those of the Magyars and Muslims? (b) How did the Magyar invasions differ from those of the Muslims and Vikings?*

---

nearly 30 years. Finally, in 843, Charlemagne's grandsons drew up the Treaty of Verdun, which split the empire into three regions. (See the map page 189.)

Although Charlemagne's empire crumbled, the Frankish ruler left a lasting legacy. He ... Christian civilization into northern ... furthered the blending of German, ... ristian traditions. He also set up ... government, and later me- ... to his example when they ... own kingdoms.

New Attacks

Even after the defeat at Tours in 732, Muslim forces kept up their pressure on Europe. In the late 800s, they conquered Sicily, which became a thriving center of Islamic culture. It was not until the mid-900s, when power struggles in the Middle East diverted attention from Europe, that Muslim attacks finally subsided.

About 896, a new wave of nomadic people, the Magyars, settled in what is today Hungary. From there, they overran eastern Europe and moved on to plunder Germany, parts of France, and Italy. Finally, after about 50 years, they were pushed back into Hungary.

The most destructive raiders, however, were the Vikings. They snapped the last threads of unity in Charlemagne's empire. These expert sailors and ferocious fighters burst out of Scandinavia, a northern region that now includes Norway, Sweden, and Denmark. They looted and burned communities along the coasts and rivers of Europe, from Ireland to Russia.

▲ *Figurehead of a Viking ship*

The Vikings were not just fierce warriors. They were traders and explorers as well. In their far-ranging voyages, they sailed around the Mediterranean Sea and crossed the Atlantic Ocean. Leif Erikson set up a short-lived Viking colony on the continent of North America in about the year 1000. Other Vikings opened trade routes that linked northern Europe to Mediterranean lands. Vikings also settled in England, northern France (Normandy), Ireland, and parts of Russia.

SECTION 1 REVIEW

1. Identify (a) Clovis, (b) Islam, (c) Charlemagne, (d) Alcuin, (e) Treaty of Verdun, (f) Vikings.

2. What resources did Europe have at the dawn of the Middle Ages?

3. (a) What group led the first wave of invasions of Europe? (b) What groups were part of the second wave of invasions? (c) What was the effect of the invasions?

4. What steps did Charlemagne take to improve government and unify his empire?

5. *Critical Thinking* **Recognizing Points of View** The term *Middle Ages* was coined by Europeans to describe the period from 500 to 1500. Do you think that other civilizations, such as that of China or Islam, use the same term for that period? Why or why not?

6. *ACTIVITY* Write a telegram of 25 words or less reporting on the battle of Tours and describing its significance.

Feudalism and the Manor Economy

Guide for Reading

- How did feudalism shape medieval society?
- What status did noblewomen have in medieval Europe?
- What was the basis of the manor economy?
- **Vocabulary** *vassal, fief, knight, chivalry, troubadour, manor, serf*

It was 1127, and Count William had just inherited the rich lands of Flanders, in Western Europe. In April, the nobles of Flanders gathered to pledge loyalty to their new lord. One by one, they knelt before him. "Will you serve me loyally?" asked William. "I will," the noble replied. He then took a solemn oath:

> ❝I promise on my faith that I will in future be faithful to Count William and will observe my [loyalty] to him completely against all persons in good faith and without deceit.❞

The count then touched the noble with a small rod. With that gesture, he granted the noble a parcel of land, including any towns, castles, or people on it.

Although the words might vary, ceremonies like this one took place all across Europe during the Middle Ages. In public, before witnesses, great nobles and lesser lords exchanged vows of loyalty and service. Those vows were part of a new political and social system that governed medieval life.

A New System of Rule

In the face of invasions by Vikings, Muslims, and Magyars, kings and emperors were too weak to maintain law and order. People needed to defend their homes and lands. In response to that basic need for protection, a new system, called feudalism, evolved.

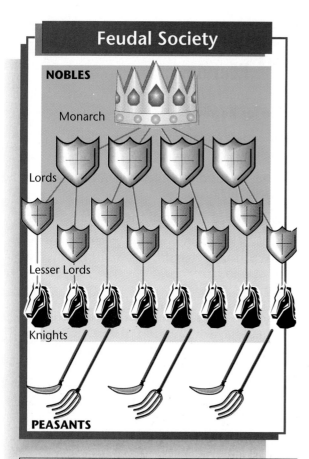

Feudal Society

NOBLES

Monarch

Lords

Lesser Lords

Knights

PEASANTS

Interpreting a Chart Under feudalism, everyone had a well-defined place in society. At the head of society was the monarch. Peasants, who made up the bulk of the population, were at the bottom.
■ *What other groups were part of feudal society?*

As you have read in Chapter 3, feudalism was a loosely organized system of rule in which powerful local lords divided their large land-holdings among the lesser lords. In exchange for land, these lesser lords, or vassals, pledged service and loyalty to the greater lord.

The relationship between lords and vassals was established by custom and tradition. A lord granted his vassal a fief (FEEF), or estate. Estates ranged from a few acres to hundreds of square miles and included peasants to work the land, as well as any towns or buildings on the land. Besides granting the estate, the lord also promised to protect his vassal.

In return, the vassal pledged loyalty to his lord. He also agreed to provide the lord with 40 days of military service each year, certain money payments, and advice.

Lords, Vassals, and Knights

Everyone had a place in feudal society, as the chart at left shows. Below the monarch were the most powerful lords—dukes and counts—who held the largest fiefs. Each of these lords had vassals, and these vassals in turn had their own vassals. In many cases, the same man was both vassal and lord—vassal to a more powerful lord above him and lord to a less powerful vassal below him.

Because vassals often held fiefs from more than one lord, feudal relationships grew very complex. A vassal who had pledged loyalty to several lords could have serious problems if his overlords quarreled with each other. What was he to do if both demanded his aid? To solve this problem, a vassal usually had a liege lord to whom he owed his first loyalty.

The World of Warriors

Feudal lords battled constantly for power, and for feudal nobles warfare was a way of life. Many nobles trained from boyhood for a future occupation as a knight, or mounted warrior.

Training for knighthood. At the age of seven, a boy slated to become a knight was sent away to the castle of his father's lord. There, he learned to ride and fight. He also learned to keep his armor and weapons in good condition. Training was difficult and discipline was strict. Any laziness was punished with an angry blow or even a severe beating.

When his training was finished, often when he was about age 21, the boy was ready to be made a knight. Kneeling before an older knight, he bowed his head. The knight struck the young man with his hand or the flat side of his sword and declared something like the following: "In the name of God, Saint Michael, and Saint George, I dub thee knight. Be valiant." After this "dubbing," the young knight took his place beside other warriors.

ISSUES *For* **TODAY** In feudal society, everyone knew his or her place. What are the benefits and drawbacks of a clearly defined social order?

As the fierce fighting of the early Middle Ages lessened in the 1100s, tournaments, or mock battles, came into fashion. A powerful lord would invite knights from the surrounding area to a tournament to enter these contests of fighting skill. At first, tournaments were as dangerous as real battles, and captured knights were held for ransom. In time, they acquired more ceremony and ritual.

Castles. During the early Middle Ages, powerful lords fortified their homes to withstand attack. Their strongholds included a keep, or wooden tower, ringed by a fence. The keep was separated from the surrounding area by a moat, or water-filled ditch.

The strongholds gradually became larger and grander. By the 1100s, royal rulers and nobles owned sprawling stone castles with high walls, towers, and drawbridges over wide moats. Wars often centered on seizing castles that commanded strategic river crossings, harbors, or mountain passes. Castle dwellers stored up food and water so that they could withstand a long siege. If attackers failed to starve the defenders into surrender, they might tunnel under the castle walls.

Role of noblewomen. Noblewomen as well as noblemen played active roles in this warrior society. The "lady" became "lord of the manor" while her husband or father was off fighting. She supervised vassals, managed the household, and performed necessary agricultural and medical tasks. Sometimes she might even have to go to war to defend her estate.

Some medieval noblewomen, like Eleanor of Aquitaine, took a hand in politics. Eleanor inherited vast lands in southwestern France. Through two marriages, she became, first, queen of France and, later, queen of England. For more than 70 years, Eleanor was a leading force in European affairs.

Women's rights to inheritance were severely restricted under the feudal system. Land was usually inherited by the eldest son in a family. Women did, however, receive land as part of their dowry, and fierce negotiations swirled around an unmarried or widowed heiress. If her husband died before her, a woman regained rights to her land.

Like their brothers, the daughters of nobles were sent to friends or relatives for training. Before her parents arranged her marriage, a young woman was expected to know how to spin, weave, and supervise servants. A few learned to read and write. As a wife, she was expected to bear many children and be dutiful and loyal to her husband.

Chivalry. In the later Middle Ages, knights adopted a code of conduct called chivalry. Chivalry required knights to be brave, loyal, and true to their word. In warfare, they had to fight fairly and be generous to their enemies. Knights, for example, agreed not to attack another knight before he had a chance to put on his armor and prepare for battle. Chivalry also dictated that warriors treat a captured knight well or even release him if he promised to pay his ransom. Chivalry had limits, though. It applied to nobles only, not to commoners.

Chivalry raised women to a new status. The code of chivalry called for women to be protected and cherished. Troubadours, or wandering poets, adopted this view. Their love songs

Knight in Armor To do battle, a knight needed armor and helmet, shield, lance, and sword. He also needed several horses, with armor and saddles. Finally, to care for the horses and equipment, he needed the services of a squire, or knight in training. **Economics and Technology** *What economic reason helps to explain why nobles and not peasants became knights?*

praised the perfection, beauty, and wit of women throughout the ages. Much later, ideas of chivalry would shape our modern ideas of romantic love.

The Manor

The heart of the medieval economy was the manor, or lord's estate. Most manors included one or more villages and the surrounding lands. Peasants, who made up the majority of medieval society, lived and worked on the manor.

Peasants and lords. Most of the peasants on a manor were serfs, who were bound to the land. Serfs were not slaves who could be bought and sold. Still, they were not free. They could not leave the manor without the lord's permission. And if the manor was granted to a new lord, the serfs went along with it.

Peasants and their lords were tied together by mutual rights and responsibilities. Peasants had to work several days a week farming the lord's domain, or lands. They also had to repair the lord's roads, bridges, and fences. Peasants paid the lord a fee when they married, when they inherited their father's acres, or when they used the local mill to grind grain. Other payments fell due at Christmas and Easter. Because money had largely disappeared from medieval Europe, they paid with products such as grain, fruit, honey, eggs, or chickens.

In return for a lifetime of labor, peasants had the right to farm several acres for themselves. They were also entitled to their lord's protection from Viking raids or feudal warfare. Although they could not leave the manor without permission, they also could not be forced off it. In theory, at least, they were guaranteed food, housing, and land.

A narrow world. The medieval manor was a small, self-sufficient world. Peasants produced almost everything they needed, from food and clothing to simple furniture and tools. Most peasants never ventured more than a few miles from their village. They had no schooling and no knowledge of the larger world.

A typical manor included a few dozen one-room huts clustered close together in a village. (★ See *Skills for Success*, page 206.) Nearby stood a water mill to grind grain, a tiny church, and the manor house. The fields surrounding the village were divided into narrow strips. Each family had strips of land in different fields so that good and bad land was shared fairly. Half the land was left fallow, or unplanted, each year, to allow the soil to regain its fertility.

Daily Life

For most peasants, life was harsh. Men, women, and children worked long hours, from sunup to sundown. During planting season, a man might guide an ox-drawn plow while his wife goaded the ox into motion with a pointed stick. Children helped plant seeds, weeded, and took care of pigs or sheep.

The peasant family ate a simple diet of black bread with vegetables such as peas, cabbage, turnips, or onions. They seldom had meat unless they poached wild game at the risk of harsh punishment. If they lived near a river, a meal might include fish. At night, the family and any cows, chickens, pigs, or sheep slept together in their one-room hut.

Feudal Justice *Feudal justice was very different from Roman ideas of law. In this illustration of a trial by ordeal, a woman walks over red-hot coals. If she is burned, she is judged guilty. If she emerges unharmed, it is held as proof that God has found her innocent.* **Continuity and Change** *What method is used to try people accused of crimes today?*

Seasons. Like farmers everywhere, European peasants worked according to the season. In spring and autumn, they plowed and harvested. In summer, they hayed. At other times, they weeded, repaired fences, and performed chores. Hunger was common, especially in late winter when the harvest was exhausted and new crops had not yet ripened. Disease took a heavy toll, and few peasants lived beyond the age of 35.

Celebrations. Despite life's grimness, peasants found occasions to celebrate, such as marriages and births. Welcome breaks came on holidays such as Christmas and Easter, when they had a week off from work.

Dozens of other festivals in the Christian calendar brought days off, too. For these times, people might butcher an animal so that they could feast on meat. There would also be dancing and rough sports, from wrestling to ball games.

Beliefs. On the sabbath, peasants might attend chapel. After services, they gossiped or danced, even though the priest might condemn their racy songs or rowdy behavior.

In medieval Europe, people believed in elves, fairies, and other nature spirits. They had faith in love potions and magic charms. Witches, they thought, could cast spells with a mere look.

Priests tried to "Christianize" these old beliefs and practices. They built churches where temples to ancient gods had once stood. Where villagers had once sacrificed to the gods of the sun and rain to ensure good crops, priests might bless the fields in the name of Christ.

SECTION 2 REVIEW

1. **Define** (a) vassal, (b) fief, (c) knight, (d) chivalry, (e) troubadour, (f) manor, (g) serf.
2. Describe three features of feudal society.
3. How did chivalry affect the status of women?
4. (a) What responsibilities did the peasant have toward the lord? (b) What responsibilities did the lord have toward the peasant?
5. *Critical Thinking* **Recognizing Causes and Effects** How did the breakdown of central authority in Europe lead to the development of feudalism?
6. *ACTIVITY* Imagine that you are a peasant on a medieval manor. Write a diary entry for a typical day of your life.

3 The Medieval Church

Guide for Reading

- How did the Church dominate life in the Middle Ages?

- How did monks and nuns influence European life?

- Why did reform movements spring up within the Church?

- **Vocabulary** *secular, sacrament, canon law, excommunication, interdict, tithe, anti-Semitism*

The Lady Hirsendis waved goodbye to her husband as he set off for Jerusalem. Then she turned to her own responsibilities, looking after the family's lands in her husband's absence. First, however, she must ride to the monastery of Marmoutier, to pray to St. Martin. She would also pay her respects to the abbot, or head of the monastery.

Religion was woven into the fabric of the medieval world. Indeed, the Middle Ages has often been called Europe's "age of faith." The commanding force behind that faith was the Christian Church.

A Spiritual and Worldly Empire

After the fall of Rome, the Christian Church split into eastern and western churches. The western church, headed by the pope, became known as the Roman Catholic Church. The Roman Catholic Church grew stronger and wealthier during the Middle Ages. In time, it not only controlled the spiritual life of Christians, but was also the most powerful secular, or worldly, force in Western Europe.

The Church hierarchy. The pope was the spiritual leader of the Roman Catholic Church. He also ruled vast lands in central Italy, known as the Papal States. As the spiritual heir and representative of Christ on Earth, the pope claimed to have authority over all secular rulers.

An army of churchmen supervised the Church's many activities. High Church officials were usually nobles. Some archbishops and

Legend	
Mostly Christian, 476	Muslim, 1050
Mostly Christian, added by 1050	⊕ Monastery

NORWAY
SWEDEN
SCOTLAND
IRELAND
NORTH SEA
DENMARK
ENGLAND
BALTIC SEA
RUSSIA
ATLANTIC OCEAN
Canterbury
GERMANY
Bingen
FRANCE
Cluny
SPAIN
ITALY
BLACK SEA
CORSICA
Assisi
PAPAL STATES
Rome
Monte Cassino
Constantinople
SARDINIA
BYZANTINE EMPIRE
SICILY
CRETE
MEDITERRANEAN SEA

0   200   400 Miles
0   200   400 Kilometers

GEOGRAPHY AND HISTORY

In the years following the fall of Rome, Roman Catholic missionaries helped spread Christianity throughout Europe.

1. **Location** On the map, locate (a) Papal States, (b) France, (c) Spain, (d) Bingen, (e) Assisi, (f) Rome.
2. **Region** (a) Name three areas of Europe that were Christian in 476. (b) Name three areas that became Christian between 476 and 1050. (c) Which area of Europe remained Muslim?
3. **Critical Thinking Understanding Sequence** What device is used on this map to demonstrate a sequence of events? Explain.

bishops had their own territories, like other feudal lords. Since they were often the only educated people, feudal rulers appointed them to administer their own governments.

Authority of the Church. Medieval Christians believed that all people were sinners, doomed to eternal suffering. The only way to avoid the tortures of hell was to participate in the sacraments, which are the sacred rituals of the Church. Through faith in Christ and participation in the sacraments, Christians could achieve salvation—eternal life in heaven. Because it decided who could participate in the sacraments, and thus who could gain salvation, the Church had absolute power in the religious life of Christians during the Middle Ages.

The Church had its own body of laws, known as canon law, and its own courts. Canon law applied to religious teachings, the behavior of the clergy, and even marriages and morals.

Anyone who refused to obey Church laws faced a range of penalties. The most severe was excommunication. People who were excommunicated could not receive the sacraments. To people who believed in the tortures of hell, such a punishment was truly terrifying. People who were excommunicated also could not be buried in sacred ground. All other Christians were required to shun them.

A powerful noble who violated Church laws could face an interdict, which excluded an entire town, region, or kingdom from participating in most sacraments and from receiving Christian burial. Even the strongest ruler was likely to give in to that pressure.

The Church and Daily Life

Most Christians had no contact with the pope or the higher clergy. They saw only their local priest, who supervised their religious life and provided comfort during times of trouble. The English poet Geoffrey Chaucer fondly described a poor town priest:

> 66Wide was his parish, with
>   houses far asunder,
>   But he would not be kept by
>   rain or thunder,
>   If any had suffered a sickness
>   or a blow,
>   From visiting the farthest,
>   high or low,
>   Plodding his way on foot, his
>   staff in hand,
>   He was a model his flock could
>   understand.99

The village church. For peasants, religion was linked to the routines of daily life. In the village church, priests baptized their children and performed their marriages. In addition, the church was a social center, where they exchanged news and gossip. In the later Middle Ages, some priests ran schools in the church.

Villagers took pride in the church building, which they decorated with care. Some churches housed relics, the bones or blood of martyrs or other holy figures. Visitors would make pilgrimages, or journeys, to pray before the relics.

The tithe. To support itself, the Church required all Christians to pay a *tithe,* or tax equal to a tenth of their incomes. The idea of a tithe had existed in ancient religions before Christianity. The Church used the tithe to help the poor.

Women and the Church. The Church taught that men and women were equal before God. On Earth, however, women were inferior to men. The Church presented women in two extreme roles. On the one hand, women were seen as "daughters of Eve," weak and easily led into sin, and thus needing the guidance of a man. On the other hand, there was the ideal woman, modest and pure in spirit, personified by Mary, "mother of God." Faced with these two extremes, the ordinary woman had little to follow in the way of a realistic role model.

The Church tried to protect women. It set a minimum age for marriage. Church courts fined men who seriously injured their wives. Yet the Church upheld a double standard, punishing women for offenses much more harshly than men.

Monks and Nuns

Both women and men might withdraw from worldly life to become nuns or monks. Behind the thick walls of monasteries and convents, they devoted their lives to spiritual goals.

The Benedictine Rule. About 530, a monk named Benedict founded the monastery of Monte Cassino in Italy. He drew up a set of rules to regulate life there. In time, the Benedictine Rule, as it became known, spread to monasteries and convents across Europe.

Under the Benedictine Rule, monks and nuns took an oath of poverty. They also took vows of chastity, or purity, and of obedience to the abbot. Their chief duties were prayer and worship of God. However, Benedict also believed in the spiritual value of manual labor, and he required monks to work in the fields or at other physical tasks.

A life of service. In a world without hospitals, public schools, or social programs, convents and monasteries provided basic social services. Monks and nuns tended the sick. They gave alms, or charity, to the poor and set up schools for children. Travelers, especially Christian pilgrims traveling to holy shrines, could find food and a night's lodging at many monasteries and convents.

Centers of learning. Monasteries and convents performed a vital cultural function by preserving the writings of the ancient world.

ART HISTORY

Illuminated Manuscript *Monks, nuns, and other skilled artisans copied books by hand and illuminated, or illustrated, each page. They decorated the letters and framed the text with intricate designs, biblical scenes, or portrayals of daily life.* **Art and Literature** *Describe the decorations on the illuminated manuscript shown here.*

Most often, monks and nuns simply copied the ancient books as a form of labor. Once copied out, the work itself—Virgil's *Aeneid,* for example—might rest unread on a monastery shelf for centuries. Still, it would be there when scholars once again took an interest in such things.

Some monks and nuns were better educated and took a more serious interest in culture. The Italian abbot Cassiodorus, for example, wrote valuable summaries of Greek and Latin works. He also taught the Latin and Greek classics to the monks who served under him.

Other monks, like the Venerable Bede in England, produced scholarly works of their own. Bede was the first to use the designations B.C. and A.D.—meaning before and after the birth of Christ—to date historical events. Bede, a historian, was concerned with the truth. But like all writers of the time, he mixed stories of magical miracles with historical fact.

Missionaries. Not all monks and nuns remained isolated from the outside world. During the early Middle Ages, men and women risked their lives to spread Christian teachings across Europe.

St. Patrick was a monk who crossed to Ireland and set up the Irish Church. Pope Gregory the Great sent another monk, St. Augustine, as a missionary to the Angles and Saxons in England. He became the first archbishop of Canterbury. Later, the Church honored some of its missionaries by declaring them saints.

Hildegard of Bingen: Adviser to Popes and Kings

The very first vision, Hildegard recalled, occurred when she was a child of three. "I kept it hidden until God in His grace willed to have it made public," she later wrote. This vision, soon followed by others, marked the beginning of an extraordinary life. Hildegard would become a composer, writer, abbess, and adviser to the great men and women of her day. Even the pope recognized her special gift as a prophet.

Commanded by God. Perhaps in response to her visions, Hildegard's parents placed her in a convent at an early age. There, she would get an education, and if she did not

marry, she might take religious vows. By the age of 14, Hildegard had made her decision: She would become a nun.

During 24 years of convent life, Hildegard followed the daily routine—reading, singing God's praises, and keeping busy copying books, weaving cloth, and doing other manual work. Then, when she was 38 years old, she was named abbess, or head of the convent.

Not long after assuming the duties of abbess, Hildegard had a new vision:

> 66 A great flash of light from heaven pierced my brain. . . . In that instant my mind was imbued with the meaning of the sacred books, the Psalter, the Gospel, and the other books of the Old and New Testament. 99

A voice accompanying the vision commanded Hildegard to "set down all things according to the secrets of their mysteries."

The Work of Nuns *Nuns like Hildegard of Bingen made important contributions to society. Besides advising kings and popes, Hildegard composed more than 80 pieces of religious music, compiled a medical book entitled* Causes and Cures, *and wrote several works criticizing corruption in the Church. Here, a group of nuns waits to receive a blessing.* **Continuity and Change** *Do members of religious orders play a social role today? Explain.*

Certain that the command came from God, Hildegard began writing the first of several books. It dealt with subjects ranging from science, medicine, and philosophy to Christian teachings and morals. Hildegard's writing, expressed in mystical terms, clearly revealed her own extensive knowledge and brilliant mind.

A sage and prophet. In 1147, Hildegard founded a new convent, near Bingen, in Germany. Even before moving to Bingen, Hildegard had gained a reputation as a sage and a prophet. Now, reports of her visions and writings spread across Europe. Popes, emperors, kings, and queens sought her advice.

Hildegard did not hesitate to speak her mind and encouraged or scolded churchmen and rulers alike. "Take care that the Highest King does not strike you down because of the blindness that prevents you from governing justly," she warned the German emperor Frederick I. To Eleanor of Aquitaine, who for some 70 years played a central role in European politics, she wrote: "Make peace with God and with men, and God will help you in your tribulations."

Growing restrictions on women. Hildegard was not the only nun to raise her voice in the early Middle Ages. Many women with inquiring minds and proud spirits entered convents. But as the Church grew more powerful, it began to restrict nuns' activities. It withdrew rights they had once had to preach the Gospel or hear confession. It frowned on too much learning for women, preferring them to accept the Church's authority. The tradition of women mystical writers continued for a while, but by the early 1400s, the increasingly heavy restrictions on women's activities made it hard for other women to earn a position of power as Hildegard had done. ▪

Reform Movements

The very success of the medieval Church brought serious problems. As its wealth and power grew, discipline weakened. The clergy tended to be worldly, and many lived in luxury. Monks and nuns ignored their vows. Married priests devoted more time to the interests of their families than to their Church duties. The growing corruption and moral decay led to demands for reform.

The monastery at Cluny. In the early 900s, the pious Abbot Berno at Cluny, a monastery in eastern France, set out to end abuses. First, he revived the Benedictine Rule. He also announced that he would not permit nobles to interfere in the running of the monastery. Finally, he filled the monastery with men who were devoted solely to religious pursuits. Other monasteries copied the Cluniac program, spreading Abbot Berno's reforms across Western Europe.

In 1073, a new pope, Gregory VII, extended the Cluniac reforms throughout the entire Church. He prohibited simony (SIHM uh nee), the selling of positions in the Church, and outlawed marriage for priests. Gregory then called on Christians to renew their faith. To end outside influence, he insisted that the Church, and not kings and nobles, choose Church officials. That policy would lead to a battle of wills with the German emperor, as you will read.

Preaching orders. A different approach to reform was taken by friars, monks who traveled widely, preaching to the poor, especially in Europe's growing towns. The first order of friars, the Franciscans, was founded by a wealthy young Italian known as Francis of Assisi. When he was about 20 years old, Francis underwent a religious conversion. Leaving his father's prosperous home, he devoted himself to preaching the Christian message and teaching by his own examples of good works.

The Spanish reformer St. Dominic also founded a preaching order of friars to work in the larger world. He, too, called for friars to live in poverty as the early Christians had. Dominic was particularly upset by the spread of heresies, religious beliefs or doctrines that differed from accepted Church teachings. The Dominicans dedicated themselves to educating people about Church doctrines and disputing the ideas of the heretics.

Some women responded to the call of reform by creating groups that were independent of the regular Church orders. One such group was the Beguines (BEHG eenz). Most convents accepted only well-born women who gave their dowry to the Church. The Beguines were made up of women who did not have sufficient financial means to enter a convent. Supporting themselves through their weaving and embroidering,

Seder Plate *Throughout Europe, Jewish communities observed their unique traditions and customs. This Seder plate belonged to a family living in Muslim Spain. At the Passover holiday each year, the plate was filled with the traditional foods of the Seder, or Passover meal.* **Diversity** *Why does one often need courage to be different from others?*

the Beguines ministered to the poor and set up hospitals and shelters.

Jews in Western Europe

Medieval Europe was home to numerous Jewish communities. After the Romans expelled them from Palestine, the Jews had scattered all around the Mediterranean. In their new homes, they preserved the oral and written laws that were central to their faith.

These Mediterranean, or Sephardic, Jews flourished particularly in Spain. The Arab Muslims who gained control of Spain in the 700s were tolerant of both Christians and Jews. Jewish culture flowered in Muslim Spain, which became a major center of Hebrew scholarship. Jews also served as officials in Muslim royal courts.

Jews spread into northern Europe as well. There, they became known as Ashkenazim, or "German" Jews. Many Christian rulers in northern Europe protected or tolerated hard-working Jewish communities, although they taxed them heavily. Early German kings gave educated Jews positions in their courts. Charlemagne, for example, appointed Isaac, a Jew, to serve as interpreter for envoys sent to the Muslim ruler Harun al Rashid in Baghdad.

Often, however, medieval Christians persecuted Jews. As the Church's power increased, it barred Jews from owning land or practicing most occupations, including trade and handicrafts. The Church also charged that Jews were responsible for the death of Jesus, thus laying the foundations for anti-Semitism, or prejudice against Jews.

In bad times, anti-Semitism increased. Christians blamed Jews for all kinds of ills, including diseases and famines. Because many Jews were moneylenders, people blamed them for their own economic hardships. As persecution worsened in Western Europe, large numbers of Jews migrated into Eastern Europe. There, they built communities that survived until modern times. (See the map on page 250.)

SECTION 3 REVIEW

1. **Identify** (a) Roman Catholic Church, (b) Benedictine Rule, (c) Cluny, (d) Francis of Assisi, (e) Dominicans, (f) Beguines.
2. **Define** (a) secular, (b) sacrament, (c) canon law, (d) excommunication, (e) interdict, (f) tithe, (g) anti-Semitism.
3. Describe three ways in which the Church shaped medieval life.
4. (a) What views did the Church hold about women? (b) How did the Church views of women change over time?
5. How did monks and nuns help build Christian civilization in Europe?
6. *Critical Thinking* **Analyzing Information** Why do you think important leaders accepted the scolding and advice of Hildegard, an "inferior" woman?
7. *ACTIVITY* When copying out old texts, monks and nuns often decorated the first letter of a paragraph and the margins of a page with brilliant designs. (See the picture on page 197.) Imagine that you are a medieval monk. Copy and decorate the Chaucer poem on page 196.

4 Economic Expansion and Change

Guide for Reading

■ How did new technologies lead to an agricultural revolution?

■ What economic and social changes occurred in the High Middle Ages?

■ What was life like in a medieval town?

■ **Vocabulary** *charter, capital, usury, guild, apprentice*

The castle of Count William of Flanders was a bustling place. Hundreds of people lived and worked there, from lords and ladies to household knights and servants. Such a large establishment had many needs. As people sought to supply them, the castle became the center of a new town. A medieval chronicler describes the process:

66There began to throng before the gate near the castle bridge, traders and merchants selling costly goods. Then came inn-keepers to feed and house those doing business with the [lord] . . . and these built houses and set up their inns . . . and the houses so increased that there grew up a town.99

The appearance of new towns was a symbol of the economic revival that began in Europe about 1000. This period of revival, which spanned from 1000 to 1300, is called the High Middle Ages. These centuries saw remarkable changes that would greatly strengthen Western Europe.

An Agricultural Revolution

By 1000, Europe's economic recovery was well underway. It had begun in the countryside, where peasants adapted new farming technologies that made their fields more productive. The result was an agricultural revolution that transformed Europe.

New technologies. By about 800, ants were using new iron plows that carved into the heavy soil of northern Europe. T were a big improvement over the old wood plows, which had been designed for the lig soils of the Mediterranean region. Also, a new kind of harness allowed peasants to use horses rather than oxen to pull the plows. Because faster-moving horses could plow more land in a day than oxen, peasants could now enlarge their fields and plant more crops.

Looking up, a peasant might have seen another new device, a windmill, turning slowly against the sky. Where there were no fast-moving streams to turn a water mill, the power of the wind had been harnessed to grind the peasants' grain into flour.

Expanding production. Other changes brought still more land into use and further increased food production. Feudal lords who wanted to boost their incomes pushed peasants to clear forests, drain swamps, and reclaim wasteland for farming and grazing.

Peasants also adopted the three-field system. They planted one field in grain, a second with legumes, such as peas and beans, and left the third fallow. The legumes restored soil fertility while adding variety to the peasant diet. Unlike the old two-field system, the new method left only a third—rather than half—of the land unplanted.

All these improvements let farmers produce more food. With more food available, the population grew. Between about 1000 and 1300, the population of Europe doubled.

Trade Revives

Europe's growing population needed goods that were not available on the manor. Peasants needed iron for farm tools. Wealthy nobles wanted fine wool, furs, and spices from Asia. As foreign invasions and feudal warfare declined, traders reappeared, criss-crossing Europe to meet the growing demand for goods.

New trade routes. Enterprising traders formed merchant companies that traveled in armed caravans for safety. They set up regular trade routes. Along these routes, merchants exchanged local goods for those from remote markets in Asia and the Middle East.

...erchants bought Chi-
...ld jewelry, and Asian
...ese goods to Venice on
...ice, traders loaded their
...s and headed north over
...hine River to Flanders. In
...ers bought the goods to
...id and the lands along the
...hern Europeans paid for the
...oducts like honey, furs, fine cloth,
...d.

...de fairs. At first, traders and customers
...t local trade fairs. These fairs took place
...ar navigable rivers or where trade routes met.

People from the surrounding villages, towns, and castles flocked to the fairs. Peasants traded farm goods and animals. As they ate and drank, they enjoyed the antics of jugglers, acrobats, or even a dancing bear. They had no money to buy the fine woolens, swords, sugar, and silks offered by the merchants, however. The customers for these luxuries were the feudal rulers, nobles, and wealthy churchmen.

New towns. The fairs closed in the autumn when the weather made roads impassable. Merchants might wait out the winter months near a castle or in a town with a bishop's palace. These settlements attracted artisans who made goods that the merchants could sell.

Slowly, these small centers of trade and handicraft developed into the first real medieval cities. Some boasted populations of 10,000, and a few topped 100,000. Europe had not seen towns of this size since Roman times.

The most prosperous cities grew up in northern Italy and Flanders. Both areas were centers of the wool trade and had prosperous textile industries. Each anchored one end of the profitable north-south trade routes across Europe.

To protect their interests, the merchants who set up a new town would ask the local lord, or if possible the king himself, for a charter, or written document that set out the rights and privileges of the town. In return for the charter, merchants paid the lord or the king a large sum of money or a yearly fee or both.

Although charters varied from place to place, they almost always granted townspeople the right to choose their own leaders and control their own affairs. Most charters also had a clause, popular with runaway serfs, that declared that anyone who lived in the town for a year and a day was free. "Town air makes free," was a common medieval saying.

A Commercial Revolution

As trade revived, money reappeared. This, in turn, led to more changes. Merchants, for example, needed money to buy goods, so they borrowed from moneylenders. In time, their need for capital, or money for investment, spurred the growth of banking houses.

New business practices. To meet the needs of the changing economy, Europeans developed new ways of doing business. For example, many merchants joined together in an organization known as a partnership. Under this setup, a group of merchants pooled their funds to finance a large-scale venture that would have been too costly for any individual trader.

Merchants also developed a system of insurance to help reduce business risks. For a small fee, an underwriter would insure the merchant's shipment. If the goods arrived safely, the merchant lost only the small insurance payment. If the shipment was lost or destroyed, the underwriter paid the merchant most of its value.

Europeans adapted other business practices from Middle Eastern merchants. Among the most important was the bill of exchange. A merchant deposited money with a banker in his home city. The banker issued a bill of exchange, which the merchant exchanged for cash in a distant city. A merchant could thus travel without carrying gold coins, which were easily stolen.

Social changes. These new ways of doing business were part of a commercial revolution that transformed the medieval economy. Slowly, they also reshaped medieval society.

The use of money, for example, undermined serfdom. Feudal lords needed money to buy fine clothes, weapons, furniture, and other goods. As a result, many peasants began selling farm products to townspeople and fulfilling their obligations to their lords by paying their rent with money rather than with labor. By 1300, most peasants in Western Europe were either tenant farmers, who paid rent for their land, or hired farm laborers.

Trade in Medieval Europe

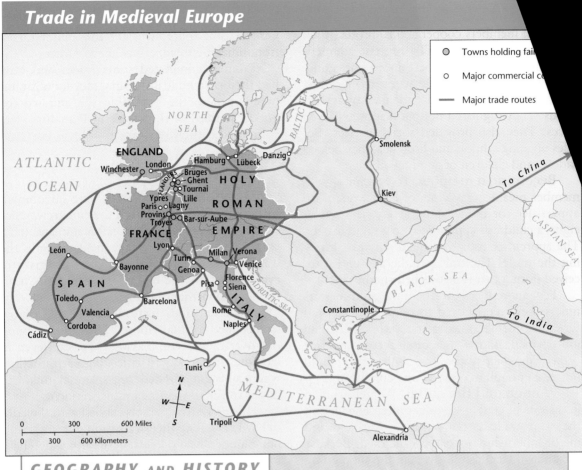

GEOGRAPHY AND HISTORY

Growing population in medieval Europe led to a need for more goods. As trade revived, trade routes multiplied and many towns hosted annual trade fairs.

1. Location On the map, locate (a) Flanders, (b) Bruges, (c) Venice.
2. Region In which two areas were most of the principal commercial centers located?
3. Critical Thinking **Linking Past and Present** What might be today's equivalent of a medieval trade fair? Explain.

In towns, the old social order of nobles, clergy, and peasants gradually changed. By 1000, a new class appeared that included merchants, traders, and artisans. They formed a middle class, standing between nobles and peasants. There were a number of independent women. In towns, they had the right to carry on trade and buy and sell their own property.

Nobles and the clergy despised the new middle class. To nobles, towns were a disruptive influence beyond their control. To the clergy, the profits that merchants and bankers made from usury (YOO zhuh ree), or lending money at interest, were immoral.

Role of Guilds

Merchant guilds, or associations, dominated life in medieval towns. They passed laws, levied taxes, and decided whether to spend funds to pave the streets with cobblestones, build protective walls for the city, or raise a new town hall.

In time, artisans came to resent the powerful merchants. They organized craft guilds. Each guild represented workers in one occupation, such as weavers, bakers, brewers, sword makers, and goldsmiths. In some towns, the struggles between craft guilds and the wealthier merchant guilds led to riots and revolts.

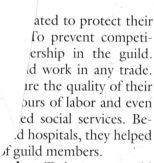

...ated to protect their ... To prevent competi- ...ership in the guild. ...d work in any trade. ...re the quality of their ...ours of labor and even ...ed social services. Be- ...d hospitals, they helped ...f guild members.

...ember. To become a guild ...any years of hard work as an ... trainee. At the age of seven or ...was apprenticed to a guild master. ...ntice usually spent seven years learn- ...rade. The only pay the apprentice re- ...during that time was bed and board.

...Few apprentices ever became guild masters ...less they were related to one. Most labored for guild members as salaried workers, called journeymen. Journeymen often accused masters of keeping their wages low so that they could not save enough to open a competing shop.

Women and the guilds. Women worked in dozens of crafts. A woman often engaged in the same trade as her father or husband and might inherit his workshop if he died. Because she knew the craft well, she kept the shop going and sometimes became a guild master herself.

Girls became apprentices in trades ranging from ribbonmaking to papermaking to surgery.

Women dominated some trades and even had their own guilds. In Paris, they far outnumbered men in the profitable silk and woolen guilds. A third of the guilds in Frankfurt were composed entirely of women.

City Life

Medieval towns and cities were surrounded by high, protective walls. As the city grew, space within the walls filled to overflowing, and newcomers had to settle in the fields outside the walls. To keep up with this constant growth, every few years the city might rebuild its walls farther and farther out.

Medieval cities were a jumble of narrow streets lined with tall houses. Upper floors hung out over the streets, making them dim even in daytime. In the largest cities, a great cathedral, where a bishop presided, or a splendid guild hall might tower above the humbler residences.

During the day, streets echoed with the cries of hawkers selling their wares and porters grumbling under heavy loads. A wealthy merchant might pass, followed by a procession of servants. At night, the unlit streets were deserted.

Artisans at Work The workers on the left are making a cabinet, while those on the right are producing tapestries. In towns all over medieval Europe, middle-class artisans specialized in a wide variety of crafts. **Continuity and Change** How do factories of today differ from medieval workshops?

Street Performers

In medieval times, as today, not all entertainers performed on a stage in a theater before a large audience. For some, the stage is a street or a square, a field or a park. Their audience consists of passersby. And their pay is the applause and donations of the crowd.

Linking Past and Present Based on the pictures below, has street entertainment changed since the Middle Ages? Explain.

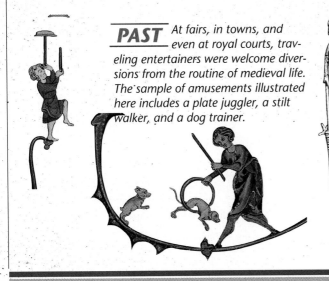

PAST At fairs, in towns, and even at royal courts, traveling entertainers were welcome diversions from the routine of medieval life. The sample of amusements illustrated here includes a plate juggler, a stilt walker, and a dog trainer.

PRESENT At New York City's Washington Square Park, a creative street performer captivates onlookers with a most unusual balancing act.

Even a rich town had no garbage collection or sewer system. Residents simply flung their wastes into the street. Larger cities might pass laws requiring butchers, for example, to dump their garbage on the edge of town. But towns remained filthy, smelly, noisy, and crowded.

Looking Ahead

By 1300, Western Europe was a different place from what it had been in the early Middle Ages. Although most people had no way of knowing it, slow but momentous changes were sending shock waves through medieval life. Trade, for example, put ideas as well as money into circulation. New riches revised the social structure. In politics, too, new forces were at work.

In the global sphere, the economic revival of the High Middle Ages was bringing Europeans into contact with civilizations much more advanced than their own. From these lands came products, ideas, and technologies that would spark an even greater transformation in how Europeans thought and lived.

SECTION 4 REVIEW

1. **Identify** High Middle Ages.
2. **Define** (a) charter, (b) capital, (c) usury, (d) guild, (e) apprentice.
3. What were two effects of the agricultural revolution that took place during the Middle Ages?
4. (a) What new ways of doing business evolved in the Middle Ages? (b) Why were they necessary?
5. How did the growth of towns affect the rigid class system of feudal times?
6. *Critical Thinking* **Synthesizing Information** Give three pieces of evidence that prove the High Middle Ages were a time of economic growth.
7. *ACTIVITY* Imagine that a growing medieval city has hired you to attract people to move there. Create an ad that describes opportunities the city provides for merchants, artisans, and peasants.

CHAPTER REVIEW AND SKILLS FOR SUCCESS

CHAPTER REVIEW

REVIEWING VOCABULARY

Review the vocabulary words in this chapter. Then, use *ten* of these vocabulary words and their definitions to create a matching quiz. Exchange quizzes with another student. Check each other's answers when you are finished.

REVIEWING FACTS

1. How did the culture of the Germanic tribes differ from that of the Romans?
2. What happened to Charlemagne's empire after his death?
3. What was the basic cause of the rise of feudalism?
4. What were the duties and rights of peasants?
5. Why was the pope a powerful figure in medieval Europe?
6. What role did monasteries and convents play in the preservation of ancient culture?
7. What improvements were made in European agriculture during the Middle Ages?
8. What social changes were caused by the commercial revolution of the Middle Ages?
9. Why were cities of the Middle Ages both filthy and smelly?

SKILLS FOR SUCCESS   INTERPRETING DIAGRAMS

Diagrams present complex information in a way that can be understood quickly. Use the diagram of a manor below to answer the questions that follow.

1. **Identify the parts of the diagram.** (a) What is the subject of the diagram? (b) What kinds of buildings does the diagram show?

2. **Draw conclusions based on the diagram.**
(a) How does the diagram support the statement that the manor was self-sufficient?
(b) How would this affect life in Europe?

Manor house

Blacksmith's shop

Lord's oven

Priest's house

Serfs' houses

Kitchen garden

Well

Mill

Church

Fallow field

Wheat field

Peas, oats, barley, and beans

REVIEWING CHAPTER THEMES

Review the "Focus On" questions at the start of this chapter. Then select *three* of those questions and answer them, using information from the chapter.

CRITICAL THINKING

1. **Linking Past and Present** Compare life on a medieval manor with life on an American farm today. Which do you think would be more self-sufficient? Why?

2. **Predicting Consequences** How do you think the weakening of the feudal system affected the Church? Explain.

3. **Recognizing Causes and Effects** As you have read on page 200, anti-Semitism increased in bad times. Why do you think this was so?

ANALYZING PRIMARY SOURCES

Use the quotation on page 201 to answer the following questions.

1. Near what large building did the town emerge?

2. What activity led to the creation of the town?

3. Was the growth of the town planned? Explain your answer.

FOR YOUR PORTFOLIO

ROLE PLAYING Work with classmates to develop a radio or TV interview show called "Youth of Medieval Times." First, have each member of the group choose a role from medieval society, such as knight or monk. Members should then do research about the everyday life of their characters, and summarize this information on information sheets. Give these sheets to a classmate who will serve as the interviewer. Finally, present your show, with the interviewer posing questions based on the information sheets and the role players answering them.

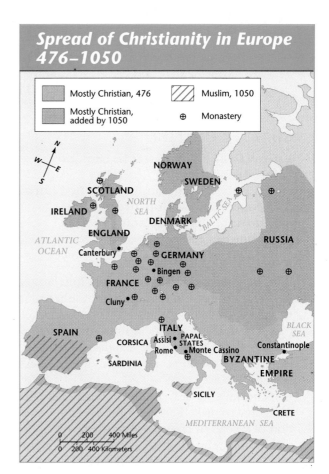

Spread of Christianity in Europe 476–1050

Mostly Christian, 476	Muslim, 1050
Mostly Christian, added by 1050	⊕ Monastery

ANALYZING MAPS

Use the map to answer the following questions.

1. Did Christianity expand into France before or after it expanded into Russia?

2. The areas of Muslim control were in which direction from the areas of Christian control?

3. Where were most of the monasteries located?

INTERNET ACTIVITY

WRITING A DIARY ENTRY Use the Internet to research daily life in early medieval Europe. Then write a diary entry from the point of view of a medieval European. Include information about how your status in medieval European society affects your tasks, beliefs, and expectations of life.

The High Middle Ages

(1050–1450)

Darkness had just fallen when four armed knights burst into Canterbury Cathedral in southern England. "Where is Thomas Becket, traitor to the king and the realm?" they shouted. Becket, the archbishop of Canterbury, stepped forward. "I am here, no traitor, but a priest. Why do you seek me?"

The knights served King Henry II. They had come to make Becket lift the excommunication of several of Henry's supporters. When the archbishop refused their demand, the knights struck him. An eyewitness reported the bloody scene that unfolded:

> 66At the third blow, [Thomas] fell on his knees and elbows, offering himself a living victim, and saying in a low voice, 'For the name of Jesus, I am ready to embrace death.' 99

News of the murder quickly reached the king. Henry was appalled. He realized that his own words had doomed the man who had once been among his closest friends.

Eight years earlier, in 1162, Henry had appointed Becket as archbishop. Once in office, Becket surprised Henry by resisting his attempts to extend royal power over the clergy. A bitter quarrel flared between the two men. Each man used his power to block the other.

At last, Henry's fury exploded. "What a pack of fools and cowards I have nourished," he cried, "that not one of them will avenge me of this turbulent priest." Four hotheaded knights took Henry at his word. Within days, Becket lay dead. And Henry, forced to live with the consequences of his careless words, had to abandon his efforts to extend royal power at the expense of the Church.

By the High Middle Ages, Western Europe had secured its borders against invaders and planted seeds of economic growth. As conditions improved, feudal monarchs like Henry II increased their power over both the nobles and the Church. They thus took the first steps on the long road toward building the modern nation-state.

FOCUS ON these themes as you read:

■ **Political and Social Systems**
How did feudal monarchs build the foundations for strong national governments?

■ **Global Interaction**
How did Western Europeans come in contact with more advanced civilizations?

■ **Art and Literature**
How did the revival of trade and the growth of towns influence medieval culture?

■ **Religions and Value Systems**
How did Christian scholars try to fit the learning of ancient Greece and the Arab world into their own system of beliefs?

■ **Continuity and Change**
How did the disasters of the late Middle Ages help set the stage for the modern age?

TIME AND PLACE

A New Stability for Europe The High Middle Ages saw the return of orderly society to Europe. As monarchs centralized their power and feudal warfare declined, towns became centers not only of new economic activity but also of a revival of culture. Here, a representative of that revival, the writer Christine de Pizan, presents one of her works to the queen of France. **Art and Literature** How would the return of order encourage cultural pursuits?

HUMANITIES LINK

Art History Chartres Cathedral, France (page 227).
Literature In this chapter, you will encounter passages from the following works of literature: "Good King Louis, you held the land under yoke" (page 214); Christine de Pizan, *The City of Ladies* (page 226); *Poem of the Cid* (page 226); Christine de Pizan, *Joan of Arc* (page 232); Geoffrey Chaucer, *The Canterbury Tales* (page 234).

1076	1096	1215	1226	1347	1429	1492
Gregory VII excommunicates Henry IV	Christians launch First Crusade	King John signs Magna Carta	Louis IX becomes king of France	Black Death breaks out in Italy	Joan of Arc leads French armies against English	Spanish complete Reconquista

1000   1100   1200   1300   1400   1500

1 Growth of Royal Power in England and France

Guide for Reading

- How did monarchs in England and France increase royal power?

- What ideas about government and law emerged in England?

- Why did royal rulers consult with representative assemblies?

- **Vocabulary** *common law, jury*

> 66We, who are as good as you, swear to you, who are no better than we, to accept you as our king and sovereign lord; provided you observe our liberties and laws; but if not, not.99

In those blunt words, the nobles of Aragon, a region in what is today Spain, pledged loyalty to their king. Like feudal nobles everywhere, they believed themselves to be the equal of the monarch and were determined to protect their privileges.

In the early Middle Ages, hundreds of feudal nobles ruled over territories of varying size. Most acknowledged a king or other overlord, but royal rulers had little power. During the High Middle Ages, as economic conditions improved, feudal monarchs started to increase their power. Bit by bit over many centuries, they built the framework for what would become the European nations of today.

Monarchs, Nobles, and the Church

In medieval Europe, kings stood at the head of society. Yet feudal monarchs had limited power. They ruled their own domains but relied on vassals for military support. Nobles and the Church had as much—or more—power than the king. Both nobles and the Church had their own courts, collected their own taxes, and fielded their own armies. They jealously guarded their rights and privileges against any effort by rulers to increase royal authority.

Crafty, ambitious, and determined rulers used various means to centralize power. They expanded the royal domain and set up a system of royal justice that undermined feudal or Church courts. They organized a government bureaucracy, developed a system of taxes, and built a standing army. Monarchs strengthened ties with the middle class. Townspeople, in turn, supported royal rulers, who could impose the peace and unity that were needed for trade and commerce.

The struggles among monarchs, nobles, and the Church lasted for centuries. Here, you will see how a few rulers in England and France moved to strengthen royal power.

Strong Monarchs in England

During the early Middle Ages, Angles, Saxons, and Vikings invaded and settled in England. Although feudalism developed, English rulers generally kept their kingdoms united.

Norman conquest. In 1066, the Anglo-Saxon king Edward died without an heir. His death triggered a power struggle that changed the course of English history. A council of nobles chose Edward's brother-in-law Harold to rule. But Duke William of Normandy, a tough, ruthless descendant of the Vikings, also claimed the English throne. The answer to the rival claims lay on the battlefield.

Duke William raised an army and won the backing of the pope. He then sailed across the English Channel. At the Battle of Hastings, William and his Norman knights triumphed over Harold. On Christmas Day 1066, William the Conqueror, as he was now called, assumed the crown of England.

William takes control. Once in power, William exerted firm control over his new lands. Like other feudal monarchs, he granted fiefs to the Church and his Norman lords, or barons, but he kept a large amount of land for himself. He monitored who built castles and where. He required every vassal to swear first allegiance to him rather than to any other feudal lord. Even though William listened to the advice of his chief nobles, he always had the last word.

To learn about his kingdom, William had a complete census taken in 1086. The result was the *Domesday Book* (pronounced doomsday), which listed every castle, field, and pigpen in England. As the title suggests, the survey was as thorough and inevitable as doomsday, believed to be God's final day of judgment that no one could escape. Information in the *Domesday Book* helped William and his successors build an efficient system of tax collecting.

Although William's French-speaking nobles dominated England, the country's Anglo-Saxon population survived. Over the next 300 years, a gradual blending occurred of Norman French and Anglo-Saxon customs, languages, and traditions.

Increasing royal authority. William's successors strengthened two key areas of government: finances and law. They created the royal exchequer, or treasury, to collect taxes. Into the exchequer flowed fees, fines, and other dues.

In 1154, an energetic, well-educated king, Henry II, inherited the throne. He broadened the system of royal justice. As a ruler, he could not simply write new laws but had to follow accepted customs. Henry, however, found ways to expand old ideas into law. He then sent out traveling justices to enforce royal laws. The decisions of the royal courts became the basis for English common law, or law that was common—the same—for all people. In time, people chose royal courts over those of nobles or the Church. Since royal courts charged fees, the exchequer benefited from the growth of royal justice.

Early juries. Under Henry II, England also developed an early jury system. When traveling justices visited an area, local officials collected a jury, or group of men sworn to speak the truth. (*Juré* in French

means "sworn on oath.") These early juries determined which cases should be brought to trial and were the ancestors of today's grand jury. Later, another jury evolved that was composed of 12 neighbors of an accused. It was the ancestor of today's trial jury.

A tragic clash. Henry's efforts to extend royal power led to a bitter dispute with the Church. Henry claimed the right to try clergy in royal courts. Thomas Becket, the archbishop of Canterbury and once a close friend of Henry's, fiercely opposed the king's move.

The conflict simmered for years. Then, as we have seen, in 1170, four of Henry's knights, believing they were doing Henry's bidding, murdered the archbishop in his own cathedral. Henry denied any part in the attack. Still, to make peace with the Church, he eased off his attempts to regulate the clergy. Becket, meantime, was honored as a martyr and declared a saint. Pilgrims flocked to his tomb at Canterbury, where miracles were said to happen.

Invasion In 1066, hundreds of Norman ships crossed the English Channel to land some 7,000 men, 3,000 horses, and cartloads of supplies on the English coast. The landing was unopposed because the Anglo-Saxon army was busy repelling a Viking invasion in the north. **Impact of the Individual** Why did Normans invade England?

Evolving Traditions of Government

Later English rulers repeatedly clashed with nobles and the Church. Most battles developed as a result of efforts by the monarch to raise taxes or to impose royal authority over traditional feudal rights. Out of those struggles evolved traditions of government that would influence the modern world.

John's troubles. Henry's son John was a clever, greedy, cruel, and untrustworthy ruler. During his reign, he faced three powerful enemies: King Philip II of France, Pope Innocent III, and his own English nobles. He lost his struggles with each.

Ever since William the Conqueror, Norman rulers of England had held vast lands in France. (See the map on page 213.) In 1205, John suffered his first setback when he lost a war with Philip II and had to give up English-held lands in Anjou and Normandy. Next, John battled with Innocent III over selecting a new archbishop of Canterbury. When John attacked the Church, the pope responded by excommunicating him. He also placed England under the interdict—as you recall, a papal order that forbade Church services in an entire kingdom. Even the strongest ruler was likely to give in to that pressure. To save himself and his crown, John had to accept England as a fief of the papacy and pay a yearly fee to Rome.

The Magna Carta. Finally, John angered his own nobles with heavy-handed taxes and other abuses of power. In 1215, a group of rebellious barons cornered John and forced him to sign the Magna Carta, or great charter. In this document, the king affirmed a long list of feudal rights. Besides protecting their own privileges, the barons included a few clauses recognizing the rights of townspeople and the Church.

The Magna Carta contained two basic ideas that in the long run would shape government traditions in England. First, it asserted that the nobles had certain rights. Over time, the rights that had been granted to nobles were extended to all English citizens. Second, the Magna Carta made clear that the monarch must obey the law. Among the most significant clauses were those that protected the legal rights of the people:

66No freeman shall be arrested or imprisoned or dispossessed or outlawed or . . . in any way harmed . . . except by the lawful judgment of his peers or by the law of the land. . . . To none will we sell, to none deny or delay, right or justice.99

The king also agreed not to raise new taxes without first consulting his Great Council of lords and clergy. Many centuries later, American colonists would claim that those words meant that any taxation without representation was unjust. In 1215, though, neither the king nor his lords could have imagined such an idea.

Development of Parliament. During the 1200s, English rulers often called on the Great Council for advice. Eventually, this body evolved into Parliament. Its name comes from the French word *parler*, meaning "to talk." As

Edward I and Parliament In this scene, King Edward I presides over Parliament. On either side of him are his vassals, the rulers of Scotland and Wales. Clergymen sit on the left and lords sit on the right. ***Political and Social Systems*** *What other social class was represented in the Model Parliament?*

Parliament acquired a larger role in government, it helped unify England.

In 1295, Edward I summoned Parliament to approve money for his wars in France. "What touches all," he declared, "should be approved by all." He had representatives of the "common people" join the lords and clergy. The "commons" included two knights from each county and representatives of the towns.

Much later, this assembly became known as the Model Parliament because it set up the framework for England's legislature. In time, Parliament developed into a two-house body: the House of Lords with nobles and high clergy and the House of Commons with knights and middle-class citizens.

Looking ahead. Like King Edward I, later English monarchs summoned Parliament for their own purposes. Over the centuries, though, Parliament gained the crucial "power of the purse." That is, it won the right to approve any new taxes. With that power, Parliament could insist that the monarch meet its demands before voting for taxes. In this way, it could check, or limit, the power of the monarch.

Royal Successes in France

Monarchs in France did not rule over a unified kingdom, like William the Conqueror did in England. Instead, the successors to Charlemagne had little power over a patchwork of territories ruled by great feudal nobles.

The Capetians. In 987, these feudal nobles elected Hugh Capet, the count of Paris, to fill the vacant throne. They probably chose him because he was too weak to pose a threat to them. Hugh's own lands, the Ile de France around Paris, were smaller than those of many of his vassals.

Hugh and his heirs slowly increased royal power. First, they made the throne hereditary, passing it from father to son. Fortunately, the Capetians enjoyed an unbroken succession for 300 years. Next, they added to their lands by playing rival nobles against each other. They also won the support of the Church.

Perhaps most important, the Capetians built an effective bureaucracy. Government officials collected taxes and imposed royal law over the king's domain. By establishing order, they

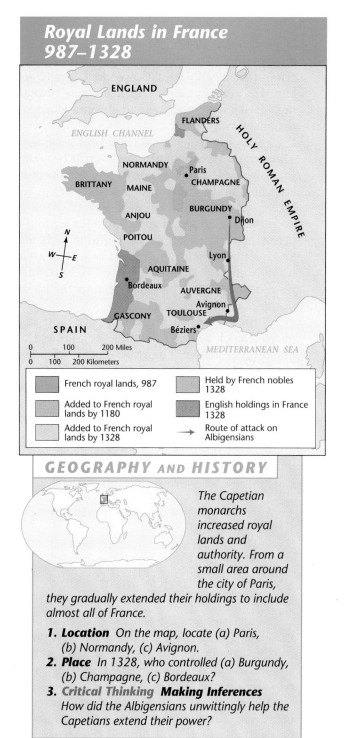

Royal Lands in France 987–1328

ENGLAND
ENGLISH CHANNEL
FLANDERS
HOLY ROMAN EMPIRE
NORMANDY
Paris
CHAMPAGNE
BRITTANY
MAINE
ANJOU
BURGUNDY
Dijon
POITOU
Lyon
AQUITAINE
AUVERGNE
Bordeaux
Avignon
GASCONY
TOULOUSE
SPAIN
Béziers
MEDITERRANEAN SEA

0   100   200 Miles
0   100   200 Kilometers

French royal lands, 987	Held by French nobles 1328
Added to French royal lands by 1180	English holdings in France 1328
Added to French royal lands by 1328	→ Route of attack on Albigensians

GEOGRAPHY AND HISTORY

The Capetian monarchs increased royal lands and authority. From a small area around the city of Paris, they gradually extended their holdings to include almost all of France.

1. **Location** On the map, locate (a) Paris, (b) Normandy, (c) Avignon.
2. **Place** In 1328, who controlled (a) Burgundy, (b) Champagne, (c) Bordeaux?
3. **Critical Thinking** **Making Inferences** How did the Albigensians unwittingly help the Capetians extend their power?

added to their prestige and gained the backing of the new middle class of townspeople.

Philip Augustus. An outstanding French king of this period was Philip II, often called Philip Augustus. A bald, red-faced man who ate and drank too much, Philip was a shrewd and able ruler. He strengthened royal government in many ways. Instead of appointing nobles to fill government positions, he used paid middle-class officials who would owe their loyalty to him. He granted charters to many new towns, organized a standing army, and introduced a new national tax.

Philip also quadrupled royal land holdings. Through trickery, diplomacy, and war, he brought English-ruled lands in Normandy, Anjou, and elsewhere under his control. He then began to take over southern France. Informed by the pope that the Albigensian (al buh JEHN see uhn) heresy had sprung up in the south, he sent his knights to suppress it and add this vast area to his domain. (See the map on page 213.) Before his death in 1223, Philip had become the most powerful ruler in Europe.

A model monarch. Perhaps the most admired French ruler of this time was Louis IX, grandson of Philip Augustus. Louis, who ascended to the throne in 1226, embodied the ideal of the perfect medieval monarch—generous, noble, and devoted to justice and the rules of chivalry. Within 30 years of his death, he was declared a saint. France's poets mourned his passing:

> **66**Good King Louis, you held the land
>   under yoke
>   To the profit of barons and of the
>   little folk . . .
>   To whom may poor men cry now in
>   their woe
>   Since the good king is dead who
>   loved them so?**99**

Saint Louis was a deeply religious man, and he pursued religious goals that were acceptable to Christians in his day. He persecuted heretics and Jews and led thousands of French knights in two wars against Muslims.

Louis did much to improve royal government. Like Charlemagne, he sent out roving officials to check on local officials. He expanded the royal courts, outlawed private wars, and ended serfdom in his lands. To ensure justice, he even heard cases himself under a tree in the royal park of Vincennes. His enormous personal prestige helped create a strong national feeling among his subjects. By the time of his death in 1270, France was an efficient centralized monarchy.

Clash with the pope. Louis's grandson, Philip IV, ruthlessly extended royal power. Always pressed for cash, he tried to collect new taxes from the French clergy. These efforts led to a head-on clash with Pope Boniface VIII.

"God has set popes over kings and kingdoms," declared the pope and forbad Philip to tax the clergy without papal consent. Philip countered by threatening to arrest any clergy who did not pay up. As their quarrel escalated, Philip sent troops to seize Boniface. The pope escaped, but he was badly beaten and died soon afterward. Shortly after, a Frenchman was elected pope. He moved the papal court to the town of Avignon (AH veen yohn) on the border of southern France, ensuring that future French rulers would control religion within their own kingdoms.

The Estates General. During this struggle with the pope, Philip rallied French support by setting up the Estates General in 1302. This body had representatives from all three estates, or classes: clergy, nobles, and townspeople. Although later French kings consulted the Estates General, it did not develop the same role that the English Parliament did. It never gained the power of the purse or otherwise served as a balance to royal power.

SECTION 1 REVIEW

1. **Identify** (a) William the Conqueror, (b) *Domesday Book,* (c) Henry II, (d) Thomas Becket, (e) Magna Carta, (f) Model Parliament, (g) Saint Louis, (h) Philip IV, (i) Estates General.
2. **Define** (a) common law, (b) jury.
3. What steps did William the Conqueror take to exert royal power in England?
4. What principles were established by the Magna Carta?
5. How did the Capetians increase royal power in France?
6. *Critical Thinking* **Linking Past and Present** How is the jury system important to us today?
7. *ACTIVITY* Write a newspaper editorial supporting or opposing the actions of *one* of the following kings: Henry II, John I, Louis IX, or Philip IV.

The Holy Roman Empire and the Church

Guide for Reading

- Why did Holy Roman emperors fail to build a unified state in Germany?

- What issues led to clashes between emperors and popes?

- What powers did the Church have at its peak?

- **Vocabulary** *crusade*

The Church, you will recall, spread its influence across Europe during the early Middle Ages. By the High Middle Ages, both popes and monarchs were extending their authority. In the early 1200s, Pope Innocent III claimed broad new powers:

> ❝The priesthood is the sun and the monarchy the moon. Kings rule over their respective kingdoms, but [the pope] rules over the whole Earth.❞

With secular rulers advancing their own claims to power, explosive conflicts erupted. The longest and most destructive struggle pitted popes against the Holy Roman emperors who ruled vast lands from Germany to Italy.

The Holy Roman Empire

In the early Middle Ages, the emperor Charlemagne had brought much of what is today the nation of Germany under his rule. (See Chapter 8.) After Charlemagne's death, Germany dissolved into a patchwork of separate states ruled by a number of powerful counts and dukes. In time, the dukes of one of those states, Saxony, began to extend their power over neighboring German lands. In 936, Duke Otto I of Saxony took the title king of Germany.

Like Charlemagne, Otto I worked closely with the Church. He appointed bishops and abbots to top government jobs. Also like Charlemagne, he took an army south into Italy to help the pope put down a rebellion by Roman nobles. In 962, a grateful pope crowned Otto emperor. Later, Otto's successors took the title Holy Roman emperor—"holy" because they were crowned by the pope, "Roman" because they saw themselves as heirs to the emperors of ancient Rome.

Emperors and nobles. The Holy Roman Empire had the potential to be the strongest monarchy in Europe. German emperors claimed authority over much of central and eastern Europe as well as parts of France and Italy. In fact, the real rulers of these lands were the emperor's vassals—hundreds of dukes, counts, archbishops, bishops, and knights. For German emperors, the challenge was to control these nobles. In the end, as you will see, it was a challenge they never met.

Conflict with the Church. The close ties between Otto and the Church held the seeds of conflict. Holy Roman emperors saw themselves as protectors of Italy and the pope. They repeatedly crossed the Alps to intervene in Italian affairs. They were tempted, too, by the desire to control the rich cities of northern Italy.

A key conflict between emperors and popes rose over who would control appointments to high Church offices. Like secular rulers in England and France, the Holy Roman emperor often decided who would become bishops and abbots. As the Cluny reforms strengthened the Church, popes attempted to end such outside interference.

Imperial Crown Holy Roman emperors first wore this jewel-encrusted gold crown around the late 900s. Some, however, claimed that Charlemagne had worn it almost two centuries earlier. **Political and Social Systems** Why do you think Holy Roman emperors wanted people to believe that the crown had been worn by Charlemagne?

Two Determined Rulers

Under the reforming pope Gregory VII, the conflict between emperors and the Church burst into flames. Gregory was one of the greatest medieval popes. He was also among the most controversial. Indeed, few Europeans of his time had a neutral view of him. Many admired and revered him. Among his enemies, however, he probably aroused more hatred and contempt than any other pope of his time.

Gregory was determined to make the Church independent of secular rulers. To do so, he banned the practice of lay investiture. Under this practice, the emperor or another lay person (a person who is not a member of the clergy) "invested," or presented, bishops with the ring and staff that symbolized their office. Only the pope, said Gregory, had the right to appoint and install bishops in office.

Pope versus emperor. Pope Gregory's ban brought an angry response from the Holy Roman emperor Henry IV. He argued that bishops held their lands as royal fiefs. Since he was their overlord, Henry felt entitled to give them the symbols of office. The feud heated up as the two men exchanged insulting notes. Meanwhile, rebellious German princes saw a chance to undermine Henry by supporting the pope.

In 1076, Gregory excommunicated Henry, freeing his subjects from their allegiance to the emperor. The pope then headed north to crown a new emperor. Faced with revolts at home, Henry was forced to make peace with the pope.

Barefoot in the snow. In January 1077, Henry crossed the icy Alps. He found the pope staying at a castle in Canossa and presented himself as a repentant sinner. Gregory later described the scene:

> 66 There, having put aside all the trappings of royalty, with bare feet and clad only in a wretched woolen garment, he [Henry] continued for three days to stand before the castle gate . . . beseeching us with tears to grant him absolution and forgiveness. 99

Gregory knew that Henry was only trying to save his throne. But according to the tradition and law of the Church, the pope, as a priest, had to forgive a confessed sinner. Gregory thus lifted the order of excommunication. Henry quickly returned to Germany and subdued his rebellious nobles. In later years, he took revenge on Gregory when he led an army to Rome and forced the pope into exile.

Concordat of Worms. The struggle over investiture dragged on for almost 50 years. Finally, in 1122, both sides accepted a treaty known as the Concordat of Worms (VOHRMS). In it, they agreed that the Church had the sole power to elect and invest bishops with spiritual authority. The emperor, however, had the right to invest them with fiefs. Although this compromise ended the investiture struggle, new battles were soon raging between popes and emperors.

REX ROGAT ABBATEM. MATHILDIM SUPPLICAT ATQ;

A Repentant Emperor In the heat of the investiture conflict, Emperor Henry IV urged Gregory VII to step down as pope, calling for him to be "damned throughout the ages." Gregory's simple, but powerful, response was, "I forbid anyone to serve him as king." Here, Henry is shown at Canossa, humbly begging the pope's forgiveness. Countess Matilda of Tuscany, who helped reconcile the pope and the monarch, is at right.
Religions and Value Systems *Do you think that the conflict between popes and emperors could have been avoided? Explain.*

New Struggles Between Popes and Emperors

During the 1100s and 1200s, ambitious German emperors sought to master Italy. The emperor Frederick I, called Barbarossa, or "red beard," dreamed of building an empire that stretched from the Baltic to the Adriatic. For years, he fought to bring the wealthy cities of northern Italy under his control. With equal energy, they resisted. By joining forces with the pope in the Lombard League, they managed to defeat Barbarossa's armies.

Barbarossa did succeed, however, in arranging a marriage between his son Henry and Constance, heiress to Sicily and southern Italy. That move entangled German emperors even more deeply in Italian affairs.

Frederick II. Sicily, a rich island kingdom in the Mediterranean, had a sophisticated court, where Muslim and Christian influences existed side by side. The child of Henry and Constance, Frederick II, was raised in this rich court. Frederick was bright and well educated, fluent in Arabic, Greek, French, and several other languages. He valued the scientific learning of the Muslim world and saw himself as a man of reason. He was also an arrogant, able, and cynical leader, willing to use any means to achieve his ends.

As Holy Roman emperor, Frederick spent little time in Germany. Instead, he pursued his ambitions in Italy. There, he clashed repeatedly and unsuccessfully with several popes. Like his grandfather, Frederick also tried but failed to subdue the cities of northern Italy.

Consequences. While Frederick was embroiled in Italy, he gave in to many demands of his German nobles. As a result, they grew increasingly independent. Although the Holy Roman Empire survived, it remained fragmented into many feudal states. The emperors thus lost control of Germany at a time when French and English rulers were building the foundations for stable, unified governments. The German people paid a high price for their emperors' ambitions: They would not achieve unity for another 600 years.

Southern Italy and Sicily, too, faced centuries of upheaval. There, popes turned to the French to overthrow Frederick's heirs. A local uprising against French rule in Sicily led to 200 years of

A Powerful Pope Innocent III led the Church to the height of power and prestige. He kept strict control over the bishops and other clergy. He asserted his authority over secular rulers. At the time of his death, Innocent was the unquestioned leader of all Christendom. **Impact of the Individual** What methods did Innocent use to exert control?

chaos as French and Spanish rivals battled for power. The region that had once been a thriving center of European culture was left in ruins.

The Church Under Innocent III

In the 1200s, the Roman Catholic Church reached its peak of power. Reforming popes like Gregory VII claimed the right to depose kings and emperors. Gregory's successors greatly expanded papal power.

The height of papal power. Innocent III, who took office in 1198, embodied the triumph of the Church. As head of the Church, he claimed supremacy over all other rulers. The pope, he said, stands "between God and man, lower than God but higher than men, who judges all and is judged by no one."

Innocent clashed with all the powerful rulers of his day. More often than not, the pope came out ahead. As you have read, when King John of England dared to appoint an archbishop of Canterbury without the pope's approval, Innocent excommunicated the king and placed his kingdom under interdict. Innocent ordered the same punishment for France when Philip II tried unlawfully to annul his marriage. The Holy Roman emperor Frederick II also felt the wrath of the powerful pope.

In 1209, Innocent, aided by Philip II, launched a brutal crusade, or holy war, against the Albigensians in southern France. The Albigensians wanted to purify the Church and return to the simple ways of early Christianity. Tens of thousands of people were slaughtered in the Albigensian Crusade.

Looking ahead. For almost a century after Innocent's death, popes pressed their claim to supremacy. During this period, though, the French and English monarchies were growing stronger. In 1296, Philip IV of France successfully challenged Pope Boniface VIII on the issue of taxing the clergy. (See page 214.) After Philip engineered the election of a French pope, the papacy entered a period of decline.

SECTION 2 REVIEW

1. **Identify** (a) Holy Roman Empire, (b) Gregory VII, (c) Henry IV, (d) Concordat of Worms, (e) Frederick II, (f) Innocent III, (g) Albigensian Crusade.
2. **Define** crusade.
3. (a) Why was the power of German emperors limited? (b) How did the ambitions of German emperors affect the Holy Roman Empire?
4. (a) Describe two issues that led to clashes between popes and Holy Roman emperors. (b) How was each resolved?
5. *Critical Thinking* **Comparing** (a) How did the political development of the Holy Roman Empire differ from that of England and France in the 1100s and 1200s? (b) What were the causes of these differences?
6. *ACTIVITY* On an outline map of Europe, label the places that you have read about in this section. Illustrate your map to show what happened in each location.

3 Europeans Look Outward

Guide for Reading

- What advanced centers of civilizations flourished around the world in 1050?
- What were the causes of the Crusades?
- How did the Crusades affect Western Europe?
- How did Ferdinand and Isabella increase royal power in Spain?

Nearly 23 weeks after setting out from his home in France, Count Stephen of Blois reached the city of Antioch in Syria. There, on March 29, 1098, he dictated a letter to his wife, Adele. "You may be very sure, dearest, that the messenger whom I send you has left me outside Antioch safe and unharmed," he began. He went on to tell of the battles he had fought and the riches he had won. Many more battles lay ahead before he and his fellow knights achieved their goal—the conquest of Jerusalem.

Stephen of Blois was among thousands of Europeans who joined the Crusades, a series of holy wars launched in 1096 by Christian Europe against Muslim lands in the Middle East. For the first time since the fall of Rome, Western Europeans were strong enough to break out of their narrow isolation and take the offensive against other lands. As they streamed eastward over the next 200 years, Western Europeans learned that the world was much larger than they had ever dreamed. Their encounters outside Europe would serve to stimulate the pace of change.

The World in 1050

In 1050, when Western Europe was barely emerging from isolation, several civilizations in the Middle East and Asia had long been major powers. You will read about these civilizations in other chapters. What follows here is an overview of the world at the time that medieval Europe was first beginning to test its strength.

PARALLELS THROUGH TIME

Good Manners

Books of etiquette, or proper social behavior, date back as far as ancient Egypt and the *Instructions of the Vizier Ptah-hotep*. (See page 23.) Since then, every society has evolved its own system of customs and manners that people are expected to observe. However, ideas about good manners vary from culture to culture and from class to class.

Linking Past and Present How does etiquette at your school cafeteria differ from etiquette at a restaurant? Do you think rules of etiquette are still necessary? Explain.

PAST During the late Middle Ages, as monarchs gained greater prestige, royal courts set the standards for good behavior. The first European etiquette books advised nobles how to behave properly at a court banquet:

> "A number of people gnaw a bone and then put it back in the dish. This is a serious offense."
>
> "Do not spit over the table in the manner of hunters."
>
> "Refrain from falling upon the dish like a swine while eating, snorting disgustingly, and smacking the lips."

PRESENT Today, guides to etiquette range from newspaper columns like "Miss Manners" to handbooks for international business travelers. Following are instructions for the proper way to call a waiter in various cultures:

> "Africa: Knock on the table."
>
> "Middle East: Clap your hands."
>
> "Japan: Extend your arm slightly upward, palm down, and flutter your fingers."

Islam: An international civilization. During Europe's Middle Ages, Islam had given rise to a brilliant new civilization. Islamic civilization reached from Spain across North Africa and the Middle East and on to the borders of India.

Muslim traders and scholars spread goods and ideas even farther afield. Trading caravans regularly crossed the Sahara to West Africa. Arab ships touched at ports on the east African coast and sailed on to India, Southeast Asia, China, and Korea. Through contacts with diverse cultures, Muslims acquired and passed on a whole range of ideas and technologies.

India and China: Ancient centers of civilization. Beyond the Muslim world lay India and China. Although it was politically divided, India was a land of thriving cities. Hindu and Buddhist traditions flourished, and wealthy princes financed the building of stunning temples and palaces. Indian mathematicians invented a numbering system, which Arabs adapted. Eventually, Western Europeans adopted these Hindu-Arabic numbers.

China had a strong, central government at a time when Europe was politically fragmented. Under the Tang and Song dynasties, China's culture flourished. Its civilization had an influence on neighboring peoples in Korea, Japan, and Southeast Asia. The Chinese made amazing advances in technology, inventing paper, printing, and gunpowder. In dozens of large cities, traders benefited from the use of coins and paper money, unknown to medieval Europeans.

African and American civilizations. In West Africa, the Soninke people were building the great trading empire of Ghana. Its merchants traded goods, especially gold, that would travel across the Sahara to North Africa, the Middle East, and even Europe.

Across the Atlantic, in Central America and southern Mexico, the Mayas had cleared the rain forests and built large cities dominated by towering temples. In Peru, too, Native Americans were carving out empires and creating great works of art, including elegant pottery, textiles, and gold jewelry. The civilizations of the Americas, however, remained outside the contacts that were taking place among Africans, Europeans, and Asians between 1050 and 1250.

Byzantine civilization. Closer to Western Europe, Byzantine civilization was a rival to Islam in the eastern Mediterranean. Although pounded by invaders, the Byzantine empire was generally prosperous and united at a time when Western Europe was weak and backward. Its scholars still studied the writings of the ancient Greeks and Romans. In the markets of Constantinople, the Byzantine capital, Byzantine and Muslim merchants mingled with traders from Venice and other Italian cities. Even Vikings made their way to this bustling city.

In the 1050s, the Seljuk Turks invaded the Byzantine empire. The Turks had migrated from Central Asia into the Middle East, where they converted to Islam. By 1071, the Seljuks had overrun most Byzantine lands in Asia Minor (present-day Turkey). The Seljuks also extended their power over Palestine and attacked Christian pilgrims to the Holy Land.*

---

*Christians called Jerusalem and other places in Palestine where Jesus had lived and taught the Holy Land. Jerusalem was also a holy place for Jews and Muslims.

The Crusades

As the Seljuk threat grew, the Byzantine emperor Alexius I sent an urgent plea to Pope Urban II in Rome. In 1095, he asked for Christian knights to help him fight the Turks. Although Roman popes and Byzantine emperors were longtime rivals, Urban agreed.

At the Council of Clermont in 1095, Urban incited French and German bishops and nobles to action. "From Jerusalem and the city of Constantinople comes a grievous report," he began. "An accursed race . . . has violently invaded the lands of those Christians and has depopulated them by pillage and fire." Urban then called for a crusade to free the Holy Land:

> 66Seize that land from [the Seljuks], and subject it to yourselves. . . . Undertake this journey eagerly for the [forgiveness] of your sins and with the assurance of everlasting glory in the kingdom of heaven.99

Taking up the cross. *Deus lo volt!* "God wills it!" roared the assembly in response to the pope's words. Soon, thousands of knights were on their way to the Holy Land. Because they sewed large crosses—*cruces* in Latin—on their tunics, they came to be called crusaders. As the crusading spirit swept through Western Europe, armies of ordinary men and women inspired by fiery preachers left for the Holy Land, too. Few returned.

Why did so many people take up the cross? Religious reasons played a large role. Yet many knights also hoped to win wealth and land. Some crusaders sought to escape troubles at home. Others yearned for adventure.

The pope, too, had mixed motives. Urban hoped to increase his power in Europe and perhaps heal the split between the Roman and Byzantine churches. (See page 242.) He also saw lands in the Middle East as an outlet for Europe's growing population. Finally, he hoped that the Crusades would set Christian knights to fighting Muslims instead of one another.

Massacre in Jerusalem. For 200 years, crusaders marched, fought, and for a time occupied parts of Palestine. Only the First Crusade came close to achieving its goals. After a long,

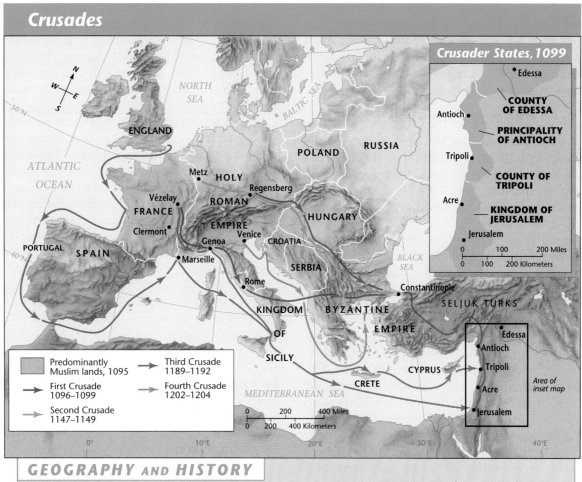

Crusades

Crusader States, 1099

- COUNTY OF EDESSA
- PRINCIPALITY OF ANTIOCH
- COUNTY OF TRIPOLI
- KINGDOM OF JERUSALEM

Legend:
- Predominantly Muslim lands, 1095
- First Crusade 1096–1099
- Second Crusade 1147–1149
- Third Crusade 1189–1192
- Fourth Crusade 1202–1204

GEOGRAPHY AND HISTORY

Urged on by Pope Urban, thousands of Europeans joined the Crusades to expel the Muslims from the Holy Land.

1. **Location** On the map, locate (a) Holy Roman Empire, (b) Kingdom of Jerusalem, (c) Constantinople.
2. **Movement** Which crusaders traveled to the Holy Land mostly by water?
3. **Critical Thinking** *Analyzing Information* Based on the map, why would it be difficult for Europeans to defend the Crusader States?

bloody campaign, Christian knights captured Jerusalem in 1099. They capped their victory with a massacre of Muslim and Jewish residents of the city.

Later crusades. The crusaders divided the captured lands into four small states. (See the map above.) The Muslims repeatedly sought to destroy these Christian kingdoms, prompting Europeans to launch new crusades. By 1187, Jerusalem had fallen to the able Muslim leader Salah al-Din, known to Europeans as Saladin. On the Third Crusade, Europeans tried but failed to retake Jerusalem. After negotiations, though, Saladin did reopen the holy city to Christian pilgrims.

Europeans also mounted crusades against other Muslim lands, especially in North Africa. All ended in defeat. During the Fourth Crusade, the crusaders were diverted from fighting Muslims to fighting Christians. After helping Venetian merchants defeat their Byzantine trade rivals in 1204, crusaders captured and looted Constantinople, the capital of the Byzantine empire itself!

Muslim armies meanwhile overran the crusader states. By 1291, they captured the last Christian outpost, the port city of Acre. As in Jerusalem 200 years earlier, the victors massacred their defeated enemies. This time, the victims were Christians.

Impact of the Crusades

The Crusades failed in their chief goal—the conquest of the Holy Land. They also left a bitter legacy of religious hatred behind them. In the Middle East, both Christians and Muslims committed appalling atrocities in the name of religion. In Europe, crusaders sometimes turned their religious fury against Jews, massacring entire communities.

The Crusades did have some positive effects, however. Beginning just as Europe was emerging from the Middle Ages, they helped to quicken the pace of changes already underway.

Increased trade. Even before the Crusades, Europeans had developed a taste for luxury goods that merchants brought from the Byzantine empire. The Crusades increased the level of trade. Returning crusaders introduced fabrics, spices, and perfumes from the Middle East to a larger market.

Merchants in Venice and other northern Italian cities built large fleets to carry crusaders to the Holy Land. They later used those fleets to open new markets in the crusader states. Even after the Muslims had recaptured Acre, Italian merchants kept these trade routes open. Our words *sugar, cotton, rice,* and *muslin,* which were borrowed from Arabic, show the range of trade goods involved.

The Church. Enthusiasm for the Crusades brought papal power to its greatest height. This period of enhanced prestige was short-lived, however. As we have seen, popes were soon involved in bitter clashes with feudal monarchs. Also, the Crusades did not end the split between the Roman and Byzantine churches. In fact, Byzantine resentment against the West hardened as a result of the Fourth Crusade.

Feudal rulers. The Crusades also helped to increase the power of feudal monarchs. Rulers won new rights to levy taxes in order to support the Crusades. Some rulers, including the French king Louis IX, led crusades, which added greatly to their prestige.

The money economy and serfdom. The Crusades further encouraged the growth of a money economy. To finance a journey to the Holy Land, nobles needed money. They allowed peasants to pay rents in money rather than grain or labor, which helped undermine serfdom.

A wider world view. Contacts with the Muslim world led Christians to realize that millions of people lived in regions they had never known existed. Soon a few curious Europeans even visited far-off places like India and China.

In 1271, a young Venetian, Marco Polo, set out for China with his merchant father and uncle. After many years in China, he returned to Venice full of stories about the wonders of Chinese civilization. Doubting Europeans called Marco Polo the "prince of liars." To them, his tales of a government-run mail service and black stones (coal) that were burned to heat homes were totally untrue.

The experiences of crusaders and of travelers like Marco Polo expanded European horizons. They brought Europe into a wider world from which it had been cut off since the fall of Rome. By the 1400s, a desire to trade directly with India and China would lead Europeans to a new age of exploration.

The Crusading Spirit and the Reconquista

The crusading spirit continued long after the European defeat at Acre. It flourished especially in Spain, where Christian warriors had been battling Muslims for centuries.

Muslims had conquered most of Spain in the 700s and carried Islamic civilization there. (See Chapter 11.) Several tiny Christian kingdoms survived in the north, however. As they slowly expanded their borders, they sought to take over Muslim lands. Their campaign to drive the Muslims from Spain became known as the Reconquista, or "reconquest."

 ISSUES For TODAY After years of isolation, Western Europeans began to renew contacts with the outside world. What effects does contact between cultures produce?

Marco Polo in China *Marco Polo served as an official of Kublai Khan, the ruler of China. He traveled throughout China and also visited Persia, Burma, Sumatra, and India. Polo's story kindled the European imagination and encouraged others to travel and explore.* **Economics and Technology** *How does this illustration portray China as a land of great wealth?*

Christian advances. Efforts by Christian warriors to expel the Muslims began in the 700s. Their first real success did not come, however, until 1085, when they recaptured the city of Toledo. During the next 200 years, Christian forces pushed slowly and steadily southward. By 1300, Christians controlled the entire Iberian Peninsula except for Granada. Muslim influences remained strong, though, and helped shape the arts and literature of Christian Spain.

Ferdinand and Isabella. In 1469, Isabella of Castile married Ferdinand of Aragon. This marriage between the rulers of two powerful kingdoms opened the way for a unified state. Using their combined forces, the two monarchs made a final push against the Muslim stronghold of Granada. In 1492, Granada fell. The Reconquista was complete.

Isabella and Ferdinand tried to impose unity on their diverse peoples. They joined forces with townspeople against powerful nobles. Isabella was determined to bring religious as well as political unity to Spain.

Under Muslim rule, Spain had enjoyed a tradition of religious toleration. Christians, Jews, and Muslims lived there in relative peace. Isabella ended that policy of toleration. Aided by the Inquisition, a Church court set up to try people accused of heresy, Isabella launched a brutal crusade against Jews and Muslims. Often, those who refused to convert to Christianity were burned at the stake.

More than 150,000 people fled into exile. The queen achieved religious unity but at a high price. Her policy destroyed two skilled, educated groups that had contributed much to Spain's economy and culture.

SECTION 3 REVIEW

1. **Identify** (a) Crusades, (b) Council of Clermont, (c) Saladin, (d) Reconquista, (e) Isabella, (f) Ferdinand, (g) Inquisition.
2. What advanced civilizations flourished around the world at the time of the First Crusade?
3. (a) Why did Europeans join the Crusades? (b) What were three results of the Crusades?
4. How did Spain achieve political and religious unity?
5. *Critical Thinking* **Analyzing Information** How did the Crusades reflect the growing strength of medieval Europe?
6. *ACTIVITY* Write two articles reporting on the First Crusade: one from the point of view of a Christian knight, another from the point of view of a Muslim living in Jerusalem.

Learning, Literature, and the Arts

Guide for Reading

- Why did a revival of learning occur in the High Middle Ages?

- How did literature reflect the changing culture of medieval Europe?

- What styles of architecture emerged in the High Middle Ages?

- **Vocabulary** *theology, scholasticism, vernacular*

By the 1100s, Europe was experiencing dynamic changes. No longer was everyone preoccupied with the daily struggle to survive. Improvements in agriculture were creating a steadier food supply. The revival of trade and growth of towns were signs of increased prosperity. Within the towns and cities of medieval Europe, a few people were acquiring wealth. In time, towns contributed a vital spark that ignited the cultural flowering of the High Middle Ages.

Medieval Universities

As economic and political conditions improved in the High Middle Ages, the need for education expanded. The Church wanted better-educated clergy. Royal rulers also needed literate men for their growing bureaucracies. By getting an education, the sons of wealthy townspeople might hope to qualify for high jobs in the Church or royal governments.

Academic guilds. By the 1100s, schools had sprung up around the great cathedrals to train the clergy. Some of these cathedral schools evolved into the first universities. They were organized like guilds with charters to protect the rights of members and set standards for training.

Salerno and Bologna in Italy boasted the first universities. Paris and Oxford soon had theirs. In the 1200s, other cities rushed to organize universities. Students often traveled from one university to another. They might study law in

Students in Class *Early universities were modeled on medieval trade guilds. In northern Europe, teachers acted as the guild masters, setting the term of study and establishing conditions for receiving a degree. In the schools of Italy, students ran the first guilds. They required teachers to start and finish lectures on time and fined them if they missed class or skipped material.* **Continuity and Change** *How does the curriculum of medieval universities compare to courses of study today?*

Bologna, medicine in Montpellier, and theology, or religion, in Paris.

Student life. University life offered few comforts. A bell wakened students at about 5 A.M. for prayers. Students then attended classes until 10 A.M., when they had their first meal of the day—perhaps a bit of beef and soup mixed with oatmeal. Afternoon classes continued until 5 P.M. Students ate a light supper and then studied until time for bed.

Since medieval universities did not have permanent buildings, classes were held in rented rooms or in the choir loft of a church. Students sat for hours on hard benches as the teacher dictated and then explained Latin texts. Students were expected to memorize what they heard.

A program of study covered the seven liberal arts: arithmetic, geometry, astronomy, music, grammar, rhetoric, and logic. To show they had mastered a subject, students took an oral exam. Earning a degree as a bachelor of arts took between three and six years. Only after several more years of study could a man qualify to become a master of arts and a teacher.

Women were not allowed to attend the universities. This exclusion seriously affected their lives. Without a university education, they could not become doctors, lawyers, administrators, church officials, or professors. They were also deprived of the mental stimulation that was an important part of university life.

Europeans Acquire "New" Learning

Universities received a further boost from an explosion of knowledge that reached Europe in the High Middle Ages. Many of the "new" ideas had originated in ancient Greece but had been lost to Western Europeans after the fall of Rome.

In the Middle East, Muslim scholars had translated the works of Aristotle and other Greek thinkers into Arabic, and their texts had spread across the Muslim world. In Muslim Spain, Jewish scholars translated these works into Latin, the language of Christian European scholars.

The challenge of Aristotle. By the 1100s, these new translations were seeping into Western Europe. There they set off a revolution in the world of learning. The writings of the ancient Greeks posed a challenge to Christian scholars. Aristotle taught that people should use reason to discover basic truths. Christians, however, accepted many ideas on faith. They believed that the Church was the final authority on all questions. How could they use the logic of Aristotle without undermining their Christian faith?

Christian scholars, known as scholastics, tried to resolve the conflict between faith and reason. Their method, known as scholasticism, used reason to support Christian beliefs. Scholastics studied the works of the Muslim philosopher Averröes (ah VEHR oh eez) and the Jewish rabbi Maimonides (mī MAHN uh deez).

These thinkers, too, used logic to resolve the conflict between faith and reason.

Thomas Aquinas. The writings of these thinkers influenced the scholastic Thomas Aquinas (uh KWĪ nuhs). In a monumental work, *Summa Theologica*, Aquinas examined Christian teachings in the light of reason. Faith and reason, he concluded, existed in harmony. Both led to the same truth, that God ruled over an orderly universe. He thus brought together Christian faith and classical Greek philosophy.

Science and mathematics. Works of science, translated from Arabic and Greek, also reached Europe from Spain and the Byzantine empire. Christian scholars studied Hippocrates on medicine and Euclid on geometry, along with works by Arab scientists. They saw, too, how Aristotle had used observation and experimentation to study the physical world.

Yet science made little real progress in the Middle Ages because most scholars still believed that all true knowledge must fit with Church teachings. It would take many centuries before Christian thinkers changed the way they viewed the physical world. (See page 364.)

In mathematics, as we have seen, Europeans adopted Hindu-Arabic numerals. This system was much easier to use than the cumbersome system of Roman numerals that had been traditional throughout Europe for centuries. In time, Arabic numerals allowed both scientists and mathematicians to make extraordinary advances in their fields.

▲ *Performing surgery*

Education for Women

Few women received a good education. An exception was Christine de Pizan (duh pee ZAHN), an Italian-born woman who came to live in the French court. De Pizan was married at 15, but her husband died before she was 25. Left with three children, De Pizan earned her living as a writer, an unusual occupation for a woman of that time.

De Pizan used her pen to examine the achievements of women. In *The City of Ladies,* she questions several imaginary characters about men's negative views of women. She asks Lady Reason, for example, whether women are less capable of learning and understanding, as men insist. Lady Reason replies:

> ❝If it were customary to send daughters to school like sons, and if they were then taught the same subjects, they would learn as thoroughly and understand the subtleties of all arts and sciences as well as sons.❞

Still, men continued to look on educated women as oddities. Women, they felt, should pursue their "natural" gifts at home, raising children, managing the household, and doing needlework, and leave books and writing to men.

Medieval Literature

While Latin was the language of scholars and churchmen, new writings began to appear in the vernacular, or the everyday languages of ordinary people, such as French, German, and Italian. These writings captured the spirit of the High Middle Ages. Medieval literature included epics about feudal warriors and tales of the common people.

Heroic epics. Across Europe, people began writing down oral traditions in the vernacular. French pilgrims traveling to holy sites loved to hear the *chansons de geste,* or "songs of heroic deeds." The most popular was the *Song of Roland,* which praises the courage of one of Charlemagne's knights who died while on a military campaign in Muslim Spain. A true feudal hero, Roland loyally sacrifices his life out of a sense of honor.

Spain's great epic, *Poem of the Cid,* also involves conflict with Islam. The Cid was Rodrigo Díaz, a bold and fiery Christian lord who battled Muslims in Spain. Calling to his warriors, he surges into battle full of zeal:

> ❝There are three hundred lances that
> each a pennant bears.
> At one blow every man of them his
> Moor has slaughtered there,
> And when they wheeled to charge
> anew as many more were slain,
> You might see great clumps of lances
> lowered and raised again. . . .
> Cried the Moor "Muhammed!" The
> Christians shouted on St. James of
> Grace,
> On the field Moors thirteen hundred
> were slain in little space.❞

Dante's journey. "In the middle of the journey of life, I found myself in a dark wood, where the straight way was lost." So begins the *Divine Comedy* by the famed Italian poet Dante Alighieri (DAHN tay al lee GYEH ree). The poem takes the reader on an imaginary journey into hell and purgatory, where souls await forgiveness. Finally, Dante describes a vision of heaven.

"Abandon all hope, all ye that enter here" is the warning Dante receives as he approaches hell. There, he talks with people from history who tell how they earned a place in hell. Humor, tragedy, and the endless medieval quest for religious understanding are all ingredients in Dante's poem.

Chaucer's wit. In *The Canterbury Tales,* Geoffrey Chaucer follows a band of English pilgrims traveling to Thomas Becket's tomb. In brilliant word portraits, he sketches a range of characters, including a knight, a plowman, a merchant, a miller, a monk, a nun, and the five-times-widowed "wife of Bath." Each character

Medieval poets often accompanied their recitations on the lute, a stringed instrument based on an Arab instrument called the al-'ud. The lute first arrived in Europe when Christians copied the instrument from their Islamic neighbors to the south.

Chartres Cathedral, France *As you walk into its Gothic immenseness, your eyes are drawn upward. High above you is the ceiling, its massive weight supported by columns, pointed arches, and ribbed vaulting. Warm sunlight filters through stained glass windows, revealing scenes of heaven and Earth, angels and saints, God and humanity. And a kaleidoscope of soft, glowing color washes over the darkness below.* **Art and Literature** *What effect do you think medieval architects were trying to achieve with Gothic cathedrals? Did they succeed? Explain.*

tells a story. Whether funny, romantic, or bawdy, each tale adds to our picture of medieval life. (★ See *Skills for Success,* page 234.)

Splendors in Stone

"In the Middle Ages," wrote French author Victor Hugo, "men had no great thought that they did not write down in stone." With riches from trade and commerce, townspeople, nobles, and monarchs indulged in a flurry of building. Their greatest achievements were the towering stone cathedrals that served as symbols of their wealth and religious devotion.

Romanesque strength. About 1000, monasteries and towns built solid stone churches that reflected Roman influences. These Romanesque churches looked like fortresses with thick walls and towers. Their roofs were so heavy that builders cut only tiny slits of windows in the walls for fear of weakening the supports. As a result, these massive structures were only dimly lit.

Gothic grace. About 1140, Abbot Suger wanted to build a new abbey church at St. Denis near Paris. He hoped that it "would shine with wonderful and uninterrupted light." Urged on by the abbot, builders developed what became known as the Gothic style of architecture. A key feature of this style was the flying buttresses, or stone supports that stood outside the church. These supports allowed builders to construct higher walls and leave space for huge stained-glass windows.

The new Gothic churches soared to incredible heights. Their graceful spires, lofty ceilings, and enormous windows carried the eye upward to the heavens. "Since their brilliance lets the splendor of the True Light pass into the church," declared a medieval visitor, "they enlighten those inside."

Soon cities all over Europe were competing to build grander, taller cathedrals. The faithful contributed money, labor, and skills to help build these monuments "to the greater glory of God."

"Bibles in stone." As churches rose, stonemasons carved sculptures to decorate them inside and out. At the same time, skilled crafts-workers, members of a guild, created the brilliant stained-glass windows that added to the splendor of medieval churches. Carvings and stained glass portrayed stories from the Bible and served as a religious education to the people, most of whom were illiterate.

SECTION 4 REVIEW

1. **Identify** (a) Thomas Aquinas, (b) Christine de Pizan, (c) *Song of Roland,* (d) *Poem of the Cid,* (e) Dante, (f) Chaucer.
2. **Define** (a) theology, (b) scholasticism, (c) vernacular.
3. How did new knowledge pose a challenge to Christian scholars?
4. What were two kinds of vernacular literature that developed in the High Middle Ages?
5. What were the characteristics of (a) Romanesque architecture, (b) Gothic architecture?
6. *Critical Thinking* **Analyzing Information** Why do you think Gothic churches are sometimes called "Bibles in stone"?
7. *ACTIVITY* Solve this problem using Roman numerals: MCMLXXX + MMCCCLX. Then, translate and solve the problem using Arabic numerals. How do you think the introduction of Arabic numerals might have affected mathematics in Western Europe?

5 A Time of Crisis

Guide for Reading

- Why was the late Middle Ages a time of decline?
- What challenges did the Church face in the late Middle Ages?
- Why did Joan of Arc become a national hero in France?

For Europeans in the late Middle Ages, the "Four Horsemen of the Apocalypse" were a fearful sight. These dreaded riders, whose images were widely portrayed on the walls of churches, symbolized famine, disease, war, and death. Their appearance, people believed, signaled the end of the world.

To Europeans in the mid-1300s, the end of the world indeed seemed to have come. The evils embodied by the Four Horsemen swept over the region. First, widespread crop failures brought famine, malnutrition, and starvation. Then plague and war deepened the crisis. Europe eventually recovered from these disasters. Still the upheavals of the 1300s and 1400s marked the end of the Middle Ages and the beginning of the early modern age.

The Black Death

In the autumn of 1347, a fleet of Genoese trading ships, loaded with grain, left the Black Sea port of Caffa and sailed for Messina, Sicily. By mid-voyage, sailors were falling sick and dying. Soon after the ships tied up at Messina, townspeople, too, fell sick and died. A medieval chronicler reported:

66Seeing what a calamity of sudden death had come to them by the arrival of the Genoese, the people of Messina drove them in all haste from their city and port. But the sickness remained and a terrible mortality ensued.99

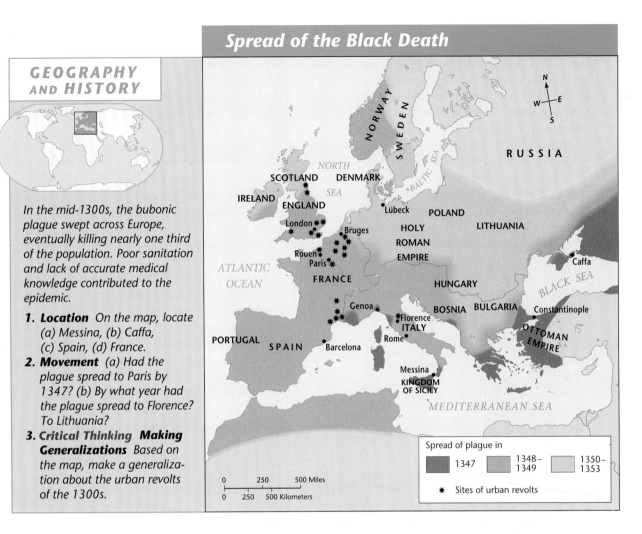

Spread of the Black Death

In the mid-1300s, the bubonic plague swept across Europe, eventually killing nearly one third of the population. Poor sanitation and lack of accurate medical knowledge contributed to the epidemic.

1. **Location** On the map, locate (a) Messina, (b) Caffa, (c) Spain, (d) France.
2. **Movement** (a) Had the plague spread to Paris by 1347? (b) By what year had the plague spread to Florence? To Lithuania?
3. **Critical Thinking Making Generalizations** Based on the map, make a generalization about the urban revolts of the 1300s.

Spread of plague in
| 1347 | 1348–1349 | 1350–1353 |

✳ Sites of urban revolts

Within months, the disease that Europeans called the Black Death was raging through Italy. By 1348, it had reached Spain and France. From there, it ravaged the rest of Europe. One in three people died, worse than any war in history.

A global epidemic. The sickness was the bubonic plague, a disease spread by fleas on rats. Bubonic plague had broken out before in Europe, Asia, and North Africa but had died down. One strain, though, had survived in the Gobi Desert of Mongolia. In the 1200s, Mongol armies conquered China and much of Asia, probably setting off the new outbreak.

In the premodern world, rats infested ships, towns, and even the homes of the rich and powerful, so no one took any notice of them. In the early 1300s, rats scurrying through crowded Chinese cities spread the plague, which killed about 35 million people there.

Fleas jumped from those rats to infest the clothes and packs of traders traveling west. As a result, the disease spread from Asia to the Middle East. Terrible reports reached Europe: "India was depopulated," wrote a chronicler. "Tartary, Mesopotamia, Syria, and Armenia were covered with dead bodies. The Kurds fled in vain to the mountains." In Cairo, one of the world's largest cities, the plague at its peak killed about 7,000 people a day.

A terrible death. The disease struck with stunning speed. "People lay ill little more than two or three days," wrote a French friar, Jean de Venette. "He who was well one day was dead the next." A few victims survived. Most did not.

Unsanitary conditions in towns and homes guaranteed that the disease would spread. Unaware of what a flea bite might mean, people paid little attention until they noticed the swellings and black bruises on their skin that promised death. Victims suffered heavy sweats and convulsive coughing. They spat blood, stank terribly, and died in agony.

Chapter 9 **229**

Social upheaval. The plague brought terror and bewilderment, since people had no way to stop the disease. Some people turned to magic and witchcraft for cures. Others plunged into wild pleasures, believing they would soon die anyway. Still others saw the plague as God's punishment. They beat themselves with whips to show they repented their sins.

Christians blamed Jews for the plague, charging that they had poisoned the wells. "The whole world," De Venette noted, "rose up against [the Jews] cruelly on this account." In the resulting hysteria, thousands of Jews were slaughtered.

Normal life broke down. The Italian poet Francesco Petrarch wrote to his brother:

> 66How will people in the future believe that there has been such a time . . . when the whole globe has remained without inhabitants? When before has it been seen that houses are left vacant, cities deserted, fields are too small for the dead, and a fearful and universal solitude [lay] over the whole Earth?99

Economic results. As the plague kept recurring in the late 1300s, the European economy plunged to a low ebb. As workers and employers died, production declined. Survivors demanded higher wages, but as the cost of labor soared, prices rose, too.

Landowners and merchants pushed for laws to limit wages. To stop rising costs, landowners converted croplands to sheep raising, which required less labor. Villagers forced off the land sought work in towns. There, guilds refused to accept new members, limited apprenticeships, and denied journeymen the chance to become masters.

Coupled with the fear of the plague, these restrictions sparked explosive revolts. Bitter, angry peasants rampaged in England, France, Germany, and elsewhere. In cities, too, artisans fought, usually without success, for more power. The plague had spread both death and social unrest. Western Europe would not fully recover from its effects for more than 100 years. ◾

Upheaval in the Church

The late Middle Ages brought spiritual crisis, scandal, and division to the Roman Catholic Church. Many priests and monks died during the plague. Their replacements faced challenging questions. "Why did God spare some and kill others?" asked survivors. The sacraments offered little comfort to people rocked by the fear of sudden death.

Divisions within the Catholic Church. The Church was unable to provide the strong leadership needed in this desperate time. In 1309, Pope Clement V had moved the papal court to Avignon on the border of southern France. (See page 214.) There it remained for about 70 years under French domination. This period is often called the Babylonian Captivity of the Church, referring to the time when the ancient Hebrews were held captive in Babylon.

The Dance of Death *The scene at left is from a set of engravings depicting the terror of the plague, by the German artist Hans Holbein, the Younger. The Black Death made no distinctions, taking men, women, and children of all backgrounds and classes.* ***Political and Social Systems*** *What social class is Death visiting in this engraving?*

In Avignon, popes reigned over a lavish court. Critics lashed out against the worldly, pleasure-loving papacy, and anticlergy sentiment grew. Within the Church itself, reformers tried to end the "captivity."

In 1378, reformers elected their own pope to rule from Rome. French cardinals responded by choosing a rival pope. For decades, two and sometimes even three popes claimed to be the true "vicar of Christ." Not until 1417 did a Church council at Constance finally end the crisis.

New heresies. With its moral authority weakened, the Church faced still more problems. Popular preachers challenged its power. In England, John Wycliffe, an Oxford professor, attacked Church corruption.

Wycliffe insisted that the Bible, not the Church, was the source of all Christian truth. He began translating the Bible into English so that people could read it themselves rather than rely on the clergy to read it. Czech students at Oxford carried Wycliffe's ideas to Bohemia— what is today the Czech Republic. There, Jan Hus led the call for reforms.

The Church responded by persecuting Wycliffe and his followers and suppressing the Hussites. Hus was tried for heresy and burned at the stake in 1415. The ideas of Wycliffe and Hus survived, however. A century later, other reformers took up the same demands.

The Hundred Years' War

On top of the disasters of famine, plague, and economic decline came a long, destructive war. Between 1337 and 1453, England and France fought a series of conflicts, known as the Hundred Years' War. The fighting devastated France and drained England.

As you have read, English rulers had battled for centuries to hold onto the French lands of their Norman ancestors. French kings, for their part, were intent on extending their own power in France. When Edward III of England claimed the French crown in 1337, war erupted anew between these rival powers. Once fighting started, economic rivalry and a growing sense of national pride made it hard for either side to give up the struggle.

English victories. At first, the English won a string of victories—at Crécy in 1346,

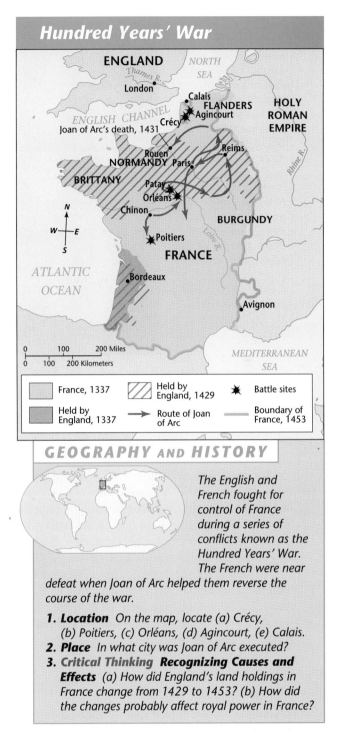

Hundred Years' War

GEOGRAPHY AND HISTORY

The English and French fought for control of France during a series of conflicts known as the Hundred Years' War. The French were near defeat when Joan of Arc helped them reverse the course of the war.

1. **Location** On the map, locate (a) Crécy, (b) Poitiers, (c) Orléans, (d) Agincourt, (e) Calais.
2. **Place** In what city was Joan of Arc executed?
3. **Critical Thinking** **Recognizing Causes and Effects** (a) How did England's land holdings in France change from 1429 to 1453? (b) How did the changes probably affect royal power in France?

Poitiers 10 years later, and Agincourt in 1415. They owed their success not to braver or more skillful knights but to the longbow wielded by English archers. This powerful new weapon was six feet long and took years to master. But it could discharge three arrows in the time a French archer with his crossbow fired just one. And its arrows pierced all but the heaviest armor.

Joan of Arc
Astonished by Joan's victories, English leaders claimed that she was aided by supernatural forces. Officials at her trial made 70 charges against her, including heresy and witchcraft. Here, Joan rallies her troops as they lay siege to the city of Paris. **Impact of the Individual** *What effect do you think Joan's execution had on the morale of French soldiers?*

The English victories took a heavy toll on French morale. England, it seemed, was likely to bring all of France under its control. Then, in what seemed to the French a miracle, their fortunes were reversed.

Joan of Arc. In 1429, a 17-year-old peasant woman, Joan of Arc, appeared at the court of Charles VII, the uncrowned king of France. She told Charles that God had sent her to save France. She convinced the desperate French king to let her lead his army against the English.

To Charles's amazement, Joan inspired the battered and despairing French troops to fight anew. In an astonishing year of campaigning, she led the French to several victories and planted the seeds for future triumphs.

The poet Christine de Pizan honored Joan's bravery and success:

66Ah, what honor to the feminine sex!
  Which God so loved that he showed
  A way to this great people
  By which the kingdom, once lost,
  Was recovered by a woman,
  A thing that men could not do.99

Joan paid for success with her life. She was taken captive by allies of the English and turned over to her enemies for trial. The English wanted to discredit her, and they had her tried for witchcraft. She was convicted and burned at the stake. That action, however, only strengthened her value to the French, who saw her as a martyr. Much later, the Church declared her a saint.

Outcomes. After Joan's death, the French took the offensive. With a powerful new weapon, the cannon, they attacked English-held castles. By 1453, the English held only the port of Calais in northwestern France.

In the end, the Hundred Years' War set France and England on different paths. The war created a growing sense of national feeling in France and allowed French kings to expand their power. During the war, English rulers turned repeatedly to Parliament for funds, which helped that body win the "power of the purse." England ended up losing its French lands, but that setback was not as disastrous for them as it appeared in 1453. With their dreams of a continental empire shattered, English rulers began looking at new trading ventures overseas.

Looking Ahead

The Hundred Years' War brought many changes to the late medieval world. The longbow and cannon gave common soldiers a new importance on the battlefield and undermined the value of armored knights on horseback. Although neither nobles nor commoners knew it

CAUSE AND EFFECT

Long-Term Causes

Growth of strong monarchs
Growth of towns and cities
Growth of representative bodies
Crusades
Increased trade
Population decline

Immediate Causes

Economic revival
New technology and agricultural productivity
Development of universities
Wider world view

WESTERN EUROPEAN EMERGENCE FROM ISOLATION

Immediate Effects

Population growth
End of feudalism
Centralized monarchies
Growth of Italian trading centers
Increased productivity

Long-Term Effects

Renaissance
Age of Exploration
Scientific Revolution
Western European colonies in Asia, Africa, and the Americas

Connections Today

Growth of strong central governments
Spread of representative government
Capitalism and powerful business classes
Influence of Western European culture around the world
Influence of technology on everyday life

Interpreting a Chart During the late Middle Ages, the chaos that had swept Europe for several hundred years gave way to an orderly society. As conditions improved, Europeans began to take a broader view of the world. ■ Select two long-term causes from the chart at left. Explain how they contributed to Western Europe's eventual emergence from isolation.

then, feudal society was changing. Knights and castles were doomed to disappear. Strong monarchs needed large armies, not feudal vassals, to fight their wars.

In the 1400s, as Europe recovered from the Black Death, other changes occurred. The population expanded and manufacturing grew. These changes, in turn, led to increased trade. Italian cities flourished as centers of shipping. They sent European cloth to the Middle East in exchange for spices, sugar, and cotton. Europeans developed new technologies. German miners, for example, used water power to crush ore and built blast furnaces to make cast iron.

The recovery of the late Middle Ages set the stage for further changes during the Renaissance, Reformation, and Age of Exploration, which you will read about in Unit 4. As Europe grew stronger, it would take a more prominent role on the global stage.

SECTION 5 REVIEW

1. **Identify** (a) bubonic plague, (b) Babylonian Captivity, (c) John Wycliffe, (d) Jan Hus, (e) Hundred Years' War, (f) Joan of Arc, (g) Charles VII.
2. What were three effects of the Black Death?
3. Why did reformers criticize the Church in the late 1300s?
4. How did new technologies affect fighting during the Hundred Years' War?
5. *Critical Thinking* **Comparing** Compare the effects of the Hundred Years' War in France and in England.
6. *ACTIVITY* Imagine that you lived in Western Europe at the time of the Black Death. Write several diary entries that reflect what life was like during the plague years.

CHAPTER REVIEW

REVIEWING VOCABULARY

Select *five* vocabulary words from the chapter. Write each word on a separate slip of paper. Then, write the definition for each word on other slips of paper. Scramble the slips and exchange them with another student. Match the words with their definitions, and then check each other's results.

REVIEWING FACTS

1. In the struggle for power among monarchs, feudal nobles, and Church officials, which group eventually gained the most political power?

2. What two important ideas were contained in the Magna Carta?

3. Why did Henry IV beg Pope Gregory VII for forgiveness?

4. What event outside Europe sparked the Crusades?

5. What were some of the results of the Crusades?

6. How did Gothic architecture differ from Romanesque architecture?

7. Explain what the Black Death was and when it occurred.

8. What were the effects of the Hundred Years' War?

SKILLS FOR SUCCESS ANALYZING LITERATURE AS HISTORICAL EVIDENCE

Works of literature often contain valuable information about the period in which they were written. Geoffrey Chaucer wrote *The Canterbury Tales* in the late 1300s. In it, he follows the adventures of a group of English pilgrims. In the excerpt below, he introduces the pilgrims.

Read the excerpt. Then, use the following steps to analyze it.

1. **Identify the source.** (a) What is the title of the work? (b) Who wrote it?

2. **Define unfamiliar words.** Use a dictionary or context clues to find the meanings of the following: (a) motley, (b) tithe, (c) learned.

3. **Study the content of the work.** (a) Which three people are described in the excerpt?

(b) Was the Merchant a successful businessman? How do you know?

4. **Analyze the source as historical evidence.** (a) What qualities of medieval knights does Chaucer list? (b) What evidence is there that the clergy were among the best-educated people in medieval Europe?

The Canterbury Tales by Geoffrey Chaucer

66There was a KNIGHT, a most distinguished man,

Who from the day on which he first began

To ride abroad had followed chivalry,

Truth, honor, generousness and courtesy. ...

There was a MERCHANT with a forking beard

And motley dress; high on his horse he sat,...

This estimable Merchant so had set

His wits to work, none knew he was in debt,

He was so stately in negotiation,

Loan bargain and commercial obligation. ...

A holy-minded man of good renown

There was, and poor, the PARSON to a town.

Yet he was rich in holy thought and work.

He also was a learned man, a clerk,

Who truly knew Christ's gospel and would preach it

Devoutly to parishioners and teach it. ...

He much disliked extorting tithe or fee,

Nay rather preferred beyond a doubt

Giving to poor parishioners round about

From his own goods and Easter offerings.99

REVIEWING CHAPTER THEMES

Review the "Focus On" questions at the start of this chapter. Then select *three* of those questions and answer them, using information from the chapter.

CRITICAL THINKING

1. **Defending a Position** Review the conflict between Pope Gregory VII and the Holy Roman emperor Henry IV. Then, cite three arguments that each man might have given to defend his position.

2. **Recognizing Causes and Effects** Construct a cause-and-effect chart for the Crusades. The chart should include both immediate and long-term effects.

3. **Synthesizing Information** Based on your readings in Chapters 8 and 9, make a chart showing the main political, economic, social, and religious developments of the early Middle Ages and the High Middle Ages. Next to each item, explain its importance.

ANALYZING PRIMARY SOURCES

Use the quotation on page 215 to answer the following questions.

1. According to the passage, who is the true ruler of Earth?

2. What did Pope Innocent III mean when he compared the priesthood to the sun and the monarchy to the moon?

3. How might monarchs have reacted to this statement by Innocent III?

FOR YOUR PORTFOLIO

WRITING ABOUT HISTORICAL FIGURES

Write a dramatic scene or a short story about an event in the life of a person in this chapter. Research to find out about the life of that person. Then write your scene or short story. When you have completed your project, write a summary explaining the importance of the person you chose.

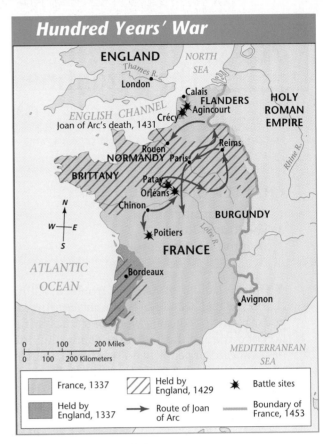

Hundred Years' War

France, 1337
Held by England, 1337
Held by England, 1429
Route of Joan of Arc
Battle sites
Boundary of France, 1453

ANALYZING MAPS

Use the map to answer the following questions.

1. Did England control more French territory in 1337 or in 1429?

2. When was the city of Avignon under English control?

3. Which of the battle sites shown on the map was farthest south?

INTERNET ACTIVITY

CREATING A DIAGRAM Use the Internet to research medieval Gothic cathedrals. Then draw a simple diagram of part of a cathedral. With your diagram, include a description of the technology used to build that section of the cathedral, or an explanation of that section's significance to medieval architects, clergy, and citizens.

The Byzantine Empire and Russia

(330–1613)

CHAPTER OUTLINE

1 The Byzantine Empire
2 The Rise of Russia
3 Shaping Eastern Europe

Prince Vladimir of Kiev was troubled. All his life, he had been loyal to the ancient Russian gods. He had dedicated wooden statues to the god of cattle and the god of the winds. But now he had heard of people who worshiped a single, all-powerful God. Should he abandon his traditional gods in favor of the God of the Jews, Christians, and Muslims? He sent agents to other lands to find out about these religions.

The ruler of the nearby Khazars had converted to Judaism. But, learning that Jews had been scattered across the Earth, Vladimir wondered if Judaism had enough worldly power. He rejected Islam because pork and alcohol were forbidden to Muslims. Roman Catholicism lost its appeal when Vladimir learned that the pope claimed authority over kings. Besides, Vladimir's agents reported that churches in Germany had little splendor.

Finally, Vladimir examined Greek Orthodox Christianity, the religion of the Byzantine empire to the south. When his agents returned from Constantinople, the Byzantine capital, they praised its glorious churches:

> 66We knew not whether we were in
> heaven or Earth. For on Earth there
> is no such splendor or such beauty,
> and we are at a loss how to describe
> it. We only know that God dwells
> there.99

Another agent reminded Vladimir, "If the Greek faith were evil, it would not have been adopted by your grandmother Olga, who was wiser than all others." Convinced, Vladimir and all his nobles tore down their wooden idols and converted to Orthodox Christianity in 988.

This story from Russia's earliest written history, *The Primary Chronicle,* mixes legend with truth. Still, Vladimir's conversion did mark a turning point in Russian history. It linked Russia to the Byzantine empire and to the cultural heritage of the eastern Roman empire.

As you have seen, the collapse of Rome left Europe divided. To the west, medieval civilization emerged. To the east, the Roman empire survived as the Byzantine empire. Byzantine civilization later influenced Eastern Europe, bringing Greek culture as well as Eastern Orthodox Christianity to the Slavic peoples.

FOCUS ON these questions as you read:

■ **Continuity and Change**
How did the Byzantine empire preserve the political and cultural heritage of Rome?

■ **Religions and Value Systems**
Why did a new form of Christianity emerge in the Byzantine empire and Russia?

■ **Political and Social Systems**
How did the rulers of Moscow build a powerful centralized Russian state?

■ **Diversity**
What peoples and cultural traditions shaped the Slavic kingdoms of Eastern Europe?

TIME AND PLACE

A Monument to Byzantine Glory *The Byzantine emperor Justinian built the Church of Hagia Sophia, or "Holy Wisdom," as part of his plan to restore the glory of Rome. Located in the city of Constantinople (present-day Istanbul), it was the largest religious structure of its day. Murals, mosaics, and sculptures adorned almost every surface of its magnificent interior.* **Continuity and Change** *What architectural features did Hagia Sophia share with earlier Roman structures?*

HUMANITIES LINK

Art History Icon of Christ and St. Maenas (page 243).
Literature In this chapter, you will encounter passages from the following works of literature: *The Primary Chronicle* (page 236); Procopius, *Secret History* (pages 240–241).

527	1019	1054	1386	1462
Reign of Justinian begins	Golden age of Kievan Russia begins	Christian schism	Poland and Lithuania unite	Ivan the Great begins reign

500   700   900   1100   1300   1500

1 The Byzantine Empire

Guide for Reading

- What were the emperor Justinian's achievements?
- Why was the Byzantine empire able to survive for so long?
- How did the Byzantine empire influence later civilizations?
- **Vocabulary** *autocrat, patriarch, icon, schism*

The teeming bazaars of Constantinople awed visitors. Rabbi Benjamin of Tudela, a Spanish traveler, saw merchants there from all over the Middle East, from Egypt—even from as far away as Russia and Hungary. "The city's daily income," he noted, "what with rent from shops and markets and taxes levied on merchants coming by sea and by land, reaches 20,000 gold pieces."

During the early Middle Ages, as the cities of the western Roman empire crumbled into ruin, Constantinople prospered. With its high walls and golden domes, it stood as the proud capital of the mighty Byzantine empire.

Heir to Rome

You will recall that, as German invaders pounded the Roman empire in the west, emperors shifted their base to the eastern Mediterranean. By 330, the emperor Constantine had rebuilt the Greek city of Byzantium, renaming it Constantinople. From this "New Rome," roads fanned out from the Balkans to the Middle East and North Africa. In time, the eastern Roman empire became known as the Byzantine empire.

Constantinople. The vital center of the empire was Constantinople. Constantine had located his capital wisely on the shores of the Bosporus, a strait that linked the Mediterranean and Black seas. The city had an excellent harbor and was guarded on three sides by water. Later emperors built an elaborate system of land and sea walls to bolster its defenses.

Equally important, Constantinople commanded the key trade routes linking Europe and Asia. For centuries, the city's favorable location made it Europe's busiest marketplace. There, merchants sold silks from China, wheat from Egypt, gems from India, spices from Southeast Asia, slaves from Western Europe, and furs from the Viking lands in the north.

At the center of the city, Byzantine emperors and empresses lived in glittering splendor. Dressed in luxurious silk, they attended chariot races at the Hippodrome, an arena built by a Roman emperor in the 200s. Crowds cheered wildly as rival charioteers careened their vehicles around and around. The spectacle was another reminder of the city's glorious Roman heritage.

A blending of cultures. After rising to spectacular heights, the Byzantine empire eventually declined to a small area around Constantinople itself. Yet it was still in existence nearly 1,000 years after the fall of the western Roman empire. As the heir to Rome, it promoted a brilliant civilization that blended ancient Greek, Roman, and Christian influences with other traditions of the Mediterranean world.

The Age of Justinian

The Byzantine empire reached its greatest size under the emperor Justinian, who ruled from 527 to 565. Justinian was determined to revive the grandeur of ancient Rome by recovering the western provinces that had been overrun by Germanic invaders. He spared no expense to achieve that dream.

Led by the brilliant general Belisarius, Byzantine armies reconquered North Africa, Italy, and southern Spain. The endless campaigns left Italy a bleeding ruin. The fighting

GLOBAL CONNECTIONS

Byzantine trade with China was sometimes disrupted by wars with Persia, which controlled the western part of the Silk Road. To bypass Persia, the emperor Justinian tried to establish other routes to China, but with limited success. Then, in 550, two Byzantine agents smuggled a supply of silkworm eggs out of China. Armed with the secrets of silkmaking, the Byzantines set up a state-owned silk industry that enriched the empire for centuries.

also exhausted Justinian's treasury and weakened his defenses in the east. In the end, the costly victories were temporary. Justinian's successors lost the bitterly contested lands in the west.

Hagia Sophia. Justinian left a more lasting monument in his buildings. To restore Roman glory, he launched a program to beautify Constantinople. His great triumph was the church of Hagia Sophia ("Holy Wisdom"). Its immense, arching dome improved on earlier Roman buildings. (See the picture on page 237.) The interior glowed with colored marble and with stunning silk curtains embroidered by local women.

Seeing this awesome church, the emperor recalled the temple King Solomon had built in Jerusalem. "Glory to God who has judged me worthy of accomplishing such a work as this!" Justinian exclaimed. "O Solomon, I have surpassed you!"

Code of laws. Justinian is best remembered for his reform of the law. Early in his reign, he set up a commission to collect, revise, and organize all the laws of ancient Rome. The result was the *Corpus Juris Civilis,* "Body of Civil Law," popularly known as Justinian's Code. This massive collection included laws passed by Roman assemblies or decreed by Roman emperors, as well as the legal writings of Roman judges and a handbook for students.

Justinian's Code had an impact far beyond the Byzantine empire. By the 1100s, it had reached Western Europe. There, both the Roman Catholic Church and medieval monarchs modeled their laws on its principles. The code thus preserved and transmitted the heritage of Roman law. Centuries later, the code also guided legal thinkers who began to put together the international law in use today.

Absolute power. To Justinian, the law was a means to unite the empire. Yet he himself was an autocrat, or sole ruler with complete authority. Like earlier Roman emperors, he had a large bureaucracy to carry out orders. Taxes from trade and industry enabled him to maintain a strong military and project Byzantine power abroad.

The emperor also had power over the Church. He was deemed Christ's co-ruler on Earth. As a Byzantine official wrote, "The em-

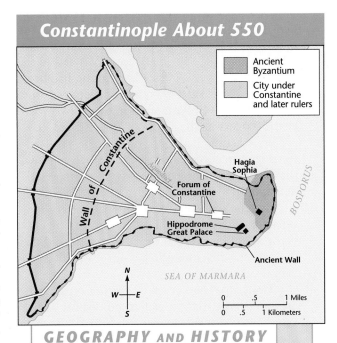

Constantinople About 550

Ancient Byzantium

City under Constantine and later rulers

Wall of Constantine

Hagia Sophia

Forum of Constantine

Hippodrome
Great Palace

Ancient Wall

BOSPORUS

SEA OF MARMARA

0   .5   1 Miles
0   .5   1 Kilometers

GEOGRAPHY AND HISTORY

The city of Constantinople was the grand capital of the Byzantine empire. Its public buildings were evidence of the wealth of the empire.

1. **Location** On the map, locate (a) Bosporus, (b) Sea of Marmara, (c) Ancient Wall, (d) Hippodrome, (e) Hagia Sophia.
2. **Interaction** How might geography have influenced the way people in Constantinople made a living?
3. *Critical Thinking* **Making Generalizations** (a) In what ways is this map more useful than the map on page 241 for learning about Constantinople? (b) In what ways is it less useful? (c) How do you account for the differences between the two maps?

peror is equal to all men in the nature of his body, but in the authority of his rank he is similar to God, who rules all." Unlike feudal monarchs in Western Europe, he combined both political power and spiritual authority.

Powerful though he was, Justinian might never have achieved his goals without the help of his wife, Theodora. The empress did more than offer advice and influence policy. In 532, her firmness helped save the throne itself.

Empress With an Iron Will

Justinian's court was in an uproar. A few days earlier, rioting had broken out between the Blues and the Greens, supporters of two rival chariot racers at the Hippodrome. Severe government action had only caused the two factions to join forces against the emperor. Now, the riot was turning into a revolt, with rebels demanding that Justinian give up the throne.

As rebels stormed the imperial palace, Justinian and his advisers huddled inside. The emperor asked his council for advice. One and all, they agreed that the safest course would be to flee the city.

Then, up rose a small woman of regal bearing. Her large, dark eyes flashed disgust at the cowardly advice of the council. Firmly, the empress Theodora spoke her mind. "Whether or not a woman should give an example of courage to men, is neither here nor there," she declared. "At a moment of desperate danger, one must do what one can."

An ambitious woman. Who was this woman whose words silenced the imperial council? Theodora had risen from humble beginnings. Her father was a bear keeper for the Hippodrome. At an early age, she herself became an actress, considered a lowly occupation. Charming, graceful, and intelligent, she led an adventurous life, traveling to Syria and Egypt. In her twenties, she settled in Constantinople, where she caught Justinian's eye. They wed in 525. Two years later, when he succeeded to the throne, she was crowned empress.

Theodora proved a shrewd, tough politician who did not hesitate to challenge the emperor's orders and pursue her own policies. She took a hand in diplomacy, trying to persuade the Persians to abide by a peace treaty. She moved quickly to help residents of Antioch after their city was destroyed in an earthquake. In addition, she championed the rights of women and set up hospitals for the poor.

At the same time, Theodora could be ruthless in pursuit of her goals. The Byzantine historian Procopius, in his *Secret History*, painted the empress as an evil, scheming monster. Those who opposed her might find themselves tossed out of office. Worse, they might disappear into her secret dungeons deep within the palace—never to be seen again.

Theodora stands firm. Now, with revolt threatening her husband's crown and her own, Theodora needed every ounce of her iron will. To her, the idea of fleeing was unthinkable. Without hesitation, she addressed Justinian and the council:

> 66If flight were the only means of safety, still I would not flee. Those who have worn the crown should never survive its loss. . . . Emperor, if you wish to flee, well and good, you have

An Influential Empress Theodora, seen in this mosaic carrying a church offering, encouraged her husband, Justinian, to protect women's rights. During their reign, new laws outlawed wife beating, enabled abused wives to sue for divorce, and permitted women to own property. **Impact of the Individual** How does this mosaic emphasize the majesty and power of Theodora?

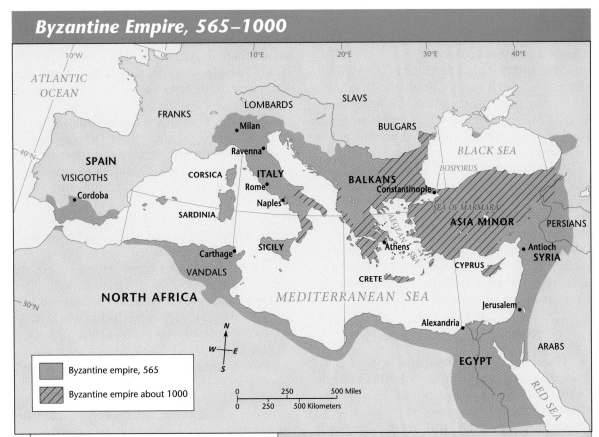

Byzantine Empire, 565–1000

Byzantine empire, 565

Byzantine empire about 1000

0   250   500 Miles

0   250   500 Kilometers

GEOGRAPHY AND HISTORY

The Byzantine empire had reached its greatest size by 565, when Justinian's reign ended. Over the next 400 years, it lost much of its territory to invading armies.

1. Location On the map, locate (a) Bosporus, (b) Asia Minor, (c) Constantinople, (d) Rome, (e) Cordoba.

2. Place What peoples lived in the areas north of the Byzantine empire?

3. Critical Thinking Comparing Compare the extent of the Byzantine empire at its height with that of the Roman empire at its height. (See the map on page 147.) What areas were common to both empires?

the money, the ships are ready, the sea is clear. But I shall stay. I accept the ancient proverb: Royal purple is the best burial sheet. **"**

Her strong words fired Justinian's resolve. He rallied his supporters and moved to crush the revolt. Within days, the emperor's armies trapped 30,000 rioters in the Hippodrome and killed them all.

By her coolness and energy, Theodora had proven her value as adviser and co-ruler to Justinian. When she died of cancer in 548, he was shattered. Although he ruled for another 17 years, the most glorious days of his reign ended with Theodora's death. ■

Changing Fortunes of Empire

The fortunes of the Byzantine empire rose and fell in the centuries after Justinian. Time and again, its skilled forces held off foreign enemies. The empire withstood attacks by Persians, Slavs, Arabs, Vikings, Mongols, and Turks.

A buffer to invaders. During the early Middle Ages, the Byzantine empire served as a buffer, protecting Western Europe from the harshest onslaught of invaders from the east. In the 600s and 700s, Arab armies overran the wealthy Byzantine provinces of Egypt and Syria before advancing on Constantinople. The city held out, eventually turning back the attackers. By resisting the Arab advance, the Byzantine empire gave the weak and divided kingdoms of Europe a measure of security.

Strengths. Although much of the Mediterranean world fell to the Arabs, the Byzantines held onto their heartland in the Balkans and in Asia Minor. The empire's greatest strengths came from a strong central government and prosperous economy.

Peasants formed the backbone of the empire, working the land, paying taxes, and providing soldiers for the military. In the cities of the empire, trade and industry flourished. While Western Europe was reduced to a barter economy, the Byzantine empire preserved a healthy money economy. The bezant, the Byzantine gold coin stamped with the emperor's image, circulated from England to China.

Byzantine Christianity

Christianity was as influential in the Byzantine empire as it was in Western Europe. But divisions grew between Byzantine Christians and Roman Catholics to the west.

Differences east and west. Since early Christian times, differences had emerged over Church leadership. Although the Byzantine emperor was not a priest, he controlled Church affairs and appointed the patriarch, or highest Church official, in Constantinople. Byzantine Christians rejected the pope's claim to authority over all Christians.

Further differences developed over time. Unlike priests in Western Europe, the Byzantine clergy retained their right to marry. Greek, not Latin, was the language of the Byzantine Church. The chief Byzantine holy day was Easter, celebrated as the day Jesus rose from the dead. Among western Christians, Christmas, the birthday of Jesus, came to receive greater emphasis.

Schism. During the Middle Ages, the two branches of Christianity drew farther apart. A dispute over the use of icons, or holy images, contributed to the split. Many Byzantine Christians prayed to images of Christ, the Virgin Mary, and the saints. In the 700s, however, a Byzantine emperor outlawed the veneration of icons, saying it violated God's commandment against worshiping "graven images."

The ban set off violent battles within the empire. The pope took a hand in the dispute, excommunicating the emperor. Although a later empress eventually restored the use of icons, the conflict left great resentment against the pope.

In 1054, other controversies provoked a schism, or permanent split, between the Eastern (Greek) Orthodox and the Roman Catholic churches. The pope and the patriarch excommunicated each other. Thereafter, contacts between the two churches were guarded and distant. They treated each other as rivals rather than branches of the same faith.

Crisis and Collapse

By the time of the schism, the Byzantine empire was declining. Struggles over succession, court intrigues, and constant wars undermined its strength. As in Western Europe, powerful local lords gained control of large areas. As the empire faltered, its enemies advanced. The Nor-

A Secret Weapon At sea, the Byzantine navy defeated the Arab fleet with the help of a secret weapon known as Greek fire. Using long metal tubes, the Byzantines fired a flaming, oily compound that ignited an enemy's wooden ship. So well did the Byzantines keep the secret of Greek fire that even today we do not know its exact formula. **Economics and Technology** Why do some nations today try to keep nuclear weapons out of the hands of other nations?

mans conquered southern Italy. Even more serious, the Seljuk Turks advanced across Asia Minor. A nomadic people out of central Asia, the Seljuks had converted to Islam in their migrations westward.

The Crusades. In the 1090s, the Byzantine emperor called for western help to fight the Seljuks, resulting in the First Crusade. (See page 220.) During later crusades, however, trade rivalry sparked violence between the Byzantine empire and Venice. Venetian merchants convinced knights on the Fourth Crusade to attack Constantinople in 1204. For three days, crusaders burned and plundered the city, sending much treasure west.

For 50 years, western Christians ruled Constantinople. Although a Byzantine emperor reclaimed the capital in the 1260s, the empire never recovered. Venetian merchants gained control of Byzantine trade, draining the wealth of the empire. More threatening, the Ottoman Turks overran most of Asia Minor and the Balkans, as you will read in Chapter 11.

The end of an empire. In 1453, Ottoman forces surrounded Constantinople. After a siege lasting two months, they stormed the broken walls. When the last Byzantine emperor was offered safe passage, he replied, "God forbid that I should live an emperor without an empire." He chose instead to die fighting.

The Ottoman ruler Muhammad II entered the city in triumph and renamed it Istanbul. The ancient Christian city became the capital of the Ottoman empire. Hagia Sophia was turned into an Islamic house of worship, and Istanbul soon emerged as a great center of Muslim culture.

The Byzantine Heritage

Although Byzantine power had faded long before, the fall of Constantinople marked the end of an era. To Europeans, the empire had stood for centuries as the enduring symbol of Roman civilization. Throughout the Middle Ages, Byzantine influence radiated across Europe. Even the Ottoman conquerors adapted features of Byzantine government, social life, and architecture.

What was the Byzantine heritage? For 1,000 years, the Byzantines built on the culture of the Hellenistic world. Byzantine civilization blended Christian beliefs with Greek science, philosophy, arts, and literature. The Byzantines also extended Roman achievements in engineering and law.

Arts. Byzantine artists made unique contributions, especially in religious art and architecture, that influenced western styles from the Middle Ages to the present. Icons, designed to evoke the presence of God, gave viewers a sense of personal contact with the sacred. Mosaics

ART HISTORY

Icon of Christ and St. Maenas *Painted in the 500s, this early Byzantine icon already displays the style of thousands of later icons. The holy figures stare directly outward, inviting the viewer into a personal relationship. Through a stained glass effect, light seems to shine through the painting. The background, halos, and the figures themselves seem to glow because the artist painted upon a background of reflecting gold paint.* **Art and Literature** *Why do you think most icons were done in the same traditional style?*

brought scenes from the Bible to glowing life. In architecture, Byzantine palaces and churches blended Greek, Roman, Persian, and other Middle Eastern styles.

The world of learning. Byzantine scholars preserved the classic works of ancient Greece. In addition, they produced their own books, especially histories.

Like the Greek historians Herodotus and Thucydides, Byzantine historians were mostly concerned with writing about their own times. Procopius, an adviser to the general Belisarius, chronicled the Byzantine campaign against Persia. As you have read, he also wrote a *Secret History* that savagely criticized Justinian and Theodora.

Anna Comnena is considered by many scholars to be the western world's first important female historian. In the *Alexiad,* she analyzed the reign of her father, Emperor Alexius I. Comnena's book portrayed Latin crusaders as greedy barbarians.

As the empire tottered in the 1400s, Greek scholars left Constantinople to teach at Italian universities. They took valuable Greek manuscripts to the West, along with their knowledge of Greek and Byzantine culture. The work of these scholars contributed to the European cultural flowering known as the Renaissance. (See Chapter 14.)

SECTION 1 REVIEW

1. **Identify** (a) Hagia Sophia, (b) *Corpus Juris Civilis,* (c) Theodora, (d) Procopius, (e) Anna Comnena.
2. **Define** (a) autocrat, (b) patriarch, (c) icon, (d) schism.
3. Choose two accomplishments of Justinian and explain the importance of each.
4. How did location contribute to the strength of the Byzantine empire?
5. Describe the legacy of Byzantine civilization.
6. *Critical Thinking* **Analyzing Information** Reread Theodora's speech on pages 240–241. What do her words suggest about her character and goals?
7. *ACTIVITY* Create a chart illustrating some of the differences between Roman Catholic and Byzantine Christianity.

The Rise of Russia

Guide for Reading

- What traditions influenced early Russia?
- How did the princes of Moscow become czars of Russia?
- What kind of government did Russian rulers develop?
- **Vocabulary** *boyar, czar*

In Russia, a patriotic monk saw a special meaning in the fall of Constantinople. The prince of Moscow, he declared, had inherited the mantle of the Roman and Byzantine emperors:

> 66The first Rome collapsed owing to its heresies. The second Rome fell victim to the Turks, but a new and third Rome has sprung up in the north, illuminating the whole universe like a sun.99

Moscow had reason to claim itself heir to the Byzantine empire. Over many centuries, Byzantine culture greatly influenced the development of Russian society.

Geography: The Russian Land

Today, Russia is the largest nation in the world. Its early history, however, began in the fertile area of present-day Ukraine. In the later Middle Ages, its political center shifted northward to the city of Moscow. From there, Russia created a huge empire that extended from Eastern Europe across Asia to the Pacific.

Russia lies on the vast Eurasian plain that reaches from Europe to the borders of China. Although mapmakers use the Ural Mountains to mark the boundary between Europe and Asia, these ancient mountains were long ago worn away to wooded hills. They posed no obstacle to the movement of peoples.

Regions. Three broad zones with different climates and resources helped shape early Russian life. The northern forests supplied lumber for building and fuel. Fur-bearing animals attracted hunters, but poor soil and a cold, snowy climate hindered farming. Farther south, a band of fertile land attracted early farmers. This region was home to Russia's first civilization.

A third region, the southern steppe, is an open, treeless grassland. It offered splendid pasture for the herds and horses of nomadic people. With no natural barriers, the steppe was a great highway, along which streams of nomads migrated from Asia into Europe.

Rivers. Russia's network of rivers provided transportation for both people and goods. The Dnieper (NEE puhr) and Volga rivers became productive trade routes. Major rivers ran from north to south, linking the Russians early on to the advanced Byzantine world in the south.

Growth of Kiev

During Roman times, the Slavs expanded into southern Russia. Like the Germanic peoples who pushed into Western Europe, the Slavs had no political organization more complex than the clan. They lived in small villages, farmed, and traded along the rivers connecting the Baltic in the north to the Black Sea.

The Varangians. In the 700s and 800s, the Vikings steered their long ships out of Scandinavia. These expert sailors were as much at home on Russian rivers as on the stormy Atlantic. The Vikings, called Varangians by later Russians, worked their way south along the rivers, trading with and collecting tribute from the Slavs. They also conducted a thriving trade with Constantinople.

Located at the heart of this vital trade network, the city of Kiev would become the center of the first Russian state. Within a few generations, the Varangians who had settled among the Slavs were absorbed into the local culture. Viking names like Helga and Waldemar became the Slavic names Olga and Vladimir.

Byzantine influences. Trade had already brought Kiev into the Byzantine sphere of influence. Constantinople later sent Christian

PARALLELS THROUGH TIME

St. Nicholas

St. Nicholas is the patron saint of Russia and Greece. He is considered the protector of children, sailors, and scholars. Thousands of churches are dedicated to him. But to many people today, he is better known as Santa Claus.

Linking Past and Present How has the tradition of "St. Nick" changed? How has it remained the same?

PAST *This Russian icon portrays the original St. Nicholas, a Christian bishop who lived in the 300s in Asia Minor. After his death, he was honored as the patron saint of children, sailors, and scholars. In many areas of Europe, children would wait eagerly for St. Nicholas to visit them on December 6, his feast day. Dressed in a bishop's red and white robes, he arrived on a donkey and brought gifts of fruit and nuts.*

PRESENT *Early Dutch settlers in America called St. Nicholas "Sinterklass." Over the years, the name evolved into "Santa Claus." By the late 1800s, the figure of Santa Claus had taken on most of the features—the white beard, jolly laugh, flying reindeer—that we know today.*

missionaries to convert the Slavs. About 863, two Greek monks, Cyril and Methodius, adapted the Greek alphabet so they could translate the Bible into Slavic languages. This Cyrillic (suh RIHL ihk) alphabet became the written script used in Russia and Ukraine to the present.

In 957, Olga, the reigning princess of Kiev, converted to Byzantine Christianity. But it was not until the reign of her grandson Vladimir that the new religion spread widely. (See page 236.) After his conversion, Vladimir married the sister of a Byzantine emperor. Soon Greek priests arrived in Kiev to preside over the mass baptisms organized by the prince.

With Byzantine Christianity came many changes. The Russians acquired a written language, and a class of educated Russian priests emerged. Russians adapted Byzantine religious art, music, and architecture. Byzantine domes capped with colorful, carved "helmets" became the onion domes of Russian churches.

Byzantine Christianity set the patterns for close ties between Church and state. Russian rulers, like the Byzantine emperor, eventually controlled the Church, making it dependent on them for support. The Russian Orthodox Church would long remain a pillar of state power.

Yaroslav. Kiev enjoyed its golden age under Yaroslav the Wise, who ruled from 1019 to 1054. To improve justice, he issued a written law code. A scholar, he translated Greek works into his language. He arranged marriages between his children and the royal families of Western Europe.

Kiev declined in the 1100s as rival families battled for the throne. Also, Russian trading cities were hurt because Byzantine prosperity faded. As Russian princes continued to squabble among themselves, Mongol invaders from central Asia struck the final blow.

The Mongol Conquest

In the early 1200s, a young leader united the nomadic Mongols of central Asia. As his mounted bowmen overran lands from China to Eastern Europe, he took the title Genghiz Khan (GEHNG gihz KAHN), "World Emperor." You will read more about the Mongols (called Tatars by the Russians) in Chapter 13. Here, we will look at their impact on Russia.

The Golden Horde. Between 1236 and 1241, Batu, the grandson of Genghiz, led Mongol armies into Russia. Known as the Golden Horde, from the color of their tents, they looted and burned Kiev and other Russian towns. So many inhabitants were killed, declared a Russian historian, that "no eye remained to weep for the dead." From their capital on the Volga River, the Golden Horde ruled Russia for the next 240 years.

The Mongols, while fierce conquerors, were generally tolerant rulers. They demanded regular payments of heavy tribute, and Russian princes had to acknowledge the Mongols as their overlords. But as long as the tribute was paid, the Mongols left Russian princes to rule without much interference.

Mongol influences. Historians have long debated how Mongol rule affected Russia. Peasants felt the burden of heavy taxes. Some fled to remote regions, while others sought protection from Mongol raids by becoming serfs of Russian nobles. Even though the Golden Horde converted to Islam, the Mongols tolerated the Russian Orthodox Church, which grew more powerful during this period. The Mongol conquest brought peace to the huge swath of land between China and Eastern Europe, and Russian merchants benefited from new trade routes across this region.

During the period of Mongol rule, Russians adopted the practice of isolating upper-class women in separate quarters. Beginning in the 1200s, women became totally subject to male authority in the household. Husbands could even sell their wives into slavery to pay family debts.

The absolute power of the Mongols served as a model for later Russian rulers. Russian princes came to develop a strong desire to centralize their own power without interference from nobles, the clergy, or wealthy merchants. Perhaps most important, Mongol rule cut Russia off from contacts with Western Europe at a time when Europeans were making rapid advances in the arts and sciences.

Moscow Takes the Lead

During the Mongol period, the princes of Moscow steadily increased their power. Their success was due in part to the city's location near important river trade routes. They also used their position as tribute collectors for the Mongols to subdue neighboring towns. When the head of the Russian Orthodox Church made Moscow his capital, the city became Russia's spiritual center as well.

As Mongol power declined, the princes of Moscow took on a new role as patriotic defenders of Russia against foreign rule. In 1380, they rallied other Russians and defeated the Golden Horde at the battle of Kulikovo. Although the Mongols continued their terrifying raids, their strength was much reduced.

Ivan the Great. The driving force behind Moscow's rising power was Ivan III, known as Ivan the Great. Between 1462 and 1505, he brought much of northern Russia under his rule. He also recovered Russian territories that had fallen into the hands of neighboring Slavic states.

Ivan built the framework for absolute rule. He tried to limit the power of the boyars, or great landowning nobles. After his marriage to Sophia-Zoë Paleologus, niece of the last Byzantine emperor, he adopted Byzantine court rituals. Like the Byzantine emperors, he used the double-headed eagle as his symbol. Ivan and his successors took the title czar, the Russian word for Caesar. "The czar," claimed Ivan, "is in nature like all men, but in authority he is like the highest God."

Ivan the Terrible. Ivan IV, grandson of Ivan the Great, further centralized royal power. He undercut the privileges of the old boyar families and granted land to nobles in exchange for military or other service. At a time when the manor system had faded in Western Europe, Ivan IV introduced new laws that tied Russian serfs to the land.

About 1560, Ivan IV became increasingly unstable, trusting no one and subject to violent fits of rage. In a moment of madness, he killed his own son. He organized the *oprichniki* (aw PREECH nee kee), agents of terror who enforced the czar's will. Dressed in black robes and

ISSUES For TODAY Russian princes were strongly influenced by the Byzantine tradition of autocratic rule. What advantages and disadvantages may result when a government is dominated by a single powerful individual?

Growth of Russia, 1300–1584

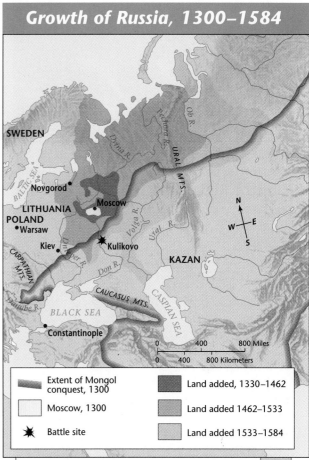

Extent of Mongol conquest, 1300

Moscow, 1300

★ Battle site

Land added, 1330–1462

Land added 1462–1533

Land added 1533–1584

GEOGRAPHY AND HISTORY

Between 1300 and 1584, Russia grew from a small area around Moscow to a large territory.

1. Location On the map, locate (a) Black Sea, (b) Ural River, (c) Danube River, (d) Caucasus Mountains, (e) Kulikovo.

2. Place During what years did Novgorod become part of Russia?

3. Critical Thinking Synthesizing Information Locate the natural feature usually considered by mapmakers to be the boundary between Europe and Asia. In 1584, was Russia mostly in Europe or mostly in Asia?

mounted on black horses, they slaughtered rebellious boyars and sacked towns suspected of disloyalty. Their saddles were decorated with a dog's head and a broom, symbols of their constant watchfulness to sweep away their master's enemies.

Ivan the Terrible *This painting of Ivan IV, done some 300 years after his death, shows how his reputation as a harsh ruler survived the centuries. Yet the czar was a man of interesting contrasts. He was a devout member of the Orthodox Church and composed original prayers and church music. He once sent the names of 3,000 of his victims to various monasteries, directing the monks to pray for their souls.* **Impact of the Individual** *What aspect of Ivan's character did the artist emphasize in this portrait? Explain.*

The czar's awesome power, and the ways he used it, earned him the title "Ivan the Terrible." When he died in 1584, he left a wounded land seething with rebellion. But he had introduced Russia to a tradition of extreme absolute power.

Looking ahead. Disputes over succession, peasant uprisings, and foreign invasions soon plunged Russia into a period of disorder. This "Time of Troubles" lasted from 1604 to 1613. Finally, the *zemsky sobor* (ZEHM skee suh BAWR), an assembly of clergy, nobles, and townsmen, chose a new czar, 17-year-old Michael Romanov. His reign established the Romanov dynasty, which would rule Russia until 1917.

In the 1600s, Russia was an emerging power. Like monarchs in France or Spain, the czars expanded national borders and centralized royal control. But Russia developed along far different lines. Byzantine influences had helped establish a strong tradition of autocratic rule. Later Russian rulers were generally more autocratic than western kings and queens. Authoritarian leaders, from Peter the Great and Catherine the Great to Joseph Stalin, would shape Russian history down to this century.

SECTION 2 REVIEW

1. **Identify** (a) Cyril and Methodius, (b) Vladimir, (c) Yaroslav, (d) Genghiz Khan, (e) Time of Troubles, (f) Michael Romanov.
2. **Define** (a) boyar, (b) czar.
3. Describe one way each of the following groups influenced Russia's development: (a) Slavs, (b) Varangians, (c) Byzantines, (d) Mongols.
4. How did the center of power in Russia shift to Moscow?
5. What methods did Ivan III and Ivan IV use to centralize their power?
6. *Critical Thinking* **Recognizing Points of View** Supporters of Ivan III called Moscow "the third Rome." (a) Why do you think they wanted to compare Moscow to Rome? (b) Do you agree that Moscow was truly the heir to Rome? Why or why not?
7. *ACTIVITY* Organize a debate on the following statement: "The only way to ensure absolute power is through the use of terror."

3 Shaping Eastern Europe

Guide for Reading

- Why did Eastern Europe develop diverse cultural traditions?

- What traditions shaped Eastern Europe in the Middle Ages?

- What threats did Eastern European kingdoms face?

- **Vocabulary** *ethnic group*

Many times in our century, people have opened their newspapers to find the news dominated by turbulent events in Eastern Europe. In 1914, a political assassination by Serbian nationalists triggered World War I. In 1938 and 1939, German aggression in Czechoslovakia and Poland sparked World War II. In 1989, revolts in Eastern European nations helped topple the Soviet empire. In the 1990s, the Balkans were again torn apart by war as rival national groups clashed in Bosnia.

The roots of such conflicts lie deep in the history of the region. As you will see, it has often been a history marked by war, revolution, and foreign conquest.

Geography: Eastern Europe

The region known as Eastern Europe is a wide swath of territory lying between German-speaking Central Europe to the west and the largest Slavic nation, Russia, to the east. Many peoples, many nations have flourished in the area over the centuries. We will now look at the diverse geography and patterns of settlement that have shaped the region.

A diverse region. To get a sense of the geography of Eastern Europe, look at the map on page 187. Traveling from north to south, your eye will pass from the chilly waters of the Baltic Sea, down across the plains of Poland, then through the mountainous Balkans. The Balkan Peninsula, a roughly triangular arm of land, juts southward into the warm Mediterranean.

Several geographic features influenced developments in Eastern Europe. Much of the region lies on the great European plain that links up with the steppes of southern Russia. As in Russia, nomadic peoples migrated across the steppe from Asia. The pressure of these migrations created frequent turmoil and slowed the growth of prosperous, stable states.

The main rivers of Eastern Europe, like the Danube or the Vistula, flow either into the Black Sea or into the Baltic. Goods and cultural influences traveled along these river routes. As a result, the Balkans in the south felt the impact of the Byzantine empire and later the Muslim Ottoman empire. By contrast, the northern regions bordering Germany and the Baltic Sea forged closer links to Western Europe.

A mix of peoples. Many groups settled in Eastern Europe. In the early Middle Ages, the Slavs spread out from a central heartland in Russia. The West Slavs filtered into what is today Poland and the Czech and Slovak republics. The South Slavs descended into the Balkans and became the ancestors of the Serbs, Croats, and Slovenes.

The Balkans were peopled by other ethnic groups as well. An ethnic group is a large group of people who share the same language and cultural heritage. Waves of Asian peoples migrated into Eastern Europe, among them the Huns, Avars, Bulgars, Khazars, and Magyars. Vikings and other Germanic people added to the mix. The result is a region of many peoples, languages, and cultural traditions.

Powerful neighboring states exercised strong cultural influences on Eastern Europe, adding further to the diversity. From the south, Byzantine missionaries carried Eastern Orthodox Christianity, as well as Byzantine culture, throughout the Balkans. At the same time, German knights and missionaries from the West spread Roman Catholic Christianity to Poland, Hungary, the Czech area, and the western Balkans. In the 1300s, the Ottomans invaded the Balkans, spreading Islam into pockets of that area. As Russian power grew, its influence also radiated to Eastern Europe.

Jewish settlements. In the late Middle Ages, Eastern Europe was a refuge for many Jewish settlers. Western European Christians launched brutal attacks on Jewish communities during the Crusades and the Black Death. To escape persecution, hundreds of Jews fled east.

Migrations and Expulsions of Jews, 1100–1650

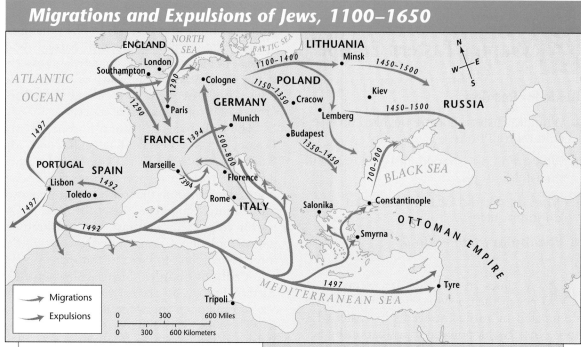

GEOGRAPHY AND HISTORY

During the Middle Ages, Jews faced restrictions on where they could live and what occupations they could pursue. When times were bad, they were often expelled by the authorities.

1. **Location** On the map, locate (a) Poland, (b) Spain, (c) Lithuania.
2. **Movement** (a) When were Jews expelled from Spain? (b) When did large numbers of Jews first migrate to Russia?
3. **Critical Thinking** **Analyzing Information** How was the movement of Jews in the Middle Ages different from the movement of the Magyars in the 900s? (See the map on page 190.)

As monarchs centralized power in England, France, and Spain, they expelled Jews from their lands, and these groups, too, migrated eastward.

In the 1300s, Polish kings followed a policy of toleration toward Jews. As a result, Jewish villages sprang up in Poland and other sparsely populated areas of Eastern Europe. Jewish peasants and scholars contributed to the economic and cultural development of Poland during this period.

Early Kingdoms

During the Middle Ages, Eastern Europe included many kingdoms, duchies (lands ruled by dukes), and principalities (lands ruled by princes). Wars constantly shifted boundaries. Sometimes, strong empires absorbed national groups. Alliances or royal marriages bound others together for a time. To get a sense of these shifting fortunes, we will look at the kingdoms of Poland, Hungary, and Serbia.

Poland. Western missionaries brought Roman Catholicism to the West Slavs of Poland in the 900s. A century later, the first Polish king was crowned. To survive, the new kingdom often had to battle German, Russian, and Mongol forces.

Poland's greatest age came after its queen Jadwiga (yahd VEE gah) married Duke Wladyslav Jagiello (vwah DIHS wahv yahg YEH loh) of Lithuania in 1386. Under the Jagiello dynasty, Poland-Lithuania controlled the largest state in Europe, an empire stretching from the Baltic to the Black Sea. Jadwiga patronized the fine university at the city of Cracow, which became a major center of science and the arts.

Unlike Russia or Western Europe, where monarchs limited the power of nobles, Polish nobles gradually gained power at the expense of the monarch. They met in a diet, or assembly, where the vote of a single noble was enough to block the passage of a law. This *liberum veto,* or "free veto," made it hard for the government to take decisive action.

Without a strong central government, Poland declined in the 1600s. It enjoyed a final moment of glory in 1683 when the Polish king Jan Sobieski (YAHN saw BYEH skee) broke the Ottoman siege of Vienna, Austria. In the next century, however, Poland disappeared from the map entirely, gobbled up by ambitious neighbors. (See page 443.)

Hungary. Hungary was settled by the Magyars who had raided Europe from the Asian steppes in the century after Charlemagne. About 970, the Magyars adopted Roman Catholic Christianity. Traditionally, Hungarians credit Stephen I with converting the entire country when he was crowned Hungary's first Christian king on Christmas Day in 1000.

Hungary was larger in the Middle Ages than it is today. Its rulers controlled present-day Slovakia, Croatia, and parts of Romania. Like King John of England, though, the Hungarian king was forced to sign a charter recognizing the rights of his nobles. Known as the Golden Bull of 1222, it strictly limited royal power.

The Mongols overran Hungary in 1241, killing about half its population. They soon withdrew, so their invasion did not have the same impact as it had on Russia. The expansion of the Ottoman Turks, though, did end Hungarian independence in 1526. Later, the Austrian Hapsburgs replaced the Ottomans as rulers of Hungary.

Serbia. During the 600s, South Slavs settled the mountainous Balkans. Serbs, Croats,

▲ *A battle between Hungarian and Mongol troops*

Slovenes, and other Slavic peoples in the Balkans had different histories during the Middle Ages. The Serbs accepted Orthodox Christianity. By the late 1100s, they had set up their own state, which reached its height under Stefan Dušan (STEH fahn DOO shahn). He battled the Byzantine empire and conquered Macedonia in the 1300s. Yet Stefan encouraged Byzantine culture and even modeled his law code on that of Justinian.

Stefan's successors lacked his political gifts, and Serbia could not withstand the Ottoman advance. At the battle of Kosovo in 1389, Serbs fought to the death, a memory still honored by their descendants. During almost 500 years of Ottoman rule, Serbs preserved a sense of their own identity.

Looking ahead. Migration, conquest, dynastic marriages, and missionary activity helped produce a tangle of overlapping claims to territories in Eastern Europe. In early modern times, large empires swallowed up much of the region. Yet whenever they had a chance, the peoples of Eastern Europe tried to recover their independence. In later chapters, we will see how the desire to rebuild separate states repeatedly ignited new turmoils.

SECTION 3 REVIEW

1. **Identify** (a) Jadwiga, (b) *liberum veto,* (c) Jan Sobieski, (d) Golden Bull of 1222, (e) Stefan Dušan.
2. **Define** ethnic group.
3. How did Eastern Europe become home to many ethnic groups?
4. What religions were introduced into Eastern Europe?
5. *Critical Thinking* **Comparing** (a) How were the histories of Poland, Hungary, and Serbia similar? (b) How were their histories different?
6. *ACTIVITY* Create flashcards for *six* of the diverse groups that settled in or influenced Eastern Europe. On one side of each card, write the name of the group. On the other side, write a sentence describing one way that group affected developments in Eastern Europe. Use the flashcards to quiz other students.

CHAPTER REVIEW

REVIEWING VOCABULARY

(a) Classify each of the vocabulary words introduced in this chapter under one of the following themes: Religions and Value Systems, Political and Social Systems, Diversity.
(b) Choose one word in each category and write a sentence explaining how that word relates to the theme.

REVIEWING FACTS

1. How was the Byzantine empire an outgrowth of the Roman empire?
2. What important split in Christianity occurred in 1054?
3. When and how did the Byzantine empire fall?
4. How did Christianity spread to Kiev?
5. What was the Golden Horde?

6. What were the accomplishments of Ivan the Great?
7. What peoples and religions are represented in Eastern Europe?
8. Why did many Jews migrate to Eastern Europe?

REVIEWING CHAPTER THEMES

Review the "Focus On" questions at the start of this chapter. Then select *three* of those questions and answer them, using information from the chapter.

CRITICAL THINKING

1. **Recognizing Points of View** Justinian and Theodora have been both condemned and admired by historians. (a) Why do you think a contemporary Byzantine historian like

SKILLS FOR SUCCESS   ORGANIZING YOUR WRITING

In the Skills for Success in Chapter 3, you learned about the writing process. (See page 66.) During the prewriting stage, you must organize your ideas in a way that will make your writing both clear and convincing.

Two of the most common ways to organize writing are cause-and-effect and comparison-and-contrast. A cause-and-effect organization can explain why an event happened or what impact an event had. A comparison-and-contrast organization can show how two events are the same and how they are different.

Imagine that you are writing essays based on the two questions below. Read the questions. Then, use the following steps to organize your writing.

> **Question A.** What events or developments led to the decline of the Byzantine empire?
>
> **Question B.** How were Russia and the Byzantine empire similar? How were they different?

1. **Identify the best method for organizing your writing.** (a) What kind of organization would you use to write an answer to question A? (b) Question B?

2. **Arrange useful information into a prewriting chart or list.** (a) List some of the causes of the decline of the Byzantine empire. (b) Prepare a chart that outlines some of the similarities and differences between Russia and the Byzantine empire.

3. **Draw conclusions that can be used as a thesis statement.** A thesis statement presents the main point in your writing. What conclusion can you draw about the chief causes of the fall of the Byzantine empire? Write your conclusions in the form of a thesis statement.

4. **Write an answer to the question based on your thesis statement.** Which details from your prewriting chart or list support your thesis statement for Question A?

Procopius might have been critical of the emperor and empress? (b) What factors might influence later historians to have different views of such historical figures?

2. **Drawing Conclusions** How might European history have been different if the Byzantine empire had fallen after the death of Justinian?

3. **Defending a Position** Autocratic rule helped the princes of Moscow and the czars of Russia create a strong central state. Do you think that great accomplishments can justify autocratic rule? Why or why not?

4. **Linking Past and Present** (a) How have long-standing ethnic differences in Eastern Europe influenced events in our own time? (b) Do you think long-standing ethnic differences have played a similar role in the development of American society? Explain.

ANALYZING PRIMARY SOURCES

Use the quotation on pages 240–241 to answer the following questions.

1. What was Theodora urging Justinian to do?

2. What did Theodora mean by the statement, "Those who have worn the crown should never survive its loss"?

3. Why would the statement quoted in question 2 never be appropriate for a leader in a democracy?

FOR YOUR PORTFOLIO

PREPARING AN ORAL REPORT Work with a partner to prepare a lecture about political and religious influences on the arts of either the Byzantine empire or Russia. First, review this chapter and list any information about links between the arts, politics, and religion. Then decide on one form of art to focus on in your lecture, such as architecture, icons, or illuminated manuscripts. Look in art books or museums or the Internet for examples of pictures to illustrate your lecture. Outline your talk and organize the pictures to go with it. Finally, present your lecture to the class.

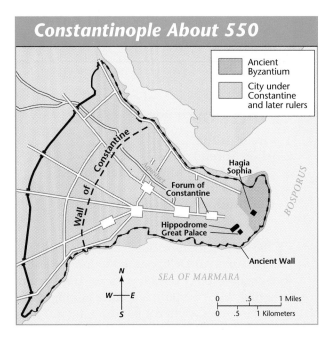

Constantinople About 550

Ancient Byzantium

City under Constantine and later rulers

Wall of Constantine
Hagia Sophia
Forum of Constantine
BOSPORUS
Hippodrome
Great Palace
Ancient Wall
SEA OF MARMARA

N W E S

0 .5 1 Miles
0 .5 1 Kilometers

ANALYZING MAPS

Use the map to answer the following questions.

1. On how many sides was Constantinople bordered by land?

2. On how many sides was the city bordered by water?

3. Which building shown on the map was located on land once occupied by the Greek city of Byzantium?

INTERNET ACTIVITY

EXPLORING HISTORICAL EFFECTS Use the Internet to research a period of Byzantine history—for example, the age of Justinian, the schism, the Crusades, or the fall of Constantinople. Then write a brief explanation of how the events of that period affected life in the Byzantine empire.

The Muslim World

(622–1650)

CHAPTER OUTLINE

The opportunity seemed perfect. In 1333, the sultan of Delhi wanted to hire educated foreigners to carry out his policies. Ibn Battuta (IHB uhn bat TOO tah), a scholar visiting India from Morocco, wanted a job. Still, he was nervous when he first met the sultan. Depending on the ruler's response, he could expect either great riches or instant dismissal. He recalled:

66 I approached the sultan, who took my hand and shook it, and continuing to hold it addressed me most kindly, saying in Persian, 'This is a blessing; your arrival is blessed; be at ease, I shall be compassionate to you and give you such favors that your fellow countrymen will hear of it and come to join you.' . . . Every time he said any encouraging word I kissed his hand, until I had kissed it seven times. 99

Ibn Battuta got the job and became a judge in the sultan's court.

Ibn Battuta was the greatest traveler of his day. By the time he reached India, he had already visited Egypt, the Middle East, the eastern coast of Africa, Asia Minor, Constantinople, and Central Asia. After eight years in India, he sailed on to Southeast Asia and China. Still later, he crossed the Sahara to tour West Africa. In all, he logged about 75,000 miles (120,700 km).

As far away as his travels took him, he rarely set foot outside what Muslims called the *Dar al-Islam*, or the "Abode of Islam." In Ibn Battuta's day, Muslim traditions linked lands from North Africa to Southeast Asia.

In 622, a major religion, Islam, emerged in Arabia. Within a few years, Arabs spread Islam across a huge empire. Although the Arab empire eventually broke apart, Islam continued to spread, creating shared traditions among diverse peoples. The Dar al-Islam also opened routes for the transfer of goods, ideas, and technologies. Muslim civilization was thus the world's first multiregional civilization. It blended elements from many cultures and pointed toward a global civilization to come.

FOCUS ON these questions as you read:

- **Religions and Value Systems**
  What are the central religious and moral teachings of Islam?

- **Diversity**
  How did Muslim rulers deal with the wide diversity among the peoples that they ruled?

- **Global Interaction**
  How did Muslim civilization create links among three continents?

- **Art and Literature**
  What artistic and literary traditions flourished in the Muslim world?

TIME AND PLACE

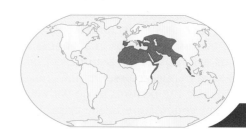

Pages From a Sacred Book *Muslim artists illuminated pages of the Quran with exquisite calligraphy and artwork. According to Muslim teachings, the Quran contains the true word of God, revealed to the prophet Muhammad. Muslims throughout the world study classical Arabic in order to read the Quran in its most sacred form.* **Diversity** *What languages had special importance for medieval Christians?*

HUMANITIES LINK

Art History Persian decorated tile (page 279).
Literature In this chapter, you will encounter passages from the following works of literature: the Quran (pages 256 and 257); Rabiah al-Adawiyya, "Oh my Lord, if I worship Thee from fear of Hell" (page 263); Omar Khayyám, *The Rubáiyát* (page 270); Baki, "Will not the King awake from sleep?" (page 278).

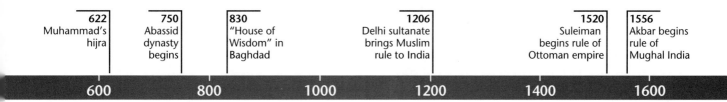

622	750	830	1206	1520	1556
Muhammad's hijra	Abassid dynasty begins	"House of Wisdom" in Baghdad	Delhi sultanate brings Muslim rule to India	Suleiman begins rule of Ottoman empire	Akbar begins rule of Mughal India

600	800	1000	1200	1400	1600

1 Rise of Islam

Guide for Reading

■ How did Muhammad become the prophet of Islam?

■ What are the basic teachings of Islam?

■ How did Islamic teachings help shape the lives of believers?

■ **Vocabulary** *hijra, caliph, mosque, hajj*

In the Arabian town of Mecca, the market-place echoed with the bargaining and bustle of business as usual. One corner, though, was hushed. There, a husky, black-bearded man was speaking to a handful of followers:

> 66In the name of God, the Compassionate, the Merciful,
> Praise be to God, Lord of the Universe,
> The Compassionate, the Merciful,
> Sovereign of the Day of Judgment!
> You alone we worship, and to You alone we turn for help.99

Some bowed their heads, moved by the beauty of Muhammad's words. His wife, Khadija (kah DEE jah), a respected merchant, had fully accepted her husband's vision. But many had their doubts. Muhammad had once been a good merchant himself. Surely, they thought, he was now mad.

In years to come, Muhammad would be recognized by millions of Muslims as the Prophet. His followers would carry the message of Islam to people on three continents and set off one of the most powerful forces in world history.

Oasis Towns and Desert Life

Islam appeared in the Arabian Peninsula, part of southwestern Asia. (See the map on page 261). The peninsula is mostly desert, but farming is possible in scattered oases and other areas where there is enough water for irrigation.

Bedouins. Many Arab clans occupied the region at the time of Muhammad. Nomadic herders, called Bedouins (BEHD oo ihnz), adapted to the conditions of the desert. Using camels, they crossed and recrossed long stretches of blistering, sandy desert in search of seasonal pasturelands. In this rugged environment, the Bedouins developed a strong tradition of hospitality and generosity toward travelers. At the same time, they acquired a strong sense of clan solidarity. Raids on scarce grazing territories led to frequent warfare. The Bedouins would form the backbone of the armies that conquered a huge empire in the 600s and 700s.

Mecca. Bedouins regularly traded with other Arabs who had settled in oasis towns like Mecca in western Arabia. This trade helped support a thriving economy. Mecca was a bustling market town at the crossroads of two main caravan routes. One route linked southern Arabia to India and to Syria and Palestine on the Mediterranean coast. The other route crossed from Mesopotamia to eastern Africa. Silks, spices, and other luxuries passed through the bazaars of Mecca.

Mecca was also a thriving pilgrimage center. Arabs came to pray at the Kaaba, an ancient shrine that Muslims today believe was built by the prophet Abraham. In Muhammed's time, though, the Kaaba housed statues of many local gods and goddesses. The pilgrim traffic brought good profits to the local merchants.

The Prophet Muhammad

Muhammad was born in Mecca about 570. Orphaned at an early age, he was raised by an uncle. In his youth, he worked as a shepherd among the Bedouins. Later, he led caravans across the desert and became a successful merchant. When he was about 25, Muhammad married Khadija, a wealthy older widow, who ran a prosperous caravan business. By all accounts, he was a devoted husband and a loving father to his daughters.

Muhammad's vision. Troubled by the idol worship of the Arabs and by the moral ills of society, Muhammad often went to a lonely desert cave to pray and meditate. There, when he was about 40, he heard a voice saying, "Proclaim." According to Muslim belief, the voice was that of the angel Gabriel.

"What shall I proclaim?" asked Muhammad doubtfully. The voice replied:

66Proclaim—in the name of your God,
　　the Creator,
Who created man from a clot of con-
　　gealed blood.
Proclaim! Your God is most generous,
He who has taught man by the pen
　　things they knew not.99

The vision left Muhammad terrified and puzzled. How could he, an illiterate merchant, become the messenger of God? But Khadija encouraged him to accept the call. She became the first convert to the faith called Islam, from the Arabic word for "submission." Muhammad devoted the rest of his life to spreading Islam. He urged people to give up their false gods and submit to the one true God.

The hijra. At first, few people listened to Muhammad. His rejection of the traditional Arab gods angered Meccan merchants who feared neglecting their idols and disrupting the pilgrim trade. In 622, faced with the threat of murder, Muhammad and his followers left Mecca for Yathrib, a journey known as the hijra. Later, Yathrib was renamed Medina, or "city of the Prophet," and 622 became the first year of the Muslim calendar.*

The hijra was a turning point for Islam. In Medina, Muhammad was welcomed by Muslim converts as ruler and lawgiver as well as God's prophet. As his reputation grew, thousands of Arabs adopted Islam. From Medina, Muslims launched attacks on Meccan caravans and defeated the Meccans in battle. Finally, in 630, Muhammad returned in triumph to Mecca, where he destroyed the idols in the Kaaba.

Death of the Prophet. In the next two years, Muhammad worked to unite the Arabs. His death in 632 plunged his followers into grief. Abu Bakr, an early convert to Islam, sternly told the faithful, "If you worship Muhammad, Muhammad is dead. If you worship God, God is alive."

Islam survived the death of its prophet. Abu Bakr was elected the first caliph, or successor to Muhammad. As you will read, under the caliphs, the message of Islam quickly spread far beyond Arabia.

---

*The Muslim calendar uses A.H. for dates after the hijra. However, this chapter, like the rest of the book, will continue to use dates based on the Christian Era calendar.

A Shrine in Mecca This ceramic tile shows the Kaaba, the most revered shrine in the holy city of Mecca. The Kaaba, a cubelike black structure, is located at the center. The surrounding courtyard can hold as many as 300,000 people. Today, as in the past, Muslim pilgrims from all over the world gather at the Kaaba to worship God and honor the prophet Muhammad. **Religions and Value Systems** Why does Mecca hold special importance to Muslims?

The Message of Islam

Like Judaism and Christianity, Islam is based on strict monotheism. Muslims believe in one all-powerful, compassionate God, whose name in Arabic is Allah. Islam also teaches that people are responsible for their own actions. "Whoever strays bears the full responsibility for straying," states the Quran (ku RAHN), the sacred text of Islam. Each individual will stand before God on the final judgment day and, depending on his or her actions, face either eternal punishment in hell or eternal bliss in paradise. Muslims recognize no official priests who mediate between the people and God.

Five Pillars. All Muslims accept five basic duties, known as the Five Pillars of Islam. The first is a declaration of faith. "There is no god but God, Muhammad is the messenger of God." Muslims believe that God had sent other prophets, including Abraham, Moses, and Jesus, but that Muhammad was the last and greatest prophet.

The second pillar is daily prayer. After a ritual washing, Muslims face the holy city of Mecca to pray. Although Muslims may pray anywhere, they often gather in houses of worship called *masjids* or mosques. The third pillar is giving charity to the poor. The fourth is fasting from sunrise to sunset during the holy month of Ramadan. The fifth pillar is the hajj, or pilgrimage to Mecca. All Muslims who are able are expected to visit the Kaaba at least once. Pilgrims wear simple clothes so that all stand as equals before God.

Some Muslims look on jihad (jee HAHD), or effort in God's service, as another duty. Jihad has often been mistakenly translated simply as "holy war." In fact, it may include acts of charity or an inner struggle to achieve spiritual peace, as well as any battle in defense of Islam.

The Quran. To Muslims, the Quran contains the sacred word of God as revealed to Muhammad. It is the final authority on all matters. The Quran not only teaches about God, but also provides a complete guide to life. Its ethical standards emphasize honesty, generosity, and social justice. It sets harsh penalties for crimes such as stealing or murder.

Muslims believe that, in its original Arabic form, the Quran is the "inimitable" word of God. Because the meaning and beauty of the Quran reside in its original language, converts to Islam learn Arabic. This shared language has helped unite Muslims from many regions.

Sharia. Over time, Muslim scholars developed an immense body of law interpreting the Quran and applying its teachings to daily life. This Islamic system of law, the Sharia, regulates moral conduct, family life, business practices, government, and others aspects of a Muslim community. Like the Quran, the Sharia helped unite the many peoples who converted to Islam.

Unlike the law codes that evolved in the west, the Sharia does not separate religious matters from criminal or civil law. It applies the Quran to all legal situations. Thus, Islam became both a religion and a way of life.

"People of the Book." As you have seen, Muslims believe in the same God as Jews and Christians, recognize many of the same prophets, and accept the idea of heaven and hell. The Quran teaches that, while Islam was God's final and complete revelation, the Torah and Bible contained partial revelation from God. To Muslims, Jews and Christians are "People of the Book," spiritually superior to polytheistic idol worshipers. Although some later Muslims overlooked Muhammad's principle of tolerance, in general, the People of the Book enjoyed religious freedom in early Muslim societies.

Women in Early Muslim Society

Before Islam, the position of women in Arab society varied. In some communities, women took a hand in many activities, including religion, trade, and warfare. Khadija, for example, owned her own business and as a widow chose to remarry. Most women, however, were under the control of a male guardian and could not inherit property. Among a few tribes, unwanted daughters were sometimes killed at birth.

Rights. Islam affirmed the spiritual equality of women and men. "Whoever does right, whether male or female," states the Quran, "and is a believer, all such will enter the Garden." The Quran prohibited the killing of daughters and ensured protection for widows. Inheritance laws guaranteed a woman a share of her parents' or husband's property. Muslim women had to consent freely to marriage and had the right to divorce, although it was harder for a woman to get a divorce than for a man. Muslim women also had the right to an education. In the early days of Islam, some Arab women participated actively in public life.

Though spiritually equal, men and women had different roles and rights. For example, the amount of an inheritance given to a daughter was less than that given to a son. The Quran

ISSUES For TODAY

For the devout Muslim, Islamic teachings guide every aspect of life. How can religious beliefs and values influence the way of life of a society?

World Religions

Religion	Origins	Holy Books	Major Beliefs	Connections Today
Hinduism	Prehistoric India	The Vedas are considered most sacred.	One God who can take many forms; goal: to achieve moksha; reincarnation; nonviolence	More than 750 million Hindus in India and Indian communities around the world
Judaism	Palestine (around 2000 B.C.)	The Torah	One God; Ten Commandments; the Torah as God's revelation and the plan for proper living	About 15 million Jews in the world, most of whom live in the United States or Israel
Buddhism	Northern India (500s B.C.)	The Tripitaka	Four Noble Truths; the Eightfold Path; goal: to reach nirvana	About 325 million Theravada and Mahayana Buddhists, mostly in Southeast Asia and East Asia
Daoism	China (500s B.C.)	Tao Te Ching Chuang Tze	Natural spontaneity; desire for harmony; sense of the absurd	Possibly as many as 480 million Daoists, mostly in China
Christianity	Palestine (A.D. 30)	The Bible	One God; Jesus, son of God and redeemer of humankind	About 2 billion Roman Catholics, Protestants, and Eastern Orthodox Christians around the world
Islam	Arabia (A.D. 622)	The Quran	One all-powerful, compassionate God; Muhammad was prophet of Islam; Five Pillars of Islam	More than 1 billion Muslims worldwide, mostly in Asia and Africa

Hundreds of millions of people practice local traditions that go back hundreds of thousands of years. These include Shinto in Japan and a variety of practices among Native Americans, Africans, and Pacific islanders.

Interpreting a Chart Muhammad began preaching the message of Islam at a time when Hinduism, Buddhism, and Christianity already dominated much of the world. Today, these four religions are the most widely practiced religions in the world. ■ Which religions on this chart emerged in Asia? How does Muhammad's role in Islam differ from Jesus Christ's role in Christianity?

permitted a man to have up to four wives if he treated them all justly. Still, few men could afford to support more than one wife.

Changes. As Islam spread, Arabs sometimes absorbed attitudes from the non-Arab peoples they conquered. In Persia and Byzantine lands, for example, Arabs adopted the practice of veiling women and secluding them in a separate part of the home. Muslims called the women's quarters the harem because it was *haram,* or forbidden, to violate it. The harem was the center of activity where women planned and carried out the indoor life of the family.

In many cities, upper-class women in particular faced restrictions. Secluded in their quarters, they were waited on by women servants and seldom ventured out. An Egyptian judge of the 1300s stated that "a woman should leave her home on three occasions only: when she is conducted to the house of her bridegroom, when her parents die, and when she goes to her own grave."

Still, as in other cultures, women's lives varied greatly according to region and class. Veiling and seclusion were not so strictly followed among lower-class city women. In rural areas, peasant women continued to contribute to the economy in many ways.

SECTION 1 REVIEW

1. **Identify** (a) Mecca, (b) Kaaba, (c) Khadija, (d) Quran, (e) Sharia, (f) People of the Book.
2. **Define** (a) hijra, (b) caliph, (c) mosque, (d) hajj.
3. How did Muhammad become the prophet of Islam?
4. (a) What are the Five Pillars of Islam? (b) How do they help unite Muslims?
5. How do the Quran and Sharia guide the lives of Muslim men and women?
6. *Critical Thinking* **Analyzing Information** Reread Abu Bakr's words about the death of Muhammad on page 257. (a) Restate his main point in your own words. (b) Why do you think he made this statement?
7. *ACTIVITY* Organize a debate around the following statement: "By and large, Arab women benefited from the rise of Islam."

2 Islam Spreads

Guide for Reading

- How did Islam spread rapidly over a wide area?
- What divisions emerged within Islam?
- Why did the Arab empire decline?
- **Vocabulary** *minaret, sultan*

Every day, more Arabs joined the forces of Amr ibn-al-As as he rode toward Alexandria, gateway to the fertile Nile Valley. The city was a Byzantine stronghold. After a year's siege, Alexandria fell. Amr told his victorious army:

    ❝The Nile floods have fallen, the spring grazing is good. There is milk for the lambs and the kids. Go out with God's blessing and enjoy the land, its milk, its flocks, and its herds. And take good care of your neighbors.❞

Inspired by the teachings of Muhammad, Arab armies surged across the Byzantine and Persian empires. In a stunningly short time, an Arabic empire reached from the Atlantic to the borders of India.

The Age of Conquest

When Muhammad died, Abu Bakr faced an immediate crisis. The loyalty of some Arab tribal leaders had been dependent on Muhammad's personal command. They now withdrew their loyalty for the Muslim state. Abu Bakr's most important contribution was to reunify the Arabs on a firmer base of loyalty to Islam itself. The reunited forces then embarked on a remarkable military campaign.

From victory to victory. Under the first four caliphs, Arab armies marched from victory to victory. They conquered great chunks of the Byzantine empire, including the provinces of Syria and Palestine with the cities of Damascus and Jerusalem. Next, they rapidly demolished the Persian empire. The Arabs then swept into Egypt.

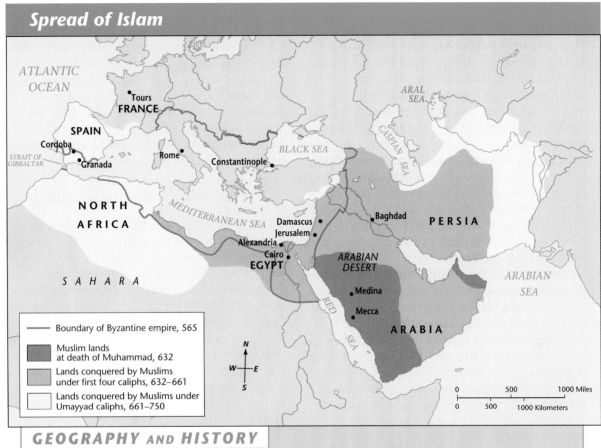

GEOGRAPHY AND HISTORY

In less than 150 years, Islam had spread from its origins in Arabia across southwest Asia and North Africa and into Europe.

1. Location On the map, locate (a) Spain, (b) Persia, (c) Cairo, (d) Byzantine empire, (e) Tours.

2. Region (a) In which period did Baghdad come under Muslim control? (b) Which city remained under the Byzantine empire? (c) Which regions were conquered in the time of the Umayyad caliphs?

3. Critical Thinking **Applying Information** By 750, Muslims controlled much of the trade of the Mediterranean world. How might the spread of Islam have contributed to this success in trade?

Later Muslim armies dashed west, defeating Byzantine forces across North Africa. In 711, they crossed the Strait of Gibraltar into Spain and pushed up the peninsula into France. At the other end of the Mediterranean, they crossed the Bosporus to besiege the Byzantine capital of Constantinople.

The breathtaking swiftness of the Arab conquests did not slow down until nearly 100 years after Muhammad's death. In 718, the Arabs abandoned the siege of Constantinople. (As you read in Chapter 10, not until 1453 did Constantinople fall to another Muslim people, the Ot-toman Turks.) In 732, the Arab push into Europe was turned back at the battle of Tours in France.

Still, Muslim and Christian forces would continue to contend in Spain for centuries. Later waves of conquest would also expand the Muslim zone much farther, especially in Asia and Africa. (See Chapters 12 and 13.)

Reasons for success. Why did the Arabs have such an astonishing series of victories? One reason was the weakness of the Byzantine and Persian empires. These longtime rivals had fought each other to exhaustion. Many people in the Fertile Crescent welcomed the Arabs as liberators from harsh Byzantine or Persian rule. Bold, efficient fighting methods also contributed to the Arab success. The Arab camel and horse cavalry, with generations of experience in desert warfare, mounted aggressive and mobile offensives that overwhelmed more traditional armies.

Perhaps the key reason for Arab success, however, was the common faith Muhammad had given his people. Islam welded a patchwork of tribes into a determined, unified state. Belief in the holiness of their faith and certainty of paradise for those who fell in battle spurred the Arab armies to victory.

Treatment of conquered people. The advancing Arabs brought many people under their rule. Muslim leaders imposed a special tax on non-Muslims, but allowed Christians, Jews, and Zoroastrians to practice their own faiths and follow their own laws. As Muslim civilization developed, many Jews and Christians played key roles as officials, doctors, and translators. In time, many non-Muslims converted to Islam.

Great Mosque of Cordoba The interior of this Spanish mosque seems like a dense forest of columns. The columns support two levels of decorated horseshoe arches that in turn support the roof above. After retaking the city of Cordoba in 1236, Christians converted the mosque into a cathedral. **Global Interaction** *What earlier civilizations used columns and arches and influenced the development of Muslim architecture?*

Many nomadic people of North Africa and Central Asia chose Islam immediately. Its message was simple and direct, and they saw its triumph as a sign of God's favor. Moreover, Islam had no religious hierarchy or class of priests. In principle, it emphasized the equality of all believers, regardless of race, sex, class, or wealth. In later centuries, Turkish and Mongol converts helped spread Islam far across Asia.

The Muslim Presence in Europe

As you have read, the Arab conquests extended to the fringes of southern and western Europe. The major areas of Muslim influence in Europe at this time were Spain and Sicily.

Spain. The Arabs and their North African allies overran Spain at the beginning of the 700s. But rivalries among princes divided Muslim Spain politically. Spanish Christian counterattacks slowly reclaimed the peninsula, gradually pushing the Moors, as Christians called North African Muslims, back into southern Spain. There, the Muslim presence remained strong until 1492. (See Chapter 9.)

For centuries, Spain was one of the most brilliant corners of the Muslim world. Princes encouraged poetry, the arts, and scholarship. At great centers of learning such as the city of Cordoba, rulers employed Jewish officials and welcomed Christian students to absorb Greek ideas at the feet of Muslim teachers. The beauty of the royal courts may still be seen today in the

Alhambra, a Muslim palace in Granada, with its elaborately decorated halls and columns, its courtyards, gardens, and reflecting pools.

Sicily. During the early Middle Ages, when Europe was weak, the Arabs seized control of Sicily and a number of other Mediterranean islands. The Arab presence was much briefer in Sicily than in Spain. Europeans soon regained the lost lands. Although Sicily was now ruled by knights from Normandy, it remained strongly Arabic in culture. Muslim officials, merchants, and farmers gave the island good government and a flourishing economy. Arab poets, philosophers, and scientists enriched the courts of Norman kings.

Movements Within Islam

Not long after Muhammad's death, divisions arose within Islam over his successor. The split between Sunni (SOO nee) and Shiite (SHEE ite) Muslims had a profound impact on later Islamic history.

Rival factions. The Sunnis felt that the caliph should be chosen by leaders of the Muslim community. Although the Sunnis agreed that the caliph should be a pious Muslim, they viewed him simply as a leader, not as a religious authority.

The Shiites, on the other hand, argued that the only true successors to the Prophet were descendants of Muhammad's daughter and son-in-law, Fatima and Ali. The Shiites believed that the descendants of the Prophet were divinely inspired. The Sunnis believed that inspiration came from the example of Muhammad as recorded by his early followers.

Ali became the fourth caliph, but he was assassinated in 661 in a struggle for leadership. Later his son, too, was killed. Many other Shiites died in battle against Sunnis, trying to install their candidates for caliph. Shiites grew to admire martyrdom as a demonstration of their faith.

Like the schism between Roman Catholic and Eastern Orthodox Christians, the division between Sunni and Shiite Muslims has survived for more than 1,300 years. Members of both branches believe in the one true God, look to the Quran for guidance, and make the hajj to Mecca. But numerous differences have emerged

Sufi Preaching *This Persian manuscript shows a group of Muslims listening reverently to the words of a visiting Sufi. Older men sit nearest to the teacher, while younger men listen from the sidelines. Women and children occupy a gallery of their own.*
Religions and Value Systems *Based on what you have read, what kind of message do you think this Sufi might be preaching?*

in such areas as religious practice, law, and daily life. Traditionally, Sunnis have been the majority branch within Islam. Today, about 90 percent of Muslims are Sunnis. Most Shiites live in Iran, Lebanon, Iraq, and Yemen. The Shiite movement itself has split into several different factions.

Sufi. A third tradition emerged with the Sufis, Muslim mystics who sought communion with God through meditation, fasting, and other rituals. Sufis were respected for their piety and miraculous powers. One of the earliest Sufis, Rabiah al-Adawiyya (RAHB ee ah al a da WEE ah), rejected marriage and devoted her life to prayer. In her poetry, she urged Muslims to worship God selflessly, without hope of reward:

66Oh my Lord, if I worship Thee from
    fear of Hell, burn me in Hell,
And if I worship Thee in hope of
    Paradise, exclude me from Paradise
But if I worship Thee for Thine own
    sake,
Then withhold not from me Thine
    eternal beauty.99

Like Christian monks and nuns, some Sufis helped spread Islam through missionary work.

They carried the faith to remote villages, where they blended local traditions and beliefs into Muslim culture.

The Arab Empire

After the death of Ali, the Umayyad (oh MĪ ad) family set up a dynasty that ruled the Islamic world until 750. From their capital at Damascus in Syria, they directed the spectacular conquests that carried Islam from the Atlantic to the Indus Valley.

Umayyads. Even as victories expanded the Arab empire, the Umayyads faced numerous problems. First, they had to adapt from desert life to ruling large cities and huge territories. To govern their empire, the Umayyads often relied on local officials, including educated Jews, Greeks, and Persians. As a result, Byzantine and Persian traditions of government influenced Arab rulers.

While conquests continued, vast wealth flowed into Umayyad hands. When conquests slowed in the 700s, economic tensions increased between wealthy Arabs and those who had less. Many Muslims criticized the court at Damascus for abandoning the simple ways of the early caliphs. Shiites hated the Umayyads because they had defeated Ali and killed his son, dishonoring the Prophet's family. Unrest also festered among non-Arab converts to Islam, who under the Umayyads had fewer rights than Arabs.

Abbassids. Discontented Muslims found a leader in Abu al-Abbas, who captured Damascus in 750. Soon after, one of his generals invited members of the defeated Umayyad family to a banquet—and killed them all. Only one Umayyad escaped to Spain, where he set up an independent caliphate at Cordoba. Abu al-Abbas then founded the Abbassid dynasty, which lasted until 1258.

The Abbassid dynasty ended Arab dominance and helped make Islam a truly universal religion. Under the early Abbassids, the empire of the caliphs reached its greatest wealth and power, and Islamic civilization enjoyed a golden age.

"City of Peace." The Abbassid caliph al-Mansur chose as the site of his new capital Baghdad, a small market town in present-day Iraq. He noted that the location offered many strategic advantages:

“It is an excellent military camp. Besides here is the Tigris to put us in touch with lands as far as China and bring us all that the seas yield.”

Under the Abbassids, Baghdad exceeded Constantinople in size and wealth.

In Baghdad, Persian traditions strongly influenced Arab life, but Islam remained the religion and Arabic the language of the empire. Poets, scholars, philosophers, and entertainers from all over the Muslim world flocked to the Abbassid court. Visitors no doubt felt that Baghdad deserved its title "City of Peace, Gift of God, Paradise on Earth."

Many gardens, dotted with fabulous fountains, gleamed in the sunlight. Above the streets loomed domes and minarets, the slender towers of mosques, from which the *muezzin*, or crier, called the faithful to prayer. In busy market courtyards, merchants sold goods from Africa, Asia, and Europe. The palace of the caliph echoed with the music of flutes, cymbals, and tambourines, and the voices of female singers.

Harun al-Rashid. From 786 to 809, the caliph Harun al-Rashid ruled an empire larger than that of his European contemporary Charlemagne. For centuries, in both Europe and the Muslim world, Harun was seen as a model ruler and as a symbol of wealth and splendor.

Many stories and legends recall Harun's fabulous wealth and his generous support of the arts. One story tells how Harun was struck by the beauty of some verses. He ordered his treasurer to pay the poet 10,000 dirhams—a vast sum of money.

The poet was overwhelmed. Bowing low, he stammered, "O prince of the faithful, your words of praise are better than my verse."

GLOBAL CONNECTIONS

Harun's court at Baghdad enjoyed friendly relations with Charlemagne's court at Aachen. Harun hoped that the Frankish king might join him in an alliance against the rival Umayyad caliphate in Spain. To that end, Harun sent Charlemagne a number of fabulous gifts, including a mechanical clock and an elephant. According to some reports, Harun also sent a chess set—perhaps the first one ever seen in Western Europe.

Delighted, the caliph again turned to his treasurer. "O Fadhl," he ordered, "give him another 100,000." The caliph would hardly miss such sums. At his death, he had an estimated billion dirhams in cash plus large stores of jewels, gold, and other treasure.

Decline of the Caliphate

Starting about 850, Abbassid control over the Arab empire fragmented. In Spain, Egypt, and elsewhere, independent dynasties ruled separate Muslim states. Cairo and Cordoba in Spain flourished as centers of religion, scholarship, and trade.

As the caliph's power faded, civil wars erupted, and Shiite rulers took over parts of the empire. Between 900 and 1400, a series of invasions added to the chaos.

Seljuks. In the 900s, the Seljuk Turks migrated into the Middle East from Central Asia. They adopted Islam and built a large empire across the Fertile Crescent. By 1055, a Seljuk sultan, or authority, controlled Baghdad, but he left the Abbassid caliph as a figurehead.

As the Seljuks pushed into Asia Minor, they threatened the Byzantine empire. As you read in Chapter 9, stories of Seljuk interference with Christian pilgrims traveling to Jerusalem led Pope Urban II to preach the First Crusade in 1095.

The Crusaders. In 1099, after a long and bloody siege, Christian crusaders captured Jerusalem, a city holy to Christians, Muslims, and Jews. For 150 years, the city passed back and forth between Muslims and Christians. The Muslim general Salah al-Din, or Saladin, ousted Christians from Jerusalem in 1187. They regained it after his death, holding it until 1244.

Christians also ruled a few tiny states in Palestine, but they were eventually expelled. In the long term, the Crusades had a much greater impact on Europe than on the Muslim world. (★ See *Skills for Success,* page 280.)

Mongols. In 1216, Genghiz Khan led the Mongols out of Central Asia across Persia and Mesopotamia. Mongol armies returned again and again. In 1258, Hulagu, grandson of Genghiz, burned and looted Baghdad, killing the last Abbassid caliph. Later, the Mongols adopted Islam. (You will read more about the Mongols in Chapter 13.)

CAUSE AND EFFECT

Long-Term Causes

Weakness of Byzantine and Persian empires
Economic and social changes in Arabia

Immediate Causes

Tribes of Arabia unified by Islam around a central message
Wide acceptance of religious message of Islam
Easy acceptance of social ideas of Islam, such as equality among believers

SPREAD OF ISLAM

Immediate Effects

Islam spreads from the Atlantic coast to the Indus Valley
Centers of learning flourish in Cairo, Cordoba, and elsewhere

Long-Term Effects

Muslim civilization emerges
Linking of Europe, Asia, and Africa through Muslim trade network
Arabic becomes shared language of Muslims
Split between Sunnis and Shiites

Connections Today

Islam is religion of nearly one fifth of world population
Millions of Muslims make pilgrimages to Mecca
Arabic is among the most widely known languages in the world

Interpreting a Chart Islam spread most dramatically in the centuries immediately following the hijra. Religion, politics, and culture all played a role in its rapid rise. ■ How does the spread of Islam help explain the wide knowledge of Arabic in today's world?

In the late 1300s, another Mongol leader, Timur the Lame, or Tamerlane, led his armies into the Middle East. Though himself a Muslim, Tamerlane's ambitions led him to conquer Muslim as well as non-Muslim lands. His armies overran Persia and Mesopotamia before invading Russia and India.

Looking ahead. As the 1200s drew to a close, the Arab empire had fragmented and fallen. Independent Muslim caliphates and states were scattered across North Africa and Spain, while a Mongol khan ruled the Muslim Middle East. After five centuries, the Dar al-Islam was as politically divided as the Christian world.

Even though the empire crumbled, Islam continued to link diverse people across an enormous area. In the future, other great Muslim empires would arise in the Middle East and India. Muslims also benefited from an advanced civilization that had taken root under the Abbassids. In the next section, you will read about the achievements of this Muslim civilization.

SECTION 2 REVIEW

1. **Identify** (a) Fatima and Ali, (b) Sufi, (c) Rabiah al-Adawiyya, (d) Umayyads, (e) Abu al-Abbas, (f) Harun al-Rashid, (g) Tamerlane.
2. **Define** (a) minaret, (b) sultan.
3. (a) What areas did Arab armies conquer? (b) Give three reasons for the rapid success of the Arab conquests.
4. What issues divided Sunni Muslims and Shiite Muslims?
5. (a) How did divisions within the Arab empire lead to the emergence of the Abbassid dynasty? (b) Why did the empire eventually break up?
6. *Critical Thinking* **Drawing Conclusions** Muhammad said, "Know ye that every Muslim is a brother to every other Muslim and that ye are now one brotherhood." How might this idea have increased the appeal of Islam to conquered peoples?
7. *ACTIVITY* Imagine that you are a Bedouin who is visiting Baghdad for the first time during the reign of Harun al-Rashid. Record in your diary how city life differs from nomadic life in the desert.

3 Golden Age of Muslim Civilization

Guide for Reading

- What were the economic strengths of the Muslim world?
- What traditions influenced Muslim arts and literature?
- What advances did Muslims make in the sciences?

One night, Caliph al-Mamun had a vivid dream. There in his chambers he came upon a balding, blue-eyed stranger sitting on the low couch.

"Who are you?" the caliph demanded.

"Aristotle," the man replied.

The caliph was delighted. He plied the great Greek philosopher with questions about ethics, reason, and religion.

Although al-Mamun soon awoke, his dream inspired him to action. He had scholars collect and translate the great works of the classical world into Arabic. By 830, the caliph had set up the "House of Wisdom," a library and university in Baghdad.

Under the Abbassids, Islam absorbed traditions from many cultures. In the process, a vital new civilization rose that flourished in cities from Damascus to Cairo to Cordoba and later to Delhi in India. The great works produced by scholars of the Abbassid golden age shaped the Muslim world just as Greek and Roman classics shaped western culture.

Society and the Economy

The Muslim empire united people from diverse cultures, including Arabs, Persians, Egyptians and other Africans, and Europeans. Later, Mongols, Turks, Indians, and people in Southeast Asia declared their faith in Islam. In time, Muslim civilization absorbed and blended many traditions.

Social classes. Muslim society was more open than that of medieval Europe. Although Arabs had held themselves apart from non-Arab

Going Shopping

Some complain that the marketplace is loud, busy, crowded. But for merchants selling their wares, shoppers looking for bargains, and people who just want to be with people, this is the place to be.

Linking Past and Present What advantages does an enclosed mall have over an open-air marketplace? Why are some open-air markets still popular?

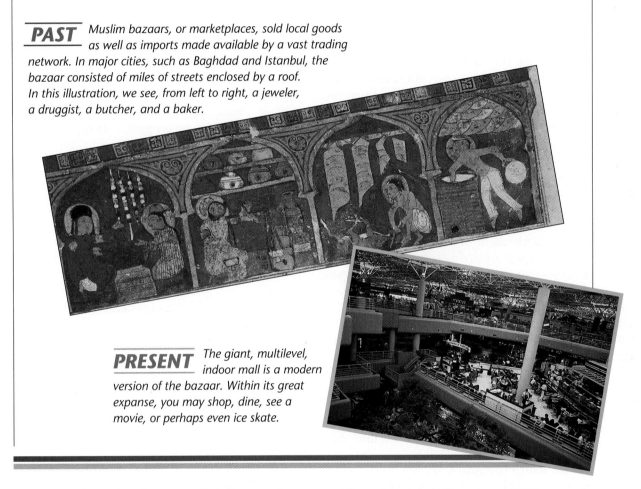

PAST *Muslim bazaars, or marketplaces, sold local goods as well as imports made available by a vast trading network. In major cities, such as Baghdad and Istanbul, the bazaar consisted of miles of streets enclosed by a roof. In this illustration, we see, from left to right, a jeweler, a druggist, a butcher, and a baker.*

PRESENT *The giant, multilevel, indoor mall is a modern version of the bazaar. Within its great expanse, you may shop, dine, see a movie, or perhaps even ice skate.*

Muslims at first, that distinction faded under the Abbassids. People could move up in society, especially through religious, scholarly, or military achievements.

As in Greece and Rome, slavery was common in the cities of the Muslim world. Slaves were brought from conquered lands in Spain, Greece, Africa, India, and Central Asia. Muslims could not be enslaved. If non-Muslim slaves converted to Islam, they did not automatically become free, but their children did. A female slave who married her owner also gained freedom.

Most slaves worked as household servants. Some were skilled artisans. The Abbassids used slave-soldiers who fought loyally for the caliph. Slaves of rulers sometimes rose to high positions in government, and a number of caliphs were the sons of slave mothers. Islamic law encouraged the freeing of slaves. Many slaves bought their freedom, often with the help of charitable donations or even state funds.

An international trade network. Merchants were honored in the Muslim world, in part because Muhammad had been a merchant.

A traditional collection of deeds and sayings of the Prophet stated:

> 66The honest, truthful Muslim merchant will stand with the martyrs on the Day of Judgment. I commend the merchants to you, for they are the couriers of the horizon and God's trusted servants on Earth. . . . If God permitted the inhabitants of Paradise to trade, they would deal in cloth and perfume. 99

Between 750 and 1350, merchants built a vast trading network across the Muslim world and beyond, spreading Islam peacefully in their wake. Camel caravans crossed the Sahara into West Africa. Muslim traders traveled the Silk Road from China. Monsoon winds carried Arab ships from East Africa to India. Everywhere Muslim traders bought and exchanged goods, creating great fortunes for the most successful.

Trade spread both products and technologies. As you have read, Arab merchants brought Arabic numerals from India to the western world. Arabs also carried sugar from India and papermaking from China. A common language and religion helped this global exchange to grow and thrive.

Extensive trade and a prosperous money economy led Muslims to pioneer new ways of doing business. They set up partnerships, bought and sold on credit, and formed banks to change currency. To make the transfer of money easier, Muslims invented the ancestors of today's bank checks. We get our word *check* from the Arabic word *sakk*.

Manufacturing. As in medieval Europe, handicraft manufacturing in Muslim cities was typically organized by guilds. The heads of the guilds, chosen by their members, often had the authority to regulate prices, weights and measures, methods of production, and the quality of the product. Most labor was done by wage workers.

Across the Muslim world, artisans produced a wealth of fine goods. Steel swords from Damascus, leather goods from Cordoba, cotton textiles from Egypt, and carpets from Persia were highly valued. Workshops also turned out fine glassware, furniture, and tapestries.

Agriculture. Outside the cities, agriculture flourished across a wide variety of climates and landforms. Muslim farmers cultivated sugar cane, cotton, dyes, medicinal herbs, fruits, vegetables, and flowers that were bought and sold in world markets.

The more arid regions of the Muslim world were basically divided into two kinds of land, "the desert and the sown." Small farming communities faced a constant scarcity of water. To improve farm output, the Abbassids organized massive irrigation projects and drained swamplands between the Tigris and Euphrates. Farmers in Mesopotamia, Egypt, and the Mediterranean coast produced grain, olives, dates, and other crops.

The deserts continued to support independent nomads who lived by herding. Still, nomads and farmers shared economic ties. Nomads bought dates and grain from settled peoples, while farming populations acquired meat, wool, and hides from the nomads.

Muslim Art

As in Christian Europe and Hindu India, religion shaped the arts of the Islamic world. Muslim artists also drew on the technical skills and styles of the many peoples with whom they came in contact.

Design and decoration. Because the Quran strictly banned the worship of idols, Muslim religious leaders forbade artists to portray God or human figures in religious art. The walls and ceilings of mosques were decorated with elaborate abstract and geometric patterns. The arabesque, an intricate design composed of curved lines that suggest floral shapes, appeared in rugs, textiles, and glassware. Muslim artists also perfected skills in calligraphy. They worked the flowing Arabic script, especially verses from the Quran,

▲ *Bronze griffin*

Dome of the Rock *Jerusalem is a holy city for Muslims, Christians, and Jews. The most revered Muslim site in Jerusalem is the Dome of the Rock. It was built in the 600s over a rock where Muslims believe Muhammad ascended into Heaven, and where Jews believe Abraham offered his son Isaac to God.* **Continuity and Change** *Why are Jews, Muslims, and Christians all familiar with the story of Abraham?*

into decorations on buildings and objects of art. (See the picture on page 255.)

In nonreligious art, some Muslim artists did paint human and animal figures. Arabic scientific works were often lavishly illustrated. Literary works and luxury objects sometimes showed stylized figures. In later periods, Persian, Turkish, and Indian artists excelled at painting miniatures to illustrate books of poems and fables.

Architecture. Muslim architects adapted the domes and arches of Byzantine buildings to new uses. In Jerusalem, they built the Dome of the Rock, a great shrine capped with a magnificent dome. Domed mosques and high minarets dominated Muslim cities in the same way that cathedral spires dominated medieval Christian cities. Outside many mosques lay large courtyards, with fountains where the faithful performed ceremonial washing before prayer.

Literature

The great work of Islamic literature was the poetic Quran itself. Scholars studied the sacred words of the Quran in Arabic and then produced their own works interpreting its meaning.

Poetry. Long before Muhammad, Arabs had a rich tradition of oral poetry, which helped bring the various Arab groups together as one culture. In musical verses, Bedouin poets chanted the dangers of desert journeys, the joys of battle, or the glories of their clans. Their most important themes, chivalry and the romance of nomadic life, recurred in Arab poetry throughout the centuries. Through Muslim Spain, these traditions came to influence medieval European literature and music.

Later Arab poets developed elaborate formal rules for writing poetry and explored both religious and worldly themes. As you have read, the poems of Rabiah al-Adawiyya expressed Sufi mysticism. Other poets praised important leaders, described the lavish lives of the wealthy, sang of the joys and sorrows of love, or conveyed nuggets of wisdom.

Persian Muslims also had a fine poetic tradition. Firdawsi (fihr DOW see) wrote in Persian using Arabic script. His masterpiece, the *Shahnamah,* or *King's Book of Kings,* tells the history of Persia in 60,000 verses. Omar Khayyám (kī YAHM), famous in the Muslim world as a scholar and astronomer, is best known to westerners for *The Rubáiyát* (ROO bī yaht). In this collection of four-line poems, he meditates on fate and the fleeting nature of life:

❝The Moving Finger writes; and having writ,
Moves on; nor all your Piety nor Wit
Shall lure it back to cancel half a line,
Nor all your Tears wash out a word of it.❞

Tales. Arab writers prized the art of storytelling. Across their empire, they gathered and adapted stories from Indian, Persian, Greek, Jewish, Egyptian, and Turkish sources. The best-known collection is *The Thousand and One Nights,* a group of tales narrated by the fictional princess Scheherezade (shu hehr uh ZAH duh). They include romances, fables, adventures, and humorous anecdotes, many set in the Baghdad of Harun al-Rashid. Later versions filtered into Europe, where millions of children thrilled to "Aladdin and His Magic Lamp" or "Ali Baba and the Forty Thieves."

The World of Learning

"Seek knowledge even as far as China," declared Muhammad. Although he could not read and write, his respect for learning set the tone for Muslim civilization. Al-Mamun and later caliphs made Baghdad into the greatest Muslim center of learning. Its vast libraries attracted a galaxy of scholars, who were well paid and highly respected. Other cities, like Cairo, Bukhara, Timbuktu, and Cordoba, had their own centers of learning.

Philosophy. Muslim scholars translated the works of the Greek philosophers, as well as many Hindu and Buddhist texts. Like later Christian thinkers in Europe, Muslim scholars tried to harmonize Greek ideas about reason with religious beliefs based on divine revelation. In Cordoba, the philosopher Ibn Rushd—known in Europe as Averroës—put all knowledge to the test of reason. His writings on Aristotle were translated into Latin and influenced Christian scholastics in medieval Europe. Ibn Khaldun set standards for the scientific study of history. He stressed the importance of studying the causes of events.

Mathematics. Muslim scholars studied both Indian and Greek mathematics before making their original contributions. The greatest Muslim mathematician was al-Khwarizmi (ahl kwah REEZ mee). His work pioneered the study of algebra (from the Arabic word *al-jabr*). In the 800s, he wrote a book that was later translated into Latin and became a standard mathematics textbook in Europe.

Astronomy. Like many scholars of the time, al-Khwarizmi made contributions in other fields. He developed a set of astronomical tables based on Greek and Indian discoveries. At observatories from Baghdad to Central Asia, Muslim astronomers studied eclipses, observed the Earth's rotation, and calculated the circumference of the Earth to within a few thousand feet. The work of Muslim astronomers and navigators helped pave the way for later explorers like Christopher Columbus.

Masters of Medicine

If you had been on the streets of Baghdad one day in the early 900s, you might have seen a puzzling sight. A well-dressed man was traveling through the city, pausing at various locations. Wherever he stopped, he hung up a piece of raw meat, then moved on. You might have been even more puzzled to learn that the man was

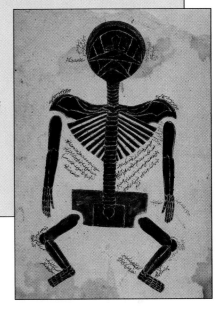

Muslim Medical Texts At hospitals in Baghdad, Cairo, and Damascus, scholars studied in libraries well stocked with medical texts like these. On the right is a page from an anatomy text. The book on the left is an Arabic translation of a Greek text on rabies. **Economics and Technology** Based on this illustration, what did Muslim physicians know about rabies?

Muhammad al-Razi—the most respected doctor in the city.

In fact, al-Razi was engaged in serious environmental research. He had been given the task of choosing the site for a new hospital. But how could he determine the healthiest location? By carefully observing the pieces of raw meat, al-Razi found his answer. He advised that the hospital be built at the place where the meat rotted most slowly!

The Muslim medical world. Building on the knowledge of Greeks, Muslims made remarkable advances in medicine and public health. Under the caliphs, physicians and pharmacists had to pass a test before they could practice. The government set up hospitals, with separate wards for women. Injured people could get quick treatment at a department similar to today's emergency room. Physicians traveled to rural areas to provide health care to those who could not get to a city, while others regularly visited jails.

As you have seen, one of the most original medical thinkers was al-Razi, head physician at Baghdad's chief hospital. He wrote many books on medicine, including a pioneering study of measles and smallpox. He also challenged accepted medical practices. Treat the mind as well as the body, he advised young doctors. If a doc-

tor made hopeful comments, he taught, patients would recover all the faster.

Equally famous was the Persian physician Ibn Sina, known in Europe as Avicenna. By the age of 16, he was already a doctor to the Persian nobility. His great work was the *Canon on Medicine,* a huge encyclopedia of what the Greeks, the Arabs, and he himself had learned about the diagnosis and treatment of disease. The book includes a list of more than 4,000 prescriptions, made with such ingredients as mercury from Spain, myrrh from East Africa, and camphor from India.

Behind these two great names stood dozens of others. Muslim eye surgeons developed a way to treat cataracts, drawing fluid out of the lenses with a hollow needle. For centuries, surgeons around the world used this method to save patients' eyesight. Arab pharmacists were the first to mix bitter medicines into sweet-tasting syrups and gums.

Knowledge moves west. A story from the Crusades illustrates the vast difference in medical knowledge between Arab and European doctors at that time. A French knight in Syria, who had severely wounded his leg, came under the care of a Lebanese doctor. Using herbs and oils, the doctor was able to ease the leg's infection.

Suddenly, a French doctor arrived on the scene and demanded to take over the treatment. The Lebanese doctor reported what happened next:

66The French doctor then said to the knight, 'Which would thou prefer, living with one leg or dying with two?' The latter replied, 'Living with one leg.' The physician said, 'Bring me a strong knight and a sharp ax.' A knight came with the ax. . . . Then the physician laid the leg of the patient on a block of wood and bade the knight strike his leg with the ax and chop it off at one blow. Accordingly he struck it— while I was looking on—one blow, but the leg was not severed. He dealt another blow, upon which . . . the patient died on the spot.99

In time, however, European physicians began to attend Muslim universities in Spain and translate Arabic medical texts. For 500 years, the works of Avicenna and al-Razi became the standard medical textbooks at European schools. ▪

SECTION 3 REVIEW

1. **Identify** (a) Dome of the Rock, (b) Omar Khayyám, (c) *The Thousand and One Nights,* (d) Averroës, (e) Muhammad al-Razi, (f) Avicenna.
2. (a) Why did trade flourish across the Muslim world? (b) How did new business methods encourage trade?
3. How did the teachings of Islam influence the arts?
4. Describe one advance made by Muslim civilization in each of the following areas: (a) mathematics, (b) astronomy, (c) medicine.
5. *Critical Thinking* **Applying Information** Muhammad taught that "the ink of the scholar is holier than the blood of the martyr." (a) What do you think he meant? (b) How might this attitude have contributed to the development of Muslim civilization?
6. *ACTIVITY* Examine the examples of Arabic calligraphy on page 255. Then, write your own first name in a similar style.

4 Muslims in India

Guide for Reading

■ What impact did the Muslim invasions have on India?

■ How did Muslim and Hindu traditions clash and blend?

■ How did Akbar strengthen Mughal rule?

The whole of India is full of gold and jewels," advisers told Sultan Mahmud of Ghazni. "And since the inhabitants are chiefly infidels and idolators, by the order of God and his Prophet, it is right for us to conquer them." In 1001, Mahmud led his armies into northern India. Smashing and looting Hindu temples, he used the fabulous riches of India to turn his capital into a great Muslim center. Later Muslim invaders did more than loot and destroy. They built a dazzling new Muslim empire in India.

The arrival of Islam brought changes to India as great as those caused by the Aryan migrations 2,000 years earlier. As Muslims mingled with Indians, each civilization absorbed elements from the other.

The Muslim Advance

As you read in Chapter 4, the Gupta empire fell about 550. India again fragmented into many local kingdoms. In the age-old pattern, rival princes battled for control of the northern plain. Despite power struggles, Indian culture flourished. Hindu and Buddhist rulers spent huge sums to build and decorate magnificent temples. Trade networks linked India to the Middle East, Southeast Asia, and China.

Although Arab armies conquered the Indus Valley in 711, they advanced no farther into the subcontinent. Then about 1000, Turkish converts to Islam pushed into India. At first, they were adventurers like Mahmud, who pillaged much of the north. In the late 1100s, though, the sultan of Ghur defeated Hindu armies across the northern plain. He made Delhi his capital. From there, his successors organized the Delhi sultanate, which lasted from 1206 to 1526. The Delhi sultanate marked the beginning of Muslim rule in northern India.

Why did the Muslim invaders triumph? They won on the battlefield in part because Turkish mounted archers had far greater mobility than Hindu forces, who rode slow-moving war elephants. Then, too, Hindu princes wasted their resources battling one another instead of uniting against a common enemy. In some places, large numbers of Hindus, especially from low castes, converted to Islam.

Delhi Sultanate

Muslim rule brought changes to Indian government and society. Sultans expanded their power over much of India, introducing Muslim traditions of government. Many Turks, Persians, and Arabs migrated to India to serve as soldiers or officials. Trade between India and the Muslim world increased. During the Mongol raids of the 1200s, many scholars and adventurers fled from Baghdad to India, bringing Persian and Greek learning. The newcomers helped create a brilliant civilization at Delhi, where Persian art and architecture flourished.

In 1398, Tamerlane invaded India. He plundered the northern plain and smashed into Delhi. "Not a bird on the wing moved," reported stunned survivors. Tens of thousands of artisans were enslaved and marched off to build Tamerlane's capital at Samarkand. Delhi, an empty shell, slowly recovered. But the sultans no longer controlled a large empire, and northern India again fragmented, this time into rival Hindu and Muslim states.

Meeting of Two Cultures

At its worst, the Muslim conquest of northern India inflicted disaster on Hindus and Buddhists. The widespread destruction of Buddhist monasteries contributed to the drastic decline of Buddhism as a major religion in India. During the most violent onslaughts, many Hindus were killed. Others may have converted to escape death. In time, though, relations became more peaceful.

Hindu-Muslim differences. The Muslim advance brought two utterly different religions

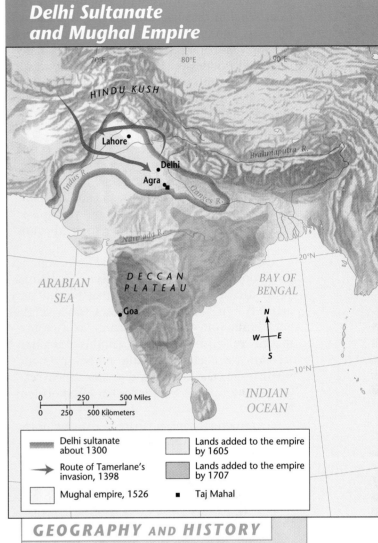

Delhi Sultanate and Mughal Empire

▬ Delhi sultanate about 1300	▭ Lands added to the empire by 1605
→ Route of Tamerlane's invasion, 1398	▨ Lands added to the empire by 1707
▭ Mughal empire, 1526	■ Taj Mahal

GEOGRAPHY AND HISTORY

Two Muslim dynasties ruled much of the Indian subcontinent. The Delhi sultanate, founded in 1206, was a powerful presence in northern India for more than 300 years. It was replaced by the Mughal dynasty in 1526.

1. **Location** On the map, locate (a) Delhi, (b) Hindu Kush, (c) Ganges River, (d) Taj Mahal.
2. **Movement** Describe Tamerlane's invasion route into India in 1398.
3. **Critical Thinking** Linking Past and Present Use the map on page 564 to name the present-day countries that now occupy the land of the Mughal empire.

and cultures face to face. Hinduism was an ancient religion that had evolved over thousands of years. Hindus recognized many sacred texts and prayed before statues representing many gods and goddesses. Islam, by contrast, was a newer faith with a single sacred text. Muslims were devout monotheists who saw the statues and carvings in Hindu temples as an offense to the one true God.

Hindus accepted differences in caste status and honored Brahmans as a priestly caste. Muslims taught the equality of all believers before God and had no religious hierarchy. Hindus celebrated religious occasions with music and dance, a practice that many strict Muslims condemned.

Interactions. Eventually, the Delhi sultans grew more tolerant of their subject population. Some Muslim scholars argued that behind the many Hindu gods and goddesses was a single god. Hinduism was thus accepted as a monotheistic religion. Although Hindus remained second-class citizens, as long as they paid the non-Muslim tax, they could practice their religion. Some sultans even left local Hindu rulers in place.

During the Delhi sultanate, a growing number of Hindus converted to Islam. Some lower-caste Hindus preferred Islam because it rejected the caste system. Other converts came from higher castes but chose to accept Islam because they accepted its monotheistic beliefs or because they served in the Muslim government. Indian merchants were attracted to Islam in part because of the strong trade network across Muslim lands.

Cultural blending. During this period, too, Indian Muslims absorbed elements of Hindu culture, such as marriage customs and caste ideas. A new language, Urdu, evolved as a marriage of Persian, Arabic, and Hindi. Local artisans applied Persian art styles to Indian subjects.

An Indian holy man, Nanak, sought to blend Muslim monotheism and Hindu beliefs. He preached "the unity of God, the brotherhood of man, the rejection of caste, and the futility of idol worship." His teachings led to the rise of a new religion, Sikhism (SEEK iz uhm), in northern India. The Sikhs later organized into military forces that clashed with the powerful Mughal rulers of India.

Mughal India

In 1526, Turkish and Mongol invaders again poured through the mountain passes in India. At their head rode Babur (BAH buhr), who claimed descent from Genghiz Khan and Tamerlane. "I placed my foot in the stirrup of resolution and my hands on the reins of confidence in God," recalled Babur in his memoirs. Just north of Delhi, Babur met a huge army led by the sultan Ibrahim. Babur's force was small but had cannons, which he put to good use.

In no time, Babur swept away the remnants of the Delhi sultanate and set up the Mughal dynasty, which ruled from 1526 to 1857. (*Mughal* is the Persian word for Mongol.) Babur and his heirs conquered an empire that stretched from the Himalayas to the Deccan.

Akbar the Great. The chief builder of the Mughal empire was Babur's grandson Akbar. During his long reign, from 1556 to 1605, he created a strong central government on the subcontinent, earning the title Akbar the Great.

Akbar was a leader of unusual abilities. Although a Muslim, he won the support of Hindu subjects through his policy of toleration. He opened government jobs to Hindus of all castes and treated Hindu princes as his partners in ruling the vast empire. He ended the tax on non-Muslims and himself married a Hindu princess.

Akbar could not read and write, but consulted leaders of many faiths, including Muslims, Hindus, Buddhists, and Christians. Like Asoka (see page 83), he hoped to promote religious harmony through tolerance:

> ❝O God, in every temple I see people that seek You. In every language I hear spoken, people praise you. If it be a mosque, people murmur the holy prayer. If it be a Christian church, they ring the bell for love of You. . . . It is You whom I seek from temple to temple.❞

By recognizing India's diversity, Akbar placed Mughal power on a firm footing. (☑ See *You Decide*, "Does Diversity Strengthen or Weaken a Society?" pages 338–339.)

Akbar strengthened his empire in other ways. To improve government, he used paid officials in place of hereditary officeholders. He

Akbar the Great
Despite his power and rank, Akbar tried to keep in touch with all the people of his empire. Hindus and Muslims, rich and poor, men and women, were all welcome to present petitions to him at his court. Here, Akbar enjoys an evening's entertainment of music and dance. **Impact of the Individual** *What might have occurred in India if Akbar's policies had been less tolerant?*

modernized the army, encouraged international trade, and introduced land reforms.

Akbar's successors. Akbar's son Jahangir (juh hahn GIR) was a weaker ruler than his father. He left most details of government in the hands of his wife, Nur Jahan. Fortunately, she was an able leader whose shrewd political judgment was matched only by her love of poetry and royal sports. She was the most powerful woman in Indian history until this century.

The high point of Mughal literature, art, and architecture came with the reign of Shah Jahan, Akbar's grandson. When his wife, Mumtaz Mahal, died at age 39, after giving birth to her fourteenth child, Shah Jahan was distraught. "Empire has no sweetness," he cried, "life itself has no relish left for me now." He then had a stunning tomb built for her, the Taj Mahal (TAHZH muh HAHL). It was designed in Persian style, with spectacular white domes and graceful minarets mirrored in clear blue reflecting pools. Verses from the Quran adorn its walls. The Taj Mahal stands as perhaps the greatest monument of the Mughal empire.

Decline. In the late 1600s, the emperor Aurangzeb resumed persecution of Hindus.

Economic hardships increased under heavy taxes, and discontent sparked revolts against Mughal rule. Against this background, as you will read, European traders began to mobilize against the once-powerful Mughal empire.

SECTION 4 REVIEW

1. **Identify** (a) Urdu, (b) Sikhism, (c) Babur, (d) Nur Jahan, (e) Taj Mahal.
2. (a) Describe the stages by which Muslims advanced into India. (b) Why were they able to conquer the subcontinent?
3. How did relations between Hindus and Muslims evolve over time?
4. What policies did Akbar follow to strengthen his empire?
5. *Critical Thinking* **Applying Information** How does the history of Muslims in India illustrate the process of cultural diffusion? (See page 17.)
6. *ACTIVITY* Using information in this chapter and Chapter 4, create a chart listing differences between Islam and Hinduism.

5 The Ottoman and Safavid Empires

Guide for Reading

- How did the Ottomans and Safavids build powerful, prosperous empires?

- How did Muslim traditions influence these empires?

- Why did culture flourish under the Ottomans and Safavids?

- **Vocabulary** *millet*

While the Mughals ruled India, two other dynasties, the Ottomans and Safavids, dominated the Middle East and parts of Eastern Europe. All three empires owed much of their success to new weapons. In 1453, Ottoman cannons blasted gaps in the great defensive walls of Constantinople. Later, muskets made a new kind of army possible, giving firepower to ordinary foot soldiers and reducing the importance of mounted warriors.

The new military technology helped the Ottomans and Safavids create strong central governments. As a result, this period from about 1450 to 1650 is sometimes called "the age of gunpowder empires."

The Ottoman Advance

The Ottomans were yet another Turkish-speaking nomadic people who had migrated from Central Asia into northwestern Asia Minor. In the 1300s, they expanded across Asia Minor and into the Balkans. Their growing forces threatened the crumbling Byzantine empire. In 1453, Muhammad II captured Constantinople, which he renamed Istanbul.

In the next 200 years, the Ottoman empire continued to expand. At its height it stretched from Hungary to Arabia and Mesopotamia and across North Africa. In 1529 and 1683, Ottoman armies besieged Vienna, sending waves of fear through Western Europe. Although they failed to take Vienna, the Ottomans ruled the largest, most powerful empire in both Europe and the Middle East for centuries.

Ottoman Culture

The Ottoman empire enjoyed its golden age under the sultan Suleiman (soo lay mahn), who ruled from 1520 to 1566. Called Suleiman the Magnificent by westerners, he was known to his people as the "Lawgiver."

A brilliant general and wise ruler, Suleiman modernized the army and conquered many new lands. He strengthened the government of the rapidly growing empire and improved its system of justice. As sultan, Suleiman had absolute power, but he ruled with the help of a grand vizier and a divan, or council. A huge bureaucracy supervised the business of government, and the powerful military kept the peace. As in other Islamic states, Ottoman law was based on the Sharia, supplemented by royal edicts. Government officials worked closely with religious scholars who interpreted the law.

Social organization. The Ottomans divided their subjects into four classes, each with its appointed role. At the top were "men of the pen"—such as scientists, lawyers, judges, and poets— and "men of the sword," soldiers who guarded the sultan and defended the state. Below them were "men of negotiation"—such as merchants, tax collectors, and artisans, who carried out trade and production—and "men of husbandry," farmers and herders who fed the community.

▲ *Jeweled gold canteen from the reign of Suleiman*

The Ottomans ruled diverse peoples who had many religions. The men of the sword and men of the pen were almost all Muslims, while the other classes included non-Muslims as well. Non-Muslims were organized into millets, or religious communities. These included Greek Christians, Armenian Christians, and Jews. Each millet had its own religious leaders who were responsible for education and some legal matters.

Janissaries. Like earlier Muslim empires, the Ottomans recruited officers for the army and government from among the huge populations of conquered peoples in their empire. The

Ottoman and Safavid Empires

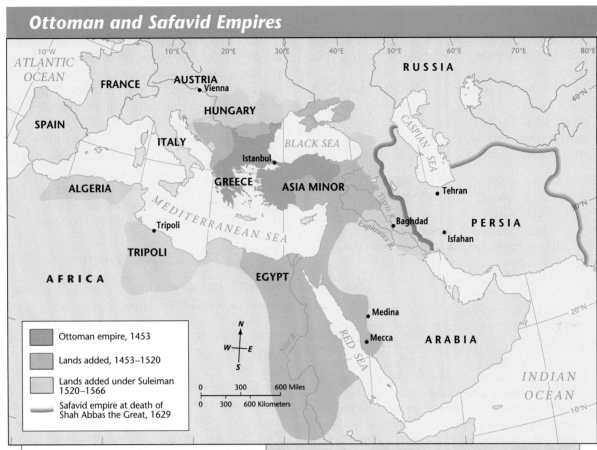

Map Legend:
- Ottoman empire, 1453
- Lands added, 1453–1520
- Lands added under Suleiman 1520–1566
- Safavid empire at death of Shah Abbas the Great, 1629

GEOGRAPHY AND HISTORY

At its height, the Ottoman empire covered vast lands in Europe, Africa, and Asia. During the same period, the Safavids controlled most of present-day Iran.

1. Location On the map, locate (a) Black Sea, (b) Nile River, (c) Istanbul, (d) Baghdad, (e) Arabia.

2. Region (a) Into what regions did the Ottoman empire expand under Suleiman? (b) What region did the Safavids control in 1629?

3. Critical Thinking **Recognizing Points of View** How do you think Russians probably felt about the growth and expansion of the Ottoman empire?

Ottomans levied a "tax" on Christian families in the Balkans, requiring them to turn over young sons to the government.

The boys were converted to Islam and put into rigorous military training at the palace school. The best soldiers won a prized place in the janissaries, the elite force of the Ottoman army. The brightest students received special education to become officials and might serve as judges, poets, or even grand vizier.

As boys were recruited into the janissaries, so non-Muslim girls were sought to act as slaves in the households of the wealthy. Most female slaves were from Eastern Europe. (The word *slave* is derived from Slav.) Slaves were accepted as members of the household and often became free on the death of their masters.

The arts and literature. The arts blossomed under Suleiman. Influenced by Persian artistic styles, Ottoman painters produced magnificently detailed miniatures and illuminated manuscripts. The royal architect Sinan, a janissary military engineer, designed hundreds of mosques and palaces. He compared his most famous building, the Selimiye Mosque at Edirne, to the greatest church of the Byzantine empire: "With God's help and the Sultan's mercy," Sinan wrote, "I have succeeded in building a dome for the mosque which is greater in diameter and higher than that of Hagia Sophia." (See page 237.)

Literature, too, thrived as Ottomans adapted Persian and Arab models to produce works in their own Turkish language. The greatest Ottoman poet was Baki, whose masterpiece was a moving lament for the death of Suleiman:

> 66Will not the King awake from sleep?
>   The dawn of day has broken.
> Will not he come forth from his tent
>   bright as heaven's display?
> Long have our eyes looked down the
>   road, and yet no news is come
> From yonder land, the threshold of his
>   majesty's array.99

A Magnificent Sultan Europeans dubbed Suleiman "the Magnificent" largely because of the splendor of his court. But they also admired his virtues as a ruler. "The Sultan himself assigns to all their duties and offices," noted a Flemish visitor, "and in doing so pays no attention to wealth or the empty claims of rank. He only considers merit. Thus, offices are filled by men capable of performing them." **Impact of the Individual** By what title was Suleiman known to his own subjects? How did he earn this title?

Decline. The Ottoman empire was a powerful force for 500 years. By the 1700s, however, European advances in both commerce and military technology were leaving the Ottomans behind. While European industry and trade pressed ahead, the aging Ottoman empire remained dependent on agriculture. Russia and other European powers chipped away at Ottoman lands, while local rulers in North Africa and elsewhere broke away from Ottoman control. From time to time, able sultans tried to revive Ottoman power, but with limited success.

The Safavid Empire

By the early 1500s, the Safavids (sah FAH weedz), a Turkish-speaking dynasty, had united a strong empire in present-day Iran. Sandwiched between two other expansionist powers, Mughal India and the Ottoman empire, the Safavids engaged in frequent warfare. Religion played a major role in the conflict. The Safavids were Shiite Muslims who enforced their beliefs throughout Iran and found sympathizers within the Ottoman empire. The Ottomans were Sunni Muslims who despised the Shiites as heretics.

Abbas the Great. The outstanding Safavid ruler, Shah Abbas the Great, revived the glory of ancient Persia. From 1588 to 1629, he centralized the government and created a powerful military force modeled on the Ottoman janissaries. Abbas used a mixture of force and diplomacy against the Ottomans. He also sought alliances with European states who had reason to fear Ottoman power.

To strengthen the economy, Abbas reduced taxes on farmers and herders and encouraged the growth of industries. While earlier Safavids had imposed their faith on the empire, Abbas tolerated non-Muslims and valued their economic contributions. He wanted to make his new capital at Isfahan (is fuh HAHN) a center of the international silk trade. Because the trade was controlled by Armenians, Abbas had thousands of Armenians brought to Isfahan. Even though they were Christians, he had a settlement built for them just outside the capital, where they could govern themselves.

Under Abbas, Isfahan flourished as a center of Persian culture. He welcomed artists, poets, and scholars to the court. Palace workshops

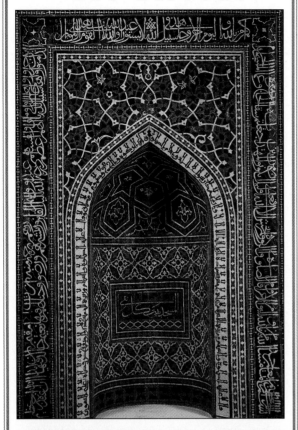

Persian Decorated Tile *The mihrab, or niche, of a mosque indicates the direction of Mecca, the focal point for Muslim prayer. This mihrab from the Safavid city of Isfahan consists of ceramic tiles fitted together to form geometric designs, floral patterns, and beautiful calligraphy. The geometric design symbolizes the logic and perfect order of God's creations.* **Art and Literature** *How does this mosaic differ from the Byzantine mosaic on page 240? What religious beliefs or customs explain these differences?*

produced magnificent porcelains, clothes, and rugs. Women and men wove intricately designed flowers and animals into marvelous garden scenes.

Abbas liked to walk the streets of Isfahan in disguise, mingling with the crowds in bazaars. Amid the cries of street vendors and swarms of traders and customers, he asked people about their problems. If he heard stories of corruption, he punished the guilty.

Decline. Safavid glory slowly faded after the death of the Shah Abbas, though the dynasty held onto power until 1722. In the late 1700s, a new dynasty, the Qajars (kah JAHRZ), won control of Iran. They made Tehran their capital and ruled until 1925. Still, the Safavids had left a lasting legacy. They planted Shiite traditions firmly in Iran and gave Persians a strong sense of their own identity.

Looking Ahead

By 1500, Islam had become the dominant faith across a large part of the world from West Africa to Southeast Asia. Islam was not a regional culture like Christian Europe, but an international culture reaching across three continents. An extraordinary diversity of peoples—Arabs, Berbers, Turks, Persians, Slavs, Mongols, Indians, and many others—answered the muezzin's call to prayer each day. This vast world was not politically united, but the Quran, the Sharia, and a network of cultural and economic ties linked Muslims across the Dar al-Islam.

Three large states dominated the Muslim world in the 1500s. The Ottomans, the Safavids, and the Mughals were reaching their peak of power. At the same time, however, the nations of Europe were undergoing a period of dynamic growth. Several of these nations would soon challenge Muslim power.

SECTION 5 REVIEW

1. **Identify** (a) janissaries, (b) Sinan, (c) Baki, (d) Isfahan.
2. **Define** millet.
3. How did the Ottomans govern a large and diverse empire?
4. Why were the Safavids and Ottomans often at war?
5. Describe one way the arts flourished under each of the following rulers: (a) Suleiman, (b) Shah Abbas.
6. *Critical Thinking* **Linking Past and Present** (a) How did the introduction of cannons and muskets affect the growth of the Ottoman and Safavid empires? (b) What changes in military technology have shaped today's world?
7. *ACTIVITY* Design a banner or write a motto that might have been used by one of the four social classes in the Ottoman empire.

CHAPTER REVIEW

REVIEWING VOCABULARY

Choose *four* vocabulary words from this chapter. Then, write a sentence for each word in which you define the word and describe its relation to the beliefs and practices of Islam.

REVIEWING FACTS

1. Where did Islam first appear?
2. List the Five Pillars of Islam.
3. Through what lands did Islam expand during the 600s and 700s?
4. How did the break between the Sunni and Shiite Muslims occur?
5. To what areas did Muslim merchants travel to trade?
6. How did Muslim scholars build on the achievements of earlier civilizations?
7. How did Islam spread to India?
8. What areas did the Ottoman empire control at its height?
9. When did Ottoman power begin declining?
10. What present-day country did the Safavids control?

SKILLS FOR SUCCESS   RECOGNIZING POINTS OF VIEW

Point of view influences the way a person describes events. For example, a person who is opposed to war of any kind can observe a battle and see only a senseless loss of life. A military veteran can observe the same battle and focus on the tactics used by both armies.

The excerpts below are from two accounts of the First Crusade. In the first, Fulcher of Chartres, a Christian chronicler, describes the crusaders' capture of the city of Antioch in southern Turkey. In the second, the Muslim historian Ibn al-Athir describes the same event. Read their accounts, then answer the following questions.

1. **Study the contents of each source.** List three points on which both writers agree.
2. **Analyze the points of view.**

(a) Why does Fulcher refer to the capture of Antioch as a "return"? (b) Why does al-Athir refer to the Muslims as "defenders"? (c) Why do the two writers give different dates for the event?

3. **Evaluate the usefulness of the sources.** Do you think that these excerpts are reliable sources of information about the Crusades? Explain.

Fulcher of Chartres:

66From this month of October, the siege of the city continued . . . until the month of June 1098. . . . God appeared to a certain Turk predestined by His grace and said to him, 'Arise, you who sleep! I command you to return the city to the Christians.' . . . The Turk . . . secretly made a plot with our men by which they should obtain the city.

On the appointed night, the Turk admitted over the wall twenty of our men by means of rope ladders. At once, without delay, the gate was opened. The Franks, who were ready, entered the city. Forty more of our soldiers who had already entered by means of the ropes slew sixty Turks.99

Ibn al-Athir:

66After the siege had been going on for a long time, the Franks made a deal with one of the men who were responsible for the towers. He was an armor-maker called Ruzbih whom they bribed. . . . The Franks sealed their pact with the armor-maker, God curse him! and made their way to the water gate. They opened it and entered the city. Another gang of them climbed the tower with ropes. At dawn, when more than 500 of them were in the city and the defenders were worn out after the night watch, they sounded their trumpets. . . . This happened in 491.99

REVIEWING CHAPTER THEMES

Review the "Focus On" questions at the start of this chapter. Then select *three* of those questions and answer them, using information from the chapter.

CRITICAL THINKING

1. **Applying Information** "If men walk in the way of God's will," declared Akbar, "interference with them would be unfair." How did Akbar's policies reflect this idea?

2. **Synthesizing Information** The Arab, Ottoman, and Safavid empires all declined after periods of strength. Review what you have read about other empires in Egypt, India, China, and Rome. (a) What forces tend to strengthen an empire? (b) What forces tend to make an empire decline?

ANALYZING PRIMARY SOURCES

Use the quotation on page 264 to answer the following questions.

1. What is the Tigris?
2. How would the Tigris "put [the Abbasids] in touch with lands as far as China"?
3. What general statement might al-Mansur have made regarding the proper location of a capital?

FOR YOUR PORTFOLIO

WRITING A DOCUMENTARY With a group of classmates, prepare a travel documentary based on the journeys of the Moroccan Muslim scholar Ibn Battuta. First, reread the introduction to this chapter and list the places Ibn Battuta visited. Then use outside sources to research the life and travels of Ibn Battuta. Make an outline for your documentary, indicating the topics you want to cover. Then write the narration for your documentary. Finally, present your visuals and commentary to the class.

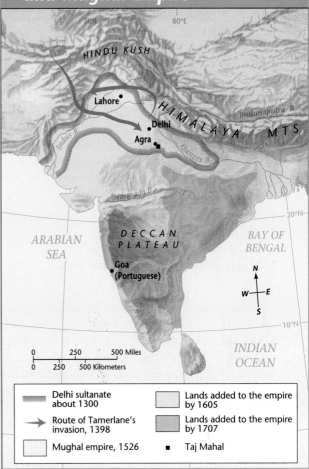

Delhi Sultanate and Mughal Empire

Delhi sultanate about 1300	Lands added to the empire by 1605
Route of Tamerlane's invasion, 1398	Lands added to the empire by 1707
Mughal empire, 1526	■ Taj Mahal

ANALYZING MAPS

Use the map to answer the following questions.

1. The Delhi sultanate included parts of which two major rivers?
2. During which period was Agra added to the Mughal empire?
3. Which part of the Indian subcontinent did not become part of the Mughal empire?

INTERNET ACTIVITY

WRITING A BIOGRAPHY Use the Internet to research the life of one of the Muslim scholars listed in the text. Then write a brief biography of that scholar, focusing on the contributions he made to his field. Include information about the scholar's most influential works.

Kingdoms and Trading States of Africa

(750 B.C.–A.D. 1586)

CHAPTER OUTLINE

1 **Early Civilizations of Africa**
2 **Kingdoms of West Africa**
3 **Trade Routes of East Africa**
4 **Many Peoples, Many Traditions**

Today, nothing remains of Kumbi Saleh but ruins in the Saharan sands. In the mid-1000s, however, the city was the capital of the wealthy West African kingdom of ancient Ghana. In his *Book of Roads and Kingdoms,* the Spanish Arab historian al-Bakri described the splendors of Kumbi Saleh. Although the Muslim writer had not visited Ghana himself, he had collected information from traders who had.

Kumbi Saleh was made up of two separate walled towns, some six miles apart. The first town was dominated by the royal palace, surrounded by a complex of domed buildings. Here, the king of Ghana sat in regal splendor, adorned in necklaces and bracelets. "And when he sits before the people," noted al-Bakri, "he puts on a high cap decorated with gold and wrapped in turbans of fine cotton." Al-Bakri then described the elaborate ceremonies when the king dispensed justice:

> 66When he gives audience to his people, to listen to their complaints and set them to rights, he sits in a pavilion around which stand his horses adorned in cloth of gold. Behind him on his right hand are the sons of the princes of his empire, splendidly clad and with gold braided into their hair. . . . The beginning of the audience is announced by the beating of a kind of drum which they call *deba,* made of a long piece of hollowed wood.99

In the second town, prosperous Muslim merchants from north of the Sahara lived in luxurious stone buildings. Lured by the gold wealth of Ghana, these merchants helped make Kumbi Saleh a bustling center of trade. As Muslims, they also helped spread their Islamic faith to West Africa. The Muslim quarter housed 12 separate mosques.

By the time Ghana reached its peak, the vast continent of Africa had already been home to a number of other civilizations. In some regions, major political powers rose despite geographic obstacles, such as poor soil or harsh climates. From the time of ancient Egypt, trade and other contacts linked parts of Africa to Europe, the Middle East, India, and other parts of Asia.

FOCUS ON these questions as you read:

■ **Geography and History**
How did geography both help and hinder the peoples of Africa?

■ **Diversity**
What conditions contributed to the development of varied cultures in Africa?

■ **Global Interaction**
How were parts of Africa tied into major trading networks?

■ **Art and Literature**
What literary and artistic traditions developed in Africa?

TIME AND PLACE

African Masks In Africa, as elsewhere, people believed that art played a vital role in society, especially when combined with music and dance. Elaborate masks, like the ones shown here, were used in political, religious, and social ceremonies. *Art and Literature* Compare these masks to the Greek sculptures on page 103. How do the artists' styles differ?

HUMANITIES LINK

Art History Benin bronze sculpture (page 293).
Literature In this chapter, you will encounter passages from the following works of literature: al-Bakri, *Book of Roads and Kingdoms* (page 282); Leo Africanus, *The History and Description of Africa* (page 289); *The Glory of Kings* (page 294); Yoruba riddles (page 301); *Sundiata* (pages 302–303).

730 B.C. Nubia conquers Egypt	**200** B.C. Axum begins to control extensive trade network		A.D. **600s** Islam spreads to North Africa	A.D. **1324** Mansa Musa's pilgrimage to Mecca	A.D. **1500** Kingdom of Kongo thrives

B.C.	800	400	B.C.	A.D.	400	1200	1600	A.D.

1 Early Civilizations of Africa

Guide for Reading

- What geographic features have influenced African life?

- What were the achievements of Nubian civilization?

- What early civilizations influenced North Africa?

- **Vocabulary** *savanna, desertification*

As the sun rose above the east bank of the Nile, workers hurried to the construction site. They had only a few hours to work in comfort before the sun turned the desert into a furnace. Still, as long as King Taharqa (tuh HAHR kuh) was determined to restore Egyptian monuments and beautify his own kingdom of Nubia, their work would continue.

An ancient inscription explains how Taharqa's artisans and architects renovated an old mud-brick temple and turned it into a spectacular monument. Set amid an artificial lake and gardens, the monument was "built of good white sandstone, excellent, hard, . . . the house being of gold, the columns of gold, the inlays thereof being of silver."

About 680 B.C., Taharqa commanded the Nile Valley from Nubia to the Mediterranean. By that time, Nubia was already 3,000 years old. Along with Egypt, it stood as one of the world's early civilizations.

Geography: The Continent of Africa

After Asia, Africa is the second largest continent, covering one fifth of all the Earth's land surface. Its geography is immensely varied, but certain features have had a major impact on its development.

Climate zones. Many outsiders, misled by movies, imagine Africa as a continent covered with thick jungles. In fact, tropical rain forests cover less than five percent of the land, mostly along the Equator. (See the map opposite.) Thick trees and roots make this region unsuitable for farming.

Africa's largest and most populated climate zone is the savanna, or grassy plains, which stretches north and south of the forest zone. The savanna generally has good soil and enough rainfall to support farming, but irregular patterns of rainfall sometimes cause long, deadly droughts. In parts of the savanna, the tsetse fly infects people and cattle with sleeping sickness. But in other parts of the savanna, cattle herding is a common occupation.

The savanna belts trail off into increasingly dry steppe zones and then into two major deserts. The blistering Sahara in the north is the world's largest desert. Although the Sahara did become a highway for migration and trade, its size and harsh terrain limited movement. The Kalahari and Namib in the south are smaller but equally forbidding.

Along the Mediterranean coast of North Africa and at the tip of southern Africa lie areas of fertile farmland. As you have read, the fertile Nile River valley offered a favorable environment to early farmers.

Movement. In addition to deserts and rain forests, other geographic features have acted as barriers to easy movement of people and goods. Although Africa is surrounded by oceans and seas, it has few good natural harbors. In addition, much of the interior is a high plateau. As rivers flow down to the coast, they cascade through a series of rapids and cataracts that hinder travel between the coast and the interior. Within the interior, though, the same rivers—including the Zambezi, Congo, and Niger—serve as open highways.

Despite geographic barriers, people did migrate, both within Africa and to neighboring continents. Like the rivers, the Great Rift Valley of East Africa served as an interior corridor. People also traveled across the savanna lands. The Red Sea and Indian Ocean linked East Africa to the Middle East and other Asian lands, while North Africa formed the southern rim of the Mediterranean world.

Resources. Since ancient times, Africa's mineral wealth has spurred trade among various regions. Salt, iron, gold, and copper were important commodities in early trade networks. In

Geography of Africa

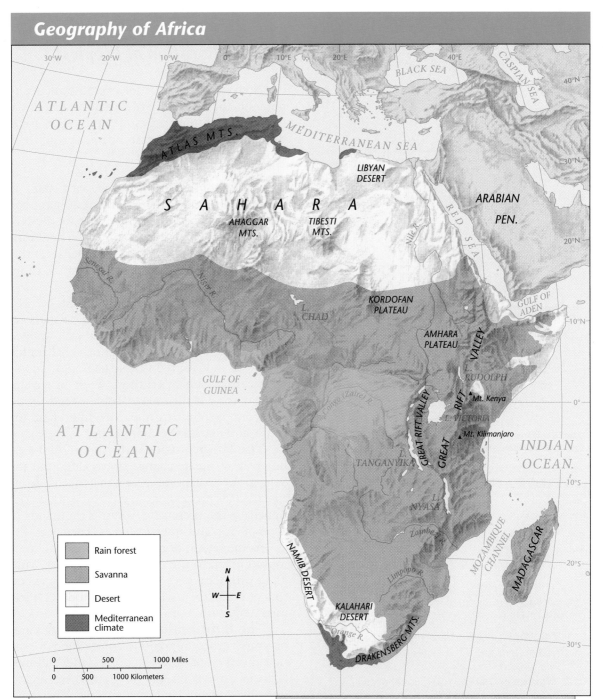

Rain forest

Savanna

Desert

Mediterranean climate

ATLANTIC OCEAN

MEDITERRANEAN SEA

BLACK SEA

CASPIAN SEA

ATLAS MTS.

LIBYAN DESERT

S A H A R A

AHAGGAR MTS.

TIBESTI MTS.

ARABIAN PEN.

RED SEA

Nile R.

Senegal R.

Niger R.

L. CHAD

KORDOFAN PLATEAU

GULF OF ADEN

GULF OF GUINEA

AMHARA PLATEAU

GREAT RIFT VALLEY

RUDOLPH

Mt. Kenya

Congo (Zaire) R.

L. VICTORIA

Mt. Kilimanjaro

INDIAN OCEAN

ATLANTIC OCEAN

L. TANGANYIKA

GREAT RIFT VALLEY

L. NYASA

Zambezi R.

MOZAMBIQUE CHANNEL

MADAGASCAR

NAMIB DESERT

Limpopo R.

N
W E
S

KALAHARI DESERT

Orange R.

DRAKENSBERG MTS.

0   500   1000 Miles

0   500   1000 Kilometers

GEOGRAPHY AND HISTORY

Africa is the second largest continent in the world. Stretching more than 5,000 miles from north to south, the continent has widely varied terrains and climates.

1. **Location** On the map, locate (a) Congo River, (b) Sahara, (c) Great Rift Valley, (d) Mount Kilimanjaro, (e) Atlas Mountains, (f) Namib Desert, (g) Kalahari Desert.

2. **Interaction** Which type of climate zone might be most attractive for people to live in? Why?

3. **Critical Thinking** **Applying Information** Why do you think the climate in most of Africa is warm throughout the year?

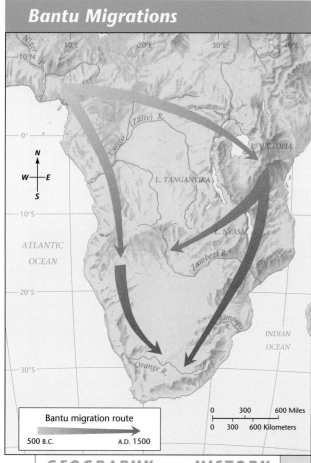

Bantu migration route

500 B.C.   A.D. 1500

| 0 | 300 | 600 Miles |
| 0 | 300 | 600 Kilometers |

GEOGRAPHY AND HISTORY

Over a period of two thousand years, Bantu peoples migrated from their place of origin to populate most of southern Africa. Today as many as one third of Africans speak a language in the Bantu family.

1. **Location** On the map, locate (a) Lake Victoria, (b) Orange River, (c) Lake Nyasa, (d) Lake Tanganyika.
2. **Movement** (a) Where did Bantu peoples originate? (b) Approximately when did Bantu peoples reach the Orange River?
3. **Critical Thinking** **Solving Problems** How have scientists learned about the Bantu migrations?

the 1800s, desire for gold and diamonds was one cause that led Europeans to seek control of territories in Africa. More recently, nations such as Nigeria and Angola have exported large quantities of oil.

Migration of Peoples

Archaeologists have uncovered evidence to pinpoint the Great Rift Valley of East Africa as the home of the earliest people. (See pages 8–9.) Gradually, their descendants spread to almost every corner of the Earth.

Stone Age cultures. In Africa, as elsewhere, Paleolithic people developed skills as hunters and food gatherers. By 5500 B.C., Neolithic farmers had learned to cultivate the Nile Valley and to domesticate animals. These early farmers settled into permanent villages that eventually supported the great civilization of ancient Egypt. (See Chapter 2.)

Farming spread across North Africa. Neolithic villages even appeared in the Sahara region, which at that time was a well-watered zone. Ancient rock paintings show a Sahara full of forests and rivers. In these paintings, people wear clothes similar to those worn by groups such as the Fulani today. Women tend crops, cook, and help move camp. Men hunt, herd the cattle, and defend the community.

The Sahara dries out. About 2500 B.C., however, a climate change slowly dried out the Sahara. As the land became parched, the desert spread. This process of desertification has continued to the present, devouring thousands of acres of cropland and pastureland each year.

As the region dried, people retreated. Some moved north to the Mediterranean coast. Mingling with local people, they became the ancestors of the Berbers who live there today. Others migrated south to the savanna or rain forests.

The Bantu migrations. Over thousands of years, other migrations contributed to the rich diversity of African peoples and cultures. Scholars have been able to trace these migrations by studying language patterns. They have learned that West African farmers and herders migrated to the south and east between about A.D. 500 and 1500. Wherever they settled, they spread their skills in farming and ironworking. Like the Indo-European peoples who migrated across Europe and Asia, these West African peoples spoke a variety of languages that derived from a common root language. (See Chapter 3.) We call this African root language Bantu.

Bantu peoples met, and often displaced, earlier groups. In central and southern Africa, for example, they forced the Khoisan (KOI sahn) into less-desirable areas, such as the Zaire rain forest or the Kalahari desert. On the east coast of Africa, Bantu-speaking peoples encountered migrants from Asia.

As people migrated across Africa, they adapted to its many climates and developed a diversity of cultures. While some were nomadic cattle herders, others cultivated grain or root crops. In several regions, farming people built great empires, as you will read.

The Nile Kingdom of Nubia

While Egyptian civilization was developing, another African civilization took shape on a wide band of fertile land among the cataracts of the upper Nile. The ancient kingdom of Nubia, also called Kush, was located in present-day Sudan. Archaeologists and historians have just begun to document the shifting tides of Nubia's 4,000-year history.

Nubia and Egypt. From time to time, ambitious Egyptian pharaohs subdued Nubia, but the Nubians always regained their independence. As a result of conquest and trade, Nubian rulers adopted many Egyptian traditions. They built palaces and pyramids modeled on Egyptian styles. They used Egyptian titles and worshiped deities like Amon-Re and Isis.

About 750 B.C., as you have read, the Nubian king Piankhi (pee AHNG kee) conquered Egypt. "Raging like a panther," he defeated his enemies "like a cloud burst," according to an inscription. For a century, Nubian kings like Taharqa ruled Egypt. But Taharqa's armies could not match the iron weapons of the invading Assyrians. Forced to retreat from Egypt, the Nubians returned south.

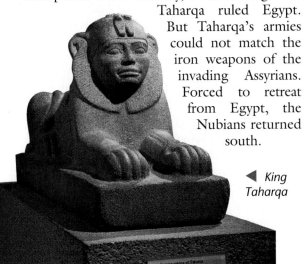

◀ *King Taharqa*

The furnaces of Meroë. By 500 B.C., Nubian rulers moved their capital to Meroë (MEHR uh wee). Meroë commanded both the north-south Nile routes and the east-west route from the Red Sea into the savanna. Along this wide trade network, Nubia sent gold, ivory, animal skins, perfumes, and slaves to the Mediterranean world and the Middle East.

Equally important, Meroë was rich in iron ore. Its furnaces, fueled by large quantities of timber, produced iron for tools and weapons. Trade may have spread iron technology across the savanna lands into West Africa. Today, giant heaps of iron waste remain as evidence of the prosperous iron industry of ancient Meroë.

Splendors and decline. Although Nubia absorbed much from Egypt, it later followed an independent course. Nubians worshiped their own gods including Apedemak, a lion-headed warrior god. At Meroë, artistic styles reflected a greater sense of freedom than Egyptian styles. Nubians also created their own system of writing, using an alphabet instead of hieroglyphics. Unfortunately, the Nubian alphabet has yet to be deciphered.

After the joint reign of King Natakamani and Queen Amanitere in the first century A.D., Nubia's golden age dimmed. Desertification may have engulfed Nubian farmlands. Finally, about A.D. 350, armies from the kingdom of Axum on the Red Sea overwhelmed Nubia. King Ezana of Axum boasted:

❝I burnt their towns, both those built of brick and those built of reeds, and my army carried off their food and copper and iron . . . and destroyed the statues in their temples.❞

As you will read later, Axum would make its own mark on this region beyond the Nile.

North Africa in the Ancient World

Early African civilizations had strong ties to the Mediterranean world. Trade linked Egypt with Greece and Mesopotamia. Later, Egypt was ruled, in turn, by the Greeks and Romans. These powers also knew of the rich civilization that lay south of Egypt and valued Nubian exports. Over time, however, Nubia lost touch with the Mediterranean world.

Ships of the Desert With the help of camels, merchants and warriors overcame the obstacles of the Sahara. Camel caravans, like those that still traverse the Sahara today, also helped Islam spread across North Africa. **Geography and History** What other domesticated animals are well suited for travel in a particular environment? Explain.

Carthage. At the opposite end of the Mediterranean, Carthage rose as a great North African power. Like Nubia, its wealth came from trade. Founded by Phoenician traders, Carthage came to dominate the western Mediterranean. Between 800 B.C. and 146 B.C., it forged an empire that stretched from the Maghreb (present-day Tunisia, Algeria, and Morocco) to southern Spain and Sicily, as well as outposts in England, France, and possibly West Africa.

As Rome expanded, territorial and trade rivalries erupted between the two powers. Despite the efforts of Hannibal, Rome eventually crushed Carthage. (See pages 132–133).

Roman rule. The Romans built roads, dams, aqueducts, and cities across North Africa. They developed its farmlands to harvest bumper crops of grain, fruit, and other foods. From North Africa, they imported lions and other fierce animals to Rome to do battle with gladiators. North Africa also provided soldiers for the Roman army. One of them, Septimius Severus, later became emperor of Rome.

Under Roman rule, Christianity spread to the cities of North Africa. St. Augustine, the most influential Christian thinker of the late Roman empire, was born in present-day Algeria. From 395 to 430, Augustine was bishop of Hippo, a city near the ruins of ancient Carthage.

The camel revolutionizes trade. By A.D. 200, camels had been brought to North Africa from Asia. These hardy "ships of the desert" revolutionized trade across the Sahara. Although daring traders had earlier made the difficult desert crossing in horse-drawn chariots, camel caravans created new trade networks. Camels could carry loads of up to 500 pounds and could plod 20 or 30 miles a day, often without water. The caravan brought great profits to merchants on both sides of the Sahara.

Spread of Islam. Further changes came in the 600s, when Arab armies carried Islam into North Africa. At first, the Arabs occupied the cities and battled the Berbers in the desert. In time, however, Berbers and Arabs joined forces to conquer Spain. Islam replaced Christianity as the dominant religion of North Africa, and Arabic replaced Latin as its language.

North Africa benefited from the blossoming of Muslim civilization. Cities like Cairo, Fez, and Marrakesh were famed for their mosques and libraries. Linked into a global trade network, North African ports did a busy trade in grain, wine, fruit, ivory, and gold. Along with their goods, Muslim traders from North Africa carried Islam into West Africa.

SECTION 1 REVIEW

1. **Identify** (a) Bantu, (b) Piankhi, (c) Taharqa, (d) Meroë, (e) St. Augustine.
2. **Define** (a) savanna, (b) desertification.
3. (a) What barriers to movement did the geography of Africa pose? (b) Describe two examples of migration in Africa.
4. How did Nubian civilization prosper?
5. Describe one way each of the following influenced North Africa: (a) the growth of the Roman empire, (b) the spread of Islam.
6. *Critical Thinking* **Linking Past and Present** (a) What effects did desertification have on African peoples? (b) How might life in the United States be affected if well-watered areas began to turn into desert today?
7. *ACTIVITY* Imagine that you are a merchant preparing to embark on a camel caravan across the Sahara. Write a diary entry describing your feelings about the journey.

2 Kingdoms of West Africa

Guide for Reading

- What role did resources and trade play in West Africa?

- How did West African rulers build powerful kingdoms?

- How did Islam influence the peoples of West Africa?

In the early 1500s, the scholar Hassan ibn Muhammad—known in the West as Leo Africanus—described the commercial wealth and bustling markets of the West African city of Timbuktu:

> 66 Here are shops of artisans and merchants, and especially such as weave linen and cotton cloth. And here do the merchants of North Africa bring the cloth of Europe. All the women of this region, except the maid-servants, go with their faces covered and sell all the necessary foods. 99

Timbuktu stood at one end of a trade network that reached north to Cairo and then across the Mediterranean Sea to Italy. Between about 800 and 1600, several powerful kingdoms won control of the prosperous Sahara trade. Among the richest West African states were Ghana, Mali, and Songhai.

The West African Landscape

As the Sahara dried out, you will recall, some Neolithic people migrated southward into the western savanna. There, farmers grew beans, melons, and a wide variety of cereal grains. Men cleared the land and prepared the fields for planting, while women did most of the weeding, transplanting, threshing, and grinding of the grain.

By A.D. 100, settled farming villages were expanding, especially along the Senegal and Niger rivers and around Lake Chad. In time, some villages grew into towns with local rulers, creating larger political units.

Trading patterns. Villagers traded any surplus food they produced. Gradually, a trade network linked the savanna to forest lands in the south and then funneled goods across the Sahara to the Mediterranean and Middle East. From West Africa, caravans crossed the Sahara carrying leather goods, kola nuts, cotton cloth, and slaves. From North Africa, Arab and Berber merchants brought silk, steel, Venetian glass beads, and horses.

Gold for salt. Two products, gold and salt, dominated the Sahara trade. Gold was plentiful in present-day Ghana, Nigeria, and Senegal. Men dug the gold-bearing soil from pits. Then, women washed the soil to extract the gold dust. The precious metal was stuffed into hollow feather quills for safe travel to the markets of North Africa and Europe.

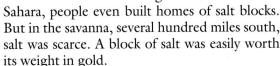

In return, West Africans received an equally valuable commodity, salt. People need salt in their diet to prevent dehydration, especially in hot, tropical areas. The Sahara had an abundance of salt. In fact, at Taghaza in the central

▲ *West African gold*

Sahara, people even built homes of salt blocks. But in the savanna, several hundred miles south, salt was scarce. A block of salt was easily worth its weight in gold.

As farming and trade prospered, cities developed on the northern edges of the savanna. Strong monarchs gained control of the most profitable trade routes.

Gold Wealth of Ghana

By A.D. 800, the rulers of the Soninke people had united many farming villages to create the kingdom of Ghana.* Ghana was located in the broad "V" made by the Niger and Senegal rivers. (See the map on page 295.) From there, the king controlled gold-salt trade routes across

---

*Ghana, meaning ruler, was the name used for the kingdom by Arab traders. The modern nation of Ghana is not located on the site of the ancient kingdom, but several hundred miles to the south.

West Africa. The two streams of trade met in the marketplaces of Ghana, where the king collected tolls on all goods entering or leaving his land. So great was the flow of gold that Arab writers called Ghana "land of gold."

King and court. As you read, the king of Ghana presided over elaborate ceremonies at his court in Kumbi Saleh. To the people, he was a semi-divine figure who dispensed justice and kept order. According to al-Bakri, the king had a huge army of foot soldiers as well as a small, well-trained cavalry.

Women in Ghana had a high status and played an active role in the economic life of the empire. Some held positions in the government. The ruler himself inherited the throne through his mother, the previous king's sister.

Influence of Islam. Muslim merchants formed their own settled communities throughout the kingdom. Islam spread slowly at first. The king employed Muslims as counselors and officials, gradually absorbing Muslim military technology and ideas about government. Muslims also introduced their written language, coinage, business methods, and styles of architecture. In time, a few city dwellers adopted Islam, but most Soninke continued to follow their own traditional beliefs.

About 1050, however, the Almoravids (al MOR uh veedz), pious Muslims of North Africa, launched a campaign to spread their form of Islam. After conquering the Maghreb and Spain, they pressed south across the Sahara. They overwhelmed Ghana, whose rulers may have converted to Islam. In the end, though, the Almoravids were unable to maintain control over such a distant land. Ghana survived, but its empire declined in the late 1100s. In time it was swallowed up by a rising new power, the West African kingdom of Mali.

Mali: Where the King Dwells

Amid the turmoil of Ghana's collapse, the Mandinke people on the upper Niger suffered a bitter defeat by a rival leader. Their king and all but one of his sons were executed. According to tradition, the survivor was Sundiata, a sickly boy regarded as too weak to be a threat. But Sundiata grew up to be a brilliant military leader. By 1250, he had crushed his enemies, won control

of the gold trade routes, and founded the empire of Mali. (📖 See *World Literature*, "Sundiata," pages 302–303.)

Mali is an Arab version of the Mandinke word meaning "where the king dwells." Sundiata and succeeding *mansas*, or kings, expanded their influence over both the gold-mining regions to the south and the salt supplies of Taghaza. Where caravan routes crossed, towns like Timbuktu mushroomed into great trading cities.

The greatest emperor of Mali was Mansa Musa (MAHN sah MOO sah), who came to the throne in about 1312. Musa expanded Mali's borders westward to the Atlantic Ocean and pushed northward to conquer many Berber cities. During Mansa Musa's 25-year reign, he worked to ensure peace and order in his empire. "There is complete and general safety throughout the land," commented Ibn Battuta when he visited Mali. "The traveler here has no more reason to fear thieves than the man who stays at home."

Musa converted to Islam and based his system of justice on the Quran. At the same time, he did not adopt all customs associated with some nearby Muslim societies. For example, women in Mali wore no veils and were not secluded within the home.

In 1324, Mansa Musa fulfilled one of the Five Pillars of Islam. Like all able Muslims, he made his pilgrimage to Mecca.

The Emperor's Hajj

 From the tall mosque in Cairo, the muezzin called faithful Egyptian Muslims to prayer. "*La ilaha illa Allah; Muhammadun rasulu Allah,*" he cried. "There is no God but God; Muhammad is the prophet of God." Today, a visitor from thousands of miles away also heard the muezzin's call. He was Mansa Musa, stopping at Egypt on his way to Mecca.

A fabulous journey. By the time he reached Cairo, the emperor had already made the difficult journey across the Sahara. He traveled in kingly style. Musa was accompanied by 500 slaves, each bearing a golden staff. His caravan boasted 100 camels heavily laden with gold.

Mansa Musa *The mapmaker Abraham Cresque drew this map of West Africa for the king of France. It shows Mansa Musa on his throne holding symbols of power and wealth. "So abundant is the gold which is found in his country," noted Cresque, "that he is the richest and most noble king in all the land."* **Economics and Technology** *How does the map indicate the economic prosperity of West Africa?*

Egyptians were awed by this fabulous display of wealth. Nor was Musa stingy about sharing it. One witness reported:

66This man spread upon Cairo the flood of his generosity: there was no person, officer of the court, or holder of any office of the Sultanate who did not receive a sum of gold from him. The people of Cairo earned incalculable sums from him, whether by buying and selling or by gifts.99

In fact, the emperor and his servants spent so lavishly that the value of gold in Cairo dropped for more than 10 years!

Musa had one moment of tension during his stopover in Cairo. An Egyptian official requested that the emperor visit the palace of the sultan. Musa balked, however, at kissing the ground before the sultan's feet. The emperor finally did agree to the custom, but said, "I will prostrate myself before God who created me and brought me into the world."

Musa at length resumed his journey to Arabia. Finally, the caravan reached Mecca. Like other pilgrims, he visited the Kaaba and prayed humbly in the city most sacred to Muslims. Then he made the long journey back across the Sahara to Mali. The hajj had taken over a year.

Results of the hajj. Through his pilgrimage, Mansa Musa showed his devotion to Islam. At the same time, he forged new trading and diplomatic ties with Muslim states such as Egypt and Morocco. Musa also returned home with scholars and artists, like as-Sahili, a poet and architect from Spain. The newcomers introduced Arab styles in the palaces and mosques of Mali.

As a result of Musa's pilgrimage, word of Mali's enormous wealth spread across the Muslim world and filtered into Europe. The news sparked the interest of European rulers in African gold, especially since they had recently begun to use gold coins.

In 1375, Abraham Cresque, a French Jewish mapmaker, included a picture of Mansa Musa on a map of West Africa. It shows the ruler wearing a gold crown and holding a solid gold nugget in one hand. To this day, that image, along with the eyewitness reports of Mansa Musa's pilgrimage, still stands as a glowing symbol of the splendors of Mali. ◾

A New Empire in the Grasslands

In the 1400s, disputes over succession weakened Mali. Subject peoples broke away, and the empire shriveled. By 1450, the wealthy trading city of Gao (GOW) had emerged as the capital of a new West African kingdom, Songhai (SAWNG hī).

Two great leaders. Songhai grew up on the bend of the Niger River in present-day Niger and Burkina Faso. Between 1464 and 1492, the soldier-king Sonni Ali used his powerful army to forge the largest state that had ever existed in West Africa. Sonni Ali brought key trade routes and wealthy cities like Timbuktu under his control. Unlike the rulers of Mali, he did not adhere to the practices of Islam. Instead, he followed traditional religious beliefs.

Soon after Sonni Ali's death, though, the emperor Askia Muhammad set up a Muslim dynasty. He further expanded the territory of Songhai and improved the government. He set up a bureaucracy with separate departments for farming, army, and the treasury. The king appointed officials to supervise each of these departments.

Like Mansa Musa, Askia Muhammad made a pilgrimage to Mecca that led to increased ties with the Muslim world. Scholars and poets from Muslim lands flocked to his court at Gao. In towns and cities across Songhai, Askia Muhammad built mosques and opened schools for the study of the Quran.

Timbuktu. By the 1400s, Timbuktu had become a leading center of learning. The city drew some of the best scholars from all over the Muslim world. Hassan ibn Muhammad described the city's intellectual life:

> 66Here are great store of doctors, judges, . . . and other learned men, that are bountifully maintained at the king's cost and charges. And hither are brought various manuscripts of books from North Africa, which are sold for more money than any other merchandise.99

Invaders from the north. Songhai prospered until about 1586, when disputes over succession led to civil war. Soon after, the ruler of Morocco sent his armies south to seize the West African gold mines. The invaders used gunpowder weapons to defeat the disunited forces of Songhai.

Like the Almoravids in Ghana, however, the Moroccans were not able to rule an empire across the Sahara. With the downfall of Songhai, this part of West Africa splintered into many small kingdoms.

Other Kingdoms of West Africa

In the period from 500 to 1500, other kingdoms flourished in various parts of West Africa. The fertile northern lands of modern-day Nigeria were home to the Hausa people, who had probably migrated there when the Sahara dried out. They were both successful farmers and traders.

Walled towns of the Hausa. By the 1300s, the Hausa had built a number of clay-walled cities. While these city-states remained independent of one another, in time they expanded into thriving commercial centers. In the cities, cotton weavers and dyers, leatherworkers, and other artisans produced goods for sale. Merchants traded with Arab and Berber caravans from north of the Sahara. Hausa goods were sold as far away as North Africa and southern Europe.

Kano was the most prosperous Hausa city-state. Its walls, 14 miles in circumference, housed a population of more than 30,000 people. Kano's greatest king, Muhammad Rumfa, was a Muslim, as were many merchants and officials. The Hausa developed a written language based on Arabic.

Many Hausa rulers were women, such as Amina of the city-state of Zaria. In the 1500s, she conquered Kano and expanded the boundary of Zaria as far as the Niger River. Under Amina, the Hausa came to dominate Saharan trade routes.

The forest kingdom of Benin. South of the savanna, Benin (beh NIN) rose in the rain forests of the Guinea coast. The forest peoples carved out farming villages and traded pepper, ivory, and later slaves to their neighbors in the savanna.

The rulers of Benin organized their kingdom in the 1300s, probably building on the achievements of earlier forest cultures. An *oba*, or king, was both a political and religious leader. Still, much power was spread among other figures, including the queen mother and a council of hereditary chiefs. A three-mile-long wall surrounded the capital, Benin City. Its broad avenues were dotted with tidy homes and a great palace.

The palace, in particular, was decorated with elaborate brass plaques and sculptures. Accord-

Benin Bronze Sculpture *This bronze from the forest kingdom of Benin shows a powerful queen mother surrounded by attendants. Benin artisans used a lost-wax process to create sculptures of bronze and brass. In this process, the sculptor formed a wax model encased within a clay shell. Molten metal was then poured into the clay shell. The melting wax ran out and was replaced with the finished metal sculpture.* **Art and Literature** *What does this sculpture suggest about the importance of the queen mother in Benin?*

ing to tradition, artisans from Ife (EE fee), an earlier forest society, had taught the people of Benin how to cast bronze and brass. Benin sculptors developed their own unique style for representing the human face and form. Their works depicted warriors armed for battle, queen mothers with upswept hairstyles, and the oba himself.

Looking ahead. Later Benin bronze works showed helmeted and bearded Portuguese merchants. These newcomers began to arrive in growing numbers in the 1500s. At first, Benin benefited from the new trade with European countries. However, as you will read in Chapter 16, increasing contacts with Europe opened the door to a booming slave trade that would have far-reaching consequences for all of West Africa.

SECTION 2 REVIEW

1. **Identify** (a) Almoravids, (b) Sundiata, (c) Sonni Ali, (d) Askia Muhammad.
2. How did the gold-salt trade develop between West Africa and North Africa?
3. How did the arrival of Muslim traders affect West Africa?
4. How did the Hausa states differ from kingdoms such as Mali or Songhai?
5. *Critical Thinking* **Recognizing Causes and Effects** (a) Describe two short-term effects of Mansa Musa's hajj. (b) What do you think was the most important long-term effect?
6. *ACTIVITY* Write an art review comparing the Benin bronze above to a piece of sculpture from an earlier chapter.

Trade Routes of East Africa

Guide for Reading

- How did the kingdom of Axum emerge as a prosperous state?

- What religious traditions influenced East Africa?

- What trade networks linked East Africa to other regions?

According to Ethiopian tradition, the first emperor of Ethiopia was the son of the Hebrew king Solomon and Makeda, the Queen of Sheba. The ancient chronicle *The Glory of Kings* tells how Makeda journeys to Jerusalem after hearing of Solomon's wisdom. "Learning is better than treasures of silver and gold," she says. The queen spends six months at Solomon's court, gathering knowledge to bring back to her people.

When Makeda is about to return to Sheba, Solomon gives her a ring and a blessing:

66May the peace of God be with thee. While I was sleeping . . . I had a vision. The sun which before my eyes was shining upon Israel, moved away. It went and soared above Ethiopia. It remained there. Who knows but that thy country may be blessed because of thee? Above all keep the truth which I have brought thee. Worship God.99

The East African kingdom of Ethiopia had proud roots in Jewish and Christian tradition. In later centuries, when other African kingdoms were coming under the influence of Islam, Ethiopia remained a center of Christianity.

Axum and Its Successors

About A.D. 350, you will recall, King Ezana of Axum conquered and absorbed the ancient kingdom of Nubia. Located southeast of Nubia, Axum extended from the mountains of modern Ethiopia to the sun-bleached shores of the Red Sea. The peoples of Axum were descended from African farmers and from traders who had immigrated from Arabia. This merging of cultures introduced Hebrew religious traditions to Axum. It also gave rise to a unique written and spoken language, Geez.

Trade. The kingdom of Axum profited from the strategic location of its two main cities, the port of Adulis on the Red Sea and the upland capital city of Axum. From about 200 B.C. to A.D. 400, Axumites commanded a triangular trade network linking Africa, India, and the Mediterranean world.

Products from the African interior such as ivory, hides, rhinoceros horn, and gold passed through the city of Axum. To Adulis came ships carrying goods from farther down the coast of East Africa, or from India across the Indian Ocean. These goods would then flow north up the Red Sea to the Mediterranean, to the Middle East, Greece, Rome, and beyond.

Christian converts. In these great centers of international trade, Greek, Egyptian, Arab, and Jewish merchants mingled with African, Indian, and other traders. As elsewhere, ideas spread along with goods. The powerful king Ezana converted to Christianity in the 300s. As the new religion took root among the people, Christian churches replaced older temples.

At first, Christianity strengthened ties between Axum and the Mediterranean world.

▲ Ethiopian rock church

Then in the 600s, Islam came to dominate North Africa, leaving Axum an isolated island of Christianity. Weakened by civil war and cut off from its harbors, Axum slowly declined.

Ethiopia, a Christian outpost. Though Axum faded, its legacy survived among people of the interior uplands. The Axumites became the ancestors of the present-day Ethiopians, who maintained their independence through the centuries. Their survival was due in part to the unifying power of their Christian faith, which gave them a unique sense of their own identity. Geography helped, too, by providing the protection of rugged, mountainous terrain.

In the early 1200s, King Lalibela had a dozen churches carved into the mountains. (See the picture on page 294.) Ethiopian chronicles affirmed that the builders had divine help:

    66Angels joined the workers, the quarry men, the stone cutters, and the laborers. The angels worked with them by day and by themselves at night. The men . . . doubted whether the angels were doing this work because they could not see them, but Lalibela knew, because the angels, who understood his virtue, did not hide from him.**99**

Over the centuries, Ethiopian Christians absorbed many traditions. They adapted traditional East African drum music and dances that are still used in church services today. They also observed Jewish holidays and dietary laws. (A separate group of Ethiopian Jews, the Falasha, survived in the mountains of Ethiopia until recent years.) Until the fall of the last emperor in 1974, Ethiopian rulers claimed descent from Solomon.

East African City-States

While Axum declined, a string of commercial cities gradually rose along the East African coast. Since ancient times, Phoenician, Greek, Roman, and Indian traders had visited this coast. In the A.D. 600s, Arab and Persian merchants set up Muslim communities under the protection of local African rulers. Later, Bantu-speaking peoples migrated into the region and adopted Islam. Other waves of Asian immigrants from as far away as Indonesia added to the rich cultural mix.

African Kingdoms and Trading States

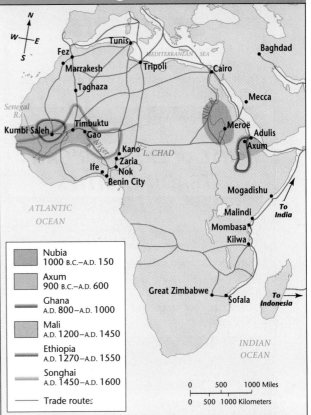

Nubia
1000 B.C.–A.D. 150

Axum
900 B.C.–A.D. 600

Ghana
A.D. 800–A.D. 1000

Mali
A.D. 1200–A.D. 1450

Ethiopia
A.D. 1270–A.D. 1550

Songhai
A.D. 1450–A.D. 1600

Trade routes

0   500   1000 Miles
0 500 1000 Kilometers

GEOGRAPHY AND HISTORY

From 1000 B.C. in Nubia to the A.D. 1400s and 1500s in Songhai, Africans built strong kingdoms in East Africa and West Africa. Many of the kingdoms developed because of profitable trade with other lands.

1. **Location** On the map, locate (a) Indian Ocean, (b) Nile River, (c) Axum, (d) Ghana, (e) Malindi.
2. **Place** (a) Why were Mombasa and Kilwa important trade centers? (b) Which West African kingdoms included the Senegal River?
3. **Critical Thinking** *Making Generalizations* Make one generalization about the African trade routes shown on the map.

Growth of trade. By A.D. 1000, port cities like Mogadishu (mahg uh DIHSH oo), Kilwa, and Sofala, and offshore islands like Zanzibar, were thriving from trade across the Indian

CAUSE AND EFFECT

Causes

- Early trade with Phoenician, Greek, Roman, Arab, Chinese, and Indian traders
- Trading communities set up by Arab and Asian immigrants on east coast

RISE OF EAST AFRICAN TRADING CITIES

Immediate Effects

- Thriving commerce in Mogadishu, Kilwa, Sofala
- Rise of strong East African city-states
- Rise of slave trade
- Introduction of crops and animals from Middle East and Asia

Long-Term Effects

- Rich mix of cultures
- Development of Swahili language

Connections Today

- Diffusion of East African culture
- Mogadishu is capital and largest city in Somalia
- Swahili is official language in Tanzania and still spoken in other East African nations
- Arab and Indian communities in East Africa today
- Strong Muslim influence in East Africa today

Interpreting a Chart *Starting in the 600s, prosperous trading cities grew up along the East African coast. The effects of this trade can still be felt in Africa.* ■ *Why are there Arab and Indian communities in East Africa today?*

Trade helped local rulers build strong city-states. A Muslim visitor described Kilwa as "one of the most beautiful and well-constructed towns in the world." Its royal palace, built of coral and cut stone, stood on a high cliff overlooking the city. In the marketplace of Kilwa, merchants offered goods from both inland and coastal regions. A thriving slave trade also developed. Thousands of Africans were seized as slaves inland and sold to Persian traders.

A blend of cultures. International trade created a rich and varied mix of cultures in the East African city-states. Bantu-speaking Africans mingled in the streets with traders from Arabia and Southeast Asia. With the spread of Islam, Middle Eastern influences grew stronger. Marriages between African women and non-African Muslim men furthered the spread of Muslim culture. A wife's property rights allowed her husband to settle and own land. Their children often gained positions of leadership.

Eventually, the blend of cultures gave rise to a new language, Swahili. Swahili fused many Arabic words onto a Bantu base and was written in Arabic script.

The Stones of Great Zimbabwe

To the south and inland from the coastal city-states, massive stone ruins sprawl across rocky hilltops near the great bend in the Limpopo River. Looming walls, a great palace, and cone-shaped towers testify to the powerful and prosperous capital of a great inland empire. Today, these impressive ruins are known as Great Zimbabwe, which means "great stone buildings."

Europeans who came upon these ruins in the 1800s thought they were the work of the ancient Phoenicians. In fact, the builders were a succession of Bantu-speaking peoples who settled in the region between 900 and 1500. The newcomers brought improved farming skills, iron, and mining methods. On the relatively fer-

ISSUES For TODAY Trading patterns encouraged a blending of diverse cultures in the city-states of coastal East Africa. How can economic links lead to cultural diffusion?

Ocean. Riding the monsoon winds, merchant vessels sailed northeast to India between April and August, and returned to East Africa between December and March.

tile land, they produced enough food to support a growing population.

Economy and government. We know little about how this civilization developed, but it probably reached its height about 1300. By then, it had tapped nearby gold resources and created profitable commercial links with coastal cities like Sofala. Archaeologists have found beads from India and porcelain from China, showing that Great Zimbabwe was part of a trade network that reached across the Indian Ocean.

Very little is known about the government in Great Zimbabwe. Scholars have suggested, however, that the ruler of Great Zimbabwe was a god-king who presided over a large court. He may have shared authority with a powerful queen mother and nine queens, each of whom had her own court. A central bureaucracy ruled an inner ring of provinces, while appointed governors had authority in more distant villages.

Decline. By 1500, Zimbabwe was in decline. Some scholars suggest that overfarming had exhausted the soil. Civil war and dwindling trade probably contributed to the breakup of Zimbabwe. By then, Portuguese traders were pushing inland to find the source of gold that reached the coast. They failed to discover the gold mines, and their intrusion helped undermine later small states that formed in the region.

SECTION 3 REVIEW

1. **Identify** (a) Queen of Sheba, (b) Ezana, (c) Geez, (d) Lalibela, (e) Swahili.
2. Why was Axum a key trading center for three continents?
3. What religious traditions came together in Ethiopia?
4. What evidence suggests that Great Zimbabwe was a center of trade?
5. *Critical Thinking* **Analyzing Information** (a) Why did Ethiopia become increasingly isolated over the centuries? (b) What might have helped it survive as an independent kingdom?
6. *ACTIVITY* Create a map showing trade networks and goods exchanged between East Africa, Asia, and the Middle East.

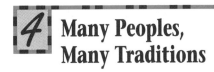

4 Many Peoples, Many Traditions

Guide for Reading

- How did African peoples adapt to different environments?
- What bonds held African societies together?
- How did art and literature strengthen African societies?
- **Vocabulary** *slash-and-burn agriculture, nuclear family, patrilineal, matrilineal, lineage, griot*

At harvest time, the Kikuyu (kee KOO yoo) people of East Africa offered an ancient prayer of thanksgiving to their traditional gods:

66Mwene-Nyaga, you who have brought us rain and have given us good harvest, let people eat grain of this harvest calmly and peacefully. . . . Guard us against illness of people or our herds and flocks so that we may enjoy this season's harvest in peace.99

In West African mosques, Muslims recited a different prayer: "Praise be to God, Lord of the Universe, the Compassionate, the Merciful."

Differing religious traditions contributed to the diversity of the vast continent of Africa. At the same time, they also formed bonds that held individual societies together.

Adapting to the Land

Bantu peoples, you will recall, gradually migrated across Africa, bringing farming skills and knowledge of ironworking to its many regions. Wherever they settled, they adapted to local environments and absorbed ideas from the peoples they encountered. Trade or other contacts brought additional changes. As a result, the ways of life of African societies varied greatly from place to place.

Hunters and food gatherers. The great Bantu migrations pushed the earliest hunting and food-gathering peoples of Africa to fringe areas. The Khoisan people, for example, adapted to the harsh desert conditions of the Kalahari by gathering edible roots and herbs and hunting small game.

Because food was scarce, these hunting-gathering people lived in small bands numbering only about 20 or 30. Their knowledge of the natural world, however, was unmatched by city dwellers or farming villagers. They could track animals across long distances and could identify the food and healing properties of many different plants.

Herding and fishing. In parts of the savanna free from the tsetse fly, some peoples raised herds of cattle. Because of limited grass for grazing, these societies were often nomadic. In general, the men herded and hunted, while the women raised food in small gardens. To protect their herds against raiders, these societies perfected skills in warfare.

Along the coasts and rivers, fish was the basic food source for some people. Most fishing peoples used nets. They traded any surplus fish for grain, animal skins, and other products made by people who lived inland. Some fishing areas had enough food resources to support large populations.

Settled farming societies. Farming communities raised a variety of crops from grains to root crops like yams or tree crops like bananas. Most farming peoples practiced a method that is today called slash-and-burn agriculture. They cleared forest and brush land with iron axes and hoes, then burned the remains, using the ash for fertilizer. Because the land lost its fertility within a few years, villagers would move on to clear other land. Eventually, after giving the soil time to renew its fertility, they might return to the abandoned fields.

Forms of Village Government

Farming peoples generally lived in tightknit communities and helped one another in tasks such as clearing the land, planting, and harvesting. Both men and women planted, but usually were responsible for different crops. Political patterns varied, depending in part on the size of the communities that the land could support. However, village governments often had similar features.

Sharing power. In these pre-urban societies, power was usually shared among a number of people rather than centralized in the hands of a single leader. In some villages, a chief had a good deal of authority, but in many others, elders made the major decisions. Sometimes, older men would supervise religious ceremonies, while younger men made decisions about war. In some places, especially in parts of West Africa, women took the dominant role in the marketplace or acted as official peacemakers in the village.

Villages often made decisions by a process known as consensus. In open discussions, people whose opinions were valued voiced their views before a general agreement was reached. The opinions of older women and men usually held the greatest weight. People also exercised authority as members of village associations. For example, religious and market associations gave women a way to voice their concerns about village matters.

Villages that were ruled by a larger kingdom like Songhai had to obey decisions made at a distant court. These villagers, like those in China or India, had to pay taxes and provide soldiers to the central government.

The kingdom of Kongo. The kingdom of Kongo, which flourished about 1500 in the forest zone of central Africa, illustrates one form of government organization. It consisted of many villages grouped into districts and provinces and governed by officials appointed by the king. Each village had its own chief, a man chosen on the basis of the descent of his mother's family.

In theory, the king of Kongo had absolute power. In fact, that power was limited. The king was chosen by a board of electors and had to govern according to traditional laws. Unlike rulers of West African states, who maintained strong standing armies, kings of Kongo depended on a system of military service that called upon men to fight only in times of need. Through local governors, the king collected taxes either in goods or in cowrie shells, a common African currency.

The organization of Kongo was just one type of African government. In many regions, people belonged to small local societies without a centralized government.

Family Patterns

In Africa, as elsewhere, the family was the basic unit of society. Patterns of family life varied. In hunting and gathering societies, for example, the nuclear family was typical, with parents and children living and working together as a unit. In other African communities, people lived in joint families. Several generations shared the same complex of houses.

Lines of descent. Family organization varied in other ways as well. Some families were patrilineal, that is, important kinship ties, such as inheritance and residence, were passed through the father's side. Other families were matrilineal, with inheritance and descent traced through the mother's side. In a patrilineal culture, a bride would move to her husband's village and become part of his family. In a matrilineal culture, the husband joined his wife's family in her village.

Matrilineal cultures also forged strong ties between brothers and sisters. Brothers were expected to protect their sisters, while sisters made their sons available to help their brothers whenever needed.

Wider ties. Each family belonged to a lineage, or group of households who claimed a common ancestor. Several lineages formed a clan that traced its descent to an even more remote and often legendary ancestor. Belonging to a particular family, lineage, or clan gave people a strong sense of community values. Elders taught both girls and boys their special roles in the community along with their clan's history and religious beliefs.

An individual's place in society was also determined by a system of age grades. An age grade included all girls or boys born in the same year. Each age grade had particular responsibilities and privileges. In the older age grades, children began to take part in village activities, which created social ties beyond the family.

Religious Beliefs

Across Africa, religious beliefs were varied and complex. Like Hindus or ancient Greeks and Romans, village Africans worshiped many gods and goddesses. Along with all ancient peoples, they identified the forces of nature with divine spirits and tried to influence those forces

Village Life This sculpted panel depicts people at work in an agricultural village. For most Africans, the activities of daily life revolved around family and community. Each individual was expected to help provide for the needs of the group. **Economics and Technology** What economic activities are depicted in this sculpture?

Traditions in Fabric

The color, weave, and pattern of a fabric often reveals its cultural origin. From the tartan plaids of Scotland to the colorful batiks of Indonesia, these unique styles form part of a cultural heritage that has been passed from generation to generation.

Linking Past and Present Why do you think clothing in kente patterns has become popular in the United States?

PAST *The sample of kente cloth below was produced by the Ashanti people of West Africa. The beautiful fabric is typically made of silk, with woven strips of multicolored design. Ashanti kings and chieftains wore kente as a symbol of their power and prestige.*

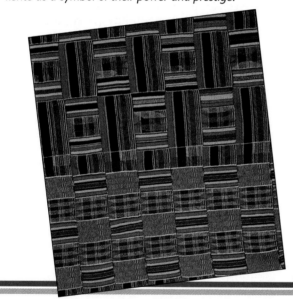

PRESENT *This New York shop has an interesting collection of African wares. Customers may purchase American-style ties, belts, and other clothing in a variety of traditional African patterns.*

through the rituals and ceremonies that they practiced.

Village elders called upon certain spirits to bring rain or good harvests. To cure illnesses or other troubles, specially trained healers mingled their skills in herbal medicine with prayers to the gods. Diviners sought advice about the future from the spirit world.

Many African peoples believed that a single, unknowable supreme being stood above all the other gods and goddesses. This supreme being was the creator and ruler of the universe and was helped by the lesser spirits, who were closer to the people. Like the Chinese, many African peoples believed that the spirits of their ancestors were present on Earth. Just as Christians in me-

dieval Europe called on the saints for help, people in Africa turned to the spirits of their departed ancestors.

Christianity and Islam, as you have seen, influenced peoples in some parts of Africa. Converts often associated the God of Christians and Muslims with their traditional supreme being. In this way, Christianity and Islam absorbed many local practices and beliefs.

African Arts

In art and architecture, African traditions extend far back in time to the ancient rock paintings of the Sahara. The pyramids of Egypt and Nubia, the rock churches of Ethiopia, and the stones of Great Zimbabwe bear lasting witness to the creative power of these early civilizations. Sadly, many wooden buildings and works of art have not survived the ages.

African artists created works in ivory, wood, and bronze. Sometimes, their work was decorative. Artisans wove and dyed cloth, inscribed jugs and bowls, and shaped bracelets and neck ornaments simply to beautify them. Much art, though, served social and religious purposes.

Art strengthened bonds within the community and linked both the makers and the users of the work. Patterns used to decorate textiles, baskets, swords, and other objects had important meanings. Often, they identified an object as the work of a particular clan or possession of royalty. Boldly patterned kente cloth was once worn only by West African rulers or members of the royal family.

In Africa, as elsewhere, much art was closely tied to religion. Statues and other objects were used in religious ceremonies. In many rituals, leaders wore impressively carved wooden masks decorated with cowrie shells or grass. Once the mask was in place, both the wearer and the viewers could feel the presence of the spiritual force it represented. As you will read, the stylized forms of African masks and other works had a dramatic influence on the development of modern art in the western world.

Literary Traditions

African societies preserved their histories and values through both oral and written literature. Ancient Egypt, Nubia, and Axum left written records of their past. Later, Arabic provided a common written language for peoples in parts of Africa influenced by Islam. African Muslim scholars gathered in cities like Timbuktu and Kilwa as well as in Cairo and other North African centers. Documents in Arabic offer invaluable evidence about law, religion, and history.

Oral traditions date back many centuries. In West Africa, griots (GREE ohs), or professional poets, recited ancient stories. They preserved both histories and traditional folk tales in the same way that the epics of Homer or Aryan India were passed orally from generation to generation.

Griots often used riddles to sharpen the wits of the audience. The following traditional riddles have been handed down by the Yoruba people of present-day Nigeria:

&& We call the dead—they answer.
We call the living—they do not answer.

Two tiny birds
Jump over two hundred trees. &&

The answer to the first riddle is "leaves." Dead leaves make noise when stepped on, but fresh ones do not. The second riddle refers to the eyes, which can see over long distances.

Histories praised the heroic deeds of famous ancestors or kings. Folk tales, which blended fanciful stories with humor and sophisticated word play, taught important moral lessons. Oral literature, like religion and art, thus fostered a sense of community and common values among peoples of Africa.

SECTION 4 REVIEW

1. **Define** (a) slash-and-burn agriculture, (b) nuclear family, (c) patrilineal, (d) matrilineal, (e) lineage, (f) griot.
2. Describe three types of African society.
3. (a) How did family patterns vary across Africa? (b) How did the age-grade system strengthen community ties?
4. How was art connected to religion in African cultures?
5. *Critical Thinking* **Analyzing Information** How might a matrilineal line of descent allow women to excercise greater authority in village affairs?
6. *ACTIVITY* Using the Yoruba riddles on this page as a model, create three riddles about the world around you.

GLOBAL CONNECTIONS

As elsewhere, much African oral literature takes the form of proverbs. Proverbs from different cultures often express similar ideas. For example, a proverb of the Fulani people of West Africa states, "A dog once burnt will leave ash-covered embers alone." The same idea has been expressed in Korea as "A cow that has been scorched by the sun will pant even on seeing the moon," and in England as "Once bitten, twice shy."

World Literature
Sundiata

Introduction *The epic of Sundiata, founder of Mali, is part of Africa's long tradition of oral literature. Like the* Mahabharata *in India or the* Iliad *in Greece, the* Sundiata *epic was passed down from memory for many centuries before being written down. This version was translated in the 1960s by Djibril Tamsir Niane, who heard the tale from a griot.*

The epic recounts the efforts of young Sundiata to reclaim his father's kingdom from his enemy Soumaoro (soo mah AWR oh), king of Sosso. In it, details of battle are mixed with praise of Sundiata's courage, his distinguished ancestors, and his supernatural powers. In the following passage, Sundiata and Soumaoro confront each other on the eve of the final battle.

Sundiata went and pitched camp at Dayala in the valley of the Niger. Now it was he who was blocking Soumaoro's road to the south. . . .

Soumaoro advanced as far as Krina, near the village of Dayala on the Niger, and decided to assert his rights before joining battle. Soumaoro knew that Sundiata also was a sorcerer, so, instead of sending an embassy, he committed his words to one of his owls. The night bird came and perched on the roof of Sundiata's tent and spoke. Sundiata in his turn sent his own to Soumaoro. Here is the dialogue of the sorcerer kings:

"Stop, young man. Henceforth I am the king of Mali. If you want peace, return to where you came from," said Soumaoro.

"I am coming back, Soumaoro, to recapture my kingdom. If you want peace you will make amends to my allies and return to Sosso where you are the king."

"I am king of Mali by force of arms. My rights have been established by conquest."

"Then I will take Mali from you by force of arms and chase you from my kingdom."

"Know, then, that I am the wild yam of the rocks; nothing will make me leave Mali."

"Know, also that I have in my camp seven master smiths who will shatter the rocks. Then, yam, I will eat you."

"I am the poisonous mushroom that makes the fearless ill."

"As for me, I am the ravenous rooster, the poison does not matter to me."

"Behave yourself, little boy, or you will burn your foot, for I am the red-hot cinder."

"But me, I am the rain that extinguishes the cinder; I am the boisterous torrent that will carry you off."

"I am the mighty silk-cotton tree that looks from on high on the tops of other trees."

"And I, I am the strangling creeper that climbs to the top of the forest giant."

"Enough of this argument. You shall not have Mali."

"Know that there is not room for two kings on the same skin, Soumaoro; you will let me have your place."

"Very well, since you want war I will wage war against you, but I would have you know that I have killed nine kings. . . ."

"Prepare yourself, Soumaoro, for it will be long before the calamity that is going to crash down upon you and yours comes to an end."

Thus Sundiata and Soumaoro spoke together. After the war of mouths, swords had to decide the issue. . . .

In the evening, to raise the men's spirits, Sundiata gave a great feast, for he was anxious that his men should wake up happy in the morning. . . . Sundiata's griot, in front of the whole army, called to mind the history of old Mali. He praised Sundiata, seated amidst his lieutenants, in this manner:

"Now I address myself to you, Sundiata, I speak to you king of Mali, to whom dethroned monarchs flock. The time foretold to you is now coming. Sundiata, kingdoms and empires are in the likeness of man; like him they are born, they grow and disappear. Each king embodies one moment of that life. Formerly, the

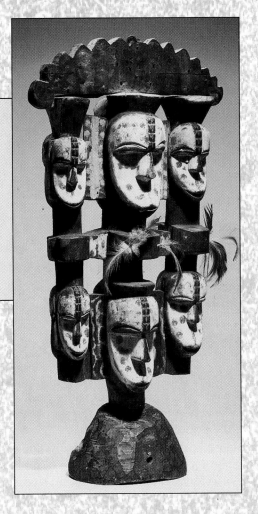

Ceremonial Headdress *Veneration of ancestors played an important role in many traditional African religions. In the* Sundiata *epic, the griot takes great pains to recount the king's exalted ancestry. Elsewhere in West Africa, headdresses like the one at the right were used in religious ceremonies. Through dance and ritual, the people thanked ancestors for successful harvests and honored great warriors of the past.* **Religions and Value Systems** *Name another culture in which veneration of ancestors played an important role.*

kings of Ghana extended their kingdom over all the lands, but the circle has closed and the kings of Ghana are nothing more than petty princes in a desolate land. Today, another kingdom looms up, powerful, the kingdom of Sosso. Humbled kings have brought their tribute to Sosso, Soumaoro's arrogance knows no more bounds and his cruelty is equal to his ambition. . . . The kingdom of Sosso is but the growth of yesterday, whereas that of Mali dates from ancient times. Each kingdom has its childhood, but Soumaoro wants to force the pace, and so Sosso will collapse under him like a horse worn out beneath its rider. . . .

"You are the outgrowth of Mali just as the silk-cotton tree is the growth of the earth, born of deep and mighty roots. To face the tempest the tree must have long roots and gnarled branches. . . . You are the son of Nare Maghan, but you are also the son of your mother Sogolon, the buffalo-woman, before whom powerless sorcerers shrank in fear. You have the strength and majesty of the lion, you have the might of the buffalo. . . .

"Tomorrow, allow me to sing the 'Song of the Vultures' over the bodies of the thousands of Sossos whom your sword will have laid low before evening."

Source: D. T. Niane, *Sundiata: An Epic of Old Mali* (Harlow, England: Longman Group Ltd., 1965).

Thinking About Literature

1. **Vocabulary** Use the dictionary to find the meanings of the following words: embassy, amends, ravenous, boisterous, torrent, embodies, tempest.
2. (a) How do Sundiata and Soumaoro conduct their war of words on the eve of the battle? (b) Describe the nature of their conversation.
3. (a) What does Sundiata's griot say about the nature of empires? (b) Why does he predict that Soumaoro is doomed to failure? (c) What importance does the griot give to Sundiata's ancestry?
4. *Critical Thinking* **Drawing Conclusions** People went to great pains to memorize lengthy epics like *Sundiata*, the *Mahabharata*, and the *Iliad*. Why do you think they felt it was important to pass down these stories?

CHAPTER REVIEW

REVIEWING VOCABULARY

Write sentences using *five* of the vocabulary words from this chapter, leaving blanks where the vocabulary words would go. Exchange your sentences with another student and fill in the blanks on each other's lists.

REVIEWING FACTS

1. What is the Sahara?
2. How did camels revolutionize trade in Africa?
3. Which products dominated the Sahara trade?
4. What were the effects of Mansa Musa's pilgrimage to Mecca?

5. How was trade important for the kingdom of Axum?
6. Why did city-states emerge in East Africa?
7. How did the consensus method of making decisions operate in African villages?
8. What were the uses of Africa's oral traditions?

REVIEWING CHAPTER THEMES

Review the "Focus On" questions at the start of this chapter. Then select *three* of those questions and answer them, using information from the chapter.

SKILLS FOR SUCCESS   MAKING PRESENTATIONS

Before you go before a group of people, you must spend time organizing your information and deciding how best to present it. You should also practice the presentation aloud.

Imagine that you have been assigned to make a presentation on African arts to a group of history students in a lower grade. The following steps can help you prepare your presentation more effectively.

1. **Make a list of questions that your presentation will answer.** (a) Look at the list of possible questions at right. Which of these should you try to answer in your presentation on African arts? (b) What sources could you use to locate information to answer these questions?

2. **Define the goal of your presentation and identify your audience.** Possible goals include presenting a point of view, persuading, entertaining, or informing. (a) What do you think would be the main goal of your presentation on African arts? (b) Who is your audience? How much knowledge do you think they have about the topic? (c) How might your answers to these questions affect your presentation?

3. **Prepare an outline and notes to guide you during the presentation.** Look back at your list of questions and arrange them in order. Then

write notes on how you want to answer the questions. Which question should you answer first during your presentation? Why?

4. **Practice your presentation aloud.** As you practice, time yourself and evaluate your delivery. Check that you are speaking clearly and at an appropriate pace. What are the dangers of speaking too quickly or too slowly?

Possible Questions to Be Answered in the Presentation

A. What materials did African artists use?
B. Why did Nubian rulers move their capital to Meroë?
C. What was the purpose of much early African art?
D. What skills did artisans of Benin develop?
E. How did African art influence modern art?
F. What are the unique qualities of African art?
G. What family patterns were found in African societies?
H. Why is it worthwhile to learn about the art of Africa?

CRITICAL THINKING

1. **Linking Past and Present** Most modern African nations regained their independence from European rule between 1957 and 1979. (a) Look at the map of modern Africa on page 562. Which nations took their names from ancient African kingdoms? (b) Why do you think these nations chose these names?

2. **Predicting Consequences** (a) Describe the process of slash-and-burn agriculture. (b) What might be some dangers of the extensive use of slash-and-burn methods?

3. **Comparing** (a) Describe three traditions that created social bonds in African communities. (b) How are these traditions similar to the traditions that create social bonds in your community? How are they different?

ANALYZING PRIMARY SOURCES

Use the quotation on page 294 to answer the following questions.

1. According to Solomon, what was the great lesson he taught Makeda?

2. What prediction did Solomon make?

3. What image did Solomon use to describe his prediction?

FOR YOUR PORTFOLIO

RECITING A TALE Play the part of an African griot and recite a traditional tale from an African culture. First, review the section titled "Literary Traditions" on page 301. Then use outside resources to find a traditional African folk tale or historical event to retell. Learn what you can about the background of the story you choose. Then read the tale or history several times until you can retell it in your own words. Practice telling the tale aloud, using different voices, facial expressions, and gestures to make it come alive. Then prepare an introduction in which you explain the origin and significance of your story. Finally, introduce your story to the class and then recite it.

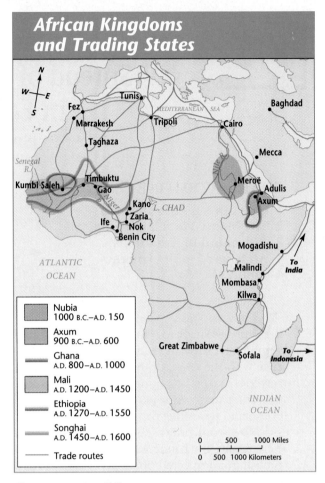

African Kingdoms and Trading States

Nubia 1000 B.C.–A.D. 150
Axum 900 B.C.–A.D. 600
Ghana A.D. 800–A.D. 1000
Mali A.D. 1200–A.D. 1450
Ethiopia A.D. 1270–A.D. 1550
Songhai A.D. 1450–A.D. 1600
Trade routes

ANALYZING MAPS

Use the map to answer the following questions.

1. Timbuktu was part of which two African kingdoms?

2. The kingdom of Nubia was located on which major river?

3. How does the map show African trade with other continents? With which other continents is trade shown?

INTERNET ACTIVITY

ANALYZING STATISTICS Use the Internet to research statistics on the economic or military strength of an early African culture. Then write a brief explanation of how these statistics show the strength or the weakness of that culture.

Spread of Civilizations in East Asia

(500–1603)

CHAPTER OUTLINE

1 **Two Golden Ages of China**
2 **The Mongol and Ming Empires**
3 **Korea and Its Traditions**
4 **An Island Empire Emerges**
5 **Japan's Feudal Age**

Many people in China distrusted the empress Wu Zhao (WOO JOW). From humble beginnings, she had risen to a position of influence with the emperor. After his death, she had ruthlessly taken power into her own hands, even unseating her own sons. No other woman had ever dared to assume the title of emperor!

Now, rival princes and Confucian scholars were raising the banner of revolt against her. Lo Binwang, a respected poet, wrote a declaration condemning the empress as a "vile character." He issued a fiery call to arms:

❝Rise, rise, all men! . . . Are your hearts dead? Does not the royal will still ring in your ears? Consider, the orphans of our emperor are left helpless and defenseless while their father's grave is hardly dry!❞

Soon, the declaration came to the attention of Wu Zhao herself. "Who wrote it?" she demanded angrily.

"Lo Binwang," replied her chief ministers. Surely, they thought, the poet would now feel Wu Zhao's wrath.

Surprisingly, the empress did not direct her anger at Lo Binwang. Rather, she berated her own ministers. Why had they failed to bring such a talented writer into her service? Like other educated Chinese, Wu prized a skilled and brilliant writer, no matter what side he was on.

In the late 600s, Wu Zhao became the only woman to rule China in her own name. Like many other rulers, she won power by combining political skill with ruthlessness. Many Chinese historians saw her as an evil adventurer. Others praised her for supporting Buddhism and recruiting able officials regardless of social standing. Her strong rule helped guide China through one of its most brilliant periods.

After the 500s, China again emerged as a united empire. "Barbarians" on the fringes of the Middle Kingdom admired and copied Chinese civilization. As a result, Chinese culture spread to neighboring lands. While Korea and Japan adopted much from China, they reshaped these traditions to fit their own distinct patterns of civilization.

FOCUS ON these questions as you read:

- **Continuity and Change**
  What traditions helped preserve Chinese civilization despite the rise and fall of dynasties?

- **Global Interaction**
  How did Chinese civilization come to influence people in Korea and Japan?

- **Political and Social Systems**
  How did Japan develop into a feudal society?

- **Art and Literature**
  What distinct literary and artistic traditions emerged in China and Japan?

TIME AND PLACE

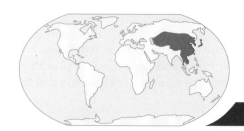

An Enlightened Ruler Emperors of the Tang dynasty helped create a golden age in China. This picture shows Ming Huang, or "Enlightened Emperor," on horseback. His achievements included reforming the political bureaucracy, restoring the canal system, and strengthening border defenses. He also established several music academies and supported the work of painters and writers. **Impact of the Individual** Why do you think this ruler was called "Enlightened Emperor"?

HUMANITIES LINK

Art History Li Ching, *Buddhist Temple in the Hills After Rain* (page 313).
Literature In this chapter, you will encounter passages from the following works of literature: Li Bo, "Beside my bed the bright moonbeams glimmer" (page 313); Li Qingzhao, "Year after year I have watched" (page 313); Marco Polo, *A Description of the World* (page 317); *Songs of the Flying Dragons* (page 322); Sei Shonagon, *The Pillow Book*, (page 326); Sogi, "To live in the world" (page 327); Kenko, *Essays in Idleness* (page 330).

668	690	960	1010	1279	1405	1603
Shilla dynasty unites Korea	Empress Wu Zhao rules China	Song golden age begins	*The Tale of Genji* written	Mongol conquest of China completed	First Ming voyages of exploration	Tokugawa Ieyasu becomes shogun

600	800	1000	1200	1400	1600

1 Two Golden Ages of China

Guide for Reading

- How did the Tang and Song dynasties restore Chinese culture and prosperity?

- How did social patterns reflect Confucian traditions?

- What were the artistic achievements of Tang and Song China?

- **Vocabulary** *tributary state, pagoda*

Slowly the artisan inscribed the Chinese characters onto a wood block. He carefully cut away the spaces between each one. One slip of the knife and the page would be ruined. With a brush, he then stroked velvety black ink onto the characters. Finally, he pressed a sheet of paper against the inked block. When he pulled it away, he had a beautifully printed page ready for binding.

The job required special attention because it was an important government order. In 932, the emperor asked for a printed copy of the Confucian classics. Using this system of woodblock printing, it would take 20 years to print all 130 volumes.

Woodblock printing was just one of the many significant inventions created in China between the 600s and 1200s. At a time when Europe was fragmented into many small feudal kingdoms, China remained a unified state under two powerful dynasties.

▲ *Emperor Tang Taizong*

The Brilliant Tang

After the Han dynasty collapsed in 220, China remained a divided land for nearly 400 years. During this period, however, China escaped the grim decay that disrupted Western Europe after the fall of Rome. Farm production expanded and technology slowly improved. Buddhism spread, while learning and the arts continued. Even Chinese cities survived. Although invaders stormed northern China, they would often adopt Chinese civilization rather than demolish it.

Meanwhile, various Chinese dynasties rose and fell in the south. Despite frequent warfare, China's impulse toward unity and the old Confucian order remained strong. During the brief Sui dynasty (589–618), Emperor Sui Wendi reconquered most Han territory and reunited the north and south. But the Middle Kingdom was not restored to its earlier glory until the rule of the Tang (618–907) and, later, the Song (960–1279) dynasties.

Building the Tang empire. The first two Tang emperors were father and son, but the son was the driving force behind the dynasty. The father, Li Yuan, was a leading general under the Sui dynasty. When the Sui began to crumble, his ambitious son Li Shimin urged him to lead a revolt. Though only 16 years old, Li Shimin was already a war hero. Father and son crushed all rivals and firmly established the Tang dynasty.

Eight years later, Li Shimin compelled his aging father to step down and mounted the throne himself, taking the name Tang Taizong. Brilliant general, government reformer, famous historian, and master of the calligraphy brush, Tang Taizong would become the most admired of all Chinese emperors.

The Tang dynasty carried empire building to greater heights, conquering territories deep into Central Asia as far as present-day Afghanistan. Chinese armies forced the neighboring lands of Vietnam, Tibet, and Korea to become tributary states. That is, while these states remained independent, their rulers had to acknowledge Chinese supremacy and send regular tribute to the Tang emperor.

The size, wealth, and advanced civilization of Tang China deeply impressed nearby peoples. As you will read, students from Korea and Japan traveled to the Tang capital of Changan to learn about Chinese government, law, and arts.

Government and the economy. Tang rulers, such as Empress Wu Zhao, restored the Han system of uniform government throughout

Porcelain Art *Most ceramics from the Tang period, like these figures, have been found in tombs. Chinese artisans made porcelain by mixing a pure white clay called kaolin with a special mineral called china stone. They then baked the clay in kilns at temperatures exceeding 2,200° Fahrenheit.* **Economics and Technology** *Why do you think Chinese porcelain has been highly prized throughout the world?*

China. They rebuilt the bureaucracy and enlarged the civil service system to recruit talented officials trained in Confucian philosophy. They also set up schools to prepare male students for the exams and developed a flexible new law code.

Under a system of land reform, the Tang emperors redistributed land to peasants. This policy weakened the power of large landowners. At the same time, it increased government revenues, since the peasants could now pay taxes.

Under the Tang, a system of canals encouraged internal trade and transportation. The largest of these, the Grand Canal, linked the Huang He and Yangzi rivers. As a result, food from farming regions in the south could be sent by water to the capital in the north. At the time, the Grand Canal was the longest waterway ever dug by human labor.

Decline. Like earlier dynasties, the Tang eventually weakened. Later Tang emperors lost China's northwestern territories in Central Asia to the Arabs. Government corruption, crushing taxes, drought, famine, and rebellions all contributed to the downward swing of the dynastic cycle. (See page 62.) In 907, a rebel general overthrew the last Tang emperor. This time, however, the chaos following the collapse of a dynasty did not last long.

Prosperity Under the Song

In 960, a scholarly general, Zhao Kuangyin (JOW koo awng YEEN), reunited much of China and founded the Song dynasty. The Song ruled 319 years, slightly longer than the Tang, However, the Song controlled less territory than the Tang had. In addition, the Song faced the constant threat of invaders in the north. In the early 1100s, the battered Song retreated south of the Huang He River. There, the Southern Song ruled for another 150 years from their new capital at Hangzhou (HAHNG JOH).

Despite military setbacks, the Song period was a golden age. Chinese wealth and culture dominated East Asia even when its armies did not. Under the Song, the Chinese economy expanded. The center of farming shifted from the millet and wheat-growing north to the rice paddies of the Yangzi and south. There, new strains of rice and improved irrigation methods helped peasants produce two rice crops a year. The rise in productivity created surpluses, allowing more people to pursue commerce, learning, or the arts.

Under the Song, as under the Tang, foreign trade flourished. Merchants arrived by land and sea from India, Persia, and the Middle East. The

QUICK STUDY

Science and Technology of Tang and Song China

Invention	Description	Diffusion	Connections Today
Mechanical clock 700s 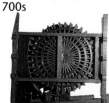	Chinese learned of water-powered clocks from Middle Easterners. Mechanical clocks used a complex series of wheels, shafts, and pins, turning at a steady rate, to tell exact time.	In early 1300s, European traders carried Chinese mechanical clocks westward.	Mechanical clocks have been largely replaced by quartz-crystal clocks. Today very accurate atomic clocks use steady frequency of energy changes in atoms to tell exact time.
Gunpowder 850	Made from mixture of saltpeter, sulfur, and charcoal, all found in abundance in China; used first in fireworks, later in weapons.	Knowledge of gunpowder and its ingredients, carried by Arab traders, reached Europe in the late 1200s.	Gunpowder is still used today with much the same formula to make deadly weapons and brilliant fireworks.
Smallpox vaccine 900s 	Small amounts of smallpox virus given to patients; the patient's own immune system then created antibodies to fight the disease; became widely used in China in the 1500s.	Idea spread to Turkish regions in the 1600s, where Europeans learned of it.	Led to later vaccines and to the science of immunology.
Block printing, 700s **Movable type,** 1040s 	Based on earlier techniques such as seals (first used in the Middle East). In block printing, a full page of characters was carved onto a wooden block. Movable type was made up of pre-cut characters that were combined to form a page.	Printing spread to Korea; later carried to Japan by Buddhist monks. May have spread to Europe with Mongol armies.	Block printing today is used mainly for book illustrations and decorative arts. Movable type is being replaced by faster electronic typesetting, which is done by computer.
Spinning wheel 1000s	A belt turned a large wheel, which then turned a spindle on which thread was wound.	Probably spread to Europe by Italians who traveled to China during Mongol dynasty.	Spindles and wheels are still used in high-speed machinery to mass produce yarn and thread.

Interpreting a Chart The Tang and Song periods were golden ages, not only for the arts, but for science and technology as well. In addition to the developments shown on this chart, the Chinese also introduced paper money and pioneered the use of arches in bridge building. Many inventions traveled westward only after many centuries. ■ *Which of the advances on this chart do you think probably had the greatest impact on history? Explain.*

Chinese built better ships, and their merchants carried goods to Southeast Asia in exchange for spices and special woods. Song porcelain has been found as far away as East Africa. To improve trade, the government issued paper money. China's cities, which had been mainly centers of government, now prospered as centers of trade. Several cities boasted populations over one million.

Three Levels of Chinese Society

Under the Tang and Song, China was a well-ordered society. The emperor ruled over a splendid court filled with aristocratic families. The court stood at the center of a huge bureaucracy from which officials fanned out to every province and county in China.

Gentry. The two main classes of Chinese society were the gentry and the peasantry. The gentry were wealthy landowners. They valued scholarship more than physical labor. Most scholar-officials at court came from this class because they alone could afford to spend years studying the Confucian classics. Only a few lucky men passed the grueling civil service exam and won the most honored positions in government. (See Chapter 4.) When not in government service, the gentry often served in the provinces as allies of the emperor's officials.

The Song scholar-gentry supported a revival of Confucian thought, searching out old Confucian texts. New schools of thinkers reinterpreted Confucian ideas that emphasized social order based on duty, rank, and proper behavior. This Confucian revival stressed traditions of the past. Although corruption and greed existed among civil servants, the ideal Confucian official was a wise, kind, selfless, virtuous scholar who knew how to ensure harmony in society.

Peasants. Most Chinese were peasants who worked the land, living on what they produced. Drought and famine were a constant threat, but better tools and new crops did improve the lives of many peasants. To add to their income, some families produced handicrafts such as baskets or embroidery. They carried these products to nearby market towns to sell or trade for salt, tea, or iron tools.

Peasants lived in small, largely self-sufficient villages that managed their own affairs. "Heaven is high," noted one Chinese saying, "and the emperor far away." Peasants relied on one another rather than on the government. When disputes arose, a village leader and council of elders put pressure on the parties to resolve the problem. Only when these efforts failed did villagers take their disputes to the emperor's county representative.

Although the joint family was the ideal, few peasants could support several generations within a household. Still, both peasants and gentry valued family ties. They conducted ceremonies to consult the spirits of their ancestors for help with family problems.

In China, even peasants could move up in society through education and government service. If a bright peasant boy received an education and passed the civil service examinations, both he and his family rose in status.

Merchants: prosperous but lowly. In market towns and cities, some merchants acquired vast wealth. Still, according to Confucian tradition, merchants had an even lower social status than peasants because their riches came from the labor of others. An ambitious merchant therefore might buy land and educate at least one son to enter the ranks of the scholar-gentry.

The Confucian attitude toward merchants affected economic policy. Some rulers favored trade and commerce but sought to control it. They often restricted where foreign merchants could live and even limited the activities of private traders. Despite restrictions, Chinese trade flourished during Song times.

Status of Women

Women seem to have had higher status in Tang and early Song times than they did later. Within the home, women were called upon to run family affairs. Wives and mothers-in-law had great authority and managed family finances, discipline, and servants. Still, within families, boys were valued more highly than girls were. To eliminate conflict within families, judges ruled that when a young woman married, she must completely become a part of her husband's family. She no longer could keep her dowry and could never remarry.

Women's subordinate position was reinforced in late Song times when the custom of

footbinding emerged. The practice probably began at the imperial court. The feet of young girls were bound with long strips of cloth, producing a lily-shaped foot about half the size of a foot that was allowed to grow normally. Tiny feet and a stilted walk became a symbol of female nobility and beauty. Footbinding was intensely painful, yet the custom survived because parents feared that a daughter with large feet would be unable to find a good husband. Eventually, the custom spread from the wealthy to the lower classes. Peasant families hoped that attractive daughters with lily feet would be able to marry into the gentry.

Not every girl in China had her feet bound. Peasants who relied on their daughters for field labor did not accept the practice, nor did some peoples like the Hakka of the southeastern mountains. Still, most women came to accept footbinding as a rite of passage. By making it impossible for women to leave home without assistance, the custom of footbinding reinforced the Confucian belief that women were "inside" people who did not do any outside work.

A Flood of Literature

Prose and poetry flowed from the brushes of Tang and Song writers. Scholars produced works on philosophy, religion, and history. Short stories that often mixed fantasy, romance, and adventure made their first appearance in Chinese literature.

Still, among the gentry, poetry was the most respected form of Chinese literature. Confucian scholars were expected to master the skills of poetry. We know the names of some 200 major and 400 minor Tang and Song poets. Their works touched on Buddhist and Daoist themes as well as on social issues. Many poems reflected on the shortness of life and the immensity of the universe.

Probably the greatest Tang poet was Li Bo (LEE BOW). A zestful lover of life and freedom, he spent most of his life moving from place to place. He wrote some 2,000 poems celebrating harmony with nature or lamenting the passage of time. In one poem, he wrote of old memories:

> 66Beside my bed the bright moonbeams
>   glimmer
> Almost like frost on the floor.
> Rising up, I gaze at the mountains
>   bathed in moonlight:
> Lying back, I think of my old home.99

A popular legend says that Li Bo drowned when he tried to embrace the reflection of the moon in a lake.

More realistic and less romantic were the poems of Li Bo's close friend Du Fu. His verses described the horrors of war or condemned the lavishness of the court. A later poet was Li Qingzhao (LEE CHING jow). The educated daughter of scholars, she wrote at a time when invasion threatened the Song dynasty. In this poem, Li Qingzhao describes the experience of women left behind when a loved one must go off to war:

> 66Year after year I have watched
>   My jade mirror. Now my rouge
> And creams sicken me.
> One more
> Year that he has not come back.
> My flesh shakes when a letter
> Comes from South of the River.99

Achievements in the Arts

A prosperous economy supported the rich culture of Tang and Song China. The splendid palaces of the emperors were long ago destroyed, but statues, paintings, and ceramics have survived.

Landscapes. Along with poetry, painting and calligraphy were essential skills for the scholar-gentry. In both of these arts they sought balance and harmony through the mastery of simple strokes and lines. The Song period saw the triumph of Chinese landscape painting. Steeped in the Daoist tradition, painters sought to capture the spiritual essence of the natural world. "When you are planning to paint," instructed a Song artist, "you must always create a harmonious relationship between heaven and earth." (See the picture at right.)

Misty mountains and delicate bamboo forests dominated Chinese landscapes. Yet Chinese painters also produced realistic, vivid

Buddhist Temple in the Hills After Rain This painting is believed to be the work of the Song artist Li Ching. Landscapes of the Song period were influenced by Confucianism, Daoism, and Buddhism. A landscape represented nature as a whole, while mountains and water had special symbolic meaning. Color was unimportant because the artist's goal was not to reproduce a realistic scene, but to convey a feeling. One artist explained, "Outwardly, nature has been my teacher, but inwardly I follow the springs of inspiration in my heart." **Art and Literature** Explain the meaning of this quotation.

portraits of emperors, like those on pages 307 and 308. Other painters created lively scenes of city life.

Sculpture and architecture. Buddhist themes dominated sculpture and influenced Chinese architecture. Sculptors created striking statues of the Buddha. In fact, these statues created such a strong impression that, today, many people picture the Buddha as a Chinese god rather than an Indian holy man. In China, the Indian stupa evolved into the graceful pagoda, a multistoried temple with eaves that curved up at the corners.

Porcelain. The Chinese perfected skills in making porcelain, a shiny, hard pottery, that was prized as the finest in the world. (See the picture on page 309.) They developed beautiful glazes to decorate vases, tea services, and other objects that westerners would later call "chinaware." Artists also produced porcelain figures of neighing camels, elegant court ladies playing polo, and bearded foreigners fresh from their travels on the Silk Road.

SECTION 1 REVIEW

1. **Identify** (a) Sui Wendi, (b) Tang Taizong, (c) Wu Zhao, (d) Grand Canal, (e) Zhao Kuangyin, (f) Li Bo.
2. **Define** (a) tributary state, (b) pagoda.
3. How did the rise of the Tang and Song dynasties benefit China?
4. (a) Describe the social structure of China under the Tang and Song dynasties. (b) Why did merchants have such a low status in the Chinese social system?
5. (a) What ideas and traditions shaped Chinese painting? (b) What themes did Chinese poets address?
6. *Critical Thinking* **Applying Information** "Distant water cannot put out a nearby fire." How does this saying reflect the nature of village government under the Tang and Song dynasties?
7. *ACTIVITY* Imagine that you are a young girl or the parent of a young girl in late Song China. Write a letter or poem in which you express your feelings about the custom of footbinding.

2 The Mongol and Ming Empires

Guide for Reading

- How did the Mongols create a world empire?
- What was the legacy of the Mongol conquest?
- How did Ming rulers reassert Chinese greatness?

In the early 1200s, the Song were threatened by a new wave of invaders from the north. You have already met the leader of this invasion. He was the brilliant Mongol chieftain Genghiz Khan, who now turned his attention to subduing China.

The Mighty Mongol War Machine

Genghiz Khan was born Temujin, or Iron-smith, in 1162. According to Mongol tradition, he was marked for greatness from the moment of his birth. His mother had been shocked to see her newborn baby holding a clump of blood in his hand. His father, a minor chief, quickly consulted a Mongol holy man. "This child," predicted the seer, "will rule the world." The prediction was not far wrong.

Early years. When Temujin was born, the Mongols were a nomadic people who grazed their horses and sheep on the steppe grasslands of Central Asia. While he was still a boy, his father was poisoned by a rival clan. Unprepared to lead his father's armies, Temujin suffered major disasters in battle. At the age of 15, he was taken prisoner. For the rest of his life, he never forgot the humiliation of being locked in a wooden collar and paraded before his enemies.

Escaping to the mountains, the youth wandered as an outcast among drifting clans. As he grew up, he acquired a reputation for courage and a genius for military leadership. He first took revenge on the clan that had enslaved him. Then, before the age of 45, he was elected

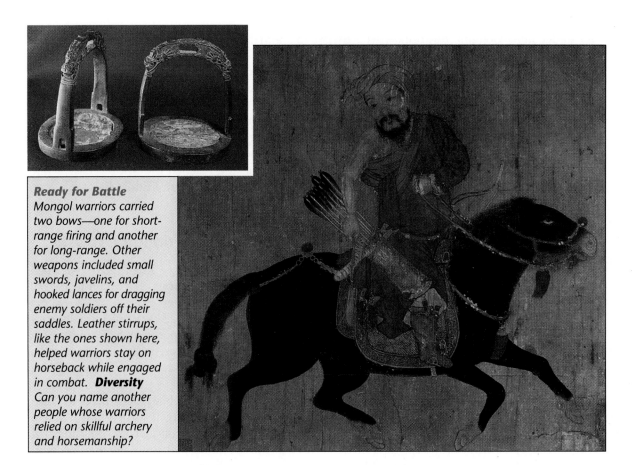

Ready for Battle
Mongol warriors carried two bows—one for short-range firing and another for long-range. Other weapons included small swords, javelins, and hooked lances for dragging enemy soldiers off their saddles. Leather stirrups, like the ones shown here, helped warriors stay on horseback while engaged in combat. **Diversity** Can you name another people whose warriors relied on skillful archery and horsemanship?

supreme ruler of all the Mongols. He was now known as Genghiz Khan, "World Emperor."

Mongols in battle. Genghiz Khan imposed strict military discipline and demanded absolute loyalty. Under his inspired leadership, Mongol armies swept to triumph. They were tough, skilled warriors who lived in the saddles of their shaggy ponies. They could travel for days at a time, eating only a few handfuls of grain and drinking mare's milk.

These highly trained, mobile armies were possibly the most skilled horsemen in the world. A later observer described the Mongols battle tactics:

66They keep hovering about the enemy, discharging their arrows first from one side and then from the other, occasionally pretending to flee, and during their flight shooting arrows backwards at their pursuers. . . . In this sort of warfare the adversary imagines he has gained a victory, when in fact he has lost the battle; for the Mongols . . . wheel about, and renewing the fight,

overpower his remaining troops. . . . Their horses are so well broken-in to quick changes of movement, that upon the signal given, they instantly turn in any direction, and by these rapid maneuvers many victories have been obtained.99

Mongol women were also great riders and fighters. Some women commanded their own military forces. Mostly, though, they took the responsibility of managing the needs of the camp, leaving the entire male population free for warfare.

As terrifying as the Mongol armies was Genghiz Khan's reputation for fierceness. He told his troops:

66The greatest joy is to conquer one's enemies, to pursue them, to seize their belongings, to see their families in tears, to ride their horses.99

Yet he could also be a generous victor. Once, an enemy soldier, standing alone against the advancing Mongols, shot Genghiz's horse out from under him. Genghiz not only spared the man's life, but rewarded his bravery by offering him a high post in the Mongol army.

On to China. As Mongol armies advanced into China, they faced the problem of attacking walled cities. They turned to Chinese and Turkish military experts to teach them to use cannon and other new weapons. Both the Mongols and Chinese launched missiles against each other from metal tubes filled with gunpowder. This use of cannon in warfare would soon spread westward to Europe.

Genghiz Khan did not live to complete the conquest of China. Still, before he died in 1227, he had shattered the settled lives of peoples across Eurasia and become the world's most successful conqueror. The domain of the "World Emperor" was indeed the largest the world had yet seen. ▪

Effects of Mongol Domination

The heirs of Genghiz Khan continued to expand the Mongol empire. For the next 150 years, they dominated much of Asia. Their furious assaults toppled empires and spread destruction from southern Russia through Muslim lands in the Middle East to China. In China, the Mongols devastated the flourishing province of Sichuan (SECH WAHN) and annihilated its great capital city of Chengdu.

Once conquest was completed, though, the Mongols were not oppressive rulers. Often, they allowed conquered people to live much as they had before—as long as they regularly paid their tribute to the Mongols.

Genghiz Khan had set an example for his successors by ruling conquered lands with tolerance and justice. Although the Mongol warrior had no use for city life, he had respect for scholars, artists, and artisans. He listened to the ideas of Confucian and Muslim scholars, Buddhist monks, Christians, Jews, and Zoroastrians.

In the 1200s and 1300s, the sons and grandsons of Genghiz Khan established peace and order within their domains. Political stability set the stage for economic growth. Under the protection of the Mongols, who now controlled the great Silk Road, trade flourished across Eurasia. A contemporary noted that Mongol rule meant that people "enjoyed such a peace

that a man might have journeyed from the land of sunrise to the land of sunset with a golden platter upon his head without suffering the least violence from anyone."

Cultural exchanges increased as foods, tools, inventions, and ideas spread along the trade routes. From China, the use of windmills and gunpowder moved westward. Techniques of papermaking reached the Middle East, while crops and trees from the Middle East were carried into East Asia.

The Yuan: A Foreign Dynasty

Although Genghiz Khan had subdued northern China, the Mongols needed nearly 70 more years to conquer the south. Genghiz Khan's grandson, Kublai (KOO blī), finally toppled the last Song emperor in 1279. From his capital at Cambulac, present-day Beijing, Kublai Khan ruled all China as well as Korea, Tibet, and Vietnam.

Government. Kublai Khan tried to keep the Mongols from being absorbed into Chinese civilizations as other conquerors of China had been. He decreed that only Mongols could serve in the military. He also reserved the highest government jobs for Mongols or other non-Chinese officials whom he employed. Still, because the Mongols were too few to control so vast an empire, Kublai allowed Chinese officials to continue to rule the provinces.

Under Mongol rule, an uneasy mix of Chinese and foreign ways developed. Kublai adopted a Chinese name for his dynasty, the Yuan (yoo AHN), and turned Cambulac into a Chinese walled city. At the same time, he had Arab architects design his palace, and many rooms reflected Mongol steppe dwellings.

Kublai Khan was an able though demanding ruler. He rebuilt and extended the Grand Canal to his new capital, but at a terrible cost in human lives. He welcomed many foreigners to his court, including the African Muslim world traveler Ibn Battuta. (See page 254.)

A western visitor. The Italian merchant Marco Polo was one of many visitors to China during the Yuan dynasty. In 1271, he left Venice with his father and uncle. He crossed Persia and Central Asia to reach China. During his stay in China, he spent 17 years in Kublai's service. He

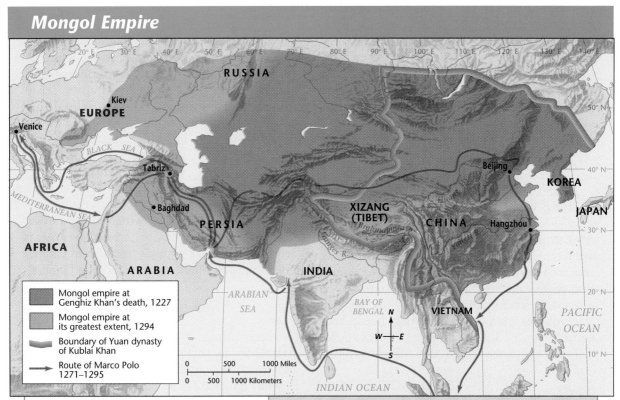

GEOGRAPHY AND HISTORY

At its height, the Mongol empire was the largest in the world. One result of the Mongol conquest of China was increased contact between China and the western world. Marco Polo's visit to China also spurred cultural exchanges.

1. **Location** On the map, locate (a) Beijing, (b) Indian Ocean, (c) Hangzhou, (d) Venice.
2. **Region** Compare the extent of the Mongol empire in 1227 to the extent of the empire in 1294.
3. **Critical Thinking** **Linking Past and Present** Look at the Atlas maps on pages 564 and 566. Identify the present-day countries through which Marco Polo would have to travel if he made his journey to Asia today.

returned to Venice by sea after visiting Southeast Asia and India.

In *A Description of the World,* Marco Polo left a vivid account of the wealth and splendor of China. Here, he describes the royal palace of Kublai Khan:

❝The palace itself has a very high roof. Inside, the walls of the halls and chambers are all covered with gold and silver and decorated with pictures of dragons and birds and horsemen and various breeds of beasts and scenes of battle. The ceiling is similarly adorned, so that there is nothing to be seen anywhere but gold and pictures. The hall is so vast and so wide that a meal might well

be served there for more than 6,000 men.❞

Polo also described the efficient royal mail system, with couriers riding swift ponies along the empire's well-kept roads. Furthermore, he reported, the city of Hangzhou was 10 or 12 times the size of Venice, one of Italy's richest city-states.

As you read, Marco Polo's book astonished readers in medieval Europe. In the next centuries, Polo's reports sparked European interest in the riches of Asia.

Other contacts. As long as the Mongol empire prospered, contacts between Europe and Asia continued. The Mongols tolerated a variety of beliefs. The pope sent Christian

Chapter 13 **317**

priests to Beijing, while Muslims set up their own communities in China. Meanwhile, some Chinese products moved toward Europe. They included gunpowder, porcelain, and playing cards.

The Ming: Restoring Chinese Rule

The Yuan dynasty declined after the death of Kublai Khan. Most Chinese despised the foreign Mongol rulers. Confucian scholars retreated into their own world, seeing little to gain from the barbarians. Heavy taxes, corruption, and natural disasters led to frequent uprisings. Zhu Yuanzhang (DZOO yoo ahn DZUHNG), a peasant leader, forged a rebel army that toppled the Mongols and pushed them back beyond the Great Wall. In 1368, he founded a new Chinese dynasty, which he called the Ming, meaning brilliant.

Early Ming rulers sought to reassert Chinese greatness after years of foreign rule. The Ming restored the civil service system, and Confucian learning again became the road to success. The civil service exams became more rigorous than ever. A board of censors watched over the bureaucracy, rooting out corruption and disloyalty.

Economic revival. Economically, Ming China was immensely productive. The fertile, well-irrigated plains of eastern China supported a population of more than 100 million. In the Yangzi Valley, peasants produced huge rice crops. Better methods of fertilizing helped to improve farming. In the 1500s, new crops reached China from the Americas, especially corn and sweet potatoes. (See Chapter 16.)

Chinese cities were home to many industries, including porcelain, paper, and tools. The Ming repaired the extensive canal system that linked various regions and made trade easier. New technologies increased output in manufacturing. Better methods of printing, for example, led to the production of a flood of books.

▲ *Ming porcelain jar*

Cultural flowering. Ming China also saw a revival of arts and literature. Ming artists developed their own styles of landscape painting and created brilliant blue and white porcelain. Ming vases were among the most valuable and popular products exported to the West.

While Confucian scholars continued to produce classical poetry, new forms of popular literature began to emerge. Ming writers composed popular novels, including *The Water Margin,* about an outlaw gang that tries to end injustice by corrupt officials. Ming writers also produced the world's first detective stories. Performing artists developed a popular tradition of Chinese opera that combined music, dance, and drama.

China and the World

Early Ming rulers proudly sent Chinese fleets into distant waters. The most extraordinary of these ventures were the voyages of the Chinese admiral Zheng He (DZUHNG HEH).

The voyages of Zheng He. In 1405, Zheng He departed at the head of a fleet of 62 huge ships and hundreds of smaller ones, carrying a crew of more than 25,000 sailors. The largest ships measured 400 feet long. Zheng He's goal was to promote trade and collect tribute from lesser powers across the "western seas."

During seven expeditions between 1405 and 1433, Zheng He explored the coasts of Southeast Asia and India and the entrances to the Red Sea and the Persian Gulf. He dropped anchor and visited many ports in East Africa, returning home with new and unfamiliar animals for the imperial zoo. One of these creatures the Chinese identified as a *qilin,* a legendary beast whose appearance was a sign of Heaven's favor. People flocked to marvel at this 15-foot-tall creature with the body of a deer, the tail of an ox, and red spots—a giraffe.

In the wake of the voyages, Chinese merchants settled in Southeast Asian and Indian trading centers. The voyages also showed local rulers the power and strength of the Middle Kingdom. Many acknowledged the supremacy of the Chinese empire.

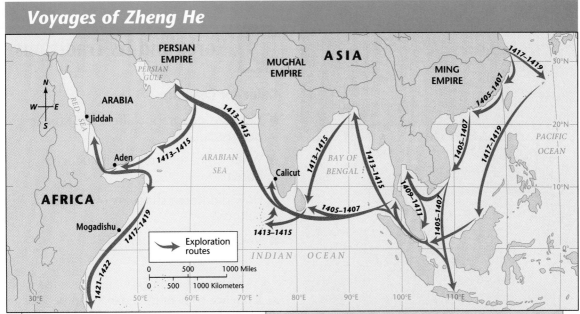

Voyages of Zheng He

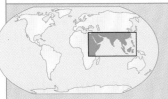
The Chinese proudly proclaimed that the Ming had unified the "seas and continents":

66The countries beyond the horizon and from the ends of the Earth have all become subjects. . . . We have crossed immense water spaces and have seen huge waves like mountains rising sky-high, and we have set eyes on barbarian regions far away . . . while our sails loftily unfurled like clouds day and night continued their course, crossing those savage waves as if we were walking on a public highway.99

Turning inward. In 1433, the year Zheng He died, the Ming emperor suddenly banned the building of seagoing ships. Later, ships with more than two masts were forbidden. Zheng He's huge ships were retired and rotted away.

Why did China, with its advanced naval technology, turn its back on overseas exploration? The fleets were costly and did not produce any profits. Also, Confucian scholars at court had little interest in overseas ventures. To them, Chinese civilization was the most successful in the world. They wanted to preserve its ancient traditions, which they saw as the source of stability. In fact, such rigid loyalty to tradition would eventually weaken China.

Less than 60 years after China halted overseas expeditions, the explorer Christopher Columbus would sail west from Spain in search of a sea route to Asia. As you will see, this voyage made Spain a major power and had a dramatic impact on the entire world. We can only wonder how the course of history might have changed if the Chinese had continued the explorations they had begun under the Ming.

Forbidden! *Ming rulers built the Forbidden City, a complex of royal buildings deep within Beijing. The dragon ramp, shown here, led to the Hall of Supreme Harmony, where the emperor received the few foreigners who were allowed inside.* **Political and Social Systems** *What does the Forbidden City suggest about the position of the Ming emperor?*

SECTION 2 REVIEW

1. Identify (a) Kublai Khan, (b) Marco Polo, (c) Zheng He.

2. Why were the Mongols successful warriors?

3. How did the Mongol conquests promote trade and cultural exchanges?

4. How did the Ming emperors try to restore Chinese culture?

5. *Critical Thinking* **Making Inferences** What does Marco Polo's awe at the glories of China suggest about the differences between China and Europe at that time?

6. *ACTIVITY* Organize a debate between Confucian scholars who want to end overseas voyages and court supporters of Zheng He.

3 Korea and Its Traditions

Guide for Reading

- How did geography affect the Korean peninsula?

- What Chinese traditions influenced Korea?

- How did Korea shape its own distinct culture?

- **Vocabulary** *hangul*

As early as Han times, China extended its influence to a ring of states and peoples on the borders of the Middle Kingdom. To the northeast, Korea lay within the Chinese zone of influence. While Korea absorbed many Chinese traditions over the centuries, it also maintained its own identity.

Geography: The Korean Peninsula

Korea is located on a peninsula that juts south from the Asian mainland with its tip pointing toward Japan. Mountains and the Yalu River separate Korea from China.

Mountains and seas. An early visitor once compared Korea's landscape to "a sea in a heavy gale." Low but steep mountains cover nearly 70 percent of the Korean peninsula. The most important range, the T'aebaek (TEH BEHK), runs from the north to the south along the eastern coast, with smaller chains branching off to form hilly areas. Since farming is difficult on the mountains, most people live along the western coastal plains, Korea's major farming region.

Korea has a 5,400-mile (8,700-km) coastline with hundreds of good harbors. In addition, the offshore waters feature thousands of islands. Since earliest times, Koreans have depended upon seafood for most of the protein in their diet. Today, South Korea has the third largest fishing industry in the world.

The impact of location. Korea's location on China's doorstep has played a key role in its development. From its powerful mainland neighbor, Korea received many cultural and

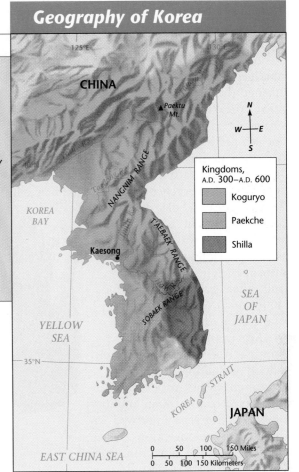

Korea occupies a peninsula jutting south from China toward the islands of Japan. In ancient times it was divided into three kingdoms whose territory extended into present-day China.

1. Location On the map, locate (a) Yalu River, (b) Han River, (c) T'aebaek range, (d) Korea Strait.

2. Region Why do most Koreans live along the western coastal plains?

3. Critical Thinking *Analyzing Information* How might the physical features of Korea have made it difficult to unite the people?

technological influences. At times, China extended political control over the peninsula. Throughout its history, Korea has also served as a cultural bridge linking China and Japan. From early times, Koreans adapted and transformed Chinese traditions before passing them on to Japan.

Despite the strong ties, the Korean language is unrelated to Chinese. The earliest Koreans probably migrated eastward from Siberia and northern Manchuria during the Stone Age. They evolved their own ways of life before the first wave of Chinese influence reached the peninsula during the Han dynasty. In 108 B.C., the Han emperor Wudi invaded Korea and set up a military colony there. From this outpost, Confucian traditions and Chinese ideas about government, as well as Chinese writing and farming methods, spread to Korea.

Korea United

Between about A.D. 300 and 600, powerful local rulers forged three separate kingdoms: Koguryo (KOH GUH REE OH) in the north, Paekche (PEHK CHEH) in the southwest, and Shilla (SHIL LAH) in the southeast. Although they shared the same language and cultural background, the three kingdoms often warred with each other or with China. Still, Chinese influences continued to arrive. Missionaries spread

Mahayana Buddhism, which took root among the rulers and nobles. Korean monks then traveled to China and India to learn more about Buddhism. They brought home the arts and learning of China.

In 668, with the support of the Tang empress Wu Zhao, the Shilla dynasty united the Korean peninsula. Unlike China, Korea had only three dynasties. The Shilla ruled from 668 to 918, the Koryo (KOR EE OH) from 918 to 1392, and the Choson (CHOH SUHN) or Yi from 1392 to 1910.

Adapting Chinese influences. Under the Shilla dynasty, Korea became a tributary state, acknowledging Chinese overlordship but preserving its independence. Over the centuries, Korea came to see its relationship to China in Confucian terms, as that of a younger brother who owed respect and loyalty to an older brother. Koreans also adopted the Confucian emphasis on the family as the foundation of the state.

Women's public roles were restricted, and their position within the family became subordinate to the male head of the household.

At the same time, Koreans adapted and modified Chinese ideas. For example, they adapted the Chinese civil service examination to reflect their own system of inherited ranks. In China, even a peasant could win political influence by passing the exam. In Korea, only aristocrats were permitted to take the test.

The Koryo dynasty. During the Koryo age, Buddhism reached its greatest influence in Korea. Korean scholars wrote histories and poems based on Chinese models, while artists created landscape paintings following Chinese principles. The Koryo dynasty built their capital at Kaesong (KEH SUNG) following the plan of the Tang capital at Changan.

Koreans used woodblock printing from China to produce a flood of Buddhist texts. Later, Korean inventors made movable metal type to print large numbers of books. Koreans improved on other Chinese inventions. They learned to make porcelain from China, but then perfected techniques of making celadon ware with an unusual blue-green glaze. Korean celadon vases and jars were prized throughout Asia. In the 1200s, when the Mongols overran Korea and destroyed many industries, the secret of making celadon was lost forever.

▲ *Celadon pitcher*

Choson: The Longest Dynasty

The Mongols occupied Korea until the 1350s. In 1392, the brilliant Korean general Yi Song-gye (EE SUNG KEH) set up the Choson dynasty. In *Songs of the Flying Dragons*, Korea's leading poets held Yi up as a model of virtue and wisdom for future rulers:

66When you have men at your beck and
    call,
When you punish men and sentence
    them,
Remember, my Lord,
His mercy and temperance.

If you are unaware of people's sorrow,
Heaven will abandon you.
Remember, my Lord,
His labor and love.99

Yi reduced Buddhist influence and set up a government based upon Confucian principles. Within a few generations, Confucianism had made a deep impact on Korean life.

Hangul. Despite Chinese influence, Korea preserved its distinct identity. In 1443, King Sejong (SEH JONG) decided to replace the Chinese system of writing. "The language of this land," he noted, "is different from China's." He had experts develop hangul, an alphabet using symbols to represent the sounds of spoken Korean.

Although Confucian scholars rejected hangul at the outset, its use quickly spread. Hangul was easier for Koreans to use than the thousands of characters of written Chinese. Its use led to an extremely high literacy rate.

Looking ahead. In the 1590s, the ambitious ruler of Japan decided to invade the Asian mainland by way of Korea. The Korean admiral Yi Sun-shin used metal-plated "turtle boats" to beat back the invaders. The Koreans sought Chinese help, and after six years of war, the Japanese gave up their quest. As the Japanese withdrew from Korea, though, they carried off many Korean artisans who took their skills to Japan.

SECTION 3 REVIEW

1. **Identify** (a) Shilla, (b) Koryo, (c) Choson, (d) Yi Song-gye, (e) Sejong.
2. **Define** hangul.
3. How did location influence the development of Korean civilization?
4. Give two examples of how Koreans adapted or modified Chinese ideas.
5. *Critical Thinking* **Analyzing Information** Today, South Korea observes Hangul Day as a national holiday. Why do you think Koreans celebrate the creation of their alphabet?
6. *ACTIVITY* Draw a poster expressing the relationship between Korea and China during the Shilla, Koryo, or Choson dynasty.

4 An Island Empire Emerges

Guide for Reading

- What geographic features influenced the early development of Japan?
- How did Chinese civilization influence Japan?
- What cultural traditions emerged at the Heian court?
- **Vocabulary** *archipelago, kami, kana*

Prince Shotoku of Japan's ruling Yamato clan wanted to create an orderly society. In 604, he completed a document that outlined ideals of behavior he felt should be followed, not only at the royal court, but throughout Japan. The prince wrote:

> 66Harmony should be valued and quarrels should be avoided. Everyone has his biases, and few men are far-sighted. Therefore some disobey their lords and fathers and keep up feuds with their neighbors. But when the superiors are in harmony with each other and inferiors are friendly, then affairs are discussed quietly and the right view of matters prevails.99

Shotoku was strongly influenced by Confucian ideas about social order. He was a devout Buddhist and an energetic student of Chinese thought.

Like Korea, Japan felt the powerful influence of Chinese civilization early in its history. At the same time, the Japanese continued to maintain their own distinct culture.

Geography: Japan, a Land Apart

Japan is located on an archipelago (ahr kuh PEHL uh goh), or chain of islands, about 100 miles (161 km) off the Asian mainland. Its four main islands—Hokkaido (hoh KĪ doh), Honshu (hahn SHOO), Kyushu (kee OO shoo), and Shikoku (shee KOH koo)—lie to the east of the Korean peninsula.

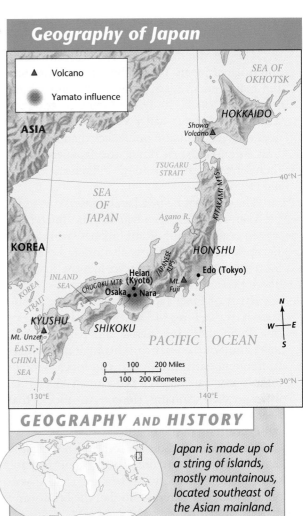

Geography of Japan

Volcano

Yamato influence

GEOGRAPHY AND HISTORY

Japan is made up of a string of islands, mostly mountainous, located southeast of the Asian mainland. In addition to its four main islands, Japan includes over 3,000 smaller islands.

1. **Location** On the map, locate (a) Hokkaido, (b) Honshu, (c) Kyushu, (d) Shikoku, (e) Kitakami Mountains, (f) Mount Fuji, (g) Sea of Japan.
2. **Interaction** Name three ways in which geography might have affected the Japanese way of life.
3. **Critical Thinking** Analyzing Information Which area was more likely to feel the influence of the Yamato clan—Osaka or Edo? Why?

Land and sea. Japan is about the size of Montana, but four fifths of its land is too mountainous to farm. As a result, most people settled in narrow river valleys and along the coastal plains. A mild climate and sufficient rainfall, however, helped Japanese farmers make the most of the limited arable land. As in ancient Greece, the mountainous terrain at first was an obstacle to unity.

The surrounding seas have both protected and isolated Japan. While it was close enough to the mainland to learn from Korea and China, Japan was too far away for China to conquer. The Japanese thus had greater freedom to accept or reject Chinese influences than did other East Asian lands. At times, the Japanese sealed themselves off from foreign influences, choosing to go their own way.

The seas that helped Japan preserve its identity also served as trade routes. The Inland Sea was an especially important link between various Japanese islands. The seas also offered plentiful food resources. The Japanese, like the Koreans, developed a thriving fishing industry.

Ring of Fire. Japan lies in a Pacific region known as the Ring of Fire, which also includes the Philippines, Indonesia, and parts of Australia and South America. This region is subject to frequent earthquakes and volcanoes. Violent underwater earthquakes can launch killer tidal waves, called tsunami (tsoo NAH mee), that sweep over the islands without warning, wiping out everything in their path.

The Japanese came to fear and respect the dramatic forces of nature. Today, as in the past, soaring Mount Fuji, with its snow-capped volcanic crater, is a sacred symbol of the beauty and majesty of nature.

Early Traditions

The people we know today as the Japanese probably migrated from the Asian mainland more than 2,000 years ago. They slowly pushed the earlier inhabitants, the Ainu, onto the northernmost island of Hokkaido.

Yamato clan. Early Japanese society was divided into uji, or clans. Each uji had its own chief and a special god or goddess who was seen as the clan's original ancestor. Some clan leaders were women, suggesting that women held a respected position in society.

By about A.D. 500, the Yamato clan came to dominate a corner of Honshu, the largest Japanese island. For the next 1,000 years, the Yamato Plain—home to the present-day cities of Nara, Kyoto, and Osaka—was the heartland of Japanese government. The Yamato set up Japan's first and only dynasty. They claimed direct descent from the sun goddess, Amaterasu.

The rising sun, therefore, become their symbol. Later Japanese emperors were revered as living gods. While this is no longer the case, the current Japanese emperor still traces his roots to the Yamato clan.

Shinto. The kami, or clan gods and goddesses, were generally nature spirits. This worship of the forces of nature became known as Shinto, meaning "the way of the gods." Shinto never evolved into an international religion like Christianity, Buddhism, or Islam. Still, its traditions have survived to the present day. Hundreds of Shinto shrines dot the Japanese countryside. These Shinto shrines are dedicated to special sites or objects such as mountains or waterfalls, ancient gnarled trees, or even oddly shaped rocks.

The Korean bridge. The Japanese language is distantly related to Korean but completely different from Chinese. During the early centuries A.D., Japan and Korea were in continuous contact with each other. Korean artisans and metalworkers settled in Japan, bringing sophisticated skills and technology. Japanese and Korean warriors crossed the sea in both directions to attack each other's strongholds. Some of the leading families at the Yamato court claimed Korean ancestors.

By about A.D. 500, missionaries from Korea had introduced Buddhism to Japan. With it came knowledge of Chinese writing and culture. This opening sparked a sudden surge of Japanese interest in Chinese civilization.

Japan Looks to China

In the early 600s, Prince Shotoku, a member of the Yamato ruling family, decided to learn about China directly instead of through Korean sources. He sent young Japanese nobles to study in China. Over the next 200 years, many students, monks, traders, and officials would visit the great court of Changan during the heyday of the Tang dynasty.

 **ISSUES For TODAY** Both Korea and Japan were part of China's "sphere of influence"—the region dominated by Chinese civilization. How can a powerful nation exert influence on its neighbors?

Imported from Tang China. Each mission spent a year or more in China—negotiating, trading, but above all studying. They returned to Japan eager to spread Chinese thought, technology, and arts. Equally important, they imported Chinese ideas about government. Like the Chinese emperor, Japanese rulers adopted the title "Heavenly Emperor" and claimed absolute power. They strengthened the central government, set up a bureaucracy, and adopted a law code similar to that of China.

In 710, the Japanese emperor built a new capital at Nara, modeled on the Tang capital at Changan. There, nobles spoke Chinese and dressed in Chinese fashion. Their cooks had to learn to cook Chinese dishes and served food on Chinese-style pottery. Tea drinking and the tea ceremony were imported from China. Japanese officials and scholars used Chinese characters to write official histories. Tang music and dances became very popular, as did gardens designed along Chinese lines.

Most changes affected only a small number of people at the court. Although Japan set up a bureaucracy like China's, it had little real authority beyond the court. In the countryside, the old clans remained strong.

As Buddhism spread, the Japanese adopted pagoda architecture. Buddhist monasteries grew rich and powerful. Confucian ideas and ethics also took root. They included the emphasis on filial piety, the relationships between superior and inferior, and respect for learning.

Selective borrowing. After the first enthusiasm for everything Chinese died down, the Japanese became more selective. They kept some Chinese ways but discarded or modified others. Japan, for example, never accepted the Chinese civil service examination to choose officials based on merit. Instead, they maintained their tradition of inherited status through family position. In the end, officials were the educated sons of nobles.

By the 800s, as Tang China began to decline, the Japanese court turned away from its model. After absorbing all they could from China, the Japanese spent the next 400 years digesting and modifying these cultural acquisitions to produce their own unique civilization. The Japanese asserted their identity by revising the Chinese system of writing and adding kana, or

Divine Protector In the 700s, Emperor Shōmu ordered Buddhist monasteries and temples to be built throughout Japan. This statue of a warrior god protected a Buddhist temple from evil spirits. **Global Interaction** How was Buddhism introduced into Japan?

phonetic symbols representing syllables. Japanese artists developed their own styles.

The Heian Period

This blend of cultures occurred from 794 to 1185. During this time, the imperial capital was in Heian (hay AHN), present-day Kyoto. There, wealthy court families like the Fujiwara wielded real power, while emperors performed traditional religious ceremonies. The Fujiwara married their daughters to the heir to the throne, thus ensuring their authority.

An elegant court. At court a sophisticated culture blossomed. Noblewomen and noblemen lived in a fairy-tale atmosphere of beautiful pavilions, gardens, and lotus pools. Elaborate rules of etiquette governed court ceremony. Courtiers dressed with extraordinary care in delicate, multicolored silk. Draping one's sleeve out a carriage window was a fine art.

Poet of the Heian Court
Lady Komachi, captured here in ink and color on paper, is one of 36 men and women considered to be the classical poets of the Heian period. Draped about her are layer upon layer of extravagant robes. Upper-class women of the time customarily powdered their faces, blackened their teeth, and wore as many as 25 layers of robes. **Art and Literature** Why do you think poets were highly honored at the Heian court?

Although men at court still studied Chinese, women were forbidden to learn the language. Still, it was Heian women who produced the most important works of Japanese literature using the new kana. Sei Shonagon, a lady-in-waiting to the empress in the late 900s, wrote *The Pillow Book.* In a series of anecdotes and personal observations, Shonagon gives vivid details of court manners, decor, and dress. In one section, she lists some pet peeves about court life:

&&One is in a hurry to leave, but one's visitor keeps chattering away. If it is someone of no importance, one can get rid of him by saying, 'You must tell me all about it next time.' But should it be the sort of visitor who commands one's best behavior, the situation is hateful indeed.&&

Lady Murasaki. The best-known Heian writer was Shonagon's rival, Murasaki Shikibu. Her monumental work, *The Tale of Genji,* is considered the world's first novel. Composed about 1010, it recounts the lives and loves of the fictional Prince Genji and his son.

In one scene, Prince Genji moves with ease through the festivities at an elaborate "Chinese banquet." After dinner "under the great cherry tree of the Southern court," the entertainment begins. Genji performs skillfully on the "thirteen stringed zither" and does the Wave Dance. But the main event is a Chinese poetry contest, which Murasaki describes in elaborate detail.

The Heian romances are haunted by a sense that beauty and love are soon gone. Perhaps this feeling of melancholy was prophetic. Outside the walls of the court, clouds of rebellion and civil war were gathering.

SECTION 4 REVIEW

1. **Identify** (a) Ring of Fire, (b) Yamato clan, (c) Amaterasu, (d) Shinto, (e) Shotoku, (f) Sei Shonagon, (g) Murasaki Shikibu.
2. **Define** (a) archipelago, (b) kami, (c) kana.
3. Describe two ways geography affected Japan.
4. (a) What aspects of Japanese life were influenced by China? (b) How did the Japanese preserve their own culture?
5. How did women influence culture at the Heian court?
6. *Critical Thinking* **Comparing** How was the Japanese development of kana similar to the Korean development of hangul?
7. *ACTIVITY* Create your own list of three dislikes written in the style of Sei Shonagon's *Pillow Book.*

5 Japan's Feudal Age

Guide for Reading

- How did feudalism develop in Japan?
- What changes took place under the Tokugawa shoguns?
- What cultural traditions emerged in feudal Japan?
- **Vocabulary** *shogun, daimyo, samurai, bushido, kabuki, haiku*

“To live in the world
Is sad enough without this rain
Pounding on my shelter.”

In this verse, the poet Sogi reveals a sense of uncertainty and despair. The 1400s, when Sogi lived, were a time of political intrigue, rebellions, and war in Japan. Yet, despite centuries of turmoil, Japanese culture blossomed.

Age of the Samurai

While the emperor presided over the splendid court at Heian, rival clans battled for control of the countryside. Local warlords and even Buddhist temples formed armed bands loyal to them rather than to the central government. As these armies struggled for power, Japan evolved a feudal system. As in the feudal world of medieval Europe, a warrior aristocracy dominated Japanese society.

Feudal society. In theory, the emperor headed Japanese society. In fact, he was a powerless, though revered, figurehead. Real power lay in the hands of the shogun, or supreme military commander. Yoritomo Minamoto was appointed shogun in 1192. He set up the Kamakura shogunate, the first of three military dynasties that ruled Japan for almost 700 years.

Often the shogun controlled only a small part of Japan. He distributed lands to vassal lords who agreed to support him with their armies in time of need. These great warrior lords were later called daimyo (DĪ myoh). They, in turn, granted land to lesser warriors called samurai, meaning "those who serve." Samurai were the fighting aristocracy of a war-torn land. (★ See *Skills for Success,* page 332.)

Bushido. Like medieval Christian knights, samurai were heavily armed and trained in the skills of fighting. They also developed their own code of values. Known as bushido (BOO shee doh), or the way of the warrior, the code emphasized honor, bravery, and absolute loyalty to one's lord.

The true samurai had no fear of death. "If you think of saving your life," it was said, "you had better not go to war at all." Samurai prepared for hardship by going hungry or walking barefoot in the snow. A samurai who betrayed the code of bushido was expected to commit *seppuku* (seh POO koo), or ritual suicide, rather than live without honor.

Women. During the age of the samurai, the position of women declined steadily. At first, some women in feudal society trained in the military arts or supervised their family's estates. A few even became legendary warriors. As fighting increased, though, inheritance was limited to sons. Unlike the European ideal of chivalry, though, the samurai code did not set women on a pedestal. Instead, the wife of a warrior had to accept the same hardships as her husband and owed the same loyalty to his overlord.

Mongol invasions. During the feudal age, most fighting took place between rival warlords, but the Mongol conquest of China and Korea also threatened Japan. When the Japanese refused to accept Mongol rule, Kublai Khan launched an invasion from Korea in 1274. After a fleet carrying 30,000 troops arrived, a typhoon wrecked many Mongol ships.

In 1281, the Mongols landed an even larger invasion force, but again a typhoon destroyed

---

GLOBAL CONNECTIONS

Samurai were trained, not only in swordsmanship and archery, but in techniques of combat without weapons. These "martial arts" probably originated among Buddhist monks in India and Tibet. They gradually spread to China, then to Korea, and finally to Japan, with each culture developing its own unique versions. In recent years, Japanese karate and Korean tae kwon do have become increasingly popular in the United States and other western countries.

much of the Mongol fleet. The Japanese credited their miraculous delivery to the *kamikaze*, (kah mih KAH zee), or divine winds. The Mongol failure reinforced the Japanese sense that they were a people set apart who enjoyed the special protection of the gods.

Order and Unity Under the Tokugawas

The Kamakura shogunate crumbled in the aftermath of the Mongol invasions. A new dynasty took power in 1338, but the level of warfare increased after 1450. To defend their castles, daimyo armed peasants as well as samurai, which led to even more ruthless fighting.

Gradually, several powerful warriors united large parts of Japan. By 1590, the brilliant general Toyotomi Hideyoshi (hee day HOH shee), a commoner by birth, had brought most of Japan under his control. He then tried, but failed, to conquer Korea and China. In 1600, the daimyo Tokugawa Ieyasu (toh kuh GAH wah ee YAY yah soo) defeated his rivals to become master of Japan. Three years later, he was named shogun. The Tokugawa shogunate ruled Japan until 1868.

Centralized feudalism. The Tokugawa shoguns were determined to end feudal warfare. They kept the outward forms of feudal society but imposed central government control on all Japan. For this reason, their system of government is called centralized feudalism.

The Tokugawas created a unified, orderly society. To control the daimyo, they required these great lords to live in the shogun's capital at Edo (Tokyo) every other year. A daimyo's wife and children had to remain in Edo full time, giving the shogun a check on the entire family. The shogun also forbade daimyo to repair their castles or marry without permission.

New laws fixed the old social order rigidly in place and upheld a strict moral code. Only samurai were allowed to serve in the military or hold government jobs. They were expected to follow the traditions of bushido. Peasants had to remain on the land. Lower classes were forbidden to wear luxuries such as silk clothing. Women, too, faced greater restrictions under the Tokugawas. One government decree sent to all villages stated:

66 The husband must work in the fields, the wife must work at the loom. Both must do night work. However good-looking a wife may be, if she neglects her household duties by drinking tea or sightseeing or rambling on the hillsides, she must be divorced. 99

Economic growth. While the shoguns tried to hold back social change, the Japanese economy grew by leaps and bounds. With peace restored to the countryside, agriculture improved and expanded. New seeds, tools, and the use of fertilizer led to greater output of crops.

Food surpluses supported rapid population growth. Towns sprang up around the castles of daimyo. Edo grew into a booming city, where artisans and merchants flocked to supply the needs of the daimyo and their families.

Trade flourished within Japan. New roads linked castle towns and Edo. Each year, daimyo and their servants traveled to and from the capital, creating a demand for food and services along the route. In the cities, a wealthy merchant class emerged. In accordance with Confucian tradition, merchants had low status. Still, Japanese merchants gained influence by lending money to daimyo and samurai. Some merchants further improved their social position by marrying their daughters into the samurai class.

Zen Buddhism

During Japan's feudal age, a Buddhist sect from China won widespread acceptance among samurai. Known in Japan as Zen, it emphasized meditation and devotion to duty. Zen had seemingly contradictory traditions. Zen monks were great scholars, yet they valued the uncluttered mind and stressed the importance of reaching a moment of "non-knowing." Zen stressed compassion for all, yet samurai fought to kill. In Zen monasteries, monks sought to experience absolute freedom, yet rigid rules gave the master complete authority over his students.

Zen beliefs shaped Japanese life in many ways. At Zen monasteries, upper-class men learned to express devotion to nature in such activities as landscape gardening. Zen Buddhists believed that people could seek enlightenment, not only through meditation, but through the precise performance of everyday tasks. For example, the elaborate rituals of the tea ceremony reflected Zen values of peace, simplicity, and love

Harmony With Nature This temple, named the Silver Pavilion, was a Zen monastery and a peaceful retreat for visiting shoguns. Zen monks served as advisers to shoguns and were the leading scholars and artists of their day. **Religions and Value Systems** How does the setting of this temple reflect Zen values?

of beauty. (See the chart below.) Zen reverence for nature also influenced the development of fine landscape paintings.

Changing Artistic Traditions

Cities such as Edo and Osaka were home to an explosion in the arts and theater. At stylish entertainment quarters, sophisticated nobles mixed with the urban middle class. Urban culture emphasized luxuries and pleasures and differed from the feudal culture that had dominated Japan for centuries.

Theater. In the 1300s, feudal culture had produced Nō plays performed on a square wooden stage without scenery. Men wore elegant carved masks while a chorus chanted important lines to musical accompaniment. The action was slow. Each movement had a special meaning. Many Nō plays presented Zen Buddhist themes, emphasizing the need to renounce selfish desires. Others recounted fairy tales or the struggles between powerful lords.

In the 1600s, towns gave rise to a new form of drama, kabuki (kuh BOO kee). Kabuki was influenced by Nō plays, but it was less refined and included comedy or melodrama in portraying family or historical events. Dressed in colorful costumes, actors used lively and exaggerated movements to convey action. Kabuki was originated by an actress and temple dancer named Okuni, who became famous for her performance of warrior roles. However, women were soon banned from performing on stage.

Literature. The feudal age produced stories like the *Tale of the Heike* about a violent conflict between two families. Another important prose work of the feudal period was *Essays in Idleness,* a loosely organized collection of 243 short essays by a Zen Buddhist priest named Kenko. In one essay, Kenko wrote of the fleeting nature of worldly things:

> **66**If we were never to fade away . . . , but linger on forever in the world, how things would lose their power to move us! The most precious thing in life is its uncertainty. What a wonderfully unhurried feeling it is to live even a single year in perfect serenity! If that is not enough for you, you might live a thousand years and still feel it was but a single night's dream.**99**

The Japanese adapted Chinese poetry models, creating miniature poems, called haiku. In only three lines—totaling 17 syllables in the Japanese language—these tiny word pictures express a feeling, thought, or idea. The poem by Sogi on page 327 is an example of haiku.

Arts. Japanese paintings often reflected the influence of Chinese landscape paintings. Yet Japanese artists developed their own styles. On magnificent scrolls, artists boldly re-created historical events, such as the Mongol invasions.

In the 1600s, the vigorous urban culture produced a flood of colorful woodblock prints to satisfy middle-class tastes. Some woodblock

---

Japanese Tea Ceremony

1 Guests pass outer gate of teahouse and enter small tea garden.

2 Guests admire landscape of garden. They wash hands and mouths at carved stone basin.

3 Guests enter tearoom through very tiny entrance. Last guest closes and locks door.

4 Guests face alcove where a scroll is displayed, containing a line of calligraphy by a Zen priest.

5 Guests seat themselves around small hearth. Host enters and serves light meal in covered bowls. After dessert, guests leave tearoom briefly.

6 Upon returning, guests find calligraphy replaced by single flower in a vase.

7 Guests are reseated. All drink from same bowl containing thick tea. Later, guests are served thin tea in individual bowls.

Interpreting a Chart *The chart above illustrates the steps of the Japanese tea ceremony, or chanoyu. By following a precise series of rituals, guests tried to leave the outside world behind. The complete ceremony could take up to four hours.* ■ *At what point is tea actually served? How might this ceremony give a sense of relief from everyday anxieties?*

PARALLELS THROUGH TIME

Musical Theater

Music, drama, and spectacle have had a long and successful partnership on the stage. When acting, singing, and dancing are combined with imaginative costumes and striking stage sets, the result is usually unbeatable entertainment.

Linking Past and Present What different types of musical theater entertain people today?

PAST In the towns of Tokugawa Japan, audiences attended kabuki programs that ran from morning till night. Kabuki captivated its fans with sensational plots, realistic dialogue, acrobatics, and swordplay. In both dramas and comedies, actors wore elaborate costumes and makeup as they told their stories through music and dance.

PRESENT Musical theater remains a popular art form in many cultures today. A summer evening is the perfect time to enjoy an Italian opera in the open air.

---

artists produced humorous prints. Their fresh colors and simple lines give us a strong sense of the pleasures of town life in Japan.

Looking Ahead

The Tokugawa shogunate brought peace and stability to Japan. Trade flourished, merchants prospered, and prosperity contributed to a flowering of culture. Still, the shoguns were extremely conservative. They tried to preserve samurai virtues and ancient beliefs.

In the 1500s, Japan faced a new wave of foreign influence. The shogun at first welcomed the outsiders, then moved to sever foreign ties. In Chapter 15, you will read about Japan's uneasy relationship with an expanding Europe.

SECTION 5 REVIEW

1. **Identify** (a) Yoritomo Minamoto, (b) Toyotomi Hideyoshi, (c) Tokugawa Ieyasu, (d) Zen.
2. **Define** (a) shogun, (b) daimyo, (c) samurai, (d) bushido, (e) kabuki, (f) haiku.
3. (a) Who held the most power in feudal Japan? (b) What values did bushido emphasize?
4. Describe three results of centralized feudalism.
5. How did the growth of towns influence Japanese arts and literature?
6. *Critical Thinking* **Analyzing Information** Why do you think the Tokugawas wanted to restrict the role of women?
7. *ACTIVITY* Write a haiku describing an aspect of the world around you.

CHAPTER REVIEW

REVIEWING VOCABULARY

Review the vocabulary words in this chapter. Then, use *seven* of these vocabulary words and their definitions to create a matching quiz. Exchange quizzes with another student. Check each other's answers when you are finished.

REVIEWING FACTS

1. Which two dynasties united China between the 600s and 1200s?
2. Describe two main classes of Chinese society.
3. Why were the Mongol armies so powerful?
4. How did Mongol rule affect Asia?
5. What lands did Zheng He visit?
6. Describe the location of Korea in relation to China and Japan.
7. What was the relationship between Korea and China during the Shilla dynasty?

8. How has Japan's island status affected its history?
9. What was the outcome of the attempted Mongol invasions of Japan?
10. How did life in Japan change under the Tokugawas?

REVIEWING CHAPTER THEMES

Review the "Focus On" questions at the start of this chapter. Then select *three* of those questions and answer them, using information from the chapter.

CRITICAL THINKING

1. **Synthesizing Information** Review what you have read about the Mongol empire in this chapter and in Chapters 10 and 11. (a) How was the Mongol period both destructive and

SKILLS FOR SUCCESS   INTERPRETING A CHART

A chart provides a great deal of information in a simple, easy-to-follow form. One common type of chart is a flowchart, which illustrates complex processes or procedures step by step. (The chart on page 330 is an example of a flowchart.) Another type of chart is an organization chart, which shows the structure of an organization or society. Lines and arrows show relationships among people or groups within the organization.

The organization chart at right illustrates the social levels of feudal society in Japan. Study the chart and then answer the questions below.

1. **Identify the parts of the chart.** (a) What is the title of the chart? (b) What do the dotted lines show?
2. **Practice reading the chart.** (a) Who occupied the highest position in Japanese feudal society? How does the chart show this? (b) Why does the chart show no lines connecting the peasants, artisans, and merchants?
3. **Draw conclusions based on the information in the chart.** (a) Using this chart, what words would you use to describe Japanese feudal society? (b) Compare this chart to the one on page 192. How was Japanese feudalism similar to European feudalism?

Feudal Society in Japan

Emperor
Held highest rank in society but had no political power

Shogun
Actual ruler

Daimyo
Large landowners

Samurai
Warriors loyal to daimyo

Peasants   **Artisans**
Three fourths of population

Merchants
Low status but gradually gained influence

constructive? (b) What do you think were the three greatest effects of the Mongol conquests across East Asia, Russia, and the Muslim world?

2. **Analyzing Fine Art** Locate three examples of porcelain in this chapter. (a) During what period was each piece made? (b) Compare the Tang figures with the Han pottery on page 93. How do they show advances in pottery techniques? (c) Based on your reading, how did celadon combine Chinese and Korean influences?

3. **Drawing Conclusions** (a) Describe the Japanese practice of selective borrowing from China. (b) How have Americans borrowed from other cultures? Give two examples. (c) What are some of the benefits and disadvantages of borrowing ideas from other cultures?

ANALYZING PRIMARY SOURCES

Use the quotation about Mongol battle tactics on page 315 to answer the following questions.

1. How did the Mongols trick their opponents in battle?

2. Why were the Mongols able to use this tactic effectively?

3. How would you describe the writer's attitude toward the Mongol warriors?

FOR YOUR PORTFOLIO

CREATING A CHART Create a chart showing areas of cultural diffusion among China, Japan, and Korea. Begin by reviewing the material in this chapter. As you review, make notes and identify the cultural areas you will need to do further research on. Then brainstorm ways to organize your chart, including headings to include (such as language, architecture, and government). Use library and other resources to add to your information on each cultural area. Then create your chart. Finally, display your finished chart in the classroom.

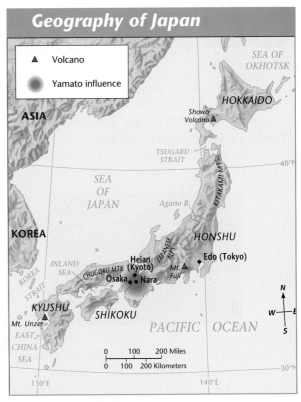

Geography of Japan

▲ Volcano

● Yamato influence

ANALYZING MAPS

Use the map to answer the following questions.

1. What body of water separates Japan and Korea?

2. What are the northernmost and southernmost of the major Japanese islands?

3. What was the former name of the current Japanese capital, Tokyo?

INTERNET ACTIVITY

CREATING A PRESENTATION Use the Internet to research an invention or technological discovery from early China during the time period discussed in this chapter. Then create and deliver a brief presentation about it. You should tell when the item or technique was invented, how it was discovered or created, and if it is still in use today.

Regional Civilizations

Chapter 8 The Rise of Europe
(500–1300)

From 500 to 1000, Europe was a fragmented, largely isolated region. Feudalism, the manor economy, and the Roman Catholic Church were dominant forces during the early Middle Ages.

- Between 400 and 700, Germanic invaders carved Europe up into small kingdoms.
- In the 800s, Charlemagne temporarily reunited much of Europe. He revived learning and furthered the blending of German, Roman, and Christian traditions.
- Feudalism, based on mutual obligations among lords and vassals, gave a strict order to medieval society.
- The Church governed the spiritual lives of Christians and was the most powerful secular force in medieval Europe.
- By the 1000s, advances in agriculture and commerce spurred economic revival.

Chapter 9 The High Middle Ages
(1050–1450)

During the High Middle Ages, economic conditions improved and learning and the arts flourished. At the same time, feudal monarchs moved to centralize their power, building a framework for the modern nation-state.

- In England and France, long-lasting traditions of royal government evolved.
- In the Holy Roman Empire, conflicts erupted between popes and secular rulers.

- European contacts with the Middle East during the Crusades revived interest in trade and exploration.
- Beginning in the 1300s, famine, plague, and war marked the decline of medieval Europe.

Chapter 10 The Byzantine Empire and Russia
(330–1613)

After the fall of Rome, the Greco-Roman heritage survived in the Byzantine empire. Byzantine civilization shaped the developing cultures of Russia and Eastern Europe.

- The Byzantine empire served as a center of world trade and a buffer between Western Europe and the Arab empire.
- Traders and missionaries carried Byzantine culture and Eastern Orthodox Christianity to Russia and Eastern Europe.
- Czars Ivan III and Ivan IV expanded the Russian empire and laid the foundation for extreme absolute power.
- Invasions and migrations created a mix of ethnic and religious groups in Eastern Europe.

Chapter 11 The Muslim World
(622–1650)

The religion of Islam emerged on the Arabian peninsula in the 600s. Muslim civilization eventually created cultural ties among diverse peoples across three continents.

- Muhammad was the prophet of Islam, a monotheistic religion. Through the Quran, the Five Pillars, and the Sharia, Islam was both a religion and a way of life.
- The Arab empire was ruled by several powerful caliphates. After 850, they were replaced by independent dynasties ruling separate Muslim states.
- Learning, literature, science, medicine, and trade flourished during the golden age of Muslim civilization.
- By the 1500s, the Mughals, Ottomans, and Safavids dominated the Muslim world with powerful empires in India, Eastern Europe, and the Middle East.

Chapter 12 Kingdoms and Trading States of Africa
(750 B.C.– A.D. 1586)

Despite geographic barriers, many civilizations rose and flourished in Africa. Kingdoms in the west and city-states in the east became important commercial and political centers.

- The Bantu migrations, contacts with Greece and Rome, and the spread of Islam contributed to Africa's diversity.
- Between 800 and 1600, a succession of powerful West African kingdoms controlled the rich Sahara trade route.
- Indian Ocean trade routes led to the growth of prosperous city-states along the East African coast.
- Art and oral literature fostered common values and a sense of community among the peoples of Africa.

Chapter 13 Spread of Civilizations in East Asia
(500–1603)

After 400 years of fragmentation, China re-emerged as a united empire and the most powerful force in East Asia. While Korea and Japan were heavily influenced by Chinese civilization, each maintained its own identity.

- China expanded and prospered under the powerful Tang and Song dynasties.
- During the 1200s and 1300s, the Mongols ruled much of Asia. After the fall of the Mongols, the Ming restored Chinese culture and later imposed a policy of isolation.
- While maintaining its own identity, Korea served as a cultural bridge linking China and Japan.
- The seas allowed Japan to preserve its unique culture while selectively borrowing religious, political, and artistic traditions from China.
- During the 1100s, Japan created a feudal society that was ruled by powerful military lords.

A Global View

How Did Regional Civilizations Expand the Scope of World History?

During the period of roughly a thousand years from 500 to 1500, sprawling regional civilizations came to dominate much of the world. Extending beyond the borders of any single empire, regional civilizations linked diverse nations within a shared culture.

Shared Cultures

Sometimes regional civilizations were based on a common religion that spread to a number of neighboring countries. Sometimes a powerful empire would influence its neighbors until they all shared a common regional culture. Sometimes geographic features, such as grassy plains or mountains, influenced all the people who lived there, producing a single regional style of civilization.

Important regional civilizations between 500 and 1500 included Christian Europe, the Muslim zone of Eurasia and North Africa, the trading states of Africa south of the Sahara, and the Chinese sphere of influence in East Asia.

Christendom and Islam

Two of the major regional civilizations that took shape during this period were based on a common religion. These were the civilizations of the Christian and Muslim zones.

Within each of these regions, diverse peoples shared powerful religious beliefs. Christians and Muslims also felt a duty to spread their religions, and the civilizations that went with them, to neighboring peoples. Both these crusading faiths thus brought cultural unity to many peoples and nations.

Christianity had already spread around the Mediterranean and westward across Europe in Roman times. During the Middle Ages, the Christian religion and related institutions spread across Eastern Europe as well. Influential medieval institutions included feudalism, the manor system, and the medieval Christian churches—Roman Catholic in the West and Greek Orthodox in the East.

The Prophet Muhammad proclaimed the Muslim faith in

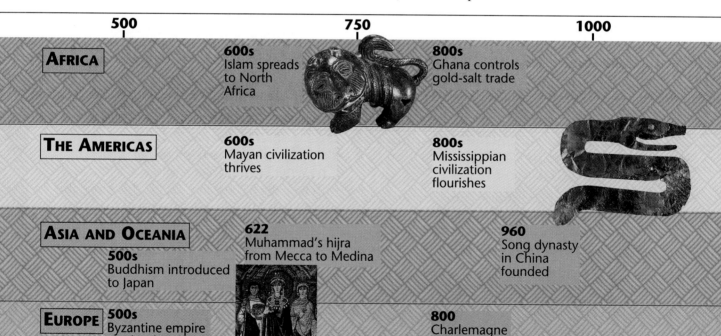

	500		750		1000
AFRICA		**600s** Islam spreads to North Africa		**800s** Ghana controls gold-salt trade	
THE AMERICAS		**600s** Mayan civilization thrives		**800s** Mississippian civilization flourishes	
ASIA AND OCEANIA	**500s** Buddhism introduced to Japan		**622** Muhammad's hijra from Mecca to Medina		**960** Song dynasty in China founded
EUROPE	**500s** Byzantine empire reaches height				**800** Charlemagne crowned emperor by pope

the 600s. Believers spread Islam far across North Africa, western Asia, and even parts of southern Europe. With the religion came literacy, cities, long-distance trade, and developments in philosophy and art. Islam thus shaped the culture of many peoples, from Muhammad's own Arabian neighbors to the nomads of the Eurasian steppes, from the kingdoms of western Africa to India and Southeast Asia.

Africa and Asia

Other regions of Africa and Asia saw the rise of other kinds of regional civilizations during this period. Across Africa, geography and trade linked many peoples, while in East Asia the influence of China imposed a common culture on a wide region.

In West Africa, peoples of the grasslands built a series of similar kingdoms and empires. All profited greatly from their commercial ties to Muslim traders from the north and the gold mines of the Guinea coast to the south. On the other side of the continent, African rulers and Muslim merchants from the north constructed a string of commercial city-states down the East African coast. These coastal trading cities linked India and China to inner Africa and the Mediterranean.

In East Asia, China's looming power continued to influence surrounding states, especially Korea and Japan. From the Chinese empire, the Japanese and Korean peoples adapted Confucian philosophy, belief in divine emperors, and the Chinese version of Buddhism,

among other things. A common civilization, often described as Confucian, thus united this vast region.

Looking Ahead

Regional civilizations were a step beyond kingdoms and empires. They brought common economic and cultural characteristics to regions that were still too large for political unification. Next, regional civilizations headed toward global interdependence. This step would be taken only after European expansion began in 1492.

ACTIVITY Choose two events and two pictures from the time line below. For each, write a sentence explaining how it relates to the themes expressed in the Global View essay.

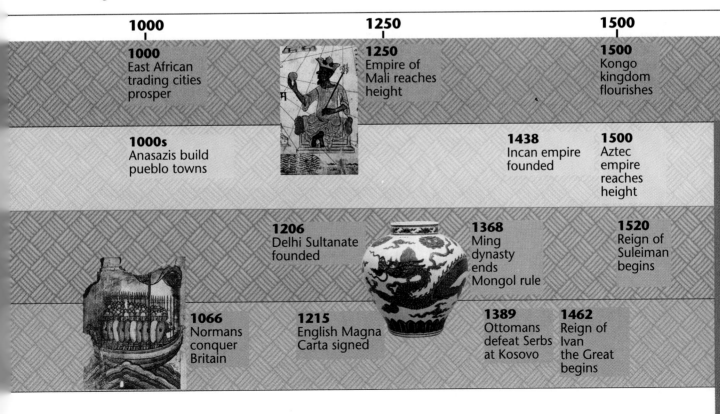

1000

1000
East African trading cities prosper

1000s
Anasazis build pueblo towns

1250

1250
Empire of Mali reaches height

1206
Delhi Sultanate founded

1066
Normans conquer Britain

1215
English Magna Carta signed

1368
Ming dynasty ends Mongol rule

1389
Ottomans defeat Serbs at Kosovo

1438
Incan empire founded

1500

1500
Kongo kingdom flourishes

1500
Aztec empire reaches height

1520
Reign of Suleiman begins

1462
Reign of Ivan the Great begins

You Decide

Exploring Global Issues

Does Diversity Strengthen or Weaken a Society?

"India has not ever been an easy country to understand," commented Indian prime minister Indira Gandhi in the 1970s. "Perhaps it is too deep, contradictory, and diverse." Many earlier rulers might have agreed with her. Although the Mughal emperor Akbar was able to strengthen his rule by accepting India's many religions, other leaders found diversity a daunting challenge and a threat to national unity.

Today, with modern technology bringing people together at a faster rate than ever before, questions remain. Should a nation encourage diversity? Or can lack of unity weaken the fabric of a society? To begin your own investigation, examine these viewpoints.

ITALY
1835

Giuseppe Mazzini, who led a movement to unite Italy into a single state, defined the ties that bind a nation:

> **❝**A nation is an association of those who are brought together by language, by given geographical conditions, or by the role assigned them by history, who acknowledge the same principles and who march together to the conquest of a single definite goal under the rule of a common body of law. . . . It is necessary that [a nation's] ideas be shown to other lands in their beauty and purity, free from any alien mixture.**❞**

MEXICO
1853

Lucas Alamán, a conservative leader, believed that religious unity was vital to his recently independent nation:

> **❝**First and foremost is the need to preserve the Catholic religion, because we believe in it and because . . . we consider it to be the only common bond that links all Mexicans when all the others have been broken.**❞**

ARGENTINA
1925

The cultures of many Latin American nations blend Native American, European, and African influences. Several paintings by Pedro Figari, including this one, *Creole Dance*, celebrate the richness of this heritage. ▶

EGYPT

1933

Taha Husayn, a respected scholar, pointed out that his nation's culture was a blend of three distinct traditions. The first came from ancient Egypt, the second from Arabian Muslims:

> **❝**As for the third element, it is the foreign element which has always influenced Egyptian life, and will always do so. It is what has come to Egypt from its contacts with the civilized peoples in the east and west . . . Greeks, and Romans, Jews and Phoenicians in ancient times, Arabs, Turks and Crusaders in the Middle Ages, Europe and America in the modern age. . . . I should like Egyptian education to be firmly based on a certain harmony between these three elements.**❞**

UNITED STATES

1935

Anthropologist Margaret Mead based her views on her observations of both American and Pacific island societies:

> **❝**If we are to achieve a richer culture, rich in contrasting values, we must recognize the whole gamut of human potentialities, and so weave a less arbitrary social fabric, one in which each diverse human gift will find a fitting place.**❞**

"CANADA IS MADE UP OF TWO DISTINCT NATIONS, JUST LIKE TWO TRAINS ON PARALLEL TRACKS THAT WILL NEVER MEET"—PREMIER RENE LEVESQUE

CANADA

1980s

This cartoon comments on long-standing tensions between French-speaking Canadians and those who speak English. Rene Levesque was a leader who called for French Quebec to break away from the rest of Canada. ▷

COMPARING VIEWPOINTS

1. Do you think Alamán would agree with Akbar's religious policies? Explain.
2. How does Mazzini's view of what strengthens a society differ from Mead's?
3. What is Husayn's attitude toward cultural diversity? Which other viewpoints here seem closest to his?
4. Which of the quotations or pictures here suggest that diversity can be dangerous to a society? In what way?

YOUR INVESTIGATION

ACTIVITY

1. Find out more about one of the viewpoints above or another viewpoint related to this topic. You might investigate:

- The attitude toward diversity in a single-culture society such as Japan or Korea.
- The ideas of nationalist leaders of the 1800s in Germany, Italy, Greece, Ireland, and other European countries.
- The contributions of immigrants to the development of the United States or Canada.
- The effects of ethnic or religious conflicts on a nation such as Yugoslavia, Nigeria, or Lebanon.
- Recent debates about multiculturalism or immigration policy in the United States.

2. Decide which viewpoint you agree with most closely and express it in your own way. You may do so in an essay, a cartoon, a poem, a drawing or painting, a song, a skit, a video, or some other way.

UNIT 4

EARLY MODERN TIMES

Art and Literature

In the forest kingdom of Benin, artisans developed skills for casting superb bronze and brass pieces. This hip plate shows three Benin warriors.

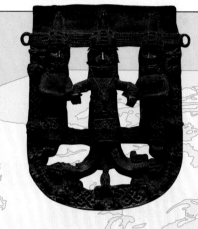

Impact of the Individual

Atahualpa was the last of the mighty Incan god-kings. He seized power from his brother in 1532 but was unable to withstand a threat from Spanish invaders.

ATLANTIC OCEAN

Tenochtitlán

PACIFIC OCEAN

Cuzco

Global Interaction

By 1500, European explorers were navigating the world's oceans. This cup honored Sir Francis Drake's feat of sailing around the globe from 1577 to 1580.

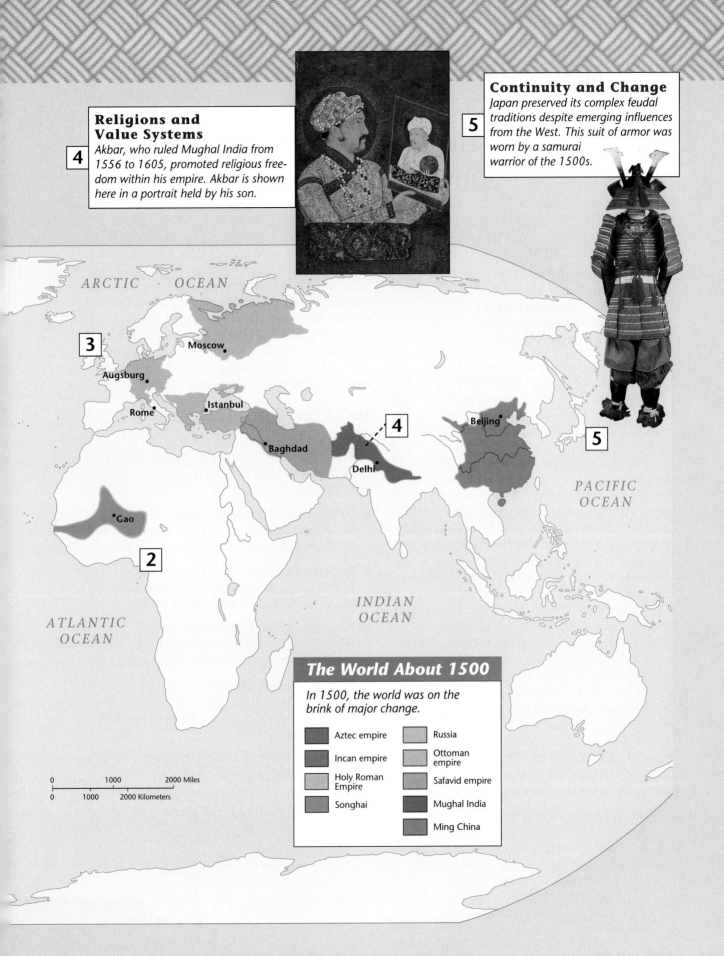

Religions and Value Systems

4 Akbar, who ruled Mughal India from 1556 to 1605, promoted religious freedom within his empire. Akbar is shown here in a portrait held by his son.

Continuity and Change

5 Japan preserved its complex feudal traditions despite emerging influences from the West. This suit of armor was worn by a samurai warrior of the 1500s.

ARCTIC OCEAN

3

Moscow

Augsburg

Rome

Istanbul

Baghdad

4

Delhi

Beijing

5

PACIFIC OCEAN

Gao

2

INDIAN OCEAN

ATLANTIC OCEAN

The World About 1500

In 1500, the world was on the brink of major change.

0   1000   2000 Miles
0   1000   2000 Kilometers

- Aztec empire
- Incan empire
- Holy Roman Empire
- Songhai
- Russia
- Ottoman empire
- Safavid empire
- Mughal India
- Ming China

The Renaissance and Reformation

(1300–1600)

CHAPTER OUTLINE

1 The Renaissance in Italy
2 The Renaissance Moves North
3 The Protestant Reformation
4 Reformation Ideas Spread
5 The Scientific Revolution

Michelangelo rushed from the Vatican. He yanked tight the straps of his saddle and flung himself onto his horse. No one treated him like that, he swore silently. Not even the pope!

Within moments, Michelangelo was galloping out Rome's northern gate, homeward bound toward Florence. As he rode, the great artist thought about the scene that had just ended in the Vatican. He could not believe that Pope Julius II had rejected the project they had planned so carefully for years. Even more humiliating, the pope had had Michelangelo thrown out by a groom!

Before long, the pope and the artist forgot their quarrel, and Julius set Michelangelo to work on an even greater project. He would create a huge mural to decorate the ceiling of the Sistine Chapel in the Vatican.

It was an enormous task. For four years, Michelangelo lay on his back on a wooden platform suspended just a few inches below the chapel ceiling. Paint dripping in his face, he painstakingly illustrated the biblical history of the world, from the Creation to the Flood. In a poem, the artist later described his ordeal:

66My stomach is thrust toward my chin,
  My beard curls up toward the sky,
  My head leans right over onto my
    back . . .
  The brush endlessly dripping onto
    my face . . .
  I am bent as a Syrian bow.99

Michelangelo was one of the towering geniuses of the Renaissance, the great period of cultural rebirth that transformed Europe between the 1300s and the 1500s. The Renaissance began in northern Italy and spread throughout Europe. It ushered in a golden age in the arts and literature and a revolution in the sciences. At the same time, divisions within the Church shattered Christian unity in the West.

FOCUS ON these themes as you read:

■ **Art and Literature**
   How did the rediscovery of classical models influence the arts and literature of the Renaissance?

■ **Religions and Value Systems**
   How did discontent with the Church lead to the Protestant Reformation?

■ **Impact of the Individual**
   How did the Renaissance create a new emphasis on individual achievement?

■ **Economics and Technology**
   What influence did the new technology of printing have on European life and culture?

■ **Continuity and Change**
   How did the Scientific Revolution transform the way people viewed the physical world?

TIME AND PLACE

A Golden Age in the Arts During the Renaissance, the rulers of Italy's many states supported the work of hundreds of artists. This family portrait by Andrea Mantegna was commissioned by the Gonzagas, rulers of Mantua in northern Italy. The Gonzagas hoped that Mantegna would make their city a leading center of the arts. **Continuity and Change** How are artists supported in our society?

HUMANITIES LINK

Art History Raphael, *The Marriage of the Virgin* (page 346).
Literature In this chapter, you will encounter passages from the following works of literature: Michelangelo, "My stomach is thrust toward my chin" (page 342); Niccolò Machiavelli, *The Prince* (page 349); William Shakespeare, *Hamlet* (page 351); Alexander Pope, *Epitaphs: Intended for Sir Isaac Newton* (page 366).

Mid-1300s	1400s	1456	Mid-1400s	1517	1545	Mid-1500s
Renaissance begins in Italy	Medici family gains influence in Florence	Gutenberg Bible is printed	Northern Renaissance begins	Luther posts 95 Theses	Council of Trent meets	Scientific Revolution begins

1300   1400   1500   1600

1 The Renaissance in Italy

Guide for Reading

- How did the Renaissance differ from the Middle Ages?

- Why did the Renaissance begin in Italy?

- What ideas influenced Renaissance scholars, artists, and writers?

- **Vocabulary** *patron, humanism, perspective*

The philosopher Marsilio Ficino smiled with pleasure as he watched the sun cast a golden glow over his native city of Florence. To Ficino, this glow symbolized the revival of art and thought that was taking place in Italy. Dipping his pen in ink, he began to write. "This century," he wrote, "like a golden age has restored to light the liberal arts, which were almost extinct: grammar, poetry, rhetoric, painting, sculpture, architecture, music." What a glorious time to be alive, he thought.

As Ficino recognized, a new age had dawned in Western Europe in the 1300s and 1400s. Europeans called it the Renaissance, meaning "rebirth."

What Was the Renaissance?

The Renaissance was a time of creativity and change in many areas—political, social, economic, and cultural. Perhaps most important, however, were the changes that took place in the way people viewed themselves and their world. Spurred by a reawakened interest in classical learning, especially the culture of ancient Rome, creative Renaissance minds set out to transform their own age. Their era, they felt, was a time of rebirth after the disorder and disunity of the medieval world.

But Renaissance Europe did not really break completely with its medieval past. After all, the Middle Ages had preserved much of the classical heritage. Latin had survived as the language of the Church and of educated people. And the mathematics of Euclid, the astronomy of Ptolemy, and the works of Aristotle were well known to late medieval scholars.

Yet the Renaissance did produce new attitudes toward culture and learning. Unlike medieval scholars, who debated the nature of life after death, Renaissance thinkers were eager to explore the richness and variety of human experience in the here and now. At the same time, there was a new emphasis on individual achievement. Indeed, the Renaissance ideal was the person with talent in many fields.

Jewel of the Renaissance Florence, situated along the banks of the Arno River, was one of the richest and most beautiful cities of Italy. Its rulers used their wealth to attract the best artists and writers of the time, and Florence came to symbolize the creative spirit of the Renaissance. **Geography and History** Why was location on a body of water important for early cities?

The Renaissance supported a spirit of adventure and a wide-ranging curiosity that led people to explore new worlds. Columbus, who sailed to the Americas in 1492, represented that spirit. So did Nicolaus Copernicus, the scientist who revolutionized the way people viewed the universe. Renaissance writers and artists, eager to experiment with new forms, were also products of that adventurous spirit.

Italian Beginnings

The Renaissance began in Italy in the mid-1300s, then spread north to the rest of Europe. It reached its height in the 1500s. Italy was the birthplace of the Renaissance for several reasons.

Why Italy? As you have read, the Renaissance was marked by a reawakened interest in the culture of ancient Rome. Since Italy was the center of ancient Roman history, it was only natural for this reawakening to start there. Architectural remains, antique statues, coins and inscriptions—all were visible reminders to Italians of the "glory that was Rome."

Italy differed from the rest of Europe in another important way. Italy's cities had survived the Middle Ages. In the north, city-states like Florence, Milan, Venice, and Genoa grew into prosperous centers of trade and manufacturing. Rome, in central Italy, and Naples in the south, along with a number of smaller city-states, also contributed to the Renaissance cultural revival.

A wealthy and powerful merchant class in these city-states further promoted the cultural rebirth. These merchants exerted both political and economic leadership, and their attitudes and interests helped to shape the Italian Renaissance. They stressed education and individual achievement. They also spent lavishly to support the arts.

Florence and the Medicis. Florence, perhaps more than any other city, came to symbolize the Italian Renaissance. Like ancient Athens, it produced a dazzling number of gifted poets, artists, architects, scholars, and scientists in a short space of time.

In the 1400s, the Medici (MEH dee chee) family of Florence organized a banking business. The business prospered, and the family expanded into wool manufacturing, mining, and other ventures. Soon, the Medicis ranked among the

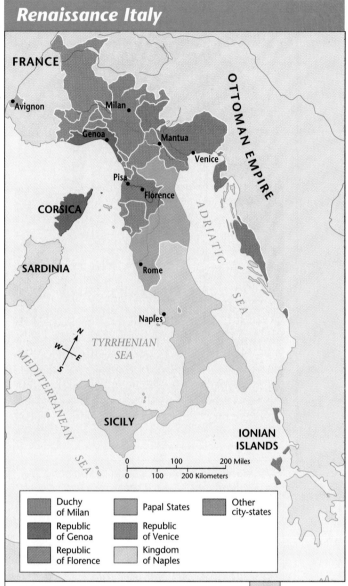

Renaissance Italy

- Duchy of Milan
- Republic of Genoa
- Republic of Florence
- Papal States
- Republic of Venice
- Kingdom of Naples
- Other city-states

GEOGRAPHY AND HISTORY

At the time of the Renaissance, Italy was made up of numerous republics, kingdoms, and city-states.

1. **Location** On the map, locate (a) Florence, (b) Duchy of Milan, (c) Papal States, (d) Rome, (e) Avignon.
2. **Place** (a) In which state was Pisa an important city? (b) Which republic controlled Corsica? (c) Who controlled Avignon?
3. **Critical Thinking Applying Information** Describe the location of the cultural center of Renaissance Italy.

The Marriage of the Virgin *In this painting, we see Raphael's skillful use of perspective and color and his knowledge of human anatomy. Raphael creates perspective with the pavement grid, which leads the viewer's eye through the open church doors to the landscape beyond. With its dome, columns, and arches, the church building is typically classical in style.* **Art and Literature** *Compare this painting to the medieval painting on page 232. What differences in style do you see?*

richest merchants and bankers in Europe. Money translated into cultural and political power. Cosimo de' Medici gained control of the Florentine government in 1434, and the family continued as uncrowned rulers of the city for many years.

Best known of all the Medicis was Cosimo's grandson Lorenzo, known as "the Magnificent." Lorenzo, who died in 1492, represented the Renaissance ideal. A clever politician, he held Florence together during difficult times. He was also a generous patron, or financial supporter, of the arts. Under Lorenzo, poets and philosophers frequently visited the Medici palace. Artists like Michelangelo learned their craft by sketching ancient Roman statues collected in the Medici gardens. Lorenzo was himself a poet, and some of his works are still featured in collections of Italian verse.

Humanism

At the heart of the Italian Renaissance was an intellectual movement known as humanism. Based on the study of classical culture, humanism focused on worldly subjects rather than on the religious issues that had occupied medieval thinkers. Humanist scholars hoped to use the wisdom of the ancients to increase their understanding of their own times.

Humanists believed that education should stimulate the individual's creative powers. They returned to the *studia humanitas,* or humanities, the subjects taught in ancient Greek and Roman schools. The main areas of study were grammar, rhetoric, poetry, and history, based on Greek and Roman texts. Humanists did not accept the classical texts without question, however. Rather, they studied the ancient authorities in light of their own experiences.

Petrarch. Francesco Petrarch (PEE trahrk), a Florentine who lived from 1304 to 1374, was an early Renaissance humanist. In monasteries and churches, he hunted down and assembled a library of Greek and Roman manuscripts. Through his efforts, as well as the efforts of others encouraged by his example, the speeches of Cicero, the poems of Homer and Virgil, and Livy's *History of Rome* again became known to Western Europeans.

Petrarch also wrote literature of his own. His *Sonnets to Laura,* love poems written in the vernacular and inspired by a woman he knew only from a distance, greatly influenced other writers of his time.

A Golden Age in the Arts

The Renaissance reached its most glorious expression in its paintings, sculpture, and architecture. Wealthy patrons played a major role in this artistic flowering. Popes and princes supported the work of hundreds of artists. Wealthy and powerful women such as Isabella d'Este of Mantua were important patrons of the arts as well.

Renaissance art reflected humanist concerns. Like artists of the Middle Ages, Renaissance artists portrayed religious figures such as Mary, Jesus, and the saints. However, they often set these figures against Greek or Roman backgrounds. Painters also produced portraits of well-known figures of the day, reflecting the humanist interest in individual achievement.

Renaissance artists studied ancient Greek and Roman works and revived many classical forms. The sculptor Donatello, for example, created a life-size statue of a soldier on horseback. It was the first such figure done since ancient times.

Roman art had been very realistic, and Renaissance painters developed new techniques for representing both humans and landscapes in a realistic way. Renaissance artists learned the rules of perspective. By making distant objects smaller than those close to the viewer, artists could paint scenes that appeared three-dimensional. They also used shading to make objects look round and real. Renaissance artists studied human anatomy and drew from live models. This made it possible for them to portray the human body more accurately than medieval artists had done.

The genius of Leonardo. Florence was home to many outstanding painters and sculptors. One of the most brilliant was Leonardo da Vinci (DAH VIHN chee), who was born in 1452. His exploring mind and endless curiosity fed a genius for invention. Today, people admire Leonardo's paintings for their freshness and realism. Most popular is *Mona Lisa*, a portrait of a woman whose mysterious smile has baffled viewers for centuries.

To produce his masterpieces, Leonardo made sketches of nature and of models in his studio. He even dissected corpses to learn how bones and muscles work. "Indicate which are the muscles and which the tendons, which become prominent or retreat in the different movements of each limb," he wrote in his notebook.

Leonardo thought of himself as an artist, but his talents and accomplishments ranged over many areas. His interests extended to botany, anatomy, optics, music, architecture, and engineering. He made sketches for flying machines and undersea boats centuries before the first airplane or submarine was actually built.

Michelangelo. Like Leonardo, Michelangelo was a many-sided genius—sculptor, engineer, painter, architect, and poet. As a young man, he shaped stone into masterpieces like the *Pietà*, which captures the sorrow of Mary as she cradles the dead Christ on her knees. *David*, Michelangelo's statue of the biblical shepherd who killed the giant Goliath, recalls the harmony and grace of ancient Greek tradition.

Raphael. A few years younger than Leonardo and Michelangelo, Raphael (RAF ee uhl) studied the works of those great masters. His paintings blend Christian and classical styles. One of his well-known works, *School of Athens,* pictures an imaginary gathering of great thinkers and scientists, including Plato, Aristotle, Socrates, and even the Arab philosopher Averroës. In typical Renaissance fashion, Raphael includes the faces of Michelangelo, Leonardo, and himself in the assembled group.

Michelangelo's Moses Michelangelo sculpted this huge statue of the prophet Moses for the tomb of Pope Julius II. Standing almost eight feet tall, the monumental sculpture took years to complete. After it was finally set up, the artist lamented, "I lost all my youth in bondage to this tomb." **Art and Literature** How does the sculpture reflect Michelangelo's attention to anatomical detail?

Raphael is probably best known, however, for his tender portrayals of the madonna, the mother of Christ.

Women artists. Some women overcame the limits on education and training to become professional artists. Sometimes, these women kept their work secret, allowing their husbands to pass it off as their own.

A few women artists did gain acceptance. In the 1500s, Sofonisba Anguissola (soh foh NIHZ bah ahn gwee SOH lah), an Italian noblewoman, won fame as a portrait painter. One of her works, *The Artist's Sisters Playing Chess,* earned her an invitation to become court painter to King Philip II of Spain. In the 1600s, Artemisia Gentileschi (ahr teh MEE zee uh jehn tee LEHS kee) created bold paintings of dramatic realism. In *Judith and the Maidservant,* she depicts the nobility of the biblical heroine Judith, who saved Israel from an invading army by killing the enemy leader.

Architecture. Renaissance architects rejected the Gothic style of the late Middle Ages as cluttered and disorderly. Instead, they adopted the columns, arches, and domes that had been favored by the Greeks and Romans. For the cathedral in Florence, Filippo Brunelleschi (broo nehl LEHS kee) created a magnificent dome, which he modeled on the dome of the Parthenon in Rome. Equally famous is Michelangelo's design for the dome of St. Peter's Church in Rome. It served as a model for many later buildings, including the United States Capitol in Washington, D.C.

Writings for the New Age

Poets, artists, and scholars mingled with politicians at the courts of Renaissance rulers. A literature of "how-to" books sprang up to help ambitious men and women who wanted to rise in the Renaissance world.

Castiglione's ideal courtier. The most widely read of these books was *The Book of the Courtier* by Baldassare Castiglione (bahl dahs SAHR ray kahs steel YOHN ay). Castiglione's ideal courtier was a well-educated, well-mannered aristocrat who has mastered many fields, from poetry to music to sports.

The ideal differed for men and women. The ideal man, wrote Castiglione, is athletic but not overactive. He is good at games, but not a gambler. He plays a musical instrument and knows literature and history but is not arrogant. The ideal woman offers a balance to men. She is graceful and kind, lively but reserved. She is pure but not prudish. She is beautiful, "for outer beauty," wrote Castiglione, "is the true sign of inner goodness."

Machiavelli's advice. Niccolò Machiavelli (mahk ee uh VEHL ee) wrote a different kind of handbook. Machiavelli had served Florence as a diplomat and had observed kings and princes in foreign courts. He also had studied ancient Roman history. In *The Prince,* published in 1513, Machiavelli combined his personal experience of politics with his knowledge of the past to offer a guide to rulers on how to gain and maintain power.

The Prince did not discuss leadership in terms of high ideals. Instead, Machiavelli took a look at real rulers in an age of ruthless power politics. He stressed that the end justifies the

The Renaissance Prince *The most important personality trait of a successful ruler, said Machiavelli in* The Prince, *was the ability to instill fear in his subjects. One leader that Machiavelli used as a model of an effective prince was Lorenzo de' Medici (left), who ruled Florence from 1469 to 1492.* **Continuity and Change** *What personality trait do you think is most important for rulers today?*

means. He urged rulers to use whatever methods were necessary to achieve their goals. On the issue of honesty in government, for example, he taught that results were more important than promises. He wrote:

66How praiseworthy it is for a prince to keep his word and live with integrity rather than craftiness, everyone understands; yet . . . those princes have accomplished most who paid little heed to keeping their promises, but who knew how craftily to manipulate the minds of men.99

Machiavelli saw himself as an enemy of oppression and corruption. But critics attacked his cynical advice, claiming that he was inspired by the devil. Later students of government, however, argued that he provided a realistic look at politics. His work continues to spark debate because it raises important ethical questions about the nature of government.

SECTION 1 REVIEW

1. **Identify** (a) Lorenzo de' Medici, (b) Francesco Petrarch, (c) Leonardo da Vinci, (d) Michelangelo, (e) Raphael, (f) Sofonisba Anguissola, (g) Filippo Brunelleschi, (h) Baldassare Castiglione, (i) Niccolò Machiavelli.
2. **Define** (a) patron, (b) humanism, (c) perspective.
3. Describe three ways in which the Renaissance differed from the Middle Ages.
4. What conditions in Italy contributed to the Renaissance?
5. How did Renaissance art reflect humanist concerns?
6. *Critical Thinking* **Linking Past and Present** In *The Prince,* Machiavelli wrote that "It is much safer to be feared than loved." (a) What did he mean by that? (b) Do you think a ruler today would be wise to follow that advice? Why or why not?
7. *ACTIVITY* Create a cover for a magazine about the Italian Renaissance. Then, write a short "Letter from the Publisher" in which you summarize the most important features of the Italian Renaissance.

2 The Renaissance Moves North

Guide for Reading

■ Why was the Renaissance delayed in northern Europe?

■ How did individual artists and writers contribute to the northern Renaissance?

■ What themes did northern humanists explore?

■ How did the printing press transform Europe?

In the mid-1300s, Europe was ravaged by the Black Death. (See page 228.) The plague reduced the population by one third and brought the economy to a standstill. Italy recovered fairly quickly and was soon the center of the creative upsurge known as the Renaissance. In northern Europe, recovery was delayed for nearly 100 years. Only after 1450 did the north enjoy the economic growth that had earlier supported the Renaissance in Italy.

Artists of the Northern Renaissance

The northern Renaissance began in the 1400s in the prosperous cities of Flanders, a region that included parts of what is today northern France, Belgium, and the Netherlands. Spain, France, Germany, and England enjoyed their great cultural rebirth 100 years later, in the 1500s.

A "German Leonardo." Albrecht Dürer traveled to Italy in 1494 to study the techniques of the Italian masters. Returning home, he employed these methods in paintings, engravings, and prints that portray the religious upheaval of his age. Through these works as well as through essays, Dürer helped to spread Italian Renaissance ideas in his homeland.

Dürer had a keen and inquiring mind. Because of his wide-ranging interests, which extended far beyond art, he is sometimes called the "German Leonardo."

Peasant Dance *Though a highly educated city dweller, Pieter Bruegel earned the nickname "peasant Bruegel" from his paintings. He painted farm people, exploring their everyday lives and customs. The villagers in this lively scene are engaged in a variety of festive activities.* **Art and Literature** *How would Bruegel's paintings be valuable to historians?*

Flemish painters. Among the many talented artists of Flanders in the 1400s, Jan and Hubert van Eyck (VAN ĪK) stand out. Their portrayals of townspeople as well as their religious scenes abound in rich details that add to the realism of their art. The van Eycks also developed oil paint. Northern artists used this new medium to produce strong colors and a hard surface that could survive the centuries.

A leading Flemish artist of the 1500s was Pieter Bruegel (PEE tuhr BROY guhl). Bruegel used vibrant colors to portray lively scenes of peasant life. Bruegel's work influenced later Flemish artists, who painted scenes of daily life rather than religious or classical themes.

In the 1600s, Peter Paul Rubens created a larger and lusher style of Flemish painting. His work blended the realistic tradition of Flemish painters like Bruegel with the classical themes and artistic freedom of the Italian Renaissance. Many of his enormous paintings portray pagan figures from the classical past. Rubens, who spoke six languages, enjoyed a successful career as a diplomat as well as a painter.

Northern Humanists

Like Italian humanists, northern European humanist scholars stressed education and a revival of classical learning. At the same time, however, they emphasized religious themes. They believed that the revival of ancient learning should be used to bring about religious and moral reform.

Erasmus. The great Dutch humanist Desiderius Erasmus used his knowledge of classical languages to produce a new Greek edition of the New Testatment and a much-improved Latin translation of the same text. Erasmus also called for a translation of the Bible into the everyday language of the people. As Erasmus explained:

❝I disagree very much with those who are unwilling that Holy Scripture, translated into the vernacular, be read by the uneducated . . . as if the strength of the Christian religion consisted in the ignorance of it.❞

Erasmus used his pen to call for reforms in the Church. He challenged the worldliness of Church practices and urged a return to early Christian traditions. In his best-known work, *The Praise of Folly,* he uses humor to expose the ignorant and immoral behavior of many people of his day, including the clergy. A Christian thinker, he taught that an individual's chief duties are to be open-minded and of good will toward others.

Sir Thomas More. Erasmus's friend the English humanist Sir Thomas More also used his pen to press for social and economic reform. In *Utopia,* More describes an ideal society, where men and women live in peace and harmony. Private property does not exist in More's utopia. No one is idle, all are educated, and justice is used to end crime rather than to eliminate the criminal. More, an English judge, was later put to death when he refused to support King Henry VIII in a controversy with the pope. (See pages 358–359.)

Literature of the Northern Renaissance

While Erasmus and More wrote mostly in Latin, many northern writers used the modern languages of their countries. In towns and cities, the middle class formed a demanding new audience for works in the vernacular. The middle class particularly enjoyed dramatic tales and comedies.

Rabelais. The French humanist François Rabelais had a varied career as a monk, physician, Greek scholar, and author. In the novel *Gargantua and Pantagruel,* written in French, he chronicles the adventures of two gentle giants, Gargantua and his son, Pantagruel. On the surface, Rabelais's book is a comic adventure of travel and war. But Rabelais uses his characters to offer opinions on a wide variety of serious subjects, such as education and religion.

Shakespeare. The towering figure of Renaissance literature was the English poet and playwright William Shakespeare. Between 1590 and 1613, he wrote 37 plays that are still performed around the world.

Shakespeare's comedies, such as *A Midsummer Night's Dream,* laugh at the follies and joys of young people in love. His history plays, such as *Richard III,* chronicle the power struggles of English kings. His tragedies show human beings crushed by powerful forces or their own weakness. In *Romeo and Juliet,* two teenagers fall victim to an old family feud. In *Othello,* a noble warrior is driven mad by jealousy, while *Macbeth* depicts an ambitious couple whose desire for political power leads them to commit murder.

Shakespeare's love of words vastly enriched the English language. More than 1,700 words appeared for the first time in his works, including *bedroom, lonely, generous, gloomy, heartsick, hurry,* and *sneak.* Also, many lines from Shakespeare's plays are still quoted today. For example, in *Hamlet,* a father gives the following advice to his son:

66To thine own self be true,
And it must follow as the night the day
Thou canst not then be false to any man.99

The Printing Press

People have always sought better, faster, and easier ways to communicate with one another. Early civilizations transformed communication by developing writing systems. Hundred of years later, the development of the printing press began another communications revolution.

Linking Past and Present How is computer technology revolutionizing the way we communicate today?

PAST In this early print shop, the workers at left set type into adjustable molds. At center, the type is inked and a sheet of paper placed over it. Finally, the worker at right uses a screw to lower and press a metal platen onto the type, thus creating the printed page.

PRESENT

High-speed automation, combined with the latest in computer technology, drives the presses in modern printing plants.

Cervantes. The Renaissance in Spain in the early 1600s produced its own great works. Best known is *Don Quixote* (DAHN kee HOH tay), by Miguel de Cervantes (suhr VAN teez), an entertaining tale that mocks romantic notions of medieval chivalry. (See page 193.)

The novel follows the adventures of Don Quixote, a foolish but idealistic knight, and his faithful servant, Sancho Panza. Quixote imagines himself involved in one dangerous adventure after another. Panza tries without success to convince the knight that the "castles" he sees are really humble inns and the "jousting knights" that he tries to fight are in fact windmills. Quixote, however, is unable to understand the modern world, which requires the skills of practical men like Sancho Panza rather than those of romantic and battle-ready knights.

The Printing Revolution

The great works of Renaissance literature reached a large audience. The reason for this was a crucial breakthrough in technology—the development of printing in Europe.

The technology. The Chinese had learned to make paper and had printed books centuries earlier. By 1300, methods of papermaking had reached Europe. By the 1400s, German engravers had developed movable type. At last, in 1456, Johann Gutenberg of Mainz, Germany, printed a complete edition of the Bible using movable metal type. With the Gutenberg Bible, the European age of printing had begun.

Printing presses sprang up in Italy, Germany, the Netherlands, and England. By 1500, they had turned out more than 20 million volumes. In the next century, between 150 and 200 million books went into circulation.

Impact. The printing revolution brought immense changes. Books printed with movable type on rag paper were cheaper and easier to produce than hand-copied works. As books became more readily available, more people learned to read and write. They also gained access to a broad range of knowledge as presses churned out books on topics from medicine and law to astrology, mining, and geography.

Printing influenced both religious and secular thought. "The preaching of sermons is speaking to a few of mankind," noted an English author, "but printing books is talking to the whole world." With printed books, educated Europeans were exposed to new ideas that greatly expanded their horizons.

The new presses contributed to the religious turmoil that engulfed Europe in the 1500s. (See Section 3.) By then, many Christians could read the Bible for themselves. As a result, the ideas of religious reformers spread faster and to a larger audience than ever before.

SECTION 2 REVIEW

1. **Identify** (a) Jan and Hubert van Eyck, (b) Albrecht Dürer, (c) Pieter Bruegel, (d) Peter Paul Rubens, (e) William Shakespeare, (f) Johann Gutenberg.
2. Why did the northern Renaissance take place nearly 100 years after the Renaissance in Italy?
3. What role did Dürer play in the spread of Renaissance ideas?
4. (a) What issues did Erasmus raise in his writings? (b) What themes did Thomas More explore in *Utopia*?
5. What were three effects of the printing revolution?
6. *Critical Thinking* **Recognizing Causes and Effects** Why do you think the cultural flowering of the Renaissance did not begin until after economic growth had taken place?
7. *ACTIVITY* Shakespeare invented new words by combining two existing words. Examples of these compound words are *eyesore, heartsick, hot-blooded, leapfrog,* and *tongue-tied.* Look up definitions of these words. Then, create five compound words of your own.

3 The Protestant Reformation

Guide for Reading

- Why did the Church face widespread criticism?
- How did Martin Luther challenge the Church?
- What role did John Calvin play in the Reformation?
- **Vocabulary** *indulgence, recant, predestination, theocracy*

During the Renaissance, the Roman Catholic Church fell on troubled times. Christians from all levels of society grew impatient with the corruption of the clergy and the worldliness of the Church. In the words of one unhappy peasant, "Instead of saving the souls of the dead and sending them to Heaven, [the clergy] gorge themselves at banquets after funerals. . . . They are wicked wolves! They would like to devour us all, dead or alive."

From such bitterness sprang new calls for reform. During the Middle Ages, the Church had renewed itself from within. (See pages 230–231.) In the 1500s, however, the movement for reform unleashed forces that shattered Christian unity in Europe. This reform movement is known as the Protestant Reformation.

Abuses in the Church

Beginning in the late Middle Ages, the Church had become increasingly caught up in worldly affairs. Popes competed with Italian princes for political power. They fought long wars to protect the Papal States against invasions by secular rulers. They intrigued against powerful monarchs who tried to seize control of the Church within their lands.

During the Renaissance, popes, like other Renaissance rulers, maintained a lavish lifestyle. When Leo X, a son of Lorenzo the Magnificent, was elected pope, he is said to have exclaimed:

"God has given us the papacy—let us enjoy it!" Like wealthy merchants, popes, too, were patrons of the arts. They hired painters and sculptors to beautify churches and spent vast sums to rebuild the cathedral of St. Peter's at Rome.

To finance such projects, the Church increased fees for religious services like marriages and baptisms. It also promoted the sale of indulgences. An indulgence was a pardon for sins committed during a person's lifetime. In the Middle Ages, the Church had granted indulgences only for good deeds, such as going on a crusade. By the late 1400s, however, an indulgence could be obtained in exchange for a money gift to the Church.

Many Christians protested such practices. In northern Europe, especially, religious piety deepened even as interest in secular things was growing. Christian humanists such as Erasmus urged a return to the simple ways of the early Christian Church. They stressed Bible study, exposed Church abuses, and rejected Church pomp and ceremony.

Luther's Protest

Protests against Church abuses continued to grow. In 1517, these protests erupted into a full-scale revolt. The man who triggered the revolt was a German monk and professor of theology named Martin Luther.

The son of a middle-class German family, Luther had been slated by his father for a career as a lawyer. As a youth, however, he had a powerful religious experience that changed his life. One day, during a violent storm, Luther was knocked to the ground by lightning. Terrified, he cried out to St. Anne for help. He promised to become a monk if he were spared.

True to his word, Luther entered a monastery. There, he prayed and fasted and tried to lead a holy life. Still, he suffered from doubts. He believed he was a sinner, doomed to eternal damnation. He also grew increasingly disillusioned with what he saw as the corruption and worldliness of the Church. At last, an incident in the town of Wittenberg prompted him to act.

Attack on indulgences. In 1517, a German priest named Johann Tetzel set up a pulpit on the outskirts of Wittenberg. With the approval of the pope, he sold indulgences to any Christian who contributed money for the new Cathedral of St. Peter in Rome. Tetzel claimed that purchase of these indulgences would assure the entrance into heaven not only of the purchasers but of their dead relatives as well. "Don't you hear the voices of your dead parents and other relatives crying out?" he demanded. " 'Have mercy on us, for we suffer great torment from which you can release us with a few [pennies].' "

To a pious man like Martin Luther, "indulgence salesman" Tetzel was the final insult. It made Luther furious to see people paying for indulgences instead of seeking true repentance.

He jeered that Tetzel's favorite jingle was, "As soon as the coin in the coffer rings, a soul from purgatory springs!"

The outraged Luther drew up his 95 Theses, a list of arguments against indulgences. In accordance with the custom of the time, he posted the list on the door of Wittenberg's All Saints Church. Among other things, he argued that indulgences had no basis in the Bible, that the pope had no authority to release souls from purgatory, and that Christians could be saved only through faith.

Martin Luther versus the Church. Almost overnight, copies of Luther's 95 Theses were printed and distributed across Europe, where they stirred up furious debate. The Church tried to persuade Luther to recant, or give up his views. Luther refused. Instead, he developed even more radical new doctrines. Before long, he was urging Christians to reject what he saw as the tyranny of Rome. Since the Church would not reform itself, he wrote, it must be reformed by secular authorities.

In 1521, the pope excommunicated Luther. Later that year, the new Holy Roman emperor, Charles V, summoned Luther to the diet, or assembly of German princes, at Worms. Luther went, expecting to defend his writings. Instead, the emperor simply ordered him to give them up. Luther refused:

> ❝I cannot and will not recant anything, for to go against conscience is neither right nor safe. . . . Here I stand. I cannot do otherwise.❞

Charles declared Luther an outlaw, making it a crime for anyone in the empire to give him food or shelter. Luther had many powerful supporters, however. One of these, Prince Frederick of Saxony, hid him at a castle in Wartburg. Luther remained in hiding for nearly a year. Throughout Germany, in the meantime, thousands hailed him as a hero. They accepted his teachings and, following his lead, renounced the authority of the pope.

Luther's teachings. At the heart of Luther's teachings were several beliefs. First, he argued that salvation could be achieved through faith alone. He thus rejected the Church doctrine that good deeds were necessary for salvation.

Second, Luther declared that the Bible was the sole source of religious truth. He denied other traditional authorities, such as Church councils or the pope.

Third, Luther rejected the idea that priests and the Church hierarchy had special powers. He talked, instead, of the "priesthood of all believers." All Christians, he said, had equal access to God through faith and the Bible. Luther translated the Bible into the German vernacular so that ordinary people could study it by themselves. Every town, he said, should have a school so that girls and boys could learn to read the Bible.

Luther called for other practices of the Catholic Church to be modified. He rejected five of the seven sacraments because the Bible did not mention them. He banned indulgences,

German Bible Before the Reformation, few people could read the Bible, which was in Latin. Then Martin Luther translated the Bible into German. The translation was a bestseller, and before long a half million copies were in print. Here, Luther's image appears on a 1574 edition of the Bible. **Religions and Value Systems** What effect do you think the Reformation had on literacy? Explain.

confession, pilgrimages, and prayers to saints. He abolished the elaborate ritual of the Catholic mass and instead emphasized the sermon. And he permitted the clergy to marry. These, and other changes, were adopted by the Lutheran churches set up by Luther's followers.

Spread of Lutheran Ideas

Luther's ideas found a fertile field in northern Germany and Scandinavia. While the new printing presses spread Luther's writings, fiery preachers denounced Church abuses. By 1530, the Lutherans were using a new name, *Protestant,* for all those who "protested" papal authority.

Widespread support. Why did Lutheranism win widespread support? Many of the clergy saw Luther's reforms as the answer to corruption in the Roman Catholic Church. A number of German princes, however, embraced Lutheran beliefs for more selfish reasons. Some saw Lutheranism as a way to throw off the rule of both the Church and the Holy Roman emperor. Others welcomed a chance to seize Church property in their territory. Still other Germans supported Luther because of feelings of national loyalty. They were tired of seeing German money used to build Roman churches or line the pockets of Italian churchmen.

The Peasants' Revolt. The peasants also took up Luther's banner. They hoped to gain his support for social and economic change as well as religious reform.

In 1524, a Peasants' Revolt erupted across Germany. The rebels demanded an end to serfdom. They also demanded other changes in their harsh lives. As the revolt grew more violent, Luther denounced it. He did not see himself as a social reformer. In fact, he urged nobles to suppress the rebellion. They did so, with great brutality, killing between 70,000 and 100,000 people and leaving 50,000 more homeless.

The Peace of Augsburg. During the 1530s and 1540s, the Holy Roman emperor Charles V tried to force Lutheran princes back into the Catholic Church. He had little success. Finally, Charles and the princes reached a settlement. The Peace of Augsburg, signed in 1555, allowed each prince to decide which religion—Catholic or Lutheran—would be followed in his lands. Most northern German states chose Lutheranism. The south remained largely Catholic.

Civil War in France The conflict between French Catholics and Protestants resulted in numerous atrocities. On St. Bartholomew's Day in 1572, Catholics massacred thousands of Huguenots in Paris. In this illustration, Huguenots destroy and loot a Catholic church. **Continuity and Change** Do religious conflicts still occur today? Explain.

John Calvin

The most important reformer to follow Martin Luther was John Calvin. Calvin had a logical, razor-sharp mind, and his ideas had a profound effect on the direction of the Protestant Reformation.

Teachings. Calvin was born in France and trained as a priest and lawyer. In 1536, Calvin published the *Institutes of the Christian Religion*. In this book, which was read by Protestants everywhere, he set forth his religious beliefs. He also provided advice on how to organize and run a Protestant church.

Like Luther, Calvin believed that salvation was gained through faith alone. He, too, regarded the Bible as the only source of religious truth. But Calvin put forth a number of ideas of his own.

Calvin taught that God was all powerful and that humans were by nature sinful. God alone, he said, decided whether an individual achieved eternal life.

Calvin preached predestination, the idea that God had long ago determined who would gain salvation. To Calvinists, the world was divided into two kinds of people—saints and sinners. Calvinists tried to live like saints, believing that only those who were saved could live truly Christian lives.

Calvin's Geneva. In 1541, Protestants in the city-state of Geneva in Switzerland asked Calvin to lead their community. In keeping with his teachings, Calvin set up a theocracy, or government run by church leaders.

Calvin's followers in Geneva came to see themselves as the new "chosen people." They were crusaders in a religious revolution whose job it was to build a truly Christian society. Calvinists stressed hard work, discipline, thrift, honesty, and morality. Citizens faced fines or other harsher punishments for offenses such as fighting, swearing, laughing in church, and dancing. Calvin closed theaters and frowned on elaborate dress. To many Protestants, this emphasis on strict morality made Calvinist Geneva seem a model community.

Like Luther, Calvin believed in religious education for girls as well as boys. Women, he felt, should read the Bible—in private. He also allowed them to sing in church, a practice that earned him criticism from some church leaders.

Spread of Calvinism. Reformers from all over Europe visited Geneva and then returned home to spread Calvin's ideas. By the late 1500s, they had planted Calvinism in Germany, France, the Netherlands, England, and Scotland. This new challenge to the Catholic Church set off bloody wars of religion across Europe.

In Germany, Calvinists faced opposition from Lutherans as well as from Catholics. In France, wars raged between French Calvinists, called Huguenots, and Catholics in the late 1500s. Calvinists in the Netherlands organized the Dutch Reformed Church. To avoid persecution, "field preachers" gave sermons in the countryside, away from the eyes of town authorities.

In Scotland, a Calvinist preacher named John Knox led a religious rebellion. He declared that "right religion takes neither [its origin] nor authority from worldly princes, but from the eternal God alone." Under Knox, Scottish Protestants overthrew their Catholic queen. They then set up the Scottish Presbyterian Church.

SECTION 3 REVIEW

1. **Identify** (a) Protestant Reformation, (b) Martin Luther, (c) Peace of Augsburg, (d) John Calvin, (e) Huguenot, (f) John Knox.
2. **Define** (a) indulgence, (b) recant, (c) predestination, (d) theocracy.
3. Why did many Christians feel that the Church needed to be reformed?
4. (a) How did Luther's ideas about Christianity differ from those of the Catholic Church? (b) Why did Luther's ideas gain widespread support?
5. (a) Identify five ideas taught by Calvin. (b) Which of these ideas were different from Luther's?
6. *Critical Thinking* **Synthesizing Information** How did the Reformation reflect humanist ideas?
7. *ACTIVITY* Make a concept map comparing the basic teachings of Roman Catholicism, Lutheranism, and Calvinism.

4 Reformation Ideas Spread

Guide for Reading

- Why did England form a new Church?
- How did the Catholic Church reform itself?
- What were the results of the Reformation?
- **Vocabulary** *annul, ghetto*

Henry III, the Catholic king of France, was deeply disturbed by the Calvinist reformers in Geneva. "It would have been a good thing," he wrote, "if the city of Geneva were long ago reduced to ashes, because of the evil doctrine which has been sown from that city throughout Christendom."

Henry was not alone in his resentment. Throughout Europe, Catholic monarchs and the Catholic Church fought back against the Protestant challenge. They also took steps to reform the Church and to restore its spiritual leadership of the Christian world.

Radical Reformers

As the Reformation continued, hundreds of new Protestant sects sprang up. These sects often had ideas that were even more radical than those of Luther and Calvin. A number of groups, for example, rejected infant baptism. Infants, they argued, are too young to understand what it means to accept the Christian faith. Only adults, they felt, should receive the sacrament of baptism. Because of this belief, these groups were known as Anabaptists.

Some Anabaptists sought radical social change, as well. Some called for the abolition of private property. Others wanted to speed up the coming of God's day of judgment, by violent means if necessary. When a group of radical Anabaptists took over the city of Munster in Germany, even Luther advised his supporters to join Catholics in suppressing the threat to the traditional order.

Most Anabaptists, however, were peaceful women and men. In an age of intolerance, they called for religious toleration and separation of church and state. Despite the harsh persecution they suffered, these groups influenced Protestant thinking in many countries. Today, Protestant denominations such as Baptists, Quakers, Mennonites, and Amish all trace their ancestry to the Anabaptists.

The English Reformation

In England, religious leaders such as John Wycliffe had called for Church reform as early as the 1300s. (See page 231.) By the 1520s, even some English clergy were toying with Protestant ideas. The final break with the Catholic Church, however, was the work not of religious leaders but of the English king Henry VIII. For political reasons, Henry wanted to end papal control over the English church.

Seeking an annulment. At first, Henry VIII stood firmly against the Protestant revolt. The pope even awarded him the title "Defender of the Faith" for a pamphlet that he wrote denouncing Luther. In 1527, however, an issue arose that set Henry at odds with the Church.

After 18 years of marriage, Henry and his wife, Catherine of Aragon, had only one surviving child, a daughter named Mary Tudor. Henry felt that England's stability depended on his having a male heir to succeed him. He decided to remarry, hoping that a new wife would bear him a son. Since Church law does not permit divorce, he asked the pope to annul, or cancel, his marriage to Catherine.

Break with Rome. Popes had freed rulers from marriages before. But the current pope did not want to offend the powerful Holy Roman emperor Charles V, Catherine of Aragon's nephew. He therefore refused Henry's request.

Henry was furious. Spurred on by his advisers, many of whom leaned toward the new Protestant teachings, he decided on a course of action. First, he would stir up English feelings against the pope. Second, he would take over the English church.

Acting through Parliament, Henry had a series of laws passed. They took the English Church from the pope's control and placed it under Henry's rule. The most notable of these laws, the Act of Supremacy passed in 1534, made Henry "the only supreme head on Earth of the Church of England."

At the same time, Henry appointed Thomas Cranmer archbishop. Cranmer annulled the king's marriage to Catherine. Henry then wed Anne Boleyn, Catherine's lady-in-waiting. Anne bore him a second daughter, Elizabeth. In the years that followed, Henry married four more times but had only one son, Edward.

The Church of England. Between 1536 and 1540, Henry shut down all convents and monasteries in England and seized their lands. This move brought new wealth to the royal exchequer. Henry shrewdly offered aristocrats and others of high standing a share of the gains, thereby securing their support for the Anglican Church, as the new Church of England was called.

But Henry was not a religious radical. Aside from making himself head of the Anglican Church and allowing the use of the English Bible, he kept most Catholic forms of worship.

When Henry died in 1547 and his 10-year-old son, Edward VI, inherited the throne, religious turmoil swept England. The young king was dominated by devout Protestants who pushed for Calvinist reforms. Thomas Cranmer drew up the *Book of Common Prayer*. It imposed a moderate form of Protestant service but preserved many Catholic doctrines. Even so, the changes sparked violence.

When Edward died in his teens, his half-sister Mary Tudor, inherited the throne. A pious Catholic, Mary was determined to make England Catholic again. She failed, but not before hundreds of Protestants had died at the stake. After Mary's death, her Protestant half-sister, Elizabeth I, became queen. Under her skillful rule, unity was restored and England became firmly established as a Protestant land.

Elizabeth I Restores Unity to England

Mary Tudor was 17 years old when Elizabeth I was born. At court, Mary treated her young half-sister kindly, frequently giving her gifts when she was a "good girl." When

Queen Elizabeth I *Though regal and often aloof, Elizabeth I took pains to court her subjects. On trips through the countryside, the royal coach often stopped so that she could thank the crowds for their loyalty. A noble she had once imprisoned later remarked: "If ever a person had the gift or the style to win the hearts of the people, it was this Queen."* **Impact of the Individual** *In what way was Elizabeth a successful politician?*

Mary became queen, however, kindness was replaced by fear. Elizabeth, Mary realized, possessed two qualities that made her dangerous to an unpopular Catholic queen. Elizabeth was Protestant and popular.

Imprisoned in the Tower. In January 1554, barely six months after Mary ascended to the throne, a plot against her was uncovered. Although she had no proof, Mary was convinced that Elizabeth was involved. She had Elizabeth arrested and imprisoned in the Tower of London.

For two months, Elizabeth waited in terror. Her own mother, Anne Boleyn, had gone to her death from the Tower, as had many other innocent victims. Would the same thing happen to her? she wondered.

Early in May, soldiers appeared. Their orders were to remove Elizabeth to the queen's manor house in the distant town of Woodstock. They assured her that there was no cause for alarm. The frightened Elizabeth, however, did not believe them. Once she was away from London, she was sure, she would be murdered.

Elizabeth's unjust imprisonment in the Tower had made her even more popular with the people. Eager crowds turned out to greet her during the four-day journey from London to Woodstock. In villages all along the route, countryfolk pressed forward to catch a glimpse of the princess and to offer her cakes and other sweets. Church bells rang to pay her homage, and onlookers cried out "God save your Grace!" as she passed.

Confined at Woodstock. At Woodstock, Elizabeth was lodged in the gatehouse, a shabby building of four rooms. Her servants were replaced by members of Queen Mary's household, and she could not talk to strangers unless a guard was present. She was not allowed paper, pen, and ink. Any books she received were first sent to London to be examined by the queen and her council for secret messages.

Mary kept Elizabeth at Woodstock for nearly a year. At last, in April 1555, she allowed her to return to court. Shortly after, Elizabeth retired to the country, where she lived until Mary's death in 1558 made her queen.

A policy of religious compromise. As queen, Elizabeth adopted a policy of religious compromise. She moved cautiously at first but gradually enforced reforms that she felt both moderate Catholics and Protestants could accept. She attacked anyone—Catholic or Protestant—who defied her.

▲ *The Lord's Prayer*

Under Elizabeth, English replaced Latin as the language of the Anglican Church service. The *Book of Common Prayer* was restored, although it was revised to make it more acceptable to Catholics. A lot of the pomp and ceremony of Catholic ritual, including the robes of the clergy, was retained. The Catholic hierarchy of bishops and archbishops was also kept, although Elizabeth acted quickly to reaffirm that the monarch was at the head of the Anglican Church.

Even though she preserved many traditional Catholic ideas, Elizabeth firmly established England as a Protestant nation. After her death, England again faced religious storms. But during her long and skillful reign, England escaped the kinds of religious wars that tore apart other European states during the 1500s. ▪

The Catholic Reformation

As the Protestant Reformation swept across northern Europe, a vigorous reform movement took hold within the Catholic Church. The leader of this movement, known as the Catholic Reformation, was Pope Paul III. During the 1530s and 1540s, he set out to revive the moral authority of the Church and roll back the Protestant tide. To end corruption within the papacy itself, he appointed reformers to key posts. They and their successors guided the Catholic Reformation for the rest of the century.

Council of Trent. To establish the direction that reform should take, the pope called the Council of Trent in 1545. It met off and on for almost 20 years. The council reaffirmed traditional Catholic views, which Protestants had challenged. Salvation comes through faith *and* good works, it declared. The Bible, while a major source of religious truth, is not the *only* source.

The council also took steps to end abuses in the Church. It provided stiff penalties for worldliness and corruption among the clergy. It also established new schools to create a better-educated clergy who could challenge Protestant teachings.

The Inquisition. To deal with the Protestant threat more directly, Pope Paul strengthened the Inquisition. As you have read, the Inquisition was a Church court set up to root out heresies during the Middle Ages. The Inquisition used secret testimony, torture, and execution to stamp out heresy. It also prepared the Index of Forbidden Books, a list of works considered too immoral or irreligious for Catholics to read. Included on the Index were books by Luther and Calvin.

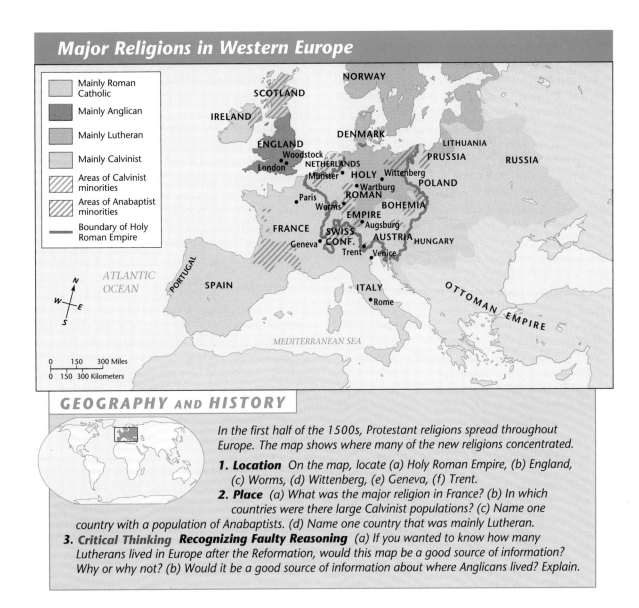

Major Religions in Western Europe

Legend:
- Mainly Roman Catholic
- Mainly Anglican
- Mainly Lutheran
- Mainly Calvinist
- Areas of Calvinist minorities
- Areas of Anabaptist minorities
- Boundary of Holy Roman Empire

Map labels: NORWAY, SCOTLAND, IRELAND, DENMARK, LITHUANIA, PRUSSIA, RUSSIA, ENGLAND, Woodstock, London, NETHERLANDS, Münster, HOLY, Wittenberg, POLAND, Wartburg, ROMAN, BOHEMIA, Paris, Worms, EMPIRE, Augsburg, FRANCE, SWISS CONF., AUSTRIA, HUNGARY, Geneva, Trent, Venice, ATLANTIC OCEAN, PORTUGAL, SPAIN, ITALY, Rome, OTTOMAN EMPIRE, MEDITERRANEAN SEA

0   150   300 Miles
0   150   300 Kilometers

GEOGRAPHY AND HISTORY

In the first half of the 1500s, Protestant religions spread throughout Europe. The map shows where many of the new religions concentrated.

1. **Location** On the map, locate (a) Holy Roman Empire, (b) England, (c) Worms, (d) Wittenberg, (e) Geneva, (f) Trent.
2. **Place** (a) What was the major religion in France? (b) In which countries were there large Calvinist populations? (c) Name one country with a population of Anabaptists. (d) Name one country that was mainly Lutheran.
3. **Critical Thinking** **Recognizing Faulty Reasoning** (a) If you wanted to know how many Lutherans lived in Europe after the Reformation, would this map be a good source of information? Why or why not? (b) Would it be a good source of information about where Anglicans lived? Explain.

Ignatius of Loyola. In 1540, the pope recognized a new religious order, the Society of Jesus, or Jesuits. Founded by Ignatius of Loyola, the Jesuit order was determined to combat heresy and spread the Catholic faith.

Ignatius was a Spanish knight raised in the crusading tradition. His military career ended abruptly when his leg was shattered in battle. During a long and painful recovery, he found comfort in reading about Christian saints who had overcome mental and physical torture. He decided to become a "soldier of God."

Ignatius drew up a strict program for the Jesuits. It included spiritual and moral discipline, rigorous religious training, and absolute obedience to the Church. Led by Ignatius, the Jesuits embarked on a crusade to defend and spread the Catholic faith throughout the world.

To further the Catholic cause, Jesuits became advisers to Catholic rulers, helping them combat heresy in their lands. They set up schools that taught humanist and Catholic beliefs and enforced discipline and obedience. Daring Jesuits slipped into Protestant lands in disguise to minister to the spiritual needs of Catholics. Jesuit missionaries spread their Catholic faith to distant lands, including Asia, Africa, and the Americas.

St. Teresa of Avila. As the Catholic Reformation spread across Europe, many Catholics experienced renewed feelings of intense faith. One woman who symbolized this religious renewal was Teresa of Avila. A daughter of a well-to-do Spanish noble family, Teresa entered a Carmelite convent in her youth. The convent routine, however, was not strict enough to satisfy her strongly religious nature. She set up her own order of Carmelite nuns. They lived in isolation, eating and sleeping very little and dedicating themselves to prayer and meditation.

Impressed by her spiritual life, her superiors in the Church asked Teresa to reorganize and reform convents and monasteries throughout Spain. Teresa was widely honored for her work, and after her death the Church made her a saint. Her mystical writings rank among the most important Christian texts of her time.

Results. Did the Catholic Reformation succeed? By the late 1500s, Rome was a far more pious city than the one Luther had visited 70 years earlier. Across Catholic Europe, piety, charity, and religious art flourished. The reforms did stop the Protestant tide and even returned some areas to the Catholic Church. Still, Europe remained divided into a Catholic south and a Protestant north.

Widespread Persecution

During this period of heightened religious passion, persecution was widespread. Both Catholics and Protestants fostered intolerance. The Inquisition executed many people accused of heresy. Catholic mobs attacked and killed Protestants. Protestants killed Catholic priests and destroyed Catholic churches. Both Catholics and Protestants persecuted radical sects like the Anabaptists.

Witch hunts. Almost certainly, the religious fervor of the times contributed to a wave of witch hunting. Those accused of being witch-

In the United States, in the town of Salem, Massachusetts, a witch hunt broke out in 1692. The panic began when two girls suffered strange fits. When coaxed to explain their behavior, they accused neighbors of casting spells over them. Soon, accusations spread like wildfire throughout the town. Before the witch hunt ended the following year, at least 200 people were named, and 20 people executed, as witches.

es, or agents of the devil, were usually women, although some men faced similar attacks. Between 1450 and 1750, tens of thousands of women and men died in the witch-hunting craze.

Scholars have offered various reasons for this savage persecution. At the time, most people believed in magic and spirits. They also saw a close link between magic and heresy.

In troubled times, people look for scapegoats. Typically, people accused of witchcraft were social outcasts—beggars, poor widows, midwives blamed for infant deaths, or herbalists whose potions and cures were seen as gifts of the devil.

In the charged religious atmosphere of the times, many people were convinced that witchcraft and devil worship were on the rise. Most victims of the witch hunts died in the German states, Switzerland, and France, all centers of religious conflict. When the wars of religion ended, the persecution of witches also declined.

Jews and the Reformation. The Reformation brought hard times to Europe's Jews. For many Jews in Italy, the early Renaissance had been a time of relative prosperity. Unlike Spain, which had expelled its Jews in 1492, Italy allowed Jews to remain and to enjoy economic and cultural well-being. Some Jews followed the traditional trades they had been restricted to in medieval times. They were goldsmiths, artists, traders, and moneylenders. Others expanded into law, government, and business. A few highly educated Jews served as advisers to powerful rulers.

Yet the pressure remained strong on Jews to convert. By 1516, Jews in Venice had to live in a separate quarter of the city, known as the ghetto. Other Italian cities set up walled ghettos for Jews.

Humanist scholars like Erasmus had sympathy for Jews. At first, Luther hoped that Jews would be converted to his teachings. When they were not, he called for them to be expelled from Christian lands and for their synagogues and books to be burned.

During the Reformation, restrictions on Jews increased. Some German princes expelled Jews from their lands. All German states confined Jews to ghettos or required them to wear a yellow badge if they traveled outside the ghetto.

CAUSE AND EFFECT

Long-Term Causes

Roman Catholic Church becomes more worldly
Humanists urge return to simple religion
Strong national monarchs emerge

Immediate Causes

Johann Tetzel sells indulgences in Wittenberg
Martin Luther posts 95 Theses
Luther translates the Bible into German
Printing press allows spread of reform ideas
Calvin and other reformers preach against
    Roman Catholic traditions
Luther calls for Jews to be expelled from
    Christian lands

PROTESTANT REFORMATION

Immediate Effects

Peasants' Revolt
Founding of Lutheran, Calvinist, Anglican,
    Presbyterian, and other Protestant churches
Weakening of Holy Roman emperor

Long-Term Effects

Religious wars in Europe for more than 100
    years
Catholic Reformation
Strengthening of the Inquisition
Jewish migration to Eastern Europe
Increased anti-Semitism

Connections Today

About one fourth of Christians are Protestant
Religious conflict in Northern Ireland

Interpreting a Chart The Protestant Reformation brought sweeping changes to Western Europe. ■ How did Johann Tetzel's sale of indulgences contribute to the onset of the Reformation? Identify one effect of the Protestant Reformation that you see today.

In the 1550s, Pope Paul IV reversed the lenient policy of Renaissance popes and restricted Jewish activity. Even Emperor Charles V, who had supported tolerance of Jews in the Holy Roman Empire, banned the migration of Jews to his colonies in the Americas. After 1550, many Jews migrated to Poland-Lithuania and to parts of the Ottoman empire, where they were allowed to prosper. Dutch Calvinists also tolerated Jews, taking in families who were driven out of Portugal and Spain.

Looking Ahead

The upheavals of the Catholic and Protestant reformations sparked wars of religion in Europe until the mid-1600s. At that time, issues of religion began to give way to issues of national power. As you will read in Chapter 17, Catholic and Protestant rulers of the mid-1600s often made decisions based on political interests rather than for purely religious reasons.

SECTION 4 REVIEW

1. **Identify** (a) Anabaptists, (b) Henry VIII, (c) Mary Tudor, (d) *Book of Common Prayer,* (e) Elizabeth I, (f) Catholic Reformation, (g) Council of Trent, (h) Inquisition, (i) Jesuits, (j) St. Teresa of Avila.
2. **Define** (a) annul, (b) ghetto.
3. (a) Describe the steps by which England became a Protestant country. (b) How did England's experience differ from that of the German states?
4. (a) What were the goals of the Catholic Reformation? (b) Did it succeed? Explain your answer.
5. (a) Why did persecution increase during the Reformation? (b) Which groups faced the greatest persecution?
6. *Critical Thinking* **Recognizing Causes and Effects** If the Catholic Church had undertaken reform earlier, do you think that the Protestant Reformation would have occurred? Explain.
7. *ACTIVITY* Prepare a script for a TV news program reporting on King Henry VIII's break with the Catholic Church.

The Scientific Revolution

Guide for Reading

- How did astronomers change the way people viewed the universe?

- What was the new scientific method?

- How did Newton's work link physics and astronomy?

- What advances were made in chemistry and medicine?

- **Vocabulary** *heliocentric, gravity*

Both the Renaissance and the Reformation looked to the past for models. Humanists turned to ancient classical ideas. Religious reformers looked to the Bible and early Christian times for inspiration. The profound change that took place in science beginning in the mid-1500s, by contrast, pointed ahead, toward a future shaped by a new way of thinking about the physical universe. We call that historic change the Scientific Revolution.

Changing Views of the World

Until the mid-1500s, European scholars accepted the idea of the ancient Greek astronomer Ptolemy that the Earth was the center of the universe. They accepted this view because it seemed to agree with common sense. It also followed the teachings of the Church. In the 1500s and 1600s, some startling discoveries radically changed the way Europeans viewed the physical world.

A revolutionary theory. In 1543, Polish scholar Nicolaus Copernicus (koh PERnuh kuhs) published *On the Revolutions of the Heavenly Spheres*. In it, he proposed a heliocentric, or sun-centered, model of the universe. The sun, he said, stood at the center of the universe. The Earth, he went on, was just one of several planets that revolved around the sun.

Most experts rejected this revolutionary theory, which contradicted both Church teachings and the teachings of Ptolemy. In Europe at the time, all scientific knowledge and many religious teachings were based on the arguments developed by classical thinkers. If Ptolemy's reasoning about the planets was wrong, they believed, then the whole system of human knowledge would also have to be questioned.

Then, in the late 1500s, the Danish astronomer Tycho Brahe (TEE koh BRAH uh) provided evidence that supported Copernicus's theory. Brahe set up an astronomical observatory. Every night for years, he carefully observed the sky, accumulating data about the movement of the heavenly bodies.

After Brahe's death, his assistant, the brilliant German astronomer and mathematician Johannes Kepler, used Brahe's data to calculate

A Home Devoted to Science Tycho Brahe named his unique home Uraniborg, or Heavenly City. It consisted of a castle, library, laboratory, observatories, and a shop for making instruments. There, Brahe and his students made observations and developed instruments that were more accurate than any previous work. *Economics and Technology* Besides science, what other academic subject is useful to astronomers?

the orbits of the planets revolving around the sun. His calculations supported Copernicus's heliocentric view. At the same time, however, they showed that the planets did not move in perfect circles, as both Ptolemy and Copernicus believed, but in another kind of orbit called an ellipse.

"It does move." Scientists of many lands built on the foundations laid by Copernicus and Kepler. In Italy, Galileo Galilei used technology developed by a Dutch lens grinder to assemble an astronomical telescope. With this instrument, he became the first person to see the mountains on the moon and sunspots. He also observed the four moons of Jupiter moving slowly around that planet—exactly, he realized, the way Copernicus said that the Earth moved around the sun.

Galileo's discoveries caused an uproar. Other scholars attacked him because his observations contradicted ancient views about the world. The Church condemned him because his ideas challenged the Christian teaching that the heavens were fixed, unmoving, and perfect.

In 1633, Galileo was brought to trial before the Inquisition. Threatened with death unless he withdrew his "heresies," Galileo agreed to publicly state that the Earth stood motionless at the center of the universe. "Nevertheless," he is said to have muttered as he left the court, "it does move."

ISSUES *For* **TODAY** Artists, writers, scholars, and scientists of the Renaissance and Reformation transformed the world with their revolutionary new ideas. What are some consequences of challenging accepted ways of thinking?

The new scientific method. Despite the opposition of religious authorities, by the early 1600s a new approach to science had emerged. Unlike most earlier approaches, it started not with Aristotle or Ptolemy or even the Bible but with observation and experimentation. Complex mathematical calculations were used to convert the observations and experiments into scientific laws. In time, this approach became known as the scientific method.

Newton Ties It All Together

As a student at Cambridge University in England, Isaac Newton devoured the works of the leading scientists of his day. By age 24, he had developed a brilliant theory to explain why the planets moved as they did. According to one story, Newton was sitting in a garden when an apple fell from a tree. He wondered whether the force that pulled that apple to the Earth might not also control the movements of planets in space.

In the next 20 years, Newton perfected his theory. Using mathematics, he showed that a single force keeps the planets in their orbits around the sun. He called this force gravity.

In 1687, Newton published *Mathematical Principles of Natural Philosophy*, explaining the law of gravity and other workings of the universe. Nature, argued Newton, follows uniform laws. All motion in the universe can be measured and described mathematically.

To many, Newton's work seemed to link physics and astronomy, to bind the new science together as gravity itself held the universe together. English poet Alexander Pope caught the spirit of what would later be called the Newtonian revolution in these lines:

> **"**Nature and Nature's Laws lay hid in night,
> God said, Let Newton be! and all was light.**"**

For over 200 years, Newton's laws held fast, until a revolution in physics in the early 1900s once more transformed the way people view the universe.

More Scientific Advances

The 1500s and 1600s saw change in areas other than astronomy. Among the most impor-

tant breakthroughs were those that occurred in chemistry and medicine.

Chemistry. Chemistry slowly freed itself from the magical notions of alchemy. Alchemists optimistically believed it was possible to transform ordinary metals into gold.

In the 1600s, Robert Boyle distinguished between individual elements and chemical compounds. He also explained the effect of temperature and pressure on gases. Boyle's work opened the way to modern chemical analysis of the composition of matter.

Medicine. Medieval physicians relied on the ancient works of Galen. Galen, however, had made many errors, in part because he had limited knowledge of human anatomy. During the Renaissance, artists like Leonardo da Vinci, as well as physicians, made new efforts to study the human body. In 1543, Andreas Vesalius published *On the Structure of the Human Body,* the first accurate and detailed study of human anatomy. Vesalius's careful and clear drawings corrected errors inherited from ancient classical authorities.

A French physician, Ambroise Paré, developed a new and more effective ointment for

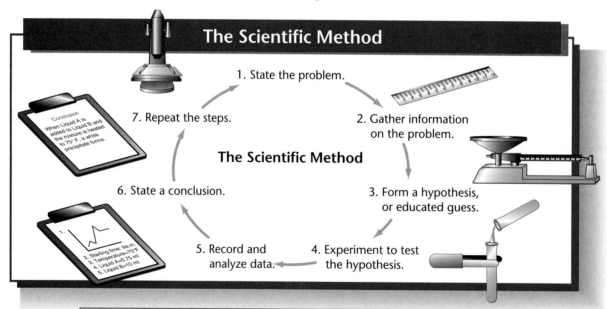

The Scientific Method

The Scientific Method

1. State the problem.

2. Gather information on the problem.

3. Form a hypothesis, or educated guess.

4. Experiment to test the hypothesis.

5. Record and analyze data.

6. State a conclusion.

7. Repeat the steps.

Interpreting a Chart The scientific method, still used by scientists today, was based on a new way of thinking. For the first time, scientists relied on objective data that they collected and measured, rather than on subjective observation. After reaching a conclusion, followers of the scientific method repeated their work at least once—and usually many times—to make sure that their findings were correct. ■ Why do you think it is important for scientists to repeat their work, as shown in Step 7?

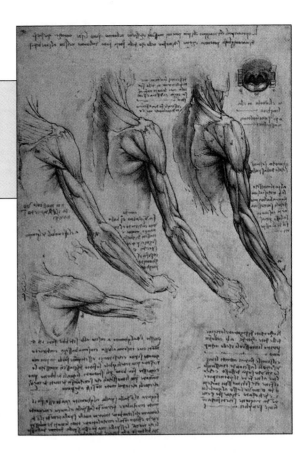

Human Anatomy *Leonardo da Vinci's drawings of human anatomy were based on dissections of more than 30 cadavers. He traced the circulatory, nervous, muscular, and skeletal systems with fair accuracy.* **Continuity and Change** *How would the practice of medicine be affected today if physicians did not have accurate knowledge of anatomy?*

preventing infection. He also developed a technique for closing wounds with stitches.

In the early 1600s, William Harvey, an English scholar, described the circulation of the blood for the first time. He showed how the heart serves as a pump to force blood through veins and arteries. These pioneering scientists opened the way for further advances.

Bacon and Descartes

The new scientific method was really a revolution in thought. Two giants of this revolution were the Englishman Francis Bacon and the Frenchman René Descartes (ruh NAY day KAHRT). Each devoted himself to the problem of knowledge.

Both Bacon and Descartes rejected Aristotle's scientific assumptions. They also challenged the scholarly traditions of the medieval universities that sought to make the physical world fit in with the teachings of the Church. Both argued that truth is not known at the beginning of inquiry but at the end, after a long process of investigation.

Bacon and Descartes differed in their methods, however. Bacon stressed experiment and observation. He wanted science to make life better for people by leading to practical technologies. Descartes emphasized human reasoning as the best road to understanding. His *Discourse on Method* begins with the statement: "I think, therefore I am." Through reason, he argued, rather than traditional sources of knowledge, people could discover basic truths.

Thinkers like Bacon and Descartes helped bring the scientific method to the pursuit of all knowledge. They also spread the idea of the possibility of human progress. With their pioneering approaches, they opened the way to the Enlightenment of the 1700s. (See Chapter 18.)

SECTION 5 REVIEW

1. **Identify** (a) Nicolaus Copernicus, (b) Tycho Brahe, (c) Johannes Kepler, (d) Galileo Galilei, (e) Andreas Vesalius, (f) William Harvey, (g) René Descartes.
2. **Define** (a) heliocentric, (b) gravity.
3. Why did each of the following challenge the heliocentric theory: (a) scholars, (b) the Church?
4. How did the new scientific method that was developed in the 1500s and 1600s differ from the traditional approach to science?
5. How did Newton explain the workings of the universe?
6. Identify three advances in medicine during the 1500s and 1600s.
7. *Critical Thinking* **Applying Information** Identify three ways in which your life would be different if the Scientific Revolution had not occurred.
8. *ACTIVITY* Review the material on Galileo Galilei on page 365. Then, with some of your classmates reenact Galileo's trial before the Inquisition.

CHAPTER REVIEW

REVIEWING VOCABULARY

Review the vocabulary words in this chapter. Then, use *ten* of these words to create a crossword puzzle. Exchange puzzles with a classmate. Complete the puzzles and then check each other's answers.

REVIEWING FACTS

1. What was the Renaissance? When did it begin?
2. Why did the Renaissance begin in the place that it did?
3. What three different kinds of plays did Shakespeare write?
4. What was the impact of the invention of the printing press?
5. What was the Protestant Reformation? When did it begin?
6. What were Luther's 95 theses?
7. How did the English Reformation occur?
8. Which groups were persecuted during the Reformation?
9. What is the scientific method?
10. What did Descartes mean by the statement, "I think, therefore I am"?

SKILLS FOR SUCCESS ANALYZING FINE ART

Works of fine art, such as paintings and sculptures, can show us what famous people looked like, what a culture's beliefs were, and what people wore. As with written sources, a historian must determine the reliability of an artwork. For example, a painter might have tried to flatter the king who was paying for a portrait by making him look more imposing than he was in real life.

At right is a section of a large painting called *Children's Games*, by Pieter Bruegel. (See page 350.) Study the painting and answer the following questions.

1. **Identify the work of art and the artist.**
   (a) What is the title of the painting? (b) Who was the artist? (c) When and where did he live?

2. **Analyze the information in the artwork.**
   (a) What is the subject of the painting?
   (b) Identify or describe the games shown in the painting.

3. **Draw conclusions based on the work of art.**
   (a) Would you consider this painting a reliable source of information? Explain. (b) Using this painting, compare children's games in Bruegel's time with children's games today.

REVIEWING CHAPTER THEMES

Review the "Focus On" questions at the start of this chapter. Then select *three* of those questions and answer them, using information from the chapter.

CRITICAL THINKING

1. **Comparing** (a) Compare and contrast the Renaissance in Italy with the Renaissance in northern Europe. (b) How would you account for the differences?

2. **Recognizing Causes and Effects** Why did England escape the kinds of religious wars that tore apart other European nations?

3. **Linking Past and Present** Modern scientists refer to the discoveries of Copernicus as the Copernican Revolution. Why do you think they use that term?

ANALYZING PRIMARY SOURCES

Use the quotation on page 351 to answer the following questions.

1. What is the meaning of the first line of the excerpt?

2. According to the speaker, what will be the result if a person is true to oneself?

3. Do you agree with the argument made in the excerpt? Explain.

FOR YOUR PORTFOLIO

WRITING A BOOK REVIEW Write a review of a book written during the Renaissance. First, make a list of the books mentioned in this chapter. Look over two or three books before selecting one to read. Your review should list the author's main points and describe how this book reflects the period in which it was written. After writing your review, present it to the class. Be ready to defend your point of view with examples from the book you read.

Renaissance Artists and Writers

Artist or Writer	Famous Work
Leonardo da Vinci (artist, 1452–1519)	*Mona Lisa*
Niccolò Machiavelli (writer, 1469–1527)	*The Prince*
Michelangelo (artist, 1475–1564)	Sistine Chapel
Raphael (artist, 1483–1520)	*School of Athens*
Miguel de Cervantes (writer, 1547–1616)	*Don Quixote*
William Shakespeare (writer, 1564–1616)	*King Lear*

ANALYZING TABLES

Use the table and information from the chapter to answer the following questions.

1. Which of the works deals with politics?

2. Which of the works concerns a man who imagines that he is a medieval knight?

3. Which of the works can be seen in the Vatican?

INTERNET ACTIVITY

WRITING A PERSUASIVE ESSAY Use the Internet to research the invention of the printing press and its effects on Renaissance Europe. Then write an essay in which you try to persuade the reader that the invention of the Internet either will or will not have a similar effect on world civilization in the future.

The First Global Age: Europe and Asia

(1415–1796)

CHAPTER OUTLINE

1 **The Search for Spices**
2 **Diverse Traditions of Southeast Asia**
3 **European Footholds in Southeast Asia and India**
4 **Encounters in East Asia**

In early July 1511, Portuguese naval commander Afonso de Albuquerque (ahl boo KEHR kuh) ordered his fleet to drop anchor off Malacca. Malacca was a rich trading port that controlled the sea route linking India, Southeast Asia, and China. To announce his arrival, Albuquerque fired a cannon salute and sounded trumpets.

The sultan of Malacca sent a message to the Portuguese. "Have you come in peace or in war?"

"Peace," replied Albuquerque. His true goal, however, was not peace, but conquest. He was determined to defeat the Muslim rulers who controlled the rich Indian Ocean spice trade and to build a Portuguese trading empire in Asia.

The fleet remained at anchor for several weeks. Then, on July 25, Albuquerque gave the order to open fire. An observer described the bombardment of Malacca:

66 [The cannonballs] came like rain, and the noise of the cannon was as the noise of thunder in the heavens and the flashes of fire of their guns were like flashes of lightning in the sky. And the noise of their guns was like that of groundnuts popping in the frying pan.99

The Portuguese took the city, killing its inhabitants and seizing its wealth. On the ruins of a mosque, Albuquerque built a fort. The sultan had fled, thinking the invaders would loot and leave. But when he heard about the fort, he realized that the Portuguese had come to stay.

Portugal was the first European power to gain a foothold in Asia. In the early 1500s, European nations explored the seas beyond Europe, hunting for an all-water trade route to Asia. In the process, they encountered two previously unknown continents, the Americas.

Although Europeans mastered the seas, they could transport few soldiers to face the mighty empires of Asia. In the 1600s, however, European strength increased and older Asian empires declined. In this chapter and the next, you will see how Europeans ushered in the first global age, bringing together many peoples and civilizations for the first time.

FOCUS ON these questions as you read:

- **Economics and Technology**
  How did technology help Europeans explore the seas and build trading empires in Asia?

- **Diversity**
  What patterns of civilizations emerged in Southeast Asia?

- **Global Interaction**
  What new global patterns resulted from the European age of exploration?

- **Continuity and Change**
  How did the first global age affect the civilizations of Asia?

TIME AND PLACE

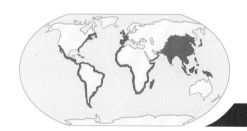

Global Trade Network *Through trade with India and East Asia, European states grew wealthy and powerful. This painting shows the busy port city of Lisbon, capital of Portugal and the home port of a global trade network. During the 1500s, Portugal used military force to gain control of trade routes on the Indian Ocean.* **Global Interaction** *How are these Portuguese ships equipped for military conquest?*

HUMANITIES LINK

Art History Japanese screen painting (page 389).
Literature In this chapter, you will encounter passages from the following works of literature: "All the male heroes bowed their heads" (page 381); Pak Chi-won, "The Story of Ho" (page 388).

1498	1511	1630s	1641	1736	1793
Da Gama rounds Africa and reaches India	Portugal seizes Malacca	Japan bars western merchants	Dutch take Malacca	Reign of Emperor Qianlong of China begins	China rejects British trade

1400	1500	1600	1700	1800

1 The Search for Spices

Guide for Reading

- Why did European nations send explorers across the oceans?

- How did technology aid European sailors?

- What countries led the way in overseas exploration?

- **Vocabulary** *cartographer, astrolabe, caravel, circumnavigate*

Today, we take pepper for granted. To Europeans of past ages, though, this spice was as valuable as gold. Ancient Romans paid as much as $125 for 12 ounces (340 g) of pepper. During the Middle Ages, the pepper in your local supermarket could have paid a year's rent. The price was measured in more than just money. As pepper traveled from Asia to Europe, each cargo cost an estimated 1,000 lives.

By the late 1400s, the desire to share in the rich spice trade of the East spurred Europeans to explore the oceans. In the hope of enormous reward, sailors risked death on long sea voyages in tiny wooden ships.

Europeans Take to the Seas

Europeans had traded with Asia long before the Renaissance. During the Middle Ages, the Crusades introduced Europeans to many luxury goods from Asia. Later, when the Mongol empire united much of Asia in the 1200s and 1300s, Asian goods flowed to Europe along complex overland trade routes. Marco Polo's tales of Chinese wealth and splendor fascinated Europeans.

The Black Death and the breakup of the Mongol empire disrupted Asian trade routes. By the 1400s, though, Europe was recovering from the plague. As its population increased, so, too, did the demand for Asian goods. The most valued trade items were spices, such as cloves, cinnamon—and, especially, pepper. In the days before refrigeration, meat spoiled quickly. Peo-ple used spices to preserve food and to add flavor to dried and salted meat. Spices were also used to make medicines and perfumes. The major source of spices was the Moluccas, an island chain in present-day Indonesia, which Europeans called the Spice Islands.

Motives. In the 1400s, Muslim and Italian merchants controlled most trade between Asia and Europe. Muslim traders brought spices and other prized goods to eastern Mediterranean ports in Egypt, Syria, and Turkey. From there, traders from Venice and other Italian cities carried the precious cargoes to European markets. Each time goods passed from one trader to another, the prices increased. Europeans wanted to cut out the Muslim and Italian middlemen and gain direct access to the riches of Asia. To do so, the Atlantic powers—first Portugal, then Spain—sought a new route to Asia that bypassed the Mediterranean.

Many sailors hoped to get rich by trading in spices or conquering rich lands. Yet the desire for wealth was not the only motive that lured men to sea. Some voyagers were still fired by the centuries-old desire to crusade against the Muslims. During the Catholic Reformation, missionaries and soldiers set out overseas to win new converts to Christianity. The Renaissance spirit of inquiry fired people's desire to learn more about the lands beyond Europe.

Improved technology. Several improvements in technology helped Europeans conquer the vast oceans of the world. Cartographers, or mapmakers, created more accurate maps and sea charts. European sailors also learned to use the astrolabe, an instrument developed by the ancient Greeks and perfected by the Arabs, to determine their latitude at sea. The chart on the next page shows some of the other technological advances that helped navigators chart long sea voyages.

Along with more reliable navigational tools, Europeans designed larger and better ships. The Portuguese developed the caravel, which combined the square sails of European ships with Arab lateen, or triangular, sails. Caravels also adapted the sternpost rudder and numerous masts of Chinese ships. The new rigging made it easier to sail across or even into the wind. Finally, European ships added more armaments, including sturdier cannons.

Technology of Ocean Navigation

Device or Improvement	Description	Importance at the Time	Connections Today
Magnetic compass (around 1000) 	A device for determining direction. A magnetic needle, floating in a dish of liquid, pointed north-south, allowing sailors to determine the direction of the ship.	Made it possible to find direction at sea, but was not very accurate; magnetic compass pointed northward but not to actual North Pole; iron in a ship could cause false readings.	Limits of magnetic compass led to development of the gyrocompass, which is not affected by magnetic force or gravity. Today it is used in ships, aircraft, and spacecraft.
Astrolabe (late 1400s) 	A device used to measure the angles of the sun and stars above the horizon. It was difficult to use accurately in rough seas.	Improvement over the former method of measuring the altitude of the sun or stars as so many "hand widths" above the horizon.	Its weaknesses led to the development of the more accurate sextant.
Mercator projection (1569) 	Map projection that shows latitude and longitude as straight lines; shapes are accurate, but size is distorted the farther one moves from the equator.	Excellent map for navigators because it showed true directions of places in relation to each other.	One of the most common types of map projections, even today. (See, for example, the map on page 995.)
Sextant (forerunner, about 1500; first sextant, 1730) 	Device for determining the altitude of the sun or stars. By comparing this altitude at different degrees of latitude, the navigator could find the latitude of the ship.	Improvement over the astrolabe because the movements of the ship did not affect the reading so much and the user did not have to look directly into the sun.	The sextant, with only slight variations, was widely used until the mid-1900s. Since World War II, other inventions, such as radar, have taken its place.

Interpreting a Chart Today, space travel would be unthinkable without the computer and the radio. In the 1400s, ocean travel would have been unthinkable without the compass and the astrolabe. Such technology allowed ships to navigate on the open seas, far out of sight of land. ■ Why was the Mercator projection an important contribution to navigation? How was navigation linked to astronomy?

Portuguese Pioneers

Portugal, a small nation on the western edge of Spain, led the way in exploration. As in Spain, Christian knights in Portugal had fought off Muslim rule. By the 1400s, Portugal was strong and stable enough to expand into Muslim North Africa. In 1415, the Portuguese seized Ceuta (SAY oo tah) on the North African coast. The victory sparked the imagination of Prince Henry, known to history as Henry the Navigator.

Mapping the coast of Africa. Prince Henry embodied the crusading drive and the new spirit of exploration. He had heard tales of a mysterious but very rich Christian African ruler, Prester John. Henry hoped to form an alliance with Prester John against the Muslims. He also wanted to find the source of African gold.

At Sagres in southern Portugal, Henry gathered scientists, cartographers, and other experts. They redesigned ships, prepared maps, and trained captains and crews for long voyages. Henry then sent out ships that slowly worked their way south to explore the coast of West Africa.

Henry died in 1460, but the Portuguese continued their quest. In 1488, Bartholomeu Dias rounded the southern tip of Africa after being blown off course by a violent storm. Despite the turbulent seas, the tip became known as the Cape of Good Hope because it opened the way for a sea route to Asia.

On to India. In 1497, Vasco da Gama led four ships around the Cape of Good Hope. As he sailed up the coast of East Africa, he took on an Indian pilot who guided him across the Indian Ocean. After a 10-month voyage, Da Gama finally reached the great spice port of Calicut on the west coast of India.

The long voyage home took a heavy toll. The Portuguese lost half their ships. Many sailors died of hunger, thirst, and scurvy, a disease caused by the lack of vitamin C during months at sea. An officer wrote:

> **66**All our people suffered from their
> gums, which grew over their teeth so
> that they could not eat. Their legs
> swelled, and other parts of the body,
> and these swellings spread until the
> sufferer died.**99**

Still, the venture proved highly profitable to the survivors. In India, Da Gama had acquired a cargo of spices that he sold at a profit of 3,000 percent.

Da Gama quickly outfitted a new fleet. In 1502, he forced a treaty of friendship on the Hindu ruler of Calicut. Da Gama then left Portuguese merchants there to buy spices when prices were low and to keep them stored near the dock until the next fleet could return to pick them up. As you will read, the Portuguese would soon seize key outposts around the Indian Ocean to create a vast trading empire.

Spain Enters the Race

The profitable Portuguese voyages spurred other European nations to seek a sea route to Asia. In the 1480s, an Italian navigator from the port of Genoa, Christopher Columbus, sought Portuguese backing for his own plan. He wanted to reach the Indies* by sailing west across the Atlantic. Like most educated Europeans, Columbus knew that the Earth was a sphere. A few weeks sailing west, he reasoned, would bring a ship to eastern Asia.

Although his plan made sense, Columbus made two errors. First, he greatly underestimated the circumference of the Earth. Second, he had no idea that two continents, North and South America, lay in his path.

Voyages of Columbus. In 1492, Columbus finally convinced Ferdinand and Isabella of Spain to finance his "enterprise of the Indies." That year, the Catholic rulers had driven the Muslims from their last stronghold in Spain. To strengthen the power of their new monarchy, they sought new sources of wealth. Like the Portuguese, the Spanish hoped to bypass the Muslim-Italian monopoly on the spice trade. Queen Isabella was also anxious to spread Christianity among the people of Asia.

On August 3, 1492, Columbus sailed west with three small ships, the *Pinta,* the *Niña,* and the *Santa María.* He carried a letter to the ruler of China and took along an interpreter who spoke Arabic. With good weather and a favorable wind, his voyage was much shorter than Da Gama's would be. Still, the crew grew anxious as provisions ran low and no land came into sight. Finally, on October 12, a lookout yelled, "Land! Land!" The tiny fleet dropped anchor in the Caribbean Sea, off what were probably the Bahamas.

Columbus spent several months cruising the islands of the Caribbean, searching for China and Japan. Since he thought he had reached the Indies, he called the people of the region Indians. In 1493, he returned to Spain to a hero's welcome. In three later voyages, Columbus remained convinced he had reached islands off the coast of East Asia. Before long, though, other

---

*The Indies, or East Indies, was the European name for a group of islands in Southeast Asia. Today, they are a part of Indonesia.

Europeans realized that he had found a route to a continent previously unknown to them.

Line of Demarcation. Spain and Portugal pressed rival claims to the islands Columbus explored. In 1493, Pope Alexander VI stepped in to keep the peace. He set a Line of Demarcation that divided the non-European world into two zones. Spain had the right to trade and explore lands west of the line. Portugal had the same rights east of the line. The next year, in the Treaty of Tordesillas (tor day SEE yahs), the two countries moved the line.

In 1500, the Portuguese captain Pedro Alvarez Cabral was blown off course as he sailed around Africa. Landing in Brazil, which lay east of the Line of Demarcation, he claimed it for Portugal. In the next chapter, you will read about the effects of these Spanish and Portuguese claims.

Naming the "New World." In 1507, a German cartographer read reports about the "New World" by an Italian sailor, Amerigo Vespucci. The mapmaker labeled the region America and the name stuck. The islands Columbus had explored in the Caribbean became known as the West Indies.

Europeans continued to seek routes around or through the Americas to Asia. In 1513, the Spanish adventurer Vasco Nuñez de Balboa, with the help of Native Americans, hacked a passage through the tropical forests of Panama. From a ridge on the west coast, he gazed at a huge body of water that he called the South Sea. Before long, another hardy explorer, Ferdinand Magellan, would rename it the Mar Pacifico, the Pacific (peaceful) Ocean.

The Quest for El Paso

A minor Portuguese noble, Magellan was only 19 when Vasco da Gama returned from his historic voyage to India. By 1511, Magellan himself had sailed around Africa to the East Indies and joined Afonso de Albuquerque in the attack on Malacca. Magellan slowly became convinced that he could find *El Paso,* a sea route through the Americas to the Indies. After Magellan had a falling out with the king of Portugal, he convinced King Charles of Spain to finance his voyage.

A bold plan. Magellan recruited sailors for a two-year voyage, but would not reveal their destination. Adventurous crew members signed on from many European nations—Spain, Portugal, the German states, the Netherlands—as well as from Africa and Southeast Asia. Among Magellan's recruits was an Italian adventurer, Antonio Pigafetta, whose journal gives us a fascinating record of the voyage.

Onto five ships Magellan loaded two years' worth of stores, including 10 tons of biscuits, 6,000 pounds of salt beef and pork, dried beans, flour, water, and wine, plus lumber, weapons, and gunpowder. He added mirrors, fishhooks, cloth, and knives as trade goods. Finally, on September 20, 1519, the ships sailed from Spain toward the "bottom of the world."

Perils at sea. As they sailed south and west, discontent surfaced. Magellan had to put down more than one mutiny. In October, storms lashed the ships. "We went up and down

Fear of the Unknown It took courage to volunteer for a long voyage. Popular tales warned that the oceans were full of dragons, sea serpents, and other monsters. This 1550 drawing contrasts the tame animals of the land with the fearsome creatures of the sea. **Continuity and Change** In popular fiction today, what unexplored regions are sometimes populated by monsters?

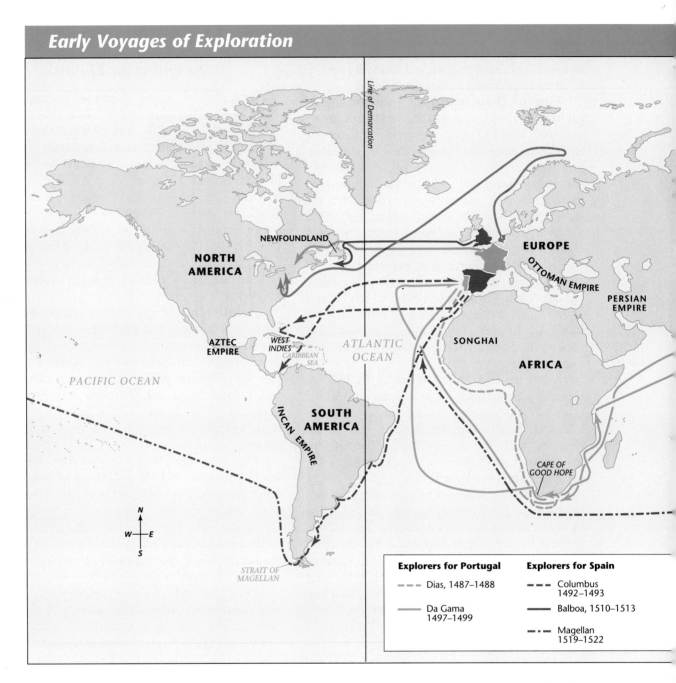

NEWFOUNDLAND

NORTH
AMERICA

EUROPE

OTTOMAN EMPIRE

PERSIAN
EMPIRE

AZTEC
EMPIRE

WEST
INDIES

CARIBBEAN
SEA

ATLANTIC
OCEAN

SONGHAI

AFRICA

PACIFIC OCEAN

INCAN EMPIRE

SOUTH
AMERICA

CAPE OF
GOOD HOPE

N
W—E
S

STRAIT OF
MAGELLAN

Line of Demarcation

Explorers for Portugal	Explorers for Spain
- - - Dias, 1487–1488	- - - Columbus 1492–1493
—— Da Gama 1497–1499	—— Balboa, 1510–1513
	-·-·- Magellan 1519–1522

in the sea until good weather came," wrote Pigafetta. Then the fleet was becalmed for weeks. Food rotted in the tropical heat.

Finally, the fleet reached the coast of South America. Slowly, they explored each bay, hoping that one would lead to the Pacific. When another mutiny erupted, Magellan left the traitors on a barren part of the coast and sailed away, ignoring their cries for mercy.

In November 1520, more than a year after leaving Spain, Magellan's ships entered a bay at the southern tip of South America. Amid brutal storms, rushing tides, and unpredictable winds, Magellan charted a tortuous passage that became known as the Strait of Magellan. "I think that there is not in the world a more beautiful country, or better strait than this one," wrote Pigafetta.

The ships emerged from this lashing into the calm Pacific Ocean. Although many wanted to return to Spain the way they had come, Magellan insisted they push on across the Pacific to the East Indies. Three more weeks, he thought, would bring them to the Spice Islands.

Violence and bloodshed. Like Columbus, Magellan had miscalculated. The Pacific

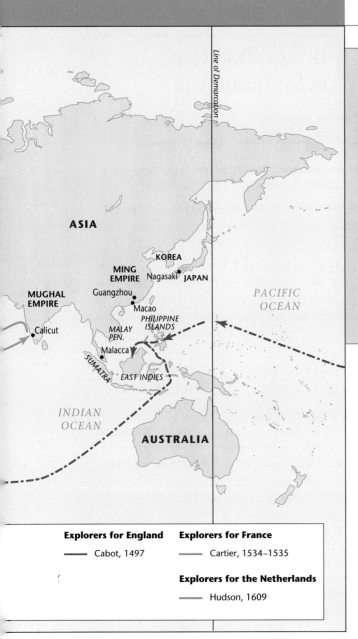

Explorers for England
—— Cabot, 1497

Explorers for France
—— Cartier, 1534–1535

Explorers for the Netherlands
– – – Hudson, 1609

GEOGRAPHY AND HISTORY

Beginning in the later 1400s, European nations sent explorers across the oceans in search of riches. Many explorers sought a Northwest Passage around the Americas, but none succeeded in finding one.

1. **Location** On the map, locate (a) Cape of Good Hope, (b) East Indies, (c) West Indies, (d) Europe, (e) Incan empire.
2. **Movement** (a) For which country did Balboa sail? Cartier? (b) Which lands did Cabot explore? Da Gama? (c) Which explorers were probably looking for the Northwest Passage?
3. **Critical Thinking** **Applying Information** Why does the Line of Demarcation appear to be two lines on the map?

was much wider than he imagined. Pigafetta described their terrible hardships:

66We remained 3 months and 20 days without taking in provisions or other refreshments and ate only old biscuit reduced to powder, full of grubs and stinking from the dirt which rats had made on it. We drank water that was yellow and stinking. We also ate the ox hides from under the mainyard which we softened by soaking in seawater for several days.99

Soon, there was an outbreak of scurvy, which killed 19 crew members. Finally in March 1521, the fleet anchored off the Philippines. It had crossed the Pacific Ocean.

Around the world. Magellan won many converts to Christianity among the Filipinos, but he unfortunately made the mistake of getting involved in local politics. In a minor battle with one ruler, he found himself trapped. He died fighting to save his comrades. "Thus we lost our mirror, light, comfort and true guide," mourned Pigafetta.

After further battles and disasters, 18 half-dead sailors aboard a single ship completed the voyage. On September 8, 1522, more than three years after setting out, they anchored off Seville. The survivors, including Pigafetta, "went in shirts and barefoot" to give thanks at a nearby shrine. This ragged band was hailed as the first people to circumnavigate, or sail around, the world.

The Search Continues

"I believe that never more will any man undertake to make such a voyage," predicted Pigafetta. But he was wrong. Although Spain and Portugal had divided the world between themselves, English, Dutch, and French explorers searched the coast of North America for a northwest passage to Asia.

Seeking a northwest passage. In 1497, King Henry VII of England had already sent a Venetian navigator named John Cabot (Giovanni Caboto) to seek a more northerly route than the one Columbus had charted. Cabot found rich fishing grounds off Newfoundland, which he claimed for England. Later the French captain Jacques Cartier explored the St. Lawrence River, while Henry Hudson, sailing for the Dutch, explored the Hudson River. Neither found the hoped-for passage to Asia, though.

The search for a northwest passage continued for centuries. In the meantime, bold sailors like Francis Drake followed Magellan's course around the stormy tip of South America.

Looking ahead. The European age of exploration marked the beginning of a period of growing global interdependence that has continued to the present day. Yet the activities of European explorers brought tragedy as well as triumph. In Chapter 16, you will read about the impact of European expansion on peoples of the Americas and West Africa.

The immediate impact of European exploration, though, was felt in Asia. When European fleets sailed toward Southeast Asia, they entered a world that had long ago developed its own cultures and trading patterns.

SECTION 1 REVIEW

1. **Identify** (a) Prince Henry the Navigator, (b) Vasco da Gama, (c) Christopher Columbus, (d) Treaty of Tordesillas, (e) Vasco Nuñez de Balboa, (f) Ferdinand Magellan.
2. **Define** (a) cartographer, (b) astrolabe, (c) caravel, (d) circumnavigate.
3. Why did European nations seek a sea route to Asia?
4. Describe how each of the following countries contributed to the conquest of the world's oceans: (a) Portugal, (b) Spain.
5. *Critical Thinking* **Making Decisions** What pros and cons would you weigh if you were a sailor trying to decide whether to sign on with Da Gama, Columbus, or Magellan?
6. *ACTIVITY* Write a proclamation or design a poster that Prince Henry might have issued to attract navigators, sailors, and other experts to his sailing school at Sagres.

2 Diverse Traditions of Southeast Asia

Guide for Reading

- How did trade help shape Southeast Asia?
- How did neighboring civilizations influence Southeast Asian cultures?
- What major states emerged in Southeast Asia?

Sandwiched between China and India, the region known today as Southeast Asia was strongly influenced by these two powerful neighbors. Yet the distinct cultures of Southeast Asia retained their own unique identities.

Geography: Mainland and Islands of Southeast Asia

Southeast Asia is made up of two major regions. The first region, mainland Southeast Asia, includes several peninsulas that jut south between India and China. Today, the mainland is home to Myanmar (MEE uhn mahr), Thailand, Cambodia, Laos, Vietnam, and part of Malaysia. The second region, island Southeast Asia, consists of more than 20,000 islands scattered between the Indian Ocean and the South China Sea. It includes the present-day nations of Indonesia, Singapore, Brunei (bru NĪ), and the Philippines.

Location. The mainland is separated from the rest of Asia by mountains and high plateaus. Still, traders and invaders did push overland into the region. The mountains also separated the four main river valleys of Southeast Asia—the Irrawaddy (ihr uh WAHD ee), Chao Phraya, Mekong, and Red. As elsewhere, the earliest civilizations emerged in these fertile river valleys.

Island Southeast Asia has long been of strategic importance. All seaborne trade between China and India had to pass through either the Malacca or Sunda straits. Whoever commanded the straits controlled rich trade routes. As you will read, the movements of people and goods between India and China would greatly influence Southeast Asia.

Growing Rice *In the river valleys and deltas of Southeast Asia, farmers have relied on rice as their staple crop. In fact, in several languages, the words for* rice *and for* food *are the same. Rice grows in* padis, *fields that are flooded by irrigation or heavy rains. These Vietnamese padis are flooded by the Mekong River.* **Geography and History** *What type of climate is needed for rice farming?*

Trade routes in the southern seas. The monsoons, or seasonal winds, shaped trading patterns in the "southern seas." Ships traveled northeast in summer and southwest in winter. Between seasons, while waiting for the winds to shift, merchants harbored their vessels in Southeast Asian ports, which became important centers of trade and culture. By the time of the Han empire, an international trade network linked East Africa and the Middle East to India, Southeast Asia, and China.

The key products of Southeast Asia were spices. In coastal towns from India to Southeast Asia, merchants bought and sold cloves, nutmeg, ginger, pepper, and other spices. Only a fraction of the spices traded in the region was destined for markets in Europe. Most cargoes went to East Asia, the Middle East, and East Africa.

Early traditions. The peoples of Southeast Asia developed their own cultures before Indian or Chinese influences shaped the region. At Bang Chiang in Thailand, archaeologists have found jars and even bronze bracelets at least 5,000 years old. This evidence is challenging old theories about when civilization began in the region.

Over the centuries, diverse ethnic groups speaking many languages settled in Southeast Asia. In isolated villages, they followed their own religious and cultural patterns. Many societies were built around the nuclear family rather than the joint families common in India and China.

Women had greater equality in Southeast Asia than elsewhere in Asia. Female merchants took part in the spice trade, gaining fame for their skill in bargaining, finance, and languages. In some port cities, they gained enough wealth and influence to become rulers. Matrilineal descent was an accepted custom in Southeast Asia, and women also had some freedom in choosing or divorcing marriage partners. Even after Indian and Chinese influences arrived, women retained their traditional rights.

Impact of India

Indian merchants and Hindu priests filtered into Southeast Asia, slowly spreading their culture. Later, Buddhist monks and scholars introduced Theravada beliefs. Following the path of trade and religion came the influence of Sanskrit writing, Indian law, government, art, architecture, and farming.

Increasing contacts. In the early centuries A.D., Indian traders settled in port cities in growing numbers. They gave presents to local rulers and married into influential families. Trade brought prosperity as merchants exchanged Indian cottons, jewels, and perfume for raw materials such as timber, spices, and gold.

In time, local Indian families exercised considerable power. Also, people from Southeast Asia visited India as pilgrims or students. As these contacts increased, Indian beliefs and ideas won widespread acceptance. Indian influence reached its peak between 500 and 1000.

Empires and Kingdoms of Southeast Asia

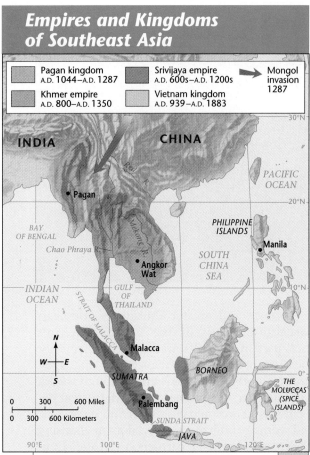

Pagan kingdom A.D. 1044–A.D. 1287	Srivijaya empire A.D. 600s–A.D. 1200s	→ Mongol invasion 1287
Khmer empire A.D. 800–A.D. 1350	Vietnam kingdom A.D. 939–A.D. 1883	

GEOGRAPHY AND HISTORY

The region we now call Southeast Asia consists of both mainland areas and thousands of islands. It was home to numerous ancient and diverse cultures.

1. **Location** On the map, locate (a) Pagan kingdom, (b) Angkor Wat, (c) Java, (d) the Moluccas, (e) Sunda Strait.
2. **Movement** (a) From what direction did the Mongol invasion come to Southeast Asia? (b) When did the Mongol invasion take place?
3. **Critical Thinking** **Understanding Sequence** Using the information on this map, and information from Section 2, make a list of events to include on a time line for Southeast Asia.

Islam. Long after Hinduism and Buddhism took root in Southeast Asia, Indians carried a third religion, Islam, into the region. By the 1200s, Muslims ruled northern India. (See Chapter 11.) From there, traders spread both Islamic beliefs and civilization throughout the islands of Indonesia and as far east as the Philippines.* Arab merchants, too, spread the new faith. The prevalence of Islam in lands surrounding the Indian Ocean helped create a stable, thriving trade network.

New Kingdoms and Empires

The blending of Indian influences with traditional ways produced a series of kingdoms and empires in Southeast Asia. Some of these states rivaled those of India.

Pagan. The kingdom of Pagan (pah GAHN) arose in the fertile rice-growing Irrawaddy Valley in present-day Myanmar. In 1044, King Anawrata (ah nuh RAH tuh) united the region. He is credited with bringing Buddhism to the Burman people. Although Buddhism had reached nearby cultures long before, Anawrata made Pagan a major Buddhist center. He filled his capital city with magnificent stupas and shrines at about the same time that people in medieval Europe were beginning to build Gothic cathedrals.

Pagan flourished for some 200 years after Anawrata's death, but fell in 1287 to conquering Mongols. When the Burmans finally threw off foreign rule to become masters of their own fate, they looked back with pride to the great days of Pagan.

The Khmer empire. Indian influences also helped shape the Khmer (kuh MEHR) empire that reached its peak between 800 and 1350. Its greatest rulers controlled much of present-day Cambodia, Thailand, and Malaysia. During its centuries of splendor, the Khmer people adapted Indian writing, mathematics, architecture, and art. Khmer rulers became pious Hindus. Like the princes and emperors of India, they saw themselves as god-kings. Most ordinary people, however, preferred Buddhism.

In the 1100s, King Suryavarman II built the great temple complex at Angkor Wat. The ruins that survive today, though overgrown with jungle and pocked by the bullets of recent wars, are among the most impressive in the world. Hundreds of carved figures tell Hindu myths and glorify the king. Although the images of Vishnu,

---

*Today, Indonesia has the largest Muslim population of any nation in the world.

▲ Temple at Angkor Wat

Shiva, and the Buddha reflect strong Indian influence, the style is uniquely Khmer.

Srivijaya. The trading empire of Srivijaya (shree vah jī yah), in Indonesia, flourished from the 600s to the 1200s. Srivijaya controlled the Malacca Strait. Both Hinduism and Buddhism reached this island empire. As elsewhere in Southeast Asia, however, the local people often blended Indian beliefs into their own forms of worship, based on nature spirits.

Later, Islam spread to Sumatra, Java, and other islands. Local rulers adopted the new religion, which cemented commercial links with other Muslim trading centers around the Indian Ocean.

Vietnam Emerges

In most of Southeast Asia, Indian influence outweighed Chinese influence. Indian traditions spread mostly through trade. China, however, sent military forces to conquer neighboring Annam, what is today northern Vietnam.

The heart of northern Vietnam was the Red River delta around present-day Hanoi. There, the river irrigated fertile rice padis, which fed a growing population. The Vietnamese had their own culture. As elsewhere in Southeast Asia, women often held positions of authority.

Chinese domination. In 111 B.C., Han armies conquered the region. China remained in control for 1,000 years. During that time, the Vietnamese absorbed Confucian ideas. They adopted the Chinese civil service system and built a government bureaucracy similar to China's. Vietnamese nobles learned to speak and read Chinese. Unlike the rest of Southeast Asia, where Theravada Buddhism had the strongest impact, Vietnam adopted Mahayana beliefs from China. Daoism also helped shape Vietnamese society.

Resistance. Despite these powerful Chinese influences, the Vietnamese preserved a strong sense of their separate identity. In A.D. 39, two noble sisters, Trung Trac and Trung Nhi, led an uprising that drove the Chinese occupiers from the land. Trung Trac set up a royal court in Melinh. She rejected Chinese influence and tried to restore a simpler form of government according to ancient Vietnamese traditions. She also abolished the hated tribute taxes that had been imposed by the Chinese.

A Han general soon crushed the revolt, but the Trung sisters refused to surrender. To this day, they are remembered as great martyrs and heroes. A Vietnamese poet of the 1400s wrote:

66All the male heroes bowed their heads
  in submission;
 Only the two sisters proudly stood up
  to avenge their country.**99**

Finally in 939, as the Tang dynasty collapsed in China, Vietnam was able to break free from Chinese rule. The Vietnamese turned back repeated Chinese efforts to reconquer their land, but did remain a tributary state of China. Ties between the two countries remained so strong that, while China was the "large dragon" of East Asia, Vietnam became known as the "smaller dragon."

SECTION 2 REVIEW

1. **Identify** (a) Pagan, (b) Anawrata, (c) Khmer, (d) Suryavarman II, (e) Trung sisters.
2. How did an international trade network emerge in the Indian Ocean?
3. What outside religious beliefs influenced the peoples of Southeast Asia?
4. Describe the relationship between Vietnam and China.
5. *Critical Thinking* **Analyzing Information** Women had an inferior social status in both India and China. Why do you think Southeast Asian women retained their equality despite Indian and Chinese influence?
6. *ACTIVITY* Create a map showing foreign influences in Southeast Asia. First, draw or trace an outline map of the region. Use arrows to show the origins and direction of influences—blue arrows for trade routes, red arrows for invasion routes. Then, show what products or ideas traveled along these routes.

3 European Footholds in Southeast Asia and India

Guide for Reading

- How did Portugal build a trading empire in Southeast Asia?

- How did the Dutch become a leading commercial power?

- Why were Europeans able to extend their influence in India after 1700?

- **Vocabulary** *sepoy, raj*

When the Portuguese arrived in the Indian Ocean, their ships were small in size and number, but they had one great advantage. The firepower of their shipboard cannons was unmatched. When the Portuguese first reached Colombo in present-day Sri Lanka, witnesses reported that they had "guns with a noise like thunder and a ball from one of them, after traversing a league, will break a castle of marble." In time, their firepower helped the newcomers win control of the existing Indian Ocean trade network.

Portugal's Empire in the East

After Vasco da Gama's voyage, the Portuguese burst into the Indian Ocean. In 1510, they seized the island of Goa off the coast of India, making it their major base. Afonso de Albuquerque then moved to end Muslim power and make the Indian Ocean a "Portuguese lake."

Trading outposts. Albuquerque burned coastal towns and crushed Arab fleets at sea. The Portuguese attacked Aden, at the entrance to the Red Sea, and took Ormuz, gateway to the Persian Gulf. The richest prize, though, was the port of Malacca, as Albuquerque knew:

> **❝**If we take this trade of Malacca away from them, Cairo and Mecca will be entirely ruined, and Venice will receive no spiceries unless her merchants go to buy them in Portugal.**❞**

In 1511, Albuquerque was successful in taking Malacca. The Portuguese massacre of the city's Muslims made the Europeans hated and feared.

In less than 50 years, the Portuguese had military and trading outposts rimming the southern seas. They seized cities on the east coast of Africa so they could resupply and repair their ships traveling to and from the Indies. For most of the 1500s, Portugal controlled the spice trade between Europe and Asia.

Matchmaking in Goa In this 1628 painting, two Indian women welcome a Portuguese settler. Many Portuguese men married local women who converted to Christianity. Their children formed the base of a new colonial society. Goa remained under Portuguese control until 1961. **Global Interaction** *Why did the Portuguese seize control of Goa?*

Endangered Species

In the fragile balance of nature, each plant and animal is especially suited to conditions in its environment. Sudden changes to that environment may threaten the survival of an entire species. In fact, scientists estimate that 99 percent of all species that ever existed—including the giant dinosaurs and the woolly mammoth—are already extinct!

Linking Past and Present Why do many individuals and governments today try to protect endangered species?

PAST *The flightless dodo bird (left) once thrived on an island in the Indian Ocean. But when the Portuguese and Dutch arrived in the 1500s, they found the placid dodo very easy to hunt. Also, the newcomers introduced rats, pigs, and dogs that ate countless dodo eggs. Within 200 years, the dodo bird was extinct.*

PRESENT *Today, world organizations keep careful track of endangered species, such as the Galapagos penguin (left) and the scarlet macaw (above). To protect them and their environment, conservationists try to limit hunting and control the introduction of new species.*

Impact. Despite their sea power, the Portuguese remained on the fringe of Asian trade. They had neither the strength nor the resources to conquer much territory on land. In India and China, where they faced far stronger empires, they merely sought permission to trade.

The intolerance of Portuguese missionaries caused resentment. In Goa, they attacked Muslims, destroyed Hindu temples, and introduced the Inquisition. Portuguese ships even sank Muslim pilgrim ships on their way to Mecca. While the Portuguese disrupted some older trade patterns, exchanges continued among Asians. Some bypassed Portuguese-controlled towns. Others traded with the newcomers.

In the late 1500s, Portuguese power declined overseas. By the early 1600s, other Europeans were vying to replace the Portuguese.

Rise of the Dutch

The Dutch were the first Europeans to challenge Portuguese domination in Asia. The land we know today as the Netherlands included a group of provinces and prosperous cities on the North Sea. The region had long been a center of handicrafts and trade. Through royal marriages, it fell under Spanish rule in the early 1500s. Later, the Protestant northern provinces won independence. (See Chapter 17.)

Sea power. In 1599, a Dutch fleet returned to Amsterdam from Asia after more than a year's absence. It carried thousands of pounds of pepper and cloves, along with other spices. Church bells rang to celebrate this "Happy Return." Those who had invested in the venture received 100 percent profit. The success of this voyage led to a frenzy of overseas activity.

By the late 1500s, their warships and trading vessels put the Dutch in the forefront of European commerce. They used their sea power to set up colonies and trading posts around the world. Like the Portuguese, the Dutch wanted to profit from the spice trade. They charted routes to bypass sea lanes under Portuguese control. At the southwestern tip of Africa, the Dutch built the Cape Town settlement, where they could repair and resupply their ships.

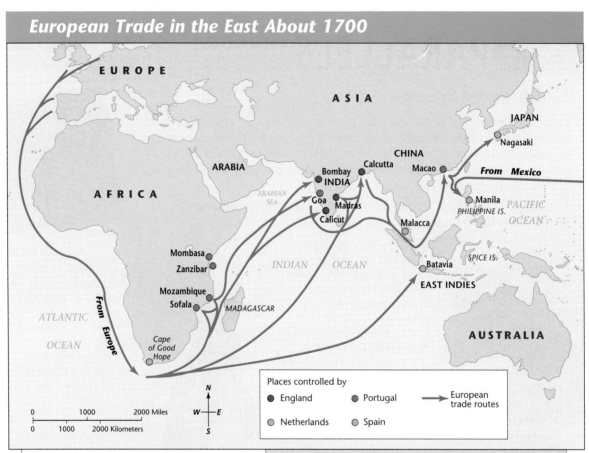

European Trade in the East About 1700

Places controlled by
- ● England
- ● Portugal
- ● Netherlands
- ● Spain
→ European trade routes

The lure of spices led first Portugal and then other European nations to explore sea routes to Asia. They gained control of coastal cities through which they carried on their trade.

1. **Location** On the map, locate (a) Spice Islands, (b) Philippine Islands, (c) Malacca, (d) Goa, (e) Sofala.
2. **Place** Which country controlled (a) Malacca? (b) Calcutta? (c) Manila?
3. **Critical Thinking** **Analyzing Information** How did Portugal's control of Zanzibar and Mozambique help its trade in India?

Dutch dominance. In 1602, a group of wealthy Dutch merchants formed the Dutch East India Company. In the next decades, the Dutch strove to make themselves the major European power in the east. In 1641, they captured Malacca from the Portuguese and opened trade with China. Before long, they were able to enforce a monopoly in the Spice Islands, controlling shipments to Europe as well as much of the trade within Southeast Asia.

The Dutch, like the Portuguese, used military force to further their trading goals. At the same time, they forged closer ties with local rulers than the Portuguese had. The Dutch generally avoided aggressive missionary activities. Many Dutch merchants married Asian women.

Trade brought the Dutch enormous wealth. At home, Dutch merchants built tall mansions along the canals of Amsterdam and hired artists like Rembrandt to paint their portraits. In the 1700s, however, the growing power of England and France contributed to a decline in the Dutch overseas trading empire.

Spain Seizes the Philippines

While the Portuguese and Dutch set up bases on the fringes of Asia, Spain took over the

Philippines. Magellan claimed the archipelago for Spain in 1521. Within about 50 years, Spain had conquered and colonized the islands. They were then named for the Spanish king Philip II. Unlike most other peoples of Southeast Asia, the Filipinos were not united. As a result, they could be more easily conquered.

In the spirit of the Catholic Reformation, Spanish priests set out to convert the Filipino people to the Christian religion. Later, missionaries moved on from the Philippines to spread Catholic teachings in East Asia.

The Philippines became a key link in Spain's overseas trading empire. The Spanish shipped silver mined in Mexico and Peru across the Pacific to the Philippines. From there, they used it to buy goods in China. In this way, large quantities of American silver flowed into the trade networks of East Asia.

Mughal India and European Traders

Before the 1700s, European traders made very little impression on India, which was enjoying one of its greatest periods of strength and prosperity. In 1526, Babur had founded the Mughal dynasty. It achieved its peak under his grandson Akbar. (See Chapter 11.) European merchants, who had reached India before the rise of the Mughals, were dazzled by India's splendid court and its many luxury goods. There seemed little that Europeans could offer of value to the Mughals.

Industry and commerce. Besides producing spices, Hindu and Muslim families across India presided over vigorous handicraft and shipbuilding industries. India was the world leader in textile manufacturing. It exported large quantities of silk and cotton, from sheer muslins to elaborate chintzes.

The Mughal empire was larger, richer, and more powerful than any in Europe. When Europeans sought trading rights, the emperors saw

ISSUES For TODAY The desire to dominate the spice trade led Europeans on a course of exploration and conquest. How can control of major resources influence political developments?

A Prized Import Indian artisans created products like this hand-painted cotton wall hanging for European markets. Indian cottons became so popular in England that, to protect the British textile industry, Parliament tried to ban them. *Global Interaction* How does this wall hanging reflect both Indian and European culture?

no threat in granting such concessions. The Portuguese and later the Dutch, English, and French built forts and warehouses in coastal towns. There they bought and shipped cargoes to Europe.

Turmoil and decline. When Akbar's successors ended his policy of religious toleration, conflicts rekindled between Hindu and Muslim princes. Civil war drained Mughal resources. Rulers then increased taxes, sparking peasant rebellions. An Indian historian at the time noted:

> **66** Tax collectors have become a scourge for the peasants. . . . Many townships that used to yield full revenue have, owing to the oppression of officials, been so far ruined and devastated that they have become forests infested by tigers and lions. **99**

Several weak rulers held the throne in the early 1700s. Corruption became widespread, and the central government collapsed.

British-French rivalry. As Mughal power faltered, French and English traders played off rival Indian princes against each other. The British and French East India companies made alliances with local officials and independent rajahs. Each company organized its own army of sepoys, or Indian troops. Well trained and disciplined, sepoy regiments helped keep order in areas ruled by the companies.

By the mid-1700s, the British and the French were locked in a global power struggle. In 1756, war between Britain and France erupted in Europe, and fighting soon spread to their lands overseas.

In India, Robert Clive, an agent of the British East India Company, used an army of British troops and sepoys to drive the French from their trading posts. The Company then forced the Mughal emperor to recognize its right to collect taxes in Bengal in the northeast. By the late 1700s, the Company had become the real ruler of Bengal. With its great wealth, the Company built forts and raised armies to spread its influence into other parts of India.

The Company often gained its ends, not only by military force, but by winning the backing of local Indian rulers. The activities of the British East India Company set the stage for the expanding British raj, or rule, to come.

SECTION 3 REVIEW

1. **Identify** (a) Afonso de Albuquerque, (b) Robert Clive.
2. **Define** (a) sepoy, (b) raj.
3. How did Portugal gain control of the spice trade?
4. How did the Dutch replace the Portuguese as the major European trading power in Asia?
5. (a) Why did Mughal power decline? (b) How did the decline help France and Britain?
6. *Critical Thinking* **Analyzing Information** How did European powers build on existing trade networks in the Indian Ocean?
7. *ACTIVITY* "Whoever is head of Malacca has his hand on the throat of Venice," noted Portuguese naval commander Afonso de Albuquerque. Draw a cartoon showing what he meant by this.

4 Encounters in East Asia

Guide for Reading

- How did shifts in power affect China and its relations with European powers?
- Why did Korea become the Hermit Kingdom?
- What policy did Tokugawa shoguns take toward foreigners?

The Europeans who reached Asia in the 1500s often made a poor impression on their hosts. The Italian traveler Niccoló Manucci told how Asians thought that Europeans "have no polite manners, that they are ignorant, wanting in ordered life, and very dirty."

Europeans, by contrast, wrote enthusiastically about China. In 1590, a visitor described Chinese artisans "cleverly making devices out of gold, silver and other metals." He was also impressed with their industries:

&6&6Their industry appears in the making of guns and gunpowder, whereof there are many rare fireworks. To these may be added the art of printing. Although their letters are many and most difficult . . . they daily publish huge multitudes of books.&9&9

Portuguese ships first reached China by way of the South China Sea during the Ming dynasty. To the Chinese, the Portuguese were "southern barbarians" who, like other foreigners, lacked the civilized ways of the Middle Kingdom.

European Trade With China

The Ming dynasty, you will recall, ended its overseas explorations in the mid-1400s. Confucian officials had little use for foreigners. "Since our empire owns the world," said a Ming document, "there is no country on this or other sides of the seas which does not submit to us."

Limits on foreign trade. Portuguese traders reached China by sea in 1514. To the Chinese, the newcomers had little to offer in exchange for silks and porcelains. European textiles, metalwork, and other goods were inferior to Chinese products. The Chinese therefore demanded payment in gold or silver.

The Ming eventually allowed the Portuguese a trading post at Macao, near Canton, present-day Guangzhou (gwahng JOH). Later, they let Dutch, English, and other Europeans trade with Chinese merchants but under strict limits. Foreigners could trade only at Canton under the supervision of imperial officials. When each year's trading season ended, they had to sail away. Europeans tried, without success, to break these restrictions.

Matteo Ricci. A few European scholars, like the brilliant Jesuit priest Matteo Ricci, did make a positive impression on Ming China. In the 1580s, Ricci learned to speak Chinese and adopted Chinese dress. His goal was to convert upper-class Chinese to Christianity. He hoped that they, in turn, would spread Christian teachings to the rest of China.

▲ Chinese fan showing foreign flags in Canton

Ricci won friends among the scholar-gentry by sharing his knowledge of the arts and sciences of Renaissance Europe. The Chinese were fascinated by new European technologies, including maps. They were also open to European discoveries in astronomy and mathematics. While Chinese rulers welcomed Ricci and other Jesuits for their learning, the priests had little success spreading their religious beliefs.

The Manchu Conquest

In the early 1600s, the aging Ming dynasty decayed. Revolts erupted, and Manchu invaders pushed through the Great Wall. The Manchus ruled a region in the northeast that had long been influenced by Chinese civilization. In 1644, victorious Manchu armies seized Beijing and made it their capital.

Qing rule. The Manchus set up a new dynasty called the Qing (CHIHNG), meaning "pure." To preserve their distinct identity, the Manchus barred intermarriage between Manchus and Chinese. Manchu women were forbidden to follow the traditional Chinese practice of footbinding. Still, the Manchus won the support of the Chinese scholar-gentry because they adopted the Confucian system of government. For each top government position, the Qing chose two people, one Manchu and one Chinese. Local government remained in the hands of the Chinese, but Manchu troops stationed across the empire ensured loyalty.

Two rulers oversaw the most brilliant age of the Qing. Kangxi (kahng SHEE), who ruled from 1661 to 1722, was an able administrator and military leader. He extended Chinese power into Central Asia and promoted Chinese culture. Kangxi's grandson Qianlong (chyehn LOHNG) had an equally successful reign from 1736 to 1796. He expanded the borders to rule the largest area in Chinese history. Qianlong retired after 60 years because he did not want to rule longer than his grandfather had.

Prosperity. The Chinese economy expanded under both emperors. New crops from the Americas, such as potatoes and corn, boosted farm output, which contributed to a population boom. China's population rose from 140 million in 1740 to over 300 million by 1800. Peace and prosperity contributed to further growth in handicraft industries, including silk, cotton, and porcelain. Internal trade grew, as did the demand for Chinese goods from all over the world.

Response to westerners. The Qing maintained the Ming policy of restricting foreign traders. Still, Europeans kept pressing to open up new cities to trade. In 1793, Lord Macartney arrived in China at the head of a British diplomatic mission. He brought samples of British-made goods to show the Chinese the advantages of trade with westerners. The Chinese thought the goods were gifts offered as tribute to the emperor and looked on them as rather crude products.

Further misunderstandings followed. The Chinese told Macartney he would have to perform the traditional kowtow, touching his head to the ground to show respect to the emperor. Macartney refused. He also offended the Chinese by speaking of the natural superiority of the English. The negotiations faltered. In the end, Qianlong did receive Macartney, but the meeting accomplished nothing. Later, in a letter to King George III of Britain, Qianlong rejected the request for trading rights. (★ See *Skills for Success*, page 390.)

At the time, Qianlong's attitude seemed justified by China's successes. After all, he already ruled the world's greatest empire. In the long run, however, his policy proved disastrous. Even then, there was much the Chinese could have learned from the West. In the 1800s, China would learn about western advances—especially in military technology—the hard way.

The Hermit Kingdom

Like China, Korea restricted outside contacts in the 1500s and 1600s. Earlier, Korean traders had far-ranging contacts across East Asia. A Korean map from the 1300s accurately outlines lands from Japan to the Mediterranean. Koreans probably acquired this knowledge from Arab traders who had visited Korea.

The Choson dynasty, you will recall, firmly embraced Confucian ethics and ideas. Like the Chinese, Koreans felt that Confucian learning was the most advanced in the world. The low status of merchants in Confucianism also led Koreans to look down on foreign traders.

Two other events led the Koreans to turn inward. The Japanese invasion in the 1590s devastated the land of Korea. Then in 1636, the Manchus conquered Korea before overrunning Ming China. When the Manchus set up the Qing dynasty in China, Korea became a tributary state, forced to acknowledge Chinese supremacy. The two invasions left Korea feeling like "a shrimp among whales."

In response, the Koreans chose isolation, excluding all foreigners except the Chinese and a few Japanese. When European sailors were shipwrecked on Korean shores, they were imprisoned. As a result, Korea became known as the Hermit Kingdom.

Even though Korea had few contacts with the world for about 250 years, this period was a great age for Korean arts and literature. In one satirical tale, "The Story of Ho," Pak Chi-won describes a poor scholar who breaks with tradition by becoming a merchant. Here, Master Ho describes doing business in an isolated country:

❝Our country has no trade with other countries, and . . . everything we use is produced and consumed in the same province. . . . With ten thousand yang, you can buy just about all of one particular item produced in the country. You can buy the whole lot, whether you load it on a cart or on a boat.❞

Tokugawa Shoguns and Foreign Traders

Unlike the Chinese or Koreans, the Japanese at first welcomed western traders. In 1543, the Portuguese reached Japan. Later came the Spanish, Dutch, and English. They arrived at the turbulent time when strong daimyo were struggling for power. The Japanese quickly acquired western firearms and built castles modeled on European designs. In fact, the new weapons may have helped the Tokugawa shoguns centralize power and impose order.

Spread of Christianity. Japan was much more open to European missionaries than China. Jesuits, like the Spanish priest Francis Xavier, found the Japanese curious and eager to learn about Christianity. A growing number of Japanese adopted the new faith. As a missionary reported, some Japanese "hang a crucifix from their shoulders or waist . . . some, who are especially kindly disposed, have memorized the *Our Father* and the *Hail Mary*, and recite them as they walk in the streets."

Closing the door. The Tokugawa shoguns, however, became increasingly hostile

GLOBAL CONNECTIONS

Qianlong was also disturbed by word of the French Revolution, which had begun in 1789. French revolutionaries spread ideas about liberty and equality and eventually toppled the monarchy. Even worse, the king of France was beheaded not long before Macartney's visit. This news confirmed Qianlong's desire to remain aloof from the West.

Japanese Screen Painting Shoguns and daimyos filled their castles with brilliant, multi-paneled screen paintings. Many screens depicted the beauties of nature. Others portrayed scenes of everyday life, including a popular series of "Southern Barbarian" screens. This screen depicts the activities of Japanese and Portuguese seafarers aboard a large ship. **Art and Literature** How did the artist create a sense of motion?

toward foreigners. After learning how Spain had seized the Philippines, they may have seen the newcomers as agents of an invading force. In addition, Japanese officials disliked the intrigues and competition among Christian missionaries. They also suspected that Japanese Christians—who may have numbered 300,000—owed their allegiance to a foreign power, the pope.

In response, the Tokugawas expelled foreign missionaries. They brutally persecuted Japanese Christians, killing many thousands. The few Christians who survived practiced their religion in secret for the next 200 years.

By 1638, the Tokugawas had barred all western merchants and forbidden Japanese to travel abroad. They outlawed the building of large ships, thereby ending foreign trade. To keep informed about world events, they permitted just one or two Dutch ships each year to trade at a small island in Nagasaki harbor. Through this tiny gateway, the Japanese did learn about some foreign ideas. They studied Dutch medical texts, for example, which they found to be more accurate than Chinese ones.

Looking ahead. Japan maintained its policy of strict isolation for more than 200 years. During this time, internal trade boomed. Cities grew in size and importance. By the late 1700s, Edo (present-day Tokyo) had a million inhabitants, more than either London or Paris.

In 1853, Japan was forced to reopen contacts with the western world. Renewed relations unleashed an extraordinary period of change that helped Japan emerge as a major world power.

SECTION 4 REVIEW

1. **Identify** (a) Matteo Ricci, (b) Manchus, (c) Kangxi, (d) Qianlong, (e) Hermit Kingdom.
2. (a) How was economic prosperity reflected in Qing China? (b) How did the Qing restrict foreign trade?
3. Why did Korea pursue a policy of isolation?
4. Why did the Tokugawa policy toward foreigners change over time?
5. *Critical Thinking* **Linking Past and Present** Why are some Americans today in favor of limiting ties to foreign countries?
6. *ACTIVITY* Write a dialogue between two officials in China, Korea, or Japan. One official should express a willingness to establish relations with European powers. The other should argue in favor of a policy of isolation.

CHAPTER REVIEW

REVIEWING VOCABULARY

Write sentences using *four* of the vocabulary words from this chapter, leaving blanks where the vocabulary words would go. Exchange your sentences with another student and fill in the blanks on each other's lists.

REVIEWING FACTS

1. What different motives led Europeans to explore the oceans?

2. What was the line of Demarcation?

3. Why was Magellan's voyage of 1519–1522 important?

4. What are the two major regions of Southeast Asia?

5. How did Christianity spread to the Philippines?

6. Which two European nations competed for influence in India?

7. What was the policy of the Ming and Qing dynasties toward foreigners?

8. What important policy did Japanese leaders follow between 1638 and 1853?

SKILLS FOR SUCCESS   RECOGNIZING BIAS

A critical reader of primary sources must be able to detect bias. **Bias** is a prejudice for or against someone or something.

As cultures came into closer contact during the first global age, both Europeans and Asians exhibited cultural biases. As you have read, many Asians viewed Europeans as dirty, ignorant, and rude. Many Europeans considered themselves more civilized than Asians.

The first reading below is from Qianlong's letter to King George III. (See page 388.) The second is from a later analysis of China by Lord Macartney. Read both excerpts and answer the following questions.

1. **Identify the source of the writing.** (a) What was Qianlong's cultural background? (b) What was Macartney's cultural background?

2. **Look for evidence of bias.** (a) What words does Qianlong use to describe England and the English? (b) What seems to be Macartney's general attitude toward China? How can you tell?

3. **Draw conclusions.** (a) What cultural attitudes influenced Qianlong's viewpoint? (b) How may Macartney's personal experiences have shaped his opinions?

Emperor Qianlong
❝You, O King, from afar have yearned after the blessings of our civilization, and in your eagerness to come into touch with our converting influence have sent an Embassy. . . .

Your Ambassador has put forward requests which completely fail to recognize the Throne's principle to 'treat strangers from afar with indulgence,' and to exercise a pacifying control over barbarian tribes the world over. . . . Nevertheless, I do not forget the lonely remoteness of your island, cut off from the world. . . . I have therefore commanded my minister to enlighten your Ambassador on the subject.❞

Lord Macartney
❝The empire of China is an old first-rate [warship], which a succession of vigilant officers has continued to keep afloat for these 150 years past, and have overawed their neighbors merely by her bulk and appearance. But whenever an insufficient man happens to have command on deck, [goodbye] to the discipline and safety of the ship. She may perhaps not sink outright. She may drift for a time as a wreck, and then be dashed to pieces on the shore. But she can never be rebuilt.❞

REVIEWING CHAPTER THEMES

Review the "Focus On" questions at the start of this chapter. Then select *three* of those questions and answer them, using information from the chapter.

CRITICAL THINKING

1. **Linking Past and Present** (a) Why were spices such valued trading goods in the 1400s? (b) What goods and resources play a similar role in the world economy today?

2. **Analyzing Information** How did European encounters with India, China, and Japan link economic, religious, and political activity? Give two examples.

3. **Identifying Alternatives** (a) Describe the policy the Tokugawa shoguns followed toward foreign merchants after 1638. (b) What other policies might they have followed instead?

ANALYZING PRIMARY SOURCES

Use the quotation on page 377 to answer the following questions.

1. What went on for three months and twenty days?

2. Why did the sailors not have access to fresh water?

3. What did the sailors do to the ox hides to make them edible?

FOR YOUR PORTFOLIO

WRITING A LETTER Write a letter of advice to European explorers, traders, missionaries, and officials on their way to Asia. Begin by choosing a European nation and a land in Asia to which people from that nation traveled. Use outside resources to learn about the region of Asia you have chosen. Then write a letter explaining to Europeans what they might encounter that would appear unfamiliar to them.

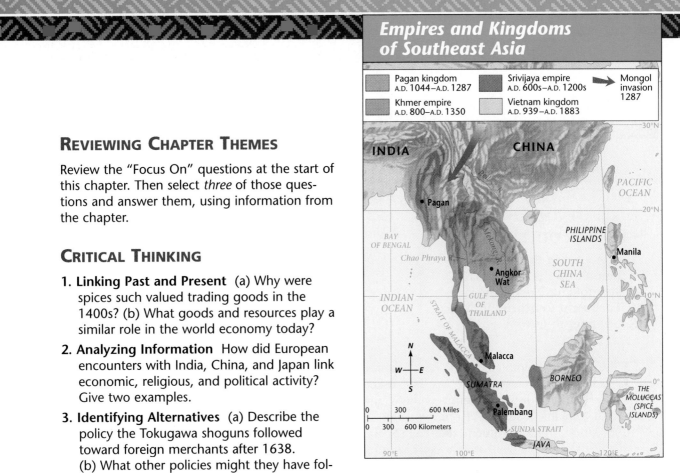

Empires and Kingdoms of Southeast Asia

| | Pagan kingdom A.D. 1044–A.D. 1287 | | Srivijaya empire A.D. 600s–A.D. 1200s | → | Mongol invasion 1287 |
| | Khmer empire A.D. 800–A.D. 1350 | | Vietnam kingdom A.D. 939–A.D. 1883 | | |

ANALYZING MAPS

Use the map to answer the following questions.

1. In which empire was Angkor Wat located?

2. What is the location of the Philippine Islands in relation to China?

3. Why did the location of the city of Malacca make the city important to Southeast Asian trade?

INTERNET ACTIVITY

WRITING NEWS REPORTS Use the Internet to research one of the European voyages that began the first global age. If possible, try to find a primary source from the voyage, such as the letters of Christopher Columbus. Then write a series of news reports that the voyager might have written if he had been able to send news flashes about his travels back to his home country.

16

The First Global Age: Europe, the Americas, and Africa

(1492–1750)

CHAPTER OUTLINE

1 Conquest in the Americas
2 Remaking the Americas
3 Struggle for North America
4 Turbulent Centuries in Africa
5 Changes in Europe

The Indians assembled on the beach, as the strangers from across the sea had asked them to do. They listened silently as the young Spanish captain read the *Requerimiento,* or "Requisition." This document, drafted in Spain, claimed the Indians' land for the Spanish king and queen, as earthly representatives of the Catholic Church. If the Indians accepted the authority of these rulers, the document stated, "all would be well." If they did not, punishment would be swift and severe:

> 66If you do not do this, . . . we shall take you and your wives and your children, and make slaves of them. . . . We shall take away your goods, and shall do you all the mischief and damage that we can, as to vassals who do not obey, and refuse to receive their lord.99

Scenes such as this were repeated across South America and the Caribbean in the early 1500s. A flood of Spanish explorers, settlers, and missionaries had followed Columbus to the Americas. Wherever they went, they claimed the land and its people for their king and Church. If native peoples resisted, the invaders imposed their will by force. As loyal Christians, they believed, it was not only their right but their *duty* to bring their civilization to the Indians.

The Spanish were the first Europeans to arrive in the Americas. Their early encounters with the native population set a pattern of interaction that would continue in the centuries to come. At the same time, Spanish explorations and colonization set in motion the modern global age. Not only did they bring into contact the peoples of Africa, Europe, and the Americas, but they began an exchange of plants, animals, institutions, values, and ideas that affects the world to this day.

FOCUS ON these questions as you read:

- **Economics and Technology**
  How did the winning of overseas empires affect the economy of Europe?

- **Global Interaction**
  What global exchanges occurred as a result of European expansion overseas?

- **Political and Social Systems**
  How were the governments of the Spanish, French, and English colonies similar? How were they different?

- **Diversity**
  How were different cultures around the world brought into contact during the 1500s and 1600s?

- **Religions and Value Systems**
  What role did Christian values and teachings play in the European colonization of the Americas?

TIME AND PLACE

A First Encounter This early encounter between the Spanish conqueror Hernan Cortés and the Aztecs of Mexico was friendly. Cortés, however, later conquered the Aztecs and seized their empire. Encounters among the peoples of Europe, Africa, and the Americas sometimes resulted in peaceful exchanges but other times led to turbulence and conflict. **Art and Literature** How did the artist suggest Cortés's violent intentions?

HUMANITIES LINK
Art History Gold ritual ornament (page 395).
Literature In this chapter, you will encounter a passage from the following works of literature: Aztec poet, "And all this happened to us" (page 395); Carlos de Sigüenza y Góngora, *The Misadventures of Alonso Ramírez* (pages 416–417).

1492	1500s	1607	1670s	1759
Columbus lands in Americas; Columbian exchange begins	Atlantic slave trade begins	English found Jamestown	Osei Tutu organizes Asante kingdom	British defeat French at Quebec

| 1500 | 1550 | 1600 | 1650 | 1700 | 1750 |

1 Conquest in the Americas

Guide for Reading

- Why did Spanish explorers travel to the Americas?

- Why were the Spanish able to conquer the Aztec and Incan empires?

- What were the results of the first encounters between the Spanish and Native Americans?

- **Vocabulary** *conquistador*

The Spanish soldiers who reached the Aztec capital of Tenochtitlán in 1519 were astonished by its size and splendor. From the emperor's palace, one soldier wrote, "we had a clear view of the three causeways by which Mexico communicated with the land, and of the aqueduct . . . which supplied the city with the finest water." They also saw the majestic temples "of the nearby cities, built in the form of towers and fortresses, . . . and others . . . all whitewashed, and wonderfully brilliant."

Within a few years, the Spanish had captured and destroyed the Aztec capital. In its place, they built a new city that became the heart of the Spanish empire in the Americas.

First Encounters

In 1492, Christopher Columbus landed in the islands that are now called the West Indies, in the Caribbean. There, he encountered the Taíno people. The Taínos lived in villages and grew corn, yams, and cotton, which they wove into cloth. They were friendly and generous toward the Spanish. Columbus reported that "they invite you to share anything they possess, and show as much love as if their hearts went with it." He further noted "how easy it would be to convert these people [to Christianity]— and to make them work for us."

Friendly relations soon evaporated. Streams of Spanish conquistadors (kahn KEES tuh dohrz), or conquerors, followed in the wake of Columbus. They settled on the islands of Hispaniola (now the Dominican Republic and Haiti), Cuba, and Puerto Rico. They seized the gold ornaments worn by the Taínos, then enslaved them to make them pan for more gold. At the same time, the newcomers forced the Taínos to convert to Christianity. Those who resisted were treated cruelly.

Meanwhile, a deadly but invisible invader was at work—disease. Europeans unknowingly carried diseases such as smallpox, measles, and influenza to which Native Americans had no immunity. These diseases spread rapidly and wiped out village after village. As a result, the Native American population of the Caribbean islands declined by as much as 90 percent in the 1500s. This cycle of disease and death was repeated in many other places across the Western Hemisphere.

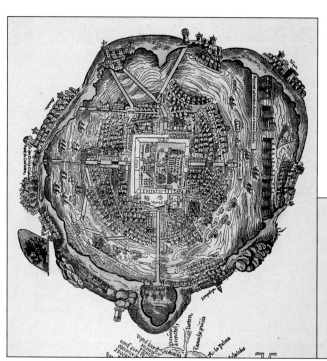

Tenochtitlán Shortly after his arrival in Mexico, Cortés sent this map of Tenochtitlán, the Aztec capital, to the Spanish king. As the map shows, the city was built on an island in the middle of a lake and connected to the mainland by broad wooden causeways, or bridges. Four major roads divided the city into quarters and led to a central plaza dominated by massive temples to the Aztec gods. **Economics and Technology** How do you think the causeways served as a defense against invaders?

The Conquistadors

From Cuba, Spanish explorers probed the coasts of the Americas. They spread stories of empires rich in gold. Attracted by the promise of riches as well as by religious zeal, a flood of adventurers soon followed. Bernal Diaz del Castillo, a Spanish soldier, later noted:

❝[The conquistadors acted] in the service of God and his Majesty, and to give light to those who sat in darkness, and also to acquire that wealth that most men covet.❞

Cortés in Mexico. Among the earliest conquistadors was Hernan Cortés. Cortés landed on the coast of Mexico in 1519 with about 600 men, 16 horses, and a few cannons. As he headed inland toward Tenochtitlán, he was helped by Malinche (mah LIHN chay), a young Indian woman who served as his translator and adviser. The Spanish called her Doña Marina. Malinche knew both the Mayan and Aztec languages, and she learned Spanish quickly.

From Malinche, Cortés learned that many conquered peoples hated their Aztec overlords. The Aztecs, you will recall, sacrificed thousands of captives to their gods each year. Malinche helped Cortés arrange alliances with these discontented groups.

Moctezuma's dilemma. Meanwhile, in Tenochtitlán, messengers brought word about the newcomers to the Aztec emperor Moctezuma. The Aztec ruler hesitated. Was it possible that the leader of the pale-skinned, bearded strangers was Quetzalcoatl, the god-king who had long ago vowed to return from the east? To be safe, Moctezuma sent gifts of gold, silver, and precious stones. At the same time, he urged the strangers not to continue to Tenochtitlán.

Cortés had no intention of turning back. Fighting and negotiating by turns, he and his men advanced steadily inland toward the capital. At last, they arrived in Tenochtitlán, where they were dazzled by the grandeur of the city and by the gold in its temples.

Fall of Tenochtitlán. Moctezuma welcomed Cortés to his capital. However, relations between the Aztecs and Spaniards soon grew strained, and the Aztecs drove the Spanish from the city. Moctezuma was killed in the fighting.

Gold Ritual Ornament *Like Native American artists throughout Central and South America, Mexican artists crafted elaborate works of gold. Their creations were rich in religious symbolism, representing gods and incorporating sacred objects and animals, such as jaguars, serpents, eagles, and suns. The golden ornament shown here probably portrays the god of the dead.* **Economics and Technology** *How do you think the fine quality of the gold work produced in Central and South America reinforced Europeans' desire to conquer the area?*

Cortés and his allies retreated to plan an assault. In 1521, in a brutal struggle, Cortés and his Indian allies captured and demolished Tenochtitlán. An unknown Aztec lamented:

❝And all this happened to us
   We saw it,
   We are amazed
   With this lamentable and sad fortune,
   We see ourselves anguished.
   Broken spears lie in the road;
   We have torn our hair with grief.
   The houses are roofless now, and their
      walls are red with blood.❞

On the ruins of Tenochtitlán, the Spanish later built Mexico City. From this new capital, Spanish forces marched out to conquer an empire across Mexico and Central America.

Pizarro in Peru. Cortés's success inspired other adventurers. Among them was Francisco Pizarro. He arrived in Peru in 1532, just after the Incan ruler Atahualpa (ah tah WAHL pah) won the throne from his brother in a bloody civil war. (See Chapter 7.)

Helped by Indian allies, Pizarro captured Atahualpa after slaughtering thousands of his followers. The Spanish demanded a huge ransom in return for the ruler's freedom. Although the Incas paid the ransom, the Spanish killed Atahualpa anyway.

Despite continuing resistance, the invaders overran the Incan heartland. From Peru, Spanish forces surged across lands once ruled by the Incas in Ecuador and Chile. Before long, Spain added much of South America to its growing empire.

▲ *Francisco Pizarro*

Reasons for Victory

Why did the mighty Aztecs and Incas fall so rapidly? How was it possible for a few hundred European soldiers to overrun huge Native American empires with populations in the millions? Several reasons explain the amazing successes of the Spanish.

1. Superior military technology was a key factor. The Spaniards' horses frightened some Indians, who had never seen animals like these. Spanish muskets and cannons—weapons of "fire and thunder"—terrorized Indian soldiers, while metal helmets and armor protected the Spanish from the Indians' arrows and spears.

2. Division and discontent among the Indians aided the Spanish. The Aztecs and Incas had defeated many rival groups to forge their empires. The Spanish played on old hatreds to make allies. In fact, Indian warriors provided Cortés and Pizarro with much of their fighting power.

3. Disease brought by the Europeans weakened the Aztecs and Incas. As tens of thousands of Indians died, the bewildered and demoralized survivors felt that their gods had deserted them. The Spanish seemed almost immune to the same diseases, which supported the idea that the gods of the conquerors were more powerful.

4. Many Indians believed that the disasters they suffered marked the end of the world. To the Aztecs, the destruction of Tenochtitlán signaled the end of the reign of the sun god. (See page 158.) "Let us die, then," the Aztecs lamented, "for our gods are already dead."

Ongoing resistance. As the pattern of disease and conquest was repeated across the Americas, Native Americans continued to resist the invaders. For years, Mayas in the Yucatan re-

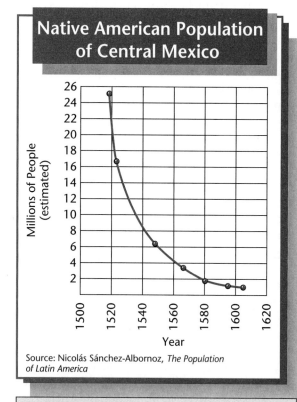

Native American Population of Central Mexico

Source: Nicolás Sánchez-Albornoz, *The Population of Latin America*

Interpreting a Chart Disease and conquest combined to drastically reduce the Native American population. This graph shows what happened to central Mexico's Native Americans after the arrival of the Spanish in 1519. ■ *How many Native Americans lived in central Mexico in 1519? How many lived there in 1605?*

gion of Central America fought Spanish rule. Long after the death of Atahualpa, revolts erupted among the Incas.

Resistance did not always take the form of military action. Throughout the Americas, Indians resisted Europeans by preserving aspects of their own culture—language, religious traditions, foods, clothing, and skills such as weaving and pottery.

Looking Ahead

Spanish conquests in the Americas would bring changes to peoples and cultures around the world. An immediate result was the flow of treasure from the Americas to Spain. The Spanish melted down gold and silver statues and ornaments taken from the Aztecs and Incas. When they depleted these sources, they forced Native Americans to mine silver from rich lodes in Peru and Mexico.

In the 1500s and early 1600s, treasure fleets sailed each year to Spain or the Spanish Philippines loaded with gold and silver. As you will read, this flood of wealth created both benefits and problems for the economy of Europe.

SECTION 1 REVIEW

1. **Identify** (a) Taínos, (b) Hernan Cortés, (c) Malinche, (d) Moctezuma, (e) Francisco Pizarro, (f) Atahualpa.
2. **Define** conquistador.
3. Describe the motives of the Spanish conquistadors.
4. (a) How did divisions within the Aztec and Incan empires help the Spanish? (b) What other reasons explain the rapid conquest of the Spanish invasion?
5. What were the effects of the Spanish conquest of the Americas?
6. *Critical Thinking* **Comparing** Compare the Spanish conquest of the Americas with the Reconquista or the Crusades. (a) How were they similar? (b) How were they different?
7. *ACTIVITY* Write a song about Cortés's arrival in Mexico from either the Aztec or Spanish point of view.

2 Remaking the Americas

Guide for Reading

- How did Spain govern its American empire?
- Why did the Spanish bring enslaved Africans to the Americas?
- What new social structure emerged in Spanish America?
- How did cultural blending reshape the Americas after 1492?
- **Vocabulary** *viceroy, plantation, encomienda, peon, peninsular, creole, mestizo, mulatto*

In order to build an American empire, the Spanish set out to impose their culture, language, religion, and way of life on millions of subjects. It was simple to erect new Spanish-style cities on top of the ruins of conquered Indian capitals. "Christianizing" Native Americans, on the other hand, turned out to be a little more complex. From the first, Christian Europeans had much to learn from the peoples that they conquered. In the end, a new culture emerged that reflected both European and Native American traditions.

Ruling the Spanish Empire

In the 1500s, Spain claimed a vast empire stretching from California to South America. In time, it divided these lands into five provinces. The most important were New Spain (Mexico) and Peru.

Spain was determined to maintain strict control over its empire. To achieve this goal, the king set up the Council of the Indies to pass laws for the colonies. He also appointed viceroys, or representatives who ruled in his name, in each province. Lesser officials and *audiencias,* or advisory councils of Spanish settlers, helped the viceroy rule. The Council of the Indies in Spain closely monitored these colonial officials to make sure they did not overstep their bounds.

The Catholic Church. To Spain, winning souls for Christianity was as important as gaining land. The Catholic Church played a key role in the colonies, working hand in hand with the government. Church leaders often served as royal officials and helped to regulate the activities of Spanish settlers. As Spain's American empire expanded, Church authority expanded along with it.

Franciscan, Jesuit, and other missionaries baptized thousands of Native Americans. In frontier regions, they built mission churches and worked to turn new converts into loyal subjects of the Catholic king of Spain. They emphasized the superiority of European culture over Native American traditions. They also introduced western clothing, the Spanish language, and new crafts such as carpentry and locksmithing.

Economy. To make the empire profitable, Spain closely controlled its economic activities, especially trade. Colonists could export raw materials only to Spain and could buy only Spanish manufactured goods. Laws forbade colonists from trading with other European nations or even with other Spanish colonies. The most valuable resources shipped from Spanish America were silver and gold.

A Mission Church Priests set up missions throughout New Spain. They encouraged Native Americans to live in the missions, where they could learn the Christian faith. Nearby forts protected the missions as well as neighboring mines and ranches. **Political and Social Systems** Why do you think Spanish missions needed military protection?

Sugar cane was introduced into the West Indies and elsewhere and quickly became a profitable resource. The cane was refined into sugar, molasses, and rum. Sugar cane, however, had to be grown on plantations, large estates run by an owner or the owner's overseer. Finding the large numbers of workers needed to make the plantations profitable was a major problem.

At first, Spanish monarchs granted the conquistadors encomiendas, the right to demand labor or tribute from Native Americans in a particular area. The conquistadors used this system to enslave Native Americans under the most brutal conditions. Those who resisted were hunted down and killed. Disease, starvation, and cruel treatment caused catastrophic declines in the population.

Bartolomé de las Casas. A few bold priests, like Bartolomé de las Casas, condemned the evils of the encomienda system. In vivid reports to Spain, Las Casas detailed the horrors that Spanish rule had brought to Native Americans and pleaded with the king to end the abuse.

Prodded by Las Casas, Spain passed the New Laws of the Indies in 1542 forbidding enslavement of Native Americans. The laws were meant to end abuses against Native Americans, but Spain was too far away to enforce them. Many Native Americans were forced to become peons, workers forced to labor for a landlord in order to pay off a debt. Landlords advanced them food, tools, or seeds, creating debts that workers could never pay off in their lifetime.

Workers from Africa. To fill the labor shortage, Las Casas urged colonists to import workers from Africa. Africans were immune to tropical diseases, he said, and had useful skills in farming, mining, and metalworking. Las Casas later regretted that advice because it furthered the brutal African slave trade. Colonists had begun bringing Africans to the Americas as early as 1502.

As demand for sugar products skyrocketed, the settlers imported millions of Africans. The newcomers were forced to work as field hands, miners, or servants in the houses of wealthy landowners. Others became peddlers, skilled artisans, artists, and mechanics.

In time, Africans and their American-born descendants greatly outnumbered European settlers in the West Indies and parts of South America. Often, they resisted slavery by rebelling or running away. In the cities, some enslaved Africans earned enough money to buy their freedom.

Social Classes

In Spanish America, the unique mix of peoples gave rise to a new social structure. At the top of colonial society were peninsulares, people born in Spain. (The term *peninsular* referred to the Iberian Peninsula, on which Spain is located.) Peninsulares filled the highest positions in both colonial governments and the Catholic Church. Next came creoles, American-born descendents of Spanish settlers. Creoles owned most of the plantations, ranches, and mines.

Other social groups reflected the mixing of populations. They included mestizos, people of Native American and European descent, and mulattoes, people of African and European descent. At the bottom of society, Native Americans and people of African descent formed the lowest social classes.

Colonial Culture

Over the centuries, the Spanish colonies developed a unique culture. It combined European, Native American, and African traditions.

Cities. Spanish settlers preferred to live in towns and cities. Mexico City grew so quickly that by 1550 it was the largest Spanish-speaking city in the world.

Colonial cities were centers of government, commerce, and European culture. Around the central plaza, or square, stood government buildings and a Spanish-style church. Broad avenues and public monuments symbolized European power and wealth. Cities were also centers of intellectual and cultural life. Architecture and painting as well as poetry and the exchange of ideas flourished.

Education. To meet the Church's need for educated priests, the colonies built universities. The University of Mexico was established as early as 1551. A dozen Spanish American universities were busy educating young men long before Harvard, the first university in the 13 English colonies, was founded in 1636.

A New Society The social structure of Spain's American empire reflected its unique blend of people. This portrait depicts a Spanish man, his Mexican wife, and their young daughter, a mestizo. **Diversity** What were the social classes of New Spain?

Women wishing an education might enter a convent. One such woman was Sor Juana Inés de la Cruz. Refused admission to the University of Mexico because she was a girl, Juana entered a convent at the age of 16. There, she devoted herself to study and the writing of poetry. She earned a reputation as one of the greatest lyric poets ever to write in the Spanish language.

Cultural blending. Although Spanish culture was dominant in the cities, the blending of diverse traditions changed peoples' lives throughout the Americas. Settlers learned Native American styles of building, ate foods native to the Americas, and traveled in Indian-style canoes. Indian artistic styles influenced the newcomers. At the same time, settlers taught their religion to Native Americans. They also introduced animals, especially the horse, that transformed the lives of many Native Americans.

Africans contributed to this cultural mix with their farming methods, cooking styles, and crops, including okra and palm oil. African drama, dance, and song heightened Christian worship services. In Cuba, Haiti, and elsewhere, Africans forged new religions that blended African and Christian beliefs.

The Portuguese in Brazil

A large area of South America remained outside the Spanish empire. By the Treaty of Tordesillas in 1494, Portugal claimed Brazil. (See the map on page 402.) Portugal issued grants of land to Portuguese nobles, who agreed to develop them and share profits with the crown. Landowners sent settlers to build towns, plantations, and churches.

Unlike Spain's American lands, Brazil offered no instant wealth from silver or gold. Early settlers clung to the coast, where they cut and exported brazilwood, used to produce a precious dye. Before long, they turned to plantation agriculture and cattle raising. They forced Indians and Africans to clear land for sugar plantations. As many as five million Africans were sent to Brazil.

The thickly forested Amazon basin remained largely unexplored by settlers. However, ruthless adventurers slowly pushed inland. They attacked and enslaved Native American peoples and claimed for themselves land for immense cattle ranches. Some even discovered gold.

As in Spanish America, a new culture emerged in Brazil that blended European, Native American, and African patterns. European culture dominated the upper and middle classes, but Native American and African influences left their mark. Portuguese settlers, for example, eagerly adopted Indian hammocks. A settler expressed his enthusiasm:

66Would you believe that a man could sleep suspended in a net in the air like a bunch of hanging grapes? Here it is a common thing . . . I tried it and will never again be able to sleep in a bed, so comfortable is the rest one gets in the net.99

Challenging Spanish Power

In the 1500s, the wealth of the Americas helped make Spain the most powerful country in Europe. As you have read, Spain controlled all trade with its American colonies. That policy annoyed other Europeans. Many English and Dutch agreed with the French king Francis I, who declared that "I should like to see Adam's will, wherein he divided the Earth between Spain and Portugal." Smugglers soon did a flourishing business with Spanish colonists.

Spanish treasure fleets also offered a tempting target to Dutch, English, and French pirates. Their ships nested among the Caribbean islands ready to pounce on Spanish galleons. Some pirates, called privateers, operated with the approval of European governments. England's Queen Elizabeth, for example, knighted Francis Drake for his daring raids on Spanish treasure ships. (📖 See *World Literature*, "The Misadventures of Alonso Ramírez," page 416.)

Like the Spanish, the Dutch, English, and French hunted for rich gold empires in the Americas and for a northwest passage around North America to Asia. In doing so, they explored the coasts and planted settlements in North America. (See Chapter 15.)

SECTION 2 REVIEW

1. **Identify** (a) Council of the Indies, (b) Bartolomé de las Casas, (c) New Laws of the Indies, (d) Sor Juana Inés de la Cruz.
2. **Define** (a) viceroy, (b) plantation, (c) encomienda, (d) peon, (e) peninsular, (f) creole, (g) mestizo, (h) mulatto.
3. (a) Describe how Spain controlled its American empire. (b) What role did the Catholic Church play in the empire?
4. (a) Why did Las Casas urge Spanish settlers to import workers from Africa? (b) What labor did enslaved Africans perform in the colonies?
5. How did the mix of peoples in Spanish America result in a new social structure?
6. Give three examples of cultural blending in Spain's American empire.
7. *Critical Thinking* **Making Decisions** The Spanish tried to fill their need for labor by enslaving first Native Americans and then Africans. How would you have solved the problem of a dependable labor supply without the use of slavery?
8. *ACTIVITY* Review what you have read about Spanish treatment of Native Americans, on page 398. Then, design a poster to rouse public opinion in Spain to protect the Indians.

3 Struggle for North America

Guide for Reading

■ What problems did settlers in New France face?

■ What traditions of government evolved in the English colonies?

■ How did the Treaty of Paris of 1763 affect North America?

■ How did Native American traditions influence European colonists?

In the 1500s and 1600s, other European powers moved into the Americas and began building settlements. France, the Netherlands, England, and Sweden joined Spain in claiming parts of North America.

At first, the Europeans were disappointed. North America did not yield gold treasure or offer a water passage to Asia, as they had hoped. Before long, though, the English and French were turning large profits by growing tobacco in Virginia, fishing off the North Atlantic coast, and trading fur from New England to Canada.

By 1700, France and England controlled large parts of North America. As their colonies grew, they developed their own governments, different from each other and from that of Spanish America.

Building New France

By the early 1500s, French fishing ships were crossing the Atlantic each year to harvest rich catches of cod off Newfoundland, Canada. Distracted by wars at home, though, French rulers at first paid little attention to Canada—New France, as they called it. Only in 1608 did Samuel de Champlain build the first permanent French settlement in Quebec. Jesuits and other

Settlers in New France *This illustrated map depicts French settlers arriving in New France. Does the map seem confusing? Try turning it upside down. You should now recognize eastern North America, from the Florida peninsula in the south to Canada in the north.* **Geography and History** *Why do you think the French mapmaker drew this map "upside down"?*

Land Claims in the Americas About 1700

HUDSON BAY

Pelts

NEWFOUNDLAND

NEW FRANCE

Whale meat, fish

NOVA SCOTIA

ENGLISH COLONIES

ATLANTIC OCEAN

LOUISIANA

Mississippi

Tobacco, grain

FLORIDA

BAHAMAS (Eng.)

GULF OF MEXICO

WEST INDIES

Sugar, tobacco

Silver

MEXICO

CARIBBEAN SEA

PACIFIC OCEAN

Gold

Silver

Tobacco, cacao, hides

GUIANA

Amazon R.

BRAZIL

Sugar, tobacco, cotton

PERU

Copper, grain

Gold, diamonds

CHILE

Meat

Silver, hides

STRAIT OF MAGELLAN

Land claims about 1700

- Dutch
- English
- French
- Portuguese
- Spanish
- → Main exports

0   750   1500 Miles
0   750   1500 Kilometers

N
W — E
S

GEOGRAPHY AND HISTORY

By the 1700s, European nations had claimed vast stretches of land in both North and South America. They used their American colonies as a steady source of raw materials for making manufactured goods.

1. **Location** On the map, locate (a) New France, (b) Louisiana, (c) Mexico, (d) Peru, (e) Brazil, (f) Chile.
2. **Movement** (a) Which raw materials were exported from the West Indies? (b) From Mexico?
3. **Critical Thinking** Synthesizing Information Based on the map and what you have read, to which European country did Brazil probably send its raw materials? Explain.

missionaries soon followed. They advanced into the wilderness, converting Native Americans to Christianity.

Slow growth. Helped by Native American allies, French fur traders traveled inland, claiming vast territory. France's American empire reached from Quebec to the Great Lakes and down the Mississippi to Louisiana and the Gulf of Mexico. (See the map at left.)

The population of New France grew slowly. Wealthy landlords owned huge tracts along the St. Lawrence River. They sought settlers to farm the land, but the harsh Canadian climate attracted few French peasants.

Many who went to New France soon abandoned farming in favor of fur trapping and trading. They faced a hard life in the wilderness, but the soaring European demand for fur ensured good prices. Fur traders and trappers learned survival and trapping skills from Native Americans. Many married Native American women. Fishing, too, supported settlers who lived in coastal villages and exported cod and other fish to Europe.

Government policy. In the late 1600s, the French king Louis XIV set out to strengthen royal power and boost tax revenues from his overseas empire. He appointed officials to oversee justice and economic activities in New France. He also sent more settlers and soldiers to North America. He even paid for unmarried women to travel to New France, where they might find husbands and help build new communities. The Catholic Louis, however, prohibited Protestants from settling in New France.

By the early 1700s, French forts, missions, and trading posts stretched from Quebec to Louisiana. Yet the population of New France remained small compared to that of the 13 English colonies expanding along the Atlantic coast.

The 13 English Colonies

The English built their first permanent colony at Jamestown, Virginia, in 1607. Its early years were filled with disaster. Many settlers died of starvation and disease. The rest survived with the help of friendly Native Americans. The colony finally made headway when the settlers started to grow and export tobacco, a crop they learned about from the Indians.

In 1620, other English settlers, the Pilgrims,* landed at Plymouth, Massachusetts. They were seeking religious freedom, rather than commercial profit. Before coming ashore, they signed the Mayflower Compact, in which they set out guidelines for governing their North American colony. It read:

> 66We, whose names are underwritten . . . having undertaken for the Glory of God, and Advancement of the Christian Faith . . . a voyage to plant [a] colony in the [Americas] . . . do enact, constitute, and frame, such just and equal Laws . . . as shall be thought most [fitting] and convenient for the general Good of the Colony.99

Today, we see this document as an important early step toward self-government.

Many Pilgrims died in the early years. Local Indians, however, taught them to grow corn and helped them survive in the new land. Soon, a new wave of Puritan immigrants arrived to establish the Massachusetts Bay Colony.

Growth. In the 1600s and 1700s, other groups and individuals founded colonies. Some, like Virginia, were commercial ventures, organized for profit. Others, like Massachusetts, Pennsylvania, and Maryland, were set up as havens for persecuted religious groups.

Geographic conditions helped shape different ways of life in the New England, middle, and southern colonies. In New England, many settlers were farmers who transferred to North America the village life they had enjoyed in England. In parts of the South, a plantation economy emerged.

Like New Spain, the English colonies needed workers to clear land and raise crops. A growing number of Africans were brought to the colonies and sold as slaves. In several mainland colonies, enslaved Africans and their descendants outnumbered Europeans.

---

*Pilgrims were a band of English Puritans, a Protestant group, who rejected the practices of the official Church of England. (See page 359.)

Government. Like the rulers of Spain and France, English monarchs asserted control over their American colonies. They appointed royal governors to oversee colonial affairs and had Parliament pass laws to regulate colonial trade. Yet compared to settlers in the Spanish and French colonies, English colonists enjoyed a large degree of self-government. Each colony had its own representative assembly elected by propertied men. The assemblies advised the royal governor and made decisions on local issues.

The tradition of consulting representative assemblies grew out of the English experience. (See page 212.) Beginning in the 1200s, Parliament had played an increasingly important role in English affairs. Slowly, too, English citizens had gained certain legal and political rights. England's American colonists expected to enjoy the same rights. When colonists later protested British policies in North America, they saw themselves as "freeborn Englishmen" defending their traditional rights.

Caught Up in Global Power Struggles

By the 1600s, Spain, France, England, and the Netherlands were competing for trade and colonies around the world. All four nations had colonies in North America, where they often fought for territory. After several naval wars with the Netherlands, the English seized the Dutch colony of New Netherland in 1664 and renamed it New York. English settlers in Georgia clashed with the Spanish in nearby Florida.

Competition was also fierce in the Caribbean region. The Dutch brought sugar production to the Caribbean from Brazil and made it a big business. The French acquired Haiti, the richest of the sugar colonies, as well as Guadeloupe and Martinique. The English took Barbados and Jamaica. In the late 1600s, the French and English Caribbean islands, worked

ISSUES For TODAY

Compared to the Spanish and French colonies, the 13 English colonies enjoyed a large degree of self-government. How are people's lives affected by the form of government under which they live?

by enslaved Africans, surpassed Brazil as the world's largest exporter of sugar. Shortly after, these little islands had surpassed the whole of North America in exports to Europe.

British-French rivalry. By the 1700s, Britain and France had emerged as bitter rivals for power around the globe. Their clashes in Europe often ignited conflicts in the Caribbean, North America, and India. The struggle came to a head when the Seven Years' War erupted in Europe in 1756. The war soon spread to India and North America. In the English colonies, it was called the French and Indian War.

Although France held more territory in North America, the British colonies had more people. Trappers, traders, and farmers from the English colonies were pushing west into the Ohio Valley, a region claimed by France. The French, who had forged alliances with the Indians, fought to oust the intruders.

During the war, a combined force of British soldiers and colonial troops launched a series of campaigns against the French in Canada and on the Ohio frontier. In 1759, the British captured

Quebec and then Montreal. Though the war dragged on until 1763, the British had won control of Canada.

The peace treaty. By the Treaty of Paris that ended the war, France ceded Canada and its lands east of the Mississippi River to Britain. As you have read, the British also forced the French out of India. The French, however, regained the rich sugar-producing islands in the Caribbean and the slave-trading outposts in Africa that the British had seized during the war.

The peace treaty ensured British dominance in North America. Yet thousands of French settlers remained in Canada and Louisiana. French culture continues to shape both areas to the present day.

Impact on Native Americans

As in Spanish America, the arrival of European settlers in North America had a profound impact on Native Americans. Some Native Americans traded or formed alliances with the newcomers. In the West, as we will see, the arrival of the horse transformed the lifestyle of buffalo-hunting Indians.

Frequently, however, clashes erupted. As settlers claimed more land, Native Americans resisted their advance. Bitter fighting resulted. In the end, superior weapons helped the English to victory. Year by year, the flood of new settlers pushed the frontier—and the Indians—slowly westward.

Disease. As elsewhere, the Native American population of North America plummeted. Disease weakened or killed large numbers. In 1608, an estimated 30,000 Algonquians lived in Virginia. By 1670, only 2,000 remained.

In New England, diseases brought by European fishing fleets wiped out entire Indian villages even before the European settlers arrived. A Pilgrim noted that Indians "had been melted down by . . . disease, whereof nine-tenths of them have died."

Legacy. While encounters with Europeans often brought disaster to Native American societies, the Indian way of life helped shape the emerging new culture of North America. Settlers adopted Native American technologies. From Indians, they learned to grow corn, beans, squash, and tomatoes and to hunt and trap forest animals. Today's Thanksgiving menu of turkey and pumpkin pie reflects Indian foods.

On the frontier, some colonists adopted Indian clothing. "It is not uncommon to see a Frenchman wearing Indian moccasins and leggings," observed a visitor to New France. At the same time, though, he might also sport "a fine ruffled shirt and a laced waistcoat."

Trails blazed by Indians became highways for settlers moving west. Across the continent, rivers like the Mississippi and mountains like the Appalachians bear Indian names. Some Europeans came to respect Native American medical knowledge. Today, many people are taking a new look at Indian religious traditions that stress respect for the natural environment.

SECTION 3 REVIEW

1. **Identify** (a) Samuel de Champlain, (b) Louis XIV, (c) Jamestown, (d) Pilgrims, (e) Mayflower Compact, (f) French and Indian War, (g) Treaty of Paris.
2. (a) Why did New France have a hard time attracting settlers? (b) What economic activities were profitable in New France?
3. What motives brought English settlers to North America?
4. (a) What European countries competed for power in North America? (b) How did Britain come to dominate the continent?
5. Describe three ways in which Native Americans influenced the emerging new culture of North America.
6. *Critical Thinking* **Synthesizing Information** Compare New France and the 13 English colonies in terms of (a) population, (b) size, and (c) government.
7. *ACTIVITY* Create a brochure to attract settlers to New France.

4 Turbulent Centuries in Africa

Guide for Reading

- What were the results of early encounters between Europeans and Africans?
- How did the Atlantic slave trade affect Africa?
- What kingdoms emerged in West Africa in the early modern age?
- What groups battled for power in southern Africa?

The first encounters between Europeans and Africans took place in the 1400s. By then, as you have read, diverse societies had emerged in Africa, and Islam, spread by Muslim traders, had become an important force on the continent. Europeans brought new influences to Africa. At the same time, the contact caused people and products from Africa to become part of the international exchanges that marked this first global age.

European Outposts in Africa

In the 1400s, Portuguese ships explored the coast of West Africa, looking for a sea route to India. They built a string of small forts along the West African coast to trade for gold, collect food and water, and repair their ships. African rulers set the terms of trade.

The Portuguese lacked the power or resources to push into the African interior. They did, however, attack the coastal cities of East Africa, such as Mombasa and Malindi, which were hubs of international trade. (See Chapter 12.) With muskets and cannons blazing, they expelled the Arabs who controlled the East African trade and took over this commerce for themselves.

The Portuguese, however, gained little profit from their victories. Trade between the interior and the coast soon dwindled. By 1600, the once prosperous East African coastal cities had sunk into poverty.

West African Carving
West African artists produced many fine carvings. This ivory salt cellar depicts Portuguese soldiers of the 1500s.
Art and Literature
Whom do you think the artist created the salt cellar for? Explain.

Other Europeans soon followed the Portuguese into Africa. The Dutch, the English, and the French established forts along the western coast of Africa. Like the Portuguese, they exchanged muskets, tools, and cloth for gold, ivory, hides, and slaves.

The Atlantic Slave Trade

In the 1500s, Europeans began to view slaves as the most important item of African trade. Slavery had existed in Africa, as elsewhere around the world, since ancient times. Egyptians, Greeks, Romans, Persians, Indians, and Aztecs often enslaved defeated foes. Our word *slave* comes from the large number of Slavs, taken from southern Russia, to work as unpaid laborers in Roman times.

The Arab empire also used slave labor, often captives taken from Africa. In the Middle East, many enslaved Africans worked on farming estates or large-scale irrigation projects. Others became artisans, soldiers, or merchants. Some rose to prominence in the Muslim world even though they were officially slaves.

European slave traders in Africa. The Atlantic slave trade began in the 1500s, to fill the need for labor in Spain's American empire. In the next 300 years, it grew into a huge and profitable business. Each year, traders shipped tens of thousands of enslaved Africans across the Atlantic to work on tobacco and sugar plantations in the Americas.

Europeans seldom took part in slave raids. Instead, they relied on African traders to bring captives from the interior to coastal trading posts. There, the captives were exchanged for textiles, metalwork, rum, tobacco, weapons, and gunpowder.

Horrors of the Middle Passage. Once purchased, Africans were packed below the decks of slave ships. For enslaved Africans, the Middle Passage,* as Europeans called the voyage, was a horror. Hundreds of men, women, and children were crammed into a single vessel. Slave ships became "floating coffins" on which up to half the Africans on board died from disease or brutal mistreatment. Sometimes, enslaved Africans committed suicide by leaping overboard. Others tried to seize control of the ship and return to Africa.

African Leaders Resist

Some African leaders tried to slow down the transatlantic slave trade or even to stop it altogether. They used different forms of resistance. But in the end, the system that supported the trade was simply too strong for them to resist. The efforts of two of these leaders are recounted below.

King Affonso speaks out. An early voice raised against the slave trade was that of Affonso I, ruler of Kongo in west-central Africa. Affonso had been born Nzinga Mbemba (uhn ZIHN gah uhm BEHM bah). As a young man, he was tutored by Portuguese missionaries, who baptized him in 1491 with the Christian name Affonso.

Impressed by his early contacts with the Portuguese, Affonso dreamed of building a modern Christian state in Kongo. After becoming king in 1505, he called on Portuguese missionaries, teachers, and technical experts to help

---

*The Middle Passage was part of a three-legged trade network that sent raw materials from the Americas to Europe, slaves from Africa to the Americas, and manufactured goods from Europe to Africa.

him develop Kongo. He sent his sons to Portugal to be educated in Christian ways.

Soon, however, Affonso grew worried. Each year, more and more Portuguese arrived in Kongo to buy slaves. They offered such high prices that government officials and local chiefs were eager to become involved in the business. Even Christian missionaries began to buy and sell Africans. In 1526, Affonso wrote in dismay to the king of Portugal:

66Merchants are taking every day our natives, sons of the land and sons of our nobles and vassals and our relatives, because the thieves and men of bad conscience . . . grab them and get them to be sold. . . . Our country is being completely depopulated.99

Affonso insisted that "it is our will that in these Kingdoms there should not be any trade of slaves nor outlet for them." Kongo, he stated, could benefit from contacts with Europe, but the trade in human lives was evil. His appeal failed, and the slave trade continued.

The almamy passes a law. In the late 1700s, another African ruler, the almamy of Futa Toro in northern Senegal, tried to halt the slave trade in his lands. Unfortunately, he enjoyed no more success than Affonso had 200 years earlier.

Since the 1500s, French sea captains had bought slaves from traders in Futa Toro. The almamy decided to put a stop to this practice. In 1788, he passed a law forbidding anyone to transport slaves through Futa Toro for sale abroad.

The sea captains were furious. They protested to the almamy and requested him to repeal the law. The almamy refused. He returned the presents the captains had sent him in hopes of winning him over to their cause. "All the riches in the world would not make me change my mind," he said.

The almamy's victory was short-lived, however. The inland slave traders simply worked out another route for bringing their captives to the coast. Weighing anchor, the French captains sailed to this new market. There, they supplied

A Profitable Business From walled compounds in this thriving West African town, Portuguese, French, English, and Dutch traders competed for shares in the highly profitable slave trade. African merchants who supplied them with slaves made large profits, too. King Affonso I of Kongo could not end the slave trade because he could not end African and European greed. **Global Interaction** Why did the Atlantic slave trade become important?

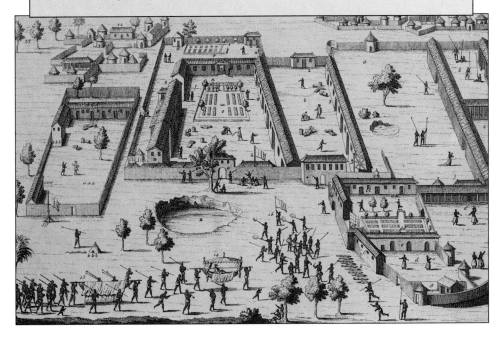

African Slave Trade

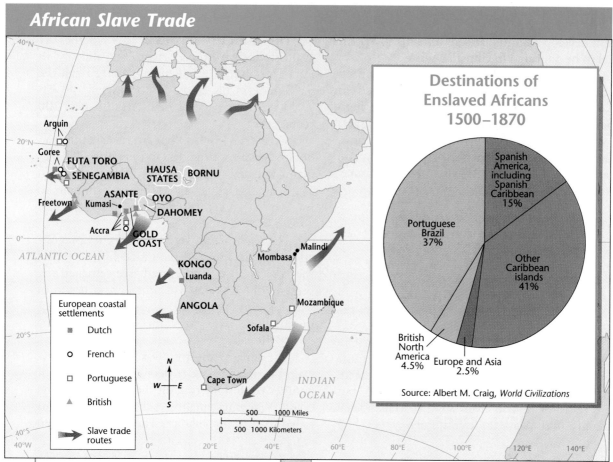

Destinations of Enslaved Africans 1500–1870

- Portuguese Brazil 37%
- Spanish America, including Spanish Caribbean 15%
- Other Caribbean islands 41%
- British North America 4.5%
- Europe and Asia 2.5%

Source: Albert M. Craig, *World Civilizations*

European coastal settlements

- ■ Dutch
- ○ French
- □ Portuguese
- ▲ British
- ⟶ Slave trade routes

GEOGRAPHY AND HISTORY

From bases along the coasts of Africa, European ships carried millions of enslaved Africans to be sold in markets in Europe, Asia, and the Americas.

1. **Location** On the map, locate (a) Accra, (b) Futa Toro, (c) Kongo, (d) Bornu, (e) Malindi.
2. **Place** (a) Name one trading settlement set up by the French. (b) Name one settlement set up by the British.
3. **Critical Thinking** **Analyzing Information** Many slaves who were first shipped to the Caribbean were later sold to slaveholders in British North America. How might this fact affect your analysis of the information on the circle graph about the proportion of slaves in British North America?

themselves with the slaves that the almamy had prevented them from buying in Senegal. There was no way the almamy could stop them. ■

Impact of the Atlantic Slave Trade

Historians are still debating the number of Africans who were affected by the Atlantic slave trade. In the 1500s, they estimate, about 2,000 enslaved Africans were sent to the Americas each year. In the 1780s, when the slave trade was at its peak, that number topped 80,000 a year. By the 1800s, when the overseas slave trade was finally stopped, an estimated 11 million enslaved Africans had reached the Americas. Another two million probably died under the brutal conditions of the voyage between Africa and the Americas.

The slave trade had other results, too. One of the most important was the loss of countless numbers of young women and men from West Africa. The region as a whole recovered from this population drain. But with their youth captured, some societies and small states disappeared forever. At the same time, there was a rise of new African states whose way of life depended on the slave trade.

Rise of New States

Among the large states that rose in West Africa in the 1600s and 1700s were Oyo, Bornu, and Dahomey. Another state, the Asante kingdom, emerged in the area occupied by modern Ghana.

The Asante kingdom. In the late 1600s, an able military leader, Osei Tutu, won control of the trading city of Kumasi. From there, he conquered neighboring peoples and organized the Asante kingdom. Osei Tutu claimed to rule by divine right. Leading chiefs served as a council of advisers but were subject to the royal will.

Officials chosen by merit rather than birth supervised an efficient bureaucracy. They managed the royal monopolies over gold mining and the slave trade. The Asante traded with Europeans on the coast, exchanging gold and slaves for firearms. But they shrewdly played off rival Europeans against each other to protect their own interests.

Islamic crusades. In the 1700s and early 1800s, an Islamic revival spread across West Africa. It began among the Fulani people in northern Nigeria.

The Fulani scholar and preacher Usman dan Fodio denounced the corruption of the local Hausa rulers, who were Muslim in name only. He called for social and religious reforms based on the Sharia, or Islamic law. In the early 1800s, Usman inspired Fulani herders and Hausa townspeople to rise up against their rulers.

Usman and his successors set up a powerful Islamic state. Under their rule, literacy increased, local wars quieted, and trade improved. Their success inspired other Muslim reform movements in West Africa. Between about 1780 and 1880, more than a dozen Islamic leaders rose to power, replacing old rulers or founding new states in the western Sudan.

Conflicts in Southern Africa

Over many centuries, you will recall, Bantu-speaking peoples had migrated into southern Africa. (See Chapter 12.) In 1652, Dutch immigrants also arrived in the region. They built Cape Town to supply ships sailing to or from the East Indies. Dutch farmers, called Boers, settled around Cape Town. Over time, they ousted or enslaved the Khoisan herders who lived there. The Boers held to a Calvinist belief that they were the elect of God and looked on Africans as inferiors.

In the 1700s, Dutch herders and ivory hunters began to push north. As they did, they battled powerful African groups like the Zulus.

Shaka. The Zulus had migrated into southern Africa in the 1500s. In the early 1800s, they emerged as a major force under a ruthless and brilliant leader, Shaka. He built on the successes of earlier leaders who had begun to organize young fighters into permanent regiments.

Between 1818 and 1828, Shaka waged relentless war and conquered many nearby peoples.

Asante Power The Asantes traded gold and slaves for European guns. With the help of these weapons, they built a large and powerful kingdom. Here, an Asante warrior stands guard before the royal armory in the palace. **Economics and Technology** How do you think the Asantes would respond to movements to end the slave trade? Explain.

He absorbed their young men and women into Zulu regiments. By encouraging rival groups to forget their differences, he cemented a growing pride in the Zulu kingdom.

Shaka's wars disrupted life across southern Africa. Groups driven from their homelands by the Zulus adopted Shaka's tactics. They then migrated north, conquering still other peoples and creating their own powerful states.

Later Shaka's half-brother took over the Zulu kingdom. About this time, the Zulus faced a new threat, the arrival of well-armed, mounted Boers migrating north from the Cape Colony.

Boers versus Zulus. In 1815, the Cape Colony passed from the Dutch to the British. Many Boers resented British laws that abolished slavery and otherwise interfered in their way of life. To escape British rule, they loaded their goods into covered wagons and started north. In the late 1830s, several thousand Boer families joined this "Great Trek."

As they traveled northward, the Boers came into contact with the Zulus. Fighting quickly broke out. At first, Zulu regiments held their own. But in the end, Zulu spears could not hold back Boers armed with guns. The struggle for control of the land would rage until the end of the century, as you will read in Chapter 25.

SECTION 4 REVIEW

1. **Identify** (a) Middle Passage, (b) Asante, (c) Usman dan Fodio, (d) Boer, (e) Shaka.
2. Describe the early contacts between Europeans and Africans in the 1500s.
3. (a) Why did the Atlantic slave trade prosper? (b) What effects did it have on Africa?
4. What steps did the Asante ruler take to ensure his power?
5. How did southern Africa become a battleground for various groups?
6. *Critical Thinking* **Solving Problems** (a) What kinds of information would historians need to determine the number of Africans involved in the slave trade? (b) Why might they have trouble finding this information?
7. *ACTIVITY* Write five questions that could be used to review the content of this section. Then, write answers to the questions.

5 Changes in Europe

Guide for Reading

- How did European explorations lead to a global exchange?
- What economic changes occurred in Europe in the 1500s and 1600s?
- What social changes took place in Europe during the 1500s and 1600s?
- **Vocabulary** *inflation, capitalism, entrepreneur, joint stock company, mercantilism, tariff*

In 1570, Joseph de Acosta visited the Americas. He wrote in amazement about the many strange forms of life that he saw there:

66[There are] a thousand different kinds of birds and beasts of the forest, which have never been known, neither in shape nor name; and whereof there is no mention made, neither among the Latins nor Greeks, nor any other nations of the world.99

To Europeans like Acosta, the Americas were so different that they believed they were a "new world." Acosta, a clergyman, even wondered if God had created the Americas at a different time from the rest of the globe.

European explorations between 1500 and 1700 brought major changes to the world. You have already seen how the arrival of Europeans affected peoples in Asia, Africa, and the Americas. Here, we will look at the impact that these explorations had on Europe itself.

A Global Exchange

When Columbus returned to Spain in March 1493, he brought with him "new" plants and animals that he had found in the Americas. He also brought back a group of Taínos, people from the West Indies. Later that year, Columbus returned to the Americas. With him were some 1,200 settlers and a collection of European animals and plants, including horses, cows, pigs, wheat, barley, and sugar cane. In this way, Columbus began a vast global exchange that would have a profound effect on the world. In addition to people, plants, and animals, it included technology and even disease. Because this global exchange began with Columbus, we call it the Columbian exchange.

New foods. From the Americas, Europeans brought home a long list of foods. Tomatoes, sweet potatoes, pumpkins, squash, beans, manioc (a root vegetable), pineapples, and peppers enriched the diet of Europeans. Tobacco and chocolate also made the voyage east to Europe. Perhaps the most important foods from the Americas, however, were corn and the potato. Easy to grow, the potato helped feed Europe's rapidly growing population. Corn spread all across Europe and to Africa and Asia, as well.

▲ *Pumpkin and pineapple: foods from the Americas*

At the same time, Europeans carried a wide variety of plants and animals to the Americas. Foods included wheat, melons, and grapes from Europe itself, and bananas, coconut palms, coffee, and sugar cane from Africa and Asia. Cattle, pigs, goats, and chickens, unknown before the European encounter, added protein to the Native American diet. Horses and donkeys introduced by the Europeans also changed the lives of Native Americans. The horse, for example, gave the nomadic peoples of western North America a new, more effective way to hunt buffalo.

Impact on population. The transfer of food crops from continent to continent took time. By the 1700s, however, corn, potatoes, manioc, beans, and tomatoes were contributing to population growth around the world, from Europe to West Africa to China. While other factors help account for the population explosion that began at this time, new food crops from the Americas were probably a key cause.

Migration of people and ideas. The Columbian exchange sparked the migration of millions of people. Each year, shiploads of European settlers sailed to the Americas. Europeans also settled on the fringes of Africa and Asia. As you have read, the Atlantic slave trade forcibly brought millions of Africans to the Americas. The Native American population, as we have seen, declined drastically in the early years of the western invasion.

The vast movement of peoples led to the transfer of ideas and technologies. Europeans and Africans brought to the Americas their beliefs and customs. In Europe and elsewhere, people adapted customs and inventions from distant lands. Language also traveled. Words such as *pajama* (from India) or *hammock* and *canoe* (from the Americas) entered European languages as evidence of the exchange.

A Commercial Revolution

The opening of direct links with Asia, Africa, and the Americas had far-reaching consequences for Europeans. Their conquest of empires in the Americas and increased trade with Asia contributed to dramatic economic changes. Among them were an upsurge in prices, known as the price revolution, and the rise of modern capitalism.

The price revolution. In the early modern age, prices began to rise in parts of Europe.

GLOBAL CONNECTIONS

In Ireland, the potato had a profound effect on the way people lived. The potato was introduced into Ireland from the Americas in the 1580s. The new crop was easy to grow and highly nutritious. Before long, Irish peasants depended on it as their main source of food. Then, in 1845, disaster struck. In a single month, a blight wiped out the entire potato crop. More than a million Irish died of starvation and disease in the famine that followed. And in a strange twist of history, tens of thousands of starving Irish left their homeland to seek a new life in the Americas—from where the potato had first come.

CAUSE AND EFFECT

Long-Term Causes

Scientific Revolution
Europeans search for a sea route to Asia

Immediate Causes

Columbus and other Europeans arrive in the Americas
Europeans bring new plants, animals, and diseases to the Americas
Europeans encounter new plants and animals in the Americas

COLUMBIAN EXCHANGE

Immediate Effects

Spanish defeat Aztec and Incan empires
Millions of Native Americans die from "European" diseases
Enslaved Africans are sent to the Americas
American foods, including corn and potatoes, are introduced into Europe

Long-Term Effects

Spread of items such as horses, corn, potatoes, and sugar around the world
Population growth in Europe, Africa, and Asia
Exchange of ideas, technology, arts, and language between Europe and the Americas
Population migration from Europe to the Americas
Growth of capitalism

Connections Today

A multicultural society in the United States
Worldwide reliance on staples such as corn and potatoes

Interpreting a Chart The arrival of Columbus in the Americas set off a global exchange of people, goods, and ideas that has continued to this day. ■ *Based on the chart, name one immediate and one long-term effect of the Columbian exchange. What effects of the Columbian exchange can you see in your life?*

The economic cycle that involves a rise in prices linked to a sharp increase in the amount of money available is today called inflation.

One cause of European inflation was the increase in population. As the population grew, the demand for goods and services rose. Because goods were scarce, sellers could raise their prices.

Inflation was also fueled by an increased flow of silver and gold. By the mid-1500s, tons of these precious metals were flowing into Europe from the Americas. Rulers used much of the silver and gold to make coins. The increased money in circulation, combined with the scarcity of goods, caused prices to rise.

Growth of capitalism. Expanded trade and the push for overseas empires spurred the growth of European capitalism, the investment of money to make a profit. Entrepreneurs, or enterprising merchants, organized, managed, and assumed the risks of doing business. They hired workers and paid for raw materials, transport, and other costs of production.

As trade increased, entrepreneurs sought to expand into overseas ventures. Such ventures were risky. Capitalist investors were more willing to take the risks when demand and prices were high. Thus, the price revolution of the early modern age gave a boost to capitalism.

Entrepreneurs and capitalists made up a new business class devoted to the goal of making profits. Together, they helped change the local European economy into an international trading system.

New business methods. Early capitalists discovered new ways to create wealth. From the Arabs, they adapted methods of bookkeeping to show profits and losses from their ventures. During the late Middle Ages, as you have read, banks sprang up, allowing wealthy merchants to lend money at interest. Capitalists also developed insurance to reduce the risk of financial disaster in dangerous ventures.

The joint stock company, also developed in late medieval times, grew in importance. It allowed people to pool large amounts of capital needed for overseas ventures. As you have read, East India companies were founded in England, France, and the Netherlands in the early 1600s. With government approval, these companies invested in trading ventures around the world.

Making a Profit

In a capitalist market system, almost anything can be traded. If demand is great, prices rise dramatically and traders earn amazing profits. When demand falls, however, traders can be completely wiped out. The trick is knowing when to buy and when to sell.

Linking Past and Present   How would supply and demand affect price?

PAST   *For Europeans of the 1600s, the tulip was a luxury item. In the Netherlands, the enormous demand for tulips attracted numerous profit-seeking investors and led to a buying frenzy that became known as tulipomania. At first, tulip prices skyrocketed. But a bust soon followed. Prices—and the dreams of many investors—crashed.*

PRESENT

Today, many young people collect baseball cards. For those who are lucky, an initial purchase price of a few dollars may result in a handsome profit in the future.

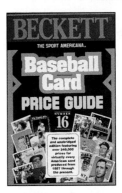

Bypassing the guilds. The growing demand for goods led merchants to find ways to increase production. Traditionally, guilds controlled the manufacture of goods. But guild masters often ran small-scale businesses without the capital to produce for large markets. They also had strict rules regulating quality, prices, and working conditions.

Enterprising capitalists devised a way to bypass the guilds. The putting out system, as it was called, was first used to produce textiles but later spread to other industries. Under the putting out system, a merchant capitalist distributed raw wool to peasant cottages. Cottagers spun the wool into thread and then wove the thread into cloth. Merchants bought the wool cloth from the peasants and sent it to the city for finishing and dyeing. Finally, the merchants sold the finished product for a profit.

The putting out system separated capital and labor for the first time. From this system controlled by merchants, the next step would be the capitalist-owned factories of the Industrial Revolution. (See Chapter 20.)

A New Economic Policy

European monarchs enjoyed the benefits of the commercial revolution. In the fierce competition for trade and empire, they adopted a new policy, known as mercantilism, aimed at strengthening their national economies.

Foreign trade. Mercantilists supported several basic ideas. They believed that a nation's real wealth was measured in its gold and silver treasure. To build its supply of gold and silver, they said, a nation must export more goods than it imported. Thomas Mun, an eager spokesman for mercantilism, endorsed this idea:

66 The ordinary means . . . to increase our wealth and treasure is by foreign trade, wherein we must ever observe this rule: to sell more to strangers [foreigners] yearly than we consume of theirs in value. 99

The role of colonies. Overseas empires were central to the mercantile system. Colonies, said mercantilists, existed for the benefit of the parent country. They should provide resources and raw materials not available in Europe. In turn, they should enrich a parent country by serving as a market for its manufactured goods.

To achieve these goals, European powers passed strict laws regulating trade with their colonies. Colonists could not set up industries to manufacture goods or buy goods from a foreign country. Also, only ships from the parent country or the colonies themselves could be used to send goods in or out of the colonies.

Increasing national wealth. Mercantilists urged rulers to adopt other policies to increase government revenues. To boost production, governments cleared wasteland, exploited mineral and timber resources, drained swamps, built roads and canals, and backed new industries. They imposed a single national currency and established standard weights and measures.

Governments also sold monopolies, or the right to operate without competition, to large producers in certain industries as well as to big overseas trading companies. Finally, governments imposed tariffs, or taxes on imported goods, to protect local industries from foreign competition.

The Lives of Ordinary People

How did these economic changes affect the average European? In general, their impact depended on a person's social class. The price revolution, for example, hurt nobles. Their wealth was in land, and they had trouble raising money to pay higher costs for stylish clothing, fancy foods, and other luxuries. Some had to sell off land, which in turn reduced their income. Merchants, however, who invested in overseas ventures acquired wealth. Yet in towns and cities the wages of hired workers did not keep up with inflation, creating poverty and discontent.

Peasants. Most Europeans were still peasants. Europe's growing involvement in the world had little immediate effect on their lives. Changes took generations, even centuries, to be felt.

Like their medieval ancestors, peasants in the 1500s and 1600s struggled through harvests, survived wars, and did their best to enjoy whatever leisure time they had. Tradition-bound peasants were often reluctant to grow foods brought from the Americas. Only in the late 1700s did German peasants begin to raise potatoes. Even then, many complained that these strange-looking tubers tasted terrible.

Growing cities. Within Europe's growing cities, there were great differences in wealth and power. Successful merchants dominated city life. Guilds, too, remained powerful. And as trade grew, another group—lawyers—gained importance for their skills in writing contracts.

Middle-class families enjoyed a comfortable life. They lived in fine homes and dressed in fine clothing. Servants cooked, cleaned, and waited on them. Other city residents, such as journeymen and other laborers, were not so lucky, often living in crowded quarters on the edge of poverty.

Family. Noble households, which had once numbered in the hundreds and included immediate and distant relatives as well as unrelated members of the court, grew smaller. Among other classes, the nuclear family made up of parents and children had long been the usual family unit.

Among middle-class families, parents took great care to plan for their children's education, careers, and marriages. They arranged marriages with an eye to financial and social advantages.

Women. European families were patriarchal, with the husband and father responsible for the behavior of his wife and children. A woman's chief roles were as wife and mother. Society stressed such womanly virtues as modesty, household economy, obedience, and caring for her family.

Sharing the Work In this Dutch painting from the 1600s, men, women, and children work together spinning and weaving wool. Most women learned to weave at home, and their work skills were highly valued in a weaver's shop. **Economics and Technology** How does this painting convey a sense of economic prosperity?

Middle-class women might help their husbands in a family business, although guilds increasingly pushed women out of many trades. Peasant women worked alongside their husbands in the fields. In towns, young girls and married women alike worked as servants.

Women had almost no property or legal rights. Very slowly after the 1600s, that situation changed. A few women from well-to-do families acquired an education. In England, several women became playwrights. Katherine Boyle, sister of the English chemist Robert Boyle, took an active role in the "new science" of the period.

Looking Ahead

In the 1500s and 1600s, Europe emerged as a powerful new force on the world scene. The voyages of exploration marked the beginning of what would become European domination of the globe. In the centuries ahead, competition for empire would spark wars in Europe and on other continents.

European expansion would spread goods and other changes throughout the world. It would also revolutionize the European economy and transform its society. The concept of "the West" itself emerged as European settlers transplanted their culture to the Americas and, later, to Australia and New Zealand.

For centuries, most Europeans knew little or nothing about the other parts of the globe. Exposure to different cultures was both unsettling and stimulating. As their horizons broadened, they had to reexamine old beliefs and customs. Educated Europeans studied the geography, histories, and cultures of other worlds, which they in turn used to create a new world of ideas.

SECTION 5 REVIEW

1. **Identify** (a) Columbian exchange, (b) putting out system.
2. **Define** (a) inflation, (b) capitalism, (c) entrepreneur, (d) joint stock company, (e) mercantilism, (f) tariff.
3. How did the voyages of Columbus lead to global exchanges of goods and ideas?
4. Explain how each of the following contributed to economic changes in Europe in the 1500s and 1600s: (a) the price revolution, (b) capitalism, (c) mercantilism.
5. Choose one social group. Explain how the lives of that group changed during the 1500s and 1600s.
6. *Critical Thinking* **Applying Information** "The treasure which is brought into the realm by the balance of our foreign trade is that money which only does abide with us, and by which we are enriched." How does this statement reflect mercantilist thinking?
7. *ACTIVITY* Create an illustrated map of the world showing the movement of items in the Columbian exchange.

World Literature
The Misadventures of Alonso Ramírez
Carlos de Sigüenza y Góngora

Introduction *One of the most noted scholars of colonial Mexico was Carlos de Sigüenza y Góngora (see GWEHN sah EE GOHN goh rah), a Jesuit priest, poet, and scientist. In 1690, he published* The Misadventures of Alonso Ramírez, *one of the first and finest seagoing adventure stories of the new global age.*

There was a real sailor named Alonso Ramírez. He told his life story to Sigüenza y Góngora, who turned it into an exciting narrative filled with pirates, exotic places, and daring exploits. The action moves from South America to Southeast Asia and India to the Caribbean. Here, Ramírez describes being kidnapped by a band of English pirates.

Before setting sail they put my 25 men on board the flagship. It was commanded by an Englishman called Master Bel. It had 80 men, 24 pieces of artillery, and 8 stone mortars all bronze. Captain Donkin was master of the second ship, and he had 70 men, 20 pieces of artillery, and 8 stone mortars. In both there were a great many shotguns, cutlasses, axes, grenades, and pots full of various foul-smelling ingredients besides grappling irons. . . .

Turning the ships toward Caponiz with mine in tow, they began with pistols and cutlasses in hand to examine me again and even to torture me. . . .

They put me and [a] companion in the hold, where we could hear above much shouting and the report of a blunderbuss. I noticed the blood on the deck after they let us out, and showing it to me they said it was that of one of my men who had died and that the same thing would happen to me if I did not respond properly to questioning. I told them humbly that they could do what they wanted with me because I had nothing to add to what I had already said.

Careful then to find out which of my companions had died, I checked and found the number the same as before, which puzzled me. I found out much later that what I had seen was the blood of a dog and that the whole episode had been feigned.

Not satisfied with what I had said, they began asking questions again in a solicitous manner of my Indian boatswain . . . and they discovered from him that there was a village and prison on the island of Caponiz. . . .

They anchored off land from a direction where they expected no trouble from the islanders. . . . Arming their canoes with sufficient men they made for land and found the inhabitants friendly. They told the islanders they only wished a safe harbor for the ships so as to add provisions and fruit, which they lacked.

Either through fear or for other motives which I did not learn about, the poor islanders agreed to this. They received clothes which had been stolen in return for pitch, fat, salted turtle meat, and other items. . . .

[*After a four-month stay, the pirates decide to leave the island.*]

Consulting over the price they should give the islanders for their hospitality, they settled it the same day they set sail by attacking at dawn those who were sleeping without precautions, and putting everyone to the knife. . . . Setting fire to the village and then hoisting colors, they boarded their ships with great rejoicing. . . .

[*The pirates sail to the port of Cicudana on the island of Borneo.*]

The pirates set to work in their canoes to sound the river bar, not only to see if larger ships might enter but to plan an attack. They were interrupted in this by a coastal sampan in which were representatives of the authorities of the place, who had come to reconnoiter. The pirates answered that they were from the

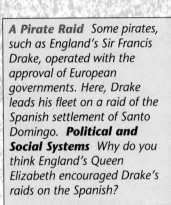

A Pirate Raid Some pirates, such as England's Sir Francis Drake, operated with the approval of European governments. Here, Drake leads his fleet on a raid of the Spanish settlement of Santo Domingo. **Political and Social Systems** Why do you think England's Queen Elizabeth encouraged Drake's raids on the Spanish?

English nation and were loaded with noble and exquisite goods to be exchanged for diamonds.

As they had received friendly treatment from this nation and saw rich samples from the ships captured [earlier], they granted a license to trade. They gave a generous gift to the governor and received permission to go up river to the town, a fourth of a league from the sea, whenever they wished.

During the three days we were there, our captors found the place to be undefended and open on all sides. Telling the Cicudanes that they could not stay for long and that they should collect their diamonds in the governor's house, where there would be a fair, they left us on board under guard and went up river at midnight well armed. They attacked the village by surprise, advancing first on the governor's house. There they sacked the building for the diamonds and other precious stones gathered there and then proceeded to do the same with other houses, which they put to the torch together with some boats they found there.

On board we could hear the clamor of the village and the shots; the mortality, as they bragged later, was considerable. This detestable treachery being carried out without injury to themselves, they brought the governor as a prisoner together with other leaders on board

with great speed, and raising the anchor they sped away. Never has there been pillage to compare to this in the high price received for so little effort. Who can say what it was worth? I saw Captain Bel with the crown of his hat heaped full of diamonds.

Source: Carlos de Sigüenza y Góngora, *The Misadventures of Alonso Ramírez,* translated by Edwin H. Pleasants (New York: The Borzoi Anthology of Latin American Literature, Volume 1, 1977).

Thinking About Literature

1. **Vocabulary** Use the dictionary to find the meanings of the following words: blunderbuss, feign, solicitous, sampan, reconnoiter, sack, mortality, pillage.
2. (a) What words does the narrator use to describe the English pirates? (b) Describe one example he gives to show their treachery.
3. How does this selection illustrate global interaction? Give three examples.
4. *Critical Thinking* **Linking Past and Present** Today, people continue to be fascinated by stories of pirates. (a) How is Sigüenza y Góngora's picture of pirates similar to that found in popular literature, movies, or television programs today? (b) Do you think this is an accurate picture of pirates? Explain.

CHAPTER REVIEW

REVIEWING VOCABULARY

Review the vocabulary words in this chapter. Then, use *ten* of these words to create a cross-word puzzle. Exchange puzzles with a class-mate. Complete the puzzles and then check each other's answers.

REVIEWING FACTS

1. How did the conquistadors treat the Native Americans they encountered?

2. What four reasons explain why the Spanish defeated the Aztecs and Incas?

3. Why were Africans brought to Spanish colonies in the Americas?

4. What parts of North America were colonized by France?

5. What part of North America was colonized by England?

6. Define the Atlantic slave trade.

7. What was the Columbian exchange?

SKILLS FOR SUCCESS USING A COMPUTERIZED CARD CATALOG

Computerized card catalogs use a system of menus and prompts to help you locate information. The screens below are examples. Follow the directions to research the slave trade.

1. **Start your search.** Look at Screen 1 below. What would you type to find information about the slave trade?

2. **Narrow your search.** Study Screen 2. How many books does the library have on the slave trade in West Africa?

3. **Select the books that relate to your topic.** Study Screen 3. Imagine you are writing a report about personal experiences of enslaved Africans. Which title would you select?

4. **Locate the books you need.** Study Screen 4. What is the call number of the book you selected?

Screen 1

```
You may search the catalog by one of
the following:

        A = Author
        T = Title
        S = Subject

Enter your search below:

>> S = slave trade
```

Screen 2

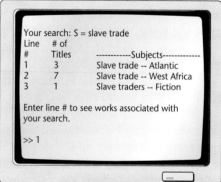

```
Your search: S = slave trade
Line    # of
#       Titles       ------------Subjects------------
1       3            Slave trade -- Atlantic
2       7            Slave trade -- West Africa
3       1            Slave traders -- Fiction

Enter line # to see works associated with
your search.

>> 1
```

Screen 3

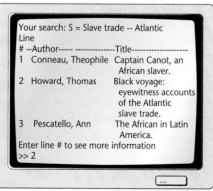

```
Your search: S = Slave trade -- Atlantic
Line
# --Author----- -------------Title-------------------
1  Conneau, Theophile  Captain Canot, an
                        African slaver.
2  Howard, Thomas      Black voyage:
                        eyewitness accounts
                        of the Atlantic
                        slave trade.
3  Pescatello, Ann     The African in Latin
                        America.
Enter line # to see more information
>> 2
```

Screen 4

```
                    (Record 2 of 3)
AUTHOR:     Howard, Thomas

TITLE:          Black voyage: eyewitness
                accounts of the Atlantic
                slave trade.

PUBLISHER:  Little, Brown (1971)

Call Number: 380.1 H     Status: Checked in

>>                     Enter ? for HELP
```

REVIEWING CHAPTER THEMES

Review the "Focus On" questions at the start of this chapter. Then select *three* of those questions and answer them, using information from the chapter.

CRITICAL THINKING

1. **Linking Past and Present** How might your life be different if France had defeated England in the Seven Years' War?

2. **Recognizing Points of View** How might each of the following people have viewed European explorations in the 1500s and 1600s: (a) a Spaniard, (b) a Native American, (c) an African?

3. **Recognizing Causes and Effects** (a) What were three causes of the expansion of the Atlantic slave trade? (b) What were three immediate effects of the slave trade on Africa? (c) What do you think might have been some long-term effects of the slave trade on Africa's later development? Explain.

ANALYZING PRIMARY SOURCES

Use the quotation on page 403 to answer the following questions.

1. What was the goal of the voyage?

2. What two motives were given for the voyage?

3. What do you think the writers meant by describing their laws as "just and equal"?

FOR YOUR PORTFOLIO

CREATING A BOARD GAME Work with a team of classmates to create an educational board game on European activities in the Americas and Africa during the first global age. Review the chapter to make a list of facts you will use in your game. Use outside sources to find additional material. Then write and design your game. You may want to assign some people to work on the board configuration, while others make the pieces, write any necessary cards, and develop the rules. Finally, play your game to see if it works. Make adjustments as necessary.

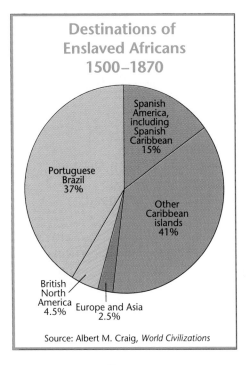

Destinations of Enslaved Africans 1500–1870

Spanish America, including Spanish Caribbean 15%

Portuguese Brazil 37%

Other Caribbean islands 41%

British North America 4.5%

Europe and Asia 2.5%

Source: Albert M. Craig, *World Civilizations*

ANALYZING GRAPHS

Use the graph to answer the following questions.

1. What percentage of enslaved Africans were *not* taken to the Americas?

2. To what single destination were the largest percentage of enslaved Africans taken?

3. What evidence of British participation in the Atlantic slave trade does the graph show?

INTERNET ACTIVITY

WRITING A BUSINESS REPORT Use the Internet to research the exports of Brazil or another European colony in the Americas during the first global age. Then write a business report describing how that colony helped increase the wealth of the colonizing nation. If possible, compare the colonial exports with the exports that area produces as an independent nation today.

The Age of Absolutism

(1550–1800)

CHAPTER OUTLINE

1 Extending Spanish Power
2 France Under Louis XIV
3 Triumph of Parliament in England
4 Rise of Austria and Prussia
5 Absolute Monarchy in Russia

"I have had an idea that will . . . give much pleasure to the people here, particularly the Queens," wrote Louis XIV, the young king of France. His plan was to throw a grand party where each guest would receive a lottery ticket for a prize of jewelry—and every ticket would be a winner.

Louis's party quickly grew into a more elaborate affair called "The Pleasures of the Enchanted Isle." Some 600 noble guests flocked to the royal palace at Versailles (ver sī) for three days of pageants, sports, ballets, dances, plays, and music. On the first day, courtiers costumed as medieval knights staged a tournament:

> "All knights, with their helmets covered in plumes of different colors and their tournament cloaks, gathered round the tournament barriers making an enchanting scene."

Later they feasted on 100 sumptuous dishes. As darkness fell, flaming torches and costumed dancers created a magical evening.

Day two featured an opera and a comedy by France's leading playwright. The king himself performed in a ballet with "incredible agility and grace." Day three ended with fireworks and music along the river. The magnificent entertainment stretched from three days to a week. At last, the costumed gods, goddesses, knights, and ladies were transformed back into French courtiers. But the extravaganza was only the first of many. The elegance of the French court became the talk of European ruling circles.

Louis XIV was more than a lavish party giver. In this chapter, you will see that he and other European monarchs created ever more powerful nations in the 1500s and 1600s. They built up their state bureaucracies and equipped powerful armies. They ensured loyalty to the crown and used their growing resources for bold ventures at home and overseas. While Spain, Portugal, and the Netherlands quickly took the lead in acquiring overseas empire, France and Britain surpassed them in the 1600s and 1700s. As they did so, the center of world civilization shifted to Europe.

FOCUS ON these questions as you read:

- **Political and Social Systems**
  How did absolute monarchs centralize their power?

- **Impact of the Individual**
  What role did individual rulers such as Louis XIV of France and Peter the Great of Russia play in shaping their nations?

- **Continuity and Change**
  How did struggles between monarchs and Parliament affect the development of Britain?

- **Art and Literature**
  How did European monarchs contribute to cultural flowering within their countries?

TIME AND PLACE

The Palace at Versailles From 1669 to 1685, Louis XIV had the vast palace of Versailles built about 10 miles from Paris. More than a cluster of luxurious buildings, the palace was an advertisement for the French monarchy. Versailles dazzled rulers in Europe and beyond, and kings from Morocco to Russia tried to imitate its splendor. ***Political and Social Systems*** Unlike medieval castles, Versailles was not protected by walls or moats. What does this suggest about France under Louis XIV?

HUMANITIES LINK

Art History Salon de la Guerre, Versailles (page 429).
Literature In this chapter, you will encounter passages from the following works of literature: Miguel de Cervantes, *Don Quixote* (page 425); Jacques Bossuet, *Universal History* (page 427); John Evelyn, Diary (pages 434–435); Jacob von Grimmelshausen, *Simplicissimus* (page 436); Alexander Pushkin, *The Bronze Horseman* (page 441).

| 1556 Hapsburg empire divided; Philip II begins rule of Spain | 1642 English civil war begins | 1685 Louis XIV revokes Edict of Nantes | 1697 Peter the Great tours Western Europe | 1756 Seven Years' War begins | 1795 Third partition of Poland |

| 1550 | 1600 | 1650 | 1700 | 1750 | 1800 |

1 Extending Spanish Power

Guide for Reading

- How did Philip II use royal power?
- How did the arts flourish during Spain's golden age?
- Why did the Spanish economy decline in the 1600s?
- **Vocabulary** *absolute monarch, divine right*

❝On 22 March 1595, ships from the Indies . . . began to discharge and deposit with the Chamber of Commerce 332 cartloads of silver, gold, and pearls of great value. On 8 April, 103 cartloads of silver and gold were unloaded.❞

In the 1500s, wealth from the Americas helped make Spain the most powerful state in Europe. American gold also paved the way for a golden age of literature and art. Yet the flood of gold and silver would eventually contribute to an economic decline.

Spain and the Hapsburg Empire

In the 1500s, Spain emerged as the first modern European power. Under Isabella and Ferdinand, Spain had expelled the last Muslim rulers and enforced religious unity. In 1492, Isabella financed Columbus's voyage, leading to the Spanish conquest of the Americas.

Wearing two crowns. The next monarch, Charles V,* ruled an even larger empire from 1519 to 1556. A grandson of Ferdinand and Isabella, Charles was also heir to the Hapsburgs, the Austrian rulers of the Holy Roman Empire and the Netherlands.

Ruling two empires involved Charles in constant warfare. He continued a long Hapsburg struggle with France over rival claims in Italy. As a devout Catholic, he also fought to sup-

---

*Within Spain, the king was known as Charles I. However, historians usually refer to him by his imperial title, Charles V.

press the Protestant movement in the German states. After years of religious warfare, however, Charles was forced to allow the German princes to make their own choice of religions. (See page 356.)

His greatest foe was the Ottoman empire. Under Suleiman, Ottoman forces advanced across central Europe to the walls of Vienna, Austria. (See page 276.) Although Austria held firm, the Ottomans occupied much of Hungary. Ottoman naval forces also challenged Spanish power in the Mediterranean.

An empire divided. Perhaps the Hapsburg empire was too scattered and diverse for any one person to rule. Exhausted and disillusioned, Charles V gave up his titles and entered a monastery in 1556. He divided his empire, leaving the Hapsburg lands in central Europe to his brother Ferdinand, who became Holy Roman emperor. He gave Spain, the Netherlands, southern Italy, and the huge Spanish overseas empire to his 29-year-old son Philip.

An Imposing Monarch

Like his father, King Philip II was hardworking, devout, and ambitious. During his long reign from 1556 to 1598, he sought to expand Spanish influence, strengthen the Catholic Church, and make his own power absolute. Thanks in part to silver from the Americas, he made Spain the foremost power in Europe.

A tireless worker. Unlike many other monarchs, Philip devoted much time to government work. He seldom hunted, never jousted, and lived as sparsely as a monk. His isolated, somber palace outside Madrid reflected Philip's character. Called the Escorial (ehs KOHR ee uhl), it served as a church, a residence, and a tomb for members of the royal family.

"It is best to keep an eye on everything," Philip often said. He plowed through a mountain of paperwork each day, making notes on even the most trivial matters. Once the Spanish ambassador to England wrote about a new kind of insect he had seen in London. "Probably fleas," Philip scribbled on the letter.

King by divine right. Like Ferdinand and Isabella, Philip further centralized royal power, making all parts of the government responsible to him. He became an absolute monarch, a

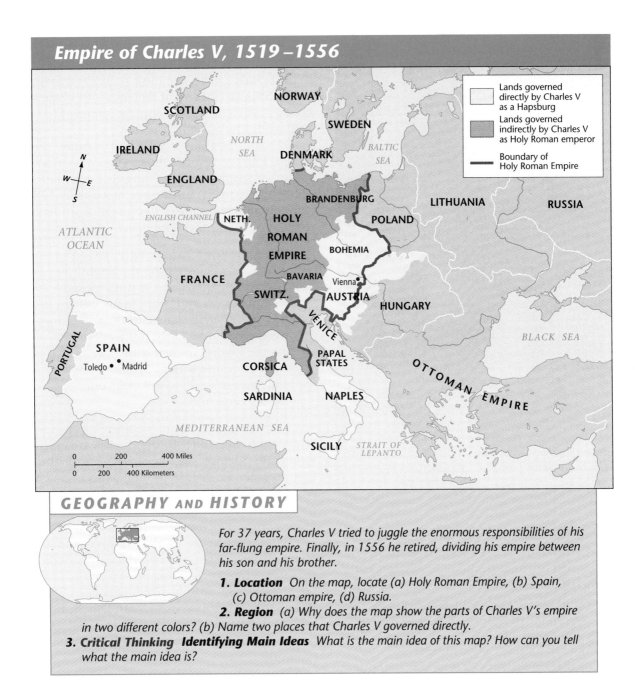

Empire of Charles V, 1519–1556

Lands governed directly by Charles V as a Hapsburg

Lands governed indirectly by Charles V as Holy Roman emperor

Boundary of Holy Roman Empire

NORWAY

SCOTLAND

SWEDEN

IRELAND

NORTH SEA

DENMARK

BALTIC SEA

ENGLAND

ENGLISH CHANNEL

NETH.

BRANDENBURG

LITHUANIA

RUSSIA

HOLY ROMAN EMPIRE

POLAND

ATLANTIC OCEAN

BOHEMIA

FRANCE

BAVARIA

Vienna

SWITZ.

AUSTRIA

HUNGARY

VENICE

BLACK SEA

PORTUGAL

SPAIN

Toledo • Madrid

PAPAL STATES

CORSICA

OTTOMAN EMPIRE

SARDINIA

NAPLES

MEDITERRANEAN SEA

SICILY

STRAIT OF LEPANTO

0   200   400 Miles

0   200   400 Kilometers

GEOGRAPHY AND HISTORY

For 37 years, Charles V tried to juggle the enormous responsibilities of his far-flung empire. Finally, in 1556 he retired, dividing his empire between his son and his brother.

1. Location On the map, locate (a) Holy Roman Empire, (b) Spain, (c) Ottoman empire, (d) Russia.

2. Region (a) Why does the map show the parts of Charles V's empire in two different colors? (b) Name two places that Charles V governed directly.

3. Critical Thinking Identifying Main Ideas What is the main idea of this map? How can you tell what the main idea is?

ruler with complete authority over the government and the lives of the people. Like other European rulers, Philip believed that he ruled by divine right. That is, he believed that his authority to rule came directly from God.

Partly as a result of the concept of divine right, Philip saw himself as the guardian of the Catholic Church. The great undertaking of his life was to defend the Catholic Reformation and turn back the Protestant tide in Europe. Within his own lands, he enforced religious unity, turning the Inquisition against Protestants and other people considered to be heretics.

The Wars of Philip II

Philip fought many wars as he advanced Spanish Catholic power throughout the world. At the battle of Lepanto in 1571, Spain and its Italian allies soundly defeated an Ottoman fleet in the Mediterranean. Although Christians hailed this as a great victory, the Ottomans remained a major power in the Mediterranean for centuries.

Revolt in the Netherlands. During the last half of his reign, Philip battled Protestant rebels in the Netherlands. At the time, the region

A Religious King This sculpture from the tomb of Philip II shows the Spanish king with members of his family. Philip was a devout Catholic. Yet his desire to rule as an absolute monarch often led him to meddle in Church policy. He even went so far as to tell Spanish bishops what they should wear! **Impact of the Individual** How does this sculpture suggest the seriousness and religious faith of Philip II?

ships. Francis Drake, the most daring Sea Dog, looted Spanish cities in the Americas. To Philip's dismay, instead of punishing the pirate, Elizabeth made him a knight!

To end English attacks and subdue the Dutch, Philip prepared a huge armada, or fleet, to carry a Spanish invasion force to England. In 1588, the Armada sailed with more than 130 ships, 20,000 men, and 2,400 pieces of artillery. A Spanish commander confidently predicted:

> **❝**It is well known that we fight in God's cause. So, when we meet the English, God will surely arrange matters so that we can grapple and board them, either by sending some strange freak of weather or, more likely, just by depriving the English of their wits. If we can come to close quarters, Spanish valor and Spanish steel . . . will make our victory certain.**❞**

The "strange freak of weather," however, favored the other side. In the English Channel, lumbering Spanish ships took losses from the lighter, faster English ships. Suddenly, a savage storm blew up, scattering the Armada. After further disasters at sea, the tattered remnants limped home in defeat.

While the defeat of the Spanish Armada ended Philip's plan to invade England, it had little short-term effect on his power. In the long term, however, Spain's naval superiority did dwindle. In the 1600s and 1700s, Dutch, English, and French fleets challenged—and surpassed—Spanish power in Europe and around the world.

The Golden Century

The century from 1550 to 1650 is often called Spain's *siglo de oro*, or "golden century," for the brilliance of its arts and literature. Philip II was a patron of the arts and also founded academies of science and mathematics.

Painters. Among the famous painters of this period was El Greco, meaning "the Greek." Born on the Greek island of Crete, El Greco had studied in Renaissance Italy before settling in Spain. He produced haunting religious pictures and striking portraits of Spanish nobles, done in a dramatically elongated style.

included 17 provinces that are today Belgium, the Netherlands, and Luxembourg. It was the richest part of Philip's empire. Protestants in the Netherlands resisted Philip's efforts to crush their faith. Both Protestant and Catholic subjects also opposed burdensome taxes and autocratic Spanish rule, which threatened their traditions of local self-government.

In the 1560s, riots against the Inquisition sparked a general uprising in the Netherlands. Savage fighting raged for decades. In 1581, the northern, largely Protestant provinces declared independence and became known as the Dutch Netherlands. They did not gain official recognition, however, until 1648. The southern, mostly Catholic provinces remained part of the Spanish empire.

The Armada sails. By the 1580s, Philip saw England's Queen Elizabeth I as his chief Protestant enemy. First secretly, then openly, Elizabeth had supported the Dutch against Spain. She even encouraged English captains, known as Sea Dogs, to plunder Spanish treasure

El Greco's use of vibrant colors influenced the work of Diego Velázquez (vuhl LAHS kehs), court painter to King Philip IV. Velázquez is perhaps best known for his portraits of Spanish royalty. In one painting, *The Maids of Honor,* he shows himself in the act of painting the portraits of several young girls.

Writers. Spain's golden century produced outstanding writers like Lope de Vega. A peasant by birth, he wrote more than 1,500 plays, including witty comedies and action-packed romances.

Miguel de Cervantes (suhr VAN tayz) wrote *Don Quixote* (dahn kee HOHT ee), the first modern novel in Europe. It pokes fun at medieval tales of chivalry. Dressed in rusty armor, the madman Don Quixote rides out on his broken-down plowhorse in search of adventure. He battles a windmill, which he thinks is a giant, and mistakes two flocks of sheep for opposing armies. Don Quixote's companion, Sancho Panza, a practical-minded peasant, expresses doubt about their quest:

66'What I can gather clearly from all this is that those adventures that we are after will bring us in the end so many misadventures that we won't know our right foot from our left. The best and wisest thing for us to do, in my humble opinion, is to go back to our village, now that it's reaping time, and look after our own affairs. . . .'

'How little you know of knighthood, Sancho,' answered Don Quixote. 'Be quiet and have patience, for a day will come when you will see with your own eyes how fine a thing it is to follow this profession. . . . What greater contentment can the world offer, or what pleasure can equal that of winning a battle and triumphing over one's enemy?'99

Don Quixote mocked the traditions of Spain's feudal past. Yet Cervantes admired both the unromantic realism of Sancho and the foolish yet heroic idealism of Don Quixote.

PARALLELS THROUGH TIME

"Living" Dolls

Mechanical dolls have fascinated people for centuries. Whether wound by key or powered by batteries, they give the magical illusion that an inanimate object has come to life.

Linking Past and Present Give other examples of how technology has affected the way children and adults play.

PAST Mechanical dolls were once the playthings of aristocrats. This elegant lady of the Spanish court was made in the late 1500s. She could walk, turn her head, and strum the cittern, a musical instrument related to the guitar.

PRESENT Computer technology has produced dolls that tell stories, imitate voices, and perform a wide range of actions. A remote control can make this Jennie Gymnast™ doll do splits, headstands, and leg kicks.

Economic Decline

In the 1600s, Spanish power slowly declined. The successors of Philip II were less able rulers than he. Economic problems were also partly to blame.

Costly overseas wars drained wealth out of Spain almost as fast as it came in. Then, too, treasure from the Americas led Spain to neglect farming and commerce. The government heavily taxed the small middle class, weakening a group that in other European nations supported royal power. The expulsion of Muslims and Jews from Spain deprived the economy of many skilled artisans and merchants. Finally, American gold and silver led to soaring inflation, with prices rising much higher in Spain than elsewhere in Europe.

Even though Spain still ruled a huge colonial empire, its strength slipped away. By the late 1600s, France had replaced Spain as the most powerful European nation.

SECTION 1 REVIEW

1. **Identify** (a) Hapsburgs, (b) *siglo de oro*, (c) El Greco, (d) Diego Velázquez, (e) Miguel de Cervantes.
2. **Define** (a) absolute monarch, (b) divine right.
3. (a) Describe three ways in which Philip II ensured absolute power. (b) How did he try to further Catholicism?
4. Why was the period from 1550 to 1650 Spain's golden age?
5. Explain three reasons why Spanish power and prosperity declined.
6. *Critical Thinking* **Recognizing Points of View** The English referred to the storm that battered the Spanish Armada as "the Protestant wind." (a) What does this nickname mean? (b) What might the Spanish have called it?
7. *ACTIVITY* Imagine that you are Charles V shortly after you have given up your throne and divided your empire. Write a letter to Philip II in which you explain the reasons for your actions and give one piece of advice about being king.

2 France Under Louis XIV

Guide for Reading

- How did wars of religion divide France?
- How did French rulers become absolute monarchs?
- What were the results of the reign of Louis XIV?
- **Vocabulary** *intendant, balance of power*

Louis XIV was an expert on power. He even wrote a book teaching his heir how to rule:

66 Consider the king in his workchamber. From it goes forth the orders that make magistrates and captains, citizens and soldiers, provinces, navies, and armies act together. He is the image of God, who from His throne in highest heaven makes all the world go. 99

By the late 1600s, Louis had become absolute monarch as well as the most powerful ruler in Europe. Yet, just 100 years earlier, France had been caught in terrible turmoil.

Rebuilding France

From the 1560s to the 1590s, religious wars between Huguenots (French Protestants) and the Catholic majority tore France apart. Leaders on both sides used the strife to further their own ambitions. Two of the noble families, the Catholic Guises and the Protestant Bourbons, hoped to replace the declining Valois dynasty on the throne.

Each side committed terrible atrocities. The worst began on St. Bartholomew's Day, August 24, 1572. As Huguenot and Catholic nobles gathered to celebrate a royal wedding, violence erupted that led to the massacre of 3,000 Huguenots. In the next few days, thousands more were slaughtered. For many, the St. Bartholomew's Day Massacre symbolized the complete breakdown of order in France.

Henry IV. In 1589, a Bourbon prince and Huguenot leader, Henry of Navarre, inherited the French throne as Henry IV. Knowing that a

Protestant would face severe problems ruling a largely Catholic land, he became Catholic. "Paris is well worth a Mass," he is supposed to have said. To protect Protestants, however, he issued the Edict of Nantes in 1598. It granted the Huguenots religious toleration and let them fortify their own towns and cities.

Henry IV then set out to heal his shattered land. His goal, he said, was not the victory of one sect over another, but "a chicken in every pot"—a good Sunday dinner for every peasant. Under Henry, the government reached into every area of life. Royal officials administered justice, improved roads, built bridges, and revived agriculture. By building the royal bureaucracy and reducing the influence of nobles, Henry laid the foundations for royal absolutism.

Richelieu. When Henry IV fell victim to an assassin in 1610, his nine-year-old son, Louis XIII, inherited the throne. For a time, nobles reasserted their power. Then, in 1624, Louis XIII appointed Cardinal Armand Richelieu (RIHSH uh loo) as his chief minister. This cunning, capable leader spent the next 18 years strengthening the central government.

Richelieu was determined to destroy the power of the nobles and the Huguenots, two groups that did not bow down to royal authority. He defeated the private armies of the nobles and destroyed their fortified castles. While reducing their independence, Richelieu tied the nobles to the king by giving them high posts at court or in the royal army. At the same time, he smashed the walled cities of the Huguenots and outlawed their armies. Yet he allowed them to continue to practice their religion.

▲ *Cardinal Richelieu*

Richelieu handpicked his able successor, Cardinal Jules Mazarin. When five-year-old Louis XIV inherited the throne in 1643, the year after Richelieu's death, Mazarin was in place to serve as the young king's chief minister. Like Richelieu, Mazarin worked tirelessly to extend royal power.

From Boy King to Sun King

Soon after Louis XIV became king, disorder again swept France. In an uprising called the Fronde, nobles, merchants, peasants, and the urban poor rebelled, each group for its own reasons. On one occasion, rioters drove the boy king from his palace. It was an experience Louis would never forget.

When Mazarin died in 1661, Louis resolved to take over the government himself. "I have been pleased to entrust the government of my affairs to the late Cardinal," he declared. "It is now time that I govern them myself."

"I am the state." Like his great-grandfather Philip II of Spain, Louis believed in divine right. He took the sun as the symbol of his power. Like the sun that stands at the center of the solar system, the Sun King was the center of the French nation. Louis is often quoted as saying, "*L'etat, c'est moi*"—"I am the state."

Bishop Jacques Bossuet (bah soo WAY), a court preacher and tutor to Louis's son, summed up the theory of divine right in his *Universal History*. As God's representative on Earth, wrote Bossuet, the king was entitled to unquestioning obedience. The king himself was responsible only to God:

❝The royal power is absolute. . . . Without this absolute authority the king could neither do good nor repress evil. It is necessary that his power be such that no one can escape him.❞

Not once during his reign did Louis XIV call a meeting of the Estates General. (See page 214.) In fact, the Estates General did not meet between 1614 and 1789. Thus, unlike the English Parliament, the Estates General played no role in checking royal power.

The business of government. Like Philip II, Louis spent many hours each day attending to government affairs. To strengthen the state, he followed the policies of Richelieu. He expanded the bureaucracy and appointed intendants, royal officials who collected taxes, recruited soldiers, and carried out his policies in the provinces. The office of intendant and other government jobs often went to wealthy middle-class men. In this way, Louis cemented ties between the middle class and the monarchy.

Under Louis XIV, the French army became the strongest in Europe. The state paid, fed, trained, and supplied up to 300,000 soldiers. Louis used this highly disciplined army to enforce his policies at home and abroad.

Colbert and the French economy. Louis found an expert organizer in his chief finance minister, Jean Baptiste Colbert (kohl BEHR). Colbert followed mercantilist policies to bolster the economy and promote trade.

Colbert had new lands cleared for farming, encouraged mining and other basic industries, and built up luxury trades such as lacemaking. To protect French manufacturers, he put high tariffs on imported goods. He also encouraged overseas colonies, such as New France in North America, and regulated trade with the colonies to enrich the royal treasury.

Colbert's policies helped make France the wealthiest state in Europe. Yet Louis XIV was often short of cash. Not even the financial genius of Colbert could produce enough income to support the huge costs of Louis's court or pay for his many foreign wars.

The Splendor of Versailles

In the countryside near Paris, Louis XIV turned a royal hunting lodge into the immense palace of Versailles. He spared no expense to make Versailles the most magnificent building in Europe. Its halls and salons displayed the finest paintings and statues, glittering chandeliers and mirrors. In the royal gardens, millions of flowers, plants, trees, and fountains were set out in precise geometric patterns.

Versailles became the perfect symbol of the Sun King's wealth and power. As both the king's home and the seat of government, it housed at least 10,000 people, from nobles and officials to servants.

Ceremonies of daily life. Louis XIV perfected elaborate ceremonies that emphasized his own importance. Each day began with "*la levée*," the king's rising, a major court occasion. High-ranking nobles competed for the honor of holding the royal wash basin or handing the king his diamond buckle shoes. At night the ceremony was repeated in reverse. Wives of nobles vied to attend upon women of the royal family.

Such ceremonies served another purpose. French nobles were descendants of the feudal lords who held power in medieval times. Left at their estates, these nobles were a threat to the power of the monarchy. By luring nobles to Versailles, Louis turned them into courtiers angling for privileges rather than warriors battling for power. Louis carefully protected their prestige and left them free from paying taxes.

Cultural flowering. The king, along with wealthy residents of Versailles and Paris, supported a "splendid century" of the arts. The king sponsored musical entertainments and commissioned plays by the best writers. Women of the court acted, played music, and danced in pageants.

The age of Louis XIV was the classical age of French drama. Jean Racine (rah SEEN) wrote tragedies based on ancient Greek myths. The

The King Dances The French nobles at Versailles put on plays and other entertainments. Often, the king himself took part. Here, Louis XIV performs in a ballet for an audience of courtiers. **Political and Social Systems** How did Louis's costume reinforce his image as king?

Salon de la Guerre, Versailles *The Salon de la Guerre, or Hall of War, is a dazzling example of an ornate artistic style called baroque. The hall is decorated with gilded bronze, carved marble, crystal, and mirrors. Oil paintings depict war through the ages. The oval sculpture in the center of the room shows Louis XIV as the Roman god of war.* **Art and Literature** *How do the images in the Salon de la Guerre glorify Louis XIV?*

actor-playwright Molière (mohl YAIR) turned out comedies such as *The Miser* that poked fun at French society to the delight of both middle-class citizens and sophisticated courtiers.

In painting, music, architecture, and decorative arts, French styles became the model for all Europe. A new form of dance drama, ballet, gained its first great popularity at the French court. As a leading patron of culture, Louis sponsored the French Academies, which set high standards for both the arts and sciences.

Successes and Failures

Louis XIV ruled France for 72 years, longer than any other monarch. During that time, French culture, manners, and customs replaced those of Renaissance Italy as the standard for European taste. In both foreign and domestic affairs, however, many of Louis's policies were costly failures.

The wars of Louis XIV. Louis XIV poured vast resources into wars to expand French borders and dominate Europe. At first, he did gain some territory. His later wars were disastrous, though, because rival rulers joined forces to check French ambitions. Led by the Dutch or the English, these alliances fought to maintain the balance of power, a distribution of military and economic power that would prevent any one nation from dominating Europe.

In 1700, Louis's grandson Philip V inherited the throne of Spain. Louis declared that France and Spain "must regard themselves as one." But neighboring powers led by England were determined to prevent this union. The War of the Spanish Succession dragged on until 1713, when an exhausted France signed the Treaty of Utrecht. Philip remained on the Spanish throne, but France agreed never to unite the two crowns.

Persecution of Huguenots. Perhaps Louis's most costly blunder was his treatment of the Huguenots. He saw the Protestant minority as a threat to religious and political unity. In 1685, he revoked the Edict of Nantes. Facing persecution, more than 100,000 Huguenots fled France. Huguenots, however, had been among the most hard-working and prosperous of Louis's subjects. Their loss was thus a serious blow to the French economy, just as the expulsion of Muslims and Jews had hurt Spain.

Looking ahead. Louis outlived his sons and grandsons. When he died in 1715, his five-year-old great-grandson inherited the throne as Louis XV. Although France was then the strongest state in Europe, years of warfare had drained the treasury. The prosperity nurtured by Colbert evaporated under the burden of bad harvests, heavy taxes, and other problems.

Louis XV was far too weak a king to deal with such problems. He neglected his duties and filled his hours with dances, hunting, and other pleasures. Meanwhile, the need for reform was growing, and he knew it. He used to quote an old French proverb, "After us, the deluge." As you will read in Chapter 19, the deluge came during the reign of the next king.

SECTION 2 REVIEW

1. **Identify** (a) St. Bartholomew's Day Massacre, (b) Edict of Nantes, (c) Fronde, (d) Versailles, (e) Molière, (f) War of the Spanish Succession.
2. **Define** (a) intendant, (b) balance of power.
3. (a) What were the effects of the French wars of religion? (b) How did Henry IV rebuild French unity?
4. Describe one way each of the following strengthened the power of the French monarchy: (a) Richelieu, (b) Louis XIV, (c) Colbert.
5. *Critical Thinking* **Applying Information** On his deathbed, Louis XIV told his heir, "I have loved war too well; do not copy me in this, nor in the lavish expenditures I have made." Why do you think Louis gave this advice?
6. *ACTIVITY* Imagine that your school is putting on a play about Louis XIV set at Versailles. You have been asked to design the set. Make a list of furniture, paintings, and other items you would want to include in the set.

3 Triumph of Parliament in England

Guide for Reading

■ What issues divided the Stuart kings and Parliament?

■ What were the causes and results of the English Civil War?

■ How did the Glorious Revolution ensure the rule of law?

■ **Vocabulary** *limited monarchy, habeas corpus*

"The most high and absolute power in the realm consists in the Parliament," wrote an English statesman in the 1560s. He was voicing a tradition that had roots in the Middle Ages. But in 1603, a monarch with far different ideas took the throne. "Kings are called gods," declared James I, "because they sit upon God's throne on Earth." Before long, the new king found himself on a collision course with Parliament.

In the 1600s, while Louis XIV perfected royal absolutism in France, England developed in a different direction. In this section, we will look at why and how the English Parliament asserted itself against royal power.

The Tudors and Parliament

From 1485 to 1603, England was ruled by the Tudor dynasty. Although the Tudors believed in divine right, they shrewdly recognized the value of good relations with Parliament. When Henry VIII broke with the Roman Catholic Church, he turned to Parliament to legalize his actions. Parliament approved the Act of Supremacy, making him head of the Church of England, and voted on his seizure of monastery lands. (See Chapter 14.)

A constant need for money also led Henry to consult Parliament frequently. Although he had inherited a bulging treasury, he quickly used up his funds fighting overseas wars. To levy new taxes, the king had to seek the approval of Parliament. Members of Parliament tended to vote as Henry's agents instructed. Still, they got used to being consulted on important matters.

Like her father, Elizabeth I both consulted Parliament and controlled it with a firm hand. Her advisers conveyed Elizabeth's wishes to Parliament and forbade discussion of certain subjects, such as foreign policy or the queen's marriage. Her skill in handling Parliament helped make "Good Queen Bess" a popular and successful ruler.

The Early Stuarts

In 1603, after a 45-year reign, Elizabeth died without a direct heir. The throne passed to her relatives the Stuarts, the ruling family of Scotland. The Stuarts were neither as popular as the Tudors nor as skillful in dealing with Parliament. They also inherited problems that Henry and Elizabeth had long suppressed. The result was a "century of revolution" that pitted the Stuart monarchs against Parliament.

A New English Bible
In 1604, James I asked a group of scholars to translate the Bible from Greek and Hebrew into English. For seven years, the committee worked on what we now call the "King James" Bible. Written in the rich language of the age of Shakespeare, it is still the best-known English version of the Bible. **Religions and Value Systems** Why would English Protestants favor an English translation of the Bible?

The royal challenge. James I, the first Stuart monarch, had agreed to rule according to English laws and customs. Soon, however, he was lecturing Parliament about divine right. "I will not be content that my power be disputed upon," he declared.

James repeatedly clashed with Parliament over money and foreign policy. He needed funds to finance his lavish court and wage wars. When members wanted to discuss foreign policy before voting funds, James dissolved Parliament and collected taxes on his own. Leaders in the House of Commons fiercely resisted the king's claim to absolute power.

James also found himself embroiled in religious disputes. At that time, English Protestants called Puritans were pressing to "purify" the Church of England of Catholic practices. Puritans wanted simpler services and a more democratic church without powerful bishops. James rejected their demands. As Puritans pushed harder for change, the king warned, "I will make them conform themselves or I will harry them out of this land or else do worse."

Parliament responds. Charles I inherited the throne in 1625. Like his father, Charles behaved like an absolute monarch. He imprisoned foes without trial and squeezed the nation for money. By 1628, though, his need to raise taxes forced Charles to summon Parliament. Before voting any funds, Parliament insisted that Charles sign the Petition of Right. It prohibited the king from raising taxes without the consent of Parliament or imprisoning anyone without just cause.

Charles did sign the petition, but he then dissolved Parliament in 1629. For 11 years, he ignored the petition and ruled without Parliament. During that time, he created bitter enemies, especially among Puritans. His Archbishop of Canterbury, William Laud, tried to force all clergy to follow strict Anglican rules, dismissing or imprisoning any who resisted. Many people felt that the archbishop was trying to revive Catholic practices.

In 1637, Charles and Laud tried to impose the Anglican prayer book on Scotland. The Calvinist Scots revolted. To get funds to suppress the Scottish rebellion, Charles finally had to summon Parliament in 1640. When it met, however, Parliament launched its own revolt.

The Long Parliament. The Parliament that Charles I summoned became known as the Long Parliament because it lasted on and off until 1653. Its actions triggered the greatest political revolution in English history. In a mounting struggle with the king, Parliament tried and finally executed his chief ministers, including Archbishop Laud. It further declared that the Parliament could not be dissolved without its consent and called for the abolition of bishops.

Charles lashed back. In 1642, he led troops into the House of Commons to arrest its most radical leaders. They escaped through a back door and soon raised their own army. The clash between them now moved to the battlefield.

The English Civil War

The civil war that followed lasted from 1642 to 1649. Like the Fronde that occurred about the same time in France, it posed a major challenge to the rise of absolute monarchs. But while the forces of royal power won in France, in England the forces of revolution triumphed.

Cavaliers and Roundheads. At first, the odds seemed to favor the Cavaliers, or supporters of Charles I. Many Cavaliers were wealthy nobles, proud of their plumed hats and fashionably long hair. Well trained in dueling and warfare, the Cavaliers expected a quick victory. But their foes proved to be tough fighters having the courage of their convictions. The forces of Parliament were composed of country gentry, town-dwelling manufacturers, and Puritan clergy. They were called Roundheads because their hair was cut close around their heads.

The Roundheads found a leader of genius in Oliver Cromwell. A Puritan member of the lesser gentry, Cromwell was a skilled general. He organized the "New Model Army" for Parliament into a disciplined fighting force. Inspired by Puritan chaplains, Cromwell's army defeated the Cavaliers in a series of decisive bat-

A Roundhead Victory The Battle of Marston Moor, fought in 1644, was a turning point in the English Civil War. Cromwell, seen here on his horse, was wounded in the neck early in the battle. However, he rallied his troops for a second attack and finally defeated the forces of King Charles I. **Continuity and Change** How would a modern battle scene differ from this one?

tles. By 1647, the king was in the hands of parliamentary forces.

Execution of a king. Eventually, Parliament set up a court to put the king on trial. It found him guilty and condemned him to death as "a tyrant, traitor, murderer, and public enemy." On a cold January day in 1649, Charles I stood on a scaffold surrounded by his foes. "I am a martyr of the people," he declared.

Showing no fear, the king told the executioner that he himself would give the sign for him to strike. After a brief prayer, Charles knelt and placed his neck on the block. Silence gripped the crowd as the executioner raised his ax. On the agreed signal, he severed the king's head with a single stroke.

The execution sent shock waves throughout Europe. In the past, kings had occasionally been murdered by rivals or died on the battlefield. But for the first time, a ruling monarch had been tried and executed by his own people. The parliamentary forces had sent a clear signal that, in England, no ruler could claim absolute power and ignore the rule of law.

The Kingless Decade

After the execution of Charles I, the House of Commons abolished the monarchy, the House of Lords, and the official Church of England. It declared England a republic, known as the Commonwealth, under the leadership of Oliver Cromwell.

Rebels in Ireland. The new republic faced many problems. Supporters of Charles II, the uncrowned heir to the throne, attacked England by way of Ireland and Scotland. Cromwell led forces into Ireland to crush the uprising. He then took stern measures against the Irish Catholic majority. In 1652, Parliament passed a law exiling most Catholics to barren land in the west of Ireland. Anyone found disobeying the order could be killed on sight.

The Levellers. Squabbles also splintered forces within the Commonwealth. One group, called Levellers, thought that poor men should have as much say in government as the gentry, lawyers, and other leading citizens. "I think that the poorest He that is in England hath a life to live as well as the greatest He," wrote one Leveller:

> 66 Every man that is to live under a
> government ought first by his own
> consent to put himself under that
> government. 99

Such ideas horrified the gentry, who dominated Parliament. Cromwell and his generals suppressed the Levellers, as well as more radical groups who threatened property ownership. As the challenges to order grew, Cromwell took the title Lord Protector in 1653. From then on, he ruled through the army.

Life in the Commonwealth

 In the 1650s, Parliament enacted a series of laws designed to make sure that Sunday was set aside for religious observance. Anyone over the age of 14 who was caught "profaning the Lord's Day" could be fined, including

> 66 Every person being in any tavern,
> tobacco-house, cellar or shop; . . .
> every person dancing or profanely
> singing or playing upon musical instruments; . . . all tailors fitting or going to
> fit any wearing apparel; and barbers
> trimming upon the day aforesaid. 99

Under the Commonwealth, Puritan preachers tried to root out godlessness and impose a "rule of saints." The English Civil War thus ushered in a social revolution as well as a political one.

Puritan morality. To the Puritans, theaters were "spectacles of pleasure too commonly expressing mirth and levity." So, like Calvin in Geneva, Cromwell closed all theaters. Puritans also frowned on lewd dancing, raged against taverns and gambling, and cut down Maypoles. Yet Puritans enjoyed many types of entertainment. While they banned music in churches, they played music at home and even joined in modest dancing.

Although Cromwell could not accept open Catholic worship, he believed in religious freedom for other Protestant groups. "What greater hypocrisy," Cromwell demanded, "than for those who were oppressed by the bishops to become the greatest oppressors themselves, so

The Orthodox true Minifter,   the Seducer and falfe Prophet.

soon as their yoke was removed?" He even welcomed Jews back to England, after more than 350 years of exile.

Schooling. Puritans felt that every Christian, rich and poor, must be able to read the Bible. To spread religious knowledge, they encouraged education for all people. (▮ See *You Decide*, What Is the Goal of Education? pages 450–451.)

By mid-century, families from all classes were sending their children to school, girls as well as boys. Students learned the alphabet from hornbooks, paddle-shaped pieces of wood with letters and words carved on them. A popular rhyme taught the alphabet through moral lessons and references to the Bible:

66**A** In **A**dam's fall,
We sinned all.

B Thy life to mend,
This **B**ook [the Bible] attend. . . .

F The idle **F**ool
Is whipt at School.99

Women. Puritans pushed for changes in marriage to ensure greater fidelity. In addition to marriages based on business interests, they encouraged marriages based on love. As in the past, women were seen mainly as caretakers of the family, subordinate to men.

Despite their lower status, some women sought new liberties. Female Levellers asserted their right to petition Parliament. "Have we not

an equal interest with the men of this nation in those liberties and securities contained in the . . . laws of the land?" they asked.

Among some radical Protestant groups, women even preached sermons. Katherine Chidley, an outspoken writer on religious matters, asserted that a husband had authority over a wife "in bodily and civil respects, but not to be a Lord over her conscience."

Still, whenever women took a public role, most men were horrified. A popular rhyme warned, "When women preach and cobblers pray/The fiends in hell make holiday."

End of the Commonwealth. Soon after Cromwell's death in 1658, the Puritans lost their grip on England. Many people were tired of military rule and strict Puritan ways. In 1660, a newly elected Parliament invited Charles II to return to England from exile.

The Puritan experiment ended in the restoration of the monarchy. Yet Puritan ideas about morality, government, equality, and education lasted. Years later, they would play an important role in shaping the United States of America. ▮

The Stuarts Restored

In late May 1660, cheering crowds welcomed Charles II back to London. John Evelyn wrote in his diary:

66This day came his Majesty, Charles the Second to London, after a sad and long exile. . . . This was also his birthday, and with a triumph of above 20,000 horse and foot [soldiers], branding their swords, and shouting with inexpressible joy; the ways strewd with flowers, the bells ringing, the streets hung with tapestry. **"**

With his charm and flashing wit, young Charles II was a popular ruler. He reopened theaters and taverns and presided over a lively court in the manner of Louis XIV. Charles restored the official Church of England, but tolerated other Protestants such as Presbyterians, Quakers, and Baptists.

Although Charles accepted the Petition of Right, he shared his father's faith in absolute monarchy and secretly had Catholic sympathies. Still, he shrewdly avoided his father's mistakes in dealing with Parliament.

Charles's brother James II inherited the throne in 1685. Unlike Charles, James flaunted his Catholic faith. He further angered his subjects by suspending laws at whim and appointing Catholics to high office. Many feared that James would restore the Roman Catholic Church. In 1688, alarmed parliamentary leaders invited James's Protestant daughter, Mary, and her Dutch Protestant husband, William III of Orange, to become rulers of England.

The Glorious Revolution

When William and Mary landed with their army late in 1688, James II fled to France. This bloodless overthrow of a king became known as the Glorious Revolution. Before they could be crowned, however, William and Mary had to accept several acts passed by Parliament that became known as the English Bill of Rights.

Limits on royal power. The Bill of Rights ensured the superiority of Parliament over the monarchy. It required the monarch to summon Parliament regularly and gave the House of Commons the "power of the purse." A king or queen could no longer interfere in Parliamentary debates or suspend laws. The bill also barred any Catholic from sitting on the throne. Under the Bill of Rights, England became a limited monarchy, a government in which a constitution or legislative body limits the monarch's powers.

The Bill of Rights formally restated the traditional rights of English citizens, such as trial by jury. It abolished excessive fines and cruel or unjust punishment. It also affirmed the principle of habeas corpus. That is, no person could be held in prison without first being charged with a specific crime. Later, the Toleration Act of 1689 granted limited toleration to Puritans, Quakers, and other Protestant dissenters, though not yet to Catholics. Still, only members of the Church of England could hold public office.

Looking ahead. What the Glorious Revolution accomplished was not democracy, but the beginnings of constitutional monarchy. English rulers still had much power, but they had to obey the law and govern in partnership with Parliament. In the age of absolute monarchy elsewhere in Europe, a limited monarchy in England was radical enough.

SECTION 3 REVIEW

1. **Identify** (a) Petition of Right, (b) Cavalier, (c) Roundhead, (d) Oliver Cromwell, (e) Leveller, (f) Bill of Rights.
2. **Define** (a) limited monarchy, (b) habeas corpus.
3. (a) How did the Tudors handle Parliament? (b) Why did the Stuarts clash with Parliament?
4. (a) Explain two causes of the English Civil War. (b) Why did many people welcome the return of the monarchy?
5. Describe two results of the Glorious Revolution.
6. *Critical Thinking* **Analyzing Information** (a) How might Puritan teachings have led some women to seek greater liberties? (b) Why do you think many men were upset by the idea of women speaking in public?
7. *ACTIVITY* Draw a political cartoon about the execution of Charles I from the point of view of either a Roundhead or a Cavalier.

ISSUES
For
TODAY

While Louis XIV strengthened absolute power in France, the Stuarts were unable to do the same in England. How do leaders achieve and maintain power?

4 Rise of Austria and Prussia

Guide for Reading

- What were the results of the Thirty Years' War?

- How did Austria and Prussia emerge as great powers?

- How did the balance of power affect European diplomacy?

Year after year, war ravaged the German states of central Europe. Bodies of victims littered fields and roads. "God send that there may be peace again," prayed a German peasant in 1638. But peace never lasted long. As the Thirty Years' War dragged on, almost every European power was sucked into the conflict.

Finally, two great German-speaking powers, Austria and Prussia, rose out of the ashes. Like Louis XIV in France, their rulers perfected skills as absolute monarchs.

The Thirty Years' War

The French philosopher Voltaire noted that, by early modern times, the Holy Roman Empire was neither holy, nor Roman, nor an empire. It was a patchwork of several hundred small, separate states that paid little heed to the emperor. Religion further divided the German states. The north was largely Protestant, while the south was Catholic. This power vacuum sparked the Thirty Years' War.

The war begins. The war had both religious and political causes. It began as a local conflict in Bohemia, the present-day Czech Republic. Ferdinand, the Hapsburg king of Bohemia, sought to suppress Protestants and to assert royal power over local nobles. In May 1618, rebellious Protestant noblemen tossed two royal officials out of a castle window in Prague. This act signaled the start of a general revolt, which Ferdinand* moved quickly to sup-

---

*The following year, Ferdinand was elected Holy Roman emperor and became known as Ferdinand II.

press. The conflict widened as both sides sought allies.

With the support of Spain, Poland, and other Catholic states, Ferdinand tried to roll back the Reformation. At first, he defeated the Bohemians and their Protestant allies. Alarmed by the Hapsburg victories, Protestant powers like the Netherlands and Sweden sent troops into Germany.

What began as a local religious struggle blazed into a European conflict. Before long, political motives outweighed religious issues. Catholic and Protestant rulers shifted alliances to suit their own interests. At one point, Catholic France led by Cardinal Richelieu joined Lutheran Sweden against the Catholic Hapsburgs of Austria.

"God have pity on us." The fighting took a brutal toll. Roving armies of mercenaries burned villages and sacked cities. "We have had blue coats and red coats and now come the yellow coats," cried the citizens of one German town. "God have pity on us." Soldiers destroyed crops and homes and killed without mercy. Jacob von Grimmelshausen captured the nightmare violence in his novel *Simplicissimus*. At one point, he describes the plunder of a fictional village by marauding soldiers:

> 66For one of [the peasants] they had taken they thrust into the baking oven and there lit a fire under him, although he had as yet confessed to no crime; as for another, they put a cord around his head and twisted it so tight with a piece of wood that the blood gushed from his mouth and nose and ears. In a word each had his own device to torture the peasants, and each peasant his several tortures.99

Murder and torture were followed by famine and disease. Wolves, not seen in settled areas since the Middle Ages, stalked the deserted streets of once-bustling villages. Perhaps one third of the population of the German states died in the Thirty Years' War.

Peace at last. Finally, in 1648, the exhausted combatants accepted a series of treaties, known as the Peace of Westphalia. Because so many powers had been involved in the conflict, the war ended with a general European peace

Europe After the Peace of Westphalia, 1648

Legend:
- Controlled by Spanish Hapsburgs
- Controlled by Austrian Hapsburgs
- Italian city-states
- Prussia
- Sweden
- Boundary of Holy Roman Empire

Map labels include: NORWAY, RUSSIA, Moscow, SCOTLAND, NORTH SEA, BALTIC SEA, IRELAND, DENMARK, POLAND, ENGLAND, London, DUTCH NETH., Berlin, SILESIA, SPANISH NETH., WESTPHALIA, SAXONY, Prague, BOHEMIA, ATLANTIC OCEAN, Paris, LORRAINE, ALSACE, BAVARIA, Vienna, AUSTRIA, HUNGARY, FRANCE, SWISS FED., Milan, BLACK SEA, PORTUGAL, SPAIN, CORSICA, PAPAL STATES, Rome, Naples, Istanbul, OTTOMAN EMPIRE, SARDINIA, MEDITERRANEAN SEA, AFRICA, SICILY, CRETE

Scale: 0–400 Miles / 0–400 Kilometers

GEOGRAPHY AND HISTORY

The horrors of the Thirty Years' War finally ended with a series of treaties called the Peace of Westphalia. The map shows who controlled various European lands after the treaties went into effect.

1. **Location** On the map, locate (a) Poland, (b) Sweden, (c) Spanish Netherlands, (d) Westphalia.
2. **Place** (a) In 1648, who controlled Bohemia? (b) What country separated the two parts of Prussia? (c) What lands did the Spanish Hapsburgs control?
3. **Critical Thinking Drawing Conclusions** How can you tell from the map that the Holy Roman Empire was not a strong, unified state?

and an attempt to settle other international problems as well.

France emerged a clear winner, gaining territory on both its Spanish and German frontiers. The Hapsburgs were big losers because they had to accept the almost total independence of all the princes of the Holy Roman Empire. The Netherlands and the Swiss Federation (present-day Switzerland) won recognition as independent states.

The Thirty Years' War left Germany divided into more than 360 separate states, "one for every day of the year." These states still formally acknowledged the leadership of the Holy Roman emperor. Yet each state had its own government, coinage, state church, armed forces, and foreign policy. Germany, potentially the most powerful nation in Europe, thus remained fragmented for another 200 years.

Hapsburg Austria

Though weakened by war, the Hapsburgs still wanted to create a strong united state. They kept the title of Holy Roman emperors, but focused their attention on expanding their own lands. To Austria, they added Bohemia, Hungary, and, later, parts of Poland and Italy.

Unity and diversity. Uniting these lands proved difficult. Divided by geography, they also included diverse peoples and cultures. By the 1700s, the Hapsburg empire included Germans, Magyars, Slavs, and others. Its people spoke many languages, including Czech, Hungarian, Polish, and Italian. In many parts of the empire, people had their own laws, assemblies, and customs.

The Hapsburgs succeeded in exerting some control over these diverse peoples. They sent German-speaking officials to Bohemia and Hungary and settled Austrians on confiscated lands in these provinces. The Hapsburgs also put down revolts in both Bohemia and Hungary. Still, the Hapsburg empire never developed a centralized system like that of France.

Maria Theresa. In the early 1700s, the emperor Charles VI faced a new crisis. He had no son. His daughter, Maria Theresa, was intelligent and capable, but no woman had yet ruled Hapsburg lands in her own name. Charles persuaded other European rulers to recognize his daughter's right to succeed him. When he died, however, many ignored their pledge. Maria Theresa later recalled:

> 66I found myself . . . without money, without credit, without army, without experience and knowledge of my own, and finally also without any counsel, because each one of them first wanted to wait and see what would develop.99

The greatest threat came in 1740, when Frederick II of Prussia seized the rich Hapsburg province of Silesia. Maria Theresa set off for Hungary to appeal for military help. The Hungarians were ordinarily unfriendly to the Hapsburgs. But she made a dramatic plea before an assembly of Hungarian nobles. According to one account, the nobles rose to their feet and shouted, "Our lives and blood for your Majesty! We will die for our monarch, Maria Theresa!" She eventually got further help from Britain and Russia.

During the eight-year War of the Austrian Succession, Maria Theresa failed to push Frederick out of Silesia. Still, she did preserve her empire and win the support of most of her people. Equally important, she strengthened Hapsburg power by reorganizing the bureaucracy and improving tax collection. She even forced nobles and clergy to pay taxes and tried to ease the burden of taxes and labor services on peasants. Many of her reforms were later extended by her son and successor, Joseph II. (See Chapter 18.)

A Large Royal Family Maria Theresa had one thing in common with most women of her day—her duties included motherhood. During her reign, she gave birth to 11 daughters and 5 sons. When her oldest son became Emperor Joseph II, she often quarreled with him about state policy. Another child, Marie Antoinette, married the king of France. **Political and Social Systems** *Why are family ties important in a monarchy?*

Prussia: Out of the Ashes

While Austria was molding a strong Catholic state, Prussia emerged as a new Protestant power. In the 1600s, the Hohenzollern (HOH uhn tsahl ern) family ruled scattered lands across north Germany. After the Peace of Westphalia, ambitious Hohenzollern rulers united their lands by taking over the states between them. Like absolute rulers elsewhere, they imposed royal power on all their subjects and reduced the independence of their nobles, called Junkers (YOON kerz).

To achieve their goals, Prussian rulers set up an efficient bureaucracy and forged one of the best-trained armies in Europe. Great emphasis was put on military values. A Prussian military leader boasted, "Prussia is not a state which possesses an army, but an army which possesses a state." The Hohenzollerns won the loyalty of the Junkers by giving them positions in the army and government. By 1740, Prussia was strong enough to challenge its rival Austria.

Frederick II. That year, young Frederick II inherited the Prussian throne. His father, Frederick William, had made sure that, from an early age, Frederick was trained in the art of war:

66His tutor must take the greatest pains to imbue my son with a sincere love for the soldier's profession and to impress upon him that nothing else in the world can confer upon a prince such fame and honor as the sword.99

In fact, young Frederick preferred playing the flute and writing poetry. Frederick William despised these pursuits and treated the young prince so badly that he decided to flee the country. Discovering these plans, Frederick William put his son in solitary confinement. A friend who had helped Frederick was beheaded while the 18-year-old prince was forced to watch.

Military successes. Frederick's harsh military training did have an effect. As king, Frederick II lost no time in using his army. As you read, he boldly seized mineral-rich Silesia from Austria, sparking the War of the Austrian Succession.

In several later wars, Frederick made brilliant use of his disciplined army, forcing all to accept Prussia as a great power. His exploits earned him the name Frederick the Great.

Keeping the Balance of Power

By 1750, the great powers of Europe included Austria, Prussia, France, England, and Russia. They formed various alliances to maintain the balance of power. As you have seen, early in the century, the Dutch and English combined to check the aggressive ambitions of Louis XIV. At times, the great powers switched partners, but two rivalries persisted. Prussia battled Austria for control of the German states, while Britain and France competed for overseas empire.

Sometimes, rivals went to war to maintain the balance of power. In the 1700s, those wars ignited worldwide conflict. The Seven Years' War, which lasted from 1756 to 1763, was fought on three continents. Prussia, Austria, Russia, France and Britain battled in Europe. As you read, Britain and France also fought in India and in North America, where the conflict was known as the French and Indian War. The Treaty of Paris ending the war gave Britain a huge empire.

SECTION 4 REVIEW

1. **Identify** (a) Peace of Westphalia, (b) Maria Theresa, (c) Frederick the Great, (d) Seven Years' War.
2. How did the Thirty Years' War affect the German states?
3. (a) What two major powers emerged at the end of the Thirty Years' War? (b) How were their goals similar or different?
4. (a) Why did European nations want to maintain a balance of power? (b) What methods did they use?
5. *Critical Thinking* **Linking Past and Present** Westphalia was the first modern peace conference. (a) Why do you think such a peace conference had to be devised? (b) How do warring nations try to settle their disputes today?
6. *ACTIVITY* Both Louis XIV and Frederick William wrote instructions for training their sons. With a partner, create your own list of rules for a successful absolute monarch in the 1600s and 1700s.

5 Absolute Monarchy in Russia

Guide for Reading

- How did Peter the Great strengthen Russia?

- What were the goals of Russian foreign policy?

- What were the results of the partition of Poland?

In the early 1600s, Russia was still a medieval state, untouched by the Renaissance and largely isolated from Western Europe. The "Time of Troubles" had plunged the state into a period of disorder and foreign invasions. (See page 248.) The election of the first Romanov czar in 1613 restored a measure of order. Not until 1682, however, did a czar emerge who was strong enough to regain the absolute power of earlier czars. He was Peter the Great, who pushed Russia on the road to becoming a great modern power.

Peter the Great

Peter, just 10 years old when he came to the throne, did not take control of the government until 1689. The young czar was a striking figure, nearly seven feet tall, with a booming laugh and a furious temper. Though he was not well educated, Peter was immensely curious. He spent hours in the "German quarter," the Moscow suburb where many Dutch, Scottish, English, and other foreign artisans and soldiers lived. There, he heard of the advanced technology that was helping Western European monarchs forge powerful empires.

Journey to the West. In 1697, Peter set out to study western technology for himself.

He spent hours walking the streets of European cities, noting the manners and homes of the people. He visited factories and art galleries, learned anatomy from a doctor, and had a dentist teach him how to pull teeth. Disguised in shabby clothes, he even worked for a time as a carpenter in a Dutch shipyard. In England, Peter was impressed by Parliament. "It is good," he said, "to hear subjects speaking truthfully and openly to their king."

Returning to Russia, Peter brought along a group of technical experts, teachers, soldiers, and nobles he had recruited in the West. He then began to reshape Russia in his large, callused hands. But convincing fellow Russians to modernize proved difficult. To impose his will, Peter became the most autocratic of Europe's absolute monarchs.

Autocrat and reformer. Peter was determined to centralize royal power. He brought all Russians under his control, including the Russian Orthodox Church. He forced the haughty boyars to serve the state in civilian or military jobs.

Under Peter, serfdom spread in Russia, long after it had died out in Western Europe. By tying peasants to land given to nobles, he ensured that nobles could serve the state. Further, he forced some serfs to become soldiers or labor on roads, canals, and other government projects.

Using autocratic methods, Peter pushed through social and economic reforms. He imported western technology, improved education, simplified the Russian alphabet, and set up academies for the study of mathematics, science, and engineering. To pay for his reforms, he adopted mercantilist policies and encouraged exports. He improved the waterways and canals, developed mining and textiles, and backed new trading companies.

Some changes had a symbolic meaning. After returning from the West, Peter insisted that noblemen shave their beards and replace their old-fashioned robes with Western European clothes. To

◀ Peter the Great

Off With Their Beards! *This famous cartoon shows Peter the Great shearing the beard off a protesting Russian boyar. To encourage men to shave, Peter imposed a tax on beards in 1705. The "beard license" at right was proof that its bearer had paid the tax and did not need to shave.* **Continuity and Change** *Why did Peter want noblemen to shave off their beards?*

largest standing army in Europe and set out to extend Russian borders.

Search for a warm-water port. In 1700, Peter began a long war against Sweden, Russia's northwestern neighbor that dominated the Baltic region. After early setbacks, Peter eventually rebuilt his army, pushed the Swedes back, and won land along the Baltic. However, Baltic seaports were frozen over in the winter. Peter therefore turned south, seeking a warm-water port that would allow Russia to trade with the West all year long.

The nearest warm-water coast was that of the Black Sea. Peter fought the Ottoman Turks to recover Russian lands north of the Black Sea. Though Peter failed in this effort, the later Russian empress Catherine the Great succeeded before the century was over.

Peter's city. The great symbol of Peter's desire to forge a modern Russia was his new capital city, St. Petersburg. Seeking to open a "window on the West," he located the city on the swampy shores of the Neva River near the Baltic coast. He forced tens of thousands of serfs to drain the swamps. Many thousands died, but Peter got his city. He then invited Italian architects and artisans to design great palaces in western style.

A hundred years later, Russia's best-known poet, Alexander Pushkin, wrote *The Bronze Horseman.* Pushkin portrays Peter as a larger-than-life ruler who is determined to tame nature at whatever cost:

> 66Here, Swede, beware. Soon by our labor
> Here a new city shall be wrought,
> Defiance to the haughty neighbor.
> Here we at Nature's own behest
> Shall break a window to the West,
> Stand planted on the ocean level;
> Here flags of foreign nations all
> By waters new to them will call
> And unencumbered we shall revel.99

Toward the Pacific. Russian traders and raiders also blazed trails across Siberia to the Pacific. Under Peter, Russia signed a treaty with Qing China, defining their common border in the east. In the early 1700s, Peter hired the Danish navigator Vitus Bering to explore what became known as the Bering Strait between

end the practice of secluding women, he held grand parties at which upper-class women and men were expected to dance together. Russian nobles resisted this radical mixing of the sexes in public.

Peter had no mercy for any who resisted the new order. When elite palace guards revolted, he had over 1,000 tortured and executed. As an example of his power, he left their rotting corpses outside the palace walls for months.

Russian Expansion

From his earliest days as czar, Peter worked to build Russian military power. He created the

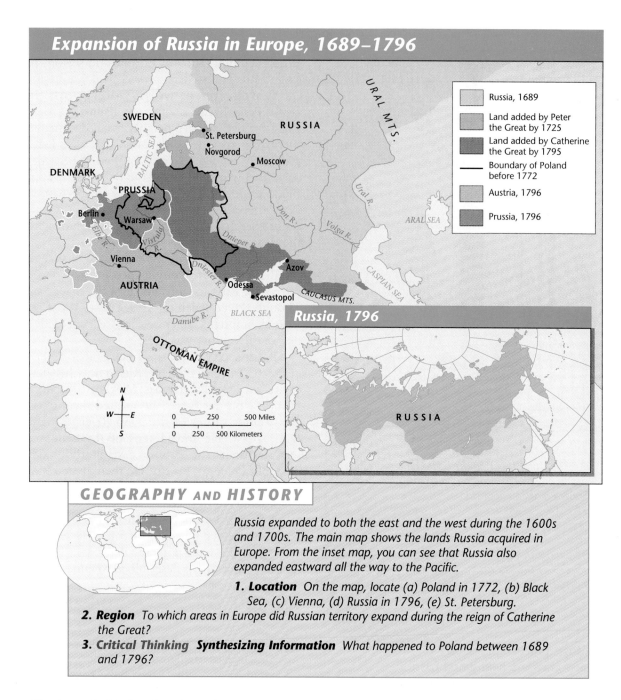

Expansion of Russia in Europe, 1689–1796

MAP LEGEND
- Russia, 1689
- Land added by Peter the Great by 1725
- Land added by Catherine the Great by 1795
- Boundary of Poland before 1772
- Austria, 1796
- Prussia, 1796

Russia, 1796

GEOGRAPHY AND HISTORY

Russia expanded to both the east and the west during the 1600s and 1700s. The main map shows the lands Russia acquired in Europe. From the inset map, you can see that Russia also expanded eastward all the way to the Pacific.

1. **Location** On the map, locate (a) Poland in 1772, (b) Black Sea, (c) Vienna, (d) Russia in 1796, (e) St. Petersburg.
2. **Region** To which areas in Europe did Russian territory expand during the reign of Catherine the Great?
3. **Critical Thinking** **Synthesizing Information** What happened to Poland between 1689 and 1796?

Siberia and Alaska. Russian pioneers crossed into Alaska and migrated as far south as California. Few Russians moved east of the Ural Mountains at this time, but on a map, Russia was already the largest country in the world, as it still is today.

Peter's legacy. When Peter died in 1725, he left a mixed legacy. He had expanded Russian territory, gained ports on the Baltic Sea, and created a mighty army. Yet many reforms died with him. Nobles, for example, soon ignored his policy of service to the state.

Like earlier czars, Peter the Great had brandished terror to enforce his absolute power. His policies contributed to the growth of serfdom, which only served to widen the gap between Russia and the West that Peter had sought to narrow.

Catherine the Great

Peter's immediate successors were ineffective rulers. Russian nobles quickly reasserted their independence. Then a new monarch took the reins of power firmly in hand. She became known to history as Catherine the Great.

Absolute rule. A German princess by birth, Catherine had come to Russia at the age of 15 to wed the heir to the Russian throne. She learned Russian, embraced the Russian Orthodox faith, and won the loyalty of the people. In 1762, her mentally unstable husband, Czar Peter III, was murdered by a group of Russian army officers. Whether or not Catherine was involved in the plot, she certainly benefited. With their support, she ascended the Russian throne herself.

Catherine proved to be an efficient, energetic empress. She reorganized the provincial government, codified laws, and began state-sponsored education for boys and girls. Like Peter the Great, she embraced western ideas. At court, she encouraged French language and customs, wrote histories and plays, and organized court performances. As you will read in the next chapter, she was also a serious student of the French thinkers who led the movement known as the Enlightenment.

Like other absolute monarchs, Catherine could be ruthless. She granted Russian nobles important rights, such as exemption from taxes, but also let them increase their stranglehold on the peasants. When peasants rebelled against the harsh burdens of serfdom, Catherine took firm action to repress them.

Catherine was determined to expand Russia's borders. After a war against the Ottoman empire, she achieved the Russian dream of a warm-water port on the Black Sea. She also took steps to seize territory from neighboring Poland.

Partition of Poland. As you read in Chapter 10, Poland had once been a great European power. However, Polish rulers were un-

able to centralize their power or diminish the influence of the Polish nobility. The divided Polish government was ill prepared to stand up to the increasing might of its neighbors Russia, Prussia, and Austria.

In the 1770s, Catherine the Great, Frederick the Great, and Emperor Joseph II of Austria hungrily eyed Poland. To avoid fighting each other, the three monarchs agreed to partition, or divide up, Poland. Poland was partitioned three times, first in the 1770s, then twice in the 1790s. By the time Austria, Prussia, and Russia had taken their final slice in 1795, the independent kingdom of Poland had vanished from the map. Not until 1918 would a free Polish state reappear.

Looking Ahead

By the mid-1700s, absolute monarchs ruled four of the five major European powers. Britain, with its strong Parliament, was the only exception. But new ideas would soon shatter the French monarchy, upset the balance of power, and revolutionize European societies. In the next chapters, you will read about how the Enlightenment, the French Revolution, the rise of Napoleon Bonaparte, and the Industrial Revolution would transform Europe.

GLOBAL CONNECTIONS

Polish patriots, such as cavalry commander Kasimir Pulaski, bravely resisted partition. In 1772, though, Russian advances forced Pulaski to flee. In France, he met Benjamin Franklin, who urged him to join the American colonists' fight for independence. Pulaski organized the first American cavalry corps and led many charges against the British. He was later killed in Georgia. Today, the people of two nations honor Pulaski as a heroic freedom fighter.

SECTION 5 REVIEW

1. **Identify** (a) St. Petersburg, (b) Vitus Bering, (c) Catherine the Great.
2. (a) List three goals of Peter the Great. (b) Explain one reform that Peter undertook to achieve each goal.
3. Why did Russian rulers seek to expand their territory in the 1700s?
4. How did Poland disappear as an independent state in the late 1700s?
5. *Critical Thinking* **Comparing** Compare the goals and policies of Peter the Great to those of *one* of the following: (a) Louis XIV, (b) Frederick II, (c) Maria Theresa.
6. *ACTIVITY* Imagine that Peter the Great wanted to learn about the latest technology and ways of life in the United States today. Draw up a list of the people he should meet and the places he should visit.

CHAPTER REVIEW

REVIEWING VOCABULARY

Choose *four* vocabulary words from this chapter. Then, write a sentence for each word in which you define the word and describe its relation to the political system of one of the major European powers.

REVIEWING FACTS

1. What was the Spanish Armada? What happened to it?
2. What caused Spain's economy to decline beginning in the 1600s?
3. Explain what the statement, "I am the state," meant regarding the French monarchy.

4. Describe the results of the English Civil War.
5. How did the Glorious Revolution limit royal power in England?
6. What was the status of Germany following the Thirty Years' War?
7. What reforms did Peter the Great carry out?
8. How and when did the kingdom of Poland lose its independence?

REVIEWING CHAPTER THEMES

Review the "Focus On" questions at the start of this chapter. Then select *three* of those questions and answer them, using information from the chapter.

SKILLS FOR SUCCESS INTERVIEWING

Before interviewers begin asking questions, they need to be well informed about the topic. Once the interview begins, the interviewer tries to go into greater depth and get as thorough information as possible. To do this, interviewers should avoid questions that can be answered by a simple yes or no.

Preparing imaginary interviews with historical figures is a good way to practice interviewing skills. The interview questions listed at right are some possible questions an interviewer who lived in the 1600s might have asked Louis XIV.

1. **Prepare a list of questions in advance.** (a) Is question D or E a better question to ask about the Huguenots? Why? (b) Would it be good interviewing to ask question B? Why or why not?

2. **Organize the questions in a logical progression.** Which question would you use as your closing question—A, E, F, or G? Explain.

3. **Anticipate responses and prepare follow-up questions.** (a) How would you expect Louis XIV to answer question E? (b) What would be a good follow-up question to this answer?

4. **Listen carefully and record the answers during the interview.** Why is it important to record answers during the interview instead of after it is over?

Interview Questions

A. What do you consider to be your greatest accomplishment and why?

B. When did you first come to power?

C. What did it feel like to assume the leadership of your nation at such a young age?

D. As a Christian, how can you justify the persecution of the Huguenots?

E. Why did you revoke the Edict of Nantes and resume the older state policy against the Huguenots?

F. Did you know that France's wars have left the nation deeply in debt?

G. Who do you think are France's greatest painters and writers today? Why?

H. What do you like best about the palace of Versailles? Why?

CRITICAL THINKING

1. **Understanding Sequence** Create a time line showing key events in Spain's history between the rise of Ferdinand and Isabella and the end of the golden age. Use events from this chapter and from Chapters 9, 14, 15, and 16.

2. **Linking Past and Present** Which aspects of Commonwealth society are part of American society today? Which are not?

3. **Recognizing Points of View** How might each of the following have viewed the reign of Peter the Great: (a) a boyar, (b) a serf, (c) a visitor from Western Europe, (d) Catherine the Great?

4. **Recognizing Causes and Effects** Review the discussion of the kingdom of Poland in Chapter 10. (a) What were the immediate causes of the partition of Poland? (b) What do you think were the long-term causes?

ANALYZING PRIMARY SOURCES

Use the quotation on page 425 to answer the following questions.

1. What was Sancho Panza afraid of?

2. What did Sancho Panza recommend that he and Don Quixote do?

3. What response did Don Quixote give?

FOR YOUR PORTFOLIO

WRITING A SPEECH Write a speech in which you introduce a European leader to a large audience. First, list important rulers from 1550 to 1800 and the lands they ruled. Choose the ruler you will introduce. Use the chapter text and outside resources to learn as much as you can about the ruler. Find at least one high-interest anecdote that you can include. Then write your speech. Include the ruler's key accomplishments and explain why he or she is important. Finally, give your speech to the class. Afterward, discuss why you think this ruler was or was not a positive force in the development of his or her nation.

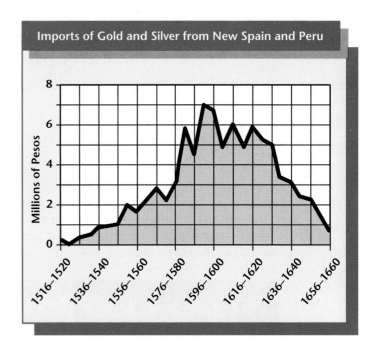

Imports of Gold and Silver from New Spain and Peru

ANALYZING GRAPHS

Use the graph to answer the following questions.

1. Summarize the information presented by the graph.

2. What was the peak value of gold and silver imports?

3. How would you expect the drop in gold and silver imports to have affected the Spanish economy?

INTERNET ACTIVITY

WRITING A BIOGRAPHY Use the Internet to research one of the absolute monarchs described in the text. Then write a brief biography of the monarch. Focus on the characteristics that made this person an example of absolutism, and on how this ruler affected the country he or she ruled. Be sure to list the sources you used in writing your biography.

Unit-in-Brief

Early Modern Times

Chapter 14 The Renaissance
and Reformation
(1300–1600)

Between the 1300s and 1500s, Europe experienced a period of cultural rebirth known as the Renaissance. During the same period, the Protestant Reformation and the Scientific Revolution reshaped European civilization.

- Beginning in Italy and later spreading to northern Europe, the Renaissance reached its most glorious expression in painting, sculpture, and architecture.
- The intellectual movement known as humanism stressed the study of classical Greek and Roman cultures and the development of the individual.
- Reformers like Martin Luther and John Calvin challenged Church corruption and eventually broke away from the Church entirely.
- In response to the Protestant Reformation, the Catholic Church undertook its own vigorous reform movement.
- Religious fervor led to widespread intolerance and persecution by both Protestants and Catholics.
- During the Scientific Revolution, startling discoveries by individuals such as Copernicus,

Newton, and Galileo changed the way Europeans viewed the physical world.

Chapter 15 The First Global Age:
Europe and Asia
(1415–1796)

Beginning in the 1500s, European powers gradually built trading empires in Asia. Thus began a period of increasing global interdependence that has continued to the present day.

- Improvements in technology helped European explorers navigate the vast oceans of the world.
- In his search for a sea route to Asia, Christopher Columbus came upon the Americas, two continents previously unknown to Europeans.
- While strongly influenced by China and India, the nations of Southeast Asia retained their own unique cultural identities.
- The desire for spices led Europeans to seek control of the Indian Ocean trade network.
- In the 1600s, the Dutch replaced the Portuguese as the major European power in Asia. In the 1700s, England and France vied for dominance.

- During the 1500s and 1600s, China and Korea restricted contact with the outside world.
- While the Japanese initially welcomed western traders, they later adopted a similar policy of isolation.

Chapter 16 The First Global Age: Europe, the Americas, and Africa
(1492–1750)

During the age of exploration, European powers built colonial empires in the Americas. New patterns of conquest and global exchange had an enormous impact on the civilizations of Africa as well.

- Spanish conquistadors vanquished the Aztec and Incan civilizations and set up a vast empire in the Americas.
- By the 1600s, Spain, France, England, and the Netherlands were competing for trade and colonies.
- The arrival of European settlers in North America brought disaster to Native Americans.
- Beginning in the 1400s, Europeans began establishing trading outposts in Africa.
- Millions of slaves were imported from Africa to meet labor needs in American colonies. The slave trade led to the fall of some African states and the rise of others.
- The Columbian Exchange was a vast global interchange of people, animals, culture, ideas, and technology.

- Beginning in the 1500s, Europe experienced a commercial revolution that brought about dramatic economic changes, including the rise of capitalism.

Chapter 17 The Age of Absolutism
(1550–1800)

During the 1500s and 1600s, European monarchs struggled to centralize their power. As they vied for the lead in overseas empire, the center of world civilization shifted to Europe.

- During the 1500s, wealth from the Americas helped make Spain the most powerful nation in Europe.
- Following a period of religious and social turmoil, Louis XIV achieved royal absolutism and helped France become the most powerful nation in Europe in the 1600s.
- Despite efforts at absolutism by several English monarchs, Parliament successfully asserted itself against royal power.
- The Thirty Years' War involved most of Europe. After the Peace of Westphalia, Prussia emerged as a new Protestant power.
- The Hapsburgs expanded Austrian territory but were unable to develop a strong centralized system.
- Peter the Great of Russia centralized royal power, embarked on a program of modernization, and sought to expand Russian territory from Europe to the Pacific.

A Global View

How Did Changes in Western Europe Help Bring About the First Global Age?

Between the 1300s and the 1600s, Europe moved out of the medieval period of relative isolation. European nations extended their economic links—and, sometimes, their military might—around the world. For these and other reasons, many historians consider this period to be the birth of the modern age.

Rebirth and Reform

The Renaissance was truly a "rebirth" of western culture. Great artists like Michelangelo and writers like Shakespeare created modern styles in the arts. During the Reformation, religious reformers like Luther and Calvin founded the modern Protestant churches. Con-

flicts between Catholic and Protestant nations would shape European politics for centuries.

Finally, the Scientific Revolution began the exploration of the physical universe by the methods of modern science. Scientists from Copernicus to Newton formulated numerous scientific laws for the first time.

Western Empires

While these changes in western culture were going on, Europeans also embarked upon an unprecedented surge of empire building. Equipped with new ships, navigational aids, and gunpowder weapons, European soldiers, traders, and missionaries spread western power around the world.

The first target of European empire builders was Asia, Europe's longtime trading partner. During the 1500s and 1600s, Europeans established scattered trading posts and colonies in India, Southeast Asia, and beyond. They brought back profitable cargoes of spices, silks, and other valuable Asian goods.

At the same time, Europeans also established a presence in Africa and the Americas. Spanish conquistadors, followed by settlers from Portugal, the Netherlands, France, and England, conquered much of the so-called New World—South America, the Caribbean islands, and North America.

1350   1450   1550

AFRICA

1300s
Kingdom of Benin flourishes

1460s
Sonni Ali founds Songhai

1500s
Zulus migrate into southern Africa

THE AMERICAS

1400s
Aztec and Incan empires expand

1492
Columbus reaches the Caribbean

1521
Fall of Tenochtitlán

ASIA AND OCEANIA

1405–1433
Voyages of Zheng He

1510
Portuguese seize Goa

1526
Mughal empire founded

EUROPE

Mid-1300s
Renaissance begins in Italy

1456
Gutenberg Bible launches age of printing

1517
Luther issues 95 Theses

These colonists shipped home gold, silver, sugar, tobacco, and other commodities.

Western people first settled on the coasts of Africa to establish way stations on the new sea route to Asia. To get laborers for their American plantations and mines, however, Europeans soon developed a brutal but lucrative trade in African slaves. The slave trade added very substantially to the working population of the Americas but cost Africa millions of human beings.

Powerful Kings and Queens

While these empires were growing overseas, the modern system of great powers was evolving in Europe itself. France became Europe's superpower in the 1600s. Louis XIV, the "Sun King," served as a model of absolute royal power. England in the 1600s, by contrast, provided an early example of more democratic rule as Parliament limited the power of monarchs.

Farther east, three states—Austria, Prussia, and Russia—emerged as great modern powers in the 1700s. The Russia of Peter the Great and the Prussia of Frederick the Great particularly emphasized strong bureaucracies and armies as instruments of royal power.

Looking Ahead

All these trends and developments had great significance for the future. Reformed religion and Renaissance art would continue to shape the cultural experience of Europeans for centuries. The Scientific Revolution, combined with the later rise of industry, would give human beings unprecedented understanding of the world they lived in.

The European great power system would build the empires and fight the wars of later centuries. Modern democratic and bureaucratic governments would grow from these early modern nation states. And the global connections first forged by European empire builders would evolve into the modern world, where people are linked by trade, travel, and international organizations.

ACTIVITY Choose two events and two pictures from the time line below. For each, write a sentence explaining how it relates to the themes expressed in the Global View essay.

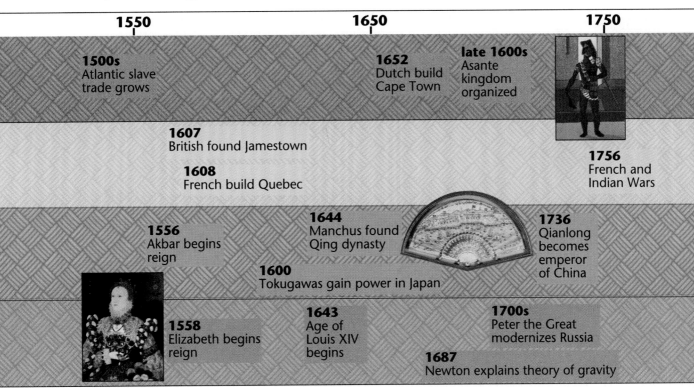

1550

1650

1750

1500s
Atlantic slave trade grows

1652
Dutch build Cape Town

late 1600s
Asante kingdom organized

1607
British found Jamestown

1608
French build Quebec

1756
French and Indian Wars

1556
Akbar begins reign

1644
Manchus found Qing dynasty

1736
Qianlong becomes emperor of China

1600
Tokugawas gain power in Japan

1558
Elizabeth begins reign

1643
Age of Louis XIV begins

1700s
Peter the Great modernizes Russia

1687
Newton explains theory of gravity

UNIT 4

You Decide

Exploring Global Issues

What Is the Goal of Education?

Like other Puritans, writer John Milton valued education. He supported a curriculum that included Greek and Latin, politics and music—even "all the locks and grips of wrestling." But he also believed that the final purpose of education was to gain knowledge of God and "out of that knowledge to love Him, to imitate Him, to be like Him."

Today, the idea of education for all is widely accepted, but educators still debate the final purpose. To begin your investigation, examine these viewpoints.

GREECE

450 B.C.

This vase painting, *Instruction in Music and Grammar at an Attic School,* illustrates the classical ideal that education should teach all arts for the development of well-rounded citizens. ▶

FRANCE

1762

Jean-Jacques Rousseau, an influential philosopher, summed up his ideas about education in his book *Emile:*

❝All men being equal, their common vocation is the profession of humanity. . . . It matters little to me, whether my pupil be designed for the army, the bar, or the pulpit. . . . To live is the profession I would teach him.❞

CUBA

1883

José Martí, a poet and political leader, turned away from classical ideas about what should be taught:

❝The schools teach classes in ancient geography, rules of rhetoric, and similar things of long ago, but in their place there should be courses in health; advice on hygiene; practical counseling; clear and simple studies of the human body, its parts, functions, ways of adjusting one to the other, economizing one's strength, and directing it well so that there will be no reason to restore it later.❞

BRITAIN

1944

Sir William Beveridge, a leading economist, argued that education was vital to a democracy:

❝Ignorance is an evil weed, which dictators may cultivate among their dupes, but which no democracy can afford amongst its citizens.❞

UNITED STATES

1954

Virginia Gildersleeve, dean of Barnard College, summed up her ideas about a well-rounded education:

❝The ability to think straight, some knowledge of the past, some vision of the future, some skill to do useful service, some urge to fit that service into the well-being of the community—those are the most vital things education must try to produce.❞

NIGERIA

1960s

After gaining independence, many African nations set up educational systems that stressed the skills needed to modernize, such as engineering or agriculture. Here, a botany student learns about plant chemistry. ▶

JAPAN

1980s

Jiro Nagai, a professor of education, listed the goals of modern Japanese schooling:

❝Citizenship education should produce citizens who (1) realize that the dignity of the individual and respect for human rights form the basis of a democratic social life; (2) have a deep love and awareness of their own nation and culture . . . ; (3) have a spirit of international understanding and cooperation. Schools in Japan are expected to develop such qualities in the nation's younger generation.❞

COMPARING VIEWPOINTS

1. Which of these viewpoints focus mainly on the needs of the individual student? Which focus on the needs of the community?
2. Which of the two pictures better illustrates Martí's point of view? Which of the pictures represents an opposing idea? Explain.
3. Which of these viewpoints seems closest to the educational goals of your own school?

YOUR INVESTIGATION

ACTIVITY

1. Find out more about other viewpoints related to this topic. You might investigate one or more of the following:
   ■ The educational and civil service system in Confucian China.
   ■ The goals of the traditional age-grade system shared by many African cultures.
   ■ The work of an educational reformer, such as Friedrich Froebel of Germany, George Dewey of the United States, or Maria Montessori of Italy.
   ■ The educational system of a totalitarian state, such as Nazi Germany or the Soviet Union under Stalin.
   ■ Current debates in the United States over "tech-prep" education or the teaching of values in schools.

2. Decide which viewpoint you agree with most closely and express it in your own way. You may do so in an essay, a cartoon, a poem, a drawing or painting, a song, a skit, a video, or some other way.

ENLIGHTENMENT AND REVOLUTION

Global Interaction

2 *From 1756 to 1763, Britain and France fought for empire in Europe, North America, and Asia. As a result of the Seven Years' War, Britain won control of Canada.*

NORTH
AMERICA

2

1

ATLANTIC
OCEAN

PACIFIC
OCEAN

SOUTH
AMERICA

N
W — E
S

**Political
and Social Systems**

1 *Colonial Latin America developed a rigid social hierarchy. This painting shows members of different Mexican social classes during the later colonial period.*

**Continuity
and Change**

3 *The Atlantic slave trade led to the decline of some West African kingdoms and the rise of others. This helmet is from the Asante kingdom, which flourished in the 1700s.*

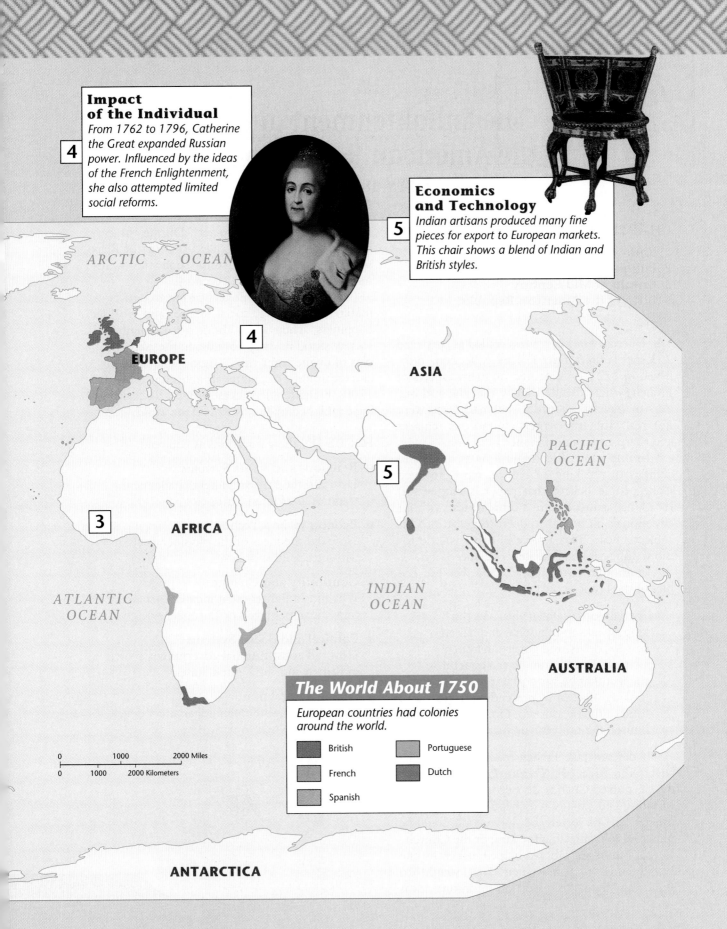

Impact of the Individual

4 From 1762 to 1796, Catherine the Great expanded Russian power. Influenced by the ideas of the French Enlightenment, she also attempted limited social reforms.

Economics and Technology

5 Indian artisans produced many fine pieces for export to European markets. This chair shows a blend of Indian and British styles.

ARCTIC OCEAN

4

EUROPE

ASIA

5

PACIFIC OCEAN

3

AFRICA

ATLANTIC OCEAN

INDIAN OCEAN

AUSTRALIA

The World About 1750

European countries had colonies around the world.

- British
- French
- Spanish
- Portuguese
- Dutch

0   1000   2000 Miles

0   1000   2000 Kilometers

ANTARCTICA

The Enlightenment and the American Revolution

(1715–1800)

CHAPTER OUTLINE

1 **Philosophy in the Age of Reason**
2 **Enlightenment Ideas Spread**
3 **Britain at Mid-Century**
4 **Birth of the American Republic**

All across France, readers smiled as they read the *Persian Letters*. This collection, published in 1721, commented on many aspects of French society. Readers knew that the authors, Persian travelers named Usbek and Rica, were not real. Still, the writers' humorous remarks and sharp criticisms of France hit home.

In one letter, Rica reports on the amazing abilities of the king of France, who can even make people believe that paper is money: "If [the king] is involved in a difficult war without any money, all he has to do is to get it into his subjects' heads that a piece of paper will do for money, they are immediately convinced of it."

In another letter, Usbek describes the nobles of the French court:

66A great lord is a man who sees the king, speaks to ministers, and has ancestors, debts, and government pensions. If, in addition, he can conceal the fact that he has nothing to do by looking busy, or by pretending to be fond of the pleasures of life, he thinks himself the most fortunate of men.99

It did not take French readers long to discover who wrote the *Persian Letters*. He was a minor noble, Charles de Secondat, Baron de Montesquieu (MAHN tehs kyoo). He had published the book secretly because people could be punished for criticizing the king or the Church.

Montesquieu's book helped usher in the Enlightenment, a movement that sought to shine the "light" of reason on traditional ideas about government and society. During the Enlightenment, sometimes called the Age of Reason, thinkers fought against superstition, ignorance, intolerance, and tyranny.

Enlightenment thinkers promoted goals of material well-being, social justice, and worldly happiness. Their ideas about government and society stood in sharp contrast to the old principles of divine-right rule, a rigid social hierarchy, and the promise of a better life in heaven. Since the 1700s, Enlightenment ideas have spread, challenging established traditions around the world.

FOCUS ON these questions as you read:

■ **Religions and Value Systems**
How did the Enlightenment challenge the traditional order in Europe?

■ **Economics and Technology**
How did the ideas of the physiocrats clash with mercantilist policy?

■ **Continuity and Change**
Why did Enlightenment ideas at first affect only the upper levels of European society?

■ **Political and Social Systems**
How did constitutional government evolve in Britain and the United States?

■ **Global Interaction**
How did Enlightenment ideas affect developments in North America?

TIME AND PLACE

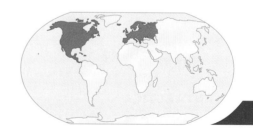

A New View of the World The first balloon flights in the late 1700s caused a sensation. By conquering gravity, balloons not only gave people a new perspective on the world but also inspired a new faith in the power of human reason. In this way, they are a perfect symbol for the European Age of Enlightenment, during which they were invented. ***Economics and Technology*** How would balloon flights provide a new perspective on the world?

HUMANITIES LINK

Art History Jean-Antoine Houdon, *Voltaire* (page 457).
Literature In this chapter, you will encounter passages from the following works of literature: Baron de Montesquieu, *Persian Letters* (page 454); Alexander Pope, "Essay on Man" (page 456); Fanny Burney, *Evelina* (pages 474–475).

| **1707** England and Scotland unite | **1719** Defoe's *Robinson Crusoe* | **1748** Montesquieu's *The Spirit of the Laws* | **1762** Rousseau's *The Social Contract* | **1781** Joseph II of Austria grants religious toleration | **1783** Treaty of Paris ends American Revolution |

| 1700 | 1720 | 1740 | 1760 | 1780 | 1800 |

1 Philosophy in the Age of Reason

Guide for Reading

■ How was the Enlightenment linked to the Scientific Revolution?

■ What ideas about government emerged during the Enlightenment?

■ What economic ideas did Enlightenment thinkers support?

■ **Vocabulary** *natural laws, social contract, natural rights, philosophe, physiocrat, laissez faire, free market*

> 66Go, wondrous creature! mount where
>   Science guides;
>   Go, measure earth, weigh air, and state
>   the tides;
>   Instruct the planets in what orbs to run,
>   Correct old Time, and regulate the
>   sun.99

Those lines by the English poet Alexander Pope celebrated the successes of humans—the "wondrous creature"—in the Scientific Revolution. By the early 1700s, European thinkers felt that nothing was beyond the reach of the human mind. Using the methods of modern science, reformers set out to study human behavior and solve the problems of society.

A World of Progress and Reason

The Enlightenment grew out of the Scientific Revolution of the 1500s and 1600s, with its amazing discoveries by thinkers like Copernicus and Newton. (See pages 364–367.) In the 1700s, other scientists expanded European knowledge. Joseph Priestley and Antoine Lavoisier (ahn TWAHN lah vwah ZYAY), for example, built the framework for modern chemistry. Edward Jenner developed a vaccine against smallpox, a disease whose path of death spanned the centuries.

Scientific successes created great confidence in the power of reason. If people used reason to find laws that governed the physical world, why not use reason to discover natural laws—laws that govern human nature? By applying scientific knowledge, inventors changed peoples' lives. Why not apply natural laws to change human society? Through the use of reason, insisted Enlightenment thinkers, they could solve every social, political, and economic problem. Heaven could be achieved here on Earth.

Two Views of the Social Contract

In the 1600s, two English thinkers, Thomas Hobbes and John Locke, set forth ideas that were to become key to the Enlightenment. Both men lived through the upheavals that shook England early in the century. (See Chapter 17.) Yet they came to very different conclusions about human nature and the purpose and nature of government.

"Nasty, brutish, and short." Thomas Hobbes set out his ideas in a work titled *Leviathan.* Hobbes argued that people were naturally cruel, greedy, and selfish. If not strictly controlled, they would fight, rob, and oppress one another. Life in the "state of nature"—without laws or other control—would be "solitary, poor, nasty, brutish, and short."

To escape that "brutish" life, said Hobbes, people entered into a social contract, an agreement by which they gave up the state of nature for an organized society. Hobbes believed that only a powerful government could ensure an orderly society. Such a government was an absolute monarchy, which could impose order and compel obedience. Not surprisingly, Hobbes had supported the Stuart kings in their struggle against Parliament.

Natural rights. John Locke had a more optimistic view of human nature. People were basically reasonable and moral, he said. Further,

GLOBAL CONNECTIONS

Growing knowledge of other cultures enriched western thought. Enlightenment thinkers were drawn to the sages of China and the gurus, or religious thinkers of India, as well as to Greek and Roman philosophers. Some saw Native American sachems, or wisemen, as great sources of wisdom, closer to nature and natural truths than western thinkers.

they had natural rights, or rights that belonged to all humans from birth. These included the right to life, liberty, and property.

In *Two Treatises of Government,* Locke argued that people formed governments to protect their natural rights. The best kind of government, he said, had limited power and was accepted by all citizens. Thus, unlike Hobbes, Locke rejected absolute monarchy and sided with Parliament in its struggle against the Stuarts.

Locke then set out a radical idea. A government, he said, has an obligation to those it governs. If a government fails its obligations or violates people's natural rights, the people have the right to overthrow the government. This right to revolution would echo through Europe, in Britain's North American colonies, and around the world in the centuries that followed.

Montesquieu's Spirit of the Laws

In the 1700s, France saw a flowering of Enlightenment thought. An early and influential thinker was the Baron de Montesquieu. Montesquieu studied the governments of Europe, from Italy to England. He read all he could about ancient and medieval Europe and learned about Chinese and Native American cultures. His sharp criticism of absolute monarchy opened the doors for later debate.

In 1748, Montesquieu published *The Spirit of the Laws.* In it, he discussed governments throughout history and wrote admiringly about Britain's limited monarchy. Montesquieu felt that the British had protected themselves against tyranny by dividing the functions and powers of government among three separate branches: the legislature, executive, and judiciary. (In fact, Montesquieu had misunderstood the British system, which did not separate powers in this way.) To him, the separation of powers was the best way to protect liberty.

Montesquieu also felt that each branch of government could serve as a check on the other two, an idea that we call checks and balances. Some 40 years after Montesquieu's book appeared in France, the ideas of separation of powers and checks and balances in government were written into the Constitution of the United States. (See page 473.)

Voltaire *Jean-Antoine Houdon, who lived from 1741 to 1828, was the greatest sculptor of his time. His work combined classical dignity with precise realism. In this statue, even though Voltaire is shown in the robes of ancient Rome, his face is starkly realistic. Houdon makes no effort to hide the ravages of old age on the features of the philosopher, who was 84 years old at the time the sculpture was begun.* **Art and Literature** *Look at the pictures on page 103. How do you think a classical Greek sculpture of Voltaire might differ from this one by Houdon? Explain.*

The World of the Philosophes

In France, a group of Enlightenment thinkers applied the methods of science to better understand and improve society. These thinkers were called philosophes, which means "lovers of wisdom."

Voltaire defends freedom of thought. Probably the most famous philosophe was François-Marie Arouet, who took the name Voltaire. "My trade," said Voltaire, "is to say what I think," and he did so throughout his long, controversial life. Voltaire used biting wit as a weapon to expose the abuses of his day. He targeted corrupt officials and idle aristocrats. Barbs flew from his pen against inequality, injustice, and superstition. He detested the slave trade and deplored religious prejudice.

Voltaire's outspoken attacks offended the government and the Catholic Church. He was imprisoned and forced into exile. He saw his books censored and burned, but he continued to defend freedom of speech. "I do not agree with a word that you say," he supposedly declared, "but I will defend to the death your right to say it." (◨ See *You Decide,* "What Limits Should There Be on Freedom of Speech?" pages 550–551.)

The Encyclopedia. Another philosophe, Denis Diderot (dee DROH), labored some 25 years to produce a 28-volume *Encyclopedia.* As the editor of this huge work, Diderot did more than just gather articles on human knowledge. His purpose was "to change the general way of thinking" by explaining the new thinking on government, philosophy, and religion. Diderot's *Encyclopedia* included articles by leading thinkers of the day, including Montesquieu and Voltaire.

▲ *Diderot's* Encyclopedia

In their *Encyclopedia* articles, the philosophes denounced slavery, praised freedom of expression, and urged education for all. They attacked divine-right theory and traditional religions. Critics raised an outcry. The French government argued that the *Encyclopedia* was an attack on public morals, while the pope threatened to excommunicate Catholics who bought or read the volumes.

Despite efforts to ban the *Encyclopedia,* as many as 20,000 copies were printed between 1751 and 1789. This work did much to shape French public opinion in the mid-1700s. When translated into other languages, it helped spread Enlightenment ideas across Europe and into the Americas.

Rousseau: A Controversial Figure

The most controversial philosophe was Jean-Jacques Rousseau (ZHAHN ZHAHK roo SOH). Rousseau was a strange, difficult man. Coming from a poor family, he never felt comfortable in the glittering social world of Enlightenment thinkers.

Rousseau believed that people in their natural state were basically good. This natural innocence, he felt, was corrupted by the evils of society, especially the unequal distribution of property. This view was later adopted by many reformers and revolutionaries.

In 1762, Rousseau set forth his ideas about government and society in *The Social Contract.* It begins: "Man is born free, and everywhere he is in chains." The chains, says Rousseau, are those of society, which controls the way people behave. He argues, however, that some social controls—control by a freely formed government, for example—are good, not evil. In consenting to form a government, he says, individuals choose to give up their self-interest in favor of the common good. Although people surrender their rights, they retain their freedom because the government is based on the consent of the governed.

Rousseau put his faith in the "general will," or the best conscience of the people. The good of the community as a whole, he said, should be placed above individual interests. He defined freedom as obedience to the law. Thus, unlike many Enlightenment thinkers who put the individual first, Rousseau felt that the individual should be subordinate to the community.

Rousseau has influenced political and social thinkers for more than 200 years. Woven through his work is a hatred of political and economic oppression. His ideas would help fan the flames of revolt in centuries to come.

Limited "Natural Rights" for Women

The Enlightenment slogan "free and equal" did not apply to women. Women did have "natural rights," said the philosophes. But unlike the natural rights of men, these rights were limited to the areas of home and family.

European Political Thinkers

Thinker	Major Ideas	Quotation	Connections Today
Thomas Hobbes *Leviathan* (1651) 	People are driven by selfishness and greed. To avoid chaos, they give up their freedom to a government that will ensure order. Such a government must be strong and able to suppress rebellion.	"The condition of man [in the state of nature] . . . is a condition of war of everyone against everyone."	Hobbes's ideas have been used to justify absolute power. To some people today, Hobbes presents a bleak but true view of how people and governments behave.
John Locke *Two Treatises of Government* (1690) 	People have a natural right to life, liberty, and property. Rulers have a responsibility to protect those rights. People have the right to change a government that fails to do so.	"Men being . . . by nature all free, equal, and independent, no one can be put out of this estate and subjected to the political power of another without his own consent."	Locke's ideas influenced authors of U.S. Declaration of Independence and French revolutionaries in the 1790s. Later, people extended his ideas to include equality for women and others.
Baron de Montesquieu *The Spirit of the Laws* (1748) 	The powers of government should be separated into executive, legislative, and judicial branches, to prevent any one group from gaining too much power.	"In order to have . . . liberty, it is necessary that government be set up so that one man need not be afraid of another."	His ideas about separation of powers greatly influenced framers of U.S. Constitution.
Jean-Jacques Rousseau *The Social Contract* (1762) 	People are basically good but become corrupted by society. In an ideal society, people would make the laws and would obey them willingly.	"Only the general will can direct the energies of the state in a manner appropriate to the end for which it was founded, i.e., the common good."	Rousseau has been hailed as a champion of democracy for his idea that political authority lies with the people. But dictators have used his ideas about the "general will" to justify their programs.

Interpreting a Chart Political and social philosophers thrived in Enlightenment Europe. Their ideas had a major impact throughout the world of their time and continue to influence developments today. ■ *Why did Montesquieu recommend separation of powers of government? How might Rousseau's ideas be used to justify dictatorship?*

By the mid-1700s, a small but growing number of women protested this view. They questioned the notion that women were by nature inferior to men and that men's domination of women was therefore part of "nature's plan." Germaine de Staël in France and Catharine Macaulay and Mary Wollstonecraft in England argued that women had been excluded from the social contract itself. Their arguments were ridiculed and often sharply condemned.

Wollstonecraft was the best known of the British female critics. She accepted that a woman's first duty was to be a good mother. At the same time, however, she felt that a woman should be able to decide what is in her own interest and should not be completely dependent on her husband. In 1792, Wollstonecraft published *A Vindication of the Rights of Woman*. In it, she called for the same education for girls and boys. Only education, she argued, could give women the tools they needed to participate equally with men in public life.

New Economic Thinking

Other thinkers, the physiocrats, focused on economic reforms. Like the philosophes, physiocrats looked for natural laws to define a rational economic system.

Laissez faire. Physiocrats rejected mercantilism, which required government regulation to achieve a favorable balance of trade. Instead, they urged a policy of laissez faire (LEHS ay FAIR), allowing business to operate with little or no government interference. Unlike mercantilists, who called for acquiring gold and silver wealth through trade, the physiocrats claimed that real wealth came from making the land more productive. Extractive industries, they said, such as agriculture, mining, and logging, produced new wealth. While mercantilists had imposed tariffs, or taxes on foreign goods, to protect local manufacturing, physiocrats supported free trade and wanted to lift all tariffs.

ISSUES For TODAY

Laissez-faire economists argue that society would be better off if the government allowed business and the marketplace to operate without interference. What is the proper role of government in a nation's economy?

Adam Smith. British economist Adam Smith greatly admired the physiocrats. In his influential work, *The Wealth of Nations*, he argued that the free market, the natural forces of supply and demand, should be allowed to operate and regulate business. He tried to show how manufacturing, trade, wages, profits, and economic growth were all linked to the forces of supply and demand. Wherever there is a demand for goods or services, he said, suppliers will seek to meet it. They do so because of the economic rewards they can get from fulfilling the demand. A strong supporter of laissez faire, Smith believed that the marketplace was better off without any government regulation. At the same time, however, he did believe that government had a duty to protect society, administer justice, and provide public works.

Adam Smith's ideas would gain increasing influence as the Industrial Revolution spread across Europe and beyond. His emphasis on the free market and the law of supply and demand would help to shape immensely productive economies in the 1800s and 1900s.

SECTION 1 REVIEW

1. **Identify** (a) Thomas Hobbes, (b) John Locke, (c) Baron de Montesquieu, (d) Voltaire, (e) Denis Diderot, (f) Jean-Jacques Rousseau, (g) Mary Wollstonecraft, (h) *The Wealth of Nations*.
2. **Define** (a) natural laws, (b) social contract, (c) natural rights, (d) philosophe, (e) physiocrat, (f) laissez faire, (g) free market.
3. How did the successes of the Scientific Revolution influence Enlightenment thinkers?
4. Describe the government favored by each of the following: (a) Hobbes, (b) Locke.
5. How were the physiocrats different from the mercantilists?
6. *Critical Thinking* **Defending a Position** Rousseau put the "general will"—the common good—over the interest of the individual. Do you agree with that position? Why or why not?
7. *ACTIVITY* Create a cartoon to illustrate the ideas of one or more of the philosophes you read about in this section.

2 Enlightenment Ideas Spread

Guide for Reading

- How did Enlightenment ideas pose a challenge to the established order?

- Why did some European rulers embrace Enlightenment ideas?

- What ideas influenced artists and writers of the Enlightenment?

- How did most people live during the Age of Reason?

- **Vocabulary** *salon, enlightened despot, baroque*

From France, Enlightenment ideas flowed across Europe, and beyond. Everywhere, thinkers examined traditional beliefs and customs in the light of reason and found them flawed. Even absolute monarchs experimented with Enlightenment ideas, although they drew back when it became clear that the changes called for by the philosophes might threaten the old order—that is, the established way of doing things.

The Challenge of New Ideas

The ideas of the Enlightenment spread quickly through many levels of society. Educated people all over Europe eagerly read not only Diderot's *Encyclopedia* but also the small, cheap pamphlets that printers churned out on a broad range of issues. At the same time, middle-class men met to discuss the new ideas in the coffeehouses that were sprouting up in Europe's major cities.

Spreading Enlightenment Ideas Printing presses helped carry the ideas of the philosophes to a growing literate middle class. Booksellers offered not only Diderot's massive Encyclopedia *but also cheaper books and pamphlets on a range of issues. Here, customers examine the wares in a local bookshop.* **Continuity and Change** *How are ideas spread today?*

Achieving a just society. As Enlightenment ideas spread, people began to challenge the old ways. More and more, they saw the need for reform to achieve a just society.

During the Middle Ages, most Europeans had accepted without question a society based on divine-right rule, a strict class system, and a belief in heavenly reward for earthly suffering. In the Age of Reason, such ideas seemed unscientific and irrational. A just society, Enlightenment thinkers taught, should ensure material well-being, social justice, and happiness in this world.

Censorship. Government and Church authorities felt they had a sacred duty to defend the old order. They believed the old order had been set up by God. To protect against the attacks of the Enlightenment, they waged a war of censorship, banning and burning books and imprisoning writers. Some writers avoided the censors by having their books printed in the few countries, like the Netherlands, that allowed

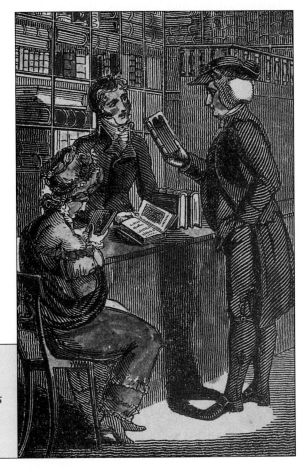

Salon de Madame Geoffrin The salon of Madame Geoffrin attracted the leading artists, writers, and thinkers of the day. Through gatherings like these, women helped to shape the tastes and manners of the Enlightenment. **Political and Social Systems** Based on the painting, did more women or men attend Madame Geoffrin's salon? Why do you think this was so?

freedom of the press. Others published their books under a false name.

Writers like Montesquieu, Voltaire, and Rousseau sometimes disguised their ideas in works of fiction. You have already seen how Montesquieu mocked French society in the *Persian Letters*. The hero of Voltaire's humorous novel *Candide* travels across Europe and even to the Americas and the Middle East in search of "the best of all possible worlds." Voltaire slyly uses the tale to expose the corruption and hypocrisy of European society. Novels like *Candide* did not suggest specific reforms but did show readers the need for change.

Salons

The new literature, the arts, science, and philosophy were regular topics of discussion in salons, informal social gatherings at which writers, artists, philosophers, and others exchanged ideas. The salon originated in the 1600s, when a group of noblewomen in Paris began inviting a few friends to their homes for poetry readings. Only the most witty, intelligent, and well-read people were invited to the salons.

By the 1700s, some middle-class women began holding salons. In the drawing rooms of these *salonières* (sah lohn YAIR), middle-class citizens could meet with the nobility on an equal footing to discuss and spread Enlightenment ideas.

The Salon in the Rue Saint Honoré

In 1713, 14-year-old Marie-Thérèse Rodet was wed to François Geoffrin (zhehf RAN), 48. Everyone said it was a good match. Monsieur Geoffrin was a rich and well-respected manufacturer who would provide a comfortable life for his young wife.

The Geoffrins settled into a house on the Rue Saint Honoré (SAHN ahn oh RAY) in Paris. In the years that followed, Madame Geoffrin gave birth to two children and dutifully cared for her home and family. The pattern of her life seemed set forever—quiet and uneventful, without much intellectual excitement.

A new world. Then one day, a neighbor invited Madame Geoffrin to attend her salon. For the first time, the young woman heard the polished conversation of learned men and women. It opened the door to a new world.

Inspired, Madame Geoffrin eventually set up her own salon in the house on Rue Saint Honoré. She entertained poets and philosophers, artists and musicians. Her husband protested, but she would not give in. For years, he sat silent and ignored at the table while her guests dined and talked. One day, someone noticed that the old man was absent and inquired about him. "It was my husband," replied Madame Geoffrin. "He is dead."

The *salonière*. By 1750, Madame Geoffrin was a leading *salonière*. In her home, she brought together the brightest and most talented people of her day. On Mondays, Geoffrin welcomed artists and musicians. The young musical genius Wolfgang Amadeus Mozart played for her guests. On Wednesdays, philosophers and poets came for discussion and dispute. Diderot was a regular at the Wednesday dinners, and Madame Geoffrin donated large sums of money to support the *Encyclopedia*.

Even visiting monarchs paid their respects at what came to be called the "kingdom" of Rue Saint Honoré. Madame Geoffrin corresponded with Catherine II of Russia and Maria Theresa of Austria. Catherine was so eager to learn what was going on that she had spies report on the conversation at Geoffrin's salon.

"Women ruled then." *Salonières* like Madame Geoffrin were often not well educated themselves. They set up salons to learn from the conversations of educated men. The *salonières* were not intimidated by such men, however. While remaining gracious, they demanded high standards of discussion. Diderot commented:

66Women accustom us to discuss with charm and clearness the driest and thorniest subjects. . . . Hence we develop a particular method of explaining ourselves easily, and this method passes from conversation into style.99

By the end of the 1700s, the influence of women's salons had ended. Later, looking back, the celebrated court painter Elisabeth Vigée Lebrun observed: "Women ruled then." 🔖

Enlightened Despots

Discussions of Enlightenment theories also enlivened the courts of Europe. Philosophes tried to convince European rulers to adopt their ideas. If they could "enlighten" the ruling classes, they thought, they could bring about reform. Some monarchs did accept Enlightenment ideas. They became enlightened despots, or absolute rulers who used their power to bring about political and social change.

Frederick the Great. As king of Prussia from 1740 to 1786, Frederick II exerted extremely tight control over his subjects. Still, he saw himself as the "first servant of the state," with a duty to work for the common good.

Frederick admired Voltaire and lured him to Berlin to develop a Prussian academy of science. When the king was not busy fighting wars, he had swamps drained and forced peasants to grow new crops such as the potato. He also had seed and tools distributed to peasants who had suffered in Prussia's wars. He tolerated religious differences, welcoming victims of religious persecution. "In my kingdom," he said, "everyone can go to heaven in his own fashion."

Frederick's reforms were directed mainly at making the Prussian government more efficient. He reorganized the civil service and simplified laws. But a "rationalized" bureaucracy also meant a stronger monarchy—and more power for Frederick himself. (★ See *Skills for Success*, page 476.)

Catherine the Great. Catherine II of Russia read the works of the philosophes and exchanged letters with Voltaire and Diderot. She praised Voltaire as someone who had "fought the united enemies of humankind: superstition, fanaticism, ignorance, trickery."

Catherine, who became empress in 1762, experimented with Enlightenment ideas. Early in her reign, she made limited reforms in law and government. She granted nobles a charter of rights and spoke out against serfdom. Still, like Frederick in Prussia, Catherine intended to give up no power. When a serf revolt broke out, she ruthlessly suppressed it. She also allied herself with the Russian nobles who opposed change. In the end, Catherine's contribution to Russia was not reform but an expanded empire.

Joseph II. The most radical enlightened despot was the Hapsburg emperor Joseph II, son and successor of Maria Theresa. An eager student of the Enlightenment, Joseph traveled in disguise among his subjects to learn of their problems. His efforts to improve their lives won him the nickname the "peasant emperor."

Maria Theresa had begun to modernize Austria's government. Joseph continued her reforms. He chose talented middle-class officials rather than nobles to head departments and imposed a range of political and legal reforms. Despite opposition, he granted toleration to Protestants and Jews in his Catholic empire. He ended censorship and attempted to bring the

Catholic Church under royal control. He sold the property of many monasteries and convents, which he saw as unproductive, and used the proceeds to build hospitals. Joseph even abolished serfdom. Like many of his reforms, however, this measure was canceled after his death.

The Arts and Literature

In the 1600s and 1700s, the arts evolved to meet changing tastes. As in earlier periods, artists and composers had to please their patrons, the men and women who commissioned works from them or gave them jobs.

Courtly art. In the age of Louis XIV, courtly art and architecture were either in classical style, in the Greek and Roman tradition, or in the grand, complex style known as baroque. (See the picture on page 429.) Baroque paintings were huge, colorful, and full of excitement. They glorified historic battles or the lives of saints. Such works matched the grandeur of European courts.

By the mid-1700s, architects and designers developed the rococo style. Unlike the heavy splendor of the baroque, rococo art was personal, refined, elegant, and charming. Furniture and tapestries featured delicate shells and flowers, as well as a European version of Chinese decorations. Portrait painters showed noble subjects in charming rural settings, surrounded by happy servants and pets.

Middle-class audiences. A new audience, the growing middle class, emerged with its own requirements. Successful merchants and town officials wanted their portraits painted, but without frills. They liked pictures of family life or realistic town or country scenes. Dutch painters such as Rembrandt van Rijn (REHM brant van RIN) conferred great dignity on merchants and other ordinary, middle-class subjects.

Trends in music. New kinds of musical entertainment evolved in the baroque era. Ballets and operas—plays set to music—were performed at royal courts. Before long, opera houses sprang up from Italy to England to amuse the paying public. The music of the period followed ordered, structured forms well suited to the Age of Reason.

Among the towering musical figures of the period was Johann Sebastian Bach. A devout German Lutheran, Bach wrote complex and beautiful religious works for organ and choirs. Another German-born composer, George Frederick Handel, spent much of his life in England. There, he wrote the *Water Music* and other pieces for King George I, as well as many operas. His most celebrated work, the *Messiah,* combines instruments and voices. Today, it is a standard at Christmas and Easter concerts.

In 1762, a six-year-old prodigy, Wolfgang Amadeus Mozart, burst onto the European scene to gain instant celebrity as a composer and performer. In his brief life, the young man from Salzburg composed an amazing variety of music with remarkable speed. His brilliant operas, graceful symphonies, and moving religious music helped define the new style of classical composition. At age 35, Mozart died in poverty, leaving a musical legacy that thrives today.

The novel. By the 1700s, literature developed new forms and a wide new audience. Middle-class readers, for example, liked stories about their own times told in plain prose. One result was an outpouring of novels, long works of prose fiction.

A number of English novelists created popular works. Daniel Defoe wrote *Robinson Crusoe,* an exciting tale about a sailor ship-

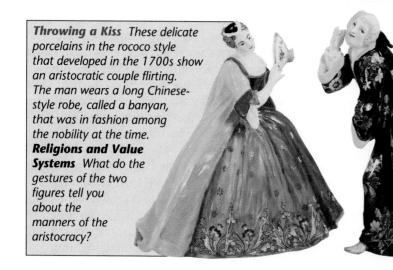

Throwing a Kiss *These delicate porcelains in the rococo style that developed in the 1700s show an aristocratic couple flirting. The man wears a long Chinese-style robe, called a banyan, that was in fashion among the nobility at the time.* **Religions and Value Systems** *What do the gestures of the two figures tell you about the manners of the aristocracy?*

Peasants Gathering Hay *Enlightenment ideas did not change life for most Europeans. The vast majority continued to live in villages and work as farmers. Here, English peasants rake hay, which was used to feed farm animals during the winter.* **Political and Social Systems** *Based on the picture, what conclusion can you draw about the role of women on the farm?*

wrecked on a tropical island. Through hard work, his own wits, and the help of an islander whom he names Friday, Crusoe survives his ordeal. In *Pamela*, Samuel Richardson used a series of letters to tell a story about a servant girl. This technique was adopted by several other authors of the period. (☐ See *World Literature,* "Evelina," pages 474–475.)

Lives of the Majority

Most Europeans were untouched by either courtly or middle-class culture. They remained what they had always been—peasants living in small rural villages. Their culture was based on centuries-old traditions that changed slowly.

Conditions west and east. Peasant life varied across Europe. Villages in Western Europe were relatively more prosperous than those in Eastern Europe. In the West, serfdom had largely disappeared. Instead, some peasants worked their own patches of land. Others were tenants of large landowners, paying a yearly rent for the land they farmed. Still others were day laborers who hired themselves out for the farm season.

In central and Eastern Europe, by contrast, serfdom was firmly rooted. In Russia, it spread and deepened in the 1700s. Peasants bound to the land owed labor services to their lords and could be bought and sold with the land. Russian landowners could also send serfs to labor in government mines or serve long terms as soldiers in the imperial armies.

Old ways survive. Despite advances, some echoes of serfdom survived in Western

Europe. In France, peasants still had to provide free labor, repairing roads and bridges after the spring floods just as their ancestors had done. In England, country squires had the right to hunt foxes across the plowed and planted fields of their tenants.

By the late 1700s, radical ideas about equality and social justice seeped into peasant villages. While some peasants eagerly sought to topple the old order, others resisted efforts to bring about change. In the 1800s, war and political upheaval as well as changing economic conditions would transform peasant life in Europe.

SECTION 2 REVIEW

1. **Identify** (a) *Candide,* (b) Joseph II, (c) Johann Sebastian Bach, (d) George Frederick Handel, (e) Wolfgang Amadeus Mozart, (f) Daniel Defoe.
2. **Define** (a) salon, (b) enlightened despot, (c) baroque.
3. (a) Describe three ways in which Enlightenment ideas spread. (b) Why did those ideas threaten the old order?
4. What were the goals of enlightened despots?
5. How did courtly tastes differ from middle-class tastes?
6. How did peasant life vary across Europe?
7. *Critical Thinking* **Analyzing Information** (a) What did Frederick II mean when he said, "In my kingdom, everyone can go to heaven in his own fashion"? (b) How did his actions reflect that idea?
8. *ACTIVITY* Imagine that you are living in Paris during the 1700s. Organize a salon to discuss a "just society." Be sure to include supporters of both the old order and Enlightenment ideas among your guests.

3 Britain at Mid-Century

Guide for Reading

- Why did Britain become a global power in the 1700s?

- What new political institutions emerged in Britain in the 1700s?

- What groups held political power in Britain?

- **Vocabulary** *constitutional government, prime minister*

66Foreign trade is . . . the honor of the kingdom, the noble profession of the merchant, . . . the supply of our wants, the employment of our poor, the improvement of our lands, the nursery of our [sailors], the walls of the kingdom, the means of our treasure, the sinews of our wars, the terror of our enemies.99

With words like these, English advocates of mercantilism preached their cause in the mid-1600s. Over the next century, Britain embraced this doctrine and built a colonial and commercial empire that reached around the world. It replaced Spain as the most successful European empire builder and outstripped the Netherlands as the foremost European trading nation. At the same time, Britain developed a constitutional monarchy, a political system somewhere between the absolute monarchies of the European continent and later democratic governments.

Global Expansion

Why did Britain, a small island kingdom on the edge of Europe, rise to global prominence in the 1700s? Here, we can look at only a few reasons for its success.

Geography. England's location made it well placed to control trade during the Renaissance. In the 1500s and 1600s, English merchants sent ships across the world's oceans and planted outposts in the West Indies, North America, and India. From these tiny settlements, England would eventually build a global empire.

Success in war. In the 1700s, Britain was generally on the winning side in European conflicts. Each victory brought valuable rewards. By the Treaty of Utrecht, France gave Britain Nova Scotia and Newfoundland in North America. (See page 429.) It also won a monopoly on the slave trade in Spanish America. The slave trade brought enormous wealth to British merchants, who invested their profits in other ventures. In 1763, the Treaty of Paris ending the Seven Years' War brought Britain all of French Canada. (See page 404.) The British East India Company pushed the French out of India.

Unlike its European rivals, Britain had no large standing army. Instead, it built up its fleet. By 1763, Britain had a more powerful navy than its greatest rival, France. With its superior naval power, it was well able to protect its growing empire and trade.

A favorable business climate. England offered a more favorable climate to business and commerce than its European rivals. Although

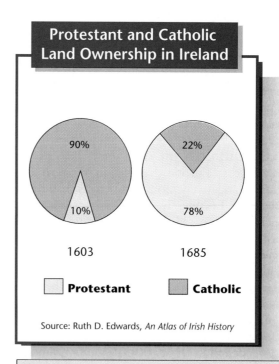

Protestant and Catholic Land Ownership in Ireland

90% / 10% — 1603

22% / 78% — 1685

Protestant / Catholic

Source: Ruth D. Edwards, *An Atlas of Irish History*

Interpreting a Chart In the 1600s, England seized land from Irish Catholics and gave it to English and Scottish settlers, who were Protestants. By the end of the century, Protestants controlled most of Ireland.
■ What percentage of Ireland's land was owned by Catholics in 1603? In 1685?

The Act of Union joined England and Scotland in the United Kingdom of Great Britain in 1707. The tiny kingdom of Wales had joined with England some 200 years earlier.

1. **Location** On the map, locate (a) Irish Sea, (b) Edinburgh, (c) London, (d) English Channel.
2. **Place** Which neighboring land was controlled by Britain but was not part of the United Kingdom in 1707?
3. **Critical Thinking** Applying Information How might it benefit England to join politically with its neighbors?

United Kingdom of Great Britain, 1707

England followed mercantilist policies, it put fewer restrictions on trade than France did. Also, while British nobles, like most nobles in Europe, looked down on trade, some did engage in business activities.

Union with Scotland. At home, England grew by merging with neighboring Scotland. In 1707, the Act of Union united the two countries in the United Kingdom of Great Britain. The union brought economic advantages to both lands. It allowed trade to pass freely between England and Scotland, creating a larger market for farmers and manufacturers. Although many Scots resented the union, growing prosperity eventually made it more acceptable. The United Kingdom also included Wales.

Ireland. England had controlled Ireland since the 1100s. In the 1600s, English rulers tried to subdue Catholic Ireland by sending Protestants from England and Scotland to settle there. They gave Protestant settlers title to Irish Catholic lands.

The Irish fiercely resisted Protestant rule. When uprisings failed, repression increased. Catholics were forbidden to own weapons, marry non-Catholics, or serve as teachers.

Growth of Constitutional Government

In the century after the Glorious Revolution (see page 435), three new political institutions arose in Britain: political parties, the cabinet, and the office of prime minister. The appearance of these institutions was part of the evolution of England's constitutional government—that is, a government whose power is defined and limited by law. Unlike the United States Constitution, which is a single written document, the British constitution is made up of all acts of Parliament over the centuries. It also includes documents such as the Magna Carta and Bill of Rights, as well as unwritten traditions that protect citizens' rights.

Political parties. Two political parties emerged in England in the late 1600s, Tories and Whigs. The conservative Tories were generally landed aristocrats who sought to preserve older traditions. They supported broad royal powers and a dominant Anglican Church. The Whigs backed the more liberal policies of the Glorious Revolution. They were more likely to reflect urban business interests, support religious toleration for Protestants, and favor Parliament over the crown. For much of the 1700s, the Whigs dominated Parliament.

Political Campaigns

Wherever there have been elections, there have also been election campaigns. Throughout history, politicians eager to win office have done whatever they could to win votes.

Linking Past and Present What methods do candidates use to win votes in the United States today? Do you think any of the same methods were used in England in the 1700s? Explain.

PAST Only men who owned land could vote in England during the 1700s. Even so, elections were a time of bustling activity. In this painting by the great British artist William Hogarth, campaigners try to win votes for their candidates outside a tavern.

PRESENT In the United States today, political campaigns are elaborate affairs, and citizens participate in events like the convention (right) mainly through television. Candidates, such as Carol Moseley-Braun (far right), however, still go out to shake hands with their supporters.

These early political parties were unlike the party organizations that we know today. They represented cliques among the rich, powerful men who served as members of Parliament. Linked by family ties or personal agreements, members pooled their votes to advance their common interests. The modern political party, representing groups of voters and with a distinct platform, did not appear until the 1800s.

The cabinet system. The cabinet was another new feature of government. In 1714, the British throne passed by hereditary right to a German Protestant prince. George I spoke no English and relied on the leaders in Parliament to help him rule. Under George I, and his German-born son George II, a handful of parliamentary advisers set policy. They were called the cabinet because they met in a small room, or "cabinet."

In time, the cabinet gained official status. It was made up of leaders of the majority party in the House of Commons. The cabinet remained in power so long as it enjoyed the support of the Commons. If the Commons voted against a cabinet decision, the cabinet resigned. This cabinet system (also called a parliamentary system) was later adopted by other countries in Europe and elsewhere around the world.

The prime minister. Heading the cabinet was the prime minister. The prime minister was the leader of the majority party in Parliament and in time the chief official of the British government. From 1721 to 1742, the able Whig leader Robert Walpole molded the cabinet into a unified body, requiring all members to agree on major issues. Although the title was not yet used, Walpole is often called Britain's first prime minister.

Politics and Society

The age of Walpole was a time of peace and prosperity. But even as Parliament and the cabinet assumed new powers, British government was far from democratic. Rather, it was an oligarchy—as you recall, a government in which the ruling power belongs to a few people.

The ruling elite. In Britain as on the continent, landowning aristocrats were seen as the "natural" ruling class. The highest nobles held seats in the House of Lords. Other wealthy landowners, along with rich business leaders in the cities, controlled elections to the House of Commons. The right to vote was limited to a relatively few male property owners, and their votes were often openly bought.

Other classes. The lives of most people contrasted sharply with those of the ruling elite. The majority made a meager living from the land. In the 1700s, even that poor existence was threatened. Wealthy landowners bought up farms and took over common lands, evicting tenant farmers and small landowners. Many landless families drifted into towns, where they faced a harsh and desperate existence.

A small but growing middle class included successful merchants and manufacturers. They controlled affairs in the towns and cities. Some improved their social standing by marrying into the landed gentry. The middle class also produced talented inventors and entrepreneurs who helped usher in the Industrial Revolution. (See Chapter 20.)

George III Reasserts Royal Power

In 1760, George III embarked on a 60-year reign. Unlike his father and grandfather, the new king was born in England. He spoke English and loved Britain. But George was eager to recover the powers the crown had lost. Following his mother's advice, "George, be a king!" he set out to reassert royal power. He wanted to end Whig domination, choose his own ministers, dissolve the cabinet system, and make the House of Commons follow his will.

Personal rule. Gradually, George found seats in Parliament for "the king's friends." Then, with their help, he set out to regain control of the government.

His troubles, however, began early in his reign. After the Seven Years' War, George and his ministers adopted a new policy: English colonists in North America must pay the costs of their own defense. When colonists protested, Parliament passed harsh measures to force them to obey. In 1775, these and other conflicts triggered the American Revolution—and disaster for Britain. (See Section 4.)

Cabinet rule restored. Britain's loss of its American colonies discredited the king. Increasingly, too, he suffered from bouts of mental illness. In the crisis of leadership that followed, cabinet rule was restored in 1788.

In the decades ahead, revolution engulfed France, and Napoleon Bonaparte's armies stormed across Europe, dragging Britain into long wars. During that time, the cabinet controlled the government. The British came to see the prime minister as their real political leader.

SECTION 3 REVIEW

1. **Identify** (a) Act of Union, (b) Tories, (c) Whigs, (d) Robert Walpole, (e) George III.
2. **Define** (a) constitutional government, (b) prime minister.
3. How did each of the following contribute to Britain's rise to global prominence in the 1700s: (a) geography, (b) success in war, (c) attitudes toward business and commerce?
4. Who made up the ruling oligarchy in Britain?
5. *Critical Thinking* **Comparing** How does the parliamentary system of government that evolved in England differ from the modern American system of government?
6. *ACTIVITY* Make a diagram showing the relationship among the English crown, prime minister, cabinet, and Parliament.

4 Birth of the American Republic

Guide for Reading

- How were the 13 English colonies part of a global empire?

- Why did colonists come to resent British rule?

- How did Enlightenment ideas influence Americans?

- What was the global impact of the American Revolution?

Early in 1776, English colonists in North America eagerly read the newly published *Common Sense*. The pamphlet called on them to declare their independence from Britain. Its author, Tom Paine, a recent immigrant from England, wrote with passion under the cool banner of reason. "In the following pages," he declared, "I offer nothing more than simple facts, plain arguments, and common sense."

In *Common Sense*, Paine echoed the themes of the Enlightenment. He rejected ancient prejudice and tyranny, while appealing to reason, natural laws, and the promise of freedom. He wrote:

> ❝'Tis repugnant to reason, to the universal order of things, to all examples from former ages, to suppose that this Continent can long remain subject to any external power.❞

Colonists hotly debated Paine's arguments. As resentment of British policies grew, however, many came to agree with his radical ideas. Soon, they set out on the dangerous and uncertain road that led to independence from British rule.

The 13 English Colonies

By 1750, a string of 13 prosperous colonies stretched along the eastern coast of North America. They were part of Britain's growing empire. Colonial cities such as Boston, New York, and Philadelphia were busy centers of commerce linking North America, the West Indies, Africa, and Europe. Colonial shipyards produced many vessels used in that global trade.

Britain applied mercantilist policies to its colonies. In the 1600s, Parliament had passed the Navigation Acts to regulate colonial trade and manufacturing. For the most part, these acts were not rigorously enforced. Smuggling was common and was not considered a crime by the colonists.

By mid-century, too, the colonies were home to diverse religions and ethnic groups. Social distinctions were more blurred than in Europe, although government and society were dominated by wealthy landowners and merchants. In politics as in much else, there was a good deal of free discussion. Colonists felt entitled to the rights of English citizens, and their colonial assemblies exercised much control over local affairs.

Ways of life differed from New England to the southern colonies. Still, colonists shared common values, respect for individual enterprise, and a growing self-confidence. They also had an increasing sense of their own destiny separate from Britain.

Growing Discontent

After 1763, relations between Britain and the 13 colonies grew strained. The Seven Years' War, called the French and Indian War in North America, had drained the British treasury. King George III and his ministers thought that the colonists should help pay for the war and for the troops still stationed on the frontier. Britain began to enforce the long-neglected laws regulating colonial trade, and Parliament passed new laws to raise taxes from the colonies.

The British measures were not burdensome. Still, colonists bitterly resented what they saw as an attack on their rights. "No taxation without representation," they protested. Since they had no representatives in Parliament, they believed, Parliament had no right to tax them. While Parliament did repeal some of the

◀ *Teapot celebrating repeal of a British tax*

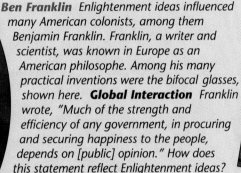

Ben Franklin *Enlightenment ideas influenced many American colonists, among them Benjamin Franklin. Franklin, a writer and scientist, was known in Europe as an American philosophe. Among his many practical inventions were the bifocal glasses, shown here.* **Global Interaction** *Franklin wrote, "Much of the strength and efficiency of any government, in procuring and securing happiness to the people, depends on [public] opinion." How does this statement reflect Enlightenment ideas?*

hated measures, in general, it asserted its right to tax.

Early clashes. A series of violent clashes intensified the crisis. In 1770, British soldiers in Boston opened fire on a crowd that was pelting them with stones and snowballs. Colonists called the death of five protesters the "Boston Massacre." In 1773, a handful of colonists staged the Boston Tea Party, hurling a cargo of recently arrived British tea into the harbor to protest a tax on tea. When Parliament passed harsh laws to punish Massachusetts, other colonies rallied to its support.

Fighting begins. In April 1775, the crisis exploded into war. The next month, as fighting spread, colonial leaders met in a Continental Congress to decide what action to take. Members included some extraordinary men: the radical yet fair-minded Boston lawyer John Adams, the Virginia planter and soldier George Washington, and such pillars of the American Enlightenment as Benjamin Franklin and Thomas Jefferson.

Declaring independence. The Congress set up a Continental Army, with George Washington in command. The following year, it took a momentous step, voting to declare independence from Britain. Young Thomas Jefferson drafted the Declaration of Independence, a document that clearly reflects the ideas of John Locke in lines such as these:

66We hold these truths to be self-evident, that all men are created equal, that they are endowed by their Creator with certain unalienable rights, that among these are life, liberty, and the pursuit of happiness. That to secure these rights, governments are instituted among men, deriving their just powers from the consent of the governed.99

The Declaration claimed that people had the right "to alter or abolish" unjust governments—a right to revolt. Jefferson carefully detailed the colonists' grievances against Britain. Because the king had trampled colonists' natural rights, he argued, the colonists had the right to rebel and set up a new government that would protect them. Aware of the risks involved, on July 4, 1776, American leaders adopted the Declaration, pledging "our lives, our fortunes, and our sacred honor" to the cause of the United States of America.

The American Revolution

At first, the American cause looked bleak. The British had professional soldiers, a huge fleet, and plentiful money. They occupied most major American cities. Also, about a third of the colonists were Loyalists who supported Britain. Many others refused to fight for either side.

The Continental Congress had few military resources and little money to pay its soldiers. Still, colonists battling for independence had some advantages. They were fighting on their own ground for their farms and towns. Although the British held New York and Philadelphia, rebels controlled the countryside.

The French alliance. A turning point in the war came with the American triumph over

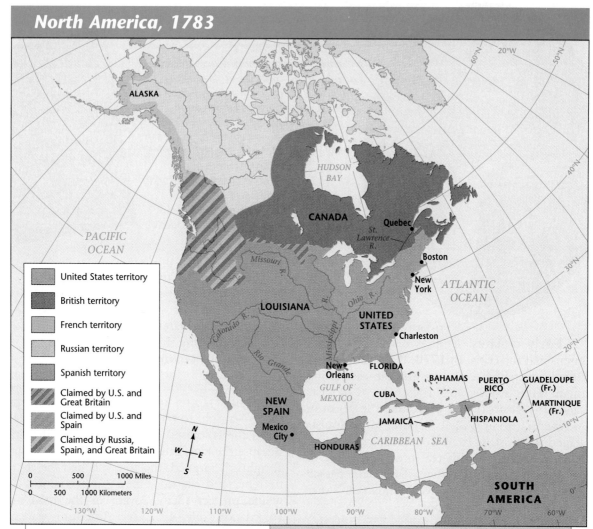

North America, 1783

Map Legend:
- United States territory
- British territory
- French territory
- Russian territory
- Spanish territory
- Claimed by U.S. and Great Britain
- Claimed by U.S. and Spain
- Claimed by Russia, Spain, and Great Britain

GEOGRAPHY AND HISTORY

In the peace treaty ending the American Revolution, Britain recognized the United States as an independent nation, stretching from the Atlantic Ocean in the east to the Mississippi River in the west. Britain still controlled Canada, to the north of the new nation.

1. Location On the map, locate (a) United States, (b) Mississippi River, (c) Canada, (d) New Spain.

2. Region (a) Who claimed Louisiana in 1783? (b) Who claimed Alaska? (c) What area was claimed by Russia, Spain, and Great Britain?

3. Critical Thinking Solving Problems What methods might the nations shown on the map use to resolve conflicting land claims?

the British in 1777 at the Battle of Saratoga. The victory convinced France to join the Americans against its old rival, Britain. The alliance brought the Americans desperately needed supplies, trained soldiers, and French warships. Spurred by the French example, the Netherlands and Spain soon added their support.

Hard times continued, however. In the brutal winter of 1777–1778, Continental troops at Valley Forge suffered from cold, hunger, and disease. Through this crisis and others, George Washington proved a patient, courageous, and determined leader able to hold the ragged army together.

Treaty of Paris. Finally in 1781, with the help of the French fleet, Washington forced the surrender of a British army at Yorktown, Virginia. With that defeat, the British war effort crumbled. Two years later, American, British, and French negotiators signed the Treaty of Paris ending the war. In it, Britain recognized the independence of the United States of America. It also accepted the new nation's western frontier as the Mississippi River.

A New Constitution

A national government set up by a document that Americans called the Articles of Confederation was too weak to rule the new United States effectively. To address this problem, the nation's leaders gathered once more in Philadelphia. During the hot summer of 1787, they hammered out the Constitution of the United States. This framework for a strong, flexible government has adapted to changing conditions for more than 200 years.

The impact of Enlightenment ideas. The framers of the Constitution had absorbed the ideas of Locke, Montesquieu, and Rousseau and had studied history. They saw government in terms of a social contract entered into by "We the People of the United States." They provided not only for an elective legislature but also for an elected president rather than a hereditary monarch.

The Constitution created a federal republic, with power divided between the federal, or national, government and the states. A central feature of the new federal government was the separation of powers among the legislative, executive, and judicial branches, an idea borrowed directly from Montesquieu. Within that structure, each branch of government was provided with checks and balances on the other branches.

The Bill of Rights, the first 10 amendments to the Constitution, recognized the idea that people had basic rights that the government must protect. They included freedom of religion, speech, and the press, as well as the rights to trial by jury and to private property.

Limited freedom. In 1789, the Constitution became law. It set up a representative government with an elected legislature to reflect the wishes of the governed.

Yet most Americans at the time did not have the right to vote. Only white men who met certain property requirements could vote. Women could not cast a ballot. Nor could African Americans—enslaved *or* free—or Native Americans. It would take many years of struggle before the right to vote and equal protection under the law were extended to all adult Americans.

Global impact. Despite its limits, the Constitution of the United States created the most liberal government of its day. From the start, the new republic shone as a symbol of freedom to European countries and to Latin America. Its Constitution would be copied or adapted by many lands throughout the world.

The Enlightenment ideals that had inspired American colonists brought changes in Europe, too. In France in 1789, a revolution in the name of liberty and equality toppled the monarchy. Before long, other Europeans took up the cry for freedom. By the mid-1800s, most absolute monarchs across Europe would see their powers greatly reduced.

SECTION 4 REVIEW

1. **Identify** (a) Navigation Acts, (b) Continental Congress, (c) George Washington, (d) Thomas Jefferson, (e) Battle of Saratoga, (f) Treaty of Paris of 1783, (g) Bill of Rights.
2. What role did the 13 colonies have in the British empire?
3. Explain why conflict between the colonists and Britain increased after 1763.
4. Give two examples of how Enlightenment ideas were reflected in each of the following: (a) the Declaration of Independence, (b) the Constitution of the United States.
5. How did the ideals of the American Revolution influence other nations?
6. *Critical Thinking* **Analyzing Information** In your own words, describe the idea of separation of powers. Then, give two examples of how your life would be different if the Constitution did not provide for separation of powers.
7. *ACTIVITY* Write a storybook for young children describing the causes, main events, and effects of the American Revolution.

World Literature

Evelina

Fanny Burney

Introduction *One of England's first female novelists was Fanny Burney. In 1778, she published* Evelina, or The History of a Young Lady's Entrance Into the World. *It tells the story of a 16-year-old woman who is sent from her small rural village to visit London. In a series of letters home, Evelina tells of her adventures in the city. The novel gives us an interesting picture of upper-middle-class life. In the following passage, Evelina describes going to her first dance in London.*

LETTER X
EVELINA TO THE REV. MR. VILLARS
Monday, April 4
We are to go this evening to a private ball, given by Mrs. Stanley, a very fashionable lady of Mrs. Mirvan's acquaintance.

We have been *a-shopping* as Mrs. Mirvan calls it, all this morning, to buy silks, caps, gauzes, and so forth.

The shops are really very entertaining, especially the [textile dealers]; there seem to be six or seven men belonging to each shop; and every one took care by bowing and smirking, to be noticed. We were conducted from one to another, and carried from room to room with so much ceremony, that at first I was almost afraid to go on.

I thought I should never have chosen a silk: for they produced so many, I knew not what to fix upon; and they recommended them all so strongly, that I fancy they thought I only wanted persuasion to buy everything they showed me. And, indeed, they took so much trouble, that I was almost ashamed I could not.

At the [hat shop], the ladies we met were so much dressed, that I should rather have imagined they were making visits than purchases. But what most diverted me was, that we were more frequently served by men than by women; and such men! so [fussy], so affected! they seemed to understand every part of a woman's dress better than we do ourselves. . . .

The dispatch with which they work in these great shops is amazing, for they have promised me a complete suit of linen [by] the evening.

I have just had my hair dressed. You can't think how oddly my head feels; full of powder and black pins, and a great cushion on the top of it. I believe you would hardly know me, for my face looks quite different to what it did before my hair was dressed. When I shall be able to make use of a comb for myself I cannot tell; for my hair is so much entangled, *frizzled* they call it, that I fear it will be very difficult.

I am half afraid of this ball tonight; for, you know, I have never danced but at school; however, Miss Mirvan says there is nothing in it. Yet, I wish it was over.

Adieu, my dear Sir, pray excuse the wretched stuff I write; perhaps I may improve by being in this town, and then my letters will be less unworthy your reading. Meantime, I am,
   Your dutiful and affectionate,
   EVELINA
P. S. Poor Miss Mirvan cannot wear one of the caps she made, because they dress her hair too large for them.

LETTER XI
EVELINA TO THE REV. MR. VILLARS
Tuesday, April 5
We passed a most extraordinary evening. A *private* ball this was called, so I expected to have seen about four or five couples; but Lord! my dear sir, I believe I saw half the world! Two very large rooms were full of company; in one were cards for the elderly ladies, and in the other were the dancers. My mamma Mirvan, for she always calls me her child, said she would sit with Maria and me till we were provided with partners, and then join the card-players.

Rich Women and Poor Lines between social classes were sharply drawn in London of the 1700s. Here, a wealthy Englishwoman and her daughters give money to a poor woman and her baby. **Diversity** How does clothing signal the difference between rich and poor in this painting?

The gentlemen, as they passed and repassed, looked as if they thought we were quite at their disposal, and only waiting for the honor of their commands; and they sauntered about, in a careless indolent manner, as if with a view to keep us in suspense. I don't speak of this in regard to Miss Mirvan and myself only, but to the ladies in general; and I thought it so provoking, that I determined in my own mind that, far from honoring such airs, I would rather not dance at all, than with anyone who would seem to think me ready to accept the first partner who would condescend to take me.

Not long after, a young man, who for some time looked at us with a kind of negligent impertinence, advanced on tiptoe towards me; he had a set smile on his face, and his dress was so foppish, that I really believed he even wished to be stared at; and yet he was very ugly.

Bowing almost to the ground with a sort of swing, and waving his hand, with the greatest conceit, after a short and silly pause, he said, "Madam—may I presume?"—and stopped, offering to take my hand. I drew it back, but could scarce forbear laughing. "Allow me, Madam," he continued, affectedly breaking off every half moment, "the honor and happiness—if I am not so unhappy as to address you too late—to have the happiness and honor—"

Again he would have taken my hand; but, bowing my head, I begged to be excused, and turned to Miss Mirvan to conceal my laughter.

He then desired to know if I had already engaged myself to [dance with] some more fortunate man? I said No, and that I believed I should not dance at all. He would keep himself, he told me, disengaged, in hopes I should relent; and then, uttering some ridiculous speeches of sorrow and disappointment, though his face still wore the same invariable smile, he retreated.

Source: Fanny Burney, *Evelina, or The History of a Young Lady's Entrance Into the World* (New York: W.W. Norton & Company, 1965).

Thinking About Literature

1. **Vocabulary** Use the dictionary to find the meanings of the following words: saunter, dispatch, indolent, provoke, condescend, foppish.
2. (a) What preparations does Evelina make for the ball? (b) Describe three things that she finds surprising or amusing.
3. What annoys Evelina about the behavior of the men at the ball?
4. *Critical Thinking* **Linking Past and Present** (a) Based on the excerpts, do you think that *Evelina* reflected the experiences of most middle-class young women of the 1700s? (b) Why would Burney's novel appeal to these young women? (c) Do similar stories appeal to young women today? Explain.

CHAPTER REVIEW AND SKILLS FOR SUCCESS

CHAPTER REVIEW

REVIEWING VOCABULARY

Select *five* vocabulary words from the chapter. Write each word on a separate slip of paper. Then, write the definition for each word on other slips of paper. Scramble the slips and exchange them with another student. Match the words with their definitions, and then check each other's results.

REVIEWING FACTS

1. According to John Locke, what should happen if a government violates people's natural rights?

2. According to Adam Smith, how should wages and prices be regulated?

3. How did Enlightenment thinkers differ from medieval thinkers regarding a just society?

4. How did Eastern and Western Europe differ regarding serfdom?

5. What areas combined to form the United Kingdom of Great Britain?

6. What was the cabinet system?

7. How did taxation create tensions between the American colonies and the British government?

8. What idea from the Baron de Montesquieu was incorporated into the United States Constitution?

REVIEWING CHAPTER THEMES

Review the "Focus On" questions at the start of this chapter. Then select *three* of those questions and answer them, using information from the chapter.

SKILLS FOR SUCCESS DISTINGUISHING FACTS FROM OPINIONS

When reading either primary or secondary sources, you must be able to distinguish facts from opinions. A **fact** is a statement that can be proved by reliable sources. An **opinion** is a judgment that reflects a person's beliefs or feelings. It may or may not be provable.

The passage at right is from a college textbook discussion of Frederick the Great of Prussia. Read the passage. Then, answer the following questions.

1. **Determine which statements are facts.**
   (a) List two statements about Frederick's economic policies that appear to be facts. (b) How could you prove that these are facts?

2. **Determine which statements are opinions.**
   (a) List two statements from the passage that are opinions. (b) How do you know that they are opinions?

3. **Determine how the writer uses facts to support his opinions.** What fact does the writer use to support his opinion that Frederick's policies as king produced "several economic absurdities"?

> ❝Viewed as a general, diplomat, and the master mechanic of Prussian administration, Frederick the Great was efficient and successful, but he was scarcely enlightened. . . .
>
> No physiocrat could have done more than Frederick to improve Prussian agriculture. From England he imported clover, crop rotation, and the iron plow, which turned up the soil more effectively than the old wooden share. . . .
>
> Frederick, however, was hostile to the doctrine of laissez faire and cut imports to the bone to save money for the support of the army. His mercantilism . . . placed a staggering burden of taxation on his subjects and produced several economic absurdities. For instance, Frederick tried to make Prussia grow its own tobacco, for which the climate was not suited. . . .❞

Source: Crane Brinton et al., *Modern Civilization* (Englewood Cliffs, NJ: Prentice Hall, 1967).

CRITICAL THINKING

1. **Synthesizing Information** Write a sentence summarizing the major ideas of each of the following thinkers: (a) John Locke, (b) Baron de Montesquieu, (c) Voltaire, (d) Mary Wollstonecraft, (e) Adam Smith.

2. **Linking Past and Present** Today, we talk about human rights rather than natural rights. Describe a human rights issue that has recently been in the news.

3. **Predicting Consequences** What do you think would be the effects of Britain's repression of Catholics in Ireland?

4. **Analyzing Information** (a) What ideas about government do you think English settlers brought with them to the Americas in the 1600s and 1700s? (b) How might those ideas have contributed to the outbreak of the American Revolution?

ANALYZING PRIMARY SOURCES

Use the quotation on page 471 to answer the following questions.

1. What three "unalienable rights" did the Declaration list?

2. According to the Declaration, what is the purpose of government?

3. What is the source of government power?

FOR YOUR PORTFOLIO

WRITING A DIARY ENTRY Write a diary entry from the point of view of someone living in Western Europe or North America during the Age of Enlightenment. To begin, review the chapter and make a list of people, ideas, and events that you might comment on. Then choose a topic for your entry, such as the publication of an important book or an event you attended. Use outside resources to add to the information in the text. Then write your diary entry, including as many details as you can to make it "authentic." Finally, share your diary entry with the class. Explain why you chose the topic you did.

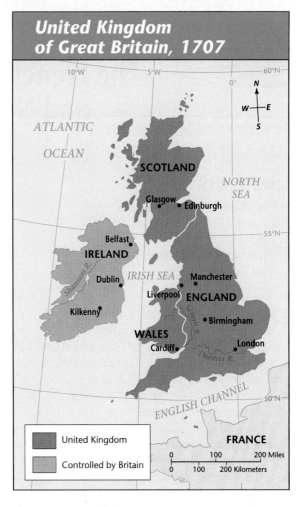

United Kingdom of Great Britain, 1707

ANALYZING MAPS

Use the map to answer the following questions.

1. Which three areas made up the United Kingdom?

2. List one city in each of those three areas.

3. What was the relationship between Ireland and Britain?

INTERNET ACTIVITY

WRITING A LETTER Use the Internet to research one of the political thinkers described in the text. Then write a letter to him explaining why you think his ideas are or are not relevant in the present day.

CHAPTER

19

The French Revolution and Napoleon

(1789–1815)

CHAPTER OUTLINE

1 On the Eve of Revolution
2 Creating a New France
3 Radical Days
4 The Age of Napoleon Begins
5 The End of an Era

Rain pounded the Parisian suburb of Versailles on the morning of June 20, 1789. In the street, delegates to the National Assembly milled about outside their meeting hall. A notice on the door announced that King Louis XVI would speak to them on a future day. But why were the doors locked?

These middle-class men had been chosen as representatives to help the king solve France's financial crisis. But they had their own plans, too. They wanted sweeping reforms of a government sadly out of touch with its people. Already they had challenged the old order by insisting that nobles and clergy meet with them.

Perhaps that demand had pushed the king too far. Did the locked door mean that he was going to forbid them to meet altogether? The delegates stood in the rain, debating what to do next. One delegate suggested that they move their meeting to an indoor tennis court nearby.

They trooped off to the tennis court. Crowds of curious spectators pushed into the galleries. Jean-Joseph Mounier (moon YAY), a leading member of the Assembly, spoke up:

> 66Let us swear to God and our country never to separate and to meet wherever circumstances might require until we have established a sound and just constitution.99

As the delegates took the oath, the crowd in the gallery cheered. They sensed that they were witnessing a revolutionary moment.

The men who took the Tennis Court Oath were children of the Enlightenment who believed that the government could be rationally reformed. Like the delegates to the American Continental Congress in 1776, they pledged their lives to freeing their country from tyranny. They had no idea that they would help trigger an upheaval considerably more radical than the American Revolution. The French Revolution ultimately destroyed an absolute monarchy and disrupted a centuries-old social system.

Between 1789 and 1815, events in France upset the balance of power across all of Europe. Most historians see the French Revolution as a major turning point that helped usher in the modern era in European politics.

FOCUS ON these questions as you read:

- **Religions and Value Systems**
  What beliefs and attitudes inspired the leaders of the French Revolution?

- **Political and Social Systems**
  How did the French Revolution reshape social and political institutions?

- **Impact of the Individual**
  How did the rise of Napoleon Bonaparte create upheaval across Europe?

- **Continuity and Change**
  What were the temporary and lasting effects of the French Revolution?

TIME AND PLACE

Storming the Bastille For centuries, French kings jailed their enemies in the Bastille, an imposing fortress in Paris. Even the great philosopher Voltaire was once held there. Its heavy cannons, high towers, and thick walls symbolized the monarch's power. But on July 14, 1789, an angry mob seized the Bastille, shaking the monarchy to its roots. **Political and Social Systems** Compare this picture to the one on page 421. How do Versailles and the Bastille represent two sides of absolute monarchy?

HUMANITIES LINK

Art History Francisco Goya, *The Third of May, 1808* (page 500).
Literature In this chapter, you will encounter passages from the following works of literature: William Wordsworth, *The Prelude* (pages 488 and 492); Edmund Burke, *Reflections on the Revolution in France* (page 488); Olympe de Gouges, *Declaration of the Rights of Woman* (page 493).

1789 French Revolution begins	1793 Reign of Terror begins	1799 Napoleon overthrows Directory	1804 Napoleon becomes emperor	1812 Napoleon invades Russia	1815 Napoleon defeated at Waterloo
1790	1795	1800	1805	1810	1815

1 On the Eve of Revolution

Guide for Reading

- What was the social structure of the old regime?

- Why did France face an economic crisis by 1789?

- Why did efforts at reform fail?

- **Vocabulary** *bourgeoisie, deficit spending*

On April 28, 1789, unrest exploded at the Réveillon (ray vay OHN) wallpaper factory in Paris. A rumor had spread that, though bread prices were soaring, the owner was planning to cut wages for his workers. Enraged workers then invaded the owner's home, leaving it in ruins.

Meanwhile, on the outskirts of the city, a group of nobles was enjoying an afternoon at the racetrack. Unaware of the trouble, they returned to Paris through the neighborhood of Réveillon's factory. An eyewitness told what happened as the aristocrats' carriages bumped through the streets:

66A troop of men stopped the people returning from the races . . . asking them whether they were for the nobles or the Third Estate [the common people] . . . insulting those it thought noble. They forced the women from their carriages and made them shout: 'Long live the Third Estate!'99

Though unpleasant, incidents like the Réveillon riots did not worry most aristocrats too much. Yes, France was facing a severe economic crisis. But a few financial reforms would certainly settle things. And rioters would get the hanging they deserved.

The nobles could not have been more wrong. The crisis went deeper than government finances. Reform would not be enough. By July, the hungry, unemployed, or poorly paid people of Paris had taken up arms. Their actions would push events further and faster than anyone could foresee.

The Old Regime

In 1789, France, like the rest of Europe, still clung to an outdated social system that had emerged in the Middle Ages. Under this *ancien regime,* or old order, everyone in France belonged to one of three classes: the First Estate, made up of the clergy; the Second Estate, made up of the nobility; or the Third Estate, the vast majority of the population.

The clergy. In the Middle Ages, the Church had exerted great influence throughout Christian Europe. In 1789, the French clergy still enjoyed enormous wealth and privilege. They owned about 10 percent of the land, collected tithes, and paid no direct taxes to the state. High Church leaders such as bishops and abbots were usually nobles who lived very well. Parish priests, however, often came from humble origins and might be as poor as their peasant congregations.

The First Estate did provide social services. Nuns, monks, and priests ran schools, hospitals, and orphanages. But during the Enlightenment, philosophes targeted the Church for reform. They pointed to the idleness of some clergy, Church interference in politics, and its intolerance of dissent. In response, many clergy condemned the Enlightenment for undermining religion and moral order.

Nobles. The Second Estate was the titled nobility of French society. In the Middle Ages, noble knights had defended the land. In the 1600s, Richelieu and Louis XIV had crushed the nobles' military power but given them other rights—under strict royal control. Those rights included top jobs in government, the army, the courts, and the Church.

At Versailles, ambitious nobles vied for royal appointments, while idle courtiers enjoyed endless entertainments. Many nobles, however, lived far from the center of power. Though they owned land, they had little money income. As a result, they felt the pinch of trying to maintain their status in a period of rising prices.

Many nobles hated absolutism and resented the royal bureaucracy that employed middle-class men in positions once reserved for the aristocracy. They feared losing their traditional privileges, especially their freedom from paying taxes.

The Third Estate. In 1789, the Third Estate numbered about 27 million people, or 98 percent of the population. It was a diverse group. At the top sat the bourgeoisie (boor zhwah ZEE), or middle class. The bourgeoisie included the prosperous bankers, merchants, and manufacturers who propped up the French economy. It also included the officials who staffed the royal bureaucracy, as well as lawyers, doctors, journalists, professors, and skilled artisans.

The bulk of the Third Estate—9 out of 10 people in France—were rural peasants. Some were prosperous landowners who hired laborers to work for them. Others were tenant farmers or day laborers. Still others owed obligations to local nobles.

The poorest members of the Third Estate were city workers. They included apprentices, journeymen, and others who worked in industries such as printing or clothmaking. Many women and men earned a living as servants, stable hands, porters, construction workers, or street hawkers of everything from food to pots and pans. A large number were unemployed. To survive, some turned to begging or crime.

Discontent. From rich to poor, members of the Third Estate resented the privileges enjoyed by their social "betters." Wealthy bourgeois families could buy political office and even titles, but the best jobs were still reserved for nobles. Urban workers earned miserable wages. Even the smallest rise in the price of bread, their main food, might mean starvation.

Peasants were burdened by taxes on everything from land to soap to salt. Though technically free, many owed fees and services that dated to medieval times, such as the corvée (kohr VAY), unpaid labor to repair roads and bridges. Peasants were also incensed when nobles, hurt by rising prices, tried to reimpose old manor dues. Also, only nobles had the right to hunt game. Peasants were even forbidden to kill rabbits that ate their crops.

In towns and cities, Enlightenment ideas led people to question the ancien regime. Why, people demanded, should the first two estates have privileges at the expense of the majority? It did not meet the test of reason! Everywhere, the Third Estate called for the privileged classes to pay their share. In 1789, the Abbé Sieyès (syay

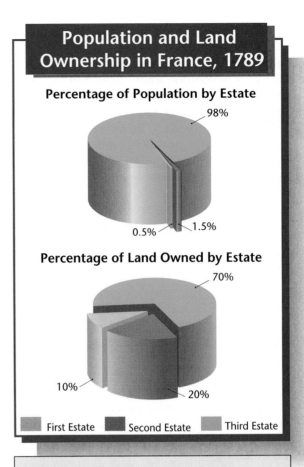

Population and Land Ownership in France, 1789

Percentage of Population by Estate

98%

0.5%   1.5%

Percentage of Land Owned by Estate

70%

10%   20%

First Estate   Second Estate   Third Estate

Interpreting a Graph Inequalities among France's three estates were a leading cause of discontent. ■ Which estate included the fewest people? Which owned the most land? Based on these graphs, what reason did the Third Estate have to be discontented?

EHS), a member of the clergy, wrote a widely read pamphlet that asked:

66What is the Third Estate?
    EVERYTHING.
What has it been in the political order
    up to now? NOTHING.
What is it asking for? To become
    SOMETHING.99

A Financial Crisis

Hand in hand with social unrest went a mushrooming financial crisis. The crisis was caused in part by years of deficit spending, that is, a government spending more money than it takes in. Louis XIV had left France deeply in debt. Wars like the Seven Years' War and the American Revolution strained the treasury even further. Costs generally had risen in the 1700s, and the lavish court soaked up millions. To bridge the gap between income and expenses, the government borrowed more and more money. By 1789, half its tax income went just to pay interest on this enormous debt.

To solve the financial crisis, the government would have to increase taxes, reduce expenses, or both. However, the nobles and clergy fiercely resisted any attempt to end their exemption from taxes.

A crumbling economy. Other economic woes added to the crisis. A general economic decline began in the 1770s. Then, in the late 1780s, bad harvests sent food prices soaring and brought hunger to poorer peasants and city dwellers.

Hard times and lack of food inflamed these people. In towns, people rioted, demanding bread. In the countryside, peasants began to attack the manor houses of the nobles. Arthur Young, an English visitor to France, witnessed the violence:

66Everything conspires to render the present period in France critical: the [lack] of bread is terrible; accounts arrive every moment from the provinces of riots and disturbances, and calling in the military, to preserve the peace of the markets.99

Failure of reform. The heirs of Louis XIV were not the right men to solve the crisis. Louis XV, who ruled from 1715 to 1774, pursued pleasure before serious business and ran up more debts. His grandson, Louis XVI, was well-meaning but weak and indecisive. He wisely chose Jacques Necker, a financial wizard, as an adviser. Necker urged the king to reduce court spending, reform government, and improve internal trade by abolishing tariffs that made trade costly. When Necker proposed taxing the First and Second estates, however, the nobles and high clergy forced the king to dismiss the would-be reformer.

As the crisis deepened, the pressure for reform mounted. Finally, the wealthy and powerful classes demanded that the king call the

A Heavy Burden In this cartoon, a priest and a nobleman stand on a stone that crushes a peasant. The words on the stone refer to taxes and other obligations that peasants traditionally owed to the government. **Political and Social Systems** What was the cartoonist saying about the relationship among France's three estates?

Estates General before making any changes. (See page 214.) French kings had not summoned the Estates General for 175 years, fearing that nobles would try to recover the feudal powers that they had lost under absolute rule. To reform-minded nobles, the Estates General seemed to offer a chance to carry out changes like the Glorious Revolution in England. It would establish a constitution to bring the absolute monarch under the control of the nobles and guarantee their privileges.

The King Takes Action

As 1788 closed, France tottered on the verge of bankruptcy. Bread riots were spreading, and nobles, fearful of taxes, were denouncing royal tyranny. A baffled Louis XVI finally summoned the Estates General to meet at Versailles in May 1789.

The cahiers. In preparation, Louis had all three estates prepare *cahiers* (kah YAY), or notebooks, listing their grievances. Many cahiers called for reforms such as fairer taxes, freedom of the press, or regular meetings of the Estates General. In one town, shoemakers denounced regulations that made leather so expensive they could not afford to

▲ *Fan celebrating the Estates General*

make shoes. Some peasants demanded the right to kill animals that were destroying their crops. Servant girls in the city of Toulouse demanded the right to leave service when they wanted and that "after a girl has served her master for many years, she receive some reward for her service."

The cahiers testified to boiling class resentments. One called tax collectors "bloodsuckers of the nation who drink the tears of the unfortunate from goblets of gold." Another one of the cahiers condemned the courts of nobles as "vampires pumping the last drop of blood" from the people. Another complained that "20 million must live on half the wealth of France while the clergy . . . devour the other half."

The Tennis Court Oath. Delegates to the Estates General from the Third Estate were elected, though only propertied men could vote. Thus, they were mostly lawyers, middle-class officials, and writers. They were familiar with the writings of Voltaire, Rousseau, and other philosophes and with the complaints in the cahiers. They went to Versailles, not only to solve the national financial crisis, but also to insist on reform.

From the beginning, the Estates General was deadlocked over the issue of voting. Traditionally, each estate had met separately and voted as a group. This system always allowed the First and Second estates to outvote the Third Estate two to one. The Third Estate wanted all three orders to meet together.

After weeks of stalemate, delegates of the Third Estate took a daring step. Saying that they represented the people of France, they transformed themselves into the National Assembly. They then invited members of the other estates to help them shape a constitution. A few days later, as you have read, the National Assembly found itself locked out of its meeting place. In fact, workers were just preparing the hall for a royal speech, but many delegates believed that the king intended to send them home. They then took the famous Tennis Court Oath, vowing not to disband until they had drawn up a constitution for France.

When some reform-minded clergy and nobles joined the National Assembly, Louis XVI grudgingly had to accept it. At the same time, royal troops gathered around Versailles and Paris. Rumor held that the king would dissolve the Assembly.

The crisis deepened in early July. The king, who had brought back Necker to help with the financial crisis, again dismissed the popular minister. Food shortages were also getting worse because of a disastrous 1788 harvest.

Storming the Bastille

On July 14, Paris seized the spotlight from the National Assembly meeting in Versailles. The streets buzzed with rumors that royal troops were going to occupy the capital. More than 800 Parisians assembled outside the Bastille, a grim medieval fortress used as a prison for political and other prisoners. The crowd was demanding weapons and gunpowder believed to be stored there.

The commander of the Bastille refused to open the gates and opened fire on the crowd. In the battle that followed, many people were killed. Finally, the enraged mob broke through the defenses. They killed the commander and five guards and released a handful of prisoners, but found no weapons.

When told of the attack, Louis XVI asked, "Is it a revolt?" "No, sire," replied a noble, "It is a revolution." The storming of the Bastille quickly became a symbol of the French Revolution. Supporters saw it as a blow to tyranny, a step toward freedom. Today, the French still celebrate July 14 as Bastille Day, the French national holiday.

SECTION 1 REVIEW

1. **Identify** (a) Jacques Necker, (b) cahiers, (c) National Assembly, (d) Bastille.
2. **Define** (a) bourgeoisie, (b) deficit spending.
3. (a) Describe the three estates of French society. (b) Why were members of each estate discontented with conditions in 1789?
4. What were the causes of the financial crisis that gripped France?
5. (a) Why did Louis XVI call the Estates General in 1789? (b) What were the results of this decision?
6. *Critical Thinking* **Applying Information** A French lawyer of the day wrote that Louis XVI "was too well intentioned not to try to remedy abuses that had shocked him, but he possessed neither the character nor the talents to control an impetuous nation in a situation that cried out for reform." (a) How does this description apply to the king's actions in 1789? (b) Do you think Louis XVI could have prevented the outbreak of revolution? Why or why not?
7. *ACTIVITY* Imagine that you belong to one of the following groups in 1789 France: nobles, high clergy, parish priests, the bourgeoisie, peasants, city workers. With two partners, write a cahier describing what you think is the chief problem facing the nation.

2 Creating a New France

Guide for Reading

■ How did popular uprisings contribute to the French Revolution?

■ What political and social reforms emerged in the early stages of the revolution?

■ How did people outside France respond to the revolution?

■ **Vocabulary** *émigré, sans-culotte*

Excitement, wonder, and fear engulfed France as the revolution unfolded at home and spread abroad. Today, historians divide this revolutionary era into four phases. The moderate phase of the National Assembly (1789–1791) turned France into a constitutional monarchy. Then, a radical phase (1792–1794) of escalating violence led to a Reign of Terror. There followed a period of reaction against extremism, known as the Directory (1795–1799). Finally, the Age of Napoleon (1799–1815) consolidated many changes brought by the revolution. In this section, you will read about the moderate start of the French Revolution.

Revolts in Paris and the Provinces

The political crisis of 1789 was punctuated by the worst famine in memory. Starving peasants roamed the countryside or flocked to the towns, where they swelled the ranks of the unemployed. As grain prices soared, even people with jobs had to spend up to 80 percent of their income on bread.

The Great Fear. In such desperate times, rumors ran wild, setting off what was later called the "Great Fear." Tales of marauders attacking villages and towns spread panic. Other rumors claimed that government troops were seizing peasant crops.

Inflamed by famine and fear, peasants unleashed their fury on nobles who were trying to reimpose medieval dues. Defiant peasants attacked the homes of nobles, burned old manor records, and stole grain from storehouses. The attacks died down after a time, but they demonstrated peasant anger with an unjust regime.

Paris in arms. Paris, too, was in turmoil. As the capital and chief city of France, it was the revolutionary center. Various factions competed for power. Moderates looked to the Marquis de Lafayette, the aristocratic "hero of two worlds" who had fought alongside George Washington in the American Revolution. Lafayette headed the National Guard, a largely middle-class militia organized in response to the arrival of royal troops in Paris. The Guard was the first group to don the tricolor, a red, white, and blue badge, which was eventually adopted as the national flag of France.

A more radical group, the Paris Commune, replaced the royalist government of the city. It could mobilize whole neighborhoods for protests or violent action to further the revolution. Newspapers and political clubs—many even more radical than the Commune—blossomed everywhere. Some demanded an end to monarchy and spread scandalous stories about the royal family and members of the court.

Liberty, Equality, Fraternity

Peasant uprisings and the storming of the Bastille stampeded the National Assembly into action. On August 4, at a stormy all-night meeting, nobles in the National Assembly voted to end their privileges. They gave up their old manorial dues, their exclusive hunting rights, their special legal status, and their exemption from taxation.

An end to special privilege. "Feudalism is abolished," announced the weary delegates at 2 A.M. The president of the Assembly later wrote:

66 This has been a night for destruction and for public happiness. We may view this moment as the dawn of a new revolution, when all the burdens weighing on the people were abolished and France was truly reborn. 99

Were the votes on the night of August 4 voluntary? Contemporary observers and historians today note that the nobles gave up nothing that they had not already lost. In the months ahead, the National Assembly turned the reforms of

Declaration of Rights *The Marquis de Lafayette presented a first draft of the Declaration of the Rights of Man and the Citizen in July 1789. Lafayette had fought for American independence and was inspired by the ideals of the new United States. The final declaration, shown here, expresses the basic beliefs of the French Revolution in 17 articles.* **Religions and Value Systems** *How does this painting glorify the value of human rights?*

August 4 into law, meeting a key Enlightenment goal—the equality of all citizens before the law.

Declaration of the Rights of Man. In late August, as a first step toward writing a constitution, the Assembly issued the Declaration of the Rights of Man and the Citizen. The document was modeled in part on the American Declaration of Independence. All men, it announced, were "born and remain free and equal in rights." They enjoyed natural rights to "liberty, property, security, and resistance to oppression." Like Locke and the philosophes, it insisted that governments exist to protect the natural rights of citizens.

The Declaration further proclaimed that all male citizens were equal before the law. Each French man had an equal right to hold public office "with no distinction other than that of

Sweet Dreams Lavish tapestries and glittering chandeliers adorned the bedchamber of Queen Marie Antoinette at Versailles. Tales of her extravagance inflamed public anger against the queen. She even had a mock peasant village built on the ground of Versailles so that she and her ladies-in-waiting could play at being milkmaids. **Art and Literature** Compare this picture to the one on page 429. How are these two rooms similar in style?

their virtues and talents." In addition, the Declaration asserted freedom of religion and called for taxes to be levied according to ability to pay. Its principles were captured in the enduring slogan of the French Revolution, "Liberty, Equality, Fraternity."

Uncertain and hesitant, Louis XVI was slow to accept the reforms of the National Assembly. Parisians grew suspicious as more royal troops arrived. Nobles continued to enjoy gala banquets while people were starving. By autumn, anger again turned to action.

Women March on Versailles

"Bread!" shouted the mob as it streamed down the road that led from Paris to Versailles.

"Bread!" In a driving rainstorm, they marched the entire 12 miles (19 km). They wanted to see the king and would not take no for an answer.

Angry mobs were not a new sight in France. What surprised many observers, however, was that this mob was made up of thousands of women. On October 5, they showed themselves as determined as the men who had stormed the Bastille three months earlier.

A group of rough-spoken market women burst into the palace at Versailles. A duchess later recalled the scene:

66 The fishmonger women cried out that they wanted to speak to the king . . . and they could be calmed only by admitting a dozen of them to the presence of that unfortunate prince. His goodness disarmed them, and their opinions were so changed by the time they returned to their companions that they ran the risk of being the victims of their fury. 99

"We'll wring her neck!" Much of the crowd's anger was directed at the queen, Marie Antoinette. She was the daughter of Maria Theresa, the Hapsburg empress of Austria. (See Chapter 17.) Ever since Marie Antoinette had married Louis, she had come under attack for being frivolous and extravagant. She eventually grew more serious and even advised the king to compromise with moderate reformers. Still, she remained a source of scandal. Enemies accused her of immorality. Early in the revolution, the radical press spread the story that she had answered the cries of hungry people for bread by saying "Let them eat cake." Though the story was untrue, it helped inflame feelings against the queen.

"Death to the Austrian! We'll wring her neck!" shouted the women who stormed Versailles. "Tear out her heart, cut off her head, fry her liver and even then it won't be all over."

Lafayette and the National Guard eventually calmed the crowd. Still, the women would not leave Versailles until the king met their most important demand—to return with them to Paris. Not too happily, the king agreed.

A triumphant procession. The next morning, the crowd marched back to Paris, led by women perched on the barrels of seized cannon. They told bewildered spectators that they were bringing back to Paris "the baker, the baker's wife, and the baker's boy"—Louis XVI, Marie Antoinette, and their son. "Now we won't have to go so far/When we want to see our king," they sang. Crowds along the way cheered the king, who now wore the tricolor.

The royal family moved into the Tuileries (TWEE luh reez) palace. For the next three years, Louis was a virtual prisoner in his own capital.

The women of Paris would continue to take action during the revolution. Elisabeth Guenard, who sympathized with the royal cause, also understood what drove the women to Versailles. "You have to be a mother," she wrote, "and have heard your children ask for bread you cannot give them to know the level of despair to which this misfortune can bring you." ◼

A Time of Reform

The National Assembly soon followed the king to Paris. Its largely bourgeois members worked to draft a constitution and to solve the continuing financial crisis.

Reorganizing the Church. To pay off the huge government debt—much of it owed to the bourgeoisie—the Assembly voted to take over and sell Church lands. In an even more radical move, it put the French Catholic Church under state control. Under the Civil Constitution of the Clergy, issued in 1790, bishops and priests became elected, salaried officials. The Civil Constitution ended papal authority over the French Church and dissolved convents and monasteries.

Reaction was swift and angry. Many bishops and priests refused to accept the Civil Constitution. The pope condemned it. Large numbers of French peasants, who were basically conservative, also rejected the changes. When the government punished clergy who refused to

To Versailles! As famine gripped Paris, poor mothers did not have enough food for their children. On October 5, 1789, thousands of women decided to bring Louis XVI to Paris, where he could no longer ignore their suffering. **Continuity and Change** *Based on this painting, in what ways do you think the march challenged traditional roles of women?*

support the Civil Constitution, a huge gulf opened between revolutionaries in Paris and the peasantry in the provinces.

A written constitution. The National Assembly completed its main task by producing a constitution. The Constitution of 1791 set up a limited monarchy in place of the absolute monarchy that had ruled France for centuries. A new Legislative Assembly had the power to make laws, collect taxes, and decide on issues of war and peace. Lawmakers would be elected by tax-paying male citizens. Still, only about 50,000 men in a population of more than 27 million could qualify as candidates to run for the Assembly.

To make government more efficient, the constitution replaced the old provinces with 83 departments of roughly equal size. It abolished the old provincial courts and reformed laws. The middle-class framers of the constitution protected private property and supported free trade. They compensated nobles for land seized by the peasants, abolished guilds, and forbade city workers to organize labor unions.

To moderate reformers, the Constitution of 1791 seemed to complete the revolution. Reflecting Enlightenment goals, it ended Church interference in government and ensured equality before the law for all citizens. At the same time, it put power in the hands of men with the means and leisure to serve in government.

The fateful flight. Meanwhile, Marie Antoinette and others had been urging the king to escape their humiliating situation. In 1791, Louis finally gave in. One night in June, a large coach lumbered north from Paris toward the border. Inside sat the king disguised as a valet, the queen dressed as a governess, the royal children, and a loyal friend pretending to be their wealthy Russian employer.

When they stopped at a small town, a former soldier who had been stationed in Paris recognized Marie Antoinette. Louis's disguise was uncovered when someone held up the new revolutionary currency with the king's face on it.

The royal family was trundled back to Paris, to the insults of the crowds. The old shouts of "Long live the King!" were replaced by cries of "Long live the Nation!" To Parisians, the king's dash to the border showed he was a traitor to the revolution.

Reaction Outside France

Events in France stirred debate all over Europe. Supporters of the Enlightenment applauded the reforms of the National Assembly. They saw the French experiment as the dawn of a new age for justice and equality. In his poem *The Prelude,* the English poet William Wordsworth later recalled how the start of the French Revolution stirred feelings of joy and hope:

❝Bliss was it in that dawn to be alive,
    But to be young was very Heaven!❞

Widespread fears. European rulers and nobles, however, denounced the French Revolution. They increased border patrols, fearing the spread of the "French plague." Fueling those fears were the horror stories that were told by émigrés (EHM ih grayz)—nobles, clergy, and others who had fled revolutionary France. Émigrés reported attacks on their privileges, property, religion, and even their lives. "Enlightened" rulers turned against French ideas. Catherine the Great of Russia burned Voltaire's letters and locked up her critics.

In Britain, Edmund Burke, who had defended the American Revolution, bitterly condemned revolutionaries in Paris. In *Reflections on the Revolution in France,* he predicted all too accurately that the revolution would become more violent:

❝Plots and assassinations will be anticipated by preventive murder and preventive confiscation. . . . When ancient opinions and rules of life are taken away, the loss cannot possibly be estimated. From that moment we have no compass to govern us.❞

Threats from abroad. Louis XVI's failed flight brought further hostile rumblings from abroad. In August 1791, the king of Prussia and the emperor of Austria—who was Marie Antoinette's brother—issued the Declaration of Pilnitz. In it, they threatened to intervene if necessary to protect the French monarchy.

The declaration may have been mostly bluff. But revolutionaries in France took the threat seriously and prepared for war. The revolution was about to enter a new, more radical phase.

War at Home and Abroad

In October 1791, the newly elected Legislative Assembly took office. Faced with crises at home and abroad, it would survive for less than a year. Economic problems fed renewed turmoil. Assignats, the revolutionary currency, dropped in value, which caused prices to rise rapidly. Uncertainty about prices led to hoarding and additional food shortages.

The sans-culottes. In Paris and other cities, working-class men and women, called sans-culottes* (sanz kyoo LAHTZ), pushed the revolution into more radical action. By 1791, many sans-culottes demanded a republic. They also wanted the government to guarantee them a living wage.

The sans-culottes found support among radical leaders in the Legislative Assembly, especially the Jacobins. A revolutionary political club, the Jacobins were mostly middle-class lawyers or intellectuals. They used pamphleteers and sympathetic newspaper editors to advance the republican cause.

From right to left. Within the Legislative Assembly, hostile factions feuded for power. Members with similar views sat together in the meeting hall. On the right sat those who felt reform had gone far enough or even wanted to turn the clock back to 1788. In the center sat supporters of moderate reform. On the left sat the Jacobins and other republicans who wanted to abolish the monarchy and pushed for other radical changes. This seating arrangement led to the modern use of the terms *right*, *center*, and *left* to describe similar political positions.

War on tyranny. Groups on the left soon held the upper hand. In April 1792, the war of words between French revolutionaries and European monarchs moved onto the battlefield. Eager to spread the revolution and destroy tyranny abroad, the Legislative Assembly declared war first on Austria, then on Prussia, Britain, and other states. The great powers expected to win an easy victory against France, a land divided by revolution. In fact, the fighting that began in 1792 lasted on and off until 1815.

---

*Sans-culottes means "without culottes," the fancy knee-breeches worn by upper-class men. Shopkeepers, artisans, and other working-class men wore trousers, not culottes.

Protecting the Revolution "I guard the nation," says the inscription on this brass-and-ivory button, below. It showed the wearer's determination to defend the revolution from threats at home and abroad. Among the most ardent revolutionaries were the sans-culottes, like the young man at right. They would help push the revolution in a more radical and violent direction. **Political and Social Systems** How does this picture suggest that the sans-culottes were determined to protect the revolution?

SECTION 2 REVIEW

1. **Identify** (a) Great Fear, (b) Marquis de Lafayette, (c) tricolor, (d) Legislative Assembly, (e) Declaration of Pilnitz, (f) Jacobins.
2. **Define** (a) émigré, (b) sans-culotte.
3. What role did the people of Paris play in the French Revolution?
4. Describe two main ideas or reforms contained in each of the following: (a) the Declaration of the Rights of Man and the Citizen, (b) the Civil Constitution of the Clergy, (c) the Constitution of 1791.
5. (a) Why did some people outside France support the French Revolution? (b) Why did other people oppose it?
6. *Critical Thinking* **Comparing** Compare the women's march on Versailles to the storming of the Bastille in terms of goals and results.
7. *ACTIVITY* In a group of five or six students, write and perform a skit about *one* of the following events: the Great Fear; the night of August 4; the women's march on Versailles; the flight and capture of the royal family.

3 Radical Days

Guide for Reading

- Why did the revolution become more radical?

- What was the Reign of Terror?

- How did the French Revolution change daily life?

- **Vocabulary** *suffrage, nationalism*

Someone who had left Paris in 1791 and returned in 1793 could have gotten lost. Almost 4,000 streets had new names. Louis XV Square was renamed the Square of the Revolution. King-of-Sicily Street, named for the brother of Louis XVI, had become the Rights of Man Street.

Renaming streets was one way that Jacobins tried to wipe out all traces of the old order. In 1793, the revolution entered a radical phase. For a year, France experienced one of the bloodiest regimes in its history as determined leaders sought to extend and preserve the revolution.

Downfall of the Monarchy

War heightened tensions in Paris, especially as dismal news arrived from the front. Well-trained Prussian forces were cutting down raw French recruits. Royalist officers deserted the French army, joining émigrés and others seeking to restore the king to power.

Outbreaks of violence. Battle disasters inflamed revolutionaries who thought the king was in league with the invaders. A crowd of Parisians invaded the Tuileries on August 10, 1792, and slaughtered the king's guards. The royal family fled to the Legislative Assembly.

A month later, citizens attacked the prisons that were holding nobles and priests accused of political offenses. These prisoners were killed, along with many ordinary criminals. Historians have disagreed about the people who carried out the "September massacres." Some call them "bloodthirsty savages," while others argue that they were patriots defending France from its enemies. In fact, most were ordinary citizens fired to fury by real and imagined grievances.

The French Republic. Backed by Paris crowds, radicals took control of the Assembly. Radicals called for the election of a new legislative body, the National Convention. Suffrage, the right to vote, was to be extended to all male citizens, not just to property owners.

The Convention that met in September 1792 was a more radical body than earlier assemblies. It voted to abolish the monarchy and declare France a republic. Deputies then drew up a new constitution for France. The Jacobins, who controlled the Convention, set out to erase all traces of the old order. They seized lands of nobles and abolished titles of nobility. All French men and women were called "Citizen." Louis XVI became Citizen Capet, from the dynasty that ruled France in the Middle Ages.

Death of a king and queen. The Convention also put Louis XVI on trial as a traitor to France. The king was convicted by a single vote and sentenced to death. On a foggy morning in January 1793, Louis mounted a scaffold in a public square in Paris. He tried to speak, but his words were drowned out by a roll of drums. Moments later, the king was beheaded.

In October, Marie Antoinette was also executed. The popular press celebrated her death. "The Widow Capet," however, showed great dignity as she went to her death. Their son, the uncrowned Louis XVII, died of unknown causes in the dungeons of the revolution.

The Convention Under Siege

By early 1793, danger threatened France on all sides. The country was at war with much of Europe, including Britain, the Netherlands, Spain, and Prussia. In the Vendée (vahn DAY) region of western France, royalists and priests led peasants in a rebellion against the government. In Paris, the sans-culottes demanded relief from food shortages and rising prices. The Convention itself was bitterly divided between Jacobins and a rival group, the Girondins.

ISSUES For TODAY

A complex blend of ideas and conditions led to the overthrow of the French monarchy. What circumstances can lead to revolution?

PARALLELS THROUGH TIME

Portraits in Wax

The custom of making wax sculptures of famous people dates to Roman times. Today, wax museums such as the legendary Madame Tussaud's in London or the Hollywood Wax Museum in Los Angeles remain popular tourist attractions.

Linking Past and Present Why do you think wax museums have fascinated people for centuries?

PAST As a young woman, Marie Tussaud ran a waxworks exhibit in Paris and taught wax carving to the royal family. During the revolution, she molded these death masks of Louis XVI and Marie Antoinette, below. Later, when she opened her famous wax museum in London, she displayed the heads in her Chamber of Horrors. At left is Madame Tussaud's own self-portrait in wax.

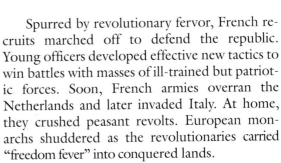

PRESENT

Today, skilled artisans continue to produce lifelike wax sculptures of celebrities like Bill Cosby (above) and Arnold Schwarzenegger (right).

Committee of Public Safety. To deal with the threats to France, the Convention created the Committee of Public Safety. The 12-member committee had almost absolute power as it battled to save the revolution. It prepared France for all-out war, ordering all citizens to join the war effort:

> ❝Young men shall go to battle. Married men shall forge arms and transport provisions. Women shall make tents and clothing and serve in hospitals. Children will make lint from old linen. And old men shall be brought to public places to arouse the courage of soldiers.❞

Spurred by revolutionary fervor, French recruits marched off to defend the republic. Young officers developed effective new tactics to win battles with masses of ill-trained but patriotic forces. Soon, French armies overran the Netherlands and later invaded Italy. At home, they crushed peasant revolts. European monarchs shuddered as the revolutionaries carried "freedom fever" into conquered lands.

Robespierre. At home, the government battled counterrevolutionaries under the guiding hand of Maximilien Robespierre (ROHBZ pyair). Robespierre, a shrewd lawyer and politician, quickly rose to the leadership of the Committee of Public Safety. Among Jacobins, his selfless dedication to the revolution earned him the nickname "the incorruptible." Enemies called him a tyrant.

Robespierre had embraced Rousseau's idea of the general will. He promoted religious toleration and sought to abolish slavery. Though cold and humorless, he was popular with the sans-culottes, who hated the old regime as much as he. He believed that France could achieve a "republic of virtue" only through the use of terror. "Liberty cannot be secured," he cried, "unless criminals lose their heads."

Reign of Terror. Robespierre was a chief architect of the Reign of Terror, which lasted from about July 1793 to July 1794. Revolutionary courts conducted hasty trials. Spectators greeted death sentences with cries of "Hail the Republic!" or "Perish the traitors!"

Perhaps 40,000 people died during the Terror. About 15 percent were nobles and clergy. Another 15 percent were middle-class citizens, often moderates who had supported the revolution in 1789. The rest were peasants and sans-culottes involved in riots or revolts against the Republic. Many were executed, including victims of mistaken identity or false accusations by their neighbors. Many more were packed into hideous prisons, where deaths were common.

The engine of the Terror was the guillotine. Its fast-falling blade extinguished life instantly. A member of the legislature, Dr. Joseph Guillotin (GEE oh tan), had introduced it as a more humane method of beheading than the uncertain ax. But the guillotine quickly became a symbol of horror. William Wordsworth, who had welcomed the start of the revolution, turned in revulsion from the Terror:

> ❝The Mother from the Cradle of her Babe,
> The Warrior from the Field, all perished, all,
> Friends, enemies, of all parties, ages, ranks,
> Head after head, and never heads enough
> For those that bade them fall.❞

Within a year, though, the Reign of Terror consumed its own. Weary of bloodshed and fearing for their own lives, the Convention turned on the Committee of Public Safety. Once the heads of Robespierre and other radicals fell, executions slowed down dramatically.

Reaction and the Directory

In reaction to the Terror, the revolution entered a third stage. Moving away from the excesses of the Convention, moderates produced another constitution, the third since 1789. The Constitution of 1795 set up a five-man Directory

---

The Guillotine *Early versions of the guillotine had been used for centuries. In the 1790s, though, it became a symbol of the Reign of Terror. Some people considered the guillotine humane because it worked swiftly and surely. Others were horrified because it made executions routine and simple, like a present-day assembly line.* **Economics and Technology** *What newer methods of capital punishment have been invented since the 1700s?*

and a two-house legislature elected by male citizens of property.

The Directory held power from 1795 to 1799. Weak but dictatorial, it faced growing discontent. Leaders lined their own pockets but failed to solve pressing problems. When rising bread prices stirred hungry sans-culottes to riot, the Directory quickly suppressed them.

As chaos threatened, politicians turned to a popular military hero, Napoleon Bonaparte. They planned to use him to advance their own goals—a bad miscalculation! Before long, Napoleon would outwit them all to become ruler of France.

Women in the Revolution

As you have seen, women of all classes participated in the revolution from the very beginning. Working-class women demonstrated and fought in street battles. In Paris and elsewhere, women formed their own political clubs. A few, like Jeanne Roland, were noted leaders. Roland supported the revolution through her writings, her salon, and her influence on her husband, a government minister.

Rights for women. Many women were disappointed when the Declaration of the Rights of Man did not grant equal citizenship to women. Olympe de Gouges (oh LAMP duh GOOZH), a journalist, demanded equal rights in her *Declaration of the Rights of Woman*:

66Woman is born free and her rights are the same as those of man. . . . All citizens, be they men or women, being equal in the state's eyes, must be equally eligible for all public offices, positions, and jobs. . . . [Women] have the right to go to the scaffold; they must also have the right to go to parliament.99

Women did gain some rights. The government made divorce easier, a move aimed at weakening Church authority. It allowed women to inherit property, to undermine the tradition of nobles leaving large estates to their oldest sons. These reforms, like others, did not last long after Napoleon gained power.

Setbacks. As the revolution progressed, women's right to express their views in public came under fire. In 1793, a committee of the National Convention declared that women did not have "the moral and physical strength necessary to practice political rights." Women's revolutionary clubs were banned.

Among the many women who became victims of the Terror were republicans like Gouges and moderates like Roland. As she mounted the steps to the guillotine, Roland cried, "O liberty, what crimes are committed in your name!"

Changes in Daily Life

By 1799, the 10-year-old French Revolution had dramatically changed France. It had dislodged the old social order, overthrown the monarchy, and brought the Church under state control.

New symbols such as the red "liberty caps" and the tricolor confirmed the liberty and equality of all male citizens. Elaborate fashions and powdered wigs gave way to the practical clothes and simple haircuts of the sans-culottes. To show their revolutionary spirit, enthusiastic parents gave their children names like Constitution, Republic, or August Tenth.

Nationalism. Revolution and war gave people a strong sense of national identity. In earlier times, people had felt loyalty to local authorities. As monarchs centralized power, loyalty shifted to the king or queen. Now, the government rallied sons and daughters of the revolution to defend the nation itself. Nationalism, an aggressive feeling of pride in and devotion to one's country, spread throughout France.

By 1793, France was a nation in arms. From the port city of Marseilles (mahr SAY), troops marched to a rousing new song:

66Come, children of the fatherland,
The glorious day has arrived.
Against us the bloody banner
Of tyranny is raised.
To arms, citizens!
Join the battalions.
Let us march, let us march!99

"La Marseillaise" (mahr say EHZ) would later become the French national anthem.

Social reform. Revolutionaries pushed for social reform, such as compulsory elementary education. The Convention set up state schools to replace religious ones and organized systems to help the poor or care for old soldiers and war widows. The government also abolished slavery in French West Indian colonies and extended religious toleration.

The Convention tried to de-Christianize France. It created a secular calendar with 1793 as the Year I of the new era of freedom. It banned many religious festivals, replacing them with secular celebrations. Huge public ceremonies boosted support for republican and nationalist ideals.

The arts. French arts moved toward a grand classical style that echoed the grandeur of ancient Rome. The leading artist of the period was Jacques Louis David (dah VEED). David immortalized such stirring events as the Tennis Court Oath and, later, the reign of Napoleon. (See the painting on page 495.) David's paintings helped shape the way future generations pictured the French Revolution.

SECTION 3 REVIEW

1. **Identify** (a) Committee of Public Safety, (b) Maximilien Robespierre, (c) Directory, (d) Olympe de Gouges, (e) "La Marseillaise," (f) Jacques Louis David.
2. **Define** (a) suffrage, (b) nationalism.
3. (a) Why did revolutionaries fear that the revolution was in danger? (b) What was their response to that danger?
4. What were three results of the Reign of Terror?
5. Describe one effect of the French Revolution on each of the following: (a) daily life, (b) the arts, (c) the rights of women.
6. *Critical Thinking* **Defending a Position** Robespierre wrote, "Terror without virtue is fatal. Virtue without terror is powerless. Terror is nothing but prompt, severe, and unbending justice." Do you agree that the Reign of Terror was necessary to defend the republic? Why or why not?
7. *ACTIVITY* Create a poster that might have been used to support or oppose *one* of the following: the goals of the Jacobins; the execution of Louis XVI or Marie Antoinette; the policies of the Committee of Public Safety; French nationalism; equal rights for women.

4 The Age of Napoleon Begins

Guide for Reading

■ How did Napoleon gain power?

■ What role did Napoleon play in furthering the French Revolution?

■ How did Napoleon build and defend his empire?

■ **Vocabulary** *plebiscite, annex, blockade*

66He was like an expert chess player, with the human race for an opponent, which he proposed to checkmate.99

Thus did Madame Germaine de Staël (STAHL), a celebrated writer and intellectual, describe Napoleon Bonaparte. Napoleon himself expressed a humbler view of his rise to power. "Nothing has been simpler than my elevation," he once observed. "It is owing to the peculiarities of the time."

From 1799 to 1815, Napoleon would dominate France and Europe. A hero to some, an evil force to others, he gave his name to the final phase of the revolution—the age of Napoleon.

The Man From Corsica

Napoleon Buonaparte (as he once spelled his name) was born on the French-ruled island of Corsica in the Mediterranean. His family were minor nobles, but had little money. At age nine, he was sent to France to be trained for a military career. When the revolution broke out, he was an ambitious 20-year-old lieutenant, eager to make a name for himself.

Napoleon favored the Jacobins and republican rule. However, he found the conflicting ideas and clashing personalities of the revolution confusing. He wrote his brother in 1793:

66Since one must take sides, one might as well choose the side that is victorious, the side which devastates, loots, and burns. Considering the alternative, it is better to eat than be eaten.99

Napoleon Crossing the Alps This portrait by Jacques Louis David glorifies Napoleon as a military hero. His fame as a general helped Napoleon become emperor. When a government is weak, he commented, the people look for a genius to save the country. Once they find him, "a great people, thronging around him, seems exultingly to proclaim, 'This is the man.'" **Impact of the Individual** Why do you think other French soldiers are barely visible in this painting?

Early successes. During the turmoil of the revolution, he rose quickly in the army. In December 1793, he drove British forces out of the French port of Toulon (too LOHN). He then went on to win several dazzling victories against the Austrians, capturing most of northern Italy and forcing the Hapsburg emperor to make peace. Hoping to disrupt British trade with India, he led a colorful expedition to Egypt in 1798. The Egyptian campaign proved disastrous, but Napoleon managed to hide stories of the worst losses from his admirers in France.

Success fed his ambition. By 1799, he moved from victorious general to political leader. That year, he helped overthrow the weak Directory and set up a three-man governing board, the Consulate. Another constitution was drawn up, but Napoleon soon took the title First Consul. In 1802, he had himself named consul for life.

GLOBAL CONNECTIONS

The Egyptian campaign was a military failure but a cultural success. Napoleon sent a commission of scientists, artists, and other scholars to collect extensive information on Egypt. Their work introduced Egyptian culture to Europe and launched a craze for Egyptian styles. More important, French troops discovered the Rosetta Stone. As you read, French scholar Jean Champollion was eventually able to use the Rosetta Stone to decipher ancient Egyptian hieroglyphics.

A self-made emperor. Two years later, Napoleon had accumulated enough power into his hands to take the title Emperor of the French. He invited the pope to preside over his coronation at Notre Dame cathedral in Paris. During the ceremony, however, Napoleon took the crown from the pope's hands and placed it on his own head. By this action, Napoleon meant to show that he owed his throne to no one but himself.

Yet at each step on his rise to power, Napoleon had held a plebiscite (PLEHB ih sīt), or ballot in which voters say yes or no to an issue. Each time, the French strongly supported him. To understand why, we must look at his policies.

France Under Napoleon

During the consulate and empire, Napoleon consolidated power, strengthening the central government. Order, security, and efficiency replaced liberty, equality, and fraternity as the slogans of the new regime.

CAUSE AND EFFECT

Long-Term Causes

Corrupt, inconsistent, and insensitive leadership
Prosperous members of Third Estate resent privileges of First and Second estates
Spread of Enlightenment ideas

Immediate Causes

Huge government debt
Poor harvests and rising price of bread
Failure of Louis XVI to accept financial reforms
Formation of National Assembly
Storming of Bastille

THE FRENCH REVOLUTION

Immediate Effects

France adopts its first written constitution
French feudalism ends
Declaration of the Rights of Man and the Citizen adopted
Monarchy abolished
Revolutionary France fights coalition of European powers
Reign of Terror

Long-Term Effects

Napoleon gains power
Napoleonic Code established
French conquests spark nationalism
French public schools set up

Connections Today

French people remain proud of Napoleon's glory days
French law reflects Napoleonic Code
Metric system, set up after revolution, in use worldwide
After centuries of power, French political and military influence declines in Europe

Interpreting a Chart *Once it began, the French Revolution moved swiftly. Its long-term causes, however, had been building up for decades.* ■ *Why is the rise of Napoleon considered a long-term effect rather than an immediate effect?*

Reforms. To restore prosperity, Napoleon modernized finance. He regulated the economy to control prices, encourage new industry, and build roads and canals. To ensure well-trained officials and military officers, he promoted a system of public schools under strict government control.

At the same time, Napoleon backed off from some social reforms of the revolution. He made peace with the Catholic Church in the Concordat of 1801. The Concordat kept the Church under state control but recognized religious freedom for Catholics. Revolutionaries who opposed the Church denounced the agreement, but Catholics welcomed it.

Napoleon won support across class lines. He encouraged émigrés to return, provided they took an oath of loyalty. Peasants were relieved when he recognized their right to lands they had bought from Church and nobles during the revolution. The middle class, who had benefited most from the revolution, approved Napoleon's economic reforms and the restoration of order after years of chaos. Napoleon also made all "careers open to talent," a popular policy among those who remembered the old aristocratic monopoly of power. Napoleon's chief opposition came from royalists on the right and republicans on the left.

Napoleonic Code. Among Napoleon's most lasting reforms was a new law code, popularly called the Napoleonic Code. It embodied Enlightenment principles such as the equality of all citizens before the law, religious toleration, and advancement based on merit.

But the Napoleonic Code undid some reforms of the French Revolution. Women, for example, lost most of their newly gained rights under the new code. The law considered women minors who could not exercise the rights of citizenship. Male heads of households regained complete authority over their wives and children. Again, Napoleon valued order and authority over individual rights.

Subduing an Empire

From 1804 to 1814, Napoleon furthered his reputation on the battlefield. He successfully faced down the combined forces of the greatest European powers. Year after year, he marshaled the military might of France to field enormous armies. He took great risks and even suffered huge losses. "I grew up on the field of battle," he once said, "and a man such as I am cares little for the life of a million men." By 1810, his Grand Empire reached its greatest extent. "We are babes in the hands of a giant," sighed Czar Alexander I of Russia.

As a military leader, Napoleon valued rapid movements and made effective use of his large armies. He developed a new plan for each battle, so opposing generals could never anticipate what he would do next. His enemies paid tribute to his leadership. Napoleon's presence on the battlefield, said one, was "worth 40,000 troops." The map on the right highlights Napoleon's most celebrated strategic victory, the Battle of Austerlitz.

The Grand Empire. Napoleon redrew the map of Europe. He annexed, or added outright, some areas to France, including the Netherlands and Belgium as well as parts of Italy and Germany. He abolished the tottering Holy Roman Empire and created a 38-member Confederation of the Rhine under French protection. He cut Prussian territory in half, turning part of old Poland into the Grand Duchy of Warsaw. And he forced alliances on European powers from Madrid to Moscow. At various times, the rulers of Austria, Prussia, and Russia reluctantly signed treaties with the "Corsican upstart," as his enemies called him. (See the map on page 499.)

Napoleon put friends and family members on the thrones of Europe. He unseated the king of Spain and placed his own brother, Joseph Bonaparte, on the throne. Napoleon also divorced his wife, Josephine, to marry a Hapsburg princess, the niece of Marie Antoinette. He and his heirs could then claim kinship with the ancient ruling families of Europe.

France versus Britain. Britain alone remained outside Napoleon's European empire. With only a small army, Britain relied on its sea power to stop Napoleon's drive to rule the continent. In 1805, Napoleon prepared to invade England. But at the Battle of Trafalgar, fought off the southwest coast of Spain, British admiral Horatio Nelson smashed a French fleet. During the battle, Nelson was fatally shot by a French sniper but lived long enough to learn of the

Battle of Austerlitz, 1805

French forces
Fake French retreat
Russian-Austrian forces
Russian-Austrian retreat
Hills
Swamps

1. French fake retreat to lure Russian-Austrian forces off Pratzen Heights.
2. Russian-Austrian forces chase French.
3. French take Pratzen Heights.
4. Russian-Austrian forces attack, but are repulsed.
5. More French troops join in to defeat Russian-Austrian forces.

GEOGRAPHY AND HISTORY

In December 1805, Napoleon's forces fought a combined Russian-Austrian army at the Battle of Austerlitz. Thanks to Napoleon's superior leadership, his outnumbered troops won an outstanding victory.

1. **Location** On the map, locate (a) Austerlitz, (b) Pratzen Heights, (c) Satschan Sea, (d) Napoleon's headquarters.
2. **Movement** How were Napoleon's troops able to defeat the Russian-Austrian forces south of Pratzen Heights?
3. *Critical Thinking* **Making Generalizations** Why is control of the high ground important in a battle?

British victory. His last words were, "Thank God, I have done my duty."

With an invasion ruled out, Napoleon tried to strike at Britain's lifeblood, its commerce. He waged economic warfare through the Continental System, which closed European ports to British goods. Britain responded with its own blockade of European ports. A blockade involves shutting off ports to keep people or supplies from moving in or out. During their long struggle, both Britain and France seized neutral ships suspected of trading with the other side. British attacks on American ships sparked anger in the United States and eventually triggered the War of 1812.

Successes and failures. In the end, Napoleon's Continental System failed to bring Britain to its knees. Although British exports declined, its powerful navy kept open vital trade routes to the Americas and India. Meanwhile, restrictions on trade hurt Europe, created a scarcity of goods, and sent prices soaring. Resentful European merchants ignored Napoleon's ban on British goods and engaged in widespread smuggling.

Still, for years the French celebrated unforgettable successes. Napoleon's triumphs boosted French nationalism. Great victory parades filled the streets of Paris with cheering crowds. To this day the glory and grandeur of the age of Napoleon are a source of pride to many French citizens.

SECTION 4 REVIEW

1. **Identify** (a) Consulate, (b) Concordat of 1801, (c) Napoleonic Code, (d) Battle of Trafalgar, (e) Confederation of the Rhine, (f) Continental System.
2. **Define** (a) plebiscite, (b) annex, (c) blockade.
3. (a) Describe Napoleon Bonaparte's rise to power. (b) Why did many French support him?
4. How did Napoleon's policies both extend and turn back the reforms of the French Revolution? Give examples.
5. (a) How did Napoleon come to dominate most of Europe? (b) Why did his efforts to subdue Britain fail?
6. *Critical Thinking* **Drawing Conclusions** Why do you think both royalists and republicans opposed Napoleon?
7. *ACTIVITY* Draw a political cartoon commenting on the rivalry between Britain and Napoleonic France, from either a British or French point of view.

The End of an Era

Guide for Reading

- What events led to Napoleon's downfall?

- What principles guided leaders at the Congress of Vienna?

- How did the Congress of Vienna seek to impose a new order on Europe?

- **Vocabulary** *guerrilla warfare, abdicate, legitimacy*

Napoleon watched the battle for the Russian city of Smolensk from a chair outside his tent. As fires lit up the walled city, he exclaimed:
"It's like Vesuvius erupting. Don't you think this is a beautiful sight?"
"Horrible, Sire," replied an aide.
"Bah!" snorted Napoleon. "Remember, gentlemen, what a Roman emperor said: 'The corpse of an enemy always smells sweet.'"
In 1812, Napoleon pursued his dream of empire by invading Russia. The campaign began a chain of events that eventually led to his downfall. Napoleon's final defeat brought an end to the era of the French Revolution.

Challenges to Napoleon's Empire

Under Napoleon, French armies spread the ideas of the revolution across Europe. They backed liberal reforms in the lands they conquered. In some places, they helped install revolutionary governments that abolished titles of nobility, ended Church privileges, opened careers to men of talent, and ended serfdom and manorial dues. The Napoleonic Code, too, was carried across Europe. French occupation sometimes brought economic benefits as well, by reducing trade barriers and stimulating industry.

Yet Napoleon's successes contained the seeds of defeat. While nationalism spurred French armies to success, it worked against them, too. Many Europeans who welcomed the ideas of the French Revolution nevertheless saw Napoleon's armies as foreign oppressors. They

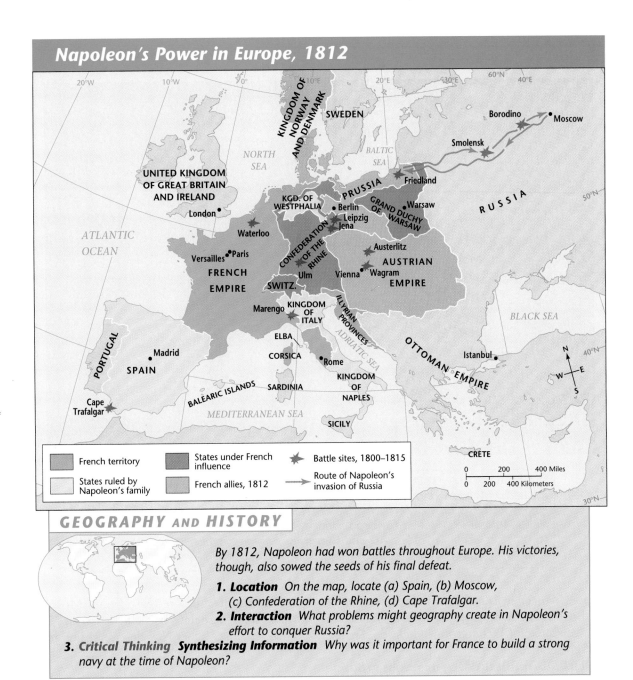

Napoleon's Power in Europe, 1812

Legend:
- French territory
- States ruled by Napoleon's family
- States under French influence
- French allies, 1812
- ★ Battle sites, 1800–1815
- → Route of Napoleon's invasion of Russia

0 200 400 Miles
0 200 400 Kilometers

GEOGRAPHY AND HISTORY

By 1812, Napoleon had won battles throughout Europe. His victories, though, also sowed the seeds of his final defeat.

1. **Location** On the map, locate (a) Spain, (b) Moscow, (c) Confederation of the Rhine, (d) Cape Trafalgar.
2. **Interaction** What problems might geography create in Napoleon's effort to conquer Russia?
3. **Critical Thinking** **Synthesizing Information** Why was it important for France to build a strong navy at the time of Napoleon?

---

resented the Continental System and Napoleon's effort to impose French culture.

From Rome to Madrid to the Netherlands, nationalism unleashed revolts against France. In the German states, leaders encouraged national loyalty among German-speaking people to counter French influence.

Resistance in Spain. Resistance to foreign rule bled French occupying forces in Spain. In 1808, Napoleon replaced the king of Spain with his own brother, Joseph Bonaparte. He also introduced liberal reforms that sought to undermine the Spanish Catholic Church. But many Spaniards remained loyal to their former king and devoted to the Church. When they resisted the invaders, well-armed French forces responded with brutal repression. Far from crushing resistance, the French reaction further inflamed Spanish nationalism.

Spanish patriots conducted a campaign of guerrilla warfare, or hit-and-run raids, against the French. (In Spanish, *guerrilla* means "little war.") Small bands ambushed French supply trains or troops before melting into the countryside. These attacks kept large numbers of French soldiers tied down in Spain, when

The Third of May, 1808 *This painting by the Spanish artist Francisco Goya shows the execution of Spaniards by Napoleon's troops. The man about to be shot throws out his arms, a martyr for the cause of liberty. The faceless French soldiers embody the inhumanity of war. Artists like Goya shifted away from the heroic, classical style of Jacques Louis David toward more emotional scenes.* **Art and Literature** *Why do you think Goya painted the scene as taking place at night? What effect does the lantern create?*

Napoleon needed them elsewhere. Eventually, the British sent an army under Arthur Wellesley, later the Duke of Wellington, to help the Spanish fight France.

Defeat in Russia. Despite revolts in Spain and elsewhere, Napoleon continued to seek new conquests. In 1812, Alexander I of Russia resigned from the Continental System. Napoleon responded by assembling his Grand Army. About 600,000 soldiers from France and other countries invaded Russia.

To avoid battles with Napoleon, the Russians retreated eastward, burning crops and villages as they went. This "scorched earth" policy left the French hungry and cold as winter came. Napoleon entered Moscow in September. He realized, though, that he could not feed and supply his army through the long Russian winter. In October, he turned homeward.

The 1,000-mile retreat from Moscow turned into a desperate battle for survival. The French general Michel Ney described the grim scene:

66The army marches covered in great snowflakes. The stragglers fall to the lances of the Cossacks. As for me, I cover the retreat. Behind files the army with broken ranks. It is a mob without purpose, famished, feverish. . . . General Famine and General Winter, rather than the Russian bullets, have conquered the Grand Army.99

Only about 100,000 soldiers of the once-proud Grand Army survived. Many died. Others deserted. Napoleon himself rushed back to Paris to raise a new force to defend France. His reputation for success, however, was shattered.

Downfall of Napoleon

The disaster in Russia brought a new alliance of Russia, Britain, Austria, and Prussia against a weakened France. In 1813, they defeated Napoleon in the Battle of the Nations at Leipzig. The next year, as his enemies closed in on France, Napoleon *abdicated,* or stepped down from power. The victors exiled him to Elba, an island in the Mediterranean. They then recognized Louis XVIII, brother of Louis XVI, as king of France.

Napoleon returns. The restoration of Louis XVIII did not go smoothly. The Bourbon king agreed to accept the Napoleonic Code and honor the land settlements made during the revolution. However, many émigrés rushed back to France bent on revenge. An economic depression and the fear of a return to the old regime helped rekindle loyalty to Napoleon.

As the victorious allies gathered for a general peace conference in Vienna, Napoleon escaped his island exile and returned to France. Soldiers flocked to his banner. As citizens cheered Napoleon's advance, Louis XVIII fled. In March 1815, the emperor of the French entered Paris in triumph.

Waterloo. Napoleon's triumph was short-lived. His star soared for only 100 days, while the allies reassembled their forces. On June 18, 1815, the opposing armies met near the town of Waterloo in Belgium. British forces under the Duke of Wellington and a Prussian army commanded by General Blücher crushed the French in an agonizing day-long battle. Once again, Napoleon was forced to abdicate and go into exile on St. Helena, a lonely island in the South Atlantic. This time, he would never return.

Legacy of Napoleon. Napoleon died in 1821, but his legend lived on in France and around the world. His contemporaries as well as historians have long debated his legacy. Was he "the revolution on horseback," as he claimed? Or was he a traitor to the revolution?

No one, though, questions Napoleon's impact on France and on Europe. The Napoleonic Code consolidated many changes of the revolution. The France of Napoleon was a centralized state with a constitution. Elections were held with expanded, though limited, suffrage. Many more citizens had rights to property and access

Retreat From Moscow This British cartoon depicts Napoleon's retreat from Moscow. Hundreds of thousands of French soldiers died during their long trek across Russia's frozen landscape. **Global Interaction** Why do you think this cartoonist made light of the suffering of Napoleon's army?

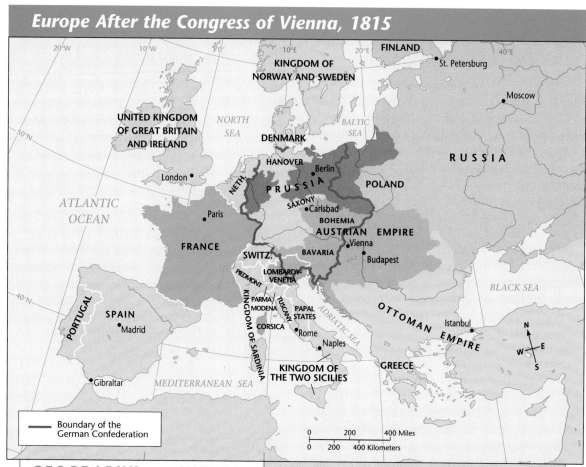

Europe After the Congress of Vienna, 1815

Boundary of the German Confederation

GEOGRAPHY AND HISTORY

At the Congress of Vienna in 1815, European leaders redrew the map of Europe. They sought to contain France and restore peace to the continent.

1. Location On the map, locate (a) German Confederation, (b) Netherlands, (c) Vienna, (d) France.

2. Place Which country was expanded by the Congress of Vienna so it could contain French ambitions to the north?

3. Critical Thinking Comparing Study the map on page 499. What new countries appeared after the Congress of Vienna?

to education than under the old regime. Still, French citizens lost many rights promised so fervently by republicans during the Convention.

On the world stage, Napoleon's conquests spread the ideas of the revolution. He failed to make Europe into a French empire. Instead, he sparked nationalist feeling across Europe. The abolition of the Holy Roman Empire would eventually help in creating a new Germany. Napoleon also had a dramatic impact across the Atlantic. In 1803, his decision to sell France's vast Louisiana Territory to the American government doubled the size of the United States and ushered in an age of American expansion.

The Congress of Vienna

After Waterloo, diplomats and heads of state again sat down at the Congress of Vienna. They faced the monumental task of restoring stability and order in Europe after 25 years of war.

Glittering spectacle. The Congress met for 10 months, from September 1814 to June 1815. It was a brilliant gathering of European leaders. Diplomats, courtiers, and royalty dined and danced, attended concerts and ballets, and enjoyed hunting parties and picnics arranged by their host, Emperor Francis I of Austria. Beneath the glittering spectacle, paid spies slipped in and out of rented palaces, anxious to find out who was saying what to whom.

Serious work. While the entertainment kept thousands of smaller players busy, the real work fell to Prince Clemens von Metternich of Austria, Czar Alexander I of Russia, and Lord Robert Castlereagh (KAS uhl ray) of Britain. Defeated France was also invited to send a representative to Vienna, Prince Maurice Talleyrand.

The chief goal of the Vienna decision makers was to create a lasting peace by establishing a balance of power and protecting the system of monarchy. Each of the leaders also pursued his own goals. Metternich, the dominant figure at the Congress, wanted to restore the *status quo* (Latin for "the way things are") of 1792. Alexander I urged a "holy alliance" of Christian monarchs to suppress future revolutions. Lord Castlereagh was determined to prevent a revival of French military power. The aged diplomat Talleyrand shrewdly played the other leaders against one another to get defeated France accepted as an equal partner.

The Vienna Settlement

Despite clashes and controversies, the diplomats at Vienna finally worked out a framework for peace. Their decisions set the stage for European politics for the next 100 years.

Balance of power. The peacemakers redrew the map of Europe. (See the map on page 502.) To contain French ambitions, they ringed France with strong countries. In the north, they added Belgium and Luxembourg to Holland to create the kingdom of the Netherlands. To prevent French expansion eastward, they gave Prussia lands along the Rhine River. They also allowed Austria to reassert control over northern Italy. This policy of containment proved fairly successful in maintaining the peace.

Stability. To turn back the clock to 1792, the architects of the peace promoted the principle of legitimacy, restoring hereditary monarchies that the French Revolution or Napoleon had unseated. Even before the Congress began, they had put Louis XVIII on the French throne. Later, they restored "legitimate" monarchs in Portugal, Spain, and the Italian states.

To protect the new order, Metternich pushed to create the Concert of Europe, a peacekeeping organization. It included all of the major European states. Leaders pledged to maintain the balance of power and to suppress any uprisings inspired by the ideas of the French Revolution.

Problems of the peace. The Vienna statesmen achieved their immediate goals. However, they failed to foresee how powerful new forces such as nationalism would shake the foundations of Europe. They redrew national boundaries without any concern for national cultures.

In Germany, they created a loosely organized German Confederation with Austria as its official head. But Germans who had battled Napoleon were already dreaming of a strong united German nation. Their dream would not come true for more than 50 years, but the story of German unification began in this period.

Looking ahead. Many people inspired by revolutionary ideals condemned the Vienna settlement. Still, the general peace lasted for a hundred years. Europe would not see war on a Napoleonic scale until 1914.

Yet the ideals of the French Revolution were not destroyed. In the next decades, its slogan and goals would inspire people in Europe and Latin America to seek equality and liberty. (See Chapter 21.) The spirit of nationalism ignited by Napoleon remained a powerful force.

SECTION 5 REVIEW

1. **Identify** (a) Waterloo, (b) Clemens von Metternich, (c) Concert of Europe.
2. **Define** (a) guerrilla warfare, (b) abdicate, (c) legitimacy.
3. How did Napoleon's success contain the seeds of his defeat?
4. (a) What were the chief goals of the Congress of Vienna? (b) Describe three actions taken to achieve these goals.
5. *Critical Thinking* **Drawing Conclusions** Do you agree that Napoleon was "the revolution on horseback"? Why or why not?
6. *ACTIVITY* Imagine that it is 1816 and you are Napoleon, Metternich, or a former French revolutionary. Write a letter in which you evaluate the events of the last 30 years.

CHAPTER REVIEW

REVIEWING VOCABULARY

Select *five* vocabulary words from the chapter. Write each word on a separate slip of paper. Then, write the definition for each word on other slips of paper. Scramble the slips and exchange them with another student. Match the words with their definitions, and then check each other's results.

REVIEWING FACTS

1. Why was there discontent with the old regime in France?
2. Why did a crowd storm the Bastille?

3. What was the slogan of the French Revolution?
4. What happened to Louis XVI and Marie Antoinette in 1793?
5. What was the Reign of Terror?
6. List the reforms that Napoleon made as leader of France.
7. How did Napoleon try to increase French power in Europe?
8. What was the result of Napoleon's invasion of Russia?
9. How did the Congress of Vienna try to restore the balance of power in Europe?

SKILLS FOR SUCCESS   IDENTIFYING RELEVANT FACTS

When researching a topic, students of history must wade through a large amount of information and decide what is relevant. Relevant information has a clear and important link to the subject under investigation.

Imagine that you are preparing a paper about the Reign of Terror. Look at the information below, and then answer the following questions.

1. **Look for *examples* and *details* relevant to your topic.** (a) Which statement illustrates that the Committee of Public Safety ruled with almost dictatorial powers? (b) Is statement B relevant to the topic? Explain.

2. **Look for information providing background and reasons relating to the topic.** (a) Which statements provide reasons why the Reign of Terror began and ended? (b) Is statement D relevant to the topic? Explain.

3. **Draw conclusions about the relevance of the information.** What are some key words, names, and dates that appear in the statements that are relevant to the Reign of Terror?

TOPIC: The Reign of Terror
A. By 1794, the supporters of the revolution began to question the need for constant executions. In July, Robespierre was arrested and executed.
B. The revolution transformed daily life in France.
C. In the face of domestic and foreign threats, the National Convention set aside the constitution and created a Committee of Public Safety with almost dictatorial powers.
D. With the help of troops loyal to him, Napoleon Bonaparte and two directors overthrew the government in 1799.
E. The National Assembly abolished feudalism and introduced sweeping religious reforms.
F. The campaign known as the Reign of Terror lasted from July 1793 to July 1794.
G. Maximilien Robespierre led the Committee of Public Safety during the Reign of Terror.
H. To uncover traitors, the Committee of Public Safety sent agents across France.
I. Between 20,000 and 40,000 French people were executed as traitors.

REVIEWING CHAPTER THEMES

Review the "Focus On" questions at the start of this chapter. Then select *three* of those questions and answer them, using information from the chapter.

CRITICAL THINKING

1. **Defending a Position** The Declaration of the Rights of Man has been called the "death certificate" of the old regime. Do you agree? Why or why not?

2. **Linking Past and Present** Most historians agree that the French Revolution was a great turning point in European history. What events and ideas that emerged during the French Revolution are still a part of our political and social views today?

ANALYZING PRIMARY SOURCES

Use the quotations on pages 488 and 492 to answer the following questions.

1. What mood did Wordsworth express in the first passage?

2. What mood did he express in the second passage?

3. What accounts for the change in Wordsworth's attitude toward the French Revolution?

FOR YOUR PORTFOLIO

CREATING A DOCUMENTARY Work with a group of four students to prepare a segment for a documentary series on the French Revolution. First, choose one of these topics: The Way It Was, The Outbreak of the Revolution, A Moderate Start, The Radicals Take Over, The Rise and Fall of Napoleon, or Peace Again. Then review the relevant pages in your textbook and consult outside sources for additional research on your segment. Note documents, maps, and other visuals to include in your segment. Work with your group to write your segment. Finally, present your segment to the class.

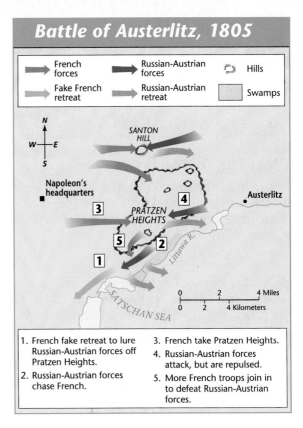

Battle of Austerlitz, 1805

French forces	Russian-Austrian forces	Hills
Fake French retreat	Russian-Austrian retreat	Swamps

1. French fake retreat to lure Russian-Austrian forces off Pratzen Heights.
2. Russian-Austrian forces chase French.
3. French take Pratzen Heights.
4. Russian-Austrian forces attack, but are repulsed.
5. More French troops join in to defeat Russian-Austrian forces.

ANALYZING MAPS

Use the map to answer the following questions.

1. In what direction from Austerlitz was Napoleon's headquarters located?

2. What was the result of the fighting at Santon Hill?

3. Which body of water did the Russian and Austrian troops cross in their retreat after the battle?

INTERNET ACTIVITY

INTERPRETING HISTORICAL SYMBOLS
Use the Internet to research one of the symbols of the French Revolution or the French republic, such as the Bastille, the Tricolor, or "La Marseillaise." Then write a brief historical analysis of the symbol. Explain how it originated, what it represented to French citizens during the revolution, and, if possible, how it appears in France today.

The Industrial Revolution Begins

(1750–1850)

CHAPTER OUTLINE

1 Dawn of the Industrial Age
2 Britain Leads the Way
3 Hardships of Early Industrial Life
4 New Ways of Thinking

On September 15, 1830, an excited crowd gathered at the bustling seaport of Liverpool, England. They had come to celebrate the opening of the Liverpool & Manchester, the world's first public steam-operated railway.

The 600 specially invited guests climbed aboard the gaily decorated trains. The engineer signaled that all was ready. Slowly, the shiny locomotives moved out of the station.

About halfway along the route, the locomotives stopped to take on water. Several passengers climbed down to get a closer look at the engines. Among them was William Huskisson, president of Britain's Board of Trade.

Suddenly, another locomotive steamed up the track. Startled guests clambered to safety. "Huskisson! For God's sake, get to your place!" shouted someone. But in his hurry, Huskisson stumbled and fell. The approaching engine ran him over and crushed his leg.

Stunned passengers lifted the injured man onto another train. The rescue locomotive roared to the nearest town. But despite a doctor's efforts, Huskisson died of his wounds.

The tragedy took the joy out of the occasion. Still, people noted the amazing speed attained by the engine carrying the wounded Huskisson. An astonished observer reported:

66The . . . engine conveyed the wounded
body of the unfortunate gentleman
a distance of about 15 miles in 25 minutes, or at the rate of 36 miles an hour.
This incredible speed burst upon the
world with the effect of a new and
unlooked-for phenomenon.99

Despite the sad events of opening day, investors flocked to the new railroad. Soon railroads were sprouting everywhere, creating fabulous fortunes for builders and speeding people and goods to distant destinations.

Steam-powered railroads were part of the enormous transformation known as the Industrial Revolution. The Industrial Revolution refers to the shift of production from simple hand tools to complex machines, and from human and animal power to steam power.

The Industrial Revolution was a crucial turning point in history. The changes that began in Western Europe 250 years ago have spread around the globe. In this chapter we will look at the early Industrial Revolution in its birthplace in Britain, from about 1750 to 1850.

FOCUS ON these questions as you read:

■ **Continuity and Change**
How did the Industrial Revolution transform traditional ways of life?

■ **Economics and Technology**
What role did capital and technology play in the Industrial Revolution?

■ **Impact of the Individual**
How did individual contributions shape the industrial age?

■ **Political and Social Systems**
Why did new social and political philosophies develop during the industrial age?

TIME AND PLACE

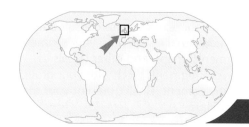

An Industrial Town *Iron and coal were key ingredients of the Industrial Revolution. Coal powered the steam engines in Europe's new factories. Iron was used in railroads, bridges, and machines. Here, blast furnaces, used to purify iron ore, light up the sky of an early industrial town.* **Continuity and Change** *Based on this picture, how do you think the Industrial Revolution changed the European landscape? Explain.*

HUMANITIES LINK

Art History Joseph Wright, *An Iron Forge* (page 511).
Literature In this chapter, you will encounter passages from the following works of literature: Alfred, Lord Tennyson, "Ode Sung at the Opening of the International Exhibition" (page 510); Charles Dickens, *Hard Times* (page 516).

| 1760s Watt improves steam engine | 1776 Smith's *Wealth of Nations* | 1800 Owen begins social reforms at New Lanark | 1830 Liverpool–Manchester Railroad opens | 1848 Marx and Engels publish *The Communist Manifesto* |

| 1750 | 1775 | 1800 | 1825 | 1850 |

1 Dawn of the Industrial Age

Guide for Reading

- What factors contributed to a second agricultural revolution?

- Why did populations soar in Europe?

- What energy sources powered the Industrial Revolution?

- **Vocabulary** *enclosure*

For thousands of years after the rise of civilization, most people lived and worked in small farming villages. A chain of events set in motion in the mid-1700s changed that way of life forever.

The Industrial Revolution started in Britain. Unlike most political revolutions, it was neither sudden nor swift. Instead, it was a long, slow, uneven process in which production shifted from simple hand tools to complex machines. New sources of power replaced human and animal power. In the 250 years since it began, the Industrial Revolution has spread from Britain to the rest of Europe and North America, and then around the globe.

A Turning Point in History

In 1750, most people worked the land, using simple handmade tools. They lived in simple cottages lit by firelight and candles. They made their own clothes and grew their own food. In nearby towns, they might exchange goods at a weekly outdoor market.

Like their peasant ancestors, these people knew little of the world that existed beyond their village. The few who left home traveled only as far as their feet or a horse-drawn cart could take them. Those bold adventurers who dared to cross the seas were at the mercy of winds that filled billowing sails.

Then the Industrial Revolution began. For growing numbers of people, the rural way of life began to disappear. By the 1850s, many country villages had grown into industrial towns and cities. Their inhabitants bought food and clothing in stores that offered a large variety of machine-made goods. They worked indoors behind a counter, desk, or factory machine. Their homes were multistory tenements.

Industrial-age travelers moved rapidly by train or steamship. Urgent messages flew along telegraph wires. New inventions and scientific "firsts" poured out each year. Between 1840 and 1855, for example, an American dentist used an anesthetic for the first time, a French physicist measured the speed of light, and a German chemist developed the Bunsen burner. Elias Howe made the first sewing machine, and a Hungarian doctor introduced antiseptic methods to reduce the risk of women dying in childbirth.

Still more stunning changes occurred in the next century, creating our familiar world of skyscraper cities and carefully tended suburbs. Cars and televisions, air travel and antibiotics, and a mass of other goods and services made their appearance.

How and why did these great changes occur? Historians point to a series of interrelated causes that helped trigger the industrialization of the West.

A New Agricultural Revolution

Oddly enough, the Industrial Revolution was made possible in part by a change in the farming fields of Western Europe. In Chapter 1, you read about an agricultural revolution some 11,000 years ago, when people learned to farm and domesticate animals. About 300 years ago, a second agricultural revolution took place. It greatly improved the quality and quantity of farm products.

Improved methods of farming. The Dutch led the way in the new agricultural revolution. In the 1600s, they built earthen walls known as dikes to reclaim land from the sea. They combined smaller fields into larger ones to

The Industrial Revolution transformed the way people lived and worked. How does technology affect the way people live?

Improved Farm Machinery
Jethro Tull's seed drill planted seeds in straight lines. Since crops planted this way grew in neat rows, they could be weeded with another new invention, the horse-drawn hoe, instead of by hand. **Continuity and Change** Does Tull's seed drill have anything in common with modern farm equipment? Explain.

This four Wheel Drill Plow, with a Seed and a Manure Hopper was first Invented in the Year 1745 and is now in Use with W.ᵐ Ellis at Little Gaddesden near Hempstead in Hertfordshire. where any person may View the same. It is so light that a Man may Draw it. but Generally drawn by a pony or little Horse.

make better use of the land and used fertilizer from livestock to renew the soil.

In the 1700s, British farmers expanded on Dutch experiments. Some farmers mixed different kinds of soils to get higher crop yields. Others tried out new methods of crop rotation. Lord Charles Townshend won the nickname "Turnip Townshend" for urging farmers to grow turnips, which restored exhausted soil. Jethro Tull invented a mechanical device, the seed drill, to aid farmers. It deposited seeds in rows rather than scattering them wastefully over the land. Another pioneer, Robert Bakewell, bred stronger horses for farmwork and fatter sheep and cattle for meat.

Educated farmers exchanged news of experiments through farm journals. King George III himself, nicknamed "Farmer George," wrote articles about his model farm near Windsor Castle.

Enclosure movement. Meanwhile, rich landowners pushed ahead with enclosure, the process of taking over and fencing off land formerly shared by peasant farmers. In the 1500s, they had enclosed land to gain pastures for sheep and increased wool output. By the 1700s, they wanted to replace the strip farms of medieval times with larger fields that could be cultivated more efficiently.

As millions of acres were enclosed, farm output rose. Profits also rose because large fields needed fewer people to work them. But such progress had a human cost. Many farm laborers were thrown out of work. Small farmers were forced off their land because they could not compete with large landholders. Villages shrank as cottagers left in search of work.

In time, jobless farmworkers migrated to towns and cities. There, they formed a growing labor force that would tend the machines of the Industrial Revolution.

The Population Explosion

The agricultural revolution contributed to a rapid growth of population. This population explosion has continued, although today, the center of growth has shifted from the western world to developing nations outside Europe.

Precise population statistics for the 1700s are rare, but those that do exist are striking. Britain's population, for example, soared from about 5 million in 1700 to almost 9 million in 1800. The population of France rose from 18 million in 1715 to 26 million in 1789. The population of Europe as a whole shot up from roughly 120 million to about 190 million in the same period. Such growth was unlike any in earlier history. Yet in the 1800s, populations would climb still higher.

The population boom of the 1700s was due more to declining death rates than to rising birthrates. The agricultural revolution reduced the risk of famine. Because they ate better, women were healthier and had stronger babies. Some deadly diseases, such as bubonic plague, had faded away. In the 1800s, better hygiene and sanitation along with improved medical care further slowed deaths from disease.

An Energy Revolution

A third factor that helped trigger the Industrial Revolution was an "energy revolution."

From the beginning of human history, the energy for work was provided mostly by the muscles of humans and animals. In time, water mills and windmills were added to muscle power.

In the 1700s, inventive minds found ways to use water power more efficiently. Giant water wheels powered machines in the first factories. People also harnessed new sources of energy. Among the most important was coal, used to develop the steam engine. In 1712, inventor Thomas Newcomen had developed a steam engine powered by coal to pump water out of mines. About 1769, James Watt improved on Newcomen's engine. Watt's steam engines would become the vital power source of the early Industrial Revolution.

Watt linked up with a shrewd partner, Matthew Boulton, who saw the potential of steam engines. He told the king of England:

66 Your Majesty, I have at my disposal what the whole world demands: something which will uplift civilization more than ever by relieving man of all undignified drudgery. I have *steam power*. 99

SECTION 1 REVIEW

1. **Identify** (a) Charles Townshend, (b) Jethro Tull, (c) Robert Bakewell, (d) Thomas Newcomen, (e) James Watt.
2. **Define** enclosure.
3. How did each of the following affect agriculture in the 1700s and 1800s: (a) new farming methods, (b) mechanical inventions, (c) enclosure?
4. Identify three causes of the population explosion in Europe in the 1700s and 1800s.
5. (a) What role did the steam engine play in the Industrial Revolution? (b) What energy source powered the steam engine?
6. *Critical Thinking* **Recognizing Causes and Effects** What were the immediate and long-term effects of the agricultural revolution?
7. *ACTIVITY* Keep a log of your activities for one week. Next to each activity, indicate how it might have been different if you lived in the pre-industrial world.

2 Britain Leads the Way

Guide for Reading

■ Why was Britain the first nation to industrialize?

■ Why were coal and iron important to the industrial age?

■ How did industrialization change the textile industry?

■ **Vocabulary** *factory, turnpike*

Visitors crowded into London's Crystal Palace in 1851. The immense structure housed the Great Exhibition, a display of the "Works of Industry of all Nations." The palace itself was specially built for the occasion. A vast cavern of glass and iron, it symbolized the triumph of the industrial age.

This early world's fair, and a second one in 1862, offered an awesome array of machines, works of art, and other exhibits. Britain's leading poet, Alfred Tennyson, wrote:

66 . . . lo! the giant aisles
  Rich in model and design;
  Harvest-tool and husbandry,
  Loom and wheel and enginery,
  Secrets of the sullen mine,
  Steel and gold, and coal and wine,
  Fabric rough or fairy-fine . . .
  And shapes and hues of Art divine!
  All of beauty, all of use
  That one fair planet can produce. 99

In the century before the exhibitions, Britain had been the first nation to industrialize. Its success became the model for others, in Europe and around the world.

Why Britain?

Why did the Industrial Revolution begin in Britain? Historians have identified a number of key factors that helped Britain take an early lead in industry.

Natural resources. Though a relatively small nation, Britain had large supplies of coal to power steam engines. It also had plentiful iron to build the new machines.

Human resources. A large number of workers were needed to mine the coal and iron, build the factories, and run the machines. The agricultural revolution of the 1600s and 1700s freed many men and women in Britain from farm labor. The population boom that resulted further swelled the available work force.

New technology. Britain had been a center of the Scientific Revolution, which had focused attention on the physical world and developed new devices for managing it. In the 1700s, Enlightenment thinkers promoted the idea of progress through technology. The *Encyclopedia* compiled by the French philosophe Diderot, for example, included articles on technology as well as on social and political reform. In the 1700s, Britain had plenty of skilled mechanics who were eager to meet the growing demand for new, practical inventions.

Technology was an important part of the Industrial Revolution, but it did not cause it. After all, other societies, such as the ancient Greeks or Chinese, had advanced technology for their time but did not move on to industrialization. Only when other necessary conditions existed, including demand and capital, did technology pave the way for industrialization.

Economic conditions—capital and demand. In the 1700s, trade from a growing overseas empire helped the British economy prosper. The business class accumulated capital, or wealth to invest in enterprises such as mines, railroads, and factories. (See page 467.) A large number of these entrepreneurs were ready to risk their capital in new ventures.

An Iron Forge *In the late 1700s, most artists ignored the Industrial Revolution, which was changing the world around them. They thought that bleak factories and banging machinery were not proper subjects for art. But factory scenes fascinated English artist Joseph Wright, whose home town of Derby was a center of industry. In this painting, a giant hammer driven by a water wheel pounds a piece of white-hot iron. The red glow of the forge tints the faces of the master, his wife, and children.* **Art and Literature** *How are the children reacting to the sight of the forge?*

At home, the population explosion boosted demand for goods. However, a growing population alone would not have resulted in increased production. General economic prosperity was also needed to enable not only the middle and upper classes but also artisans and farmers to afford the new consumer goods.

Political and social conditions. Britain had a stable government that supported economic growth. It built a strong navy to protect its empire and overseas trade. Although members of the upper class tended to look down on business and business people, they did not reject the great wealth produced by the new entrepreneurs.

Technology of the British Industrial Revolution

Invention	Description	Impact	Connections Today
Improved steam engine (James Watt) 	Improved version of steam engine that used coal rather than water power. First used to pump water from mines and to forge iron. By the late 1780s, powered machines in cotton mills.	Steam engines provided power for early Industrial Revolution. They led to the factory system, early assembly lines, and rapidly growing production.	Steam engines are still used today to power giant ocean liners, pile drivers, and electric generators.
Spinning mule (Samuel Crompton) 	Spinning device that combined the features of the spinning jenny, which made it possible to spin many threads at one time, and the water frame, which could produce strong cotton threads.	Produced stronger, finer thread; helped create demand for factories; supply of thread exceeded weavers' ability to use; this spurred invention of better weaving machines.	Today's spinning machines use computers to ensure strong and even threads. They can spin even the coarsest natural fibers, such as hemp and flax.
Steam-powered locomotive (George Stephenson) 	Steam-powered vehicle used to pull a train. The "iron horse" moved faster and could haul heavier loads than a horse could.	Revolutionized transportation. Created demand for iron for rails and trains; created jobs building and running railroads; linked people far and wide.	Railroads, powered by electricity and diesel fuel, carry tons of freight and millions of passengers each year. High-speed passenger trains in Europe and Japan can reach 185 mph.
Dynamo (Michael Faraday)	Electric generator that worked by rotating a coil of wire between the poles of a magnet, which created electric current.	Development of electric power was critical to later industrial developments. By late 1800s, other inventors had found ways to use electric power to run machines and light up whole cities.	All electric generators and transformers work on the principle of Faraday's dynamo. In the 1990s, the U.S., Russia, and China together produced and used 42 percent of the world's total electric power.

Interpreting a Chart Beginning in the mid-1700s, inventors in Britain applied scientific principles to practical problems. The technological advances that they made helped trigger the Industrial Revolution.
■ Review the definition of the Industrial Revolution on page 506. How does each of the inventions on the chart fit that definition?

Religious attitudes also played a role in the growth of British industry. Many entrepreneurs came from religious groups that encouraged thrift and hard work. At the same time, for many people, worldly problems had become more important than concern about life after death. Thus, inventors, bankers, and other risk-takers felt free to devote their energies to material achievements.

The Age of Iron and Coal

New technologies in the iron industry were key to the Industrial Revolution. Iron was needed for machines and steam engines. Producing high-quality iron, however, required large quantities of fuel, which in the past had most often been wood. Over the centuries, Britain had cleared most of its trees. In the 1700s, the British turned to coal for fuel.

The Darby family of Coalbrookdale were leaders in developing Britain's iron industry. In 1709, Abraham Darby began to use coal instead of wood for smelting iron, that is, separating iron from its ore. When he discovered that coal gave off impurities that damaged the iron, Darby found a way to remove the impurities from coal.

Darby's experiments led him to produce better-quality and cheaper iron. His son and grandson improved on his methods. In 1779, his grandson, Abraham Darby III, made the world's first cast iron bridge. In the years that followed, high-quality iron found more and more uses, especially after the world turned to building railroads.

GLOBAL CONNECTIONS

The Industrial Revolution in Britain had an unforeseen impact on the United States. American planters supplied raw cotton for the British textile industry. However, they could not keep up with demand until the invention of the cotton gin in 1793 speeded up the processing of the cotton. The "gin" changed everything. With enormous profits to be made, American planters wanted more slaves to plant and pick more cotton. A vicious cycle followed. Slaves planted cotton. Planters earned profits by selling the cotton and then bought more land and more slaves to earn more profits. In this way, slavery became entrenched in the American economy.

Revolutionary Changes in the Textile Industry

Important changes also took place in Britain's largest industry—textiles. Indeed, it was in this industry that the Industrial Revolution first took hold.

The early industry. In the 1600s, cotton cloth imported from India had become increasingly popular. British merchants tried to organize a cotton cloth industry at home. They developed the putting out system. (See page 413.) They distributed imported raw cotton to peasant families who spun it into thread and then wove the thread into cloth. Skilled artisans in the towns finished and dyed the cloth.

Under the putting out system, production was slow. As the demand for cloth grew, inventors came up with a string of remarkable devices that revolutionized the British textile industry. (See the chart on page 512.)

Major inventions. Among the inventions was John Kay's flying shuttle. Using Kay's device, weavers worked so fast that they soon outpaced spinners. James Hargreaves solved that problem by producing the spinning jenny in 1764, which spun many threads at the same time.

A few years later, Richard Arkwright invented the waterframe, using water power to speed up spinning still further. Arkwright, who had begun life as a barber, was typical of Britain's hard-working and highly disciplined entrepreneurs. An observer noted:

> 66[Arkwright] commonly labored in his [many] concerns from five o'clock in the morning till nine at night; and when considerably more than fifty years of age . . . he encroached upon his sleep, in order to gain an hour each day to learn English grammar.99

The first factories. The new machines doomed the old putting out system of manufacturing. They were too large and expensive to be operated at home. Instead, manufacturers built long sheds to house the machines. At first, they located the sheds near rapidly moving streams, which provided water power to run the machines. Later, machines were powered by steam engines.

British Cotton Trade About 1850

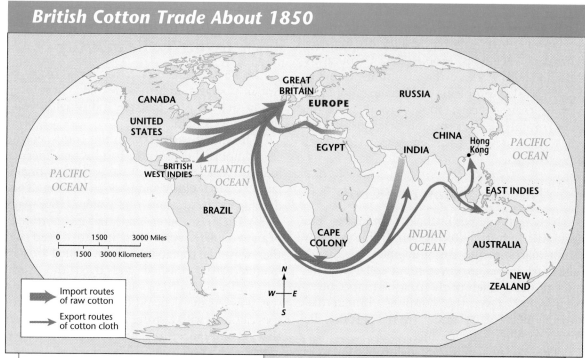

GEOGRAPHY AND HISTORY

As the textile industry grew, Great Britain needed ever-increasing supplies of raw cotton for its mills. It also sought out new markets for finished cotton cloth.

1. **Location** On the map, locate (a) Great Britain, (b) United States, (c) British West Indies.
2. **Movement** (a) Name two overseas sources that supplied raw cotton to Britain. (b) Name two overseas markets to which Britain exported its cotton cloth.
3. **Critical Thinking** **Predicting Consequences** What might have happened to the British cotton industry if Britain had lost control of its colony in India?

Spinners and weavers came each day to work in these first factories—as these places that brought together workers and machines to produce large quantities of goods came to be called. Early observers were awed at the size and output of these establishments. As a writer of the 1800s commented:

66Those vast brick buildings, . . . towering to the height of 70 or 80 feet, . . . now perform labors which formerly employed whole villages. In the steam loom factories, the cotton is carded, roved, spun, and woven into cloth, and the same [amount] of labor is now performed in one of these structures which formerly occupied the industry of an entire district.99

Revolution in Transportation

As factories sprang up and production increased, entrepreneurs needed faster and cheaper methods of moving goods from place to place. In the 1700s, individuals made improvements in local systems of transportation. Some capitalists invested in turnpikes, which were privately built roads that charged a fee to travelers who used them. Others had canals dug to link rivers or connect inland towns to coastal ports. Engineers also built stronger bridges and upgraded harbors to help the rapidly expanding overseas trade.

On land. The great revolution in transportation, however, was the invention of the steam locomotive. It was this invention that made possible the growth of railroads.

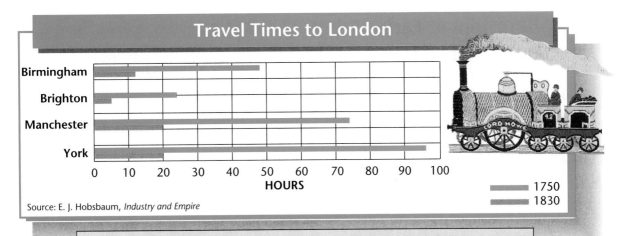

Travel Times to London

Birmingham
Brighton
Manchester
York

HOURS
0 10 20 30 40 50 60 70 80 90 100

■ 1750
■ 1830

Source: E. J. Hobsbaum, *Industry and Empire*

Interpreting a Graph Advances in transportation during the Industrial Revolution greatly reduced travel time between major cities. ■ About how long did it take to travel between London and Birmingham in 1750? In 1830? What invention made this increased speed possible?

In the early 1800s, pioneers like George Stephenson developed steam-powered locomotives to pull carriages along rails. As we saw on page 506, the world's first major rail line, from Liverpool to Manchester in England, opened in 1830. In the following decades, railroads got faster and railroad building boomed. By 1870, rail lines crisscrossed Britain, Europe, and eastern North America.

On sea. Other inventors applied steam power to improve shipping. Scottish builders made the first paddle wheel steamboats to pull barges along canals. In 1807, an American, Robert Fulton, used Watt's steam engine to power the *Clermont* up the Hudson River. Fulton's steamboat traveled at a record-breaking speed of more than five miles an hour!

Designing steamships for ocean voyages was more difficult. The coal needed for the voyage took up much of the cargo space. But by the late 1800s, steam-powered freighters with iron hulls were carrying 10 to 20 times the cargo of older wooden ships.

Looking Ahead

As the Industrial Revolution got under way, it triggered a chain reaction. In response to growing demand, inventors developed machines that could produce large quantities of goods more efficiently. As the supply of goods increased, prices fell. Lower prices made goods more affordable and thus created more consumers who further fed the demand for goods.

The Industrial Revolution did more than change the way goods were made. It affected people's whole way of life. In the 1800s, a tidal wave of economic and social changes swept the industrializing nations of the world.

SECTION 2 REVIEW

1. **Identify** (a) Abraham Darby, (b) John Kay, (c) James Hargreaves, (d) Richard Arkwright, (e) Robert Fulton.
2. **Define** (a) factory, (b) turnpike.
3. Describe five factors that contributed to the Industrial Revolution in Britain.
4. Explain how each of the following was key to industrialization: (a) coal, (b) iron, (c) better methods of transportation.
5. How did the Industrial Revolution transform the textile industry?
6. *Critical Thinking* **Analyzing Information** Explain how each of the following helped contribute to demand for consumer goods in Britain: (a) population explosion, (b) general economic prosperity.
7. *ACTIVITY* Create a concept map that shows the major causes of the Industrial Revolution and how they were related.

3 Hardships of Early Industrial Life

Guide for Reading

- How did the factory system change workers' lives?

- What problems did the industrial working class face?

- What were the costs and benefits of the Industrial Revolution?

- **Vocabulary** *urbanization*

The Industrial Revolution brought great riches to most of the entrepreneurs who helped set it in motion. For the millions of workers who crowded into the new factories, however, the industrial age brought poverty and harsh living conditions. In *Hard Times,* the British novelist Charles Dickens describes a typical factory town and the people who live in it:

❝It was a town of machinery and tall chimneys, out of which interminable serpents of smoke trailed themselves forever and ever. . . . It had a black canal in it, and a river that ran purple with ill-smelling dye. [It was] inhabited by people . . . who all went in and out at the same hours, . . . to do the same work, and to whom every day was the same as yesterday and tomorrow, and every year the counterpart of the last and the next.❞

In time, reforms would curb many of the worst abuses of the early industrial age in Europe and the Americas, and people at all levels of society would benefit from industrialization. Until then, working people could look forward only to lives marked by dangerous working conditions; unsafe, unsanitary, and overcrowded housing; and unrelenting poverty.

The New Industrial City

The Industrial Revolution brought rapid urbanization, or a movement of people to cities. Changes in farming, soaring population growth, and an ever-increasing demand for workers led masses of people to migrate from farms to cities. Almost overnight, small towns around coal or iron mines mushroomed into cities. Other cities grew up around the factories that entrepreneurs built in once-quiet market towns. In these new, overcrowded urban centers, misery festered.

The market town of Manchester numbered 17,000 people in the 1750s. Within a few years, it exploded into a center of the textile industry. Its population soared to 40,000 by 1780 and 70,000 by 1801. Visitors described the "cloud of coal vapor" that polluted the air, the pounding noise of steam engines, and the filthy stench of its river "filled with waste dye-stuffs."

In Manchester, as elsewhere, a gulf divided the urban population. The wealthy and the middle class lived in pleasant neighborhoods. Vast numbers of poor, however, struggled to survive in foul-smelling slums. They packed into tiny rooms in tenement buildings. No light filtered through the dark, narrow alleys. They had no running water, only community pumps. There was no sewage or sanitation system, and wastes and garbage rotted in the streets. Cholera and other diseases spread rapidly. In time, reformers pushed for laws to improve conditions in city slums.

The Factory System

The heart of the new industrial city was the factory. There, the technology of the machine age imposed a harsh new way of life on workers.

Rigid discipline. The factory system differed greatly from farmwork. In rural villages, people worked hard, but their work varied according to the season. In factories, workers faced a rigid schedule set by the factory whistle. "While the engine runs," said an observer, "people must work—men, women, and children are yoked together with iron and steam."

Working hours were long. Shifts lasted from 12 to 16 hours. Weary workers suffered accidents from machines that had no safety devices. They might lose a finger, a limb, or even their lives. Workers were exposed to other dangers, as well. Coal dust destroyed the lungs of miners, while textile workers constantly breathed air filled with lint. If workers were sick or injured, they lost their jobs.

Women workers. Women made up much of the new industrial work force. Employers often preferred women workers to men. They thought women could adapt more easily to machines and were easier to manage than men. More important, they were able to pay women less than men, even for the same work.

Factory work created special problems for women. Their new jobs took them out of their homes for 12 hours or more a day. They then returned to crowded slum tenements to feed and clothe their families, clean, and cope with sickness and other problems. Family life had been hard for poor rural cottagers. In industrial towns, it was even grimmer.

Child labor. Factories and mines hired many boys and girls. Nimble-fingered and quick-moving children changed spools in textile mills. Others clambered through narrow mine shafts, pushing coal carts.

Since children had helped with farmwork, parents accepted the idea of child labor. And the wages the children earned were needed to help support the family. One mother told investigators of her 10-year-old child who worked in the mines from six in the morning until eight at night. "It would hurt us," she said, "if children were prevented from working till [they were] 11 or 12 years old, because we've not jobs enough to live now as it is."

Employers often hired orphans, making deals with local officials who were glad to have the children taken off their hands. Orphans worked long hours for a minimum of food. Overseers beat children accused of idling. A few enlightened factory owners did provide basic education and a decent life for child workers. More often, though, children, like their parents, were slaves to the machines.

Patience Kershaw's Life Underground

The horrors of child labor were slowly exposed in the 1830s and 1840s, when British lawmakers looked into abuses in factories and mines. Government commissions heard about children as young as five years old working in factories. Some died. Others were stunted in growth or had twisted limbs. Most remained uneducated.

A 12-hour workday. From 17-year-old Patience Kershaw, members of the Ashley Mines Commission heard about life in the coal mines:

> ❝My father has been dead about a year. My mother is living and has 10 children, 5 lads and 5 lasses. The oldest is about 30, the youngest is 4. Three lasses go to mill. All the lads are [coal miners].❞

Kershaw's sisters had started in the mines but switched to mill work. One changed jobs when her legs swelled from standing in the cold water that covered the mine floor.

Kershaw herself worked in the mines. Her job was "hurrying"—pushing carts of coal to the surface of the mine:

> ❝I go to [the mine] at 5 o'clock in the morning and come out at 5 in the evening. . . . I hurry in the clothes I have now got on, trousers and ragged jacket. The bald place upon my head is made by [pushing] the corves [carts

Working Underground Thousands of children worked in Britain's coal mines during the Industrial Revolution. In the cramped, narrow mine shafts, children crawled on all fours, pushing coal carts or dragging them behind. *"Some places are scarcely fit for a dog to go in, not being more than from two feet and a half to a yard in height,"* one young miner said. **Economics and Technology** Why did many parents resist efforts to end child labor?

full of coal]. . . . I hurry the corves a mile and more underground and back. . . . I wear a belt and chain . . . to get the corves out.**,,**

Kershaw said that the men she worked with beat her if she did not work quickly enough. And "the boys sometimes pull me about. I am the only girl in the pit. There are about 20 boys and 15 men."

Efforts at reform. Like many other working poor, Kershaw had entered the mines as a small child. In a tangle of underground tunnels, men, women, and children mined coal to fuel the engines of the Industrial Revolution.

Kershaw probably never saw the Ashley Mines Commission report. Besides, since she had never attended school, she could not have read it in any case. But in 1842, her testimony shocked many people in Britain. Slowly, Parliament passed laws to regulate the employment of children in mines and factories. ▪

The Working Class

In rural villages, farm families had ties to a community where they had lived for generations. When they moved to the new industrial cities, they felt lost and bewildered. In time, though, factory and mine workers developed their own sense of community.

Protests. As the Industrial Revolution began, weavers and other skilled artisans resisted the new "labor-saving" machines that were costing them their jobs. They smashed machines and burned factories. Such rioters in England were called Luddites after a mythical figure, Ned Ludd, who supposedly destroyed machines in the 1780s.

Protests met harsh repression. Luddites were hanged or sent to penal colonies in Australia. When workers held a rally in Manchester in 1819, soldiers charged the crowd, killing a dozen and injuring hundreds more. For years, workers were forbidden to form labor unions to bargain for better pay and working conditions. Strikes were outlawed.

Spread of Methodism. Many working-class people found comfort in a new religious movement. In the mid-1700s, John Wesley had been the leader of a religious revival and founded the Methodist Church. Wesley stressed the need for a personal sense of faith. He urged Christians to improve their lot by adopting sober, moral ways.

Methodist meetings featured hymns and sermons promising forgiveness of sin and a better life to come. Methodist preachers took this message of salvation into the slums. There, they sought to rekindle self-confidence and hope among the working poor. They set up Sunday schools where followers not only studied the Bible but also learned to read and write. Methodists helped channel workers' anger away from revolution and toward social reform.

Worker Protests *On a hot August day in 1819, workers in the industrial city of Manchester gathered to hear several reformers speak. Suddenly, soldiers attacked the crowd, killing a dozen people and wounding hundreds more.* **Art and Literature** *Do you think the artist who created this cartoon sympathized with the workers or the soldiers? Explain.*

Frankenstein

In 1816, a teenager named Mary Shelley (below left) had a nightmare vision that "so possessed my mind that a thrill of fear ran through me." Shelley's nightmare inspired her to write *Frankenstein*, a novel about a scientist who tries to make a human being but creates a monster instead. The story reflected the fear of many Europeans during the Industrial Revolution that humans were using technology to tamper with nature.

Linking Past and Present Why did people during the Industrial Revolution worry that technology had gone too far? Are those concerns still valid today?

PAST *In Shelley's novel, the monster is not a grunting brute. Instead, he is an intelligent but hideously ugly and evil creature who reads poetry and argues cleverly with Victor Frankenstein, his creator. "Why," he piteously asks, "did you form a monster so hideous that even you turned from me in disgust?"*

PRESENT *The story of Frankenstein and his monster has continued to capture the popular imagination. A silent movie based on the tale was made in 1910, and a film featuring Boris Karloff (above right) as the monster was one of the biggest hits of the 1930s. Mel Brooks made* Young Frankenstein, *a spoof on the original story, in the 1970s, and in 1994 still another version starring Robert De Niro was released.*

FRANKENSTEIN,
BY
MARY W. SHELLEY.

The New Middle Class

Those who benefited most from the Industrial Revolution were the entrepreneurs who set it in motion. This new middle class came from several groups. Some were merchants who invested their profits in factories. Others were inventors or skilled artisans who turned their technological know-how into a ticket to a better life. Some rose from "rags to riches," a pattern that the age greatly admired.

Middle-class families lived in solid, well-furnished homes. They dressed well and ate large meals. Middle-class men made their influence felt in Parliament, where they opposed any effort to regulate factories or legalize labor unions.

As a sign of their new standard of living, middle-class women were encouraged to become "ladies." They took up "ladylike" activities, such as drawing, embroidery, or playing the piano. A "lady" did not work outside the home. She was also discouraged from doing the physical labor of housework. The first thing a family's new wealth acquired was a maid servant. The family then set about educating their daughters to provide a happy, well-furnished home for their future husbands. Sons learned to become businessmen.

The new middle class valued hard work and the determination to "get ahead." They had confidence in themselves and often little sympathy for the poor. If they thought of the faceless millions in the factories and mines, they generally supposed the poor to be responsible for their own misery. Some believed the poor were so lazy or ignorant that they could not "work their way up" out of poverty.

Benefits and Problems

Since the 1800s, people have debated whether the Industrial Revolution was a blessing or a curse. The hardships brought by the early industrial age were terrible. Said English writer Thomas Carlyle, "Something [ought] to be done."

In time, "something" would be done. Reformers pressed for laws to improve working conditions. Unions won the right to bargain with employers for better wages and hours. Eventually, working-class men gained the right to vote, which gave them po-litical power. Some workers founded political parties and movements that sought swifter, more radical solutions.

Despite the social problems created by the Industrial Revolution—low pay, unemployment, dismal living conditions—the industrial age did bring material benefits. As demand for mass-produced goods grew, new factories opened, creating more jobs. Wages rose so that workers had enough left after paying rent and buying food to buy a newspaper or visit a music hall. As the cost of railroad travel fell, people could visit family in other towns. Horizons widened, opportunities increased.

Industrialization continues to spread around the world today. Often, it begins with great suffering. In the end, it produces more material things for more people.

SECTION 3 REVIEW

1. **Identify** (a) Luddite, (b) John Wesley, (c) Methodism.
2. **Define** urbanization.
3. Describe working conditions in an early factory.
4. What special problems did factory work create for women?
5. How did the conditions of the early industrial age improve over time?
6. *Critical Thinking* **Comparing** Compare the life of a farmworker with that of a factory worker in the early industrial age.
7. *ACTIVITY* Write five questions for an interview with Patience Kershaw.

4 New Ways of Thinking

Guide for Reading

- What economic ideas helped shape the industrial age?
- What reforms did individual thinkers urge?
- How was socialism linked to the Industrial Revolution?
- **Vocabulary** *utilitarianism, socialism, communism, proletariat*

Everywhere in his native England, Thomas Malthus saw the effects of the population explosion—crowded slums, hungry families, and widespread misery. After careful study, in 1798 he published an "Essay on the Principle of Population." Poverty and misery, he concluded, were unavoidable because the population was increasing faster than the food supply. Malthus wrote:

66The power of population is [far] greater than the power of the Earth to produce subsistence for man.99

Malthus was one of many thinkers who tried to understand the staggering changes taking place in the early industrial age. As heirs to the Enlightenment, these thinkers looked for natural laws that governed the world of business and economics. Their ideas would influence governments in the years ahead.

Laissez-Faire Economics

During the Enlightenment, physiocrats argued that natural laws should be allowed to operate without interference. As part of this philosophy, they believed that government should not interfere in the free operation of the economy. In the early 1800s, middle-class business leaders embraced this laissez-faire, or "hands-off," approach.

Legacy of Adam Smith. The prophet of laissez-faire economics was Adam Smith. (See page 460.) Smith believed that a free market—

the unregulated exchange of goods and services—would eventually help everyone, not just the rich.

The free market, Smith said, would produce more goods at lower prices, making them affordable by everyone. A growing economy would also encourage capitalists to reinvest profits in new ventures. Supporters of this free enterprise capitalism pointed to the successes of the industrial age, in which government had played no part.

Malthus on population. Like Smith's *Wealth of Nations,* Thomas Malthus's writings on population shaped economic thinking for generations. As you have read on page 520, Malthus grimly predicted that population would outpace the food supply. The only checks on population growth, he said, were war, disease, and famine. As long as population kept increasing, he went on, the poor would suffer. He thus urged families to have fewer children.

In the early 1800s, many people accepted Malthus's bleak view. It was too pessimistic, however. Although the population boom continued, the food supply grew even faster. As the century progressed, living conditions for the western world also slowly improved. And then people did begin having fewer children. In the 1900s, population growth ceased to be a problem in western countries, though it still afflicted some nations elsewhere.

Ricardo on wages. Another influential British economist, David Ricardo, agreed with Malthus that the poor had too many children. In his "iron law of wages," Ricardo noted that when wages were high, families had more children. But more children increased the supply of labor, which led to lower wages and higher unemployment. Like Malthus, Ricardo held out no hope for the working class to escape poverty. Because of such gloomy predictions, economics became known as the "dismal science."

Neither Malthus nor Ricardo was a cruel man. Yet both opposed any government help for the poor. To these supporters of laissez-faire economics, the best cure for poverty was not government relief but the unrestricted "laws of the free market." Individuals, they felt, should be left to improve their lot through thrift, hard work, and limiting the size of their family.

The Utilitarians

Others revised laissez-faire doctrines to justify some government intervention. By 1800, Jeremy Bentham was preaching utilitarianism, the idea that the goal of society should be "the greatest happiness for the greatest number" of its citizens. To Bentham, laws or actions should be judged by their "utility." Did they provide

Overcrowding in a London Slum *Thomas Malthus warned that the population explosion was causing widespread misery throughout England. Here, French artist Gustave Doré captures the squalor and overcrowded conditions of a London slum.* **Political and Social Systems** *What did Malthus recommend as a solution to the problems of the early industrial age?*

more pleasure (happiness) than pain? He strongly supported individual freedom, which he believed ensured happiness. At the same time, he saw the need for government to intervene under certain circumstances.

Bentham's chief follower, John Stuart Mill, also argued that actions are right if they promote happiness and wrong if they cause pain. He reexamined the idea that unrestricted competition in the free market was always good. Often, he said, it favored the strong over the weak.

Although he believed strongly in individual freedom, Mill wanted the government to step in to improve the hard lives of the working class. He further called for giving the vote to workers and women. These groups could then use their political power to win reforms. Mill and other utilitarians worked for reforms in many areas, from child labor to public health.

Most middle-class people rejected Mill's ideas. Only in the later 1800s were his views slowly accepted. Today's democratic governments, however, have absorbed many ideas from Mill and the utilitarians.

Emergence of Socialism

While the champions of laissez-faire economics praised individual rights, other thinkers focused on the good of society in general. They condemned the evils of industrial capitalism, which they believed had created a gulf between rich and poor. To end poverty and injustice, they offered a radical solution—socialism. Under socialism, the people as a whole rather than private individuals would own and operate the "means of production"—the farms, factories, railways, and other large businesses that produced and distributed goods.

Socialism grew out of the Enlightenment faith in progress, its belief in the basic goodness of human nature, and its concern for social justice. The goal of socialists was a society that operated for the welfare of all the people. In a socialist society, one reformer predicted:

66 There will be no war, no crime, no administration of justice, as it is called, no government. Besides there will be neither disease, anguish, melancholy,

nor resentment. Every man will seek . . . the good of all. 99

The Utopians. Early socialists tried to build self-sufficient communities in which all work was shared and all property was owned in common. When there was no difference between rich and poor, they felt, fighting between people would disappear. These early socialists were called Utopians, after Thomas More's ideal community. (See page 351.) The name implied that they were impractical dreamers. However, the Utopian Robert Owen did set up a model community to put his ideas into practice.

Robert Owen. A poor Welsh boy, Owen became a successful mill owner. Unlike most self-made industrialists at the time, he refused to use child labor. He campaigned vigorously for child labor laws and encouraged labor unions.

Owen insisted that the conditions in which people lived shaped their character. To prove his point, he set up his factory in New Lanark, Scotland, as a model village. He built homes for workers, opened a school for children, and generally treated employees well. He showed that an employer could offer decent living and working conditions and still run a profitable business. By the 1820s, many people were visiting New Lanark to observe Owen's reforms.

The "Scientific Socialism" of Karl Marx

In the 1840s, Karl Marx, a German philosopher, condemned the ideas of the Utopians as unrealistic idealism. He put forward a new theory, "scientific socialism," which he claimed was based on a scientific study of history.

As a young man in Germany, Marx agitated for reform. Forced to leave his homeland because of his radical ideas, he lived first in Paris and then settled in London. He teamed up with another German socialist, Friedrich Engels, whose father owned a textile factory in England.

In 1848, Marx and Engels published a pamphlet, *The Communist Manifesto.* "A spectre is haunting Europe," it began, "the spectre of communism." Communism is a form of socialism that sees class struggle between employers and employees as inevitable.

Marxism. In the *Manifesto*, Marx theorized that economics was the driving force in history. The entire course of history, he argued, was "the history of class struggles" between the "haves" and "have-nots." The "haves" have always owned the means of production and thus controlled society and all its wealth. In industrialized Europe, Marx said, the "haves" were the bourgeoisie, or middle class. The "have-nots" were the proletariat, or working class.

According to Marx, the modern class struggle pitted the bourgeoisie against the proletariat. In the end, he predicted, the proletariat would triumph. It would then take control of the means of production and set up a classless, communist society. In such a society, the struggles of the past would end because wealth and power would be equally shared.

Marx despised capitalism. He believed it created prosperity for a few and poverty for many. He called for an international struggle to bring about its downfall. "Working men of all countries," he urged, "unite!"

Impact. At first, Marxist ideas had little impact. In time, however, they would have worldwide effects. In Western Europe, socialist political parties emerged. Many of them absorbed Marxist ideas, including the goal of a classless society.

In the late 1800s, Russian socialists embraced Marxism, and the Russian Revolution of 1917 set up a communist-inspired government. (See Chapter 28.) Later, revolutionaries around the world would adapt Marxist ideas to their own ends.

Weaknesses. Marx claimed his ideas were based on scientific laws. However, many of the assumptions on which he based his theories were wrong. He predicted that the misery of the proletariat would touch off a world revolution. Instead, by 1900, the standard of living of the working class improved. As a result, Marxism lost much of its appeal in industrially developed western countries.

Marx also predicted that workers would unite across national borders to wage class warfare. Instead, nationalism won out over working-class loyalty. In general, people felt stronger ties to their own countries than to the international communist movement.

Champion of the Working Class *Karl Marx was a social philosopher and revolutionary. He argued that history was a struggle between the classes that would end with the victory of the working class.*
Global Interaction *Marx was born in Germany but lived for more than 30 years in London. How might living in London during the industrial age have influenced Marx's ideas?*

SECTION 4 REVIEW

1. **Identify** (a) Thomas Malthus, (b) "iron law of wages," (c) John Stuart Mill, (d) Utopians, (e) *The Communist Manifesto*.
2. **Define** (a) utilitarianism, (b) socialism, (c) communism, (d) proletariat.
3. (a) Which group of people supported the free-market ideas of Adam Smith? (b) Why?
4. How did Utopian socialists propose to end the miseries brought by the Industrial Revolution?
5. (a) Describe Karl Marx's view of history. (b) How have events challenged that view?
6. *Critical Thinking* **Linking Past and Present** Choose *one* economic or political theory discussed in this section. Then, analyze it in relation to life today.
7. *ACTIVITY* Make a chart outlining the main ideas of the individuals discussed in this section. Then, compare *two* of them.

CHAPTER REVIEW

REVIEWING VOCABULARY

Review the vocabulary words in this chapter. Then, use *five* of these vocabulary words and their definitions to create a matching quiz. Exchange quizzes with another student. Check each other's answers when you are finished.

REVIEWING FACTS

1. How did the enclosure movement affect people?

2. What new source of energy helped trigger the Industrial Revolution?

3. List three reasons why the Industrial Revolution began in Britain.

4. What inventions improved transportation on land and on sea?

5. Why did large numbers of people migrate to cities?

6. What benefits and problems did the Industrial Revolution create?

7. List the government reforms sought by John Stuart Mill.

8. Why did Marx's prediction of a proletarian revolution not come true?

SKILLS FOR SUCCESS   RECOGNIZING FAULTY REASONING

Whenever you participate in a discussion or a debate, you begin your argument with a **premise**, or statement that is the basis for your argument. You then build on your premise by adding specific arguments. You try to reach a **conclusion** that is so sound that the other side will agree with you.

Many people, however, employ faulty reasoning during discussions. Three common types of faulty reasoning are (1) attacking your opponents rather than their arguments, (2) incorrectly stating cause-and-effect relationships, and (3) using circular arguments, or giving a conclusion that simply restates your premise.

In the dialogue at right, several students are discussing the Industrial Revolution. Read the dialogue, and follow the steps to identify the faulty reasoning.

1. **Identify personal attacks.**
   (a) Which student is focusing on the person rather than on the argument? (b) Why is this faulty reasoning?

2. **Identify incorrect statements of cause-and-effect relationships.** (a) What argument does Student B use to criticize the Industrial Revolution? (b) Why is this faulty reasoning?

3. **Identify circular arguments.** (a) Which student uses circular reasoning to support his or her argument? (b) How is this circular reasoning?

Student A: "I don't see how anyone can question the benefits of the Industrial Revolution. Without it, think of all the machines and scientific advances we wouldn't have today."

Student B: "I don't agree. After all, the Industrial Revolution caused a lot of suffering. In 1860, shortly after the Industrial Revolution, the Civil War broke out in the United States. Later came World War I in Europe."

Student C: "But the Industrial Revolution also produced labor unions and the middle class."

Student D: "Your reasoning is all wrong. Those changes were produced by reformers who could see that all these new machines were just taking advantage of people."

Student E: "I'd expect *you* to make a statement like that. After all, you still use a pencil and paper to do your homework. You just don't like machines!"

REVIEWING CHAPTER THEMES

Review the "Focus On" questions at the start of this chapter. Then select *three* of those questions and answer them, using information from the chapter.

CRITICAL THINKING

1. **Recognizing Causes and Effects** Why were the agricultural revolution and the energy revolution necessary to the Industrial Revolution?

2. **Analyzing Political Cartoons** Study the political cartoon on page 518. (a) What is the subject of the cartoon? (b) Who are the men on horseback? (c) Who are the people under attack? (d) What do you think was the artist's purpose in creating the cartoon?

3. **Defending a Position** Do you think that the negative social consequences of the Industrial Revolution could have been avoided? Use material from the chapter to defend your position.

ANALYZING PRIMARY SOURCES

Use the quotations on pages 510, second column, and 516 to answer the following questions.

1. What is the mood of each quotation?

2. What picture did each writer present of the Industrial Revolution?

3. How might you account for the difference between the two views?

FOR YOUR PORTFOLIO

CONDUCTING A CLASS DEBATE Work with classmates as part of a team to debate topics related to the chapter. Begin by reviewing the rules for formal debates. Assign two teams to each topic that the class wants to debate. Next, work with your team to prepare arguments for your side. As each pair of teams holds its debate, the rest of the class serves as an audience.

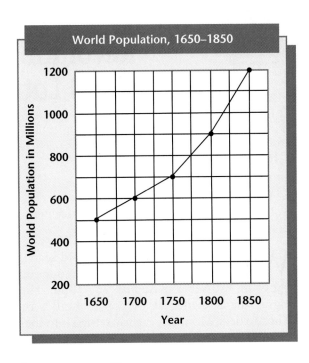

World Population, 1650–1850

ANALYZING GRAPHS

Use the graph as well as information from the chapter to answer the following questions.

1. What happened to world population during the period shown in the graph?

2. By how many people did world population rise between 1650 and 1700? Between 1800 and 1850?

3. By what year had the world population of 1700 doubled?

4. What were some causes of the population growth shown in the graph?

INTERNET ACTIVITY

WRITING AN OPINION PAPER Use the Internet to research primary or secondary sources on the daily life of factory workers during the Industrial Revolution. Then write an opinion paper explaining why you do or do not think that the benefits of living in an industrialized nation today outweigh the negative social consequences of the Industrial Revolution.

Revolutions in Europe and Latin America

(1790–1848)

CHAPTER OUTLINE

1 An Age of Ideologies
2 To the Barricades!
3 Latin American Wars of Independence

Was it possible that an opera could spark a revolution? The answer was a resounding "Yes" in Brussels on August 25, 1830. That night, the audience at the opera house, the Théâtre de la Monnaie, eagerly settled into their seats. They had come to see a popular new opera, *La Muette de Portici*. But was their real interest in the opera's music or in its political content?

The opera is set in Naples, Italy. The year is 1647, and Naples is under Spanish rule. The hero, a young fisherman named Masaniello, yearns to free his country. In the second act, he sings of his love for his land:

> 66Sacred love of country
>   Restore to us our daring and
>   our pride!
>   My country gave me life
>   And I shall give it liberty.99

The Belgian audience listened raptly to Masaniello's words. For 15 years, since the Congress of Vienna, Belgians had been forced to live under Dutch rule. As the tenor lingered over the last lines of the aria, the audience rose to their feet and joined their voices to his.

Outside, crowds of students and workers took up the patriotic song. Within hours, the demonstrations in Brussels turned into riots and then into a full-scale revolt against Dutch rule. Within days, the Belgians had successfully ejected the Dutch from their land. By year's end, they had won independence.

The Brussels revolt was part of a wave of violent uprisings that swept Western Europe in the first half of the 1800s. Across the continent, minor incidents flared into revolution. This "age of revolutions," as it is sometimes called, was fueled by the political ideas of the French Revolution and the economic problems caused by the Industrial Revolution.

In the aftermath of the Congress of Vienna, the great powers sought to silence liberal and nationalist demands. But simmering discontent erupted in three major revolutionary outbreaks—in the 1820s, 1830, and 1848. Rebels, divided by class interests, were soon crushed. Still, the uprisings sent a chilling message to rulers across Europe. The winds of liberalism and nationalism also swept across the Atlantic, igniting wars of independence in Latin America.

FOCUS ON these questions as you read:

- **Political and Social Systems**
  How were revolutionaries seeking to change the European political and social system?

- **Economics and Technology**
  How did economic changes contribute to revolutionary unrest in Europe?

- **Continuity and Change**
  How were the revolutions of the early 1800s an outgrowth of the French Revolution?

- **Global Interaction**
  How did events and ideas in Europe affect the people of Latin America?

TIME AND PLACE

The Spirit of Revolution *In 1830 and again in 1848, the streets of European cities seethed with rebellion. As in 1789, the revolts began in Paris and spread across the continent. In time, the revolutionary spark jumped the Atlantic and ignited uprisings in the Americas. Here, a French crowd storms the barricades.* **Art and Literature** *Do you think the painter supported the rebels? Explain.*

HUMANITIES LINK

Art History Honoré Daumier, *"You Have the Floor"* (page 532).
Literature In this chapter, you will encounter passages from the following works of literature: Daniel Auber, Eugène Scribe, Germaine Delavigne, *La Muette de Portici* (page 526); Stendhal, *The Charterhouse of Parma* (page 528).

1804	1810	1824	1830	1848
Haiti declares independence from France	Mexican Revolution begins	Latin American wars for independence end	Belgium begins fight for independence	Revolutions take place throughout Europe

| 1790 | 1800 | 1810 | 1820 | 1830 | 1840 | 1850 |

1 An Age of Ideologies

Guide for Reading

- How did the goals of conservatives and liberals differ?

- How did nationalism pose a challenge to the old order?

- Why was Europe plagued by constant unrest after 1815?

- **Vocabulary** *ideology, universal manhood suffrage, autonomy*

The Conservative Order European conservatives were determined to preserve the old order. At the heart of that order was the monarchy, symbolized by the Hapsburg coat of arms shown here. **Political and Social Systems** What other institutions were part of the old order?

A "revolutionary seed" had been planted in Europe, warned Prince Clemens von Metternich. The ideas spread by the French Revolution and Napoleon Bonaparte, he believed, not only threatened Europe's monarchs. They also undermined its basic social values:

> 66Kings have to calculate the chances of their very existence in the immediate future. Passions are let loose and [join] together to overthrow everything that society respects as the basis of its existence: religion, public morality, laws, customs, rights, and duties, all are attacked, confounded, overthrown, or called in question.99

At the Congress of Vienna, the European powers had sought to uproot that "revolutionary seed." Other voices, however, kept challenging the order imposed in 1815. The clash of people with opposing ideologies, or systems of thought and belief, plunged Europe into a period of turmoil that lasted more than 30 years.

Preserving the Old Order

The Congress of Vienna was a clear victory for conservative forces. Who were these forces? And what did they want?

Conservatives included monarchs and members of their government, noble landowners, and church leaders. They supported the political and social order that had come under attack during the French Revolution. They had

benefited in many ways from the old order. Conservative ideas also appealed to peasants, who wanted to preserve traditional ways.

Goals. The conservatives in 1815 had very different goals from conservatives in the United States today. Conservatives of the early 1800s wanted to turn back the clock to the way things had been before 1789. They wanted to restore to power the royal families that had lost their thrones when Napoleon swept across Europe. They accepted the hierarchy of social classes. The lower classes, they felt, should respect and obey their social superiors. Conservatives also backed an established church—Catholic in Austria and the southern European countries, Orthodox in Eastern Europe, and Protestant in Britain, the Netherlands, Prussia, and the Scandinavian lands.

Attitude toward change. Conservatives believed that talk about natural rights and constitutional government could lead only to chaos, as it had in France in 1789. If change had to come, they argued, it must come slowly. A character in a novel by the French writer Stendhal expresses the conservative view:

> 66The words *liberty, justice,* and *happiness of the greatest number* are criminal. They give men's minds a habit of discussion. Man ends by distrusting . . . the authority of the princes set up by God.99

Conservatives equated their own interests with peace and stability for all people. Conservative leaders like Metternich opposed freedom of the press. They urged monarchs throughout Europe to suppress revolutionary ideas and crush protests in their own countries. Metternich also proposed that monarchs should step in to defeat successful revolutions in neighboring lands. (★ See *Skills for Success*, page 544.)

The Liberal Challenge

Challenging the conservatives at every turn were the liberals. In the early 1800s, liberals embraced Enlightenment ideas spread by the French Revolution. They spoke out against divine-right monarchy, the old aristocracy, and established churches. They defended the natural rights of individuals to liberty, equality, and property.

Because liberals spoke mostly for the bourgeoisie, or middle class, their ideas are sometimes called "bourgeois liberalism." Liberals included business owners, bankers, and lawyers, as well as politicians, newspaper editors, writers, and others who helped to shape public opinion.

Political ideas. Liberals wanted governments to be based on written constitutions and separation of powers. They called for rulers elected by the people and responsible to them. Thus, most liberals favored a republican form of government over a monarchy, or at least wanted the monarch to be limited by a constitution.

The liberals of the early 1800s saw the role of government as limited to protecting basic rights such as freedom of thought, speech, and religion. They believed that only male property owners or others with a financial stake in society should have the right to vote. Only later in the century would liberals throw their support behind the principle of universal manhood suffrage, giving all adult men the right to vote, and social reforms. John Stuart Mill, an influential English liberal, was a notable exception, who urged equal rights for women.

Economic views. Liberals strongly supported the laissez-faire economics of Adam Smith and David Ricardo. (See page 460.) They saw the free market as an opportunity for capitalist entrepreneurs to succeed. As capitalists and often employers, liberals had different goals from those of workers laboring in factories, mines, and other enterprises of the early Industrial Revolution.

Nationalist Stirrings

Another challenge to Metternich's conservative order came from nationalists. Like liberalism, nationalism was an outgrowth of the Enlightenment and the French Revolution. Also like liberalism, it ignited a number of revolts against established rule.

Goals. For centuries, European rulers had won or lost lands in war. They exchanged territories and the people who lived in them like pieces in a game. Regions also passed back and forth with various marriages between royal families. As a result of all this land swapping, by 1815 Europe had several empires that included many nationalities. The Austrian, Russian, and Ottoman empires, for example, each included diverse peoples.

Unifying and gaining independence for people with a common national heritage became a major goal of nationalists in the 1800s. Each national group, they believed, should have its own state.

While nationalism gave people with a common heritage a sense of identity and a goal—establishment of their own homeland—it also had negative effects. It often bred intolerance and led to persecution of national or ethnic minorities.

Revolts in the Balkans. The Balkans, in southeastern Europe, were home to many ethnic groups. In the early 1800s, several Balkan peoples rebelled against the Ottomans, who had ruled them for more than 300 years.

The first Balkan people to revolt were the Serbs. In two major rebellions between 1804 and 1817, the Serbs suffered terrible defeats. In the end, however, they achieved autonomy, or self-rule, within the Ottoman empire. The bitter

ISSUES *For* **TODAY**

Conservatives in the 1800s tried to preserve the old social order by holding back the forces of change. How can the need for social and political change be balanced with the desire for a stable society?

struggle fostered a sense of Serbian identity. A revival of Slavic literature and culture added to the sense of nationhood.

Independence for the Greeks. In 1821, the Greeks, too, revolted, seeking to end centuries of Ottoman rule. At first, the Greeks were badly divided. But years of suffering in long, bloody wars of independence helped shape a national identity.

Leaders of the rebellion justified their struggle as "a national war, a holy war, a war the object of which is to reconquer the rights of individual liberty." They appealed for support to Western Europeans, who admired ancient Greek civilization.

The Greeks won sympathy in the West. In the late 1820s, Britain, France, and even conservative Russia forced the Ottomans to grant independence to some Greek provinces. By 1830, Greece was independent. The European powers, however, pressured the Greeks to accept a German king, a move meant to show that they did not support revolution. Still, liberals were enthusiastic, while nationalists everywhere saw reasons to hope for a country of their own.

Challenges to the Old Order

Several other challenges to the Vienna settlement erupted in the 1820s. Revolts occurred along the southern fringe of Europe. In Spain, Portugal, and the Italian states, rebels demanded constitutional governments.

Metternich urged conservative rulers to crush the uprisings. A French army marched into Spain to suppress a revolt, while Austrian forces crossed the Alps to smash Italian rebels.

Troops dampened the fires of liberalism and nationalism in western and southern areas of Europe, but could not smother them. In the next decades, sparks would flare anew. Added to liberal and nationalist demands were the goals of the new industrial working class. By the mid-1800s, social reformers and agitators were urging workers to support socialism or some other way of reorganizing property ownership, further contributing to the unrest of this period.

Greek Independence *Inspired by the nationalism that was sweeping Europe, the Greeks proclaimed independence. For a decade, they battled their Ottoman rulers. At last, after the British, French, and Russians intervened, the Turks granted Greece independence. Here, a victorious Greek soldier raises the national flag over a defeated enemy.* **Art and Literature** *Compare this painting with that on page 527. How does each represent the spirit of nationalism?*

SECTION 1 REVIEW

1. **Identify** (a) conservatives, (b) liberals, (c) nationalists.
2. **Define** (a) ideology, (b) universal manhood suffrage, (c) autonomy.
3. (a) Which groups backed conservative ideas? Why? (b) How did the political goals of conservatives differ from those of liberals?
4. How did nationalists threaten the system set up by Metternich?
5. *Critical Thinking* **Applying Information** How did ideologies like liberalism and nationalism contribute to unrest?
6. *ACTIVITY* Create a series of political cartoons expressing the point of view of each of the following groups: (a) conservatives, (b) liberals, (c) nationalists.

To the Barricades!

Guide for Reading

■ Why did revolts break out in France in 1830 and 1848?

■ How did revolutions in France affect other parts of Europe?

■ Why did the revolts of 1830 and 1848 generally fail to achieve their goals?

The quick suppression of liberal and nationalist uprisings in the 1820s did not end Europe's age of revolutions. "We are sleeping on a volcano," warned Alexis de Tocqueville, a liberal French leader who saw widespread discontent. "Do you not see that the Earth trembles anew? A wind of revolution blows, the storm is on the horizon."

In 1830 and 1848, Europeans saw street protests explode into full-scale revolts. As in 1789, the upheavals began in Paris and radiated out across the continent.

France After the Restoration

When the Congress of Vienna restored Louis XVIII to the French throne, he prudently issued a constitution, the Charter of French Liberties. It created a two-house legislature and allowed limited freedom of the press. Still, while Louis was careful to shun absolutism, the king retained much power.

Efforts at compromise. Louis's efforts at compromise satisfied few people. Ultraroyalists, supporters on the far right, despised constitutional government and wanted to restore the old regime. The "ultras" included many high clergy and émigré nobles who had returned to France after the Revolution.

The ultras faced bitter opposition from other factions. Liberals wanted to extend suffrage and win a share of power for middle-class citizens like themselves. On the left, radicals yearned for a republic like that of the 1790s. And in working-class slums, men and women wanted what they had wanted in 1789—a decent day's pay and bread they could afford.

The July revolution. When Louis XVIII died in 1824, his brother, Charles X, inherited the throne. Charles, a strong believer in absolutism, rejected the very idea of the charter. In July 1830, he suspended the legislature, limited the right to vote, and restricted the press.

Liberals and radicals responded forcefully to the king's challenge. In Paris, angry citizens threw up barricades across the narrow streets. From behind them, they fired on the soldiers and pelted them with stones and roof tiles. Within days, rebels controlled Paris. The revolutionary tricolor flew from the towers of Notre Dame cathedral. A frightened Charles X abdicated and fled to England.

With the king gone, radicals wanted to set up a republic. Moderate liberals, however, insisted on a constitutional monarchy. The Chamber of Deputies, the lower house of the French legislature, chose Louis Philippe as king. He was a cousin of Charles X and in his youth, had supported the revolution of 1789.

The "citizen king." The French called Louis Philippe the "citizen king" because he owed his throne to the people. Louis got along well with the liberal bourgeoisie. Like them, he dressed in a frock coat and top hat. Sometimes, he strolled the streets, shaking hands with well-wishers. Liberal politicians and professionals filled his government.

Under Louis Philippe, the upper bourgeoisie prospered. Louis extended suffrage, but only to France's wealthiest citizens. The vast majority of the people still could not vote. Louis Philippe's other policies also favored the middle class at the expense of the workers.

The French Revolution of 1848

In the 1840s, discontent grew. Radicals formed secret societies to work for a French republic. Utopian socialists called for an end of private ownership of property. (See Chapter 20.) Even liberals denounced Louis Philippe's government for corruption and called for expanded suffrage.

Toward the end of the decade, an economic slump shut down factories. Harvests were poor. People lost their jobs and bread prices soared. Scandals involving high officials filled the newspapers. As in 1789, Paris was ripe for revolution.

La Caricature (Journal) N.º 216.

"You have the floor; explain yourself!"

"You Have the Floor" The political cartoons of French artist Honoré Daumier combine masterful line drawings with a sharp wit. His works were immensely influential in calling attention to the social injustices of the time. In this drawing, Daumier depicts a court scene. The defendant, mouth gagged and arms pinned down by his prosecutors, stands before the judge. The judge snarls, "You have the floor; explain yourself!" **Art and Literature** What do the judge's words mean? Based on the cartoon, what is Daumier's view of the French justice system?

"February Days." In February 1848, when the government took steps to silence critics and prevent public meetings, angry crowds took to the streets. During the "February Days," iron railings, overturned carts, paving stones, and toppled trees again blocked the streets of Paris. Church bells rang alarms, while women and men on the barricades sang the revolutionary "La Marseillaise." A number of demonstrators clashed with royal troops and were killed.

As the turmoil spread, Louis Philippe abdicated. A group of liberal, radical, and socialist leaders proclaimed the Second Republic. (The First Republic had lasted from 1792 until 1804, when Napoleon became emperor.)

From the start, deep differences divided the new government. Middle-class liberals were interested in political reforms such as constitutions. Socialists wanted far-reaching social and economic change that would help hungry workers. In the early days of the new republic, the socialists forced the government to set up national workshops to provide jobs for the unemployed.

"June Days." By June, however, upper- and middle-class interests had won control of the government. They saw the national workshops as a waste of money, and they shut them down.

Furious, workers took to the streets of Paris, rallying to the cry "Bread or Lead!" This time, however, bourgeois liberals turned violently against the protesters. Peasants, who feared that socialists might take their land, also attacked the rioting workers. At least 1,500 people were killed before the government crushed the rebellion.

The fighting of the "June Days" left a bitter legacy. The middle class both feared and distrusted the left, while the working class nursed a deep hatred for the bourgeoisie.

Louis Napoleon. Toward the end of the year, the National Assembly, dominated by forces who wanted to restore order, issued a constitution for the Second Republic. It created a strong president and a one-house legislature. But it also gave the vote to all adult men, the widest suffrage in the world at the time. Nine million Frenchmen now could vote, compared to only 200,000 who had that right before.

When elections for president were held, the overwhelming winner was Louis Napoleon, nephew of Napoleon Bonaparte. The "new" Napoleon attracted the working classes by presenting himself as a man who cared about social issues such as poverty. At the same time, his famous name, linked with order and authority as well as with France's past glories, helped him with conservatives.

Once in office, Louis Napoleon used his position as a steppingstone to greater power. By 1852, he had proclaimed himself emperor, taking the title Napoleon III. (He was the third Napoleon because the son of Napoleon I, Napoleon II, had died in his youth without ever ruling France.) Thus ended the short-lived Second Republic.

Like his celebrated uncle, Louis Napoleon used a plebiscite to win public approval for his seizure of power. A stunning 90 percent of voters supported his move to set up the Second Empire. Many saw a monarchy as more stable than a republic. Millions of French also recalled the glory days of Napoleon Bonaparte and hoped that his nephew would restore the magic. A few voters even thought he was the old Napoleon, miraculously still alive and returned from exile!

In fact, Napoleon III, like Louis Philippe, ruled at a time of rapid economic growth. For the bourgeoisie, the early days of the Second Empire brought prosperity and contentment. In time, however, Napoleon III would embark on foreign adventures that brought down his empire and ended France's long leadership in Europe.

"Europe Catches Cold"

In both 1830 and 1848, the revolts in Paris inspired uprisings elsewhere in Europe. As Metternich said, "When France sneezes, Europe catches cold." Most uprisings were suppressed. But here and there, rebels did force changes on conservative governments. Even when they failed, they frightened rulers badly enough to encourage reform later in the century.

Belgium. The one notable success for Europe's revolutionaries in 1830 took place in Belgium. In 1815, the Congress of Vienna had united the Austrian Netherlands (present-day Belgium) and the Kingdom of Holland under the Dutch king. The Congress had wanted to create a strong barrier against French expansion.

The Belgians resented the new arrangement. The Belgians and Dutch had different languages, religions, and economic interests. The Belgians were Catholic, while the Dutch were Protestant. The Belgian economy was based on manufacturing; the Dutch, on trade.

In 1830, news of the Paris uprising that toppled Charles X ignited a revolutionary spark in Belgium. Students and workers threw up barri-

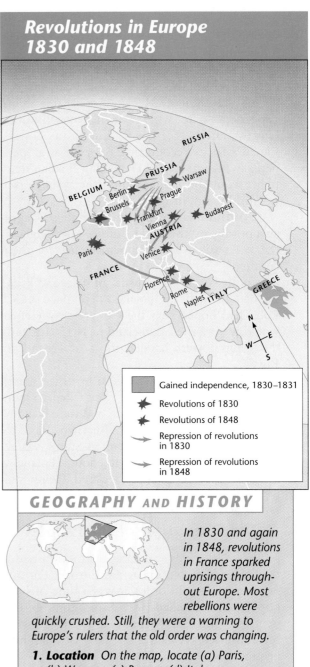

Revolutions in Europe 1830 and 1848

Gained independence, 1830–1831

★ Revolutions of 1830

★ Revolutions of 1848

→ Repression of revolutions in 1830

→ Repression of revolutions in 1848

GEOGRAPHY AND HISTORY

In 1830 and again in 1848, revolutions in France sparked uprisings throughout Europe. Most rebellions were quickly crushed. Still, they were a warning to Europe's rulers that the old order was changing.

1. **Location** On the map, locate (a) Paris, (b) Warsaw, (c) Prague, (d) Italy.
2. **Place** (a) Which countries gained independence in 1830 and 1831? (b) Name two places where revolutions took place in 1830. In 1848.
3. **Critical Thinking** **Making Inferences** How can you tell from the map that the revolution in Budapest was unsuccessful?

cades in Brussels, the capital. The Dutch king turned to the other European powers for help. Britain and France, however, believing they would benefit from the separation of Belgium and Holland, supported Belgian demands for independence. The conservative powers—Austria, Prussia, and Russia—were too busy putting down revolts of their own to become involved.

As a result, in 1831, Belgium became an independent state with a liberal constitution. Shortly after, the major European powers signed a treaty recognizing Belgium as a "perpetually neutral state." Protecting Belgian neutrality would be an important issue at the outset of World War I, in 1914.

Poland. Nationalists in Poland also staged an uprising in 1830. But, unlike the Belgians, the Poles failed to win independence for their country.

In the late 1700s, Russia, Austria, and Prussia had divided up Poland. (See page 443.) Poles had hoped that the Congress of Vienna would restore their homeland in 1815. Instead, the great powers handed most of Poland to Russia.

In 1830, Polish students, army officers, and landowners rose in revolt. They failed to gain widespread support, however, and were brutally crushed by Russian forces. Survivors fled to Western Europe and the United States, where they kept alive the dream of freedom. "Poland is not yet lost," they proudly declared, "while still we live."

The Springtime of the Peoples

In 1848, revolts in Paris again unleashed a tidal wave of revolution across Europe. For opponents of the old order, it was a time of such hope that they called it the "springtime of the peoples." Michael Bakunin, a young Russian revolutionary, recalled the feeling of unlimited possibilities:

> **66**It seemed as if the entire world was turned upside down. The improbable became commonplace, the impossible possible. . . . If someone had said, 'God has been driven from heaven and a republic has been proclaimed there,' . . . no one would have been surprised.**99**

Sources of discontent. Revolution in France was the spark that touched off the revolts. But grievances had been piling up for years.

Unrest came from many sources. Middle-class liberals wanted a greater share of political power for themselves, as well as protections for the basic rights of all citizens. Workers demanded relief from the miseries of the spreading Industrial Revolution. And nationalists of all classes ached to throw off foreign rule. By 1848, discontent was so widespread that it was only a matter of time before it exploded into full-scale revolution.

Metternich falls. In the Austrian empire, revolt first broke out in Vienna, taking the government by surprise. Metternich, who had dominated Austrian politics for more than 30 years, tried to suppress the students who took to the streets. But when workers rose up to support the students, Metternich resigned and fled in disguise. The Austrian emperor promised reform.

▲ Metternich flees in disguise

Revolution quickly spread to other parts of the empire. In Budapest, Hungarian nationalists led by Louis Kossuth demanded an independent government. They also called for an end to serfdom and a written constitution to protect basic rights. In Prague, the Czechs made similar demands. Overwhelmed by events, the Austrian government agreed to the reforms.

Any gains were short-lived, however. The Austrian army soon regained control of Vienna and Prague. With Russian help, Austrian forces also smashed the rebels in Budapest. Many were imprisoned or executed or forced into exile.

Revolution in Italy. Uprisings also erupted in the Italian states. Nationalists wanted to end domination of Italy by the Austrian Hapsburgs. As elsewhere, nationalist goals were linked to demands for liberal reforms such as constitutional government. Workers suffering economic hardships demanded even more radical changes.

Italy in Revolt Throughout Italy, nationalists rose up to end Austrian domination. Here, rebels in Venice hurl cobblestones at well-armed Austrian forces. **Political and Social Systems** What other goals did Italian nationalists pursue?

From Venice in the north to Naples in the south, Italians set up independent republics. Revolutionaries even expelled the pope from Rome and installed a nationalist government.

Before long, however, the forces of reaction surged back here, too. Austrian troops ousted the new governments in northern Italy. A French army restored the pope to power in Rome. In Naples, local rulers betrayed their promises to the rebels, canceling the reforms they had reluctantly accepted.

Turmoil in the German states. In the German states, university students passionately demanded national unity and liberal reforms. Economic hard times and a potato famine brought peasants and workers into the struggle. Workers destroyed the machines that threatened their livelihood, while peasants burned the homes of wealthy landowners.

Women, too, plunged into the struggle. A German woman explained her reasons for fighting alongside her husband:

❝You know it was not [enthusiasm for] war that called me, but love. Yet I must confess—hate, too, a burning hate generated in the struggle against tyrants and oppressors of sacred human rights.❞

In Prussia, liberals forced King Frederick William IV to agree to a constitution written by an elected assembly. Within a year, though, he dissolved the assembly. Later, he issued his own constitution keeping power in his own hands or those of the upper classes.

Frankfurt Assembly. Throughout 1848, delegates from many German states met in the Frankfurt Assembly. "We are to create a constitution for Germany, for the whole land," declared one leader with boundless optimism.

Divisions soon emerged. Delegates debated endlessly on such topics as whether the new Germany should be a republic or a monarchy, and whether or not to include Austria in a united German state. Finally, the assembly offered Prussia's Frederick William IV the crown of a united Germany. To their dismay, the conservative king rejected the offer because it came not from the German princes but from the people—"from the gutter," as he described it. By early 1849, the assembly was dissolved, under threat from the Prussian military.

Outside the assembly, liberals clashed with workers whose demands were too radical for middle-class reformers to accept. Conservative forces rallied, dousing the last flames of revolt.

GLOBAL CONNECTIONS

The defeat of liberal forces in Europe in 1848 had a profound effect on the other side of the world. By the 1850s, Japan would begin to emerge from centuries of self-imposed isolation. Seeking to modernize, the new leaders of Japan looked to Europe for examples. The nation that they chose as a model was the conservative, militaristic Germany that had emerged after the defeat of the liberals in 1848. As a result, modern Japan, like Germany after 1848, was marked by political conservatism and emphasis on a strong military.

Chapter 21 **535**

Hundreds were killed. Many more went to prison. And thousands of Germans left their homeland, most for the cities of the United States.

Looking Ahead

By 1850, the flickering light of rebellion faded, ending the age of liberal revolution that had begun in 1789. Why did the uprisings fail? In general, revolutionaries did not have mass support. In Poland in 1830, for example, peasants did not take part in the uprising. In 1848, a growing gulf divided workers seeking radical economic change and liberals pursuing moderate political reform.

By mid-century, Metternich was gone from the European scene. Still, his conservative system remained in force. In the decades ahead, liberalism, nationalism, and socialism would win successes not through revolution but through political activity. Ambitious political leaders would unify Germany and Italy. Workers would campaign for reforms through unions and the ballot box, as they increasingly won the right to vote.

SECTION 2 REVIEW

1. **Identify** (a) Charter of French Liberties, (b) Charles X, (c) Louis Philippe, (d) Louis Napoleon, (e) Louis Kossuth, (f) Frankfurt Assembly.
2. (a) What were the causes of the French revolution of 1830? (b) What were its effects?
3. How was the French revolution of 1848 really two revolutions?
4. Why did conservative leaders in Europe fear news of revolutions in France?
5. Why did most revolts in the 1830s and 1840s fail?
6. *Critical Thinking* **Identifying Alternatives** Do you think that European rulers could have prevented nationalist revolts by allowing reforms? Why or why not?
7. *ACTIVITY* Create a "docudrama" for television based on the "February Days" and "June Days" during the French revolution of 1848.

3 Latin American Wars of Independence

Guide for Reading

- What were the long-term causes of the revolutions in Latin America?
- How did Haiti's struggle for freedom differ from independence fights in other parts of Latin America?
- How did Mexico and the nations of South America win independence?

Like many wealthy Latin American* creoles, young Simón Bolívar (boh LEE vahr) was sent to Europe to complete his education. There, he became a strong admirer of the ideals of the French Revolution.

One afternoon, Bolívar and his Italian tutor sat talking about freedom and the rights of ordinary people. Bolívar's thoughts turned to his homeland, held as a colony by Spain. He fell on his knees and swore a solemn oath:

66I swear before God and by my honor never to allow my hands to be idle nor my soul to rest until I have broken the chains that bind us to Spain.99

In later years, Bolívar would fulfill his oath, leading the struggle to liberate northern South America from Spain. Elsewhere in Latin America, other leaders organized independence movements. By 1825, most of Latin America had been freed from colonial rule.

Climate of Discontent

By the late 1700s, the revolutionary fever that gripped Western Europe had spread to Latin America. There, discontent was rooted in

---

*Latin America refers to the regions in Middle and South America colonized by Europeans, especially the Spanish, French, and Portuguese, whose languages are rooted in Latin. It includes Spanish-speaking countries from Mexico to Argentina, Portuguese-speaking Brazil, and French-speaking Haiti.

the social, racial, and political system that had emerged during 300 years of Spanish rule.

Ethnic and social hierarchy. Spanish-born peninsulares dominated Latin American political and social life. Only they could hold top jobs in government and the Church. Many creoles—the European-descended Latin Americans who owned the haciendas, ranches, and mines—bitterly resented their second-class status. Merchants fretted under mercantilist policies that tied the colonies to Spain. "Commerce ought to be as free as air," declared one colonial merchant.

Meanwhile, a growing population of mestizos and mulattoes were angry at being denied the status, wealth, and power that were available to whites. Native Americans suffered economic misery under the Spanish, who had conquered the lands of their ancestors. In the Caribbean region and parts of South America, masses of enslaved Africans who worked on plantations longed for freedom.

Beyond dissatisfaction with Spanish rule, the different classes had little in common. In fact, they distrusted and feared one another. At times, they worked together against the Spanish. But once independence was achieved, the creoles, who had led the revolts, dominated the governments.

Enlightenment ideas. In the 1700s, educated creoles read the works of Enlightenment thinkers such as Voltaire, Rousseau, and Montesquieu. They watched colonists in North America throw off British rule. Translations of the Declaration of Independence and the Constitution of the United States even circulated among the creole elite.

Women actively participated in the exchange of ideas. In some cities, women hosted and attended salons, called *tertulias,* where independence and revolution were discussed.

During the French Revolution, young creoles like Simón Bolívar traveled in Europe and were inspired by the ideals of "liberty, equality, and brotherhood." Still, while Enlightenment ideas and revolutions in other lands touched off debates, most creoles were reluctant to act.

Napoleon. The spark that finally ignited widespread revolt in Latin America was Napoleon's invasion of Spain in 1808. Napoleon ousted the Spanish king and placed his brother

Social Classes in Latin America These portraits, both by Edouard Pingret, paint contrasting pictures of life in colonial Latin America. The wealthy women at top are probably peninsulares, Spanish-born settlers who dominated political and social life. At the opposite end of the social scale was the Native American woman, at bottom. This inequality between classes fed discontent and in time resulted in uprising. **Diversity** What other classes made up the social hierarchy in Latin America?

Joseph on the Spanish throne. Latin American leaders saw Spain's weakness as an opportunity to reject foreign domination and demand independence from colonial rule.

Haiti's Struggle

Even before Spanish colonists hoisted the flag of freedom, revolution had erupted elsewhere in Latin America, in a French-ruled colony on the island of Hispaniola. Haiti, as it is now called, was France's most valued possession in the 1700s.

In Haiti, French planters owned great sugar plantations worked by nearly a half million enslaved Africans. The sugar trade was hugely profitable, but conditions for enslaved workers were horrendous. Many were cruelly overworked and underfed. Haiti also had a population of both free and enslaved mulattoes. Free mulattoes, however, had few rights and were badly treated by the French.

In the 1790s, revolutionaries in France were debating ways to abolish slavery in the West Indies. However, debating the issue in Paris did not help enslaved Haitians gain their freedom. Embittered by suffering and inspired by talk of liberty and equality, they took action. In 1791, a slave revolt exploded in northern Haiti. Under the able leadership of Toussaint L'Ouverture (too SAN loo vuhr TYOOR), Haitians would fight for freedom and pave the way for throwing off French rule.

Toussaint L'Ouverture

 Toussaint L'Ouverture was born into slavery in Haiti. But his father, the son of a noble West African family, had only recently been brought to the West Indian island. He taught the boy to take pride in his African heritage.

Toussaint learned to speak both French and the African language of his ancestors. Thanks to a kind master, he also learned to read. He pored over stories of slave revolts in ancient Rome and of military heroes like Julius Caesar.

In time, Toussaint read the works of the French philosophes. One passage, in particular, impressed him:

66Nations of Europe, your slaves need neither your generosity nor your advice to break the . . . yoke that oppresses them. All they need is a brave leader. Who will he be? There is no doubt that he will appear. He will come and raise the sacred standard of liberty.99

Toussaint determined to be that "brave leader" and bring his people to liberty.

The uprising begins. When a slave revolt broke out in 1791, Toussaint was nearly 50 years old. His intelligence and military skills soon earned him the position of leader.

The struggle was long and complex. Toussaint's army of former slaves faced many enemies. Mulattoes, promised high pay, joined French planters against the rebels. France,

Toussaint L'Ouverture *A self-educated former slave, Toussaint L'Ouverture led Haitians in a revolt against French rule. Although Toussaint was captured and killed, his followers eventually won independence. In 1820, Haiti became a republic, the only nonslave nation in the Western Hemisphere.*
Impact of the Individual *Compare this portrait with the portrait of Napoleon on page 495. What impression is each artist trying to create?*

Spain, and Britain each sent armies to Haiti. The fighting took more lives than any other revolution in the Americas.

An inspiring commander. Although untrained, Toussaint was a brilliant general. He was also an inspiring commander. On the eve of one crucial battle, he issued this stirring call to his army:

> 66Do not disappoint me. Prove yourselves men who know how to value liberty and how to defend it. . . . We are fighting so that liberty—the most precious of all earthly possessions—may not perish. We are fighting to preserve it for ourselves, for our children, for our brothers, for our fellow citizens.99

Rebuilding. By 1798, Toussaint had achieved his goal—enslaved Haitians had been freed. And even though Haiti was still a French colony, Toussaint's forces controlled most of the island.

Toussaint set about rebuilding the country, which had been destroyed by long years of war. By offering generous terms, he won the support of French planters. He set out to improve agriculture, expand trade, and give Haiti a constitution. He even tried to heal rifts between classes by opening his government to whites and mulattoes as well as Africans.

Renewed struggle. In France, meantime, Napoleon Bonaparte rose to power. He determined to regain control over Haiti. In 1802, he sent a large army to the island.

Toussaint again took up arms, this time to fight for full independence. His guerrilla forces were aided by a deadly ally, yellow fever, which took a growing toll on the invaders. In April 1802, with soldiers dying at the rate of a hundred a day, the French agreed to a truce, or temporary peace.

"The tree of black liberty." Shortly after, a trusted French friend lured Toussaint to his house, where he betrayed him. Soldiers seized the Haitian leader and hustled him in chains onto a French warship. As the ship sailed, Toussaint told the captain:

> 66In overthrowing me, the French have only felled the tree of black liberty in Haiti. It will shoot up again, for it is deeply rooted, and its roots are many.99

Ten months later, in a cold mountain prison in France, Toussaint died. But Haiti's struggle for freedom continued. In 1804, Haitian leaders declared independence. With yellow fever destroying his army, Napoleon abandoned Haiti. In the years ahead, rival Haitian leaders fought for power. Finally, in 1820, Haiti became a republic, the only nonslave nation in the Western Hemisphere. ▮

A Call to Freedom in Mexico

The slave revolt in Haiti frightened creoles in Spanish America. While they wanted power themselves, most had no desire for economic or social changes that might threaten their way of life. In 1810, however, a creole priest in Mexico, Father Miguel Hidalgo (hih DAHL goh), raised a cry for freedom that would echo across the land.

El Grito de Dolores. Father Hidalgo presided over the poor rural parish of Dolores. On the morning of September 16, 1810, he rang the church bells summoning the people to prayer. When they gathered, he startled them with an urgent appeal. We do not know his exact words, but his message is remembered:

> 66My children, will you be free? Will you make the effort to recover the lands stolen from your forefathers by the hated Spaniards 300 years ago?99

Father Hidalgo's speech became known as "el Grito de Dolores"—the cry of Dolores. It called the people of Mexico to fight for "Independence and Liberty."

Poor Mexicans rallied to Father Hidalgo. A ragged army of poor mestizos and Native Americans marched to the outskirts of Mexico City. At first, some creoles supported the revolt. However, they soon rejected Hidalgo's call for an end to slavery and his plea for reforms to improve conditions for Native Americans. They felt that these policies would cost them power. They also believed that the Indians deserved their lot in life.

After some early successes, the rebels faced growing opposition. Less than a year after he

National Flags

For most of history, flags were emblems of an army or a royal family. With the rise of nationalism, however, national flags began to emerge. Today, each nation has a flag whose design represents the ideals of its people.

Linking Past and Present Why do you think designing a flag is often one of the first things a new nation does?

PAST *Each new nation of Latin America adopted its own flag. The yellow-blue-red flag of Venezuela symbolized the gold of the Americas separated from Spain by the blue ocean. Argentina borrowed its blue-white-blue flag from fleets that attacked Spanish ports during the colonial era.*

PRESENT *These flags represent nations that gained independence since 1945. The Star of David on the Israeli flag symbolizes the quest for a Jewish homeland. The shield and crossed spears of Kenya's flag recall its proud struggle for independence.*

issued the "Grito," Hidalgo was captured and executed, and his followers scattered.

José Morelos. Another priest picked up the banner of revolution. Father José Morelos was a mestizo who called for wide-ranging reform. He wanted to improve conditions for the majority of Mexicans, abolish slavery, and give the vote to all men. For four years, Morelos led rebel forces before he, too, was captured and shot in 1815.

Spanish forces, backed by conservative creoles, hunted down the surviving guerrillas. They had almost succeeded in ending the rebel movement when events in Spain had unexpected effects on Mexico.

Independence achieved. In Spain in 1820, liberals forced the king to issue a constitution. This alarmed Agustín de Iturbide (ee toor BEE day), a conservative creole in Mexico. Iturbide feared that the new Spanish government might impose liberal reforms on the colonies as well.

Iturbide had spent years fighting Mexican revolutionaries. Suddenly in 1821, he reached out to them. Backed by creoles, mestizos, and Native Americans, he overthrew the Spanish viceroy. Mexico was independent at last.

Iturbide took the title Emperor Agustín I. Soon, however, liberal Mexicans toppled the would-be monarch and set up the Republic of Mexico.

Although Mexico was free of Spanish rule, the lives of most people changed little. Military leaders dominated the government and ruled by force of arms. The next 100 years would see new struggles to improve conditions for Mexicans. These struggles would be even more complicated by the intervention of foreign powers, including the United States.

New Republics in Central America

Spanish-ruled lands in Central America declared independence in the early 1820s. Iturbide tried to add these areas to his Mexican empire. After his overthrow, local leaders set up a republic called the United Provinces of Central America.

The union was short-lived. It soon fragmented into the separate republics of Guatemala, Nicaragua, Honduras, El Salvador, and Costa Rica. Like Mexico, the new nations faced many social and economic problems.

Revolutions in South America

In South America, Native Americans had rebelled against Spanish rule as early as the 1700s. These rebellions had limited results, however. It was not until the 1800s that discontent among the creoles sparked a widespread drive for independence.

An early challenge. The strongest challenge by Native Americans was led by Tupac Amaru, who claimed descent from the Incan royal family. He demanded that the government end the brutal system of forced Indian labor. Spanish officials rejected the demand for reform.

In 1780, Tupac Amaru organized a revolt. A large army crushed the rebels and captured and killed their leader. But the revolt did have effects. The Spanish king ordered officials to look into the system of forced labor and eventually abolished it.

▲ Simón Bolívar

A long struggle. In the early 1800s, widespread discontent began to surface among other South Americans. Educated creoles like Simón Bolívar, whom you read about at the beginning of the section, had applauded the French and American revolutions. They dreamed of winning their own independence.

In 1808, when Napoleon Bonaparte occupied Spain, Bolívar and his friends saw it as a signal to act. Bolívar by then had returned to South America. In 1810, he led an uprising that established a republic in his native Venezuela.

Bolívar's new republic was quickly toppled by conservative

CAUSE AND EFFECT

Long-Term Causes

European domination of Latin America
Spread of Enlightenment ideas
American and French revolutions
Growth of nationalism in Latin America

Immediate Causes

Creoles, mestizos, and Indians resent colonial rule
Revolutionary leaders emerge
Napoleon invades Spain and ousts Spanish king

INDEPENDENCE MOVEMENTS IN LATIN AMERICA

Immediate Effects

Toussaint leads slave revolt in Haiti
Colonial rule ends in much of Latin America
Attempts made to rebuild economies

Long-Term Effects

18 separate republics set up
Continuing efforts to achieve stable democratic governments and to gain economic independence

Connections Today

Numerous independent nations in Latin America
Ongoing efforts to bring prosperity and democracy to people in Latin America

Interpreting a Chart *By 1825, most of Latin America had become independent. Growth of nationalism and discontent with colonial rule played a role in bringing about the independence movements.* ■ *What was one immediate effect of Latin American independence movements? Which effect of independence movements in Latin America continues to this day?*

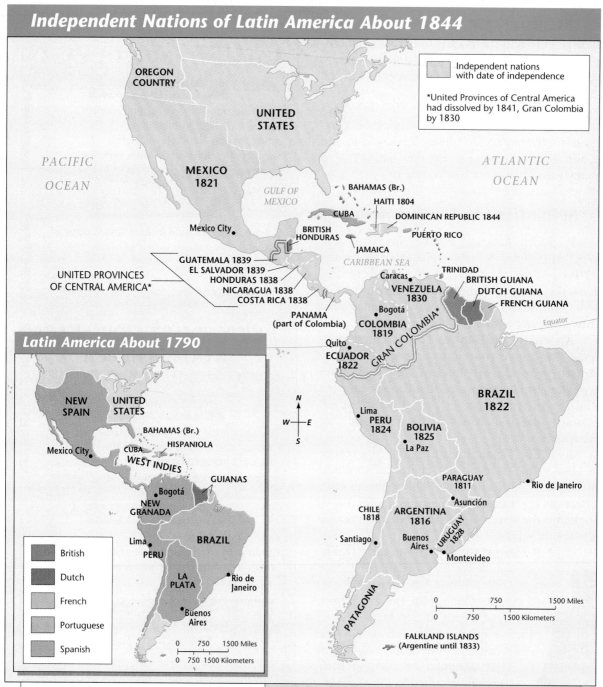

Independent Nations of Latin America About 1844

OREGON COUNTRY

UNITED STATES

PACIFIC OCEAN

ATLANTIC OCEAN

Independent nations with date of independence

*United Provinces of Central America had dissolved by 1841, Gran Colombia by 1830

MEXICO 1821

GULF OF MEXICO

Mexico City

BAHAMAS (Br.)

HAITI 1804

CUBA

DOMINICAN REPUBLIC 1844

PUERTO RICO

BRITISH HONDURAS

JAMAICA

GUATEMALA 1839
EL SALVADOR 1839
HONDURAS 1838
NICARAGUA 1838
COSTA RICA 1838

UNITED PROVINCES OF CENTRAL AMERICA*

CARIBBEAN SEA

Caracas

TRINIDAD

BRITISH GUIANA
DUTCH GUIANA
FRENCH GUIANA

PANAMA (part of Colombia)

VENEZUELA 1830

Bogotá

COLOMBIA 1819

GRAN COLOMBIA*

Equator

Quito

ECUADOR 1822

BRAZIL 1822

Lima

PERU 1824

BOLIVIA 1825

La Paz

PARAGUAY 1811

Rio de Janeiro

Asunción

CHILE 1818

ARGENTINA 1816

Buenos Aires

URUGUAY 1828

Santiago

Montevideo

PATAGONIA

N W E S

0   750   1500 Miles
0   750   1500 Kilometers

FALKLAND ISLANDS
(Argentine until 1833)

Latin America About 1790

NEW SPAIN

UNITED STATES

BAHAMAS (Br.)

Mexico City

CUBA

HISPANIOLA

WEST INDIES

GUIANAS

Bogotá

NEW GRANADA

BRAZIL

Lima

PERU

LA PLATA

Rio de Janeiro

Buenos Aires

British
Dutch
French
Portuguese
Spanish

0   750   1500 Miles
0   750   1500 Kilometers

GEOGRAPHY AND HISTORY

In the late 1700s, Europeans controlled most of Latin America. Wars of independence erupted across the region, however, and by the mid-1800s, a number of new nations had been born.

1. **Location** (a) On the main map, locate the following: Mexico, Gran Colombia, Haiti. (b) On the inset map, locate the following: La Plata, New Spain.

2. **Place** (a) Which countries had been carved out of New Granada by 1844? (b) Which independent countries had been part of New Spain?

3. **Critical Thinking Synthesizing Information** In a sentence, summarize the information shown on these two maps. Then, explain why the mapmaker needed to include an inset map.

forces. For years, civil war raged in Venezuela. The revolutionaries suffered many setbacks, and twice Bolívar was forced into exile on the island of Haiti.

Then, Bolívar conceived a daring plan. He would march his army across the Andes and attack the Spanish at Bogotá, the capital of the viceroyalty of New Granada (present-day Colombia). First, he cemented an alliance with the hard-riding *llañeros*, or Venezuelan cowboys. Then in a grueling campaign, he led an army through swampy lowlands and over the snow-capped mountains. Finally, in August 1819, he swooped down to take Bogotá from the surprised Spanish.

Other victories followed. By 1821, Bolívar had freed Caracas, Venezuela. "The Liberator," as he was now called, then moved south into Ecuador, Peru, and Bolivia. There, he joined forces with another great South American leader, José de San Martín.

San Martín. Like Bolívar, San Martín was a creole. He was born in Argentina but went to Europe for military training. In 1816, this gifted general helped Argentina win freedom from Spain. He then joined the independence struggle in other areas. He, too, led an army across the Andes, from Argentina into Chile. He defeated the Spanish in Chile before moving into Peru to strike further blows against colonial rule.

Bolívar and San Martín tried to work together, but their views were too different. In 1822, San Martín stepped aside, letting Bolívar's forces win the final victories against Spain.

Dreams and disappointments. The wars of independence had ended by 1824. Bolívar now worked tirelessly to unite the lands he had liberated into a single nation, called Gran Colombia. Bitter rivalries, however, made that impossible. Before long, Gran Colombia split into three countries: Venezuela, Colombia, and Ecuador.

Bolívar faced another disappointment as power struggles among rival leaders triggered violent civil wars. Spain's former South American colonies faced a long struggle to achieve stable governments—and an even longer one for democracy. Before his death in 1830, a discouraged Bolívar wrote, "We have achieved our independence at the expense of everything else."

Contrary to his dreams, no social revolution took place. South America's common people had simply changed one set of masters for another.

Independence for Brazil

No revolution or military campaigns were needed to win independence for Brazil. When Napoleon's armies conquered Portugal, the Portuguese royal family fled to Brazil. During his stay in Brazil, the Portuguese king introduced many reforms, including free trade.

When the king returned to Portugal, he left his son Dom Pedro to rule Brazil. "If Brazil demands independence," the king advised Pedro, "proclaim it yourself and put the crown on your own head."

In 1822, Pedro followed his father's advice. He became emperor of an independent Brazil. He accepted a constitution that provided for freedom of the press and religion as well as an elected legislature. Brazil remained a monarchy until 1889, when social and political turmoil led it to become a republic.

SECTION 3 REVIEW

1. **Identify** (a) Toussaint L'Ouverture, (b) Miguel Hidalgo, (c) el Grito de Dolores, (d) José Morelos, (e) Agustín de Iturbide, (f) Tupac Amaru, (g) Simón Bolívar, (h) José de San Martín, (i) Dom Pedro.
2. How did the colonial class system contribute to discontent in Latin America?
3. (a) What was the first step on Haiti's road to independence? (b) What role did Toussaint L'Ouverture play in Haiti's struggle?
4. Why did creoles in Mexico refuse to support Hidalgo or Morelos?
5. (a) What was Bolívar's goal for South America? (b) Did he achieve his goal? Explain.
6. *Critical Thinking* **Comparing** Compare the ways Mexico and Brazil achieved independence.
7. *ACTIVITY* Imagine that you have been hired by the French government. Create a "wanted" poster for the capture of Toussaint L'Ouverture.

21 CHAPTER REVIEW AND SKILLS FOR SUCCESS

CHAPTER REVIEW

REVIEWING VOCABULARY

Review the following vocabulary from this chapter: *ideology, universal manhood suffrage, autonomy, nationalism, peninsular, creole, mulatto, mestizo.* Write sentences using each of these terms, leaving blanks where the terms would go. Exchange your sentences with another student and fill in the blanks on each other's lists.

REVIEWING FACTS

1. What were the goals of the conservatives of the early 1800s?

2. What were the goals of the liberals of that period?

3. What was the goal of nationalists?

4. What sources of discontent led to revolts across Europe in 1848?

5. Describe the outcome of the 1848 rebellions.

6. How did Toussaint L'Ouverture aid the cause of Haitian independence?

7. When and how did Mexico gain independence from Spain?

8. How did Mexico's independence change the lives of its people?

SKILLS FOR SUCCESS   IDENTIFYING IDEOLOGIES

An **ideology** is a system of thought that seeks to define the proper nature of government and society. Liberalism, conservatism, and capitalism are examples of ideologies.

The statements below reflect basic ideas of conservatism and liberalism, two opposing ideologies of the 1800s. Read the statements, and then follow the steps to identify the ideology each statement represents.

1. **Identify the subject of the statement.** (a) What is the main subject of Prince Metternich's statement? Of Jeremy Bentham's statement? (b) How are the two subjects related?

2. **List the major points of the statement.** (a) What rule does Metternich believe should guide change in gov-

ernment? (b) According to Bentham, what should be the goal of government?

3. **Identify the speaker's ideology.** (a) According to Metternich, from whom do kings get their power? (b) According to Bentham, from whom should a government get its power? (c) What ideology does each speaker represent? Explain.

Prince Clemens von Metternich
❝I am a true friend to order and public peace. As such . . . I am absolutely convinced that the governments ruled by kings must . . . stop the rioting and social unrest. By taking whatever steps are necessary, the kings will fulfill the duties which God . . . has given them power to do.

[O]ne rule guides how governments and citizens should behave when it comes to change. This rule declares 'that no one should ever dream of changing or reforming society when emotions are out of control.' ❞

Adapted from Prince Metternich, *Secret Memorandum for Alexander I,* December 15, 1820.

Jeremy Bentham
❝In every society, a government should work for the greatest happiness of the greatest number of citizens. . . . What we have now are governments by kings which work for the greatest happiness for themselves. . . . A king has no reason to see that his subjects are happy and content . . . since his subjects have no say in whether he will be ruler or not. . . . Under a representative democracy [in which men elect their government leaders], the goal is the greatest happiness of the greatest number. ❞

Adapted from Jeremy Bentham, *Constitutional Code for the Use of All Nations,* 1827, 1830.

REVIEWING CHAPTER THEMES

Review the "Focus On" questions at the start of this chapter. Then select *three* of those questions and answer them, using information from the chapter.

CRITICAL THINKING

1. **Recognizing Causes and Effects** How did ideologies like liberalism and nationalism contribute to unrest in Europe in the 1800s?

2. **Analyzing Information** You have read Metternich's comment, "When France sneezes, Europe catches cold." What did he mean?

3. **Synthesizing Information** (a) Identify the major goal of the following leaders: Toussaint L'Ouverture, Miguel Hidalgo, Simón Bolívar. (b) Did each achieve his goal? Explain.

ANALYZING PRIMARY SOURCES

Use the quotation on page 528, first column, to answer the following questions.

1. Restate the first sentence of the excerpt in your own words.

2. What things, according to Metternich, were under attack?

3. From reading this excerpt, what do you think was Metternich's attitude toward public "passions"?

FOR YOUR PORTFOLIO

CREATING A HISTORICAL COMIC BOOK Work with a group of classmates to produce a comic book about the age of revolution in Europe and Latin America. Begin by selecting an event from this chapter as the subject. Then assign some members to do research, others to write dialogue, and so on. With the group, outline the story you will tell. Then, after research is completed, have the writers and artists set down the story and assemble the comic book.

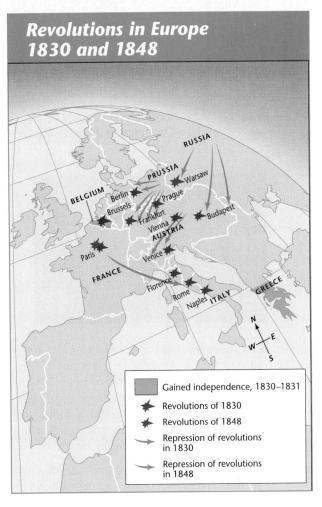

Revolutions in Europe 1830 and 1848

■	Gained independence, 1830–1831
★	Revolutions of 1830
✦	Revolutions of 1848
→	Repression of revolutions in 1830
→	Repression of revolutions in 1848

ANALYZING MAPS

Use the map to answer the following questions.

1. In which year was there a revolution in Warsaw?

2. Which city witnessed revolutions in both 1830 and 1848?

3. Were there revolutions in Great Britain in 1830 or 1848? How do you know?

INTERNET ACTIVITY

WRITING A SPEECH Use the Internet to research the independence movement of a Spanish colony in Latin America. Then write a speech calling for that colony's independence from Spain.

Unit-in-Brief

Enlightenment and Revolution

Chapter 18 The Enlightenment and the American Revolution (1715–1800)

The Enlightenment was a movement in Western Europe and North America that sought to discover natural laws and apply them to social, political, and economic problems. Since the 1700s, Enlightenment ideas have spread around the world, creating upheaval and change as they have challenged established traditions.

- Enlightenment thinkers called philosophes applied the methods of science to their efforts to understand and improve society.
- The ideas of thinkers such as Locke, Montesquieu, and Rousseau would later justify revolutions and inspire principles of representative government.
- Physiocrats rejected mercantilism in favor of laissez-faire economics.
- Despite a growing middle class, most Europeans remained peasants who lived in small rural villages, untouched by Enlightenment ideas.
- England established a constitutional monarchy and built the most powerful commercial empire in the world.
- After years of growing dissent, Britain's North American colonies won independence in the American Revolution.
- Inspired by Enlightenment ideas, the United States adopted a constitution that would serve as a model for other democratic nations.

Chapter 19 The French Revolution and Napoleon (1789–1815)

Between 1789 and 1815, the French Revolution destroyed an absolute monarchy and disrupted a social system that had existed for over a thousand years. These events ushered in the modern era in European politics.

- France was burdened by an outdated social class system, a severe financial crisis, and a monarchy too indecisive to enact reforms.
- In 1789, dissatisfied members of the middle class called for a constitution and other reforms. Meanwhile, hunger and social resentment sparked rioting among peasants and poor city dwellers.
- In the first phase of the French Revolution, moderates attempted to limit the power of the monarchy and guarantee basic rights.
- In 1793, as enemies outside France denounced the revolution, radicals executed the king and queen and began a Reign of Terror.
- From 1799 to 1815, Napoleon Bonaparte consolidated his power within France and subdued the combined forces of the greatest powers of Europe.
- Under Napoleon, French armies spread the ideas of revolution across Europe.
- In 1815, the Congress of Vienna sought to undo the effects of the French Revolution and the Napoleonic era.

Chapter 20 The Industrial Revolution Begins (1750–1850)

During the 1700s, production began to shift from simple hand tools to complex machines and new sources of energy replaced human and animal power. Known as the Industrial Revolution, this transformation marked a crucial turning point in history and changed the lives of people all over the world.

- An agricultural revolution contributed to a population explosion that, in turn, fed the growing industrial labor force.
- Abundant resources and a favorable business climate allowed Britain to take an early lead in industrialization.
- New sources of energy, such as coal and steam, fueled factories and paved the way for faster means of transporting people and goods.
- A series of remarkable inventions revolutionized the British textile industry and led to the creation of the first factories.
- Rapid urbanization and the rise of the factory system at first created dismal living and working conditions.
- Laissez-faire economists, utilitarians, and socialists put forth their own ideas for solving the problems of industrial society.
- Karl Marx promoted communism, a radical form of socialism that would have a worldwide influence.

Chapter 21 Revolutions in Europe and Latin America (1790–1848)

With the Congress of Vienna, the great powers sought to return to the political and social order that had existed prior to 1789. However, in the early 1800s, a wave of violent uprisings swept across Western Europe and Latin America, fueled by the political ideas of the French Revolution and the economic problems of the Industrial Revolution.

- Two opposing ideologies emerged in Europe. Liberals embraced Enlightenment ideas about democracy and individual rights, while conservatives sought to preserve the old political and social order.
- Nationalism inspired independence movements among peoples with a shared heritage but also bred intolerance and persecution of minorities.
- In 1830 and 1848, ideological tensions and social inequalities sparked uprisings in France and elsewhere in Europe. Although most of these democratic revolutions were suppressed, they served to hasten reform later in the century.
- In Latin America, discontent with foreign domination led to a series of independence movements that freed most of the region from colonial rule by 1825.

A Global View

How Did the New Ideas of the Enlightenment Lead to a Wave of Democratic Revolutions?

During the later 1700s and the early 1800s, new ideas brought revolutionary changes in western society and government. The Enlightenment, the American and French revolutions, and the Industrial Revolution all made this period a turning point in western history.

Ideas and Machines

Voltaire, Rousseau, and other thinkers of the French Enlightenment urged radical changes in government. They proposed limitations on governmental power and favored enlightened rule dedicated to the welfare of the people. Their ideas were partly inspired by the example of France's powerful neighbor across the English Channel. British monarchs actually shared power with Parliament, which included elected representatives of at least some of the people.

The Industrial Revolution also made key contributions to social change. In the beginning, industrialization created a poverty-stricken new working class. The demands of this class for improved living conditions would lead to major political changes in later years. At the same time, however, increased productivity would bring great material wealth.

Revolutions in Europe

In the late 1700s, France, Europe's greatest power, confronted many economic, social, and political problems. These problems finally exploded in the French Revolution of 1789.

During the tumultuous years that followed, revolutionaries who were inspired by the ideas of the Enlightenment overthrew the French monarchy. They stripped the Church of its power and the ruling aristocracy of its land. Leaders like Robespierre also launched a savage Reign of Terror, which claimed the lives of thousands of people.

Out of this revolutionary chaos, a new ruler rose to power. Napoleon Bonaparte greatly strengthened the French government and conquered most of Europe. An alliance of all the other great powers finally

	1750	1775	1800

AFRICA

Late 1700s
Islamic revival in Africa

1788
Futa Toro passes law against slave trade

THE AMERICAS

1763
Britain wins control of Canada

1775
American Revolution begins

1789
United States Constitution takes effect

ASIA AND OCEANIA

1756
Seven Years' War affects India

1770
Cook claims Australia for Britain

1793
Emperor Qianlong rejects British trade

EUROPE

1751
Diderot publishes *Encyclopedia*

1764
Spinning jenny invented

1789
French Revolution begins

defeated him at Waterloo in 1815.

Though the French Revolution had failed, the problems that had caused it persisted. As a result, Europeans rose in revolt in many lands in 1830 and 1848. Though most of these revolutions also failed, they made the need for reform clear.

Revolutions in the Americas

More successful revolutions blazed up in Europe's American colonies. In both North and South America, Enlightenment ideas and economic grievances drove the colonists to revolt. Once free of European control, the former colonists established republics with elected governments rather than hereditary monarchies.

The first American revolution began in 1775 in Britain's North American colonies. After a hard struggle, George Washington and his colleagues freed the 13 colonies. The United States Constitution gave the new nation a republican government which guaranteed the rights of the people.

The United States experiment in democracy helped inspire revolutions in Spain's Latin American colonies. By 1825, a string of independent Spanish-speaking republics stretched from Argentina to Mexico. During this period, Haiti gained independence from France, while Brazil broke away from Portugal.

In the Americas as in Europe, most people did not yet have the right to vote. Still, most of two continents had been freed from European rule.

Looking Ahead

By the mid-1800s, most of the world was still ruled by autocratic monarchs, and Europe's remaining overseas colonies had no democratic rights. Still, the "age of democratic revolutions" left a legacy of accelerating change. Enlightenment political ideas would develop further over the next two centuries. Europe and the Americas would continue to build increasingly democratic governments, and democratic ideas would begin to spread beyond the West.

ACTIVITY Choose two events and two pictures from the time line below. For each, write a sentence explaining how it relates to the themes expressed in the Global View essay.

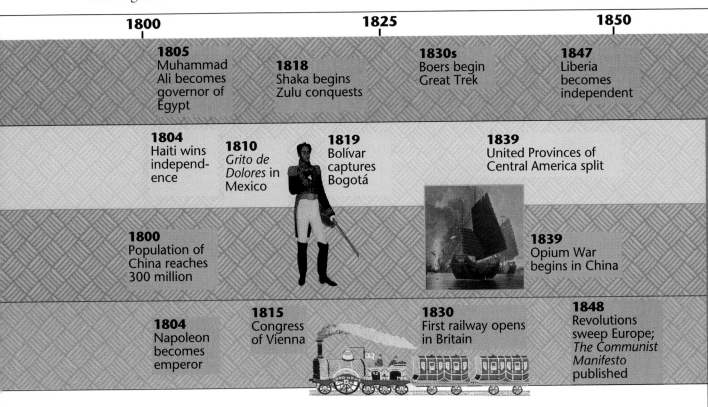

1800	1825	1850

1805 Muhammad Ali becomes governor of Egypt

1818 Shaka begins Zulu conquests

1830s Boers begin Great Trek

1847 Liberia becomes independent

1804 Haiti wins independence

1810 *Grito de Dolores* in Mexico

1819 Bolívar captures Bogotá

1839 United Provinces of Central America split

1800 Population of China reaches 300 million

1839 Opium War begins in China

1804 Napoleon becomes emperor

1815 Congress of Vienna

1830 First railway opens in Britain

1848 Revolutions sweep Europe; *The Communist Manifesto* published

UNIT 5

You Decide

Exploring Global Issues

What Limits Should There Be on Freedom of Speech?

"I do not agree with a word that you say, but I will defend to the death your right to say it." Whether or not Voltaire said these exact words, he passionately believed in this idea. Since then, people everywhere have quoted these words to uphold the right to free speech.

But are there limits to freedom of speech? And, if so, what are they? To begin your investigation, examine these viewpoints.

ENGLAND

1859

In his influential work *On Liberty,* the philosopher John Stuart Mill stated his belief that democracy required the free exchange of ideas:

66If all mankind minus one were of one opinion, and only one person were of the contrary opinion, mankind would be no more justified in silencing that one person, than he, if he had the power, would be justified in silencing mankind.99

UNITED STATES

1919

Supreme Court justice Oliver Wendell Holmes gave a famous definition of the limits of free speech in the case of *Schenck* v. *United States:*

66The most stringent protection of free speech would not protect a man in falsely shouting fire in a theater and causing a panic.99

FRANCE

1940

During wartime, democratic governments have restricted free speech in the interests of security. "Silence," warns this poster from World War II. "The enemy hears your secrets." ▶

SILENCE

L'ENNEMI..
GUETTE VOS CONFIDENCES

CHINA

1957

Mao Zedong founded a government in China based on the ideas of the communist philosopher Karl Marx:

66What should our policy be towards non-Marxist ideas? As far as unmistakable counterrevolutionaries and saboteurs of the socialist cause are concerned, the matter is easy. We simply deprive them of their freedom of speech.99

IRAN

1979

The same year he was overthrown, Shah Muhammad Reza Pahlavi had denounced the dangers of uncontrolled free speech:

66Freedom of thought, freedom of thought! Democracy, democracy! With five-year-old children going on strike and parading through the streets? That's democracy? That's freedom of thought?99

SOUTH AFRICA

1980s

In the face of protests from the black majority, the minority government of South Africa took many measures to limit free speech, including censoring news reports like this one. ▶

dela!" echoed through the stadium as the wife of Nelson Mandela, the long-imprisoned black leader, arrived. ███
███ she told the workers. ███
███ ███ Union leaders have asked miners to stay away from the pits this Wednesday as a gesture of protest and mourning

CANADA

1985

The criminal code of Canada outlaws public remarks against religious, racial, or ethnic groups:

66Every one who, by communicating statements other than in private conversation, willfully promotes hatred against any identifiable group is guilty of . . . an indictable offense and is liable to imprisonment for a term not exceeding two years.99

COMPARING VIEWPOINTS

1. Which of the viewpoints represented here seems to place the fewest restrictions on freedom of speech?
2. Mao Zedong and the shah of Iran were both authoritarian dictators. How are their viewpoints similar or different?
3. When should free speech in a democracy be restricted according to Holmes? According to the poster? According to the Canadian criminal code?

YOUR INVESTIGATION

ACTIVITY

1. Find out more about other viewpoints related to this topic. You might investigate one or more of the following:

- The Alien and Sedition acts, enacted in the United States in 1798.
- Wartime censorship in Allied nations during World War I.
- Restrictions on free speech in Iran since the overthrow of the shah.
- The contrasting policies toward dissent of Soviet leaders Leonid Brezhnev and Mikhail Gorbachev.
- Recent debates in the United States about forms of "symbolic speech," such as flag burning.

2. Decide which viewpoint you agree with most closely and express it in your own way. You may do so in an essay, a cartoon, a poem, a drawing or painting, a song, a skit, a video, or some other way.

A Look Ahead: The Modern Era

Industrialism and a New Global Age

Life in the Industrial Age (1800–1910)

From the mid-1800s, industrialism spread rapidly across Europe to North America and beyond. This second Industrial Revolution transformed the economies of the world and solidified patterns of life familiar to us today.

- By the mid-1800s, other western nations, particularly Germany and the United States, were challenging Britain's position as the world's industrial giant.
- Steel, electricity, and advances in communications and transportation marked the second Industrial Revolution.
- By the late 1800s, "big business" came increasingly to dominate the industrial world.
- With the spread of industry, a more complex social structure, dominated by middle-class values, evolved. Although the poor continued to endure harsh conditions, the overall standard of living for workers improved.
- Artistic movements such as romanticism, realism, and expressionism reflected various responses to social and technological changes.

Nationalism Triumphs in Europe (1800–1914)

The 1800s saw an upsurge of nationalism in Europe. Nationalism unified some countries and sparked divisiveness and conflict in others.

- Between 1862 and 1890, Otto von Bismarck molded the German states into a powerful empire. To strengthen the empire, Bismarck promoted economic development, aggressive foreign policy goals, and domestic reforms.
- Although nationalist forces unified Italy in 1870, a long history of fragmentation created a host of problems for the new state.
- Nationalist feelings among diverse ethnic groups in Eastern Europe created widespread unrest and helped hasten the decline of the Ottoman and Hapsburg empires.
- Reluctant to surrender absolute power, Russian czars of the 1800s swung between reform and repression.

Growth of Western Democracies (1815–1914)

In Britain, France, and the United States, reformers struggled for an extension of democratic rights and social change. Although many inequalities persisted, these efforts paved the way for great improvements in the quality of life.

- The British Parliament passed a series of reforms designed to help those whose labor supported the new industrial society. Suffrage was extended to all male citizens, prompting women to seek the vote as well.

- Following its defeat in the Franco-Prussian War and a fierce internal revolt, France established the Third Republic, which instituted a series of important reforms.
- By 1900, the United States had become the world's leading industrial giant, a global power, and a magnet for immigrants seeking freedom and opportunity.

The New Imperialism (1800–1914)

During the 1800s, European powers embarked on a period of aggressive expansion known as the Age of Imperialism. Despite fierce resistance, these powers brought much of the world under their control between 1870 and 1914.

- The Industrial Revolution gave western powers both the means and the motives to seek global domination.
- With little regard for traditional patterns of settlement, European powers partitioned almost the entire African continent.
- Taking advantage of the slowly crumbling Ottoman empire, Britain, France, and Russia competed to extend their influence over Algeria, Egypt, and other Ottoman lands.
- Britain set up a profitable system of colonial rule, controlling over 60 percent of India.
- Western powers carved out spheres of influence along the Chinese coast. China unsuccessfully tried to resist foreign influence with belated efforts at modernization and reform.

- By the early 1900s, leaders in many colonized regions were forging their own nationalist movements.

New Global Patterns (1800–1914)

Imperialism resulted in a global exchange that profited industrial nations but disrupted local economies in Africa, Asia, and Latin America. Radical changes reshaped the lives of both subject peoples and westerners.

- As a defense against western imperialism, Japan transformed itself into a modern industrial power and set out on its own imperialist path.
- By 1900, western powers had claimed most islands in the Pacific and divided up most of Southeast Asia.
- The British colonies of Canada, Australia, and New Zealand won independence relatively quickly.
- Although Latin American nations struggled to set up stable governments and economies, a pattern of military rule and economic dependency emerged.
- The United States created its own sphere of influence in the Western Hemisphere.
- Europeans forced subject peoples to accept western ideas about government, technology, and culture.

World Wars and Revolutions

World War I and Its Aftermath (1914–1919)

Many forces—including nationalism, militarism, and imperialist rivalries—propelled Europe into World War I. This massive conflict engulfed much of the world for four years and ushered in a new age of modern warfare.

- Two huge alliances emerged in Europe: the Central Powers, dominated by Germany and Austria-Hungary, and the Allies, led by France, Britain, and Russia.
- Although the assassination of Archduke Francis Ferdinand in 1914 ignited World War I, historians agree that all the major powers share blame for the conflict.
- Trench warfare and new weapons contributed to a stalemate on the Western Front.
- In 1917, the United States entered the war, allowing the Allies to achieve victory.
- The Paris peace conference imposed heavy penalties on Germany and redrew the map of Eastern Europe.

Revolution in Russia (1917–1939)

V. I. Lenin and his successors transformed czarist Russia into the communist Soviet Union. This experiment in single-party politics and a state-run economy would exert a powerful influence over the modern world for almost 75 years.

- In March 1917, political, social, and economic conditions in Russia sparked a revolution that overthrew the czar and paved the way for more radical changes.

- After leading the Bolsheviks to power in October 1917, Lenin hoped to build the classless, communist state envisioned by Karl Marx.
- Lenin's successor, Stalin, imposed "five-year plans" to build industry and farm output.
- Stalin created a totalitarian state, employing censorship, propaganda, and terror to ensure personal power and push the Soviet Union toward modernization.

Nationalism and Revolution Around the World (1914–1939)

Between 1919 and 1939, the desire for democracy and self-determination contributed to explosive struggles in many regions. New leaders in Africa, Latin America, and Asia built liberation movements that would change the world.

- The Mexican Revolution opened the door to social and economic reforms.
- Latin American leaders promoted economic nationalism, seeking to end dependence on the industrial powers.

- In Africa, a new generation of leaders called for an end to imperialism and reaffirmed traditional cultures.
- Arab nationalism gave rise to Pan-Arabism, a movement which sought to end foreign domination and unite Arabs in their own state.
- In India, Gandhi led a campaign of nonviolent resistance to British rule.
- In China, foreigners extended their spheres of influence. Later, communists and nationalists engaged in civil war.
- During the 1920s and 1930s, extreme nationalism and economic upheaval set Japan on a militaristic and expansionist path.

Crisis of Democracy in the West
(1919–1939)

After World War I, western nations worked to restore prosperity and ensure peace. At the same time, political and economic turmoil in the 1920s and 1930s challenged democratic traditions and led to the rise of powerful dictators.

- The Great Depression of the 1930s created financial turmoil and widespread suffering throughout the industrialized world.
- Scientific discoveries, new trends in literature and the arts, and social changes all contributed to a sense of uncertainty.
- Three systems of government—democracy, communism, and fascism—competed for influence in postwar Europe.
- In Italy, Mussolini and his Fascist party took advantage of economic and political unrest to win power in the 1920s.

- In Germany, Hitler rose to power by appealing to extreme nationalism, anti-Semitism, anti-communism, and resentment of the Treaty of Versailles. In the 1930s, he turned Germany into a totalitarian Nazi dictatorship.

World War II and Its Aftermath
(1931–1949)

Between 1939 and 1945, nations all over the globe fought World War II, the largest and most costly conflict in history. The war shifted the balance of world power from Western Europe to the United States and the Soviet Union.

- The Axis powers—Germany, Italy, and Japan—embarked on a course of aggression in the late 1930s. At first, France and Britain adopted a policy of appeasement but finally declared war when Hitler invaded Poland.
- The Axis at first enjoyed an unbroken string of victories in Europe.
- During the Holocaust, the Nazis systematically killed more than six million Jews, as well as millions of other people the Nazis considered undesirable.
- The Soviet Union and the United States joined the war on the Allied side. Allied victories in North Africa and Europe eventually led to the defeat of Germany.
- To force a Japanese surrender, the United States employed a powerful new weapon, the atomic bomb.
- World War II was followed by the Cold War, which pitted the western democracies, led by the United States, against the communist bloc, dominated by the Soviet Union.

555

The World Today

The World Since 1945: An Overview
(1945–Present)

Since the end of World War II, the world has changed rapidly. While we cannot yet determine the long-term impact of events of the recent past, we can identify political, social, and economic trends that have shaped the postwar years.

- The collapse of western colonial empires led to the emergence of nearly 100 new countries, mostly in Africa and Asia.
- Nuclear weapons, terrorism, and human rights are enduring issues in an increasingly interdependent world.
- Complex economic ties link the rich nations of the global North and the poor nations of the global South.
- Urbanization, modernization, women's movements, and technology have brought dramatic social changes.
- Technology has revolutionized agriculture and medicine and helped create a global, westernized popular culture.

Europe and North America
(1945–Present)

Within a framework of growing regional cooperation, Western Europe enjoyed tremendous economic growth after World War II. At the same time, the Cold War pitted the West, led by the United States, against the Soviet Union and its allies.

- In the postwar era, Western European nations expanded social programs and introduced the welfare state. By the 1980s, an economic slowdown forced cuts in social programs.
- The United States led world opposition to communism, extended civil rights, and pursued economic prosperity.
- Efforts to reform inefficiencies in government and the economy led to the collapse of the Soviet Union.
- After shaking off Soviet domination, nations of Eastern Europe faced economic challenges and ethnic conflicts.

East Asia and Southeast Asia
(1945–Present)

China, Japan, and other Asian nations have achieved varying degrees of success in their efforts to modernize. Several of these nations enjoy growing trade and other ties, linking the nations of the Pacific Rim from Asia to the Americas.

- After World War II, Japan introduced democratic reforms and by the 1960s had emerged as an economic superpower.
- Under communist rule, the People's Republic of China achieved modest economic gains while sacrificing individual political freedoms.

- The "Asian tigers"—Taiwan, Hong Kong, Singapore, and South Korea—vaulted into the class of newly industrialized nations.
- Cold War tensions sparked long, devastating conflicts in Korea, Vietnam, and Cambodia.

South Asia and the Middle East (1945–Present)

In South Asia and the Middle East, nations cast off western rule and set out to modernize. They have often confronted similar challenges—from religious strife and border conflicts to urbanization and population growth.

- Upon achieving independence, India built on the legacy of British rule to create the world's largest democracy.
- Ethnic and religious rivalries have fueled ongoing conflict among people of South Asia.
- When secular governments in the Middle East did not yield promised improvements, some reformers rejected western models and called for a reaffirmation of Islamic values.
- The long Arab-Israeli struggle and other conflicts have focused world attention on the Middle East.

Africa (1945–Present)

Leaders of new African nations set out to build strong central governments, achieve economic growth, and raise standards of living. They have faced a variety of obstacles, including economic dependency and political instability.

- After independence, many new nations experienced military or one-party rule but have since introduced multiparty democracy.
- African nations experimented with different economic systems, including socialism and mixed economies.

- After decades of conflict, South Africa abandoned its system of apartheid in the 1990s and made a transition to democratic rule.
- In Africa, as elsewhere, modernization and urbanization have disrupted traditional cultures and ways of life.

Latin America (1945–Present)

Despite setbacks, Latin American nations have tried to sustain economic growth and overcome a legacy of poverty and social inequality. Marxism, military rule, and the Roman Catholic Church have been continuing influences in the region.

- In the postwar period, poverty and uneven distribution of wealth fed social unrest in many nations.

- Latin America was a focus of Cold War politics, especially after a communist revolution in Cuba in 1959.
- Through trade, investment, and military intervention, the United States was a dominant force in Latin America.
- Although Mexico enjoyed economic gains in agriculture and manufacturing, most people remained in poverty.
- Argentina and Brazil experienced economic growth and long periods of military rule.

REFERENCE

Contents

ATLAS

DOCUMENTS

GLOSSARY

CONNECTIONS CHARTS

INDEX

SECTION

Historical Documents

ATLAS

DOCUMENTS

GLOSSARY

CONNECTIONS CHARTS

INDEX

The World: Political

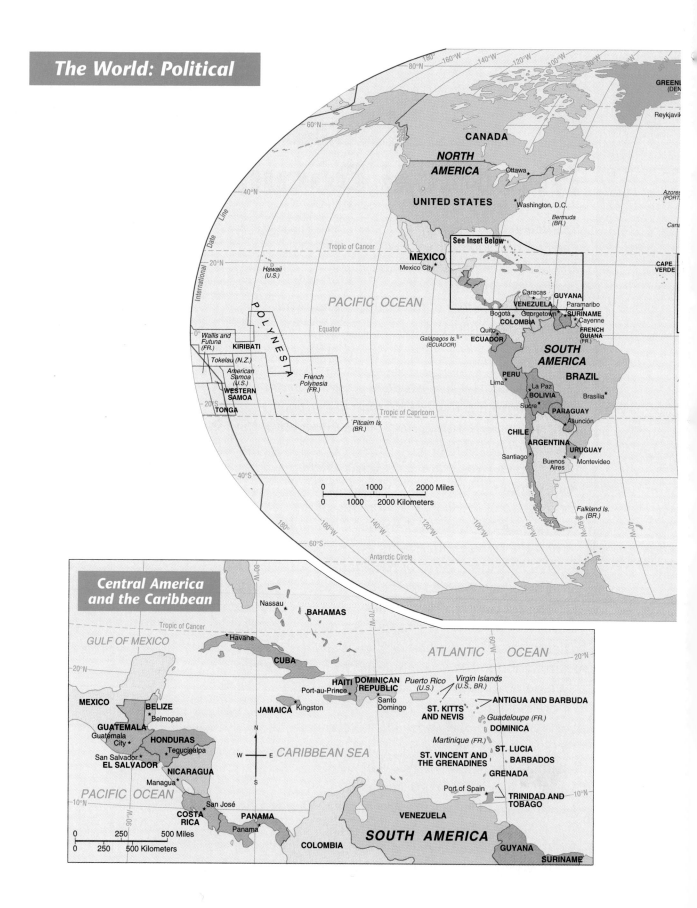

Central America and the Caribbean

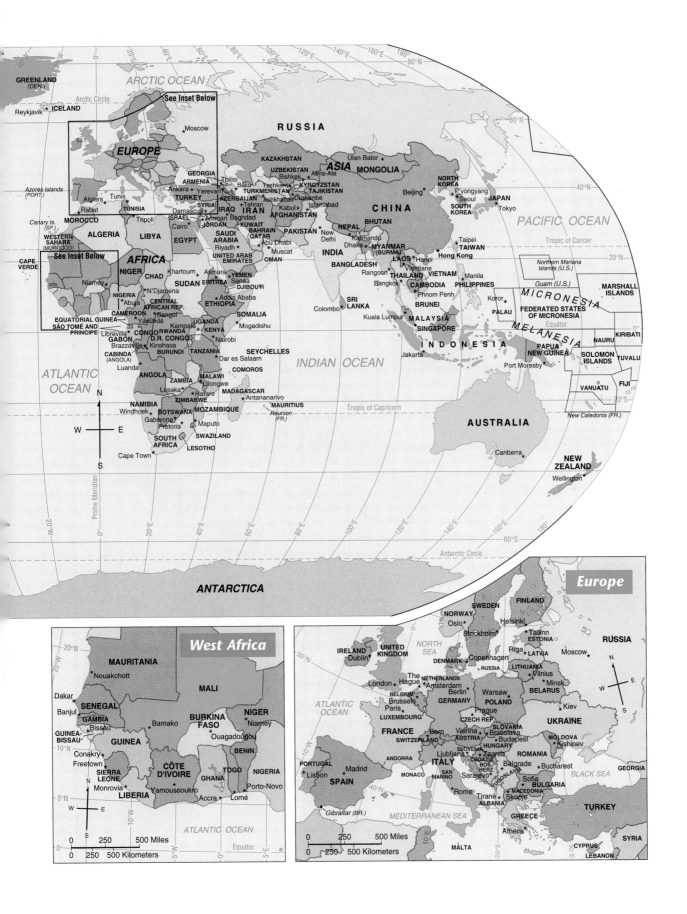

GREENLAND
(DEN.)

ARCTIC OCEAN

Reykjavik · ICELAND

Arctic Circle

See Inset Below

Moscow

RUSSIA

EUROPE

60°N

KAZAKHSTAN

ASIA

MONGOLIA

Ulan Bator

NORTH
KOREA

40°N

UZBEKISTAN

GEORGIA
ARMENIA   Tbilisi   Baku   Bishkek   KYRGYZSTAN
Ankara   Yerevan   TURKMENISTAN   TAJIKISTAN
Azores Islands   TURKEY   AZERBAIJAN   Ashkhabad   Dushanbe
(PORT.)   SYRIA   IRAN   Kabul   Islamabad

Beijing   P'yongyang   Seoul   JAPAN
SOUTH   Tokyo
KOREA

PACIFIC OCEAN

Algiers   Tunis   Damascus   IRAQ   Tehran   AFGHANISTAN
Rabat   TUNISIA   ISRAEL   Amman   Baghdad
MOROCCO   Tripoli   JORDAN   Cairo   KUWAIT   PAKISTAN   New   Katmandu   MYANMAR
Delhi   Dhaka   (BURMA)

CHINA

NEPAL   BHUTAN

Taipei   TAIWAN

Tropic of Cancer

Northern Mariana
Islands (U.S.)

20°N

WESTERN
SAHARA   ALGERIA   LIBYA   EGYPT   SAUDI   BAHRAIN   QATAR
(MOROCCO)   ARABIA   Riyadh   Abu Dhabi   INDIA
CAPE   UNITED ARAB   Muscat
VERDE   See Inset Below   EMIRATES   OMAN
AFRICA   BANGLADESH   LAOS   Hanoi
Hong Kong   Guam (U.S.)   MARSHALL
ISLANDS
NIGER   CHAD   Khartoum   Asmara   YEMEN   Manila
Niamey   SUDAN   ERITREA   Sanaa   DJIBOUTI   THAILAND   VIETNAM   MICRONESIA
NIGERIA   N'Djamena   Addis Ababa   Rangoon   CAMBODIA   PHILIPPINES
Abuja   CENTRAL   ETHIOPIA   Bangkok   Phnom Penh   Koror   FEDERATED STATES
AFRICAN REP.   Bangui   SRI   BRUNEI   PALAU   OF MICRONESIA
EQUATORIAL GUINEA   CAMEROON   UGANDA   SOMALIA   Colombo   LANKA   KualaLumpur   MALAYSIA   MELANESIA
SÃO TOMÉ AND   Yaoundé   Kampala   KENYA   Mogadishu   SINGAPORE   NAURU   KIRIBATI
PRINCIPE   Libreville   CONGO   RWANDA   Nairobi   PAPUA   SOLOMON
GABON   D.R. CONGO   INDONESIA   NEW GUINEA   ISLANDS   TUVALU
Brazzaville   Kinshasa   TANZANIA   Jakarta
CABINDA   BURUNDI   Dar es Salaam   INDIAN OCEAN   Port Moresby
(ANGOLA)   Luanda   SEYCHELLES   VANUATU   FIJI

ATLANTIC
OCEAN

N

W   E

S

ANGOLA   ZAMBIA   MALAWI   COMOROS
Lusaka   Liongwe   New Caledonia (FR.)
NAMIBIA   ZIMBABWE   MOZAMBIQUE   MADAGASCAR   MAURITIUS
Windhoek   BOTSWANA   Harare   Antananarivo   Reunion   Tropic of Capricorn   20°S
Gaborone   Pretoria   (FR.)
SOUTH   Maputo   AUSTRALIA
AFRICA   SWAZILAND
Cape Town   LESOTHO
Canberra   NEW
ZEALAND
Wellington

60°S

Antarctic Circle

ANTARCTICA

Europe

SWEDEN   FINLAND
NORWAY
Oslo   Helsinki
Stockholm   RUSSIA
IRELAND   UNITED   NORTH   Tallinn   ESTONIA
Dublin   KINGDOM   SEA   DENMARK   Copenhagen   Riga   LATVIA   Moscow
The   NETHERLANDS   RUSSIA   LITHUANIA
London   Hague   Amsterdam   Berlin   Vilnius   Minsk
ATLANTIC   BELGIUM   GERMANY   Warsaw   BELARUS
OCEAN   Brussels   POLAND
Paris   Prague   Kiev
LUXEMBOURG   CZECH REP.   UKRAINE
FRANCE   Bern   Vienna   SLOVAKIA
SWITZERLAND   AUSTRIA   Bratislava   MOLDOVA
Ljubljana   HUNGARY   Budapest   Kishinev
ANDORRA   SLOVENIA   Zagreb   ROMANIA
PORTUGAL   ITALY   CROATIA   Belgrade   Bucharest   GEORGIA
Lisbon   Madrid   BOS.   YUGOSLAVIA
SAN   HERZ.   Sarajevo   BLACK SEA
MONACO   MARINO   Sofia   BULGARIA
SPAIN   Rome   Tirane   MACEDONIA   Skopje
Gibraltar (BR.)   ALBANIA   TURKEY
MEDITERRANEAN SEA   GREECE
Athens   SYRIA
MALTA   CYPRUS   LEBANON

West Africa

MAURITANIA
Nouakchott
MALI
Dakar
SENEGAL
Banjul   Bamako   NIGER
GAMBIA   Bissau   BURKINA   Niamey
GUINEA-   FASO
BISSAU   GUINEA   Ouagadougou   BENIN
Conakry
Freetown   CÔTE   NIGERIA
SIERRA   D'IVOIRE   GHANA   TOGO
LEONE   Yamoussoukro   Porto-Novo
Monrovia   Accra   Lomé
LIBERIA

ATLANTIC OCEAN

0   250   500 Miles
0   250   500 Kilometers

0   250   500 Miles
0   250   500 Kilometers

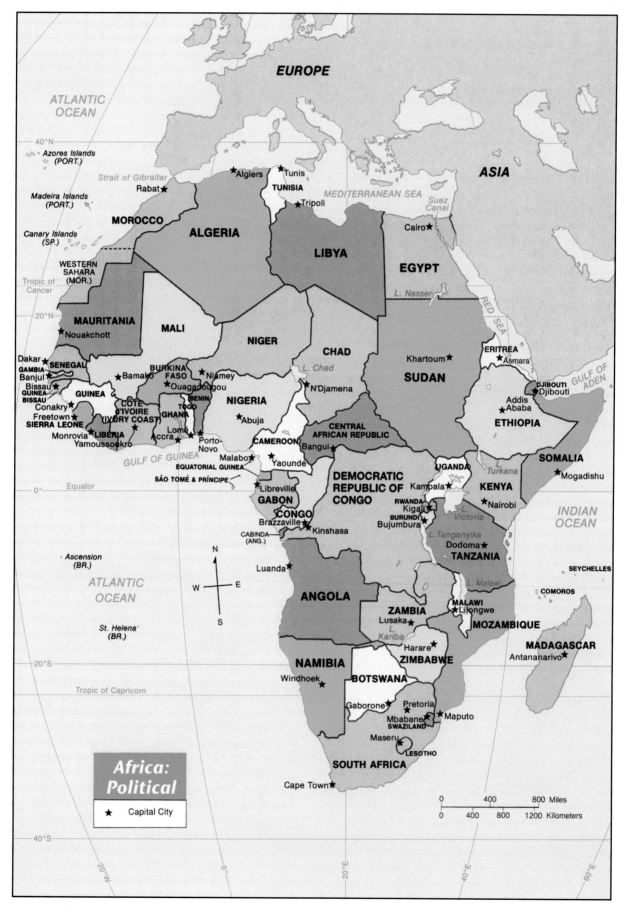

EUROPE

ATLANTIC
OCEAN

ASIA

40°N

Azores Islands
(PORT.)

Strait of Gibraltar

Algiers★ ★Tunis

MEDITERRANEAN SEA

Suez
Canal

Madeira Islands
(PORT.)

Rabat ★

TUNISIA

★Tripoli

Canary Islands
(SP.)

MOROCCO

ALGERIA

LIBYA

Cairo★

Tropic of
Cancer

WESTERN
SAHARA
(MOR.)

EGYPT

L. Nasser

RED SEA

20°N

MAURITANIA

Nouakchott★

MALI

NIGER

CHAD

Khartoum★

ERITREA
★Asmara

Dakar★
GAMBIA
Banjul★
Bissau★
GUINEA-
BISSAU
Conakry★
Freetown★
SIERRA LEONE
Monrovia★
Yamoussoukro★

SENEGAL

★Bamako

BURKINA
FASO
Ouagadougou★

★Niamey

L. Chad

N'Djamena★

SUDAN

DJIBOUTI
Djibouti★

GULF OF
ADEN

GUINEA

CÔTE
D'IVOIRE
(IVORY COAST)
GHANA
LIBERIA

BENIN
TOGO
Lomé★
Accra★

NIGERIA

★Abuja

Addis
Ababa★

ETHIOPIA

Porto-
Novo

CAMEROON

CENTRAL
AFRICAN REPUBLIC

GULF OF GUINEA

Malabo★

Bangui★

SOMALIA
★Mogadishu

EQUATORIAL GUINEA

SÃO TOMÉ & PRÍNCIPE

Yaoundé★

UGANDA

L.
Turkana

Equator

0°

Libreville★

GABON

DEMOCRATIC
REPUBLIC OF
CONGO

Kampala★

KENYA
★Nairobi

INDIAN
OCEAN

CONGO

Brazzaville★

RWANDA
Kigali★
BURUNDI
Bujumbura★

L.
Victoria

Ascension
(BR.)

CABINDA
(ANG.)

★Kinshasa

L. Tanganyika

Dodoma★

SEYCHELLES

ATLANTIC
OCEAN

Luanda★

TANZANIA

COMOROS

St. Helena
(BR.)

ANGOLA

L. Malawi

MALAWI
Lilongwe★

ZAMBIA
Lusaka★

MOZAMBIQUE

MADAGASCAR
Antananarivo★

20°S

L.
Kariba

NAMIBIA

Windhoek★

Harare★

ZIMBABWE

Tropic of Capricorn

BOTSWANA

N

W   E

S

Africa:
Political

Gaborone★

Pretoria★

Mbabane★ ★Maputo
SWAZILAND

★ Capital City

Maseru★

SOUTH AFRICA

LESOTHO

0   400   800 Miles

0   400   800   1200 Kilometers

Cape Town★

40°S

20°W

0°

20°E

40°E

60°E

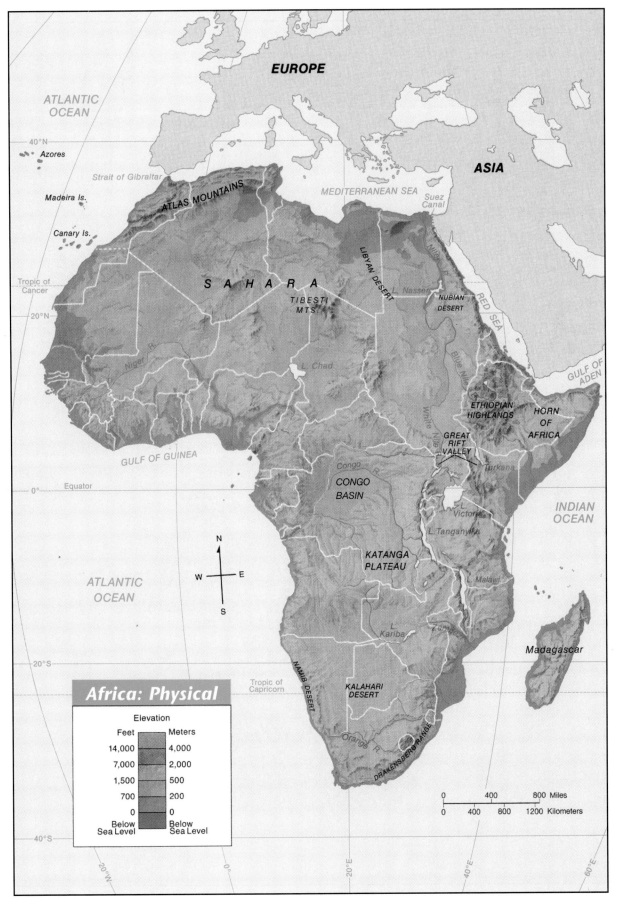

ATLAS

EUROPE

ASIA

ATLANTIC
OCEAN

40°N

Azores

Strait of Gibraltar

MEDITERRANEAN SEA

Suez
Canal

Madeira Is.

ATLAS MOUNTAINS

Canary Is.

Tropic of
Cancer

S A H A R A

LIBYAN DESERT

L. Nasser

RED SEA

GULF OF
ADEN

20°N

TIBESTI
MTS.

NUBIAN
DESERT

Nile R.

Blue Nile

Niger R.

L. Chad

White Nile

ETHIOPIAN
HIGHLANDS

HORN
OF
AFRICA

GULF OF GUINEA

GREAT
RIFT
VALLEY

Turkana

INDIAN
OCEAN

Congo R.

Equator

0°

CONGO
BASIN

L.
Victoria

L. Tanganyika

N

KATANGA
PLATEAU

W   E

ATLANTIC
OCEAN

Malawi

S

Madagascar

L.
Kariba

Zambezi

20°S

NAMIB DESERT

Tropic of
Capricorn

KALAHARI
DESERT

Africa: Physical

Orange R.

DRAKENSBERG RANGE

Elevation

Feet	Meters
14,000	4,000
7,000	2,000
1,500	500
700	200
0	0
Below Sea Level	Below Sea Level

0   400   800 Miles

0   400   800   1200 Kilometers

40°S

20°W

0°

20°E

40°E

60°E

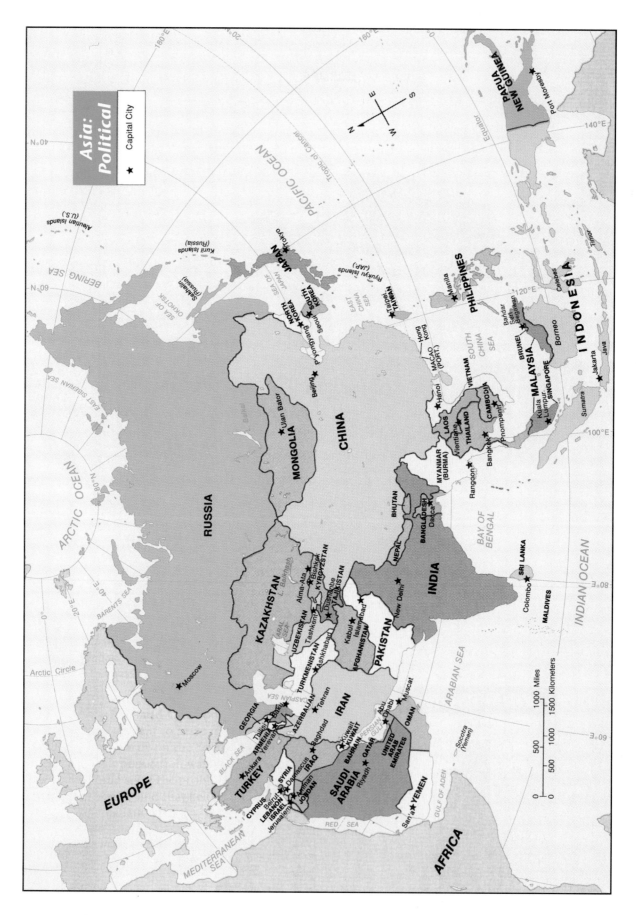

Asia:
Political

★ Capital City

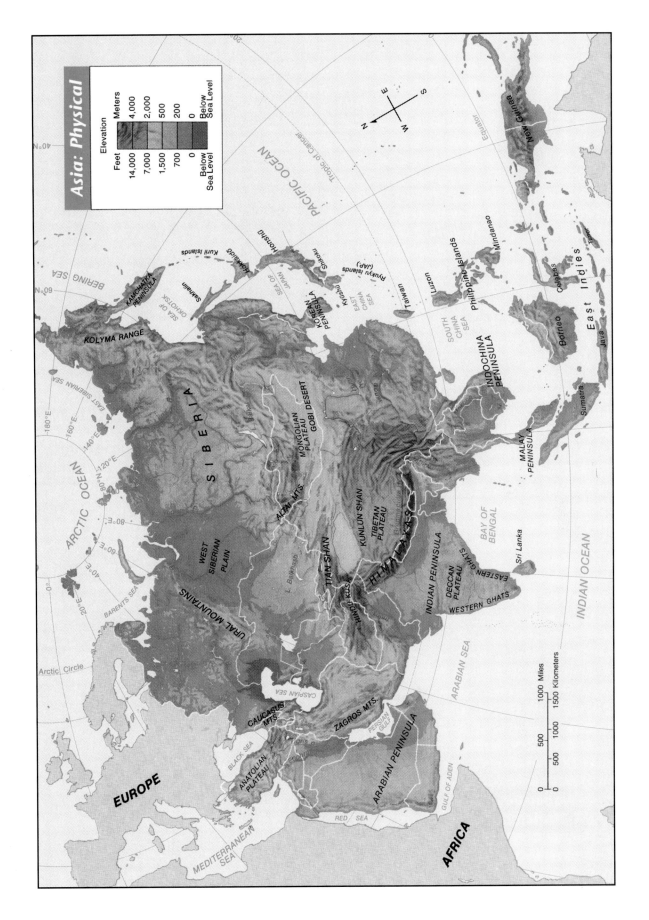

Asia: Physical

Elevation

Feet	Meters
14,000	4,000
7,000	2,000
1,500	500
700	200
0	0
Below Sea Level	Below Sea Level

PACIFIC OCEAN

Tropic of Cancer

New Guinea

E
N — S
W

Equator

Mindanao

BERING SEA

SEA OF OKHOTSK

Kamchatka PENINSULA

Kuril Islands

Hokkaido

Sakhalin

Honshu

Shikoku

Ryukyu Islands (JAP.)

Kyushu

EAST CHINA SEA

Taiwan

Luzon

Philippine Islands

Celebes

Timor

East Indies

KOLYMA RANGE

KOREAN PENINSULA

SEA OF JAPAN

SOUTH CHINA SEA

Borneo

Java

SIBERIA

EAST SIBERIAN SEA

MONGOLIAN PLATEAU

GOBI DESERT

INDOCHINA PENINSULA

Sumatra

ARCTIC OCEAN

L. Baikal

ALTAI MTS.

KUNLUN SHAN

TIBETAN PLATEAU

MALAY PENINSULA

WEST SIBERIAN PLAIN

TIAN SHAN

HIMALAYAS

INDIAN PENINSULA

BAY OF BENGAL

EASTERN GHATS

DECCAN PLATEAU

Sri Lanka

INDIAN OCEAN

L. Balkhash

HINDU KUSH

WESTERN GHATS

BARENTS SEA

URAL MOUNTAINS

Arctic Circle

CASPIAN SEA

CAUCASUS MTS.

ZAGROS MTS.

PERSIAN GULF

ARABIAN SEA

BLACK SEA

ANATOLIAN PLATEAU

ARABIAN PENINSULA

EUROPE

GULF OF ADEN

MEDITERRANEAN SEA

RED SEA

AFRICA

0   500   1000 Miles
0   500   1000   1500 Kilometers

ICELAND
★ Reykjavik

Arctic Circle

NORWEGIAN SEA

Faroe Islands
(DEN.)

Shetland Islands
(BR.)

BARENTS SEA

FINLAND

GULF OF BOTHNIA

NORWAY

Oslo ★

SWEDEN

★ Stockholm

Helsinki ● St. Petersburg

Tallinn

ESTONIA

RUSSIA

Moscow ★

Riga
★
LATVIA

ATLANTIC
OCEAN

SCOTLAND

N.
IRELAND

Dublin
★

IRELAND

UNITED
KINGDOM

WALES   ENGLAND

London ★

NORTH SEA

DENMARK
Copenhagen ★

BALTIC SEA

RUSSIA

LITHUANIA
Vilnius ★

Minsk ★

BELARUS

Kiev
★

NETHERLANDS
The
Hague ★ ● Amsterdam

Brussels ●

BELGIUM

Berlin ★

POLAND

Warsaw ★

UKRAINE

ENGLISH CHANNEL

LUXEMBOURG

GERMANY

Prague ●

CZECH REPUBLIC

SLOVAKIA

★ Bratislava

MOLDOVA
● Kishinev

Paris ●

BAY OF
BISCAY

FRANCE

SWITZERLAND
★
Bern

LIECHTENSTEIN

Vienna
●
AUSTRIA

Budapest
★

HUNGARY

Ljubljana
★

SLOVENIA

Zagreb
★

CROATIA

Belgrade
★

ROMANIA

Bucharest
★

BLACK
SEA

ITALY

SAN
MARINO

BOSNIA -
HERZEGOVINA

Sarajevo ●

SERBIA

YUGOSLAVIA

MONTENEGRO

Sofia
★

BULGARIA

Istanbul ●

Bosporus

PORTUGAL

SPAIN

Madrid ★

ANDORRA

MONACO

Corsica
(FR.)

VATICAN
CITY

Rome ★

ADRIATIC SEA

ALBANIA

Tirane ●

F.Y.R. OF
MACEDONIA

Skopje
★

TURKEY

Lisbon
★

40°N

Sardinia
(IT.)

Balearic Islands
(SP.)

GREECE

AEGEAN
SEA

Strait of
Gibraltar

Gibraltar
(BR.)

MEDITERRANEAN   SEA

Sicily

Athens ★

MALTA

Crete

AFRICA

N

W ● E

S

**Europe:
Political**

★ Capital City

● Major City

0   200   400 Miles

0   200   400   600 Kilometers

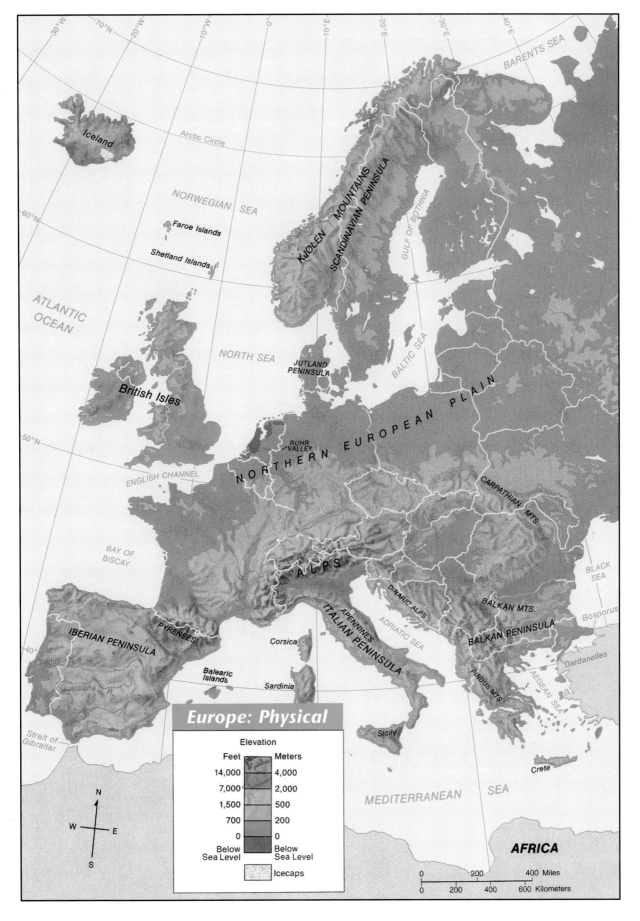

Europe: Physical

Elevation

Feet		Meters
14,000		4,000
7,000		2,000
1,500		500
700		200
0		0
Below Sea Level		Below Sea Level

Icecaps

N
W E
S

30°W
70°N
20°W
10°W
0°
10°E
20°E
30°E
40°E

Arctic Circle

Iceland

BARENTS SEA

NORWEGIAN SEA

60°N

Faroe Islands

Shetland Islands

KJØLEN MOUNTAINS
SCANDINAVIAN PENINSULA

GULF OF BOTHNIA

ATLANTIC OCEAN

NORTH SEA

BALTIC SEA

British Isles

JUTLAND PENINSULA

50°N

RUHR VALLEY

NORTHERN EUROPEAN PLAIN

Vistula

CARPATHIAN MTS.

ENGLISH CHANNEL

Danube

BLACK SEA

BAY OF BISCAY

A L P S

DINARIC ALPS

BALKAN MTS.

Bosporus

IBERIAN PENINSULA

PYRENEES

Corsica

APENNINES
ITALIAN PENINSULA

ADRIATIC SEA

BALKAN PENINSULA

Dardanelles

40°

Tagus R.

Balearic Islands

Sardinia

PINDUS MTS.

AEGEAN SEA

Guadiana R.

Strait of Gibraltar

Sicily

Crete

MEDITERRANEAN   SEA

AFRICA

0   200   400 Miles
0   200   400   600 Kilometers

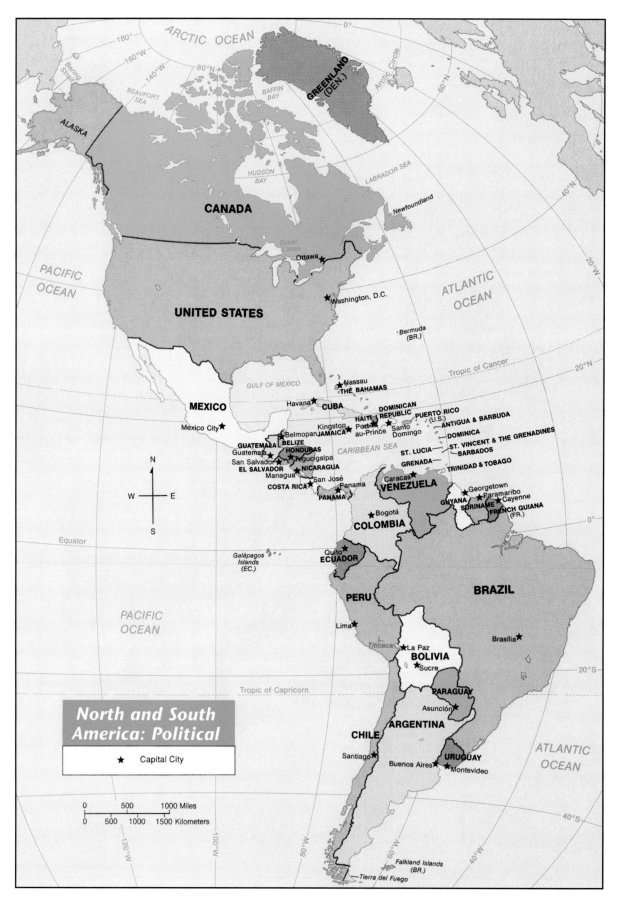

ARCTIC OCEAN

180°

160°W

140°W

80°N

BAFFIN
BAY

60°N

GREENLAND
(DEN.)

Arctic Circle

ALASKA

BEAUFORT
SEA

Bering
Strait

PACIFIC
OCEAN

HUDSON
BAY

CANADA

Great
Lakes

LABRADOR SEA

Newfoundland

40°N

Ottawa ★

ATLANTIC
OCEAN

20°W

UNITED STATES

★ Washington, D.C.

Bermuda
(BR.)

20°N

Tropic of Cancer

GULF OF MEXICO

★ Nassau
THE BAHAMAS

MEXICO

Havana ★

CUBA

DOMINICAN
REPUBLIC

PUERTO RICO
(U.S.)

ANTIGUA & BARBUDA

Mexico City ★

Kingston

HAITI
Port-
au-Prince

Santo
Domingo

DOMINICA

Belmopan ★

JAMAICA

ST. VINCENT & THE GRENADINES

GUATEMALA

BELIZE

CARIBBEAN SEA

ST. LUCIA
BARBADOS

Guatemala

HONDURAS

San Salvador

Tegucigalpa

GRENADA

TRINIDAD & TOBAGO

EL SALVADOR

NICARAGUA

Managua

Caracas ★

N

San José

Panama

VENEZUELA

Georgetown

W   E

COSTA RICA

Panama

GUYANA

Paramaribo

Cayenne

SURINAME

FRENCH GUIANA
(FR.)

S

PANAMA

★ Bogotá

0°

COLOMBIA

Equator

Galápagos
Islands
(EC.)

Quito ★

ECUADOR

PERU

BRAZIL

PACIFIC
OCEAN

Lima ★

Brasília ★

L.
Titicaca

★ La Paz

20°S

BOLIVIA

★ Sucre

Tropic of Capricorn

PARAGUAY

Asunción ★

**North and South
America: Political**

ARGENTINA

CHILE

★ Capital City

Santiago ★

URUGUAY

Buenos Aires ★

ATLANTIC
OCEAN

Montevideo

0   500   1000 Miles

40°S

0   500 1000 1500 Kilometers

120°W

100°W

80°W

Falkland Islands
(BR.)

60°W

40°W

Tierra del Fuego

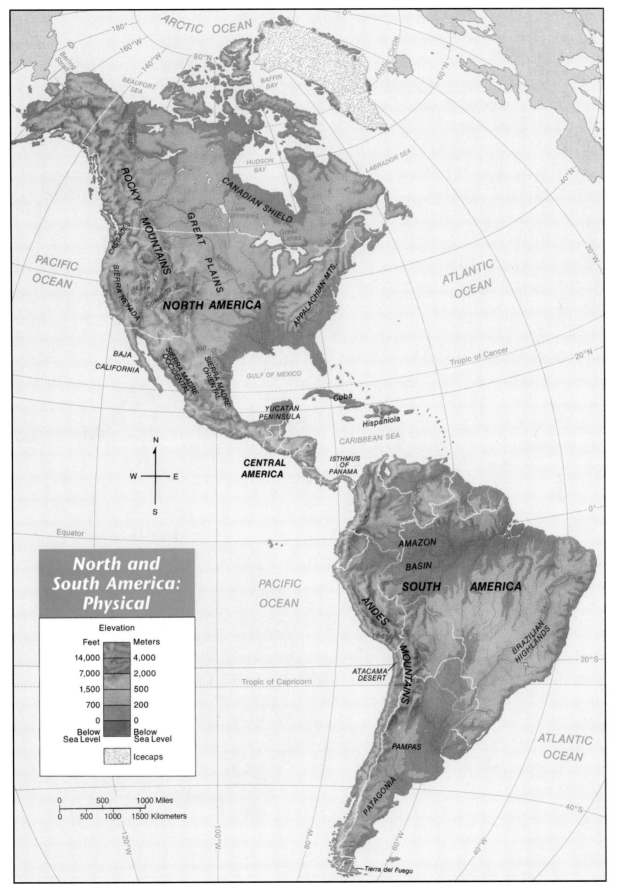

North and South America: Physical

Elevation

Feet		Meters
14,000		4,000
7,000		2,000
1,500		500
700		200
0		0
Below Sea Level		Below Sea Level

Icecaps

0   500   1000 Miles
0   500   1000   1500 Kilometers

ARCTIC OCEAN
BEAUFORT SEA
Bering Strait
Yukon R.
Mackenzie
BAFFIN BAY
HUDSON BAY
LABRADOR SEA
Lake Winnipeg
CANADIAN SHIELD
ROCKY MOUNTAINS
GREAT PLAINS
Great Lakes
St. Lawrence R.
CASCADES
SIERRA NEVADA
Missouri R.
Great Salt Lake
Colorado R.
NORTH AMERICA
APPALACHIAN MTS.
PACIFIC OCEAN
ATLANTIC OCEAN
BAJA CALIFORNIA
SIERRA MADRE OCCIDENTAL
SIERRA MADRE ORIENTAL
Rio Grande
Tropic of Cancer
GULF OF MEXICO
Cuba
YUCATÁN PENINSULA
Hispaniola
CARIBBEAN SEA
N
W   E
S
CENTRAL AMERICA
ISTHMUS OF PANAMA
Equator
AMAZON BASIN
SOUTH AMERICA
ANDES MOUNTAINS
Amazon R.
São Francisco R.
BRAZILIAN HIGHLANDS
Titicaca
PACIFIC OCEAN
ATACAMA DESERT
Tropic of Capricorn
PAMPAS
PATAGONIA
ATLANTIC OCEAN
Tierra del Fuego

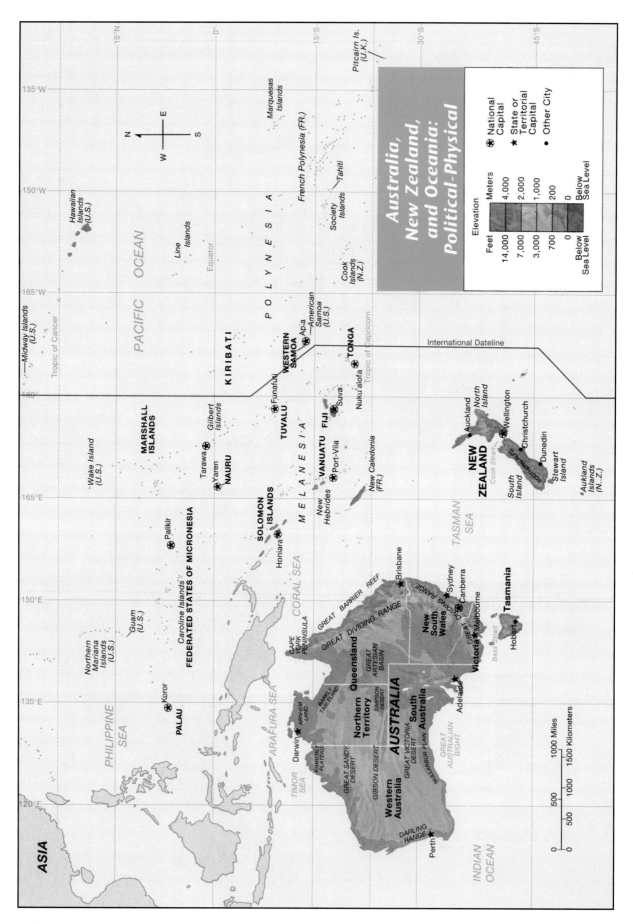

Australia, New Zealand, and Oceania: Political-Physical

Elevation

Feet	Meters
14,000	4,000
7,000	2,000
3,000	1,000
700	200
0	0
Below Sea Level	Below Sea Level

⊛ National Capital
★ State or Territorial Capital
• Other City

UNDERSTANDING MAP PROJECTIONS

Geographers and historians use globes and maps to represent the Earth. A globe is like a small model of the Earth. It shows major geographic features, representing the landmasses and bodies of water accurately. However, a globe is not always convenient to use. A map, on the other hand, which can be printed on a piece of paper or in a book, is a more convenient way to show the Earth. Unfortunately, no map can be an exact picture of the Earth because all maps are flat and the Earth's surface is curved.

Mapmakers have developed many ways of showing the curved Earth on a flat surface. Each of these ways is called a map projection. The three maps on this page show different types of map projections—each with its advantages and disadvantages.

The Robinson projection shows correct shapes and sizes of landmasses for most parts of the world. They are commonly used today by geographers. You will find numerous Robinson projections in this book. They appear at the beginning of each unit, beside the time line at the beginning of each chapter, and as a locator map beneath most other maps in the book.

The Mercator projection, one of the earliest projections developed, accurately shows the directions north, south, east, and west. As you can see, the parallels and meridians are straight lines intersecting each other at right angles. This makes it easy to plot distances on the map. As a result, Mercator projections are useful for showing sailors' routes and ocean currents. Sizes become distorted, however, as you move farther away from the equator.

The Interrupted projection shows the sizes and shapes of landmasses accurately. However, the interruptions in the oceans make it difficult to measure distances and judge directions across water.

Map Projections

Robinson Projection

Mercator Projection

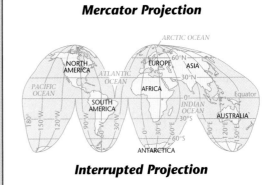

Interrupted Projection

GEOGRAPHY AND HISTORY

Map projections enable mapmakers to show the curved Earth on a flat page. Each of the projections shown here has its advantages and disadvantages.

1. **Location** *On the maps, locate (a) North America, (b) Africa, (c) Australia.*
2. **Region** *(a) On an Interrupted projection, which continent is divided into sections? Why is it divided? (b) List three pages in this textbook on which you can find a Robinson projection.*
3. **Critical Thinking** **Comparing** *Locate Antarctica on the Robinson and Mercator projections. On which map is its size shown more accurately? Explain why this is so.*

DOCUMENT IN BRIEF

In this letter Ptah-hotep describes rules of behavior that he believes will help his son live a successful life.

Instruction of Ptah-hotep

Ptah-hotep, who lived around 2450 B.C. in Egypt, was a vizier, or chief minister, to a pharaoh during the Old Kingdom. In the excerpt below, Ptah-hotep describes some practical rules for behavior that he believes will help his son live a successful life.

Be not arrogant because of your knowledge, and be not puffed up because you are a learned man. Take counsel with the ignorant as with the learned, for the limits of art cannot be reached, and no artist is perfect in his skills. . . .

If you are a leader, commanding the conduct of many, seek out every good aim, so that your policy may be without error. A great thing is truth, enduring and surviving; it has not been upset since the time of Osiris. He who departs from its laws is punished. It is the right path for him who knows nothing. Wrongdoing has never brought its venture safe to port. Evil may win riches, but it is the strength of truth that it endures long. . . .

If you want your conduct to be good, free from every evil, then beware of greed. It is an evil and incurable sickness. No man can live with it; it causes divisions between fathers and mothers, and between brothers of the same mother; it parts wife and husband; it is a gathering of every evil, a bag of everything hateful. A man thrives if his conduct is right. He who follows the right course wins wealth thereby. But the greedy man has no tomb. . . .

If you are a worthy man sitting in the council of his lord, confine your attention to excellence. Silence is more valuable than chatter. Speak only when you know you can resolve difficulties. He who gives good counsel is an artist, for speech is more difficult than any craft. . . .

If you listen to my sayings, then all your affairs will go forward. . . . If the son of a man accepts what his father says, no plan of his will fail. . . . Failure follows him who does not listen. . . .

▲ Egyptian tomb painting

ANALYZING THE DOCUMENT

Use the excerpt above to answer the following questions.

1. Which of the following is the best summary of the fourth paragraph?

   A Speak only when you have something helpful to say.

   B Achieve excellence so that you may council the lord.

   C Remain silent while in the council of the lord.

   D Give good counsel in order to gain wealth.

2. The author wishes his son to listen to his advice so that he will —

   A be greedy.

   B be sick.

   C be successful.

   D be arrogant.

3. **Critical Thinking: Making Inferences**
   What does Ptah-hotep mean by the phrase, "the greedy man has no tomb"?

The Epic of Gilgamesh

The Epic of Gilgamesh is a collection of tales about a hero named Gilgamesh written about 2000 B.C. The main themes of the poem are the unpredictability of the gods and the inevitability of death. These themes may be a reflection of life in Sumer, where the flooding of the Tigris and Euphrates was both unpredictable and devastating.

In this epic poem Gilgamesh comes to realize that death is the common lot of all people, even fearless heroes.

Utnapishtim says to him, to Gilgamesh. . . .
"About a plant I will tell thee. . . .
Its thorns will prick thy hands just as does the rose.
If thy hands obtain the plant, thou wilt attain [eternal] life."
No sooner had Gilgamesh heard this, . . .
He tied heavy stones to his feet.
They pulled him down into the deep and he saw the plant.
He took the plant, though it pricked his hands.
He cut the heavy stones from his feet.
The sea cast him up upon its shore.
Gilgamesh says to him, to Urshanabi, the boatman:
"Urshanabi, this plant is a plant apart,
Whereby a man my regain his life's breath. . . .
Its name shall be 'Man Becomes Young in Old Age.'
I myself shall eat it
And thus return to the state of my youth."
Gilgamesh saw a well whose water was cool.
He went down into it to bathe in the water.
A serpent snuffed the fragrance of the plant;
It came up from the water and carried off the plant,
Going back to shed its slough [skin].
Thereupon Gilgamesh sits down and weeps.
His tears running down over his face.
He took the hand of Urshanabi, the boatman:
"For whom, Urshanabi, have my hands toiled?
For whom is being spent the blood of my heart?
I have not obtained a boon [benefit] for myself.
For the serpent have I effected a boon!"

▲ Gilgamesh holding a lion

ANALYZING THE DOCUMENT

Use the excerpt above to answer the following questions.

1. What does Utnapishtim tell Gilgamesh about?

   A a boatman named Urshanabi

   B a plant that brings eternal life

   C a well with cool water

   D a serpent who carries away youth

2. At the end of the poem, Gilgamesh weeps because—

   A the serpent has shed its skin.

   B he has toiled with his hands for too long.

   C he has failed to find everlasting life and must accept death.

   D he has eaten all of the plant.

3. *Critical Thinking:* Synthesizing Information What physical characteristic of snakes leads the author to choose it as the creature who benefits from the plant?

◆ DOCUMENT
IN BRIEF

Hammurabi's Code is a set of laws based on the principle of "an eye for an eye" and "a tooth for a tooth."

The Code of Hammurabi

Hammurabi's Code, written about 1750 B.C., is a series of 282 laws decreed by Hammurabi, the ruler of the city of Babylon. The laws were written down so that people and judges would have a consistent set of rules to follow in settling disputes and imposing penalties. Although some of the penalties seem cruel by today's standards, they did provide a more orderly system of government than unrestricted personal vengeance.

1. *If a man bring an accusation against another man, charging him with murder, but cannot prove it, the accuser shall be put to death.*

22. *If a man practice robbery and is captured, that man shall be put to death.*

23. *If the robber is not captured, the man who has been robbed shall, in the presence of god, make an itemized statement of his loss, and the city and the governor in whose province and jurisdiction the robbery was committed shall compensate him for whatever was lost.*

53. *If a man neglects to maintain his dike and does not strengthen it, and a break is made in his dike and the water carries away the farmland, the man in whose dike the break has been made shall replace the grain which has been damaged.*

117. *If a man be in debt and sell his wife, son, or daughter, or bind them over to service, for three years they shall work in the house of their purchaser or master; in the fourth year they shall be given their freedom.*

195. *If a son strike his father, they shall cut off his hand.*

196. *If a man destroy the eye of another man, they shall destroy his eye.*

199. *If he destroy the eye of a man's slave or break a bone of a man's slave, he shall pay one-half his price.*

200. *If a man knock out the tooth of a man of his own rank, they shall knock out his tooth.*

206. *If a man strike another man in a quarrel and wound him, he shall swear, "I struck him without intent," and he shall pay for the physician.*

229. *If a builder build a house for a man and does not make its construction sound, and the house which he has built collapses and causes the death of the owner of the house, the builder shall be put to death.*

▲ Babylon's King Hammurabi

ANALYZING THE DOCUMENT

Use the excerpts above to answer the following questions.

1. Which of the following statements best describes the penalties in Hammurabi's Code?

   A Punishment should be equal to the crime or offense.

   B Punishment should be greater than the crime or offense.

   C Punishment should be decided by the judge and the victim.

   D Punishment should be swift.

2. According to the excerpts above, which of the following statements was true of the society in which these laws were written?

   A Children were required to be obedient to their fathers.

   B Builders were not responsible for their work.

   C Governors were not responsible for robberies in their cities.

   D People could not be sold as slaves or servants.

3. *Critical Thinking:* Drawing Conclusions In what ways do you think law number 23 above would influence a governor's actions?

Confucius: *Analects*

The *Analects* are a collection of 497 verses recorded by Confucius' followers long after his death (perhaps in the fourth century B.C.). Confucius' teachings emphasize duty and responsibility as a means of ensuring social order and good government.

> *T*he Master said, He who rules by moral force is like the pole-star, which remains in its place while all the lesser stars do homage to it.
>
> The Master said, If out of the three hundred Songs I had to take one phrase to cover all my teaching, I would say 'Let there be no evil in your thoughts.'
>
> Mêng Wu Po asked about the treatment of parents. The Master said, Behave in such a way that your father and mother have no anxiety about you, except concerning your health.
>
> Tzu-kung asked about the true gentleman. The Master said, He does not preach what he practices till he has practiced what he preaches.
>
> The Master said, A gentleman can see a question from all sides without bias. The small man is biased and can see a question only from one side.
>
> The Master said, Yu, shall I teach you what knowledge is? When you know a thing, to recognize that you know it, and when you do not know a thing, to recognize that you do not know it. That is knowledge.
>
> Chi K'ang-tzu asked whether there were any form of encouragement by which he could induce the common people to be respectful and loyal. The Master said, Approach them with dignity, and they will respect you. Show piety towards your parents and kindness towards your children, and they will be loyal to you. Promote those who are worthy, train those who are incompetent; that is the best form of encouragement.

The *Analects* are a collection of sayings that emphasize education and self-sacrifice as the keys to becoming a superior person.

DOCUMENTS

▲ Confucius and his students

ANALYZING THE DOCUMENT

Use the excerpts above to answer the following questions.

1. According to the excerpts, which one saying did Confucius pick to best summarize his teachings?

   A Be kind to your father and mother.

   B Let there be no evil in your thoughts.

   C Do not preach what you do not practice.

   D A gentleman can see a question from all sides without bias.

2. Confucius describes a gentleman as one who—

   A is knowledgeable.

   B is respectful and loyal.

   C can understand more than one point of view on a question or issue.

   D can distinguish those who are worthy from those who are incompetent.

3. *Critical Thinking:* **Identifying Main Ideas** Use your own words to describe Confucius' definition of knowledge.

◆ **DOCUMENT IN BRIEF**

This speech by the Athenian leader Pericles is one of the most famous defenses of democracy of all time.

Thucydides: *History of the Peloponnesian War*

This excerpt from Thucydides' *History of the Peloponnesian War* records a speech made by the Athenian leader Pericles in honor of those who died fighting Sparta in the first year of the war (431 B.C.). In the speech, Pericles describes the superior qualities of Athenian democracy as compared to life in Sparta.

For our government is not copied from those of our neighbors: we are an example to them rather than they to us. Our constitution is named a democracy, because it is in the hands not of the few but of the many. But our laws secure equal justice for all in their private disputes, and our public opinion welcomes and honors talent in every branch of achievement, not for any sectional reason but on grounds of excellence alone. And as we give free play to all in our public life, so we carry the same spirit into our daily relations with one another . . .

We are lovers of beauty without extravagance, and lovers of wisdom without unmanliness. Wealth to us is not mere material for vainglory but an opportunity for achievement; and poverty we think it no disgrace to acknowledge but a real degradation to make no effort to overcome. Our citizens attend both to public and private duties, and do not allow absorption in their own various affairs to interfere with their knowledge of the city's. We differ from other states in regarding the man who holds aloof from public life not as 'quiet' but as useless; we decide or debate, carefully and in person, all matters of policy, holding, not that words and deeds go ill together, but that acts are foredoomed to failure when undertaken undiscussed. For we are noted for being at once adventurous in action and most reflective beforehand. Other men are bold in ignorance, while reflection will stop their onset. But the bravest are surely those who have the clearest vision of what is before them, glory and danger alike, and yet notwithstanding go out to meet it. . . . In a word I claim that our city as a whole is an education to Greece, and that her members yield to none, man by man, for independence of spirit, many-sidedness of attainment, and complete self-reliance in limbs and brain.

▲ Athena, goddess of wisdom

ANALYZING THE DOCUMENT

Use the excerpt above to answer the following questions.

1. Pericles defines democracy as a system based on—

   A equal justice for all.

   B the say of all people, not just a few.

   C beauty and wisdom.

   D free play in public life.

2. According to Pericles, a good citizen is one who—

   A participates fully in public debate.

   B is quiet during public debate.

   C acts boldly without being delayed by discussion.

   D attends exclusively to his own business.

3. *Critical Thinking:* **Synthesizing Information** What does Pericles mean when he states that Athens is "an education to Greece"?

Aristotle:
The Politics

DOCUMENT IN BRIEF

The Politics describes the characteristics of an ideal state as well as practical matters relating to the preservation and improvement of government.

The Greek philosopher Aristotle (384–322 B.C.), was a student of Plato. Like Plato, Aristotle was suspicious of democracy, which he thought could lead to mob rule. Instead, Aristotle favored rule by a single strong and virtuous leader. In this excerpt from *The Politics,* Aristotle outlines the forms of government and discusses the strengths and weaknesses of each form.

First let us consider what is the purpose of a state and how many forms of government there are by which human society is regulated. We have already said, earlier in this treatise . . . that man is by nature a political animal. And therefore men, even when they do not require one another's help, desire to live together all the same, and are in fact brought together by their common interests. . . . Well-being is certainly the chief end of individuals and of states. . . .

The conclusion is evident: governments which have a regard to the common interest are constituted in accordance with strict principles of justice, and are therefore true forms; but those which regard only the interest of the rulers are all defective and perverted forms. For they are despotic, whereas a state is a community of free men. . . .

We call that form of government in which one rules, and which regards the common interest, kingship or royalty; that in which more than one, but not many, rule, aristocracy. It is so called, either because the rulers are the best men, or because they have at heart the best interest of the state and of the citizens. But when the citizens at large administer the state for the common interest, the government is called by the generic name—constitutional government. . . .

Of the above-mentioned forms, the perversions are as follows: of royalty, tyranny; of aristocracy, oligarchy; of constitutional government, democracy. For tyranny is a kind of monarchy which has in view the interest of the monarch only; oligarchy has in view the interest of the wealthy; democracy, of the needy; none of them the common good of all.

▲ Democracy crowning the people of Athens

ANALYZING THE DOCUMENT

Use the excerpt above to answer the following questions.

1. The form of government in which more than one, but not many, rule is known as—

   A kingship or royalty.

   B aristocracy.

   C constitutional government.

   D tyranny.

2. Which of the following does Aristotle describe as the corrupt form of aristocracy?

   A tyranny

   B oligarchy

   C monarchy

   D democracy

3. *Critical Thinking:* Identifying Main Ideas
   What does Aristotle mean when he states that "man is by nature a political animal"?

Asoka: *Edicts*

▲ Pillar of Asoka

During his rule of Maurya India beginning in 268 B.C., Asoka converted to Buddhism, rejected violence, and resolved to rule by moral example. Asoka had stone pillars set up across India announcing laws, or edicts, and describing the just actions of his government. The following are excerpts from several of the pillars.

This world and the other are hard to gain without great love of Righteousness, great self-examination, great obedience, great circumspection, great effort. Through my instruction respect and love of Righteousness daily increase and will increase. . . . For this is my rule— to govern by Righteousness, to administer by Righteousness, to please my subjects by Righteousness, and to protect them by Righteousness.

Whoever honors his own [religion] and disparages another man's, whether from blind loyalty or with the intention of showing his own [religion] in a favorable light, does his own [religion] the greatest possible harm. Concord is best, with each hearing and respecting the other's teachings. It is the wish of the [king] that members of all [religions] should be learned and should teach virtue.

All the good deeds that I have done have been accepted and followed by the people. And so obedience to mother and father, obedience to teachers, respect for the aged, kindliness . . . to the poor and weak, and to slaves and servants, have increased and will continue to increase. . . . And this progress of Righteousness . . . has taken place in two manners, by enforcing conformity to Righteousness, and by exhortation [urging or pleading]. I have enforced the law against killing certain animals and many others, but the greatest progress of Righteousness . . . comes from exhortation in favor of noninjury to life and abstention from killing living beings.

I have done this that it may endure . . . as long as the moon and sun, and that my sons and my great-grandsons may support it; for by supporting it they will gain both this world and the next.

ANALYZING THE DOCUMENT

Use the excerpt above to answer the following questions.

1. The excerpt provides evidence that Asoka favored—

   A animal sacrifices.

   B war.

   C daily rituals.

   D religious tolerance.

2. Based on the passage you can tell that Asoka was probably—

   A a vegetarian.

   B a monk.

   C a dictator.

   D a judge.

3. *Critical Thinking:* **Drawing Conclusions** Which of his actions does Asoka view as the best promotion of Righteousness? Why do you think this is so?

Magna Carta

A group of barons forced King John of England to sign the Magna Carta at Runnymede in 1215. The barons were tired of the king's military campaigns and heavy taxes. The purpose of the document was to limit the power of the monarch and to secure rights such as trial by jury, due process of law, and protection against the arbitrary taking of life, liberty, or property. Below are excerpts from 5 of its 63 articles.

DOCUMENTS

2. *We also have granted to all the freemen of our kingdom, for us and for our heirs [those who inherit a title or property] forever, all the underwritten liberties, to be had and holden by them and their heirs, of us and our heirs forever. . . .*

12. *No scutage [tax] or aid shall be imposed in our kingdom, unless by the general council of our kingdom; except for ransoming our person, making our eldest son a knight and once for marrying our eldest daughter; and for these there shall be paid no more than a reasonable aid.*

14. *And for holding the general council of the kingdom concerning the assessment of aids, except in the three cases aforesaid, and for the assessing of scutage, we shall cause to be summoned the archbishops, bishops, abbots, earls, and greater barons of the realm, singly by our letters. And furthermore, we shall cause to be summoned generally, by our sheriffs and bailiffs all others who hold of us in chief, for a certain day, that is to say, forty days before their meeting at least, and to a certain place. And in all letters of such summons we will declare the cause of such summons. And summons being thus made, the business shall proceed on the day appointed, according to the advice of such as shall be present, although all that were summoned come not.*

39. *No freeman shall be taken or imprisoned, or diseised [deprived], or outlawed, or banished, or in any way destroyed . . . unless by the lawful judgment of his peers, or by the law of the land.*

40. *We will sell to no man, we will not deny to any man, either justice or right.*

▲ King Edward I and the Great Council

ANALYZING THE DOCUMENT

Use the excerpt above to answer the following questions.

1. In article 2 the king grants the rights described in the document to—

   A only those freemen who have heirs.

   B his own heirs.

   C all freemen and their heirs for all time.

   D all freemen currently living in England.

2. Article 14 forces the king to consult a great council before raising new taxes. The article also prevents the king from—

   A holding unannounced meetings or meetings on short notice.

   B summoning the general council to make laws regarding taxation.

   C consulting with the general council before calling a meeting.

   D summoning the sheriffs and bailiffs.

3. **Critical Thinking: Making Inferences**
   What does article 40 imply about royal corruption during this period of English history?

◆ DOCUMENT
  IN BRIEF

In his *Discourses*, Machiavelli describes methods for establishing and preserving republics.

Niccolò Machiavelli: *Discourses*

Niccolò Machiavelli (1469-1527) is best known for a system of power politics in which "the ends justify the means," as described in his book *The Prince*. However, in his book *Discourses on the First Ten Books of Titus Livy*, Machiavelli concludes that the best-governed state is ruled by the people rather than by a ruthless prince.

*I*n short, to bring this topic to conclusion, I say that, just as princely forms of government have endured for a very long time, so, too, have republican forms of government; and that in both cases it has been essential for them to be regulated by laws. For a prince who does what he likes is a lunatic; and a populace which does what it likes is unwise. If, therefore, it be a question of a prince subservient to the laws and of a populace chained up by laws, more virtue will be found in the populace than in the prince; and if it be a question of either of them loosed from control by the law, there will be found fewer errors in the populace than in the prince, and these of less moment and much easier to put right. For a licentious [disregarding rules] and turbulent populace, when a good man can obtain a hearing, can easily be brought to behave itself; but there is no one to talk to a bad prince, nor is there any remedy except the sword. . . .

When the populace has thrown off all restraint, it is the not the mad things it does that are terrifying, nor is it of present evils that one is afraid, but of what may come of them, for amidst such confusion there may come to be a tyrant. In the case of bad princes it is just the opposite: it is present evils that are terrifying, but for the future there is hope, since men are convinced that the evil ways of a bad prince may make for freedom in the end. . . . The reason why people are prejudiced against the populace is because of the populace anyone may speak ill without fear and openly, even when the populace is ruling. But of princes people speak with the utmost trepidation and the utmost reserve.

▲ Lorenzo de Médici, Renaissance Prince

ANALYZING THE DOCUMENT

Use the excerpt above to answer the following questions.

1. Machiavelli states that the only way to bring an unruly prince under the law is to—

   A obtain a hearing.

   B use physical combat.

   C discuss the people's legal rights.

   D choose a tyrant.

2. Machiavelli concludes that the greatest threat posed by an unlawful populace is—

   A the rise of a dictator.

   B the violence of the mob.

   C the loss of a prince.

   D the destruction of property.

3. *Critical Thinking:* **Making Inferences** Why do you think Machiavelli believes that the populace is more subject to criticism than a prince?

King Affonso I:
Letter to King John of Portugal

DOCUMENT IN BRIEF

In his letter to the king of Portugal, King Affonso of Kongo pleads with the king to end the slave trade.

In 1490, the Portuguese converted the son of a Kongo king to Christianity and then helped him to assume his father's throne. The king, born Nzinga Mbemba, was renamed Affonso. King Affonso soon realized that his relationship with Portugal had extremely negative consequences, as can be seen from his letter in 1526 to King John of Portugal.

Sir, Your Highness of Portugal should know how our Kingdom is being lost in so many ways. This is caused by the excessive freedom given by your officials to the men and merchants who are allowed to come to this Kingdom to set up shops with goods and many things which have been prohibited by us. Many of our vassals, whom we had in obedience, do not comply because they have the things in greater abundance than we ourselves. It was with these things that we had them content and subjected under our jurisdiction, so it is doing a great harm not only to the service of God, but to the security and peace of our Kingdoms and State as well.

And we cannot reckon how great the damage is, since the mentioned merchants are taking every day our natives, sons of the land and the sons of our noblemen and vassals and our relatives. The thieves and men of bad conscience grab them wishing to have the things and wares of this Kingdom which they are ambitious of; they grab them and get them to be sold. And so great, Sir, is the corruption and licentiousness that our country is being completely depopulated, and your Highness should not agree with this nor accept it as in your service. And to avoid it we need from those your Kingdoms no more than some priests and a few people to teach in schools, and no other goods except wine and flour for the holy sacrament.

That is why we beg of Your Highness to help and assist us in this matter, commanding your factors that they should not send here either merchants or wares, because it is <u>our will that in these kingdoms there should not be any trade of slaves nor outlet for them.</u> Concerning what is referred to above, again we beg of Your Highness to agree with it. . . .

▲ West African ivory carving of Portuguese soldiers

ANALYZING THE DOCUMENT

Use the excerpt above to answer the following questions.

1. Which of the following best describes the author's purpose for writing this letter?

   A to ask the king for money to help in ending the slave trade

   B to inform the king of the abuses taking place and to ask for his help in ending them

   C to inform the king about the extent of trade taking place in the kingdom

   D to ask the king for an explanation for why people are being enslaved

2. What does Affonso request of King John in the last paragraph?

   A that he not send any merchants or wares

   B that he send teachers

   C that he send priests

   D that he pray for Affonso

3. *Critical Thinking:* Recognizing Causes and Effects According to King Affonso, how have the Portuguese affected his kingdom and state?

DOCUMENTS

DOCUMENT IN BRIEF

Bernal Díaz's history provides an account of the Aztec capital of Tenochtitlán before the Spanish conquest.

DOCUMENTS

Bernal Díaz: *The True History of the Conquest of New Spain*

Bernal Díaz del Castillo (c. 1492-1581) accompanied Hernan Cortés on his conquest of the Aztecs in present-day Mexico. Díaz wrote his history many years later to refute what he viewed as inaccurate accounts of the conquest. The following excerpt describes a meeting between Cortés and Moctezuma, the Aztec king, in the Aztec city of Tenochtitlán.

When we climbed to the top of the great [temple] there was a kind of platform, with huge stones where they put the poor Indians to be sacrificed, and an image like a dragon and other evil figures, with a great deal of blood that had been shed that day. Moctezuma, accompanied by two priests, came out from an oratory dedicated to the worship of his cursed idols. . . .

Then Moctezuma took him [Cortés] by the hand and bade him look at his great city and at all the other cities rising from the water, and the many towns around the lake. . . .

There we stood looking, for that large and evil temple was so high that it towered over everything. From there we could see all three of the causeways that led into Mexico. . . .

We saw the fresh water that came from Chapultepec, which supplied the city, and the bridges on the three causeways, built at certain intervals so the water could go from one part of the lake to another, and a multitude of canoes, some arriving with provisions and others leaving with merchandise. We saw that every house in this great city and in the others built on the water could be reached only by wooden drawbridges or by canoe. We saw temples built like towers and fortresses in these cities, all white-washed; it was a sight to see. . . .

After taking a good look and considering all that we had seen, we looked again at the great square and the throngs of people, some buying and others selling. The buzzing of their voices could be heard more than a league away. There were soldiers among us who had been in many parts of the world, in Constantinople and Rome and all over Italy, who said that they had never before seen a market place so large and so well laid out, and so filled with people.

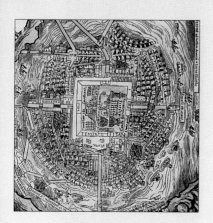

▲ Tenochtitlán

ANALYZING THE DOCUMENT

Use the excerpt above to answer the following questions.

1. The scene described in this excerpt is of—

   A a view of Tenochtitlán's market and surroundings from the top of a tall temple.

   B an indoor temple with many statues.

   C a view of Tenochtitlán's temple from the market place.

   D a view of the markets in Rome.

2. Which of the following best describes the author's view of the Aztecs?

   A generous and busy

   B evil and prosperous

   C loving and kind

   D athletic and loud

3. *Critical Thinking:* **Recognizing Points of View** Which words and phrases in the excerpt above reveal the author's opinion of the Aztec's religion?

The English Bill of Rights

When the Catholic king, James II, was forced from the English throne in 1688, Parliament offered the crown to his Protestant daughter Mary and her husband William of Orange. But Parliament insisted that William and Mary submit to a Bill of Rights. This document, a continuation of the struggle between the crown and Parliament, sums up the powers that Parliament had been seeking since the Petition of Right in 1628.

◆ DOCUMENT IN BRIEF

The English Bill of Rights ensured the superiority of Parliament over the king and queen.

Whereas, the late King James II. . .did endeavor to subvert and extirpate [eliminate] the Protestant religion and the laws and liberties of this kingdom. . .and whereas the said late King James II having abdicated the government, and the throne being vacant. . . .

The said lords [Parliament] . . . being now assembled in a full and free representative [body] of this nation . . . do in the first place . . . declare:

1. *That the pretended power of suspending of laws or the execution of laws by regal authority without consent of Parliament is illegal. . . .*

4. *That levying money for or to the use of the crown by pretense of prerogative [right] without grant of Parliament . . . is illegal;*

5. *That it is the right of the subjects to petition the king, and all commitments and prosecutions for such petitioning are illegal.*

6. *That . . . raising or keeping a standing army within the kingdom in time of peace, unless it be with consent of Parliament, is against law. . . .*

8. *That election of members of Parliament ought to be free. . . .*

9. *That the freedom of speech and debates or proceedings in Parliament ought not to be impeached [challenged] or questioned in any court or place out of Parliament. . . .*

10. *That excessive bail ought not to be required, nor excessive fines imposed, nor cruel and unusual punishments inflicted. . . .*

13. *And that, for redress of all grievances and for the amending, strengthening, and preserving of the laws, Parliaments ought to be held frequently. . . .*

ANALYZING THE DOCUMENT

Use the excerpts above to answer the following questions.

1. This Bill of Rights required the monarch to—

   A raise money for paying the members of Parliament.

   B summon Parliament regularly.

   C cancel laws he or she considered unjust.

   D keep a standing army to defend the country.

2. Which of the following statements best summarizes these excerpts from the Bill of Rights?

   A The King's powers are limited by the Parliament.

   B The Parliament's powers are limited by the monarch.

   C The Parliament's duty is to amend laws.

   D The King's powers are unlimited.

3. *Critical Thinking:* **Making Inferences** Why do you think the members of Parliament included item 9 above? Why do you think this item was important?

DOCUMENTS

DOCUMENT IN BRIEF

In this essay Locke states that the primary purpose of government is to protect the natural rights of people.

John Locke:
Two Treatises on Government

English philosopher John Locke (1632-1704) published *Two Treatises on Government* in 1690. In the writings Locke holds that all people possess natural rights, including property and personal freedom. Locke also states that governments hold their power only with the consent of the people. Locke's ideas heavily influenced revolutions in America and France.

*B*ut though men, when they enter into society give up the equality, liberty, and executive power they had in the state of Nature into the hands of society . . . the power of the society or legislative constituted by them can never be supposed to extend farther than the common good. . . . [W]hoever has the legislative or supreme power of any commonwealth, is bound to govern by established standing laws, promulgated and known to the people, and not by extemporary decrees, by indifferent [unbiased] and upright judges, who are to decide controversies by those laws; and to employ the force of the community at home only in the execution of such laws, or abroad to prevent or redress foreign injuries and secure the community from inroads and invasion. And all this to be directed to no other end but the peace, safety, and public good of the people. . . .

The reason why men enter into society is the preservation of their property; and the end while they choose and authorize a legislative is that there may be laws made, and rules set, as guards and fences to the properties of all the society, . . .

Whensoever, therefore, the legislative [power] shall transgress this fundamental rule of society, and either by ambition, fear, folly, or corruption, endeavor to grasp themselves, or put into the hands of any other, an absolute power over the lives, liberties, and estates of the people, by this breach of trust they forfeit the power the people had put into their hands for quite contrary ends, and it devolves [passes] to the people; who have a right to resume their original liberty, and by the establishment of a new legislative (such as they shall think fit), provide for their own safety and security, which is the end which they are in society. . . .

▲ John Locke

ANALYZING THE DOCUMENT

Use the excerpts above to answer the following questions.

1. Which of the following groups has the final authority of government in Locke's opinion?

   A the legislature

   B the prince

   C the people

   D the judges

2. Which of the following statements best summarizes the excerpts above?

A People should give up their fundamental rights in order to establish absolute monarchies.

B People establish governments in order to set and enforce laws. If a government does not do this, the people may abolish it.

C Most legislative powers are corrupt.

D Judges may need to act outside the law.

3. ***Critical Thinking:*** **Making Inferences**
According to Locke, what do people give up when they enter into a society ? Why do you think people do this?

Jean-Jacques Rousseau:
The Social Contract

DOCUMENT IN BRIEF

In consenting to form a government, Rousseau says, individuals choose to give up their self-interest in favor of the common good.

In *The Social Contract*, Rousseau (1712-1778) proposes an ideal society formed through a "social contract," and based on the natural will of the people. Rousseau believed that people in their natural state were basically good but were corrupted by the evils of society. The first lines of *The Social Contract*, "Man is born free, but is everywhere in chains," reflect this idea.

" *Find a form of association that defends and protects the person and goods of each associate with all the common force, and by means of which each one, uniting with all, nevertheless obeys only himself and remains as free as before."* This is the fundamental problem which is solved by the social contract. . . .

[F]irst of all, since each one gives his entire self, the condition is equal for everyone, and since the condition is equal for everyone, no one has an interest in making it burdensome for the others. . . .

If, then, everything that is not the essence of the social compact is set aside, one will find that it can be reduced to the following terms: Each of us puts his person and all his power in common under the supreme direction of the general will; and in a body we receive each member as an indivisible part of the whole.

Instantly, in place of the private person of each contracting party, this act of association produces a moral and collective body, composed of as many members as there are voices in the assembly, which receives from this same act its unity, its common self, its life, and its will. This public person, formed thus by the union of all the others, formerly took the name <u>City</u>, and now takes that of <u>Republic</u> or <u>body politic</u>, which its members call <u>State</u> when it is passive, <u>Sovereign</u> when active, <u>Power</u> when comparing it to similar bodies. As for the associates, they collectively take the name <u>People</u>; and individually are called <u>Citizens</u> as participants in the sovereign authority, and <u>Subjects</u> as subjects to the laws of the State. . . .

▲ Jean-Jacques Rousseau

ANALYZING THE DOCUMENT

Use the excerpt above to answer the following questions.

1. The "social contract" provides a solution to the problem of finding a form of government in which—

   A people's differences can be solved peacefully.

   B people remain as free as they were without government.

   C people are not subject to unjust laws.

   D minorities are protected.

2. The *Republic* or *body politic* is defined as the—

   A assembly.

   B collective body that comes into being when people dissolve the social contract.

   C collective body that comes into being when private persons enter the social contract.

   D moral and collective body appointed by the king.

3. *Critical Thinking:* **Drawing Conclusions**
   Why does Rousseau believe that people are safe putting themselves under the direction of the "general will"?

This declaration, written in 1789 in France, states the natural rights of citizens and establishes the equality of all citizens before the law.

Declaration of the Rights of Man and of the Citizen

The French National Assembly issued this document in 1789 after having overthrown the established government in the early stages of the French Revolution. The document was modeled in part on the English Bill of Rights and on the American Declaration of Independence.

Therefore the National Assembly recognizes and proclaims, in the presence and under the auspices of the Supreme Being, the following rights of man and of the citizen:

1. *Men are born and remain free and equal in rights. Social distinctions may be founded only upon the general good.*

2. *The aim of all political association is the preservation of the natural and imprescriptible [inviolable] rights of man. These rights are liberty, property, security, and resistance to oppression.*

4. *Liberty consists in the freedom to do everything which injures no one else. . . .*

5. *Law can only prohibit such actions as are hurtful to society. . . .*

6. *Law is the expression of the general will. Every citizen has a right to participate personally, or through his representative, in its formation. It must be the same for all, whether it protects or punishes. All citizens, being equal in the eyes of the law, are equally eligible to all dignities and to all public positions and occupations, according to their abilities, and without distinction except that of their virtues and talents.*

7. *No person shall be accused, arrested, or imprisoned except in the cases and according to the forms prescribed by law.*

9. *As all persons are held innocent until they shall have been declared guilty, if arrest shall be deemed indispensable, all harshness not essential to the securing of the prisoner's person shall be severely repressed by law.*

11. *The free communication of ideas and opinions is one of the most precious of the rights of man. Every citizen may, accordingly, speak, write, and print with freedom. . . .*

13. *A common contribution is essential for the maintenance of the public [military] forces and for the cost of administration. This should be equitably distributed among all the citizens in proportion to their means.*

▲ Declaration of Rights

ANALYZING THE DOCUMENT

Use the excerpts above to answer the following questions.

1. Which article above specifically protects citizens from police brutality and torture?

   A 5   B 6
   C 9   D 11

2. Which of the following describes the tax policy set forth in this document?

A All citizens pay the same amount of tax.

B Only citizens in the military pay taxes.

C All citizens pay taxes in proportion to their wealth.

D There should be no taxes imposed on citizens.

3. **Critical Thinking: Applying Information** Give one real-life example of each of the four natural rights listed under article 2 above.

Olympe de Gouges:
Declaration of the Rights of Woman and the Female Citizen

DOCUMENT IN BRIEF

In this document French journalist Olympe de Gouges demands equal rights for women.

DOCUMENTS

Born Marie Gouze, Olympe de Gouges did not believe the Declaration of the Rights of Man had gone far enough. In 1791 she wrote the Declaration of the Rights of Woman demanding equal rights for women. De Gouges was guillotined in 1793 in part because of her royalist politics and in part because of her ideas about women's rights.

1. *Woman is born free and lives equal to man in her rights. . . .*

2. *The purpose of any political association is the conservation of the natural and imprescriptible rights of woman and man; these rights are liberty, property, security, and especially resistance to oppression.*

6. *The law must be the expression of the general will; all female and male citizens must contribute either personally or through their representatives to its formation. It must be the same for all. . . .*

7. *No woman is an exception; she is accused, arrested, and detained in cases determined by law. Women, like men, obey this rigorous law.*

9. *Once any woman is declared guilty, complete rigor is [to be] exercised by the law.*

10. *No one is to be disquieted for his very basic opinions; woman has the right to mount the scaffold; she must equally have the right to mount the rostrum, provided that her demonstrations do not disturb the legally established public order.*

16. *No society has a constitution without the guarantee of rights and the separation of powers; the constitution is null if the majority of individuals comprising the nation have not cooperated in drafting it.*

17. *Property belongs to both sexes whether united or separate. . . . Woman, wake up; the tocsin [alarm bell] of reason is being heard throughout the whole universe; discover your rights. . . . When will you cease to be blind? What advantage have you received from the Revolution? A more pronounced scorn, a more marked disdain. . . . The reclamation of your patrimony [inheritance], based on the wise decrees of nature—what have you to dread from such a fine undertaking?*

▲ Women's march on Versailles

ANALYZING THE DOCUMENT

Use the excerpts above to answer the following questions.

1. Which of the above articles specifically states a woman's right to speak publicly?

    A 2   B 6

    C 7   D 10

2. Why does de Gouges state that the constitution is not valid?

A Women have not cooperated in drafting it.

B It does not guarantee property rights to women.

C Women are not treated with respect.

D Women are subject to unjust arrest.

3. ***Critical Thinking:* Recognizing Causes and Effects** Why do you think de Gouges included article 9 above which implies that women should not be given special treatment if found guilty of a crime?

DOCUMENT IN BRIEF

In this decree Miguel Hidalgo calls for an end to slavery and an end to heavy taxes on the poor in Mexico.

Miguel Hidalgo:
Decree of Hidalgo

Father Miguel Hidalgo of Mexico called for freedom from Spanish rule in 1810. The following decree, also issued in 1810 from Guadalajara, Jalisco, was an attempt to gain additional support for the uprising from Native Americans, blacks, and mestizos. In the end, Hidalgo's rebellion failed because creoles feared that more rights for Native Americans and an end to slavery would cost them power. Less than one year after the start of the uprising, Hidalgo was captured and executed, and his followers scattered.

From the happy moment that the valiant American nation took up arms to shake off the heavy yoke that has oppressed it for three centuries, one of the principal objectives has been to extinguish such duties that cannot advance its fortune, especially those which in these critical circumstances do not well serve that end or provide for the real need of the kingdom in meeting the costs of the struggle, so therefore there is now put forward here the most urgent remedy in the following declarations:

1. *That all owners of slaves shall give them their freedom before the end of ten days, under penalty of death, which shall be applied to those who violate this article.*

2. *That from now on the collection of tributes according to caste [race] shall cease, as shall exactions that are demanded of the Indians.*

3. *That all legal business, documents, letters and actions can be on common paper, with the requirement of the seal totally abolished.*

▲ Mural by Diego Rivera (Hidalgo is the white-haired man at the center)

ANALYZING THE DOCUMENT

Use the excerpt above to answer the following questions.

1. Item 2 above calls for an end to—

   A slavery.

   B collection of any taxes.

   C collection of taxes based on race.

   D all business transactions with Indians.

2. What does "the seal" probably symbolize in item 3 above?

   A approval from Spanish authorities

   B a postage stamp

   C a special type of paper

   D Native American traditions

3. *Critical Thinking:* **Defending a Position**
   Describe some of the "natural rights" Hidalgo could have listed in his decree as explanations for why he wished to abolish slavery, taxes based on race, and the requirement of the seal.

Simón Bolívar:
Address to the Congress of Venezuela

In this address Simón Bolívar offers the Venezuelan Congress advice on what type of government to establish in Venezuela.

DOCUMENTS

Encouraged by the revolutions in British North America and France, colonists in Spanish South America soon began to create a force for independence. Simón Bolívar was one of the leaders of this movement. The excerpt below, from Bolívar's Address to the Second National Congress of Venezuela, was given in 1819.

Subject to the threefold yoke of ignorance, tyranny, and vice, the American people have been unable to acquire knowledge, power, or [civic] virtue. The lessons we received and the models we studied, as pupils of such pernicious teachers, were most destructive. . . .

If a people, perverted by their training, succeed in achieving their liberty, they will soon lose it, for it would be of no avail to endeavor to explain to them that happiness consists in the practice of virtue; that the rule of law is more powerful than the rule of tyrants, because, as the laws are more inflexible, everyone should submit to their beneficent austerity; that proper morals, and not force, are the bases of law; and that to practice justice is to practice liberty. Therefore, Legislators, your work is so much the more arduous, inasmuch as you have to reeducate men who have been corrupted by erroneous illusions and false incentives. Liberty, says Rousseau, is a succulent morsel, but one difficult to digest. . . .

Legislators, meditate well before you choose. Forget not that you are to lay the political foundation for a newly born nation which can rise to the heights of greatness that Nature has marked out for it if you but proportion this foundation in keeping with the high plane that it aspires to attain. Unless your choice is based upon the peculiar . . . experience of Venezuelan people—a factor that should guide you in determining the nature and form of government you are about to adopt for the well-being of the people . . . the result of our reforms will again be slavery.

▲ Simón Bolívar

ANALYZING THE DOCUMENT

Use the excerpt above to answer the following questions.

1. According to Bolívar, the people of Latin America—

   A have not been well prepared for self-government by the Spanish.

   B have been well prepared for self-government by the Spanish.

   C have been ruled well by the Spanish.

   D have little desire for self-government.

2. Bolívar states that a government will be most effective if it—

   A adheres closely to theories of good government.

   B imitates the structure of other successful governments.

   C is molded to fit the character of the nation for which it is built.

   D is based on the rule of law.

3. **Critical Thinking: Defending a Position** Would you describe Bolívar as practical or idealistic? Use examples from the excerpt to defend your opinion.

◆ **DOCUMENT IN BRIEF**

In this interview Gandhi explains the ideas behind his nonviolent method of passive resistance.

Mohandas Gandhi: *Hind Swaraj*

Mohandas Gandhi led a successful, peaceful revolution in India against British rule. In the following excerpt from his book *Hind Swaraj (Indian Home Rule)*, published in 1938, Gandhi explains the ideas behind his nonviolent method of passive resistance in the form of an imaginary conversation between an editor and a reader.

EDITOR: *Passive resistance is a method of securing rights by personal suffering; it is the reverse of resistance by arms. When I refuse to do a thing that is repugnant to my conscience, I use soul-force. For instance, the Government of the day has passed a law which is applicable to me. I do not like it. If by using violence I force the Government to repeal the law, I am employing what may be termed body-force. If I do not obey the law and accept the penalty for its breach, I use soul-force. It involves sacrifice of self.*

Everybody admits that sacrifice of self is infinitely superior to sacrifice of others. Moreover, if this kind of force is used in a cause that is unjust, only the person using it suffers. He does not make others suffer for his mistakes. . . . No man can claim that he is absolutely in the right or that a particular thing is wrong because he thinks so, but it is wrong for him so long as that is his deliberate judgment. It is therefore meet [proper] that he should not do that which he knows to be wrong, and suffer the consequence whatever it may be. This is the key to the use of soul-force.

READER: *You would then disregard laws—this is rank disloyalty. We have always been considered a law-abiding nation. You seem to be going even beyond the extremists. They say that we must obey the laws that have been passed, but that if the laws be bad, we must drive out the lawgivers even by force.*

EDITOR: *Whether I go beyond them or whether I do not is a matter of no consequence to either of us. We simply want to find out what is right and to act accordingly. The real meaning of the statement that we are a law-abiding nation is that we are passive resisters. When we do not like certain laws, we do not break the heads of law-givers but we suffer and do not submit to the laws.*

▲ Mohandas Gandhi

ANALYZING THE DOCUMENT

Use the excerpt above to answer the following questions.

1. What is the goal of a person who practices passive resistance?

   A to bring about peaceful reform or change

   B to gain support for violence

   C to discover truth

   D to injure wrongdoers

2. The author defines soul-force as—

   A weapons used for peaceful purposes.

   B refusal to obey a law that is unjust and accepting the penalty.

   C obeying all laws while working to overthrow the lawmakers.

   D trying to determine what is right.

3. ***Critical Thinking:* Understanding Sequence** What does Gandhi mean when he says that a person using soul force "does not make others suffer for his mistakes"?

Franklin D. Roosevelt:
The Four Freedoms

DOCUMENT IN BRIEF

In this speech Franklin D. Roosevelt describes the four "essential human freedoms": freedom of speech and worship, and freedom from want and fear.

Franklin D. Roosevelt delivered the following address to Congress in January 1941 after having been elected to a third term as president of the United States. In the speech he described the "four freedoms" which he hoped would be secured throughout the world. As he spoke, most of Europe had already fallen to Hitler's tyranny and Great Britain was struggling against the threat of German invasion.

In the future days, which we seek to make secure, we look forward to a world founded upon four essential human freedoms.

The first is freedom of speech and expression—everywhere in the world.

The second is freedom of every person to worship God in his own way—everywhere in the world.

The third is freedom from want—which translated into world terms, means economic understandings which will secure to every nation a healthy peace time life for its inhabitants—everywhere in the world.

The fourth is freedom from fear—which translated into world terms, means a worldwide reduction of armaments to such a point and in such a thorough fashion that no nation will be in a position to commit an act of physical aggression against any neighbor—anywhere in the world. . . .

Since the beginning of our American history we have been engaged in change—in a perpetual peaceful revolution—a revolution which goes on steadily, quietly adjusting itself to changing conditions—without the concentration camp or the quick-lime in the ditch. The world order which we seek is the cooperation of free countries, working together in a friendly civilized society.

This nation has placed its destiny in the hands and heads and hearts of its millions of free men and women; and its faith in freedom under the guidance of God. Freedom means the supremacy of human rights everywhere. Our support goes to those who struggle to gain those rights or keep them. Our strength is in our unity of purpose.

To that high concept there can be no end save victory.

▲ Franklin D. Roosevelt

ANALYZING THE DOCUMENT

Use the excerpt above to answer the following questions.

1. Being able to make a living and support one's family is an example of—

    A freedom of speech.

    B freedom of worship.

    C freedom from want.

    D freedom from fear.

2. Roosevelt thinks the nation's strength comes from—

    A citizens worshipping together.

    B citizens working together for a common purpose.

    C its support for other nations.

    D carrying out peaceful revolutions.

3. ***Critical Thinking:* Applying Information** Describe some of the specific actions that would be necessary to secure Roosevelt's description of "freedom from fear."

DOCUMENT IN BRIEF

The Universal Declaration of Human Rights sets forth the basic liberties and freedoms to which all people are entitled.

The Universal Declaration of Human Rights

The General Assembly of the United Nations adopted this declaration on December 10, 1948. They hoped that it would become a standard by which liberty and freedom could be judged throughout the world.

Article 1   *All human beings are born free and equal in dignity and rights. They are endowed with reason and conscience and should act towards one another in a spirit of brotherhood.*

Article 2   *Everyone is entitled to all the rights and freedoms set forth in this Declaration, without distinction of any kind, such as race, colour, sex, language, religion, political or other opinion, national or social origin, property, birth or other status. . . .*

Article 3   *Everyone has the right to life, liberty and security of person.*

Article 4   *No one shall be held in slavery or servitude. . . .*

Article 5   *No one shall be subjected to torture or to cruel, inhuman or degrading treatment or punishment.*

Article 9   *No one shall be subjected to arbitrary arrest, detention or exile.*

Article 13   *Everyone has the right to freedom of movement. . . .*

Article 18   *Everyone has the right to freedom of thought, conscience and religion. . . .*

Article 19   *Everyone has the right to freedom of opinion and expression. . . .*

Article 20   *Everyone has the right to freedom of peaceful assembly and association. . . .*

Article 23   *Everyone has the right to work, to free choice of employment, to just and favourable conditions of work and to protection against unemployment.*

Article 25   *Everyone has the right to a standard of living adequate for the health and well-being of himself and of his family, including food, clothing, housing and medical care and necessary social services, and the right to security in the event of unemployment, sickness, disability, widowhood, old age or other lack of livelihood. . . .*

Article 26   *Everyone has the right to education. Education shall be free, at least in the elementary and fundamental stages.*

▲ Vietnamese refugee

ANALYZING THE DOCUMENT

Use the excerpts above to answer the following questions.

1. Which of the following articles grants a person the right to leave and return to their country?

   A Article 4

   B Article 5

   C Article 13

   D Article 18

2. Which of the following articles grants a person the right to live free from hunger?

   A Article 1

   B Article 9

   C Article 23

   D Article 25

3. **Critical Thinking:** Drawing Conclusions In what ways might the existence of this declaration benefit people living under an oppressive government?

Mao Zedong:
The People's Democratic Dictatorship

In this speech, given in 1949 on the anniversary of the founding of the Communist Party, Mao Zedong explains the philosophy that guided China under his leadership. Mao's ideas were heavily influenced by the communist philosopher Karl Marx.

Who are the "people"? At the present stage in China, they are the working class, the peasantry, the petty bourgeoisie and the national bourgeoisie.

Under the leadership of the working class and the Communist Party, these classes unite to create their own state and elect their own government so as to enforce their dictatorship over the henchmen of imperialism—the landlord class and bureaucratic capitalist class. . . . The people's government will suppress such persons. It will only permit them to behave themselves properly. It will not allow them to speak or act wildly. Should they do so, they will be instantly curbed and punished. The democratic system is to be carried out within the ranks of the people, giving them freedom of speech, assembly and association. The right to vote is given only to the people, not to the reactionaries.

These two things, democracy for the people and dictatorship for the reactionaries, when combined, constitute the people's democratic dictatorship.

Why must things be done in this way? Everyone is very clear on this point. If things were not done like this, the revolution would fail, the people would suffer and the state would perish. . . .

Our present task is to strengthen the people's state apparatus—meaning principally the people's army, the people's police and the people's courts—thereby safeguarding national defence and protecting the people's interests. Given these conditions, China, under the leadership of the working class and the Communist Party, can develop steadily from an agricultural into an industrial country and from a New Democratic into a Socialist and, eventually, Communist society, eliminating classes and realizing universal harmony.

▲ Mao Zedong

ANALYZING THE DOCUMENT

Use the excerpt above to answer the following questions.

1. Who are the "reactionaries"?

   A the peasants

   B the bourgeoisie

   C the landlords and capitalists

   D the working class

2. According to Mao, the Communist Party represents the interests of—

   A the landlords.

   B the capitalists.

   C the imperialists.

   D the working class.

3. *Critical Thinking:* **Making Inferences** Why do you think the "people's government" denies some groups of people the right to free speech?

Kwame Nkrumah: *Autobiography*

Kwame Nkrumah led the people of Gold Coast in their quest for independence from Britain. After succeeding in 1957, Nkrumah became the first prime minister and renamed the country Ghana. In this excerpt from his *Autobiography*, Nkrumah speaks of the need to establish economic independence as a means of maintaining political independence.

Independence for the Gold Coast was my aim. It was a colony, and I have always regarded colonialism as the policy by which a foreign power binds territories to herself by political ties, with the primary object of promoting her own economic advantage. No one need be surprised if this system has led to disturbances and political tension in many territories. There are few people who would not rid themselves of such domination if they could. . . .

I saw that the whole solution to [our] problem lay in political freedom for our people, for it is only when a people are politically free that other races can give them the respect that is due them. It is impossible to talk of equality of races in any other terms. No people without a government of their own can expect to be treated on the same level as people of independent sovereign states. It is far better to be free to govern or misgovern yourself than to be governed by anybody else. . . .

Once freedom is gained, a greater task comes into view. All dependent territories are backward in education, in science, in agriculture, and in industry. The economic independence that should follow and maintain political independence demands every effort from the people, a total mobilization of brain and manpower resources. What other countries have taken three hundred years or more to achieve, a once dependent territory must try to accomplish in a generation if it is to survive.

ANALYZING THE DOCUMENT

Use the excerpt above to answer the following questions.

1. How does the author define colonialism?

    A a balanced political alliance

    B a balanced economic alliance

    C a ruling country helping residents of a colony

    D a ruling country interested in its own economic gain

2. Nkrumah viewed political independence as a means of gaining—

    A respect from other sovereign states.

    B great personal wealth.

    C a better system of education.

    D better resources.

3. **Critical Thinking: Recognizing Causes and Effects** Nkrumah states that newly independent countries must establish economic independence with great speed if they are to survive. Give reasons to support this statement.

Andrei Sakharov:
Nobel Peace Prize Lecture

DOCUMENT IN BRIEF

In this lecture Sakharov states that intellectual freedom is essential to progress and human rights.

Andrei Sakharov was a Soviet physicist and a leading Soviet dissident. He was awarded the Nobel Peace Prize in 1975 for his efforts to limit nuclear testing, end human rights abuses, and protect intellectual freedom. Because of his outspokenness he was exiled in a remote Soviet city from 1980 to 1986.

Peace, progress, human rights—these three goals are indissolubly linked: it is impossible to achieve one of them if the others are ignored. This idea provides the main theme of my lecture. . . .

I am convinced that international trust, mutual understanding, disarmament, and international security are inconceivable without an open society with freedom of information, freedom of conscience, the right to publish, and the right to travel and choose the country in which one wishes to live. I am also convinced that freedom of conscience, together with other civic rights, provides both the basis for scientific progress and a guarantee against its misuse to harm mankind, as well as the basis for economic and social progress. . . .

We cannot reject the idea of a spreading use of the results of medical research or the extension of research in all its branches, including bacteriology and virology, neurophysiology, human genetics, and gene surgery, no matter what potential dangers lurk in their abuse and the undesirable social consequences of this research. . . . It is quite clear that in the hands of irresponsible bureaucratic authorities operating secretly, all this research may prove exceptionally dangerous, but at the same time it may prove extremely important and necessary to mankind, if it is carried out under public supervision and discussion and socio-scientific analysis. . . .

Freedom of conscience, the existence of an informed public opinion, a pluralistic system of education, freedom of the press, and access to other sources of information—all these are in very short supply in the socialist countries. . . . At the same time these conditions are a vital necessity, not only to avoid all witting or unwitting abuse of progress, but also to strengthen it.

▲ Andrei Sakharov

ANALYZING THE DOCUMENT

Use the excerpt above to answer the following questions.

1. Sakharov states that scientific research must continue despite the risks that its findings may be misused because—

   A it may prove to be extremely important to people.

   B it is human nature to want to explore the unknown.

   C bureaucratic authorities depend on it.

   D it may lead to mutual international understanding.

2. In this excerpt, an "open society"—

   A encourages optimism.

   B allows a free flow of ideas.

   C allows authorities to operate secretly.

   D sees progress as a vital necessity.

3. *Critical Thinking:* **Identifying Main Ideas** What roles do public opinion, freedom of the press, and access to information play in protecting against the misuse of technology?

DOCUMENTS

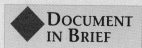

▲ Lech Walesa

Lech Walesa:
Nobel Peace Prize Lecture

Lech Walesa organized an independent trade union in Poland known as Solidarity. After a successful strike by Solidarity members in 1980, the Communist Polish government granted the workers many new rights and higher wages. A year later, however, the gains were withdrawn and Solidarity was outlawed. Lech Walesa was awarded the Nobel Peace Prize in 1983 for his work promoting freedom in Poland. This lecture was delivered at a time when Solidarity was still illegal.

May I repeat that the fundamental necessity in Poland is now understanding and dialogue. I think that the same applies to the whole world: we should go on talking, we must not close any doors or do anything that would block the road to an understanding. And we must remember that only peace built on the foundations of justice and moral order can be a lasting one.

In many parts of the world the people are searching for a solution which would link the two basic values: peace and justice. The two are like bread and salt for mankind. Every nation and every community have the inalienable right to these values. No conflicts can be resolved without doing everything possible to follow that road. Our times require that these aspirations which exist the world over must be recognized.

Our efforts and harsh experiences have revealed to the world the value of human solidarity. Accepting this honourable distinction I am thinking of those with whom I am linked by the spirit of solidarity.

—first of all, of those who in the struggle for the workers' and civic rights in my country paid the highest price—the price of life;

—of my friends who paid for the defence of "Solidarity" with the loss of freedom, who were sentenced to prison terms or are awaiting trial;

—of my countrymen who saw in the "Solidarity" movement the fulfillment of their aspirations as workers and citizens, who are subjected to humiliations and ready for sacrifices, who have learn[ed] to link courage with wisdom and who persist in loyalty to the cause we have embarked upon;

—of all those who are struggling throughout the world for workers' and union rights, for the dignity of a working man, for human rights.

ANALYZING THE DOCUMENT

Use the excerpt above to answer the following questions.

1. Walesa feels that the Polish workers' efforts have taught the world the value of—

   A justice.

   B peace.

   C human solidarity.

   D hard work.

2. What were the members of Solidarity struggling for?

   A government loyalty

   B shorter prison terms

   C workers' and civic rights

   D bread and salt

3. **Critical Thinking: Defending a Position**
   Do you agree with the idea that the only way to build a lasting peace is to establish justice?

Octavio Paz:
Latin America and Democracy

Octavio Paz, a Mexican poet, philosopher, and diplomat, won the Nobel Prize for Literature in 1990. The following excerpt is from his book, *One Earth, Four or Five Worlds: Reflections on Contemporary History*.

DOCUMENT IN BRIEF

In this essay Paz states that democracy is necessary for social and economic reform in Latin America.

DOCUMENTS

*L*atin American democracy was a late arrival on the scene, and it has been disfigured and betrayed time and time again. It has been weak, hesitant, rebellious, its own worst enemy, all too eager to worship the demagogue, corrupted by money, riddled with favoritism and nepotism [appointing relatives]. And yet almost everything good that has been achieved in Latin America in the last century and a half has been accomplished under democratic rule, or, as in Mexico, a rule heading toward democracy. A great deal still remains to be done. Our countries need changes and reforms, at once radical and in accord with the tradition and the genius of each people. In countries where attempts have been made to change the economic and social structures while at the same time dismantling democratic institutions, injustice, oppression, and inequality have become stronger forces than ever. The cause of the workers requires, above all else, freedom of association and the right to strike, yet this is the very first thing that their liberators strip them of. Without democracy, changes are counterproductive; or, rather, they are not changes at all.

To repeat again, for on this point we must be unyielding: changes are inseparable from democracy. To defend democracy is to defend the possibility of change; in turn, changes alone can strengthen democracy and enable it to be embodied in social life. This is a tremendous, twofold task. Not only for Latin Americans: for all of us. The battle is a worldwide one. What is more, the outcome is uncertain, dubious. No matter: the battle must be waged.

ANALYZING THE DOCUMENT

Use the excerpt above to answer the following questions.

1. The author states that workers need—

   A higher wages.

   B. democracy.

   C change.

   D freedom of association and the right to strike.

2. Which of the following is the *best summary* of the passage?

   A Democracy is the best system for change.

   B Democracy is too flawed to be successful.

   C Democratic institutions cannot be dismantled.

   D Reforms must be made in keeping with the people's traditions.

3. ***Critical Thinking:*** **Recognizing Causes and Effects** According to the author, how have nondemocratic attempts at reform influenced Latin America?

▲ Mikhail Gorbachev

Mikhail Gorbachev: *Perestroika*

Mikhail Gorbachev's economic and political reforms paved the way for the independence of Eastern Europe, the breakup of the Soviet Union, and the end of the Cold War. In the following speech delivered in 1989, Gorbachev asks the people of the Soviet Union to maintain confidence in the changes brought about by perestroika despite the difficulties and criticisms of the program.

Good evening, comrades, I am here to talk to you about our current affairs. The situation in the country is not simple. We all know and feel this. Everything has become entangled in a tight knot: Scarcity on the consumer goods market, conflicts in ethnic relations, and difficult and sometimes painful processes in the public consciousness, resulting from the overcoming of distortions and from the renewal of socialism. People are trying to understand where we have found ourselves at the moment, evaluating the pluses and minuses of the path we have covered during the last four-plus years, the development of democracy and the pace of the economic and political reforms. . . .

Some are ready to give up perestroika and return to the past. Others, who consider themselves "active reformers," want to head perestroika onto the path of rash decisions and hasty projects, prompted by ambition rather than concern for real progress. . . .

True, perestroika is meeting with many difficulties. But it is radical change, a revolution in the economy and in policy, in the ways of thinking and in people's consciousness, in the entire pattern of our life. Besides, we have not been able to avoid mistakes in our practical actions in the course of perestroika. But perestroika has opened up realistic opportunities for society's renewal, for giving society a new quality and for creating truly humane and democratic socialism. It has returned to the great nation a sense of dignity and given the Soviet people a sense of freedom. It is a powerful source of social, spiritual, and, I should say, patriotic energy for decades to come.

That is why we must do everything to continue perestroika on the basis of the ideas and principles proclaimed by the party. And we must not allow those who are using the difficulties we have met to impose on society doubts about the correctness of the path we have chosen.

ANALYZING THE DOCUMENT

Use the excerpt above to answer the following questions.

1. Gorbachev states that the "active reformers" want to—

   A return to the past.

   B end the policy of perestroika.

   C speed up the pace of reforms under perestroika.

   D further debate the policy of perestroika.

2. Which of the following statements best *summarizes* this excerpt?

   A Perestroika imposes too many reforms on society.

   B Perestroika is a great source of dignity.

   C Perestroika must continue despite mistakes and criticism.

   D Perestroika does not allow for enough freedom.

3. *Critical Thinking:* **Recognizing Bias** How does Gorbachev discredit the ideas of "active reformers" in this excerpt?

Vaclav Havel:
New Year's Address

◆ DOCUMENT IN BRIEF

In this speech Havel calls citizens to be active participants in their new democracy.

DOCUMENTS

Vaclav Havel was a leading dissident and human rights activist in communist-led Czechoslovakia. When the "democracy movement" swept through Eastern Europe in 1989, Havel was elected president. In the following speech delivered on January 1, 1990, Havel asks the citizens of Czechoslovakia to accept responsibility for their past and to move forward in building a democracy.

Our country is not flourishing. The enormous creative and spiritual potential of our nations is being wasted. Entire branches of industry produce goods that are of no interest to anyone, while we lack the things we need. . . . We now have the most contaminated environment in all of Europe. . . .

But all this is not even the main problem. The worst thing is that we live in a contaminated moral environment. We have fallen morally ill because we became used to saying one thing and thinking another. We have learned not to believe in anything, to ignore each other, to care only about ourselves. Notions such as love, friendship, compassion, humility, or forgiveness have lost their depth and dimensions. . . . Only a few of us managed to cry out loud that the powers-that-be should not be all-powerful. . . .

We have all become used to the totalitarian system and accepted it as an immutable fact, thus helping to perpetuate it. In other words, we are all . . . responsible for the creation of the totalitarian machinery. . . .

Why do I say this? It would be very unwise to think of the sad legacy of the last forty years as something alien or something inherited from a distant relative. On the contrary, we have to accept this legacy as something we have inflicted on ourselves. If we accept it as such, we will understand that it is up to all of us, and only us, to do something about it. We cannot blame the previous rulers for everything—not only because it would be untrue, but also because it could weaken our sense of duty, our obligation to act independently, freely, sensibly, and quickly. Let us not be mistaken: even the best government in the world, the best parliament, and the best president cannot do much on their own. And in any case, it would be wrong to expect a cure-all from them alone. Freedom and democracy, after all, require everyone to participate and thus to share responsibility.

ANALYZING THE DOCUMENT

Use the excerpt above to answer the following questions.

1. What does Havel mean by "contaminated moral environment"?

    A People are dishonest and disinterested.

    B People are disrespectful of the environment.

    C People are unwise and unruly.

    D People have no respect for the law.

2. According to Havel, why must everyone participate in the new democracy?

    A to correct the wrongs of the past

    B to share responsibility

    C to prevent totalitarianism

    D to prevent environmental pollution

3. *Critical Thinking:* **Recognizing Causes and Effects** Why does Havel want people to accept responsibility for the totalitarian machinery of the past?

◆ DOCUMENT
IN BRIEF

In this speech Vargas Llosa describes what is needed to sustain democracy in Latin America.

Mario Vargas Llosa: *Latin America, The Democratic Option*

In this speech delivered in 1990, Peruvian writer Mario Vargas Llosa (1936–) describes the changes that are needed to maintain and extend democracy in Latin America.

*T*he democratization of Latin America, even though it has today an unprecedented popular base, is very fragile. To maintain and extend this popular base, governments will have to prove to their citizens that democracy means not only the end of political brutality but progress—concrete benefits in areas such as labor, health, and education, where so much remains to be done. But, given Latin America's current economic crisis, when the prices of its exports are hitting record lows and the weight of its foreign debt is crushing, those governments have virtually no alternative but to demand that their citizens—especially the poor—make even greater sacrifices than they've already made. . . . A realistic and ethically sound approach that our creditors could take would be to demand that each debtor nation pay what it can without placing its stability in jeopardy. . . .

If we want democracy to take hold in our countries, our most urgent task is to broaden it, give it substance and truth. Democracy is fragile in so many countries because it is superficial, a mere framework within which institutions and political parties go about their business in their traditionally arbitrary, bullying way. . . .

Perhaps the hardest struggle we Latin Americans will have will be against ourselves. Centuries of intolerance, of absolute truths, of despotic governments, weigh us down—and it won't be easy to shake that burden off. The tradition of absolute power that began with our pre-Columbian empires, and the tradition that might makes right that the Spanish and Portuguese explorers practiced, were perpetuated in the nineteenth century, after our independence, by our caudillos [military dictators] and our oligarchies, often with the blessing or direct-intervention of foreign powers.

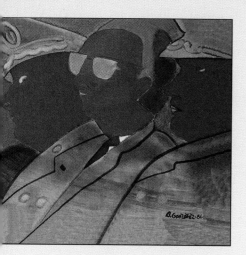

▲ *The Parrots,* by Colombian artist Beatriz González

ANALYZING THE DOCUMENT

Use the excerpt above to answer the following questions.

1. The author states that democratic governments in Latin America have to provide—

   A real improvements in labor, health, and education.

   B higher incomes.

   C less bureaucracy.

   D greater income from exports.

2. The author states that many democratic governments are fragile because—

   A they lack authoritative governments.

   B they do not always act democratically.

   C they lack international support.

   D they lack strong political parties.

3. ***Critical Thinking:*** **Identifying Main Ideas**
   In the last paragraph the author describes what he thinks may be the greatest obstacle to democracy in Latin America. Restate the main idea of that paragraph in your own words.

Aung San Suu Kyi:
Freedom from Fear

DOCUMENT IN BRIEF

In this essay Aung San Suu Kyi describes the roles of fear and courage when living under an oppressive government.

Aung San Suu Kyi, leader of Burma's National League for Democracy and winner of the Nobel Peace Prize, has worked courageously for human rights and democracy in Burma. Because of her opposition to Burma's ruling military junta, she was held under house arrest from 1989 to 1995 and again in 1997.

Fearlessness may be a gift but perhaps more precious is the courage acquired through endeavour, courage that comes from cultivating the habit of refusing to let fear dictate one's actions, courage that could be described as 'grace under pressure'—grace which is renewed repeatedly in the face of harsh, unremitting pressure.

Within a system which denies the existence of basic human rights, fear tends to be the order of the day. Fear of imprisonment, fear of torture, fear of death, fear of losing friends, family, property or means of livelihood, fear of poverty, fear of isolation, fear of failure. A most insidious [more dangerous than seems evident] form of fear is that which masquerades as common sense or even wisdom, condemning as foolish, reckless, insignificant or futile the small, daily acts of courage which help to preserve man's self-respect and inherent human dignity. It is not easy for a people conditioned by fear under the iron rule of the principle that might is right to free themselves from the enervating [weakening] miasma [pollution] of fear. Yet even under the most crushing state machinery courage rises up again and again, for fear is not the natural state of civilized man.

The wellspring [source] of courage and endurance in the face of unbridled power is generally a firm belief in the sanctity of ethical principles combined with a historical sense that despite all setbacks the condition of man is set on an ultimate course for both spiritual and material advancement. . . . It is man's vision of a world fit for rational, civilized humanity which leads him to dare and to suffer to build societies free from want and fear. Concepts such as truth, justice and compassion cannot be dismissed as trite [meaningless] when these are often the only bulwarks [defenses] which stand against ruthless power.

ANALYZING THE DOCUMENT

Use the excerpt above to answer the following questions.

1. According to the author, why do people work against all odds to build societies free from want and fear?

   A because they have a dream of a just world

   B because they dismiss truth and justice as trite

   C because they are powerless

   D because they wish to gain courage

2. What are the sources of courage according to the author?

   A power and history

   B belief in ethical principles and a sense that progress is inevitable

   C belief in truth and compassion

   D power and endurance

3. *Critical Thinking:* **Applying Information** Describe one or more examples of a person refusing to let fear dictate his or her actions.

DOCUMENTS

Nelson Mandela: *Glory and Hope*

Nelson Mandela delivered this speech after having been elected president in South Africa's first multiracial elections in 1994. Knowing that the injustices of apartheid would not be easily erased, Mandela asked the people to work together for peace and justice.

Today, all of us do, by our presence here, and by our celebrations . . . confer glory and hope to newborn liberty.

Out of the experience of an extraordinary human disaster that lasted too long must be born a society of which all humanity will be proud.

Our daily deeds as ordinary South Africans must produce an actual South African reality that will reinforce humanity's belief in justice, strengthen its confidence in the nobility of the human soul and sustain all our hopes for a glorious life for all. . . .

The time for the healing of the wounds has come. . . .

The time to build is upon us.

We have, at last, achieved our political emancipation. We pledge ourselves to liberate all our people from the continuing bondage of poverty, deprivation, suffering, gender and other discrimination.

We have triumphed in the effort to implant hope in the breasts of the millions of our people. We enter into a covenant that we shall build the society in which all South Africans, both black and white, will be able to walk tall, without any fear in their hearts, assured of the inalienable right to human dignity—a rainbow nation at peace with itself and the world. . . .

We understand it still that there is no easy road to freedom.

We know it well that none of us acting alone can achieve success.

We must therefore act together as a united people, for national reconciliation, for nation building, for the birth of a new world.

Let there be justice for all. Let there be peace for all. Let there be work, bread, water, and salt for all. . . . The sun shall never set on so glorious a human achievement!

▲ Nelson Mandela

ANALYZING THE DOCUMENT

Use the excerpt above to answer the following questions.

1. In this speech Mandela is celebrating—

   A the birth of a new, free nation.

   B decades of peace and justice in South Africa.

   C years of racial justice.

   D the end of violence.

2. Which of the following best summarizes the excerpt?

   A We must find work for all South Africans.

   B We must not take the path of violence.

   C We must now finish the work of freedom that we have started.

   D We must correct the evils of the past through severe punishments.

3. *Critical Thinking:* Making Inferences
   Having achieved political freedom, what further "freedoms" does Mandela call for in his speech?

Harry Wu: *The Outlook for China, Human Rights*

DOCUMENT IN BRIEF

In this speech Wu describes the state of communism in China and the country's system of forced labor camps.

Author and human rights activist Harry Wu was imprisoned in China for 19 years because of his criticisms of the Communist regime. The excerpt below is from a speech Wu delivered in 1996.

Sometimes people ask me, "What are you fighting for?" And my answer is quite simple. I want to see the word laogai in every dictionary in every language in the world; I want to see the laogai ended. . . .

The economic boom made possible by capitalism makes profits for both the West and China. But despite the huge profits earned by China's external trade, ordinary people enjoy only a tiny part. The communist government puts most of the profits into upgrading its weapons systems, into internal and external political activities, and into maintaining the nation's political stability. . . .

Today, a specter is hovering over Mainland China—capitalism. Communism is dead; it is no longer believed in by the Chinese in general nor even by the majority of Communist Party members. The "capitalistic" economic boom has made the superstructure of the communist regime appear pretty on the outside, but its pillars are heavily damaged. Looming in front of China are some huge crises.

At the core of the human rights question in China today is China's fundamental machinery for crushing human beings physically, psychologically and spiritually: the laogai camp system, of which we have identified 1,100 camps. It is also an integral part of the national economy. Its importance is illustrated by some basic facts: one third of China's tea is produced in laogai camps; 60 percent of China's rubber vulcanizing chemicals are produced in a single laogai camp in Shanghai; the first and second chain hoist works in the country to receive direct export authority are laogai camps in Zhejiang Province; one of the largest and earliest exporters of hand tools is a camp in Shanghai; an unknown but significant amount of China's cotton crop is grown by prisoners. I could go on and on and on. . . . The laogai is not simply a prison system, it is a political tool for maintaining the Communist Party's totalitarian rule.

▲ A call for democracy in China

ANALYZING THE DOCUMENT

Use the excerpt above to answer the following questions.

1. What is a laogai?

   A a labor camp for prisoners

   B a warehouse for exports

   C a chemical plant

   D a tea or cotton plantation

2. The "damaged pillars" described in the second paragraph are a symbol of—

   A the noncommunist leadership.

   B the communist regime's lack of true support by the people.

   C the economy of the country.

   D the Chinese prison system.

3. ***Critical Thinking:*** **Synthesizing Information** Why do you think the author describes the laogai as "a political tool for maintaining the Communist Party's totalitarian rule"?

GLOSSARY

This Glossary defines many important terms and phrases. Some terms are phonetically respelled to aid in pronunciation. See the Pronunciation Key below for an explanation of the respellings. The page number following each definition is the page on which the term or phrase is first discussed in the text. All terms that appear in blue type in the text are included in this Glossary.

PRONUNCIATION KEY When difficult terms or names first appear in the text, they are respelled to aid in pronunciation. A syllable in small capital letters receives the most stress. The key below lists the letters used for respelling. It includes examples of words using each sound and shows how they are respelled.

SYMBOL	EXAMPLE	RESPELLING
a	hat	(hat)
ay	pay, late	(pay), (layt)
ah	star, hot	(stahr), (haht)
ai	air, dare	(air), (dair)
aw	law, all	(law), (awl)
eh	met	(meht)
ee	bee, eat	(bee), (eet)
er	learn, sir, fur	(lern), (ser), (fer)
ih	fit	(fiht)
ī	mile	(mīle)
ir	ear	(ir)
oh	no	(noh)
oi	soil, boy	(soil), (boi)
oo	root, rule	(root), (rool)
or	born, door	(born), (dor)
ow	plow, out	(plow), (owt)
u	put, book	(put), (buk)
uh	fun	(fuhn)
yoo	few, use	(fyoo), (yooz)
ch	chill, reach	(chihl), (reech)
g	go, dig	(goh), (dihg)
j	jet, gently, bridge	(jeht), (JEHNT lee), (brihj)
k	kite, cup	(kīt), (kuhp)
ks	mix	(mihks)
kw	quick	(kwihk)
ng	bring	(brihng)
s	say, cent	(say), (sehnt)
sh	she, crash	(shee), (krash)
th	three	(three)
y	yet, onion	(yeht), (UHN yuhn)
z	zip, always	(zihp), (AWL wayz)
zh	treasure	(TREH zher)

A

abdicate to give up a high office (p. 501)

absolute monarch ruler with complete authority over the government and lives of the people he or she governs (p. 422)

acropolis (uh KRAHP uh lihs) hilltop fortress of an ancient Greek city-state (p. 108)

ahimsa (uh HIM sah) Hindu belief in nonviolence (p. 79)

alchemy (AL kuh mee) medieval science whose aim was to transform ordinary metals into gold (p. 92)

annex to add a territory onto an existing state or country (p. 497)

annul to cancel or invalidate (p. 358)

anti-Semitism prejudice against Jews (p. 200)

apartheid policy of strict racial separation in South Africa; abolished in 1989 (p. 602)

apprentice young person learning a trade from a master (p. 204)

aqueduct in ancient Rome, bridgelike stone structure that carried water from the hills into the cities (p. 142) ▲

archaeology (ahr kee AHL uh jee) study of the lives of early people through examination of their physical remains (p. 4)

archipelago (ahr kuh PEHL uh goh) chain of islands (p. 323)

aristocracy in Greek city-states, government headed by a privileged minority or upper class (p. 109)

artifact object made by human beings (p. 4)

artisan skilled craftworker (p. 14)

astrolabe instrument used to determine latitude by measuring the position of the stars (p. 372) ▲

atman (AHT muhn) in Hindu belief, a person's essential self (p. 78)

autocrat ruler who has complete authority (p. 239)

autonomy self-rule (p. 529)

B

balance of power distribution of military and economic power that prevents any one nation from becoming too strong (p. 429)

baroque ornate style of art and architecture popular in the 1600s and 1700s (p. 464)

barter economy system in which one set of goods or services is exchanged for another (p. 40)

bias prejudice for or against someone or something (p. 390)

bishop in the early Christian Church, a high-ranking Church official with authority over a local area, or diocese (p. 147)

blockade the shutting off of a port to keep people or supplies from moving in or out (p. 498)

bourgeoisie (boor zhwah ZEE) the middle class (p. 481)

boyar landowning noble in Russia under the czars (p. 247)

brahman according to Aryan belief, the single spiritual power that resides in all things (p. 55)

bureaucracy system of managing government through departments run by appointed officials (p. 14)

bushido (BOO shee doh) code of conduct for samurai during the feudal period in Japan (p. 327)

GLOSSARY

C

caliph successor to Muhammad as political and religious leader of the Muslims (p. 257)

calligraphy beautiful handwriting (p. 61)

canon law body of laws of a church (p. 196)

capital money for investment (p. 202)

capitalism economic system in which the means of production are privately owned and operated for profit (p. 412)

caravel improved type of sailing ship in the 1400s (p. 372)

cartographer mapmaker (p. 372)

caste in traditional Indian society, unchangeable social group into which a person is born (p. 55)

cataract waterfall (p. 22)

charter in the Middle Ages, a written document that set out the rights and privileges of a town (p. 202)

chivalry code of conduct for knights during the Middle Ages (p. 193)

circumnavigate to travel all the way around the Earth (p. 377)

city-state political unit made up of a city and the surrounding lands (p. 16)

civil law body of law dealing with private rights of individuals (p. 38)

clan group of families with a common ancestor (p. 60)

colony territory settled and ruled by people from another land (p. 42)

comedy in ancient Greece, play that mocked people or social customs (p. 120)

common law system of law based on court decisions that became accepted legal principles (p. 211)

communism form of socialism advocated by Karl Marx; according to Marx, class struggle was inevitable and would lead to the creation of a classless society in which all wealth and property would be owned by the community as a whole (p. 522)

conquistador (kahn KEES tuh dor) name for the Spanish explorers who claimed lands in the Americas for Spain in the 1500s and 1600s (p. 394)

constitutional government a government whose power is defined and limited by law (p. 467)

consul in ancient Rome, official from the patrician class who supervised the government and commanded the armies (p. 131)

covenant binding agreement (p. 44)

creole person in Spain's colonies in the Americas who was an American-born descendant of Spanish settlers (p. 399)

crusade holy war (p. 218)

cultural diffusion the spread of ideas, customs, and technologies from one people to another (p. 17)

cuneiform (kyoo NEE uh form) wedge-shaped writing of the ancient Sumerians and other ancient peoples (p. 35) ▲

czar title of the ruler of the Russian empire (p. 247)

D

daimyo (DĪ myoh) warrior lords directly below the shogun in feudal Japan (p. 327)

deficit spending situation in which a government spends more money than it takes in (p. 481)

delta triangular area of marshland formed by deposits of silt at the mouth of some rivers (p. 22)

democracy government in which the people hold ruling power (p. 110)

demotic system of ancient Egyptian writing, simpler than hieroglyphics, that was developed for everyday use (p. 29)

desertification process by which fertile or semi-desert land becomes desert (p. 286)

dharma (DAHR muh) in Hindu belief, an individual's religious and moral duties (p. 79)

diaspora (dī AS puh ruh) the scattering of the Jewish people from their homeland in Palestine (p. 45)

GLOSSARY

dictator ruler who has complete control over a government; in ancient Rome, a leader appointed to rule for six months in times of emergency (p. 131)

direct democracy system of government in which citizens participate directly rather than through elected representatives (p. 114)

dissident someone who speaks out against the government (p. 595)

divine right belief that a ruler's authority comes directly from God (p. 423)

dynastic cycle rise and fall of Chinese dynasties according to the Mandate of Heaven (p. 62)

dynasty ruling family (p. 23)

E

émigré (EHM ih gray) person who flees his or her country for political reasons (p. 488)

empire group of states or territories controlled by one ruler (p. 16)

enclosure in England in the 1700s, the process of taking over and fencing off public lands (p. 509)

encomienda right the Spanish government granted to its American colonists to demand labor or tribute from Native Americans (p. 398)

enlightened despot absolute ruler who uses his or her power to bring about political and social change (p. 463)

entrepreneur person who assumes financial risks in the hope of making a profit (p. 412)

ethics moral standards of behavior (p. 45)

ethnic group large group of people who share the same language and cultural heritage (p. 249)

excommunication exclusion from the Roman Catholic Church as a penalty for refusing to obey Church laws (p. 196)

F

factory place in which workers and machines are brought together to produce large quantities of goods (p. 514)

feudalism (FYOOD uhl ihz uhm) loosely organized system of government in which local lords governed their own lands but owed military service and other support to a greater lord (p. 62)

fief (FEEF) in the Middle Ages, an estate granted by a lord to a vassal in exchange for service and loyalty (p. 192)

filial piety respect for parents (p. 90)

free market market in which goods are bought and sold without restrictions (p. 460)

G

geography study of people, their environments, and their resources (p. 6)

ghetto separate section of a city where members of a minority group are forced to live (p. 362)

glacier thick sheet of ice that covered parts of the Earth during the ice age (p. 9)

gravity force that tends to pull one mass or object to another (p. 365)

griot (GREE oh) professional storyteller in early West Africa (p. 301)

guerrilla warfare fighting carried on through hit-and-run raids (p. 499)

guild in the Middle Ages, association of merchants or artisans who cooperated to protect their economic interests (p. 203)

H

habeas corpus principle that a person cannot be held in prison without first being charged with a specific crime (p. 435)

haiku form of Japanese poetry that expresses a feeling, thought, or idea in three lines, or 17 syllables (p. 330)

hajj pilgrimage to Mecca that all Muslims are expected to make at least once in their lifetime (p. 258)

hangul alphabet that uses symbols to represent the sounds of spoken Korean (p. 322)

heliocentric based on the belief that the sun is the center of the universe (p. 364)

heresy religious belief that is contrary to the official teachings of a church (p. 148)

hierarchy (HĪ uhr ahr kee) system of ranks (p. 34)

hieroglyphics (hī er oh GLIHF ihks) form of picture writing developed by the ancient Egyptians (p. 29)

hijra Muhammad's flight from Mecca to Medina in 622 (p. 257)

historian person who studies how people lived in the past (p. 5)

humanism intellectual movement at the heart of the Italian Renaissance that focused on worldly subjects rather than on religious issues (p. 346)

I

icon holy image of Christ, the Virgin Mary, or a saint venerated in the Eastern Orthodox Church (p. 242) ▲

ideograph symbol that represents a thought or an idea (p. 61)

ideology system of thought and belief (p. 528)

indulgence in the Roman Catholic Church, pardon for sins committed during a person's lifetime (p. 354)

inflation economic cycle that involves a rise in prices linked to a sharp increase in the amount of money available (p. 412)

intendant official appointed by French king Louis XIV to govern the provinces (p. 428)

interdict in the Roman Catholic Church, excommunication of an entire region, town, or kingdom (p. 196)

J

joint family family organization in which several generations share a common dwelling (p. 88)

joint stock company private trading company in which shares are sold to investors to finance business ventures (p. 412)

jury group of people sworn to make a decision in a legal case (p. 211)

K

kabuki (kuh BOO kee) form of Japanese drama developed in the 1600s (p. 330)

kami spirit who was believed to be the original ancestor of an early Japanese clan (p. 324)

kana in the Japanese writing system, phonetic symbols representing syllables (p. 325)

karma in Hindu belief, all the actions that affect a person's fate in the next life (p. 79)

kiva large underground chamber used by the Anasazi for religious ceremonies (p. 170)

knight noble in Europe who served as a mounted warrior for a lord in the Middle Ages (p. 192)

L

laissez faire policy allowing business to operate with little or no government interference (p. 460)

latitude distance north or south of the Equator (p. 6)

legion basic unit of the ancient Roman army, made up of about 5,000 soldiers (p. 132)

legislature lawmaking body (p. 111)

legitimacy the principle by which monarchies that had been unseated by the French Revolution or Napoleon were restored (p. 503)

limited monarchy government in which a constitution or legislative body limits the monarch's powers (p. 435)

lineage group claiming a common ancestor (p. 299)

loess fine windblown yellow soil (p. 59)

longitude distance east or west of the Prime Meridian (p. 6)

M

manor during the Middle Ages in Europe, a lord's estate, which included one or more villages and the surrounding lands (p. 194)

martyr person who suffers or dies for his or her beliefs (p. 146)

matrilineal term for a family organization in which kinship ties are traced through the mother (p. 299)

mercantilism policy by which a nation sought to export more than it imported in order to build its supply of gold and silver (p. 413)

mercenary soldier serving in a foreign army for pay (p. 151)

messiah savior sent by God (p. 144)

mestizo person in Spain's colonies in the Americas who was of Native American and European descent (p. 399)

millet in the Ottoman empire, a religious community of non-Muslims (p. 276)

minaret slender tower of a mosque, from which Muslims are called to prayer (p. 264)

monarchy government in which a king or queen exercises central power (p. 108)

monopoly complete control of a product or business by one person or group (p. 95)

monotheistic believing in one God (p. 44)

monsoon seasonal wind; in India, the winter monsoon brings hot, dry weather and the summer monsoon brings rain (p. 50)

mosque Muslim house of worship (p. 258)

mulatto person in Spain's colonies in the Americas who was of African and European descent (p. 399)

mummification (muhm mih fih KAY shuhn) practice of preserving the bodies of the dead (p. 27)

mystic person who devotes his or her life to seeking spiritual truths (p. 55)

N

nationalism feeling of pride in and devotion to one's country (p. 493)

natural laws rules that govern human nature (p. 456)

natural rights rights that belong to all humans from birth (p. 457)

nirvana in Buddhism, union with the universe and release from the cycle of rebirth (p. 80)

nomad person who moves from place to place in search of food (p. 9)

nuclear family family unit consisting of parents and children (p. 299)

O

oligarchy government in which ruling power belongs to a few people (p. 109)

oracle bone bone used by priests in Shang China to predict the future (p. 61) ▲

oral history collection of people's remembrances about a time or an event (p. 444)

P

pacifism opposition to all war (p. 590)

pagoda multistoried Buddhist temple (p. 314)

papyrus (puh PĪ ruhs) plant that grows along the banks of the Nile; used by the ancient Egyptians to make a paperlike material (p. 29)

patriarch in the Byzantine empire, highest church official in a major city (p. 242)

patriarchal describing a family headed by the father or oldest male (p. 88)

patrician member of the landholding upper class in ancient Rome (p. 131)

patrilineal term for a family organization in which kinship ties are traced through the father (p. 299)

patron person who provides financial support for the arts (p. 346)

peninsular member of the highest class in Spain's colonies in the Americas (p. 399)

GLOSSARY

peon worker forced to labor for a landlord in order to pay off a debt (p. 398)

perestroika restructuring of the Soviet government and economy in the 1980s (p. 598)

perspective artistic technique used to give drawings and paintings a three-dimensional effect (p. 347)

phalanx in ancient Greece, a massive formation of heavily armed foot soldiers (p. 109)

pharaoh (FAIR oh) title of the rulers of ancient Egypt (p. 23)

philosophe member of a group of Enlightenment thinkers who tried to apply the methods of science to the improvement of society (p. 457)

physiocrat an Enlightenment thinker who searched for natural laws to explain economics (p. 460)

pictogram drawing used to represent a word (p. 16)

plantation large estate run by an owner or overseer and worked by laborers who live there (p. 398)

plebeian (plee BEE uhn) member of the lower class in ancient Rome, including farmers, merchants, artisans, and traders (p. 131)

plebiscite ballot in which voters have a direct say on an issue (p. 495)

polis city-state in ancient Greece (p. 108)

polytheistic believing in many gods (p. 14)

pope head of the Roman Catholic Church (p. 147)

potlatch ceremonial dinners given by wealthy Native Americans of the Northwest Coast (p. 173)

predestination idea that God long ago determined who will gain salvation (p. 357)

prehistory period of time before writing systems were invented (p. 4)

primary source firsthand information about people or events of the past, such as that found in a diary or legal document (p. 100)

prime minister head of the cabinet in a parliamentary government; usually the leader of the largest party in the legislature (p. 469)

proletariat the working class (p. 523)

prophet spiritual leader believed to be interpreting God's will (p. 45)

Q

quipu knotted strings used by Incan officials for record keeping (p. 166)

R

raj British rule of India (p. 386)

rajah elected chief of an Aryan tribe in ancient India (p. 55)

recant to give up one's views or beliefs (p. 355)

reincarnation in Hinduism, belief in the rebirth of the soul in another bodily form (p. 79)

republic system of government in which officials are chosen by the people (p. 130)

rhetoric art of skillful speaking (p. 116)

S

sacrament sacred ritual of the Roman Catholic Church (p. 196)

salon informal social gathering at which writers, artists, and philosophers exchanged ideas; originated in France in the 1600s (p. 462)

samurai member of the warrior class in Japanese feudal society (p. 327)

sans-culotte (sanz kyoo LAHT) working-class men and women who called for radical action in France during the French Revolution (p. 489)

satrap governor of a province in the Persian empire (p. 40)

savanna grassy plain with irregular patterns of rainfall (p. 284)

schism permanent division in a church (p. 242)

scholasticism in medieval Europe, school of thought that used logic and reason to support Christian belief (p. 225)

scribe in ancient civilizations, specially trained person who knew how to read and write and kept records (p. 16)

secondary source information about the past that is not based on direct experience (p. 100)

sect small religious group (p. 145)

secular having to do with worldly, rather than religious, matters (p. 195)

sepoy Indian soldier who served in an army set up by the French or English East India company (p. 386)

serf in medieval Europe, peasant bound to the lord's land (p. 194)

shogun in Japanese feudal society, supreme military commander who held more power than the emperor (p. 327)

silt rich soil carried by flooding rivers (p. 22)

slash-and-burn agriculture farming method in which forest and brush are cut down and burned to create planting fields (p. 298)

social contract agreement by which people give up their freedom to a powerful government in order to avoid chaos (p. 456)

socialism system in which the people as a whole rather than private individuals own all property and operate all businesses (p. 522)

steppe sparse, dry grassland (p. 17)

strait narrow water passage connecting two bodies of water (p. 105)

stupa large domelike Buddhist shrine (p. 85)

subcontinent large landmass that juts out from a continent (p. 50)

suffrage the right to vote (p. 490)

sultan Muslim ruler (p. 265)

T

tariff tax on imported goods (p. 414)

technology tools and skills people use to meet their basic needs (p. 4)

theocracy government run by church leaders (p. 357)

theology the study of religion (p. 224)

tithe payment to a church equal to one tenth of a person's income (p. 197)

tragedy in ancient Greece, a play that focused on human suffering and usually ended in disaster (p. 120)

tribune official in ancient Rome who was elected by the plebeians to protect their interests (p. 132)

tributary state independent state that has to acknowledge the supremacy of another state and pay tribute to its ruler (p. 308)

tribute payment that conquered peoples were forced to make to their conquerors (p. 162)

troubadour wandering poet in Europe in the Middle Ages (p. 193)

turnpike privately built road that charges a fee to travelers who use it (p. 514)

tyrant in ancient Greece, ruler who gained power by force (p. 110)

U

universal manhood suffrage right of all adult men to vote (p. 529)

urbanization movement of people from rural areas to cities (p. 516)

usury (YOO zhuh ree) practice of lending money at interest (p. 203)

utilitarianism idea that the goal of society should be to bring about the greatest happiness for the greatest number of people (p. 521)

V

vassal in medieval Europe, a lord who was granted land in exchange for service and loyalty to a greater lord (p. 192)

vernacular everyday language of ordinary people (p. 226)

veto power to block a government action (p. 132)

viceroy representative who ruled one of Spain's provinces in the Americas in the king's name (p. 397)

vizier chief minister who supervised the business of government in ancient Egypt (p. 23)

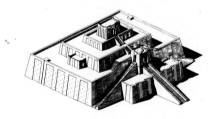

Z

ziggurat (ZIHG oo rat) pyramid-temple dedicated to the chief god or goddess of an ancient Sumerian city-state (p. 33)

CONNECTIONS WITH PRENTICE HALL LITERATURE

Topic	Author	Work/Genre	See Prentice Hall Literature *World Masterpieces*
Unit 1 Early Civilizations			
The Egyptian Empire, pages 24–25	unknown	I Think I'll Go Home and Lie Very Still (poetry)	page 33
Sumerian Civilization, pages 32–34	unknown	Enkindu's Dream of the Underworld (epic poetry)	page 19
A Covenant With God, pages 44–45	unknown	The Story of the Flood (biblical)	page 47
The Vedic Age, pages 53–55	unknown	The Mystery of the Brahman (hymn)	page 162
Unit 2 Empires of the Ancient World			
Hinduism: Unity and Diversity, pages 78–79	unknown	Numskull and the Rabbit (fable)	page 184
The Wisdom of Confucius, pages 90–91	unknown	I Beg of You, Chung Tze (poetry)	page 220
The Age of Homer, pages 105–107	Homer	The Quarrel of Achilleus and Agamemnon (epic poetry)	page 335
Unit 3 Regional Civilizations			
The Age of Charlemagne, pages 188–189	unknown	Song of Roland (epic poetry)	page 569
Lords, Vassals, and Knights, page 192	Chrétien de Troyes	The Grail (epic poetry)	page 602
Strong Monarchs in England, pages 210-211	Marie deFrance	The Lay of the Werewolf	page 612
The Brilliant Tang, pages 308–309	Li Bo (Li Po)	The River-Merchant's Wife: A Letter (poetry)	page 234
The Heian Period, pages 325–326	Sei Shonagon	The Pillow Book (sketches)	page 296
Unit 4 Early Modern Times			
Humanism, page 346	Francesco Petrarch	Laura (poetry)	page 676
Literature of the Northern Renaissance, pages 351–352	Christopher Marlowe	The Tragical History of the Life and Death of Dr. Faustus (play)	page 700
The Golden Century, pages 424–425	Miguel de Cervantes Saavedra	The Adventures of Don Quixote (fiction)	page 695
Unit 5 Enlightenment and Revolution			
A World of Progress and Reason, page 456	Jonathan Swift	A Modest Proposal (satirical essay)	page 801
Liberty, Equality, Fraternity, pages 485–486	Victor Hugo	The Expiation (poetry)	page 890
France After the Restoration, page 531	Charles Baudelaire	The Albatross (poetry)	page 905

CONNECTIONS CHARTS

CONNECTIONS WITH PRENTICE HALL SCIENCE

Topic	See Prentice Hall *Biology* or Prentice Hall *Chemistry*: *Connections to Our Changing World*

Unit 1 Early Civilizations

The First Farmers, pages 10–11 (planting seeds)	*Biology*, Seed Development, pages 540–542
Geography: The Nile Valley, page 22 (deserts)	*Biology*, Deserts, page 1015

Unit 2 Empires of the Ancient World

Golden Age of the Guptas, pages 85–87 (vaccinations)	*Biology*, Immunity, pages 973–975
Hellenistic Civilization, pages 124–125 (illnesses and cures)	*Biology*, What Is a Disease? pages 953–954

Unit 3 Regional Civilizations

A Land of Great Potential, page 186 (minerals)	*Biology*, Minerals, pages 847–858
The Black Death, pages 228–230 (plague)	*Biology*, How Is Infectious Disease Spread? page 954

Unit 4 Early Modern Times

More Scientific Advances, pages 366–367 (scientific method)	*Chemistry*, Scientific Method, pages 7–13
Bacon and Descartes, page 367 (blood circulation)	*Biology*, Blood, pages 905–907

Unit 5 Enlightenment and Revolution

A New Agricultural Revolution, pages 508–509 (soils)	*Biology*, Types of Soil, pages 487–488
The Age of Iron and Coal, page 513 (coal)	*Chemistry*, The Energy Crisis, pages 59–60

INDEX

INDEX

Eyck, Jan and Hubert van, 350
Ezana, king of Axum, 287, 294

Factory system, 514, 516–17
Family: African, 299, *p299*; Chinese, 311–12; in early modern age, 414; in India, 88–89, *p89*; joint family, 88–89; matrilineal family, 299, 379; medieval, 193, 194–95, 197; nuclear family, 299; patrilineal family, 299; Roman empire, 138–39
Faraday, Michael, *c512*
Faxian, 85
February days (France, 1848), 532
Ferdinand II, Holy Roman emperor, 436, *n436*
Ferdinand, king of Spain, 223, 374, 422
Fertile Crescent, 32, *m32*; Assyrian empire, 38–40, *m39*; contributions of, *c41*; Hammurabi, 37, *p37*, 574; Persian empire, *m39*, 40–42, 97; Roman empire influenced by, 141; Sargon, 37, *See also* Jews.
Feudalism: beginnings, 191–92; in China, 62; chivalry, 193–94; daily life, 194–95; in Japan, 327–31, *p328–29*, *c330*, *p331*, *c332*; noblewomen, 193; religion, 195–96; social structure, 192–93, *c192*, *p193*, 194; warfare, 192–93, *p193. See also* High Middle Ages; Manor system; Middle Ages.
Fez, 288, *m295*
Ficino, Marsilio, 344
Fief, 192, 210, 216
Filial piety, 90, 91, 98, 325
Firdawsi, 270
Fishing industry: Japanese, 324; Korean, 320
Five Pillars of Islam, 257–58, 290
Flanders, 202, 349
Florence, 344, *p344*, 345–46, *m345*
Flying buttress, 228
Footbinding, 312, *p312*, 387
Forbidden City, *p320*
Four Freedoms, The

(Roosevelt), 591
"Four Horsemen of the Apocalypse," 228
France: African slave trade, 406, 407–08, *m408*; Albigensian heresy, *m213*, 214, 218; American Revolution, 471–72, 482, 485; American settlements, 401–02, *p401*, *m402*, 404–05, *m472*; Arab land, 261, *m261*; bubonic plague, 229, *m229*; Calvinism, 357, *m361*; Cardinal Richelieu, 427, *p427*, 428, 480; after Congress of Vienna, *m502*, 503, 531; constitution, 483, 485, 488, 490, 492–93, 495; European balance of power, 439; expansionism, 420; exploration voyages, 378; Franco-Prussian War, 489, 490; French and Indian War, 404, *p404*, 439, 482; Haitian independence, 538–39, *m542*; Hapsburg conflict in Italy, 422; Henry IV, 426–27; Holy Roman Empire, *m213*; Huguenots, *p356*, 357, 426–27, 429–30; Hundred Years' War, 231–32, *m231*; in India, 386, 404, 439; Italian conflicts, 491, 495, 497, *m499*; Joan of Arc, *m231*, 232, *p232*; July revolution, 531; Louis XIV, 420, *p421*, 426–30, *p427–29*; Magyar invasion, 190, *m190*; Napoleon Bonaparte, 494–503, *p495*, *m497*, *m499*, *p500-01*, *m502*, 528; under Napoleon III, 532–33; Palace at Versailles, 420, *p421*, 428–29, *p428–29*; pirate ships, 400; population explosion, 509; Republic: First, 532; Republic: Second, 532; restoration of Louis XVIII, 531; revolution of 1824, 531; revolution of 1848, 526 531–32, *p532*, 534; revolution, 473, 478, *p479*, 480–94, *c481*, *p482–83*, *p485–87*, *p489*, *p492*, *c496*, 504; royal power, *p209*, 213–14, *m213*; St. Bartholomew's Day

Massacre, *p356*, 426; serfdom, 465; Sicily ruled by, 217; in South America, *m542*; Southeast Asian trade, 386; Thirty Years' War, 436–37, *m437. See also* Estates General; French Revolution; Napoleon Bonaparte.
Francis I, emperor of Austria, 502
Francis I, king of France, 400
Franciscan order, 199, 398
Francis of Assisi, 199
Franco-Prussian War, 489, 490
Frankenstein (Shelley), 519, *p519*
Frankfurt Assembly, 535–36
Franklin, Benjamin, 471, *p471*
Franks, 184, *p186*, 187, 188–90, *m189*
Frederick I, German emperor, 199, 217
Frederick II, German emperor, 217, 218
Frederick II (Frederick the Great), king of Prussia, 438, 439, 443, 463, 476
Frederick of Saxony, 355
Frederick William IV, king of Prussia, 439, 535
Freedom from Fear (Aung San Suu Kyi), 601
Free market, 460, 520–21, 529
French and Indian War, 404, *p404*, 439, 466, 469, 470, 482
French East India Company, 386
French Revolution, 443; causes and effects of, *c496*, 528, 536; Committee of Public Safety, 491; Directory, 492–93, 495; empire, 496–98, *m497*; financial crisis, 481–83, *p482*; during French wars, 489, *p489*, 490; impact on daily life, 493–94; land distribution, *c481*; Louis XVI execution, 490; march on Versailles, 486–87, *p487*; monarchy overthrown, 490; National Assembly, 478, 483, 485, 487–88; National Convention, 490–92; 493;

old regime, 480–81, *c481*; phases of, 484; reform attempts, 483, *p483*; Reign of Terror, *p492*, 492, 504; Robespierre, 491–92; storming the Bastille, *p479*, 483–84; uprisings, 484–85; women of, 486–87, *p487*, 493
Fujiwara family, 325
Fulani, 409, 934
Fulcher of Chartres, 280
Fulton, Robert, 515
Fur trade, 402
Futa Toro, 407, *m408*

Galen (Claudius Galenus), 142, 366
Galileo Galilei, 365
Gama, Vasco da, 374, *m376–77*, 382
Gandhi, Indira, 338
Gandhi, Mohandas, 590
Ganges River, 50, *m51*, 53, 55, 82
Gao, 291, 292, *m295*
Gao Zu, Chinese emperor, 94, 99
Gargantua and Pantagruel (Rabelais), 351
Gaul, *m136*, *m147*, *m150*, 187
Gautama, Siddhartha, 79–80, *p80*, 90
Geez language, 294
Geneva, 357, 358
Genghiz Khan, 246, 265, 274, 314–16
Genoa, 345, *m345*
Gentileschi, Artemisia, 348
Geoffrin, Marie-Thérèse, 462–63, *p462*
Geographic setting: Africa, 284–86, *m285*, 289; Americas, 158–59, *m159*; ancient Egypt, *m23*, *m25*; Assyrian, Persian empires, *m39*, 40; Balkans, *m187*, 249; China, 58–59, *m59*, 95–97, *m95*, *m380*; Eastern Europe, *m187*, 249; Europe, Middle Ages, 186, *m187*; Great Britain, 466, *m467*; Greece, 107–08, *m108*, 113–14, *m113*, 122–23, *m123*; and history, 68, *p7*; India, 50–53, *m51*, *m54*, 55, *m84*, *m380*; Indus Valley, 50–51, *m51*; Italy, 130; Japan, 323–24, *m323*;

INDEX

INDEX

(continued from page ii)

from "The Second Coming" is reprinted with the permission of **Simon & Schuster, Inc. and A. P. Watt Ltd.** from *The Poems of W. B. Yeats: A New Edition,* edited by Richard J. Finneran. Copyright © 1924 by Macmillan Publishing Company, renewed 1952 by Bertha Georgia Yeats. Excerpts from *Mothers and Shadows* (Readers International, 1985), translated by Jo Labanyi from *Conversación al sur* (Mexico City: Siglo XXI, 1981). Reprinted by permission of **Siglo XXI Editores.** Excerpts from "Gonzalez Videla," from *Canto General* by Pablo Neruda, translated/ edited by Jack Schmitt. Copyright © 1991 Fundacion Pablo Neruda, Regents of the University of California. Used by permission of the publisher, the **University of California Press.** Excerpt from "Black Woman," by Léopold Senghor. Copyright © 1964, 1973, 1979, 1984, and 1990 by Éditions du Seuil, by permission of **George Borchardt, Inc.** Reprinted from *The Collected Poetry* by Léopold Sédar Senghor, translated with an Introduction by Melvin Dixon (**The University Press of Virginia,** Charlottesville, Virginia, 1991). Excerpts from *The Metamorphoses* by Publius Ovidius Naso, translated by Horace Gregory. Translation copyright © 1958 by The Viking Press, Inc., renewed 1986 by Patrick Bolton Gregory. Used by permission of **Viking Penguin, a division of Penguin Books USA Inc.**

Note: Every effort has been made to locate the copyright owner of material reprinted in this book. Omissions brought to our attention will be corrected in subsequent printings.

ART CREDITS

Visual Research: Photosearch
Contributing Artists: Alfred G. Assin, Tammara L. Newnam, Carol Richmond
Freelance desktop page layout: David Rosenthal, Rose Sievers

PHOTOGRAPHIC CREDITS

Front Cover: left © G. Dagli Orti; right © Peter Beck/The Stock Market
Back Cover: background © G. Dagli Orti; left inset © G. Dagli Orti; right inset © Peter Beck/ The Stock Market
Interior: title page background and left inset © G. Dagli Orti; right inset © Peter Beck/The Stock Market **iii** background and left inset © G. Dagli Orti; right inset © Peter Beck/The Stock Market **v** top Dez & Jen Bartlett/Bruce Coleman, Inc.; middle © Archiv/Photo Rsearchers, Inc.; bottom Dragon Head, late Zhou dynasty. Courtesy of the Freer Gallery of Art, Smithsonian Institution, Washington, D.C. (32.14) **vi** top Archaeological Museum, Sarnath/Robert Harding Picture Library; middle, top © Boltin Picture Library; middle,bottom Scala/Art Resource, NY; bottom © Boltin Picture Library **vii** left Scala/Art Resource, NY; top, right © Boltin Picture Library; bottom, right © Jose Fuste Raga/The Stock Market **viii** left (detail) Asian Art Museum of San Francisco. Avery Brundage Collection (B60 D23); top, right Scala/Art Resource, NY; bottom, right © 1993 Jason Lauré **ix** top Private Collection Great Britain; middle, top Bibliothèque Nationale de Cartes et Plans/The Bridgeman Art Library, London; middle,bottom The Huntington Library; bottom Archivo Fotographico Oronoz, Madrid **x** top Courtesy of the Peabody Essex Museum, Salem, Mass.; middle, top Musée Carnavalet, Paris/ Giraudon/The Bridgeman Art Library, London; middle,bottom Archiv für Kunst und Geschichte, Berlin; bottom © Jean-Loup Charmet **xi** bottom Excerpts from *Women in Revolutionary Paris 1789–1795,* translated by Darline Gay Levy, Harriet Branson Applewhite, and Mary Durham Johnson. (Urbana: University of Illinois Press, 1979) **xii** right Bodleian Library, Oxford (Douce MM 668) **xiii** top Nehru Memorial Museum and Library, New Delhi; middle © The London Transport Museum; bottom By permission of the Trustees of the Overlord Embroidery. The Overlord Embroidery is on display at the D-Day Museum, Portsmouth, England; bottom Philadelphia Museum of Art: Given by Mr and Mrs. Herald Paumgarten **xiv** (detail) Kunsthistorisches Museum, Vienna **xix** Verrocchio, Lorenzo de'Medici, Samuel H. Kress Collection, © 1994 Board of Trustees, National Gallery of Art, Washington. Photo Philip A. Charles **xx** (detail) The Louvre/The Bridgeman Art Library, London/ **xxv** top, left Board of Trustees of the National Museums and Galleries on Merseyside (Lady Lever Art Gallery, Port Sunlight); top, right Archiv für Kunst und Geschichte, Berlin; bottom, left JB/Keystone/Hulton Deutsch Collection Ltd.; bottom, right © Tomas Muscionico/Contact Press Images **xxvi** top © Michael Fogden/Animals Animals; bottom © Tom Owen Edmunds/The Image Bank **xxvii** top © Michael Holford; middle © Buu-Hires/Gamma Liaison International; bottom © Palomo/ Cartoonists & Writers Syndicate **xxviii** top, left © André Held; top, middle © Liu Heung Shing/Contact Press Images; top, right (detail) From the collection of Hebrew Union College Skirball Museum, Eric Hockley Photographer; bottom, left Lauros-Giraudon/Art Resource, NY; bottom, middle (detail) Copyright British Museum (PS 192184); bottom, right © Esaias Baitel/Gamma Liaison International **xxix** top, left © Michael Holford; top, right © Jonathan Wallen/ Harry N. Abrams, Inc.; middle, left The Science Museum/Science & Society Picture Library; middle, right Whipple Museum of the History of Science; bottom, left Imperial War Museum/E.T. Archive; bottom, right © Somerville/ Cartoonists & Writers Syndicate **xxx** top, left © Michael Holford; top, middle University of British Columbia/The Bridgeman Art Library, London; top, right Library of Congress; bottom, left © Justin Kerr/Brooklyn Museum; bottom,middle Copyright British Museum; bottom, right Werner Forman Archive, Smithsonian Institution, Washington/Art Resource, NY **xxxi** top, left (detail) The Louvre/The Bridgeman Art Library, London; top, middle Photo Bibliothèque Nationale, Paris; top, right Collection of the National Palace Museum. Taipei, Taiwan, Republic of China; middle, center Bibliothèque Nationale/The Bridgeman Art Library, London; bottom, left; bottom, middle Walker Art Gallery; Diplomatic Reception Rooms, United States Department of State; The Bridgeman Art Library, London; bottom, right (detail) Collection: Congreso Nacional, Salón Eliptico. Photographer: Carlos German Rojas. Courtesy of the Foundation Gallery of National Art, Republic of Venezuela **xxxii** top © Punch/Rothco; bottom, left Nationalmuseet, Copenhagen/The Bridgeman Art Library, London; bottom, right Atkinson Art Gallery/The Bridgeman Art Library, London **xxxiii** top, left Victoria & Albert Museum/Art Resource, NY; top, right Scala/Art Resource, NY; bottom © Elke Walford/Hamburger Kunsthalle, Hamburg **xxxiv** top The Field Museum, Chicago, IL. Photo, Diane Alexander White; bottom © Superstock **1** top, left The Metropolitan Museum of Art, Gift of Norbert Schimmel Trust, 1989. (1989.281.12); top, right Bequest of Alfred F. Pillsbury/The Minneapolis Institute of Arts (50.46.14); bottom © Boltin Picture Library; **3** Dez & Jen Bartlett/Bruce Coleman, Inc. **5** © 1993 Comstock **6** © Punch/Rothco **7** top © Geoffrey Clifford/Woodfin Camp & Associates, Inc.; bottom Novosti Press/The Image Bank **9** © 1985 David L. Brill/Dr. Owen Lovejoy and students, Kent State University **10** © Frank Fournier/Woodfin Camp & Associates, Inc. **11** C. M. Dixon **13** © David A. Harvey/ Woodfin Camp & Associates, Inc. **15** top,left *Ornament,* China, 5th century b.c., late Eastern Zhou dynasty. Courtesy of the Freer Gallery of Art, Smithsonian Institution, Washington, D.C. (30.27); top,right *Choker # 59,* 1980, Mary Lee Hu. Collection of Virginia K. Lewis, Richmond, VA. Courtesy, American Craft Museum. Photo: George Erml; bottom,left The Corning Museum of Glass; bottom,right *Bridal Beads,* 1992, William Harper, Collection: Susan and Steven Turner, Tallahassee, FL. **16** The Kon-Tiki Museum, Oslo **19** © Sygma **21** © Brian Drake/Photo Researchers, Inc. **24** Art Resource, NY **27** *Mummified Cat,* The Louvre © Photo Réunion des Musées Nationaux **28** top The Metropolitan Museum of Art, Rogers Fund, 1912 and 1919 (12.182.72); bottom © William Albert Allard/Magnum Photos, Inc. **30** © Archiv/Photo Researchers, Inc. **33** top © George Gerster/Comstock, Inc.; bottom-inset Copyright British Museum (E. 554) **35** © Michael Holford **36** © Michael Holford **37** (detail) The Louvre/The Bridgeman Art Library, London **40** Scala/Art Resource, NY **41** top and top-2 © Michael Holford; top-3 Erich Lessing/Art Resource, NY; bottom-3 The Metropolitan Museum of Art, Purchase, H. Dunscombe Colt Gift, 1961 (61.62); bottom-2 British Museum/The Bridgeman Art Library, London; bottom © Boltin Picture Library; **43** By permission of The British Library **44** (detail) From the collection of Hebrew Union College Skirball Museum, Eric Hockley Photographer. **49** *Dragon Head,* late Zhou dynasty. Courtesy of the Freer Gallery of Art, Smithsonian Institution, Washington, D.C. (32.14) **52** top,left © Jehangir Gazdar/Woodfin Camp & Associates, Inc.; top,right © Jehangir Gazdar/Woodfin Camp & Associates, Inc.; bottom,left Simon and Schuster; bottom,right The Seal of Cotton is a registered servicemark/ trademark of Cotton Incorporated **57** National Museum of India, New Delhi/The Bridgeman Art Library, London **60** © Michael Holford **61** Photo: Wan-go Weng Inc. Archive **65** left Copyright British Museum (PS 164193); right Copyright British Museum (PS 164193) **68** left Dez & Jen Bartlett/Bruce

Coleman, Inc.; right © Brian Drake/Photo Researchers, Inc. **69** *Dragon Head*, late Zhou dynasty. Courtesy of the Freer Gallery of Art, Smithsonian Institution, Washington, D.C. (32.14) **70** top Art Resource, NY; bottom, left © Jehangir Gazdar/Woodfin Camp & Associates, Inc.; bottom, right Photo: Wango Weng Inc. Archive **71** Top © Boltin Picture Library; bottom, left © Michael Holford; bottom, right Scala/Art Resource, NY **72** Archiv für Kunst und Geschichte, Berlin **73** © Mirror Syndication International/ Hulton Deutsch Collection Ltd. **74** top The Metropolitan Museum of Art, Rogers Fund, 1908. (08.202.47); middle The Metropolitan Museum of Art, Gift of Nathan Cummings, 1964. (64.228.45); bottom © Rapa-Explorer **75** left Copyright British Museum; right Robert Harding Picture Library **77** (detail) Copyright British Museum (PS 192184) **78** Lauros-Giraudon/Art Resource, NY **80** Leo de Wys Inc./W. Hille **83** left Archaeological Museum, Sarnath/Robert Harding Picture Library; right © Viren Desai/Dinodia Picture Agency **86** © Marc Bernheim/ Woodfin Camp & Associates, Inc. **88** SEF/Art Resource, NY **89** Los Angeles County Museum of Art, From the Nasli and Alice Heeramaneck Collection, Museum Associates Purchase **91** Giraudon/ The Bridgeman Art Library, London **92** Copyright British Museum (PS 190954) **93** The Metropolitan Museum of Art, Lent by Charlotte C. and John C. Weber. Photograph by Lynton Gardiner **94** Robert Harding Picture Library **96** top © 1994 Denman Waldo Ross Collection, Courtesy, Museum of Fine Arts, Boston (25.10-13); bottom © The Uncle Nonamé Cookie Company **97** (detail) Copyright British Museum (PS 167832) **98** The Metropolitan Museum of Art **103** left © Boltin Picture Library; right (detail) H.L.Pierce Fund. Courtesy, Museum of Fine Arts, Boston (04.283) **105** © Michael Holford **106** left C. M. Dixon; right The Kobal Collection, NY **110** C. M. Dixon **111** © Michael Holford **112** © Boltin Picture Library **115** left Gjon Mili, *Life Magazine* © Time Warner; right American School of Classical Studies at Athens: Agora Excavations. **117** Scala/Art Resource, NY **119** © Michael Holford **120** The Art Museum, Princeton University. Museum purchase, Caroline G. Mather Fund. Photographer: Bruce White **122** Kunsthistorisches Museum, Vienna **124** Nimatallah/Art Resource, NY **129** C. M. Dixon **133** Scala/Art Resource, NY **134** © Michael Hol-

ford **137** © Michael Holford/Collection of the British Museum **139** top, left John G. Ross/Art Resource, NY; top, right © Butch Martin/The Image Bank; center, left Scala/Art Resource, NY; center, right © Juan Silva/The Image Bank; bottom, right © Gabe Palmer/The Stock Market **140** © Michael Holford/Collection of the British Museum **141** © Leonard Von Matt/ Photo Researchers, Inc. **142** © Michael Holford **145** © André Held **146** Scala/Art Resource, NY **149** The Walters Art Gallery, Baltimore **153** The Metropolitan Museum of Art, Rogers Fund, 1920. (20.192.17) **157** Bob Schalkwijk/Museo Amparo, Puebla, Mexico **160** © Boltin Picture Library **161** top (detail) Otis Imboden, © National Geographic Society; bottom, left © Duomo; bottom, right Sportslight/Bridgette Gordon **162** left © Boltin Picture Library; right © Justin Kerr **164** Museum für Völkerkunde, Vienna inv. nr. 43.380 **165** (detail) © Loren McIntyre **167** © Mario Corvetto/ Comstock Inc. **168** © Loren McIntyre **171** Peabody Museum, Harvard University. Photo: Hillel Burger **172** top University of British Columbia/The Bridgeman Art Library, London; top-2 Copyright British Museum; top-3 © Justin Kerr/Brooklyn Museum; middle © Michael Holford; bottom-3 Werner Forman Archive, Smithsonian Institution, Washington/Art Resource, NY; bottom-2 Reproduced by permission of the Canadian Museum of Civilization, Negative no. S93-9725; bottom The University Museum, University of Pennsylvania (neg. # T4-303) **176** top Copyright British Museum (PS 192184); bottom, left © Boltin Picture Library; bottom, right H.L.Pierce Fund. Courtesy, Museum of Fine Arts, Boston (04.283) **177** left C. M. Dixon; right Bob Schalkwijk/ Museo Amparo, Puebla, Mexico **178** top Copyright British Museum (PS 133392); bottom, left © Boltin Picture Library; bottom, right Robert Harding Picture Library **179** top (detail) Otis Imboden, © National Geographic Society; bottom, left © Michael Holford; bottom, right SEF/Art Resource, NY **180** Historical Museum Moscow, Russia/E. T. Archive **181** © Alon Reininger/Contact Press Images **182** top *Pair of Earrings*, Aztec or Mixtec, The Nelson-Atkins Museum of Art, Kansas City, Missouri (Purchase: Nelson Trust) 62-37/1,2; bottom, left The Metropolitan Museum of Art, Henry G. Leberthon Collection, Gift of Mr. and Mrs. A. Wallace Chauncey, 1957

(57.61.16); bottom, right © André Held **183** left Adros Studio - Rome; right Courtesy of Inner Mongolia Museum, Huhehaote, PRC. Photography by Marc Carter. © Natural History Museum of Los Angeles County **185** © Leonard von Matt/Photo Researchers, Inc. **186** © Pierre Belzeaux/ Photo Researchers, Inc. **191** © University Museum of National Antiquities, Oslo, Norway. Photo: Eirik Irgens Johnsen **193** © Boltin Picture Library **194** Emil Bauer, Bamberg/ The Historisches Museum, Bamberg/ Bayerische Staatgemäldesammlung **197** © Lambeth Palace Library/The Bridgeman Art Library, London **198** (detail) Fitzwilliam Museum, University of Cambridge/The Bridgeman Art Library, London **200** © Israel Museum, Jerusalem **204** left C.M. Dixon; right C.M.Dixon **205** left Bibliothèque Municipale , Saint Omer; middle,left The Trinity College Library, Cambridge; middle,right Glazier Collection, The Pierpont Morgan Library, New York. G.24, f.40 detail; right © Peter Miller/The Image Bank **209** By permission of The British Library, London (Harley ms 4431) **211** Photo Bibliothèque Nationale, Paris **212** The Royal Collection ©1994 Her Majesty Queen Elizabeth II **215** © Meyer/Kunsthistorisches Museum, Vienna **216** Biblioteca Vaticana/ Archiv für Kunst und Geschichte, Berlin **217** (detail) Scala/Art Resource, NY **219** left © Bill Holden/Leo de Wys, Inc.; right British Library/The Bridgeman Art Library, London **223** Bibliothèque Nationale/Archiv für Kunst und Geschichte, Berlin **224** Giraudon/Art Resource, NY **225** Giraudon/Art Resource, NY **227** left © Kim Hart/Black Star; right inset © Jose Fuste Raga/The Stock Market **230** Bodleian Library, Oxford (Douce MM 668) **232** Bibliothèque Nationale/The Bridgeman Art Library, London **237** © Erich Lessing/Magnum Photos, Inc. **240** (detail) Scala/Art Resource, NY **242** (detail) Archivo Fotographico Oronoz, Madrid **243** *Icon of Christ and St. Maenas*, Photo Jacqueline Hyde © Réunion des Musées Nationaux **245** left Beniaminson/Art Resource, NY; right Courtesy Karen McCready and Jean-Yves Noblet **248** Archiv für Kunst und Geschichte, Berlin **251** (detail) Austrian National Library, Vienna **255** Giraudon/Art Resource, NY **257** © Michael Holford **259** top The Metropolitan Museum of Art, Purchase, 1962, Mr. and Mrs. John D. Rockefeller Gift (62.265); top-2 © Sid Bernstein/ Photo Researchers, Inc.; top-3 The

Metropolitan Museum of Art, Rogers Fund, 1919. (19.186) Photograph by Lynton Gardiner; bottom-2 Scala/Art Resource, NY; bottom Victoria & Albert Museum/Art Resource, NY **262** © Robert Frerck/Odyssey Productions, Chicago **263** (detail) Bodleian Library, Oxford (MS. Ouseley Add. 24 folio 55v.) **267** top (detail) Topkapi Sarayi Museum, Istanbul/Ergun Cagatay/ Tetragon; bottom © Everett C. Johnson/Leo de Wys, Inc. **268** Scala/Art Resource, NY **269** top © M. Reichenthal/The Stock Market; inset © Marvin E. Newman **271** left *Mad dog biting man. Leaf from an Arabic translation of the Materia Medica*, Dioscorides. Courtesy of the Freer Gallery of Art, Smithsonian Institution, Washington, D.C. (53.91); right By permission of the British Library [1.0. 1379 (Ethé 2296) Folio 34] **275** (detail) Courtesy of the Board of Trustees of the Victoria & Albert Museum/The Bridgeman Art Library, London **276** Topkapi Sarayi Museum, Istanbul/Ergun Cagatay/ Tetragon **278** Topkapi Sarayi Museum, Istanbul/Ergun Cagatay/ Tetragon **279** The Metropolitan Museum of Art, Harris Brisbane Dick Fund, 1939. (39.20) **283** left Robert Harding Picture Library; right © Boltin Picture Library **287** Copyright British Museum **288** © Tom Owen Edmunds/The Image Bank **289** top © Boltin Picture Library; bottom © Boltin Picture Library **291** Photo Bibliothèque Nationale, Paris **293** (Sammlung) Collection H. Meyer, 1918 Inv. Nr. 98.155, Museum für Völkerkunde, Vienna **294** © Luis Villota/The Stock Market **299** © 1993 Jason Lauré **300** left Copyright British Museum; right © Ken Karp **303** Fowler Museum of Cultural History, UCLA, Los Angeles, CA **307** (detail) Arthur M. Sackler Gallery, Harvard University, Cambridge **308** Collection of the National Palace Museum. Taipei, Taiwan, Republic of China **309** Copyright British Museum **310** top Science Museum/Michael Holford; top-2 © Uniphoto, Inc.; middle Photo Bibliothèque Nationale, Paris; bottom-2 © Jonathan Wallen/Harry N. Abrams, Inc.; bottom Giraudon/Art Resource, NY **312** left *Lady playing Double Sixes*, Style of Chou Fang. Courtesy of the Freer Gallery of Art, Smithsonian Institution, Washington, D.C. (39.37/60.4); right Courtesy of Glenn Roberts Collection **313** *A Solitary Temple Amid Clearing Peaks*, attributed to Li Ch'eng, The Nelson-Atkins Museum of Art, Kansas City, Missouri (Purchase: Nelson Trust) 47-71 **315** left © G.

Mandel/ Artephot; right The Bridgeman Art Library, London 318 The Metropolitan Museum of Art, Gift of Robert E. Tod, 1937. (37.191.1) 320 © Dave Bartruff/ Artistry International 322 Asian Art Museum of San Francisco Avery Brundage Collection (B60 D23) 325 Laurie Platt Winfrey, Inc. 326 (detail) Asian Art Museum of San Francisco. Avery Brundage Collection (B60 D23) 328 Werner Forman/Art Resource, NY 329 © John Bryson/The Image Bank 331 left © Paolo Curto/The Image Bank; right (detail) Gift of Oliver Peabody, Courtesy, Museum of Fine Arts, Boston (79.468) 334 top, left © Leonard von Matt/Photo Researchers, Inc.; top, right By permission of The British Library, London (Harley ms 4431); bottom © Erich Lessing/Magnum Photos, Inc. 335 top Giraudon/Art Resource, NY; middle Arthur M. Sackler Gallery, Harvard University, Cambridge; bottom, left Robert Harding Picture Library; bottom, right © Boltin Picture Library 336 top © Boltin Picture Library; middle Peabody Museum, Harvard University. Photo: Hillel Burger; bottom Scala/ Art Resource, NY 337 top (detail) Photo Bibliothèque Nationale, Paris; bottom, left Photo Bibliothèque Nationale, Paris; bottom, right The Metropolitan Museum of Art, Gift of Robert E. Tod, 1937. (37.191.1) 338 *Creole Dance*, Pedro Figari, The Museum of Modern Art, New York. Gift of the Honorable and Mrs. Robert Woods Bliss. 339 Donato - Toronto Sun, Canada/Rothco Cartoons 340 top Copyright Museum of Mankind, British Museum, London; middle *Atahualpa, Inca Emperor*, unknown artist, oil on paper, #4056.313. The Thomas Gilcrease Institute of American History and Art Tulsa, Oklahoma; bottom Collection of Plymouth City Museum and Art Gallery 341 left Musée Guimet, Paris/Giraudon; right The Metropolitan Museum of Art, Rogers Fund, 1904. (04.4.2) Photograph by Schecter Lee 343 Scala/Art Resource, NY 344 Scala/Art Resource, NY 346 Scala/Art Resource, NY 347 Scala/Art Resource, NY 348 *Verrocchio*, Lorenzo de'Medici, Samuel H. Kress Collection, © 1994 Board of Trustees, National Gallery of Art, Washington. Photo Philip A. Charles. 350 Erich Lessing/Art Resource, NY 351 Archiv für Kunst und Geschichte, Berlin 352 left Folger Shakespeare Library, Wahington, DC; right © Walter Bibikow/The Image Bank 354 left David Lees,

Florence; right David Lees, Florence 355 Private Collection Great Britain 356 Bibliothèque Nationale, Paris/ Bulloz 359 Walker Art Gallery/The Bridgeman Art Library, London 360 Folger Shakespeare Library, Washington, DC 364 Archiv für Kunst und Geschichte, Berlin 365 left © Deutsches Museum, Munich; right The Bettmann Archive 367 Windsor Castle, Royal Library/ Archiv für Kunst und Geschichte, Berlin 368 (detail) Kunsthistorisches Museum, Vienna 371 Giraudon/Art Resource, NY 373 top Whipple Museum of the History of Science; top-2 Bibliothèque Nationale de Cartes et Plans/The Bridgeman Art Library, London; bottom-2 By permission of The British Library, Courtesy of The Harvard College Library; bottom © Artephot 375 Archiv für Kunst und Geschichte, Berlin 379 © Peter M. Fisher/The Stock Market 381 Leo deWys, Inc. 382 Biblioteca Casenatense, Rome 383 left © George Bernard/Science Photo Library/Photo Researchers, Inc.; top,right © Stephen Dalton/Photo Researchers, Inc.; bottom, right © George Holton/Photo Researchers, Inc. 385 By Courtesy of the Board of Trustees of the Victoria & Albert Museum 387 Mr. and Mrs. Rafi Y. Mottahedeh (Otto Nelson)/Laurie Platt Winfrey, Inc. 389 Philadelphia Museum of Art: Given by Mrs. G. Brinton Roberts. Photo, Graydon Wood 393 Archiv für Kunst und Geschichte, Berlin 394 The Granger Collection, New York 395 © Boltin Picture Library 396 © Loren McIntyre 398 © Catherine Ursillo/Photo Researchers, Inc. 399 Museo de America, Madrid/The Bridgeman Art Library, London 401 The Huntington Library 404 (detail) National Archives Canada, Ottawa(C-92420) 406 Nationalmuseet, Copenhagen/The Bridgeman Art Library, London 407 Photo Bibliothèque Nationale, Paris 409 (detail) Royal Commonwealth Society Collection/ Cambridge University Library 411 top Linnean Society, London/The Bridgeman Art Library, London; bottom Archiv für Kunst und Geschichte, Berlin 413 left The Metropolitan Museum of Art, Rogers Fund, 1968 (68.66); top,right © Richard Hutchings/Photo Researchers, Inc.; bottom,right Edgewater Book Company, Inc., Cleveland, Ohio. Photo, Ken Karp 415 © Erich Lessing/Art Resource, NY 417 Rare Books and Manuscripts Division. The New York Public Library. Astor, Lenox and Tilden Foundations. 421 Archiv für Kunst und Geschichte, Berlin 424 Archivo Fotographico Oronoz, Madrid 425

left Kunsthistorisches Museum, Vienna; right Corporate Communications/Mattel Toys 427 Lauros-Giraudon/Art Resource, NY 428 Archiv für Kunst und Geschichte, Berlin 429 Giraudon/Art Resource, NY 431 left Rare Books and Manuscripts Division. The New York Public Library. Astor, Lenox and Tilden Foundations; right (detail) National Library of Scotland, Edinburgh/The Bridgeman Art Library, London 432 Cromwell Museum, Huntington 434 The Mansell Collection Limited 438 Archiv für Kunst und Geschichte, Berlin 440 Archiv für Kunst und Geschichte, Berlin 441 top Archiv für Kunst und Geschichte, Berlin; bottom Photo Bibliothèque Nationale, Paris 446 left Scala/Art Resource, NY; right Giraudon/ Art Resource, NY 447 left and right Archiv für Kunst und Geschichte, Berlin 448 top, left Museum für Völkerkunde, Vienna. inv. nr. 43.380; top, right Biblioteca Casenatense, Rome; bottom Folger Shakespeare Library, Washington, DC 449 top (detail) Royal Commonwealth Society Collection/ Cambridge University Library; middle Mr. and Mrs. Rafi Y. Mottahedeh (Otto Nelson)/Laurie Platt Winfrey, Inc.; bottom Walker Art Gallery/The Bridgeman Art Library, London 450 Bildarchiv Preussischer Kulturbesitz 451 © Mark and Evelyne Bernheim/Woodfin Camp & Associates, Inc. 452 top, left Rare Books and Manuscripts Division. The New York Public Library. Astor, Lenox and Tilden Foundations; top, right Rare Books and Manuscripts Division. The New York Public Library. Astor, Lenox and Tilden Foundations; bottom, left (detail) Nacional de Historia, Chapultepec Castle, Mexico City/Laurie Platt Winfrey, Inc.; bottom,right Museum of Mankind, British Museum/Michael Holford 453 left Collection of Countess Bobrinskoy/Michael Holford; right By Courtesy of the Board of Trustees of the Victoria & Albert Museum 455 The Bridgeman Art Library, London 457 Giraudon/Art Resource, NY 458 Archiv für Kunst und Geschichte, Berlin 459 top,left Archiv für Kunst und Geschichte, Berlin; top-2,left Philip Mould, Historical Portraits Ltd./The Bridgeman Art Library, London; top-2, right Division of Rare and Manuscript Collections, Carl A. Kroch Library, Cornell University; top,right Burghley House, Stamford, Lincolnshire/The Bridgeman Art Library, London; bottom,left Private Collection/The Bridgeman Art Library, London; bottom-2, left © Roger-Viollet; bottom-2,right © Édi-

tions Tallandier; bottom,right © Éditions Tallandier 461 © Hulton Deutsch Collection Ltd 462 © Erich Lessing/ Archiv für Kunst und Geschichte, Berlin 464 The Metropolitan Museum of Art, The Jack and Belle Linsky Collection, 1982. (1982.60.311-.312) 465 Board of Trustees of the National Museums and Galleries on Merseyside (Lady Lever Art Gallery, Port Sunlight) 468 top Sir John Sloane Museum/The Bridgeman Art Library, London; bottom,left © Wally McNamee/Sygma; bottom,right © Steve Leonard/Black Star 470 Courtesy of the Peabody Essex Museum, Salem, Mass. 471 left Diplomatic Reception Rooms, United States Department of State; right © John Lewis Stage/The Image Bank 475 Philadelphia Museum of Art: Given by Mr. and Mrs. Herald Paumgarten 479 Musée Carnavalet, Paris/Archiv für Kunst und Geschichte, Berlin 482 Carnavalet/Art Resource, NY 483 © Musée Carnavalet/Bulloz, Paris 485 Giraudon/The Bridgeman Art Library, London 486 © Agence Top, Paris 487 Édimedia, Paris 489 left © Phototheque des Musées de la ville de Paris © 1996 Artists Rights Society (ARS), New York/SPADEM, Paris; right Musée Carnavalet, Paris/Giraudon/ The Bridgeman Art Library, London 491 top, left © A.C. Cooper/ Madame Tussaud's Wax Museum; top, right © Hollywood Wax Museum; bottom, left © A.C. Cooper/ Madame Tussaud's Wax Museum; bottom, right © A.C. Cooper/ Madame Tussaud's Wax Museum 492 © Erich Lessing/Musée Carnavalet, Paris/Archiv für Kunst und Geschichte, Berlin 495 Napoleon Bonaparte crossing the Saint Bernard, © Melmaison/Réunion des Musées Nationaux 500 Giraudon/Art Resource, NY 501 © Éditions Tallandier, Paris 507 The Science Museum/Science & Society Picture Library 509 University of Reading © Rural History Centre 511 Broadlands Trust, Hants/The Bridgeman Art Library, London 512 top The Science Museum/Science & Society Picture Library; middle,top The Science Museum/Science & Society Picture Library; middle,bottom Archiv für Kunst und Geschichte, Berlin; bottom The Science Museum/Science & Society Picture Library 515 Rebus, Inc. 517 Archiv für Kunst und Geschichte, Berlin 518 Mary Evans Picture Library, London 519 top The Bettmann Archive; bottom, left Bodleian Library, Oxford [Shelley Relics (d)]; bottom,middle Princeton University Libraries; bottom, right © Everett Collection **521** Archiv für Kunst und Geschichte, Berlin **523** Karl Marx Museum, Trier/E.T. Archive **527** Musée du petit palais, Paris/Giraudon/The Bridgeman Art Library, London **528** Anne S. K. Brown Military Collection, Brown University Library **530** © Jean-Loup Charmet **532** Babcock Bequest, Courtesy, Museum of Fine Arts, Boston (14.4187) **534** Austrian National Library, Vienna **535** Correr Museum, Venice/E.T. Archive **537** top Collection of the National Bank of Mexico. Photo: Rafael Doniz. Courtesy Formento Cultural Banamex; bottom Collection of the National Bank of Mexico. Photo: Rafael Doniz. Courtesy Formento Cultural Banamex **538** © Jean-Loup Charmet **540** top and bottom left Courtesy of the Flag Research Center; top, right Associated Press/Topham/Image Works; bottom, right Courtesy of the Israel Consulate **541** (detail) Collection: Congreso Nacional, Salón Eliptico. Photographer: Carlos German Rojas. Courtesy of the Foundation Gallery of National Art, Republic of Venezuela **546** left The Bridgeman Art Library, London; right Musée Carnavalet, Paris/Archiv für Kunst und Geschichte, Berlin **547** left The Science Museum/Science & Society Picture Library; right Musée du petit palais, Paris/Giraudon/The Bridgeman Art Library, London **548** top, left Rare Books and Manuscripts Division. The New York Public Library. Astor, Lenox and Tilden Foundations; top, right Diplomatic Reception Rooms, United States Department of State; bottom Édimedia, Paris **549** top, left Collection: Congreso Nacional, Salón Eliptico. Photographer: Carlos German Rojas. Courtesy of the Foundation Gallery of National Art, Republic of Venezuela; top, right E.T. Archive; bottom Rebus, Inc. **550** Poster Photo Archives, Posters Please Inc., New York © 1996 Artists Rights Society (ARS), New York/ADAGP, Paris **551** © P. Durand/Sygma **552** left Bury Art Gallery & Museum, Lancs./The Bridgeman Art Library, London; top, right Archiv für Kunst und Geschichte, Berlin; bottom, right The Royal Collection © Her Majesty Queen Elizabeth II **553** left © National Maritime Museum, London; right Gallery Kabutoya, Japan **554** top, left © Rudolf Wakonigg/Landesmuseum für Kunst und Kultergeschichte, Münster; top, right Scala/Art Resource, NY; bottom Thames and Hudson, London **555** left *The Persistence of Memory*, Salvador Dali, The Museum of Modern Art, New York © 1996 Demart Pro Arte, Geneva/Artists Rights Society (ARS), New York; right Imperial War Museum, London **556** left Collection of the University of Fort Hare, De Beers Centenary Art Gallery, South Africa; top, right *Central Savings*, Richard Estes, The Nelson-Atkins Museum of Art, Kansas City, Missouri (Gift of the Friends of Art) F75-13. © 1996 Richard Estes/Licensed by VAGA, New York, NY, Marlborough Gallery, New York, NY; bottom, right Minick/Jiao **557** left © Wasma'a Chorbachi; top, right © Robert Frerck/ Odyssey Productions; bottom, right © 1991, The Children's Museum of Indianapolis. From the Caplan Collection of The Children's Museum of Indianapolis

HISTORICAL DOCUMENT ACKNOWLEDGMENTS

572 Excerpts from *Instruction of Ptah-hotep* based on the translation by F. L. Griffith in *A Library of the World's Best Literature*, XIII, 5329-5340. **573** Excerpts from *The Epic of Gilgamesh* from *Ancient Near Eastern Texts Relating to the Old Testament*, ed. James B. Pritchard, 3rd rev. ed. with Supplement. Copyright ©1969 by Princeton University Press. Translated by E. A. Speiser. **574** Excerpts from *The Code of Hammurabi* based on the translation by Robert F. Harper, *The Code of Hammurabi* (Chicago: The University of Chicago Press, 1904). **575** Excerpts from *The Analects of Confucius*, translated and annotated by Arthur Waley. Copyright © by Unwin Hyman, an imprint of HarperCollins Publishers Limited. **576** Excerpts from Thucydides' *History of the Peloponnesian War,* translated by Alfred Zimmern in *The Greek Commonwealth: Politics and Economics in Fifth-Century Athens*, 4th ed. (Oxford: 1924). **577** Excerpts from *Aristotle, Nicomachean Ethics,* translated by Martin Ostwald. Copyright ©1962 by Macmillan Publishing Company. **578** Excerpts from Asoka's edicts from *Sources in Indian Tradition*, Volume I, edited by William Theodore de Bary. **581** Excerpts from *The African Past and the Coming of the European*, edited by Leon E. Clark (New York: Praeger Publishers, 1970). **582** Excerpts from *The Bernard Diaz Chronicles*, translated by Albert Idell, translation copyright © 1956 by Albert Idell. Used by permission of Doubleday, a division of Bantam Doubleday Dell Publishing Group, Inc. **587** Excerpts from *Women in Revolutionary Paris 1789–1795*, translated by Darline Gay Levy, Harriet Branson Applewhite, and Mary Durham Johnson. (Urbana: University of Illinois Press, 1979). **588** Excerpt from *The Course of Mexican History* by Michael C. Meyer and William L. Sherman. (New York: Oxford University Press, 1979). **589** Excerpts from *Simón Bolívar, Selected Writings*, edited by Harold A. Bierck, Jr., translated by Lewis Bertrand. (New York: The Colonial Press, Inc., 1951). **590** Excerpts from *Hind Swaraj or Indian Home Rule* by M.K. Gandhi. (Navajivan Pulishing House, 1938). **592** Excerpts from *The Universal Declaration of Human Rights,* United Nations Publication No. 63.1.13 (New York: The United Nations, 1963). **593** Excerpts from *On People's Democratic Dictatorship*, by Mao Tse-tung. (Peking: Foreign Language Press, 1950). **594** Excerpts from *The Autobiography of Kwame Nkrumah*. Copyright © Panaf Books, London. **595** Excerpts from Andrei Sakharov, Nobel Prize Lecture, Copyright © The Nobel Foundation, 1975. **596** Excerpts from Lech Walesa, Nobel Prize Lecture, Copyright © The Nobel Foundation, 1983. **597** Excerpts from *One Earth, Four or Five Worlds: Reflections on Contemporary History* by Octavio Paz. English translation copyright © 1985 by Harcourt Brace Jovanovich, Inc. **598** Excerpts from *Perestroika* by Mikhail Gorbachev, as appeared in *Vital Speeches of the Day*, September 11, 1989. **599** Excerpts from *New Year's Day Address* by Vaclav Havel. Reprinted by permission of *Uncaptive Minds*, a publication of the Institute for Democracy in Eastern Europe. **600** Excerpts from *Latin America: The Democratic Option*, by Mario Vargas Llosa. Copyright ©1987 by *Harper's Magazine*. All rights reserved. Reproduced from the June issue by special permission. **601** Excerpts from *Freedom from Fear and Other Writings* by Aung San Suu Kyi, Forward by Vaclav Havel, translated by Michael Aris. Translation copyright © 1991 by Aung San Suu Kyi and Michael Aris. Used by permission of Penguin, a division of Penguin Books USA Inc. **602** Excerpts from *Glory and Hope* by Nelson Mandela, as appeared in *Vital Speeches of the Day*, May 10, 1994. **603** Excerpts from *The Outlook for China, Human Rights* by Harry Wu, as appeared in *Vital Speeches of the Day*, March 27, 1996

Note: Every effort has been made to locate the copyright owner of material reprinted in this book. Omissions brought to our attention will be corrected in subsequent printings.

Stop the Presses

On this page you will find a number of recent events that, because of deadlines, could not be included in the main body of the text. Each item is followed by a text heading and page numbers for background information.

WORLD MOURNS DEATHS OF PRINCESS DIANA AND MOTHER TERESA

Two of the world's best-known women died within days of each other in 1997. On August 31, Princess Diana, age 36, was killed in an automobile accident in Paris. Less than a week later, Mother Teresa, age 87, died of a heart attack in Calcutta.

Princess Diana, the former wife of Britain's Prince Charles, had campaigned for many charitable organizations and in support of causes such as banning land mines. (See "Nations Sign Treaty Banning Land Mines," below.) Mother Teresa, founder of the relief organization Missionaries of Charity, had been awarded the 1979 Nobel Peace Prize for her work in India and elsewhere.

World reaction to the deaths reflected the influence of modern communications technology. Millions of people around the world viewed the funerals of the two women on television. Many people also sent messages of condolence by electronic mail.

CHINESE COMMUNIST PARTY REAPPOINTS LEADER

In September 1997 the Chinese Communist Party reelected Jiang Zemin to a new five-year term as head of the party, which rules the People's Republic of China. Party leaders also demoted several rivals of Jiang. These results strengthened Jiang's leadership and signaled continued party support for economic reforms, especially the growth of private enterprise. China began moving away from a strict socialist system in the early 1980s under leader Deng Xiaoping.

TENSIONS RISE BETWEEN ISRAELIS AND PALESTINIANS

Rising bitterness on both sides in the Israeli-Palestinian dispute threatened to undermine the peace process during 1997. Israelis, shocked by a series of deadly terrorist attacks against Israeli civilians, called on Palestinian leader Yasir Arafat to crack down on Palestinian militants. Palestinians, meanwhile, bitterly criticized Israeli leader Benjamin Netanyahu for failing to halt construction of Jewish settlements in disputed lands.

NATIONS SIGN TREATY BANNING LAND MINES

On September 17, 1997, representatives of roughly 100 countries meeting in Oslo, Norway, approved a treaty banning the use of anti-personnel land mines. Millions of land mines are buried in nations such as Cambodia, Afghanistan, and Angola. These hidden explosives kill or cripple thousands of civilians each year.

The treaty banning land mines was scheduled to be signed formally in Ottawa, Canada, in December 1997, and would take effect after governments in 40 nations had ratified it. The United States joined several other nations in refusing to sign the treaty. President Clinton explained that American military forces rely on land mines for defense in places such as South Korea.